# Fodor's

# COMPLETE GUIDE TO THE NATIONAL PARKS OF THE WEST

1st Edition

**Where to Stay and Eat for All Budgets**

**Must-See Sights and Local Secrets**

**Ratings You Can Trust**

Fodor's Travel Publications   New York, Toronto, London, Sydney, Auckland
**www.fodors.com**

**FODOR'S COMPLETE GUIDE TO THE NATIONAL PARKS OF THE WEST**
**Editors:** Debbie Harmsen & Michael Nalepa

**Editorial Production:** Eric B. Wechter
**Editorial Contributors:** John Blodgett, Maria Burwell, Martha Schindler Connors, Cheryl Crabtree, Michelle Delio, Jennifer Edwards, Paul Eisenberg, Dustin Floyd & Tom Griffith, Lois Friedland, Veronica Hill, Constance Jones, Shannon M. Kelly, Christina Knight, Jill Koch, Janet Lowe, Carrie Miner, Janna Mock-Lopez, Molly Moker, Riley Morton, Candy Moulton, Debbie Olsen, Jennifer Paull, Gary Peterson, Marge Peterson, Holly S. Smith, Amanda R. Theunissen, Christine Vovakes, Bobbi Zane
**Maps and Illustrations:** Mark Stroud, *cartographer*; Bob Blake and Rebecca Baer, *map editors*
**Design:** Fabrizio La Rocca, *creative director*; Guido Caroti, *art director*; Ann McBride, *designer*; Melanie Marin, *senior picture editor*
**Production/Manufacturing:** Robert B. Shields
**Cover Photo** (Black Canyon of the Gunnison, Colorado): Chris Howes/Wild Places Photography/ Alamy

ISBN 978–1–4000–1627–3

ISSN 1532–9771

## SPECIAL SALES
This book is available at special discounts for bulk purchases for sales promotions or premiums. Special editions, including personalized covers, excerpts of existing books, and corporate imprints, can be created in large quantities for special needs. For more information, write to Special Markets/ Premium Sales, 1745 Broadway, MD 6-2, New York, New York 10019, or e-mail specialmarkets@ randomhouse.com.

## AN IMPORTANT TIP & AN INVITATION
Although all prices, opening times, and other details in this book are based on information supplied to us at press time, changes occur all the time in the travel world, and Fodor's cannot accept responsibility for facts that become outdated or for inadvertent errors or omissions. So **always confirm information when it matters,** especially if you're making a detour to visit a specific place. Your experiences—positive and negative—matter to us. If we have missed or misstated something, **please write to us.** We follow up on all suggestions. Contact the National Parks of the West editors at editors@fodors.com or c/o Fodor's at 1745 Broadway, New York, NY 10019.

PRINTED IN THE UNITED STATES OF AMERICA

10 9 8 7 6 5 4 3 2 1

# CONTENTS

# CONTENTS

# CONTENTS

# ABOUT THIS BOOK

## What's Inside

For each of the national parks of the West our expert writers have gathered comprehensive information on everything within the park and on the towns and attractions nearby. We have included as many sights, activities, lodging and dining options, and practical details as space allows, focusing on delivering to you the kind of in-depth, first-hand knowledge that you won't get elsewhere. Our first three chapters introduce you to the park experience, provide insight on the National Park System, and provide tips on how to best plan for and make the most of your visits to these national treasures. Following the individual park chapters is a back-of-the-book section with driving tours and campground charts to further help you in making a park trip a memorable, hassle-free vacation.

## Our Ratings

Sometimes you find terrific travel experiences and sometimes they just find you. But usually the burden is on you to select the right combination of experiences. That's where our ratings come in.

As travelers we've all discovered a place so wonderful that its worthiness is obvious. And sometimes that place is so unique that superlatives don't do it justice: you just have to be there to know. These sights, properties, and experiences get our highest rating, **Fodor's Choice,** indicated by orange stars throughout this book.

Black stars highlight sights and properties we deem **Highly Recommended,** places that our writers, editors, and readers praise again and again for consistency and excellence.

By default, there's another category: any place we include in this book is by definition worth your time, unless we say otherwise. And we will.

Disagree with any of our choices? Care to nominate a place or suggest that we rate one more highly? Visit our feedback center at www.fodors.com/feedback.

## Budget Well

Hotel and restaurant price categories from ¢ to **$$$$** are defined in the opening pages of each chapter. For attractions, we always give standard adult admission fees; reductions are usually available for children, students, and senior citizens. Want to pay with plastic? **AE, D, DC, MC, V** following restaurant and hotel listings indicate whether American Express, Discover, Diner's Club, MasterCard, and Visa are accepted.

### Many Listings
- ★ Fodor's Choice
- ★ Highly recommended
- ⊠ Physical address
- ✛ Directions
- ⊕ Mailing address
- ☏ Telephone
- 🖷 Fax
- ⊕ On the Web
- ✉ E-mail
- 🎫 Admission fee
- ☉ Open/closed times
- ⊟ Credit cards

### Hotels & Restaurants
- 🏨 Hotel
- ⌧ Number of rooms/campsites
- ⚲ Facilities
- ⅼⓄⅼ Meal plans
- ✕ Restaurant
- ⚑ Reservations
- 🛆 Dress code
- ⚲ Smoking
- 🎶 BYOB
- ✕🏨 Hotel with restaurant that warrants a visit

### Outdoors
- ⅼ Golf
- ⚠ Camping

### Other
- ☺ Family-friendly
- ⓘ Contact information
- ⇨ See also
- ⌧ Branch address
- ☞ Take note

# ABOUT THIS BOOK

### Restaurants

Unless we state otherwise, restaurants are open for lunch and dinner daily. We mention dress only when there's a specific requirement and reservations only when they're essential or not accepted—it's always best to book ahead.

### Hotels

Hotels have private bath, phone, TV, and air-conditioning and operate on the European Plan (aka EP, meaning without meals), unless we specify that they use the Continental Plan (CP, with a Continental breakfast), Breakfast Plan (BP, with a full breakfast), or Modified American Plan (MAP, with breakfast and dinner) or are all-inclusive (including all meals and most activities). We always list facilities but not whether you'll be charged an extra fee to use them, so when pricing accommodations, find out what's included.

### Campgrounds

For many visitors, camping is a central part of the national park experience. In our Where to Stay sections, we list most of the developed, frontcountry campgrounds in the park, as well as many primitive and backcountry sites, plus some of the best campgrounds outside the parks. We also have a section in back, "Campgrounds at a Glance," with campground charts for all 37 parks in this book. You can see what each campground has to offer, including such facilities as showers and fire rings, seasonal closings, and how much a campsite costs. When applicable, we also explain the park's backcountry camping opportunities and policies for permits and fire safety.

| WHAT IT COSTS | | | | | |
|---|---|---|---|---|---|
| | $$$$ | $$$ | $$ | $ | ¢ |
| RESTAURANTS | over $30 | $21–$30 | $13–$20 | $8–$12 | under $8 |
| HOTELS | over $200 | $151–$200 | $101–$150 | $50–$100 | under $50 |
| CAMPING | over $50 | $36–$49 | $18–$35 | $10–$17 | under $10 |

Restaurant prices are per person for a main course at dinner. Hotel prices are per night for two people in a standard double room in high season, excluding taxes and service charges. Camping prices are for a standard (no hookups, pit toilets, fire grates, picnic tables) campsite per night. Prices and price categories are in U.S. dollars except for the three Canadian parks in this book—Banff, Jasper, Waterton—in which the dollars represent Canadian dollars.

# Welcome to the Parks

Double Arch, Arches National Park

## WORD OF MOUTH

"All across the nation. . . people are starting out for their vacations in national and state parks. Those people will put up at roadside camps or pitch their tents under the stars, with an open fire to cook by, with the smell of the woods, and the wind in the trees. They will forget the rush and the strain of all the other long weeks of the year, and, for a short time at least, the days will be good for their bodies and good for their souls."

–Franklin D. Roosevelt

# NATIONAL TREASURES

"I went to the woods because I wished to live deliberately," wrote Henry David Thoreau, " . . . to front only the essential facts of life, and see if I could learn what it had to teach, and not, when I came to die, discover that I had not lived. . . I wanted to live deep and suck out all the marrow of life."

For many, a trip to the national parks is just that: a deliberate departure from measured daily life; an escape to a place where one can breathe life in deeply—a "seize the day," if you will. In a society overwrought with constant man-made stimulation—billboards, sound bites, a flood of unsolicited mail—something deep within the human spirit cries out for tranquility, for a place where the stimulation is not an intrusion that distracts and drains us, but a delightful diversion that invigorates us and fills us with wonder.

With their bigger-than-life panoramas, the more than three dozen western national parks covered in this guide are particularly good at awakening the senses and igniting the imagination. Whether it's the bubbling mud pots and steaming fumaroles at Yellowstone, the raging Colorado River pushing through the Grand Canyon, or the quiet nibblings and ambulations of mule deer, black bears, and big horn sheep at Yosemite, the stirrings of creation remind us that there is a refreshing alternate reality outside our brick-and-mortar-confined existences.

A visit to a western national park is more than a retreat. It is a great adventure. You can explore new terrain, encounter creatures great and small—think hungry grizzly, scrappy marmot—and add more knowledge to your noggin through naturalist talks and ranger walks.

It's an adventure for youngsters as well. At a national park, children may see their first snake or bald eagle, have their first romp through sand dunes, and experience their first night of camping, complete with marshmallows toasted over the fire and a sky above studded with stars.

If you, or your family, want mega action, the parks offer that, too. Float the Rio Grande at Big Bend, rock climb at Joshua Tree, wheel around in your 4x4 at Capitol Reef, or strap on some snowshoes or cross-country skis and tackle the powder at Grand Teton.

Any way you look at it, you can definitely live deliberately.

## WHAT'S NEW AT THE PARKS

**New Annual Pass.** In January 2007, the "America the Beautiful National Park and Federal Recreational Land Pass" debuted. The $80 pass is good for admittance into public lands run by the National Park Service, U.S. Forest Service, Fish and Wildlife Service, Bureau of Land Management, and Bureau of Land Reclamation.
**New NPS Director.** In October 2006, Mary Bomar was sworn in as the director of the National Park Service, replacing Fran Mainella, who resigned.
**Oceans to Receive Greater Protection.** In 2006, NPS launched its Ocean Park Stewardship Action Plan to restore and maintain the agency's more than 5,100 miles of beaches, coral reefs, kelp forests, wetlands, and other marine resources.
**Parks Budget Increase.** In February 2007, the Bush Administration presented a $2.4-billion budget for the parks, an all-time high. At the time of this writing, Congress had yet to approve it.

# NATIONAL PARK SERVICE THEN & NOW

### Go West, Young Man

A romantic image of the West has gripped the American psyche since the nation's birth. As the frontier shifted from the Ohio River Valley to the great plains to the Rocky Mountains and finally to the Pacific, the land just over the horizon promised freedom, open space, self-sufficiency, and adventure. Manifest Destiny, gold rushes, and the Homestead Act of 1862—which offered 160-acre parcels of land to anyone 21 years or older with $18—spurred settlers, prospectors, soldiers, and laborers to tame the American West.

### Vocal Pioneers

During this unprecedented land-grab, interest in preserving scenic western lands and archaeological sites emerged, as well as a national sense of responsibility for the wilderness. While exploring the Dakotas in 1832, painter George Catlin noted the potential for loss of wildlife and wilderness. He wrote that it could be preserved "by some great protecting policy of government. . . in a magnificent park."

The tipping point came three decades later. In 1864, in the midst of the Civil War, President Lincoln set aside Yosemite Valley and the Mariposa Grove of giant sequoias as a public trust to preserve the land for future generations. This revolutionary federal preservation concept was just the beginning. When a handful of would-be entrepreneurs explored Yellowstone in 1870, dreaming up the possibilities for development of this fairyland they'd found, a lawyer, Cornelius Hedges, made the bold suggestion that they preserve this geologically astounding land rather than capitalize on it.

Whatever persuasive prose Hedges used is not certain, but persuade them he did. A year later, one of these explorers was in the House of Representatives promoting the park plan. Also lobbying for Yellowstone were artist Thomas Moran, photographer William H. Jackson, and U. S. Geology Survey director Ferdinand Hayden, who'd been appointed by Congress to lead an expedition to Yellowstone to validate the rumors of its other-worldly features. Congress was more than convinced of its merits to be preserved, and in early 1872, President Ulysses S. Grant signed into law the bill creating Yellowstone National Park, the first and oldest national park in the world.

## NATIONAL PARKS TIMELINE

| | |
|---|---|
| 1872 | Yellowstone National Park becomes the world's first national park. |
| 1890 | Sequoia, Yosemite, and General Grant (later part of Kings Canyon) become national parks. |
| 1902 | President Theodore Roosevelt establishes his first of five parks, Crater Lake. |
| 1903 | President Roosevelt makes Wind Cave the country's seventh national park, and the first dedicated to preserving a cave. |

# NATIONAL PARK SERVICE THEN & NOW

The 1890s saw the creation of several more national parks, as well as the Forest Reserve Act of 1891, which led to our first national forests. In 1906 the Antiquities Act passed, which allowed presidents to name national monuments. President Theodore Roosevelt established Devils Tower as the first such monument, making Wyoming the home of both the first national park and first national monument.

## The Birth of the National Park System

Pioneering conservationists like John Muir and Robert Underwood Johnson—who together founded the Sierra Club in 1892—advocated for further preservation of Western treasures. Muir, who is often called the father of the National Park System, greatly influenced Theodore Roosevelt, who went on to establish five national parks.

By 1916 the Interior Department oversaw 14 national parks. In order to streamline the management of the national parks and monuments, President Woodrow Wilson approved legislation creating the National Park Service. The mission of the new agency under the Interior Department was "to conserve the scenery and the natural and historic objects and the wild life therein and to provide for the enjoyment of the same in such manner and by such means as will leave them unimpaired for the enjoyment of future generations."

While Washington made these lands protected, railroads made visiting them a reality. Thousands traveled west to such national parks as Grand Canyon, Glacier, Yosemite Valley, and Crater Lake, and stayed in the extravagant lodges constructed by the railroad companies.

## Growing Pains

The parks initially had operated on the premise of preservation and visitor enjoyment, but by 1932, the park concept had expanded to include educational components with the formation of the NPS's Naturalist Division. The naturalists were assigned to interpret park features to the public through educational outreaches. The park system had also begun to rethink its wildlife management practices.

The 1930s also brought a core of hardy workers to the nation's parks and forests as part of FDR's Works Progress Administration during the Great Depression. A total of 41 work camps were set up.

| | |
|---|---|
| 1906 | Congress selects Mesa Verde as a national park. It is the first cultural park in the system. |
| 1916 | President Woodrow Wilson signs the Organic Act, creating the National Park Service. |
| 1919 | The Grand Canyon goes from a national monument to a national park. |
| 1933 | President Franklin Delano Roosevelt develops the Civilian Conservation Corps. The corps worked in national parks and forests, planting three billion trees in nine years. |
| 1951 | The arrowhead becomes the official National Park Service emblem. The sequoia tree and |

| | |
|---|---|
| | bison represent vegetation and wildlife, the mountains and water represent scenic and recreational values, and the arrowhead represents historical and archaeological values. |
| 1967 | Congress established the National Park Foundation as a separate, fund-raising arm for the parks. |
| 1984 | The fossils of one of the oldest dinosaurs ever unearthed were found in Petrified Forest National Park. |
| 1987 | Annual recreational visitors to the parks hits an all time high: 287,244,998. |

As the country's population continued to grow, and society learned more about the environment and the effects of the Industrial Revolution, there was a need to take additional steps to retain pristine wilderness and historic areas. Congress addressed this in the 1960s and early '70s with a host of legislative measures: the Wilderness Act (1964), National Historic Preservation Act (1966), Clean Air Act (1967), Wild and Scenic Rivers Act (1968), National Environmental Policy Act (1969), and the Endangered Species Act (1973).

## The NPS Today

The National Park Service now manages nearly 400 natural, cultural, and recreational sites on some 84.4 million acres. These sites include national parks as well as monuments, memorials, historic parks, and national preserves. The NPS defines these lands as follows:

**National Park:** A natural place, generally large in size, that possesses an array of attributes, including an outstanding example of a particular type of resource, great opportunities for public use and enjoyment (or for scientific study), and a high degree of unsoiledness. It may also be historically significant.

**National Historic Park:** A historic site that extends beyond single properties.

**National Historic Site:** Usually containing a single historical feature directly associated with its subject. Derived from the Historic Sites Act of 1935, a number of historic sites were established by secretaries of the Interior, but most have been authorized by acts of Congress.

**National Monument:** A landmark, structure, or other object of historic or scientific interest situated on lands owned or controlled by the government.

**National Memorial:** Commemorative of a historic person or episode.

**National Preserve:** An area having characteristics associated with national parks, but in which oil and gas exploration and extraction, hunting, and trapping are allowed. Many existing national preserves, without sport hunting, would qualify for national park designation.

**National Recreation Area:** Centered on either water- or urban-based recreation. Urban parks combine scarce open spaces with the preservation of significant historic resources and important natural areas

---

| | |
|---|---|
| 1988 | Devastating fires raged through Yellowstone, spreading to 793,000 of the park's 2.2 million acres. One of the fires, which consumed over 410,000 acres, was caused by a discarded cigarette. |
| 1994 | Death Valley and Joshua Tree national monuments each become national parks. |
| 2001 | President Bush announces the National Parks Legacy Project to provide funds to restore and improve park facilites and landscapes, and increase park trails. |
| 2004 | Great Sand Dunes becomes the newest national park. |
| 2007 | Congress is presented with a record $2.4-billion budget for the parks, plus a $100-million donation match program as part of President Bush's National Park's Centennial Initiative. |

# NATIONAL PARK SERVICE THEN & NOW

in a location that can provide outdoor recreation for large numbers of people.

## Hot Issues

More than a century ago, conservationists were instrumental in establishing the parks as preserved areas; their efforts continue today, as the environmental and cultural landscape presents a host of challenges to these preserved areas. Overcrowding, noise and light pollution, and wildlife management loom large on the horizon. And of course, funding is consistently a concern. Here are a few of the issues facing the National Park Service today:

**Pollution.** Standing in a pristine natural paradise like Yellowstone or the Grand Canyon, pollution will probably be the furthest thing from your mind—but the problem encompasses more than just visible smog. As development encroaches on the parks, it brings the bright lights of the city one step closer to the wilderness. The resulting light pollution causes dimmer skies with fewer stars, which can be disappointing for visitors and deadly for disoriented birds who mistake the urban glow for moonlight and fly into buildings. Meanwhile, noise pollution, much of it from aircraft, threatens to break the silence that many visitors seek in the parks. This is especially true at the Grand Canyon. There are also other factors putting the parks' air, water, and land at risk. High ozone levels in Sequoia National Park, for example, can cause respiratory irritation and are damaging Jeffrey pines.

**Attendance.** As the parks compete with an ever-expanding range of entertainment options, attendance has been on the decline. A major challenge for the coming century will be attracting an increasingly busy, plugged-in population to visit the wilderness. Paradoxically, the most popular parks are facing the opposite problem—making

sure huge seasonal crowds don't negatively impact the wilderness.

**Migration Patterns.** Managing wildlife is an increasingly complex responsibility. The parks' animal inhabitants don't recognize boundaries: Elk stray into the areas around Rocky Mountain, and wolves hunt beyond the confines of Yellowstone, killing animals on nearby ranches.

**Funding.** Tight budgets force the parks to consider alternative revenue sources, including corporate sponsorships. And while you won't be seeing "McDonald's Grand Canyon" or "Half Dome, brought to you by Coca-Cola" anytime soon, adding a corporation's name to even a bench introduces advertisements into a previously commercial-free zone.

## What's Next for the NPS

The National Park Service is looking forward to its centennial celebration in 2016. President George W. Bush has a vision for the parks called "Centennial Challenge," which he launched in spring 2001 with the National Parks Legacy Project. It earmarks funding for capital improvements at the parks. Since then, 6,000 park improvements have been completed or are underway. One such initiative was the state-of-the-art visitor center at Yellowstone that opened in 2006. It was the first major facility improvement at that park in 30 years. However, operating budgets at the parks have suffered greatly the past several years. That is set to change with President Bush's new National Park's Centennial Initiative, which calls for up to $3 billion in funds over the next 10 years.

*Acknowldegments:* We thank the Department of the Interior for their helpful resources, including *A Brief History of the National Park Service.*

# THE
# ROOSEVELT
# TOUCH

**WITHOUT THEODORE ROOSEVELT AND FRANKLIN ROOSEVELT,** many of America's natural treasures would have ceased to exist. A generation apart, the two men were moved by the dire state of their nation to ramrod monumental changes in how the country preserved its outdoor wonders.

For Theodore, it was his disappointment in the disappearance of the bison and rampant misuse of the land in the western United States. For Franklin, it was the necessity of providing work for an unemployed population; work that could help save the country's ravaged forestland. Both men, through sheer force of will, drove their ideals into law.

Theodore, who believed America had an almost divine responsibility for proper stewardship of its ample resources, brought his conservation leanings to the presidency in 1901. As part of his revolutionary administration, he established the U.S. Forest Service, along with 150 national forests; the first national wildlife refuge; 51 bird preserves; four game preserves; five national parks; and 18 national monuments, including four that became national parks—Grand Canyon, Petrified Forest, Lassen Peak, and Mount Olympus (Olympic). His foresight accounted for more than half of the lands to be managed by the National Park Service when it was created in 1916—seven years after his presidency ended.

Franklin, who believed the president was called to lead with character and morality, thought it imperative to rescue the country from the throes of the Great Depression. One solution was the provision of jobs on public works. Almost immediately after Franklin's inauguration in 1933, the Civilian Conservation Corps was de-veloped. Over nine years, it employed 5 percent of American males and planted about 3 billion trees. The corps was instrumental in suppressing forest fires, clearing campgrounds, constructing roads and trails, controlling floods and soil erosion, and eradicating undesirable plants. The CCC also enabled the National Park Service to improve existing public lands, establish new national parks, and guide the development of a system of state parks. Seven states gained their first state parks through the CCC's efforts, and at the project's end in 1942, a total of 711 state parks had been established. Additionally, Franklin added his Hyde Park, N.Y., home to the NPS holdings.

Though the inspiration for each differed, their contributions were similar, as are their legacies. They stand as giants among American presidents and as standard-bearers for government-aided conservation.

–Gary Peterson

---

**DYNAMIC DUO**

**TEDDY**
**Lifespan:** 1858–1919
**Saying:** "Speak softly and carry a big stick."
**Regulated:** Railroads
**Unique qualities:** Youngest president (age 42); won Nobel Peace Prize (for mediating the Russo-Japanese War)

**FDR**
**Lifespan:** 1882–1945
**Saying:** "The only thing we have to fear, is fear itself."
**Regulated:** Wall Street
**Unique qualities:** Only president with polio; only four-term president; established the WPA (Works Progress Administration)

by Marge
Peterson

# GREAT LODGES
# OF THE NATIONAL PARKS

Union Pacific helped finance lodges at Bryce and Zion, Northern Pacific was behind the hotels in Yellowstone, and the Great Northern Railway built Glacier Park Lodge, many Glacier Hotels, and the Prince of Wales Hotel. Today, the rails don't drive tourism to the parks all that much. But the lodges still do. And you don't have to be wealthy to stay in one.

**"IF YOU BUILD IT, THEY WILL COME"** could apply to the railroad companies who laid track in the early 1900s to lure wealthy Easterners westward. But these scrappy companies took the declaration an inspired step further by building luxury hotels at the end of the line.

*Architects felt guests would be happy as long as the lodges had creature comforts.*

The Atchison, Topeka, and Santa Fe Railway finished a 65-mile railroad spur from Williams, Arizona, to the South Rim of the Grand Canyon and built the spectacular Arizona lodge El Tovar.

What makes them great? Unlike previous wilderness accommodations that were built like city hotels so guests would feel safe, these new lodges incorporated materials from the environment like the lodgepole pines and Rhyolite stone used in building Old Faithful Inn. As long as these nature-inspired structures had creature comforts, which then, and in some cases now—doesn't include in-room televisions—architects felt guests would be happy.

*Opposite:* Balconies claw skyward in the Old Faithful Inn's 76-foot high lobby. *This page:* Rocking on the deck of El Tovar, on the Grand Canyon's South Rim.

# TOP LODGES

## El Tovar, Grand Canyon

"In the Grand Canyon, Arizona has a natural wonder, which, so far as I know, is in kind unparalleled throughout the rest of the world," said Teddy Roosevelt in 1903, speaking from the area where the El Tovar would open two years later. "What you can do is to keep it for your children, your children's children, and for all who come after you, as one of the great sights which every American if he can travel at all should see."

Set atop the South Rim of the Grand Canyon, El Tovar so blends into the landscape, with its stone, wood, and earthy tones, that it looks almost like another tier of the multilayered, multihued canyon. With the elegance of a European villa and warm atmosphere of a rustic log cabin, it is arguably the most luxurious of the lodges.

Opened in 1905, El Tovar was named for Spanish explorer Don Pedro de Tobar (the "b" was changed to "v" to avoid the mispronunciation "to the bar") and was designed by architect Charles Whittlesey. Built for $250,000, it had 95 rooms, electricity, indoor plumbing, steam heat, solariums, and lounges. Originally, Jersey cows and poultry grazed on site, and greenhouses provided fresh herbs and flowers for guests feasting in the dining room. One of its most famous diners and overnight guests was **Teddy Roosevelt** *(pictured)*, who came to dinner in muddy boots and dusty riding gear—or so says local lore. In addition to Roosevelt, seven other presidents have stayed here. For its 100th birthday, the hotel received a $4.6 million restoration.

**Ahwahnee, Yosemite**

Blending into a backdrop of granite cliffs, the elegant Ahwahnee Lodge *(above)*, which opened in 1927, is six stories tall with three wings in a "Y" layout. NPS Director Stephen Mather believed that attracting wealthy, influential folks into Yosemite would lend support and congressional funding to the national parks system.

Architect Gilbert Stanley Underwood was commissioned to build a first-class fireproof hotel that blended in with the landscape. In order to resist fire, concrete was formed within timbers and then dyed to resemble redwood. The motifs and patterns found in the basketry of the local Indian tribes were used on the ceiling beams, stained-glass windows, and concrete floors. Luminaries who have signed the lodge guest book include Franklin and Eleanor Roosevelt, John F. Kennedy, Queen Elizabeth, and Clark Gable.

## Old Faithful, Yellowstone

Shock and awe may best describe the re-action of people entering the lobby of Old Faithful Inn *(below)* in Yellowstone Park. Its 76-foot high lobby has four levels of balconies with supports created with gnarled branches from a tangle of trees reaching the ceiling. Construction costs of $140,000 were financed by the North-ern Pacific Railroad and the Yellowstone Park Association. Wings were added to the hotel in 1915 and 1927—it would be difficult to duplicate the inn's construc-tion today, since cutting down trees, gath-ering wood, and quarrying rock inside the park are now illegal.

The park's most famous geyser, Old Faithful, is less than 100 yards from the inn. Approximate times for the geyser's eruptions are posted in the lobby.

### WHAT TO EXPECT

Some lodges were built more than 100 years ago, when rooms and beds were smaller. However, the difference in room size is more than offset by the huge amount of public space offered on the properties. The availability of television and Internet access varies from lodge to lodge.

### Bryce Canyon Lodge

Bryce Canyon Lodge *(above)* was the second structure built in the Union Pa-cific's Loop Tours building program, which included Cedar Breaks, Zion, the North Rim of the Grand Canyon, and a stop at Kaibab National Forest. In a grove of ponderosa pines within walking distance of the rim, the lodge opened in 1925 with 70 guest rooms, three deluxe suites, one studio room, and 40 log cab-ins. The property was known for its sing-aways, where employees lined up in front of the lodge and sang a farewell to de-parting guests. When plans to build an-other lodge on the rim didn't materialize, a gift shop, soda fountain, barbershop, and auditorium were added.

### Glacier Park Lodge

An eclectic interior design with towering tree trunks highlights Glacier Park Lodge *(below right and page 22)*. Samuel L. Bartlett was the architect of record, but Louis Hill, president of the Great Northern Railway, controlled every aspect of the design. Hill patterned the lodge, which opened in 1913, after the Oregon Forestry Building he saw at the Lewis & Clark Exposition in Portland. He had 60 Douglas firs (40 feet high and 40 inches in diameter) shipped in from the Northwest for the colonnade.

When rail passengers arrived at Glacier Park Station, they saw Indian teepees scattered across the lawn as part of a show presented to visitors, colorful banks of flowers, and the majestic lodge, all set against the backdrop of Glacier National Park.

The park and lodge were heavily promoted. On top of the half a million dollars it took to build and furnish Glacier Park Lodge, Hill spent $300,000 on artists, filmmakers, calendars, playing cards, and a special train car with a public exhibit. The *New York Times* said, "Next to Col. Roosevelt, L.W. Hill is about the best advertising man in the United States."

### Crater Lake Lodge

When Crater Lake Lodge *(above)* opened in 1915, it was anything but grand: The exterior was covered in tarpaper, fiberboard separated the guest rooms, bathrooms were shared, and electricity seldom worked. But visitors loved it anyway because of the lake view. Due to its structural defects, the $30,000 building was closed to the public in 1989. Public admiration swayed Congress to grant $15 million for renovations, and the lodge was completely rebuilt and reopened in May 1995. Perched on the rim of a defunct caldera filled with cobalt blue water, the lodge has a fanstastic deck as well as an architectural trademark, a massive stone fireplace.

## Lake Louise & Banff Springs

In the late 1800s, William Cornelius Van Horne, general manager of the Canadian Pacific Railway, said, "Since we can't export the scenery, we will have to import the tourists." And so they did. The railroad developed Fairmont Banff Springs Hotel (*right*) and the Fairmont Chateau Lake Louise, both of which opened their doors in 1890.

While the great lodges of America's national parks have a comfortable hunting-lodge aura, the Banff and Lake Louise accommodations have a stately, opulent ambience.

Fairmont Banff Springs, a mile walk from downtown Banff, is styled after a Scottish baronial castle. Combining the best of the past with the amenities sought by modern-day travelers, the hotel offers tennis, golf, bowling, horseback rides, indoor and outdoor swimming, and one of the largest spas in Canada.

Surrounded by snow-tipped mountain peaks and the majestic Victorian Glacier, Chateau Lake Louise is on the shore of pristine Lake Louise, where you can hike, downhill or cross-country ski, cycle, and canoe.

## OTHER GREAT LODGES

**Belton Chalet**–Glacier National Park

**Grand Canyon Lodge**–North Rim, Grand Canyon National Park

**Lake McDonald Lodge**–Glacier National Park

**Many Glacier Hotel**–Glacier National Park

**Paradise Inn**–Mount Rainier National Park (closed for renovation until May 2008)

**Prince of Wales Hotel**–Waterton Lakes National Park

**Sperry and Granite Park Chalets**–Glacier National Park

**Zion Park Lodge**–Zion National Park

### TO RESERVE A ROOM

Reservations should be made six months to a year in advance directly with the lodge's Internet sites; however, you can always check for last-minute cancellations. Be wary of other Internet reservation services that charge a non-refundable fee of up to 12 percent to book the lodging.

**DID YOU KNOW?**

Visitors to Glacier can take a tour that includes stays at four of the park's great lodges. The Douglas fir support pillars in the lobby of Glacier Park Lodge (shown here), are over 40 feet tall. When it first opened, the Blackfeet natives called it "Omahkoyis," meaning "Big Tree Lodge."

Moraine Lake, Banff National Park

**WORD OF MOUTH**

"We need the tonic of wilderness."

–Henry David Thoreau

# WHAT'S
# WHERE

| ARCHES | |
|---|---|
|  | **Location:** Southeastern Utah<br>**Known for:** The largest concentration of natural sandstone arches.<br>**Biggest crowds:** Spring and fall<br>**Accessibility:** Many of the arches can be viewed from your car.<br>**Why kids like it:** Walking through rock windows and playing in sand dunes is like taking a trip to Mars.<br>**What hikers say:** Awe-inspiring scenery and thrilling walks on the tops of sandstone fins make this place hard to forget.<br><br>Only four hours from Salt Lake City, this southern Utah park is easy to visit. Canyonlands National Park and the deep chasm of Dead Horse Point State Park are nearby, as is Moab, the adventure mecca of the West, which has world-class white-water rafting on the Colorado River, rock climbing, four-wheeling, and mountain biking. You can also view ancient Native American rock art nearby. |

UTAH

| BADLANDS | |
|---|---|
|  | **Location:** Southwestern South Dakota<br>**Known for:** Eroded buttes and spires that cast amazing shades of red and yellow across the South Dakota prairie.<br>**Biggest crowds:** Early August<br>**Accessibility:** Located just off Interstate 90, Badlands National Park offers a breathtaking loop tour with scenic overlooks and beautiful picnic areas.<br>**Why kids like it:** Seeing a real missile silo is cool!<br>**What hikers say:** The best way to view this unworldly area is up-close and personal on the hiking trails.<br><br>Journeying to Badlands National Park is like stepping onto another planet. With its unique and colorful buttes and spires, the area offers scenery that even the world's greatest artists would struggle to recreate. |

SOUTH DAKOTA

| BANFF | |
|---|---|
|  | **Location:** Alberta, Canada<br>**Known for:** Stunning mountain scenery, wildlife, and natural hot springs.<br>**Biggest crowds:** July and August<br>**Accessibility:** An extensive road network allows access to hiking trails, ski resorts, glaciers, lakes, and other attractions.<br>**Why kids like it:** Interpretive programs help kids learn about bears, wolves, fire, photography, human history, and outdoor adventure.<br>**What hikers say:** Great trails for beginners and experienced backcountry hikers alike lead to spectacular scenic vistas and natural wonders. |

ALBERTA

Canada's first national park—the third in the world—Banff is located 80 mi (128 km) west of Calgary, Alberta, encompassing 2,564 square mi (6,641 square km) of valleys, mountains, glaciers, forests, meadows, and rivers. Visit during the summer months to see wildlife and hike mountain trails, or come in winter for some of the world's best skiing. When you're done, visit the bustling Banff townsite, which is packed with shops and restaurants.

## BIG BEND

TEXAS

**Location:** Southwestern Texas
**Known for:** Limitless skies and lots of space.
**Biggest crowds:** Thanksgiving, Christmas, and spring break
**Accessibility:** The prettiest sites, like the Chisos Mountains, are accessible by road.
**Why kids like it:** Rangers routinely throw star-viewing parties, and there's a hot spring to swim in.
**What hikers say:** With 800,000 acres to traverse as they please, solitude-seekers will experience Nirvana here.

Located about 300 mi south of El Paso and 430 mi west of San Antonio, this enormous park is best known for its size, its remote location, and the Rio Grande River, which forms its southern border. Visitors can experience the rough beauty of the Chisos Mountains, which form the park's center, or hike through desert, forest, or river valley in a silence broken only by wildlife.

## BLACK CANYON OF THE GUNNISON

COLORADO

**Location:** Western Colorado
**Known for:** A river gorge with sheer cliffs as deep as 2,722 feet (at Warner Point).
**Biggest crowds:** Summer (especially July)
**Accessibility:** Numerous overlooks can be reached via South Rim and North Rim roads.
**Why kids like it:** It's a long, long way down to the river.
**What hikers say:** Hiking trails to the inner canyon are strenuous, unmarked, and unmaintained—but their beauty is unmatched.

Approximately 250 mi southwest of Denver, Black Canyon of the Gunnison is located between Curecanti National Recreation Area and Gunnison Gorge National Conservation Area, an incredible paradise for outdoor enthusiasts. There is no public transportation available within the park, and since there isn't a bridge connecting the two sides of the canyon, it can take upwards of three hours to drive from one to the other.

# WHAT'S
# WHERE

## BRYCE CANYON

UTAH

**Location:** Southern Utah
**Known for:** Bright, red-orange rocks in bizarre shapes.
**Biggest crowds:** July through September
**Accessibility:** You can view much of the park from scenic overlooks along the road.
**Why kids like it:** Exploring the hoodoos is like wandering through a giant maze.
**What hikers say:** You'll see some amazing colors at sunrise and sunset at the naturally carved-out amphitheaters.

Just 4½ hours from Las Vegas and Salt Lake City, this 36,000-acre park is located near Zion, Capital Reef, Arches, and Canyonlands national parks. It's also not too far from the Grand Canyon in Arizona; Utah's Kodachrome Basin State Park, featuring sand pipes once thought to be geysers; Grand Staircase-Escalante National Monument, with its labyrinths of slot canyons; and Red Canyon, a favorite Butch Cassidy hideout.

## CANYONLANDS

UTAH

**Location:** Southeastern Utah
**Known for:** Biking on White Rim Road, whitewater rafting, and canyons as far as the eye can see.
**Biggest crowds:** Spring and fall
**Accessibility:** It's easy to see three mountain ranges and countless canyons.
**Why kids like it:** They'll almost be able to see home from here—no matter where home is!
**What hikers say:** You'll find some of the best hikes in the world here.

Canyonlands is one of the least visited national parks in the country, a place to find solitude as bald eagles and red-tail hawks float above you. Just four hours from Salt Lake City, the park is home to world-class whitewater rafting on the Colorado River, as well as great mountain biking, four-wheeling, rock-climbing, and hiking.

## CAPITOL REEF

UTAH

**Location:** Southern Utah
**Known for:** The 100-mile long Waterpocket Fold.
**Biggest crowds:** Spring and early summer
**Accessibility:** Many of the park's historic sites are close to the road.
**Why kids like it:** Picking fruit in the orchards at historic Fruita and seeing mule deer up close.
**What hikers say:** A huge backcountry plus light traffic equals solitude and beauty.

Capitol Reef is 378 square mi of solitude; its distance from major cities keeps visitation relatively low compared to Bryce Canyon and Zion national parks. Most people who make the trek here focus their visit on historic Fruita village and the Scenic Drive, but there's much more to see here.

## CARLSBAD CAVERNS

NEW MEXICO

**Location:** Southwestern New Mexico
**Known for:** 300,000 diving, dipping, sonar-blipping bats.
**Biggest crowds:** Late May through early August
**Accessibility:** You'll need to head underground to see the park's true highlights—three of Carlsbad's largest caverns are fully lit and inset with audio guides, and several guided tours are available to less-visited portions.
**Why kids like it:** Watching a swarm of bats leave the caverns for a night of insect hunting.
**What hikers say:** While most of the hiking is underground, the above-ground sights—such as rocks shaped like bones, straws, mushrooms, and faces—are spectacular.

Carlsbad Caverns is famous for its hordes of hungry bats and bizarre underground formations. Visitors reach the caverns via an elevator that plunges 75 stories down to a veritable Underworld of shadows and eerily twisted rock. The park is 27 mi from the town of Carlsbad, which holds both the Pecos River and the Living Desert Zoo and Gardens.

## CHANNEL ISLANDS

CALIFORNIA

**Location:** Southern California
**Known for:** Pristine land- and seascapes with an exceptional variety of marine and terrestrial plants and animals—145 species here are found nowhere else on the planet.
**Biggest crowds:** Holidays and summer weekends
**Accessibility:** Visitors must travel to the islands by boat or plane.
**Why kids like it:** They get to meet lots of California critters, like dolphins, sea lions, whales, and rare birds.
**What hikers say:** You can trek into blissfully uncrowded, serene, wilderness areas—with miles of trails and spectacular views from nearly every vantage point.

This five-island park, which includes a nautical mile of underwater preserve surrounding each island, is the ultimate destination for nature lovers who want to really "get away from it all." Although it's just 60 mi northwest of Los Angeles, the Channel Islands are worlds away from the urban sprawl and tangled freeways on the mainland. The park is accessible by

# WHAT'S
# WHERE

boat from harbors in Ventura and Oxnard (about an hour north of Los Angeles) and Santa Barbara (about 1½ hours north of Los Angeles); trips take from 45 minutes to three hours plus, depending on the island you're visiting. There are no phones, no services, and no cars here, but you can hike, kayak, snorkel, dive, fish, swim, camp, and commune with nature.

## CRATER LAKE

OREGON

**Location:** Southern Oregon
**Known for:** Being the seventh deepest lake in the world.
**Biggest crowds:** July and August
**Accessibility:** The park has a short summer tourist season; access during most other times is contingent upon road conditions.
**Why kids like it:** You can take a cool boat ride in the middle of the caldera.
**What hikers say:** Talk about seclusion! So many trails, so little time.

Crater Lake is a geologic marvel and a hiker's paradise. The star of the park is the 21-square-mi sapphire blue expanse of the nation's deepest lake, which draws visitors from around the world. The area's volcanic past is apparent everywhere, and the park is filled with the unhurried, untamed, and untouched essence of solitude. There are no major towns around the lake, and Crater Lake Village is non-commercialized.

## DEATH VALLEY

CALIFORNIA

**Location:** Southern California
**Known for:** Breathtaking vistas, blasting 120-degree heat, mysterious moving rocks, and being the lowest point in the Western hemisphere.
**Biggest crowds:** Late fall through early spring (though rarely crowded even then)
**Accessibility:** You'll need a vehicle to get around the vast park; 4x4s are required on some back-country roads.
**Why kids like it:** The park has a *Star Wars* feel to it—which makes sense, since this was the location for the film's Tattoine (desert planet) scenes.
**What hikers say:** Don't venture out into this park without adequate clothing, sun protection, food, and water—even in the winter. The desert is very unforgiving.

The largest national park in the contiguous United States, Death Valley is a vast, lonely, beautiful place. This desert landscape is surrounded by majestic mountains, dry lake beds, and other ge-

ological wonders. From Furnace Creek Visitors Center, Baker is about 113 mi to the southeast, Las Vegas is about 141 mi to the east, and Los Angeles is roughly 294 mi southwest.

## GLACIER-WATERTON

MONTANA

**Location:** Southwestern Alberta, Canada, and northwestern Montana

**Known for:** Great hiking, and for being the world's first international peace park, created as a symbol of goodwill between Canada and the United States.

**Biggest crowds:** Early July through mid-September

**Accessibility:** The Going to the Sun Road, a national historic civil engineering landmark, has unparalleled views of both sides of the Continental Divide.

**Why kids like it:** There are plenty of short hikes that lead to scenic spots, fun boat trips to enjoy, and excellent interpretive programs in both national parks.

**What hikers say:** Voted "Best Overall National Park" by readers of *Backpacker* magazine, Glacier National Park is world-renowned for its backcountry trails and wilderness areas. There are 730 mi (1,175 km) of hiking trails in Glacier, and another 114 mi (183 km) in Waterton.

The rugged mountains that weave their way through the Continental Divide seem to have glaciers in every hollow, melting into tiny streams, raging rivers, and ice-cold mountain lakes.

## GRAND CANYON

ARIZONA

**Location:** Northwestern Arizona

**Known for:** Unsurpassed natural wonder.

**Biggest crowds:** Summer and spring break

**Accessibility:** The popular Rim Trail and all the viewpoints along the South Rim are accessible by wheelchair.

**Why kids like it:** The mule rides, the river rafting, the fossil walks . . .and perhaps watching Grandma scream when she sees a snake or scorpion.

**What hikers say:** Camping at the bottom under the stars is a once-in-a-lifetime experience.

The Grand Canyon, one of nature's longest-running works in progress, both exalts and humbles the human spirit. You can view the spectacle from the South Rim, but the North Rim is the rim less traveled. Don't just peer over the edge—take the plunge into the canyon on a mule train, on foot, or on a raft trip.

# WHAT'S
# WHERE

## GRAND TETON

WYOMING

**Location:** Northwestern Wyoming
**Known for:** Jagged mountain peaks and diverse wildlife.
**Biggest crowds:** July and August
**Accessibility:** Much of the park can be viewed from roadside overlooks.
**Why kids like it:** They can see wild animals and experience the mountains on foot, on horseback, or from a boat.
**What hikers say:** Grand Teton has trails for every skill level, from simple strolls around mountain lakes to steep treks.

You might think Grand Teton National Park would suffer in comparison to its larger, more historic neighbor to the north—Yellowstone—but when you see the Tetons rising out of Jackson Hole, you realize that the park is its own spectacular destination. Jackson Hole, the valley to the east of the Tetons, is home to world-class skiing—there are literally thousands of ways to get down the slopes. The town of Jackson, located within the valley, maintains its small-town charm while serving as the area's cultural center.

## GREAT BASIN

NEVADA

**Location:** Southern Nevada
**Known for:** The Lehman Caves and ancient bristlecone pines.
**Biggest crowds:** Summer
**Accessibility:** A scenic drive leads to Lehman Caves and 13,063-foot Wheeler Peak.
**Why kids like it:** The Lehman Caves are unlike anything they've ever seen.
**What hikers say:** This is a great place for solitary backcountry experiences.

Roughly 4 hours from both Las Vegas and Salt Lake City, Great Basin is one of the nation's least-visited national parks, attracting fewer than 100,000 visitors each year. There isn't even an entry fee—but don't let any of this give the wrong impression; the park may be off the beaten path, but it still contains plenty of natural wonders.

## GREAT SAND DUNES

COLORADO

**Location:** Southern Colorado
**Known for:** Its land-locked towering sand dunes
**Biggest crowds:** June through August
**Accessibility:** The road only goes from the park entrance to the visitor center; you'll want to walk or hike the dunes.
**Why kids like it:** They can play in the sand, build sand castles, and slide down the dunes on saucers.

**What hikers say:** Climb the High Dune for the most scenic view of the dunes; walk in the Preserve to trek on wooded trails to a fabulous view of 13,000-foot mountains.

South-central Colorado's Great Sand Dunes National Park and Preserve stretches from the mountain watersheds to the wetlands, encompassing massive dunes, plus unique hydrological and geological systems. The nation's newest national park—designated on September 13, 2004—is much bigger than the original national monument that only included the dunes. Six mountains in the Sangre de Cristo mountains, which all top out more than 13,000 feet above sea level, are also in the preserve. The park is about five hours from Denver via I-25; Highway 285 offers a more scenic route through the mountains.

## GUADALUPE MOUNTAINS

TEXAS

**Location:** West Texas
**Known for:** Several lofty peaks, including the tallest in Texas.
**Biggest crowds:** Spring break and fall (though rarely crowded even then)
**Accessibility:** It's easy to access the park from the highway, and guides are available for all of the popular trails. You can see the mountains from the highway.
**Why kids like it:** It's home to more than 300 types of birds.
**What hikers say:** Eighty miles of trails wind through the park, leading up and down rocky terrain and through lush foliage.

This rugged park is one of the least-visited in the country, but it draws thousands of visitors from surrounding states every fall, when the hardwoods of McKittrick Canyon burst into flaming color. Serious hikers make the pilgrimage here to scale 8,479-foot Guadalupe Peak. The park is located 110 miles northeast of El Paso; it's also not far from the famed Carlsbad Caverns, 40 miles north.

## JASPER

ALBERTA

**Location:** Southwestern Alberta, Canada
**Known for:** Being largest of the Canadian Rocky Mountain National Parks at 4,200 square mi (10,878 square km)—and one of the largest protected mountain ecosystems in the world.
**Biggest crowds:** July and August
**Accessibility:** Wildlife, scenery, and natural areas can be easily viewed from roads and viewpoints.
**Why kids like it:** Modern amusements pale in comparison to spotting elk, bighorn sheep, or black bears and learning about nature, wildlife, mountains, and lakes.

# WHAT'S WHERE

**What hikers say:** The park's 746 mi (1,200 km) of hiking trails take you to scenic viewpoints, past raging waterfalls, through wildflower-carpeted meadows, and to the Columbia Icefield, one of the largest accumulations of snow and ice south of the arctic circle.

Sir Arthur Conan Doyle put it well when he wrote the following in the Jasper Park Lodge's visitor's book in 1923: "A New York man reached heaven, and as he passed the gate, Peter said, 'I'm sure you will like it.' A Pittsburgh man followed and Peter said, 'It will be a very great change for you.' Finally there came a man from Jasper Park. 'I'm afraid,' said Peter, 'that you will be disappointed.' "

## JOSHUA TREE

CALIFORNIA

**Location:** Southern California
**Known for:** World-class rock climbing, stunning desert scenery.
**Biggest crowds:** October through May
**Accessibility:** Much of the park can be seen from the roads that wind through its interior. Nature trails at Cap Rock, Oasis of Mara (adjacent to the visitor center), and Bajada are wheelchair accessible, as is Keys View overlook. There is an accessible campsite at Jumbo Rocks Campground.
**Why kids like it:** Giant piles of rocks are great places to play hide and seek—and encounter some strange critters.
**What hikers say:** Inspiring desert views lurk around almost every bend on the park's hiking trails.

Due to its proximity to major urban areas, 794,000-acre Joshua Tree National Park is one of the most visited in the United States. One of three desert national parks in California, Joshua Tree lies 140 mi east of Los Angeles, 175 mi northeast of San Diego, and 215 mi southwest of Las Vegas. Come to Joshua Tree to enjoy brilliant wildflower displays, starry nights, and solitude.

## LASSEN VOLCANIC

CALIFORNIA

**Location:** Northern California
**Known for:** Mt. Lassen, a dormant volcano that last erupted in 1915—plus roiling mud pots, hissing steam vents, and other geothermal activity.
**Biggest crowds:** Mid-July through mid-September
**Accessibility:** You can take in stunning views of Mt. Lassen—plus many of the park's major geological features—from the main road. Miles of hiking trails lead to waterfalls, meadows, and geothermal areas like Bumpass Hell.

**Why kids like it:** Anything that simultaneously belches and emits a sulphury "rotten egg" smell is very, very cool.

**What hikers say:** Whether you hike Mt. Lassen on a clear day or scale it with a guide under a full moon, the experience is unforgettable.

About 250 mi northeast of San Francisco, Lassen Volcanic National Park's spectacular geologic wonders and geothermal activity make it one of the most unusual—and intriguing—parks to visit. You'll find more than 150 mi of hiking trails, countless mountain lakes and streams, and canyon overlooks, plus wildlife and wildflowers galore.

## MESA VERDE

COLORADO

**Location:** Southwestern Colorado

**Known for:** Hundreds of ancestral Puebloan cliff dwellings.

**Biggest crowds:** Mid-June through August

**Accessibility:** You can see some of the park from scenic road overlooks, but taking a guided hike is your best bet.

**Why kids like it:** You don't see clusters of ancient stone houses on cliffs every day!

**What hikers say:** Be aware that hiking is restricted, and you're sometimes required to have a ranger as a guide.

Located in the Four Corners region—the junction of Colorado, Arizona, Utah, and New Mexico—Mesa Verde is far enough away from major cities that the night skies blaze with stars. Denver is around 400 mi away; Phoenix is about 450 mi from the park; Salt Lake City is 372 mi to the northwest; and Albuquerque is 267 mi to the south.

## MOUNT RAINIER

WASHINGTON

**Location:** Southwestern Washington

**Known for:** Being—some say—the most magical mountain in America.

**Biggest crowds:** July through September

**Accessibility:** You can drive up winding mountain roads to view the summit cone or the wildflowers that carpet the alpine meadows. Hop onto the trails to walk through a wilderness of enormous trees and ancient glaciers.

**Why kids like it:** Visiting an active volcano is really cool!

**What hikers say:** Enjoy more than 240 mi of maintained trails—or seek real adventure by summiting Mt. Rainier.

The fifth highest mountain in the lower 48, Mt. Rainier is so massive that the summit is rarely visible—but when conditions

# WHAT'S WHERE

are right, the image of the entire mountain is unforgettable. Skirted around the base of Rainier are cathedral-like groves of Douglas fir, western hemlock, and western red cedar—some more than 1,000 years old. Massive glaciers and dozens of thundering waterfalls are accessible from the road or via short hikes.

## NORTH CASCADES

WASHINGTON

**Location:** Northwestern Washington
**Known for:** Stunning, snow-covered mountain panoramas and pine-ringed glacial lakes.
**Biggest crowds:** Snowmelt through early September, especially weekends and holidays
**Accessibility:** Highway 20 runs between the park's north and south units; Lake Chelan towns can only be reached by boat or floatplane. Note that park access is limited from November to April.
**Why kids like it:** Wildlife sightings are frequent, and many trails and activities are geared toward youngsters of all ages.
**What hikers say:** Every season brings visual thrills: spring wildflowers, summer waterfalls, autumn leaves, and winter snows. The stretch of Cascade peaks provides endless challenges for hikers of all levels.

This 505,000-acre expanse of montane wilderness contains more than half of the glaciers in the U.S., as well as glistening Lake Chelan, Lake Ross, and the Stehekin River. Outdoor adventure opportunities abound, from kayaking and whitewater rafting expeditions to treks along nearly 400 mi of trails. Historic pioneer homesteads and logging sites dot the park, bringing 19th-century history to life.

## OLYMPIC

WASHINGTON

**Location:** Northwestern Washington
**Known for:** Temperate rainforests, rugged coastal expanses, Sol Duc hot springs, and skiing at Hurricane Ridge.
**Biggest crowds:** June through September
**Accessibility:** Spread over several separate sections of the Olympic Peninsula, the park is easily accessible via the central Highway 101 ring road.
**Why kids like it:** The broad Hoh Rainforest trails are lined with ideal climbing sites at massive fallen logs and knotted stumps, and the west-coast beaches are natural playgrounds filled with sea stacks and tide pools.
**What hikers say:** With rainforest, mountain, and beach tracks—plus hot springs along the way—every day brings a new ad-

venture. Be on the lookout for elk, deer, bears, bald eagles, and other wildlife on the trails.

Centered on Mount Olympus and framed on three sides by water, this 922,651-acre park covers much of Washington's forest-clad Olympic Peninsula. The region is still mostly undeveloped, except for a handful of small towns around Highway 101; unpaved side roads connect this thoroughfare with interior campgrounds and coastal tracks. The park is about two hours west of Seattle and two hours northwest of Olympia.

ARIZONA

**Location:** Northeastern Arizona
**Known for:** Fallen and fossilized trees.
**Biggest crowds:** Rarely crowded
**Accessibility:** Much of the park is viewable from scenic road overlooks and short, paved hikes.
**Why kids like it:** Fossilized trees look like they're made of colored rock.
**What hikers say:** Seeing the park on foot is better than from the car, and most trails are short and paved.

Just three hours from Albuquerque and four hours from Phoenix, this 218,533-acre park is near Canyon De Chelly National Monument, where you can see ancient Native American housing and other artifacts; it's also not too far from the Grand Canyon.

CALIFORNIA

**Location:** Northern California
**Known for:** Giant coast redwoods, the tallest trees in the world.
**Biggest crowds:** Mid-June through early September
**Accessibility:** Highway 101 traverses the park north to south. Numerous secondary roads—many with unpaved sections—spool off the highway to hiking trails.
**Why kids like it:** Parts of the park feel positively prehistoric, the kind of place where kids can imagine their favorite dinosaurs coming to life.
**What hikers say:** You can hike from forests to the sea, through some of the most spectacular scenery you'll ever encounter.

Located about 300 mi north of San Francisco, Redwood National Forest has five visitors centers along a 40-mi corridor. The national park encompasses three state parks and is now a World Heritage Site and International Biosphere Reserve. Over 200 mi of trails, ranging from easy to strenuous, allow visitors to see these spectacular trees in their primitive environ-

# WHAT'S WHERE

ments. Roosevelt elk are a common site in the park, and gray whales migrate along the coast in winter and spring.

## ROCKY MOUNTAIN

COLORADO

**Location:** North-central Colorado
**Known for:** Alpine lakes and scenic peaks.
**Biggest crowds:** Summer
**Accessibility:** The park's shuttle will take you to the main sites.
**Why kids like it:** There are elk everywhere.
**What hikers say:** Remember to pace yourself, since you're at a higher elevation—but the views are definitely worth it.

The wildlands and alpine tundra of Rocky Mountain National Park are just 45 mi northwest of Boulder. Inhabited by black bears, elk, and bighorn sheep, the park has miles and miles of trails to hike, scads of 14,000-foot peaks to climb, and mountain streams and lakes to fish. Estes Park, on the banks of the Big Thompson and Fall rivers, abuts the park's eastern entrance, while Grand Lake is Rocky Mountain's considerably less-developed western gateway.

## SAGUARO

ARIZONA

**Location:** Southeastern Arizona
**Known for:** One of the densest stands of Saguaro cacti in the Sonoran Desert.
**Biggest crowds:** December through April (though rarely crowded even then)
**Accessibility:** Two scenic loop drives wind through desert lowlands and saguaro forests.
**Why kids like it:** Towering saguaros, crazy-looking critters, and indecipherable rock art make for fantastic adventures in an alien world.
**What hikers say:** Short day hikes in both districts of the park give visitors a chance to spot the desert's elusive wildlife.

The saguaro cactus, the largest of its kind in the United States, is predominantly found in southern Arizona in the western Sonora (a few of the desert giants can be found just outside the political border in California). Some of the densest saguaro forests are protected at Saguaro National Park, which is split into two districts west and east of Tucson; the better collection is found in the more interesting west district. The east district offers a paved loop road popular with cyclists, as well as extensive backcountry trails leading into the Saguaro Wilderness Area and the Rincon Mountains.

## SEQUOIA AND KINGS CANYON

**Location:** Central California
**Known for:** Groves of giant sequoias and craggy Kings River Canyon.
**Biggest crowds:** Summer (especially weekends)
**Accessibility:** You can reach about 20 percent of park land via road, including major sights such as the General Sherman Tree and Grant Grove.
**Why kids like it:** They can run around the biggest trees they've ever seen.
**What hikers say:** Stunning and secluded back-country trails meander into the hills from the floor of Kings River Canyon.

Two parks administered as one, Sequoia and Kings Canyon are perched on the western face of the southern Sierra Nevada, south of Yosemite National Park and east of Death Valley National Park. Here, ancient evergreens tower above the jagged mountain slopes, which are studded with massive granite rock formations. Cars enter the parks only from the west, via winding, steep two-lane roads: Highway 180 from Fresno and Highway 198 from Visalia. The parks are a five-hour drive from either Los Angeles or San Francisco.

## THEODORE ROOSEVELT

**Location:** Western North Dakota
**Known for:** After the untimely death of his wife, Theodore Roosevelt spent every opportunity he could on his ranch near the park that now bears his name.
**Biggest crowds:** July and August (though rarely crowded even then)
**Accessibility:** Scenic drives wind through the park's North and South units.
**Why kids like it:** There are lots of animals to see, including wild horses, elk, and bison.
**What hikers say:** The park's south unit is known for its unique hiking trails.

Theodore Roosevelt National Park's South Unit is the more commonly visited of the park's two sections. The southern entrance is located off Interstate 94 in Medora, a walkable town with museums, gift shops, and a beautiful and challenging golf course; it's also home to the world-famous Medora Musical.

# WHAT'S
# WHERE

## WIND CAVE

SOUTH DAKOTA

**Location:** Southwestern South Dakota

**Known for:** Having one of the largest caves in the world, with approximately 95 percent of the world's known boxwork formations (3–D calcite honeycomb patterns on cave walls and ceilings).

**Biggest crowds:** Early August

**Accessibility:** You can easily view the beautiful Black Hills and the grassland prairie, but to get the park's full effect, you'll need to head into the caves.

**Why kids like it:** Exploring underground caves!

**What hikers say:** There's great hiking here—both above and below ground.

Bounded by Black Hills National Forest to the West and windswept prairie to the east, Wind Cave National Park, in southwestern South Dakota, encompasses the transition between two distinct ecosystems: mountain forest and mixed grass prairie. You'll have a blast exploring the park's underground caves or viewing the abundant wildlife here.

## YELLOWSTONE

WYOMING

**Location:** Northwestern Wyoming (and parts of Idaho and Montana)

**Known for:** Extreme and consistent seismic activity, resulting in the world's most extraordinary geysers and hot springs.

**Biggest crowds:** Mid-July through mid-August

**Accessibility:** Driving in and around Yellowstone will take you past snow-capped peaks and creek-carved canyons.

**Why kids like it:** Visiting Old Faithful, the most famous active geyser, is awesome!

**What hikers say:** Enjoy day hiking through over 2.2 million acres of wilderness on over 1,100 miles of trails.

Yellowstone National Park, the oldest national park in the world, covers some 3,845 square miles of beauty and wilderness. Best known for its gushing geysers and flowing hot springs, Yellowstone National Park is an eclectic mix of all that mother nature has to offer.

## YOSEMITE

CALIFORNIA

**Location:** Central California

**Known for:** Glacier-carved Yosemite Valley, ringed by soaring granite cliffs and shimmering waterfalls.

**Biggest crowds:** Summer

**Accessibility:** Dozens of famed features lie along paved roads. A free shuttle on the valley's flat floor links attractions and services.

**Why kids like it:** There are tons of ranger programs and campfires in summer, and a kids' ski school and ice skating in winter.

**What hikers say:** You can leave the crowds behind and head for the high country trails around Tuolumne Meadows and along Tioga Road.

Spectacular Half Dome, lofty Yosemite Falls, and mind-blowing views of the southern Sierra Nevada are a few reasons why this is one of America's most-visited national parks. North of Sequoia and Kings Canyon National Parks and south of Lake Tahoe, Yosemite has 800 mi of hiking trails in an area the size of Rhode Island. Traffic arriving from San Francisco (four hours away), Los Angeles (six hours away), and other points west and south funnels in on three busy two-lane highways; from the east, only Highway 120 crosses the Sierra into the park, but it's closed late fall through spring.

**ZION**

UTAH

**Location:** Southern Utah

**Known for:** Sheer 2,000-foot cliffs and river-carved canyons.

**Biggest crowds:** April through October

**Accessibility:** Scenic drive leads to many features and easily-accessible trails.

**Why kids like it:** Swimming and tubing the Virgin River is a great antidote for the summer heat.

**What hikers say:** Hiking the Narrows and the Subway are life-list activities.

Just 2½ hours from Las Vegas and 5 hours from Salt Lake City, Zion National Park is located right next to hospitable Springdale, which is full of amenities and charm. From here you can travel quickly to Red Canyon and Bryce Canyon National Park, as well as Kanab—known as "Little Hollywood" for all of the Westerns filmed there over the years.

# THE BEST OF THE NATIONAL PARKS

## Best Parks for Accessibility

The best way to get an in-depth look at the parks is by exploring them on foot, horseback, or via some other mode of transportation, but sometimes time or physical conditioning prevents this from happening. The main sites at the following parks aren't too far off the beaten path—many are even visible from the comfort of your car.

- **Bryce.** An 18-mi road with numerous overlooks and a handful of spurs provides fabulous views of this park's famous red-orange hoodoos and points beyond. If you want to journey beyond the overlooks, several nearby trailheads offer quick escapes into the park's interior.

- **Mesa Verde.** Once the main park road passes the Morefield Campground, it forks, and the two branches lead to the archaeological treasures of the Wetherill and Chapin Mesas, respectively. Most sites are close enough to be viewed from the road, but short trails lead in for a closer look.

- **Petrified Forest.** Whether you enter from the north or the south entrance, the 28-mi park road leads to both visitor centers and a handful of quick and easy trails that meander among petrified trees. You can view most of the park's better known sites from your car.

## Best Parks for Burning Calories

The national parks are great places for a workout. Whether you walk, run, ski, row, or bike, you'll rarely have an excuse not to keep up with your exercise regimen while you're on vacation here. Hard-core fitness junkies should check out the following parks, which are particularly well-suited for extreme exertion.

- **Black Canyon of the Gunnison.** The Painted Wall, Colorado's tallest vertical wall at 2,250 feet, is just one of the major rock faces that attract the cream of the climbing crop to this rugged park, known for its dizzying heights. Most areas are best attempted by advanced and expert climbers, but less-skilled enthusiasts can try their hands at the Marmot Rocks bouldering area.

- **Canyonlands.** Three distinct areas, or districts—Island in the Sky, The Maze, and The Needles—comprise this popular but spacious national park; each one offers plenty of opportunities to put boot sole to sandstone and become totally immersed in sun and solitude. The Maze is your best bet for getting away from it all—you can only reach it by driving at least 20 miles on lonely dirt roads.

- **Mount Rainier.** Mt. Rainier is encircled by the aptly named Wonderland Trail—a whopping 93-mi trek that takes 10–14 days to complete. It's as rugged as it is long; elevation gains and losses of 3,500 feet in a day are not uncommon. Snow hangs around higher elevations into June and even July, and rain can appear at almost any time. The faint of heart and tender of sole should tramp elsewhere.

## Best Parks for Cultural History

When you're surrounded by such overwhelming natural beauty and so many opportunities to take part in outdoor activities, it's easy to overlook the parks' cultural attractions. But it would be a shame to miss out on a history lesson during your visit, whether it's touring an ancient dwelling, witnessing a historical reenactment, or visiting a great American icon.

- **Mesa Verde.** Established in 1906, Mesa Verde was the first national park to "preserve the works of man," according to President Theodore Roosevelt. The ancestral Pueblo people lived here from AD 600 to AD 1300, and to date more than 4,000 archaeological sites—including 600 cave dwellings—have been unearthed. Today, researchers continue to discover and catalogue artifacts at Mesa Verde on a regular basis.

- **Petrified Forest.** The roots at this park aren't just from its ancient trees: the area's human history and culture extend back more than 10,000 years, from pre-historic people to the more modern travelers of Route 66. You can still see petroglyphs scratched and carved into stone by the ancestors of the Hopi, Zuni, and Navajo.

- **Theodore Roosevelt.** It's fitting that Theodore Roosevelt—a major proponent of preservation who signed into law five national parks—should have a national park named in his honor. This North Dakota gem contains land that was once part of Roosevelt's Dakota Territory ranch. Visitors can step inside the former president's log cabin or peruse the visitor center's wide selection of books, posters, audio recordings, and videos dedicated to telling his many stories.

## Best Parks for Day Trippers

Some urbanites are fortunate to live just a short drive away from a national park. For those who live elsewhere, these gateway cities are served by major airports with plenty of car rental agencies, making a trip to a nearby park a surprisingly quick getaway.

- **Grand Canyon.** The popular South Rim—the destination of roughly 90 percent of the 5 million people who visit this park each year—is within 300 mi of both Phoenix and Las Vegas. If you're driving from Vegas, the far quieter (but no less stunning) North Rim, often closed due to snow right into May, is even closer.

- **Joshua Tree.** A quick two or three hour drive east from the urban sprawl of Los Angeles brings you to the junction of the Mojave and Colorado deserts. Joshua Tree National Park, named for extensive stands of the gnarled tree, is home to one of the finest wildflower displays in Southern California each spring.

- **Saguaro.** You'll find the largest concentration of the towering saguaro cactus, famed emblem of the desert southwest, just minutes east of Tucson. Unlike many parks, summer is actually the low season here, due to the intense heat. For those who don't mind sweating, lodging rates are highly discounted this time of year.

# THE BEST OF THE NATIONAL PARKS

## Best Parks for Fun & Funky Activities

All of the national parks exist for a reason: to protect something that was deemed worthy of recognition and preservation. Still, a few have such unusual and unique features that they stand out from the rest.

- **Carlsbad Caverns.** From mid-May to mid-October, watch thousands of bats spiral up into the evening sky from deep within the earth as they set out on their nightly hunt.

- **Crater Lake.** Take a boat tour on the clearest, deepest lake in the United States (and the seventh deepest in the world). Formed by volcanic activity, Crater Lake's deepest point is 1,943 feet down, and the sapphire-blue water is so clear that sunlight can penetrate to a depth of 400 feet.

- **Lassen Volcanic.** Though dormant since 1921, activity around volcanic Lassen Peak makes it clear that there's still a lot going on beneath the ground. Fumaroles, mudpots, and bubbling hot springs dot the landscape. It's a fun and sometimes smelly place to explore, but beware of the scalding water.

## Best Parks for Getting a Taste of the Wild West

The American West isn't as wild as it once was, but you can find traces of its storied past. From small preserved towns to vast desert spaces, it's still possible to feel like you've stepped into a Western movie.

- **Badlands.** Few words conjure up images of the old, Wild West better than the word "Badlands"—except maybe "Deadwood," a town 100 mi northwest of the park. Once an infamous gold camp, the entire town has been named a National Historic Landmark since undergoing a $150 million facelift. Naturally, gambling is legal here. And if all of that isn't enough to satisfy your inner cowboy, a nearby cemetary is the final resting place of Wild Bill Hickok and Calamity Jane.

- **Zion.** Thirty miles southeast of Zion's east entrance is the small city of Kanab, Utah, famously known as "Little Hollywood" for all the old westerns shot in its environs. Downtown hotels still highlight the rooms where John Wayne and other film stars slept. This area of southern Utah has also served as the backdrop for many Jeep commercials.

- **Death Valley.** Death Valley is not the most hospitable place—at least during certain times of the year—but the climate isn't as horrible as the park's reputation would suggest. Still, the name and the location have long epitomized the very idea of the desert in American literature, film, and television.

## Best Parks for Grinning and "Bearing" It

One of the parks' greatest attractions is their wildlife, and few animals attract as much attention as black and Grizzly bears. Cubs are cute and playful, but they shouldn't be approached—Mama is often close and will view you as a threat to her little ones. Still, when seen from a safe distance, bears serve as great reminders of the wildness that the national parks are meant to preserve and protect.

- **Glacier.** There are so many black and Grizzly bears in this part of Montana that they often come onto people's property, getting inside homes and causing general mayhem—though attacks on humans are rare.

- **Yellowstone.** The inspiration for fictional Jellystone Park and its anthropomorphic bears Yogi and Boo-Boo, Yellowstone is home to the greatest concentration of Grizzly bears in the lower 48.

- **Yosemite.** American black bears are the only bruins left in Yosemite (the California Grizzly was hunted to extinction in the early 20th century), but they are rarely seen.

## Best Parks for Inspiration

It's hard to not be inspired when you're at a national park. Natural wonders, peace and quiet, and ancient sites will likely leave you awestruck, no matter where you visit. These three parks, however, have left their mark on some famous visitors, impacting their subsequent work.

- **Glacier.** It took a lot to impress pioneering naturalist John Muir, who once called "this precious reserve" "the best care-killing scenery on the continent."

- **North Cascades.** Jack Kerouac, Gary Snyder, and Philip Whalen, fixtures of the Beat scene, all worked as National Park Service fire lookouts in the 1950s at Desolation Peak in North Cascades. Portions of Kerouac's *Desolation Angels* and *The Dharma Bums* chronicle his experiences on the mountain.

- **Yosemite.** Ansel Adams' repeated visits to Yosemite provided him with the intimate understanding necessary to pre-visualize many of the famous images he captured here. His exposures of Half Dome are particularly noteworthy, and are among his best known works.

# THE BEST OF THE NATIONAL PARKS

## Best Parks for Leaving Your Cell Phones Behind

Cell phones are great for staying in contact, but sometimes they offer *too* much connection to the outside world. The scenery at these parks (and their lack of service coverage) may inspire you to turn off your phone and focus on the wonders around you.

- **Capitol Reef.** Remote and wide-open Cathedral Valley, accessible by crossing the Fremont River in a high-clearance vehicle, is filled with stunning monoliths and silence. First-come, first-served primitive backcountry campsites provide a base for exploration.

- **Great Basin.** Among America's least visited National Parks, Great Basin is also one of the most beautiful. Tucked away in southeastern Nevada, far from major population centers, the park is a great place to hide from life and work back home.

- **Rocky Mountain.** Sometimes numbers say a lot. With more than 114 named mountains measuring 10,000 feet or higher, 350 mi of hiking trails, and countless far-reaching vistas, Rocky Mountain has plenty to keep you occupied (and off the phone).

## Best Parks for Not Roughing It

Getting away from it all means different things to different people. If your ideal escape involves lounging in a spa rather than roughing it in the backcountry, check out these parks.

- **Banff.** There are over 100 places to stay in the Lake Louise area of Canada's Banff National Park, from cozy motels to stunning lodges. And who needs to hike when you can take in the mountain views while savoring a fine dinner, relaxing at a spa, or sipping a glass of wine next to the fireplace?

- **Grand Teton.** Nearby Jackson and Jackson Hole feature some of the finest real estate in the country, so it's no surprise that visitors to Grand Teton have some prime lodging, shopping, dining, and spa options.

- **Zion.** After a full day of exploring the Zion backcountry, rejuvenate yourself in the nearby town of Springdale, which has a plethora of restaurants and fine hotels, lodges, and B&Bs. Enjoy magnificent vistas of the parks' massive cliffs as you soak in the hot tub to ease your achy joints.

## Best Parks to Pitch a Tent in

The national parks offer myriad options for sleeping close to nature, whether you rest your head on the plush bunks of an RV or beneath a tree separated from the stars by just a thin sheet of nylon. The facilities may vary, but many campers agree that the best way to see the parks is to get out into the undeveloped wilderness.

- **Canyonlands.** The Maze, one of Canyonlands' three distinct districts, is a backcountry camper's heaven. Named for its labyrinth-like canyons, there's room to explore for days. Remote access via long dirt roads ensures that crowds are non-existent.

- **Olympic.** Don't be deterred by the very real threat of rain at this mossy, misty, and wonderfully undeveloped national park. With the Pacific Ocean and temperate rain forests to the west and craggy peaks scattered throughout its interior, Olympic is a backpacker's delight.

- **Yosemite.** Beyond the Yosemite Valley and iconic sites like Half Dome, this park has a huge, almost secret backcountry perfect for backpackers and horseback riders wishing to embark on extended trips. In fact, 94.5 percent of the park is undeveloped wilderness.

## Best Parks for Romantics

One of the marks of a great relationship is the ability to travel together. Each of these national parks is a destination well-suited for celebrating your bond with that special someone.

- **Banff.** There is no shortage of escapist lodging at Banff, regardless of your budget or interests. There are over 100 accommodation options around Lake Louise alone, from cozy little cottages to large, historic lodges. And when you're not gazing into each other's eyes, you can stare at the breathtaking mountain scenery.

- **Channel Islands.** The mountains that dot this park off the coast of California are often obscured by mists, and animals found nowhere else on earth add to the park's otherworldly feel. The Pacific Ocean is the main attraction here: play on its beaches, ply its waters on a kayak, or tour it by boat as you enjoy an island escape for two—albeit one totally different than a typical Caribbean trip.

- **Grand Canyon.** For couples who don't mind sweating a little to get to a romantic destination, the Grand Canyon offers the quintessential Western camping experience. Sleeping at the base of this massive canyon under a clear black sky blazing with bright stars is something to add to your life's to-do list.

# THE BEST OF THE NATIONAL PARKS

## Best Parks for Scenic Drives

Car-bound tourists often get a bum rap, but let's be honest—even if you're exploring a park on foot, you have to get to the trailhead first. And sometimes the road there is amazing in its own right.

- **Glacier.** Even the hardiest hiker will admit that there's something special about speeding along a road named Going-to-the-Sun. Every year the local newspapers chronicle the road's opening for the season, when big snowplows finally clear its high passes. The 50-mi stretch of road crosses the Continental Divide at Logan Pass, and is one of America's most beautiful drives.

- **Redwood.** Keeping your eyes on the road can be a challenge when you're passing 300-foot-tall trees. The 8-mi Coastal Drive is especially wonderful, offering views of the Pacific Ocean and access to a section of the Coastal Trail—with turnouts for picnicking and gawking in wonder at majestic redwoods.

- **Rocky Mountain National Park.** The 48-mi Trail Ridge Road is the world's highest continuously paved road, with a maximum elevation of 12,183 feet. Connecting the park's east and west entrances, the road crosses the Continental Divide at Milner Pass and can take up to two months to clear of snow for its Memorial Day opening. The entire drive can be done in a couple hours, but allow more time to stop and gaze out from the many turnouts.

## Best Parks for Desert Solitaire

America's national parks run the gamut in terms of cultural, geographic, and geological attractions, but the desolate, arid environs offer a unique experience often colored by our nation's romantic notion of the desert. If you're seeking peace and quiet, you'll likely to find it here.

- **Arches.** Edward Abbey wrote his seminal *Desert Solitaire,* the book that defined the term, while stationed here as a park ranger in the 1960s. Though most often seen by car these days, Arches has an uncrowded backcountry that Abbey—were he alive—would argue is the best way to experience the place anyhow.

- **Big Bend.** Even in West Texas—a region known for wide open and silent spaces—Big Bend is quite remote. Among the least visited of the nation's national parks, it was dubbed "el despoblado," the unpopulated place, by early Spanish explorers, and has changed little since then. This is a great place to lose yourself among cacti and sprawling mountains.

- **Death Valley.** With its inhospitable environment and foreboding name, Death Valley has come to epitomize the desert of the American Southwest. It only attracts one million visitors a year, mainly outside the scorching summer months—but even in the high season the park's vast 5,300 square mi of space guarantee peace and solitude.

## Best Parks for Spotting Bald Eagles

It may sound clichéd, but you'll never forget the first time you see a bald eagle in person, soaring on the wing or diving into an icy stream to spear a fish. The national icon's white head and tail, set against a dark body, are not its only points of distinction—eagles are huge, far larger than even the biggest hawk. You can view these amazing birds at many of the national parks, but visit one of the following for your best chance at a sighting.

- **North Cascades.** Bald eagles are so much a part of this region that a festival is held in their honor every December along the Upper Skagit River, where hundreds of the regal birds gather during winter. Highlights include Native American music and dancing and bluegrass workshops.

- **Olympic.** A coastal section of this park protects a stunning 65-mi stretch of Pacific Ocean coastline, providing an ideal environment for the fish-loving bald eagle. Another fish-lover, the osprey, is also commonly found here—and from a distance, these birds look a lot like bald eagles. Up close, there's is no resemblance whatsoever, so consult your binoculars to be sure.

- **Yellowstone.** As much a part of Yellowstone as the Grizzly bear, bald eagles can usually be seen in the vicinity of Yellowstone Lake—though you may see them in the park's interior as well.

## Best Parks for Train Travel

Traveling by train to and from a national park is a rare treat, harkening back to the days when most visitors arrived by riding the rails. Fortunately, two of the nation's grandest and most historic national parks are still fully accessible via rail from a handful of major metropolitan areas.

- **Glacier.** Amtrak's Empire Builder stops at the east and west sides of Glacier on its way from Chicago to either Seattle or Portland. Shuttle service is available from either station to lodging in the park (with a prior reservation). The train also stops to the west in Whitefish, Montana, where there are additional lodging options.

- **Grand Canyon.** Grand Canyon Railway offers a variety of daily train services from Williams, Arizona, to the park's South Rim. The adults-only Sunset Limited runs during weekends in the fall, allowing passengers to witness one of Grand Canyon's unmatched sunsets while enjoying appetizers and full bar service. From November through January, The Polar Express train reenacts the classic children's book (make sure to reserve far in advance). Amtrak's Southwest Chief stops in Williams on its Chicago-to-Los Angeles run, making Grand Canyon one of the only national park's fully accessible by rail transportation.

## If You Like

**BEACHES**
Channel Islands
Olympic

**BIRDS**
Big Bend
Great Sand Dunes
Mount Rainier
Rocky Mountain
Theodore Roosevelt

**BISON**
Grand Teton
Great Sand Dunes
Rocky Mountain
Theodore Roosevelt

**BOATING**
Big Bend
Channel Islands
Glacier/Waterton
Grand Canyon
Grand Teton
Lassen Volcanic
North Cascades
Olympic
Redwood
Theodore Roosevelt
Yellowstone
Yosemite

**CAVES & CAVERNS**
Carlsbad Caverns
Great Basin
Sequoia & Kings Canyon
Wind Cave

**CLIMBING**
Arches
Black Canyon of the
  Gunnison
Canyonlands
Capitol Reef
Grand Teton
Joshua Tree
Mount Rainier
North Cascades
Olympic
Rocky Mountain
Sequoia & Kings
  Canyon
Yosemite
Yellowstone
Zion

**FISHING**
Big Bend
Black Canyon of the
  Gunnison
Capitol Reef
Channel Islands
Crater Lake
Glacier/Waterton Lakes
Grand Canyon
Grand Teton
Great Basin
Lassen Volcanic
Mount Rainier
North Cascades
Olympic
Redwood
Rocky Mountain
Sequoia & Kings Canyon
Theodore Roosevelt
Yellowstone
Yosemite

**GEOLOGICAL GREATS**
Arches
Bryce Canyon
Crater Lake
Grand Canyon
Petrified Forest
Yellowstone

**GLACIERS & ICEFIELDS**
Banff
Glacier/Waterton
Grand Teton
Jasper
Mount Rainier
North Cascades
Olympic

**GRAND GEYSERS**
Crater Lake
Death Valley
Lassen Volcanic
Mount Rainier
Olympic
Yellowstone

**HORSEBACK RIDING**
Banff
Glacier
Lassen Volcanic
Mount Rainier
Olympic

Rocky Mountain
Theodore Roosevelt
Yosemite

**MAJESTIC MOUNTAINS**
Big Bend
Capitol Reef
Glacier
Grand Teton
Guadalupe Mountains
North Cascades
Olympic
Rocky Mountain
Sequoia/Kings Canyon
Yosemite

**TERRIFIC TREES**
Joshua Tree
North Cascades
Olympic
Petrified Forest
Redwood
Sequoia & Kings Canyon
Yosemite

**VOLCANOES**
Crater Lake
Death Valley
Lassen Volcanic
Mount Rainier
Yellowstone

**WATERFALLS**
Banff
Crater Lake
Jasper
Great Sand Dunes
Lassen Volcanic
Mount Rainier
Olympic
Yellowstone
Yosemite

**WINTER RECREATION**
Bryce Canyon
Mount Rainier
Olympic
Rocky Mountain
Yellowstone
Yosemite
Zion

# Planning Your Visit

## 3

Flyfishing at Schwabaker beaver pond on the Snake River in Grand Teton National Park

**WORD OF MOUTH**

"To the body and mind which have been cramped by noxious work or company, nature is medicinal and restores their tone."

–Ralph Waldo Emerson

# EXPERIENCING THE PARKS

Once you've selected a park—the where—and have chosen a time you're going to go—the when—you're ready to start addressing the how: How will you experience the park? Will you go with a tour group? Will you go as a family and pitch a tent? Will you rough it by day but then be pampered at night? Will you try new activities, such as rock climbing or stargazing?

There are many options to choose from as you plan your park getaway. While the individual park chapters will help you in determining specific park activities, the following pages shed light on some of the offerings available throughout the national park system's western areas.

We've also included some helpful tips and information so you can prepare for all manner of excursions to the parks.

Plus, at the end of the chapter there's a hefty field guide of geological terms to educate you before you go so you can better appreciate all that you'll see.

# PARK PASSES

If you're going to be visiting several national parks at one time, or over the course of a year, invest in one of the national parks and federal recreational lands passes. Each pass admits the card holder as well as all other persons in your vehicle (or up to three others at places that charge per person rather than per vehicle) to any national park and other designated federal recreational lands, such as U.S. Forests.

- The $80 **America the Beautiful Annual Pass** is valid for a year from the date of purchase. To buy the pass online, visit http://store.usgs.gov/pass (or link to it off www.fodors.com); to order by phone, call 888/275–8747, ext. 1.

- If you're 62 or older, you can purchase the **America the Beautiful Senior Pass** instead for $10. Not only does it cost less money, it is valid for a lifetime. You must, however, purchase it in person at one of the national parks or other federal recreational areas.

- Those with permanent disabilities are entitled to the free **America the Beautiful Access Pass.** You must show documentation of your disability in order to receive the pass, and it can only be obtained in person. It is valid for a lifetime.

- Volunteer 500 or more service hours in the park and you'll be eligible for the **America the Beautiful Access Volunteer Pass.** It is valid for one year from the date of acquisition.

All passes are non-transferable, and you need to have photo identification with you when presenting your pass. *Note: The Golden Eagle, Golden Age, and Golden Access passes have been discontinued. These passes can still be used for park en-* trance if they are still valid according to the pass's original provisions.

---

### FREE ADMISSION

A handful of parks have no admission fee:
- Channel Islands
- Great Basin*
- North Cascades
- Redwood
- Wind Cave*

*\* Cave tours have a fee.*

---

- For Canada parks you can purchase a **Discovery Pass,** which allows entrance to Canada's 27 participating national parks and national historic sites for a year, or the **Annual National Parks Pass** for national parks only. Purchase the pass in person when you visit the park. Individual and family passes are available. See www.pc.gc.ca for details.

# FAMILY FUN

## Top 5 Tips

**1. Plan ahead.** Rooms and campsites fill up fast, so make your reservations as early as you can, says Kathy Kupper, a public affairs specialist with the National Parks Service. Many parks will have every room and campsite booked several months in advance (weekends are especially popular). Kupper recommends booking at least six months ahead, and more if you plan to visit one of the more popular parks, such as Grand Canyon, Grand Tetons, Rocky Mountain, Yellowstone, and Yosemite. If you plan on staying outside the park, check with the hotels you're considering as far ahead as you can, as these places can fill up fast as well. You also can go online. All of the National Parks have a Web site—links to all of them are at the National Park Service page, www.nps.gov. Many of the parks' pages have a "For Kids" link.

**2. Get the kids involved.** It might seem easier to do the planning yourself, but you'll probably have a better time—and your kids definitely will—if you involve them, says Steve Zachary, a ranger and education specialist at Lassen Volcanic National Park in California. No matter how old they are, children ought to have a good idea of where you're going and what you're about to experience. "It builds excitement beforehand, and lets the kids feel as if they've got a say in what you're doing." Zachary, who has traveled extensively through the national parks with his two sons, recommends discussing the park's various attractions and giving your kids a few choices.

**3. Know your children.** Consider your child's interests, says Zachary. This will help you plan a vacation that's both safe and memorable (for all the right reasons). For starters, if you have kids under four, be honest with yourself about whether the national park itself is age appropriate. Parents are notorious for projecting their awe for majestic scenery and overall enthusiasm for sightseeing on their younger kids, who might be more interested in cataloging the snacks in the hotel room's minibar. Likewise, Zachary says, be realistic about your child's stamina and ability. "I've seen parents who want to climb up to the volcano with their 10-year-old, but they live at sea level and the kid has never been hiking. This is a 2½-mi hike at 7,000 feet. In the end, nobody has any fun and the kid now hates hiking." A better option for many kids would be an easier hike that lets them see the volcano from a distance—and enjoy the experience.

**4. Pack wisely.** Be sure you're bringing kid-sized versions of the necessities you'll pack for yourself: Depending on the park you're visiting (and the activities you're planning), that might include sturdy hiking shoes, sunglasses, sunscreen, and insect repellant. You'll almost certainly need a few layers of clothing and plenty of water and snacks. Kids can be more susceptible to heat stress and dehydration than adults, meaning they need plenty of water when exercising. The American Academy of Pediatrics recommends giving your child about five ounces of water or another beverage every 20 minutes during strenuous exercise; studies show that kids are more willing to take flavored drinks than plain water.

**5. Develop a Plan B.** National parks are natural places, meaning they change dramatically with the seasons and the weather. So you should decide on alternate activities if Mother Nature isn't cooperative. And if you've already talked with your kids about your options, you can pick a new plan that appeals to everyone.

## Budgeting Your Trip

Like most vacations, a trip to a national park can be as frugal, or as fancy, as you like. Here are a few things to consider:

**Getting In.** Individual admission to the national parks ranges from free to $25, depending on the park (see our Essentials section at the end of each park chapter to learn individual rates). You also can buy an America the Beautiful Pass for $80, which will get you, and everyone in your group, into any national park (as well as other federal recreation areas) for one year.

**Sleeping.** You can make a reservation to camp at many parks online via http://reservations.nps.gov. Or call 800/365–2267 (800/436–7275 for Yosemite). Less than half of the parks charge for camping; the cost is typically under $20 per night. In many parks, you also can stay at a lodge, where prices run from $100 to $500 a night. There are also usually several accommodation options outside each park.

**Eating.** All of the in-park concessions are run by companies under contract with the National Parks Service, meaning their prices are set by the government. "It's more than you might spend elsewhere, but it's not too terrible," says Kupper. You also can bring in your own food and eat at one of the park's picnic areas.

**Entertainment.** The wonders of the park are entertainment enough for many youngsters, but the many sports and outdoor activities, from hiking and bicycling to horseback riding and cave touring, depending on the park, help children stay active while exploring the park. Many park visitor centers also have films; some parks, such as Grand Canyon and Zion, even have IMAX movies. Cost for these offerings varies, ranging from free to a couple

hundred dollars for something like a whitewater rafting trip.

**Souvenirs.** All of the parks have gift shops, and many stock items that are actually useful. For example, you'll find things like kid-sized binoculars, fanny packs, and magnifying glasses, all of which can make your child's visit even more enjoyable (and valuable). You can call ahead to see what's available, or just budget a few dollars to cover one item (maybe something you might have bought for your child anyway, like a disposable camera).

> ### SAMPLE BUDGET FOR FAMILY OF 4
>
> Here is an idea of what a family of four might spend on a three-day trip to Grand Canyon National Park, during which they stay and eat all their meals within the park. Depending on your accommodations and dining out options, the total you spend can vary dramatically.
>
> **Admission:** $25 per car; admission covers seven days in the park.
>
> **Lodging:** Rooms in one of the in-park lodges on the popular South Rim range from approximately $50 to $300 a night. Total for three nights: $150 to $900, or more if you have older children in a separate room. Tent camping in the park averages $15 per night. Total: $45.
>
> **Meals:** Dining options in the park range from no-frills snack bars to upscale restaurants. Per-meal costs range from $10 to $40 or more. Total (12 meals per day for three days): $360 to $1,440, or less, if cooking meals over your campfire or packing sack lunches.
>
> **TOTAL COST:** $430 to $2,365

# FAMILY FUN

## Kids Programs

About 300 of the 390 U.S. national parks are part of the Junior Ranger Program, which offers school-age kids the opportunity to learn about the park by filling out a short workbook or participating in an activity such as taking a hike with a park ranger. After completing the program, kids get a badge (or a pin or patch, depending on the park). For availability, check with the ranger station or visitor center when you arrive; some parks also put their Junior Ranger booklets online.

In addition to the Junior Ranger Program, kids can find a variety of activities designed just for them. Some parks, such as Sequoia, loan "Discovery Packs," backpacks filled with kid-friendly tools like magnifying glasses. Call ahead for availability.

Many parks also have general-interest programs that kids love. For example, Rocky Mountain National Park offers "Skins and Skulls," where visitors can touch a bear's fur and a marmot's skull, among other things, says Kyle Patterson, Public Information Officer for the park. "It helps kids—and adults—understand and explore in a hands-on, yet totally safe, way."

When you're through with the organized activities and are ready to head off on your own, remember that kids often take a shorter view of things than adults do, meaning they may need to be reminded once in awhile of why you're there and what lies ahead. A parent in Oregon recounts, "When I was hiking with my kids in Yosemite and they started to get whiny, I'd tell then, 'Hey guys, think of how much fun we're going to have at this swimming hole!' We'd also play games like I Spy." Other kids might like a scavenger hunt.

## Camping with Kids

A night in a tent under the stars is the highlight of many kids' trips to a national park. Making sure it's a pleasant experience, however, takes some preparation. While a camping novice may know to bring along the essentials of sunscreen, drinking water, and insect repellant, one seasoned camper suggests some things you may not have thought about.

A Cub Scouts pack leader and mother of three boys advises that you **check the weather forecast—and your tent—before you go.** "We actually had a family who brought a brand-new tent, that hadn't even been taken out of the box until they got to the campground, only to discover while trying to assemble it that the door was defective so it didn't zip closed. Imagine the mosquito bites they had in the morning!" She also suggests that you **choose your tent site and companions carefully.** "Trust me," she says, "you don't want to pitch your tent next to someone who snores all night!"

She says one essential you "gotta have" when venturing out into the world of tents and campfires is your own toilet paper (no explanation necessary). "And, of course," she adds, **"don't forget the marshmallows!"**

---

### WEB SITES FOR KIDS

- www.smokeybear.com
- www.symbols.gov/woodsy/toolbox/
  woodsy-kids.shtml
- www.nps.gov/learn
- www.doi.gov/kids/index.html
- www.pc.gc.ca/apprendre-learn/
  jeunes-youths/index_e.asp

# WHAT TO PACK

Everyone will have varied packing lists, of course, but here are 10 things to include among your luggage essentials.

**Binoculars.** Many of the parks are a bird-watcher's dream. A pair of binos will help you spot feathered friends as well as large mammals. 10 × (power) is a good combination for magnification, field of view, and steadiness. If the magnification is higher, the field of view is smaller, and your hand movements will prevent you from seeing well, unless you use a tripod.

**Clothes for both warm and cold weather.** Days can often be warm while nights turn chilly, so dress in layers. In cold or wet-weather hiking, synthetics such as fleece and wool are the way to go. In these fabrics your feet will stay much drier and toastier than with a cotton-blend variety.

**Comfortable shoes or sturdy hiking boots.** Be sure to break them in first. Also consider ankle support, which helps for unpaved trails.

**Digital camera.** It lets you see right away how your picture will appear. Be sure it has plenty of memory.

**Insect repellant.** If you're hiking near water and camping at night, a good bug spray can help keep your trip from being a swatting marathon. The level of DEET indicates the longevity of its effectiveness.

**Journal.** When your jaw drops at the sight of a glorious vista, and your head clears from all the fresh air, you may find some thoughts of inspiration longing to be penned. Consider a weatherproof one (sporting goods stores should have them).

**Long pants and shirts.** When hiking, especially in higher altitudes and areas with poison ivy, it's wise to wear long pants and shirts to minimize exposed skin.

**Skin moisturizer & lip balm.** At many parks you'll be in higher altitudes and drier climates.

**Snacks and water.** National parks by their nature are remote, and some are very lacking in services. Bring plenty of healthy snacks with you, as well as water.

**Sunglasses, sunscreen, and hat.** The higher elevation means the sun gets to you more quickly, so protect your skin, eyes, and scalp. Look for those marked UV Protection and Polarized.

For extended hiking trips, pick up a good topographical map. Also invest in a hiking stick if you have bad knees. If you're hiking in the backcountry, also pack a water filter.

---

## FIRST-AID KIT MUSTS

Be sure to carry a good first-aid kit with you while exploring the outdoors. A solid kit should include a first-aid manual, aspirin (or ibuprofen), adhesive bandages, butterfly bandages, sterile gauze pads, one-inch wide adhesive tape, an elastic bandage, antibacterial ointment, antiseptic cream, antihistamines, razor blades, tweezers, a needle, scissors, calamine lotion, and moleskin for blisters.

# OH STARRY NIGHT

## TIPS FOR STARGAZING IN THE PARKS

## Constellations

Constellations are stories in the sky—many depict figures from Greek mythology, including the zodiac. Brush up on a few of these tales before your trip, and—armed with the star chart (*right*)—you'll be an instant source of nighttime entertainment.

The stars appear to rotate around Polaris, the North Star, in fixed positions relative to each other. To get your celestial bearings, first find the bright stars of the Big Dipper. An imaginary line drawn through the two stars at its end (away from the handle) will hit Polaris. You can also follow the path of the dipper's handle and "Arc Arcturus" to the bright star in the constellation Bootes.

Myriad astronomy books and websites have additional star charts; *National Geographic* has a cool interactive version with images from the Hubble Space Telescope (www.nationalgeographic.com/stars/chart).

## Planets

Stars twinkle, planets don't (since they're so much closer to earth, the atmosphere doesn't distort their light as much). Planets are also bright, which makes them fairly easy to spot. Unfortunately, we can't show their positions on this star chart, since planets orbit the sun and move in relation to the stars. To search for planets, visit a stargazing website (http://stardate.org/ or www.space.com/spacewatch) before your trip.

The easiest planet to spot is Venus, the brightest object in the night sky besides the moon. Look for it just before sunrise or just after sunset; it'll be near the point where the sun is rising or setting. Like the moon, Venus goes through phases—check it out through a pair of binoculars. You can also spot Mars, Jupiter, Saturn, and Mercury—with or without the aid of binoculars.

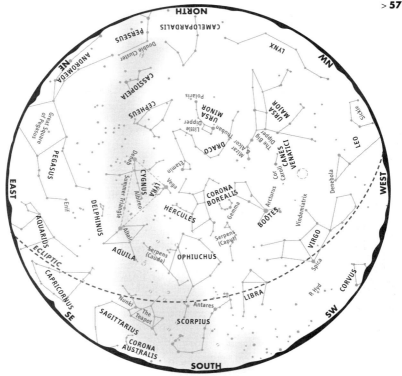

## Meteors

It's hard to match the magic of a meteor shower, the natural firework display that occurs as the earth passes through a cloud of comet debris. These pieces of space junk—most the size of a grain of sand—hit our atmosphere at high speeds, and the intense friction produces brief but brilliant streaks of light.

Since the planet passes through the same patches of interstellar rubbish each year, it's easy to roughly predict when the major meteor showers will occur. Notable ones include the Perseids (mid-August), the Orionids (late October), the Leonids (mid-November), and the Geminids (mid-December). Each shower is named after the point in the sky where meteors appear to originate. If you're not visiting during a shower, don't worry—you can spot meteors any time of the year.

## Satellites

Right now, there are about 2,500 satellites (operative and inoperative) orbiting the Earth—and you can catch a glimpse of one with a little practice. Satellites look like fast-moving, non-blinking points of light; the best way to spot one is to lie on your back and scan the sky for movement. Be on the lookout for satellites an hour or two before or after sunset (though you may see them at other times as well).

You can take the guesswork out of the search with a few cool online tools (www.nasa.gov or www.heavens-above.com). Select your location, and these websites will help you predict—down to the minute—when certain objects will be streaking overhead. It's especially worthwhile to use these sites to look for the two brightest satellites: the International Space Station and the space shuttle.

# ROCK CLIMBING Q & A

Curious about the sport of rock climbing? The national parks are prime venues for this adventurous, adrenaline-pumping pursuit.

Answering our questions about rock climbing is Coley Gentzel, a climbing guide and the program coordinator for the **American Alpine Institute (AAI)** (✉ 1515 12th St., Bellingham, WA 98225 ☎ 360/671–1505 ⊕ www.aai.cc), one of the premier rock-climbing schools in the United States.

## Is rock climbing safe?

Contrary to popular belief, rock climbing is remarkably safe. A greater number of accidents occur in skiing, river rafting, even hiking, than rock climbing. The consequences for errors, mistakes, and a lack of adequate training in rock climbing are severe, and so most people consider the sport very dangerous. That said, most people participating in the activity know what they are doing and know how to carry out proper safety procedures to protect themselves and others.

## What's a safe age to begin?

To push one's physical and mental limits within the sport, it is best to start as young as possible in order to develop strength and technique during formative years. Those who want to pursue the sport recreationally, but aren't interested in climbing progressively harder and harder climbs, can start any time. In our introductory programs, we see children from age 10 and up, seniors well over 60, and every age in between.

With indoor climbing walls, a generally safe and controlled environment, kids can start climbing (with some adult assistance) as soon as they are able to walk and scramble around. For types of climbing that involve moderate rope handling and basic techniques, climbers need to be able to

think critically and perform more involved physical processes. Children ages 10–14 are generally capable and confident with these things. For outdoor lead climbing that involves complex anchor and rope-work scenarios, climbers tend to be 16 years and older. On the flip side, we work with folks in their 50s and even 60s who are getting into rock climbing for the first time, and they tend to learn quickly.

## What shape should you be in?

Any shape at all really. What sort of shape you are in physically will dictate what type and how much rock climbing you are able to do, but there are climbs suitable for all ability levels. Ideally, would-be-climbers will have a good base of general cardio fitness, good balance, and have decent arm and leg strength. You do not need to be able to do a pull-up. Grip strength is helpful for more difficult climbs, but problems with strength can often be overcome with technique.

## But, where are the nets?

There are no nets because climbers use a special climbing rope and protective gear and anchors to secure themselves and prevent any injury in an event of a fall. Generally speaking, if a climber falls off while climbing, he will fall from 0 to 15 feet before his rope stops the fall.

Most people don't feel fear after a little bit of climbing because they learn to trust their gear. Also, fear eases with more time and exposure to the sensation of being off the ground. (Note: A good guide can pick climbs that have less exposure and are in more friendly positions for climbers who may have a more acute fear of heights.)

## Does it damage the rocks?

Certain types of climbing can leave marks on the rock. Generally speaking, there are two forms of climbing. The first is traditional-style rock climbing in which climbers place removable pieces of protection in the rock, which are extracted when they are done climbing, effectively not disturbing or affecting the rock at all. The other type is sport climbing, in which small anchors are permanently drilled into the rock for climbers to clip. This type of climbing leaves lasting marks on the rock. Most climbing venues have designated sport and traditional areas; most national parks either limit or restrict the use of fixed anchors and permanent alteration of the rocks.

### What gear do you need?

You don't need much at all to get started if you go with a qualified instructor. The basics are a harness, helmet, and rock shoes (all of which can be rented), plus the rope and anchoring devices that the instructor provides.

When you have skill and knowledge to climb on your own, there are hundreds of pieces of gear that can be used in rock climbing; not all are required in every instance or every time you climb.

To get started with *sport climbing*, a person would need the following:

- rock climbing shoes (special sticky, rubber, tight-fitting shoes)
- a harness
- a chalk bag
- 12 to 15 quick draws (two carabiners attached by a length of webbing)
- a climbing rope
- 30 feet of webbing, cordage, or anchor material
- a belay device
- a helmet
- 5–10 carabiners and 2–3 locking carabiners

For *traditional climbing* one would need all of the above as well as:

- spring-loaded camming devices covering all size ranges
- a selection of chocks (also called stoppers and nuts) covering all size ranges
- a selection of shoulder and double-length slings
- 15–20 additional carabiners

In both cases, a climber must have proper training in how to use these instruments.

### Anything else to add?

The great thing about rock climbing is that you don't need a lot of gear or time to get started. You can get your first experience by giving it a day, half day, or even a few hours. Most people that get a taste of it become totally hooked. Like a lot things in life, when you learn to do it right, it's much easier than it looks, and the rewards are far greater than you would initially guess. It's fun, it builds self-confidence, and it gives you an amazing sense of accomplishment.

---

### MOUNTAINEERING

The national parks of the West are a great training ground for potential mountaineers who want to climb higher peaks in Alaska, the Andes, or the Himalayas. Booking a 2–4 day Mount Rainier summit climb with experienced guides is a great start. The remote peaks of North Cascades and Olympic national parks also are good bets, providing a true wilderness experience.

Mountaineering can involve heavy traveling in the mountains, usually with the aim of reaching a summit. Mountaineers often employ rock climbing to reach their objectives, but they will rarely search for the most difficult and technical routes to ascend (as rock climbers often do). Mountaineering includes glacier and snow climbing as well, and is usually a multi-day activity.

# TAKE A TOUR

Whether you want an experienced guide for an active-sport trip, or an educational but leisurely program that takes the planning out of your hands, tours can be ideal for all ages and life situations—families, outdoor enthusiasts, and retirees.

Listed here are a few tour companies worth checking out. They often combine outdoor activities with educational components; trip lengths vary.

## Adventure Trips

Many trip organizers specialize in only one type of activity; however, a few companies guide different kinds of active trips. (In some cases, these larger companies also act essentially as a clearinghouse or agent for smaller trip outfitters.) Be sure to sign on with a reliable outfitter; getting stuck with a shoddy operator can be disappointing, uncomfortable, and even dangerous. Some sports—white-water rafting and mountaineering, for example—have organizations that license or certify guides, and you should be sure that the guide you're with is properly accredited.

**Backroads** ⊠ 801 Cedar St. Berkeley, CA 94710-1800 ☎ 510/527-1555 or 800/462-2848 ⊕ www.backroads.com. **The Great Canadian Adventure Co** ⊠ 6714 101 Ave., Edmonton, AB T6A 0H7 ☎ 780/424-9034 ⊕ www.adventures.ca. **REI Adventures** ⊠ 6750 S. 228th St., Kent, WA 98032 ☎ 800/622-2236 ⊕ www.rei.com/adventures. **Off the Beaten Path** ⊠ 7 E. Beall St., Bozeman, MT 59715 ☎ 800/445-2995 ⊕ www.offthebeatenpath.com. **Sierra Club Outings** ⊠ 85 2nd St., San Francisco, CA 94105 ☎ 415/977-5500 ⊕ www.sierraclub.org. **Trek America** ⊠ Box 189, Rockaway, NJ 07866 ☎ 973/983-1144 or 800/221-0596 ⊕ www.trekamerica.com. **Timberline Adventures** ⊠ 7975 E. Harvard, Suite J, Denver, CO 80231 ☎ 303/759-3804 or 800/417-2453 ⊕ www.timbertours.com. **The World Outdoors** ⊠ 2840 Wilderness Pl. Suite D, Boulder, CO 80301 ☎ 303/413-0938 or 800/488-8483 ⊕ www.theworldoutdoors.com.

## Senior Tours

Those in their golden years can participate in special tours. Some of them are quite adventurous, such as Elderhostel's grandparent-grandchild river rafting cruise down Grand Canyon's Colorado River.

**Elderhostel** ⊠ 11 Ave. de Lafayette, Boston, MA 02111 ☎ 877/426-8056 ⊕ www.elderhostel.org. **Walking The World** ⊠ Box 1186, Fort Collins, CO 80522 ☎ 970/498-0500 or 877/340-9255 ⊕ www.walkingtheworld.com.

## Single-Park Tours

If you want to concentrate solely on one park, contact the park directly to learn about organized tours they may have.

**Glacier Park Inc.** (⊠ P.O. Box 2025, Columbia Falls, MT 59912 ☎ 406/892-2525 ⊕ www.glacierparkinc.com) offers week-long excursions specifically in Glacier and Waterton that includes meals, expert narration on rides in the vintage Ford jammers, and time for play away from the group.

**Grand Canyon Tour Co.** (⊠ 4343 N. Rancho Dr., Ste. 230, Las Vegas NV 89130 ☎ 702/655-6060 or 800/222-6966 ⊕ www.grandcanyontourcompany.com) provides tours of the park from Las Vegas.

**The Yellowstone Association Institute** (⊠ Yellowstone National Park ☎ 307/344-2293 ⊕ www.YellowstoneAssociation.org) offers guided tours and trips in Yellowstone, ranging from backcountry expeditions to "Lodging and Learning" experiences within the comfort of park lodging. Some are specifically for families.

## Tours with Accessibility

**Access Tours** (⊠ Box 499, Victor, ID 83455 ☎ 800/929-4811 ⊕ www.accesstours.org) leads nine-day trips for people who use wheelchairs or walk slowly and can customize trips for groups of four or more.

# CAPTURING THE PARKS ON FILM

Today's digital cameras make it difficult to take a truly lousy picture, but there are still some things even the best models can't do without your expertise. The tips below (some of them classic photography techniques) won't turn you into the next Ansel Adams, but they might prevent you from being upstaged by your 5-year-old with her own digital camera.

**The Golden Hours:** The best photos are taken when most of us are either snoozing or eating dinner—about an hour before and after sunrise and sunset. When the light is gentle and golden, your photos are less likely to be over-exposed and filled with harsh shadows and squinting people.

**Divide to Conquer:** You can't go wrong with the Rule of Thirds. When you're setting up a shot, mentally divide your LCD into nine squares and place the primary subject where two squares intersect. (If all this talk of imaginary lines makes your head spin, just remember not to automatically plop your primary focal point in the center of your photos).

**Lock Your Focus:** To get a properly focused photo, press the shutter button down halfway and wait a few seconds before pressing down completely. (On most cameras, a light or a cheery beep will indicate that you're good to go.)

**Circumvent Auto Focus:** If your camera isn't focusing on your desired focal point, center the primary subject smack in the middle of the frame and depress the shutter button halfway, allowing the camera to focus. Then compose your photo properly (moving your focal point out of center), and press the shutter all the way down.

**Jettison the Jitters:** Shaky hands are the most common cause of out-of-focus photos. If ice water doesn't run through your veins, invest in a tripod or put the camera on something steady—such as a wall, a bench, or a rock—when you shoot. If all else fails, lean against something sturdy to brace yourself.

**Consider the Imagery:** Before you press that shutter button, take a moment or two to consider *why* you're shooting what you're shooting. Once you've determined this, start setting up your photo. Look for interesting lines that curve into your image—such as a path, the shoreline, or a fence—and use them to create the impression of depth. You can also avoid flat images by photographing people with their bodies or faces positioned at an angle to the camera.

**Ignore All the Rules:** Sure, thoughtful contemplation and careful technique are likely to produce brilliant images—but there are times when you just need to capture the moment. If you see something wonderful, grab your camera and just get the picture. If the photo turns out to be blurry, off-center, or over- or under-exposed, you can always Photoshop it later.

For more tips, visit www.fodors.com/focus.

# STAYING HEALTHY, PLAYING IT SAFE

### Altitude Sickness

Altitude sickness can result when your body is thrown into high elevations without having time to adjust. When you're at a mile (5,280 feet) or more, and especially when you're higher than 8,500 feet, you may feel symptoms of altitude sickness: shortness of breath, light-headedness, nausea, fatigue, headache, and trouble sleeping. To help your body adjust to the new elevation, drink lots of water, avoid alcohol, and wait a couple days before attempting vigorous activity. If your conditions are severe, last several days, or worsen, seek medical attention. Altitude sickness can develop into serious conditions, and even lead to death. Some people find breathing extra oxygen (from a tank) while they sleep helps.

### Animal Bites

Rangers will tell you that rattlesnakes are more scared of us than we are of them. But should they decide to lash out at you with their venomous fangs, stay calm (panic and a lot of movement can spread the poison). Have someone else get medical help for you right away. Likewise, if you are bitten by a wild animal, seek medical attention immediately. You may need a rabies or tetanus shot.

### Hypothermia

When your body gets too cold for too long, hypothermia can develop. Symptoms are chilliness and fatigue, shivering, and lack of mental clarity. If someone you're traveling with develops hypothermia, the National Park Service offers this advice: Seek shelter, remove any wet clothes from them, and wrap them in warm blankets. It also helps for you to get into the blankets with them so they can pull from your body heat. Hot beverages and high-energy bars also help.

### Safety Concerns

America's national parks have been set aside to preserve some of the most outstanding landscapes in the world. This is nature at its finest, and in raw form. This means that although parks are wonderful venues for families, providing experiences they'll remember for a lifetime, it's important that children realize that national parks are not theme parks or zoos. They need to respect and take caution with the surroundings. Here are some safety tips to keep in mind:

**Don't feed the animals.** Animals in some of the larger national parks are used to humans being around and may not flee at your presence. But this doesn't mean you should feed them. It is unhealthy for them to eat people food, and because it further acclimates them to humans, it can lead to them being more aggressive, and thus more dangerous, to future visitors.

**Register at trailheads.** If there's a notebook where you can write down your name and the time you're starting your hike, jot it down so park personnel know where you are should inclement weather or another danger occur. Also, don't hike alone, especially in bear country.

**Practice fire safety.** Check with the visitor center on campfire rules, and never build fires in the backcountry: One breath of wind can carry a cinder for miles and plant it on dry grasslands just ready to blaze. When cooking over your campfire, clear the ground around it first of dry leaves and grass, keep the fire inside the pit, throw used matches into the fire, and keep a pot of water or sand nearby. Don't start a fire when you're alone, and never leave it unattended. It goes without saying that you should never cook in your tent or any poorly ventilated area.

# MORE TIPS & TIDBITS

## Camera Care

■ If you're flying, don't pack film or equipment in checked luggage, where it is much more susceptible to damage.

■ Keep film out of the sun and heat.

■ Check the rules at Native American reservations near national parks before you take photographs. In many cases you must purchase a permit.

## Discounts for Seniors

To qualify for age-related discounts, don't wait until you've used a service. Mention your senior-citizen status up front when booking hotel reservations and before you're seated in restaurants. Have identification on hand to back up your claim.

## Maps

If you plan to do a lot of hiking or mountaineering, especially in the backcountry, invest in detailed maps and a compass. Topographical maps are sold in well-equipped outdoor stores (REI and Cabela's, for example). Maps in different scales are available from the U.S. Geological Survey. To order, call 303/202–4700 or 888/275–8747; you'll need to first request the free index and catalog, from which you can find and order the specific maps you need.

## Pets in the Park

Generally, pets are allowed only in developed areas of the national parks, including drive-in campgrounds and picnic areas. *They must be kept on a leash at all times.* With the exception of guide dogs, pets are not allowed inside buildings, on most trails, on beaches, or in the backcountry. They also may be prohibited in areas controlled by concessionaires. Some national parks have kennels; call ahead to learn the details if there's availability. Some of the na-

tional forests (www.fs.fed.us) surrounding the parks have camping and are more lenient with pets.

## Traveling with Disabilities

Most national parks have at least some accessible visitor centers, restrooms, campsites, and trails. If you're bringing a guide dog, it's best to get authorization ahead of time, and write down the name of the person with whom you spoke.

---

### PARK RESOURCES

#### ORGANIZATIONS

**National Park Conservation Association.** This organization raises awareness of the parks through public, media, and government education. ✉ *1300 19th St. NW, Ste. 300, Washington, D.C. 20036* ☎ *202/223–6722* ⊕ *www.npca.org.*

**National Park Foundation.** This is a nonprofit, fund-raising arm of the National Park Service. ✉ *11 Dupont Circle NW, 6th Flr., Washington, D.C. 20036* ☎ *202/238–4200* ⊕ *www.nationalparks.org.*

**National Park Service.** ✉ *1849 C St. NW Washington, D.C. 20240* ☎ *202/208–6843* ⊕ *www.nps.gov.*

**Parks Canada.** ✉ *25 Eddy St., Hull QC K1A 0M5* ☎ *888/773–8888* ⊕ *www. Parkscanada.gc.ca.*

#### PUBLICATIONS

**National Parks Camping Guide.** ✉ *Superintendent of Documents, U.S. Government Printing Office, Washington, D.C. 20402* ☎ *800/365–2267* ▱ *$3.50.*

# FIELD GUIDE: COMMON GEOLOGY AND TERRAIN TERMS

Some of the parks' greatest assets are the unique landscapes and bizarre geological features you'll see; many are found in only a handful of places on the planet. As you explore these strange new lands, refer to this geological glossary for more information about the forces that shaped the awesome sites around you. By the end of your trip, you'll be able to tell the difference between a syncline, an anticline, and a monocline!

## Alluvial Fans

(B) Cloudbursts in the desert cause water to rush down the faces of barren mountains and hills. Since it cannot be easily absorbed into the dry, packed soil, the water fans out into rivulets and streams, leaving behind indelible grooves. Look for these distinctive features in Death Valley and the Mojave Desert.

## Anticline

Movements of the Earth's crust produce an anticline when they push originally horizontal rock layers upward in one spot. The anticline slopes downward from the crest.

## Arch

(A) This type of window in a rock wall forms either through erosion, when wind and sand wear away the rock face, or through the freezing action of water. When water enters spaces or joints in a rock and freezes there, the expansion of the ice can crack off chunks of rock.

## Badlands

(C) Much of the sedimentary rock that eroded from the Black Hills was deposited in South Dakota's Badlands, along with ash from the volcanoes in the Yellowstone area. Water flowed over the landscape and carved out huge buttes and cliffs in a process that continues to this day. In the relatively soft, half-hardened rocks, the

elements carved drainage channels with a distinctive V shape, creating a network of ravines and ridgelines. These formations are devoid of vegetation because erosion carries off seeds and roots. The amphitheater at Bryce Canyon National Park is another example of badlands.

### Basin

**(D)** A basin is like a giant syncline, or dip in the earth. Within a basin there are usually smaller anticlines and synclines. The Great Basin is an example of a geologic basin.

### Biological Soil Crusts

Also known as cryptobiotic soil crust, this black, bumpy, stuff covers the ground throughout canyon country. It is composed of cyanobacteria, green algae, lichens, fungi, and mosses that form a living cover on the ground. The crust stabilizes the soil and allows plants to germinate and root. If it's destroyed or damaged, new plant life cannot grow. It takes an estimated 50 to 250 years for this living organism to repair itself.

### The Black Hills

South Dakota's Black Hills began as a mountainous landscape covered with limestone and shale sedimentary rock, but this covering gradually eroded away, exposing a granite face. Much of the sedimentary rock that eroded from the Black Hills was deposited in the Badlands.

### Bridge

**(G)** If a window through a rock is created by water flowing beneath it, it is called a bridge. You can see many natural bridges in canyon country, such as Hickman Bridge at Capitol Reef National Park.

### Butte

A butte is what remains when a mesa erodes. You can see good examples of this formation in Monument Valley, Arizona.

# FIELD GUIDE: COMMON GEOLOGY AND TERRAIN TERMS

## Caldera

Although it is the largest and deepest example, the bowl-shaped depression in which Crater Lake lies is only one of many along the Pacific Rim. Created when volcanoes blow their tops, small caldera remnants lie atop Mount Rainier and Mount Baker, and a bigger one remains on Mount St. Helens, where its side blew out in 1980.

## Canyon

(H) A canyon forms when water and wind erode soft layers of the Earth's rock crust. The hardness of the rock determines the shape of the canyon: A narrow, or slot, canyon generally results when the rock is the same composition all the way down and water runs through the crack. A step-like canyon such as the Grand Canyon forms when alternating soft and hard layers are eroded by wind and water, with a river cutting a narrow groove in the bottom of the canyon.

## Caves

Though they differ somewhat in their geology, caves—natural underground chambers that open to the surface—give you an opportunity to descend below the Earth and learn about the forces of heat and water upon rocks and minerals. Crystal Cave in Sequoia National park has excellent examples of stalactites and stalagmites. In South Dakota, Jewel Cave and Wind Cave, each with more than 100 mi of mapped passageway, rank as fourth and seventh longest in the world, respectively, and each is home to incredibly rare specimens. In New Mexico, Carlsbad Caverns' extensive cave system includes the Big Room, which has a 225-foot high ceiling.

## The Continental Divide

The Continental Divide of North America is a ridge that crosses the continent from north to south, separating water flowing east and water flowing west. The divide follows the crest of the Rockies through Glacier, Yellowstone, and Rocky Mountain national parks.

## Desert Pavement

High winds can scour away soil and small pebbles to leave behind bare rock, the desert pavement found in areas such as the plains of Big Bend National Park.

## Desert Varnish

This dark brown or black coating seems to drip down canyon walls as if from a spilled can of paint. Windblown dust or rain containing iron and manganese creates the color. Ancestral Puebloans and other ancient Native Americans scratched drawings called petroglyphs into the desert varnish.

## Fault Zones

Shifting underground land masses such as those of California's famous San Andreas Fault have helped create many of Joshua Tree National Park's upper elevations, including the Pinto Mountains on the northern border and the Little San Bernardino Mountains on the southwest side. This same geologic upheaval has shifted and cracked underground rocks, damming up the flow of groundwater and forcing it to the surface, making precious moisture available to wildlife and plants.

## Fossil Reef

(F) Much of the desert region of Texas and New Mexico shares a common geologic past, when a warm, shallow inland sea covered a large area. As the sea evaporated, a 400-mi-long limestone reef was deposited, made up of sediment, dead plants, and the skeletons of tiny sea creatures. Movement in the Earth's surface later

thrust the reef upward, helping to shape the Guadalupe Mountains. One of the largest and most visible examples of fossil reef is Capitan Reef in Guadalupe Mountains National Park, which attracts geologists from around the world.

## Geothermal Features

Hissing geysers, burbling mud pots, and boiling cauldrons have fascinated travelers ever since mountain man John Coulter described them to an unbelieving public in 1810. Today, these "freaks of a fiery nature," as Rudyard Kipling described them, are still clearly visible in Yellowstone National Park. Geysers, hot springs, and fumaroles are created when superheated water rises to the earth's surface from a magma chamber below. In the case of geysers, the water is trapped under the surface until the pressure is so great that it bursts through. Mud pots are a combination of hot water, hydrogen sulfide gas, and dissolved volcanic rock. The mixture looks like a hot, smelly, burping pudding.

## Glaciers

Heavy snow compacted by centuries of accumulation forms the distinctive blue, dense ice of a glacier. Incremental movement, usually inches a year, is what distinguishes a glacier from a snowfield; most of the glaciers in the contiguous United States are in Washington and Oregon, and most are receding due to global warming.

## Hot Springs

Past the eastern escarpment of the Sierra, evidence of the region's volcanic history remains in the giant caldera of the high-mountain desert. Hot springs issue from the earth and form small- to medium-size pools in the ground, some of which are suitable for bathing. If you should stumble upon one, never jump in without first test-

ing the water's temperature. The locals keep many of the springs secret, but in some places people have piped the hot waters into developed pools. While driving on U.S. 395, look for road signs pointing the way to numerous hot springs.

## Laccolithic Mountains

Throughout canyon country, many mountain ranges seem to rise suddenly out of the flat earth, with no transitional foothills. These ranges are generally located over faults in the earth's crust. They formed as molten rock, or magma, flowed up from below, and hardened under layers of sedimentary rock. Erosion and other geologic forces subsequently exposed the volcanic rock in the form of mountains. Among canyon country's laccolithic ranges are the La Sal Mountains near Moab, Utah; the Abajo Mountains near Canyonlands National Park's Needles District; and the La Plata and Ute mountains near Mesa Verde National Park; as well as Navajo Mountain near Monument Valley Tribal Park, Arizona.

## Mesa

A mesa, or hill with a smooth, flat, table-like top (mesa means "table" in Spanish), is a clear example of how hard rock stands higher and protects the soft rock beneath. A single mesa may cover hundreds of square miles of land. At the Island in the Sky District of Canyonlands National Park and at Mesa Verde you are standing on top of a mesa.

## Monocline

The most notable geologic feature of the Colorado Plateau, a monocline is a bit like half an anticline (see above). The layers of rock on either side of a monocline are mostly level, but they bend downward like a step. Pioneers often called them "reefs"

# FIELD GUIDE: COMMON GEOLOGY AND TERRAIN TERMS

because the formations were a barrier to passage through the area. The Waterpocket Fold in Capitol Reef National Park is a most dramatic example of a monocline. Another example is the Monument Upwarp, which extends from Kayenta, Arizona, to the confluence of the Green and Colorado rivers in Canyonlands National Park. There are many smaller anticlines and synclines along the Upwarp.

## Monument

This general term applies to geologic formations that are much taller than they are wide, or to formations that resemble man-made structures. You can see many examples of the first type of monument in Capitol Reef National Park's Cathedral Valley; in Monument Valley, Arizona; and in the White Rim Monument Basin area at Canyonlands National Park. Monuments that fall into the second category include the Sinking Ship in Bryce Canyon National Park and the Three Penguins at Arches National Park.

## Petrified Wood

If you want to know what the desert Southwest used to look like, picture the Florida Everglades populated with giant dragonflies and smaller species of dinosaurs. Arizona's Petrified Forest offers a glimpse of the once lush, tropical world. Stumps and logs from the ancient woodland are now turned to rock because they were immersed in water and sealed away from the air, so normal decay did not occur. Instead, the preserved wood gradually hardened as silica, or sand, filtered into its porous spaces, almost like cement. Erosion was among the geological processes that exposed the wood.

## Plains

Once home to vast herds of bison that blackened the prairie for miles, the grasslands across the nation's center today serve as America's breadbasket, supplying much of the nation and parts of the world with dairy products, grain, seeds, cattle, poultry, and pork.

## Playa

Dry, salt-encrusted lake beds known as playas commonly lie in the low points of arid Southwestern valleys. You can see examples in the Sonoran Desert near Tucson.

## The Rocky Mountains

The Rocky Mountain chain reaches from northwestern Canada down through Washington, Idaho, Montana, Wyoming, Colorado, Utah, and into New Mexico. The huge mountains are thought to have been raised by massive tectonic plates colliding, pushing the Earth's crust upwards. The soft rocks eroded and were split by deep fault zones, exposing the harder granite for which the mountains are known. Later, during several ice ages, glaciers carved sheer walls and sharp peaks into the mountains, which are what you see now in Glacier, Yellowstone, Grand Teton, and Rocky Mountain national parks.

## Sand Dunes

The sand dunes that you occasionally come across in canyon country have been deposited by winds. Wind blowing past rock formations will pick up grains of sand. If the wind then passes through a natural channel like a window or a slot canyon, it will lose speed when the channel ends and the sand will drop onto the ground. Plants cannot grow in these dry, windy spots, so the wind continues to deposit sand, and a dune forms. Two good examples in canyon country are at Coral Pink Sand Dunes State Park near Zion National Park, and on Route 24 near Capitol Reef National Park.

### Sea Stacks

Perched offshore, from San Francisco to Vancouver, Canada, sea stacks are rock headlands and pinnacles. They are composed of basalt and other volcanic material and have been separated from the mainland by the Pacific's erosive force. Some West Coast sea stacks rise more than 100 ft above the surf, and with breakers surging onto and around them, they are highly photogenic. Some of the best are found from Eureka, CA to Port Orford, OR; and from Queets to Neah Bay, WA. Sea caves and arches are rarer.

### Sierra Nevada

The Sierra Nevada mountain range is marked by a gentle rise on the west side and a sharp drop-off on the east side. The land east of the crest sank dramatically by several thousand feet, resulting in the eastern escarpment having no foothills. Moisture from the Pacific cools as the air rises up the mountains, eventually condensing and falling as rain or snow. So little water is left in the air by the time it crosses the range that the giant valleys and deserts to the east remain dry much of the year. Gaps in the crest, like Donner Pass on I–80 near Lake Tahoe, hint that large rivers once flowed westward to the ocean. The Pacific Crest Trail, which travels from Mexico to Canada, follows the line of the Sierra crest.

### Spheroidal Weathering

The desert's boulder gardens, such as Joshua Tree National Park's Wonderland of Rocks, originated when molten rock seeped up from beneath the Earth's underground crust and into the fissures or joints of other types of rock. When the magma cooled and hardened, its expansion caused the rock around it to split apart. The rounded, stacked, and blocky boulders were then shaped by wind and rain into near-spheres.

### Spire

As a butte erodes, it may become one or more spires. There are many buttes and spires in Utah's national parks.

### Syncline

A syncline is a troughlike downfold in the rock layers of the earth's crust, with its sides dipping in toward the axis. You can see synclines and anticlines as you drive throughout canyon country.

### Volcanoes

The volcanoes of the West Coast, such as Mount Rainier, Crater Lake, Mount Hood, and Mount Baker, are not, as commonly believed, dormant. Instead, most are described as "episodically active," as Mount St. Helens was in 1980 (at this writing, the volcano was actually experiencing a low-key eruption that started in 2004). At one time, the Sierra was a much lower mountain range, with peaks of only about 3,000 feet. When volcanic activity began, the flow of lava thrust the mountains upward from below and spilled out over the surface, hardening into new top layers of rock. Evidence of the region's volcanic history is most visible in the area around Mount Lassen, where you can see recent manifestations of the geological forces of volcanism.

### Window

(E) One of the more intriguing landforms you will encounter while touring canyon country are large openings in solid rock walls. These are known as arches or bridges, depending on what created the opening. Together, the two types of forms are called windows.

# Arches
# National Park

## WORD OF MOUTH

"You can't see *anything* from a car; you've got to get out and walk, better yet crawl, on hands and knees, over the sandstone and through the thornbush and cactus. When traces of blood begin to mark your trail you'll see something, maybe."

–Edward Abbey, *Desert Solitaire*

# WELCOME TO ARCHES

## TOP REASONS TO GO

★ **Unique Terrain:** There's nowhere else on Earth that looks like this.

★ **Memorable Snapshots:** You have to have a picture of Delicate Arch at sunset.

★ **Treasures Hanging in the Balance:** Landscape Arch is the longest open span in the world. Come quick! Due to its delicate nature, it could fall before you see it.

★ **Fiery Furnace:** A hike through this maze of rock walls and fins is sure to make you fall in love with the desert and appreciate nature at its most spectacular.

★ **Window to Nature:** The park has the largest collection of natural arches in the world—more than 2,000. They make great frames through which to view moonrises, mountains, and more.

Balanced Rock

**1 Devils Garden.** About 18 mi from the visitor center, this is the end of the road in Arches. Trails lead to Landscape Arch and numerous other natural rock windows. This area also has picnic tables, the park's only campground, and an amphitheater for campfire programs.

**2 Fiery Furnace.** This forbiddingly named area is so labeled because its orange spires of rock look much like tongues of flame, especially in the late-afternoon sun. About 14 mi inside from the visitor center, it's the site for ranger-guided walks.

**3 The Windows.** Reached on a spur 9²/₁₀ mi from the visitor center, this area of the park is where visitors with little time stop. Here you can see many of the park's natural arches from your car or on an easy rolling trail.

Delicate Arch

**4 Petrified Dunes.** Just a tiny pull-out about 5 mi from the visitor center, this scenic stop is where you can take pictures of acres and acres of petrified sand dunes.

**5 Courthouse Towers.** The Three Gossips, Sheep Rock, and Tower of Babel are the rock formations to see here. Enter this section of the park 3 mi past the visitor center. The Park Avenue Trail winds through the area, which was named for its steep walls and towers that look like buildings.

Bighorn Sheep

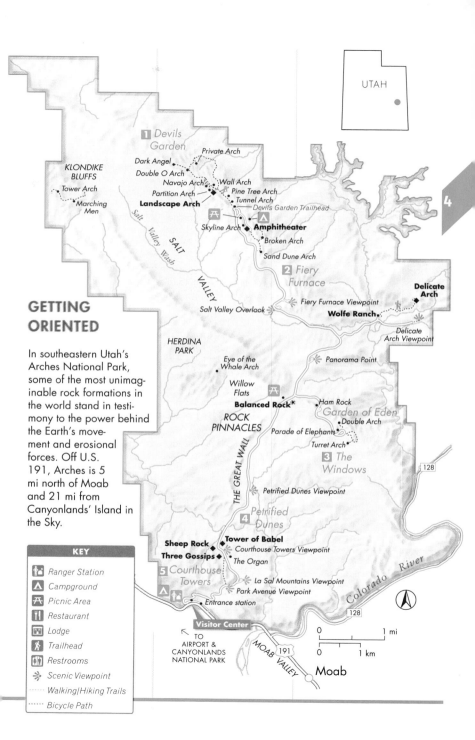

UTAH

**1** Devils Garden

KLONDIKE BLUFFS

Private Arch

Dark Angel
Double O Arch
Navajo Arch · Wall Arch
Partition Arch · Pine Tree Arch
**Landscape Arch** · Tunnel Arch
Devils Garden Trailhead

Tower Arch

Marching Men

Skyline Arch **Amphitheater**

Broken Arch

Sand Dune Arch

SALT VALLEY WASH

SALT

VALLEY

**2** Fiery Furnace

Salt Valley Overlook

Fiery Furnace Viewpoint

**Delicate Arch**

**Wolfe Ranch**

Delicate Arch Viewpoint

HERDINA PARK

Eye of the Whale Arch

Panorama Point

Willow Flats

**Balanced Rock**

Ham Rock

Garden of Eden

ROCK PINNACLES

Parade of Elephants

Double Arch

Turret Arch

**3** The Windows

128

**GETTING ORIENTED**

In southeastern Utah's Arches National Park, some of the most unimaginable rock formations in the world stand in testimony to the power behind the Earth's movement and erosional forces. Off U.S. 191, Arches is 5 mi north of Moab and 21 mi from Canyonlands' Island in the Sky.

Petrified Dunes Viewpoint

**Petrified Dunes**

THE GREAT WALL

**4**

Sheep Rock
**Three Gossips** ♦

**Tower of Babel**
Courthouse Towers Viewpoint
The Organ

La Sal Mountains Viewpoint

**5** Courthouse Towers

Colorado River

Park Avenue Viewpoint

Entrance station

128

**KEY**

🏕 Ranger Station
🛖 Campground
🌲 Picnic Area
🍴 Restaurant
🏨 Lodge
🥾 Trailhead
🚻 Restrooms
🎇 Scenic Viewpoint
······ Walking/Hiking Trails
······ Bicycle Path

**Visitor Center**

← TO AIRPORT & CANYONLANDS NATIONAL PARK

MOAB VALLEY

191

Moab

0          1 mi
0          1 km

# ARCHES PLANNER

## When to Go

**The busiest times of year at Arches are spring and fall.** In the spring, wildflowers bloom and temperatures are in the 70s. The crowds thin in summer as the thermostat approaches 100°F in July and then soars beyond that for about four weeks. In August, sudden, dramatic cloudbursts create rainfall for part of the day.

Fall brings everybody back because the weather is perfect—clear, warm days, and crisp, cool nights. October is the only autumn month that gets much rain, but even that isn't much, considering how little rain falls in the desert: an average of only 8 inches a year.

Snow seldom falls in the valley beneath the La Sal Mountains, and when it does, Arches is a photographer's paradise, as snow drapes slickrock mounds and natural rock windows. From December through February, you can hike any of the trails in nearly perfect solitude.

AVG. HIGH/LOW TEMPS.

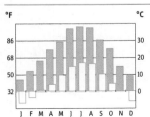

Note: Extreme highs at Arches often exceed 100°F during July and August.

## Flora & Fauna

As in any desert environment, the best time to see wildlife in Arches is early morning or evening. Summer temperatures keep most animals tucked away in cool places, though lizards crawl around all day, so if you happen to be in the right place at the right time you'll spot one of the beautiful, turquoise-necklace-collared lizards. It's more likely you'll see the Western whiptail. Mule deer, jackrabbits, and small rodents are usually active in cool morning hours or near dusk. You may spot a lone coyote foraging day or night. The park protects a small herd of desert bighorns, and some of their tribe are often seen early in the morning grazing beside U.S. 191 south of the Arches entrance. If you are fortunate enough to encounter bighorn sheep, do not approach them. They have been known to charge human beings who attempt to get too close. The park's mule deer and small mammals such as chipmunks are very used to seeing people and may allow you to get close—but don't feed them.

## Getting There & Around

Interstate 70 is the speedway that gets you across Utah. To dip southeast toward Moab, you need to veer off the interstate onto U.S. 191, a main artery running all the way to the Arizona border. Alternatively, you can take Route 128, Colorado River Scenic Byway, traveling just east of Arches. On either road services can be far apart.

The nearest airport is Grand County Airport, also known as Canyonlands Field (☎ 435/259–7419), 18 mi north of Moab. Flights are very limited. The nearest train "station" is a solitary Amtrak stop in Green River, about 60 mi northwest of Moab. For train inquiries, call Amtrak (☎ 800/872–7245).

Branching off the main, 18-mi park road are two spurs, a 2½-mi one to The Windows section and a 1⁹⁄₁₀-mi one to the Delicate Arch trailhead and viewpoint. There are several four-wheel-drive roads in the park; always check at the visitor center for conditions before attempting to drive them. U.S. 191 tends to back up mid-morning to early afternoon. There's likely to be less traffic at 8 AM or sunset.

**4**

By Janet Lowe    The red rock landscape of Arches National Park awakens the spirit and challenges the imagination: balanced rocks teeter unthinkably on pedestals; sandstone arches—of which there are more than 2,000—frame the sky with peekaboo windows; and formations like the Three Penguins greet you at points throughout the 73,379-acre park. Far from a beige-tone palette with the occasional cactus, the desert here is adorned with a rich tapestry of colors: red, orange, purple, pink, creamy ivory, deep chocolate, and even shades of turquoise. The Fiery Furnace burns like a wildfire at sunset, and acres of petrified sand dunes rise across the horizon.

## Scenic Drives

**Arches Main Park Road.** Although they are not formally designated as such, the main park road and its two short spurs are scenic drives, and you can see much of the park from your car. The main road takes you through Courthouse Towers, where you can see Sheep Rock and the Three Gossips, then alongside the Great Wall and the Petrified Dunes. A drive to The Windows section takes you to Double Arch, North and South windows, and Turret Arch; you can see Skyline Arch along the roadside as you approach the campground. The road to Delicate Arch is not particularly scenic, but it allows you hiking access to one of the park's main features. Allow about two hours to drive the 36-mi round-trip, more if you explore the spurs and stop at viewpoints.

## What to See

### Historic Site
**Wolfe Ranch.** Built in 1906 out of Fremont cottonwoods, this rustic one-room cabin housed the Wolfe family after their first cabin was lost to a flash flood. In addition to the cabin you can see remains of a root

cellar and a corral. Nearby is a Ute rock-art panel by the Delicate Arch trailhead. About 150 feet past the footbridge and before the trail starts to climb, you can see images of bighorn sheep as well as some smaller images believed to be dogs. To reach the panel, follow the narrow dirt trail along the rock escarpment to the interpretive sign. ⊠ *12⁹⁄₁₀ mi from the park entrance, 1²⁄₁₀ mi off the main road.*

## Scenic Stops

**Balanced Rock.** One of the park's favorite sights, this rock has remained mysteriously balanced on its pedestal for who knows how long. The formation's total height is 128 feet, with the huge balanced rock rising 55 feet above the pedestal. A short loop (³⁄₁₀ mi) around the base gives you an opportunity to stretch your legs and take photographs. ⊠ *9¹⁄₅ mi from the park entrance on the main road.*

**Fodor'sChoice**
★

**Delicate Arch.** The familiar symbol of Arches National Park, if not for the entire state of Utah, Delicate Arch is tall enough to shelter a four-story building. The arch is a remnant of an Entrada sandstone fin; the rest of the rock has eroded and now frames the La Sal Mountains in the background. You can drive a couple of miles off the main road to view the arch from a distance, or you can hike right up to it. The trail is a moderately strenuous 3-mi round-trip hike. ⊠ *13 mi from the park entrance, 2¹⁄₅ mi off the main road.*

**Double Arch.** In The Windows section of the park, Double Arch has appeared in several Hollywood movies, including *Indiana Jones and the Last Crusade.* Less than ¼ mi from the parking lot, the spectacular rock formation can be reached in about 10 minutes. ⊠ *11⁷⁄₁₀ mi from the park entrance on the main road.*

★ **Landscape Arch.** This natural rock opening competes with Kolob Arch at Zion for the title of largest geologic span in the world. Measuring 306 feet from base to base, it appears as a delicate ribbon of rock bending over the horizon. In 1991, a slab of rock about 60 feet long, 11 feet wide, and 4 feet thick fell from the underside, leaving it even thinner. You can reach it by walking a rolling, gravel 1³⁄₅-mi-long trail. ⊠ *Devils Garden, 18 mi from park entrance on main road.*

**Sand Dune Arch.** Kids love the trail to this arch because erosion has created a giant sandbox beneath the namesake arch. While it's an easy trail, remember that sand is difficult to walk in. A cautionary note: do not climb or jump off the arch; rangers have dealt with several accidents involving people who have done so. The trail intersects with the Broken Arch Trail, so if you visit both arches, it's 1½-mi round-trip. ⊠ *16 mi from the park entrance on the main road.*

**Skyline Arch.** A quick walk from the parking lot gives you closer views and better photos of the arch. The short trail is ²⁄₅ mi round-trip and

## ARCHES IN ONE DAY

Pack snacks, lunch, and plenty of water before you head into the park. If possible, take the Fiery Furnace walk with a ranger. If you have two or three days at Arches, your chances of getting in on the walk are better. You can sign up at the visitor center in advance, so make that your first stop. The one-day itinerary below is based on what to do if you can't take the walk or what to do on a different day. On the day of your Fiery Furnace walk, you can fill in your spare time with a walk on the **Park Avenue** trail.

Start early, while the day is still cool, with a 3-mi round-trip hike on the **Delicate Arch Trail.** The route is strenuous but richly rewarding. Pause for a healthy snack before heading for **Landscape Arch,** the second of the park's two must-see arches. To get there you must hike through **Devils Garden,** a great spot for morning photography. If

you're accustomed to hiking you might next hike out to **Double O,** a trip that is well worth the effort but that can be tough after the hike to Delicate Arch—especially in July or August. If you do hike to Double O, take your lunch with you and have a picnic in the shade of a juniper or in a rock alcove. Don't forget to pack out every scrap of paper and food. By the time you return you'll be ready to see the rest of the park by car, with some short strolls on easy paths.

In the mid- to late afternoon, drive to **Balanced Rock** for photos, then on to **The Windows.** Wander around on the easy gravel paths for more great photo ops. Depending on what time the sun is due to set, go into town for dinner before or after you drive out to Delicate Arch or the Fiery Furnace—or to the **La Sal Mountain Viewpoint**—and watch the sun set the rocks on fire.

only takes a few minutes to travel. ✉ *16½ mi from the park entrance on the main road.*

**The Windows.** Many people with limited time to spend in the park drive to this area. Here you can see a large concentration of natural windows and walk a path that winds beneath them. ✉ *11⁷⁄₁₀ mi from the park entrance, 2½ mi off the main road.*

### Visitor Center

**Arches Visitor Center.** Just opened in 2006, it's definitely worth the time for a look-see. Take time to view the 15-minute park film, *Secrets of the Red Rock,* and shop the bookstore for trail guides, books, and maps. Exhibits inform you about geology, natural history, and ancestral Puebloan presence in the Arches area, while interactive displays orient you to the park. There is water in vending machines outside. ✉ *At the park entrance* ☎ *435/719–2299* ☺ *Hours vary but generally 8 AM–5 PM daily, with extended hours late spring through early fall.*

## Sports & the Outdoors

Arches lies in the middle of the adventure capital of the world. Slick sandstone surfaces, known locally as "slickrock," make for some of the world's

## GOOD READS

**A Naturalist's Guide to Canyon Country** by David Williams and Gloria Brown is an excellent, compact field guide for both Arches and Canyonlands.

**Best Easy Day Hikes: Arches and Canyonlands** by Bill Schneider is a pocket-size trail guide that should boost your confidence on the trails.

**Canyon Country Wildflowers** by Damian Fagan can help you name the colorful blossoms you see during wildflower season (spring and early summer).

**Desert Solitaire** by Edward Abbey is a classic every visitor should read.

**Exploring Canyonlands and Arches National Parks** by Bill Schneider provides comprehensive advice on hiking trails, backcountry roads, and trip planning.

**Hiking Guide to Arches National Park** by Damian Fagan details all of the park's hiking trails.

**Into the Mystery: A Driving Tour of Moab Area Rock** by Janet Lowe offers insight into ancient Native American rock art.

best mountain biking. Thousand-foot sandstone walls draw rock climbers from across the globe—climbers should inquire at the visitor center about restrictions. There's no better place for hiking; you can choose from shady canyons or feel like you are on top of the world as you traverse red rock fins that reach for the sky. Moab outfitters can set you up for any sport you may have a desire to try.

### Bicycling

There's outstanding mountain biking all around Arches, but the park proper is not the best place to explore on two wheels. Bicycles are only allowed on established roads and since there are no shoulders, cyclists share the roadway with drivers and pedestrians gawking at the scenery. If you do want to take a spin in the park, try Willow Flats Road, the old entrance to the park. The road is about 6½-mi long one way and starts directly across from the Balanced Rock parking lot. It's a pretty ride on dirt and sand through slickrock, pinyon, and juniper country. Stay on the road with your bicycle or chance steep fines. For bike rentals and expeditions ⇨ Outfitters & Expeditions box.

### Bird-watching

Within the park you'll definitely see plenty of the big, black, beautiful raven. Look for them perched on top of a picturesque juniper branch or balancing on the bald knob of a rock. The noisy black-billed magpie populates the park, as do the more melodic canyon and rock wrens. Lucky visitors will spot a red-tailed hawk and hear its distinctive call.

### Four-Wheeling

With thousands of acres of Bureau of Land Management lands nearby, it's hardly necessary to use the park's limited trails for four-wheel adventures. You can, however, go backcountry in Arches on the Willow Flats Road and the Salt Valley Road—just don't set out without first stopping at the visitor center to learn of current conditions. The Salt Valley Road is very sandy, requiring special driving skills. For guided 4 × 4 trips, ⇨ Outfitters & Expeditions box.

## Hiking

Getting out on the trails will surely cause you to fall in love with this Martian landscape. But remember, you are hiking in a desert environment. Many people succumb to heat and dehydration because they do not drink enough water. You need a gallon per day per person. For guided trips, ⇨ Multisport under Outfitters & Expeditions box.

EASY   **Balanced Rock Trail.** You'll want to stop at Balanced Rock for photo opportunities, so you may as well walk the easy, partially paved trail around the famous landmark. This is one of the most accessible trails in the park and is suitable for small children and folks who may have difficulty walking. Allow 15 minutes for the $\frac{3}{10}$ mi round-trip walk. ⊠ *Approximately 9 mi from the park entrance.*

**Broken Arch Trail.** An easy walk across open grassland, this loop trail passes Broken Arch. The arch gets its name because it appears to be cracked in the middle, but it's not really broken. The trail is 2 mi round-trip; allow about an hour. ⊠ *End of Sand Dune Arch trail, $\frac{3}{10}$ mi off the main park road, 11 mi from the park entrance.*

**Double Arch Trail.** Near the Windows Trail is this relatively flat trail that leads you to two massive arches that make for great photo opportunities. Although only $\frac{1}{2}$ mi round-trip, you get a good taste of desert flora and fauna. ⊠ *$2\frac{1}{2}$ mi from the main road on the Windows Section spur road.*

**Park Avenue Trail.** Walk under the gaze of Queen Nefertiti, a giant rock formation that some observers think has Egyptian-looking features. The nearby rock walls resemble a New York City skyline—hence the name Park Avenue. The trail is fairly easy, with only a short hill to navigate. It's a 2 mi round-trip, or, if you are traveling with companions you can have one of them pick you up at the Courthouse Towers Viewpoint, making it a 1-mi trek downhill. Allow about 45 minutes for the one-way journey. ⊠ *On the main road, 2 mi from the park entrance.*

**Sand Dune Arch Trail.** Your kids will return to the car with shoes full of sand at this giant sandbox in the desert. It's a shady, quick hike that everyone in the family will enjoy. Set aside 30 minutes for this $\frac{2}{5}$-mi walk. ⊠ *On the main road, about $15\frac{1}{2}$ mi from the park entrance.*

**Windows Trail.** One of everyone's favorite stops in the park also gives you an opportunity to get out and enjoy the desert air. Here you'll see three giant openings in rock and walk on a trail that leads you right through the holes. Allow about an hour on this gently inclined 1-mi round-trip hike. ⊠ *On the main road, $9\frac{1}{2}$ mi from the park entrance.*

MODERATE
Fodor'sChoice
★   **Devils Garden Trail.** If you want to take a longer hike in the park, head out on this network of trails, where you can see a number of arches. You will reach Tunnel and Pine Tree arches after only $\frac{2}{3}$ mi on the gravel trail, and Landscape Arch is $\frac{4}{5}$ mi from the trailhead. Past Landscape Arch the trail changes dramatically, increasing in difficulty with many short,

# OUTFITTERS & EXPEDITIONS

### BICYCLING

**Chile Pepper Bikes.** For bicycle rentals, repairs, and espresso, stop here before you hit the trails. ⊠ 550½ N. Main St., Moab ☎ 435/259-4688 or 888/677-4688 ⊕ www.chilebikes.com.

**Rim Cyclery.** For full-suspension bike rentals and sales, solid advice on trails and parts, equipment, and gear, head to the oldest bike shop in town. ⊠ 94 W. 100 South, Moab ☎ 435/259-5333 or 888/304-8219 ⊕ www.rimcyclery.com.

**Rim Tours.** Reliable, friendly, and professional, this outfit can take you on a great guided mountain-bike tour. ⊠ 1233 S. U.S. 191, Moab ☎ 435/259-5223 or 800/626-7335 ⊕ www.rimtours.com.

**Western Spirit Cycling.** This place offers fully supported, go-at-your-own-pace multiday bike tours throughout the region. Guides versed in the geologic wonders of the area cook up meals worthy of the scenery each night. ⊠ 478 Mill Creek Dr., Moab ☎ 435/259-8732 or 800/845-2453 ⊕ www.westernspirit.com.

### FOUR-WHEELING

**Coyote Land Tours.** Let this company take you to backcountry where you could never wander on your own. Their big Mercedes Unimog vehicles cover some rough terrain while you sit back and enjoy the sites. ⊠ 397 N. Main St., Moab ☎ 435/259-6649 ⊕ www.coyotelandtours.com.

**Highpoint Hummer Tours.** If you'd rather let someone else do the driving for your off-road experience, try these friendly folks who tour the backcountry near Moab in open-air Hummer vehicles. They offer two- and four-hour "high" adventure trips plus "low" adventure tours for the more timid traveler. ⊠ 281 N. Main St., Moab ☎ 435/259-2972 or 877/486-6833 ⊕ www.highpointhummer.com.

### MULTISPORT

**Adrift Adventures.** This outfitter can get you out on the Colorado or Green rivers for either daylong or multiday raft trips. Adrift also offers a unique combination horseback ride and river trip, movie-set tour, rock-art tours, and other 4X4 excursions. ⊠ 378 N. Main, Moab ☎ 435/259-8594 or 800/874-4483 ⊕ www.adrift.net.

**Coyote Shuttle.** If you need a ride to or from your bicycle trailhead or river trip, call the Coyote. These folks also do shuttles to and from Green River for the train and bus service there. ⊠ 397 N. Main, Moab ☎ 435/259-8656 ⊕ www.coyoteshuttle.com.

**Moab Adventure Center.** Contact this reputable company for a short trip on the Colorado River, a Hummer tour, scenic flight, national park tour, or rubber kayak rental. Its shop also sells gear and clothing. ⊠ 225 S. Main St., Moab ☎ 435/259-7019 or 888/622-4097 ⊕ www.moabadventurecenter.com.

**NAVTEC.** A fast little boat engineered by this outfit gets you down the Colorado River and through Cataract Canyon in one day. They also offer trips lasting up to six days, as well as 4X4 trips and raft rentals. ⊠ 321 N. Main St., Moab ☎ 435/259-7983 or 800/833-1278 ⊕ www.navtec.com.

## RIVER EXPEDITIONS

**Canyon Voyages Adventure Co.** An excellent choice for a day trip on the Colorado River is this friendly, professional company. It's also the only company that operates a kayak school for those who want to learn how to run the rapids on their own, and you can rent rafts and kayaks here. Inside the booking office is a great shop that sells river gear, outdoor clothes, hats, sandals, and backpacks. ⊠ *211 N. Main St., Moab* ☎ *435/259-6007 or 800/733-6007* ⊕ *www.canyonvoyages.com.*

**Holiday River Expeditions.** You can rent a canoe or book a raft trip on the Green and Colorado rivers at this reliable company with decades of river experience. ⊠ *1055 E. Main St., Green River* ☎ *800/624-6323* ⊕ *www.bikeraft.com.*

**Tex's Riverways.** The folks at Tex's will take very good care of you when you rent a canoe for a self-guided trip, and they can shuttle you to and from the Green or Colorado rivers. ⊠ *691 N. 500 West, Moab* ⊕ *www.texsriverways.com.*

steep climbs. You will encounter some heights as you inch your way across a long rock fin. The trail is marked with rock cairns, and it's always a good idea to locate the next one before moving on. Along the way to Double O Arch, 2 mi from the trailhead, you can take short detours to Navajo and Partition arches. A round-trip hike to Double O takes from two to three hours. For a longer hike, include Dark Angel and/or return to the trailhead on the primitive loop. This is a difficult route through fins with a short side trip to Private Arch. If you hike all the way to Dark Angel and return on the primitive loop, the trail is 7⅕ mi round-trip. Allow about five hours for this adventure, take plenty of water, and watch your route carefully. ⊠ *18 mi from the park entrance on the main road.*

**Tower Arch Trail.** In a remote, seldom-visited area of the park, this trail takes you to a giant rock opening. If you look beneath the arch you will see a 1922 inscription left by Alex Ringhoffer, who "discovered" this section of the park. Reach the trail by driving to the Klondike Bluffs parking area via a dirt road that starts at the main park road across from Broken Arch. Check with park rangers for road conditions before attempting the drive. Allow from two to three hours for this hike. ⊠ *24½ mi from the park entrance, 7⁷⁄₁₀ mi off the main road.*

DIFFICULT    **Delicate Arch Trail.** Seeing the park's most famous freestanding arch up
★    close takes some effort. The 3-mi round-trip trail ascends a steep slick-rock slope that offers no shade—it's very hot in summer. What you find at the end of the trail is, however, worth the hard work. You can walk under the arch and take advantage of abundant photo ops, especially at sunset. In spite of its difficulty, this is a very popular trail. Allow anywhere from one to three hours for this hike, depending on your fitness level and how long you plan to linger at the arch. The trail starts at Wolf Ranch. ⊠ *13 mi from the park entrance, 2⅕ mi off the main road.*

★    **Fiery Furnace Hiking.** Rangers strongly suggest taking the guided hike through this area before you set out on your own, as there is no marked trail. A hike here is a challenging but fascinating trip through rugged ter-

## People in the Park

### OLD DOC WILLIAMS

A commemorative site in the park is named for Dr. John Williams, a dedicated local doctor and outdoorsman who loved to hike in Arches. Doc Williams, who lived to 103, was the first doctor to set up shop in Moab, back in 1896. So appreciated was his presence that area health commissioners named him county health officer and paid him $150 a year to serve the community. Locals, especially Native Americans, who came to his office and drug store would often receive a treat—sugar or a bit of hard candy. If the store was closed, folks gathered around his house and watched through the windows until Mrs. Williams brought out a loaf of home-baked bread.

rain into the heart of Arches. The trail occasionally requires the use of hands and feet to scramble up and through narrow cracks and along narrow ledges above drop-offs. To hike this area on your own you must get a permit at the visitor center ($2). If you're not familiar with the Furnace you can easily get lost and cause resource damage, so watch your step and use great caution. ⊠ *Off the main park road, about 15 mi from the visitor center.*

### Horseback Riding

Horseback riding is very restricted in the park. Horses are not allowed in the campground and must be fed a special diet for a period of time before taking them into the park. Check with the NPS for regulations. For group rides, ⇨ Multisport under Outfitters & Expeditions box.

### Rock Climbing

Fodor'sChoice
★

Rock climbers travel from across the country to scale the sheer red rock walls of Arches National Park and surrounding areas. Most climbing routes in the park require advanced techniques. Permits are not required, but you are responsible for knowing park regulations and restricted routes. One popular route in the park is Owl Rock in the Garden of Eden (about 10 mi from the visitor center), which ranges in difficulty from 5.8 to 5.11 on a scale that goes up to 5.13+. Many climbing routes are available in the Park Avenue area, about 2⅓ mi from the visitor center. These routes are also extremely difficult climbs. New climbing policies were put in place in 2006; before climbing, it's imperative that you stop at the visitor center and talk with a ranger.

## Educational Offerings

### Programs & Tours

For more information on current schedules and locations of park programs, contact the visitor center (☎ 435/719–2299) or check the bulletin boards located throughout the park.

**Campfire Program.** Every evening mid-March through October, a park ranger presents a program around the campfire at Devils Garden Campground. It's a great way to learn about subjects such as mountain lions, the Colorado River, human history in Arches National Park, or the night life of animals. ⊠ *Devils Garden Campground Amphitheater, 17⁷/₁₀ mi from the park entrance, ½ mi off the main Rd.* ◻ *Free* ⊙ *Mid-Mar.–Oct., nightly at 9.*

★ **Fiery Furnace Walk.** Join a park ranger on a two- or three-hour walk through a mazelike labyrinth of rock fins and narrow sandstone canyons. You'll see arches that can't be viewed from the park road and spend time listening to the desert. You should be relatively fit and not afraid of heights if you plan to take this moderately strenuous walk. Wear sturdy hiking shoes, sunscreen, and a hat, and bring at least a quart of water. Walks into the Fiery Furnace are usually offered twice a day (hours vary) and leave from Fiery Furnace viewpoint. Tickets may be purchased for this popular activity up to seven days in advance at the visitor center. ⊠ *Fiery Furnace trailhead, about 15 mi from the visitor center off the main park Rd.* ◻ *$10 adults, $5 children 7–12* ⊙ *Mid-Mar.–Oct., daily.*

**Guided Walks.** You can really get to know Arches National Park by joining these walks with park rangers. Many of the walks explore The Windows section of the park, but they also visit other areas of the park. Topics include geology, desert plants, and the survival tactics of animals. Check at the visitor center or on park bulletin boards for times, topics, and locations. ◻ *Free.*

**Junior Ranger Program.** Kids 6–12 can pick up a Junior Ranger booklet at the visitor center. It's full of activities, word games, drawings, and educational material about the park and the wildlife. To earn your Junior Ranger badge you must complete the booklet, attend a ranger program or watch the park slide program, and gather a bag of litter or bring 20 aluminum cans to be recycled. ☎ *435/719–2299* ◻ *Free.*

**NEED A LIFT?** Call Roadrunner Shuttle for rides to the airport or for a river or bike shuttle. They'll even take you to Salt Lake City or Grand Junction, Colorado, to catch a plane. ☎ 435/259-9402 ⊕ www.roadrunnershuttle.com.

# WHAT'S NEARBY

## Nearby Towns & Attractions

### Nearby Towns

Near the Colorado River in a beautiful valley between red rock cliffs, with the La Sal Mountains rising to 12,000 feet just 20 mi away, **Moab** is the major gateway to both Arches and Canyonlands national parks. The primarily non-Mormon community in southern Utah has been steadily gaining momentum as an arts destination, with new galleries popping up each year. The town is an interesting, eclectic place to visit, especially if you're looking for fine restaurants with good wine lists, abundant shopping, and varied lodging. Also here you'll find the area's greatest number of sports outfitters to help you enjoy the parks.

The next-closest town to Arches, about 47 mi to the northwest, is **Green River.** Unlike hip Moab, this sleepy little town is more traditional and off the tourists' radar screen. The fragrance of fresh canteloupe, watermelon, and honeydew fills the air each September (Melon Days celebrates the harvest with family-fun activities on the third weekend of September), and Crystal Geyser erupts for 30 minutes every 14 to 16 hours.

## Nearby Attractions

**Courthouse Wash.** Although this rock-art panel fell victim to a sad and unusual case of vandalism in 1980, when someone scoured the petroglyphs and pictographs that had been left by four cultures, you can still see ancient images if you take a short walk from the parking area on the left-hand side of the road. ⊠ *U.S. 191, about 2 mi south of Arches National Park entrance.*

**John Wesley Powell River History Museum.** Here you can see what it was like to travel down the Green and Colorado rivers in the 1800s. A series of interactive displays tracks the Powell Party's arduous, dangerous 1869 journey. The center also houses the River Runner's Hall of Fame, a tribute to those have followed in Powell's wake. An art gallery reserved for works thematically linked to river exploration is also onsite. ⊠ *885 E. Main St., Green River* ☎ *435/564–3427* ☜ *$2 per person, $5 per family* ⊙ *Apr.–Sept., daily 8–8; Oct.–Mar., daily 9–5.*

**Sego Canyon.** About 39 mi from Moab, this is one of the most dramatic and mystifying rock-art sights in the area. On the canyon walls you can see large, ghostlike rock-art figures etched by Native Americans approximately 4,000 years ago. There's also art left by the Ute Indians 400–700 years ago. This canyon is a little out of the way, but well worth the drive. ⊠ *About 4 mi off I–70 exit 185, Thompson Springs.*

⇨ Canyonlands National Park chapter for additional area listings.

# Area Activities

## Sports & the Outdoors

BIRD-WATCHING   **Scott M. Matheson Wetlands Preserve.** The best place around for bird-watching, this desert oasis is home to hundreds of species of birds, including such treasures as the Pied-billed Grebe, the Cinnamon Teal, and the Northern Flicker. It's also a great place to spot beaver and muskrat playing in the water. The preserve is home to three bat species: the Western pipistrel, the pallid bat, and the hoary bat. A boardwalk winds through the preserve to a viewing shelter. ⊠ *Near the intersection of 500 West and Kane Creek Blvd.* ☎ *435/259–4629.*

GOLF   **Moab Golf Course** is undoubtedly one of the most beautiful in the world.
★   The 18-hole course has lush greens set against a red rock sandstone backdrop, a lovely visual combination that's been know to distract even the most focused golfer. ⊠ *2705 S. East Bench Rd.* ☎ *435/259–6488* ☜ *Greens fees: $37 for 18 holes, including cart rental.*

RAFTING   **Fisher Towers.** On the Colorado River northeast of Arches and very near Moab, you can take one of America's most scenic—yet unintimidating—river-raft rides. This is the perfect place to take the family or to learn to kayak with the help of an outfitter. The river rolls by the red Fisher Towers as they rise into the sky in front of the La Sal Mountains. A day trip on this stretch of the river will take you about 15 mi. Outfitters offer full- or half-day adventures here. ⊠ *17 mi upriver from Rte. 128 near Moab.*

## FESTIVALS & EVENTS

**FEB.** **Western Stars Cowboy Poetry Gathering.** Cowboy poets and singers come to town Presidents' Day weekend. On tap are a dutch-oven cookoff, horse- and mule-shoeing demonstrations, traditional Western dancing and crafts, barrel racing, and Western art shows. ☎ *435/259-6272.*

**APR.** **Jeep Safari.** Every year during Easter week thousands of four-wheel-drive vehicles descend on Moab to tackle some of the toughest backcountry roads in America. ☎ *435/259-7625.*

**MAY** **Moab Arts Festival.** Artists gather at Moab's Swanny City Park to show their wares, including pottery, photography, and paintings. The festival is small enough to be fun and prices are affordable. ☎ *435/259-2742* ⊕ *www. moabartsfestival.org.*

**JUNE** **PRCA Rodeo.** Cowboys come to try their luck on thrashing bulls and broncs at this annual Western tradition. ☎ *435/259-6226.*

**JULY** **Moab Music Festival.** Listen to world-class music—primarily classical, jazz, and traditional—under the dome in the red rocks near Arches, or attend a special river concert 30 mi downstream on the Colorado River, outside Canyonlands. Musicians from all over the globe perform, and it's one event truly worth driving great distances to attend. ☎ *435/259-7003* ⊕ *www.moabmusicfest.org/.*

**NOV.** **Moab Folk Music Festival.** Folk music aficionados from all over the country gather for this outdoor concert series. ☎ *435/260-2488* ⊕ *www.moabfolkfestival.com.*

**DEC.** **Electric Light Parade.** If you visit Arches or Canyonlands in early December, you will avoid the crowds and also be in Moab for this fun—and often silly—local event. Merchants, clubs, and other organizations build whimsical floats with Christmas lights for a nighttime parade down Main Street. A **Holiday Arts and Crafts Fair** highlights the talents of many local and regional artists. ☎ *435/259-7814.*

### Arts & Entertainment

**Moab Artists Studio Tour.** Moab's artists, many of whom are inspired by the dramatic landscape nearby, open their studios to show and sell their art during this October event. ☎ *435/259–8631.*

**Moab Arts and Recreation Center.** The hub of arts activities in Moab, the center hosts art exhibits featuring local artists every other month as well as concerts and exercise classes. ✉ *111 E. 100 N, Moab* ☎ *435/259–6272.*

ART GALLERIES **Lema Kokopelli Gallery.** These folks have built a reputation for fair prices on a giant selection of Native American jewelry and art. Everything for sale here is authentic. ✉ *70 N. Main St., Moab* ☎ *435/259–5055.*

**Overlook Gallery** Take home a lasting treasure from your visit to canyon country by purchasing art at this elegant little gallery. Just a short walk from Main Street, this side street offers some great surprises in local art. ⊠ *82 E. Center, Moab* ☎ *435/259–3861.*

**Tom Till Gallery.** Stop here to buy stunning original photographs of Arches and Canyonlands by one of the nation's best-loved landscape photographers. ⊠ *61 N. Main St., Moab* ☎ *435/259–9808.*

## Shopping

**Arches Book Company.** You can't beat the warm ambience or friendly service at this popular bookstore. Every title you'd want, from the top best sellers to local authors, is here, along with your favorite coffee drink. Sit in the window, read a book, chat with locals, and watch people pass by as you sip an espresso. ⊠ *78 N. Main St., Moab* ☎ *435/259–0782* ⊕ *www.archesbookcompany.com.*

**Western Image.** A fun place to browse for a flavor of the Old West, you'll find antiques, Western art, cowboy hats, boots, belts, coins, badges, and other classy souvenirs. ⊠ *79 N. Main St., Moab* ☎ *435/259–3006.*

## Scenic Drive

**Colorado River Scenic Byway—Route 128.** One of the most scenic drives in the country is Route 128, which intersects U.S. 191 3 mi south of Arches. The 37-mi highway runs along the Colorado River northeast to Interstate 70. The drive from Moab to I-70 takes about an hour.

# WHERE TO STAY & EAT

### About the Restaurants

Since most people come to Arches to play outside, casual is the modus operandi for dining. Whether you select an award-winning Continental restaurant in Moab or a tavern in Green River, you can dress comfortably in shorts or jeans. But don't let the relaxed attire fool you. There are some wonderful culinary surprises waiting for you, often with spectacular views as a bonus. In the park itself, there are no dining facilities and no snack bars. Supermarkets, bakeries, and delis in downtown Moab will be happy to make you a sandwich to go.

### About the Hotels

There has been an explosion of overnight accommodations in the Arches area, and southeast Utah in general, during the past decade. Though there are no hotels or cabins in the park itself, in the surrounding area, every type of lodging is available, from economy chain motels to B&Bs and high-end, high-adventure resorts. It's important to know when popular events are held, however, as accommodations can, and do, fill up weeks ahead of time.

### About the Campgrounds

Campgrounds in and around Moab range from sprawling RV parks with every amenity you could dream of to quaint, shady retreats near a babbling brook. The Devils Garden Campground is a wonderful spot to call home for a few days, though it is often full and does not provide an RV dump station. Another favorite is the Dead Horse State Park Campground, which is popular with RV campers ( ⇨ Canyonlands National Park). The most centrally located campgrounds are in Moab and will generally provide services needed by RV travelers.

## Where to Eat

### In the Park

PICNIC AREAS **Balanced Rock.** The view is the best part of this picnic spot. There are no cooking facilities or water, but there are tables. If you sit just right you might find some shade under a small juniper; otherwise, this is an exposed site. Pit toilets are nearby. ⊠ *Opposite the Balanced Rock parking area, 9²/₁₀ mi from the park entrance on the main road.*

**Devils Garden.** There are grills, water, picnic tables, restrooms, and depending on the time of day, some shade from large junipers and rock walls. It's a good place for lunch before or after you go hiking. ⊠ *On the main road, 18 mi from the park entrance.*

### Outside the Park

★ **$$–$$$** ✕**Center Café.** This little jewel in the desert has a courtyard for outdoor dining. The mood inside is Spanish Mediterranean, made even more lovely by the fireplace. From grilled black Angus beef tenderloin with caramelized onion and Gorgonzola, or roasted eggplant lasagna with feta cheese and Moroccan olive marinara, there is always something here to make your taste buds go "ah." This treasure has been named "Best Restaurant in Southern Utah" more than once. Be sure to ask for the impressive wine list. ⊠ *60 N. 100 West, Moab* ☎ *435/259–4295. $16–$28* ⊟ *D, MC, V* ☉ *Closed Dec. and Jan. No lunch.*

**$$–$$$** ✕**Sorrel River Grill.** The most scenic dining experience in the area is 17 mi down the road from Moab at the Sorrel River Ranch. Outdoor dining makes the most of views over the Colorado River, the La Sal Mountains, and the red rock spires and towers that surround the ranch. The seasonal menu changes regularly for the freshest ingredients. Plenty of veggie entrées round out the menu. ⊠ *Mile Marker 17.5, Rte. 128, Moab* ☎ *435/259–4642. $15–$27* ⊟ *AE, MC, V* ☉ *No lunch.*

**$–$$$** ✕**Buck's Grill House.** For a taste of the American West, try the buffalo
Fodor'sChoice meat loaf or elk stew served at this popular dinner spot. The steaks are
★ thick and tender, and the gravies will have you licking your fingers. A selection of Southwestern entrées, including duck tamales and buffalo chorizo tacos, round out the menu. Vegetarian diners don't despair; there are some tasty choices for you, too. A surprisingly good wine list will complement your meal. Outdoor patio dining accompanied by the trickle of a waterfall will end your day perfectly. ⊠ *1393 N. U.S. 191, Moab* ☎ *435/259–5201. $8–$28* ⊟ *D, MC, V* ☉ *Closed Sat. after Thanksgiving–mid-Feb. No lunch.*

**$–$$$** ✕**Sunset Grill.** Housed in the cliff-side home of former uranium kingpin Charlie Steen, this restaurant is a Moab landmark. The views into the valley and of the Colorado River are magnificent, especially at sunset. The salmon is always reliable and the steaks are generously cut and juicy. ⊠ *900 N. Main St., Moab* ☎ *435/259–7146. $12–$24* ⊟ *AE, D, MC, V* ☉ *Closed Sun. No lunch.*

**$-$$** ✕ **Jail House Café.** Breakfast here will keep you going long into the afternoon, and since that's all that's offered, it will just have to do. From eggs Benedict to waffles, the menu is guaranteed to fill you up. Housed in what was once the county courthouse, the building held prisoners in the past. Plan your time carefully if you dine here; this is not fast food. ✉ *101 N. Main St., Moab* ☎ *435/259–3900. $9–$13* ▭ *MC, V* ◷ *No lunch or dinner. Closed Nov.–Mar.*

**$-$$** ✕ **Moab Brewery.** The hot spot for lunch and dinner, and a great brew, you have a wide selection of menu choices here. Entrées include fresh salads, creative sandwiches, and hot soups. You can't go wrong with fish, beef, poultry, or vegetarian—try the gyros salad for a taste of the Mediterranean. ✉ *686 S. Main St., Moab* ☎ *435/259–6333. $8–$14* ▭ *AE, D, MC, V.*

**¢-$$** ✕ **Isabella's Pizzeria.** The best pizza in Moab is served at this family-owned restaurant. Microbrew on tap tastes good after a day in the desert. ✉ *471 S. Main St., Moab* ☎ *435/259–6446. $6–$17* ▭ *MC, V.*

**¢-$$** ✕ **La Hacienda.** This family-run local favorite serves good south-of-the-border meals at an equally good price. The helpings are generous and the service is friendly—and yes, you can order a margarita. You can also get breakfast here, but they don't open until 11 AM. ✉ *574 N. Main St., Moab* ☎ *435/259–6319. $6–$14* ▭ *AE, D, MC, V.*

**¢-$$** ✕ **Moab Diner.** For breakfast, lunch, and dinner this is the place where old-time Moabites go. A mixture of good old-fashioned American food and Southwestern entrées gives you plenty to choose from. ✉ *189 S. Main St., Moab* ☎ *435/259–4006. $7–$14* ▭ *D, MC, V.*

★ **¢-$** ✕ **Ray's Tavern.** Ray's is something of a Western legend and a favorite hangout for river runners. Stop here for great tales about working on the river as well as the best all-beef hamburger in two counties. ✉ *25 S. Broadway, Green River* ☎ *435/564–3511. $6–$8* ▭ *AE, D, MC, V.*

## Where to Stay

### In the Park

CAMPGROUNDS & RV PARKS

★ **$** ⚠ **Devils Garden Campground.** This small campground is one of the most unusual—and gorgeous—in the National Park System, and in the West, for that matter. Sites, which are tucked away into red rock outcroppings, are available on a first-come, first-served basis during the off-season, but March through October, when the campground gets full, campers are required to pre-register for a site; this can be done at the visitor center between 7:30 and 8 AM, or at the campground entrance station after 8 AM. Also, March through October, up to 28 of the campsites can be reserved in advance (at least four but no more than 240 days prior) by contacting National Recreation Reservation Service (NRRS) via phone (☎ 877/444–6777) or online (⊕ www.ReserveUSA.com); there is a $9 booking fee. ✉ *18 mi from the park entrance on the main park Rd.* ☎ *435/719–2299, 435/259–4351 group reservations, 877/444–6777 NRRS reservations* ⊟ *435/259–4285* ⌨ *52 sites* ⚥ *Flush toilets, drinking water, fire grates, picnic tables. $15* ▭ *No credit cards.*

### Outside the Park

★ **$$$$** ▦ **Sorrel River Ranch.** This luxury ranch about 24 mi from Arches is the ultimate getaway. On the banks of the Colorado River, all rooms offer either a river view or mountain view. No matter which way you look in a landscape studded with towering red cliffs, buttes, and spires, the vista is spectacular. Rooms are furnished with hefty log beds, tables, and chairs, along with Western art and Native American rugs. For an extra cost relax in the spa with aromatherapy and a pedicure, go river rafting or mountain biking, or take an ATV out for a spin. ⊠ *Mile Marker 17.5, Rte. 128, Box K, Moab 84532* ☎ *435/259–4642 or 877/359–2715* 🖷 *435/259–3016* ⊕ *www.sorrelriver.com* ⇱ *27 suites, 32 rooms* ♨ *Restaurant, kitchen, VCR (some), Wi-Fi, pool, gym, tennis court, laundry facilities, no smoking. $279–$529* ▭ *AE, MC, V.*

**\$\$–\$\$\$\$** 🏨 **Gonzo Inn.** When creating this eclectic inn the owners gave careful attention to design, color, and art. The furnishings are all decidedly contemporary, using much metal and steel, and some rooms have fireplaces. The pool, hot tub, and courtyard overlook a shady, pretty pathway that winds for 2 mi along Mill Creek. ⊠ *100 W. 200 South, Moab 84532* ☎ *435/259–2515 or 800/791–4044* 🖷 *435/259–6992* ⊕ *www. gonzoinn.com* ⇱ *21 rooms, 22 suites* ♨ *Kitchen (some), pool, some pets allowed, no-smoking rooms. $135–$299* ▭ *AE, D, MC, V.*

☺ **\$\$–\$\$\$\$** 🏨 **Canyonlands Inn.** The best asset of this reliably comfortable and clean motel is its ideal location in the center of downtown Moab. It's within a few footsteps of many restaurants and shops, and within easy reach of the Mill Creek Parkway foot and bicycle trail. The kids will enjoy the pool and can cool off in the bubbling water feature. ⊠ *16 S. Main St., Moab 84532* ☎ *435/259–2300* 🖷 *435/259–2301* ⊕ *www. canyonlandsinn.com* ⇱ *46 rooms; 30 suites* ♨ *Refrigerator, pool, gym. $120–$229* ▭ *AE, D, MC, V.*

**\$\$–\$\$\$\$** 🏨 **Sunflower Hill Bed and Breakfast.** Tucked away on a quiet street, this turn-of-the-20th-century dwelling is operated by a family who make their guests feel truly welcome. Antiques and farmhouse treasures, well-tended gardens, and pathways make it seem like you're in the country. The full, buffet-style breakfast features a vegetable frittata, side meats, and home-baked pastries. ⊠ *185 N. 300 E, Moab 84532* ☎ *435/259–2974 or 800/662–2786* ⊕ *www.sunflowerhill.com* ⇱ *9 rooms, 3 suites* ♨ *Pool, no room phones, laundry facilities, cable TV, VCR (some), no smoking. $135–$205* ▭ *AE, D, MC, V.*

★ **\$\$\$** 🏨 **Red Cliffs Adventure Lodge.** You can have it all at this gorgeous, classically Western property. The Colorado River rolls by right outside your door, canyon walls reach for the sky in all their red glory, and you can gaze at it all from your private riverfront patio. Rooms are decidedly Western in flavor, with log furniture, lots of wood and saltillo tile. Added attractions include an on-site winery, a movie memorabilia museum, and guided rafting, hiking, biking, and horseback-riding adventures into the desert. You can hook up to high-speed Internet in your room. ⊠ *Milepost 14, Rte. 128, Moab 84532* ☎ *435/259–2002 or 866/812–2002* ⊕ *www.redcliffslodge.com* ⇱ *100 rooms, 1 suite* ♨ *Restaurant, room service, ethernet, kitchen, VCR, pool, gym, laundry facilities. $169, $269 suite* ▭ *AE, D, MC, V.*

**\$\$–\$\$\$** 🏨 **Adobe Abode.** A lovely B&B near the nature preserve, this one-story inn surrounds you with solitude. When you're not out exploring, you can unwind in a picture-perfect common room with fireplace and Southwest decor. ⊠ *778 W. Kane Creek Blvd., Moab 84532* 🕾 *435/259–7716* ⊕ *www.adobeabodemoab.com* ⟿ *5 rooms, 1 suite* ⟡ *Hot tub. $109–$169* ▤ *AE, D, MC, V.*

**$$–$$$**  🏨 **Cedar Breaks.** Some of the best lodging values in the area are rental condominiums, such as this in-town condo complex. Each unit has two bedrooms and its own balcony or patio that overlooks a grassy lawn. Moab Lodging, which takes the reservations for these units, also handles cozy little neighborhood apartments available for one night or many. ⊠ *50 E. Center St., Moab, 84532* 🕾 *435/259–5125 or 800/505–5343* 🖷 *435/259–6079* ⊕ *www.moabutahlodging.com* ⟿ *6 units* ⟡ *Kitchenettes, in-room VCRs, outdoor hot tub, laundry facilities, some pets allowed (fee); no smoking. $102–$167* ▤ *AE, MC, V.*

**$$**  🏨 **Dream Keeper Inn.** Serenity is just a wish away at this B&B in a quiet
**FodorśChoice**  Moab neighborhood, on large, shady grounds filled with flower and veg-
★  etable gardens. The rooms line a hallway in the ranch-style home, and each opens onto the pool, patio, and courtyard area, where you may want to have your morning coffee. Or, you may prefer to have breakfast in the sunny indoor dining area. Some rooms have jetted tubs. ⊠ *191 S. 200 East, Moab 84532* 🕾 *435/259–5998 or 800/505–5343* 🖷 *435/259–3912* ⊕ *www.dreamkeeperinn.com* ⟿ *6 rooms* ⟡ *Refrigerator, VCR, pool, no kids under age 15, no smoking. $100–$145* ▤ *AE, D, MC, V.*

**$**  🏨 **Green River Comfort Inn.** Right off Interstate 70, this reliable motel is convenient if you're only stopping for the night. There's a restaurant directly across the street. Rooms have a somewhat contemporary look, but mainly the decor is modern motel. ⊠ *1065 E. Main St., Green River 84525* 🕾 *435/564–3300* 🖷 *435/564–3299* ⊕ *www.choicehotels.com* ⟿ *55 rooms, 3 suites* ⟡ *Refrigerator (some), Wi-Fi, pool, gym, laundry facilities. $60–$80* ▤ *AE, D, DC, MC, V* ⏀❘ *CP.*

**CAMPGROUNDS &**  ⟁ **Canyonlands Campground.** Although this camping park is in down-
**RV PARKS**  town Moab, you get the feeling you are in a shady retreat. Because it's
↺ **$$–$$$**  downtown, all local amenities are convenient. ⊠ *555 S. Main St., Moab 84532* 🕾 *435/259–6848 or 888/522–6848* ⟿ *111 sites with hookups; 31 tent sites; 8 cabins* ⟡ *Grills, flush toilets, full hookups, partial hookups (electric and water), dump station, drinking water, guest laundry, showers, picnic tables, electricity, public telephone, general store, service station, swimming (pool), play area. $19–$39* ▤ *AE, D, MC, V.*

↺ **$–$$**  ⟁ **Moab Valley RV and Campark.** Near the Colorado River, with a 360-
**FodorśChoice**  degree view, this campground seems to get bigger and better every year.
★  Just 2 mi from Arches National Park, it's convenient for sightseeing, river rafting, and all types of area attractions and activities. On-site you can pitch some horseshoes, perfect your putting, or soak in the hot tub. Kids and parents alike will enjoy all the playgrounds, including a giant chess- and checkboard. Parents can let the kids loose to play without worry in this gated campground. The place is spotlessly clean, with everything from tent sites to cottages. ⊠ *1773 N. U.S. 191, Moab 84532* 🕾 *435/259–4469* ⊕ *www.moabvalleyrv.com* ⟿ *108 sites (62 with with full hook-ups, 7 with water and electric only, 39 tent sites); 33 cabins* ⟡ *Grills, flush toilets, full hookups, dump station, drinking water, guest laundry, showers,*

*picnic tables, electricity, public telephone, general store, play area, swimming (pool). $17–$26 camping sites, $34–$65 cabins* ⊟ *MC, V.*

★ $  ⛺ **Up the Creek Campground.** This neighborhood campground lies under big cottonwoods on the banks of Mill Creek. Even though you are near downtown, you'll feel like you're in the woods—the campground has walk-in tent sites only. ⊠ *210 E. 300 South, Moab 84532* ☎ *435/259–6995* ⇗ *20 sites* ♿ *Grills, flush toilets, drinking water, showers, picnic tables. $10 per person* ⊙ *Mid-Mar.–Oct.*

¢–$  ⛺ **Bureau of Land Management Campgrounds.** There are 342 sites at 18 different BLM campgrounds near Arches and Canyonlands national parks. Most of these are in the Moab area near Arches and Canyonlands' Island in the Sky District, along the Route 128 Colorado River corridor, on Kane Creek Road, and on Sand Flats Road. All sites are primitive and those mentioned below have no water. Campsites go on a first-come, first-served basis. They are all open year-round. Credit cards are not accepted. ☎ *435/259–6111* ⊕ *www.blm.gov/utah/moab.*

**Big Bend.** Both RVs and tents can camp at this spot next to the Colorado River near Arches. There are large cottonwoods for shade and you can hear the river rumble through the red rock canyons. ⊠ *7⁴/₁₀ mi from U.S. 191 on Rte. 128* ⇗ *23 sites* ♿ *Pit toilets. $10.*

**Goose Island Campground.** This area on the river road near Arches is suitable for RVs and tents. You can dip your toes in the Colorado River while you lounge under a cottonwood—but the river is dangerous, so don't swim without a life jacket. ⊠ *1¹/₁₀ mi from U.S. 191 on Rte. 128* ⇗ *18 sites* ♿ *Pit toilets. $10.*

**Moonflower Camping Area.** A favorite of tent campers because of the quiet and solitude, these sites are all walk-in. There's a large panel of ancient Native American petroglyphs at the mouth of Moonflower Canyon. ⊠ *3 mi from Hwy. 191 on Kane Creek Rd., Moab* ⇗ *8 sites* ♿ *Pit toilets. $5.*

**Sand Flats Recreation Area.** The largest of the campgrounds near Arches, this spot is tucked back in the slickrock near the bike trail of the same name. Juniper and pinyon provide a little shade and the La Sal Mountains loom in the distance. During certain times of the year, most notably Spring Break, this is a favorite of young folks with boom boxes, beer, and bicycles, so unless you're looking for a party atmosphere it's best to avoid this campground in March and early April. ⊠ *2 mi east of Moab on Sand Flats Rd., Moab 84532* ⇗ *143 sites* ♿ *Pit toilets. $8.*

# ARCHES ESSENTIALS

ACCESSIBILITY Not all park facilities meet federally mandated ADA standards, but as visitation to Arches climbs, the park is making efforts to increase accessibility. Visitors with mobility impairments can access the visitor center, all restrooms throughout the park, and one campsite (#7) at the Devils Garden Campground. The Park Avenue Viewpoint is a paved path with a slight decline near the end, and both Delicate Arch and Balanced Rock viewpoints are partially hard surfaced.

ADMISSION FEES Admission to the park is $10 per vehicle and $5 per person on foot, motorcycle, or bicycle, good for seven days. A $25 local park pass grants you admission to both the Arches and Canyonlands parks for one year.

ADMISSION HOURS The Park is open year-round, 24/7. It's in the Mountain time zone.

ATMS/BANKS There are no ATMs in the park. The nearest ATM and full-service bank is in Moab.
🏧 **Wells Fargo Bank** ✉ 4 N. Main St., Moab. **Zions Bank** ✉ 300 S. Main St., Moab.

AUTOMOBILE SERVICE STATIONS Head to Moab for fuel, oil and tire changes, and auto-repair work.
🏧 **American Car Care Center/Chip's Grand Tire** ✉ 312 N. Main St., Moab ☎ 435/259-7909. **Certified Ford Domestic Repair Service** ✉ 500 S. Main St., Moab ☎ 435/259-6107. **Moab Chevron** ✉ 817 S. Main, Moab ☎ 435/259-0500. **Walker Phillips 66 Service Station** ✉ 299 S. Main St., Moab ☎ 435/259-6030.

EMERGENCIES In the event of a fire or a medical emergency, or to reach law enforcement, dial 911 or contact a park ranger (on hand at the visitor center during operating hours). There are no first-aid stations in the park; report to the visitor center for help.

LOST AND FOUND For lost-and-found, stop by the park's visitor center.

PERMITS Permits are required for backcountry camping and for hiking without a park ranger in the Fiery Furnace. You can purchase a Fiery Furnace permit ($2 per person for adults, $1 for kids 7–12) at the visitor center.

POST OFFICES There is no mail drop at Arches National Park. The nearest full-service post office is in Moab.
🏧 **Moab Branch Post Office** ✉ 50 E. 100 North, Moab 84532 ☎ 435/259-7427.

PUBLIC TELEPHONES You can find a public telephone only at the park's visitor center. Cell-phone reception is available intermittently in the park.

RELIGIOUS SERVICES There are no chapel or other religious services in the park.

RESTROOMS You can find public restrooms at the visitor center, Devils Garden Campground, and Balanced Rock picnic area, as well as trailheads.

SHOPS & GROCERS There is no place within the park itself to get basic groceries or camping supplies, but several stores in Moab sell groceries and supplies for camping, climbing, and hiking.
🏧 **Dave's Corner Market** ✉ 401 Mill Creek Dr., Moab ☎ 435/259-6999. **Walker Drug Co.** ✉ 290 S. Main St., Moab ☎ 435/259-5959.

### NEARBY TOWN INFORMATION
🏧 **Green River Information Center.** ✉ 885 E. Main St., Green River 84525 ☎ 435/564-3427. 🏧 **Moab Information Center.** ✉ 84 N. 100 E. Center St. (at intersection of Center and Main), Moab 84532 ☎ 435/259-8825 or 800/635-6622 ⊕ www.discovermoab.com.

### VISITOR INFORMATION
🏧 **Arches National Park** ✉ N. U.S. 191, Moab, UT 84532 ☎ 435/719-2299, 435/719-2200, 435/719-2391 for the hearing-impaired ⊕ www.nps.gov/arch.

# Badlands National Park

Badlands National Park

## WORD OF MOUTH

"I've been about the world a lot, and pretty much over our own country, but I was totally unprepared for that revelation called the Dakota Bad Lands . . . What I saw gave me an indescribable sense of mysterious elsewhere—a distant architecture, an endless supernatural world more spiritual than earth but created out of it."

–Frank Lloyd Wright

# WELCOME TO BADLANDS

## TOP REASONS TO GO

★ **Here a fossil, there a fossil:** From the mid-1800s, the Badlands area has welcomed paleontologists, researchers, and fossil hunters who have discovered the remnants of numerous species from ancient days.

★ **A world of wildlife:** Badlands National Park is home to a wide array of wildlife: antelope, deer, black-footed ferret, prairie dogs, rabbits, coyotes, foxes, and badgers.

★ **Ready at a moment's notice:** The Minuteman Missile Silo, located at the entrance to the park, represents the only remaining intact components of a nuclear-missile field that consisted of 150 Minuteman II missiles, 15 launch control-centers, and covered over 13,500 square mi of southwestern South Dakota.

★ **Stars Aplenty:** Due to its remote location, Badlands National Park contains some of the clearest and cleanest air in the country, which makes it perfect for viewing the night sky.

**1 North Unit.** This is the most easily accessible of the three units and attracts the most visitors. It includes the Badlands Wilderness Area.

590

Scenic

589

44

Sheep Mountain Table

Pine Ridge Indian Reservation Boundary

27

**3**

STRONGHOLD UNIT

Stronghold Table

40

2

Visitor Center

TO WOUNDED KNEE

**2 Palmer Creek Unit.** This is the most isolated section of the park—no recognized roads pass through its borders. You must obtain permission from private landowners to pass through their property (contact the White River Visitor Center on how to do so). If you plan on exploring here, count on spending two days—one day to hike in and one day out.

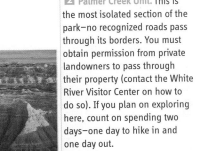

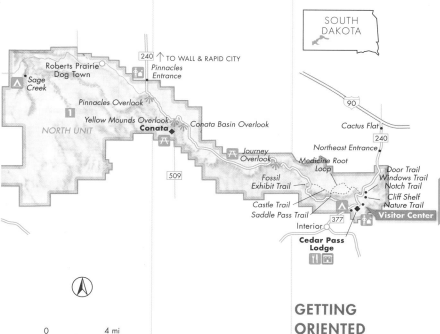

SOUTH DAKOTA

240 ↑ TO WALL & RAPID CITY

Roberts Prairie Dog Town

Pinnacles Entrance

Sage Creek

Pinnacles Overlook

90

Yellow Mounds Overlook

**Conata**

Conata Basin Overlook

Cactus Flat

**1**

**NORTH UNIT**

240

Journey Overlook

Northeast Entrance

509

Medicine Root Loop

Fossil Exhibit Trail

Door Trail

Windows Trail

Notch Trail

Cliff Shelf Nature Trail

**5**

Castle Trail

Saddle Pass Trail

377

**Visitor Center**

Interior

**Cedar Pass Lodge**

# GETTING ORIENTED

The park is divided into three units: the North Unit, and the southern Stronghold and Palmer units. The two southern units are within Pine Ridge Indian Reservation and are jointly managed by the National Park Service and the Oglala Sioux Tribe. Much of the southern units are accessible only on foot or horseback, or by a high-clearance four-wheel drive or ATV.

0        4 mi

0        4 km

**2**

**PALMER CREEK UNIT**

TO WOUNDED KNEE

**3 Stronghold Unit.** This was used as a gunnery range for the United States Air Force and the South Dakota National Guard from 1942 until the late 1960s. Discarded remnants and unexploded ordnance make this area potentially dangerous, so mind your step here. If you do find fragments of this era, do not handle them. Report the location to a ranger.

**KEY**

- Ranger Station
- Campground
- Picnic Area
- Restaurant
- Lodge
- Trailhead
- Restrooms
- Scenic Viewpoint
- ····· Walking/Hiking Trails
- ······ Bicycle Path

# BADLANDS PLANNER

## When to Go

Most visitors frequent the park between Memorial Day and Labor Day. Fortunately, **the park's vast size and isolation prevents it from ever being too packed, except possibly the first week of August,** when hundreds of thousands of motorcyclers flock to the Black Hills for the annual Sturgis Motorcycle Rally. On the flip side, it's possible to drive Badlands Loop Road in winter without seeing more than one or two other vehicles. In summer, temperatures typically hover around 90°F—though it can get as hot as 116°F—and sudden mid-afternoon thunderstorms are not unusual. It rarely rains for more than 10 or 15 minutes (the average annual rainfall is 15 inches). Autumn weather is generally sunny and warm. Snow usually appears by late October. Winter temperatures can drop to as low as -40°F. Early spring is often wet, cold, and unpredictable, and freak snowstorms appear as late as April. By May the weather usually stabilizes, bringing pleasant 70°F days.

AVG. HIGH/LOW TEMPS.

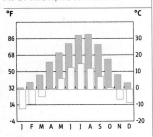

## Flora & Fauna

Little grows among the sharp rock formations and sandy buttes of the badlands. Most of the park, however, is made up of mixed-grass prairies, where more than 460 species of hardy grasses and wildflowers flourish in the warmer months, such as prairie coneflower, yellow plains prickly pear, pale-green yucca, buffalo grass, and side oats grama. Trees and shrubs are few and far between, confined largely to dry creek beds. The most common are Rocky Mountain junipers, which give the Cedar Pass area its name, and Plains cottonwoods.

For wildlife viewing, keep a sharp lookout around sunrise and sunset. It's not unusual to see herds of pronghorn antelope and mule deer dart across the flat plateaus, American bison grazing along the buttes, prairie dogs barking warnings, and sharptail grouse running through the tall grass, as golden eagles, turkey vultures, and hawks soar on the updrafts.

## Getting There & Around

In southwestern South Dakota, Badlands National Park is 70 mi east of Rapid City and 73 mi northeast of Wind Cave National Park. It is accessed via exit 110 or 131 off Interstate 90, or Route 44 east to Route 377.

Badlands is one of the least developed places on Earth, and few roads, paved or otherwise, pass within park boundaries. Badlands Loop Road (Route 240) is the only one that intersects Interstate 90. It's well maintained and rarely crowded. Portions of Route 44 and 27 run at the fringes of the badlands, connecting the visitor centers and Rapid City. Some roads through the park are unpaved, and should be traveled with care when wet. Sheep Mountain Table Road, a 7-mi road carved out by homesteaders in the early 20th century, is the only public road into the Stronghold Unit of the park. It's impassable when wet, with deep ruts—sometimes only high-clearance vehicles can get through. Off-road driving is prohibited. There's plenty of free parking at the visitor centers, scenic overlooks, and trailheads.

By T. D. Griffith
& Dustin D.
Floyd

So stark and forbidding are the chiseled spires, ragged ridgelines, and deep ravines of South Dakota's badlands that Lieutenant Colonel George Custer once described them as "hell with the fires burned out." Although a bit more accessible than the underworld, the landscape is easily the strangest in the Great Plains. Ruthlessly ravaged over the ages by wind and rain, the 380 square mi of wild terrain continue to erode and evolve, sometimes visibly changing shape in a few days. Prairie creatures thrive on the untamed territory, and fossils are in abundance.

## Scenic Drive

For the average visitor, a casual drive is the essential means by which to see Badlands. To do the scenery justice, drive slowly, and don't hesitate to get out and explore on foot when the occasion calls for it.

★ **Badlands Loop Road.** The simplest drive is on two-lane Badlands Loop Road (Route 240). The drive circles from exit 110 off Interstate 90 through the park and back to the interstate at exit 131. Start from either end and make your way around to the various overlooks along the way. Pinnacles and Yellow Mounds overlooks are outstanding places to examine the sandy pink- and brown-toned ridges and spires distinctive to the badlands. At a certain point the landscape flattens out slightly to the north, revealing spectacular views of mixed-grass prairies. In the rugged Cedar Pass area, the drive takes you past some of the park's best trails.

## What to See

### Historic Sites

**The Big Pig Dig.** Daily, from June through August, paleontologists dig for fossils and field questions from curious visitors at this site named

## BADLANDS IN ONE DAY

With a packed lunch and plenty of water, arrive at the park via the northeast entrance (off I-90 at exit 131), and follow Route 240 (Badlands Loop Rd.) southwest toward the **Ben Reifel Visitor Center.** You can pick up park maps and information here, and also pay the park entrance fee (if the booth at the entrance was closed).

Next, stop at the **Big Badlands Overlook,** just south of the northeast entrance, to get a good feel for the landscape. As you head toward the visitor center, hike one of the trails you'll pass, or if you prefer guided walks, head down to the Fossil Exhibit Trail, where you can join the Fossil Talk at 10:30 AM (with repeats at 1:30 and 3:30 PM), usually available from early June to mid-August. The badlands are one of the richest fossil fields in the world, and along the trail are examples of six extinct creatures, now protected under clear plastic domes. After your walk, drive to the **Journey Overlook,** up on the right. Here you can enjoy a packed lunch amid grassy prairies, with the sharp, rocky badland formations all around you.

After lunch, continue driving along Badlands Loop Road, stopping at the overlooks for views and a hike or two. Near the Conata Picnic Area, you'll find the **Big Pig Dig,** a fossil site still being excavated by paleontologists. At the junction with **Sage Creek Rim Road,** turn left and follow it along the northern border of the 100-square-mi **Badlands Wilderness Area,** home to hundreds of bison. If the road is dry, take a 5-mi side trip down Sage Creek Rim Road to **Roberts Prairie Dog Town,** inhabited by a huge colony of the chattering critters. Children love watching these small rodents, which bark warning calls and dive underground if you get too close to their colony. The park is less developed the farther you travel on Sage Creek Rim Road, allowing you to admire the sheer isolation and untouched beauty of badlands country. Hold out for a glorious sunset over the shadows of the nearby Black Hills.

for a large fossil originally thought to be of a prehistoric pig (it actually turned out to be a small, hornless rhinoceros). ⊠ *Conata Picnic Area, 17 mi northwest of the Ben Reifel Visitor Center.*

**Stronghold Unit.** With few paved roads and no campgrounds, the park's southwest section is difficult to access without a four-wheel-drive or high-clearance vehicle. However, if you're willing to trek, the unit's isolation provides a rare opportunity to explore badlands rock formations and prairies completely undisturbed. From 1942 to 1968 the U.S. Air Force and South Dakota National Guard used much of the Stronghold Unit as a gunnery range. If you see unexploded ordnance (UXO) while hiking in the Stronghold Unit, steer clear of it and find another route—however, note the location so you can report it to a ranger later. ⊠ *North and west of White River Visitor Center; entrance off Hwy. 27.*

**Stronghold Table.** This 3-mi-long plateau is reached only by crossing a narrow land bridge just wide enough to let a wagon pass. It was here, just

## People in the Park

### PETER NORBECK

Much of the credit for setting aside South Dakota's badlands as public lands is owed to politician Peter Norbeck. Convinced that the state's badlands formations were more distinctive than those in other parts of the American West, Norbeck began lobbying for a new national park almost immediately after he was elected to the U.S. Senate in 1920. Political maneuvering tied up the proposal in Congress for nearly 10 years, and land issues delayed the measure for another decade. Finally, on March 4, 1929, the region was declared Badlands National Monument by President Calvin Coolidge. It was promoted to a national park in 1978.

**5**

before the Massacre at Wounded Knee in 1890, that some 600 Sioux gathered to perform one of the last known Ghost Dances, a ritual in which the Sioux wore white shirts that they believed would protect them from bullets. Permission from private landowners is required to gain access to the table; contact the White River Visitor Center for details. ⊠ *Within Stronghold Unit.*

### Scenic Stops

★ **Badlands Wilderness Area.** Covering about 25% of the park, this 100-square-mi area is part of the United States' largest prairie wilderness. About two-thirds of the Sage Creek region is mixed-grass prairie, making it the ideal grazing grounds for bison, pronghorn, and many of the park's other native animals. The Grassy Tables Overlook 2 mi northwest on Sage Creek Rim Road and the Pinnacles Overlook 1 mi south of the Pinnacles entrance are the best places to get an overview of the wilderness area. Feel free to park beside the road and hike your own route into the untamed, unmarked prairie—just remember that all water in this region is unfit for drinking. ⊠ *25 mi northwest of Ben Reifel Visitor Center.*

**Big Badlands Overlook.** From this spot just south of the northeast entrance, 90% of the park's 1 million annual visitors get their first views of the White River Badlands. ⊠ *5 mi northeast of Ben Reifel Visitor Center.*

**Roberts Prairie Dog Town.** Once a homestead, the site today contains one of the (if not "the") largest colony of black-tailed prairie dogs in the country. ⊠ *5 mi west of Badlands Loop Rd. on Sage Creek Rim Rd.*

**Yellow Mounds Overlook.** Contrasting sharply with the whites, grays, and browns of the badlands pinnacles, the mounds viewed from here greet you with soft yet vivid yellows, reds, and purples. ⊠ *16 mi northwest of the Ben Reifel Visitor Center.*

### Visitor Centers

**Ben Reifel Visitor Center.** This is the park's main information hub and is open year-round. Definitely stop here first to pick up brochures and maps. June through August, a 22-minute video about Badlands geology and wildlife runs continually. The facility is named for a Sioux activist and the first

Lakota to serve in Congress. ⊠ *On Badlands Loop Rd., near Hwy. 377 junction, just over 8 mi from northeast entrance* ☎ *605/433–5361* ⊘ *June 4–Aug. 19, daily 7 AM–8 PM; Aug. 20–Sept. 9, daily 8–6; Sept. 10–June 3, daily 9–4.*

**White River Visitor Center.** Open only three months out of the year, this small center serves almost exclusively serious hikers and campers venturing into the Stronghold or Palmer units. If you're heading into one of the southern units, stop here for maps and details about road and trail conditions. The center is located on the Pine Ridge Indian Reservation. ⊠ *25 mi south of Hwy. 44 via Hwy. 27* ☎ *605/455–2878* ⊘ *June–Aug., daily 10–4.*

## Sports & the Outdoors

Pure, unspoiled, empty space is the greatest asset of Badlands National Park, and it can only be experienced to its highest degree if you're on foot. Spring and autumn are the best times of the year to do wilderness exploring, since the brutal extremes of summer and winter can—and do—kill. Before you venture out, make sure you have at least one gallon of water per person per day, and be prepared to take shelter from freak late afternoon thunderstorms, which can strike without warning.

### Air Tours

OUTFITTER & EXPEDITIONS **Black Hills Baloons.** This company provides amazing bird's-eye views of some of the Black Hills' most picturesque locations. Reservations are essential. ⊙ *Box 210, Custer 57730* ☎ *605/673–2520* ✉ *$225–$500* ⊕ *www.blackhillsballoons.com.*

### Bicycling

Bicycles are permitted only on designated roads, which may be paved or unpaved. Flat-resistant tires are recommended.

**Sheep Mountain Table Road.** This 7-mi dirt road in the Stronghold Unit is ideal for mountain biking, but should be biked only when dry. The terrain is level for the first 3 mi; then it climbs the table and levels out again. At the top you can take in great views of the area. ⊠ *About 14 mi north of the White River Visitor Center.*

OUTFITTER **Two Wheeler Dealer Cycle and Fitness.** This family-owned and -operated outfitter stocks more than 1,000 new bikes for sale or rent. Service is exceptional here, and you can get trail and route information for Badlands National Park and the Black Hills. ⊠ *100 East Blvd. N, Rapid City* ☎ *605/343–0524* ⊕ *www.twowheelerdealer.com.*

### Bird-watching

More than 215 bird species have been recorded in the area, including pelicans, cormorants, swans, golden and bald eagles, falcons, cranes, doves, and cuckoos. Established roads and trails are the best places from which to watch for nesting species. The Cliff Shelf Nature Trail and the Castle Trail, which both traverse areas with surprisingly thick vegetation, are especially good locations. You may even catch sight of a rare burrowing owl at the Roberts Prairie Dog Town. Bring along binoculars.

## Hiking

Fossil Exhibit Trail and Cliff Shelf Nature Trail are must-dos, but even these popular trails are primitive, so don't expect to see bathrooms or any hiking surfaces other than packed dirt and gravel. Because the weather here can be so variable, rangers suggest that you be prepared for anything. Wear sunglasses, a hat, and long pants, and have rain gear available. It's illegal to interfere with park resources, which includes everything from rocks and fossils to plants and artifacts. Stay at least 100 yards away from wildlife. Due to the dry climate, open fires are never allowed. Tell someone if you're going to embark on a multiday expedition. If you have a cell phone with you, assume it won't get a signal in the park. But most importantly, be sure to bring your own water. Sources in the park are few and far between, and none of them are drinkable. If you're going into the wilderness, bring a gallon of water per person per day. For day hikes, rangers suggest you drink at least a quart per person per hour.

EASY **Fossil Exhibit Trail.** Fossils of early mammals are displayed under glass along this ¼-mi length trail, which is wheelchair accessible. Since October 2006, the trail has new fossil casts that are touchable. Give yourself at least an hour to fully enjoy this popular hike. ⊠ *5 mi northwest of the Ben Reifel Visitor Center on Hwy. 240.*

Fodor'sChoice
★

**Window Trail.** This 200-yard round-trip trail ends at a natural hole in a rock wall. Looking though, you'll see more of the distinctive badlands pinnacles and spires. ⊠ *2 mi north of the Ben Reifel Visitor Center.*

MODERATE **Cliff Shelf Nature Trail.** This ½-mi loop winds through a wooded prairie
★ oasis in the middle of dry, rocky ridges and climbs 200 feet to a peak above White River Valley for an incomparable view. Look for chipmunks, squirrels, and red-wing blackbirds in the wet wood, and eagles, hawks, and vultures at hilltop. Even casual hikers can complete this trail in far less than an hour, but if you want to observe the true diversity of wildlife present here, stay longer. ⊠ *1 mi east of the Ben Reifel Visitor Center.*

**Notch Trail.** One of the park's more interesting hikes, this 1½-mi round-trip trail takes you over moderately difficult terrain and up a ladder. Winds at the notch can be fierce, but it's worth lingering for the view of the White River Valley and the Pine Ridge Indian Reservation. If you take a couple of breaks and enjoy

> ### MULTIDAY TRIP TIPS
>
> Before you begin a multiday visit to the badlands, stock up on enough water and food; both resources are hard to come by in the park. This is especially true in the backcountry, where water is so laden with silt and minerals that it's impossible to purify. Also bring along a compass, topographical map, and rain gear.

5

## TOURS

**Affordable Adventures Badlands Tour.** Take a seven-hour narrated tour through the park and surrounding badlands for $100 per person. Tours can easily be customized. ✉ *Box 546, Rapid City 57709* ☎ *605/342-7691* ⊕ *www.enetis.net/~carol* 🖃 *$100* ⊙ *Year-round.*

**Golden Circle Tours.** This company gives a seven-hour, narrated van tour out of Custer to several venues, including Mount Rushmore, Crazy Horse Monument, and Custer State Park. Other Black Hills tours are available. ✉ *40 5th St. N., Custer* ☎ *605/673-4349* ⊕ *www. goldencircletours.com* 🖃 *$59 for main tour* ⊙ *Apr. 15–Oct. 15, weather permitting.*

**Gray Line of the Black Hills.** This outfit offers bus tours from Rapid City to Mount Rushmore, Black Hills National Forest, Custer State Park, and Crazy Horse Monument. ✉ *1600 E. St. Patrick St., Rapid City* ☎ *800/456-4461* ⊕ *www. blackhillsgrayline.com* 🖃 *$35–$63* ⊙ *Apr. 15–Oct. 5.*

**Mount Rushmore Tours.** Beginning at Fort Hayes on the *Dances with Wolves* film set and then moving to Mount Rushmore, Custer State Park, and Crazy Horse Monument, this nine-hour trip around the Black Hills includes a cowboy show plus breakfast and dinner. ✉ *2255 Fort Hayes Dr., Rapid City* ☎ *888/343-3113* ⊕ *www.rushmoretours.com* 🖃 *$64* ⊙ *Mid-May–Oct.*

the views, you'll probably want to plan on spending a little more than an hour on this hike. ✉ *2 mi north of the Ben Reifel Visitor Center.*

DIFFICULT **Saddle Pass Trail.** This route, which connects with Castle Trail and Medicine Root Loop, is a steep, ¼-mi climb up and down the side of "The Wall," an impressive rock formation. Plan on spending about an hour on this climb. ✉ *2 mi west of the Ben Reifel Visitor Center.*

**Badlands Wilderness Area.** If you want a challenge, you might consider trekking this 100-square-mi parcel of grassy steppes and rocky canyons east of the highway and south of Sage Creek Rim Road, near the Pinnacles entrance. There are no services here and very few visitors. Before venturing out, check in with park staff at one of the visitor centers. ✉ *25 mi northwest of Ben Reifel Visitor Center on Hwy. 240.*

### Horseback Riding

★ The park has one of the largest and most beautiful horse-riding territories in the state. Riding is allowed in most of the park except for some marked trails, roads, and developed areas. The mixed-grass prairie of the Badlands Wilderness Area is especially popular with riders. Note that the weather in the Badlands Wilderness Area can be very unpredictable. Only experienced riders or people accompanied by experienced riders should venture far from more developed areas. Potable water for visitors and animals is a rarity. Riders must bring enough water for themselves and their stock. Only certified weed-free hay is approved in the park. Horses are not allowed to run free. All visitors with horses should contact park officials for other restrictions that may apply.

OUTFITTER ★ **Gunsel Horse Adventures.** Gunsel arranges pack trips into the badlands, Black Hills National Forest, and Buffalo Gap National Grassland. The four-day trips are based in one central campsite and are all-inclusive; you bring your own sleeping bag and personal effects (seven- and 10-day trips are also available).

> **GEAR UP!**
>
> **Scheels All Sports** is an all-purpose outfitter. Whether it's for golf, paintball, biking, or hiking, Scheels offers top-of-the-line equipment at only slightly inflated prices. ⊠ *480 Rushmore Mall, 2200 N. Maple Ave., Rapid City* ☎ *605/342–9033* ⊕ *www. scheelssports.com.*

Reservations are essential. ✉ *Box 1575, Rapid City 57709* ☎ *605/343–7608* ⊕ *www.gunselhorseadventures.com* ✉ *$250 per day.*

## Educational Offerings

In addition to what's listed here, there are many programs available for visitors of all ages to the park. Pick up information at a visitor center.

### Ranger Programs

All ranger programs and activities are free.

**Evening Program.** Watch a 40-minute outdoor audiovisual presentation on various aspects of the badlands. The shows typically begin around 9 PM. Check with a ranger for exact times and topics. ⊠ *Cedar Pass Campground amphitheater* ☉ *Mid-June–mid-Aug., daily.*

**Fossil Talk.** What were the badlands like many years ago? These protected fossil exhibits will inspire and answer all your questions. ⊠ *Fossil Exhibit Trail, 5 mi west of the Ben Reifel Visitor Center* ☉ *Mid-June–mid-Aug., daily 10:30 AM, 1:30 PM, 3:30 PM.*

**Geology Walk.** Learn the geologic story of the White River badlands in a 45-minute walk. The terrain can be rough in places, so be sure to wear hiking boots or sneakers—a hat is a good idea, too. ⊠ *Door/Window trail parking, 2 mi east of the Ben Reifel Visitor Center* ☉ *Mid-June–mid-Aug., daily 8:30 AM.*

**Junior Ranger Program.** Children ages 7–12 may participate in this 45-minute adventure, typically a short hike, game, or other hands-on activity focused on badlands wildlife, geology, or fossils. Parents are welcome. ⊠ *Cedar Pass Campground amphitheater* ☎ *605/433–5361* ☉ *June–Aug., daily 10:30 AM.*

# WHAT'S NEARBY

Badlands National Park is situated off Interstate 90 with two separate entrances. Located 50 mi east of the Black Hills (and Rapid City, the largest community on this side of the state), Badlands allows travelers a unique stop in a highly dense area of national parks, monuments, and memorials. Its close proximity to national treasures such as Mount

## Wounded Knee Massacre

IN LATE DECEMBER 1890 the men of the Seventh Cavalry, armed with a federal mandate (and some light artillery), intercepted a group of 350 Lakota in southwest South Dakota with the intention of disarming them and marching them to Nebraska, where they would be forced onto scattered reservations. The disarming process was remarkably peaceful—that is, until soldiers approached a warrior named Black Coyote. According to several accounts, Black Coyote wouldn't relinquish his weapon without compensation. Somehow, a weapon was discharged, and at least one soldier ordered the troops to open fire. Fearful of an impending attack, the cavalry did so, even bringing their artillery to bear on the Lakota camp. Warriors scrambled to retrieve their seized rifles to re-arm themselves. By the time the smoke had cleared, about 150 Lakota and 25 U.S. soldiers lay dead. While most of the remaining Lakota managed to escape, the majority perished in the elements, the victims of a sudden blizzard. When a burial party returned to the site after the storm, they found the frozen and contorted bodies of nearly 300 Lakota, mostly women and children, which they placed in a common grave.

Newspapers and government officials referred to the confrontation as a battle, but it was none other than wholesale slaughter. Within a year, the army had awarded 23 Medals of Honor to members of the Seventh Cavalry for valor shown in the carnage (modern-day activists are seeking to have them rescinded). The American people were incensed, however, and from this point on, any government-led extermination of the Indian people ended.

Rushmore National Memorial, Wind Cave National Park, Jewel Cave National Monument, and Custer State Park allow visitors to take in a wealth of sightseeing excursions in a relatively small area.

## Nearby Towns & Attractions

### Nearby Towns

Built against a steep ridge of badland rock, **Wall** was founded in 1907 as a railroad station, and is today the town nearest to Badlands National Park. Wall is home to the world-famous Wall Drug Store. **Pine Ridge,** about 35 mi south of the Stronghold Unit, is on the cusp of Pine Ridge Indian Reservation. With 2,800 square mi, the Oglala Sioux reservation is second in size only to Arizona's Navajo Reservation. **Rapid City,** in the eastern buttes of the Black Hills, is South Dakota's second-largest city and a good base from which to explore the Black Hills National Forest, the badlands 70 mi to the east, and Mount Rushmore and Wind Cave National Park, to the south 25 mi and 50 mi respectively.

### Nearby Attractions

For attractions in Rapid City and the Black Hills, *see* the Wind Cave National Park chapter.

**FodorśChoice** ★ **Mount Rushmore National Memorial.** One of the nation's most popular attractions, the giant likenesses of Washington, Jefferson, Lincoln, and Theodore Roosevelt lie just 65 mi west of Badlands. For more on Mount Rushmore, *see* Wind Cave National Park chapter. ⊠ *Rte. 244, Keystone* ☎ *605/574–2523* ⊕ *www.nps.gov/moru* ⊡ *Parking $8* ⊙ *The monument is open daily year-round; the facilities and museums have varying hours.*

★ **Wall Drug Store.** This South Dakota original got its start by offering free ice water to road-weary travelers. Today its four dining rooms seat 520 visitors. The walls are covered with art for sale. A life-size mechanical Cowboy Orchestra and Chuckwagon Quartet greet you in the store, and in the Wall Drug backyard you'll see an animated T-rex and replicas of Mount Rushmore and a native village. The attached mall has 14 shops. ⊠ *510 Main St., Wall* ☎ *605/279–2175* ⊕ *www.walldrug.com* ⊡ *Free* ⊙ *Memorial Day–Labor Day, daily 6 AM–10 PM; Labor Day–Memorial Day, daily 6:30–6.*

**Wounded Knee Historical Site.** A solitary stone obelisk commemorates the site of the December 29, 1890 massacre at Wounded Knee, the last major conflict between the U.S. military and American Indians. Only a handful of visitors make pilgrimages to the remote site today, which is simple and largely unchanged from its 1890 appearance. ⊠ *12 mi northwest of Pine Ridge, along U.S. 18* ⊡ *Free* ⊙ *24/7 year-round.*

**Wounded Knee: The Museum.** This modern facility interprets the history of the December 29, 1890 Wounded Knee Massacre through interactive exhibits with historical photos and documents. ⊠ *207 10th Ave., Wall* ☎ *605/279–2573* ⊙ *Apr.–mid-Oct., daily 8:30 AM–5:30 PM.*

---

## WHERE TO STAY & EAT

### About the Restaurants

For its lack of comparative sophistication, the grub in the restaurants surrounding Badlands National Park is typically very good. You'll probably never have a better steak—beef or buffalo—outside this area. You should also try cuisine influenced by American Indian cooking. The most popular (and well-known) is the Indian taco, made from spiced meat and flat bread. In the park itself there's only one restaurant. You'll find the most choices in Wall.

> **FAMILY PICKS**
>
> Nearly every area attraction is family oriented—kids especially love the **Fossil Exhibit Trail, Badlands Loop Tour, Robert's Prairie Dog Town, Mount Rushmore,** and **Wall Drug.** There are also great, family-friendly tours. It's difficult to single out one tour operator as being more kid friendly than another, but **Mount Rushmore Tours** probably deserves it, if only for the cowboy show at Fort Hayes. If you're looking for history, the owner of **Golden Circle** is a retired teacher who does an excellent job of touching on geology, paleontology, and Western and Native American history.

## FESTIVALS & EVENTS

JAN.–FEB. **Black Hills Stock Show and Rodeo.** Watch world-champion wild-horse races, bucking horses, timed sheepdog trials, draft-horse competitions, and steer wrestling during this two-week-long professional rodeo at the Rushmore Plaza Civic Center in Rapid City. The stockman's banquet and ball are not to be missed. ☎ *605/355–3861.*

MAR. **Badlands Quilters Weekend Getaway.** A three-day display of the region's finest hand- and machine-made quilts, plus quilting classes, demonstrations, and sales, are held in Wall's community center. ☎ *605/279–2945.*

JUNE–AUG. **Red Cloud Indian Art Show.** Native American artists' paintings and sculptures are the focus of this 11-week exhibition, beginning on the second Sunday in June, at the Red Cloud Indian School in Pine Ridge. ☎ *605/867–5491.* **Fee Free Day.** Each year on August 25th, the park opens its doors to all for free. Special programs are held all day at the Ben Reifel Visitor Center. ☎ *605/433–5361.* **Oglala Nation Powwow and Rodeo.** This traditional powwow and rodeo is hosted by the Oglala Sioux tribe at the Powwow Grounds on Pine Ridge's west side. ☎ *605/867–5821.*

### About the Hotels

There are very few lodging options in and near the park, and if you're determined to bed down within park boundaries, you have only one choice: Cedar Pass Lodge. It's rustic but comfortable and inexpensive.

The rustic-but-comfy formula is repeated by the area's few motels, hotels, and inns. Most are chain hotels in Wall, grouped around the interstate. Whether you stay inside or outside the park, don't worry about making reservations far in advance, except during the first full week of August, when the entire region is inundated with more than half a million motorcyclists for the annual Sturgis Motorcycle Rally.

### About the Campgrounds

Pitching a tent and sleeping under the stars is one of the greatest ways to fully experience Badlands National Park. You'll find two relatively easy-access campgrounds within park boundaries, but only one has any sort of amenities. The second is little more than a flat patch of ground with some signs. Unless you desperately need a flush toilet to have an enjoyable camping experience, you're just as well off hiking into the wilderness and choosing your own campsite. The additional isolation will be well worth the extra effort. You can set up camp anywhere that's at least ½ mi from a road or trail.

The handful of campgrounds located outside the park typically have more of the accoutrements of civilization. Fires may be allowed at private campgrounds outside the park, but they are never allowed within park boundaries, and the rule is rigorously enforced.

## Where to Eat

### In the Park

**$–$$** ✕ **Cedar Pass Lodge Restaurant.** Cool off within dark, knotty-pine walls under an exposed-beam ceiling, and enjoy a hearty meal of steak, trout, or Indian tacos and fry bread. ⊠ *1 Cedar St. (Rte. 240), Interior* ☎ *605/ 433–5460. $8–$18* ▭ *AE, D, MC, V* ☾ *Closed Nov.–Mar.*

PICNIC AREAS **Bigfoot Pass/Journey Overlook.** There are only a handful of tables here and no water, but the incredible view makes it a lovely spot to have lunch. Restrooms are available. ⊠ *7 mi northwest of the Ben Reifel Visitor Center on Badlands Loop Rd.*

**Conata Picnic Area.** A dozen covered picnic tables are scattered over this area, which rests against a badlands wall ½ mi south of Badlands Loop Road. There's no potable water, but there are bathroom facilities. The Conata Basin area is to the east, and Sage Creek area is to the west. ⊠ *15 mi northwest of the Ben Reifel Visitor Center on Conata Rd.*

### Outside the Park

For restaurants in Rapid City and the Black Hills, *see* Wind Cave National Park.

**¢–$$** ✕ **Cactus Family Restaurant and Lounge.** Delicious hotcakes and pies await you at this full-menu restaurant in downtown Wall. In summer you'll find a roast-beef buffet large enough for any appetite. ⊠ *519 Main St., Wall* ☎ *605/279–2561. $7–$15* ▭ *D, MC, V.*

**¢–$** ✕ **Western Art Gallery Restaurant.** This large restaurant in the Wall Drug store displays more than 200 original oil paintings, all with a Western theme. Try a hot beef sandwich or a buffalo burger. The old-fashioned soda fountain has milk shakes and homemade ice cream. ⊠ *510 Main St., Wall* ☎ *605/279–2175* ⊕ *www.walldrug.com/dining.htm. $4–$11* ▭ *AE, D, MC, V.*

## Where to Stay

### In the Park

★ **¢–$** ▦ **Cedar Pass Lodge.** Each small, stucco, white cabin has two twin beds and views of the badlands peaks. A gallery at the lodge displays the work of local artists, and the gift shop is well stocked with local crafts, including turquoise and beadwork. There are also hiking trails on the premises. ⊠ *1 Cedar St. (Hwy. 240), Interior 57750* ☎ *605/433–5460* ☎ *605/433–5560* ⊕ *www.cedarpasslodge.com* ⇌ *24 cabins* ⚖ *Restaurant, some pets allowed, no phone, no TV, no- smoking rooms. $47–$85* ▭ *AE, D, MC, V* ☾ *Closed Oct.–Apr.*

CAMPGROUNDS & ⚠ **Cedar Pass Campground.** Although it has only tent sites, this is the
RV PARKS park's most developed campground, and it's near the Ben Reifel Visitor Center, Cedar Pass Lodge (which sells ice), and a half-dozen hiking
★ **$** trails. It's undergoing a face-lift; new features will include paved interior roads, a new dump station, and improved facilities. ⊠ *Hwy. 377, ¼ mi south of Badlands Loop Rd.* ☎ *605/433–5361* ⊕ *www. cedarpasslodge.com* ⇌ *96 sites* ⚖ *Flush toilets, pit toilets, dump sta-*

*tion, drinking water, public telephone, ranger station* ⚑ *Reservations not accepted. $10* ⊟ *No credit cards* ⊙ *Mid-Apr.–mid-Oct.*

¢ ⚑ **Sage Creek Primitive Campground.** The word to remember here is primitive. If you want to get away from it all, this lovely, isolated spot surrounded by nothing but fields and crickets is the right camp for you. There are no designated campsites, and the only facilities are pit toilets and horse hitches. ⊠ *25 mi west of Badlands Loop Rd. on Sage Creek Rim Rd.* ☎ *No phone* ⚭ *Pit toilets. Free.*

## Outside the Park

For lodging in Rapid City and the Black Hills, *see* Wind Cave National Park chapter.

**$–$$** ⊡ ⚑ **Badlands Ranch and Resort.** This 2,000-acre ranch is just outside the national park, complete with gazebo, duck ponds, picnic areas, and a bonfire site. The ranch house has a Jacuzzi tub. Hunting guides are provided in season. Also on the grounds is an RV park with 35 hookup sites. ⊠ *Hwy. 44, HCR 53, Box 3, Interior 57750* ☎ *605/433–5599 or 877/433–5599* 🖷 *605/433–5598* ⊕ *www.badlandsranchandresort. com* ⇆ *4 rooms, 7 cabins* ⚭ *Picnic area, pool, kitchen, pond, play area, no-smoking rooms. $52–$108* ⊟ *AE, D, MC, V.*

**$–$$** ⊡ **Coyote Blues Village B&B.** This European-style lodge on 30 Black Hills acres (12 mi north of Hill City) displays an unusual mix of antique furnishings and contemporary art. Hearty Swiss-American breakfasts include homemade bread. Some rooms have a private deck with a hot tub. A creek runs through the property. There is no smoking inside the inn. ⊠ *Off U.S. 385, Hill City 57745* ☎ *605/574–4477 or 888/253–4477* 🖷 *605/574–2101* ⊕ *www.coyotebluesvillage.com* ⇆ *9 rooms* ⚭ *Refrigerator, gym, no-smoking rooms. $80–$150* ⊟ *D, MC, V.*

**$** ⊡ **Badlands Budget Host Motel.** Every room in this motel has views of the Buffalo Gap National Grasslands, 1 mi away. You can have breakfast and dinner on the premises. ⊠ *Rte. 377, Interior 57750* ☎ *605/433–5335 or 800/388–4643* ⇆ *21 rooms* ⚭ *Restaurant, room service, pool, laundry facilities, some pets allowed. $50–$58* ⊟ *D, MC, V.*

**$** ⊡ **Badlands Inn.** At this inn where every room faces Badlands National Park, awaken to a panoramic view of the sunrise over Vampire Peak. ⊠ *Rte. 377, Interior 57750* ☎ *605/433–5401* ⊕ *www.badlandsinn.com* ⇆ *22 rooms* ⚭ *Some pets allowed, no-smoking rooms. $53–$67* ⊟ *AE, D, MC, V* ⊙ *Closed Nov.–Mar.*

CAMPGROUNDS &
RV PARKS

☾ **$$** ⚑ **Badlands/White River KOA.** This campground's green, shady sites spread over 31 acres are pleasant and cool after a day among the dry rocks of the national park. White River and a small creek border the property on two sides. Cabins and cottages are also available. ⊠ *4 mi south of Interior on Hwy. 44, Interior 57750* ☎ *605/433–5337* ⊕ *www. koa.com* ⚭ *Flush toilets, full hookups, partial hookups (electric and water), dump station, drinking water, showers, fire grates, picnic tables, public telephone, general store, play area, swimming (pool)* ⇆ *144 sites (44 with full hookups, 38 with partial hookups), 62 tent sites. $25 tent sites, $26 partial hookups, $32 full hookups* ⊟ *MC, V* ⊙ *Mid-Apr.–early Oct.*

# BADLANDS ESSENTIALS

ACCESSIBILITY The visitor centers and Cedar Pass Lodge are all fully wheelchair accessible. Two trails—the Fossil Exhibit Trail and the Window Trail—have reserved parking and are accessible by ramp, although they are quite steep in places. The Door, Cliff Shelf, and Prairie Wind trails are accessible by boardwalk. Cedar Pass Campground has two fully accessible sites, plus many other sites that are sculpted and easily negotiated by wheelchair users. The campground's office and amphitheater also are accessible. The Bigfoot picnic area has reserved parking, ramps, and an accessible pit toilet.

ADMISSION FEES The entrance pass is $7 per person or $15 per vehicle, and is good for seven days. A $30 annual pass allows admission to the park for an entire year.

ADMISSION HOURS The park is open 24/7 year-round. It is in the Mountain time zone.

ATM/BANKS The park has no ATMs. ⚐ **Cedar Pass Lodge (ATM only)** ✉ 1 Cedar St. [Rte. 240], Interior ☎ 605/433–5460, and the nearest full-service bank is in Wall: **Black Hills Federal Credit Union** ✉ 605 Main St., Wall ☎ 605/279–2350 or **First Western Bank** ✉ 418 Main St., Wall ☎ 605/279–2141.

AUTOMOBILE SERVICE STATIONS ⚐ **Badlands Automotive** ✉ 216 4th Ave., Wall ☎ 605/279–2827 does general auto repair. **DE's Tire & Muffler** ✉ 216 W. 7th Ave., Wall ☎ 605/279–2168 does tires and muffler repair and some general auto repairs. **Harvey's Cowboy Corner** ✉ Rte. 44 at Rte. 377, Interior ☎ 605/433–5333 has fuel only. **Wall Auto Livery Amoco** ✉ 311 S. Blvd., Wall ☎ 605/279–2325 offers fuel, a car wash, and general auto repairs.

EMERGENCIES In case of a fire or medical emergency, call 911. Rangers can provide basic first aid. For assistance, call 605/433–5361, or go to either visitor center or the Pinnacles entrance ranger station. The nearest large hospital is 50 mi away in Rapid City; it has an air ambulance service.

LOST AND FOUND The park's lost-and-found is at the Ben Reifel Visitor Center.

PERMITS A backcountry permit isn't required for hiking or camping in Badlands National Park, but it's a good idea to check in at park headquarters before setting out on a backcountry journey. Backpackers may set up camps anywhere except within a half mile of roads or trails.

POST OFFICES ⚐ **Interior Post Office** ✉ 1 Main St., Interior 57750 ☎ 605/433–5345.

PUBLIC TELEPHONES You'll find pay phones at the Ben Reifel Visitor Center, Cedar Pass Lodge, and Cedar Pass Campground. Usually near the interstate you can pick up a cell-phone signal, but within the majority of the park there is no service.

RELIGIOUS SERVICES There are no religious services in the park.

RESTROOMS There are public restrooms at picnic areas, campgrounds, the visitor centers, the Door/Window/Notch and Fossil Exhibit trailheads, and Cedar Pass Lodge.

SHOPS & GROCERS Some limited groceries and supplies can be found at Cedar Pass Lodge. ⚐ **Badlands Grocery** ✉ 10 Main St., Interior ☎ 605/433–5445, 2 mi south of the Ben Reifel Visitor Center.

## NEARBY TOWN INFORMATION
⚐ **Oglala Sioux Tribe (Pine Ridge)** 🖝 Box 570, Kyle, SD 57764 ☎ 605/455–2584. **Rapid City Chamber of Commerce, and Convention and Visitors Bureau** ✉ 444 Mt. Rushmore Rd. N, Rapid City, SD 57701 ☎ 605/343–1744 or 800/487–3223 ⊕ www.rapidcitycvb.com. **Wall–Badlands Area Chamber of Commerce** ✉ 501 Main St., Wall, SD 57790 ☎ 605/279–2665 or 888/852–9255 ⊕ www.wall-badlands.com.

## VISITOR INFORMATION
⚐ **Badlands National Park** 🖝 Box 6, Interior, SD 57750 ☎ 605/433–5361 ⊕ www.nps.gov/badl.

# Banff National Park

Camping, Banff National Park

**WORD OF MOUTH**

"A sudden splendour of illumination poured over the field as the sun rose above a mountain, and in a moment, as if by magic, the frost crystals melted away into pendant drops of heaven's own distillation. Beads of clear water dripping from leaves and tinted petals, made tremulous light flashings like the sparkle of diamonds and rubies . . ."

–Author Walter D. Wilcox

# WELCOME TO BANFF

## TOP REASONS TO GO

★ **Scenery:** Visitors are often unprepared for the sheer scale of the Canadian Rockies. Scattered between the peaks are glaciers, forests, valleys, meadows, rivers, and the bluest lakes of the planet.

★ **Spectacular ski slopes:** Lake Louise Mountain Resort is Canada's largest single ski area, with skiing on four mountain faces, 4,200 skiable acres, and 113 named trails—and that's only one of the three ski resorts in Banff.

★ **Trails galore:** More than 1,000 mi (1,600 km) of defined hiking trails in the park lead to scenic lakes, alpine meadows, glaciers, forests, and deep canyons.

★ **Banff Upper Hot Springs:** Relax in naturally hot mineral springs as you watch snowflakes swirl around you, or gaze at the stars as you "take the waters" on a cool summer's evening.

★ **Icefields Parkway:** One of the most scenic drives on the continent, this 143-mi (230-km) roadway links Banff and Jasper.

**1** **Icefields Parkway.** There are many sites to be seen along this spectacular 143-mi (230-km) stretch of road. The Crowfoot Glacier, Bow Pass, Mistaya Canyon, Saskatchewan Crossing, and the Columbia Icefield are the primary highlights in the Banff section.

**2** **Lake Louise, Moraine Lake & the Bow Valley Parkway.** Backed by snowcapped mountains, fantastically ice-blue, Lake Louise is one of the most photographed lakes in the world. Lake Louise, Moraine Lake and the Valley of the Ten Peaks, and stunning Johnston Canyon are highlights of this region.

Downhill Skiing, Lake Louise

**3** **Banff Townsite.** The Banff Townsite is the hub of the park and is the place to go to find shops, restaurants, hotels, and other facilities. Highlights of the town site: Banff Information Centre, Canada Place, Whyte Museum, Banff Centre, Upper Hot Springs Pool, Sulphur Mountain Gondola, Lake Minnewanka, Vermillion Lakes, and the Hoodoos.

ALBERTA

## GETTING
## ORIENTED

Areas of majestic beauty fill the 2,564 square mi (6,641 square km) of Banff National Park. Bordered by Jasper National Park to the north, Kootenay and Yoho national parks to the west, the Bighorn Wildland Recreation Area to the east, and Kananaskis Country and Peter Lougheed Provincial Park to the south, Banff is at the center of a huge block of protected wilderness.

6

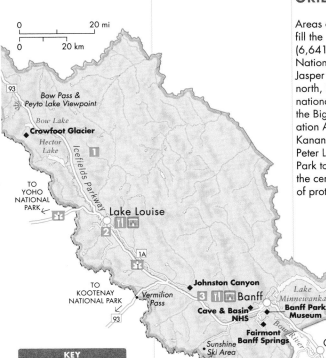

| 0 | | 20 mi |
| 0 | | 20 km |

93
Bow Pass & Peyto Lake Viewpoint
Bow Lake
● **Crowfoot Glacier**
Hector Lake
Icefields Parkway
1
TO YOHO NATIONAL PARK
Lake Louise
2
1A
TO KOOTENAY NATIONAL PARK
Vermilion Pass
93
**Johnston Canyon**
3 Banff
Lake Minnewanka
**Cave & Basin NHS**
**Banff Park Museum**
**Fairmont Banff Springs**
Bow River
Canmore
Sunshine Ski Area
TO CALGARY →

| KEY | |
|---|---|
| 🏕 | Ranger Station |
| ⛺ | Campground |
| 🌲 | Picnic Area |
| 🍴 | Restaurant |
| 📷 | Lodge |
| 🚶 | Trailhead |
| 🚻 | Restrooms |
| ⇗ | Scenic Viewpoint |
| ····· | Walking/Hiking Trails |
| ······ | Bicycle Path |

# BANFF NATIONAL PARK PLANNER

## When to Go

Banff National Park is an all-season destination. Visit in summer to hike the mountain trails or go in winter to enjoy some of the world's best skiing. Millions of people visit the park every year with the vast majority traveling during July and August, the warmest and driest months in the park. **If you can visit in late spring (May to June) or early fall (September) you will be in shoulder season when prices are lower, crowds are fewer, and the temperatures are usually still comfortable.** The downside to an off-season visit is the fact that you miss the summer interpretive programs and the wildflowers that reach their peak from early July to mid-August.

Both of the park's information centers are open all year, with extended hours during the summer months.

## Flora & Fauna

Awesome forces of nature combined to thrust wildly folded sedimentary and metamorphic rock up into ragged peaks and high cliffs. Add glaciers and snowfields to the lofty peaks, carpet the valleys with forests, mix in a generous helping of small and large mammals, wildflowers, rivers, and crystal-clear lakes, and you've got the recipe for Banff National Park.

This diverse topography has resulted in three complex life zones in Banff: montane, subalpine, and alpine. Each zone has characteristic physical environments along with its own species of plants and animals. The montane zone features valleys and grasslands as well as alders, willows, birches, and cottonwoods. The Douglas firs and lodgepole pines that cover the lower slopes of the mountains are also in the montane zone. Subalpine forest extends from the montane to about 6,500 feet and is made up of mostly spruce and pine trees. The fragile alpine zone is found at the highest elevations in the park. The rocky terrain and cold howling winds mean far fewer plants and animals can survive there.

Most of the wildlife is found in the montane life zone where bighorn sheep, deer, elk, and caribou abound. Moose and mountain goats can also be seen, as well as the occasional mountain black bear. Many other animals make their home in the park, including carnivores such as grizzly bears, wolves, coyotes, and cougars. It's common to see smaller mammals such as squirrels, marmots, muskrats, porcupines, and beavers. Birds commonly spotted are grouse, larks, finches, ptarmigans, bald eagles, golden eagles, loons, and Canada geese.

AVG. HIGH/LOW TEMPS.

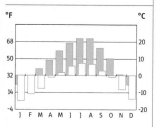

## Getting There & Around

Banff National Park, in west-central Alberta, is located 80 mi (128 km) west of Calgary, 250 mi (401 km) southwest of Edmonton, and 530 mi (850 km) east of Vancouver. The closest international airports are in Calgary and Edmonton. Major airlines serve both airports.

A car allows the most flexible travel in the Canadian Rockies, and the easiest way to get from Calgary to Banff is by car on the Trans-Canada Highway 1. Use Icefields Parkway (Hwy. 93) to get from Jasper to Banff. International car rental agencies are available at Edmonton and Calgary airports and in Banff, Lake Louise, and Jasper.

**Greyhound Canada Transportation** (☎ 800/661–8747 or 800/231–2222 in the U.S.) provides regular bus service from Calgary, Edmonton, and Vancouver to Banff and Lake Louise. **Brewsters Transportation and Tours** (☎ 800/661–1152) provides transportation between Calgary International Airport and Banff.

For travel within the towns of Banff and Lake Louise, there is a public transit system as well as several local taxi companies to choose from. Public buses also run between Banff and Lake Louise, and in the winter there is a ski shuttle service that picks up at most area hotels and transports guests to the park's three ski resorts.

## Family Picks

**Canada Place.** At Canada Place you can see what it feels like to step into a real birch-bark canoe or participate in fun games and programs designed to teach you more about Canada. It's free and there are many hands-on activities.

**Athabasca Glacier.** This glacier is the most accessible one in the park, and a short walk leads you right to its toe. You can explore the free displays at the Icefield Centre and even take an ice explorer vehicle onto the ice. (Note: Do not allow children to venture onto the ice without a trained guide!)

**Canoe adventure.** Rent a canoe at Lake Minnewanka, Moraine Lake, or Lake Louise and learn to paddle like early explorers once did.

**Enjoy the view.** You can't beat the views from the Banff Gondola during the steep eight-minute ride to the 7,500-foot summit of Sulphur Mountain. From the main deck you can hike the short distance to the summit of Sanson Peak and perhaps catch sight of grazing bighorn sheep.

**Adrenaline rush.** Try white-water rafting in summer or dogsledding and skiing in winter. The local ski hills have excellent children's programs.

6

By Debbie
Olsen

Comparing mountains is a subjective and imprecise business. Yet few would deny that the Canadian Rockies are one of the most extravagantly beautiful ranges on Earth. The mountains and vast stretches of wilderness that make up the birthplace of Canada's first national park offer stunning scenery of glaciers, lakes, valleys, and snowcapped mountain peaks. Large mammals such as deer and elk can be observed in all seasons from the roadside.

You can soak up the rugged alpine scenery, hike on more than 1,000 mi of trails, tour the region by automobile or tour bus, watch wildlife, soak in hot springs, visit historic sites, and enjoy fine dining and shopping in the town sites of Banff or Lake Louise. The winter months are ideal to enjoy outdoor sports like ice-skating, dogsledding, sleigh rides, and cross-country and downhill skiing.

*Note that all prices in this chapter are in Canadian dollars, unless stated otherwise.*

## Scenic Drives

**Bow Valley Parkway.** Formerly known as Highway 1A, this scenic drive between Banff and Lake Louise leads to Hillsdale Meadows, Johnston Canyon, Castle Mountain, and Baker Creek. There are plenty of viewpoints and picnic sites along the way.

 **Icefields Parkway.** The Icefields Parkway stretches 138 mi (230 km) and connects Banff National Park with Jasper National Park. It is an absolute highlight of the Canadian Rockies (⇨ Icefields Parkway box).

**Lake Minnewanka Loop.** It's easy to spend the day along this 15-mi (25-km) loop. Traveling clockwise, you can explore Lower Bankhead and Upper Bankhead, an abandoned coal mine and mining community. Just 2 mi (3 km) farther you come to Lake Minnewanka, the largest lake in the park at 12 mi (20 km). Boat and fishing rentals are available at the lake. Further along are more lakes and picnic areas.

## BANFF IN ONE DAY

Start your day early with a visit to the **Banff Information Centre,** where you can pick up maps and information on the major sites. Buy lunch provisions and drive to beautiful **Lake Louise**. Walk the flat shoreline trail and venture upward along the **Lake Agnes Trail** to the Teahouse (or turn back once you get a satisfyingly lofty view of Lake Louise). On the drive back to Banff town, stop at Johnston Canyon and allow an hour for the easy round-trip hike to the dramatic waterfall. Have dinner in Banff or at **Fairmont Banff Springs Hotel,** a National Historic Site. After supper, explore the hotel's interior before finishing off the day with an evening dip in the **Banff Upper Hot Springs.**

**Mount Noquay Drive.** The highlight of this 4-mi (6½-km) route is the viewpoint near the top over the Banff town site. Bighorn sheep and mule deer are often sighted along the twisting road. Trailheads at the top lead to Stoney Squaw Summit and Cascade Amphitheatre.

**Tunnel Mountain Drive.** On the east side of Banff, Tunnel Mountain Drive makes a scenic 3-mi (5-km) loop. It's closed in winter, but just off the drive, the **hoodoos**—fingerlike, eroded rock formations—are accessible year-round (signs on Banff's main street direct you to the hoodoos).

## What to See

### Historic Sites

**Banff Park Museum.** This National Historic Site, made for the 1893 World Exhibition in Chicago, is western Canada's oldest natural-history museum. ⊠ *91 Banff Ave., north of the bridge* ☎ *403/762–1558* ⊕ *www.pc.gc.ca* ⌕ *C$4* ⊙ *Mid-May–Sept., daily 10–6; Oct.–mid-May, daily 1–5.*

★ **Banff Upper Hot Springs.** The sulfur pool of hot springwater can be soothing, invigorating, or both. Lockers, bathing suits (circa 1920s or modern), and towels can be rented, and spa services are available. ⊠ *Mountain Ave., 2 mi (3 km) south of downtown (or a 20-min hike up a steep trail from the Fairmont Banff Springs parking area)* ☎ *403/762–1515, 800/ 767–1611, 403/760–2500 for spa bookings* ⊕ *www.hotspring.ca* ⌕ *C$7.50* ⊙ *Mid-May–mid-Sept., daily 9 AM–11 PM; mid-Sept.–mid-May, Sun.–Thurs. 10–10, Fri. and Sat. 10 AM–11 PM.*

**Cave and Basin National Historic Site.** This was given national park protection in 1885, becoming the birthplace of the Canadian Rockies park system. Two interpretive trails explain the area's geology and plant life, while hands-on interpretive displays offer information on the wildlife and history of the national park. You can take a guided tour of the cave daily mid-May through September and weekends throughout the rest of the year. A boardwalk leads to a marsh where the warm springwater supports tropical fish illegally dumped into the waters many years ago. ⊠ *Cave Ave., 1 mi (2 km) west of downtown* ☎ *403/762–1566* ⊕ *www.*

CLOSE UP

# Icefields Parkway

POWERFULLY RUGGED MOUNTAIN scenery, glaciers, waterfalls and icefalls, and wildlife: the Icefields Parkway reveals all of these and more as it snakes its way between Lake Louise and Jasper.

There aren't any gas stations along the route, so be sure to check the gas gauge before setting out. Although you could drive this winding road in three to four hours, it's more likely to be a full-day trip when you add in stops. The road rises to near the tree line at several points, and the weather can be chilly and unsettled at these high elevations, even in midsummer, so it's a good idea to bring warm clothing along.

Elk, moose, deer, and bighorn sheep are fairly common along this route, and occasionally you can see bears and mountain goats. In summer, alpine wildflowers carpet Bow Pass and Sunwapta Pass.

The most dramatic scenery is in the north end of Banff National Park and the south end of Jasper National Park, where ice fields and glaciers become common on the high mountains flanking the route (ice fields are massive reservoirs of ice; glaciers are the slow-moving rivers of ice that flow from the ice fields). Scenic overlooks and signposted hiking trails abound along the route.

At 6,787 feet, **Bow Summit** (✉ 25 mi [40 km] north of Lake Louise, 118 mi [190 km] south of Jasper) is the highest drivable pass in the national parks of the Canadian Rockies. On the south side of the pass is Bow Lake, source of the Bow River, which flows through Banff. You may wish to stop for lunch or supper at **Simpson's**

**Num-Ti-Jah Lodge** (✉ 25 mi [40 km] north of Lake Louise on Hwy. 93 ☎ 403/522-2167 ⊕ www.num-ti-jah. com) at Bow Lake. This rustic lodge with simple guest rooms specializes in excellent regional Canadian cuisine. Outside, walking paths circle the lake. Above Bow Lake hangs the Crowfoot Glacier, so named because of its resemblance to a three-toed crow's foot. At least that's how it looked when it was named at the beginning of the 20th century. In the Canadian Rockies, glaciers, including Crowfoot, have been receding. The lowest toe completely melted away 50 years ago, and now only the upper two toes remain. On the north side of Bow Pass is **Peyto Lake;** its startlingly intense aqua-blue color comes from the minerals in glacial runoff. Wildflowers blossom along the pass in summer, but note that it can be covered with snow as late as May and as early as September.

The short (1½ mi [2 ½ km]), steep **Parker Ridge Trail** is one of the easiest hikes in the national parks to bring you above the tree line. There's an excellent view of the Saskatchewan Glacier, where the river of the same name begins, though you've got to make it to the top of the ridge to get the view. Snowbanks can persist into early summer, but carpets of wildflowers cross the trail in late July and August. Stay on the path to keep erosion to a minimum. The signposted trailhead is about 2½ mi (4 km) south of the boundary between Banff and Jasper parks.

**Sunwapta Pass** (✉ 76 mi [122 km] north of Lake Louise, 67 mi [108 km] south of Jasper) marks the border between Banff and Jasper national parks. Wildlife is most visible in spring and autumn after a snowfall, when herds of bighorn sheep come to the road to lick up the salt used to melt snow and ice. At 6,675 feet, Sunwapta is the second-highest drivable pass in the national parks. Be prepared for a series of hairpin turns as you switchback up to the pass summit.

The **Athabasca Glacier** (⊠ 79 mi [127 km] north of Lake Louise, 64 mi [103 km] south of Jasper) is a 4½-mi (7-km) tongue of ice flowing from the immense Columbia Icefield almost to the highway. A century ago the ice flowed over the current location of the highway; signposts depict the gradual retreat of the ice since that time. Several other glaciers are visible from here; they all originate from the Columbia Icefield, a giant alpine lake of ice covering 125 square mi (325 square km), whose edge is visible from the highway. You can hike up to the toe of the glacier, but venturing further without a trained guide is extremely dangerous because of hidden crevasses. **Athabasca Glacier Ice Walks** offers three-, five-, and six-hour guided walks (C$36–C$45), which can be reserved at the Icefield Centre or through Jasper Adventure Centre, in Jasper. You can also take a trip onto the Athabasca Glacier on **Brewster Tours' Ice Explorers,** which have been modified to drive on ice (tickets are available at the Icefield Centre for C$29.86).

**The Icefield Centre** opposite Athabasca Glacier houses interpretive exhibits, a gift shop, and two dining facilities (one cafeteria style, one buffet style). The summer midday rush between 11 and 3 can be intense. There are 32 hotel rooms, available from early May to mid-October. Book through **Brewster's Transport** in Banff. ⊠ *Opposite Athabasca Glacier on Hwy. 93, 79 mi (127 km) north of Lake Louise, 64 mi (103 km) south of Jasper* ☎ *877/423-7433* ⊕ *www.brewster.ca* ⊠ *Free* ⊙ *Late May–mid-June and Sept.–early Oct., daily 10–5; mid-June–Aug., daily 10–7.*

As you continue north from the Icefield Centre through Jasper National Park towards the Jasper townsite, you'll see some of the most spectacular scenery in the Canadian Rockies. One of the most stunning sites is the **Stutfield Glacier,** (57 mi [95 km] south of Jasper Townsite). The glacier stretches down 3,000 feet of cliff face, forming a set of double icefalls visible from a roadside viewpoint. Continuing along the parkway, you'll pass the access to spectacular **Sunwapta Falls,** 33 mi (57 km) south of the town of Jasper. You'll also want to stop at **Athabasca Falls,** 19 mi (31 km) south of Jasper Townsite. These powerful falls are created as the Athabasca River is compressed through a narrow gorge, producing a violent torrent of water. The falls are especially dramatic in early summer. Trails and overlooks provide good viewpoints.

**6**

*pc.gc.ca* ☎ *C$4* ⊙ *Mid-May–Sept., daily 9–6; Oct.–mid-May, weekdays 11–4, weekends 9:30–5.*

★ **Fairmont Banff Springs.** This hotel, 1 mi (2 km) south of downtown Banff, is the town's architectural showpiece and a National Historic Site. Built in 1888, the hotel is easily recognized by its castlelike exterior. Heritage Hall, a small, free museum above the Grand Lobby, has rotating exhibits on the area's history. ⊠ *405 Spray Ave.* ☎ *403/762–2211.*

**Fairmont Château Lake Louise.** The massive hotel, opened in 1890, overlooks blue-green Lake Louise and the Victoria Glacier. The hotel is also a departure point for several moderately strenuous, well-traveled hiking routes. The most popular hike (about 2 mi, or 3 km) is to Lake Agnes. The tiny lake hangs on a mountain-surrounded shelf that opens to the east with a bird's-eye view of the Beehives and Mount Whitehorn. ⊠ *Lake Louise Dr.* ☎ *403/522–3511.*

## Scenic Stops

☾ **Banff Gondola.** Views during the steep eight-minute ride to and from the 7,500-foot summit are spectacular. From the upper gondola terminal you can hike the short distance to the summit of Sanson Peak and perhaps catch sight of grazing bighorn sheep, or visit the gift shop or the reasonably priced restaurant. The gondola is south from the center of Banff; you can catch a public Banff transit bus. ⊠ *Mountain Ave., 2 mi (3 km) south of downtown (lower terminal next to Upper Hot Springs)* ☎ *403/762–5438 or 403/762–2523* ⊕ *www.banffgondola.com* ☎ *C$22.50 round-trip* ⊙ *Early May–early Sept., daily 7:30 AM–9 PM; early Sept.–mid-Oct., daily 8:30–6:30; mid-Oct.–early Dec., daily 8:30–4:30; early Dec.–early May, daily 10–4.*

☾ **Canada Place.** With its splendid summertime flower gardens, this is a
Fodor'sChoice   pleasant place for an after-dinner stroll. It stands at the south end of
★   Banff Avenue, across a stone bridge over the Bow River. Inside are interactive activities for children and adults. ⊠ *1 Cave Ave.*

☾ **Lake Louise Sightseeing Gondola.** Ride this to an alpine plateau for a stunning view that includes more than a dozen glaciers. The deck of the Whitehorn Tea House (open June through September for breakfast and lunch) is a good place to eat. In winter, there's a buffet dinner package that includes entertainment and a torchlight ski descent. Free 30- to 90-minute, naturalist-led hikes go to the top of the mountain; schedules vary. ⊠ *Hwy. 1 (Lake Louise exit)* ☎ *403/522–3555* ⊕ *www. skilouise.com* ☎ *C$22* ⊙ *May, daily 9–4; June and Sept., daily 8:30–6; July and Aug., daily 8–6.*

> **READ ALL ABOUT IT**
>
> *The Mountain Guide* is distributed by parks staff upon entry to Banff National Park. It contains maps and good general park information such as points of interest, safety messages, programs and events, camping information and fees. If you want to use it for advance planning, it is also available on the Parks Canada Web site (⊕ www. pc.gc.ca/jasper).

★ **Moraine Lake.** This beauty, 7 mi (11 km) south of Lake Louise, is a photographic highlight of Banff National Park. Set in the Valley of the Ten Peaks, the lake reflects the snow-clad mountaintops that rise abruptly around it. The lake is a major stop for tour buses as well as a popular departure point for hikers. Visit early or late in the day to avoid crowds. Moderate hiking trails lead from the lodge at Moraine Lake into some spectacular alpine country. Call ahead for special trail restrictions.

From June through September, you can rent a canoe from the office of **Moraine Lake Lodge** (☎ 403/522–3733 ⊕ www.morainelake.com). ⊠ *Moraine Lake Rd. off Great Divide Hwy.* ☎ *403/760–1305 for hiking information.*

### Visitor Centers

**Banff Information Centre.** Park wardens and staff have excellent information on camping, hiking, programs, and sightseeing. ⊠ *224 Banff Ave., Banff* ☎ *403/762–1550* ⊕ *www.pc.gc.ca* ⊙ *Jan.–mid-May, daily 9–5; mid-June–Aug., daily 8–8; mid-May–mid-June and Sept., daily 8–6.*

**Banff Lake Louise Tourism.** Located in the same building as the Banff Information Centre, this information desk can provide you with information on hotels, restaurants, and services in the towns of Banff and Lake Louise. ⊠ *224 Banff Ave.* ☎ *403/762–8421* ⊕ *www.BanffLakeLouise. com* ⊙ *Jan.–mid-May, daily 9–5; mid-June–Aug., daily 8–8; mid-May–mid-June and Sept., daily 8–6.*

**Lake Louise Visitor Centre.** Stop here to get maps and information about area attractions and trails. The Banff Lake Louise Tourism desk can provide information on area accommodations and amenities, and you can purchase educational books and other materials from the Friends of Banff National Park. ⊠ *Village of Lake Louise next to Samson Mall* ☎ *403/ 522–3833* ⊕ *www.pc.gc.ca* ⊙ *Jan.–Apr., daily 9–5; mid-June–mid-Sept, daily 8–8; May–mid-June and mid-Sept–end of Sept., daily 8–6.*

## Sports & the Outdoors

### Air Tours

OUTFITTERS & EXPEDITIONS **Alpine Helicopters.** Helicopter sightseeing and heli-hiking in the Canadian Rockies are the specialty for this company. ⊠ *91 Bow Valley Tr., Canmore* ☎ *403/678–4802* ⊕ *www.alpinehelicopters.com.*

**CMH.** This company can arrange heli-hiking, heli-mountaineering, and heli-skiing with accommodation in remote mountain lodges. ⌂ *Box 1660, Banff* ☎ *403/762–7100 or 800/661–0252* ⊕ *www.cmhski.com.*

### Bicycling

The biking season typically runs from May through October and the more than 118 mi (189 km) of trails include ones suitable for beginners and advanced bikers. Bikers and hikers often share the trails in the park, with hikers having the right-of-way. Those who wish to enjoy free riding or down-hilling should go to nearby areas like Calgary's Canada Olympic Park, Fernie, or Golden.

OUTFITTERS & EXPEDITIONS **Backtrax Bike Rentals.** Backtrax also sells accessories, clothing, and equipment and has a repair shop on-site. Backtrax also arranges one-

to four-hour guided interpretive bike tours on local Banff trails, which are suitable for any age or physical ability. ⊠ *225 Bear St., Banff* ☎ *403/762–8177.*

⇨ Multisport Outfitters & Expeditions box for additional equipment shops.

## Bird-watching

Birdlife is abundant in the montane and wetland habitats of the lower Bow Valley and more than 260 species of birds have been recorded in the park. Come in the spring to observe the annual migration of waterfowl, including common species of ducks and Canada geese as well as occasional tundra swans, cinnamon teal, Northern shovelers, white-winged and surf scoters, and hooded and common Mergansers. Bald eagles are also seen regularly. Come in mid-October if you want to observe the annual migration of golden eagles along the "super flyway" of the Canadian Rockies. Interpreters and guides are on hand to explain the phenomenon.

## Boating

Lake Minnewanka, near town, is the only place in Banff National Park that allows private motorboats. Aluminum fishing boats with 8-horsepower motors can be rented at the dock (call Lake Minnewanka Boat Tours, *see below*).

Rafting options range from scenic float trips to family-friendly white-water excursions on the Kananaskis River to the intense white water of the Kicking Horse River, with its Class IV rapids.

OUTFITTERS & EXPEDITIONS **Canadian Rockies Rafting.** Scenic floats and thrilling white-water rafting tours on the Bow and Kananaskis rivers are available with these local experts. Pickups in Banff and Canmore are included. ⌂ *Box 8082, Canmore* ☎ *403/678–6535 or 877/226–7625.*

**Hydra River Guides.** This is where you want to go for real thrills. The guides here take you through the Class IV rapids on the Kicking Horse River. ⊠ *211 Bear St., Banff* ☎ *403/762–4534 or 800/644–8888* ⊕ *www.banffadventures.com.*

**Kootenay River Runners.** A variety of boating trips, ranging from scenic raft floats on the Toby or Kananaskis rivers to Class IV white-water rafting on the Kicking Horse, are available through this outfitter. A unique Voyageur Canoe Experience is also an option. ⊠ *110 Banff Ave., Banff* ☎ *403/762–5385 or 800/599–4399* ⊕ *www.kootenayriverrunners.com.*

Ↄ **Lake Minnewanka Boat Tours.** In summer, this operator offers 1½-hour, C$30 tours on the lake. ⌂ *P.O. Box 2189, Banff* ☎ *403/762–3473* ⊕ *www.minnewankaboattours.com.*

Ↄ **Rocky Mountain Raft Tours.** This company specializes in one- and two-hour float trips on the Bow River, starting at $24. They also rent canoes. ⌂ *Box 1771, Banff* ☎ *403/762–3632.*

## Fishing

You can experience world-class trout fishing on the Bow River in Banff and enjoy fishing for trophy lake trout on Lake Minnewanka and several other mountain lakes. You will need a National Park fishing permit to fish within the park and must follow strict fishing regulations, including no use of live bait. Some waterways are permanently closed to anglers, while others are open only at certain times per year. Before heading out on your own, read the regulations or speak to the park staff.

OUTFITTERS &
EXPEDITIONS

**Alpine Anglers.** A full-service fly shop, spin- and fly-rod rentals, float trips, and a fly-fishing guide service are available through this company. ✉ *208 Bear St., Banff* ☎ *403/762–8223* ⊕ *www.alpineanglers.com.*

**Banff Fishing Unlimited.** Bow River floats and walk and wades are available in summer and ice fishing in winter. If you want to go for the big ones, charter a boat on Lake Minnewanka. ⌂ *Box 8281, Canmore* ☎ *403/762–4936* ⊕ *www.banff-fishing.com.*

**Hawgwild Fly Fishing Guides.** Learn how to fly-fish with a local guide. ⌂ *Box 2534, Banff* ☎ *403/760–2446* ⊕ *www.flyfishingbanff.com.*

**Tightline Adventures.** Daylong and multiday fly-fishing trips can be arranged through this company. ✉ *129 Banff Ave., Banff* ☎ *403/762–4548* ⊕ *www.tightlineadventures.com.*

**Upper Bow Fly Fishing Company.** Enthusiasm is caught not taught at this company where both beginners and advanced fly fishers are catered to. ⌂ *Box 2772, Banff* ☎ *403/762–8263* ⊕ *www.upperbowflyfishing.com.*

## Hiking

The trail system in Banff National Park allows you to access the heart of the Canadian Rockies. The scenery is spectacular and you can see wildlife such as birds, squirrels, deer, and sheep along many of the trails. Make noise as you travel the trails, so you don't surprise a bear or other large animal. Also, prepare for any and all weather conditions by dressing in layers and bringing at least ½ gallon of drinking water along per person on all full-day hikes. Get a trail map at the information center. Some of the more popular trails have bathrooms or outhouses at the trailhead. Dogs should be leashed at all times. ⇨ Multisport Outfitters & Expeditions box for guided hikes.

EASY

**Bow River HooDoos Trail.** This 3-mi (4⁸⁄₁₀-km) trail feels as if it is a world away from the busy town site. The trail starts at the Bow Falls Overlook on Tunnel Mountain Drive and leads through meadows and forests and past sheer cliffs until you reach the hoodoos.

**Discovery Trail and Marsh Trail.** On a hillside above the Cave and Basin Centennial Centre, this ½-mi (⁸⁄₁₀-km) boardwalk takes you past the vent of the cave to a spring flowing out of the hillside. Interpretive signage explains the geology and history of the Cave and Basin. Follow the Marsh Trail to get a good view of the lush vegetation that is fed by the mineral water and to see the birdlife. Along the boardwalk are telescopes, benches, and interpretive signage as well as a bird blind on the marsh itself. Wheelchairs have limited access to the boardwalk.

**Fenland Trail.** It will take about an hour round-trip to walk the 1-mi (2-km) trail that slowly changes from marsh to dense forest. Watch

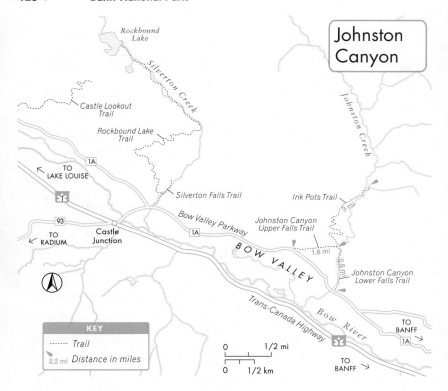

for beavers, muskrat, and waterfowl. The trail is popular with joggers and cyclists.

MODERATE  **Boom Lake Trail.** This 3²/₁₀-mi (5-km) hike climbs through a forest of pine, fir, and spruce. Surrounded by mountains and glaciers, the waters of the lake are crystal clear. The trail will take a half day round-trip. The trailhead is on Highway 93 South, 4½-mi (7 km) west of Castle Junction.

**Castle Lookout Trail.** Outstanding views of Castle Mountain and the mountains above the Bow River Valley are the highlight of this 2³/₁₀-mi (3⁷/₁₀ km) one-way trail that is somewhat steep.

Fodor'sChoice  **Johnston Canyon Trail.** Rushing water has carved a path through this lime-
★  stone canyon that is a must-see stop. The first ⁷/₁₀ mi (1¹/₁₀ km) is a paved walkway that leads to the 33-foot Lower Falls. From here a slightly more rugged 1¾-mi (2⁷/₁₀-km) trail leads to the almost-100-foot Upper Falls and a 3 mi (5 km) trail to the Ink Pots. The Ink Pots are six green pools filled with springwater. It will take four to five hours to complete the return trip.

★  **Lake Agnes Teahouse Trail.** Off Lake Louise, this 4½-mi (7-km) trail has stunning views of Lake Agnes and Mirror Lake. The trail passes through an old-growth forest and comes up the right side of a waterfall before ending at a teahouse where you can stop for dessert. It will take four hours or more to make the return trip along this trail.

DIFFICULT **Cory Pass Loop Trail.** This six-hour, 8-mi (13-km) hike is one of the most difficult hikes in the park and is only recommended for experienced hikers who are able to trace a difficult route. Hikers are rewarded with awesome views. The return route loops around Mt. Edith and descends the Edith Pass Trail. The trailhead is located at the Fireside picnic area at the eastern end of the Bow Valley Parkway.

**Sulphur Mountain Summit Trail.** This well-maintained trail crisscrosses underneath the gondola on Sulphur Mountain and climbs from the parking lot to the summit. You may choose to hike up and take the gondola down, but you should check schedules first. A restaurant and cafeteria are located at the summit along with a viewing platform and interpretive signage. It will take four hours to hike the trail round-trip.

> **FAMILY PICKS**
>
> **Adrenaline rush.** Try white-water rafting in summer or dogsledding and skiing in winter—local ski hills have excellent children's programs.
>
> **Athabasca Glacier.** A short walk leads you right to the toe of the glacier. You also can take an ice explorer vehicle onto the ice. (Note: Do not allow children to venture onto the ice without a trained guide.)
>
> **Canada Place.** At Canada Place you can see what it feels like to step into a real Voyageur birch-bark canoe or participate in fun games and programs designed to teach you more about Canada. The hands-on activities make it fun, and the best part is that it's free.

## Horseback Riding

Experiencing the Canadian Rockies on horseback takes you back to the era of Banff's early explorers. One-hour, half-day, full-day, and multi-day guided trips within the park are offered by several outfitters. Make your reservations well in advance, especially during the peak summer months and for multiday journeys. Hourly rides start at $34 per person. Short-term boarding is available in Canmore and a few other communities outside Banff.

OUTFITTERS & EXPEDITIONS **Brewsters Mountain Pack Tours.** Experience the "Cowboy Way of Life" by moving cattle and doing chores on overnight trips. ✑ *Box 964, Banff* ☎ *403/762–3953 or 800/691–5085* ⊕ *www.brewsteradventures.com.*

**Holiday on Horseback.** Arrangements for hourly or daily rides, as well as lessons, can be made by contacting this company, which operates out of three different locations in Banff (the main stable is located at the Fairmont Banff Springs). They also offer carriage rides in summer and sleigh rides in winter. ⊠ *132 Banff Ave., Banff* ☎ *403/762–4551 or 800/ 661–8352* ⊕ *www.horseback.com.*

**Lake Louise Stables.** The folks here can arrange trail rides, from one-hour to half- and full-day rides. The stables are a five-minute walk from the Fairmont Château Lake Louise. ☎ *403/762–5454* ⊕ *www. brewsteradventures.com.*

## MULTISPORT OUTFITTERS & EXPEDITIONS

**Abominable Ski & Sportswear** rents and sells ski and snowboarding equipment in winter and bikes and accessories in summer. ⊠ 229 Banff Ave., Banff ☎ 403/762–2905.

**Banff Adventures Unlimited** can book you at almost all of the area activities. They also rent bikes. ⊠ 211 Bear St., Banff ☎ 403/762–4554 ⊕ www.banffadventures.com.

**Canadian Mountain Experience** can arrange excursions such as snowmobiling, dog-mushing, and heli-skiing. ⊘ Box 8598, Canmore ☎ 403/609–3535 ⊕ www.canadianmountain.com.

**Chute High Adventures.** Mountain climbing, rock climbing, ice climbing, and guided hiking can be arranged through this company. ⊘ Box 1876, Banff ☎ 403/762–4068.

**Discover Banff Tours Ltd.** offers guided sightseeing, wildlife safaris, nature walks, ice walks, and snowshoeing adventures. ⊠ 215 Banff Ave, Main Level, Sundance Mall, Banff ☎ 403/760–5007 or 877/565–9372 ⊕ www.banfftours.com.

**Great Divide Nature Interpretation.** Guided interpretive hikes and snowshoeing trips are the specialty at this outfitter. ⊘ Box 343, Lake Louise ☎ 403/522–2735 ⊕ www.greatdivide.ca.

**Mountain Edge** stocks equipment and clothing, and you can rent downhill skis, snowboards, and helmets. ⊠ Lake Louise Ski Area, off Lake Louise Dr. ☎ 403/522–3555.

**Mountain Magic Equipment** offers three floors of hiking, climbing, skiing, running, and biking gear and a 30-foot indoor climbing wall for testing equipment. This is Canada's largest independent climbing outfitter. ⊠ 224 Bear St. ☎ 403/762–2591.

**White Mountain Adventures.** Daily guided hikes, backpacking, and heli-hiking can be arranged through this company. In winter, you can try snowshoeing, cross-country skiing, or a guided ice walk. ⊠ #7 107 Boulder Crescent, Canmore ☎ 403/678–4099 or 800/408–0005 ⊕ www.whitemountainadventures.com.

**Yamnuska Inc.** Canada's largest mountain-guide company offers programs for groups and individuals. ⊠ 200, 50 Lincoln Park, Canmore ☎ 403/678–4164 ⊕ www.yamnuska.com.

### Swimming

☾ **Banff Centre.** Amenities here include a 25-meter swimming pool, a wading pool, an outdoor sundeck, climbing wall, fitness center, gymnasium, and squash center, as well as fitness classes. ⊠ St. Julien Rd. (on Tunnel Mountain), Banff ☎ 403/762–6450 ⊕ www.banffcentre.ca ☒ C$4.25 ☾ Weekdays 6 PM–9 PM; weekends 11 AM–9 PM.

☾ **Douglas Fir Resort.** There are two indoor waterslides, a whirlpool, a steam room, and an indoor pool. ⊠ 525 Tunnel Mountain Rd., Banff ☎ 403/

*762–5591 or 800/661–9267* ⊕ *www.douglasfir.com* ✉ *C$8* ⊙ *Weekdays 4 PM–9:30 PM; weekends and holidays 10 AM–9:30 PM.*

### Winter Sports

Whether you're driving a dogsled across a frozen lake, ice climbing, snowshoeing, skiing at one of the world's top mountain ski resorts, or simply taking in the northern lights, there's no shortage of winter activities to choose from.

CROSS-COUNTRY SKIING
**Banff Alpine Guides.** Ski tours into Banff's backcountry are available with this outfitter. ✉ *Box 1025, Banff* ☎ *403/678–6091.*

**White Mountain Adventures.** Ski tours and lessons are available throughout the Bow Valley for beginner and intermediate skiers. ✉ *#7 107 Boulder Crescent, Canmore* ☎ *403/678–4099.*

DOWNHILL SKIING
★ ☾
**Lake Louise Ski Area.** The downhill terrain is large and varied, with a fairly even spread of novice, intermediate, and expert runs spread across three mountains and north-facing back bowls. The vertical drop is 3,257 feet; there are 105 runs, 11 lifts, and a terrain park. ✉ *Off Lake Louise Dr., Lake Louise* ☎ *403/522–3555* ⊕ *www.skilouise.com.*

**Ski Banff/Lake Louise Sunshine.** A good bargain is the $195, three-day pass from Ski Banff/Lake Louise Sunshine which allows you to ski at Sunshine Village, Ski Banff at Norquay, and Lake Louise. It includes free shuttle service to the slopes. You can purchase the pass at the ski areas or at many shops in Banff. ☎ *403/762–4561* ⊕ *www.skibig3.com.*

**Sunshine Village.** Five miles (8 km) west of the town of Banff, the terrain offers options for all levels of skiers. The vertical drop is 3,514 feet, and there are 103 trails and 12 lifts. ✉ *Off Hwy. 1, Banff* ☎ *403/762–6500 or 877/542–2633* ⊕ *www.skibanff.com.*

SKI & SNOWBOARD EQUIPMENT
Skis and snowboards can be rented on the slopes or at many shops in town, concentrated along Bear Street and Banff Avenue.

**Ultimate Banff.** Rent ski and snowboard equipment and take advantage of the shop's free hotel delivery. ✉ *206 Banff Ave.* ☎ *403/762–0547 or 866/SKI–RIDE* ⊕ *www.ultimatebanff.com.*

For additional equipment shops, ⇨ Multisport Outfitters & Expeditions box.

## Educational Offerings

There are a wide range of park interpretive programs in Banff. At the Banff Information Centre and at Cave and Basin, there are slide shows and presentations throughout the year. In the summer months you can enjoy campground interpretive programs, guided hikes, bicycle tours, film showings, and adventure games at Banff Avenue square.

☾ Fodor'sChoice ★
**Canada Place.** This center celebrates Canada's land, people, history, and accomplishments with interactive displays, hands-on activities, interpretive displays, educational games, and programs designed to help children and adults learn more about Canada. ✉ *1 Cave Ave.*

**Friends of Banff National Park.** This nonprofit group provides roving naturalist programs, guided hikes, and junior naturalist programs designed especially for children. The junior naturalist programs take place at Tunnel Mountain Campground, Johnston Canyon Campground, Two Jack Lakeside Campground, and Lake Louise Campground Theatre. ⊠ *224 Banff Ave., Banff* ☎ *403/762–8918* ✉ *Free or nominal fee* ⊕ *www. friendsofbanff.com.*

★ ⟲ **Mountain World Heritage Theatre.** Each summer Parks Canada's troupe of professional actors put on entertaining and educational performances for park guests. Tickets are available at The Friends of Jasper store, DO Travel, and at the door. For showtimes, check at the information center. ⊠ *Jasper Heritage Railway Station* ☎ *403/760–1338* ✉ *$10* ⊙ *July and Aug.*

## Arts & Entertainment

### Arts Venues

Most of the cultural activity in the Canadian Rockies takes place in and
★ around Banff, and the hub of that activity is **Banff Centre** (⊠ St. Julien Rd. [on Tunnel Mountain] ☎ 403/762–6100, 800/413–8368 in Alberta and British Columbia ⊕ www.banffcentre.ca), which consists of 16 buildings spread across 43 acres. The center presents a performing-arts grab bag throughout the year of pop and classical music, theater, and dance. The season peaks in summer with the monthlong **Banff Arts Festival,** with concerts, performances, films, and discussions. Within the center, the **Walter Phillips Gallery** (☎ 403/762–6281 ✉ Free ⊙ Tues., Wed., and Fri.–Sun. noon–5, Thurs. noon–9) showcases contemporary artwork by Canadian and international artists.

# WHAT'S NEARBY

About 15 mi (24 km) southeast of Banff Townsite, **Canmore** became a modest boomtown with the 1988 Olympics. It attracts a mix of tourists, residents who seek a mountain lifestyle, and commuters from Calgary who feel the hour-long commute is a fair trade-off for living in the mountains. Canmore makes a good base for exploring both Kananaskis Country and Banff National Park, without the crowds or cost of Banff.

Three provincial parks make up the 1,600-square-mi (4,200-square-km) recreational region known as **Kananaskis Country,** whose northern entrance is 16 mi (26 km) southeast of Canmore. The area includes grand mountain scenery, though perhaps not quite a match for that in the adjacent national parks. You can take part in the same activities you'd find in the national parks, and Kananaskis allows some activities that are prohibited within the national-park system, such as snowmobiling, motorized boating, off-road driving, and mountain biking. The main route through Kananaskis Country is Highway 40, also known as the Kananaskis Trail. It runs north–south through the front ranges of the Rockies. Only the northern 25 mi (40 km) of the road remain open from December 1 through June 15, in part because of the extreme conditions of Highwood Pass (at 7,280 feet, the highest drivable pass in Canada), and in part to protect winter wildlife habitats in Peter Lougheed Provincial Park and southward. Highway 40 continues south to join Highway

## FESTIVALS & EVENTS

**JAN. Ice Magic ice-sculpting contest.** On weekends, beginning the third Friday in January, ice carvers from around the world compete in this annual competition held at various locations in Lake Louise. This free exhibition remains on display until the first of March, weather permitting. ☎ *403/762–8421.*

**Banff–Lake Louise Winter Festival.** Begins on the third Friday in January and runs for 10 days. Winter sports are the highlight of the festival that also features outdoor events, nightly bar activities, and a town party. ☎ *403/762–8421.*

**APR. Easter at Sunshine Village.** Easter egg hunts, church service at the top of the strawberry chairlift, and visits by the Easter Bunny. ☎ *403/762–6508.*

**JUNE–AUG. Banff Summer Arts Festival.** Every summer the Banff Centre presents film screenings, visual-art displays, theater, opera, dance, and musical productions. ☎ *403/762–6300.*

**JULY Canada Day Celebration.** Canada Day means free admission to the national park and big celebrations in Canmore and Banff including a parade, fireworks, and live music. ☎ *403/762–0285.*

**NOV.–DEC. Santa Claus Parade.** Banff welcomes the Christmas season with a parade, treats, and photos with Santa in Central Park. On Christmas Day Santa skis at the three area ski resorts. ☎ *403/762–8421.*

541, west of Longview. Access to East Kananaskis Country, a popular area for horseback trips, is on Highway 66, which heads west from the town of Priddis.

## Area Activities

### Sports & the Outdoors

Many of the outfitters and operators who run tours in Banff National Park are based in Canmore, so if you're staying here, you can often join the tour from Canmore rather than having to drive to the park. *See* the Park section of this chapter for tours and activities within the park. Equipment for activities can be rented at most sports shops in Canmore.

GOLF **Kananaskis Country Golf Course.** This is one of the premier golf courses in the Canadian Rockies, with two 18-hole, par-72 links. ⊠ *Off Hwy. 40* ☎ *403/591–7272 or 877/591–2525.*

**Silvertip Golf Course.** This 18-hole, par-72 golf course offers spectacular elevation changes and views of the valley and mountains from most holes. ⊠ *1000 Silvertip Trail* ☎ *403/678–1600 or 877/877–5444.*

SPELUNKING **Canmore Caverns Ltd.** If you have ever wanted to don a headlamp and explore an undeveloped cave, Canmore Caverns can arrange a suitable caving experience. They supply the equipment and you bring the enthusiasm. Children should be at least nine years of age to participate. ☎ *403/678–8819* ⊕ *www.canadianrockies.net/wildcavetours.*

WATER SPORTS    **Blast Adventures.** Unique guided kayak adventures using inflatable kayaks

☾    on white water are available with this company. Transportation from Banff or Canmore is included. ⊠ *120 B Rundle Dr., Canmore* ☎ *403/ 609–2009 or 888/802–5278* ⊕ *www.blastadventures.com.*

WINTER SPORTS    **Canmore Nordic Centre.** Built for the 1988 Olympic Nordic skiing events,

★ ☾    Canmore Nordic Centre has 43 mi (70 km) of groomed cross-country trails in winter that become mountain-biking trails in summer. Some trails are lighted for night skiing, and a 1-mi (1½-km) paved trail is open in summer for roller skiing and rollerblading. This state-of-the-art facility is in the northwest corner of Kananaskis Country, south of Canmore. In late January, the annual **Canmore International Dogsled Race**—a two-day event—takes place here, attracting more than 100 international teams. ⊠ *1988 Olympic Way* ☎ *403/678–2400* ⊠ *Trails free Apr.–Oct., C\$7.50 per day Nov.–Mar.* ☉ *Lodge: daily 9–5:30; some trails illuminated until 9* PM.

**Nakiska.** The site of the 1988 Olympic alpine events, Nakiska is 45 minutes southeast of Banff and has wide-trail intermediate skiing and a sophisticated snowmaking system. The vertical drop is 2,412 feet, and there are four lifts. ⊠ *Off Hwy. 40, Kananaskis Village* ☎ *403/591–7777.*

# WHERE TO STAY & EAT

## About the Restaurants

Eating out is, for the most part, a casual affair with an emphasis on good fresh food served in large quantities. Trout, venison, elk, moose, and bison appear on the menus of even many modest establishments. Prices everywhere are slightly inflated.

## About the Hotels

The lodgings in Banff compose an eclectic list that includes backcountry lodges without electricity or running water, campgrounds, hostels with shared bathroom facilities, standard roadside motels, quaint B&B's, supremely luxurious hotels, and historic mountain resorts. Most accommodations do not provide meal plans, but some include breakfast.

With just a few exceptions, room rates are often highest from mid-June to late September and between Christmas and New Year's. In many cases, the best accommodation rates can be found during the months of October to mid-November and May to mid-June when rates can drop by as much as 50%. Lodgings in this chapter are listed with their peak-season rates. Check in advance for off-season rates.

If you want to save money, consider staying in nearby Canmore and in Kananaskis Country.

## About the Campgrounds

Parks Canada operates 13 campgrounds in Banff National Park (not including backcountry sites for backpackers and climbers). The camping season generally runs from mid-May through October, although the Tunnel Mountain and Lake Louise campgrounds remain open year-round. Hookups are available at most of the campgrounds and at 4 of the 31 Kananaskis Country campgrounds. Prices for a one-night stay range from C$9 to C$33. A fire permit is required to use a fire pit. In some cases the permit is purchased separately and in others it's included in the rates. Banff and Lake Louise participate in a reservation system that allows visitors to prebook campsites at Tunnel Mountain and Lake Louise campgrounds for a fee of C$11. The other campgrounds in the park operate on a first-come, first-served basis. To reserve a campsite, visit: ⊕ www.pc.gc.ca or call ☎ 905/426–4648 or 877/737–3783. For backcountry camping in Banff or Lake Louise, call Lake Louise Backcountry Trails Office at ☎ 403/522–1264. Numerous privately run campgrounds can be found outside park boundaries.

## Where to Eat

### In the Park

★ $$$$ ✕ **Banffshire Club.** The Scottish influence in the region becomes immediately apparent when you enter the exclusive Banffshire Club, with its vaulted ceilings, oak paneling, tartan drapes, and reproduction Stuart-era furniture. Entrées include roast young partridge with truffles, and pecan-crusted caribou. Staff members are all sommelier trained to help you choose from the extensive wine cellar. A jacket is required; loaners are available from the maître d' if necessary. Fixed-price menus start at C$110 and tasting menus go up to C$310 per person including wine pairings. ✉ *Fairmont Banff Springs, 405 Spray Ave., Banff* ☎ *403/762–6860* ⊕ *www.fairmont.com* ⌲ *Reservations essential* ⌂ *Jacket required.* C$85–C$130 ▭ *AE, D, DC, MC, V* ⊘ *No lunch.*

★ $$$$ ✕ **Eden.** Luxurious decor and magnificent mountain views form the backdrop for a dinner of regionally influenced French cuisine. There are four fixed dining options, but the main courses constantly change; previous entrées have included pan-seared venison loin and oxtail ravioli. The prix-fixe menu (C$125) includes five to eight courses and is paired with Canadian or international wine. ✉ *Rimrock Resort Hotel, 100 Mountain Ave., Banff* ☎ *403/762–1865* ⊕ *www.rimrockresort.com.* C$125 ▭ *AE, D, DC, MC, V* ⊘ *No lunch.*

$$$$ ✕ **Post Hotel.** Here is one of the true epicurean experiences in the Canadian Rockies. A low, exposed-beam ceiling and a stone, wood-burning hearth in the corner lend a warm, in-from-the-cold atmosphere; white tablecloths and fanned napkins provide an elegant touch. The combination of modern and classic dishes leads to daring regionally inspired fresh market cuisine. Look for innovative dishes prepared with fresh fish, game, or Alberta beef. The Post is one of only four restaurants in Canada to receive the *Wine Spectator* Grand Award with a 1,500-label wine list and an incredible cellar that contains almost 30,000 bottles of wine. For a unique dining experience with a group of six or more, ask to dine in the private cellar dining room. ✉ *200 Pipestone Rd., Lake Louise* ☎ *403/522–3989 or 800/661–1586* ⌲ *Reservations essential.* C$32–C$48 ▭ *AE, MC, V.*

Fodor'sChoice ★

$$$–$$$$ ✕ **Bow Valley Grill.** Serving breakfast, lunch, and dinner in a relaxed dining room overlooking the Bow Valley, this is one of the most popular restaurants in the Fairmont Banff Springs hotel. You can choose between

à la carte or buffet dining. There's a tantalizing selection of rotisserie-grilled meats, salads, and seafood, plus bread from an on-site bakery. During the summer months, buffet lunch comes with a guided historic hotel tour. ⊠ *Fairmont Banff Springs, 405 Spray Ave., Banff* ☎ *403/762–6860* ⊕ *www.fairmont.com. C$21–C$38* ⊟ *AE, D, DC, MC, V.*

**$$$–$$$$** ✕ **Mount Fairview Dining Room.** Set beneath the high ceilings and inside the log-and-stone framework of Deer Lodge, this fine-dining establishment has large picture windows and a rustic look. The specialty is regionally inspired, Rocky Mountain cuisine. Elk, caribou, and bison top out the menu choices. There is an extensive wine list. ⊠ *109 Lake Louise Dr., Lake Louise* ☎ *403/522–4202 or 800/661–1595. C$23–C$37* ⊟ *AE, D, DC, MC, V.*

**$$$–$$$$** ✕ **Waldhaus.** Fondues are a specialty at this German restaurant. The braised beef short ribs, duck with cider sauce, trout, and Wiener schnitzel are also popular. The downstairs pub serves the same menu items, except for the fondues. In summer, a barbecue lunch is held on the terrace. The savory barbecued entrées—steaks, salmon, or chicken breast on salad—are greatly enhanced by the views. ⊠ *Fairmont Banff Springs, 405 Spray Ave., Banff* ☎ *403/762–6860* ⚍ *Reservations essential. C$23–C$34* ⊟ *AE, D, DC, MC, V* ⊘ *No lunch Sept.–May.*

**$$$–$$$$** ✕ **Walliser Stube.** For something different, try this Swiss wine bar with warm cherrywood and a large selection of fondues. Choose from bison, tuna, or ostrich in broth; classic cheese; beef; and five chocolate dessert fondues. ⊠ *Fairmont Château Lake Louise, Lake Louise Dr., Lake Louise* ☎ *403/522–3511 Ext. 1817. C$27–C$42* ⊟ *AE, D, DC, MC, V.*

**$$–$$$$** ✕ **Giorgio's Trattoria.** The exotic pizzas are cooked in a wood-burning oven—try the pizza *mare* (of the sea), with tiger shrimp, cilantro, sun-dried tomatoes, and roasted garlic. A popular pasta dish is *roselline di pasta* (ham-and-mozzarella-filled pasta roses in a creamy tomato sauce). Sponge-painted walls, Philippine mahogany tables, and detailed ironwork create an elegant look. ⊠ *219 Banff Ave., Banff* ☎ *403/762–5114. C$15–C$38* ⊟ *AE, MC, V* ⊘ *No lunch.*

**$$–$$$$** ✕ **Ticino.** The distinctive Swiss dishes of Ticino, the southernmost province of Switzerland, reflect a definite Italian influence, as does the fare at this eponymous wood-beam and stucco restaurant. Fondue is a house specialty: the *mar-e-mont* (Italian for "ocean and mountain") is a beef-and-shrimp fondue you cook yourself in hot broth. Baked salmon, beef medallions, panfried veal, and lamb are other offerings. For dessert, try the Swiss chocolate dessert fondue. ⊠ *High Country Inn, 415 Banff Ave., Banff* ☎ *403/762–3848. C$14–C$33* ⊟ *AE, DC, MC, V* ⊘ *No lunch.*

**$$–$$$** ✕ **Saltlik, A Rare Steakhouse.** AAA steaks are cooked in an infrared oven to preserve flavor and tenderness. Other items include rotisserie grilled chicken, fish, and salads. The atmosphere is fun and casual and the decor is trendy and innovative. The dining room has a vaulted ceiling and a fireplace, and there are eight beers on tap in the lounge. ⊠ *221 Bear St., Banff* ☎ *403/762–2467. C$17–C$28* ⊟ *AE, MC, V.*

**$$–$$$** ✕ **Typhoon.** This intimate, café-style restaurant serves an eclectic mix of Thai, Indian, and other southeast Asian dishes. Always tasty and fresh, the soup of the day—often fragrant with the scent of lemongrass and coconut milk—comes in a huge bowl. The dinner menu includes chicken curry in a green-chili and coconut-milk sauce, tiger prawns with vegetables and noodles, and pot stickers. Dinner is served until 11 PM, appetizers until 1 AM. You can also indulge in a superb martini at the long granite-top bar. ⊠ *211 Caribou St., Banff* ☎ *403/762–2000. C$16–C$30* ▭ *AE, MC, V.*

🐾 ¢–$ ✕ **Laggan's Mountain Bakery and Deli.** Local work crews, mountain guides, and park wardens come to this small coffee shop in the Samson Mall for an early-morning muffin and cup of coffee. Laggan's sells excellent baked goods, especially the sweet poppy-seed breads made from organic grains. It's a good place to pick up a sandwich if you're driving north on the Icefields Parkway. ⊠ *Samson Mall off Hwy. 1, Lake Louise* ☎ *403/522–2017. C$5–C$8* ▭ *No credit cards.*

PICNIC AREAS **Bow Lake picnic area.** Situated on the shores of stunning Bow Lake, on the Icefields Parkway, this picnic area has a kitchen shelter, 5 tables, toilets, and fireboxes. ⊠ *Icefields Pkwy. at the edge of Bow Lake.*

**Cascade picnic area.** There are 60 tables, flush toilets, a kitchen shelter, and fireplaces at this picnic site, located on Lake Minnewanka Road. ⊠ *Off Lake Minnewanka Rd.*

**Fireside picnic area.** Located on the Bow Valley Parkway, this picnic area has picnic tables and toilets nearby. ⊠ *Off Bow Valley Pkwy.*

★ 🐾 **Lake Minnewanka picnic area.** This popular picnic area has three picnic shelters, 35 tables, flush toilets, two fire rings and six fireplaces. Hike, rent a boat or try your luck at fishing. ⊠ *6 mi (10 km) from Banff on the Minnewanka Loop.*

**Moraine Lake picnic area.** One of the most beautiful lakes in the Canadian Rockies is the setting for this picnic area located near Lake Louise. There are two kitchen shelters, eight tables, and toilets at this site. ⊠ *Off Moraine Lake Rd., 3 mi (5 km) from the village of Lake Louise.*

### Outside the Park

$$–$$$$ ✕ **Chez Francois.** This fine-dining restaurant is a favorite of food critics, locals, and the French ski team when they are visiting the Rockies. Chef-owner Jean-Francois Gouin transforms locally grown organic produce and fresh fish and meats into innovative French cuisine. Try the lobster bisque or the orange-braised duck. Sample some freshly prepared sorbet for dessert. ⊠ *Next to Best Western Green Gables Inn, 1602 Bow Valley Tr., Canmore* ☎ *403/678–6111. C$16–C$32* ▭ *AE, MC, V.*

## Where to Stay

### In the Park

🐾 $$$$ ▤ **Banff Rocky Mountain Resort.** Numerous outdoor facilities are a draw at this family-friendly resort 3 mi (5 km) east of Banff. Inside the chalet-style building, rooms are bright, with white walls, wall-to-wall carpeting, and blond-wood trim. All have fireplaces and most have kitchenettes with microwave ovens. Off-season rates decrease by 40%. ⊠ *1029 Banff Ave., at Tunnel Mountain Rd., Box 100, T1L 1A2* ☎ *403/762–5531 or 800/661–9563* ▤ *403/762–5166* ⊕ *www.rockymountainresort.*

com ↰ *171 suites* ↳ *Kitchen (some), dial-up, tennis courts, pool, gym, bicycles, no a/c.* *C$269* ⊟ *AE, D, DC, MC, V.*

**$$$$** ⊡ **Deer Lodge.** Built in 1921 as a log teahouse, this spot 15 minutes (on foot) from the shores of Lake Louise, has always been a popular destination. Guest rooms were added in 1925, and the frequent renovations since then have preserved most of the original rustic charm of the stone-and-log architecture. Feather comforters and teahouse-era antiques decorate the rooms; the older rooms are small but bright with the most historic charm. Relax around the central fireplace, with a book in one of the hotel's many nooks and crannies, or in the rooftop hot tub, complete with stunning mountain views. Rates decrease off-season. ⊠ *109 Lake Louise Dr., Box 100, Lake Louise T0L 1E0* ☎ *403/522–3747 or 800/661–1595* 🖷 *403/522–4222* ⊕ *www.crmr.com* ↰ *73 rooms* ↳ *Restaurant, no a/c, no phone (some), no TV.* *C$225–C$305* ⊟ *AE, DC, MC, V.*

**$$$$** ⊡ **Fairmont Banff Springs.** The building of this massive castle-like hotel by the Canadian Pacific Railway in 1888 marked the beginning of
Fodor'sChoice Banff's tourism boom. The hotel retains its historic elegance and mag-
★ nificent views of the Bow River and surrounding peaks, but now includes modern amenities that make for a luxurious lodging experience. Pampering is an art at the world-class Willow Stream spa. Restaurants, bars, and lounges of varying formality and cuisine create a small culinary universe. In summer about 200 rooms per night are reserved for individual travelers on inclusive resort packages. If the hotel is the focus of your visit to Banff, these packages represent good value. Rates decrease substantially off-season. ⊠ *405 Spray Ave., Box 960, T1L 1J4* ☎ *403/762–2211 or 800/441–1414* 🖷 *403/762–5755* ⊕ *www.fairmont. com* ↰ *770 rooms, 70 suites* ↳ *10 restaurants, room service, ethernet, Wi-Fi, golf course, tennis courts, pools, gym, spa, bars, concierge, some pets allowed.* *C$449* ⊟ *AE, D, DC, MC, V.*

**★ $$$$** ⊡ **Fairmont Château Lake Louise.** There's a good chance that no hotel—anywhere—has a more dramatic view out its back door. Terraces and lawns reach to the famous aquamarine lake, backed by the Victoria Glacier. Guest rooms have neocolonial furnishings, and some have terraces. The hotel began as a wooden chalet in 1890 but was largely destroyed by fire in 1924. It was soon rebuilt into the present grand stone-facade structure. The many dining choices range from family dining in the Brasserie to night-on-the-town elegance in the Fairview Dining Room (jacket required for dinner in summer). ⊠ *Lake Louise Dr., Lake Louise T0L 1E0* ☎ *403/522–3511 or 800/441–1414* 🖷 *403/522–3834* ⊕ *www. fairmont.com* ↰ *433 rooms, 54 suites* ↳ *5 restaurants, ethernet, Wi-Fi, pool, gym, spa, laundry service, parking (fee), some pets allowed, no a/c (some).* *C$350* ⊟ *AE, D, DC, MC, V.*

**★ $$$$** ⊡ **Post Hotel.** A bright red roof and log construction make this hotel a model of rustic elegance. Rooms come in 15 configurations, from standard doubles to units that have a sleeping loft, balcony, fireplace, and whirlpool tub. The deluxe suites have a king-size bed and a large living room with a river-stone fireplace. For old-fashioned, in-the-mountains romance try one of the three streamside log cabins. Furnishings are solid Canadian pine throughout. The restaurant is regularly rated as one of the best in the Canadian Rockies. Room rates decrease by about 40%

off-season. ⊠ *200 Pipestone Rd., Lake Louise T0L 1E0* ☎ *403/522–3989 or 800/661–1586* 🖷 *403/522–3966* ⊕ *www.posthotel.com* ⋤ *69 rooms, 26 suites, 3 cabins* ⌂ *Restaurant, Wi-Fi, pool, gym, spa, no a/c.* *C$305–C$400* ⊟ *AE, MC, V.*

★ $$$$ ⛱ **Rimrock Resort Hotel.** Luxury and natural splendor coexist in harmony at this 11-story hotel perched on the steep slope of Sulphur Mountain, with a gondola and hot springs nearby. The Grand Lobby has a 25-foot ceiling, giant windows, a balcony facing the Rockies, and an oversize marble fireplace. Nearly all rooms have views of the Bow Valley, though the views from the lower floors are compromised by trees. Off-season rates drop by 50%. You can catch a Banff transit bus or a shuttle to the Banff Townsite. ⊠ *100 Mountain Ave., Box 1110, T1L 1J2* ☎ *403/762–3356 or 800/661–1587* 🖷 *403/762–4132* ⊕ *www.rimrockresort.com* ⋤ *345 rooms, 6 suites* ⌂ *2 restaurants, ethernet, pool, gym, spa, concierge, no a/c.* *C$255–C$555* ⊟ *AE, D, DC, MC, V.*

$$–$$$$ ⛱ **Johnston Canyon Resort.** Situated near the trailhead for Johnston Canyon, these rustic cabins have a sense of seclusion you won't find in the busy town site. Several excellent hikes are nearby. There are fireplaces in most of the cabins. The cabins are also pet-friendly. ⊠ *Hwy. 1A (halfway between Banff and Lake Louise)* ⛫ *Box 875, Banff T0L 0C0* ☎ *403/762–2971* 🖷 *403/762–0868* ⊕ *www.johnstoncanyon.com* ⋤ *36 cabins* ⌂ *Restaurant, kitchen (some), refrigerator, some pets allowed, no a/c, no phone, no TV.* *C$129–C$284* ⊟ *MC, V.*

$$$ ⛱ **High Country Inn.** There's nothing fancy here—just clean, simple, comfortable motel rooms, many with a balcony. Cedar-covered walls give some rooms a touch of regional character. Ask for a room in the back, away from the Banff Avenue traffic. A deluxe Continental breakfast is included in the rate and includes items like pastry, fruit, cereal, and hot waffles. Rates decrease by 50% off-season. ⊠ *419 Banff Ave., Box 700, T1L 1A7* ☎ *403/762–2236, 800/661–1244 in Canada* 🖷 *403/762–5084* ⊕ *www.banffhighcountryinn.com* ⋤ *70 rooms* ⌂ *Restaurant, VCR, pool, no a/c.* *C$171* ⊟ *AE, MC, V* ⛉ *CP.*

$$$ ⛱ **Lake Louise Inn.** Five buildings hold a variety of accommodations, from small budget rooms to two-bedroom condo units, some with a balcony, fireplace, and kitchenette. A shuttle to the mountain and multiday ski packages are winter amenities. Rates decrease by 50% off-season. ⊠ *210 Village Rd., Lake Louise T0L 1E0* ☎ *403/522–3791 or 800/661–9237* 🖷 *403/522–2018* ⊕ *www.lakelouiseinn.com* ⋤ *232 rooms, 12 suites, 39 condos* ⌂ *Restaurant, room service, kitchen (some), pool, no a/c.* *C$159* ⊟ *AE, DC, MC, V.*

$$$ ⛱ **Skoki Lodge.** A 7-mi (11-km) hike or ski jaunt from the Lake Louise ski area, Skoki is the kind of backcountry lodge you must work to reach. The high-alpine scenery of the valley makes the trek well worth the effort, as does the small lodge itself, built in 1930. The log walls and big stone fireplace epitomize coziness, but don't expect private baths, running water, or electricity. Tasty home-style meals are included; reserve far in advance. There's a minimum two-day stay. ⛫ *Box 5, Lake Louise T0L 1E0* ☎ *403/522–3555* 🖷 *403/522–2095* ⊕ *www.skoki.com* ⋤ *6 rooms without bath, 3 cabins* ⌂ *Restaurant, no a/c, no phone, no TV.*

**6**

*C$159–C$180* ⊟ *AE, MC, V* ⊙ *Closed mid-Sept.–mid-Dec., Jan., mid-Apr.–mid-June* ⦿ *FAP.*

¢–$ ⊡ **HI Banff Alpine Centre.** This hostel is one of the best accommodation values in the park. You can purchase packages that include lift tickets in winter or adventure activities in the summer. The hostel has an activities program, but activities are designed for the young adults who tend to stay here and are generally not appropriate for children. ⊠ *801 Hidden Ridge Way T1L 1B5* ☎ *403/670–7580 or 866/762–4122* ⊕ *www.banffvoyagerinn.com* ⬟ *216 beds, cabins and family rooms* ⚭ *Restaurant, kitchen, no a/c. C$27–C$88* ⊟ *MC, V.*

CAMPGROUNDS & RV PARKS

$$ ⚠ **Castle Mountain Campground.** This campground is located in a beautiful wooded area close to a small store, a gas bar, and a restaurant. ⊠ *21 mi (34 km) from Banff on Bow Valley Pkwy.* ☎ *403/762–1550* ⬟ *43 sites* ⚭ *Flush toilets.* ⚮ *Reservations not accepted C$24* ⊟ *AE, MC, V* ⊙ *Open mid-May–early Sept.*

$$ ⚠ **Johnston Canyon Campground.** This campground is located across from Johnston Canyon. The scenery is spectacular and wildlife is abundant in the area. A small creek flows right by the camping area. ⊠ *15½ mi (25 km) from Banff on Bow Valley Pkwy.* ☎ *403/762–1550* ⬟ *132 sites* ⚭ *Showers, flush toilets.* ⚮ *Reservations not accepted C$24* ⊟ *AE, MC, V* ⊙ *Open early June–mid-Sept.*

★ ⚙ $$ ⚠ **Lake Louise Campground.** This forested area next to the Bow River is open year-round but in early spring and late fall tents and soft-sided trailers are not permitted in order to protect both people and bears. A protective electrical fence with a Texas gate surrounds the campground. There are plenty of hiking and biking trails nearby. ⊠ *½ mi (1 km) from Lake Louise Village and 2½ mi (4 km) from the Lake* ☎ *877/737–3783* ⬟ *399 sites* ⚭ *Partial hookups (electric), flush toilets, showers, dump station, fire pits. C$24–C$32* ⊟ *AE, MC, V.*

★ ⚙ $$ ⚠ **Tunnel Mountain Campground.** Situated close to the town site, this campground has a great view of the valley, hoodoos, and the Banff Springs golf course. There are 321 full-service sites in the trailer court, 188 power-only sites in Village II, and 618 nonserviced sites in Village I. ⊠ *1½ mi (2½ km) from Banff Townsite on Tunnel Mountain* ☎ *877/737–3783* ⬟ *1,127 sites* ⚭ *Full hookups, showers, flush toilets, fire pits. C$24–C$33* ⊟ *AE, MC, V* ⊙ *Open mid-May–early Oct.*

$$ ⚠ **Two Jack Main Campground.** This secluded camp is situated in a beautiful wooded area with lots of wildlife. You can explore the ruins of the coal-mining town of Bankhead, located nearby. If you want showers, stay at Two Jack Lakeside Campground right across the road. ⊠ *7½ mi (12 km) from Banff on the Minnewanka Loop* ☎ *403/762–1550* ⬟ *380 sites* ⚭ *Flush toilets.* ⚮ *Reservations not accepted C$24* ⊟ *AE, MC, V* ⊙ *Open mid-May–early Sept.*

## Outside the Park

⚙ $$$$ ✕⊡ **Delta Lodge at Kananaskis.** Now part of the Kananaskis Village built for the 1988 Olympics, this hotel started life as a Canadian Pacific luxury hotel. Rooms are large and lavish—many have fireplaces, hot tubs, and sitting areas. Several restaurants, skewed toward elegance, serve everything from pizza and burgers to haute cuisine. For casual dining, try the Fireweed Grill, which serves a buffet-style breakfast; burgers for lunch; and chicken, salmon, beef tenderloin, and lamb chops for dinner. ⊠ *Hwy. 40, 17 mi (28 km) south of Hwy. 1, Kananaskis Village T0L 2H0* ☎ *403/591–7711 or 888/244–8666* 🖷 *403/591–7770.*

**$$–$$$$** 🛏 **Rocky Mountain Ski Lodge.** Several motels in Canmore provide lower-price alternatives to Banff. Of these, Rocky Mountain Ski Lodge is a notch above the rest. It's really three separate motel properties rolled into one. Slanting, exposed wood-and-beam ceilings give a chaletlike feel to otherwise simple decor. Rooms in the older section have kitchenettes, but the style is more '60s American than Swiss chalet. Rates drop by 40% off-season. ⊠ *1711 Bow Valley Tr., at Hwy. 1A, Box 8070, Canmore T1W 2T8* ☎ *403/678–5445, 800/665–6111 in Canada* 🖷 *403/678–6484* ⊕ *www.rockyski.ca* ⤳ *82 rooms* ⚐ *Kitchen (some), VCR (some), Wi-Fi, laundry facilities.* *C$110–C$205* ▭ *AE, DC, MC, V.*

**CAMPGROUNDS &** ⚠ **Sundance Lodges Campground.** This campground has tent sites, RV **RV PARKS** sites, tepee camping, and old-fashioned trapper's tents. It's a quiet, se- **$$–$$$$** cluded campground designed for peace and tranquility. There are no electrical hookups, but there are outlets in the washroom. There is a small fee for pets. 🕭 *Box 190, Kananaskis Village T0L 2H0* ⊕ *www.sundancelodges.com* ☎ *403/591–7122* ⤳ *30 sites, 12 tepees, 18 trapper's tents* ⚐ *General store, showers, pit toilets, guest laundry, public telephone, fire pits, drinking water.* *C$21–C$69* ▭ *MC, V.*

# BANFF ESSENTIALS

**ACCESSIBILITY** Both visitor information centers are fully accessible and many of the campgrounds are also wheelchair accessible. There are also several trails in the park that are wheelchair accessible and Banff Transit operates one fully accessible shuttle. To find out specifics on accessible campgrounds and trails, call the information center at ☎ 403/762–1550.

**ADMISSION FEES** A park entrance pass is C$8.90 per person or C$17.80 maximum per vehicle per day. An annual pass will cost C$62.40 per adult or C$123.80 per family or group. Larger buses and vans pay a group commercial rate. If you're planning to stay a week or more, your best bet is an annual pass.

**ADMISSION HOURS** The park is open 24/7 year-round. It's in the Mountain time zone.

**ATMS/BANKS** There are at least a dozen ATMs in Banff Townsite, but only the CIBC ATM will allow you to withdraw money from a Visa card.
🏧 **CIBC Bank** ⊠ 98 Banff Ave., Banff ☎ 403/762-3317.

**AUTOMOBILE SERVICE STATIONS** You can buy propane in Lake Louise, but not in Banff. There are two gas stations in Lake Louise and five in Banff. There are also several companies that offer automobile repair service. The Petro-Canada station in Banff is a full-service station with gas sales and automotive repairs.

**EMERGENCIES**
🚑 **Ambulance, Fire, Police (RCMP)** ☎ 911.
**Banff Mineral Springs Hospital** ☎ 403/762-2222. **Lake Louise Medical Clinic** ☎ 403/522-2184. **Park Wardens** ☎ 403/762-4506.

**6**

LOST AND FOUND Contact the Banff National Park Information Centre for information about lost items (☎ 403/762-1550).

PERMITS Permits are required for backcountry camping and other activities in the park. Backcountry camping permits ($8.90 per day), day-use permits ($6.90 per day), fire permits ($7.90 per day), dumping station permits ($6.90 per day), and fishing permits ($8.90 per day) are available at the park visitor information center or at some campgrounds. In some cases a fire permit is included in your camping fees.

### POST OFFICES

🚹 **Banff Post Office** ✉ 204 Buffalo St., Banff ☎ 403/762-2586.

PUBLIC TELEPHONES Public telephones can be found at the information centers, most hotels and bars, and at several key spots around the town site of Banff and the Village of Lake Louise. Cell-phone service is sometimes unpredictable.

RESTROOOMS Public restrooms are located throughout the park at all major day-use areas, in the visitor's center on Banff Avenue, and near the mall in the downtown area. Some day-use areas have flush toilets, while others have public outhouses or dry toilets.

### SHOPS & GROCERS

🚹 **Canada Safeway** ✉ 318 Marten St., Banff ☎ 403/762-5378. **Keller Foods** ✉ 122 Bear St., Banff ☎ 403/762-3663.

### NEARBY TOWN INFORMATION

🚹 **Tourism Canmore** ✉ 907-7th Ave., Canmore 🕭 Box 8608, T1W 2V3 ☎ 403/678-1295 or 866/CANMORE (226-6673) ⊕ www.tourismcanmore.com.

### VISITOR INFORMATION

🚹 **Banff National Park** 🕭 Box 900, Banff T1L 1K2 Alberta Canada ☎ 403/762-1550 ⊕ www.pc.gc.ca.

# Big Bend National Park

**WORD OF MOUTH**

"I'd rather be broke down and lost in the wilds of Big Bend, any day, than wake up some morning in a penthouse suite high above the megalomania of Dallas or Houston."

–Environmental writer Edward Abbey

# WELCOME TO BIG BEND

## TOP REASONS TO GO

★ **Varied Terrain:** Visit gilded desert, a fabled river, bird-filled woods, and mountain spirals all in the same day.

★ **Wonderful Wildlife:** Catch sight of the park's extremely diverse number of animals, including several dozen shy mountain lions and about the same number of lumbering bears.

★ **Bird-watching:** Spy a pied-billed grebe or another member of the park's more than 400 bird species, including the Lucifer hummingbird and the unique-to-this-area pato Mexicano (Mexican duck).

★ **Hot spots:** Dip into the natural hot springs (105°F) near the Rio Grande Village.

★ **Mile-high Mountains:** Lace up those hiking boots and climb the Chisos Mountains, reaching 8,000 feet skyward in some places and remaining cool even during the most scorching Southern summer.

Bobcat

**1 North Rosillos.** Dinosaur fossils have been found in this remote, northern portion of the park. Made up primarily of back roads, this is where nomadic warriors traveled into Mexico via the Comanche Trail.

**2 Chisos Basin.** This bowl-shaped canyon amid the Chisos Mountains is at the heart of Big Bend. It's the place to watch a sunset and begin a hike.

**3 Castolon.** Just east of the Santa Elena Canyon, this historic district was once used by ranchers and the U.S. military, earning it a place on the National Register of Historic Places.

**4 Rio Grande Village.** Tall, shady cottonwoods highlight the park's eastern entrance along the Mexican border and Rio Grande. It's popular with RVers and bird-watchers.

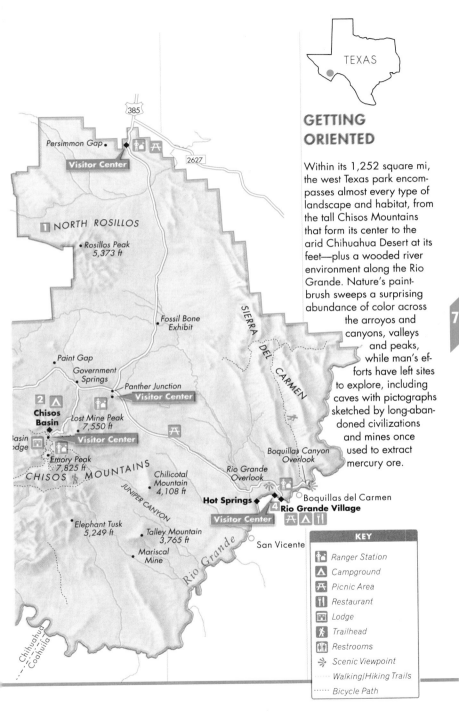

TEXAS

## GETTING ORIENTED

Within its 1,252 square mi, the west Texas park encompasses almost every type of landscape and habitat, from the tall Chisos Mountains that form its center to the arid Chihuahua Desert at its feet—plus a wooded river environment along the Rio Grande. Nature's paintbrush sweeps a surprising abundance of color across the arroyos and canyons, valleys and peaks, while man's efforts have left sites to explore, including caves with pictographs sketched by long-abandoned civilizations and mines once used to extract mercury ore.

7

Persimmon Gap

**Visitor Center**

385

2627

**1 NORTH ROSILLOS**

• Rosillos Peak
  5,373 ft

SIERRA DEL CARMEN

• Fossil Bone
  Exhibit

• Paint Gap

• Government
  Springs

Panther Junction
**Visitor Center**

**2** **Chisos Basin**

Basin Lodge

Lost Mine Peak
7,550 ft

**Visitor Center**

• Emory Peak
  7,825 ft

CHISOS MOUNTAINS

JUNIPER CANYON

Chilicotal
Mountain
4,108 ft

Rio Grande
Overlook

Boquillas Canyon
Overlook

**Hot Springs** ◆ ◆ **4 Rio Grande Village**
**Visitor Center**    ○ Boquillas del Carmen

• Elephant Tusk
  5,249 ft

• Talley Mountain
  3,765 ft

○ San Vicente

Mariscal
Mine

Rio Grande

Chihuahua
Coahuila

| KEY | |
|---|---|
| 🚺 | Ranger Station |
| ⛺ | Campground |
| 🪑 | Picnic Area |
| 🍴 | Restaurant |
| 🏠 | Lodge |
| 🥾 | Trailhead |
| 🚻 | Restrooms |
| ☀ | Scenic Viewpoint |
| ⋯ | Walking/Hiking Trails |
| ⋯ | Bicycle Path |

# BIG BEND PLANNER

## When to Go

Because the park is so vast, **there is never a bad time to make a Big Bend foray—except during Thanksgiving, Christmas, and spring break.** During these holidays, competition for rooms at the Chisos Mountain Lodge and campsites are fierce; if you're coming during these times of the year, reserve campsites and rooms up to a year in advance.

Depending on the season, Big Bend sizzles or drizzles, steams up collars or chills fingertips. Many shun the park in the summer, because temperatures skyrocket (up to 120°F in some areas), and the Rio Grande dips. If you're planning on visiting though, the lull will benefit you: rafting and other expeditions will be more personalized, and some expenses (food, excursions, etc.) might also be lower. And during those scorching summer days, the Chisos Mountains keep their cool with lots of shade and temperatures that top out in the 80s.

In the winter; temperatures rarely dip below 30°F. During those few times the mercury takes a dive, visitors might be rewarded with a rare snowfall.

## Flora & Fauna

Because Big Bend contains habitats as diverse as spent volcanos, slick-sided canyons, and the Rio Grande, it follows that species here are extremely diverse, too. Among the park's most notable residents are endangered and threatened species like the agave cactus–eating Mexican long-nosed bat, shadow-dappled peregrine falcon and fat-bellied horned lizard (Texans call them horney toads).

More than 400 species of birds wing throughout the park. Many are tops on birder lists, including the endangered black-capped vireo and the turkey vulture, which boasts a 6-foot wingspan.

In the highlands several dozen mountain lions lurk, while black bears loll in the crags and valleys. Your chances of spotting the reclusive creatures are greater in the early morning, but overall, sightings of the two predators are rare. If you do spot either, don't run away. Instead, stand tall, shout, and look as scary as possible.

If the winged, furred, and legged denizens of Big Bend are watch-worthy, so, too, are the plants populating the region. Supremely adapted to the arroyos, valleys, and slopes, the plants range from the endangered but brightly-colored Hedgehog cactus (found only in the Chisos) to the towering rasp of the giant dagger yucca. Also here are 65 types of cacti, the most in any of the national parks. So be careful where you tread—cactus spines are designed to defend.

### AVG. HIGH/LOW TEMPS.

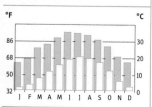

## Getting There & Around

Big Bend is 39 mi south of Marathon, off U.S. 385; 76 mi south of Alpine, off Route 118; and 50 mi east of Presidio, off Route 170. The nearest airport is in Midland, 3½ hours north of the park. The bus takes you as far as Marathon, and the train as far as Alpine.

Paved park roads have twists and turns, some very extreme in higher elevations; RVs and trailers longer than 20 feet should avoid the Ross Maxwell Scenic Drive on the park's west side and the Chisos Basin road into higher elevations in the central portion of the park. Four-wheel-drive vehicles are needed for many of the backcountry, dirt roads. At parking areas, take valuables with you. Some outfitters provide shuttle services in the immediate area and within the park.

## Border Crossings

If you want to go to Mexico, don't do it via the Rio Grande river. Terrorism threats have beefed up security, and if caught, you could face fines and imprisonment. The nearest crossing is in Presidio. You can enter Mexico by bus, cab, foot, or car—but note that if you drive, you must have a permit ($15), Mexican auto insurance (which costs up to $150 for six months), and a tourist card for each person in the vehicle ($15 each). ⇨ What's Nearby.

| WHAT TO BRING TO MEXICO | WHAT *NOT* TO BRING TO MEXICO |
|---|---|
| ■ **A passport.**<br><br>■ **Additional documentation.** Just in case, bring photo ID such as your driver's license or voter-registration card.<br><br>■ **Your own water.** Although border towns are used to catering to U.S. tourists, their water supplies do not meet U.S. standards and have been shown to be laced with arsenic and other harmful compounds. | ■ **Drugs.** Border patrol agents use drug-sniffing dogs on many cars leaving the park, and Mexican officials may search cars at customs.<br><br>■ **Ammo or guns.**<br><br>■ **Large amounts of cash.** It makes you a target.<br><br>■ **Flashy accessories.** Don't wear expensive jewelry or flaunt nice cameras. |

## Festivals & Events

FEB. **Texas Cowboy Poetry Gathering.** Ranchers and cowboys congregate at Sul Ross State University to regale audiences with original poetry and washtub-bass tributes to singers like Bob Wills. ✉ *Alpine* ☎ *432/837-8194* ⊕ *www.cowboypoetry.org.*

JUNE–AUG. **Texas Glider Rally.** The endless blue skies and chubby white clouds of West Texas attract motorless flying machines that soar in air; instruction and rides are offered. ✉ *Marfa Municipal Airport, Marfa* ☎ *800/667-9464* ⊕ *www.flygliders. com.*

SEPT. **Big Bend Balloon Rally.** Twenty to 30 brightly splashed hot-air balloons create Kodak moments as they ascend Alpine skies each Labor Day weekend. When the sun goes down, the balloons light up, and the flames are choreographed to music. ✉ *Alpine* ☎ *432/837-7486.*

NOV. **Alpine Gallery Night.** Each year, the peculiar mix of ranching and artist culture that inhabits Alpine overflows the galleries and seeps into the town's main drag, Holland Avenue. Musicians play at the train depot, barbecue vendors crowd the streets, and local artists display their works in many downtown businesses. ✉ *Alpine* ☎ *800/561-3735* ⊕ *www.alpinegallerynight.com.* **Terlingua International Chili Championship.** Top chili chefs spice up cooling weather with four days of chili cooking, bragging, and gathering at Rancho CASI, on the north side of Highway 170, 11 mi east of Lajitas. Some of the prize-winning cooks dole out samples. ✉ *Terlingua* ☎ *214/392-3499* ⊕ *www.chili. org/terlingua.html.*

**7**

By Jennifer
Edwards

Cradled in the warm, southwestern elbow of Texas, the 801,163 acres of Big Bend National Park hang suspended above the deserts of northern Mexico. From the craggy, bald Chisos Mountains rising 8,000 feet to the flat and stark plains of the Chihuahua Desert, Big Bend is one of the nation's most geographically diverse parks, with the kind of territory that inspired Hollywood's first Western sets. Visitors can ride the rapids of the Rio Grande, trek through the classic, Old West landscape, and marvel at the moonscape that skirts Boquillas, Mexico.

## Scenic Drive

**Fodor's**Choice **Ross Maxwell Scenic Drive.** This route takes you 30 mi through pyramid-
★ shape volcanic mountains. If you don't mind a little grate in your gait from the gravel that blankets the road, you can make this drive a loop by starting out at the west park entrance and turning southwest onto Old Maverick Road (unpaved) for 12⁸⁄₁₀ mi to the Santa Elena Canyon overlook—where you can get a taste of the lowland desert.

## What to See

### Historic Sites

**Castolon Historic District.** Adobe buildings and wooden shacks serve as reminders of the farming and military community of Castolon. The Magdalena House has historical exhibits. ⊠ *At end of the Ross Maxwell Scenic Dr., southwest portion of park* ☎ *432/477–2225 ranger station.*

🖑 **Hot Springs.** Hikers soak themselves in the 105°F waters here, alongside the Rio Grande, while petroglyphs (rock paintings) coat the canyon walls nearby. The remains of a post office, motel, and bathhouse point to the old commercial establishment operating here in the early 1900s. ⊠ *15 mi southeast of Panther Junction, near Rio Grande Village.*

## BIG BEND IN ONE DAY

You'll be able to drive the paved roads of the park in one day, but don't short yourself; you'll miss most striking parts if you don't hike at least one of the many trails. Two not to miss are the trails through the rifts and boulders of **Santa Elena Canyon** and the rocky pinnacles of the **Chisos Mountain Basin.**

Access the Santa Elena trailhead from the junction of **Ross Maxwell Scenic Drive** and **Old Maverick Road** at the northwestern rim of the park. From there, take the **Santa Elena Canyon Trail** (1⁷⁄₁₀ mi round-trip). You'll have to wade Terlingua Creek, and then enter the canyon, where you'll see gargantuan rocks, singular rock formations, and the Rio Grande sandwiched between sheer cliffs. Back at the trailhead, take **Ross Maxwell Scenic Drive** 30 mi north and turn east at Santa Elena Junction.

Drive to the **Chisos Mountains Basin Junction** and turn south. This scenic drive will take you to the heart of Big Bend, where you can linger for a short, less-than-a-half mile hike along the **Window View Trail.** Visit the gift shop and restaurant, or settle in for a picnic lunch at a campground table near the **Chisos Basin Visitor Center.**

Drive north back to the junction, turn east and drive 23 mi to **Rio Grande Village.** Stroll through the tall, shady cottonwoods in the picnic area, and you'll likely see many varieties of birds, including speedy roadrunners. If you have the time, follow the signs to the natural hot spring and take a dip.

Before calling it a day, drive east to the **Boquillas Canyon** overlook and view the Mexican village of Boquillas on the south side of the Rio Grande.

### Scenic Stops

★ **Chisos Basin.** Panoramic vistas, a restaurant with an up-close view of the mountains, and glimpses of the Colima warbler (found only in Big Bend) await in this forested area. Also here are hiking trails, a lodge, campground, store, and gift shop. ⊠ *Off Chisos Basin Rd., 7 mi southwest of Chisos Basin Junction and 9 mi southwest of Panther Junction.*

★ **Santa Elena Canyon.** The finale of a short hike (1⁷⁄₁₀ mi round-trip), is a spectacular view of the Rio Grande and cliffs that rise 1,500 feet to create a natural box. ⊠ *30 mi southwest of Santa Elena Junction via Ross Maxwell Scenic Dr.; 14 mi southwest of Rte. 118 via Old Maverick Rd.*

### Visitor Centers

**Castolon Visitor Center.** Here you find some of the most hands-on exhibits the park has to offer, with touchable fossils, plants, and implements used by the farmers and miners who settled here in the 1800s and early 1900s. ⊠ *In the Castolon Historic District, southwest side of the park, at the end of the Ross Maxwell Scenic Dr.* ☎ 432/477–2271 ۞ *Nov.–May, daily 10–noon and 1–5.*

Fodor'sChoice **Chisos Basin Visitor Center.** The center is one of the more highly equipped,
★ as it offers an interactive computer exhibit, a bookstore, camping sup-

---

## GOOD READS

**Naturalist's Big Bend**, by Roland H. Wauer and Carl M. Fleming, paints a picture of the park's diverse plants and animals, and traces the hidden places in Big Bend.

**Big Bend, The Story Behind the Scenery**, by Carol E. Sperling and Mary L. Van Camp, is rife with colorful photos illustrating the park's history and geology.

For gleeful, wondering, and awestruck thoughts on the Big Bend wilderness, check out **God's Country or Devil's Playground**, which collects the writing of nearly 60 authors.

The Natural History Association's **Road Guide ($1.95)** gives in-depth information on the web of paved and improved dirt roads running through the park—and the views you can see from them. Find it on sale at park visitor centers.

Three newspapers are also published in and around the park. **The Big Bend Gazette ($1)**, a monthly independent; *The Big Bend Sentinel* (75¢) is a newsy weekly that prints on Thursday in Marfa; and the National Park Service puts out the 16-page **Big Bend Paisano** (free) in the spring, fall and summer. The paper is available at visitor centers and on the park's Web site, ⊕ www.nps.gov/bibe/Paisano/index.htm.

---

plies, picnic fare, and some produce. There are plenty of nods to the wild, with natural resource and geology exhibits and a larger-than-life representation of a mountain lion. ⊠ *Off Chisos Basin Rd., 7 mi southwest of Chisos Basin Junction and 9 mi southwest of Panther Junction* ☎ *432/477–2264* ☉ *Nov.–Mar., daily, 9–3:30, closed for lunch and on Christmas Day; Apr.–Oct., daily, 9 a.m.–4:30 p.m., closed for lunch.*

**Panther Junction Visitor Center.** The park's main visitor center was set to undergo a face-lift at the time of this writing. Planned construction includes an enlarged bookstore and new, touchable exhibits on the park's mountain, river, and desert environments. Nearby, a gas station offers limited groceries such as chips, premade sandwiches, and picnic items. ⊠ *30 mi south of U.S. 385 junction leading to north park boundary* ☎ *432/477–1158* ☉ *Daily 8–6, reduced hours Christmas Day.*

**Persimmon Gap Visitor Center.** Complete with exhibits and a bookstore, this center is the northern boundary gateway into miles of flatlands that surround the heart of Big Bend. Dinosaur fossils have been found here; none are on display in the center, but the **Fossil Bone Exhibit** is on the road between Persimmon Gap and Panther Junction. ⊠ *3 mi south of U.S. 385 junction* ☎ *432/477–2393* ☉ *Daily 9–4:30, closed for lunch.*

**Rio Grande Village Visitor Center.** Opening days and hours are sporadic here, but if you do find this center open, then view videos of Big Bend's geologic and natural features at its minitheater. There are also exhibits dealing with the Rio Grande. ⊠ *22 mi southeast of Panther Junction* ☎ *432/477–2271* ☉ *Daily 8:30–4. Closed May through Oct.*

## Sports & the Outdoors

Spectacular scenery plus nearly 300 mi of road spell adventure for hikers, bikers, horseback riders, or those simply in need of a ramble on foot or by Jeep. A web of dusty, unpaved roads lures experienced hikers deep into the back country, while paved roads make casual walks easier. Because the park has over half of the bird species in North America, birding ranks high. Boating is also popular, since some of the park's most striking features are accessible only via the Rio Grande.

### Bicycling

Mountain biking the backcountry roads can be so solitary that you're unlikely to encounter another human being. However, the solitude also means you should be extraordinarily prepared for the unexpected with ample supplies, especially water (summer heat is brutal, and you're unlikely to find shade except in forested areas of Chisos Basin). Biking is recommended only during the cooler months (October through April).

On paved roads, a regular road bike should suffice, but you'll have to bring your own—outfitters tend to only stock mountain bikes. Off-road cycling is not allowed in the park. For an easy ride on mostly level ground, try the 14-mi (one way) unpaved **Old Maverick Road** on the west side of the park off Route 118. For a challenge, take unpaved **Old Ore Road** for 26⁴⁄₁₀ mi from the park's north area to near Rio Grande Village on the east side. ⇨ Multisport Outfitters box for bike rentals and expeditions.

### Bird-watching

Situated on north-south migratory pathways, Big Bend is home to at least 434 species of birds—more than any other national park. In fact, the birds that flit, waddle, soar, and swim in the park represent more than half the species of birds found in North America, including the Colima warbler, found nowhere else. To glimpse darting hummingbirds, turkey vultures, and golden eagles, try the Chisos Mountains. To spy woodpeckers, scaled quail (distinctive for dangling crests), and the famous Colima, look to the desert scrub. And for cuckoos, cardinals, and screech owls, you must prowl along the river. Rangers lead birding talks; ⇨ Ranger Programs under the Educational Offerings.

FodorsChoice ★ **Rio Grande Village.** Considered the best birding habitat in Big Bend due to its moist environment, this river wetland has summer tanagers and vermilion flycatchers among many other species. The trail's a good one for kids, and a portion is wheelchair accessible. ⊠ *22 mi southeast of Panther Junction.*

OUTFITTERS & EXPEDITIONS **Big Bend Birding Expeditions.** Join custom guided and regularly scheduled tours. ⊠ *On East Terlingua Ranch Rd., east of Texas 118* ⌂ *P.O. Box 638, Terlingua 79852* ☎ *888/531–2223.*

### Boating & Rafting

The 118 mi of the Rio Grande River that border the park form its backbone, defining the vegetation, landforms, and animals found at the park's southern rim. By turns shallow and deep, the river flows through stunning canyons and picks up speed over small and large rapids.

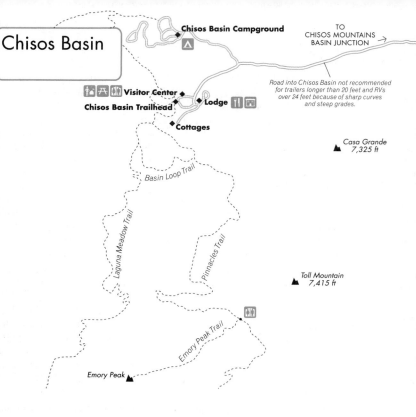

Chisos Basin

Chisos Basin Campground

TO
CHISOS MOUNTAINS
BASIN JUNCTION

Visitor Center
Chisos Basin Trailhead
Lodge
Cottages

Road into Chisos Basin not recommended
for trailers longer than 20 feet and RVs
over 24 feet because of sharp curves
and steep grades.

Casa Grande
7,325 ft

Basin Loop Trail

Laguna Meadow Trail

Pinnacles Trail

Toll Mountain
7,415 ft

Emory Peak Trail

Emory Peak

The river can be traversed in several ways, from guided rafting tours to more strenuous kayak and canoe expeditions. In general, rafting trips spell smoother sailing for families, though thrills are inherent when soaring over the river's meringue-like tips and troughs. It's also pretty safe; no fatalities have been reported in several years.

Area outfitters rent rafts, canoes, kayaks, and inflatable kayaks (nicknamed "duckies") for when the river is low. They also offer guided trips and specialty packages. Trips last anywhere from a couple of hours to several days, and cost in the tens of dollars to thousands of dollars. Personalized river tours are available all year long, and since this is the Lone Star State, they might include gourmet rafting tours that end with beef Wellington and live country music. Though many of the rafting trips are relatively smooth, thus safe for younger boaters, be sure to tell the equipment rental agent or guide if a party member weighs less than 100 pounds or more than 200, since special life jackets may be needed.

If you choose to bring your own watercraft, leave the Jet Skis at home; no motorized vehicles are allowed on the river. A river-use permit, which is free, is required; it also allows you to camp at sites along the river. Obtain permits from a visitor center or at the self-administered station at Lajitas (Barton Warnock Environmental Education Center).

For floats combined with guided trips, ⇨ Multisport Outfitters box.

### Fishing

You can cast a line into the Rio Grande all year long for free, as long as you obtain a permit from one of the park visitor centers. You cannot use jug lines, traps, or other nontraditional fishing methods.

### Hiking

Each of the park's zones has its own appeal. The east side offers easy mountain hikes, border canyons, lush vegetation, limestone aplenty, and sandy washes with geographic spectacles. West-side trails go down into striking scenery in the Santa Elena Canyon and up into towering volcanic land forms. Descend into gorges and springs or ascend into the must-see scenic windows of Grapevine Hills. The heart of the park has abandoned mines, scrub vegetation surrounding the Chisos, and deserts lying just below soaring Chisos Mountain aeries. Be sure to carry enough drinking water—a gallon per person daily (more when extremely hot). ⇨ Multisport Outfitters box for guided hiking expeditions.

EASY

★ ☾ **Chihuahuan Desert Nature Trail.** A windmill and spring form a desert oasis, a refreshing backdrop to a ½-mi flat trail; wild doves are abundant, the hike is pleasant, and kids will do just fine. While you're there, keep an eye out for the elf owl, one of the sought-after birds on the Big Bend's "Top 10" list. ⊠ *Dugout Wells, 5 mi southeast of Panther Junction.*

☾ **Rio Grande Village Nature Trail.** This ¾-mi trail is considered one of the best spots in the park to see rare birds, and the variety of other wildlife isn't in short supply either. Keep a lookout for coyotes, javelinas (they look like wild pigs), and other mammals. Expect high traffic. Restrooms are nearby and the trail can be done in less than an hour. The first ¼ mi is wheelchair accessible. ⊠ *22 mi southeast of Panther Junction.*

MODERATE **The Lost Mine Trail.** Set aside about two hours to leisurely explore the nature of the Chisos Mountains along this elevation-climbing trail. It starts at 5,400 feet, one of the highest elevations in the park, and climbs to an even higher vantage point. Though the air is thinner, all but the smallest kids should enjoy this trail because of the sweeping cliff view at the end of the first mile. The entire length is 4⁸⁄₁₀ mi round-trip. ⊠ *Begin at mi marker 5 on the Basin Rd.*

DIFFICULT **Chisos Basin Loop Trail.** A forested area and higher elevations give you some sweeping views of the lower desert and distant volcanic mountains. The elevation in the pass where the 1⁶⁄₁₀-mi round-trip hike begins is 5,400 feet; the highest point on the trail is 7,825 feet. What makes this trail difficult is not the length, but the climb. Set aside about an hour. ⊠ *7 mi southwest of Chisos Basin Junction.*

**Hot Springs Trail.** An abandoned motel and bathhouse foundation are sights along this 2-mi hike. The Rio Grande is heard at every turn, and trees shelter the way. Temperatures can soar to 120°F, so hike it during cooler months. ⊠ *22 mi southeast of Panther Junction.*

Fodor'sChoice
★ **Santa Elena Canyon Trail.** A 1⁷⁄₁₀-mi round-trip crosses Terlingua Creek and takes hikers to a view of steep cliffs jutting above the Rio Grande. Try to end up there near sunset, when the dying sun stains the cliffs a rich red-brown chestnut—its beauty can inspire poetry. It's a moderate-

## MULTISPORT OUTFITTERS

**Big Bend River Tours.** Exploring the Rio Grande is their specialty. Tours include rafting, canoeing, and hiking and horseback trips combined with a river float. ⬧ *P.O. Box 317, Terlingua, TX 79852* ☎ *800/545-4240* ⊕ *www.bigbendrivertours.com.*

**Desert Sports.** From rentals—bikes, boats, rafts, and inflatable kayaks—to experienced guides for mountain-bike touring, boating, and hiking, this outfitter has it covered. ✉ *P.O. Box 448, Terlingua* ☎ *432/371-2727 or 888/989-6900* ⊕ *www.desertsportstx.com.*

**Far Flung Adventures.** Call these pros for personalized trips via rafts and 4x4s. Trips include gourmet rafting tours with cheese and wine served on checkered tablecloths along the river. ✉ *P.O. Box 377, Terlingua* ☎ *800/839-7238* ⊕ *www.farflungoutdoorcenter.com.*

**Red Rock Outfitters.** This outfitter sells clothing and gear, and leads river rafting, canoeing, horseback riding, and mountain biking excursions, plus gives bird-watching tours. ✉ *HC 70 Box 400, Lajitas* ☎ *432/424-5170.*

to-difficult trail, and worth every bead of sweat. ✉ *8 mi west of Castolon, accessible via Ross Maxwell Scenic Dr. or Old Maverick Rd.*

### Horseback Riding

At Big Bend, guides give horseback tours, and visitors can bring their own horses. The going might be slow in some parts, as horses aren't allowed on paved roads. Trips range from two hours to several days. If you're bringing your own horses, call any visitor center at least a day ahead of time to get a permit. You may camp with your horse at any of the park's primitive campsites but not in the developed areas. A campsite with corrals near Panther Junction may be reserved (no longer than 10 weeks' notice) by calling ☎ 432/477-1158.

OUTFITTERS & EXPEDITIONS **Lajitas Stables.** Guided tours include participation in an honest-to-goodness, brand-to-hide cattle drive. You can also foray into the Mexican state of Chihuahua, via horse, on a 4–5 day trip. ✉ *P.O. Box 6, Terlingua* ☎ *888/508-7667 or 432/424-3238* ⊕ *www.lajitasstables.com.*

## Educational Offerings

### Classes & Seminars

**Big Bend Natural History Association Seminars.** One- to two-day seminars cover subjects such as wildflowers, geology, and desert survival. Class size is limited, generally from 5 to 15. Register in advance. ✉ *Held at locations throughout the park* ☎ *877/839-5377* 🖃 *Fees vary.*

### Ranger Programs

**Birding Talks.** Rangers lead two-hour birding tours; binoculars are needed. ✉ *Chisos Basin Visitor Center* ☎ *432/477-2264* ◷ *Daily 9–4:30 (varies by season), closed for lunch.*

**Interpretive Activities.** Ranger-guided events include daily slide shows, talks, and walks on natural and cultural history. Check visitor centers and campground bulletin boards for event postings, or call ☎ *432/477–2251.*

**Junior Ranger Program.** This self-guiding program, for kids 7 to 15, is taught via a $2 booklet of nature-based activities (available at visitor centers). Upon completion of the course, kids are given a Junior Ranger badge or patch, a certificate, and a bookmark. ☎ *432/477–2251.*

# WHAT'S NEARBY

Just as many of Big Bend's zones are geographically isolated, the park itself is isolated among hundreds upon hundreds of miles of West Texas desert and scrub. The nearest metropolis is El Paso, about 320 mi away, while the nearest sizeable cities are Odessa and Midland, 210 and 240 mi to the northeast. Those who fancy a border crossing also can choose from a couple of Mexican destinations.

## Nearby Towns & Attractions

### Nearby Towns

**Marathon,** just 50 mi to the north, is one of the closest towns to Big Bend. Once a shipping hub, the 500-population town still contains reminders of its Old West railroad days. **Alpine,** a town of about 6,000, hunkers down among the Davis Mountains, about 70 mi north of the park. The town is known for its extensive college agriculture program at Sul Ross University. It also attracts celebrities like Will and Jada Pinkett-Smith, who have been spotted at its historic Holland Hotel. About 26 mi west of Alpine is **Marfa,** a 2,000-population, middle-of-nowhere West Texas city known for its spooky, unexplained "Marfa lights," attributed to everything from atmospheric disturbances to imagination. Once the headquarters of quicksilver mining (now defunct), **Terlingua,** population 25, is just 5 mi from the park's west entrance on Highway 118. To the east 5 mi is **Study Butte** (pop. 100), which also has its roots in the old quicksilver mining industry. Follow Highway 170 west from Terlingua for 13 mi and you come upon the flat-rock formations of the tiny (pop. 50) **Lajitas.** Once a U.S. Cavalry outpost, Lajitas, which means (loosely) "tableland with little flat stones," has been converted to a resort area offering plenty of golf and tennis. The border town of **Presidio,** 70 mi from the park's west exit, is regarded as the gateway to northern Mexico. Across the border from Presidio is **Ojinaga, Mexico,** famous for its party-like atmosphere. A railroad beginning in Ojinaga can take you to Copper Canyon, a striking series of

| FAMILY PICKS |
| --- |

**Cowboy Poetry.** Cowboys and cowgirls congregate and relate poetry about their lives and loves.
**Star Parties.** Guides at McDonald Observatory lead observers on a tour of the celestial bodies that illuminate the West Texas sky.
**Overnight Rafting Trips.** During Spring Break, Far Flung Outdoor Center sometimes offers overnight rafting trips open only to families with children under 12. The trips include short hikes, goggles for stargazing, and canoe instruction.

7

canyons that run down the west side of the Sierra Tarahumara.

It's easy to cross the border. From Presidio, hop a bus, hail a cab, park and walk, or drive your vehicle across. Many people choose public transportation or walking, because in order to drive your car into Mexico, you must have a permit ($15), Mexican auto insurance (up to $150 for six months), and a tourist card ($15 per person). Bring your passport. For details, see the Department of State's Web site ( ⊕ www.travel.state.gov/travel/tips).

| CAUTION |  |
|---|---|
| If you try to enter the United States from Mexico through Big Bend National Park, you are subject to thousands in fines, one year's imprisonment, or both. | |

### Nearby Attractions

**Barton Warnock Environmental Education Center.** A self-guided walking tour takes you through indoor and outdoor exhibits, providing insight into cultural history and natural resources of the Big Bend area. It's a good way to become oriented to Chihuahuan Desert plant life before touring Big Bend. In the summer, the center offers Desert Garden Tours. ⊠ *Off Rte. 170, 1 mi east of Lajitas, Terlingua* ☎ *432/424–3327* 🖅 *$3; $14 per group for the Desert Garden Tours* ⊙ *Daily 8–4:30.*

**Big Bend Ranch State Park.** As a southwest buffer to Big Bend National Park, this rugged desert wilderness extends along the Rio Grande across 280,280 acres from southeast of Lajitas to Presidio. You can hike, backpack, raft, and even round up longhorn steers on the annual cattle drive put on by the park in March or April of each year. ⊠ *Entrance road at Fort Leaton, 4 mi southeast of Presidio off Rte. 170, Presidio* ☎ *432/229–3416* 🖅 *$3 entrance fee, $3 activity fee* ⊙ *Year-round; centers are open daily, 8–5.*

☺ **McDonald Observatory Visitors Center.** There's plenty to do here: Check out exhibits, examine sunspots and flares safely via film, or peer into the research telescopes. After night fall, the observatory offers "star parties." ⊠ *Hwy. 118 north through Alpine and Fort Davis, Fort Davis* ☎ *432/426–3540* ⊕ *http://mcdonaldobservatory.org* 🖅 *$8 for adults, $7 for kids. Star Party: $10 for adults, $8 for kids, or $40 a family.*

**Museum of the Big Bend.** A renovation and expansion of this West Texas haven for art lovers and cowboy poets was still underway at the writing of this book, but the museum remains open. The museum's 5,000 feet of space holds exhibits on cowboys and conquistadors, including an annual show on ranching handiwork (see saddles, reins, and spurs) held in conjunction with the Cowboy Poetry Gathering each February. ⊠ *Sul Ross State University Campus, Alpine* ☎ *432/837–8143* 🖅 *Free, donations accepted* ⊙ *Tues.–Sat. 9–5, Sun. 1–5.*

## Area Activities

### Sports & the Outdoors

Big Bend is all about playing outdoors in every way, and outside the park the fun continues with activites like golf, horseback riding, fishing,

# Bluebonnets: the Pride of Texas

*"The bluebonnet is to Texas what the shamrock is to Ireland, the cherry blossom to Japan, the lily to France, the rose to England, and the tulip to Holland."*

–Historian Jack Maguire

EVER SINCE MEN FIRST EXPLORED the prairies of Texas, the bluebonnet has been revered. Native Americans wove folktales around this bright bluish-violet flower; early-day Spanish priests planted it thickly around their newly established missions; and the cotton boll and cactus competed fiercely with it for the state flower–the bluebonnet won the title in 1901.

Nearly half a dozen varieties of the bluebonnet–distinctive for flowers resembling pioneers' sunbonnets–

exist throughout the state. From mid-January until late March, at least one of the famous flowers carpets Big Bend National Park: the Big Bend (also called Chisos Bluebonnet) has been described as "the most majestic" species, as its deep-blue flower spikes can shoot up to three feet in height. The Big Bend bluebonnets can be found beginning in late winter on the flats of the park as well as along the El Camino del Rio (Highway 70), which follows the Rio Grande between Lajitas and Presidio, Texas.

For information on viewing the bluebonnets at their peak, March through May, call the Texas Department of Transportation Hotline ☏ 800/452-9292.

–Marge Peterson

---

hunting, and more. For details about area activities, contact the town visitor centers; ⇨ Nearby Town Information in Essentials.

## Arts & Entertainment

While recreation and the outdoor adventures are alive inside the park, the arts are vibrant outside it. Activities include live poetry readings and Cinco de Mayo festivals that fill up streets and shut down towns.

ART GALLERIES ★ The **Chinati Foundation** (✉ P.O. Box 1135, Marfa ☏ 432/729–4362 ⊕ www.chinati.org) changes its exhibits regularly and has a well-attended annual open house. People fly from all over the country to see the collection, and the foundation conducts tours of its huge contemporary-art holdings by appointment. Getting to the museum can be tricky, so call for directions or visit the Web site.

**Marfa Studio of Arts** (✉ 106 E. San Antonio, Marfa ☏ 432/729–4616 ⊕ www.marfastudio.org) offers a long list of arts classes, and has a gallery filled with local art pieces. Tours are by appointment, but the gallery and store stay open Tues–Sat 1 PM to 5 PM.

DANCE HALLS ★ **Railroad Blues,** a cozy wooden bar thick with atmosphere and Texas music, is home to live music artists, kooky characters, and live, spontaneous dancing. Watch couples two-step and see if you can pick it up, too. Acts generally go on at 10 PM on weekends. *✉ 504 W. Holland Ave., Alpine ☏ 432/837–3103. ⊕ www.railroadblues.com.*

## Shopping

Alpine's main drag, **Holland Avenue** is lined with shops. You can have a triple shot of espresso, pick up a local painting, browse books, fill up your gas tank, and shop for groceries. Nearby Marfa offers shopping downtown, but the best finds are off the town square. **The Brown Recluse** (✉ 111 W. San Antonio ☎ 866/731–1811), is a used bookstore that serenades shoppers with music on vinyl and offers some killer *juevos con nopalitos* (eggs and cactus) and coffee that's roasted in the store.

# WHERE TO STAY & EAT

### About the Restaurants

One word sums up dining in the park: casual. You can wear jeans and sneakers to the one park restaurant, which serves American-style fare. Outside the park, Alpine and Marfa have the biggest selection.

### About the Hotels

At the only hotel in the park, the Chisos Basin Mountain Lodge, visitors can select from a freestanding cabin or a hotel room, both within a pace or two of spectacular views—Chisos sunsets are not to be missed. It's fun to stay here because it's close to trails, and has a nice little gift shop and the park's only restaurant. Even if you don't stay here, go just to see the stunning view through the wall-sized dining room windows.

The Big Bend area retains its grand historic hotels, like the glamorous Paisano Hotel in Marfa and the Holland Hotel in Alpine, but it also boasts the Lajitas Resort and some more moderately priced hotels.

### About the Campgrounds

The park's copious campsites are separated, roughly, into two categories—front country and backcountry. Each of its four front-country sites has toilet facilities at a minimum. You can reserve a spot at these popular places from November 15 to April 15, and rangers recommend doing so as far in advance as possible. During the times in between, sites are given on a first-come, first-served basis. Make reservations by phone at ☎ 877/444–6777 or online at ⊕ www.reserveusa.com.

Far more numerous are the primitive backcountry sites, which have no amenities and are generally inaccessible via RV. Free permits, obtained from the visitor center, are needed to camp there.

## Where to Eat

### In the Park

¢–$$  ✕ **Chisos Mountains Lodge Restaurant.** Views of the imposing Chisos Mountains are a pleasant accompaniment to nicely prepared (but not fancy) fare such as chicken-fried steak and hamburgers. The view is great and the salad bar isn't bad and there is a takeout hiker's lunch. Try the firm Imperial shrimp, raised not far from the park. ✉ *7 mi southwest of Chisos Basin Junction and 9 mi southwest of Panther Junction* ☎ *432/477–2291. $6–$14* ☐ *AE, D, DC, MC, V.*

PICNIC AREAS

Fodor's Choice
★

**Rio Grande Village Area.** There are half a dozen tables scattered under cottonwoods south of the store. Half a mile away at Daniels Ranch are two tables and a grill. Wood fires aren't allowed; charcoal and propane cooking are okay. ⊠ *2 mi southeast of Panther Junction.*

**Santa Elena Canyon Area.** Two tables sit in the shade next to the parking lot at the trailhead. There is a vault toilet. ⊠ *8 mi west of Castolon, accessible via Ross Maxwell scenic drive or Old Maverick Rd.*

**Chisos Basin Area.** There are about half a dozen tables scattered near the parking lot as well as a few grills. The tables provide an awesome view of the Chisos mountains. ⊠ *Off Chisos Basin Rd., 7 mi southwest of Chisos Basin Junction and 9 mi southwest of Panther Junction.*

**Persimmon Gap Area.** Quiet and remote, this new picnic area has tables shaded by metal roofs called ramadas. There are no grills; there is a pit toilet. ⊠ *North Big Bend, 4 mi south of U.S. 385 junction.*

### Outside the Park

$–$$$  ✕ **Candilila Cafe and Thirsty Goat Saloon.** Steaks and scrumptious country cooking are the specialty of this restaurant with wagon wheels and Old West decor. Glass walls give unobstructed views of sunsets and the nearby golf course. ⊠ *Lajitas Resort, off Rte. 170, 25 mi west of park entrance, Lajitas* ☎ *432/424–5010. $8.50–$30* ▭ *AE, D, DC, MC, V.*

☺ ¢–$$  ✕ **Edelweiss Restaurant.** Opened in 2003 by a native German brewmeister, the restaurant in the Holland Hotel offers ales that are as authentic as the spaetzel and schnitzel. There are standard choices like hamburgers, plus there's a kids' menu. ⊠ *209 W. Holland Ave., Alpine* ☎ *800/535–8040. $6–$15* ▭ *AE, D, DC, MC, V.*

¢–$$  ✕ **La Trattoria.** By day this small café offers espressos, white coffee (a concoction with twice the caffeine), and a lunch menu of light sandwiches and hot entrées. By night there's beer, wine, and an expanded menu. The homemade oatmeal cookies are a tasty dessert. ⊠ *202 W. Holland Ave., Alpine* ☎ *432/837–2200. $3–$15* ▭ *AE, D, DC, MC, V.*

★ ☺ ¢–$$  ✕ **Pizza Foundation.** This funky gas station turned hip pizza joint will appeal to most park visitors, and especially families, because of its casual atmosphere, good-smelling interior, and, most of all, the quality pizza the Rhode Island–native owners turn out. Kids will dig the fun pizza names such as the Faux Caeser, as well as several varieties of limeade, including blueberry and melon. ⊠ *100 E. San Antonio St., Marfa* ☎ *432/729–3377. $3–$15* ▭ *AE, D, DC, MC, V.*

## Where to Stay

### In the Park

☺ $$  ▦ **Chisos Mountains Lodge.** Views of desert peaks and staying in the cooler, forested section of Big Bend's higher elevations more than make up for the spartan rooms. With ranger talks just next door at the visitor center, miles of easy hiking paths, and plenty of wildlife, this is a great place for kids. Make advance reservations during busy times, such as Thanksgiving and spring break—up to a year's lead time is not out of the question. Guests can rent a TV/VCR and movies. ⊠ *7 mi southwest of Chisos Basin Junction and 9 mi southwest of Panther Junction* ☎ *432/*

7

*477–2291*  *72 rooms* *Restaurant, some pets allowed, no phone, no TV. $100–$118* *AE, D, DC, MC, V.*

**$**   **Chisos Basin Campground.** Scenic views and cool shade are the highlights here. Steep grades and twisting curves mean trailers longer than 20 feet and RVs longer than 25 feet are not recommended. *7 mi southwest of Chisos Basin Junction* *432/477–2251* *65 sites* *Grills, flush toilets, drinking water, picnic tables, food service, public telephone, general store, ranger station. $10* *No credit cards.*

**$**   **Cottonwood Campground.** This Castolon-area campground is a popular bird-watching spot. The grounds are generator free. *Off Ross Maxwell Scenic Dr., 22 mi southwest of Santa Elena Junction* *432/477–2251* *31 sites* *Grills, pit toilets, drinking water, picnic tables, general store, ranger station. $10* *No credit cards.*

★ $   **Rio Grande Village Campground.** A shady oasis, this campground is a birding "hot spot." It's also a great site for kids and seniors, due to the ease of accessing facilities. RV parking is available. *22 mi southeast of Panther Junction* *432/477–2251* *100 RV and tent sites* *Grills, flush toilets, dump station, drinking water, guest laundry, showers, picnic tables, public telephone, general store, service station, ranger station. $10* *No credit cards.*

$   **Rio Grande Village RV Park.** Often full during holidays, this is one of the best sites for families because of the toilet facilities, minitheater, and closeness of the Hot Spring, which is fun to swim in at night. Register at the Rio Grande Village Store (22 mi southeast of Panther Junction). Only 30-amp electrical connections are available. You must have a 3-inch sewer connection to stay here. *22 mi southeast of Panther Junction* *432/477–2293* *25 RV sites* *Grills, flush toilets, dump station, drinking water, guest laundry, picnic tables, electricity, public telephone, general store, service station, ranger station. $10* *AE, D, MC, V* *Reservations not accepted.*

## Outside the Park

**$$$–$$$$**
**Fodor's**Choice
★   **Lajitas Resort.** This is the nicest place to eat, shop, and overnight within 25 mi of the park. Various theme motels and lodging options are available (under the same ownership) in this revived ghost town converted into a classy, Old West–style resort community alongside the Rio Grande. Conveniences within walking distance of Lajitas include a restaurant, lounge, and golf course. Make reservations well in advance of holidays and spring break. Some visitors have noted that service here can lag behind the reputation. *Off Rte. 170, 25 mi west of park entrance, Lajitas 79852* *432/424–5000, 877/525–4827 reservations* *72 rooms, 16 suites, 2 cottages* *3 restaurants, kitchen (some), refrigerator (some), golf course, tennis court, pool, spa, bicycles, bar, laundry service. $155–$685* *AE, D, DC, MC, V.*

**$$–$$$$**
**Fodor's**Choice
★   **Hotel Paisano.** Once the playground of Liz Taylor, Rock Hudson, and James Dean, who stayed here while filming *Giant*, the Paisano has kept its glamour with beautiful Mediterranean architecture and a fountain in the center. It's located amid downtown Marfa's quirky buildings and just down the street from the historic courthouse. *207 N. Highland*

*St., Marfa 76534* ☎ *432/729–3669* 🖷 *432/729–3779* ↩ *41 rooms* △ *Pool, no phone, Wi-Fi. $99–$210* ▤ *AE, D, MC, V.*

**$–$$$$** 🏨 **Gage Motel.** Cowboy, Indian, and Hispanic cultures are reflected in room furnishings in this historic hotel, built in the 1920s in the tiny community of Marathon. The expertly crafted gardens and courtyards are worth viewing, even if you aren't a guest. Some rooms do not have private baths. A few rooms have fireplaces. Massage therapy is offered. ✉ *Off U.S. 385, 40 mi north of park boundary, Marathon 79842* ☎ *432/386–4206* 🖷 *432/386–4510* ↩ *44 rooms, 9 with bathrooms down the hall, 3 houses* △ *Restaurant, kitchen (some), refrigerator (some), pool, bar, some pets allowed, no phone (some), no TV (some). $69–$330* ▤ *AE, D, MC, V.*

**¢–$$$** 🏨 **Holland Hotel.** Once just a stop on the transcontinental railroad, the Holland Hotel is now a historic landmark in downtown Alpine. Still hung with its original, vertical sign, the hotel is set on the town's main, bustling drag—just doors down from a quaint café and across from a coffee shop. Choose from a light-filled penthouse at the top of the motel, a 1,000-square-foot loft, or clean, basic rooms on the second and third floor. ✉ *207–209 W. Holland Ave., Alpine 79830* ☎ *432/386–4206* 🖷 *432/837–7346* ↩ *14 rooms* △ *No phone (some), ethernet, kitchen (some). $45–$195* ▤ *AE, D, MC, V* ⑩ *BP.*

# BIG BEND ESSENTIALS

**7**

**ACCESSIBILITY** Visitor centers and some campsite and restrooms at Rio Grande Village and Chisos Basin are wheelchair accessible. A TDD line (432/477–2370) is available at park headquarters at Panther Junction Visitor Center. Wheelchair-accessible hiking trails include the Founder's Walk and Panther Path at Panther Junction; Window View Trail at Chisos Basin; and Rio Grande Village Nature Trail boardwalk. The Rio Grande and Chisos Basin amphitheaters also are accessible.

**ADMISSION FEES** It costs $15 to enter at the gate. Camping fees in developed campgrounds are $10 nightly and free in primitive areas (backcountry permits required).

**ADMISSION HOURS** The park never closes. Visitor centers may be closed Christmas Day. The park is in the Central time zone.

**ATMS/BANKS** The park has no ATMs.
🖪 **Quicksilver Branch Bank** ✉ At intersection of Rte. 118 and Rte. 170, Study Butte/Terlingua ☎ 432/371–2211.

**AUTOMOBILE SERVICE STATIONS** There are two Chevron gas stations in the park: the one at Panther Junction does minor work (oil and tires), and the Rio Grande Village one offers gas, and propane for camp stoves.
🖪 **Panther Junction Chevron** ✉ 26 mi south of park north entrance ☎ 432/477–2294. **Rio Grande Village Chevron** ✉ 22 mi southeast of Panther Junction ☎ 432/477–2293. **Terlingua Auto** ✉ Off Highway 170 in the Terlingua business district, Terlingua, Texas 79852 ☎ 432/371–2223.

**EMERGENCIES** Dial 911 or 432/477–1188. Medical services are just outside the park in tiny communities along Route 170.
🖪 **Big Bend Regional Medical Center** ✉ 2600 N. Highway 118 Alpine, Texas 79830 ☎ 432/371–2536.

**LOST AND FOUND** The park's lost and found is at Panther Junction Visitor Center.

**PERMITS** Mandatory backcountry camping, boating, and fishing permits are available for free at visitor centers.

POST OFFICES Visitors can post their letters and cards each weekday at the Panther Junction post office. There's also a mail drop at the Chisos Basin store.

PUBLIC TELEPHONES Public telephones can be found at the visitor centers. Cell phones do not often work in the park.

RELIGIOUS SERVICES No regular services are held within the park. Nearby communities hold Christian services; Odessa and Midland have Jewish and Islamic services also.

RESTROOMS The visitor centers have public restrooms.

SHOPS & GROCERS Two shops at the Chisos Basin Junction in the park sell some of the basics for meals and camping.
🚹 **Chisos Basin Store and Post Office** ⊠ 7 mi south of Chisos Basin Junction ☎ 432/477-2291 ⊙ Daily 9-9. **Chisos Mountain Lodge Gift and Photo Shop** ⊠ 7 mi south of Chisos Basin Junction ☎ 432/477-2291 ⊙ Daily, 7-9. **La Harmonia Company Store** ⊠ 35 mi southwest of Panther Junction at Castolon, 22 mi southwest of Santa Elena Junction ☎ 432/477-2222 ⊙ Daily 10-1

and 1:30-6. **Rio Grande Village Store** ⊠ 22 mi southeast of Panther Junction ☎ 432/477-2293 ⊙ Daily 9-6.

## NEARBY TOWN INFORMATION
🚹 **Alpine Chamber of Commerce** ⊠ 106 N. 3rd St., Alpine, TX 79830 ☎ 800/561-3735 or 432/837-2326 ⊕ www.alpinetexas.com. **Big Bend Chamber of Commerce** ⊠ Hwy. 170 at Terlingua Creek (Box 607), Terlingua, TX 79842 ☎ 432/386-4516 ⊕ www.bigbendchamber.com. **Lajitas Resort** ⌂ HC 70, Box 400, Lajitas, TX 79852 ☎ 800/944-9907 or 432/424-3471 ⊕ www.lajitas.com. **Marathon Chamber of Commerce** ⊠ 105 Hwy. 90 W, Marathon, TX 79842 ☎ 432/386-4516 ⊕ www.marathontexas.net. **Marfa Chamber of Commerce** ⊠ 207 N. Highland St., Marfa, TX 79843 ☎ 800/650-9696 ⊕ www.marfacc.com. **Presidio Chamber of Commerce** ⌂ P.O. Box 2497, Presidio, TX 79845 ☎ 432/229-3199 ⊕ www.presidiotx.org/visitors.html.

## VISITOR INFORMATION
🚹 **Big Bend National Park** ⌂ Box 129, Big Bend National Park, TX 79834 ☎ 432/477-2251 ⊕ www.nps.gov/bibe.

# Black Canyon
# of the Gunnison
# National Park

8

## WORD OF MOUTH

"Here, we find the narrower and deeper portions of the canyon with sheer, perpendicular walls of varicolored granite. Towers, pinnacles, spires, and other fantastic rock formations greet the eye with an ever new challenge, as sunshine and shadow play their part in the creation of this ever-changing pageant of rugged grandeur and majestic beauty."

—Minister and Park Founder Mark Warner

# WELCOME TO BLACK CANYON

Gunnison Canyon

## TOP REASONS TO GO

★ **Sheer of heights:** Play it safe, but edge as close to the canyon rim as you dare and peer over into the abyss as much as 2,700 feet below.

★ **Rapids transit:** Paddle Class V rapids if you can handle 50°F water and the occasional portage past untamable sections of the Gunnison River.

★ **Fine fishing:** Fish the rare waters known as Gold Medal Water. Of the 9,000 mi of trout streams in Colorado, only 168 mi have this "gold medal" distinction.

★ **Triple-park action:** Check out Curecanti National Recreation Area and Gunnison Gorge National Conservation Area, which bookend Black Canyon.

★ **Cliff-hangers:** Climb the Painted Wall—Colorado's tallest vertical wall at 2,250 feet—and other challenging rock faces.

Black Canyon of the Gunnison

0     1 mi
0     1 km

*Warner Point*

*High Point*

**1** East Portal. The only way you can get down to the river via automobile in Black Canyon is on the steep East Portal Road. In next-door Curecanti National Recreation Area, there's fishing in the waters that flow beyond the Gunnison Diversion Dam.

| KEY | |
|---|---|
| 🏠 | Ranger Station |
| ⛺ | Campground |
| 🍴 | Picnic Area |
| 🍴 | Restaurant |
| 🏨 | Lodge |
| 🚶 | Trailhead |
| 🚻 | Restrooms |
| ⇶ | Scenic Viewpoint |
| ----- | Walking/Hiking Trails |
| ····· | Bicycle Path |

**2** North Rim. If you want to access this side of the canyon from the south, expect a drive of three hours as you wind around the canyon. The area's remoteness and difficult location mean the campground here rarely fills during the summer months. A small ranger station is here.

**3** South Rim. This is the main area of the park. The park's only visitor center is here. The South Rim Road closes at Gunnison Point in the winter, when skiers and snowshoers take over.

Fishing in the Black Canyon

COLORADO

## GETTING ORIENTED

Black Canyon of the Gunnison is a park of extremes—great depths, narrow widths, tall cliffs, and steep descents. It is not a large park, but the region as a whole offers incredible scenery and unforgettable experiences for those with the stamina and the gumption to tackle the terrain.

8

North Rim Road
(closed in winter)

North Vista Trail

North Rim
Ranger Station

**North Rim Campground**
**Chasm View**
**Painted Wall**
**View**

The Narrows View

Cedar Point

Devils
Lookout

Balanced Rock View

Dragon
Point

Island Peaks View

Sunset
View

Pulpit Rock
Overlook

Kneeling Camel View

Mesa

Inclinado

Vernl

Mesa

South Rim Road

Gunnison Point

**Visitor Center**

Tomichi Point

**South Rim**
**◆ Campground**

TO
HWY 50 &
MONTROSE

347

East Portal Road

Gunnison

River

East Portal

CURECANTI
NATIONAL
RECREATION
AREA

Crystal
Dam

# BLACK CANYON OF THE GUNNISON PLANNER

## When to Go

Summer is the busiest season, with July experiencing the greatest crowds. **A spring or fall visit gives you two advantages: fewer people and cooler temperatures**—in summer, especially in years with little rainfall, daytime temperatures often reach into the 90s. A winter visit to the park brings even more solitude, as campgrounds are shut down and only about 2 mi of South Rim Road are plowed.

November through February is when the snow hits, with 9 to 24 inches of the white stuff each month on average; January typically experiences the most snow (about 2 feet). The months of April and May, and September through November are the rainiest, with a monthly average of 1⁷⁄₁₀ to 2²⁄₁₀ inches of rain. June is generally the driest month, with only about 1 inch of rain on average.

Temperatures at the bottom of the canyon tend to be 8 degrees warmer than at the rim.

## Flora & Fauna

You may spot peregrine falcons nesting in May and June, or other birds of prey such as red-tailed hawks, Cooper's hawks, and golden eagles circling overhead at any time of year. In summer, turkey vultures join the flying corps, and in winter, bald eagles.

Mule deer, elk, and the very shy bobcat also call the park home. In spring and fall, you may see a porcupine among pinyon pines on the rims. Listen for the high-pitched chirp of the yellow-bellied marmot, which hangs out on sunny, rocky outcrops. Though rarely seen, mountain lions and black bears also live in the park.

## Getting There & Around

In southwest Colorado, Black Canyon of the Gunnison is sandwiched between Gunnison and Montrose. Both towns have small airports.

The park has three roads. South Rim Road, reached by Route 347, is the primary thoroughfare and winds along the canyon's South Rim. From about late November to early April, depending on snow conditions, the road is not plowed past the visitor center at Gunnison Point. North Rim Road, reached by Route 92, is usually open from May through Thanksgiving; in winter the road is unplowed. The serpentine East Portal Road descends abruptly to the Gunnison River on the park's south side. The road is usually open from the beginning of May through the end of November, again depending upon snowfall. Because of the grade, vehicles or vehicle–trailer combinations longer than 22 feet are not permitted.

The park has no public transportation.

### AVG. HIGH/LOW TEMPS.

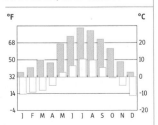

By John
Blodgett

Black Canyon of the Gunnison River is one of Colorado's, and indeed the West's, most awe-inspiring wonders. A vivid testament to the powers of erosion, the 2,722-foot-deep gash in the Earth's crust is 1,000 feet across at its rim but then narrows to only 40 feet across at the bottom. The steep angles of the cliffs make it difficult for sunlight to fully break through during much of the day, and ever-present shadows bounce off the canyon walls, leaving some places in almost perpetual darkness—nearly pitch-black at night and a sort of dusk with tunnel vision during the day. No wonder it's called the "Black Canyon."

**8**

## Scenic Drives

Two scenic rim roads offer deep and distant views into the canyon. The various hikes into the canyon are steep and strenuous, not to mention relatively unmarked. They are not for the faint of heart.

**East Portal Road.** The only way to access the Gunnison River from the park by car is via this paved route, which drops approximately 2,000 feet down to the water in only 5 mi, giving it a steep, 16% grade. (Vehicles longer than 22 feet are not allowed on the road; if you're towing a trailer, you can unhitch it at a parking area near the entrance to South Rim campground.) The bottom is actually in the adjacent Curecanti National Recreation Area. A tour of East Portal Road, with a brief stop at the bottom, takes about 45 minutes.

**North Rim Road.** Black Canyon's North Rim is less frequented, but no less spectacular: The walls are nearly vertical. To reach the 15½-mi North Rim Road, take the signed turnoff from Route 92 in Crawford. The road is paved for about the first 4 mi; the rest is gravel. After 11 mi, turn left at the intersection (North Rim Campground is to the right). There are six overlooks as the road snakes along the rim's edge. Kneeling Camel, 4½ mi out at road's end, provides the broadest view of the canyon. Set aside about two hours for a tour of the North Rim.

**South Rim Road.** This paved 7-mi stretch from Tomichi Point to High Point is the park's main road. The drive follows the canyon's level South Rim; 12 overlooks are accessible from the road, most via short gravel trails. Several short hikes onto the rim also begin roadside. Allow between two and three hours round-trip.

> ### BRIDGE OVER THE RIVER GUNNISON?
>
> A bridge that would span the canyon's two rims was proposed in the 1930s. The bad news is that it was never built, so it'll take you 2–3 hours to drive from one rim around to the other. The good news: Unforgettable scenery.

## What to See

The vast depths that draw thousands of visitors each year to Black Canyon have also historically prevented any extensive human habitation from taking root, so cultural attractions are lacking here. But what the park lacks in historic sites, it more than makes up with in scenic attractions.

### Scenic Stops

★ **Chasm View.** From this heart-in-your-throat viewpoint, the canyon walls plummet 1,820 feet to the river, but are only 1,100 feet apart at the top. As you peer down into the depths, keep in mind that this section is where the Gunnison River descends at its steepest rate, dropping 240 feet within the span a mile. ⊠ *3½ mi from South Rim Visitor Center on South Rim Rd.*

**Narrows View.** Look upriver from this North Rim overlook and you'll be able to see into the canyon's narrowest section, just a slot really, with only 40 feet between the walls. The canyon is also taller (1,725 feet) here than it is wide at the rim (1,150 feet). ⊠ *North Rim Rd., first overlook past the ranger station.*

★ **Painted Wall.** Best seen from Painted Wall View along South Rim Road, this is Colorado's tallest cliff, 2,250-feet high. Pinkish swathes of pegmatite (a crystalline, granitelike rock) give the cliff a marbled appearance. ⊠ *3⁷⁄₁₀ mi from South Rim Visitor Center off South Rim Rd.*

### Visitor Centers

**North Rim ranger station.** This small facility on the park's North Rim provides information and assistance when North Rim Road is open. ⊠ *North Rim Rd., 11 mi from Rte. 92 turnoff* ☎ *970/641–2337* ☾ *Memorial Day–Labor Day, daily 8–6.*

**South Rim Visitor Center.** The park's only visitor center has interactive exhibits as well as two orientation videos: One details the geology and history of the canyon, the other includes the history of the Gunnison Water Diversion Tunnel and flora and fauna in the park. ⊠ *1½ mi from the entrance station on South Rim Rd.* ☎ *970/249–1914 Ext. 423* ☾ *Memorial Day–Labor Day, daily 8–6; Labor Day–Memorial Day, daily 8:30–4.*

## BLACK CANYON IN ONE DAY

Pack a lunch and head to the canyon's South Rim, beginning with a stop at the **visitor center.** Before getting back into the car, take in your first view of Black Canyon from **Gunnison Point,** adjacent to the visitor center. Then set out on a driving tour of the 7-mi **South Rim Road,** allowing the rest of the morning to stop at the various viewpoints that overlook the canyon. Don't miss **Chasm View** and **Painted Wall View,** and be sure to stretch your legs along the short ($\frac{7}{10}$-mi round-trip) **Cedar Point Nature Trail.** If your timing is good, you'll reach **High Point,** the end of the road, around lunchtime.

After lunch, head out on **Warner Point Nature Trail** for an hour hike ($1\frac{1}{2}$ mi round-trip). Then retrace your drive along South Rim Road back to the visitor center.

## Sports & the Outdoors

Recreational activities in Black Canyon run the gamut, from short and easy nature trails to world-class rock climbing and kayaking. The cold waters of the Gunnison River are well known to trout anglers, and though horseback riding is limited to one trail in the park, you can at least get right up to the canyon rim and gaze far below.

### Bicycling

Bikes are not permitted on any of the trails, but cycling along South Rim Road or mountain biking on the unpaved North Rim Road is a great way to view the park. No shops rent bikes in the immediate vicinity.

### Bird-watching

The sheer cliffs of Black Canyon, though prohibitive for human habitation, provide diverse habitat for birds. Cliff dwellers such as peregrine falcons and white-throated swifts revel in the dizzying heights, while at river level the American dipper is a common sight as it forages for food in the rushing waters. Canyon wrens, which nest in the cliffs, are more often heard than seen, but their hauntingly beautiful song is the epitome of canyon country. Great horned owls and Steller's jays frequent the canyon rims. Best for birding: spring and early summer.

### Boating & Rafting

The spectacular 14-mi stretch of the Gunnison River that passes through the park is so narrow in some sections that the rim seems to be closing up above your head. The river is one of the premier kayak challenges in North America, with Class IV and Class V rapids, and portages required around bigger drops. Early visitors to the canyon declared this section unnavigable, and the fact that a few intrepid kayakers make the journey today is somewhat amazing. Once you're downstream from the rapids, the canyon opens up into what is called the Gunnison Gorge. The rapids ease considerably, and the trip becomes more of a quiet float

8

on Class I to Class III water. The Gunnison Gorge National Conservation Area is under the jurisdiction of the Bureau of Land Management. Rafting is not allowed on the Gunnison River through the national park. However, several outfitters offer guided raft trips in the Gunnison Gorge National Conservation Area to the west.

### Fishing

★ The three dams built upriver in Curecanti National Recreation Area have created prime trout fishing. In fact, the section of Gunnison River that goes through the park is designated Gold Medal Water, with abundant rainbows, browns, and

> #### GOOD READS
>
> **The Gunnison Country** by Duane Vandenbusche is almost 500 pages of historical photographs and essays on the park.
> **The Essential Guide to Black Canyon of the Gunnison National Park** by John Jenkins is considered one of the park's definitive guides.
> The **South Rim Driving Tour Guide** is enlivened by David Halpern's evocative black-and-white images.
> **A Kid's Guide to Exploring Black Canyon of the Gunnison** by Renee Skelton is perfect for the 6–12 set.

lakes. Certain restrictions apply: only artificial flies and lures are permitted, and a Colorado fishing license is required for people ages 16 and older. Rainbow trout are catch-and-release only, and there are size and possession limits on brown trout (check at the visitor center). Most anglers access the river from the bottom of East Portal Road; an undeveloped trail goes along the riverbank for about ¾ mi.

### Hiking

All trails can be hot in summer and most don't receive much shade, so bring water and wear a hat. Dogs are permitted, on leash, on Rim Rock, Cedar Point Nature, and Chasm View Nature trails. Hiking into the inner canyon, while doable, is not for the faint of heart—or step. Six named routes lead down to the river, but they are not maintained or marked. In fact, the park staff won't even call them trails; they refer to them as "controlled slides." These super-steep, rocky routes vary in one-way distance from 1 to 2¾ mi, and the descent can be anywhere from 1,800 to 2,702 feet. Your reward, of course, is a rare look at the bottom of the canyon and the fast-flowing Gunnison. ■ TIP→ **Don't attempt an inner-canyon hike without plenty of water (the park's recommendation is four quarts per person).** For descriptions of the routes, and the necessary permit to hike them, stop at the visitor center or North Rim ranger station. Dogs are not permitted in the inner canyon.

EASY **Cedar Point Nature Trail.** This short (⁷⁄₁₀ mi round-trip) interpretive trail leads out from South Rim Road to two overlooks. It's an easy stroll, and signs along the way detail the surrounding plants. ⊠ *South Rim Rd., 4²⁄₁₀ mi from South Rim Visitor Center.*

**Chasm View Nature Trail.** The park's shortest trail (³⁄₁₀ mi round-trip) starts at North Rim Campground and offers an impressive 50-yard walk right along the canyon rim as well as an eye-popping view downstream of Painted Wall and Chasm View, 1,100 feet across on the South Rim. ⊠ *North Rim Campground, 11¼ mi from Rte. 92.*

## FESTIVALS & EVENTS

**JULY–AUG. Main in Motion.** From 6–8 PM every Thursday in the summer, Main Street in Montrose is the place to be. Street performers and other artisans join restaurants and shops to make for a pleasant evening stroll. ☎ *970/249-6295.*

**JULY Colorful Colorado Car, Truck, and Rod Show.** Hosted by Black Canyon Classics, this annual car show features downtown cruises, a drive-in movie, and three days' worth of ogling sheet metal. ☎ *970/249-6051.*

**Rim Rock Trail.** Mostly flat and exposed to the sun, this 1-mi round-trip nature trail has a bird's-eye view into the canyon. Pick up an interpretative pamphlet, which corresponds to markers along the route, at the visitor center or the campground trailhead. ⊠ *Begin at the Tomichi Point overlook or the trailhead near Loop C in South Rim Campground.*

MODERATE **Deadhorse Trail.** Despite its somewhat sinister name, Deadhorse Trail (5- to 6-mi round-trip) is actually an easy-to-moderate hike, starting on an old service road from the Kneeling Camel View. The trail's farthest point provides the park's easternmost viewpoint. From this overlook, the canyon is much more open, with pinnacles and spires rising along its sides. If you want to give yourself a bit of a scare, take the mile-long loop detour, about halfway through the hike. (The detour isn't marked— just look for the only other visible trail). At the two informal overlooks, you'll be perched—without guardrails—atop the highest cliff in this part of the canyon. Make sure to keep your children by your side at all times. ⊠ *At the end of North Rim Rd.*

**North Vista Trail.** The trail begins at North Rim ranger station. The moderate round-trip hike to and from Exclamation Point is 3 mi; a more difficult foray to the top of 8,563-foot Green Mountain (a mesa, really), with about 800 feet of elevation gain, is 7 mi round-trip. You'll hike along the North Rim; keep an eye out for especially gnarled pinyon pines— the North Rim is the site of some of the oldest groves of pinyons in North America, between 400 and 700 years old. ⊠ *North Rim Rd., 11 mi from Rte. 92 turnoff.*

Fodor'sChoice **Warner Point Nature Trail.** The 1½-mi round-trip hike starts from High ★ Point. You'll enjoy fabulous vistas of the San Juan and West Elk Mountains and Uncompahgre Valley. Warner Point, at trail's end, has the steepest drop-off from rim to river: a dizzying 2,702 feet. ⊠ *At the end of South Rim Rd.*

DIFFICULT **Oak Flat Trail.** This 2-mi loop trail is the most demanding of the South Rim hikes, as it brings you about 300 feet below the canyon rim. In places, the trail is narrow and crosses some steep slopes, but you won't have to navigate any steep drop-offs. Oak Flat is the shadiest of all the South Rim trails; small groves of aspen and thick stands of Douglas fir along the loop offer some respite from the sun. ⊠ *Begins and ends just west of the South Rim Visitor Center.*

8

## Horseback Riding

Don't take the name "Deadhorse Trail" literally, because horses are permitted *only* on this easy-to-moderate 5-mi loop that begins east of North Rim Road. Horses are not allowed on the South Rim. They are allowed only in the North Rim Campground or on the North Rim Road during transport in a trailer.

Black Canyon of the Gunnison has no facilities geared toward horses, and only one outfitter runs trips into the park. If you bring your own horse, go to the end of North Rim Road and park your trailer at Kneeling Camel Overlook. No permit is required.

OUTFITTERS & EXPEDITIONS **Elk Ridge Trail Rides.** The only outfitter allowed to guide rides in Black Canyon, Elk Ridge offers a four-hour ride to the canyon rim. Riders must be at least 8 years old and can weigh no more than 230 pounds. ⌧ *10203 Bostwick Park Rd., Montrose* ☎ *970/240–6007* ⊕ *www. elkridgetrailrides.com* ⊗ *May–Sept., weather permitting.*

## Rock Climbing

Fodor'sChoice
★
Climbing Black Canyon's cliffs is one of Colorado's premier big-wall challenges for advanced rock climbers. Some routes can take several days to complete, with climbers sleeping on narrow ledges or "portaledges." Though there's no official guide to climbing in the park, reports from climbers are on file at the South Rim Visitor Center. Nesting birds of prey may lead to wall closures at certain times of the year.

If you want to get in some easier climbing, head for the Marmot Rocks bouldering area, about 100 feet south of South Rim Road between Painted Wall and Cedar Point overlooks (park at Painted Wall). Four boulder groupings offer a variety of routes rated from easy to very difficult; a pamphlet with a diagrammed map of the area is available at the South Rim Visitor Center.

OUTFITTERS & EXPEDITIONS **Crested Butte Mountain Guides.** Advanced climbers can take a full-day guided tour for $250. ⌧ *218 Maroon Ave., Crested Butte* ☎ *970/349–5430 or 877/455–2307* ⊕ *www.crestedbutteguides.com* ⊗ *Year-round.*

**Skyward Mountaineering.** Intermediate to advanced climbers can take a one-, three-, or five-day guided tour. ⌧ *Ridgway* ☎ *970/209–2985* ⊕ *www.skywardmountaineering.com* ⊗ *Mar.–Nov.*

## Winter Sports

From late November to early April, South Rim Road is not plowed past the visitor center, offering park guests a unique opportunity to cross-country ski or snowshoe on the road. It's possible to ski or snowshoe on the unplowed North Rim Road too, but it's about 4 mi from where the road closes, through sagebrush flats to the canyon rim.

OUTFITTERS & EXPEDITIONS **Guided Snowshoe Walks.** In winter, the park offers ranger-led snowshoe walks, usually once a day on weekends. Tours leave from the South Rim Visitor Center and go along the rim for about 2 mi, often on Rim Rock

Trail. A limited supply of snowshoe gear is available for use at no charge. Call ahead to reserve equipment and a space on a tour. ☎ *970/ 249–1914 Ext. 423.*

## Educational Offerings

Educational activities at the park focus on keeping children occupied, some for a good part of the summer.

### Ranger Programs

Kids ages 5 to 12 can participate in the park's **Junior Ranger Program,** which provides an activities booklet that children can follow while exploring the park. Third and fourth graders can take part in the **Annual Advanced Junior Ranger Camp,** an eight-week summer program that exposes students to the park via games, hikes, and science experiments.

# WHAT'S NEARBY

While not totally out of the way, Black Canyon of the Gunnison and its two neighboring recreation playgrounds are far enough removed from civilization (i.e., big cities) so as to preserve a sense of getting-away-from-it-all isolation. It's a good 250 mi from Denver, and 240 mi from Colorado Springs, and touristy towns such as Durango and Telluride are respectively 120 mi and 80 mi away. Colorado National Monument is about 85 mi distant.

## Nearby Towns & Attractions

### Nearby Towns

The primary gateway to Black Canyon is **Montrose,** 15 mi northeast of the park. The legendary Ute chief, Ouray, and his wife, Chipeta, lived near here in the mid-19th century. Today, Montrose straddles the important agricultural and mining regions along the Uncompahgre River, and its traditional downtown is a shopping hub. Montrose may be the official gateway to the park, but the closest town to Black Canyon's North Rim is the 11-mi-away **Crawford,** a small hillside enclave amid the sheep and cattle ranches of the North Fork Valley with a small downtown area. Northeast on Route 92 (20 mi) is **Paonia,** a unique and charming blend of the old and new West. Here, career environmentalists and hippie types who have escaped the mainstream mingle with longtime ranchers, miners, and fruit growers. Eleven miles northwest of Crawford on Route 92 is the small ranching and mining community of **Hotchkiss.** The trappings and sensibilities of the Old West are here, be it cowboy bars and fields of livestock or the annual summertime rodeo.

### Nearby Attractions

**Crawford State Park.** The focus of this 337-acre park is Crawford Reservoir, created in 1963 when a dam was built to increase the supply of irrigated water to the surrounding ranches and farms. Boating and waterskiing are permitted on the reservoir, as are swimming and fishing (the lake is stocked with rainbow trout). The park has a 1-mi handicapped-accessible hiking trail along with the primitive ½-mi Indian Fire

8

Nature Trail by the reservoir on the park's west side. ✉ *1 mi south of Crawford, off Hwy. 92* ☎ *970/921–5721* ⊕ *parks.state.co.us/Parks/crawford* 🎟 *$5* ⊙ *Daily, year-round.*

★ **Curecanti National Recreation Area.** Curecanti, named for a Ute Indian chief, covers 40 mi of striking eroded volcanic landscape along U.S. 50. Three reservoirs were created by dams constructed in the 1960s: Morrow Point, Crystal Dam, and Blue Mesa, Colorado's largest man-made lake at almost 20-mi long. You can go boating (paid permit required), windsurfing, fishing, and swimming in all three. Camping, horseback riding, and hiking (leashed pets are allowed on all trails) are also available. Three visitor centers along U.S. 50 have more information. ✉ *20 mi east of Montrose off U.S. 50* ☎ *970/641–2337* ⊕ *www.nps.gov/cure* ⊙ *Daily, year-round* 🎟 *$15 entrance fee at East Portal entrance only.*

> **TOP FAMILY PICKS**
>
> **Cimarron Visitor Center.** See a vintage, circa-1882 railroad trestle, which is listed on the National Register of Historic Places.
> **Main in Motion.** Be entertained by street-corner performers and strolling musicians during this Thursday evening event every summer in downtown Montrose.
> **Morrow Point Boat Tour.** Relax and check out Morrow Point Reservoir on this 90-minute tour.

At the western entrance to the recreation area, about 15 mi from Black Canyon, the **Cimarron Visitor Center** displays vintage railroad cars, an 1882 trestle listed on the National Register of Historic Places, and a reconstruction of a railroad stockyard. ☎ *970/249–4074* ⊙ *Memorial Day–Labor Day, daily 9–4* 🎟 *Free.*

**Ute Indian Museum and Ouray Memorial Park.** The museum commemorates the life of Ute Indian chief Ouray, famous for his patience and diplomacy when dealing with resettlement by whites, and the life of his wife, Chipeta, and depicts the history of the Ute tribe with artifacts and dioramas. Chipeta's grave is also here, 2 mi south of Montrose. ✉ *17253 Chipeta Rd., Montrose* ☎ *970/249–3098* 🎟 *$3* ⊙ *Mid-May–mid-Oct., Mon.–Sat. 9–4:30, Sun. 11–4:30; mid-Oct.–mid-May., Mon.–Sat. 8:30–5.*

## Area Activities

### Sports & the Outdoors

BOATING **Lake Fork Marina** and **Elk Creek Marina.** These two marinas on Blue Mesa Reservoir rent all types of boats and slips. If you have your own boat, there's a ramp at both marinas. ✉ *West side of the lake, Montrose* ☎ *970/641–3048 or 970/641–0707* ⊕ *www.bluemesares.com.*

FISHING Guided fishing tours operate out of Elk Creek Marina. Common catches include brown, brook, rainbow, and lake trout.
**Blue Mesa Reservoir.** This outfitter charges $300 per day for 1-2 people. ✉ *15 mi west of Gunnison on U.S. 50* ☎ *877/258–6372* ⊕ *www.bluemesares.com.*

HIKING For information on backcountry hiking in the Uncompaghre Plateau and other nearby wilderness areas, contact the district office of the Grand

CLOSE UP

## Colorado National Monument

SHEER RED-ROCK CLIFFS open to 23 mi of steep canyons and thin monoliths that sprout as high as 450 feet from the floor of the **Colorado National Monument.** President William Howard Taft declared this 32-square-mi tract of rugged, ragged terrain a national monument in 1911 after an eccentric named John Otto built trails where many thought would be impossible. Otto went on to become the monument's first custodian. Cold Shivers Point is just one of the many dramatic overlooks along **Rim Rock Drive.**

There are more than a dozen short and backcountry trails that range in length from ¼ mi to 8½ mi. An easy 30-minute stroll with sweeping canyon views, **Otto's Trail** greets hikers with breezes scented by sagebrush and juniper, which stand out from the dull red rock and sand. The trail leads to stunning, sheer drop-offs. **Serpents Trail,** with more than 50 switchbacks, ascends several hundred feet and takes about two hours to complete.

Scheduled programs, such as guided walks and campfire talks, are posted at the **Visitor Center** (☎ 970/858–3617 ⊘ Memorial Day–Labor Day, daily 8–6; Labor Day–Memorial Day, daily 9–5). Maps and trail information are also available. Rock climbing is popular at the monument, as is horseback riding, cross-country skiing, biking, and camping. ✉ *About 4 mi south of Fruita on Hwy. 340* ☎ *970/858–3617* ⊕ *www.nps.gov/ colm* ✉ *$7 per week per vehicle. Visitors entering on bicycle, motorcycle, or on foot pay $4 for weekly pass* ⊘ *Daily.*

Mesa, Uncompahgre, and Gunnison National Forests. ✉ *2250 U.S. 50, Delta* ☎ *970/874–6600* ⊕ *www.fs.fed.us/r2/gmug.*

## Shopping

The **Russell Stover Factory Outlet** (✉ 220 Stover Ave., Montrose ☎ 970/ 249–5372) sells chocolates made right across the street. The store is south of downtown Montrose off U.S. 550. Pack a picnic lunch for the Black Canyon via the **Uncompahgre Farmer's Market** (✉ Centennial Plaza, intersection of Main and Uncompahgre Sts., Montrose ☎ 970/323–5756) open late spring–early fall, Wednesday and Saturday 8:30–1. In late summer, keep your eyes peeled for locally grown sweet corn.

# WHERE TO STAY & EAT

### About the Restaurants

The park itself has no eateries, but nearby towns have choices ranging from traditional American to an eclectic café and bakery.

### About the Hotels

Black Canyon is devoid of hotels. Smaller hotels, some excellent B&Bs, and rustic lodges are nearby, as are a few of the larger chains.

## About the Campgrounds

There are two campgrounds in the national park. The smaller North Rim Campground is first-come, first served, and is closed in the winter. South Rim Campground is considerably larger, and has a loop that's open year-round. Reservations are accepted in South Rim Loops A and B Power hookups only exist in Loop B, and vehicles more than 35 feet long are discouraged from either campground. At both of the park's drive-to campgrounds there's a limit of eight people per site, and camping is limited to 14 days. Water has to be trucked up to the campgrounds, so use it in moderation; it's shut off in mid- to late September. Generators are not allowed at South Rim and are highly discouraged on the North Rim. Nearby communities such as Montrose have RV parks with more amenities, and Crawford State Park has options that include a boat ramp.

# Where to Eat

## In the Park

PICNIC AREAS   There are a variety of picnic areas at Black Canyon of the Gunnison, all with pit toilets; all are closed when it snows.

**East Portal.** This picnic area accommodates large groups. There are tables, fire grates, bathrooms, and a large shaded shelter. ⊠ *East Portal Rd. at the Gunnison River.*

**High Point.** When the sun is unforgiving, this overlook offers more shade than most of the other picnic areas. There are tables and bathrooms but no fire grates. ⊠ *West end of South Rim Rd.*

**North & South Rim campgrounds.** Feel free to use unoccupied camping sites for a picnic lunch. There are tables, fire grates, and bathrooms. ⊠ *North Rim: West end of North Rim Rd.; South Rim: About 1 mi east of South Rim Visitor Center on South Rim Rd.*

**Pulpit Rock.** There are tables and bathrooms at this overlook. ⊠ *Two mi west of South Rim Visitor Center.*

**Sunset View.** On the way to High Point, the picnic area at this overlook is ideal for an afternoon break. There are tables and bathrooms but no fire grates. ⊠ *About 1 mi east of High Point on South Rim Rd.*

## Outside the Park

¢–$$$   ✕**Camp Robber.** This small, bistro-style restaurant serves Montrose's most creative cuisine. Try entrées such as tortilla-crusted fresh red snapper, green-chili pistachio-crusted pork medallions, and spicy shrimp pasta. At lunch, salads, sandwiches (mesquite-grilled chicken cordon bleu), or blue-corn enchiladas fuel hungry hikers. ⊠ *1515 Ogden Rd., Montrose* ☎ *970/240–1590. $7–$25* ▭ *AE, MC, V* ☻ *No dinner Sun.*

¢–$$   ✕**La Cabaña at Sicily's Italian Restaurant.** This is the place to come for pizza and calzones, as well as traditional Italian favorites such as manicotti, chicken marsala, and shrimp scampi. Homemade desserts include cheesecake, key lime pie, and German chocolate cake. ⊠ *1135 E. Main St., Montrose* ☎ *970/252–8200. $7–$16* ▭ *AE, D, DC, MC, V.*

¢–$$   ✕**Zack's Bar-B-Q.** On Saturday nights, local ranching families flock to Zack's for the tastiest barbecue around; choose from ham, beef, chicken, or ribs. Steak and catfish dinners are also available Friday through Sunday nights. Breakfast here is worthy, too. ✉ *721 E. Bridge St., Hotchkiss* ☎ *970/872–3199. $4–$16* ▭ *AE, MC, V* ☸ *Closed Mon.*

## Where to Stay

### In the Park

CAMPGROUNDS & RV PARKS

★ **$–$$**

🏕 **South Rim Campground.** Stay on the canyon rim at this main campground right inside the park entrance. The RV hookups are in Loop B, and those sites are priced higher. It's possible to camp here year-round, but the loops are not plowed, so you'll have to hike in with your tent. ✉ *South Rim Rd., 1 mi from the visitor center* ⇶ *65 tent sites, 23 camper sites* ♨ *Pit toilets, partial hookups (electric), drinking water, fire grates, picnic tables, public telephone. $12–$18 for Loop B* ▭ *No credit cards.*

**$**

🏕 **North Rim Campground.** This small campground, nestled amid pinyon and juniper, offers the basics along the quiet North Rim. ✉ *North Rim Rd., 11¼ mi from Rte. 92* ⇶ *13 sites* ♨ *Pit toilets, drinking water, fire grates, picnic tables, ranger station. $12* ▭ *No credit cards* ☸ *May–Oct.*

### Outside the Park

**$$$**

FodorsChoice

★

🏨 **Leroux Creek Inn.** This sophisticated B&B has five Southwestern-style guest rooms—each with private tiled bath—within the adobe house, which keeps them blessedly cool during summer. A deck overlooks the inn's 47 acres, which include a vineyard. Dinner prepared by one of the owners is available by advance request. No smoking is allowed inside. ✉ *1220 3100 Rd., Hotchkiss 81419* ☎ *970/872–4746* ⊕ *www.lerouxcreekinn.com* ⇶ *5 rooms* ♨ *Wi-Fi, no a/c, no phone, no kids under 16, no-smoking rooms. $155–$175* ▭ *MC, V.*

**$–$$$**

🏨 **Country Lodge.** This homey, family-friendly motel has knotty-pine walls, a garden courtyard with pool and hot tub, and two separate play areas for older and younger kids. A newer three-bedroom log cabin with full kitchen and washer-dryer is available for nightly rentals in summer. ✉ *1624 E. Main St. (U.S. 50), Montrose 81401* ☎ *970/249–4567* ☎ *970/ 249–3082* ⊕ *www.countryldg.com* ⇶ *22 rooms* ♨ *Kitchen (some), refrigerator (some), pool, Wi-Fi. $80, $170 cabin* ▭ *AE, D, DC, MC, V.*

★ **$$**

🏨 **Bross Hotel.** The brick Bross Hotel, on a quiet, shady street in downtown Paonia, was opened in 1906 by the local deputy sheriff. Rooms have turn-of-the-20th-century antiques and handmade quilts. Common areas include a parlor and a spacious lounge with board games. No smoking is allowed inside. ✉ *312 Onarga St., Paonia 81428* ☎ *970/527– 6776* ☎ *970/527–7737* ⊕ *www.paonia-inn.com* ⇶ *10 rooms* ♨ *Dial-up, Wi-Fi, no a/c, no-smoking rooms. $115* ▭ *DC, MC, V.*

CAMPGROUNDS & RV PARKS

**$–$$**

🏕 **Cedar Creek RV Park.** This close-to-town park in Montrose has a miniature golf course and a shop with RV supplies. You can pitch a tent along Cedar Creek, but there are no individual tent sites ✉ *126 Rose La., Montrose 81401* ☎ *970/249–3884 or 877/425–3884* ⊕ *www.cedarcreekrv. com* ⇶ *8 tent sites, 47 camper sites with full hookups, 16 with partial hookups* ♨ *Flush toilets, full hookups, partial hookups (electric and water), dump station, drinking water, guest laundry, showers, fire pits, picnic tables, public telephone, play area. $17–$27* ▭ *D, MC, V.*

**$**

🏕 **Crawford State Park.** The park has two campgrounds, Clear Fork and Iron Creek. Both are alongside Crawford Reservoir. You'll have to pay

**8**

the $5 park admission fee as well as the camping fee. You can reserve a campsite for an extra $8 online or by calling 800/678–2267. ⊠ *1 mi south of Crawford off Hwy. 92* ⌂ *Box 147, Crawford 81415* ☎ *970/ 921–5721* ⊕ *parks.state.co.us/Parks/crawford* ☉ *Apr.–mid-Nov.* ⊟ *No credit cards except when placing a phone or online reservation.*

# BLACK CANYON ESSENTIALS

ACCESIBILITY South Rim Visitor Center is accessible to people with mobility impairments, as are most of the sites at South Rim Campground. Drive-to overlooks on the South Rim include Tomichi Point, the alternate gravel viewpoint at Pulpit Rock (the main one is not accessible), Chasm View (gravel), Sunset View, and High Point. Balanced Rock (gravel) is the only drive-to viewpoint on the North Rim. None of the park's hiking trails is accessible by car.

ADMISSION FEES Entrance fees are $15 per week per vehicle. Visitors entering on bicycle, motorcycle, or on foot pay $7 for a weekly pass.

ADMISSION HOURS The park is open 24/7 year-round. It's in the Mountain time zone.

ATMS/BANKS The park has no ATMs. 🏧 **Community First National Bank** ⊠ 401 E. Main St., Montrose ☎ 970/249-1111.

AUTOMOBILE SERVICE STATIONS 🏧 **Supermart** has fuel. ⊠ 938 S. Townsend Ave., Montrose ☎ 970/240-4612.

EMERGENCIES In the event of a medical or police emergency, dial 911. Medical assistance is available at the South Rim Visitor Center and, in summer, at the North Rim ranger station. Report fires to either of those locations.

LOST AND FOUND The park's lost and found is at South Rim Visitor Center and North Rim ranger station (summer only).

PERMITS To access the inner canyon, whether for hiking, climbing, camping, or kayaking, you must pick up a backcountry permit (no fee) at South Rim Visitor Center, North Rim ranger station, or East Portal ranger station in Curecanti National Recreation Area.

POST OFFICES 🏧 **Montrose Post Office** ⊠ 321 S. 1st St., Montrose 81401 ☎ 970/249-6654.

PUBLIC TELEPHONES There are public telephones at South Rim Visitor Center and South Rim Campground. Cell-phone reception is unreliable and sporadic.

RELIGIOUS SERVICES There are no religious services in the park.

RESTROOMS Public restrooms are at South Rim Visitor Center and South Rim Campground; Tomichi Point, Pulpit Rock, Sunset View, and High Point overlooks; North Rim ranger station and North Rim Campground; and Kneeling Camel viewpoint.

SHOPS & GROCERS There are no places in the park to buy groceries or camping supplies. 🏧 **City Market** ⊠ 128 S. Townsend Ave., Montrose ☎ 970/249-3405. **Safeway** ⊠ 1329 S. Townsend Ave., Montrose ☎ 970/249-8822.

## NEARBY TOWN INFORMATION
🏧 **Crawford Area Chamber of Commerce** ⌂ Box 22, Crawford, CO 81415 ☎ 970/921-4000 ⊕ www.crawfordcountry.org. **Hotchkiss Chamber of Commerce** ⌂ Box 158, Hotchkiss, CO 81419 ☎ 970/872-3226 ⊕ www.hotchkisschamber.com. **Montrose Visitors and Convention Bureau** ⊠ 1519 E. Main St., Montrose, CO 81402 ☎ 970/252-0505 or 800/873-0244 ⊕ www.visitmontrose.net. **Paonia Chamber of Commerce** ⌂ Box 366, Paonia, CO 81428 ☎ 970/527-3886 ⊕ www.paoniachamber.com.

## VISITOR INFORMATION
🏧 **Black Canyon of the Gunnison National Park** ⊠ 102 Elk Creek, Gunnison, CO 81230 ☎ 970/641-2337 ⊕ www.nps.gov/blca.

# Bryce Canyon National Park

Bryce Amphitheater, Bryce Canyon National Park

**WORD OF MOUTH**

"It's a helluva a place to lose a cow."

–Pioneer Ebenezer Bryce

9

# WELCOME TO BRYCE

## TOP REASONS TO GO

★ **Hoodoos Galore:** Bryce Canyon attracts visitors for its hundreds, if not thousands, of brightly colored, limestone spires, more commonly known as hoodoos.

★ **Famous Fresh Air:** To say the air around Bryce Canyon is rarified is not an exaggeration. With some of the clearest skies anywhere, the park offers views that, on a clear day, extend 200 mi and into three states.

★ **Spectacular Sunrises & Sunsets:** The deep orange and crimson hues of the park's hoodoos are intensified by the light of the sun at either end of the day.

★ **Getting into the Zone(s):** Bryce Canyon's elevation range—2,000 feet—is such that it spans three climatic zones: spruce/fir forest, ponderosa pine forest, and pinyon pine/juniper forest. The result is a park rich in biodiversity.

★ **Gaspworthy Geology:** A series of horseshoe-shaped amphitheaters comprise much of the park, and are the focus of most scenic turnouts.

Spire in Bryce Canyon

**1** Bryce Amphitheater. Here is the park's densest collection of attractions, including the historic Bryce Canyon Lodge and the points Sunrise, Sunset, and Inspiration. Paria View looks far south into Grand Staircase-Escalante National Monument.

**2** Under-the-Rim Trail. Though it more or less parallels most of the scenic drive and accesses many popular sites, from Bryce Point to the vicinity of Swamp Canyon, this trail is the best way to reach the Bryce Canyon backcountry. A handful of primitive campgrounds line the route.

Hoodoo Towers

Inspiration Point at Bryce Canyon

**3** Rainbow and Yovimpa Points. The end of the scenic road, but not of the scenery, here you can hike a trail to see some ancient bristlecone pines and look south into Grand Staircase-Escalante National Monument.

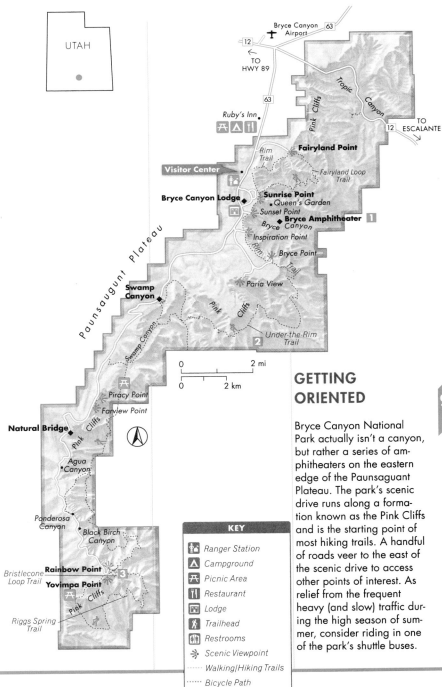

UTAH

Bryce Canyon Airport | 63

12

TO
HWY 89

63

TO
ESCALANTE | 12

Ruby's Inn

Tropic Canyon

Pink Cliffs

**Fairyland Point**

Rim Trail

**Visitor Center**

Fairyland Loop Trail

**Bryce Canyon Lodge** ◆

**Sunrise Point**

Queen's Garden

Sunset Point

**Bryce Amphitheater** ◆ [1]

Bryce Canyon

Inspiration Point

Rim Trail

Bryce Point

Paunsaugunt Plateau

Paria View

**Swamp Canyon** ◆

Pink Cliffs

Swamp Canyon

Under-the-Rim Trail [2]

0        2 mi

0        2 km

Piracy Point

Farview Point

**Natural Bridge** ◆

Pink Cliffs

*Agua Canyon*

*Ponderosa Canyon*

Black Birch Canyon

Bristlecone Loop Trail

**Rainbow Point** [3]

**Yovimpa Point**

Pink Cliffs

Riggs Spring Trail

## KEY

| 🛈 | Ranger Station |
|---|---|
| ▲ | Campground |
| ☐ | Picnic Area |
| 🍴 | Restaurant |
| 🖼 | Lodge |
| 🚶 | Trailhead |
| 👥 | Restrooms |
| ※ | Scenic Viewpoint |
| ----- | Walking/Hiking Trails |
| ...... | Bicycle Path |

## GETTING ORIENTED

9

Bryce Canyon National Park actually isn't a canyon, but rather a series of amphitheaters on the eastern edge of the Paunsaugant Plateau. The park's scenic drive runs along a formation known as the Pink Cliffs and is the starting point of most hiking trails. A handful of roads veer to the east of the scenic drive to access other points of interest. As relief from the frequent heavy (and slow) traffic during the high season of summer, consider riding in one of the park's shuttle buses.

# BRYCE CANYON PLANNER

## When to Go

Around Bryce Canyon National Park and the nearby Cedar Breaks National Monument area, elevations approach and surpass 9,000 feet, making for temperamental weather, intermittent and seasonal road closures due to snow, and downright cold nights well into June. At this altitude, the warm summer sun is perfectly balanced by the coolness of the alpine forests during the day.

**If you choose to see Bryce Canyon in July, August, or September, you'll be visiting with the rest of the world.** During these months, traffic on the main road can get crowded with cars following slow-moving RVs, so consider taking one of the park buses from the visitor center. Also in summer, lodging may be difficult to find.

**If it's solitude you're looking for, come to Bryce any time between October and March.** The snow may be flying, but imagine the multi-hued rocks under an icing of white. Strap on snowshoes or cross-country skis, and you might just have a trail all to yourself.

AVG. HIGH/LOW TEMPS.

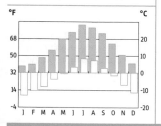

## Flora & Fauna

Due to elevations approaching 9,000 feet, many of Bryce Canyon's 400 plant species are unlike those you'll see at less lofty places. Look at exposed slopes and you might catch a glimpse of the gnarled, 2,000-year-old bristlecone pine. More common, and far younger, are the Douglas fir, ponderosa pine, and the quaking aspen, most striking in its bright golden fall color. No fewer than three kinds of sagebrush—big, black, and fringed—grow here, as well as the blue columbine.

Their reputation as a pest among Southern Utah ranchers notwithstanding, the Utah prairie dog is designated a threatened species. Be cautious around them. Though cute and seemingly approachable, they might bite if you get too close, and the bacteria that causes bubonic plague has been found on their fleas. Other animals include elk, black-tailed jackrabbits, and the desert cottontail. Below 7,000 feet, black bear have been seen in the trees, but infrequently. It's far more likely you'll see the soaring forms of golden and bald eagles, or perhaps a peregrine falcon diving into the amphitheaters at speeds approaching 200 mph.

## Getting There & Around

The closest major cities to Bryce Canyon are Salt Lake City and Las Vegas, each about 270 mi away. The nearest commercial airport is 80 mi west in Cedar City, Utah. The park is reached via Route 63, just 3 mi south of the junction with Highway 12.

You can see the park's highlights by driving along the well-maintained road running the length of the main scenic area. Bryce has no restrictions on automobiles, but in the summer you may encounter heavy traffic and full parking lots. A shuttle bus system operates from mid-May through September. It is free, though you still must pay the park entrance fee. The shuttle departs from the staging area off Highway 12 about 3 mi north of the park entrance every 10 to 15 minutes. Stops include Best Western Ruby's Inn, the North Campground, the visitor center, and all major overlooks in the northern portion of the park.

By John
Blodgett

A land that captures the imagination and the heart, Bryce
Canyon is a favorite among Utah's national parks. The park
was named for Ebenezer Bryce, a pioneer cattleman and
the first permanent settler in the area. His description of
the landscape not being hospitable to cows has oft been
repeated. Even more than his famous quote, however, Bryce
Canyon is known for its fanciful "hoodoos," best viewed
at sunrise or sunset, when the light plays off the red rock.

In geological terms, Bryce is actually an amphitheater, not a canyon. The
hoodoos in the amphitheater took on their unusual shapes because the
top layer of rock—"cap rock"—is harder than the layers below it. If
erosion undercuts the soft rock beneath the cap too much, the hoodoo
will tumble—but Bryce will never be without hoodoos, because as the
amphitheater's rim recedes, new hoodoos are formed.

## Scenic Drive

Fodor'sChoice
★

**Main Park Road.** One of the delights of Bryce Canyon National Park is
that much of the park's grandeur can be experienced from scenic overlooks along its main thoroughfare, which meanders 18 mi from the park
entrance south to Rainbow Point. Allow two to three hours to travel
the entire 36 mi round-trip. The road is open year-round, but may be
closed temporarily after heavy snowfalls to allow for clearing. Major
overlooks are rarely more than a few minutes' walk from the parking
areas, and many let you see more than 100 mi on clear days. All overlooks lie east of the road—to keep things simple (and left turns to a minimum), you can proceed to the southern end of the park and stop at the
overlooks on your northbound return. Trailers are not allowed beyond
Sunset Campground. Day users may park trailers at the visitor center
or other designated sites; check with park staff for parking options. RVs
can drive throughout the park, but vehicles longer than 25 feet are not
allowed at Paria View.

9

## What to See

### Historic Site

**Bryce Canyon Lodge.** Gilbert Stanley Underwood designed this lodge, built in 1924, for the Union Pacific Railroad. The National Historic Landmark has been faithfully restored, right down to the lobby's huge limestone fireplace and log and wrought-iron chandelier, plus bark-covered hickory furniture made by the same company that created the originals. Inside the historic building are a restaurant and a gift shop, as well as plenty of information on park activities. Guests of the lodge stay in the numerous log cabins on the wooded grounds. ⇨ *See* Where to Stay & Eat In the Park. ⊠ *2 mi south of park entrance* ☎ *435/834–5361.*

### Scenic Stops

**Agua Canyon.** When you stop at this overlook in the southern section of the park, pick out among the hoodoos the formation known as the Hunter, which actually has a few small hardy trees growing on its cap. The play of light and colorful contrasts are especially noticeable here. ⊠ *12 mi south of park entrance.*

★ **Fairyland Point.** At the scenic overlook closest to the park entrance (look for the sign marking the route off the main park road), there are splendid views of Fairyland Amphitheater and its delicate, fanciful forms. The Sinking Ship and other formations stand before the grand backdrop of the Aquarius Plateau and distant Navajo Mountain. ⊠ *1 mi off main park road, 1 mi north of visitor center.*

**Inspiration Point.** Not far at all (³⁄₁₀ mi) east along the Rim Trail from Bryce Point is Inspiration Point, site of a wonderful panorama and one of the best places in the park to see the sunset. ⊠ *5½ mi south of park entrance on Inspiration Point Rd.*

★ **Natural Bridge.** Despite its name, this formation is actually an arch carved in the rock by rain and frost erosion; true natural bridges must be bored out by streams and rivers. Pine forests are visible through the span of the arch. ⊠ *11 mi south of park entrance.*

**Rainbow and Yovimpa Points.** While Rainbow Point's orientation allows a view north along the southern rim of the amphitheater and east into Grand Staircase–Escalante National Monument, the panorama from Yovimpa Point spreads out to the south; on a clear day you can see as far as 100 mi to Arizona. The Bristlecone Loop Trail connects the two viewpoints and leads through a grove of bristlecone pine trees. There are informative displays on flora, fauna, and geological history at Rainbow Point. ⊠ *18 mi south of park entrance.*

★ **Sunrise Point.** Named for its stunning views at dawn, this overlook is a popular stop for summer crowds and is the starting point for the Queen's Garden Trail and the Fairyland Loop Trail. You have to descend the Queen's Garden Trail to get a regal glimpse of **Queen Victoria,** a hoodoo that appears to sport a crown and glorious full skirt. The trail is marked clearly but is moderately strenuous. ⊠ *2 mi south of park entrance near Bryce Canyon Lodge.*

## BRYCE CANYON IN ONE DAY

Begin your day at the **visitor center** to get an overview of the park and to purchase books and maps. Watch the video and peruse exhibits about the natural and cultural history of Bryce. Thus informed, drive to the historic **Bryce Canyon Lodge.** From here, stroll along the relaxing **Rim Trail,** then drive the 18-mi **Main Park Road,** stopping at the overlooks along the way. Allowing for traffic, and if you stop at all 13 overlooks, this drive will take you between two and three hours.

If you have the time and energy for a hike, the easiest route into the amphitheater is the **Queen's Garden Trail** at Sunrise Point. A short,

rolling hike along the **Bristlecone Loop Trail** at Rainbow Point rewards you with spectacular views and a cool walk through a forest of bristlecone pines. If you don't have time to drive the 18 mi to the end of the park, skip Bryce Canyon Lodge and drive 2 mi from the visitor center to **Inspiration Point** and the next 2 mi to **Bryce Point.**

End your day with sunset at Inspiration Point and dinner at Bryce Canyon Lodge (you'll want to have made your reservations that morning). As you leave the park, stop at **Ruby's Inn** for Native American jewelry, souvenirs for the kids, and snacks for the road.

**Sunset Point.** Bring your camera and plenty of film to watch the late-day sun paint its magic on the hoodoos here. See **Thor's Hammer,** a delicate formation similar to a balanced rock when you hike 521 feet down into the amphitheater on the Navajo Loop Trail. ⊠ *2 mi south of park entrance near Bryce Canyon Lodge.*

### Visitor Center

**Bryce Canyon Visitor Center.** You can visit with park rangers, watch a video about Bryce Canyon, study exhibits, or shop for informative books, maps, and other materials at this spacious visitor center. First aid, emergency, and lost-and-found services are offered here, and rangers dole out backcountry permits. If you want coffee, head to nearby Ruby's Inn. ⊠ *1 mi south of park entrance* ☎ *435/834–5322* ⊕ *www.nps.gov/brca* ☉ *Oct.–June, daily 8–4:30; July–Sept., daily 8–8.*

## Sports & the Outdoors

Most visitors explore Bryce Canyon by car, and though many stick only to the easiest of trails, there are plenty of other ways in which to enjoy Bryce Canyon. At these elevations, it gets warm in the summer but rarely uncomfortably hot, so hiking farther into the depths of the park is not difficult so long as you don't pick a hike that is beyond your abilities.

### Air Tours

OUTFITTERS & EXPEDITIONS

**Bryce Canyon Airlines & Helicopters.** For a once-in-a-lifetime view of park, join professional pilots and guides for a helicopter ride over it. Flights depart from Ruby's Inn Heliport. You can swoop over the amphitheater for as long as 15 minutes to more than an hour. Small air-

> ## GOOD READS
>
> **Bryce Canyon Auto and Hiking Guide** by Tully Stoud includes information on the geology and history of the area.
>
> Supplement the free park map with **Bryce Canyon Hiking Guide**, which includes an amphitheater hiking map and aerial photo.
>
> To prepare kids ages 5–10 for a trip to the park, consider ordering the 32-page **Kid's Guide to Bryce Canyon**.
>
> Books are available at the visitor center or by contacting **Bryce Canyon Natural History Association** (☎ 435/834–4601 or 888/362–2642).

plane tours and charter services are also available. ☎ *435/834–5341* ⊕ *www.rubysinn.com/bryce-canyon-airlines.html* ✉ *$55–$225.*

## Bird-Watching

More than 170 bird species have been identified in Bryce. Violet green swallows and white-throated swifts are common, as are Steller's jays, American coots, Rufous hummingbirds, and mountain bluebirds. You may even see golden eagles above the pink rocks of the amphitheater. The best time for avian variety is May through July, during migration.

## Hiking

To get up close and personal with the park's hoodoos, set aside a half day to hike into the amphitheater. Just about any hike that descends below the rim is moderately strenuous (and no below-rim trails are paved). The uneven terrain calls for sturdy hiking boots. In summer, consider hiking in the morning to avoid the day's warmest temperatures and strongest sun. Keep in mind that if you're not used to exercising at elevation, you can fall victim to altitude sickness. For trail maps, information, and ranger recommendations, stop at the visitor center. Bathrooms are located at most trailheads but not down in the amphitheater.

EASY **Bristlecone Loop Trail.** Hike through dense spruce and fir forest to exposed cliffs where ancient bristlecone pines somehow manage to survive the elements; some of the trees here are more than 1,700 years old. You might see yellow-bellied marmots and blue grouse, critters not found at lower elevations in the park. The popular 1-mi trail takes about an hour to hike. ⊠ *Rainbow Point, 18 mi south of park entrance.*

**Queen's Garden Trail.** This hike is the easiest into the amphitheater and therefore the most crowded. Allow two to three hours to hike the 2 mi down and back. ⊠ *Sunrise Point, 2 mi south of park entrance.*

MODERATE **Navajo Loop Trail.** A steep descent via a series of switchbacks leads to Wall Street, a narrow canyon with high rock walls and towering trees. The trail's end brings Thor's Hammer into view. Allow one to two hours on this 1½-mi trail. ⊠ *Sunset Point, 2 mi south of park entrance.*

★ **Navajo/Queen's Garden Combination Loop.** By walking this extended 3-mi loop, you can see some of the best of Bryce; it takes two to three hours. The route passes fantastic formations and an open forest of pine and juniper on the amphitheater floor. Descend into the amphitheater from Sunset Point on the Navajo Trail and ascend via the less demanding Queen's Garden Trail; return to your starting point via the Rim Trail. ⊠ *Sunset and Sunrise points, 2 mi south of park entrance.*

DIFFICULT **Fairyland Loop Trail.** Hike into whimsical Fairyland Canyon on this strenuous but uncrowded 8-mi trail. It winds around hoodoos, across trickles of water, and finally to a natural window in the rock at Tower Bridge, 1½ mi from Sunrise Point and 4 mi from Fairyland Point. The pink-and-white badlands and hoodoos surround you the whole way. Allow four to five hours round trip. You can pick up the loop at Fairyland Point or Sunrise Point. ⊠ *Fairyland Point, 1 mi off main park road, 1 mi south of park entrance; Sunrise Point, 2 mi south of park entrance.*

**Peekaboo Loop.** For a good workout, hike this steep trail past the Wall of Windows and the Three Wise Men. Horses use this trail in spring, summer, and fall and have the right-of-way. Start at Bryce, Sunrise, or Sunset Point and allow three to four hours to hike either the 5-mi or 7-mi loop. ⊠ *Bryce Point, 2 mi off main park road, 5½ mi south of park entrance; Sunrise and Sunset points, 2 mi south of park entrance.*

**Riggs Spring Loop Trail.** One of the park's more rigorous day hikes, or a relaxed overnighter, this 9-mi trail between Yovimpa and Rainbow points takes about four to five hours to hike. ⊠ *Yovimpa and Rainbow points, 18 mi south of park entrance.*

**Trail to the Hat Shop.** Once you reach the end you understand how the trail got its name. Hard gray caps balance precariously atop narrow pedestals of softer, rust-colored rock. Allow three to four hours to travel this strenuous 4-mi round-trip trail. ⊠ *Bryce Point, 2 mi off main park road, 5½ mi south of park entrance.*

**Under-the-Rim Trail.** This is how serious backpackers immerse themselves in the landscape of Bryce. Starting at Bryce Point, the trail travels 22½ mi to Rainbow Point, passing through the Pink Cliffs, traversing Agua Canyon and Ponderosa Canyon, and taking you by several springs. Most of the hike is on the amphitheater floor, characterized by up-and-down terrain among stands of ponderosa pine; the elevation change totals about 1,500 feet. Four trailheads along the main park road allow you to connect to the Under-the-Rim Trail and cover its length as a series of day hikes. Allow at least two days to hike the route in its entirety. Obtain a backcountry permit at the visitor center if you intend to stay in the amphitheater overnight. Also inquire about the current availability of water along the trail. ⊠ *Access from Bryce Point, Swamp Canyon, Ponderosa Canyon, and Rainbow Point.*

## Horseback Riding

Few activities conjure up the Old West like riding a horse, and Bryce Canyon offers plenty of opportunities to see the sights from the saddle. Many of the park's hiking trails were first formed beneath the hooves of cattle wranglers, and their modern-day counterparts now guide tourists over these and other trails. Area outfitters prefer reservations, and will sometimes cancel rides if not enough people sign up. Minimum rider age and max-

imum rider weight vary according to the chosen ride (anywhere from half an hour to a full day or more in length), but typically those under the age of 7 and over the weight of 230 pounds are prohibited.

| FUN FLORA FACT |
|---|
| The bulb of the sego lily, Utah's state flower, used to feed Mormon settlers when food was scarce. |

OUTFITTERS & EXPEDITIONS **Canyon Trail Rides.** Via horse or mule descend to the floor of the Bryce Canyon amphitheater. Most who take this expedition have no riding experience, so don't hesitate to join in. A two-hour ride ambles along the amphitheater floor to the Fairy Castle before returning to Sunrise Point. The half-day expedition follows Peekaboo Trail, winds past the Fairy Castle and the Alligator, and passes the Wall of Windows before returning to Sunrise Point. To reserve a trail ride, call or stop by their desk in the lodge. ⊠ *Bryce Canyon Lodge* ☎ *435/679–8665.*

**Ruby's Red Canyon Horseback Rides.** Retrace trails taken by outlaw Butch Cassidy in Red Canyon. Rides last from half an hour to all day. ⊠ *Best Western Ruby's Inn* ☎ *866/782–0002.*

## Winter Sports

Unlike Utah's other national parks, Bryce Canyon usually receives plenty of snow, making it a popular cross-country ski area. The park's 2½-mi Fairyland Ski Loop is marked but ungroomed, as is the 5-mi Paria Loop, which runs through ponderosa forests into long, open meadows.

The National Park Service lends out snowshoes free of charge at the visitor center; just leave your driver's license or a major credit card with a ranger. You can snowshoe on the rim trails but not below the rim.

OUTFITTERS & EXPEDITIONS **Best Western Ruby's Inn.** The property grooms a 31-mi private trail that connects to an ungroomed trail in the park. Rental equipment is available. ⊠ *Rte. 63, 1 mi north of park entrance* ☎ *435/834–5341.*

# Educational Offerings

## Programs and Tours

**Bryce Canyon Scenic Tours.** Enjoy a scenic two-hour tour of Bryce Canyon with knowledgeable guides who describe the area's history, geology, and flora and fauna. Choose from a sunrise tour, sunset tour, or general tour of the park. Specialized or private tours can also be arranged. ☎ *435/834–5351 or 866/834–0043* ⊕ *www.brycetours. com* ✉ *$26 and up.*

**Campfire and Auditorium Programs.** Bryce Canyon's natural diversity comes alive in the park's two campgrounds at Bryce Canyon Lodge. Lectures, slide programs, and audience participation introduce you to geology, astronomy, wildlife, history, and many other topics related to Bryce Canyon and the West. ☎ *435/834–5322.*

## Ranger Programs

The base of operations for all ranger activities is the visitor center, located 4½ mi south of the intersection of highways 12 and 63. Admis-

Central
Bryce Canyon

Visitor Center
North
General store
Corral
Sunrise Point
Queens Garden
Lodge
Thors Hammer
Sunset Point
Sunset
Wall Street
Navajo Loop Trail
Inspiration Point
Rainbow Gate
Road closed from here to Rainbow Point during winter storms
TO
RAINBOW POINT
Fairyland Loop Trail
Chinese Wall
Queens Garden Trail
Rim Trail
Bryce Creek
BRYCE CANYON
The Cathedral
Peekaboo Loop Trail
The Alligator
Peekaboo Loop Trail
Rim Trail
Wall of Windows
Bryce Point

0        1/2 mi
0        1/2 km

sion is free, but meeting times and locations vary. Stop by the visitor center or call 435/834–5322 for more information.

**Canyon Hike.** Take an early morning walk among the hoodoos of Queen's Garden or Navajo Loop Trail. A ranger points out the formations and explains some of the amphitheater's features as you go. The hike is 2- to 3-mi long and takes two to three hours to complete.

**Geology Talk.** Rangers relate the geologic story of Bryce Canyon in short sessions held at various times and locations around the park.

**Junior Ranger Program.** Running from Memorial Day to Labor Day; children ages 6 to 12 can sign up at the park visitor center. Activities vary, but a session might involve learning about geology and wildlife using arts and crafts and games. Schedules of events and topics are posted at the visitor center, Bryce Canyon Lodge, and campground bulletin boards.

**Moonlight Hike.** Three times a month, at or near full moon, rangers lead this two-hour hike. You must make reservations in person at the visitor center on the day of the hike.

**Rim Walk.** Stroll along the gorgeous rim of Bryce Canyon with a park ranger on a 1-mi, 1½-hour outing.

## Shopping

**Ruby's General Store.** Shopping at Ruby's souvenir heaven is an integral part of the Bryce Canyon experience. This large, lively store is open year-round, and is packed with everything imaginable emblazoned with the park's name, from thimbles to sweatshirts. Native American arts and crafts, Western wear, camping gear, groceries, and sundries are plentiful. There is a large selection of children's toys and trinkets. ⊠ *Rte. 63, north of the park* ☎ *435/834–5341.*

# WHAT'S NEARBY

Bryce Canyon is a bit off the beaten path, often a side trip for those who visit Zion National Park to the southwest and far from major roads or large cities (Both Las Vegas and Salt Lake City are approximately 270 mi away). Many people check out Bryce Canyon without exploring its environs. Those who have the extra time and gumption to explore will be rewarded, however. Nearby small towns offer good choices for lodging, especially during the busy summer season. The expansive and remote Escalante Grand Staircase National Monument is about an hour to the northeast, and Red Canyon offers spectacular, bright red-rock formations and a paved bike path.

## Nearby Towns & Attractions

### Nearby Towns

Decent amenities, inexpensive lodging (mainly strip motels), and an excellent location 24 mi northwest of Bryce Canyon on U.S. 89 make **Panguitch** a comfortable launching pad for area recreation. The town is noted for the distinctive brick architecture of its early homes and outbuildings, and for the original facades of some of its late-19th-century Main Street commercial structures. Northeast of Bryce 47 mi, **Escalante** has modern amenities and a state park like nothing else in Utah, and is a western gateway to the Grand Staircase–Escalante National Monument. If you're traveling through southwestern Utah on Interstate 15, **Cedar City** will be your exit to Bryce. The largest city you'll encounter in this part of Utah, it's 78 mi from Bryce Canyon. The city's claims to fame are its popular Utah Shakespearean Festival and a major state university, and it's also steeped in Mormon pioneer heritage.

### Nearby Attractions

**Dixie National Forest.** This expansive forest stretches for 170 mi across Utah, with elevations from only 2,800 feet at St. George to over 11,000 feet on Boulder Mountain. Recreational opportunities include horseback riding, fishing, canoeing, swimming, and waterskiing at one of the lakes, streams, and reservoirs. There are 26 campgrounds within the forest; some are free, others require fees. ⊠ *Dixie National Forest Headquarters, 82 N. 100 East, Cedar City* ☎ *435/865–3700, 800/280–2267 for campground information* ⊕ *www.fs.fed.us/dxnf* ☒ *Free* ☉ *Daily.*

**Escalante Petrified Forest State Park.** This park 48 mi east of Bryce Canyon off Route 12 was created to protect a huge repository of fossilized

CLOSE UP

# Grand Staircase—Escalante National Monument

In 1996, President Bill Clinton designated 1.7 million acres in south-central Utah as **Grand Staircase–Escalante National Monument,** the first monument to be administered by the Bureau of Land Management instead of the National Park Service. Its three distinct sections—the Grand Staircase, the Kaiparowits Plateau, and the Canyons of the Escalante—offer remote backcountry experiences hard to find elsewhere in the lower 48. Waterfalls, Native American ruins and petroglyphs, shoulder-width slot canyons, and improbable colors all characterize this wilderness. Straddling the northern border of the monument, the small towns of Escalante and Boulder offer access, outfitters, lodging, and dining. The route that connects them, Highway 12, is one of the most scenic stretches of road in the Southwest.

Larger than most national parks, this formidable monument is popular with backpackers, hikers, canyoneers, and hard-core mountain-bike enthusiasts. You can explore the rocky landscape, including slot canyons and wilderness, via dirt roads with a four-wheel-drive vehicle; most roads depart from Highway 12. Views into the monument are most impressive from Highway 12 between Escalante and Boulder. Calf Creek Falls is an easy 6-mi round-trip hike from the trailhead at Calf Creek Recreation Area (on Highway 12 north of Escalante). At the end of your walk, a large waterfall explodes over a cliff hundreds of feet above. It costs nothing to visit the park, but fees apply for camping and backcountry permits. ✉ *318 N. 100 East, Kanab* ☎ *435/644-6400* ⊕ *www.ut.blm.gov/monument* ▣ *Free* ☉ *Daily.*

**9**

wood and dinosaur bones. Learn all about petrified wood, which is easily spotted along two short interpretive trails. There's an attractive swimming beach at the park's Wide Hollow Reservoir, which is also good for boating, fishing, and birding. ✉ *710 N. Reservoir Rd., Escalante* ☎ *435/826-4466* ⊕ *www.stateparks.utah.gov* ▣ *$5* ☉ *Daily.*

**Kodachrome Basin State Park.** As soon as you see it, you'll understand why the park earned this name from the National Geographic Society. The sand pipes seen here cannot be found anywhere else in the world. Hike any of the trails to spot some of the 67 pipes in and around the park. The short Angels Palace Trail takes you quickly into the park's interior, up, over, and around some of the badlands. ✉ *7 mi southeast of Cannonville on Cottonwood Canyon Rd.* ☎ *435/679-8562* ⊕ *www. stateparks.utah.gov* ▣ *$6* ☉ *Year-round.*

## Area Activities

### Sports & the Outdoors

For permits and detailed information on outdoor activities in the area, contact the **Escalante Interagency Visitor Center** (✉ 755 W. Main St., Escalante ☎ 435/826-5499 ☉ Daily 7:30-5:30).

## FESTIVALS & EVENTS

**FEB.** **Bryce Canyon Winter Fest.** This event at Ruby's Best Western Inn features cross-country ski races, snow-sculpting contests, and ski archery. ☎ *435/834–5341 or 866/ 866–6616.*

**JUNE** **Panguitch Valley Balloon Rally.** Watch two dozen or more colorful hot-air balloons rise into the air at Panguitch and float over canyon country. ☎ *866/590–4134* ⊕ *www.panguitchballoons.com.* **Quilt Walk Festival.** During the bitter winter of 1864, Panguitch residents were on the verge of starvation. A group of men from the settlement set out over the mountains to fetch provisions from the town of Parowan, 40 mi away. When they hit waist-deep snowdrifts they were forced to abandon their oxen. Legend says the men, frustrated and ready to turn back, laid a quilt on the snow and knelt to pray. Soon they realized the quilt had kept them from sinking into the snow.

Spreading quilts before them as they walked, leapfrog style, the men traveled to Parowan and back, returning with lifesaving provisions. This three-day event commemorates the event with quilting classes, a tour of Panguitch's pioneer homes, crafts shows, and a dinner-theater production in which the story is acted out. ☎ *435/676–8585.*

**JUNE–OCT.** **Utah Shakespearean Festival.** This world-class festival in Cedar City features several stage productions as well as a greenshow, with jugglers, puppet shows, and folks dressed in Elizabethan period costume. ☎ *435/586–7880 or 800/752–9849.*

**JULY** **Panguitch Pioneer Day Celebration.** At one of the biggest Pioneer Day celebrations in the state, Panguitch does it right with an invitational rodeo, parade, historical program, barbecue, children's races, and dancing. ☎ *435/676–8585 or 800/444–6689.*

Hikers, bikers, anglers, and photographers are all served by **Excursions of Escalante,** where tours are custom-fit to your schedule and needs. All necessary gear is provided, and tours last from four hours to eight days. ✉ *125 E. Main St., Escalante* ☎ *800/839–7567* ⊕ *www.excursions-escalante.com* ☽ *Mid-Apr.–mid-Nov. or by appointment.*

BICYCLING   A good long-distance mountain-bike ride in the isolated Escalante region follows the 44-mi **Hell's Backbone Road** from Escalante to Boulder. The grade is steep, but the views of Box Death Hollow make it all worthwhile. The road leaves from the center of town.

FISHING   Reportedly, **Panguitch Lake** takes its name from a Paiute Indian word meaning "big fish." They may not all be big, but several types of trout are plentiful, and ice fishing is popular in winter. Watch out that a bald eagle doesn't take your catch. ✉ *17 mi south of Panguitch on Rte. 143* ☎ *435/676–2649* ⊕ *www.panguitchlake.com.*

### Arts & Entertainment

ART GALLERY   A husband-and-wife team opened **Sculptured Furniture, Art and Ceramics** (✉ 1540 W. Hwy. 12, Escalante ☎ 435/826–4631

⊕ www.sculpturedfurnitureartandceramics.com), a gallery and workshop set amid petrified wood, gardens, and dinosaur bones.

## Scenic Drives & Vistsas

FodorsChoice **Highway 12 Scenic Byway.** Keep your camera handy and steering wheel
★ steady along this route between Escalante and Loa, near Capitol Reef National Park. Though the highway starts at the intersection of U.S. 89, west of Bryce Canyon, the stretch that begins in Escalante is one of the most spectacular. The road passes through Grand Staircase–Escalante National Monument and on to Capitol Reef along one of the most scenic stretches of highway in the United States. Be sure to stop at the scenic overlooks; almost every one will give you an eye-popping view. Don't get distracted, though; the paved road is twisting and steep, and at times climbs over a hogback with sheer drop-offs on both sides.

**U.S. 89/Utah's Heritage Highway.** Winding north from the Arizona border all the way to Spanish Fork Canyon an hour south of Salt Lake City, U.S. 89 is known as the Heritage Highway for its role in shaping Utah history. At its southern end, Kanab is known as "Little Hollywood," having provided the backdrop for many famous Western movies and TV commercials. The town has since grown considerably to accommodate tourists who flock here to see where Ronald Reagan once slept and Clint Eastwood drew his guns. Other towns north along this famous road may not have the same notoriety in these parts, but they do provide a quiet, uncrowded, and inexpensive place to stay near Zion and Bryce Canyon national parks. East of Kanab, U.S. 89 runs along the southern edge of the Grand Staircase–Escalante National Monument.

# WHERE TO STAY & EAT

9

### About the Restaurants

Dining options in the park proper are limited to Bryce Canyon Lodge; the nearby Ruth's Inn complex is your best eating bet close by. The restaurants in nearby locales tend to be of the meat-and-potatoes variety.

### About the Hotels

Lodging options in Bryce Canyon include both rustic and modern amenities, but all fill up fast in summer. The big advantage of staying here is proximity, though Bryce Canyon Lodge also has views.

Southwestern Utah is steeped in pioneer heritage, and you'll find many older homes that have been refurbished as bed-and-breakfast inns. The area also has its share of older independent motels in some of the smaller towns. The high season is summer and it's best to make reservations when traveling during that time. If you are willing to find a room upward of an hour away, perhaps with fewer amenities, you may be surprised not only by same-day reservations in some cases, but also much lower room rates. Panguitch has some particularly good options for budget and last-minute travelers.

### About the Campgrounds

Campgrounds in Bryce Canyon fill up fast, especially during the summer, and are family friendly. All are drive-in, except for the handful of backcountry sites that only backpackers and gung-ho day hikers ever see. Most are first-come, first-served during the high season, but call to inquire about those available for reservation. Most of the area's state parks have camping facilities, and Dixie National Forest contains many wonderful sites. Campgrounds may close seasonally because of lack of services (one loop of North Campground remains open year-round), and roads may occasionally close in winter while heavy snow is cleared.

## Where to Eat

### In the Park

$$ ✕ **Bryce Canyon Lodge.** Set among towering pines, this rustic old lodge is the only place to dine within the park. Many menu items change each year. Try anything with the tomatillo sauce, and stick with the simpler dishes. Reservations are essential at dinner. ⊠ *About 2 mi south of the park entrance* ☎ *435/834–5361* ⊕ *www.brycecanyonlodge.com* ⌕ *Reservations essential. $13–$20* ⊟ *AE, D, DC, MC, V* ☺ *Closed Nov.–Mar.*

PICNIC AREAS   **North Campground.** This area, a shady, alpine setting among ponderosa pine, has picnic tables and grills. ⊠ *About ¼ mi from visitor center.*

**Yovimpa Point.** At the southern end of the park, this shady, quiet spot looks out onto the 100-mi vistas from the rim. There are tables and restrooms. ⊠ *18 mi south of the park entrance.*

### Outside the Park

$$–$$$$ ✕ **Milt's Stage Stop.** Locals and an increasing number of tourists have
Fodor'sChoice   discovered the terrific food at this dinner spot in beautiful Cedar Canyon,
★   about 78 mi from Bryce Canyon. It's known for its rib-eye steak, prime rib, and fresh seafood dishes. In winter, deer feed in front of the restaurant as a fireplace blazes away inside. A number of hunting trophies decorate the rustic building's interior, and splendid views of the surrounding mountains delight patrons year-round. ⊠ *UT Rte. 14, 5 mi east of town in Cedar Canyon, Cedar City* ☎ *435/586–9344. $14–$42* ⊟ *AE, D, DC, MC, V* ☺ *No lunch.*

$–$$ ✕ **Cowboy Blues.** Walk back into the Old West for basic but good American food in this rustic restaurant adorned with ranching memorabilia. Steaks, ribs, and Utah trout dominate the dinner menu, while lunch serves tried-and-true sandwiches, salads, and burgers. A full liquor license, a rarity in these parts, allows beer, wine, and cocktails to be served here. ⊠ *530 W. Main St., Escalante* ☎ *435/826–4577. $8–$16* ⊟ *AE, D, MC, V.*

$–$$ ✕ **Harold's Place.** About 15 mi west of Bryce Canyon, on Highway 12 at the entrance to Red Canyon, stands this establishment designed to resemble a log cabin. The large menu includes a variety of steaks, lamb, seafood, pastas, and salads. Try Harold's Favorite for breakfast and get eggs any way you like, potatoes, your choice of meat, and a bottomless cup of coffee, all for seven bucks. ⊠ *3066 Rte. 12, 7 mi east from Panguitch* ☎ *435/676–2350. $9–$16* ⊟ *MC, V* ☺ *Closed Nov.–Mar. No lunch.*

¢–$$  ✕ **Bryce Canyon Restaurant.** Known for homemade soups like tomato-broccoli and corn chowder, and for fresh berry and cream pies, this homey, antiques-filled restaurant 6 mi northwest of the park serves quality comfort food. ⊠ *Hwy. 12, about 15 mi west of Tropic* ☎ *800/892–7923* ⊕ *www.brycecanyonmotel.com. $5–$16* ⊟ *AE, D, DC, MC, V.*

¢–$$  ✕ **Fosters Family Steakhouse.** With a stone fireplace and picture windows, Fosters is a clean, relatively quiet, modern steak house, and one of the most pleasant restaurants in the area. The menu features prime rib, steaks, and basic chicken and seafood dishes. Beer is the only alcohol served. ⊠ *Rte. 12, 2 mi west of the junction with Rte. 63* ☎ *435/834–5227. $6–$18* ⊟ *AE, D, MC, V* ⊘ *Closed Mon.–Thurs. in Jan.*

¢  ✕ **Esca-Latte Coffee Shop & Pizza Parlor.** Fuel up for your hike with the best coffee in town. When you're spent after a day of exploration, there's no better place to sit back and relax with friends. Try a turkey sub or pizza with a cold draft microbrew, or do the salad bar. When dining on the patio, watch hummingbirds fight the wind at the feeders. ⊠ *310 W. Main St., Escalante* ☎ *435/826–4266. $3–$7* ⊟ *D, MC, V.*

## Where to Stay

### In the Park

$$  ▣ **Bryce Canyon Lodge.** A few feet from the amphitheater's rim and trail-heads is this rugged stone-and-wood lodge. You have your choice of suites on the lodge's second level, motel-style rooms in separate buildings (with balconies or porches), and cozy lodgepole-pine cabins, some with cathedral ceilings and gas fireplaces. Reservations are hard to come by, so call several months ahead. Horseback rides into the park's interior can be arranged in the lobby. Reservations are essential for dinner at the lodge restaurant. ⊠ *2 mi south of park entrance, 84717* ☎ *435/834–5361 or 888/297–2757* 🖷 *435/834–5464* ⊕ *www.brycecanyonlodge. com* ⇥ *70 rooms, 3 suites, 40 cabins* ♨ *Restaurant, no a/c, no TV, non-smoking. $135* ⊟ *AE, D, DC, MC, V* ⊘ *Closed Nov.–Mar.*

**Fodor's**Choice
★

CAMPING & RV PARKS

$  ⛺ **North Campground.** A cool, shady retreat in a forest of ponderosa pines, this is a great home base for your exploration of Bryce Canyon. You're near the general store, Bryce Canyon Lodge, trailheads, and the visitor center. Some reservations are accepted, but generally sites are available on a first-come, first-served basis; the campground usually fills by early afternoon July through September. ⊠ *Main park road, ½ mi south of visitor center* ☎ *435/834–5322* ⇥ *107 sites, 47 for RVs* ♨ *Flush toilets, dump station, drinking water, fire grates, picnic tables, public telephone, general store. $10* ⊟ *No credit cards* ⊘ *Daily.*

$  ⛺ **Sunset Campground.** This serene alpine campground is within walk-ing distance of Bryce Canyon Lodge and many trailheads. All sites are filled on a first-come, first-served basis. The campground fills by early afternoon in July, August, and September, so get your campsite before you sightsee. Reservations not accepted. ⊠ *Main park road, 2 mi south of visitor center* ☎ *435/834–5322* ⇥ *101 sites, 49 for RVs* ♨ *Flush toilets, dump station, drinking water, fire grates, picnic tables, public tele-phone, general store. $10* ⊟ *No credit cards* ⊘ *May–Oct.*

9

## Outside the Park

★ $$ ⊞ **Best Western Ruby's Inn.** North of the park entrance and housing a large restaurant and gift shop, this is "Grand Central Station" for visitors to Bryce. Rooms vary in age, with sprawling wings added as the park gained popularity. All of the guest rooms are consistently comfortable and attractive, however. Centered between the gift shop and restaurant, the lobby of rough-hewn log beams and poles sets a Southwestern mood. There's a liquor store on-site. ⊠ *Rte. 63, 1 mi south of Rte. 12, Bryce 84764* ☎ *435/834–5341 or 866/866–6616* 🖷 *435/834–5265* ⊕ *www.rubysinn.com* ➽ *383 rooms, 2 suites* ♨ *2 restaurants, dial-up, pools, laundry facilities.* *$105–$150* ☰ *AE, D, DC, MC, V.*

★ $$ ⊞ **Escalante's Grand Staircase Bed & Breakfast Inn.** Rooms have skylights, tile floors, log furniture, and murals reproducing area petroglyphs. You can relax on the outdoor porches or in the library, or make use of the rental bikes to explore the adjacent national monument. ⊠ *280 W. Main St., Escalante 84726* ☎ *435/826–4890 or 866/826–4890* ⊕ *www. escalantebnb.com* ➽ *8 rooms* ♨ *Internet, Wi-Fi, bicycles, no kids under 10.* *$112–$139* ☰ *D, MC, V* ⦿ *BP.*

$ ⊞ **Bard's Inn Bed and Breakfast.** Rooms in this turn-of-the-20th-century house 78 mi from Bryce Canyon are named after heroines in Shakespeare's plays. There are wonderful antiques throughout and handcrafted quilts grace the beds. A full breakfast includes home-baked breads, such as nutmeg-blueberry muffins, fruit, juices, and oven-shirred eggs. ⊠ *150 S. 100 West St., Cedar City 84720* ☎ *435/586–6612* ⊕ *www.bardsbandb. com* ➽ *7 rooms* ♨ *No phone.* *$80–$100* ☰ *AE, MC, V.*

$ ⊞ **Bryce Canyon Pines.** This quiet, no-surprises motel complex is tucked into the woods 6 mi from the park entrance. Most of the rooms have excellent mountain views. There's a campground on the premises. ⊠ *6 mi northwest of park entrance on Hwy. 12, Bryce 84764* ☎ *800/892–7923* 🖷 *435/834–5330* ⊕ *www.brycecanyonmotel.com* ➽ *51 rooms* ♨ *Restaurant, pool.* *$75* ☰ *AE, D, DC, MC, V.*

$ ⊞ **Bryce Valley Inn.** Rest your head in this down-to-earth motel in the tiny town of Tropic. The accommodations are clean, and a small gift shop sells Native American crafts. ⊠ *199 N. Main St. (Rte. 12), Tropic 84776* ☎ *435/679–8811 or 800/442–1890* 🖷 *435/679–8846* ⊕ *www. brycevalleyinn.com* ➽ *65 rooms* ♨ *Restaurant, laundry facilities, some pets allowed, no-smoking rooms.* *$70–$80* ☰ *AE, D, MC, V.*

ℭ ¢–$ ⊞ **Marianna Inn.** Choose from one-, two-, three-, and four-bed rooms at this clean, family-friendly motel; those with whirlpool baths are $25 extra. You can barbecue on one of the grills and eat your meal on the covered patio. Relax afterward on a hammock or in the summer-only outdoor spa. ⊠ *699 N. Main St., Panguitch 84759* ☎ *435/676–8844* 🖷 *435/676–8340* ⊕ *www.mariannainn.com* ➽ *34 rooms* ♨ *Some pets allowed, no-smoking rooms.* *$40–$75* ☰ *AE, D, DC, MC, V.*

¢–$ ⊞ **Panguitch Inn.** This quiet inn occupies a 100-year-old, two-story building a few blocks from downtown restaurants and shops. Rooms are simple and no-frills, but clean. ⊠ *50 N. Main St., Panguitch 84759* ☎ *435/676–8871* ⊕ *www.panguitchinn.com* 🖷 *435/676–8340* ➽ *25 rooms* ♨ *Some pets allowed, no-smoking rooms, no a/c.* *$40–$75* ☰ *AE, D, DC, MC, V.*

¢  ☒ **Circle D Motel.** Basic but clean and comfortable, this motel will accommodate those traveling solo in a single room for as little as $30 a night. ⊠ *475 W. Main St., Escalante 84726* ☎ *435/826–4297* ☒ *435/826–4402* ⊕ *www.utahcanyons.com/circled.htm* ⇋ *25 rooms* ⅏ *Refrigerator, some pets allowed. $45* ▭ *AE, D, MC, V.*

¢  ☒ **Escalante Outfitters.** Stay here if you're on a budget and don't care about amenities. The seven log bunkhouse cabins share a single bath house. Barbecue grills are available. ⊠ *310 W. Main St., Escalante 84726* ☎ *435/826–4266* ⊕ *www.escalanteoutfitters.com* ⇋ *7 double-occupancy cabins* ⅏ *Café, grocery, no a/c, no TV. $45* ▭ *D, MC, V.*

CAMPGROUND & RV FACILITIES
**$$**
**Fodor's**Choice
★

⚠ **Best Western Ruby's Inn Campground and RV Park.** North of the park's entrance, sites here sit amid pine and fir trees. ⊠ *Rte. 63, 1 mi off Hwy. 12, Bryce* ☎ *866/866–6616* ⇋ *200 sites; 5 cabins, 8 tepees* ⅏ *Grills, flush toilets, full hookups, dump station, drinking water, guest laundry, showers, picnic tables, electricity, public telephone, general store, swimming (pool). $18–$29* ▭ *AE, D, DC, MC, V* ☉ *Apr.–Oct.*

☾ **$$**  ⚠ **Bryce Valley KOA.** On the quiet side of Bryce, this campground has the lowest (and warmest) elevation of any camping spot near the park. Everything you need for a quiet night of sleep and comfort is here. There's a cooking pavilion for group get-togethers. ⊠ *Hwy. 12 at the Kodachrome Basin turnoff, Cannonville* ☎ *435/679–8988 or 888/562–4710* ⊕ *www.koa.com* ⇋ *65 RV sites, 20 tent sites, 5 cabins* ⅏ *Grills, flush toilets, full hookups, dump station, drinking water, guest laundry, showers, fire grates, picnic tables, electricity, public telephone, general store, play area, swimming (pool). $18–$28* ▭ *AE, D, MC, V* ☉ *Mar.–Nov.*

**$–$$**  ⚠ **Red Canyon RV Park.** In red-rock country very similar to that of Bryce Canyon, this desert campground is 16 mi northwest of the national park. Besides RV sites, primitive and full-service cabins are available. ⊠ *Rte. 12, 1 mi east of U.S. 89, Panguitch* ☎ *435/676–2690* ⊕ *www.redcanyon.net/rc_rvpark/* ⇋ *45 sites, 8 cabins* ⅏ *Flush toilets, full hookups, dump station, drinking water, showers, fire grates, electricity, public telephone. $11–$25* ▭ *AE, D, MC, V* ☉ *Apr.–Oct.*

**$–$$**  ⚠ **Riverside Resort.** As its name suggests, many of the sites here are on the banks of the Sevier River, making this a great spot to call home for a few days. You can play or fish in the river, and a large meadow accommodates overflow tent camping. A small motel is on-site. ⊠ *15 mi south of Panguitch on U.S. 89, Hatch 84735* ☎ *435/735–4223 or 800/824–5651* ⊕ *www.riversideresort-utah.com* ⇋ *65 full hookups, unlimited tent camping* ⅏ *Grills, flush toilets, dump station, drinking water, showers, electricity, public telephone, general store, play area, swimming (river). $15 tent sites, $26 full hookups* ▭ *D, MC, V.*

★ **$**  ⚠ **Escalante Petrified Forest State Park Campground.** All of the sites here accommodate tents and RVs. The 130-acre Wide Hollow Reservoir attracts many boaters and swimmers. ⊠ *710 N. Reservoir Rd., Escalante 84726* ☎ *435/826–4466 or 800/322–3770* ⊕ *www.stateparks.utah. gov* ⇋ *22 sites* ⅏ *Flush toilets, dump station, drinking water, showers, fire grates, swimming (lake). $15* ▭ *No credit cards.*

¢  ⚠ **Red Canyon.** This primitive campground in Dixie National Forest is surrounded by pine trees in a brilliant red-rock canyon. ⊠ *Hwy. 12, 8 mi northwest of the park entrance, Panguitch* ☎ *435/676–9300*

**9**

⊕ *www.fs.fed.us/dxnf* ⤳ *37 tent/RV sites* ⚸ *Flush toilets, dump station, drinking water, showers, fire grates, ranger station. $9* ⊟ *No credit cards* ⊘ *May or June–Oct. (weather permitting).*

---

# BRYCE CANYON ESSENTIALS

ACCESSIBILITY Most park facilities were constructed between 1930 and 1960. Some have been upgraded for handicap accessibility, while others can be used with some assistance. Because of the park's natural terrain, only a ½-mi section of the Rim Trail between Sunset and Sunrise points is wheelchair accessible. The 1-mi bristlecone Loop Trail at Rainbow Point has a hard surface and could be used with assistance, but several grades do not meet standards. Handicapped parking is marked at all overlooks and public facilities. Accessible campsites are available at Sunset Campground.

ADMISSION FEES The entrance fee is $20 per vehicle for a seven-day pass and $10 for pedestrians, bicyclists or shuttle riders. An annual Bryce Canyon park pass costs $30. This pass can also be used on the park shuttle.

ADMISSION HOURS The park is open 24/7, year-round. It's in the Mountain time zone.

ATMS/BANKS Ruby's Inn has an ATM. The nearest bank is in Panguitch.
🚹 **Ruby's Inn** ✉ Rte. 63, 1 mi north of the park entrance, Bryce 🕾 435/834–5341. **Zions Bank** ✉ 90 E. Center St., Panguitch 🕾 435/676–8855.

AUTOMOBILE SERVICE STATIONS Just outside the park you can fuel up, get your oil and tires changed, and have car repairs done.
🚹 **Bryce Canyon Towing** ✉ 1 mi north of the park on Rte. 63, Bryce 🕾 435/834–5232. **Tesoro at Ruby's Inn** ✉ Rte. 63, 1 mi north of the park entrance, Bryce 🕾 435/834–5341.

EMERGENCIES In an emergency, dial 911. To contact park police or if you need first aid, go to the visitor center or speak to a park ranger. (In the summer only, there is also first aid at Bryce Canyon Lodge.) The nearest hospital is in Panguitch.

LOST AND FOUND The park's lost-and-found is at the visitor center.

PERMITS A $5 backcountry permit, available from the visitor center, is required for camping in the park's interior, allowed only on Under-the-Rim Trail and Rigg's Spring Loop, both south of Bryce Point. Campfires are not permitted.

POST OFFICE You can mail letters and buy stamps from Bryce Canyon Lodge. Ruby's Inn also offers a full-service post office.
🚹 **Ruby's Inn Post Office** ✉ Rte. 63, 1 mi north of the park entrance, Bryce 84764 🕾 435/834–8088 ⊘ Weekdays 8:30–4:30, Sat. 8:30–12:30.

PUBLIC TELEPHONES Bryce Canyon Lodge, Bryce Canyon Pines General Store, Ruby's Inn, Sunset Campground, and the visitor center all have public telephones. Cell-phone reception generally is available in the park.

RELIGIOUS SERVICES Nondenominational and Mormon services are held at Bryce Canyon Lodge. Check bulletin boards at the visitor center for times.

RESTROOMS Bryce Canyon Lodge, Bryce Canyon Pines General Store, the south end of North Campground, Ruby's General Store, Ruby's Inn, Sunset Campground, Sunset Point, the visitor center, and Yovimpa Point all have public restrooms.

## NEARBY TOWN INFORMATION
🚹 **Garfield County Travel Council (Escalante, Panguitch)** ✉ 55 S. Main St., Panguitch 84759 🕾 435/676–1160 or 800/444–6689 ⊕ www.brycecanyoncountry.com. **Iron County Travel Council (Cedar City)** ✉ 581 N. Main, Box 1007, Cedar City 84720 🕾 800/354–4849 ⊕ www.scenicsouthernutah.com.

## VISITOR INFORMATION
🚹 **Bryce Canyon National Park** ✍ Box 170001, Bryce, UT 84717 🕾 435/834–5322 or 888/362–2642 ⌨ 435/834–4102 ⊕ www.nps.gov/brca.

# Canyonlands National Park

Hiking in the Fisher Towers, Canyonlands National Park

## WORD OF MOUTH

"When thinking of these rocks one must not conceive of piles of boulders or heaps of fragments, but of a whole land of naked rock, with giant forms carved on it: cathedral-shaped buttes, towering hundreds of thousands of feet, cliffs that cannot be scaled, and canyon walls that shrink the river into insignificance, with vast, hollow domes and tall pinnacles and shafts set on the verge overhead; and all highly colored—buff, gray, red, brown, and chocolate."

–John Wesley Powell

# WELCOME TO CANYONLANDS

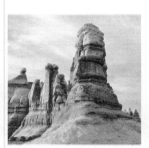

Colorado River

## TOP REASONS TO GO

★ **Solitude:** Take time for reflection in this rarely crowded park.

★ **Radical rapids:** Experience some white-water adventure in Cataract Canyon on the Colorado River.

★ **Native American artifacts:** View rock art and ancestral Puebloan dwellings in the park.

★ **Last Hold Out for Wilderness:** Walk, raft, or drive through some of this country's wildest, most untouched country.

★ **Bighorn sheep:** Snap a photo of them grazing along the roadway.

**1** Island in the Sky. From any of the overlooks here you can see for miles and look down thousands of feet to canyon floors. Chocolate-brown canyons are capped by white rock, and deep-red monuments rise nearby.

**2** Needles. Pink, orange, and red rock is layered with white rock and stands in spires and pinnacles around grassy meadows. Extravagantly red mesas and buttes interrupt the horizon, as in a picture postcard of the Old West.

**3** The Maze. Only the most-adventurous visitors walk in the footsteps of Butch Cassidy in this area, for it is accessible only by four-wheel-drive vehicles.

**4** Rivers. The park's waterways are as untamed and undammed as when John Wesley Powell explored them in the mid-1800s.

**5** Horseshoe Canyon. This unit, separate from the main park, is just northwest of the Glen Canyon Recreation Area. The famous rock art panel "Great Gallery" is the reward at the end of a long hike.

## GETTING ORIENTED

In southeastern Utah, Canyonlands National Park is divided into three distinct land districts and the river district, so it can be a little daunting to visit. Unless you have several days, you will need to choose between the Island in the Sky or the Needles districts.

Chesler Park

Great Gallery

| KEY | |
|---|---|
| 🏕️ | Ranger Station |
| ⛺ | Campground |
| 🍽️ | Picnic Area |
| 🍴 | Restaurant |
| 🏨 | Lodge |
| 🥾 | Trailhead |
| 🚻 | Restrooms |
| ⛰️ | Scenic Viewpoint |
| ⋯⋯ | Walking/Hiking Trails |
| ⋯⋯ | Bicycle Path |

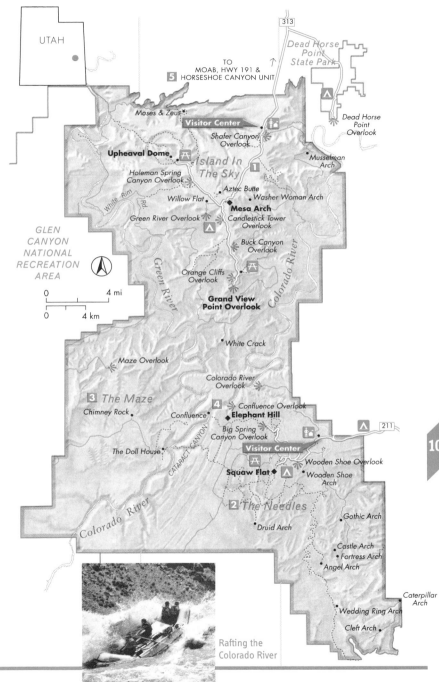

UTAH

TO
MOAB, HWY 191 &
HORSESHOE CANYON UNIT
**5**

313

*Dead Horse
Point
State Park*

*Dead Horse
Point
Overlook*

*Moses & Zeus*

**Visitor Center**

*Shafer Canyon
Overlook*

**Upheaval Dome**

*Island In
The Sky*

*Musselman
Arch*

1

*Holeman Spring
Canyon Overlook*

*Aztec Butte*

*Willow Flat*

*Washer Woman Arch*

*White Rim Rd.*

**Mesa Arch**

*Candlestick Tower
Overlook*

*Green River Overlook*

GLEN
CANYON
NATIONAL
RECREATION
AREA

*Green River*

*Buck Canyon
Overlook*

*Orange Cliffs
Overlook*

**Grand View
Point Overlook**

*Colorado River*

0        4 mi

0        4 km

*White Crack*

*Maze Overlook*

*Colorado River
Overlook*

**3** *The Maze*

*Chimney Rock*

*Confluence*

**4**

*Confluence Overlook*

**Elephant Hill**

*Big Spring
Canyon Overlook*

211

*The Doll House*

*CATARACT CANYON*

**Visitor Center**

*Wooden Shoe Overlook*

**Squaw Flat**

*Wooden Shoe
Arch*

10

*Colorado River*

**2** *The Needles*

*Gothic Arch*

*Druid Arch*

*Castle Arch*
*Fortress Arch*
*Angel Arch*

*Caterpillar
Arch*

*Wedding Ring Arch*

*Cleft Arch*

Rafting the
Colorado River

# CANYONLANDS PLANNER

## When to Go

**The busiest times of year for the park is spring and fall.** Compared to most national parks, Canyonlands is seldom crowded, but in spring backpackers and four-wheelers populate the trails and roads. During Easter week, some of the four-wheel-drive trails are used for Jeep Safari, an annual event drawing some 15,000 visitors to town.

The crowds thin out in summer as the thermostat approaches 100° in July and then soars beyond that for about four weeks. It's a great time to get out on the Green or Colorado rivers winding through Canyonlands. October can be rainy season, but the region only receives an annual rainfall of 8 inches.

The well-kept secret is that winter is the best time in the park. Crowds are gone, roads are good, and snow-capped mountains stand in the background. Winter at Canyonlands is one of nature's most memorable shows, with red rock dusted white and low-floating clouds partially obscuring canyons and towers.

AVG. HIGH/LOW TEMPS.

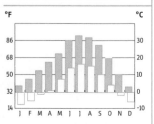

## Flora & Fauna

Your chances of seeing wildlife are fairly good in Canyonlands because there are fewer people and less traffic to scare the animals away. Cool mornings and evenings are the best time to spot them, especially during the summer when the heat keeps them in cool, shady areas. Mule deer are nearly always seen along the roadway as you enter the Needles District, and you'll no doubt see jackrabbits and small rodents darting across the roadway. Approximately 250 bighorns populate the park in the Island in the Sky District, and the Maze shelters about 100 more. If you happen upon one of these regal animals, do not approach it even if it is alone, as bighorn sheep are skittish by nature and easily stressed. Also report your sighting to a ranger.

## Getting There & Around

Off U.S. 191, Canyonlands' Island in the Sky is 21 mi from Arches National Park and 32 mi from Moab on Route 313 west of U.S. 191; the Needles District is reached via Route 211, west of U.S. 191. The nearest airport is Grand County Airport, also know as Canyonlands Field (☎ 435/259–7419), 18 mi north of Moab. Flights are very limited. The nearest train "station" is a solitary Amtrak stop in Green River, about 60 mi northwest of Moab.

Before starting a journey to any of Canyonlands' three districts, make sure your gas tank is topped off, as there are no services inside the park. Island in the Sky is 32 mi from Moab, Needles District is 80 mi from Moab, and the Maze is more than 100 mi from Moab. The Island in the Sky road from the district entrance to Grand View Point is 12 mi, with one 5-mi spur to Upheaval Dome. The Needles scenic drive is 10 mi with two spurs about 3 mi each. Roads in the Maze, suitable only for rugged, high-clearance, four-wheel-drive vehicles, wind for hundreds of miles through the canyons. Within the parks, safety and courtesy mandate that you always park only in designated pullouts or parking areas.

By Janet Lowe

While Arches looks like Mars, Canyonlands resembles the moon. Mushroomlike rock formations rise randomly out of the ground, twisting into all manner of shapes: spires, buttes, pinnacles, and mesas. It's a desert landscape, but it's not devoid of water or color. The Green and Colorado rivers traverse the canyons, where the rich browns, verdant greens, and fresh yellows of the pinyon-juniper forests complement the deep reds, baby pinks, bright oranges, and milky whites of the rocks. The park's dirt roads appeal to mountain bikers, and the rising rapids of Cataract Canyon challenge rafters.

## Scenic Drives

**Island in the Sky Park Road.** This 12-mi long road connects to a 5-mi side road to the Upheaval Dome area. You can enjoy many of the park's vistas by stopping at the overlooks—get out of your car for the best views. Once you're at the park, allow about two hours to explore.

**Needles District Park Road.** You'll feel you've driven into a picture postcard as you roll along the park road in the Needles District. Red mesas and buttes rise against the horizon, blue mountain ranges interrupt the rangelands, and the colorful red and white needles stand like soldiers on the far side of grassy meadows. The drive, about 10 mi one way, takes about half an hour.

## What to See

### Historic Sites

Ⓒ **Cowboy Line Camp.** The remnants here include furniture and camp gear. The artifacts are found on the **Cave Springs Trail,** which is short but requires some ladder climbing and sloping slickrock navigating. ⊠ *On Cave Springs Rd., 2³⁄₁₀ mi from the park entrance, Needles.*

10

## CANYONLANDS IN ONE DAY

Your day begins with a choice: Island in the Sky or Needles. If you want expansive vistas looking across southeast Utah's canyonlands, head for the Island, where you stand atop a giant mesa. If you want to drive and walk among the canyonland's needles and buttes, Needles is your destination. If you have a second or third day in the area, consider contacting an outfitter to take you on a 4x4 adventure.

■ TIP→ **Before venturing into the park, top off your gas tank, pack a picnic lunch, and stock up on plenty of water.**

### A DAY IN ISLAND IN THE SKY
Make your first stop along the main park road at **Shafer Canyon Overlook.** A short walk takes you out on a finger of land with views of the canyon over both sides. From here you can see Shafer Trail hugging the wall below.

Drive next to **Mesa Arch.** Grab your camera and water bottle for the short hike out to the arch perched on the cliff's edge. After your hike, continue on the main park road to **Grand View Point.** Stroll along the edge of the rim, and see how many

landmarks you can spot in the distance. Have your lunch at the Grand View Point picnic area. Afterward, turn back toward the visitor center but take a left on Upheaval Dome Road. Stop at Island in the Sky Campground so you can see the Green River from the nearby overlook.

Lastly, head to the Upheaval Dome parking lot to stretch your legs with a hike up to the first **Upheaval Dome** viewpoint. If you still have energy, time, and a little sense of adventure, continue to the second overlook.

### A DAY IN NEEDLES
If you can stay overnight as well, then begin today by setting up camp at one of the Needles' wonderful campgrounds. Then hit the **Joint Trail,** or any of the trails that begin from Squaw Flat Campground, and spend the day hiking in the backcountry of the park. (Or, if you really want to cram a lot in, begin the morning with a brief but terrific little hike to **Cave Springs** before tackling a lengthier trail.) Attend the **campfire program** tonight and sleep under more stars than you've seen in a long time.

**Shafer Trail.** This road was probably first established by ancient Native Americans, but in the early 1900s ranchers used it to drive cattle into the canyon. Originally narrow and rugged, it was upgraded during the uranium boom, when miners hauled ore by truck from the canyon floor. You can see the road's winding route down canyon walls from Shafer Canyon Overlook. Today, Shafer Trail is used by daring four-wheelers and energetic mountain bikers. It descends 1,400 feet to the White Rim and another 700 feet to the Colorado River. ⊠ *On the main road, less than 1 mi from the park entrance, Island in the Sky.*

### Scenic Stops
★ **Grand View Point.** At the end of the main road of Island in the Sky, don't miss this 360-degree view that extends all the way to the San Juan

Mountains in Colorado on a clear day. ⊠ *On the main road, 12 mi from entrance, Island in the Sky.*

★ **Mesa Arch.** Even though it can be crowded, you simply can't visit Island in the Sky without taking the quick ½-mi walk to Mesa Arch. The arch is above a cliff that drops nearly 1,000 feet to the canyon bottom. Views through the arch of Washerwoman Arch and surrounding buttes, spires, and canyons make this a favorite photo opportunity. ⊠ *On the main road, 6 mi from the park entrance, Island in the Sky.*

> ### MEET ME AT SUNSET
>
> Sunset is one of the picture-perfect times in Canyonlands, as the slanting sun shines over the vast network of canyons that stretch out below Island in the Sky. A moonlight drive to Grand View Point can also give you lasting memories as the moon drenches the white sandstone in light. Likewise, late afternoon color in the spires and towers at the Needles District is a humbling, awe-inspiring scene.

**Pothole Point Trail.** This is an especially good stop after a rainstorm, which fills the potholes with water. Stop to study the communities of tiny creatures, including fairy shrimp, that thrive in the slickrock hollows. Along the way, discover dramatic views of the Needles and Six Shooter Peak, too. The easy ⁶⁄₁₀-mi round-trip walk takes about 45 minutes. There's no shade, so wear a hat. ⊠ *On the main road, about 9 mi from the park entrance, Needles.*

**Upheaval Dome.** This colorful, mysterious crater is one of the many wonders of Island in the Sky. Some geologists believe it to be an eroded salt dome, but others have theorized that it is an eroded meteorite impact dome. To see it, you'll have to walk a short distance to the overlook. ⊠ *On Upheaval Dome Rd., 11 mi from the park entrance, Island in the Sky.*

### Visitor Centers

**Hans Flat Ranger Station.** This remote spot is nothing more than a stopping point for permits, books, and maps before you venture into the Maze District of Canyonlands. To get here, you must drive 46 mi on a dirt road that is sometimes impassable to two-wheel-drive vehicles. There's a pit toilet, but no water, food, or services of any kind. ⊠ *46 mi east of Rte. 24; 21 mi south and east of the Y-junction and Horseshoe Canyon kiosk on the dirt road, Maze* ☎ *435/259–2652* ☻ *Daily 8–4:30.*

**Island in the Sky Visitor Center.** Stop and watch the orientation film and then browse the bookstore for information about the Canyonlands region. Exhibits explain animal adaptations and park history. ⊠ *Past the park entrance on the main park road, Island in the Sky* ☎ *435/259–4712* ☻ *Daily 8–5 with expanded hours Apr.–Oct.*

**Needles District Visitor Center.** This gorgeous building that blends into the landscape is worth seeing, even if you don't need the books, trail maps, or other information available inside. ⊠ *Less than 1 mi from the park entrance on the main park road, Needles* ☎ *435/259–4711* ☻ *8–5 daily.*

## Sports & the Outdoors

Canyonlands is one of the world's best destinations for adrenaline junkies. You can rock climb, mountain bike treacherous terrain, tackle

**10**

world-class white-water rapids, and make your 4x4 crawl over steep cliffs along precipitous drops. Compared to other national parks, Canyonlands allows you to enjoy an amazing amount of solitude while having the adventure of a lifetime.

### Air Tours

OUTFITTERS & EXPEDITIONS **Slickrock Air Guides.** This company's regional tours give you an eagle's-eye view of the park, and you'll walk away with new respect and understanding of the word "wilderness." ⊠ *Canyonlands Air Field (also known as Grand County Airport), N. U.S. 191, near Moab* ☎ *435/259–6216 or 866/259–1626* ⊕ *www.slickrockairguides.com.*

### Bicycling

**White Rim Road.** Mountain bikers all over the world like to brag that they've ridden this 112-mi road around Island in the Sky. The trail's fame is well-deserved: it traverses steep roads, broken rock, and ledges as well as long stretches that wind through the canyons and look down onto others. There's always a good chance you'll see bighorn sheep here, too. Permits are not required for day use, but if you're biking White Rim without an outfitter you'll need careful planning and backcountry reservations (make them as far in advance as possible through the reservation office, 435/259–4351). Information about permits can be found at www.nps.gov/cany. There's no water on this route. White Rim Road starts at the end of Shafer Trail near Musselman Arch. ⊠ *Off the main park road about 1 mi from the entrance, then about 11 mi on Shafer Trail; or off Potash Rd. (Rte. 279) at the Jug Handle Arch turnoff about 18 mi from U.S. 191, then about 5 mi on Shafer Trail, Island in the Sky.*

*See* ➪ Four-Wheeling in this chapter for more routes.

OUTFITTERS & EXPEDITIONS **Nichols Expeditions.** These professional outfitters take about a dozen multiday bike trips a year into the backcountry of Canyonlands National Park. Departure dates and routes are predetermined, so contact them for a schedule. ⊠ *497 N. Main St., Moab* ☎ *435/259–3999 or 800/648–8488* ⊕ *www.nicholsexpeditions.com.*

For additional bike outfitters, ➪ Outfitters & Expeditions box, Arches National Park, Chapter 4.

### Bird-watching

Without getting on the Colorado River, you can see a variety of wrens, including the Rock wren, Canyon wren, and Bewick's wren. Blue-gray gnatchatchers are fairly common in the summer, along with the Solitary vireo and Black-throated gray warbler and Virigina's warbler. You'll have the most fun spotting the American kestrel or peregrine falcon and watching golden and bald eagles soar overhead. The common raven is everywhere you look, as are the common magpie and a variety of jays. Once on the Colorado River, you'll stand a chance of glimpsing the elusive White-faced ibis, and you'll almost certainly see a great blue heron swooping along the water or standing regally on a sandbar.

### Boating & River Expeditions

Seeing Canyonlands from the river is a great and rare pleasure. Long stretches of calm water on the Green River are perfect for lazy canoe trips. In Labyrinth Canyon, north of the park boundary, and in Stillwater Canyon, in the Island in the Sky District, the river is quiet and calm and there's plenty of shoreside camping. The Island in the Sky leg of the Colorado River, from Moab to its confluence with the Green River and downstream a few more miles to Spanish Bottom, is ideal for canoeing and for rides with an outfitter in a large, stable jet boat. If you want to take a self-guided flat-water float trip in the park you must obtain a $20 permit, which you have to request by mail or fax. Make your upstream travel arrangements with a shuttle company before you request a permit. For permits, contact the park reservation office (☎ 435/259–4351).

Below Spanish Bottom, about 64 mi downstream from Moab, 49 mi from the Potash Road ramp, and 4 mi south of the confluence, the Colorado churns into the first rapids of legendary Cataract Canyon. Home of some of the best white water in the United States, this piece of river between the Maze and the Needles District rivals the Grand Canyon stretch of the Colorado River for adventure. During spring melt-off these rapids can rise to staggering heights and deliver heart-stopping excitement. The water calms down a bit in summer but still offers enough thrills for most people. Outfitters will take you for the ride of your life in this wild canyon, where the river drops more steeply than anywhere else on the Colorado River (in ¾ mi, the river drops 39 feet). You can join an expedition lasting anywhere from one to six days, or you can purchase a $30 permit for a self-guided trip from park headquarters.

**OUTFITTERS & EXPEDITIONS**

**Oars.** This company can take you rafting on the Colorado River and four-wheeling in the parks. For those not into white water they also offer a calm-water ride on the Colorado. ⊠ *543 N. Main St., Moab* ☎ *435/259–5865 or 800/342–5938* ⊕ *www.oarsutah.com.*

**Sheri Griffith Expeditions.** This longtime Moab outfitter offers trips through the white water of Cataract, Westwater, and Desolation canyons, on the Colorado and Green rivers. Expeditions include river trips for women, writers, and families, as well as luxurious expeditions that make roughing it more comfortable. ⊠ *2231 S. U.S. 191, Moab* ☎ *435/259–8229 or 800/332–2439* ⊕ *www.griffithexp.com.*

**Tag-A-Long Expeditions.** This company holds more permits with the National Park Service and has been taking people into the white water of Cataract Canyon and Canyonlands longer than any other outfitter in Moab. They also run four-wheel-drive expeditions into the backcountry of the park and calm-water excursions on the Colorado River. They are the only outfitter allowed to take you into the park via both water and 4x4. Trips run from a half day to six days. ⊠ *452 N. Main St., Moab* ☎ *435/259–8946 or 800/453–3292* ⊕ *www.tagalong.com.*

For additional boating outfitters and rental companies, ⇨ Outfitters & Expeditions box, Arches National Park, Chapter 4.

## Four-Wheeling

Nearly 200 mi of challenging backcountry roads lead to campsites, trailheads, and natural and cultural features in Canyonlands. All of the roads require high-clearance, four-wheel-drive vehicles, and many are

**10**

inappropriate for inexperienced drivers. Especially before you tackle the Maze, be sure your four-wheel-drive skills are well honed and you can make basic road and vehicle repairs. Carry at least one full-size spare tire, extra gas, extra water, a shovel, a high-lift jack, and—October through April—chains for all four tires. Double-check to see that your vehicle is in top-notch condition, for you definitely don't want to break down in the interior of the park: towing expenses can exceed $1,000. For overnight four-wheeling trips you must purchase a $30 permit; reserve it in advance by contacting the Backcountry Reservations Office (☎ 435/259–4351). Vehicular traffic traveling uphill has the right-of-way. Check at the visitor center for current road conditions before going into the backcountry. You must carry a washable, reusable toilet with you in the Maze district and carry out all waste. For guided 4x4 trips, ⇨ Outfitters & Expeditions box in the Arches National Park chapter.

★ **Elephant Hill.** This Needles route is so difficult—steep grades, loose rock, and stair-step drops—that many people get out and walk . In fact, you can walk it faster than you can drive it. From Elephant Hill trailhead to Devil's Kitchen it's 3 ½ mi; from the trailhead to the Confluence Overlook, it's a 16-mi round-trip and requires at least eight hours. ⊠ *Off the main park road, 7 mi from the park entrance, Needles.*

**Flint Trail.** This remote, rugged road is the most used road in the Maze District, but don't let that fool you into thinking it's smooth sailing. It's very technical with 2 mi of switchbacks that drop down the side of a cliff face. You reach Flint Trail from the Hans Flat Ranger Station, which is 46 mi from the closest paved road (Rte. 24 off I–70). From Hans Flat to the end of the road at the Doll House it's 41 mi, a drive that takes about seven hours one way. From Hans Flat to the Maze Overlook it's 34 mi. The Maze is not generally a destination for a day trip, so you'll have to purchase an overnight backcountry permit for $30. ⊠ *Hans Flat Ranger Station (46 mi east of Rte. 24, Maze).*

★ **White Rim Road.** Winding around and below the Island in the Sky mesa top, the dramatic 112-mi White Rim Road offers a once-in-a-lifetime driving experience. As you tackle Murphy's Hogback, Hardscrabble Hill, and more formidable obstacles, you will get some fantastic views of the park. A trip around the loop takes two to three days and you must make reservations almost a year in advance for an overnight campsite—unless you manage to snap up a no-show or cancellation. For reservation information call the Backcountry Reservation Office (435/259–4351). White Rim Road starts at the end of Shafer Trail near Musselman Arch. ⊠ *Off the main park road about 1 mi from the entrance, then about 11 mi on Shafer Trail; or off Potash Rd. (Rte. 279) at the Jug Handle Arch turnoff about 18 mi from U.S. 191, then about 5 mi on Shafer Trail; Island in the Sky.*

## Hiking

Canyonlands National Park is a good place to saturate yourself in the intoxicating colors, smells, and textures of the desert. Many of the trails are long, rolling routes over slickrock and sand in landscapes dotted with juniper, pinyon, and sagebrush. Interconnecting trails in the Needles District provide excellent opportunities for weeklong backpacking excursions. The Maze trails are primarily accessed via four-wheel-drive vehicle. In the separate Horseshoe Canyon area, Horseshoe Canyon Trail takes a considerable amount of effort to reach, as it is more than 100 mi from Moab, 32 mi of which are a bumpy, and often sandy, dirt road.

EASY **Aztec Butte Trail.** Chances are good you'll enjoy this hike in solitude. It begins level, then climbs up a steep slope of slickrock. The highlight of the 2-mi round-trip hike is the chance to see ancestral Puebloan granaries. ⊠ *On Upheaval Dome Rd., about 6 mi from the park entrance, Island in the Sky.*

**Grand View Point Trail.** If you're looking for a level walk with some of the grandest views in the world, stop at Grand View Point and wander the 2-mi trail along the cliff edge. Most people just stop at the overlook and drive on, so the trail is not as crowded as you might think. On a clear day you can see up to 100 mi to the Maze and Needles districts of the park, the confluence of the Green and Colorado rivers, and each of Utah's major laccolithic mountain ranges: the Henrys, Abajos, and La Sals. ⊠ *On the main park road, 12 mi from the park entrance, Island in the Sky.*

Fodor'sChoice **Mesa Arch Trail.** By far the most popular trail in the park, this ⅔-mi loop ★ acquaints you with desert plants and terrain. The highlight of the hike is a natural arch window perched over an 800-foot drop below. The vistas of the rest of the park are nothing short of stunning. ⊠ *6 mi from the Island in the Sky Visitor Center.*

**Slickrock Trail.** If you're on this trail in summer, make sure you're wearing a hat, because you won't find any shade along the 2⁴/₁₀-mi round-trip trek across slickrock. This is one of the few front-country sites where you might see bighorn sheep. ⊠ *On the main park road, about 10 mi from the park entrance, Needles.*

**Whale Rock Trail.** If you've been hankering to walk across some of that pavement-smooth stuff they call slickrock, the hike to Whale Rock will make your feet happy. This 1-mi round-trip adventure, complete with handrails to help you make the tough 100-foot climb, takes you to the very top of the whale's back. Once you get there, you are rewarded with great views of Upheaval Dome and Trail Canyon. ⊠ *On Upheaval Dome Rd., 11 mi from the park entrance, Island in the Sky.*

MODERATE **Cave Spring Trail.** One of the best, most diverse trails in the park takes ★ ☾ you past a historic cowboy camp and Native American petroglyphs. About half of the trail is in shade, as it meanders under overhangs. Slanted, bumpy slickrock make this hike more difficult than others, and two ladders make the ⁶/₁₀-mi round-trip walk even more of an adventure. Allow about 45 minutes. ⊠ *Off the main park road on Cave Springs Rd., 2³/₁₀ mi from the park entrance, Needles.*

DIFFICULT **Chesler Park Loop.** Chesler Park is a grassy meadow dotted with spires and enclosed by a circular wall of colorful "needles." One of Canyonlands' more popular trails leads through the area to the famous Joint Trail. The trail is 6 mi round-trip to the viewpoint. ⊠ *Elephant Hill trailhead, off the main park road, about 7 mi from the park entrance, Needles.*

**10**

★ **Horseshoe Canyon Trail.** You arrive at this detached unit of Canyonlands National Park via a washboarded, two-wheel-drive dirt road. Park at the lip of the canyon and hike 6½ mi round-trip to the Great Gallery, considered by some to be the most significant rock-art panel in North America. Ghostly life-size figures in the Barrier Canyon style populate the amazing panel. The hike is moderately strenuous, with a 750-foot descent. Allow at least six hours for the trip and take a gallon of water per person. There's no camping allowed in the canyon, although you can camp on top near the parking lot. ⊠ *32 mi east of Rte. 24, Maze.*

**Syncline Loop Trail.** Are you up for a long, full day of hiking? Try this 8-mi trail that circles Upheaval Dome. You not only get great views of the dome, you actually make a complete loop around its base. Stretches of the trail are rocky, rugged, and steep. ⊠ *On Upheaval Dome Rd., 11 mi from the park entrance, Island in the Sky.*

## Rock Climbing

Canyonlands and many of the surrounding areas draw climbers from all over the world. Permits are not required, but because of the sensitive archaeological nature of the park, it's imperative that you stop at the visitor center to pick up regulations pertaining to the park's cultural resources. Popular climbing routes include Moses and Zeus towers in Taylor Canyon, and Monster Tower and Washerwoman Tower on the White Rim Road. Like most routes in Canyonlands, these climbs are for experienced climbers only.

For climbing outfitters, ⇨ Outfitters & Expeditions box, Arches National Park.

# Educational Offerings

## Programs & Tours

For more information on current schedules and locations of park programs, contact the visitor centers (☎ 435/259–4712 Island in the Sky, 435/259–4711 Needles) or check the bulletin boards throughout the park. Note that programs change periodically and may sometimes be cancelled because of limited staffing.

**Campfire Program.** You can enrich your visit to Canyonlands by attending a campfire program. Topics include wildlife, cultural and natural history of the park, Native American legends, cowboy history, and geology. Check with the visitor centers or park bulletin boards for details. ⊠ *Willow Flat Campground, Island in the Sky; Squaw Flat Campground, Needles* ☎ *Free* ☉ *½ hour after sunset.*

**Grand View Point Overlook Talk.** By attending this session you can learn something about the geology that created Canyonlands or the rich mining history of the region. Check at the visitor centers for times and locations. ⊠ *Grand View Point, 12 mi from the park entrance on the main park road, Island in the Sky* ☎ *$10 per vehicle* ☉ *Apr.–Oct., daily.*

**Junior Ranger Program.** Kids 6–12 can pick up a Junior Ranger booklet at the visitor centers. It's full of activities, word games, drawings, and educational material about the park and the wildlife. To earn the Ju-

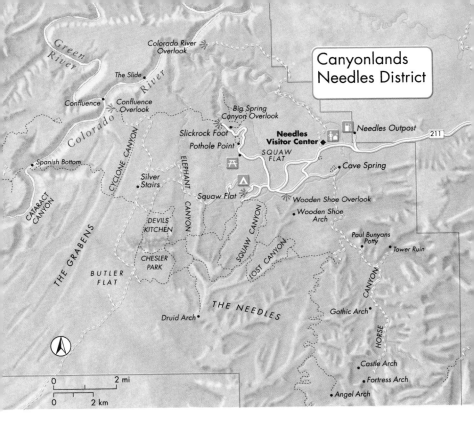

Canyonlands
Needles District

nior Ranger badge, they must complete the booklet, attend a ranger program, or watch the park slide program, and gather a bag of litter or bring 20 aluminum cans to be recycled. ☎ 435/259–4712 *Island in the Sky*, 435/259–4711 *Needles* 🖂 *Free*.

# WHAT'S NEARBY

Moab is the major gateway to both Arches and Canyonlands national parks, with the most outfitters, shops, and lodging options of the area. *See* ⇨ Arches National Park chapter for more on Moab. A handful of communities, which are much smaller and with fewer amenities, are scattered around the Needles and Island in the Sky districts along U.S. 191.

## Nearby Towns & Attractions

### Nearby Towns

Roughly 55 mi south of Moab is **Monticello.** Convenient to the Needles District, it lies at an elevation of 7,000 feet, making it a cool summer refuge from the desert heat. In winter, it gets downright cold and sees deep snow. **Blanding,** 21 mi south of Monticello, prides itself on old-fashioned conservative values. By popular vote there's a ban on the sale of liquor, beer, and wine, so the town has no state liquor store and its restaurants do not serve alcoholic beverages. About 25 mi south of Blanding, tiny **Bluff** is doing its best to stay that way. It's a great place to stop if you aren't looking for many amenities but value beautiful scenery, silence, and starry nights. Bluff is the most common starting point for trips on the San Juan

---

**UP, UP, AND AWAY**

In January, colorful balloons congregate in Bluff and take to the skies over the San Juan River and all of Utah's Canyonlands during **Bluff International Balloon Festival** (☏ 435/672–2303).

---

River, which serves as the northern boundary for the Navajo Reservation; it's also a wonderful place to overnight if you're planning a visit to Hovenweep National Monument, about 30 mi away.

### Nearby Attractions

*See* ⇨ Arches National Park chapter for additional area listings.

**Dead Horse Point State Park.** One of the finest state parks in Utah overlooks a sweeping oxbow of the Colorado River, some 2,000 feet below, and the upside-down landscapes of Canyonlands National Park. Dead Horse Point itself is a small peninsula connected to the main mesa by a narrow neck of land. As the story goes, cowboys used to drive wild horses onto the point and pen them there with a brush fence. Some were accidentally forgotten and left to perish. Facilities at the park include a modern visitor center and museum, a 21-site campground with drinking water, and an overlook. ✉ *34 mi west from Moab at the end of Rte. 313* ☏ *435/259–2614, 800/322–3770 for campground reservations* ⊕ *www.stateparks.utah.gov* ▭ *$7 per vehicle* ⊙ *Daily 8–6.*

★ **Edge of the Cedars State Park.** Tucked away on a backstreet in Blanding is one of the nation's foremost museums dedicated to the ancestral Puebloan Indians. The museum displays a variety of pots, baskets, spear points, and such. Interestingly, many of these artifacts were donated by pot hunters—archaeological looters. Behind the museum, you can visit an actual Anasazi ruin. ✉ *660 W. 400 North St., Blanding* ☏ *435/678–2238* ⊕ *www.stateparks.utah.gov* ▭ *$5 per vehicle* ⊙ *May–Sept., daily 8–8; Oct.–Apr., daily 9–5.*

**Hovenweep National Monument.** If you're headed south from Canyonlands and have an interest in ancestral Puebloan culture, a visit to this monument is a must. It's a little out of the way along a remote stretch of the Utah-Colorado border southeast of Blanding, but seeing the unusual tower structures (which may have been used for astronomical observation) is worth the effort. A ½-mi walking tour, or a more rigorous 1½-mi hike into the canyon, takes you to the ancient dwellings. A 32-site campground is available for overnighters in tents or small vehicles. ✉ *Rte. 262, 28 mi east of U.S. 191* ☏ *970/562–4282* ⊕ *www.nps.gov/hove* ▭ *$6* ⊙ *Daily 8 AM–sunset.*

**Natural Bridges National Monument.** When visitor Elliot McClure came to Natural Bridges National Monument in 1931, his car slowly disintegrated. First his headlights fell off. Next, his doors dropped off. Finally, his bumpers worked loose, and the radiator broke away. Today a drive to the three stone bridges is far less hazardous. All roads are paved and a scenic 9-mi route takes you to stops that overlook Sipapu, Owachomo, and Kachina bridges. There's also a 13-site primitive campground. Natural Bridges is a drive of about 100 mi southwest from the Needles District of Canyonlands National Park. ⊠ *Rte. 275 off Rte. 95* ☎ *435/692–1234* ⊕ *www.nps.gov/nabr* ⊠ *$6 per vehicle* ☉ *Daily 7 AM–sunset.*

★ **Newspaper Rock Recreation Site.** One of the West's most famous rock-art sites, this large panel contains Native American etchings that accumulated on the rock over the course of 2,000 years. Apparently, early pioneers and explorers to the region named the site Newspaper Rock because they believed the rock, crowded with drawings, constituted a written language with which early people communicated. Archaeologists now agree the petroglyphs do not represent language. This is one of many "newspaper rocks" throughout the Southwest. ⊠ *Rte. 211, about 15 mi west of U.S. 191.*

**Wilson Arch.** Between Arches and the Needles District of Canyonlands, this giant roadside arch makes a great photo stop. In Moab, you can still find historical photos of an airplane flying through this arch. No one has tried the stunt lately, probably because it's now illegal. ⊠ *U.S. 191, 23 mi south of Moab.*

## Shopping

**Comb Ridge Trading Post.** This absolute gem of a trading post is right on the highway. Here you will find arts and crafts by local Navajo artisans as well as a few well-chosen collectibles. ⊠ *680 S. U.S. 191, Bluff* ☎ *435/672–2415.*

**Thin Bear Indian Arts.** This tiny trading post has operated in the same spot for 29 years. Authentic jewelry, rugs, baskets and pottery are for sale. ⊠ *1944 S. Main St., Blanding* ☎ *435/678–2940.*

## Scenic Drives

**Colorado Riverway Scenic Byway—Route 279.** If you're interested in Native American rock art, this scenic drive along the Colorado River is a perfect place to spend a couple of hours. If you start late in the afternoon, the cliffs will be glowing orange as the sun sets. Along the first part of the route are signs reading "Indian Writings." Park only in designated areas to view the petroglyphs on the cliff. At the 18-mi marker you'll see Jug Handle Arch on the cliff side of the road. A few miles later the road turns to four-wheel-drive only into the Island in the Sky District. Allow about two hours round-trip for the drive.

# WHERE TO STAY & EAT

## About the Restaurants

There are no dining facilities in the park itself. Needles Outpost, just outside the entrance to the park's Needles District, offers a snack bar with hamburgers and a small grocery store for picnicking necessities. Restaurants in Monticello and Blanding offer simple meals, and most do not serve alcohol. Your best bet for a variety of dining experiences, from microbreweries to fine dining or good home cooking, is in Moab. For Moab listings, ⇨ Arches National Park chapter. Moab delis and bakeries also can prepare fresh-made sandwichs to go.

### About the Hotels

There is no lodging inside Canyonlands. The towns of Monticello and Blanding offer basic motels, both family owned and national chains. Bluff also has motels and B&Bs and offers a quiet place to stay.

### About the Campgrounds

Canyonlands campgrounds are some of the most beautiful in the National Park System. At the Needles District, campers will enjoy fairly private campsites tucked against red rock walls and dotted with pinyon and juniper trees. At Island in the Sky, starry nights and spectacular vistas make the small campground an intimate treasure. Hookups are not available in either of the park's campgrounds; however, the sites are long enough to accommodate units up to 28 feet long. There are no RV dump stations in the park. Bureau of Land Management (BLM) campgrounds between Moab and Monticello take a bit of a drive to get to but the solitude and privacy may be worth it. There are fewer opportunities for camping once you are in Monticello and Blanding. The best place to camp near Bluff is Sand Island Campground, 2 mi south of town.

For dining and lodging in Moab, ⇨ Where to Stay & Eat *in* Arches National Park, chapter 4.

## Where to Eat

### In the Park

PICNIC AREAS **Grand View Point.** Stopping here for a picnic lunch might be one of your more memorable vacation events. It's a gorgeous spot in which to recharge your energy and stretch your legs. There are picnic tables, grills, restrooms, and a little shade, if you sit near a juniper or pinyon. ⊠ *12 mi from park entrance on the main road, Island in the Sky.*

**Needles District Picnic Area.** The most convenient picnic spot in the Needles District is a sunny location right near the roadway. There is one picnic table, but there are no grills, restrooms, water, or other amenities. ⊠ *About 5 mi from the park visitor center, Needles.*

**Upheaval Dome.** Charming is a word that comes to mind to describe this picnic area nestled among the pinyon and juniper trees at the trailhead. There are no real vistas here, but the location is convenient to the Syncline Loop and Upheaval Dome trails. Amenities consist of picnic tables, grills, and restrooms without running water. ⊠ *11 mi from the park entrance on Upheaval Dome Rd., Island in the Sky.*

### Outside the Park

$$ ✕ **Cow Canyon Trading Post.** Tiny but absolutely charming, this restaurant next to a classic trading post serves three dinner entrées daily. Meals are creative and diverse, with a touch of ethnic flair. There's usu-

ally a grilled meat with plenty of fresh vegetables, and you can enjoy beer or wine with your meal. ☒ *U.S. 191 and Rte. 163, Bluff* ☎ *435/ 672–2208. $14–$20* ▤ *AE, MC, V* ⊘ *Closed Nov.–Mar. No lunch.*

¢–$$  ✕ **Homestead Steak House.** The folks here specialize in authentic Navajo fry bread and Navajo tacos. The popular—and big!—sheepherder's sandwich, is made with the fry bread and comes with your choice of beef, turkey, or ham and all the trimmings. No alcohol is served. ☒ *121 E. Center St., Monticello* ☎ *435/678–3456. $6–$18* ▤ *AE, D, MC, V* ⊘ *No breakfast on weekends.*

## Where to Stay

### In the Park

CAMPGROUNDS &  △ **Needles Outpost.** You may need to stop here for gas, supplies, or an
RV PARKS  icy drink and good meal after hiking, and you can also camp here. This
$  privately run campground isn't as pretty or private as the others in and near Needles, but a chat with the owners will be a guaranteed hoot. ☒ *Rte. 211 about 1½ mi inside the park entrance, Needles* ☎ *435/979–4007* ⤳ *23 sites* ⚙ *Flush toilets, dump station, drinking water, showers, fire grates, food service, service station. $15* ▤ *AE, D, MC, V* ⊘ *Mid-Mar.–Oct.*

★ $  △ **Squaw Flat Campground.** Squaw Flat is one of the best campgrounds in the National Park System. The sites are spread out in two different areas, giving each site almost unparalleled privacy. Each site has a rock wall at its back, and shade trees. The sites are filled on a first-come, first-served basis. ☒ *About 5 mi from the park entrance off the main road, Needles* ☎ *435/259–7164* ⤳ *25 sites* ⚙ *Flush toilets, drinking water, fire pits, picnic tables. $10* ▤ No credit cards.

¢  △ **Willow Flat Campground.** From this little campground on a mesa top, you can walk to spectacular views of the Green River. Most sites have a bit of shade from juniper trees. To get here you have to travel down a rough, washboarded road with tight and tricky turns. Only two sites are really suitable for RVs. It is filled on a first-come, first-served basis only. ☒ *About 9 mi from the park entrance off the main park road, Island in the Sky* ☎ *435/259–4712* ⤳ *12 sites* ⚙ *Pit toilets, drinking water, fire pits, picnic tables. $5* ▤ No credit cards.

### Outside the Park

$–$$  ⊡ **Desert Rose Inn and Cabins.** Bluff's largest motel is truly a rose in the
Fodor'sChoice  desert. It's an attractive log-cabin-style structure with a front porch that
★  gives it a nostalgic touch, and all rooms are spacious and clean with uncommonly large bathrooms. The cabins have small refrigerators and microwaves. ☒ *701 W. U.S. 191, Bluff 84512* ☎ *435/672–2303 or 888/ 475–7673* 🖷 *435/672–2217* ⊕ *www.desertroseinn.com* ⤳ *30 rooms, 6 cabins.* ⚙ *Refrigerator (some), ethernet, laundry facilities. $99–$125* ▤ *AE, D, MC, V.*

$  ⊡ **Days Inn.** One of the largest properties in Monticello, this is also one of the nicest, with a heated indoor pool and a hot tub that's just what the doctor ordered for soaking adventure-weary bodies. ☒ *549 N. Main St., Box 759, Monticello 84535* ☎ *435/587–2458* 🖷 *435/587– 2191* ⤳ *43 rooms* ⚙ *Refrigerator (some), pool. $64–$82* ▤ *AE, D, DC, MC, V.*

10

**$** 🏨 **Recapture Lodge.** Known for its friendliness, this popular and region-ally famous inn runs guided tours into the surrounding canyon country and presents nightly slide shows about local geology, art, and history. The plain motel rooms offered at good prices book up fast, so be sure to call ahead for reservations. ⊠ *U.S. 191, Box 309, Bluff 84512* ☎ *435/672–2281* 🖷 *435/672–2284* 🗩 *28 rooms* ⚐ *Pool. $52–$60* ⊟ *AE, D, MC, V.*

**¢–$** 🏨 **The Monticello Inn.** Quiet and well maintained, with basic and clean rooms, this motel is a bargain. ⊠ *164 E. U.S. 491, Monticello 84535* ☎ *435/587–2274 or 800/657–6622* 🖷 *435/587–2175* 🗩 *26 rooms* ⚐ *Refrigerator, ethernet, Wi-Fi. $38–$59* ⊟ *AE, D, MC, V.*

CAMPGROUNDS &  🛆 **Bureau of Land Management Campgrounds.** There are 342 sites at 18
RV PARKS  different BLM campgrounds near Arches and Canyonlands. Most of these
**$**  are in the Moab area along the Route 128 Colorado River corridor, on Kane Creek Road, and on Sand Flats Road. *See* ⇨ Arches National Park chapter 4, Where to Stay & Eat. All sites are primitive. Campsites go on a first-come, first-served basis. They are all open year-round. Credit cards are not accepted. ☎ *435/259–6111* ⊕ *www.blm.gov/utah/moab.*

🛆 **Hatch Point Campground.** If it's solitude you're looking for and you're not concerned with convenience (to get here you have to drive 32 mi south of Moab on U.S. 191, then 24 mi more on a road that includes 9 mi of gravel), this out-of-the-way place might have your name on it. You're within short walks or drives of stunning overlooks into Canyonlands' Needles District. Red and white slickrock will be the view from your site and pinyon or juniper will provide your shade. There's no water November–mid-April. ⊠ *24 mi west of U.S. 191 from the Canyon Rims turnoff* 🗩 *10 sites* ⚐ *Pit toilets, drinking water. $10.*

🛆 **Sand Island Campground.** The special charm of this campground is its proximity to the San Juan River. You'll also be surrounded by giant cottonwood trees. ⊠ *3 mi west of Bluff on U.S. 191* 🗩 *27 sites* ⚐ *Pit toilets, drinking water, fire grates, picnic tables. $10.*

🛆 **Wind Whistle Campground.** Close to the Needles District of Canyonlands, this small campground is tucked into a pinyon and juniper forest amid red rocks. Tight turns on the access road make this a less-than-ideal destination for RVs. There's no water November–mid-April. ⊠ *6 mi west of the Canyon Rims turnoff from U.S. 191* 🗩 *17 sites* ⚐ *Pit toilets, drinking water. $10.*

★ **$** 🛆 **Dead Horse Point State Park.** A favorite of almost everyone who has ever camped here, either in RVs or tents, this mesa-top campground fills up a little later in the day than the national park campgrounds. It's impressively set near the edge of a 2,000-foot cliff above the Colorado River. If you want to pay for your stay with a credit card you must do so during business hours (8–6 daily); otherwise you must pay in cash. ⊠ *Rte. 313, 18 mi off U.S. 191 (right outside the entrance to Canyonlands National Park)* ☎ *435/259–2614, 800/322–3770 reservations* ⊕ *www. stateparks.utah.gov* 🗩 *21 sites* ⚐ *Flush toilets, dump station, drinking water, picnic tables, public telephone, ranger station. $15 (plus $7 park entrance fee)* ⊟ *MC, V.*

# CANYONLANDS ESSENTIALS

ACCESSIBILITY There are currently no trails in Canyonlands that are accessible to people in wheelchairs, but Grand View Point and Buck Canyon Overlook at Island in the Sky are wheelchair accessible. The visitor centers at the Island in the Sky and Needles districts are also accessible, and the park's pit toilets are accessible with some assistance.

ADMISSION FEES Admission is $10 per vehicle and $5 per person on foot, motorcycle, or bicycle, good for seven days. Your Canyonlands pass is good for all the park's districts. There's no entrance fee to the Maze District of Canyonlands. A $25 local park pass grants you admission to both Arches and Canyonlands for one year.

ADMISSION HOURS Canyonlands National Park is open 24 hours a day, seven days a week, year-round. It is in the Mountain time zone.

ATMs/Banks The park has no ATM. **Wells Fargo Bank** ⊠ 4 N. Main St., Moab ⊠ 16 S. Main St., Monticello. **Zions Bank** ⊠ 300 S. Main St., Moab.

AUTOMOBILE SERVICE STATIONS **Car Care Center** does repairs. ⊠ 217 N. Main St., Monticello ☎ 435/678-3705. **Out West Food & Fuel** has fuel only, no repairs. ⊠ 17 N. Main St., Monticello ☎ 435/587-2555.

EMERGENCIES In the event of a fire or a medical emergency, dial 911 or contact a park ranger. There are no first-aid stations in the park; report to the visitor center for assistance. The closest hospitals are in Moab and Monticello. To reach law enforcement, dial 911 or contact a park ranger (at the visitor center during operating hours).

LOST AND FOUND For lost-and-found, stop by a visitor center.

PERMITS You need a permit for overnight backpacking, four-wheel-drive camping,

mountain-bike camping, four-wheel-drive day use in Horse and Lavender canyons (Needles District), and river trips. You can get information on the Canyonlands reservation and permit system by visiting the park's Web site at ⊕ www.nps.gov/cany or by calling the reservations office at ☎ 435/259-4351.

POST OFFICES There is no postal service at the park. **Moab Branch Post Office** ⊠ 50 E. 100 N, Moab ☎ 435/259-7427. **Monticello Branch Post Office** ⊠ 197 S. Main St., Monticello ☎ 435/587-2294.

PUBLIC TELEPHONES You can find public telephones at the park's visitor centers, as well as at Hans Flat Ranger Station in the Maze District. Cell-phone reception may be available in some parts of the park, but not reliably so.

RELIGIOUS SERVICES There are no chapel or other religious services in the park.

RESTROOMS In Island in the Sky, public restrooms are at the visitor center, Willow Flat Campground, Grand View Point, and Upheaval Dome trailhead. In the Needles District, you can find facilities at the visitor center, Squaw Flat Campground, and Big Spring Canyon Overlook Trail. In the Maze, the Hans Flat Ranger Station has restrooms, and at Horseshoe Canyon you can find relief at the trailhead. The only flush toilet is at the Needles Visitor Center; the rest are vault toilets.

Shops & Grocers Needles Outpost, just outside the park boundary, is the place to get basic groceries and camping supplies—but it won't likely have everything you need. **Blue Mountain Foods** ⊠ 64 W. Central, Monticello ☎ 435/587-2451. **Needles Outpost** ⊠ Rte. 211 about 1½ mi inside the park entrance, Needles ☎ 435/979-4007.

**10**

**NEARBY TOWN INFORMATION**
🛈 Blanding Chamber of Commerce ✉ Box 792, Blanding 84511 ☎ 435/678-2791 or 800/574-4386 ⊕ www.blandingutah.org. **Blanding Visitor Center** ✉ N. U.S. 191, Blanding 84511 ☎ 435/678-3662. **San Juan County Community Development and Visitor Services (Bluff and Monticello)** ✉ 117 S. Main St., Box 490, Monti-cello 84535 ☎ 435/587-3235 or 800/574-4386 ⊕ www.canyonlands-utah.com.

**VISITOR INFORMATION**
🛈 **Canyonlands National Park** ✉ 2282 W. Re-source Blvd., Moab, UT 84532 ☎ 435/719-2313, 435/259-4351 Backcountry Reservation Office ⊕ www.nps.gov/cany.

# Capitol Reef National Park

Devil's Garden in Capitol Reef National Park

**WORD OF MOUTH**

"The colors are such as no pigments can portray. So luminous are they that the light seems to flow or shine out of the rock rather than to be reflected from it."

–Clarence Dutton, 19th-century geologist

# WELCOME TO CAPITOL REEF

Gifford Farmhouse in Fruita

## TOP REASONS TO GO

★ **The Waterpocket Fold:** See an excellent example of a monocline—a fold in the Earth's crust with one very steep side in an area that is otherwise horizontal. This one's almost 100-mi long.

★ **No crowds:** Experience the best of Southern Utah weather, rock formations, and wide-open spaces without the crowds of nearby parks such as Zion and Bryce Canyon.

★ **Fresh fruit:** Pick apples, pears, apricots, and peaches in season at the pioneer-planted orchards at historic Fruita. These trees still produce plenty of fruit.

★ **Rock art:** View ancient pictographs and petroglyphs left by the Fremont people, who lived in this area from 700 to 1300 AD.

★ **Pioneer artifacts:** Buy faithfully reproduced tools and utensils like those used by Mormon pioneers, at the Gifford Homestead.

Chimney Rock

**1 Fruita.** This historic pioneer village is at the heart of what most people see of Capitol Reef. The one and only park visitor center nearby is the place to get maps, and travel and weather information. The scenic drive through Capitol Gorge provides a view of the Golden Throne.

**2 Cathedral Valley.** The views are stunning and the silence deafening in the park's remote northern section. High-clearance vehicles are required, as is a crossing of the Fremont River. Driving in this valley is next to impossible when the Cathedral Valley Road is wet, so ask at the visitor center about current weather and road conditions.

**3 Muley Twist Canyon.** At the southern reaches of the park, this canyon is accessed via Notom-Bullfrog Road from the north, and Burr Trail Road from the west and southeast. High-clearance vehicles are required for much of it.

## GETTING ORIENTED

At the heart of this 378-square-mi park is the massive natural feature known as the Waterpocket Fold, which runs roughly northwest to southeast along the park's spine. Capitol Reef itself is named for a formation along the fold near the Fremont River. A historic pioneer settlement, the green oasis of Fruita is easily accessed by car, and a 9-mi scenic drive provides a good overview of the canyons and rock formations that populate the park. Colors here range from deep, rich reds to sage greens to crumbling gray sediments. The absence of large towns nearby ensures that night skies are brilliant starscapes.

Springtime blossoms

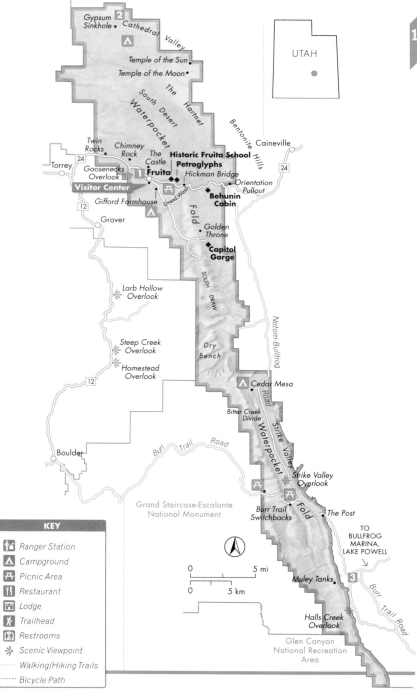

UTAH

Gypsum Sinkhole • 2 Cathedral Valley

Temple of the Sun •

Temple of the Moon •

The Hartnet

South Desert Waterpocket

Bentonite Hills

Caineville

24

Twin Rocks •

Chimney Rock •

The Castle •

Historic Fruita School Petroglyphs

Torrey

24

Goosenecks Overlook

1 Fruita

Hickman Bridge •

Orientation Pullout

Visitor Center

Behunin Cabin

Grand Wash

Fold

12

Gifford Farmhouse

Golden Throne •

Grover

Capitol Gorge

SOUTH DRAW

Larb Hollow Overlook

Steep Creek Overlook

Dry Bench

12

Homestead Overlook

Cedar Mesa

Notom-Bullfrog

Bitter Creek Divide

Waterpocket

Strike Valley Overlook

Boulder

Burr Trail Road

The Post

Strike Valley Fold

Burr Trail Switchbacks

TO BULLFROG MARINA, LAKE POWELL

Grand Staircase-Escalante National Monument

Muley Tanks

3

Burr Trail Road

Halls Creek Overlook

Glen Canyon National Recreation Area

**KEY**

🧍 Ranger Station

⛺ Campground

🏕 Picnic Area

🍴 Restaurant

🏨 Lodge

🥾 Trailhead

🚻 Restrooms

⚹ Scenic Viewpoint

····· Walking/Hiking Trails

······ Bicycle Path

0 — 5 mi

0 — 5 km

# CAPITOL REEF PLANNER

## When to Go

**Spring and early summer bring the most visitors to the park.** Folks clear out in the height of summer as temperatures reach the mid-90s, and then early fall brings people back to the park for the apple harvest and crisp autumn temperatures. Still, the park could seldom be called crowded—though the campground does fill daily throughout spring, summer, and fall. Trails remain fairly unpopulated year-round, perhaps because of the difficult nature of many of them. You're not bound to get wet, since annual rainfall is only about 7 inches. When it does rain, devastating flash floods can wipe out park roads and leave you stranded. Snowfall is usually light, especially at lower elevations.

Spring is undoubtedly one of the most beautiful times to visit this region, but weather can be unpredictable, and sudden, short-lived snowstorms are not uncommon. Although summer days can be uncomfortably hot and winter storms potentially fierce, central Utah has a generally moderate climate with four distinct seasons.

AVG. HIGH/LOW TEMPS.

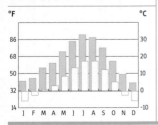

## Flora & Fauna

The golden rock and rainbow cliffs are at their finest at sunset, when it seems as if they are lighted from within. That's also when mule deer wander through the orchards near the campground. The deer are quite tame, but do not feed them; their digestive systems are harmed by people food. Many of the park's animals move about only at night to escape the heat of the day, but pinyon jays and black-billed magpies flit around the park all day. The best place to see wildlife is near the Fremont River, where animals are drawn to drink. Ducks and small mammals such as the yellow-bellied marmot live nearby. Desert bighorn sheep also live in Capitol Reef, but they are elusive. Your best chance of spotting the sheep is during a long hike deep within the park. If you should encounter a sheep, do not approach it, as they've been known to charge human beings.

## Getting There & Around

Though far from big cities, there are a variety of approaches to Capitol Reef country. The main high-speed arteries through the region are Interstates 70 and 15, but any route will require travel of some secondary roads such as U.S. 50, U.S. 89, Highway 24, or Route 72. All are well-maintained, safe roads that bisect rich agricultural communities steeped in Mormon history (such as the nearby towns of Bicknell and Loa). Interstate 15 is the fastest way through central Utah, but U.S. 89 and the local roads that feed onto it will give you a more direct path into Utah's past and present-day character. Highway 24 runs across the middle of Capitol Reef National Park, so even those traveling between points west and east of the park with no intention of touring the park get a scenic treat on their way. Once inside the park, there is no shuttle service like at nearby Zion and Bryce Canyon national parks.

11

By John
Blodgett

Your senses will be delighted by a visit to Capitol Reef National Park. Here, you are saturated in colors that are more dramatic than anywhere else in the West. The dominant Moenkopi rock formation is a rich, red-chocolate hue. Deep blue-green juniper and pinyon stand out against it. Other sandstone layers are gold, ivory, and lavender. Sunset brings out the colors in an explosion of copper, platinum, and orange, then dusk turns the cliffs purple and blue. The texture of rock deposited in ancient inland seas and worn by subsequent erosion is pure art.

The park preserves the Waterpocket Fold, a giant wrinkle in the earth that extends a hundred miles between Thousand Lake Mountain and Lake Powell. When you climb high onto the rocks or into the mountains, you can see this remarkable geologic wonder and the jumble of colorful cliffs, massive domes, soaring spires, and twisting canyons that surround it. It's no wonder Native Americans called this part of the country the "land of sleeping rainbow."

But your eyes will not be alone in their joy. The fragrance of pine and sage rises from the earth, and canyon wrens sing to you as you sit by the water. Flowing across the heart of Capitol Reef is the Fremont River, a narrow little creek that can turn into a swollen, raging torrent during desert flash floods. The river sustains cottonwoods, wildlife, and verdant valleys rich with fruit. During the harvest, your sensory experience is complete when you bite into a perfect ripe peach or apple from the park's orchards. Your soul, too, will be gratified here. You can walk the trails in relative solitude and enjoy the beauty without confronting crowds on the roads or paths. All around you are signs of those who came before: ancient Native Americans of the Fremont culture, Mormon pioneers who settled the land, and other courageous explorers who traveled the canyons. It is a rare thrill to feel the past overtake the present.

## CAPITOL REEF IN ONE DAY

Pack a picnic lunch, snacks, and cold drinks to take with you, because there are no restaurants in the park. As you enter the park, look to your left for Chimney Rock; in a landscape of spires, cliffs, and knobs, this deep-red landmark is unmistakable. Start your journey at the **visitor center**, where you can study a three-dimensional map of the area, watch the short slide show, and browse the many books and maps related to the park. Then head for the park's scenic drive, stopping at the **Fruita Historic District** to see some of the sites associated with the park's Mormon history. Stop at the **Historic Gifford Farmhouse** for a tour and a visit to the gift shop. As you continue on with your tour, check out the **Fremont Indian Petroglyphs,** and if you feel like some exertion, take a hike on the Hickman Bridge Trail. From the trail (or if you skip the hike, from Highway 24 about 2 mi east of the visitor center), you'll see **Capitol Dome.** Along this stretch of Highway 24 stop to see the old **Fruita School House,** the **petroglyphs,** and the **Behunin Cabin.** Next you'll have to backtrack a few miles on Highway 24 to find the **Goosenecks Trail.** At the same parking lot you'll find the trailhead for **Sunset Point Trail;** take this short hike in time to watch the setting sun hit the colorful cliffs.

## Scenic Drive

**Capitol Reef Scenic Drive.** This paved road starts at the visitor center and winds its way through the Fruita Historic District and colorful sandstone cliffs into Capitol Gorge; a side street, Grand Wash Road, provides access into the canyon. At Capitol Gorge, the route becomes unpaved, and road conditions may vary because of weather and amount of use. Check with the visitor center before entering Capitol Gorge. Capitol Reef Scenic Drive, called simply Scenic Drive by locals, is 9 mi long, with about the last quarter of it unpaved.

*See* ⇨ Four-Wheeling in the Sports & the Outdoors section for the **Cathedral Valley Scenic Backway** drive.

## What to See

### Historic Sites

★ ☾ **Fruita Historic District.** In 1880 Nels Johnson became the first homesteader in the Fremont River Valley, building his home near the confluence of Sulphur Creek and the Fremont River. Other Mormon settlers followed and established small farms and orchards near the confluence, creating the village of Junction. The orchards thrived, and in 1902 the settlement's name was changed to Fruita. The orchards are preserved and protected as a Rural Historic Landscape.

An old **blacksmith shop** (⊠ Scenic Dr., less than 1 mi south of visitor center) exhibits tools, farm machinery and harnesses dating from the late 1800s, and Fruita's first tractor.

**Pioneer Register.** Travelers passing through Capitol Gorge in the 19th and early 20th centuries etched the canyon wall with their names and the date they passed. Across the canyon from the Pioneer Register and about 50 feet up are signatures etched into the wall by an early United States Geologic Survey crew. It's illegal to write or scratch on the canyon walls today. You can reach the register via an easy 1-mi hike from the end of the road. ⊠ *Off Scenic Dr., 9 mi south of the visitor center.*

## Scenic Stops

**Capitol Gorge.** At the entrance to this gorge Scenic Drive becomes unpaved. The narrow, twisting road on the floor of the gorge was a route for pioneer wagons traversing this part of Utah starting in the 1860s. After every flash flood, pioneers would laboriously clear the route so wagons could continue to go through. The gorge became the main automobile route in the area until 1962, when Highway 24 was built. The short drive to the end of the road leads to some interesting hiking trails. ⊠ *Scenic Dr., 9 mi south of the visitor center.*

**Chimney Rock.** Even in a landscape of spires, cliffs, and knobs, this deep-red landform is unmistakable. ⊠ *Hwy. 24, about 3 mi west of the visitor center.*

☻ **Fremont Indian Petroglyphs.** Nearly 1,000 years ago the Capitol Reef area was occupied by the Fremont Indians, whose culture was tied closely to the ancestral Puebloan culture. Fremont rock art can be identified by the large trapezoidal figures often depicted wearing headdresses and ear baubles. ⊠ *Hwy. 24, 1²/₁₀ mi east of the visitor center.*

**The Waterpocket Fold.** A giant wrinkle in the earth that extends almost 100 mi between Thousand Lake Mountain and Lake Powell, the Waterpocket Fold is not to be missed. You can glimpse the fold by driving south on Scenic Drive—after it branches off Highway 24—past the Fruita Historic District, but for complete immersion enter the park via the 66-mi Burr Trail from the town of Boulder. Travel through the southernmost reaches of the park requires a substantial amount of driving on unpaved roads. It's accessible to most vehicles during dry weather; check at the visitor center for road conditions and recommendations.

## Visitor Center

Watch a film, talk with rangers, or peruse the many books, maps, and materials offered for sale in the bookstore. Towering over the center is the Castle, one of the park's most prominent rock formations. ⊠ *Hwy. 24, 11 mi east of Torrey* ☎ *435/425–3791* ☉ *May–Sept., daily 8–6; Oct. and mid-Apr.–May, daily 8–5; Nov.–mid-Apr., daily 8–4:30.*

# Sports & the Outdoors

The main outdoor activity at Capitol Reef is hiking. There are trails for all levels. Remember: whenever you venture into the desert—that is, wherever you go in Capitol Reef—take, and drink, plenty of water.

## Bicycling

Bicycles are allowed only on established roads in the park. Since Highway 24 is a state highway and receives a substantial amount of through traffic, it's not the best place to pedal. Scenic Drive is better, but the road is narrow, and you have to contend with drivers dazed by the beautiful surroundings. Four-wheel-drive roads are certainly less traveled, but they are often sandy, rocky, and steep. You cannot ride your bicycle in washes or on hiking trails. ⇨ Multisport Outfitters & Expeditions box.

**Cathedral Valley Scenic Backway.** In the remote northern end of the park you can enjoy solitude and a true backcountry ride on this trail. You'll be riding on surfaces that include dirt, sand, bentonite clay, and rock, and you will also ford the Fremont River; you should be prepared to encounter steep hills and switchbacks, wash crossings, and stretches of deep sand. Summer is not a good time to try this ride, as water is very difficult to find and temperatures may exceed 100°F. The entire route is about 60 mi long; during a multiday trip you can camp at the primitive campground with five sites, about midway through the loop. ✉ *Off Hwy. 24 at Caineville, or at River Ford Rd., 5 mi west of Caineville on Hwy. 24.*

**South Draw Road.** This is a very strenuous ride that traverses dirt, sand, and rocky surfaces, and crosses several creeks that may be muddy. It's not recommended in winter or spring because of deep snow at higher elevations. If you like fast downhill rides, though, this trip is for you—it will make you feel like you have wings. The route starts at an elevation of 8,500 feet on Boulder Mountain and ends 15 mi later at 5,500 feet in the Pleasant Creek parking area at Scenic Drive's end. ✉ *At the junction of Bowns Reservoir Rd. and Hwy. 12, 13 mi south of Torrey.*

## Four-Wheeling

You can explore Capitol Reef in a 4×4 on a number of exciting backcountry routes. Road conditions can vary greatly depending on recent weather patterns. Spring and summer rains can leave the roads muddy, washed out, and impassable even to four-wheel-drive vehicles. Always check at the park visitor center for current conditions before you set out, and take water, supplies, and a cell phone with you. ⇨ Multisport Outfitters & Expeditions box for guided four-wheeling trips.

**Cathedral Valley Scenic Backway.** The north end of Capitol Reef, along this backcountry road, is filled with towering monoliths, panoramic vistas, and a stark desert landscape. The area is remote and the road through it unpaved, so do not enter without a high-clearance vehicle, some planning, and a cell phone. The drive through the valley is a 58-mi loop that you can begin at River Ford Road off Highway 24. From there, the loop travels northwest, giving you access to Glass Mountain, South Desert, and Gypsum Sinkhole. Turning southeast at the sinkhole, the loop takes you past the side road that accesses the Temples of the Moon and Sun, then becomes Caineville Wash Road before ending at Highway 24, 7 mi east of your starting point. Caineville Wash Road has two water crossings. Including stops, allow a half day for this drive. ■ TIP➔ **If your time is limited, you may want to tour only the Caineville Wash Road, which takes about two hours.** At the visitor center you can check for road conditions and pick up a self-guided auto tour brochure for $1. ✉ *River Ford Rd., 11⁷⁄₁₀ mi east of visitor center on Hwy. 24.*

### DID YOU KNOW?

With its amazing rock structures, Southern Utah is like walking into an episode of the Flintstones. Arches—such as Metate Arch in Grand Staircase-Escalante National Monument (shown here)—develop when wind, sand, and water wear away the sandstone surface.

## Hiking

Many park trails include steep climbs, but there are a few easy-to-moderate hikes. A short drive from the visitor center takes you to a dozen trails, and a park ranger can advise you on combining trails or locating additional routes. ⇨ Multisport Outfitters & Expeditions box for hiking trips.

EASY **Goosenecks Trail.** This nice little walk gives you a good introduction to the land surrounding Capitol Reef. You'll enjoy the dizzying views from the overlook. It's only ²⁄₁₀ mi round-trip. ✉ *Hwy. 24, about 3 mi west of the visitor center.*

**Grand Wash Trail.** At the end of unpaved Grand Wash Road you can continue on foot through the canyon to its end at the Fremont River. You're bound to love the trip. This flat hike takes you through a wide wash between canyon walls. It's an excellent place to study the geology up close. The round-trip hike is 4½ mi; allow two to three hours for your walk. Check at the ranger station for flash-flood warnings before entering the wash. ✉ *Hwy. 24, east of Hickman Bridge parking lot, or at end of Grand Wash Rd., off Scenic Dr. about 5 mi from visitor center.*

> ### GEOLOGY BEHIND THE PARK'S NAME
>
> When water wears away layers of sandstone, basins can appear in the rock. These are called waterpockets. The 100-mi-long Waterpocket Fold—a massive rift in the Earth's crust, where geothermal pressure pushed one side 7,000 feet higher than the other—is full of these waterpockets. Early explorers with seafaring backgrounds called the fold a reef, since it was a barrier to travel. Some of the rocks, due to erosion, also have dome-like formations resembling capitol rotundas.

**Sunset Point Trail.** The trail starts from the same parking lot as the Goosenecks Trail. Benches along this easy, ⁷⁄₁₀-mi round-trip invite you to sit and meditate surrounded by the colorful desert. At the trail's end, you will be rewarded with broad vistas into the park; it's even better at sunset. ✉ *Hwy. 24, about 3 mi west of visitor center.*

MODERATE **Capitol Gorge Trail and the Tanks.** Starting at the Pioneer Register, about
★ a mile from the Capitol Gorge parking lot, is a trail that climbs to the Tanks. After a scramble up about ²⁄₁₀ mi of steep trail with cliff dropoffs, you can look down into the Tanks and can also see a natural bridge below the lower tank. Including the walk to the Pioneer Register, allow an hour or two for this interesting little hike. ✉ *At end of Scenic Dr., 9 mi south of visitor center.*

🐾 **Cohab Canyon Trail.** Children particularly love this trail for the geological features and native creatures, such as rock wrens and Western pipistrelles (canyon bats), that you see along the way. One end of the trail is directly across from the Fruita Campground on Scenic Drive, and the other is across from the Hickman Bridge parking lot. The first ¼ mi from Fruita is pretty strenuous, but then the walk becomes easy except for turnoffs to the overlooks, which are strenuous but short. Along the way you'll find miniature arches, skinny side canyons, and honeycombed patterns on canyon walls where the wrens make nests. The trail is 3²⁄₁₀ mi round-trip to the Hick-

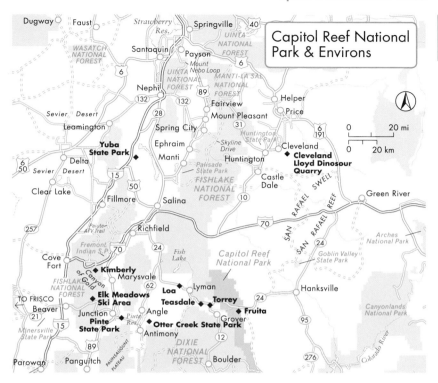

**Capitol Reef National Park & Environs**

man Bridge parking lot. The Overlook Trail adds 2 mi to the journey. Allow one to two hours to overlooks and back; allow two to three hours to Hickman Bridge parking lot and back. ⊠ *About 1 mi south of visitor center on Scenic Dr., or about 2 mi east of visitor center on Hwy. 24.*

**Fremont River Trail.** What starts as a quiet little stroll beside the river turns into an adventure. The first ½ mi of the trail is wheelchair accessible as you wander past the orchards next to the Fremont River. After you pass through a narrow gate, the trail changes personality and you're in for a steep climb on an exposed ledge with drop-offs. The views at the top of the 770-foot ascent are worth it as you look down into the Fruita Historic District. The trail is 2½ mi round-trip; allow two hours. ⊠ *Near amphitheater off Loop C of Fruita Campground, about 1 mi from visitor center.*

**Golden Throne Trail.** As you hike to the base of the Golden Throne, you may be fortunate enough to see one of the park's elusive desert bighorn sheep. You're more likely, however, to spot their small, split-hoof tracks in the sand. The trail itself is 2 mi of gradual elevation gain with some steps and drop-offs. The Golden Throne is hidden until you near the end of the trail, then suddenly you find yourself looking at a huge sandstone monolith. If you hike near sundown the throne burns gold, salmon, and platinum. The round-trip hike is 4 mi and you should allow two to

## MULTISPORT OUTFITTERS & EXPEDITIONS

**Hondoo Rivers & Trails.** Fast gaining a reputation for high-quality, educational trips into the backcountry of Capitol Reef National Park, these folks pride themselves on delivering a unique, private experience. From May to October, the company offers adventures on horseback, on foot, or via four-wheel-drive vehicle in Capitol Reef and the mountains and deserts surrounding it. Trips are designed to explore geologic landforms, seek out wildflowers in season, and to encounter free-roaming mustangs, bison, and bighorn sheep when possible. Single- or multiday trips can be arranged. ⊠ *90 E. Main St., Torrey* ☎ *435/425–3519 or 800/332–2696* ⊕ *www.hondoo.com.*

**Wild Hare Expeditions.** For a real taste of Capitol Reef backcountry, take a hiking, biking, or 4×4 expedition with this enthusiastic outfitter. Guides will teach you more in one fun day about geology, wildlife, and land ethics than you thought possible. ⊠ *116 W. Main St., Torrey* ☎ *435/425–3999 or 888/ 304–4273.*

three hours. ⊠ *At end of Capitol Gorge Rd., at Capitol Gorge trailhead, 9 mi south of visitor center.*

Fodor'sChoice
★

**Hickman Bridge Trail.** This trail is a perfect introduction to the park. It leads to a natural bridge of Kayenta sandstone, which has a 135-foot opening carved by intermittent flash floods. Early on, the route climbs a set of steps along the Fremont River, and as the trail tops out onto a bench, you'll find a slight depression in the earth. This is what remains of an ancient Fremont pit house, a kind of home that was dug into the ground and covered with brush. The trail splits, leading along the right-hand branch to a strenuous uphill climb to the Rim Overlook and Navajo Knobs. Stay to your left to see the bridge, and you'll encounter a moderate up-and-down trail. As you continue up the wash on your way to the bridge, you'll notice a Fremont granary on the right side of the small canyon. Allow about 1½ hours to walk the 2-mi round-trip. The walk to the bridge is one of the most popular trails in the park, so expect lots of company along the way. ⊠ *Hwy. 24, 2 mi east of visitor center.*

DIFFICULT

**Chimney Rock Trail.** You're almost sure to see ravens drifting on thermal winds around the deep red Mummy Cliff that rings the base of this trail. This loop trail begins with a steep climb to a rim above Chimney Rock. The trail is 3½ mi round-trip, with a 600-foot elevation change. Allow three to four hours. ⊠ *Hwy. 24, about 3 mi west of visitor center.*

### Horseback Riding

Many areas in the park are closed to horses and pack animals, so it's a good idea to check with the visitor center before you set out with your animals. Day use does not require a permit, but you need to get one for overnight camping with horses and pack animals. Hondoo Rivers & Trails and Wild Hare Expeditions run horseback tours into the national park. ⇨ Multisport Outfitters & Expeditions box. Unless you ride with a park-licensed outfitter, you have to bring your own horse, as no rentals are available.

## Educational Offerings

### Ranger Programs

From May to September, ranger programs, including guided walks and talks as well as evening programs in the Fruita Campground amphitheater, are offered at no charge. You can obtain current information about park events at the visitor center or campground bulletin boards.

**Evening Program.** Learn about Capitol Reef's geology, Native American cultures, wildlife, and more at a free lecture, slide show, or other ranger-led activities. A schedule of programs is offered from May to September nightly, ½ hour after sunset. A schedule of topics and times is posted at the visitor center. ⊠ *Amphitheater, Loop C, Fruita Campground, about 1 mi from visitor center on Scenic Dr.* ☎ *435/425–3791.*

**Junior Ranger Program.** Each child who participates in this self-guided program completes a combination of activities in the Junior Ranger booklet, attends a ranger program, interviews a park ranger, and/or picks up litter. ⊠ *At the visitor center* ☎ *435/425–3791* ⊠ *$1.50.*

**Ranger Talks.** Each day at the visitor center rangers give brief talks on park geology. Times change, so check at the center for a current schedule. ⊠ *At the visitor center* ☎ *435/425–3791* ⊠ *Free* ⊙ *May–Sept., daily.*

# WHAT'S NEARBY

## Nearby Towns & Attractions

### Nearby Towns

Probably the best home base for exploring the park, the pretty town of **Torrey,** just outside the park, has lots of personality. Giant old cottonwood trees make it a shady, cool place to stay, and the townspeople are friendly and accommodating. A little farther west on Highway 24, tiny **Teasdale** is a charming settlement cradled in a cove of the Aquarius Plateau. **Bicknell** lies another few miles west of Capitol Reef. Not much happens here, making it a wonderfully quiet place to rest your head. The Wayne County seat of **Loa,** 10 mi west of Torrey, was settled by pioneers in the 1870s. If you head south from Torrey instead of west, you can take a spectacular 32-mi drive along Highway 12 to **Boulder,** a town so remote that its mail was carried on horseback until 1940. Nearby is Anasazi State Park. In the opposite direction, 51 mi east, is **Hanksville,** more a crossroads than anything else.

### Nearby Attractions

**Anasazi State Park.** Anasazi is a Navajo word interpreted to mean "ancient enemies." What the Anasazi called themselves we don't know, but their descendants, the Hopi people, prefer the term ancestral Puebloan. This state park is dedicated to the study of that mysterious culture, with a largely unexcavated dwelling site, an interactive museum, and a reproduction of a pueblo. ⊠ *460 N. Hwy. 12, Boulder* ☎ *435/335–7308*

---

## GOOD READS

**Capitol Reef: Canyon Country Eden** by Rose Houk is an award-winning collection of photographs and lyrical essays on the park.

**Dwellers of the Rainbow, Fremont Culture in Capitol Reef National Park** by Rose Houk offers a brief background of the Fremont culture in Capitol Reef.

**Explore Capitol Reef Trails** by Marjorie Miller and John Foster is a comprehensive hiking guide.

**Geology of Capitol Reef National Park** by Michael Collier teaches the basic geology of the park.

**Red Rock Eden** by George Davidson tells the story of historic Fruita, its settlements, and orchards.

---

⊕ *www.stateparks.utah.gov* ✉ *$3 per person* ☉ *Memorial Day–Labor Day, daily 8–6; Labor Day–Memorial Day, daily 9–5.*

↺ **Goblin Valley State Park.** All of the landscape in this part of the country is strange and surreal, but Goblin Valley takes the cake as the weirdest of all. It's full of hundreds of gnome-like rock formations colored in a dramatic orange hue. Short, easy trails wind through the goblins, which delight children. ✉ *Hwy. 24, 12 mi north of Hanksville* ☎ *435/564–3633* ⊕ *www.stateparks.utah.gov* ✉ *$6 per vehicle* ☉ *Daily 8 AM–sunset.*

**San Rafael Swell.** About 80 mi long and 30 mi wide, this massive fold and uplift in the Earth's crust rises 2,100 feet above the desert. The Swell, as it is known locally, is northeast of Capitol Reef, between Interstate 70 and Highway 24. You can take photos from several viewpoints. ✉ *BLM San Rafael Resource Area, 900 North and 700 East, Price* ☎ *435/637–4584.*

---

# Area Activities

## Sports & the Outdoors

FISHING   Sitting at an elevation of 8,800 feet is Fish Lake, which lies in the heart of its namesake, 1.4-million-acre **Fishlake National Forest**. The area has several campgrounds and wonderful lodges. The lake is stocked annually with lake and rainbow trout, mackinaw, and splake. A large population of brown trout are native to the lake. The Fremont River Ranger District office can provide all the information you need on camping, fishing, and hiking in the forest. *Fremont River Ranger District office* ✉ *138 S. Main St., Loa* ☎ *435/836–2811* ⊕ *www.fs.fed.us/r4/fishlake.*

**Boulder Mountain Adventures & Alpine Angler's Flyshop.** This outfitter has a stellar reputation for personalized attention during fly-fishing trips into the high backcountry around Capitol Reef, as well as 4×4 and horseback tours. ✉ *310 W. Main St., Torrey* ☎ *435/425–3660 or 888/484–3331* ⊕ *www.fly-fishing-utah.net.*

## Arts & Entertainment

The **Robbers' Roost** ( ✉ 185 W. Main St., Torrey ☎ 435/425–3265) is part coffee bar, part bookstore, and part performance space, all contained in the late Utah writer Ward Roylance's practically pyramid-shape house. The Roost, whose name comes from Butch Cassidy's hidecut region, is an excellent place to stop to browse, talk about trails, or find out what's going on around town.

ART GALLERIES   The pleasing **Gallery 24** (✉ 135 E. Main St., Torrey ☎ 435/425–2124) sells contemporary fine art from Utah-based artists that includes sculpture, handcrafted furniture, folk art, photography, and ceramics.

## Shopping

Unique and unexpected, the nifty **Flute Shop** (✉ 2650 S. Hwy. 12, 4 mi south of junction of Hwy. 12 and Hwy. 24 ☎ 435/425–3144) is open year-round and sells Native American-style flutes and gifts.

## Scenic Drives

★ **Burr Trail Scenic Backway.** Branching east off Highway 12 in Boulder, Burr Trail travels through the Circle Cliffs area of Grand Staircase–Escalante National Monument into Capitol Reef. The views are of backcountry canyons and gulches. The road is paved between Boulder and the eastern boundary of Capitol Reef. It leads into a hair-raising set of switchbacks—not suitable for RVs or trailers—that ascends 800 feet in ½ mi. Before attempting this route, check with the Capitol Reef Visitor Center for road conditions. From Boulder to its intersection with Notom-Bullfrog Road the route is 36 mi long.

Fodor'sChoice **Utah Scenic Byway 12.** Named as one of only 20 All-American Roads in ★ the United States by the National Scenic Byways Program, Highway 12 is not to be missed. The 32-mi stretch between Torrey and Boulder winds through alpine forests and passes vistas of some of America's most remote and wild landscape. It is not for the faint of heart or those afraid of narrow, winding mountain roads.

**Utah Scenic Byway 24.** For 62 mi between Loa and Hanksville, you'll cut right through Capitol Reef National Park. Colorful rock formations in all their hues of red, cream, pink, gold, and deep purple extend from one end of the route to the other. The closer you get to the park the more colorful the landscape becomes. The vibrant rock finally gives way to lush green hills and the mountains west of Loa.

# WHERE TO STAY & EAT

### About the Restaurants

There is not even a snack bar within Capitol Reef, but dining options exist close by in Torrey, where you can find everything from one of Utah's best restaurants serving high-end Southwestern cuisine to basic hamburger joints offering up consistently good food.

### About the Hotels

There are no lodging options within Capitol Reef, but you'll have no problem finding clean and comfortable accommodations no matter what your budget in nearby Torrey and not far beyond in Bicknell and Loa. Drive farther into the region's towns, and you are more likely to find locally owned low- to moderate-price motels and a few nice bed-and-breakfasts. Reservations are recommended in summer.

### About the Campgrounds

Campgrounds in Capitol Reef fill up fast between Memorial Day and Labor Day, though that goes mainly for the super-convenient Fruita Campground and not the more remote backcountry sites. Most of the area's state parks have camping facilities, and the region's two national forests offer many wonderful sites.

## Where to Eat

### In the Park

PICNIC AREA **Gifford Farmhouse.** In a grassy meadow with the Fremont River flowing by, this is an idyllic, shady spot in the Fruita Historic District for a sack lunch. Picnic tables, drinking water, grills and a convenient restroom make it perfect. ⊠ *1 mi south of visitor center on scenic Dr.*

### Outside the Park

**$$–$$$** ✕ **Cafe Diablo.** This popular Torrey restaurant keeps getting better, and
Fodor'sChoice indeed is one of the state's best. Saltillo-tile floors and matte-plaster white
★ walls are a perfect setting for the Southwestern art that lines the walls in this intimate restaurant. Innovative Southwestern entrées include fire-roasted pork tenderloin, artichoke and sun-dried tomato tamales, and local trout crusted with pumpkin seeds and served with a cilantro-lime sauce. The rattlesnake cakes, made with free-range desert rattler and served with ancho-rosemary aioli, are delicious. ⊠ *599 W. Main St. (Hwy. 24), Torrey* ☎ *435/425–3070* ⊕ *www.cafediablo.net. $17–$28* ⊟ *AE, D, MC, V* ☉ *Closed mid-Oct.–mid-Apr. No lunch.*

★ **$–$$$** ✕ **Hell's Backbone Grill.** One of the best restaurants in Southern Utah, this remote spot is worth the drive from any distance. The menu is inspired by Native American, Western Range, Southwestern, and Mormon pioneer recipes. The owners, who are also the chefs, use only fresh, organic foods that have a historical connection to the area. Because they insist on fresh foods, the menu changes weekly. ⊠ *20 N. Hwy. 12, Boulder* ☎ *435/335–7464* ⊕ *www.hellsbackbonegrill.com. $12–$22* ⊟ *AE, D, MC, V* ☉ *Closed Nov.–Mar.*

**$–$$** ✕ **Capitol Reef Café.** For standard fare that will please everyone in the family, visit this unpretentious restaurant. Favorites include the 10-vegetable salad and the flaky fillet of locally caught rainbow trout, and the breakfasts are both delicious and hearty. Numerous vegetarian offerings make for a refreshing break from beef and beans. ⊠ *360 W. Main St. (Hwy. 24), Torrey* ☎ *435/425–3271* ⊕ *www.capitolreefinn.com $10–$19* ⊟ *AE, D, MC, V* ☉ *Closed Nov.–Mar.*

**¢** ✕ **Stan's Burger Shack.** This is the traditional pit stop between Lake Powell and Capitol Reef, featuring great burgers, fries, and shakes—and the only homemade onion rings you'll find for miles and miles. ⊠ *140 S. Hwy. 95, Hanksville* ☎ *435/542–3330. $5–$7* ⊟ *AE, D, MC, V.*

---

**FAMILY PICKS**

**Anasazi State Park.** Learn how the ancestral Puebloans lived.
**Bicknell International Film Festival.** Time your visit so you can attend the opening parade.
**Goblin Valley State Park.** Play hide-and-seek among the strange orange rock formations.

## Where to Stay

### In the Park

CAMPGROUNDS & RV PARKS

FodorsChoice
★

⟨⟨ $

▲ **Fruita Campground.** Near the orchards and the Fremont River, this shady campground is a great place to call home for a few days. The sites nearest the river or the orchards are the very best. Loop C is most appropriate for RVs, although the campground has no hookups. In summer, the campground fills up early in the day. ⊠ *Scenic Dr., about 1 mi south of the visitor center* ☏ *435/425–3791* ⇌ *71 sites* ⟨ *Grills, flush toilets, drinking water, picnic tables* ⟨ *Reservations not accepted. $10* ▭ *No credit cards.*

¢ ▲ **Cathedral Valley Campground.** You'll find this primitive campground, about 30 mi from Highway 24, in the park's remote northern district. The only way here is via a high-clearance road that should not be attempted when wet. ⊠ *Hartnet Junction, on Caineville Wash Rd.* ☏ *435/425–3791* ⇌ *6 tent sites* ⟨ *Grills, pit toilets, picnic tables.* ⟨ *Reservations not accepted. Free.*

¢ ▲ **Cedar Mesa Campground.** Wonderful views of the Waterpocket Fold and Henry Mountains surround this primitive campground in the park's southern district. The road to the campground does not require a high-clearance vehicle, but it's not paved and you should not attempt to drive it if the road is wet. ⊠ *Notom-Bullfrog Rd., 22 mi south of Hwy. 24* ☏ *435/425–3791* ⇌ *5 tent sites* ⟨ *Grills, pit toilets, picnic tables.* ⟨ *Reservations not accepted. Free.*

### Outside the Park

$–$$$$

✕▦ **Fish Lake Lodge.** This large, lakeside lodge built in 1932 exudes rustic charm and character and has great views. It houses the resort's restaurant, gift shop, game room, and even a dance hall. Guests stay in cabins that sleep 2 to 18 people. The larger houses are excellent for family reunions. Some of the lodgings are quite rustic. The larger cabins are the newest, but all focus on function rather than cute amenities. The lodge, general store, and restaurant are closed from early September to late May; cabins are available year-round. An RV park also has 24 sites for $20 a night, May–October. ⊠ *HC80, Rte. 25, Loa 84701* ☏ *435/638–1000* ⊟ *435/638–1001* ⊕ *www.fishlake.com* ⇌ *45 cabins* ⟨ *Restaurant, kitchen, no TV (some), no a/c. $100–$725* ▭ *D, MC, V.*

$$–$$$$

FodorsChoice
★

▦ **Lodge at Red River Ranch.** You'll swear you've walked into one of the great lodges of Western legend when you walk through the doors at Red River Ranch. The great room is decorated with wagon-wheel chandeliers, Native American rugs, leather furniture, and original Frederick Remington sculptures. Guest rooms are meticulously and individually decorated with fine antiques and art; each has a fireplace and most have a patio or balcony overlooking the grounds. ⊠ *2900 W. Hwy. 24, Box 22, Teasdale 84773* ☏ *435/425–3322 or 800/205–6343* ⊟ *435/425–3329* ⊕ *www.redriverranch.com* ⇌ *15 rooms* ⟨ *Restaurant, no a/c, no TV, no-smoking rooms. $140–$225* ▭ *AE, DC, MC, V.*

$$–$$$

▦ **SkyRidge Bed and Breakfast.** Each of the inn's windows offers an exceptional year-round view of the desert and mountains surrounding Capitol Reef National Park. The walls are hung with the works of local artists, and unusual furniture—each piece chosen for its look and feel—makes the guest rooms and common areas both stimulating and comfortable. Breakfasts here, which might have you feasting on apple-stuffed croissants or homemade cinnamon rolls, are excellent, and you are served evening hors d'oeuvres as well. ⊠ *950 E. Hwy. 24, Box 750220, Torrey 84775* ☎ *435/425–3222 or 800/448–6990* 🖷 *435/425–3222* ⊕ *www.skyridgeinn.com* 🖅 *6 rooms* ⚒ *Restaurant, VCR, ethernet, Wi-Fi. $109–$159* ▭ *AE, MC, V.*

★ **$–$$** 🏨 **Boulder Mountain Lodge.** If you're traveling between Capitol Reef and Bryce Canyon national parks, don't miss this wonderful lodge along scenic Highway 12. A 5-acre pond on the pastoral grounds is a sanctuary for ducks, coots, and other waterfowl, and horses graze in a meadow opposite. Large, modern rooms with balconies or patios offer gorgeous views of the wetlands. The main lodge contains a great room with fireplace, and there's a fine art gallery and remarkably good restaurant on the premises. The service and care given to guests here is impeccable. ⊠ *Hwy. 12 at Burr Trail, Boulder 84716* ☎ *435/335–7460 or 800/556–3446* 🖷 *435/335–7461* ⊕ *www.boulder-utah.com* 🖅 *20 rooms* ⚒ *Wi-Fi, some pets allowed, no-smoking rooms. $92–$130* ▭ *D, MC, V.*

★ **$–$$** 🏨 **Muley Twist Inn.** This gorgeous B&B sits on 30 acres of land, with expansive views of the colorful landscape that surrounds it. A wraparound porch, contemporary furnishings, and classical music drifting through the air add to a stay here. ⊠ *125 S. 250 West, Teasdale 84773* ☎ *435/425–3640 or 800/530–1038* 🖷 *435/425–3640* ⊕ *www.rof.net/yp/muley/index.html* 🖅 *5 rooms* ⚒ *No a/c, no TV, no-smoking rooms. $99–$119* ▭ *AE, MC, V* ⊘ *Nov.–Mar.*

**$** 🏨 **The Snuggle Inn.** On the second floor of a row of shops on Main Street, this hostelry has the feel of an old-time hotel. The rooms are spacious, with modern decorations and touches like Internet access. Each room has a pillow-top queen bed. For families, there's a sofa bed in one room. The suite has two separate bedrooms, a living room, and a full kitchen. ⊠ *55 S. Main St., Loa 84747* ☎ *435/836–2898* 🖷 *435/836–2700* ⊕ *www.thesnuggleinn.com* 🖅 *4 rooms, 1 suite* ⚒ *Kitchen (some), Wi-Fi; no a/c. $60–$85* ▭ *AE, D, DC, MC, V.*

**$** 🏨 **Wonderland Inn.** This hilltop motel has an incredible view as well as spacious rooms. A nearby RV park is under the same management; it has full and partial hookups with plenty of grass and shade. ⊠ *Hwy. 12 and Hwy. 24, Torrey 84775* ☎ *435/425–3775 or 800/458–0216* 🖷 *435/425–3212* ⊕ *www.capitolreefwonderland.com* 🖅 *50 rooms* ⚒ *Pool, Wi-Fi. $64–$72* ▭ *AE, D, MC, V.*

**¢–$** 🏨 **Rim Rock Inn.** Situated on a bluff with outstanding views into the desert, this motel was the first one built to accommodate visitors to Capitol Reef. Under energetic management it has been completely renovated, so rooms are clean and ample—and a good bargain, to boot. The on-site restaurant is a local favorite. ⊠ *2523 E. Hwy. 24, Torrey 84775* ☎ *888/447–4676* ⊕ *www.therimrock.net* 🖅 *19 rooms* ⚒ *Restaurant. $49–$79* ▭ *AE, MC, V* ⊘ *Closed Dec.–Feb.*

**¢** 🏨 **Sunglow Motel & Restaurant.** This well-maintained and inexpensive motel is right in the heart of Bicknell. Try the buttermilk and oatmeal pie at the restaurant next door—and don't knock the sounds of Pickle Pie and Pinto Bean Pie, for they are legendary, and rightfully so. ⊠ *91 E. Main*

## FESTIVALS & EVENTS

JULY **Bicknell International Film Festival.** *Don't* get out your best black beret to attend this event—it's a spoof on the serious film festivals that you read about. It begins with the world's fastest parade, a 60-mph procession that starts in Torrey and ends in Bicknell. Past themes have included "UFO Flicks," "Japanese Monster Movies," and "Viva! Elvis." The 2006 festival featured "three of the best bad B movies ever made about the circus," and attendees were encouraged to dress like clowns. ☎ *435/425-3123.*

AUG. **Wayne County Fair.** The great American county fair tradition is at its finest in Loa. Horse shows, turkey shoots, and the Tilt-a-Whirl are all standards, as is a rodeo and a parade. Look at handmade quilts and other crafts, see agricultural exhibits, play games, and eat plenty of good food while you spend a day at the fair. ☎ *435/836-2662.*

SEPT. **Art from the Land Workshop.** The Entrada Institute, a nonprofit organization committed to educating people about the Capitol Reef region, sponsors this annual three-day affair, which celebrates creativity and culture through art exhibits, readings, and writing workshops. ☎ *435/425-3265.*

*St., Bicknell 84715* ☎ *435/425-3821* 🖶 *435/425-3821* 🌐 *www. sunglowpies.com* ⤳ *15 rooms* ⌂ *Restaurant, cable TV. $25–$34* ▭ *AE, D, MC, V.*

CAMPGROUNDS &
RV PARKS
**$–$$$$**

⌂ **Thousand Lakes RV Park and Campground.** This is one of the area's most popular RV parks. There's lots of grass and shade, and the level 22-acre site provides good views of the surrounding red cliffs. The cabins come either bare-bones or with bath, microwave, refrigerator, and TV. There's free wireless Internet access. ✉ *1050 W. Rte 24, Torrey 84775* ☎ *435/425-3500 or 800/355-8995* 🖶 *435/425-3510* 🌐 *www. thousandlakesrvpark.com* ⤳ *46 full hookups, 12 partial hookups, 9 tent sites, 7 cabins* ⌂ *Grills, flush toilets, full hookups, partial hookups (water and electricity), dump station, drinking water, guest laundry, showers, fire pits, picnic tables, electricity, public telephone, general store, play area, swimming (pool). $14 tent sites, $19 partial hookups, $20 full hookups, $30–$95 cabins* ▭ *D, MC, V* ☉ *Apr.–Oct.*

$
⌂ **Fish Lake Campgrounds.** There are four Forest Service campgrounds in the Fish Lake area, about 7–15 mi northwest on Route 25 or Route 72. All are comfortable and well maintained. The two best are **Doctor Creek** and **Mackinaw.** Doctor Creek is a short drive from Fish Lake in a grove of aspen and pine. Mackinaw sits on a hill overlooking Fish Lake, giving campers a good view of the surrounding basin. The showers here are a rarity in Forest Service campgrounds. ✉ *Fremont River Ranger District Office, 138 S. Main St., Loa 84747* ☎ *435/836-2811 or 877/444-6777 (reservations)* 🌐 *www.reserveamerica.com* ⤳ *60 tent sites at Mackinaw, 30 tent sites at Doctor Creek* ⌂ *Pit toilets, dump station (Doctor Creek only), drinking water, showers (Mackinaw only). $13* ▭ *AE, D, MC, V (for online or phone reservations only)* ☉ *May–Oct.*

¢ ⚠ **Sunglow Campground.** Managed by the U.S. Forest Service, this secluded little campground is next to red cliffs in a pinyon forest. All of the sites are suitable for moderately sized RVs or tents, but RVers should know that the campground's roads are narrow and winding with some tight turns. ✉ *Hwy. 24, 1 mi east of Bicknell, Bicknell 84747* ☎ *435/ 836–2811* ⤵ *7 sites* ⌂ *Pit toilets, drinking water* ⚱ *Reservations not accepted. $5* ▭ *No credit cards* ☉ *May–Oct.*

# CAPITOL REEF ESSENTIALS

ACCESSIBILITY Like many of the undeveloped Western national parks, Capitol Reef doesn't have many trails that are accessible to people in wheelchairs. The visitor center, museum, slide show, and restrooms are all accessible, as is the campground amphitheater where evening programs are held. The Fruita Campground Loop C restroom is accessible, as is the boardwalk to the petroglyph panel on Highway 24, 1 2⁄10 mi east of the visitor center.

ADMISSION FEES There is no fee to enter the park, but it's $5 per vehicle to drive on Scenic Drive beyond Fruita Campground; this fee is good for one week.

ADMISSION HOURS The park is open year-round. It is in the Mountain time zone.

ATMS/BANKS The nearest ATM is at the travel plaza at the junction of Highways 24 and 12 in Torrey.

AUTOMOBILE SERVICE STATIONS
ⓘ **GoWest Lodge Travel Center** ✉ 2424 E. Hwy. 24, Torrey ☎ 435/425–3956, **Stan's Chevron** ✉ 350 S. Hwy. 95, Hanksville ☎ 435/542–2017, or **Wonderland Texaco** ✉ Hwys. 12 and 24, Torrey ☎ 435/425–3345. Other services include **Blackburn Sinclair and Towing** ✉ 178 E. Main St., Bicknell ☎ 435/425–3432, **Brian Auto Parts and Service** ✉ 233 S. Main, Loa ☎ 435/836–2343, and **M & D Auto Parts & Repair** ✉ 390 W. 100 N, Bicknell ☎ 435/425–3280.

EMERGENCIES Dial 911, contact a park ranger, or report to the visitor center. For park police, dial 435/425–3791. The nearest 24-hour medical center is the Beaver Valley Hospital in Beaver.

LOST AND FOUND It's at the visitor center.

PERMITS Backcountry camping permits are free; pick up at the visitor center.

POST OFFICES
ⓘ **Torrey Contract Post Office** ✉ 75 W. Main, Torrey ☎ 435/425–3716.

PUBLIC TELEPHONES They're at the visitor center and at Fruita Campground. Cell-phone reception is best near the visitor center and campground areas.

RELIGIOUS SERVICES There are no religious services in Capitol Reef.

RESTROOMS Restrooms are available at the visitor center, Fruita Campground, and Chimney Rock and Hickman Bridge trail-heads.

SHOPS & GROCERS
ⓘ **Austin's Chuckwagon General Store.** ✉ 12 W. Main St., Torrey ☎ 435/425–3288.

**NEARBY TOWN INFORMATION**
ⓘ **Capitol Reef Country Travel Council (Bicknell, Hanksville, Loa, Teasdale, Torrey)** ⓘ Box 7, Teasdale 84773 ☎ 800/858–7951 ⊕ www.capitolreef.org. **Garfield County Tourism Office (Boulder)** ✉ 55 S. Main St., Panguitch 84759 ☎ 800/444–6689 ⊕ www.brycecanyoncountry.com.

**VISITOR INFORMATION**
ⓘ **Capitol Reef National Park** ✉ HC 70 Box 15, Torrey, UT 84775 ☎ 435/425–3791 ⊕ www.nps.gov/care.

# Carlsbad Caverns National Park

Twin Domes, Carlsbad Caverns

**WORD OF MOUTH**

"The more I thought of it the more I realized that any hole in the ground which could house such a gigantic army of bats must be a whale of a big cave."

–Jim White, cowboy, from *Jim White's Own Story: The Discovery and History of Carlsbad Caverns*

# WELCOME TO CARLSBAD CAVERNS

## TOP REASONS TO GO

★ **300,000 hungry bats:** Every night and every day, bats wing to and from the caverns in a swirling, visible tornado.

★ **Take a guided tour through the underworld:** Plummet 75 stories underground, and step into enormous caves hung with stalactites and bristling with stalagmites.

★ **Living Desert Zoo and Gardens:** More preserve than zoo, this 1,500-acre park houses scores of rare species, including endangered Mexican wolves and Bolson tortoises, and now boasts a new black bear exhibit.

★ **Birding at Rattlesnake Springs:** Nine-tenths of the park's 330 bird species, including roadrunners, golden eagles, and acrobatic cave swallows, visit this green desert oasis.

★ **Pecos River:** The Pecos River, a Southwest landmark, flows through the nearby town of Carlsbad. The river is always soothing, but gets festive for holiday floaters when riverside homeowners lavishly decorate their homes.

**1** Bat Flight. Cowboy Jim White discovered the caverns after noticing that a swirling cloud of bats appeared there each morning and evening. White is long gone, but the 300,000-member bat colony is still here, snatching up 3 tons of bugs a night. Watch them leave at dusk from the amphitheater located near the park visitor center.

**2** Carlsbad Caverns Big Room Tour. Travel 75 stories below the surface to visit the Big Room, where you can traipse beneath a 255-foot-tall ceiling and take in immense and eerie cave formations. Located directly beneath the Carlsbad National Park Visitor Center, the room can be accessed via quick-moving elevator or the natural cave entrance.

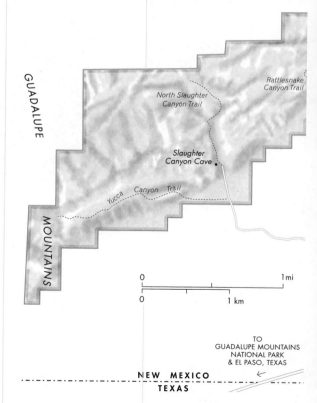

GUADALUPE

MOUNTAINS

Rattlesnake Canyon Trail

North Slaughter Canyon Trail

Slaughter Canyon Cave

Yucca Canyon Trail

0      1 mi
0      1 km

TO GUADALUPE MOUNTAINS NATIONAL PARK & EL PASO, TEXAS

NEW MEXICO

TEXAS

**3** Living Desert Zoo and Gardens. Endangered river cooters, Bolson tortoises, and Mexican wolves all roam in the Living Desert Zoo and Gardens. You can also skip alongside roadrunners and slim wild turkeys in the park's aviary, or visit a small group of cougars. The Living Desert is located within the town of Carlsbad, New Mexico, 23 mi to the north of the park.

**4** The Pecos River. In the 25,000-soul town of Carlsbad, a river runs through it—the Pecos River, that is. The river, a landmark of the Southwest, skims through town and makes for excellent boating, waterskiing, and fishing in some places. In the winter, residents gussy up dozens of riverside homes for the holiday season.

NEW MEXICO

## GETTING ORIENTED

To get at the essence of Carlsbad Caverns National Park, you have to delve below the surface—literally. Most of the park's key sights are underground in a massive network of caves (there are 113 in all, although not all are open to visitors; a variety of tours leave from the visitors center). The park also has a handful of trails above ground, where you can experience the Chihuahuan Desert and some magnificent geological formations.

TO CARLSBAD ↗
**3** **4**

Walnut Canyon Desert Dr.

**2** • Cavern Entrance
👫🏕 Visitor Center
**1**

Whites City

**5** Rattlesnake Springs
👫🏕 ♦ 418

62
180

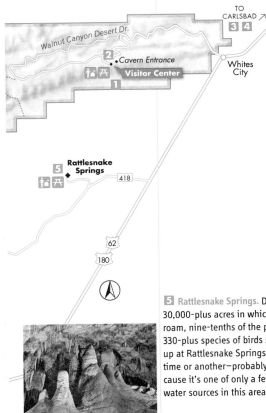

**5** Rattlesnake Springs. Despite 30,000-plus acres in which to roam, nine-tenths of the park's 330-plus species of birds show up at Rattlesnake Springs at one time or another—probably because it's one of only a few water sources in this area.

| KEY | |
|---|---|
| 👫 | Ranger Station |
| 🔺 | Campground |
| 🏕 | Picnic Area |
| 🍴 | Restaurant |
| 🏨 | Lodge |
| 🚶 | Trailhead |
| 🚻 | Restrooms |
| ⇗ | Scenic Viewpoint |
| ⋯⋯ | Walking/Hiking Trails |
| ⋯⋯ | Bicycle Path |

# CARLSBAD CAVERNS PLANNER

## When to Go

Carlsbad Caverns remains evergreen throughout the year. While the desert above may alternately bake or freeze, the caverns remain in the mid-50s. Fantastical formations don't change with the seasons either. If you're coming to see the Mexican free-tailed bat, however, your best bet is to come between spring and late fall.

GETTING THERE & AROUND

Carlsbad Caverns is 27 mi southwest of Carlsbad, New Mexico, and 35 mi north of Guadalupe Mountains National Park via U.S. 62/180. From El Paso, Texas, take U.S. 62/180 east and north 154 mi. (The nearest full-service airport is in El Paso.) The 9½-mi Walnut Canyon Desert Drive loop is one-way. This scenic drive on a curvy, gravel road is not recommended for motor homes or trailers. Be alert for wildlife such as mule deer crossing roadways, especially during early morning or evening hours.

AVG. HIGH/LOW TEMPS.

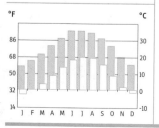

## Flora & Fauna

Without a doubt, the park's most prominent and popular residents are Mexican free-tailed bats. These bats have bodies that barely span a woman's hand, yet sport wings that would cover a workingman's boot. Female bats give birth to a single pup each year, which usually weighs more than a quarter of what an adult bat does. Their tiny noses and big ears enable them to search for the many tons of bugs they consume over their lifetime. Numbering nearly a third of a million, these tiny creatures are the park's mascot.

Famous fanged flyers aside, there is much more wildlife to recommend in the park. One of New Mexico's best birding areas is at Rattlesnake Springs. Summer and fall migrations give you the best chance of spotting the most varieties of the more than 330 species of birds. The golden eagle is one infrequent visitor. You might even get the thrill of glimpsing a brilliant, gray-and-crimson vermilion flycatcher.

If you're out walking, be wary of different rattlesnake species such as banded-rock and diamondbacks. Snakes generally appear in summer. If you see one, don't panic. Rangers say they are more scared of us than we are of them. Just don't make any sudden moves, and slowly walk away or back around the vipers.

This area is also remarkable because of its location in the Chihuahuan Desert, which sprouts unique plantlife. There are thick stands of raspy-leaved yuccas, as well as the agave (mescal) plants that were once a revered food source for the ancient Mescalero Apaches. The leaves of this leggy plant are still roasted in sand pits by Apache elders during traditional celebrations. The ceremony is open to the public at the nearby **Living Desert Zoo and Gardens**.

In spring, thick stands of yucca plants unfold yellow flowers on their tall stalks. Blossoming cacti and desert wildflowers are one of the natural wonders of Walnut Canyon. You'll see bright red blossoms adorning ocotillo plants, and sunny yellow blooms sprouting from prickly pear cactus.

12

By Jennifer
Edwards

On the surface, Carlsbad Caverns National Park is deceptively normal—but all bets are off once visitors set foot in the elevator, which plummets 75 stories underground. The country beneath the surface is part silky darkness, part subterranean hallucination. The snaky, illuminated walkway seems less like a trail and more like a foray across the river Styx and into the Underworld. Within more than 14 football fields of subterranean space are hundreds of formations that alternately resemble cakes, soda straws, ocean waves, and the large, leering face of a mountain troll.

## Scenic Drive

**Walnut Canyon Desert Drive.** This scenic drive begins ½ mi from the visitor center. It travels 9½ mi along the top of a ridge to the edge of Rattlesnake Canyon and sinks back down through upper Walnut Canyon to the main entrance road. The backcountry scenery on this one-way gravel loop is stunning; go late in the afternoon or early in the morning to enjoy the full spectrum of changing light and dancing colors. Along the way, you'll be able to see Big Hill Seep's trickling water, the tall, flowing ridges of the Guadalupe Mountain range, and maybe even some robust-looking mule deer.

## What to See

### Scenic Stops

Fodor'sChoice
★

**The Big Room.** With a floor space equal to about 14 football fields, this underground focal point of Carlsbad Caverns clues visitors in to just how large the caverns really are. The White House could fit in just one corner of the Big Room, and wouldn't come close to grazing the 255-foot ceiling. The 1-mi loop walk on a mostly level, paved trail is self-guided.

An audio guide is also available from park rangers for a few dollars. ⊠ *At the visitor center* ⊒ *$6; free for kids under 15* ⊙ *Memorial Day–Labor Day, daily 8:30–5 (last entry into the Natural Entrance is 3:30); Labor Day–Memorial Day, daily 8:30–3:30 (last entry into the Natural Entrance is 2).*

**Natural Entrance.** A self-guided, paved trail leads from the natural cave entrance. The route is winding and sometimes slick from water seepage aboveground. A steep descent of about 750 feet takes you about a mile through the main corridor and past features such as the Bat Cave and the Boneyard. Iceberg Rock is a 200,000-ton boulder that dropped from the cave ceiling eons ago. After about a mile, you'll link up underground with the 1-mi Big Room trail and return to the surface via elevator. ⊠ *At the visitor center* ⊒ *$6* ⊙ *Memorial Day–Labor Day, daily 8:30–3:30; Labor Day–Memorial Day, daily 9–2.*

> ### FLYING BLIND
>
> Bats use a type of sonar system called echolocation to orient themselves and locate their insect dinners at night. About fifteen species of bats live in Carlsbad Caverns, although the Mexican freetail is the most predominant.

**Rattlesnake Springs.** Enormous cottonwood trees shade the picnic and recreation area at this cool oasis near Black River. The rare desert wetland harbors butterflies, mammals, and reptiles, as well as 90% of the park's 330 bird species. Overnight camping and parking are not allowed. Take U.S. 62/180 5½ mi south of White's City and turn west onto Route 418 for 2½ mi. ⊠ *Rte. 418.*

### Visitor Center

A 75-seat theater offers an engrossing film about the different types of caves, as well as an orientation video that explains cave etiquette. Some of the rules include staying on paths so you don't get lost; keeping objects and trash in your pockets and not on the ground; and not touching the formations. Besides laying down the ground rules, visitor center exhibits offer a primer on bats, geology, wildlife, and the ancient people that once lived in the Carlsbad Cavern area. Friendly rangers staff an information desk, where tickets and maps are sold. Two gift shops also are on the premises. ⊠ *7 mi west of park entrance at White's City, off U.S. 62/180* ☎ *505/785–2232* ⊙ *Labor Day–Memorial Day, daily 8–5; Memorial Day–late Aug., daily 8–7.*

## Sports & the Outdoors

### Bird-watching

From warty-headed turkey vultures to svelte golden eagles, about 330 species of birds have been identified in Carlsbad Caverns National Park. The best place to bird-watch in the park (and maybe the state) is Rattlesnake Springs. Ask for a checklist at the visitor center and then start looking for red-winged blackbirds, white-throated swifts, northern flickers, and pygmy nuthatches. Keep your eyes peeled for red-tailed hawks and greater roadrunners, which wing and run swiftly.

## CARLSBAD CAVERNS IN ONE DAY

In a single day, visitors can easily view both the eerie, exotic caverns and the volcano of bats that erupt from the caverns each morning and evening. Unless you're attending the annual Bat Breakfast, when visitors have the morning meal with rangers and then view the early morning bat return, you'll probably want to sleep past sunrise and then stroll into the caves first.

For the full experience, begin by taking the **Natural Entrance Route Tour,** which allows visitors to trek into the cave from surface level. This tour winds past the Boneyard, with its intricate ossifications, and a 200,000-ton boulder called the Iceberg. After 1¼ mi or about an hour, the route links up with the **Big Room Route.** If you're not in good health or are traveling with young children, you might want to skip the Natural Entrance and start with the Big Room Route, which begins at the foot of the elevator. This underground walk extends 1¼ mi on level, paved ground, and takes about 1½ hours

to complete. If you have made reservations in advance or happen upon some openings, you also can take the additional **King's Palace** guided tour for 1 mi and an additional 1½ hours. At 83 stories deep, the Palace is the lowest rung the public can visit. By this time, you will have spent four hours in the cave. Take the elevator back up to the top. If you're not yet tuckered out, consider a short hike along the sunny, self-guided ½-mi **Desert Nature Walk** by the visitor center.

To picnic by the birds, bees, and water of **Rattlesnake Springs,** take U.S. 62/180 south from White's City 5½ mi, and turn back west onto Route 418. You'll find old-growth shade trees, grass, picnic tables, and water. Many varieties of birds flit from tree to tree. Return to the Carlsbad Caverns entrance road and take the 9½-mi Walnut Canyon Desert Drive loop. Leave yourself enough time to return to the **visitor center** for the evening bat flight.

**Rattlesnake Springs** is a natural wetland with old-growth cottonwoods, offering one of the better bird habitats in New Mexico. Because southern New Mexico is in the northernmost region of the Chihuahuan Desert, you're likely to see birds that can't be found anywhere else in the United States outside extreme southern Texas and Arizona. If you see a flash of crimson, you might have spotted a vermilion flycatcher. Wild turkeys also flap around this oasis. ⊠ *Rte. 418 2½ mi west of U.S. 62/180, 5½ mi south of White's City.*

### Caving

Carlsbad Caverns is famous for the beauty and breadth of its inky depths, as well as for the accessibility of some of its largest caves. All cave tours are ranger-led, so safety is rarely an issue in the caves, no matter how remote. There are no other tour guides in the area, nor is there an equipment retailer other than the Wal-Mart located in Carlsbad, 23 mi away. Depending on the difficulty of your cave selection (Spider Cave is the hardest to navigate), you'll need at most knee pads, flashlight batteries, sturdy pants, hiking boots with ankle support, and some water.

Fodor'sChoice
★

## DID YOU KNOW?

Tinajas (pronounced tin-ah-hah; Spanish for "earthen jar") are erosion-carved waterholes in slick-rock canyons. You can reach Big Bend's Ernst Tinaja (pictured here) via a 1 4/10-mi hike off Old Ore Road. It's deeper than it looks—up to 20-25 feet.

## Hiking

Deep, dark, and mysterious, the Carlsbad Caverns are such a park focal point that the 30,000-plus acres of wilderness above them has gone largely undeveloped. This is great news for people who pull on their hiking boots when they're looking for solitude. What you'll find are rudimentary trails that criss-cross the dry, textured terrain and lead up to elevations of 6,000 feet or more and often take a half day or more to travel. At least one, **Guadalupe Ridge Trail,** is long enough that it calls for an overnight stay. Walkers who just want a little dusty taste of desert flowers and wildlife should try the ½-mi **Desert Nature Walk.**

> ### A LONG WAY DOWN
>
> The newest discovery in Carlsbad Caverns National Park is **Lechuguilla Cave,** the deepest limestone cave in the United States. Scientists began mapping the cave network in 1986, and though they've located more than 112 mi of caverns extending to a depth of more than 1,600 feet, much more of this area along the park's northern border remains to be investigated. Lechuguilla is not open to the public, but an exhibit describing it can be viewed at the visitor center.

Finding the older, less well-maintained trails can be difficult. Pick up a topographical map at the visitor center bookstore, and be sure to pack a lot of water. There's none out in the desert, and you'll need at least a gallon per person per day. The high elevation coupled with a potent sunshine punch can deliver a nasty sunburn, so be sure to pack SPF 30 sunblock and a hat, even in winter. You can't bring a pet or a gun, but you do have to bring a backcountry permit if you're camping. They're free at the visitor center.

EASY **Desert Nature Walk.** While waiting for the night bat-flight program, try taking the ½-mi self-guided hike. The paved trail is wheelchair-accessible and an easy jaunt for even the littlest ones. The payoff is great for everyone, too: a big, vivid view of the desert basin. ⊠ *Off the cavern entrance trail, 200 yards east of the visitor center.*

**Rattlesnake Canyon Overlook Trail.** A ¼-mi stroll off Walnut Canyon Desert Drive offers a nice overlook of the greenery of Rattlesnake Canyon. ⊠ *Mile marker 9 on Walnut Canyon Desert Dr.*

MODERATE **Old Guano Road Trail.** Meander a little more than 3½ mi one-way on mostly flat terrain. Near the end, the trail dips sharply toward White's City campground, where it ends. Give yourself about half a day to complete the walk. Depending on the temperature, this walk can be taxing. Drink lots of water. ⊠ *The trailhead is at the Bat Flight Amphitheater, near the Natural Cave entrance and visitor center.*

**Rattlesnake Canyon Trail.** Rock cairns loom over this trail, which descends from 4,570 to 3,900 feet as it winds into the canyon. Allow half a day to trek down into the canyon and make the somewhat strenuous climb out; the total trip is about 6 mi. ⊠ *Mile marker 9 on Walnut Canyon Desert Dr.*

## OUTFITTERS & EXPEDITIONS

**12**

### CAVING

Spelunkers who wish to explore both developed and wild caves are in luck; park rangers lead visitors on six different tours, including the **The Hall of the White Giant** and **Spider Cave,** known for its tight twists and grimy climbs. Reservations are required at least a day in advance. If you're making reservations 21 days or more before your visit, you can send a check; 20 days or less, and you must pay by credit card over the phone or Web site. ⊕ *www.nps.gov/archive/cave/tour-gui.htm* ☎ *800/967–2283.*

Those who'd rather go it alone outside the more-established caverns can get permits and information about 10 backcountry caves from the **Cave Resources Office** (☎ 505/785–2232 Ext. 363). Make sure to heed rangers' advice for these remote, undeveloped, nearly unexplored caves.

Fodor'sChoice ★ **Yucca Canyon Trail.** Sweeping views of the Guadalupe Mountains and El Capitan give allure to this trail. Drive past Rattlesnake Springs and stop at the park boundary before reaching the Slaughter Canyon Cave parking lot. Turn west along the boundary fence line to the trailhead. The 6-mi round-trip begins at the mouth of Yucca Canyon, and climbs up to the top of the escarpment. Here you'll find the panoramic view. Most people turn around at this point; the hearty can continue along a poorly maintained route that follows the top of the ridge. The first part of the hike takes half a day. If you continue on, the hike takes a full day. ⊠ *Rte. 418, 10 mi west of U.S. 62/180.*

DIFFICULT **Guadalupe Ridge Trail.** This long, winding ramble follows an old road all the way to the west edge of the park. Because of its length (about 12 mi), an overnight stay in the backcountry is suggested. The hike may be long, but for serious hikers, the close-and-personal views into Rattlesnake and Slaughter canyons are more than worth it—not to mention the serenity of being miles and miles away from civilization. ⊠ *Follow Desert Loop Dr. 4⁸⁄₁₀ mi to the trailhead.*

**North Slaughter Canyon Trail.** Beginning at the Slaughter Canyon parking lot, the trail traverses a heavily vegetated canyon bottom into a remote part of the park. As you begin hiking, look off to the east (to your right) to see the dun-colored ridges and wrinkles of the Elephant Back formation, the first of many dramatic limestone formations visible from the trail. The route travels 5½ mi one way, with the last 3 mi steeply climbing onto a limestone ridge escarpment. Allow a full day for the round-trip. ⊠ *Rte. 418, 10 mi west of U.S. 62/180.*

## Educational Offerings

### Ranger Programs

Fodor'sChoice ★ **Evening Bat Flight Program.** In the amphitheater at the Natural Cave Entrance (off a short trail from main parking lot) a ranger discusses the park's batty residents before the creatures begin their sundown exodus.

The bats aren't on any predictable schedule, so times are a little iffy. ⊠ *Natural Cave Entrance, at the visitor center* 🎫 *Free* ☉ *Mid-May–mid-Oct., nightly at sundown.*

**Hall of the White Giant.** Plan to squirm through some tight passages for long distances to access a very remote chamber, where you'll see towering, glistening white formations that explain the name of this feature. This strenuous, ranger-led tour lasts about four hours. Steep drop-offs might elate you—or make you queasy. Wear sturdy hiking shoes, and pick up four AA batteries for your flashlight before you come. Visitors must be at least 12 years old. ⊠ *At the visitor center* ☎ *800/967–2283* 🎫 *$20* ⛏ *Reservations required* ☉ *Tour Sat. at 1.*

**King's Palace.** Throughout King's Palace, you'll see leggy "soda straws" large enough for a giant to sip and multitiered curtains of stone—sometimes by the light of just a few flashlights. The mile-long walk is on a paved trail, but there's one very steep hill. This ranger-guided tour lasts about 1½ hours and gives you the chance to experience a blackout, when all lights are extinguished. While advance reservations are highly recommended, this is the one tour you might be able to sign up for on the spot. Children under 4 aren't allowed on this tour. ⊠ *At the visitor center* ☎ *800/967–2283* 🎫 *$8* ☉ *Tours Labor Day–Memorial Day, daily 10 and 2; Memorial Day–Labor Day, daily 10, 11, 2, and 3.*

★ **Slaughter Canyon Cave.** Discovered in the 1930s by a local goatherder, this cave is one of the most popular secondary sites in the park, about 23 mi southwest of the main Carlsbad Caverns and visitor center. Both the hike to the cave mouth and the tour will take about half a day, but it's worth it to view the deep cavern darkness as it's punctuated only by flashlights and, sometimes, head lamps. From the Slaughter Canyon parking area, give yourself 45 minutes to make the steep ½-mi climb up a trail leading to the mouth of the cave. Arrange to be there a quarter of an hour earlier than the appointed time. You'll find that the cave consists primarily of a single corridor, 1,140 feet long, with numerous side passages.

You can take some worthwhile pictures of this cave. Wear hiking shoes with ankle support, and carry plenty of water. You're also expected to bring your own two D-cell flashlight. Children under age 6 are not permitted. It's a great adventure if you're in shape and love caving. ⊠ *End of Rte. 418, 10 mi west of U.S. 62/180* ☎ *800/967–2283* 🎫 *$15* ⛏ *Reservations required* ☉ *Tours Memorial Day–Labor Day, daily 10 and 1; post-Labor Day–Dec., weekends at 10; Jan.–Memorial Day, weekends 10 and 1.*

**Spider Cave.** Visitors may not expect to have an adventure in a cavern system as developed and well stocked as Carlsbad Caverns, but serious cavers and energetic types have the chance to clamber up tight tunnels, stoop under overhangs, and climb up steep, rocky pitches. This backcountry cave is listed as "wild," a clue that you might need a similar nature to attempt a visit. Plan to wear your warm, but least-favorite clothes as they'll probably get streaked with grime. You'll also need soft knee

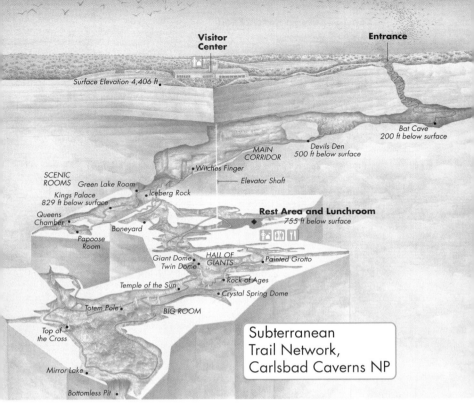

**Visitor Center**

**Entrance**

Surface Elevation 4,406 ft

Bat Cave
200 ft below surface

Devils Den
500 ft below surface

MAIN CORRIDOR

Witches Finger

SCENIC ROOMS
Green Lake Room

Elevator Shaft

Kings Palace
829 ft below surface

Iceberg Rock

Queens Chamber

**Rest Area and Lunchroom**
755 ft below surface

Boneyard

Papoose Room

Giant Dome
Twin Dome

HALL OF GIANTS

Painted Grotto

Temple of the Sun

Rock of Ages

Crystal Spring Dome

Totem Pole

BIG ROOM

Top of the Cross

Mirror Lake

Bottomless Pit

Subterranean Trail Network, Carlsbad Caverns NP

pads, 4 AA batteries, leather gloves, and water. The gloves and pads are to protect you on long, craggy clambers and the batteries are for your flashlight. It will take you half a day to complete this ranger-led tour noted for its adventure. Visitors must be at least 12 years old and absolutely not claustrophobic. ⊠ *Meet at visitor center* ☎ *800/967–2283* ✉ *$20* ♿ *Reservations required* ☉ *Tour Sun. at 1.*

## WHAT'S NEARBY

### Nearby Towns

On the Pecos River, with 2¾ mi of beaches and picturesque riverside pathways, **Carlsbad, New Mexico,** seems suspended between the past and the present. It's part university town, part Old West, with a robust Mexican kick. The Territorial town square, a block from the river, encircles a Pueblo-style country courthouse designed by New Mexican architect John Gaw Meem. Also near the park is **White's City**. Seven miles east of the caverns, it's grown from a tiny outpost to a small outpost. This privately owned town is the closest place to Carlsbad Caverns and contains dining and lodging options, plus the essentials.

## FAMILY PICKS

**Fiesta Drive-In Theater.** The Fiesta is one of only two drive-ins in New Mexico, and the movies it plays seem enhanced by the dry, silent desert that majestically surrounds the screen.

**Granny's Opera House.** Granny's is typical of some of the small community theaters in the Southwest where both audience involvement and littering aren't just tolerated, they're encouraged. And all that mess-making sure helps knock the edge off a long, stressful road trip.

**Lake Carlsbad Recreation Area.** The hundred-plus acres of green, green grass beckon picnic blankets and invite naps beneath shady trees. Kids will get a kick out of watching the ducks paddle away from personal watercraft and boats.

**Living Desert Zoo and Gardens State Park.** Can you really pass up the beautiful African carrion lily, or the swift and slick endangered river cooters (a type of turtle)—or the chance to jabber with the real-life roadrunners and wild turkeys that live in the zoo's walk-in aviary?

**Pecos River flume.** This aqueduct near the Carlsbad Spring is an oddity that Ripley's Believe It or Not once called "The River that Crosses Itself," since it carries Pecos River water across the Pecos River.

## Nearby Attractions

**Brantley Lake State Park.** In addition to 42,000-acre Brantley Lake, this park 12 mi north of Carlsbad offers primitive camping areas, nature trails, a visitor center, more than 51 fully equipped campsites, and fine fishing. You can boat here, too. ⊠ *County Rd. 30 (Capitan Reef Rd.), 5 mi off U.S. 285, Carlsbad* ☎ *505/457–2384* ⊕ *www.emnrd.state.nm. us* ☞ *$4 per vehicle.*

**Carlsbad Museum and Arts Center.** Here you'll find Pueblo pottery, Native American artifacts, and early cowboy and ranch memorabilia along with exhibitions of contemporary art. The real treasure, though, is the McAdoo Collection, with works by painters of the Taos Society of Artists. ⊠ *418 W. Fox St. Carlsbad* ☎ *505/887–0276* ☞ *Free* ☉ *Mon.–Sat. 10–5.*

**Granny's Opera House.** Ready to shed your inhibitions and whoop it up? During the hour-long old-fashioned melodramas, you can boo at the villain, throw popcorn, cheer on the heroes, tune up your vocal cords for a sing-along, and be pulled onstage by the actors. Performance times can vary, so call ahead. ⊠ *13 Carlsbad Caverns Hwy.* ☎ *505/785–2291* ☞ *$7.50, includes popcorn.*

★ ♻ **Living Desert Zoo and Gardens State Park.** This park contains impressive plants and animals native to the Chihuahuan Desert. The Desert Arboretum has hundreds of exotic cacti and succulents, and the Living Desert

Zoo—more a reserve than a traditional zoo—is home to mountain lions, deer, elk, wolves, bison, and endangered Mexican wolves, which are more petite than their snarly kin. Nocturnal exhibits and dioramas let you in on the area's nighttime wildlife, too. Though there are shaded rest areas, restrooms, and water fountains, in hot weather it's best to visit during the early morning or early evening, when it's cooler. ✉ *1504 Miehls Dr., off U.S. 285* ☎ *505/887–5516* 🎟 *$3 for the tour* ☉ *Late May–early Sept., daily 8–8; early Sept.–late May, daily 9–5; last admission 1½ hrs before closing.*

| GOOD READS |
| --- |
| **Jim White's Own Story** by early explorer Jim White tells of this cowboy's exploits into the heart of Carlsbad Caverns, before it was developed as a national park. **Bats of Carlsbad Caverns,** by various experts, helps debunk myths about bats (including myths about bats gulping up human blood). For an entertaining bat primer, go to the National Park Service web site (⊕ www.nps.gov/archive/cave/teacherguide/fs.bats.htm). |

## Area Activities

### Sports & the Outdoors

BOATING & FISHING   The **Lake Carlsbad Recreation Area** offers boat ramps, boating, and fishing; there are no admission fees. ✉ *Along Riverside and Park drives in Carlsbad* ☎ *505/885–6262* ⊕ *www.cityofcarlsbadnm.com/* ☉ *Open daily; swimming area open Memorial Day weekend through Labor Day.*

There's another boat ramp at Brantley Lake State Park ⇨ full listing in Nearby Attractions. ⚠ **If you fish here, rangers advise practicing catch and release, since the fish seem to be suffering from higher-than-average levels of DDT.**

### Arts & Entertainment

The **Fiesta Drive-In Theater** (✉ 401 W. Fiesta, Carlsbad ☎ 505/885–4126 ⊕ www.fiestadrivein.com) offers three reasonably current movie selections. For current shows, hours, and prices, check out the Web site. **Lucy's Mexicali Restaurant & Entertainment Club** (☎ 505/887–7714) has bands on the weekend. On Saturday, popular country-and-western bands play at the **Silver Spur Lounge** (☎ 505/887–2851) in the Best Western Stevens Inn, a favored local hangout where dancing takes place all week long.

# WHERE TO STAY & EAT

### About the Restaurants

Choice isn't an issue inside Carlsbad Caverns National Park because there are just three dining options—the surface-level café, the underground restaurant, and the bring-it-in-yourself option. Luckily, everything is reasonably priced (especially for being located inside a national park).

### About the Hotels

The only overnight option within the arid, rugged park is to make your own campsite in the backcountry, at least half a mi from any trail.

Outside the park, however, options expand. White's City, which is less than 10 mi to the east of the park, contains two motels. Both are near the boardwalk that connects shopping and entertainment options.

In Carlsbad, there are even more choices, but many of them aren't as appealing as they once were. The hotels here are aging and not particularly well maintained, so don't expect a mint on your pillow. Most are clean, however, if not opulent.

## About the Campgrounds

Backcountry camping is by permit only (no campfires allowed) in the park; free permits can be obtained at the visitor center, where you can also pick up a map of areas closed to camping. You'll need to hike to campsites. There are no vehicle or RV camping areas in the park. Commercial sites can be found in White's City and Carlsbad.

# Where to Eat

## In the Park

¢–$ ✕ **Carlsbad Caverns Restaurant.** This comfy, diner-style restaurant has the essentials—hamburgers, sandwiches, and hot roast beef. ✉ *Visitor center, 7 mi west of U.S. 62/180 at the end of the main park road.* ☎ *505/785–2281. $3–$10* ▱ *AE, D, MC, V* ☯ *Closes at 5 in winter, 6:30 in summer.*

¢–$ ✕ **Underground Lunchroom.** Grab a treat, soft drink, or club sandwich for a quick break. ✉ *Visitor center, 7 mi west of U.S. 62/180 at the end of the main park Rd.* ☎ *505/785–2281. $3–$10* ▱ *AE, D, MC, V* ☯ *Closes 3:30 in winter, 5 in summer; no dinner.*

PICNIC AREAS There are only a couple of places to picnic in the park. The best by far is at **Rattlesnake Springs**. There are about a dozen picnic tables and grills here, and drinking water and chemical toilets are available. ✉ *Rte. 418, 2½ mi west of U.S. 62/180.* There are also a few picnic tables in the shade by the **visitor center.**

## Outside the Park

$–$$ ✕ **Velvet Garter Restaurant and Saloon.** This eatery dishes up steaks, chicken, shrimp, and Italian and Mexican food in an Old West atmosphere. You won't find gourmet meals here, but it's a convenient place for a decent meal if you don't want to drive an additional 20 mi north to Carlsbad. There's also a full-service bar. ✉ *26 Carlsbad Caverns Hwy. White's City* ☎ *505/785–2291. $10–$18* ▱ *AE, D, MC, V.*

★ ¢–$ ✕ **Bamboo Garden Restaurant.** This is possibly the best Chinese food in southern New Mexico. Kung pao chicken is among the highlights, but there are also favorites like sweet-and-sour pork and cashew shrimp. Surroundings are pleasant but not elegant. ✉ *1511 N. Canal St. Carlsbad* ☎ *505/887–5145. $4–$12* ▱ *MC, V* ☯ *Closed Mon.*

★ ¢–$ ✕ **La Fonda.** For decades, residents of Carlsbad and Roswell have driven to this modest Mexican restaurant to dine on celebrated specialties like the Guadalajara (beef, cheese, and guacamole on a corn tortilla). Artesia is 26 mi north of the park. ✉ *206 W. Main St., Artesia* ☎ *505/746–9377. $5–$10* ▱ *AE, D, MC, V.*

★ ¢–$ ✕ **Lucy's Mexicali Restaurant & Entertainment Club.** "The best margaritas and hottest chile in the world" is the motto of this family-owned Mexican food oasis. All the New Mexican staples are prepared here, plus some not-so-standard items such as chicken fajita burritos, Tucson-style chimichangas, and brisket *carnitas* (beef brisket or chicken sautéed with chilies and seasonings). Low-fat and fat-free Mexican dishes and 12 microbrewery beers are served—or try Lucy's original Mexicali beer with a slice of orange. Live entertainment is offered on weekends. ⊠ *701 S. Canal St. Carlsbad* ☎ *505/887–7714. $4–$11* ⊟ *AE, D, DC, MC, V.*

## Where to Stay

### In the Park

CAMPGROUNDS &
RV PARKS

Backcountry camping only is allowed. *See* About the Campgrounds.

### Outside the Park

$ 🏨 **Best Western Cavern Inn.** This Territorial-style, two-story motor inn just outside the Carlsbad Caverns entrance has rooms with Southwestern decor. Under the same ownership next door is the hacienda-style **Best Western Guadalupe Inn**, notable for its tidy landscaping and private spa; it has 42 rooms and Southwestern furnishings. All guests are free to use the water park, open May through September, which features two 150-foot waterslides. ⊠ *17 Carlsbad Caverns Hwy., look for large registration sign on south side of road, White's City 88268* ☎ *505/785–2291 or 800/228–3767* 🖨 *505/785–2283* ⤳ *63 rooms* ⚲ *Pool, spa, Wi-Fi, some pets allowed. $80–$99* ⊟ *AE, D, DC, MC, V* ⓧ *BP.*

★ $ 🏨 **Best Western Stevens Inn.** This is widely known as the best-maintained hotel in town. Etched glass and carved wooden doors add a touch of elegance, and prints of Western landscapes decorate the spacious rooms. Prime rib and steaks are served in the evening at the motel's Flume Room Restaurant and Coffee Shop, which opens at 5:30 AM daily. ⊠ *1829 S. Canal St., Box 580, Carlsbad 88220* ☎ *505/887–2851 or 800/730–2851* 🖨 *505/887–6338* ⤳ *222 rooms* ⚲ *Restaurant, kitchen (some), refrigerator (some), Wi-Fi, pool, bar, laundry facilities, airport shuttle, some pets allowed, no-smoking rooms. $69–$99* ⊟ *AE, D, DC, MC, V* ⓧ *BP.*

$ 🏨 **Days Inn.** Rooms at this motel on the south side of town (it's the closest motel to Carlsbad Caverns) have Southwestern decor, king-size beds, and sofa beds. Convenient to the park, service is decent and rooms are clean. ⊠ *3910 National Parks Hwy., Carlsbad 88220* ☎ *505/887–7800, 800/329–7466 central reservations* 🖨 *505/885–9433* ⤳ *42 rooms, 8 suites* ⚲ *Pool, airport shuttle, some pets allowed. $69–$89* ⊟ *AE, D, DC, MC, V* ⓧ *CP.*

¢–$ 🏨 **Ocotillo Inn.** This clean and comfortable—if a bit nondescript—motel is locally owned and operated, and just a mile from the municipal airport. High points include a landscaped patio with a pool and a sundeck about as large as an aircraft hangar. The Café in the Park serves free Continental breakfasts to guests. ⊠ *3706 National Parks Hwy., Carlsbad 88220* ☎ *505/887–2861 or 800/321–2861* 🖨 *505/887–2861* ⤳ *120 rooms* ⚲ *Restaurant, pool, bar, laundry service, airport shuttle, some pets allowed, no-smoking rooms. $49–$89* ⊟ *AE, D, DC, MC, V* ⓧ *CP.*

# CARLSBAD CAVERNS ESSENTIALS

ACCESSIBILITY Portions of the paved Big Room trails in Carlsbad Caverns are accessible to wheelchairs. A map defining appropriate routes is available at the visitor center information desk. Individuals with walkers should ask for guidelines at the information desk. Strollers are not permitted on trails (use a baby pack instead). Individuals who may have difficulty walking should access the Big Room via elevator. From the underground lunchroom area, they should be able to step out at least a portion of a way on a trail to view some of the formations. Individuals in wheelchairs or who are otherwise mobility impaired should not take the Natural Entrance Route because the trail is steep and winding. The TDD number is 888/530–9796.

ADMISSION FEES No fee is charged for parking or to enter the aboveground portion of the park. It costs $6 to descend into Carlsbad Cavern either by elevator or through the Natural Entrance. Costs for special tours range from $7 to $20 plus general admission.

ADMISSION HOURS The park is open year-round, except Christmas Day. From Memorial Day weekend through Labor Day, tours are conducted from 8:30 to 5; the last entry into the cave via natural entrance is at 3:30, and the last entry into the cave via the elevator is at 5. From Labor Day until Memorial Day weekend tours are conducted from 8:30 to 3:30; the last entry into the cave via natural entrance is at 2, and the last entry into the cave via the elevator is at 3:30. Carlsbad is in the Mountain Time Zone.

ATMS/BANKS The park has no ATM.
🏨 **Best Western Cavern Inn** ✉ 17 Carlsbad Caverns Hwy., White's City ☎ 505/785–2291.

AUTOMOBILE SERVICE STATIONS
🏨 **White's City 24-Hour Texaco** ✉ 17 Carlsbad Caverns Hwy., White's City ☎ 505/785–2291.

EMERGENCIES In the event of a medical emergency, dial 911, contact a park ranger, or report to the visitor center. To contact park police dial 505/785–2232. Carlsbad Caverns has trained emergency medical technicians on duty and a first-aid room. White's City has emergency medical technicians available to respond to medical emergencies. A full-service hospital is in nearby Carlsbad.

LOST AND FOUND The park's lost-and-found is at the Visitor Center information desk.

PERMITS All hikers are advised to stop at the visitor center information desk for current information about trails; those planning overnight hikes must obtain a free backcountry permit. Trails are poorly defined but can be followed with a topographic map. Dogs are not allowed in the park, but a kennel is available at the park visitor center.

POST OFFICES There is a mailbox at the visitor center. Stamps can be purchased in the gift shops.
🏨 **White's City Post Office** ✉ Carlsbad Caverns Hwy., White's City 88268 ☎ 505/785–2220 ⏲ Weekdays 8–noon and 12:30–4:30, Sat. 8–noon.

PUBLIC TELEPHONES Public telephones are at the visitor center—handy, because cell phones only work about 10% of the time.

RESTROOMS Public restrooms are at the park visitor center, inside the visitor center restaurant, and near the underground lunchroom.

## TOWN INFORMATION
🏨 **Carlsbad Chamber of Commerce** ✉ 302 S. Canal St., Carlsbad, NM 88220 ☎ 505/887–6516 ⊕ www.carlsbadchamber.com. **White's City Inc.** ✉ 17 Carlsbad Caverns Hwy., White's City, NM 88268 ☎ 505/785–2291 or 800/228–3767 ⊕ www.whitescity.com.

## VISITOR INFORMATION
🏨 **Carlsbad Caverns National Park** ✉ 3225 National Parks Hwy., Carlsbad, NM 88220 ☎ 505/785–2232, 800/967–2283 reservations for special cave tours, 800/388–2733 cancellations ⊕ www.nps.gov/cave.

# Channel Islands National Park

Christy Beach, Santa Cruz Island, Channel Islands National Park

**WORD OF MOUTH**

"An island always pleases my imagination, even the smallest, as a small continent and integral portion of the globe."

–Henry David Thoreau

# WELCOME TO
# CHANNEL ISLANDS

## TOP REASONS
## TO GO

★ **Rare flora and fauna:**
The Channel Islands are
home to 145 species of
terrestrial plants and animals found nowhere else
on Earth.

★ **Time travel:** With no
cars, phones, or services,
these undeveloped islands
provide a glimpse of what
California was like hun-
dreds of years ago. This
pristine wilderness is close
to the mainland, yet worlds
away from hectic modern
life.

★ **Underwater adventures:**
The incredibly healthy
channel waters rank among
the top 10 diving destinations on the planet—but
you can also visit the kelp
forest virtually via an underwater video program.

★ **Marvelous marine mam-
mals:** More than 30 species
of seals, sea lions, whales,
and other marine mammals
ply the park's waters at various times of year.

★ **Sea cave kayaking:**
Paddle around otherwise
inaccessible portions of the
park's 175 mi of gorgeous
coastline—including one of
the world's largest sea
caves.

**1** Anacapa. Tiny Anacapa is a
five-mile stretch of three islets,
with towering cliffs, caves, natural bridges, and rich kelp
forests.

**2** San Miguel. Isolated,
windwept San Miguel has an
ancient caliche forest and hundreds of archaeological sites.
More than 30,000 pinnipeds
(seals and sea lions) hang out
on the island's beaches during
certain times of year.

Santa Ynez Peak
4,298 ft

*Santa    Barbara*

Harris Point
Cuyler Harbor
West Point
*Santa Cruz Channel*
Cabrillo Monument
Lester Ranch site
Carrington Point
Point Bennett
*San Miguel Passage*
Tyler Bight
**2** *San Miguel Island*
Sandy Point
**Vail & Vickers Ranch**
Bechers Bay
**Torrey Pines**
**5** *Santa Rosa Island*
Soledad Peak
1,574 ft
East Point
Johnsons Lee
South Point

*P A C I F I C       O C E A N*

**3** Santa Barbara. Six miles of
scenic trails criss-cross this tiny
island, known for its excellent
wildlife viewing and native
plants. It's a favorite destination
for diving, snorkeling, and
kayaking.

CALIFORNIA

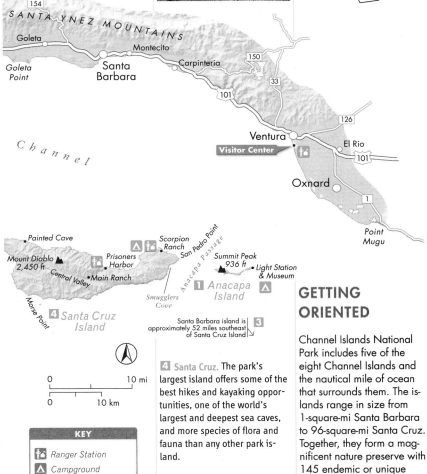

13

**4 Santa Cruz.** The park's largest island offers some of the best hikes and kayaking opportunities, one of the world's largest and deepest sea caves, and more species of flora and fauna than any other park island.

**5 Santa Rosa.** Campers love to stay on Santa Rosa, with its myriad hiking opportunities, stunning white-sand beaches, and rare grove of Torrey pines. It's also the only island accessible by plane.

## GETTING ORIENTED

Channel Islands National Park includes five of the eight Channel Islands and the nautical mile of ocean that surrounds them. The islands range in size from 1-square-mi Santa Barbara to 96-square-mi Santa Cruz. Together, they form a magnificent nature preserve with 145 endemic or unique species of plants and animals. Half the park lies underwater, and the surrounding channel waters are teeming with life, including dolphins, whales, seals, sea lions, and seabirds.

**KEY**

- Ranger Station
- Campground
- Picnic Area
- Restaurant
- Lodge
- Trailhead
- Restrooms
- Scenic Viewpoint
- ----- Walking/Hiking Trails
- ...... Bicycle Path

0        10 mi
0      10 km

# CHANNEL ISLANDS PLANNER

## When to Go

Channel Islands National Park records about 620,000 visitors each year, but most never venture beyond the visitor center in Ventura. Still, make your transportation arrangements as soon as possible if you plan to travel to the islands on holidays or summer weekends, when hotels tend to fill up.

The rains usually come from December through March—but this is also the best time to spot gray whales in the channel, and nearby hotels offer considerable discounts. In the late spring, thousands of migratory birds descend on the islands to hatch their young, and wildflowers carpet the slopes. The warm, dry summer months are the best time to go camping, and humpback and blue whales arrive to feed from late June through early fall.

The water temperature is nearly always cool, so bring a wet suit if you plan to spend much time in the ocean, even in the relatively warm months of August and September. Be prepared for fog, high winds, and rough seas any time of the year.

AVG. HIGH/LOW TEMPS.

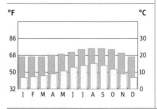

## Flora & Fauna

Often called the North American Galapagos, the Channel Islands are home to species found nowhere else on Earth: mammals such as the island fox and the Anacapa deer mouse, birds like the island scrub-jay, and plants like the Santa Barbara live-forever. Other species, such as the Santa Rosa Torrey pine and the island oak, have evolved differently from their counterparts on the mainland. It all adds up to a living laboratory not unlike the one naturalist Charles Darwin discovered off the coast of South America 200 years ago.

## Getting There & Around

Channel Islands National Park is located in the Santa Barbara Channel, south of Santa Barbara and southwest of Oxnard and Ventura. To get to the islands, you first need to get to a harbor or an airport. U.S. Highway 101 and Amtrak trains link all neighboring cities and harbors, providing access to the park. To reach the Channel Islands National Park Visitor Center (on the mainland in Ventura) by car, exit in Ventura at Seaward Boulevard or Victoria Avenue and follow the signs to Ventura Harbor/Spinnaker Drive. In Santa Barbara, exit U.S. Highway 101 at Castillo Street and head south to Cabrillo Boulevard, then turn right for the harbor entrance. If you arrive by train in either Santa Barbara, Ventura, or Oxnard, take a taxi or hop aboard a waterfront shuttle bus.

Anacapa Island is 12 mi (about 1 hour) from Channel Islands Harbor in Oxnard. Santa Cruz Island lies 20 mi (1 to 1½ hours) from the Channel Islands Visitor Center in Ventura Harbor. Santa Rosa Island is 46 mi (2½ to 3 hours) from Ventura; San Miguel is 58 mi (3½ to 4 hours) from the city. It takes 2½ to 3 hours to reach Santa Barbara Island, 55 mi offshore.

Private vehicles are not permitted on the islands. Transportation to and from the mainland is provided by private companies (see Transportation Options box). Most scheduled day trips are to a single island, so island-hopping is not an option unless you charter a boat or take a multiday trip.

13

By Cheryl
Crabtree

On crystal-clear days the craggy peaks of Channel Islands National Park are easy to see from the mainland, jutting from the Pacific in such sharp detail it seems you could reach out and touch them. The islands really aren't that far away—a high-speed boat will whisk you to the closest ones in less than an hour—yet very few people ever visit them. Those fearless, adventurous types who do will experience one of the most splendid land-and-sea wilderness areas on the planet.

## What to See

### The Islands

★ **Anacapa Island.** Although most people think of it as an island, Anacapa is actually comprised of three narrow islets. The tips of these volcanic formations nearly touch but are inaccessible from one another except by boat. All three islets have towering cliffs, isolated sea caves, and natural bridges; Arch Rock, on East Anacapa, is one of the best-known symbols of Channel Islands National Park. Wildlife viewing is the reason most people come to East Anacapa—particularly in summer when seagull chicks are newly hatched and sea lions and seals lounge on the beaches.

The compact **museum** on East Anacapa tells the history of the island and houses, among other things, the original lead-crystal Fresnel lens from the island's lighthouse (circa 1937). If you come in summer, you can also learn about the nearby kelp forests by talking with underwater rangers via microphone and camera on Tuesday, Wednesday, and Thursday afternoons at 2; these sessions are broadcast live at the visitor center. Depending on the season and the number of desirable species lurking about there, a limited number of boats travel to Frenchy's Cove, at West Anacapa, where there are pristine tide pools where you might see anemones, limpets, barnacles, mussel beds, and colorful marine

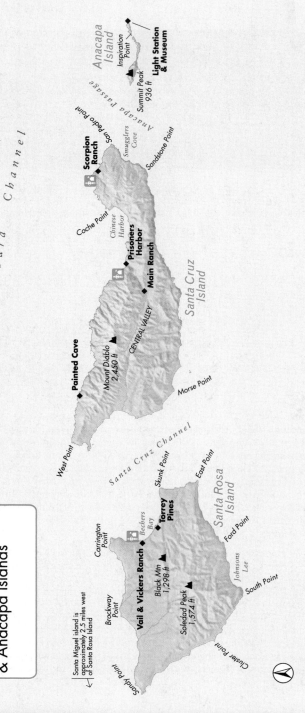

# Santa Rosa, Santa Cruz & Anacapa Islands

Ventura is approximately 28 miles
Northeast of Prisoners Harbor, Santa Cruz Island

Santa Barbara island is
approximately 52 miles southeast
of Santa Cruz Island

Santa Miguel Island is
approximately 2.5 miles west
of Santa Rosa Island

*Santa    Barbara    Channel*

*PACIFIC    OCEAN*

*Anacapa Island*

Inspiration Point

Summit Peak
936 ft

**Light Station
& Museum**

*Anacapa Passage*

San Pedro Point

Smugglers
Cove

Sandstone Point

**Scorpion
Ranch**

Coche Point

Chinese
Harbor

**Prisoners
Harbor**

**Main Ranch**

*Santa Cruz
Island*

**Painted Cave**

Mount Diablo
2,450 ft

CENTRAL VALLEY

Morse Point

West Point

*Santa Cruz Channel*

Skunk Point

**Torrey
Pines**

Bechers
Bay

Carrington
Point

**Vail & Vickers Ranch**

Black Mtn
1,298 ft

Soledad Peak
1,574 ft

Brockway
Point

Sandy Point

Cluster Point

South Point

*Johnsons
Lee*

Ford Point

East Point

*Santa Rosa
Island*

0          5 mi

0          5 km

algae). The rest of West Anacapa is closed to protect nesting brown pelicans, and trips to Middle Anacapa Island require a ranger escort.

**San Miguel Island.** The westernmost of the Channel Islands, San Miguel is frequently battered by storms sweeping across the North Pacific. The 15-square-mi island's wild, windswept landscape is lush with vegetation. Point Bennett, at the western tip, offers one of the world's most spectacular wildlife displays when more than 30,000 pinnipeds (seals and sea lions) hit its beach. Explorer Juan Rodríguez Cabrillo was the first European to visit this island; he claimed it for Spain in 1542. Legend holds that Cabrillo died on one of the Channel Islands—no one knows where he's buried, but there's a memorial to him on a bluff above Cuyler Harbor.

**Santa Barbara Island.** At about 1 square mi, Santa Barbara is the smallest of the Channel Islands. It's also the southernmost island in the chain, nearly 35 mi from the others. Triangular in shape, Santa Barbara's steep cliffs—which offer a perfect nesting spot for the Xantus's murrelet, a rare seabird—are topped by twin peaks. In spring, you can enjoy a brilliant display of yellow coreopsis.

With exhibits on the region's natural history, the small **museum** is a great place to learn about the wildlife on and around the islands. ⊠ *Santa Barbara Island* 🕾 *No phone* ⊗ *Daily 10–5.*

**Santa Cruz Island.** Five miles west of Anacapa, 96-square-mi Santa Cruz is the largest of the Channel Islands. The National Park Service manages the easternmost 25% of the island; the rest is owned by the Nature Conservancy, which requires a permit to land. When your boat drops you off on the 70 mi of craggy coastline, you'll find two rugged mountain ranges with peaks soaring to 2,500 feet and deep canyons traversed by streams. This landscape is the habitat of a remarkable variety of flora and fauna—more than 600 types of plants, 140 kinds of land birds, 11 mammal species, five varieties of reptiles, and three amphibian species live here. Bird-watchers may want to look for the endemic scrub-jay, which is found nowhere else in the world.

★ The largest and deepest sea cave in the world, **Painted Cave,** lies along the northwest coast of Santa Cruz. Named for the colorful lichen and algae that cover its walls, Painted Cave is nearly ¼ mi long and 100 feet wide. In spring a waterfall cascades over the entrance. Kayakers may encounter seals or sea lions cruising alongside their boats inside the cave.

Remnants of a dozen Chumash villages can be seen on the island. The largest of these villages, at the eastern end of the island, occupied the area now called **Scorpion Ranch.** The Chumash mined extensive chert deposits on the island for tools to produce shell-bead money, which they traded with people on the mainland. Remnants of the early-1900s ranching era can also be seen in the restored historic buildings, equipment, and adobe ovens that produced bread for the entire island.

**Santa Rosa Island.** Located between Santa Cruz and San Miguel, Santa Rosa is the second largest of the Channel Islands. The island has a rel-

## CHANNEL ISLANDS IN ONE DAY

If you have just a few hours or one day to visit Channel Islands National Park, view the exhibits at the **Channel Islands Visitor Center** in Ventura and cruise over to **East Anacapa,** where you'll have sweeping views of Santa Cruz Island and the mainland—provided it's not too foggy. Hiking is the primary activity here, especially in spring when fields of sunny coreopsis flowers bloom. Wander through Western gull rookeries, or peer down from steep cliffs and watch the antics of sea lions and seals. Alternatively, you can zip out to Scorpion Landing or Prisoner's Harbor on Santa Cruz Island on a high-speed catamaran for more extended hiking, snorkeling, or kayaking.

atively low profile, broken by a central mountain range rising to 1,589 feet. The coastal areas range from broad sandy beaches to sheer cliffs. The island is home to about 500 species of plants, including the rare Torrey pine. Three unusual mammals—the endemic island fox, spotted skunk, and deer mouse—make their home here. They hardly compare to the mammoths that once roamed the island; a nearly complete skeleton of a 6-foot-tall pygmy mammoth was unearthed in 1994. The oldest dated human remains in North America—the Arlington Springs Woman (estimated to be 13,000 years old)—were also discovered here.

The island was once home to the **Vail and Vickers Ranch,** where sheep and cattle were raised from 1901 to 1998. You can see what the operation was like by viewing the historic ranch buildings, barns, equipment, and the wooden pier where cattle were brought onto the island.

### Visitor Centers

**Channel Islands National Park Robert J. Lagomarsino Visitor Center.** The park's main visitor center has a museum, a bookstore, a three-story observation tower with telescopes, and exhibits about the islands. There's also a tide pool where you can see sea stars clinging to rocks, anemones waving their colorful, spiny tentacles, and a brilliant orange garibaldi darting around. The center also has full-size reproductions of a male northern elephant seal and the pygmy mammoth skeleton unearthed on Santa Rosa Island in 1994. Rangers lead various free public programs describing park resources on weekends and holidays at 11 and 3; they can also give you a detailed map and trip-planning packet if you're interested in visiting the actual islands. ⊠ *1901 Spinnaker Dr., Ventura* ☎ *805/658–5730* ⊕ *www.nps.gov/chis* ☉ *Daily 8:30–5.*

**Outdoors Santa Barbara Visitor Center.** The small office in the Santa Barbara Harbor provides maps and other information about Channel Islands National Park, Channel Islands National Marine Sanctuary, and Los Padres National Forest. The same building houses the Santa Barbara Maritime Museum. Volunteers staff the center; call ahead to verify hours. ⊠ *113 Harbor Way, Santa Barbara* ☎ *805/884–1475* ⊕ *http://outdoorsb.noaa.gov/* ☉ *Daily 11–5.*

## Sports & the Outdoors

### Diving

Some of the best snorkeling and diving in the world can be found in the cool waters surrounding the Channel Islands. In the relatively warm water around Anacapa and eastern Santa Cruz, photographers can get great shots of rarely seen giant black bass swimming among the kelp forests. Here you'll also find a reef covered with red brittle starfish. If you're an experienced diver, you might swim among five species of seals and sea lions, or try your hand at spearing rockfish or halibut near San Miguel and Santa Rosa. The best time to scuba dive is in the summer and fall, when the water is often clear up to a 100-foot depth. ⇨ Outfitters & Expeditions box for equipment rentals and dive operators.

| BRAVING THE ELEMENTS |
| --- |
| High winds can come without notice here, particularly on the outer islands of Santa Rosa and San Miguel. Carry a warm jacket and wear sunscreen, sunglasses, and a wide-brim hat that you can tie to your head. |

**13**

### Hiking

The terrain on most of the islands ranges from flat to moderately hilly. There are no services (and no public phones; cell-phone reception is dicey) on the islands—you'll have to bring all your own food, water (except on Santa Cruz and Santa Rosa), and supplies.

For guided hiking expeditions, ⇨ Outfitters & Expeditions box.

EASY **Cuyler Harbor Beach.** This easy walk takes you along a 2-mi-long white sand beach on San Miguel. The eastern section is occasionally cut off by high tides. ⊠ *San Miguel Campground, San Miguel Island.*

**Historic Ranch.** This easy ½-mi walk on Santa Cruz Island takes you to a historic ranch where you can see remnants of a cattle ranch. ⊠ *Scorpion Beach, Santa Cruz Island.*

★ ☙ **Inspiration Point.** This 1½-mi hike along flat terrain takes in most of East Anacapa; there are great views from Inspiration Point and Cathedral Cove. ⊠ *Landing Cove, Anacapa Island.*

**Water Canyon.** Starting at Santa Rosa Campground, this 2-mi walk along a white-sand beach includes some exceptional beachcombing. Frequent strong winds can turn this easy hike into a fairly strenuous excursion, so be prepared. If you extend your walk into Water Canyon, you'll follow animal paths to a lush canyon full of native vegetation. ⊠ *Santa Rosa Campground, Santa Rosa Island.*

MODERATE **Cavern Point.** This moderate 2-mi hike takes you to the bluffs northwest
☙ of Scorpion harbor on Santa Cruz, where you'll take in magnificent coastal views and see pods of migrating gray whales from December through March. ⊠ *Santa Cruz Campground, Santa Barbara Island.*

**Elephant Seal Cove.** This moderate to strenuous walk takes you across Santa Barbara to a point where you can view magnificent elephant seals from steep cliffs. ⊠ *Landing Cove, Santa Barbara Island.*

## TRANSPORTATION OPTIONS

**Channel Islands Aviation.** Channel Islands Aviation provides half-day excursions, surf fishing, and camper transportation year-round, flying from Camarillo Airport, about 10 mi east of Oxnard, to an airstrip on Santa Rosa. They will also pick up groups of six or more at Santa Barbara Airport. ⊠ *305 Durley Ave., Camarillo* ☎ *805/987-1301* ⊕ *www.flycia.com* 🖃 *$130 per person; $200 per person if camping.*

**Island Packers.** Sailing from Ventura and Oxnard, Island Packers' two 64-foot high-speed catamarans zip over to Santa Cruz Island—with stops at Anacapa Island—daily in summer, less frequently the rest of the year. Island Packers also visits the other

islands three or four times a month (most frequently in the spring, summer, and fall) and provides transportation for campers. ⊠ *3600 S. Harbor Blvd., Oxnard* ☎ *805/642-1393* ⊠ *1691 Spinnaker Dr., Ventura* ☎ *805/642-1393* ⊕ *www.islandpackers.com* 🖃 *$32–$62.*

**Truth Aquatics.** Truth Aquatics departs from the Santa Barbara Harbor for single- and multiday scuba trips and multiday hiking excursions to all of the Channel Islands. ⊠ *301 W. Cabrillo Blvd., Santa Barbara* ☎ *805/962-1127* ⊕ *www.truthaquatics.com* 🖃 *$100 for scuba day trips; onboard all-inclusive overnight trips average $150 per day.*

Fodor'sChoice ★ **Prisoners Harbor.** Taking in quite a bit of Santa Cruz, this moderate to strenuous 3-mi trail to Pelican Cove is one of the best hikes in the park. You must be accompanied by a ranger or Island Packers staff, or secure a permit (call 949/263-0933, Ext. 36 or visit www.tnccalifornia.org; allow 15 days to process your application), as the hike takes you through Nature Conservancy property. ⊠ *Prisoners Harbor, Santa Cruz Island.*

**Torrey Pines.** This moderate 5-mi loop climbs up to Santa Rosa's grove of rare Torrey pines and offers stellar views of Becher's Bay and the channel. ⊠ *Santa Rosa Campground, Santa Rosa Island.*

DIFFICULT **East Point.** This strenuous 12-mi hike along beautiful white-sand beaches yields the opportunity to see rare Torrey pines. Some beaches are closed between March and September, so you'll have to remain on the road for portions of this hike. ⊠ *Santa Rosa Campground, Santa Rosa Island.*

**Lester Ranch.** This short but strenuous 2-mi hike leads up a spectacular canyon filled with waterfalls and lush native plants. At the end of a steep climb to the top of a peak, you'll be rewarded with views of the historic Lester Ranch and the Cabrillo Monument. (If you plan to hike beyond the Lester Ranch, you'll need a hiking permit; call 805/658-5730.) ⊠ *San Miguel Campground, San Miguel Island.*

**Point Bennett.** Rangers conduct 15-mi hikes across San Miguel to Point Bennett, where more than 30,000 pinnipeds can be seen. ⊠ *San Miguel Campground, San Miguel Island.*

## OUTFITTERS & EXPEDITIONS

### DIVING

**Peace Dive Boat.** Ventura Harbor-based Peace Dive Boat runs single and multiday live-aboard diving adventures near all the Channel Islands. ✉ 1567 Spinnaker Dr., Ventura ☎ 866/924-2025, 805/650-3483 ⊕ www.peaceboat.com 🍽 Day trips start at $75.

**Spectre Dive Boat.** The Spectre runs single-day diving trips to Anacapa, Santa Cruz, Santa Rosa, and San Miguel. Fees include three or four dives, air, and food. ✉ 1575 Spinnaker Dr., Suite 105B-75, Ventura ☎ 866/225-3483 or 805/486-4486 ⊕ http://calboatdiving.com 🍽 $78-$110.

**Truth Aquatics.** Trips to the Channel Islands lasting a day or more can be arranged through this Santa Barbara operator. You live aboard the boats on multiday trips; all meals are provided. ✉ 301 Cabrillo Blvd., Santa Barbara ☎ 805/962-1127 ⊕ www.truthaquatics.com 🍽 $101-$600.

### HIKING

**Truth Aquatics.** Truth Aquatics serves all the park's islands for multiday overnight trips that include naturalist-led hikes (you sleep and eat on board the 65-foot twin-engine single-hull vessels). ✉ 301 W. Cabrillo Blvd., Santa Barbara ☎ 805/962-1127 or 805/963-3564 ⊕ www.truthaquatics.com 🍽 $340-$475 ⊙ Call for times and dates.

### KAYAKING

**Adventours Outdoor Excursions.** Guides lead regular weekend kayak trips to Anacapa and East Santa Cruz Island; they can also arrange custom packages. ✉ 726 Reddick Ave., Santa Barbara ☎ 877/467-2148 or 805/899-2929 ⊕ www.adventours.com 🍽 $175 and up for day trip ⊙ Call for schedule.

**Aquasports.** This highly regarded company offers guided one-, two-, and three-day trips to Scorpion Landing on Santa Cruz and one-day trips to Santa Barbara Island for beginner to expert kayakers. Cross-channel passage, instruction, equipment, and guides are included. ✉ 111 Verona Ave., Goleta ☎ 800/773-2309 or 805/968-7231 ⊕ www.islandkayaking.com 🍽 $175-$340 ⊙ Call for times and dates; advance reservations recommended.

**Channel Islands Kayak Center.** This company rents kayaks and offers one-day guided kayak and snorkeling trips. Excursions include transportation, equipment, and guides. ✉ 1691 Spinnaker Dr., Ventura ☎ 805/644-9699 ✉ 3600 Harbor Blvd., Oxnard ☎ 805/984-5995 ⊕ www.cikayak.com 🍽 $170.

**Paddle Sports.** You can take a one-day trip to one of the five islands, or overnight multi-day excursions to several islands. All trips include equipment, instruction, and transportation across the channel. ✉ 117B Harbor Way, Santa Barbara ☎ 805/899-4925 ⊕ www.kayaksb.com 🍽 $184-$500.

### WHALE-WATCHING

**Island Packers.** Depending on the season, you can take a three-hour or all-day whale-watching tour from either Ventura or Channel Islands harbors. ✉ 1691 Spinnaker Dr., Ventura ☎ 805/642-1393 ⊕ www.islandpackers.com 🍽 $26-$60.

13

### Kayaking

The most remote parts of Channel Islands are accessible only by a sea kayak. Some of the best kayaking in the park can be found on Anacapa, Santa Barbara, and the eastern tip of Santa Cruz. Anacapa has plenty of sea caves, tidal pools, and even natural bridges you can paddle beneath. Brown pelicans, cormorants, and storm petrels nest in Santa Barbara's steep cliffs; you'll find one of the world's largest colonies of Xantus' murrelets here as well, and you can also get up close and personal with seals and sea lions. Santa Cruz has plenty of secluded beaches to explore, as well as seabird nesting sites and seal and sea lion rookeries. You can land at any of the islands, but permits are required for the western side of Santa Cruz. There are no public moorings around the islands, so it's recommended that one person stay aboard the boat at all times. You'll find the best kayaking from July through September or October, when the waters calm down. Santa Barbara Island is an exception; the best months to kayak here are April through June—after that, the southerly swells make smooth kayaking difficult. Outfitters offer tours year-round, but high seas may cause trip cancellations between December and March. The operators listed below hold permits from the National Park Service to conduct kayak tours—if you choose a different company, verify that it holds the proper permits. ⇨ Outfitters & Expeditions box for kayak rentals and guided tours.

### Whale-watching

About a third of the world's cetacean species (27 to be exact) can be seen in the Santa Barbara Channel. In July and August, humpback and blue whales feed off the north shore of Santa Rosa. From late December to April, up to 10,000 gray whales pass through the Santa Barbara Channel on their way from Alaska to Mexico and back again. ⇨ Outfitters & Expeditions box for whale-watching expeditions.

## Educational Offerings

### Guided Tours

🐚 **Channel Islands Live Underwater Video Program.** Watch live as divers armed with video cameras explore the undersea world of the kelp forest off Anacapa Island; images are transmitted to monitors located on the dock at Landing Cove and in the main visitor center. You'll see bright red sea stars, spiny sea urchins, and brilliant orange garibaldis. You can even ask the divers questions via interactive lines. ⊠ *Landing Cove, Anacapa Island* 🎦 *Free* ☉ *Summer, Tues.–Thurs. at 2.*

### Ranger Programs

**Interpreting the Language of the Park.** Presentations by different rangers

---

**GOOD READS**

You can find a handful of books about this little-known gem in the Channel Islands Visitor Center in Ventura, including **California's Channel Islands: 1001 Questions Answered** by Marla Daily, **Channel Islands National Park** by Susan Lamb, and **Channel Islands National Park** by Tim Hauf. In addition, **Island of the Blue Dolphins** by Scott O'Dell is a good book that will help kids to get acquainted with the park.

focus on the park's rich history; topics include everything from tidal pools and marine life to shipwrecks and the area's cultural history. These presentations are held at the Channel Islands Visitor Center. ⊠ *1901 Spinnaker Rd., Ventura* ☎ *805/658–5730* ⊕ *www.nps.gov/chis* ▱ *Free* ⊙ *Weekends and holidays at 3* PM.

**Tidepool Talk.** Explore the area's marine habitat without getting your feet wet. Rangers at the Channel Islands Visitor Center demonstrate how animals and plants adapt to the harsh conditions found in tidal pools of the Channel Islands. ⊠ *1901 Spinnaker Rd., Ventura* ☎ *805/658–5730* ⊕ *www.nps.gov/chis* ⊙ *Weekends and holidays at 11* AM.

# WHAT'S NEARBY

## Nearby Towns

With a population of more than 100,000, **Ventura** is the main gateway to Channel Islands National Park. It's a classic California beach town filled with interesting restaurants, a wide range of accommodations, and miles of clean, white beaches. South of Ventura is **Oxnard,** a community of 162,000 boasting a busy harbor and uncrowded beaches. Known for its Spanish ambience, **Santa Barbara** has a beautiful waterfront set against a backdrop of towering mountains. Here you'll find glistening palm-lined beaches, whitewashed adobe structures with red-tile roofs, and plenty of genteel charm.

## Nearby Attractions

Fodor'sChoice ★ **Mission Santa Barbara.** Widely referred to as the "Queen of Missions," this is one of the most beautiful and frequently photographed buildings in coastal California. ⊠ *2201 Laguna St., Santa Barbara* ☎ *805/682–4149* ⊕ *www.sbmission.org* ▱ *$4* ⊙ *Daily 9–5.*

**Santa Barbara Museum of Natural History.** The gigantic skeleton of a blue whale greets you at the entrance of this complex, where major draws include a planetarium, space-related activities and exhibits, a gem and mineral display, and dioramas illustrating Chumash Indian history and culture; many exhibits have interactive components. ⊠ *2559 Puesta del Sol Rd., Santa Barbara* ☎ *805/682–4711* ⊕ *www.sbnature.org* ▱ *$8* ⊙ *Daily 10–5.*

**Stearns Wharf.** Built in 1872, historic Stearns Wharf is Santa Barbara's most visited landmark. Expansive views of the mountains, cityscape, and harbor unfold from every vantage point on the three-block-long pier, which has shops and restaurants. ⊠ *Cabrillo Blvd. at the foot of State St., Santa Barbara* ☎ *805/897–2683 or 805/564–5531.*

> **FAMILY PICKS**
>
> - Hop on a harbor water taxi and make friends with a sea lion.
> - Hunt for tide-pool treasures at the beach or the **Ty Warner Sea Center.**
> - Pedal a boat through Venetian-style canals near Channel Islands Harbor.

**Ty Warner Sea Center.** A branch of the Santa Barbara Museum of Natural History, the Sea Center specializes in Santa Barbara Channel marine life and conservation. A fascinating, hands-on marine science laboratory lets you participate in experiments, projects, and exhibits. The two-story glass walls open to stunning ocean, mountain, and city views. ⊠ *211 Stearns Wharf, Santa Barbara* ☎ *805/962–2526* ⊕ *www. sbnature.org* ⊴ *$7* ⊙ *Daily 10–5.*

# WHERE TO STAY & EAT

## About the Restaurants

Out on the islands, you won't have any trouble deciding where to dine—there are no restaurants, no snack bars, and in some cases, no potable water. Pack a fancy picnic or a simple sandwich—and don't forget it in your car or hotel room unless you want to starve. If you want to eat a quick meal before or after your island trip, each of the harbors has a number of decent eateries nearby.

Back on the mainland, though, it's a dining gold mine. Santa Barbara has a longstanding reputation for culinary excellence, and a "foodie" renaissance in recent years has transformed Ventura into a dining destination—with dozens of new restaurants touting nouvelle cuisine made with organic produce and meats. Fresh seafood is a standout, whether it's prepared simply in wharf-side hangouts or incorporated into sophisticated bistro menus. Dining attire is generally casual, though slightly dressy casual wear is the custom at pricier restaurants.

## About the Hotels

It's easy to choose where to stay in the park—your only option is sleeping in your tent in a no-frills campground. If you hanker for more creature comforts, you can splurge on a bunk and meals on a park concessionaire dive boat.

There's a huge range of lodging options on the mainland, from seaside camping to posh international resorts. The most affordable options are in Oxnard, Ventura, and Carpinteria, a small seaside community between Santa Barbara and Ventura. Despite rates that range from pricey to downright shocking, Santa Barbara's numerous hotels and bed-and-breakfasts attract thousands of patrons year-round. Wherever you stay, be sure to make reservations for the summer and holiday weekends (especially Memorial Day, Labor Day, and Thanksgiving) well ahead of time; it's not unusual for coastal accommodations to fill completely during these busy times. Also be aware that some hotels double their rates during festivals and other events.

## About the Campgrounds

Camping is the best way to experience the natural beauty and isolation of Channel Islands National Park. Unrestricted by tour schedules, you'll have plenty of time to explore mountain trails, snorkel in the kelp forests, or kayak into sea caves. Campsites are primitive, with no water (except on Santa Rosa and Santa Cruz) or electricity; enclosed camp stoves must be used. Campfires are not allowed on the islands, and you must carry all your gear and pack out all trash. Campers must arrange transportation to the islands before reserving a campsite (and yes, park personnel do check). You can get specifics on each campground and reserve a campsite ($15 per night) by contacting the **National Park Service Reservation System** (☎ 800/365–2267 ⊕ http://reservations.nps.gov) up to five months in advance.

**13**

## Where to Eat

### In Channel Islands National Park

**Picnic Areas.** Picnic tables are available on all the islands except San Miguel. You can also picnic on some of the beaches of Santa Cruz, Santa Rosa, and San Miguel; be aware that high winds are always a possibility on Santa Rosa and San Miguel.

### Outside the Park

**$$–$$$** ✕ **The Whale's Tail.** This popular seafood house in Channel Islands Harbor includes a casual upstairs shellfish bar with indoor/outdoor seating and a more formal main dining room downstairs; practically all the tables let in waterfront views. Fresh fish is delivered to the restaurant's dock daily. ⊠ *3950 Bluefin Circle, Channel Islands Harbor, Oxnard* ☎ *805/985–2511* ⚛ *Reservations essential. $20–$28* ▤ *AE, MC, V.*

**$$** ✕ **Brophy Bros.** The outdoor tables at this casual harborside restaurant have perfect views of the marina and mountains. The staff serves enormous, exceptionally fresh fish dishes—don't miss the seafood salad and chowder. This place is hugely popular, but be aware that it can be crowded and loud, especially on weekend evenings. ⊠ *119 Harbor Way, Santa Barbara* ☎ *805/966–4418. $14–$19* ▤ *AE, MC, V.*

**$–$$** ✕ **Andria's Seafood.** The specialties at this casual, family-oriented restaurant are fresh fish-and-chips and homemade clam chowder. After placing your order at the counter, you can sit outside on the patio and enjoy the view of the harbor and marina. ⊠ *1449 Spinnaker Dr., Suite A, Ventura Harbor Village* ☎ *805/654–0546. $9–$15* ▤ *MC, V.*

**$–$$** ✕ **Cabo Seafood Grill and Cantina.** A crowd of locals in the know gathers at this lively restaurant and bar close to downtown Oxnard for south of the border seafood specialties served with fresh handmade tortillas. The rainbow-hued dining rooms and patio are casual and cheery. If you're not a seafood fan, try the *carne asada* (marinated strips of beef) or one of the large combination plates. ⊠ *1041 S. Oxnard Blvd., Oxnard* ☎ *805/487–6933. $9–$15* ▤ *AE, D, DC, MC, V.*

**★ ¢–$** ✕ **La Super-Rica Taqueria.** Praised by Julia Child, this food stand with a patio on the east side of town serves some of the spiciest and most authentic Mexican dishes between Los Angeles and San Francisco. Portions are on the small side, so order several dishes and share. ⊠ *622 N. Milpas, at Alphonse St., Santa Barbara* ☎ *805/963–4940. $4–$8* ▤ *No credit cards.*

## Where to Stay

### In Channel Islands

CAMPING & RV
FACILITIES

**$**    **Del Norte Campground.** This campground on Santa Cruz, the newest on the islands, offers backpackers sweeping ocean views from its 1,500-foot perch. It's accessed via a 3½-mi hike through a series of canyons and ridges. ⊠ *Scorpion Beach landing* ☎ *800/365–2267* ⊕ *http://reservations.nps.gov* ⟿ *4 sites* ⚭ *Pit toilets, picnic tables. $15* ▭ *D, MC, V.*

**$**    **East Anacapa Campground.** You'll have to walk ½ mi and ascend more than 150 steps to reach this open, treeless camping area above Cathedral Cove. ⊠ *East Anacapa landing* ☎ *800/365–2267* ⊕ *http://reservations.nps.gov* ⟿ *7 sites* ⚭ *Pit toilets, picnic tables, ranger station. $15* ▭ *D, MC, V.*

**$**    **San Miguel Campground.** Accessed by a steep 1-mi hike through a lush canyon, this campground is on the site of the Lester Ranch; the Cabrillo Monument is nearby. Be aware that strong winds and thick fog are common on this remote island. ⊠ *Cuyler Harbor landing* ☎ *800/365–2267* ⊕ *http://reservations.nps.gov* ⟿ *9 sites* ⚭ *Pit toilets, picnic tables, ranger station. $15* ▭ *D, MC, V.*

**$**    **Santa Barbara Campground.** This seldom-visited campground perched on a cliff above Landing Cove is reached via a challenging ½-mi uphill climb. Three-day trips are permitted. ⊠ *Landing Cove* ☎ *800/365–2267* ⊕ *http://reservations.nps.gov* ⟿ *10 sites* ⚭ *Pit toilets, picnic tables, ranger station. $15* ▭ *D, MC, V.*

**★ $**    **Santa Cruz Scorpion Campground.** In a grove of eucalyptus trees, this campground is near the historic buildings of Scorpion Ranch. It's accessed via an easy, ½-mi, flat trail from Scorpion Beach landing. ⊠ *Scorpion Beach landing* ☎ *800/365–2267* ⊕ *http://reservations.nps.gov* ⟿ *40 sites* ⚭ *Pit toilets, drinking water, picnic tables. $15* ▭ *D, MC, V.*

**$**    **Santa Rosa Campground.** Backcountry beach camping for kayakers is available on this island; it's a 1½-mi flat walk to the campground. There's a spectacular view of Santa Cruz Island across the water. ⊠ *Bechers Bay landing* ☎ *800/365–2267* ⊕ *http://reservations.nps.gov* ⟿ *15 sites* ⚭ *Toilets, showers (cold), drinking water, picnic tables. $15* ▭ *D, MC, V.*

### Outside the Park

**★ $$$$**    **San Ysidro Ranch.** John and Jackie Kennedy spent their honeymoon at this romantic hideaway, and Oprah sends her out-of-town guests here. Guest cottages are scattered among groves of orange trees and flower beds; all have down comforters and fireplaces, and many have private outdoor spas—one even has its own pool. Seventeen miles of hiking trails crisscross 500 acres of open space surrounding the property, and the resort's Stonehouse Restaurant and Plow & Angel Bistro are Santa Barbara institutions. ⊠ *900 San Ysidro La., Montecito 93108* ☎ *805/565–1700 or 800/368–6788* 🖷 *805/565–1995* ⊕ *www.sanysidroranch.com* ⟿ *40 cottages* ⚭ *2 restaurants, room service, refrigerator, DVD, ethernet, WiFi, pool, gym, bar, some pets allowed; no-smoking rooms. $599* ▭ *AE, DC, MC, V* ☞ *2-day minimum stay on weekends, 3 days on holiday weekends.*

**$$–$$$**    **Franciscan Inn.** Part of this Spanish-Mediterranean motel, a block from the harbor and West Beach, dates back to the 1920s. The friendly staff and range of cheery, spacious country-themed rooms—from singles to mini- and family suites—make this a good choice for families. ⊠ *109 Bath St., Santa Barbara 93101* ☎ *805/963–8845* 🖷 *805/564–3295* ⊕ *www.franciscaninn.com* ⇗ *48 rooms, 5 suites* ⚬ *Kitchen (some), refrigerator (some), VCR, pool, laundry facilities, no-smoking rooms.* *$115–$175* ⊟ *AE, DC, MC, V* ⎥❍⎥ *CP.*

**$–$$** ▦ **Clocktower Inn.** In the heart of downtown, this inn is next to Mission San Buenaventura, the Historical Museum, and the area's many boutique shops. Rooms are done up in soft Southwestern colors, and many have private patios, fireplaces, carved headboards, desks, leather chairs, and armoires. Continental breakfast and access to a fitness studio are complimentary. ⊠ *181 E. Santa Clara, Ventura 93001* ☎ *805/652–0141 or 800/727–1027* 🖷 *805/643–1432* ⊕ *www.clocktowerinn.com* ⇗ *50 rooms* ⚬ *Restaurant, room service, ethernet, no-smoking rooms.* *$99–$139* ⊟ *AE, D, DC, MC, V* ⎥❍⎥ *CP.*

**$–$$** ▦ **Motel 6 Santa Barbara Beach.** This basic but comfortable motel—the first Motel 6 in existence—sits a half block from East Beach amid fancier hotels. It's an incredible bargain for the location, and it fills up quickly; book months in advance if possible. Two sister properties in Carpinteria, 12 mi south of Santa Barbara and 1 mi from the beach, offer equally comfortable rooms at even lower rates. ⊠ *443 Corona Del Mar Dr., Santa Barbara 93103* ☎ *805/564–1392 or 800/466–8356* 🖷 *805/963–4687* ⊕ *www.motel6.com* ⇗ *51 rooms* ⚬ *Refrigerator (some), dial-up, pool, some pets allowed, no-smoking rooms.* *$89–$112* ⊟ *AE, D, DC, MC, V.*

**$** ▦ **Channel Islands Inn and Suites.** This hacienda-style hotel is set amid soaring palm trees. Spacious, modern rooms are filled with Shaker- and mission-style furnishings. ⊠ *1001 E. Channel Islands Blvd., Oxnard 93033* ☎ *805/201–6000 or 800/344–5998* 🖷 *805/486–1374* ⊕ *www. channelislandsinn.com* ⇗ *92 rooms* ⚬ *Refrigerator, VCR, ethernet, pool, gym, laundry facilities, some pets allowed.* *$89–$99* ⊟ *AE, D, DC, MC, V* ⎥❍⎥ *BP.*

# CHANNEL ISLANDS ESSENTIALS

**ACCESSIBILITY** The Channel Islands Visitor Center is fully accessible. The islands themselves have few facilities and are not easy to navigate by individuals in wheelchairs or those with limited mobility. Limited wheelchair access is available on Santa Rosa Island via air transportation.

**ADMISSION FEES** There is no fee to enter Channel Islands National Park, but there is a $15 per day fee for staying in one of the campgrounds. The cost of taking a boat to the park varies depending on which operator you choose.

**ADMISSION HOURS** The islands are open every day of the year. Channel Islands Visitor Center is closed Thanksgiving and Christmas. Channel Islands National Park is located in the Pacific Time Zone.

**ATMS/BANKS**
❂ **Santa Barbara Bank and Trust** ⊠ 583 W. Channel Islands Blvd., near Channel Islands Harbor, Port Hueneme ☎ 805/965–5594. **Santa Barbara Bank and Trust** ⊠ 1960 Cliff Dr., Santa Barbara ☎ 805/965–5594.

AUTOMOBILE SERVICE STATIONS
🅵 **Channel Islands Chevron** ✉ 1960 Victoria Ave., near Channel Islands Harbor, Oxnard ☎ 805/985–1592. **Chevron** ✉ 920 S. Seaward Blvd., at Harbor Blvd. near Ventura Harbor, Ventura ☎ 805/642–9138. **Seaside Gas** ✉ 134 S. Milpas St., Santa Barbara ☎ 805/965–2249.

EMERGENCIES In the event of an emergency, contact a park ranger on patrol or call 911.

LOST AND FOUND The park's lost-and-found is at Channel Islands Visitor Center.

PERMITS Permits are not required to visit Channel Islands, with the exception of Middle Anacapa (call 805/658–5711 for information). Boaters who want to land on the Nature Conservancy preserve on Santa Cruz Island should call 949/263–0933 Ext. 36 or visit www.tnccalifornia.org; allow 15 days to process your application. To hike on San Miguel, call 805/658–5711. Anglers require a state fishing license. For details, call the California Department of Fish and Game at 916/653–7664. Twelve Marine Protected Areas (MPAs) with special resource protection regulations surround the islands, so be sure to read the guidelines before you depart. Contact park headquarters for information.

POST OFFICES
🅵 **Oxnard Main Post Office** ✉ 1961 North C St., Oxnard 93030 ☎ 805/278–7615 or 800/275–8777.

**Santa Barbara Main Post Office** ✉ 836 Anacapa St., Santa Barbara 93102 ☎ 805/564–2226 or 800/275–8777. **Ventura Main Post Office** ✉ 675 E. Santa Clara St., Ventura 93001 ☎ 805/643–8057 or 800/275–8777.

PUBLIC TELEPHONES Public telephones are available near the Channel Islands Visitor Center. There are no public phones on the islands.

RESTROOMS Public restrooms are available at the Channel Islands Visitor Center and at the campgrounds on all five islands.

**NEARBY TOWN INFORMATION**
🅵 **Oxnard Convention and Visitors Bureau** ✉ 200 W. 7th St., Oxnard 93030-7154 ☎ 805/385-7545 or 800/269-6273 🌐 www.visitoxnard.com. **Santa Barbara Conference and Visitors Bureau and Film Commission** ✉ 1601 Anacapa St., Santa Barbara 93101-1909 ☎ 805/966-9222 or 800/676-1266 🌐 www.santabarbaraca.com. **Ventura Visitors and Convention Bureau** ✉ 89 S. California St., Suite C, Ventura 93001 ☎ 805/648-2075 or 800/483-6214 🌐 www.ventura-usa.com. **Hot Spots** ☎ 805/564-1637 or 800/793-7666 🌐 www.hotspotsusa.com provides room reservations and tourist information for destinations in Ventura and Santa Barbara counties.

**VISITOR INFORMATION**
🅵 **Channel Islands Visitor Center** ✉ 1901 Spinnaker Dr., Ventura, CA 93001 ☎ 805/658-5730 🌐 www.nps.gov/chis ⊙ Daily 8:30-5.

# Crater Lake National Park

Crater Lake, Crater Lake National Park

## WORD OF MOUTH

"An overmastering conviction came to me that this wonderful spot must be saved, wild and beautiful, just as it was, for all future generations, and that it was up to me to do something."

–William Gladstone Steel, "Father of Crater Lake"

# WELCOME TO CRATER LAKE

Wizard Island on Crater Lake

## TOP REASONS TO GO

★ **The lake:** Experience the extraordinary rich, sapphire blue of the country's deepest lake close-up as you cruise inside the caldera basin.

★ **Native land:** Enjoy the rare luxury of interacting with totally unspoiled terrain.

★ **The night sky:** Billions of stars glisten in the pitch-black darkness of an unpolluted sky.

★ **Splendid hikes:** Accessible trails wind past colorful bursts of wildflowers gently swaying in the summer breeze.

★ **Camping at its best:** Pitch a tent or pull up a motor home at Mazama Campground, which is beautifully situated, guest-friendly, and well-maintained.

The Pinnacles.

**1** Crater Lake. The focal point of the park, this non-recreational, scenic destination is known for its deep blue hue.

**2** Wizard Island. Visitors can take boat rides to this protruding land mass rising from the western section of Crater Lake; it's a great place for a hike or a picnic.

**3** Mazama Village. This is your best bet for stocking up on snacks, beverages, and fuel in the park; it's about five miles from Rim Drive.

**4** Cleetwood Cove Trail. The only safe, designated trail to hike down the caldera and reach the lake's edge is on the rim's north side off Rim Drive.

## GETTING ORIENTED

Crater Lake National Park covers 183,224 acres. Located in Southern Oregon less than 100 miles from the California border, it's surrounded by several Cascade Range forests, including the Winema and Rogue River National Forests. The closest neighboring towns are each approximately 60 miles from the lake, with Roseburg to the Northwest, and Medford and Klamath Falls to the South.

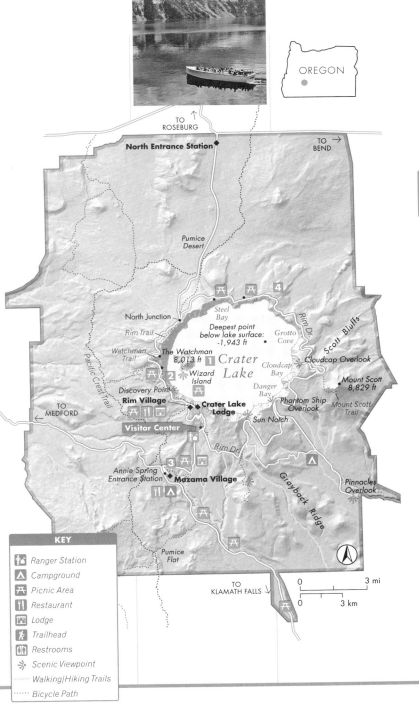

OREGON

TO
ROSEBURG

North Entrance Station

TO
BEND

14

Pumice
Desert

Steel
Bay

Deepest point
below lake surface:
-1,943 ft

Grotto
Cove

4

North Junction

Rim Trail

Watchman
Trail

The Watchman
8,013 ft

1

Crater
Lake

Rim Dr.

Scott Bluffs

Cloudcap Overlook

Wizard Island

Cloudcap
Bay

Mount Scott
8,829 ft

Pacific Crest Trail

2

Discovery Point

Rim Village

Danger
Bay

Mount Scott
Trail

Crater Lake
Lodge

Phantom Ship
Overlook

Visitor Center

Sun Notch

TO
MEDFORD

Rim Dr.

Annie Spring
Entrance Station

3

Mazama Village

Grayback Ridge

Pinnacles
Overlook

Pumice
Flat

TO
KLAMATH FALLS

KEY

🏕 Ranger Station
⛺ Campground
🎋 Picnic Area
🍴 Restaurant
🏠 Lodge
🚶 Trailhead
🚻 Restrooms
✳ Scenic Viewpoint
······ Walking/Hiking Trails
······ Bicycle Path

0       3 mi
0       3 km

# CRATER LAKE PLANNER

## When to Go

Most of the park is only accessible in late June–early July through mid-October. The rest of the year, snow blocks all park roadways and entrances except Highway 62 and the access road to Rim Village from Mazama Village. Rim Drive is typically closed because of heavy snowfall from mid-October to mid-July, and you could encounter icy conditions any month of the year, particularly in early morning. Crater Lake receives more snowfall–an annual average of 44 feet–than any other national park except for Mount Rainier. For a real-time view of weather conditions at the rim, log onto the Crater Lake Lodge crater cam at www.craterlakelodges.com/cratercam.htm.

**The park's high season is July and August.** September and early October–which can be delightful–tend to draw smaller crowds. From October through June, the entire park virtually closes due to heavy snowfall and freezing temperatures. The road is kept open just to the rim in winter, except during severe weather.

AVG. HIGH/LOW TEMPS.

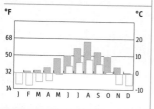

## Flora & Fauna

Two primary types of fish swim beneath the surface of Crater Lake: kokanee salmon and rainbow trout. It's estimated that hundreds of thousands of kokanee inhabit the lake, but since boating and recreational access is so limited, they elude many would-be sportsman. Trout—including bull, Eastern brook, rainbow, and German brown—also swim in the park's many streams and rivers; but they usually remain elusive because these waterways flow near inaccessibly steep canyons.

Remote canyons also shelter the park's elk and deer populations, which can sometimes be seen at dusk and dawn feeding at forest's edge. Black bears and pine martens—cousins of the short-tailed weasel—also call Crater Lake home. Birds such as three-toed–and hairy woodpeckers, California gulls, red-tailed hawks, and great horned owls are more commonly seen in the summer in the forests below the lake.

## Good Reads

*Crater Lake National Park: A Global Treasure,* by former park rangers Ann and Myron Sutton, celebrates the park's first 100 years with stunning photography, charts, and drawings. Ron Warfield's *A Guide to Crater Lake National Park and The Mountain That Used to Be* gives a useful and lushly illustrated overview of Crater Lake's history and physical features. The National Park Service uses Stephen Harris's *Fire Mountains of the West* in its ranger training; the detailed handbook covers Cascade Range geology. *Wildflowers of the Olympics and Cascades,* by Charles Stewart, is an easy-to-use guide to the area's flora and fauna. Also, be sure to pick up a copy of the park newspaper, *Reflections,* upon arrival.

14

By Janna
Mock-Lopez

The pure, untrammeled blue of Crater Lake never fails to astound at first sight. The 21-square-mi lake was created 7,700 years ago after the eruption of Mt. Mazama. Days after the eruption, the mountain collapsed on an underground chamber emptied of lava. Rain and snowmelt filled the caldera, creating a sapphire-blue lake so clear that sunlight penetrates to a depth of 400 feet (the lake is 1,943 feet deep). Today it's both the clearest and deepest lake in the United States—seventh deepest in the world.

## Scenic Drive

★ **Rim Drive.** The 33-mi loop around the lake is the main scenic route, affording views of the lake and its cliffs from every conceivable angle. The drive alone takes up to two hours; frequent stops at overlooks and short hikes can easily stretch this to a half day. Be aware that Rim Drive is typically closed due to heavy snowfall from mid-October to mid-June, and icy conditions can be encountered any month of the year, particularly in early morning. ⊠ *Rim Dr. leads from Annie Spring entrance station to Rim Village, where the drive circles around the rim; it's about 4½ mi from the entrance station to Rim Village. To get to Rim Drive from the park's north entrance at Rte. 230, follow the North Crater Lake access road for about 10 mi.*

## What to See

For most visitors, the star attractions of Crater Lake are the lake itself and the breathtakingly-situated Crater Lake Lodge. Other park highlights include the natural, unspoiled beauty of the forest and the geological marvels that you can access along the 33-mile Rim Drive.

### Historic Site

Fodor'sChoice **Crater Lake Lodge.** First built in 1915, this classic log-and-stone struc-
★  ture still boasts the original lodgepole pine pillars, beams, and stone fire-

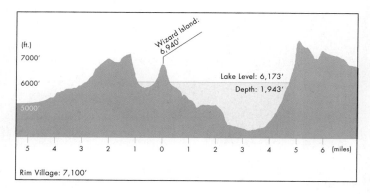

places. The lobby, fondly referred to as the Great Hall, serves as a warm, welcoming gathering place where you can play games, socialize with a cocktail, or gaze out of the many windows to view spectacular sunrises and sunsets by a crackling fire. ⊠ *Rim Village just east of Rim Visitor Center.*

## Scenic Stops

**Cloudcap Overlook.** The highest road-access overlook on the Crater Lake rim, Cloudcap has a westward view across the lake to Wizard Island and an eastward view of Mt. Scott, the volcanic cone that is the park's highest point, just 2 mi away. ⊠ *2 mi off Rim Dr., 13 mi northeast of Steel Information Center.*

**Discovery Point.** This overlook marks the spot where prospectors first spied the lake in 1853. Wizard Island is just northeast, close to shore. ⊠ *Rim Dr., 1½ mi north of Rim Village.*

**Mazama Village.** In summer a campground, motor inn, amphitheater, gas station, post office, and small store are open here. ⊠ *Mazama Village Rd. near Annie Spring entrance station* ☎ *541/830–8700* ⊕ *www.nps. gov/crla* ☉ *June–Sept., daily 8–6.*

**Phantom Ship Overlook.** From this point you can get a close look at Phantom Ship, a rock formation that resembles a small boat. ⊠ *Rim Dr., 7 mi northeast of Steel Information Center.*

**Pinnacles Overlook.** Ascending from the banks of Sand and Wheeler creeks, unearthly spires of eroded ash resemble the peaks of fairy-tale castles. Once upon a time, the road continued east to a former entrance. A path now replaces the old road and follows the rim of Sand Creek, (affording more views of pinnacles) to where the entrance still stands. ⊠ *5 mi northeast of Steel Information Center.*

## CRATER LAKE IN ONE DAY

Begin your tour at **Steel Information Center,** where interpretive displays and a short video introduce you to the story of the lake's formation and its unique characteristics. Then begin your circumnavigation of the crater's rim by heading northeast on **Rim Drive,** allowing an hour to stop at overlooks—check out the Phantom Ship rock formation in the lake below—before you reach **Cleetwood Cove Trail** trailhead, the only safe and legal access to the lake. Hike down the trail to reach the dock, and hop aboard one of the concessionaire **tour boats** for an almost-two-hour tour around the lake. If you have time, add on a trip to **Wizard Island** for a picnic lunch.

Back on Rim Drive, continue around the lake, stopping at **The Watchman** for a short but steep hike to this peak above the rim, which affords not only a splendid view of the lake, but a broad vista of the surrounding southern Cascades. Wind up your visit at **Crater Lake Lodge**—allow an hour just to wander the lobby of the 1915 structure perched on the rim. Dinner at the lodge restaurant, overlooking the lake and the Cascade sunset, caps the day.

**14**

**Sun Notch.** It's a moderate ¼-mi hike through wildflowers and dry meadow to this overlook, which has views of Crater Lake and Phantom Ship. Mind the steep edges. ✉ *E. Rim Dr., 4 mi northeast of Steel Information Center.*

★ **Wizard Island.** To get here you've got to hike down Cleetwood Cove Trail (and back up upon your return) and board the tour boat for a 1¾-hour ride. Definitely bring a picnic. ✉ *Cleetwood Cove Trail, Wizard Island dock* ☎ *541/830–8700* ☉ *Late June–mid-Sept., daily.*

### Visitor Centers

**Rim Visitor Center.** In summer you can obtain park information here, take a ranger-led tour, or stop into the nearby Sinnott Memorial, with a small museum and a 900-foot view down to the lake's surface. In winter, snowshoe walks are offered on weekends and holidays. The Rim Village Gift Store and cafeteria are the only services open in winter. ✉ *Rim Dr. on the south side of the lake, 7 mi north of Annie Spring entrance station* ☎ *541/594–3090* ⊕ *www.nps.gov/crla* ☉ *Late June–Sept., daily 9:30–5.*

**Steel Information Center.** The information center is part of the park's headquarters; you'll find restrooms and a first-aid station here. There's also a small post office and a shop that sells books, maps, and postcards. In the auditorium, an ongoing 18-minute film, *The Crater Lake Story,* describes Crater Lake's formation. ✉ *Rim Dr., 4 mi north of Annie Spring entrance station* ☎ *541/594–3100* ⊕ *www.nps.gov/crla* ☉ *Mid-Apr.–early Nov., daily 9–5; early Nov.–mid-Apr., daily 10–4.*

## Sports & the Outdoors

### Fishing

Fishing is allowed in the lake, but you may find the experience frustrating—in such a massive body of water, the problem is finding the fish. Try your luck near the Cleetwood Cove boat dock, or take poles on the boat tour and fish off Wizard Island. You don't need a state fishing license, but help protect the lake's pristine waters by only using artificial bait as opposed to live worms.

### Hiking

EASY **Castle Crest Wildflower Trail.** The 1-mi creek-side loop in the upper part of Munson Valley is one of the park's flatter and less demanding hikes. Wildflowers burst into full bloom here in July. ⊠ *Across the street from Steel Information Center parking lot, Rim Dr.*

**Godfrey Glen Trail.** Head down from the rim through Munson Valley to reach the parking area for this 2-mi loop that runs between Steel Information Center and the Castle Crest Wildflower Trail. It'll take you through an excellent example of what geologists term a hanging valley—the place where one valley hangs over a lower valley, with a cliff and a waterfall between them. Deer are frequently seen here, and flowers are abundant. ⊠ *2 mi off Rim Dr., 2⁷⁄₁₀ mi south of Steel Information Center.*

MODERATE **Annie Creek Canyon Trail.** Annie Creek is strenuous but still easy compared to some of the steep rim hikes, such as the Cleetwood Trail. The 2-mi loop threads through Annie Creek Canyon, providing views of the narrow cleft scarred by volcanic activity. This is a good spot to look for flowers and deer. ⊠ *Mazama Campground, Mazama Village Rd., near Annie Spring entrance station.*

**Cleetwood Cove Trail.** This 1-mi strenuous hike descends 700 feet down nearly vertical cliffs along the lake to the boat dock. ⊠ *Cleetwood Cove trailhead, N. Rim Dr., 11 mi north of Rim Village.*

**The Watchman Trail.** This is the best short hike in the park. Though it's less than a mile each way, the trail climbs more than 400 feet—not counting the steps up to the actual lookout, which has great views of Wizard Island and the lake. ⊠ *Watchman Overlook, 3⁷⁄₁₀ mi northwest of Rim Village on W. Rim Dr.*

DIFFICULT **Boundary Springs Trail.** If you're up for a challenge, consider a trip along this 8-mi trail. Easing down the gradually sloping northwestern shoulders of old Mt. Mazama, the path angles toward Pumice Desert and ends up at Boundary Springs, one of the sources of the Rogue River. To avoid the return trip, many hikers arrange to be picked

> **SERIOUS SAFETY**
>
> There is only one safe way to reach Crater Lake's edge: the Cleetwood Cove Trail from the north rim. The rest of the inner caldera is steep and composed of loose gravel, basalt, and pumice—extremely dangerous, in other words. That's why all hiking and climbing are strictly prohibited inside the rim, and rangers will issue citations for violations.

up at Lake West, a campground outside the park that is easily accessible via Route 230. ✉ *Pacific Crest Trail parking lot, north access road 2 mi north of Rim Dr., 8 mi south of the park's north entrance station.*

**Fodor'sChoice**
★
**Mt. Scott Trail.** This 2½-mi trail takes you to the park's highest point—the top of Mt. Scott, the oldest volcanic cone of Mt. Mazama, at 8,929 feet. It will take the average hiker 90 minutes to make the steep uphill trek—and about 45 minutes to get down. The trail starts at an elevation of about 7,450 feet, so the climb is not extreme but does get steep in spots. Views of the lake and the broad Klamath Basin are spectacular. ✉ *14 mi east of Steel Information Center, across E. Rim Dr. from the road to Cloudcap Overlook.*

**Pacific Crest Trail.** You can hike a portion of the Pacific Crest Trail, which extends from Mexico to Canada and winds through the park for more than 30 mi. For this prime backcountry experience, catch the trail about a mile east of the north entrance road, where it shadows the road along the west rim of the lake for about 6 mi, then descends down Dutton Creek to the Mazama Village area. An online brochure offers further details. ✉ *Pacific Crest Trail parking lot, north access road 2 mi north of Rim Dr., 8 mi south of the park's north entrance station* ⊕ *www.nps.gov/crla/brochures/pct.htm.*

## Educational Offerings

### Ranger Programs

**Boat Tours.** The most extensively used guided tours in Crater Lake are on the water, aboard launches that carry 49 passengers on a one-hour, 45-minute tour accompanied by a ranger. The boats circle the lake and make a brief stop at Wizard Island, where you can get off if you like. The first of seven tours leaves the dock at 10 AM; the last departs at 4:00 PM. After Labor Day, the schedule is reduced. To get to the dock you must hike down Cleetwood Cove Trail, a 1-mi walk that drops 700 feet; restrooms are available at the top and bottom of the trail. ✉ *Cleetwood Cove Trail, off north Rim Dr., 10 mi north of Rim Village* ☎ *541/830–8700* 🖃 *$25* ☉ *July–mid-Sept., daily.*

**Junior Ranger Program.** Junior Ranger booklets and badges are available at Steel Information Center and Rim Visitor Center. ☎ *541/594-3090.*

# WHAT'S NEARBY

## Nearby Towns

Three small cities serve as gateways to Crater Lake—each a 1½- to 2-hour drive to the park. Klamath Lake, the largest freshwater lake in Oregon, is anchored at its south end by the city of **Klamath Falls**, population 20,000. With year-round sunshine, Klamath Falls is home to acres of parks and marinas from which to enjoy water sports and bird-watching. **Roseburg**'s location at the west edge of the southern Cascades led to its status as a timber-industry center—still the heart of the town's economy—but its site along the Umpqua River has also drawn fishermen here for years. **Ashland,** one of the premier destinations in the Northwest, is a charming small city set in the foothills of the Siskiyou Mountains. The foundation of the city's appeal is its famed Shakespeare Festival and its dozens of fine small inns, shops, and restaurants.

## Nearby Attractions

Fodor'sChoice
★ **Klamath Basin National Wildlife Refuge Complex.** Sometimes as many as 1,000 bald eagles make Klamath Basin their rest stop, amounting to the largest wintering concentration of these birds in the contiguous United States. The largest number of migratory birds also congregate in the Klamath Basin, 24 mi south of Klamath Falls on the California–Oregon border. Although winter is eagle season, dozens of different birds can be seen here any time of year. Call for a seasonal viewing appointment. ✉ *4009 Hill Rd., 20 mi south of Klamath Falls via U.S. 97 or Rte. 39, Tulelake, CA* ☎ *530/667–2231* ⊕ *www.fws.gov/ klamathbasinrefuges/* 🎟 *Free (fee for tours)* ☉ *Weekdays 8–4:30, weekends 10–4.*

Fodor'sChoice
★ **Oregon Caves National Monument.** The marble caves, large calcite formations, and huge underground rooms that are the main attraction here are quite rare in the West. The surrounding valley holds an old-growth forest with some of the state's largest trees. Guided tours take place on the hour. ✉ *Caves Highway (Rte. 46), Cave Junction* ☎ *541/592–2100* ⊕ *www.nps.gov/orca* 🎟 *$8.50* ☉ *Late May–mid-Sept., daily 9–7; mid-Mar.–late May and mid-Sept.–Dec., daily 10–4.*

# WHERE TO STAY & EAT

### About the Restaurants

There are several casual eateries and a few convenience stores within the park, but for fantastic upscale dining on the caldera's rim, head to the Crater Lake Lodge.

### About the Hotels

Crater Lake's summer season is relatively brief, and the park's main lodge is generally booked with guest reservations a year in advance. If you don't snag one, check availability as your trip approaches—cancellations are always possible. Outside the park are options in Prospect, Klamath, Roseburg, or Ashland.

### About the Campgrounds

Both tent campers and RV enthusiasts will enjoy the heavily wooded and well-equipped setting of Mazama Campground. Drinking water, showers, and laundry facilities help ensure that you don't have to rough it too much. Lost Creek Campground is much smaller, with fewer provisions and a more "rustic" Crater Lake experience.

## Where to Eat

### In Crater Lake

**$–$$$** ✕ **Dining Room at Crater Lake Lodge.**
Fodor's Choice ★ Virtually the only place where you can dine well once you're in the park, the culinary emphasis here is on fresh, regional Northwest cuisine. The dining room is magnificent, with a large stone fireplace and views out over the clear blue waters of Crater Lake. The evening menu is the main attraction, with tempting delights such as wildflower Alaskan salmon or hazelnut-crusted halibut fillets. An extensive wine list tops off the gourmet experience. ⊠ *Crater Lake Lodge, Rim Village* ☎ *541/594–2255* ⚒ *Reservations essential. $12–$28* ☰ *AE, D, MC, V* ☉ *Closed mid-Oct.–mid-May.*

> ### SHAKESPEARE IN ORE.
>
> More than 100,000 Bard-loving fanatics descend on Ashland (89 mi from Crater Lake) for the annual Oregon Shakespeare Festival. Plays run from February to November in three theaters; peak season is July, August, and September. ☎ *541/482–4331.*

**$–$$** ✕ **Annie Creek Restaurant.** It's family-style buffet dining here, and pizza and pasta are the main features. The outdoor seating area is surrounded by towering pine trees. ⊠ *Mazama Village Rd., near Annie Spring entrance station* ☎ *541/594–2255 Ext. 4533. $8–$15* ☰ *AE, D, MC, V* ☉ *Closed mid-Oct.–mid-June.*

PICNIC AREAS **Godfrey Glen Trail.** Located in a small canyon abuzz with songbirds, squirrels, and chipmunks, this picnic area has a south-facing, protected location. The half-dozen picnic tables here are in a small meadow; there are also a few fire grills and a pit toilet. ⊠ *On Rim Dr., 1 mi east of Annie Spring entrance station.*

**Rim Drive.** About a half dozen picnic-area turnouts encircle the lake; all have good views, but they can get very windy. Most have pit toilets, and a few have fire grills, but none have running water. ⊠ *Rim Dr.*

**Rim Village.** This is the only park picnic area with running water. The tables are set behind the visitor center, and most have a view of the lake below. There are flush toilets inside the visitor center. ⊠ *Rim Dr. on the south side of the lake, 7 mi north of Annie Spring entrance station.*

**Route 62.** Set in the fir, spruce, and pine forests of the Cascades' dry side, the three picnic areas along this route have tables, some fire grills, and pit toilets, but no drinking water. Picnickers who mind traffic noise should head farther into the park. ⊠ *Rte. 62; 2, 4, and 7 mi southeast of Annie Spring entrance station.*

**Vidae Falls.** In the upper reaches of Sun Creek, the four picnic tables here enjoy the sound of the small falls across the road. There is a vault toilet, and a couple of fire grills. ⊠ *Rim Dr., 2½ mi east of Steel Information Center, between the turnoffs for Crater Peak and Lost Creek.*

**Wizard Island.** The park's best picnic venue is on Wizard Island; pack a picnic lunch and book yourself on one of the early morning boat tour departures, reserving space on an afternoon return. There are no formal picnic areas and just pit toilets, but there are plenty of sunny, protected spots where you can have a quiet meal and appreciate the astounding scene that surrounds you.

## Outside the Park

**$$–$$$$** ✕ **Chateaulin.** One of southern Oregon's most romantic restaurants occupies an ivy-covered storefront a block from the Oregon Shakespeare Festival Center. Chef David Taub dispenses French food, local wine, and impeccable service with equal facility. During outdoor theater season (from April to November), late night dining is offered to satisfy postplay hunger. Try the pan-roasted rack of lamb or the Black Angus filet mignon. ⊠ *50 E. Main St., Ashland* ☎ *541/482–2264. $14–$33* ⊟ *AE, D, MC, V* ☺ *No lunch.*

**$$–$$$** ✕ **Winchester Inn Restaurant and Wine Bar.** The only thing more imaginative than the restaurant's menu is the impressive list of Pacific Northwest and French wines. This historic home was built in 1886, and its high-windowed dining rooms are set among cottage-style gardens. Seasonal selections include locally grown specialties such as wine-poached seafood, and filet mignon with anise, lemon zest, and crushed red pepper. Sunday brunch shines with the inn's signature homemade scones. ⊠ *35 S. 2nd St., Ashland* ☎ *541/488–1113. $16–$22* ⊟ *AE, D, MC, V* ☺ *No lunch. Closed Jan; call for seasonal hours of operation.*

**$–$$$** ✕ **Rocky Point Resort.** The setting—poised on a point overlooking Upper Klamath Lake—draws diners to this spot. Guests lucky enough to snag a window table spend as much time ogling the lake and mountain views as the menu, which offers a mainstream selection of steaks, sandwiches, and seafood. ⊠ *28121 Rocky Point Rd., Klamath Falls* ☎ *541/356–2287. $12–$25* ⊟ *D, MC, V* ☺ *Closed Mon. Memorial Day through Labor Day; weekend dinner only Labor Day–late Oct.; closed Nov.–Mar.; weekend dinner only Mar.–Memorial Day.*

# Where to Stay

## In Crater Lake

**$$–$$$$** ⊞ **Crater Lake Lodge.** The period feel of this 1915 lodge on the caldera's rim is reflected in its lodgepole pine columns, gleaming wood floors, and stone fireplaces in the common areas. With magnificent lake views—and the all-too-brief tourist season at Crater Lake—rooms at this popular spot are often booked a year in advance. Plan ahead, as this is the only "in-park" place to stay by the lake. ⊠ *Rim Village, east of Rim Visitor Center* ☎ *541/830–8700* 🖷 *541/830–8514* ⊕ *www.craterlakelodges.com* ⇨ *71 rooms* ♢ *Restaurant, no phone, no TV. $130–$250* ⊟ *AE, D, MC, V* ☺ *Closed mid-Oct.–mid-May.*

**$$** ⊞ **The Cabins at Mazama Village.** In a wooded area 7 mi south of the lake, this complex is made up of several A-frame buildings. All of the modest rooms have two queen beds and a private bath. These rooms fill up fast, so book early. A convenience store and gas station are nearby in the village. ⊠ *Mazama Village, near Annie Spring entrance station* ☎ *541/830–8700* 🖷 *541/830–8514* ⇨ *40 rooms* ♢ *No phone, no TV. $110* ⊟ *AE, D, MC, V* ☺ *Closed mid-Oct.–May.*

CAMPGROUNDS    ⚠ **Mazama Campground.** Crater Lake National Park's major visitor ac-
**$$**     commodation, aside from the famed lodge on the rim, is set well below
     the lake caldera in the pine and fir forest of the Cascades. Not far from
     the main access road (Hwy. 62), it offers convenience more than out-
     door serenity—although adjacent hiking trails lead away from the road-
     side bustle. About half the spaces are pull-throughs, some with electricity,
     but no hookups are available. The best tent spots are on some of the
     outer loops above Annie Creek Canyon. ✉ *Mazama Village, near Annie
     Spring entrance station* ☎ *541/830–8700* ⌁ *211 sites* ♿ *Flush toilets,
     dump station, drinking water, guest laundry, showers, fire grates, pub-
     lic telephone. $18–$23* ▭ *AE, D, MC, V* ⊙ *Mid-June–mid-Oct.*

**$**    ⚠ **Lost Creek Campground.** The small, remote sites here are usually
     available on a daily basis. In July and August, arrive early to secure a
     spot. Lost Creek is for tent campers only; RVs must stay at Mazama.
     ✉ *Grayback Dr. and Pinnacles Rd.* ☎ *541/594–3090* ⌁ *16 sites*
     ♿ *Flush toilets, drinking water, fire grates* ⊘ *Reservations not accepted*
     ▭ *$10* ⊙ *July–mid-Sept.*

### Outside the Park

**$$–$$$$**    ▦ **Running Y Ranch Resort.** Golfers rave about the Arnold Palmer–de-
     signed course here, which wends its way through a juniper-and-pon-
     derosa–shaded canyon overlooking Upper Klamath Lake. Hiking,
     biking, horseback riding, sailing, fishing, and wildlife watching are some
     of the prime activities. Rooms in the main lodge are spacious and mod-
     ern; the two- to three-bedroom town houses have a plethora of ameni-
     ties, such as built-in entertainment centers and outdoor hot tubs.
     ✉ *5500 Running Y Rd., 5 mi north of Klamath Falls, Klamath Falls
     97601* ☎ *541/850–5500 or 888/850–0275* 🖷 *541/850–5593* ⊕ *www.
     runningy.com* ⌁ *83 rooms* ♿ *Golf course, tennis courts, laundry
     service. $149–$289* ▭ *AE, D, DC, MC, V.*

**$–$$**    ▦ **Prospect Historic Hotel Bed and Breakfast.** Noted individuals such as
★      Theodore Roosevelt, Zane Grey, Jack London, and William Jennings
     Bryan have stayed here (in rooms that now bear their names). Located
     28 mi southwest of the park entrance on Highway 62, the main house
     has quaint, country-style guest accommodations, and the elegant Din-
     ner House restaurant serves hearty pasta, chicken, and steak dishes to
     guests and the public from May through October. Behind the main
     house are clean, well-equipped motel units. ✉ *391 Mill Creek Dr.,
     Prospect 97536* ☎ *541/560–3664 or 800/944–6490* 🖷 *541/560–3825*
     ⌁ *Main house 10 rooms, motel 14 rooms* ♿ *Refrigerator, some pets
     allowed. $60–$125* ▭ *D, DC, MC, V.*

**$–$$**    ▦ **Red Lion Inn.** The rooms in this chain hotel are bright and comfort-
     able, and the adjacent 24-hour full-service restaurant offers room serv-
     ice. It's located across the street from the Klamath County Event Center.
     ✉ *3612 S. 6th St., Klamath Falls, 97603* ☎ *541/882–8864* 🖷 *541/884–
     2046* ⊕ *www.redlion.com* ⌁ *100 rooms, 8 suites* ♿ *Restaurant, Wi-
     Fi, refrigerator (some), pool, bar, laundry facilities, laundry service.
     $89–$109* ▭ *AE, D, DC, MC, V.*

**14**

# CRATER LAKE ESSENTIALS

ACCESSIBILITY All the overlooks along Rim Drive are accessible to those with impaired mobility, as are Crater Lake Lodge, the facilities at Rim Village, and Steel Information Center. A half-dozen accessible campsites are available at Mazama Campground.

ADMISSION FEES Admission to the park is $10 per vehicle, good for seven days.

ADMISSION HOURS Crater Lake National Park is open 24 hours a day year-round; however, snow closes most park roadways October through June. The park is located in the Pacific Time Zone.

ATMS/BANKS
🛈 **Village Gift Shop** ⊠ Mazama Village Rd., near Annie Spring entrance station ☎ 541/594–3090 ⊘ Closed Nov.–late May.

AUTOMOBILE SERVICE STATIONS
🛈 **Mazama Village** ⊠ Mazama Village, near Annie Spring entrance station ☎ 541/594–3090 ⊘ Closed Nov.–late May.

EMERGENCIES Dial 911 for all emergencies in the park. Park police are based at park headquarters, next to Steel Information Center.

LOST AND FOUND The park's lost-and-found is at the ranger station next to Steel Information Center.

PERMITS Backcountry campers and hikers must obtain a free wilderness permit at Rim Visitor Center or Steel Information Center for all overnight trips.

POST OFFICE
🛈 **Steel Information Center** ⊠ Crater Lake Post Office, Rim Dr., Crater Lake 97604 ☎ 541/594–3090.

PUBLIC TELEPHONES AND RESTROOMS There are public telephones and restrooms at Steel Information Center, Rim Village, Crater Lake Lodge, and the Mazama Village complex. There are also restrooms at the top and bottom of Cleetwood Cove Trail and at many of the park's picnic areas.

SHOPS & GROCERS
🛈 **Diamond Lake Resort.** ⊠ Rte. 138, 25 mi north of Crater Lake ☎ 541/793-3333 or 800/733-7593. **Mazama Camper Store.** ⊠ Mazama Village Rd., near Annie Spring entrance station ☎ 541/830-8700 ⊘ Closed Oct.–May.

**NEARBY TOWN INFORMATION**
🛈 **Ashland Chamber of Commerce** ⊠ 110 E. Main St., Box 1360, Ashland 97520 ☎ 541/482–3486 ⊕ www.ashlandchamber.com. **Klamath County Chamber of Commerce** ⊠ 507 Main St., Klamath Falls 97603 ☎ 541/884–5193 ⊕ www.klamath.org. **Klamath County Department of Tourism** ⊠ 507 Main St., Box 1867, Klamath Falls 97601 ☎ 541/884–5193 or 800/445-6728 ⊕ www.klamathcounty.net. **Roseburg Visitors and Convention Bureau** ⊠ 410 S.E. Spruce St., Box 1262, Roseburg 97470 ☎ 541/672-9731 or 800/444-9584 ⊕ www.visitroseburg.com.

**VISITOR INFORMATION**
🛈 **Crater Lake National Park** ✑ Box 7, Crater Lake, OR 97604 ☎ 541/594-3090 ⊕ www.nps.gov/crla.

# Death Valley National Park

Sand Dunes, Death Valley National Park

**WORD OF MOUTH**

"The valley we call Death isn't really that different from much of the rest of the desert West. It's just a little deeper, a little hotter, and a little drier. What sets it apart more than anything else is the mind's eye. For it is a land of illusion, a place in the mind, a shimmering mirage of riches and mystery and death. These illusions have distorted its landscape and contorted its history."

–Richard E. Lingenfelter, *Death Valley & The Amargosa: A Land of Illusion*

# WELCOME TO DEATH VALLEY

## TOP REASONS TO GO

★ **Weird science:** Death Valley's Racetrack is home to moving boulders, an unexplained phenomenon that has scientists baffled.

★ **Lowest spot on the continent:** Stand on the lowest spot in North America at Badwater, 282 feet below sea level.

★ **Wildflower explosion:** During the spring, the desert landscape is ablaze with greenery and colorful flowers, especially south of Badwater and north of Ashford Mill.

★ **Ghost towns:** Death Valley is renowned for its Wild West heritage and is home to dozens of crumbling settlements, including Ballarat, Cerro Gordo, Chloride City, Greenwater, Harrisburg, Keeler, Leadfield, Panamint City, Rhyolite, and Skidoo.

★ **Natural wonders:** From canyons to sand dunes to salt flats and dry lake beds, Death Valley serves up plenty of geological treasures.

**1 Central Death Valley.** Furnace Creek sits in the heart of Death Valley—if you only have a short time in the park, this is where you'll want to start. You can visit gorgeous Golden Canyon, Zabriskie Point, the Salt Creek Interpretive Trail, and Artist's Drive, among other popular points of interest.

**2 Northern Death Valley.** For more action, stay in Beatty, Nevada, where you can gamble in the casino by night and play in the park by day. Be sure to stop by Rhyolite Ghost Town on Highway 374 before entering the park and exploring Moorish Scotty's Castle, colorful Titus Canyon, crumbling Keane Wonder Mine, and jaw-dropping Ubehebe Crater.

**3 Southern Death Valley.** This is a desolate area, but there are plenty of sights that help convey Death Valley's rich history. Don't miss the Dublin Gulch Caves, or the famous Amargosa Opera House, where aging ballerina Marta Beckett still wows the crowds.

Mule Train

**4 Western Death Valley.** Panamint Springs Resort is a nice place to grab a meal and get your bearings before moving on to quaint Darwin Falls, smooth rolling sand dunes, bee-hive shaped Wildrose Charcoal Kilns, and historic Stovepipe Wells Village. On the way in, stop at Cerro Gordo Ghost Town, where you can view restored buildings dating back to 1867.

NEVADA
CALIFORNIA

Visitor Center
Scottys Castle
Ubehebe Crater
Grapevine
Mesquite Spring

The Racetrack

PANAMINT RANGE

TO LONE PINE

Panamint Dunes
Panamint Springs

Father Crowley Point

Darwin Falls

Darwin

178
TO RIDGECREST

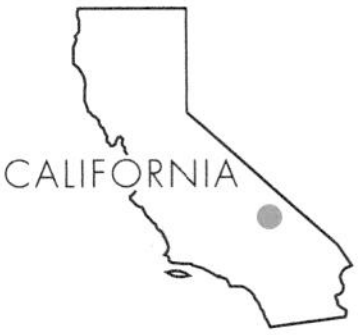
CALIFORNIA

# GETTING ORIENTED

Death Valley National Park covers 5,310 square mi, ranges from 6 to 60 mi wide, and measures 140 mi north to south. Within the park, the Panamint Range parallels Death Valley to the west, the Amargosa Range to the east. Nearly all of the park lies in southeastern California, with a small eastern portion crossing over into Nevada.

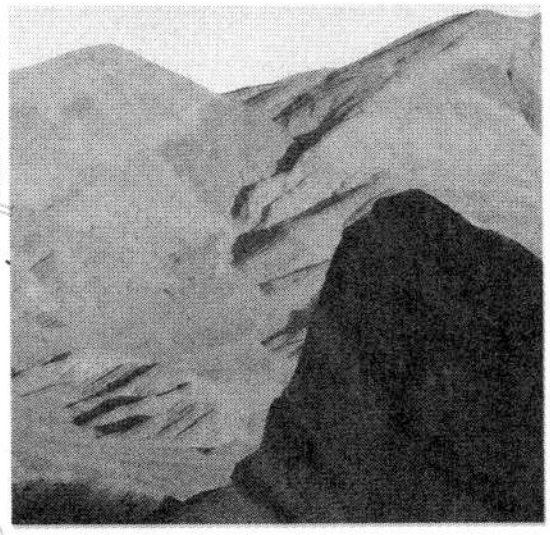
Zabriskie Point

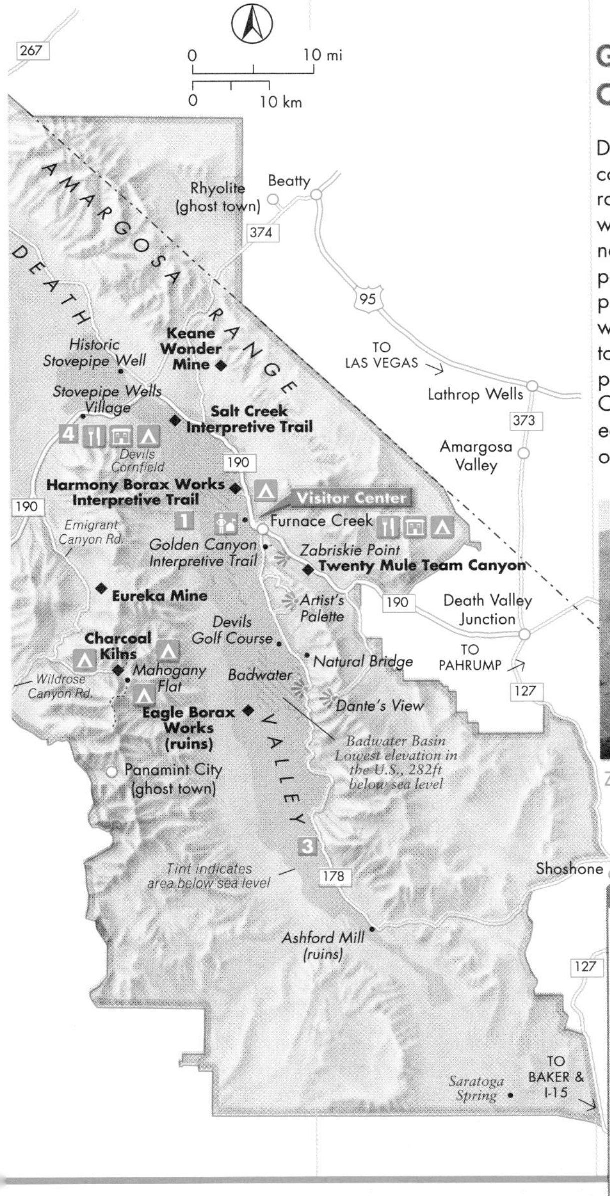
267
0
10 mi
0
10 km
AMARGOSA RANGE
DEATH VALLEY
Rhyolite (ghost town)
Beatty
374
95
TO LAS VEGAS
Lathrop Wells
373
Amargosa Valley
Keane Wonder Mine
Historic Stovepipe Well
Stovepipe Wells Village
4
Salt Creek Interpretive Trail
Devils Cornfield
190
Harmony Borax Works Interpretive Trail
Visitor Center
190
1
Furnace Creek
Emigrant Canyon Rd.
Golden Canyon Interpretive Trail
Zabriskie Point
Twenty Mule Team Canyon
Eureka Mine
Artist's Palette
190
Death Valley Junction
Devils Golf Course
Charcoal Kilns
Natural Bridge
TO PAHRUMP
Wildrose Canyon Rd.
Mahogany Flat
Badwater
127
Dante's View
Eagle Borax Works (ruins)
Badwater Basin Lowest elevation in the U.S., 282ft below sea level
Panamint City (ghost town)
3
Tint indicates area below sea level
178
Shoshone
Ashford Mill (ruins)
127
TO BAKER & I-15
Saratoga Spring

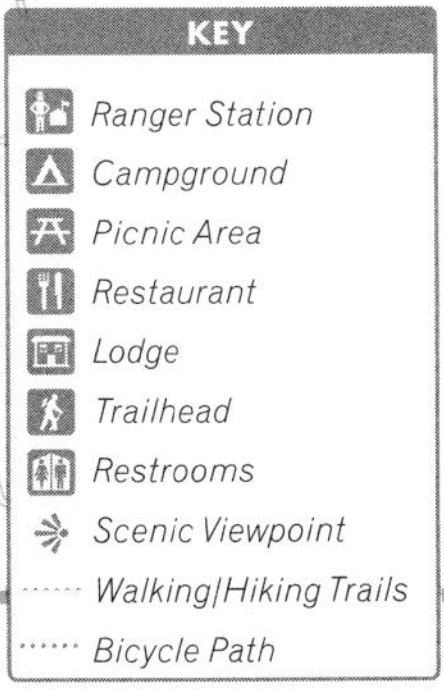
KEY
Ranger Station
Campground
Picnic Area
Restaurant
Lodge
Trailhead
Restrooms
Scenic Viewpoint
Walking/Hiking Trails
Bicycle Path

# DEATH VALLEY PLANNER

## When to Go

**Most of the park's one million annual visitors still come between late fall and early spring,** taking advantage of moderate temperatures and the lack of rainfall. During these cooler months you will need to book a room in advance, but don't worry: the park never feels crowded. If you visit during summer, believe everything you've ever heard about desert heat–it can be brutal. The dry air wicks moisture from the body without causing a sweat, so remember to drink plenty of water. Bring sunglasses, a hat, and sufficient clothing to block the sun's rays and the wind. Because there's little vegetation to soak up the rain and keep the soil together, flash floods are common; sections of roadway can be flooded or washed away. The wettest month of the year is February, when the park receives an average of $^{3}/_{10}$ inch of rain. You can check the park's daily weather report online at www.nps.gov/deva/planyourvisit/weather.htm.

AVG. HIGH/LOW TEMPS.

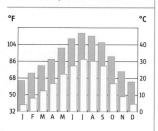

## Flora & Fauna

There's a general misconception that Death Valley National Park consists of mile upon endless mile of flat desert sands, scattered cacti, and an occasional cow skull. Many people don't realize that across the valley floor from Badwater—the lowest point in the Western Hemisphere—Telescope Peak towers 11,049 feet above sea level. The extreme topography of Death Valley is a lesson in geology. Two hundred million years ago seas covered the area, depositing layers of sediment and fossils. Between 3.5 million and 5 million years ago faults in the Earth's crust and volcanic activity pushed and folded the ground, causing mountain ranges to rise and the valley floor to drop. The valley was then filled periodically by lakes, which eroded the surrounding rocks into fantastic formations and deposited the salts that now cover the floor of the basin.

Most animal life in Death Valley (58 mammal, 37 reptile, 347 bird, and 6 amphibian species) is found near the limited sources of water. The bighorn sheep spend most of their time in the secluded upper reaches of the park's rugged canyons and ridges. Coyotes can often be seen lazing in the shade next to the golf course and have been known to run onto the fairways to steal a golf ball. The only native fish in the park is the pupfish, which grows to slightly longer than 1 inch. In winter, when the water is cold, the fish lie dormant in the bottom mud, becoming active again in spring. Because they are wary of large moving shapes, you must stand quietly over a pool at Salt Creek to see them.

Botanists say there are more than 1,000 species of plants here (21 exist nowhere else in the world), though many annual plants lie dormant as seeds for all but a few months in spring, when rains trigger a bloom. The rest congregate around limited sources of water. Most of the low-elevation vegetation grows around the oases at Furnace Creek and Scotty's Castle, where oleanders, palms, and salt cedar grow. At higher elevations you will find pinyon, juniper, and bristlecone pine.

# Getting There & Around

It can take more than three hours to cross from one side of the park to another, so it's important to choose an entrance point that makes sense for what you want to see. If you're driving from Los Angeles, enter through the western portion along Highway 395; enter from the north at Beatty, Nevada, or via the central entrance at Death Valley Junction if you're coming from Las Vegas. Travelers from Orange County, San Diego, and the Inland Empire should access the park via I-15 north at Baker.

Distances can be deceiving within the park: what seems close can be very far away. Much of the park can be toured on regularly scheduled bus tours, but these often don't allow time for hikes to sites not seen from the road, such as Salt Creek, Golden Canyon, and Natural Bridge. The best option is to drive to a number of the sites, get out of the car, and walk.

When driving in Death Valley, reliable maps are a must, as signage is often limited or, in some places, nonexistent. Other important accessories include a compass, a mobile phone (though these don't always work in remote areas), and extra food and water (3 gallons per person per day is recommended, plus additional radiator water). If you're able to take a four-wheel drive vehicle, bring it: many of Death Valley's most spectacular canyons are otherwise inaccessible. Be aware of possible winter closures or driving restrictions due to snow.

The **California State Department of Transportation Hotline** (☎ 916/445–7623 or 800/427–7623 ⊕ www.dot.ca.gov) has updates on Death Valley road conditions. The **California Highway Patrol** (☎ 760/256–1727 near Barstow, 760/872–5900 near Bishop ⊕ http://cad.chp.ca.gov/) offers the latest traffic incident information.

## GOOD READS

The Death Valley Natural History Association sells a variety of books on the area and publishes a pamphlet outlining a self-guided tour of Golden Canyon, which costs 50¢ and is available from the association or the bookstore at the visitor center. The association also sells a waterproof, tear-proof topographical map of the entire park, for $10. Additional topo maps covering select areas are $4.75 each and available at the visitor center or from the **Death Valley Natural History Association** (☎ 760/786–2146 or 800/478–8564).

# Festivals & Seasonal Events

**MAR. Diaz Lake Trout Derby.** The first Saturday of the month, you can take a shot at the "big one" in this fully stocked lake at 3,700 feet above sea level. Admission is free. ☎ 760/876–4444.

**APR. Shoshone Desert Art Show.** Admission is free for this annual arts-and-crafts show and sale weekend. ☎ 760/852–4254 or 775/727–5460.

**MAY Bishop Mule Days.** Headline entertainment includes top country music stars, steer roping, barbecues, country dances, and the longest-running nonmotorized parade in the U.S. Admission is free. ☎ 760/872–4263 ⊕ www.muledays.org.

**SEPT. Lone Pine Film Festival.** Every weekend of Columbus Day, this sleepy little town pays tribute to its Hollywood history with a three-day festival of tours, films, lectures, and Old West celebrity guests. ☎ 760/876–9103 ⊕ www.lonepinefilmfestival.org.

**NOV. Death Valley 49er Encampment Days.** Originally a centennial celebration held in 1949 to honor the area's first European visitors, this event annually draws thousands of people to the park from around the world. The weeklong celebration includes art shows, organized seminars and walks, demonstrations, and dances. ⊕ www.deathvalley49ers.org. **Shoshone Old West Days.** Just outside of Death Valley National Park, this annual festival celebrates Wild West heritage with live music, arts and crafts, competitions and contests, children's activities, and plenty of hot and hearty food. ☎ 760/852–4524.

15

By Veronica Hill

The desert is no Disneyland. With its scorching summer heat and vast, sparsely populated tracts of land, it's not often at the top of the list when most people assemble their "must-see" list of California attractions. But the natural riches of Death Valley—the largest national park outside Alaska—are overwhelming: rolling waves of sand dunes, black cinder cones thrusting up hundreds of feet from a blistered desert floor, riotous sheets of wildflowers, bizarrely shaped Joshua trees basking in the orange glow of a sunset, and a silence that is both dramatic and startling.

## Scenic Drive

★ **Artist's Drive.** This 9-mi, one-way route skirts the foothills of the Black Mountains and provides colorful views of the changing landscape. Once inside the palette, the huge expanses of the valley are replaced by the intimate, small-scale natural beauty of pigments created by volcanic deposits. It's a quiet, lonely drive. Reach by heading north off Badwater Road.

## What to See

### Historic Sites

**Charcoal Kilns.** Ten stone kilns, each 30 feet high and 25 feet wide, stand as if on parade in a line up a mountain. The kilns, built by Chinese laborers in 1879, were used to burn wood from pinyon pines to turn it into charcoal. The charcoal was then transported over the mountains into Death Valley, where it was used to extract lead and silver from the ore mined there. If you hike nearby Wildrose Peak, you will be rewarded with terrific views of the kilns. ⊠ *Wildrose Canyon Rd., 37 mi south of Stovepipe Wells.*

**Harmony Borax Works.** Death Valley's mule teams hauled borax from here to the railroad town of Mojave, 165 mi away. The teams plied the route until 1889, when the railroad finally arrived in Zabriskie. Constructed in 1883, one of the oldest buildings in Death Valley houses the Borax Museum, 2 mi south of the borax works. Originally a miners' bunkhouse, the building once stood in Twenty Mule Team Canyon. Now it displays mining machinery and historical exhibits. The adjacent structure is the original mule-team barn. ⊠ *Harmony Borax Works Rd., west of Hwy. 190, 2 mi north of Furnace Creek* ☉ *Daily 9–4:30.*

FodorśChoice
★ **Keane Wonder Mine.** The tram towers and cables from the old mill used to process gold from Keane Wonder Mine are still here, leading up to the crumbling mine, which is a steep 1-mi hike up the mountain. A nearby path leads north to Keane Wonder Spring. ⊠ *Access road off Beatty Cutoff Rd., 17½ mi north of Furnace Creek.*

★ ☾ **Scotty's Castle.** This Moorish-style mansion, begun in 1924 but never completed, takes its name from Walter Scott, better known as Death Valley Scotty. An ex-cowboy, prospector, and performer in Buffalo Bill's Wild West Show, Scotty always told people the castle was his, financed by gold from a secret mine. In reality, there was no mine, and the house belonged to a Chicago millionaire named Albert Johnson, whom Scott had finagled into investing in the fictitious mine. The house functioned for a while as a hotel and still contains works of art, imported carpets, handmade European furniture, and a tremendous pipe organ. Costumed rangers re-create life at the castle circa 1939. Try to arrive for the first tour of the day to avoid a wait, which can be up to two hours. Check out the Underground Mysteries Tour, which takes you through a ¼-mile tunnel in the castle basement. ⊠ *Scotty's Castle Rd. (Hwy. 267), 53 mi north of Salt Creek Interpretive Trail* ☎ 760/786–2392 ⊕ *www. nps.gov/deva* ☞ *$11* ☉ *Daily 8:30–5, tours daily 9–5.*

### Scenic Stops

★ **Artist's Palette.** So called for the brilliant colors of its volcanic deposits, this is one of Death Valley's most magnificent sights. Artist's Drive, the approach to the area, is one-way heading north off Badwater Road, so if you're visiting Badwater, come here on the way back. The drive winds through foothills of sedimentary and volcanic rocks. Within the palette, the huge expanses of Death Valley are replaced by intimate, small-scale natural beauty. ⊠ *11 mi south of Furnace Creek, off Badwater Rd.*

**Badwater.** This shallow sodium chloride pool lies in an expanse of desolate salt flats. At 282 feet below sea level, Badwater is the lowest spot on land in the Western Hemisphere—and also one of the hottest. ⊠ *Badwater Rd., 19 mi south of Furnace Creek.*

FodorśChoice
★ **Dante's View.** This lookout is more than 5,000 feet up in the Black Mountains. In the dry desert air you can see across most of 110-mi-wide Death Valley. The view is astounding: you can see the highest and lowest spots in the contiguous United States from the same vantage point. The tiny blackish patch far below is Badwater, at 282 feet below sea level; on the western horizon is Mt. Whitney, which rises to 14,496 feet. ⊠ *Dante's View Rd. off Hwy. 190, 35 mi from Badwater, 20 mi south of Twenty Mule Team Canyon.*

15

## DEATH VALLEY IN ONE DAY

If you begin the day in Furnace Creek, you can see many different sights without doing much driving. Bring plenty of water with you, and some food in case you get hungry in a remote location. Get up early and drive the 20 mi on Badwater Road to **Badwater,** which looks out on the lowest point in the Western Hemisphere and is a dramatic place to watch the sunrise. Returning north, stop at Natural Bridge, a medium-size conglomerate rock formation that has been hollowed at its base to form a span across the canyon, and then at the **Devil's Golf Course,** so named because of the large pinnacles of salt present here. Detour to the right onto **Artist's Drive,** a 9-mi one-way,

northbound route that passes **Artist's Palette.** The reds, yellows, oranges, and greens come from minerals in the rocks and the earth. Four miles north of Artist's Drive you will come to the **Golden Canyon Interpretive Trail,** a 2-mi round-trip that winds through a canyon with colorful rock walls. Just before Furnace Creek, take Highway 190 3 mi east to **Zabriskie Point,** overlooking dramatic, furrowed red-brown hills and the **Twenty Mule Team Canyon.** Return to Furnace Creek, where you can have lunch and visit the museum at the Furnace Creek Visitor Center. Heading north from Furnace Creek, pull off the highway and take a look at the **Harmony Borax Works.**

**Darwin Falls.** Named for Dr. Darwin French, who explored this desert wilderness in 1860, the 80-foot Darwin Falls are a unique sight in the arid, unforgiving desert. This rocky landscape, accented with trees and moss, pours down into a cool plunge pool. (Swimming is not permitted.) ⊠ *Hwy. 190, 1 mi west of Panamint Springs. Exit south on the signed dirt road and travel 2½ mi to the parking area.*

**Devil's Golf Course.** Thousands of miniature salt pinnacles carved into surreal shapes by the desert wind dot this wildly varied landscape. The salt was pushed up to the earth's surface by pressure created as underground salt- and water-bearing gravel crystallized. In some spots, perfectly round holes descend into the ground. ⊠ *Badwater Rd., 13 mi south of Furnace Creek. Turn right onto dirt road and drive 1 mi.*

**Golden Canyon.** Just South of Furnace Creek, these glimmering mountains are perhaps best known for their role in the original *Star Wars.* The canyon is a fine hiking spot, with gorgeous views of the Panamint Mountains, ancient dry lake beds, and alluvial fans. ⊠ *From the Furnace Creek Visitor Center, drive 2 mi south on Hwy. 190, then 2 mi south on Hwy. 178 to the parking area. The lot has an informational kiosk with trail guides.*

★ **Racetrack.** Getting here involves a 27-mi journey over rough and almost nonexistent dirt road, but the trip is worth the reward. Where else do rocks move on their own? This phenomenon has baffled scientists for years. No one has actually seen the rocks in motion, but theory has it that when it rains, the hard-packed lake bed becomes slippery enough that gusty winds push the rocks along—sometimes for several hundred yards. When the mud dries, a telltale trail remains. The trek to the Racetrack can be made in a passenger vehicle, but high clearance is suggested. ⊠ *From Ubehebe Crater, 27 mi west on the dirt road.*

**Sand Dunes at Mesquite Flat.** These dunes, made up of minute pieces of quartz and other rock, are ever-changing products of the wind-rippled hills, with curving crests and a sun-bleached hue. The dunes are the most photographed destination in the park, and you can see them at their best at sunrise and sunset. There are no trails, so roam where you please. Keep your eyes open for animal tracks—you may even spot a coyote or fox. Bring plenty of water, and note where you parked your car: It's easy to become disoriented in this ocean of sand. If you lose your bearings, climb to the top of a dune and scan the horizon for the parking lot. ⊠ *19 mi north of Hwy. 190, northeast of Stovepipe Wells Village.*

**Stovepipe Wells Village.** This tiny 1926 town, the first resort in Death Valley, takes its name from the stovepipe that an early prospector left to indicate where he found water. The area contains a motel, restaurant, grocery store, campgrounds, and landing strip. Off Highway 190, on a 3-mi gravel road southwest, are the multicolor walls of **Mosaic Canyon.** ⊠ *Hwy. 190, 2 mi from Sand Dunes, 77 mi east of Lone Pine.*

★ **Titus Canyon.** Titus Canyon is a popular 28-mi drive from Beatty south along Scotty's Castle Road. Along the way you'll pass Leadville Ghost Town, petroglyphs at Klare Spring, and spectacular limestone and dolomite narrows at the end of the canyon. Toward the end, a two-section of gravel road will lead you into the mouth of the canyon. ⊠ *Access road off Scotty's Castle Rd., 33 mi northwest of Furnace Creek.*

**Twenty Mule Team Canyon.** This canyon was named for the 20-mule teams that, between 1883 and 1889, carried 10-ton loads of borax through the burning desert. At places along the loop road off Highway 190, the soft rock walls reach high on both sides, making it seem like you're on an amusement-park ride. Remains of prospectors' tunnels are visible here, along with some brilliant rock formations. ⊠ *20 Mule Team Rd., off Hwy. 190, 4 mi south of Furnace Creek, 20 mi west of Death Valley Junction.*

**Ubehebe Crater.** At 500 feet deep and ½ mi across, this crater resulted from underground steam and gas explosions 3,000 years ago. Volcanic ash spreads out over most of the area, and the cinders lie as deep as 150 feet near the crater's rim. You'll get superb views of the valley from here, and you can take a fairly easy hike around the west side of the rim to Little Hebe Crater, one of a smaller cluster of craters to the south and west. ⊠ *N. Death Valley Hwy., 8 mi northwest of Scotty's Castle.*

★ **Zabriskie Point.** Although only about 710 feet in elevation, this is one of Death Valley's most scenic spots, overlooking a striking panorama of wrinkled, multicolor hills. It's a great place to watch the sunrise. ⊠ *Hwy. 190, 5 mi south of Furnace Creek.*

## Visitor Centers

**Beatty Information Center.** This is the first stop you can make coming in from Las Vegas on Route 95. Here, you can pick up maps and information about Death Valley, or learn about its natural and cultural history in one of several exhibits. ⊠ *Rte. 95, 120 mi north of Las Vegas* ☎ *775/553–2200* ⊕ *www.nps.gov/deva* ☽ *Daily 8–6.*

**Furnace Creek Visitor Center and Museum.** The exhibits and artifacts here provide a broad overview of how Death Valley formed; you can pick up maps at the bookstore run by the Death Valley Natural History Association. This is also the place to sign up for ranger-led walks (available November through April) or check out a live presentation about the valley's cultural and natural history. The center offers 12-minute slide shows about the park every 30 minutes. ⊠ *Hwy. 190, 30 mi northwest of Death Valley Junction* ☎ *760/786–3200* ☽ *Daily 8–6.*

**Scotty's Castle Visitor Center and Museum.** If you visit Death Valley, you'll likely make a stop here at the main ticket center for Scotty's Castle living-history tours. Here you'll also find exhibits, books, self-guided tour pamplets, and displays about the castle's creators, Death Valley Scotty and Albert M. Johnson. Fuel up with gasoline, sandwiches, or souvenirs before heading back out to the park. ⊠ *Rte. 267, 53 mi northwest of Furnace Creek and 45 mi northwest of Stovepipe Wells Village* ☎ *760/ 786–2392* ⊕ *www.nps.gov/deva* ☽ *Daily 7:30–5.*

## Sports & the Outdoors

### Bicycling

There are no bike rentals in the park, but mountain biking is permitted on any of the back roads open to the public. A free flier with suggested bike routes is at the Furnace Creek Visitor Center. Bicycle Trail, a 4-mi round-trip trek from the visitor center to Mustard Canyon, is a good place to start, as is Desolation Canyon, an easy 2-mi round-trip trail 4 mi south of Badwater Road. For a better workout, try the moderate 6-mi round-trip journey to Keane Wonder Mine, which begins 17 mi north of the Beatty cutoff road, or the 10-mi round-trip journey to Big Four Mine, starting 9½ mi south of Badwater Road. ⇨ Outfitters & Expeditions box for bicycle tours.

### Bird-watching

Approximately 347 bird species have been identified in Death Valley. The best place to see the park's birds is along the Salt Creek Interpretive Trail, where you can spot ravens, common snipes, killdeer, spotted sandpipers, and great blue herons. Along the fairways at Furnace Creek Golf Club, you can see kingfishers, peregrine falcons, hawks, Canada geese, yellow warblers, and the occasional golden eagle—just remember to stay off the greens. Scotty's Castle attracts wintering birds from around the globe, who are attracted to its running water, shady trees, and shrubs. Other good spots to find birds are at Saratoga Springs, Mesquite Springs, Travertine Springs, and Grimshaw Lake near Tecopa. You can download a bird checklist, divided by season, at www.nps.gov/ deva/Birdlist.htm. Rangers at Furnace Creek Visitor Center often lead birding walks through Salt Creek between November and March.

### Four-Wheeling

Maps and SUV guidebooks for four-wheel-drive and other backcountry roads (including the popular Cottonwood/Marble canyons, Racetrack, Eureka Dunes, Saratoga Springs, Warm Springs Canyon) are offered at the Furnace Creek Visitor Center. Remember: never travel alone and be sure to pack plenty of water and snacks. Driving off established roads is strictly prohibited in the park. ⇨ Outfitters & Expeditions box for guided four-wheeling expeditions.

**Butte Valley.** This 21-mi road in the park's southwest part climbs from 200 feet below sea level to 4,000 feet. The geological formations along the drive reveal the development of Death Valley. ⊠ *Trailhead on Warm Spring Canyon Rd., 50 mi south of Furnace Creek Visitor Center.*

**Hunter Mountain.** From Teakettle Junction to the park boundary, this 20-mi road climbs from 4,100 feet to 7,200 feet, winding through a pinyon-and-juniper forest. This route may be closed or muddy in winter and spring. ⊠ *Trailhead 28 mi southwest of Scotty's Castle.*

**Warm Springs Canyon.** This route takes you past Warm Springs talc mine and through Butte Valley, over Mengel Pass and toward **Geologists Cabin,** a charming and cheery little cabin where you can spend the night (if nobody else beats you to it!). The cabin, which sits under a cottonwood tree, has a fireplace, table and chairs, and a sink. Further up the road, the cabins at Mengel's Home and Russell Camp are also open for public use. Keep the historic cabins clean and to restock any items that you use. ⊠ *Warm Springs Canyon Rd., off Hwy. 190/Badwater Rd.*

### Golf

**Furnace Creek Golf Club.** Play 9 or 18 holes at the lowest golf course in the world. The club rents clubs and carts, and greens fees are reduced for Furnace Creek Ranch or Furnace Creek Inn guests. In winter, reservations are essential. ⊠ *Hwy. 190, Furnace Creek* ☎ *760/786–2301* 🖼 *$28–$55* ⊙ *Tee times 6 AM–3:30 PM; pro shop 6 AM–5 PM.*

### Hiking

Plan to hike before or after midday (when the sun is hottest). Carry plenty of water, wear protective clothing, and keep an eye out for tarantulas, black widows, scorpions, snakes, and other potentially dangerous creatures. Some of the best trails are unmarked; ask locals for directions. ⇨ Outfitters & Expeditions box for guided expeditions.

EASY **Darwin Falls.** This lovely 2-mi round-trip hike rewards you with a refreshing waterfall surrounded by thick vegetation and a rocky gorge. FodorsChoice No swimming or bathing is allowed, but it's a beautiful place for a picnic. Adventurous hikers can scramble higher toward more rewarding views of the falls. ⊠ *Access the 2-mi graded dirt road and parking area off Hwy. 190, 1 mi west of Panamint Springs Resort.*

★ **Natural Bridge Canyon.** The somewhat rough 2-mi access road has interesting geological features in addition to the bridge itself. It's ½-mi roundtrip. ⊠ *Access road off Badwater Rd., 15 mi south of Furnace Creek.*

**Salt Creek Interpretive Trail.** This trail, a ½-mi boardwalk circuit, loops through a spring-fed wash. The nearby hills are brown and gray, but

**DID YOU KNOW?**

Rocks at Death Valley's Racetrack move on their own! Though you won't see stones zipping along, the telltale trails are easy to spot. The wind actually blows rocks—some of them weighing over 700 pounds—across the surface of super-slick mud that coats the dry lakebed after rainstorms.

# OUTFITTERS & EXPEDITIONS

Reserve well in advance for all tours.

### BICYCLING

Mountain bike into the heart of Death Valley during a six-day adventure through the national park with **Spirit of the Mojave Mountain Biking Tour** (Escape Adventures; ☎ 800/596-2953 or 702/838-6966). The 110-mi journey includes accommodations (both camping and inns). Tours are $995 per person; bikes, tents, sleeping bags, helmets, and other gear may be rented for an additional price. Tours are available February–April and October only.

### FOUR-WHEELING

The 10-hour **Death Valley SUV Tour** (Death Valley Tours; ☎ 800/719-3768) departs from Las Vegas and takes you on a fully narrated whirl through Death Valley in a four-wheel-drive Jeep. Tours ($205 per person) depart Monday and Wednesday at 7 AM and include free pickup from designated hotels. Bottled water and snacks are provided, and camera rentals, tripods, and film are available for an additional fee.

### HIKING

Available during the spring months, **Death Valley National Park and Red Rock Canyon Hiking Tour** (Death Valley Tours; ☎ 800/719-3768 ⊕ www.deathvalleytours.net) is a six-day adventure that begins in Las Vegas. All transportation, permits, park fees, meals, snacks, beverages, first aid, and camping gear is included in the fee. Tours are $1,230 per person.

Join an experienced guide and spend six days exploring Death Valley's most popular sights with

**Death Valley National Park and Red Rock Hiker** (Escape Adventures; ☎ 800/596-2953 or 702/838-6966 ⊕ www.escapeadventures.com). The tour ($995), offered October and February–April, also spends two days in Red Rock Canyon National Conservation Area. For an additional fee, you can rent hiking shoes, tents, sleeping bags, trekking poles, water bottles, and more. The price includes a stay at Furnace Creek Inn.

### HORSEBACK & CARRIAGE RIDES

Set off on a one- or two-hour guided horseback or carriage ride ($10–$60) from **Furnace Creek Ranch** (✉ Hwy. 190, Furnace Creek ☎ 760/786-2345 Ext. 339). The rides traverse trails with views of the surrounding mountains, where multicolor volcanic rock and alluvial fans form a background for date palms and other vegetation. Evening carriage rides take passengers around the golf course and Furnace Creek Ranch. Cocktail rides, with champagne, margaritas, and hot spiced wine, are available. It's open October–May only.

### MOTORCYCLE TOURS

Sign up for a guided **Death Valley Dualsport Tour** (Adventure Motorcycle (AdMo) Tours; ☎ 760/249-1105). The four-day tour ($1,530) through Death Valley on a rented Suzuki DR-Z400S (or your own) bike covers about 400 mi of terrain through Death Valley National Park. The tours, which run October–May, include bike rental, gasoline, snacks, hotel accommodations for three nights, and a professional tour guide. To join, you should have a motorcycle driver's license, health insurance, and protective gear.

the floor of the wash is alive with aquatic plants such as pickerelweed and salt grass. The stream and ponds here are among the few places in the park to see the rare pupfish, the only native fish species in Death Valley. Animals such as bobcats, fox, coyotes, and snakes visit the spring, and you may also see ravens, common snipes, killdeer, and great blue herons. ⊠ *Off Hwy. 190, 14 mi north of Furnace Creek.*

★ **Titus Canyon.** The narrow floor of Titus Canyon is made of hard-packed gravel and dirt, and it's a constant, moderate uphill walk. Klare Spring and some petroglyphs are 5½ mi from the mouth of the canyon, but you can get a feeling for the area on a shorter walk.

MODERATE  **Fall Canyon.** This is a 3½-mi one-way hike from the Titus Canyon parking area. First, walk ½ mi north along the base of the mountains to a large wash, then go 2½ mi up the canyon to a 35-foot dry fall. You can continue by climbing around to the falls on the south side. ⊠ *Access road off Scotty's Castle Rd., 33 mi northwest of Furnace Creek.*

🐾 **Mosaic Canyon.** A gradual uphill trail (4 mi round-trip) winds through the smoothly polished walls of this narrow canyon; there are dry falls to climb at the upper end. ⊠ *Access road off Hwy. 190, ½ mi west of Stovepipe Wells Village.*

DIFFICULT  **Keane Wonder Mine.** Allow two hours for this 2-mi round-trip trail, which
Fodor'sChoice  follows an out-of-service aerial tramway to the mine. The way is steep,
★  but the views of the valley are spectacular. Do not enter the tunnels or hike beyond the top of the tramway—it's dangerous. The trailhead is 2 mi down an unpaved and bumpy access road. ⊠ *Access road off Beatty Cutoff Rd., 17½ mi north of Furnace Creek.*

**Telescope Peak Trail.** This 14-mi round-trip begins at Mahogany Flat Campground. The steep trail winds through pinyon, juniper, and bristle-cone pines, with excellent views of Death Valley and Panamint Valley. Ice axes and crampons may be necessary in winter—check at the Furnace Creek Visitor Center. It takes a minimum of eight hours to hike to the top of the 11,049-foot peak and return. Getting to the peak is a strenuous endeavor; take plenty of water and only attempt it in fall unless you're an experienced hiker. ⊠ *Off Wildrose Rd., south of Charcoal Kilns.*

## Educational Offerings

### Guided Tours

**Death Valley & Scotty's Castle Adventure Tour.** This 11-hour luxury motor coach tour of the park passes through its most famous landmarks. Tours include lunch and hotel pickup from designated Las Vegas–area hotels. ☎ *800/719–3768 Death Valley Tours, 800/566–5868 or 702/233-1627 Look Tours ⌑ $205 ☉ Tues., Fri., and Sun. at 7 AM.*

**Furnace Creek Visitor Center tours.** This center has the most tour options, including a weekly 2-mi Harmony Borax Walk and guided hikes to Keane Wonder Mine, Mosaic Canyon, and Golden Canyon. Less strenuous options include wildflower walks, birding walks, geology walks, and Furnace Creek Inn historical tour. The center also offers orientation programs every half hour, daily from 8 to 6. ⊠ *Furnace Creek Visitor Center, Rte. 190, 30 mi northwest of Death Valley Junction* ☎ *760/786–2331.*

15

**Gadabout Tours.** Take multiday trips through Death Valley from Ontario, California. ✉ *Sheraton Ontario Airport, 428 N. Vineyard Ave., Ontario, 91764* ⌚ *700 E. Tahquitz Canyon Way, Palm Springs, 92262* ☎ *760/325–5556 or 800/952–5068* ⊕ *www.gadabouttours.com.*

### Ranger Programs

☾ **Junior Ranger Program.** Children can join this program at any of the three visitor centers, where they can pick up a workbook and complete up to 15 projects (based on their age) to earn a souvenir badge.

## Arts & Entertainment

### Entertainment

**Marta Becket's Amargosa Opera House.** An artist and dancer from New York, Becket first visited the former railway town of Amargosa while on tour in 1964. Three years later she returned to town and bought a boarded-up theater that sat amid a group of rundown mock–Spanish colonial buildings. To compensate for the sparse audiences in the early days, Becket painted a Renaissance-era Spanish crowd on the walls and ceiling, turning the theater into a trompe l'oeil masterpiece. Now in her late 70s, Becket performs her blend of ballet, mime, and 19th-century melodrama to sellout crowds. After the show you can meet her in the adjacent gallery, where she sells her paintings and autographs her books. There are no performances mid-May through September. Reservations are required. ✉ *Rte. 127, Death Valley Junction* ☎ *760/852–4441* ▣ *$15* ☉ *Oct.–May (through Mother's Day weekend).*

# WHAT'S NEARBY

## Nearby Towns & Attractions

### Nearby Towns

Founded at the turn of the 20th century, **Beatty** sits 16 mi east of the California-Nevada border on Death Valley's northern side. Named for a single pine tree found at the bottom of the canyon of the same name, **Lone Pine**, on the park's west side, is where you'll find Mt. Whitney, the highest peak in the continental United States, at 14,496 feet. The nearby Alabama Hills have been used in many movies and TV scenes, including segments in *The Lone Ranger.* Down south, unincorporated **Shoshone,** a very small town at the edge of Death Valley, started out as a mining town. The area, dotted with tamarisk trees and date palms, is home to a natural warm-springs pool fed by an underwater river.

### What to See

★ ☾ **Ancient Bristlecone Pine Forest.** Here you can see some of the oldest living trees on earth, some of which date back more than 40 centuries. At the **Schulman Grove Visitor Center** (☎ 760/873–2500 ⊕ www.fs.fed. us/r5/inyo/about), open 8–4:30 weekdays, late May–October, you can learn about the bristlecone and take a walk to the 4,700-year-old Methuselah tree. ✉ *North from Independence on Hwy. 395, turn onto Hwy. 168 and follow signs 31 mi* ▣ *$3.*

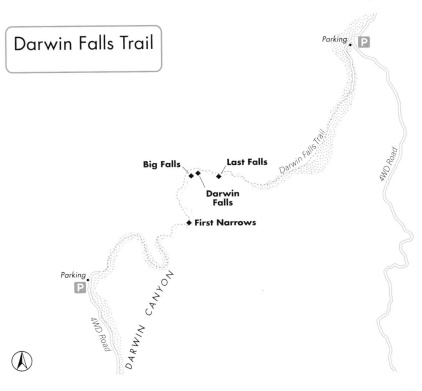

## Darwin Falls Trail

Parking

**Big Falls**    **Last Falls**

**Darwin Falls**

Darwin Falls Trail

4WD Road

**First Narrows**

Parking

DARWIN CANYON

4WD Road

15

**Ballarat Ghost Town.** This crusty, dusty town saw its heyday between 1897 and 1917. It's watched over by two lonely but lovable caretakers, George Novak and his son, Rocky, who run a working store-museum where you can grab a cold soda and hear a story or two before exploring the crumbling landscape. Ballarat's more infamous draw is **Barker Ranch,** accessible with four-wheel drive, where convicted murderer Charles Manson and his "family" were captured after the 1969 Sharon Tate murder spree. ⊠ *From Hwy. 395, exit SR-178 and travel 45 mi to the historic marker; Ballarat is 3½ mi from the pavement* ☎ *No phone.*

**Cerro Gordo Ghost Town.** Discovered by Mexican miner Pablo Flores in 1865, Cerro Gordo was California's biggest producer of silver and lead, raking in almost $13 million before it shut down in 1959. Today, the privately owned ghost town offers overnight accommodations in the **Belshaw House** for $150 per night (up to five people), billing itself the only "bed and cook your own breakfast ghost town in the world." Visit during the summer months, as its 8,300-foot elevation proves impassable during the winter. A four-wheel drive is recommended for the steep road into the ghost town. Admission includes a tour if arranged in advance. Guests are forbidden to take artifacts from the area or explore nearby mines. ⊠ *From Hwy. 395 at Lone Pine, take Hwy. 136 for 13 mi to Keeler, then travel 7½ miles up Cerro Gordo Road. From Panamint Springs, travel 31 mi* *west on Hwy. 190 until it merges with Hwy. 136; travel 5 more miles to Cerro Gordo Rd.* $5 760/876–5030 ⊕ *www.cerrogordo.us.*

**Manzanar National Historic Site.** A reminder of an ugly episode in U.S. history, the former Manzanar War Relocation Center is where some 10,000 Japanese-Americans were confined behind barbed-wire fences between 1942 and 1945. Today not much remains of Manzanar but a guard post, the auditorium, and some concrete foundations. But you can drive the one-way dirt road

---

**FAMILY PICKS**

- Look for pupfish at Salt Creek.
- Ride a piece of cardboard down the Sand Dunes.
- Explore the caves of Dublin Gulch in Shoshone.
- Take a tour on horseback at Furnace Creek Ranch.
- Venture through a real-live ghost town at Cerro Gordo or Rhyolite.

---

past the ruins to a small cemetery, where a monument stands. Signs mark where the barracks, a hospital, school, and fire station once stood. An 8,000-square-foot interpretive center has exhibits and a 15-minute film. ✉ *Hwy. 395, 11 mi north of Lone Pine* 760/878–2932 ⊕ *www.nps.gov/manz* *Free* ⊙ *Daily 9–4:30.*

**Fodor'sChoice** **Petroglyph Canyons.** Guided tours conducted by the Maturango Museum ★ are the only way to see these amazing spectacles. The two canyons, commonly called Big Petroglyph and Little Petroglyph, are in the Coso Mountain range on the million-acre U.S. Naval Weapons Center at China Lake. Each of the canyons holds a superlative concentration of ancient rock art, the largest of its kind in the Northern Hemisphere. Thousands of well-preserved images of animals and humans are scratched or pecked into dark basaltic rocks. Children under 10 are not allowed on the tour. The military requires everyone to produce a valid driver's license, social security number, passport, and vehicle registration before the trip (nondrivers must provide a birth certificate). ✉ *Tours depart from Maturango Museum, 100 E. Las Flores Ave., Ridgecrest 93555* 760/375–6900 ⊕ *www.maturango.org* $35 ⊙ *Tours Feb.–June and Sept. or Oct.–early Dec.; call for tour times.*

☺ **Randsburg.** The Rand Mining District first boomed when gold was dis-
**Fodor'sChoice** covered in the Rand Mountains in 1895. Along with neighboring set-
★ tlements, it grew further due to the success of the Yellow Aster Mine, which yielded $3 million worth of gold before 1900. Rich tungsten ore, used in World War I to make steel alloy, was discovered in 1907, and silver was found in 1919. Randsburg is one of the few gold-rush communities not to have become a ghost town; the tiny city jail is among the original buildings still standing in this town with a population under 100. In nearby Johannesburg, 1 mi south of Randsburg, spirits are said to dwell in the stunning Old West cemetery in the hills above town. ✉ *Hwy. 395, near the junction with Rte. 14.*

☺ **Rhyolite.** Though it's not within the boundary of Death Valley National
**Fodor'sChoice** Park, this Nevada ghost town, named for the silica volcanic rock nearby,
★ is still a big draw. Around 1904, Rhyolite's Montgomery Shoshone Mine caused a financial boom, and fancy buildings sprung up all over

town. Today you can still explore many of the crumbling edifices. The Bottle House, built by miner Tom Kelly out of almost 50,000 Adolphus Busch beer bottles, is a must-see. ⊠ *Hwy. 374, 35 mi north of Furnace Creek Visitor Center and 5 mi west of Beatty, NV* ☎ *No phone.*

**Shoshone Museum.** The museum chronicles the local history of Death Valley and houses a unique collection of period items, and minerals and rocks from the area. The building also houses the Death Valley Chamber of Commerce and functions as the visitor center for the southeastern entrance to Death Valley. ⊠ *Rte. 127, Shoshone* ☎ *760/852–4414* ⊕ *www.shoshonevillage.com* ⊠ *Free* ☉ *Daily 8–4.*

# WHERE TO STAY & EAT

### About the Restaurants

Inside the park, if you're looking for a special evening out in Death Valley, head to the Furnace Creek Dining Room, where you'll be spoiled with fine wines and gourmet fare such as rattlesnack empanadas or a juicy New York steak. It's also a great spot to start the day with a hearty gourmet breakfast. Most other spots within the park are mom-and-pop type places with basic American fare. Outside the park, dining choices are much the same, with little cafés and homey diners serving up coffee shop–style burgers, chicken, and steaks.

### About the Hotels

It's difficult to find lodging anywhere in Death Valley that doesn't have breathtaking views of the park and surrounding mountains. Most accommodations, aside from Furnace Creek Inn, are homey and rustic. Rooms fill up quickly during the fall and spring seasons, and reservations are required about three months in advance for prime weekends.

Outside the park, head to Beatty or Amargosa Valley in Nevada for a bit of nightlife and casino action. The western side of Death Valley, along the eastern Sierras, is a gorgeous setting, though it's quite a distance from Furnace Creek. Here, you can stay in the historic Dow Villa Motel, where John Wayne spent many a night, or head farther south to the ghost towns of Randsburg or Cerro Gordo for a true Wild West experience.

### About the Campgrounds

Backcountry camping is allowed in areas that are at least 2 mi from maintained campgrounds and the main paved or unpaved roads, and ¼ mi from water sources. You will need a high-clearance or a 4x4 vehicle to reach these locations. For your own safety, fill out a voluntary backcountry registration form so the rangers will know where to find you.

You may build fires in the fire grates that are available at all campgrounds except Sunset and Emigrant. Fires may be restricted during summer at Thorndike, Mahogany Flat, and Wildrose (check with rangers about current conditions). Wood gathering is prohibited at all campgrounds. A limited supply of firewood is available at general stores in Furnace Creek and Stovepipe Wells, but since prices are high and supplies limited, you're better off bringing your own if you intend to camp. Camping is prohibited in the historic Inyo, Los Burro, and Ubehebe Crater

**15**

areas as well as day-use spots including Aguerberry Point Road, Cottonwood Canyon Road, Racetrack Road, Skidoo Road, Titus Canyon Road, Wildrose Road, and West Side Road.

## Where to Eat

### In the Park

**$$$**
Fodor'sChoice
★

✕ **Inn Dining Room.** Fireplaces, beamed ceilings, and spectacular views provide a visual feast to match the inn's ambitious menu. Dishes may include such desert-theme items as rattlesnake empanadas and crispy cactus, and simpler fare such as cumin-lime shrimp, lamb, and New York strip steak. An evening dress code (no jeans, T-shirts, or shorts) is enforced. Lunch is served October–May only, but you can always have afternoon tea, an inn tradition since 1927. Breakfast and Sunday brunch are also served. ⊠ *Furnace Creek Inn Resort, Hwy. 190, Furnace Creek* 🕾 *760/786–2345* ⊕ *www.furnacecreekresort.com* ⌖ *Reservations essential. $25–$28* ⊟ *AE, D, DC, MC, V* ⊘ *No lunch June–Sept.*

☺ **$$$**
✕ **Wrangler Buffet and Steakhouse.** This casual, family-style restaurant has a buffet for breakfast and lunch, and steak house favorites for dinner. It's slightly more formal than the other restaurant at the Furnace Creek Resort, the Forty-Niner Cafe. ⊠ *Furnace Creek Ranch, Hwy. 190, Furnace Creek* 🕾 *760/786–2345* ⊕ *www.furnacecreekresort.com. $24–$29* ⊟ *AE, D, DC, MC, V* ⊘ *No buffet lunch Nov. 25–Dec. 22, but the coffee shop still serves lunch.*

**$$–$$$**
✕ **Panamint Springs Resort Restaurant.** This is a great place for steak and a beer, or pasta and a salad. In summer, evening meals are served outdoors on the porch, which has spectacular views of Panamint Valley. Breakfast and lunch are also served. ⊠ *Hwy. 190, 31 mi west of Stovepipe Wells* 🕾 *775/482–7680* ⌖ *Reservations essential. $15–$25* ⊟ *AE, D, MC, V.*

**$$–$$$**
✕ **Toll Road Restaurant.** There are wagon wheels in the yard and Old West artifacts on the interior walls at this restaurant in the Stovepipe Wells Village hotel. A stone fireplace heats the dining room. A full menu, with steaks, chicken, fish, and pasta, is served October–mid-May; breakfast and dinner buffets are laid out during summer. ⊠*Hwy. 190, Stovepipe Wells* 🕾*760/786–2604. $14–$25* ⊟ *AE, D, DC, MC, V* ⊘ *No lunch mid-May–Oct.*

☺ **¢–$$**
✕ **Forty-Niner Cafe.** This casual coffee shop serves typical American fare for breakfast, lunch, and dinner. The restaurant is done up in a rustic mining style with whitewashed pine walls, vintage map-covered tables, and prospector-branded chairs. Past menus and old photographs decorate the walls. ⊠ *Furnace Creek Ranch, Hwy. 190, Furnace Creek* 🕾 *760/786–2345* ⊕ *www.furnacecreekresort.com. $7–$18* ⊟ *AE, D, DC, MC, V.*

**¢–$**
✕ **19th Hole.** Overlooking the world's lowest golf course (214 feet below sea level), this open-air spot serves hamburgers, hot dogs, chicken, and sandwiches. There is drive-through service for golfers in carts. ⊠ *Furnace Creek Golf Club, Hwy. 190, Furnace Creek* 🕾 *760/786–2345. $6–$10* ⊟ *AE, D, DC, MC, V* ⊘ *Closed June–Sept. No dinner.*

### Outside the Park

★ **$–$$**
✕ **Café C'est Si Bon.** This funky little café and cyber lounge serves up delectable treats like homemade croissants slathered with homemade

fruit preserves, Thai iced tea, and wafer-thin crêpes stuffed with Gorgonzola, Armenian feta, and smooth Brie cheeses. ⊠ *Rte. 127, Shoshone* ☏ *760/852–4307. $10–$18* ⊟ *MC, V* ⊘ *Closed Tues.*

¢–$$  ✕ **Mt. Whitney Restaurant.** A boisterous family-friendly restaurant with a game room and 50-inch television, this place serves the best burgers in town—but in addition to the usual beef variety, you can choose from ostrich, venison, and buffalo burgers. ⊠ *227 S. Main St., Lone Pine* ☏ *760/876–5751. $7–$13* ⊟ *D, MC, V* ⊘ *Closed Sun. No lunch.*

★ ⟳ $  ✕ **Miner's Union Restaurant and General Store.** Built as Randsburg's Drug Store in 1896, this popular biker and family spot is one of the area's few surviving ghost-town buildings with original furnishings intact, such as tin ceiling, light fixtures, and a 1906 marble-and-stained-glass soda fountain. You can still enjoy a phosphate soda from that same fountain, cool down with a draft beer, or lunch on the signature Yellow Aster sandwich and blueberry milkshake. ⊠ *35 Butte Ave., Randsburg* ☏ *760/ 374–2180* ⊕ *www.minersunion.com. $8–$10* ⊟ *AE, D, MC, V.*

**15**

# Where to Stay

## In the Park

During the busy season (November–March) you should make reservations for lodgings within the park at least one month in advance.

$$$$  ✕▦ **Furnace Creek Inn.** Built in 1927, this adobe-brick-and-stone lodge

Fodor'sChoice  is nestled in one of the park's greenest oases. A warm mineral stream

★  gurgles across the property, and its 85°F waters feed into a swimming pool. The rooms are decorated in earth tones, with old-style furnishings. The top-notch Furnace Creek Inn Dining Room ($$$) serves desert-theme dishes such as rattlesnake empanadas and crispy cactus, as well as less exotic fare such as cumin-lime shrimp, lamb, and New York strip steak. Afternoon tea has been a tradition since 1927. ⊠ *Furnace Creek Village, near intersection of Hwy. 190 and Badwater Rd.* ⌂ *Box 1 Death Valley, 92328* ☏ *760/786–2345* ⎙ *760/786–2361* ⊕ *www. furnacecreekresort.com* ⇆ *66 rooms* ⟳ *Restaurant, room service, dial-up, tennis courts, pool, bar. $240–$375* ⊟ *AE, D, DC, MC, V* ⊘ *Closed mid-May–mid-Oct.*

$$–$$$  ✕▦ **Furnace Creek Ranch.** Originally crew headquarters for the Pacific Coast Borax Company, the four buildings here have motel-type rooms that are good for families. The best ones overlook the green lawns of the resort and the surrounding mountains. The property is adjacent to a golf course with its own team of pros, and also has a general store and a campground. The family-style Wrangler Steak House and Forty-Niner Cafe (⇨ *above*) serve American fare in simple surroundings. ⊠ *Hwy. 190, Furnace Creek* ⌂ *Box 1 Death Valley, 92328* ☏ *760/786–2345 or 800/528–6367* ⎙ *760/786–2423* ⊕ *www.furnacecreekresort. com* ⇆ *224 rooms* ⟳ *Restaurant, room service, dial-up, tennis courts, pool, bar. $105–$182* ⊟ *AE, D, DC, MC, V.*

$–$$  ▦ **Stovepipe Wells Village.** If you prefer quiet nights and an unfettered view of the night sky and nearby sand dunes, this property is for you. No telephones break the silence here, and only the deluxe rooms have televisions and some refrigerators. Rooms are simple yet comfortable and provide wide-open desert vistas. The Toll Road Restaurant ( ⇨ *above*) serves American breakfast, lunch, and dinner favorites, from omelets and sandwiches to burgers and steaks. RV campsites with full hookups ($23) are available on a first-come, first-served basis. ⊠ *Hwy. 190, Stovepipe Wells* ⌖ *Box 559 Death Valley, 92328* ☎ *760/786–2387* 🖷 *760/786–2389* ⊕ *www.stovepipewells.com* 🖃 *83 rooms* ⚭ *Some phones, some refrigerators, restaurant, bar, pool, some pets allowed, no-smoking rooms. $87–$107* ▭ *AE, D, MC, V.*

$ 🏨 **Panamint Springs Resort.** Ten miles inside the west entrance of the park, this low-key resort overlooks the sand dunes and peculiar geological formations of the Panamint Valley. It's a modest mom-and-pop-style operation with a wraparound porch and rustic furnishings. One room has a king-size bed, and two of the rooms accommodate up to six people. A pay phone, a gas pump, and a grocery store are on the premises. The resort uses satellite telephones to link to the outside world, so it is sometimes difficult to reach the property via phone. ⊠ *Hwy. 190, 28 mi west of Stovepipe Wells* ⌖ *Box 395 Ridgecrest, 93556* ☎ *775/482–7680* ⊕ *www.deathvalley.com* 🖷 *775/482–7682* 🖃 *14 rooms, 1 cabin* ⚭ *Restaurant, bar, some pets allowed, some a/c, no phone, no TV, no-smoking rooms. $79–$94* ▭ *AE, D, MC, V.*

CAMPGROUNDS &  🏕 **Furnace Creek.** This campground, 196 feet below sea level, has some
RV PARKS  shaded tent sites. Pay showers, a laundry, and a swimming pool are at
$$  nearby Furnace Creek Ranch. Reservations are accepted for stays between mid-October and mid-April; at other times sites are available on a first-come, first-served basis. Two group campsites can accommodate 40 people each. ⊠ *Hwy. 190, Furnace Creek* ☎ *301/722–1257, 800/365–2267 reservations* ⊕ *http://reservations.nps.gov* 🖃 *136 tent/RV sites* ⚭ *Flush toilets, dump station, drinking water, fire grates, picnic tables, public telephone, ranger station. $18* ▭ *AE, D, MC, V. Credit cards accepted for reservations only; otherwise, no credit cards.*

$–$$  🏕 **Panamint Springs Resort.** Part of a complex that includes a motel and cabin, this campground is surrounded by cottonwoods. The daily fee includes use of the showers and restrooms. ⊠ *Hwy. 190, 28 mi west of Stovepipe Wells* ☎ *775/482–7680* 🖷 *775/482–7682* 🖃 *11 full-hookup RV sites, 26 tent sites, 30 water-only sites* ⚭ *Flush toilets, full hookups, partial hookups (water), dump station, drinking water, showers, fire grates, picnic tables, public telephone, general store, service station (gas only). $15–$30* ▭ *AE, D, MC, V.*

$–$$  🏕 **Stovepipe Wells Village.** This is the second-largest campground in the park. Like Sunset, this area is little more than a giant parking lot, but pay showers and laundry facilities are available at the adjacent motel. ⊠ *Hwy. 190, Stovepipe Wells* ☎ *760/786–2387* 🖃 *190 tent, 14 RV sites with full-hookups* ⚭ *Flush toilets, dump station, drinking water, public telephone, general store, swimming (pool)* ⚑ *Reservations not accepted. $12–$23* ▭ *No credit cards* ⊙ *Mid-Oct.–mid-Apr.*

$  🏕 **Mesquite Springs.** There are tent and RV spaces here, some of them shaded, but no RV hookups. No generators are allowed. Since Mesquite Springs is the only campground on the north end of the park, it attracts younger campers intent on getting away from the crowds. ⊠ *Access road 2 mi south of Scotty's Castle* ☎ *No phone* 🖃 *30 tent/RV sites* ⚭ *Flush* *toilets, dump station, drinking water, fire grates, picnic tables* ⚿ *Reservations not accepted. $12* ☰ *No credit cards.*

**$** ⚿ **Sunset Campground.** This campground is a gravel-and-asphalt RV city. Hookups are not available, but you can walk across the street to the showers, laundry facilities, and swimming pool at Furnace Creek Ranch. Many of Sunset's denizens are senior citizens who migrate to Death Valley each winter to play golf and tennis or just to enjoy the mild, dry climate. No fires are allowed here. ⊠ *Sunset Campground Rd., 1 mi north of Furnace Creek* ☎ *760/786–2331* ⊕ *www.nps.gov/deva* ↵ *1,000 tent/RV sites* ⚿ *Flush toilets, dump station, drinking water, public telephone, ranger station, play area* ⚿ *Reservations not accepted. $12* ☰ *No credit cards* ☾ *Mid-Oct.–mid-Apr.*

★ **$** ⚿ **Texas Spring.** This campsite south of the Furnace Creek Visitor Center has good facilities and is a few dollars cheaper than Furnace Creek. No generators are allowed. In spring, not all sites may be available for RV use. ⊠ *Off Badwater Rd., south of the Furnace Creek Visitor Center* ☎ *800/365–2267* ↵ *92 tent/RV sites* ⚿ *Flush toilets, dump station, drinking water, fire grates, picnic tables* ⚿ *Reservations not accepted. $14* ☰ *No credit cards* ☾ *Mid-Oct.–mid-Apr.*

★ **¢** ⚿ **Mahogany Flat.** If you have a four-wheel-drive vehicle and want to scale Telescope Peak, the park's highest mountain, you might want to sleep at one of the few shaded spots in Death Valley, at a cool 8,133 feet. It's the most scenic campground, set among pinyon pines and junipers, with a view of the valley. ⊠ *Off Wildrose Rd., south of Charcoal Kilns* ☎ *No phone* ↵ *10 tent sites* ⚿ *Pit toilets, fire grates, picnic tables. Free* ⚿ *Reservations not accepted* ☾ *Mar.–Nov.*

**¢** ⚿ **Thorndike.** Folks who visit the park in summer often travel to this alpine campground high in the Panamint Mountains. During certain road conditions, you may need a four-wheel-drive vehicle. ⊠ *½ mi east of Charcoal Kilns* ☎ *No phone* ↵ *6 tent/RV sites* ⚿ *Pit toilets, fire grates, picnic tables* ⚿ *Reservations not accepted. Free* ☾ *Mar.–Nov.*

**¢** ⚿ **Wildrose.** Since it's on a paved road at a lower elevation (4,100 feet) than nearby Mahogany Flat, Wildrose is less likely to be closed because of snow in winter. The view here is not as spectacular as that from Mahogany Flat, but it does overlook the northern end of the valley. ⊠ *Wildrose Canyon Road, 37 mi south of Stovepipe Wells* ☎ *No phone* ↵ *23 tent/RV sites* ⚿ *Pit toilets, drinking water (Apr.–Nov. only), fire grates, picnic tables. Free* ⚿ *Reservations not accepted.*

## Outside the Park

**$–$$** ▦ **Dow Villa Motel and Hotel.** John Wayne slept here, and you can, too. Built in 1923 to cater to the film industry, Dow Villa is in the center of Lone Pine. Some rooms have views of the mountains; both buildings are within walking distance of just about everything in town. There are in-room coffeemakers and whirlpool tubs, though some of the guest rooms share bathrooms. Pets are allowed only in smoking rooms. Many units have an Old West feel, and are decorated with antique furniture and pictures of John Wayne or Mt. Whitney. ⊠ *310 S. Main St., Lone Pine 93545* ☎ *760/876–5521 or 800/824–9317* ⊕ *www.dowvillamotel.com* ↵ *91 rooms* ⚿ *Refrigerator, VCR, some ethernet, some Wi-Fi, pool, no-smoking rooms. $56–$130* ☰ *AE, D, DC, MC, V.*

# DEATH VALLEY ESSENTIALS

ACCESSIBILITY All of Death Valley's visitor centers, contact stations, and museums are accessible to all visitors. The campgrounds at Furnace Creek, Sunset, and Stovepipe Wells have wheelchair-accessible sites. The grounds at Scotty's Castle are accessible to the mobility impaired, and the guided tour of the main house has provisions for a wheelchair lift to the upper floors. Highway 190, Badwater Road, Scotty's Castle Road, and paved roads to Dante's View and Wildrose provide access to the major scenic viewpoints and historic points of interest.

ADMISSION FEES The entrance fee is $20 per vehicle and $10 for those entering on foot, bus, bike, or motorcycle. The payment, valid for seven consecutive days, is collected at the park's entrance stations and at the visitor center at Furnace Creek. (If you enter the park on Highway 190, there is no entrance station; remember to stop by the visitor center to pay the fee.) Annual park passes, valid only at Death Valley, are $40.

ADMISSION HOURS Most facilities within the park remain open year-round, daily 8–6.

ATMS/BANKS
🔁 **Furnace Creek Ranch Registration Office** ⊠ Hwy. 190, north of the Furnace Creek Visitor Center. **Stovepipe Wells Village** ⊠ Hwy. 190, 23 mi northwest of Furnace Creek.

AUTOMOBILE SERVICE STATIONS
🔁 **Furnace Creek Gas Station** ⊠ Hwy. 190, Furnace Creek ☎ 760/786–2232. **Scotty's Castle Gas Station** ⊠ Scotty's Castle, Hwy. 190, 53 mi northwest of Furnace Creek ☎ 760/786–2325. **Stovepipe Wells Gas Station** ⊠ Hwy. 190, Stovepipe Wells ☎ 760/786–2578.

EMERGENCIES For all emergencies, call 911. Note that cell phones don't work in many parts of the park.

LOST AND FOUND The park's lost-and-found is at the Furnace Creek Visitor Center.

PERMITS Though a permit is not required for groups of fewer than 15 people, if you're planning an overnight visit to the backcountry, complete a registration form at the Furnace Creek Visitor Center. Backcountry camping is allowed in areas that are at least 2 mi from maintained campgrounds and the main paved or unpaved roads, and ¼ mi from water sources. Most abandoned mining areas are restricted to day use.

POST OFFICES
🔁 **Death Valley Post Office** ⊠ Hwy. 190, ½ mi south of the Furnace Creek Visitor Center, Death Valley 92328 ☎ 760/786–2223.

PUBLIC TELEPHONES You'll find public telephones at Furnace Creek Visitor Center and Stovepipe Wells ranger station, as well as at the park's gas stations and lodgings.

RESTROOMS Flush toilets are available at many of the campgrounds throughout the park and at Scotty's Castle. There are public restrooms at Furnace Creek Visitor Center and Stovepipe Wells ranger station.

**NEARBY TOWN INFORMATION**
🔁 **Beatty Chamber of Commerce** ⊠ 119 E. Main St., Beatty, NV 89003 ☎ 775/553–2424 ⊕ www.governet.net/nv/as/bea. **Death Valley Chamber of Commerce** ⊠ 118 S. Rte. 127, Box 157, Shoshone, 92384 ☎ 760/852–4524 🖷 760/852–4414 ⊕ www.deathvalleychamber.org. **Lone Pine Chamber of Commerce** ⊠ 126 S. Main St., Box 749, Lone Pine, 93545 ☎ 760/876–4444 or 877/253–8981 ⊕ www.lonepinechamber.org. **Shoshone Development** 🖃 Box 67, Shoshone, 92384 ☎ 760/852–4224 🖷 760/852–4250 ⊕ www.shoshonevillage.com.

**VISITOR INFORMATION**
🔁 **Death Valley National Park** 🖃 Box 579, Death Valley, 92328 ☎ 760/786–2331, 760/786–3225 TDD 🖷 760/786–3283 ⊕ www.nps.gov/deva. **Death Valley Natural History Association** 🖃 Box 188, Death Valley, 92328 ☎ 760/786–2146 or 800/478–8564.

# Glacier & Waterton Lakes National Parks

Hikers at Piegan Pass, Glacier National Park

## WORD OF MOUTH

"Get off the tracks at Belton Station [now West Glacier], and in a few minutes you will find yourself in the midst of what you are sure to say is the best care-killing scenery on the continent."

–John Muir

# WELCOME TO GLACIER & WATERTON

## TOP REASONS TO GO

★ **Witness the Divide:** The rugged mountains that weave their way through Glacier and Waterton along the Continental Divide seem to have glaciers in every hollow melting into tiny streams, raging rivers, and icy-cold lakes.

★ **Just Hike It:** There are hundreds of miles of trails that cater to hikers of all levels—from all-day hikes to short strolls. It's little wonder the readers of *Backpacker Magazine* rated Glacier the number-one backcountry hiking park in America.

★ **Go to the Sun:** Crossing the Continental Divide at the 6,646-foot-high Logan Pass, Glacier's Going-to-the-Sun Road is a spectacular drive.

★ **View the Wildlife:** This is one of the few places in North America where all native carnivores, including grizzlies and wolves, still survive. Bighorn sheep, mule deer, coyotes, grizzly bears, and black bears can often be seen from roadways.

**1** Waterton Lakes. The Canadian national park is the meeting of two worlds: the flatlands of the prairie and the abrupt upthrust of the mountains. In this juncture of worlds, the park squeezes into a relatively small area (200 square mi) an unusual mix of wildlife, flora, and climate zones.

**2** West Glacier. Known to the Kootenai people as "sacred dancing lake," Lake McDonald is the largest glacial water basin lake in Glacier National Park.

**3** Logan Pass. At 6,646 feet, this is the highest point on the Going-to-the-Sun Road. From mid-June to mid-October, a 1½-mi boardwalk leads to an overlook that crosses an area with lush meadows and wildflowers.

**4** East Glacier. St. Mary Lake and Many Glacier are the major highlights of the eastern side of Glacier. Services and amenities are located at both sites.

**5** Backcountry. This is some of the most incredible terrain in North America and provides the right combination of beautiful scenery and isolation. Although Waterton is a much smaller park, its backcountry trails connect with hiking trails in both Glacier and British Columbia's Akamina-Kishinena Provincial Park.

## GETTING ORIENTED

In the rocky northwest corner of Montana, Glacier National Park encompasses 1.2 million acres (1,563 square mi) of untrammeled wilds. Within the park, there are 37 named glaciers (which are ever-so-slowly diminishing), 200 lakes, and 1,000 mi of streams. Neighboring Waterton Lakes National Park, across the border in Alberta, Canada, covers another 130,000 acres. In 1932, the parks were unified to form the Waterton-Glacier International Peace Park—the first international peace park in the world—in recognition of the two nations' friendship and dedication to peace.

MONTANA

Polebridge

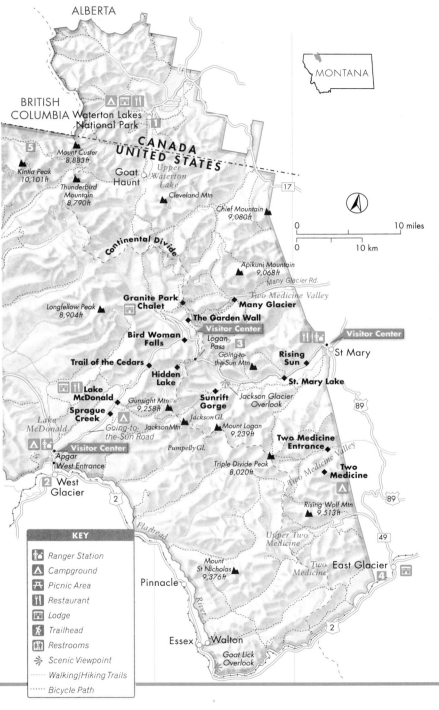

ALBERTA

MONTANA

BRITISH
COLUMBIA  Waterton Lakes
National Park

CANADA
UNITED STATES

5

Mount Custer
8,883ft

Kintla Peak
10,101ft

ThunderBird
Mountain
8,790ft

Goat
Haunt

Upper
Waterton
Lake

Cleveland Mtn

Chief Mountain
9,080ft

17

0                    10 miles
0              10 km

Continental Divide

Longfellow Peak
8,904ft

Granite Park
Chalet

The Garden Wall

Bird Woman
Falls

Trail of the Cedars

Lake
McDonald

Sprague
Creek

Lake
McDonald

Apgar
West Entrance

Apikuni Mountain
9,068ft

Many Glacier Rd.

Two Medicine Valley

Many Glacier

Visitor Center

Logan
Pass

3

Going-to-
the-Sun Mtn

Rising
Sun

St. Mary Lake

Hidden
Lake

Gunsight Mtn
9,258ft

Going-to-
the-Sun Road

JacksonMtn

Sunrift
Gorge

Jackson GI.

Jackson Glacier
Overlook

Mount Logan
9,239ft

Pumpelly GI.

Visitor Center

St Mary

89

Two Medicine
Entrance

Two
Medicine

Triple Divide Peak
8,020ft

Two Medicine Valley

89

2   West
Glacier

2

Rising Wolf Mtn
9,513ft

Upper Two
Medicine

49

KEY

👫 Ranger Station
⛺ Campground
⛱ Picnic Area
🍴 Restaurant
🏠 Lodge
🚶 Trailhead
🚻 Restrooms
⚜ Scenic Viewpoint
----- Walking|Hiking Trails
...... Bicycle Path

Flathead

Pinnacle

Mount
St Nicholas
9,376ft

River

Two
Medicine

East Glacier

4

Essex   Walton

Goat Lick
Overlook

2

# GLACIER & WATERTON PLANNER

## When to Go

Of the 2 million annual visitors to Glacier and 400,000 annual visitors to Waterton, **the vast majority drive through the gates between July 1 and September 15,** when the streams are flowing and wildlife is roaming. Spring and fall are the quiet seasons, but they're becoming increasingly popular. By October, snow forces the closing of most park roads.

Snow removal on the alpine portion of Going-to-the-Sun Road is usually completed by mid-June; the opening of Logan Pass at the road's summit marks the summer opening at Glacier, while Canada's Victoria Day in late May marks the beginning of the season in Waterton.

### AVG. HIGH/LOW TEMPS.

GLACIER

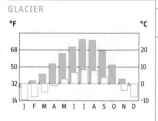

WATERTON LAKES

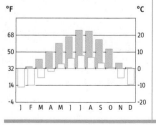

## Getting There & Around

On the east, U.S. 89 accesses Many Glacier and St. Mary, Route 49 reaches Two Medicine. On the west, U.S. 2 goes to West Glacier. The nearest airports are in Great Falls and Kalispell, Montana.

The roads in both parks are either paved or gravel and deteriorate from moisture freezing and thawing. Drive slowly and anticipate that rocks and wildlife may be around the corner. Road reconstruction is part of the park experience as there are only a few warm months in which road crews can complete projects. Scenic pullouts are frequent; watch for other vehicles pulling in or out, and watch for children in parking areas. Most development and services center around St. Mary Lake on the east, and Lake McDonald on the west.

Glacier Park, Inc. operates a shuttle along the Going-to-the-Sun Road July 1 to Labor Day. Buses make stops at major trailheads, campgrounds, and other developed areas between Lake McDonald Lodge and Rising Sun Motor Inn. For schedules and fares call ☎ 406/226–5666 or see ⊕ www.glacierparkinc.com. To get between the parks, take Chief Mountain Highway.

## Border Crossings

A passport is required of everyone in your vehicle in order to cross the Canadian/U.S. border in either direction. Kids traveling with only one parent need a notarized letter from the other parent giving permission to enter Canada or the United States. If you are traveling with pets, you need proof of immunizations to cross the border in either direction. *Landed residents of Canada and non-U.S. and non-Canadian citizens from a visa-waiver country or with a valid visitor visa entering the United States from Canada must pay $6 (cash only) at the border for a required I94 form, available at the Port of Entry.*

For information about United States Customs, call 406/335–2611; for Canadian Customs, 403/344–3767.

## Flora & Fauna

In summer, a profusion of new flowers, grasses, and budding trees covers the landscape high and low. Spring attracts countless birds, from golden eagles riding thermals north to Canada and Alaska, to rare harlequin ducks dipping in creeks. Snow-white mountain goats, with their wispy white beards and curious stares, are seen in alpine areas, and sure-footed bighorn sheep graze the high meadows in the short summers. The largest population of grizzly bears in the lower 48 states live in the wild in and around the park. Feeding the animals is illegal.

Visiting Glacier in winter makes for easy tracking of many large animals like moose, elk, deer, mountain lions, wolf, lynx, and their smaller neighbors the snowshoe hare, pine marten, beaver, and muskrat.

In park lakes, sportfishing species include burbot (ling), northern pike, whitefish, grayling, cutthroat, rainbow, lake (Mackinaw), kokanee salmon, and brook trout.

## Tours

**Glacier Park, Inc.** schedules driver-narrated van tours that cover most of the park accessible by road. The tour of Going-to-the-Sun Road is a favorite, with plenty of photo opportunities at roadside pullouts. Some of the tours are conducted in "Jammers," vintage 1936 red buses with roll-back tops. Short trips and full-day trips are available. Reservations are essential. ✐ *Box 2025 Columbia Falls, MT 59912* ☎ *406/892–2525 or 403/236–3400* ⊕ *www.glacierparkinc.com* ✉ *$40–$65* ⊙ *June–Sept.*

## Safety Tips

**Never approach a bear or any other park animal, no matter how cute, cuddly, and harmless it appears.** If you encounter a bear, don't run. Back away slowly and assume a nonthreatening posture. If a brown or grizzly bear charges, drop into the fetal position, protect your head and neck, and do not move. It's the opposite if you encounter a black bear or mountain lion: act aggressively, throw rocks or sticks, and try to look large by holding up a pack or branches. If attacked, fight back, aiming for the nose.

**To minimize the risk of contact with bears and mountain lions,** hike only during the day, hike in groups, and make lots of noise by singing, talking loudly, and clapping hands, especially near blind corners and streams.

**Check for ticks** after walking through shrubs and high grasses. They are a problem especially in the spring.

**Prepare for winter storms** with survival kits that include snow tires or chains, a shovel and window scraper, flares or a reflector, a blanket or sleeping bag, a first-aid kit, sand, gravel or traction mats, a flashlight with extra batteries, matches, a lighter and candles, paper, nonperishable foods, drinking water, and a tow chain or rope.

**16**

By Debbie Olsen

The massive peaks of the Continental Divide in Northwest Montana are the backbone of Glacier National Park and its sister park in Canada, Waterton Lakes, which together make up the International Peace Park. From their slopes, melting snow and alpine glaciers yield the headwaters of rivers that flow west to the Pacific Ocean, north to the Arctic Ocean, and southeast to the Atlantic Ocean via the Gulf of Mexico. Coniferous forests, thickly vegetated stream bottoms, and green-carpeted meadows provide homes and sustenance for all kinds of wildlife.

# GLACIER NATIONAL PARK

## Scenic Drives

★ **Going-to-the-Sun Road.** This magnificent, 50-mi highway—a National Historic Civil Engineering Landmark—crosses the crest of the Continental Divide at Logan Pass and traverses the towering Garden Wall. The Federal Highway Administration and the park have embarked on a multiyear road rehabilitation, which will see this narrow, curving highway undergo structural repair. In 2007, while work is underway, a shuttle system will allow access for visitors.

**Many Glacier Road.** This 12-mi drive enters Glacier on the northeast side of the park, west of Babb, and travels along Sherburne Lake for almost 5 mi, penetrating a glacially carved valley surrounded by mountains. It passes through meadows and a scrubby forest of lodgepole pines, aspen, and cottonwood. The farther you travel up the valley, the more clearly you'll be able to see Grinnell and Salamander glaciers. The road passes Many Glacier Hotel and ends at the Swift Current Campground. It's usually closed from October to May.

# GOING-TO-THE-SUN ROAD

Going-to-the-Sun Road, arguably the most beautiful drive in the country, connects Lake McDonald on the west side of Glacier with St. Mary Lake on the east. Turnoffs provide views of the high country and glacier-carved valleys. The sights below are listed in order from west to east.

**The Garden Wall.** An abrupt and jagged wall of rock juts above the road and is visible for about 10 mi as it follows Logan Creek from just past Avalanche Creek Campground to Logan Pass. ✉ *24–34 mi from West Glacier.*

**Logan Pass.** At 6,660 feet, this is the highest point in the park accessible by motor vehicle. It presents unparalleled views of both sides of the Continental Divide and is frequented by mountain goats, bighorn sheep, and grizzly bears. It is extremely crowded in July and August. ✉ *34 mi from West Glacier, 18 mi from St. Mary.*

**Hidden Lake Overlook.** Take a walk from Logan Pass up to see the crystalline Hidden Lake, which often still has ice clinging to it in early July. It's a 1½-mi hike on an uphill grade, partially on a boardwalk that protects the abundant wildflowers. ✉ *1½ mi from Logan Pass, Going-to-the-Sun Rd.*

**Jackson Glacier Overlook.** On the east side of the Continental Divide, you come into view of Jackson Glacier looming in a rocky pass across the upper St. Mary River valley. If it isn't covered with snow, you'll see sharp peaks of ice. The glacier is shrinking and may disappear in another 100 years. ✉ *5 mi east of Logan Pass.*

**St. Mary Lake.** When the breezes calm, the lake mirrors the snowcapped peaks that line the St. Mary Valley. The Sun Point Nature Trail follows the lake's shore 1 mi each way. You can buy an interpretive brochure for 50¢ at the trailhead on the north side of the lake, then drop it off at the box at the trail's end to be recycled. ✉ *1 mi west of St. Mary.*

■ TIP➔ **The drive is susceptible to frequent delays in summer. To avoid traffic jams and parking problems, take the road early in the morning or late in the evening (when the lighting is ideal for photography and wildlife is most likely to appear).** Vehicle size is restricted to under 21 feet long, 10 feet high, and 8 feet wide, including mirrors, between Avalanche Creek Campground and Sun Point. From late October to late May or June, deep snows close most of Going-to-the-Sun Road. During 2007 road construction take the shuttle.

If you don't want to drive the Going-to-the-Sun Road, consider making the ride in a Jammer, an antique red bus operated by **Glacier Park, Inc.** (☎ 406/892–2525 ⊕ www.glacierparkinc.com). The drivers double as guides, and they can roll back the tops of the vehicles to give you improved views. Reservations are required.

**16**

## What to See

### Historic Sites

**Apgar.** On the southwest end of Lake McDonald, this tiny hamlet has a few stores, an ice-cream shop, motels, ranger buildings, a campground, and a historic schoolhouse. From November to mid-May, no services remain open, except the weekend-only visitor center. ⊠ *2 mi north of the west entrance.*

The **Apgar Discovery Cabin,** across the street from the Apgar Visitor Center, is filled with animal posters, kids' activities, and maps. ☎ *406/888–7939* ⊗ *Mid-June–Labor Day, daily 1:30–3.*

### Scenic Stops

⇨ Going-to-the-Sun Road box for stops along that road.

**Goat Lick Overlook.** Mountain goats frequent this natural salt lick on a cliff above the Middle Fork of the Flathead River. ⊠ *2½ mi east of Walton Ranger Station on U.S. 2.*

**Grinnell and Salamander Glaciers.** These glaciers formed about 4,000 years ago as one ice mass. In 1926 they broke apart and have been shrinking ever since. The best viewpoint is reached by the 5½-mi Grinnell Glacier Trail from Many Glacier. ⊠ *5½ mi from Swiftcurrent Campground on Grinnell Glacier Trail.*

**Lake McDonald.** This beautiful 10-mi long lake is accessible year-round on Going-to-the-Sun Road. Take a boat ride to the middle for a view of the surrounding glacier-clad mountains. You can go fishing and horseback riding at either end, and in winter, snowshoe or cross-country ski. ⊠ *2 mi from the west entrance at Apgar.*

**Running Eagle Falls (Trick Falls).** Cascading near Two Medicine, this is actually two different waterfalls from two different sources. In spring, when the water level is high, the upper falls join the lower falls for a 40-foot drop into Two Medicine River; in summer, the upper falls dry up, revealing the lower 20-foot falls that start midway down the precipice. ⊠ *2 mi east of the Two Medicine entrance.*

**Two Medicine Valley.** Rugged, often windy, and always beautiful, the valley is a remote 9-mi drive from Route 49 and is surrounded by some of the park's most stark, rocky peaks. On and around the valley's lake you can rent a canoe, take a narrated boat tour, camp, and hike. Be aware that bears frequent the area. The road is closed from late October through late May. ⊠ *Two Medicine entrance, 9 mi east of Hwy. 49* ☎ *406/888–7800, 406/257–2426 boat tours.*

### Visitor Centers

**Apgar Visitor Center.** This is a great first stop if you're entering the park from the west. Here you can get all kinds of information, including maps, permits, books, and the *Junior Ranger* newspaper. You can plan your route on a large relief map to get a glimpse of where you're going. In winter, the rangers offer free snowshoe walks—they provide the snowshoes, too. ☎ *406/888–7800* ⊗ *Mid-May–Oct., daily 8–8; Nov.–mid-May, weekends 9–4.*

## GLACIER IN ONE DAY

It's hard to beat the **Going-to-the-Sun Road** for a one-day trip in Glacier National Park. This itinerary takes you from west to east—if you're starting from St. Mary, take the tour backwards. First, however, call Glacier Park Boat Tours (☎ 406/257–2426) to make a reservation for the **St. Mary Lake or Lake McDonald boat tour,** depending on where you end up. Then, drive up Going-to-the-Sun Road to **Avalanche Creek Campground,** and take a 30-minute stroll along the fragrant **Trail of the Cedars.** Afterward, continue driving up—you can see views of waterfalls and wildlife to the left and an awe-inspiring, precipitous drop to the right. At the summit, **Logan Pass,** your arduous climb is rewarded with a gorgeous view of immense peaks, sometimes complemented by a herd of mountain goats. Stop in at the **visitor center,** then take the 1½-mi **Hidden Lake Trail** up to prime wildlife-viewing spots. Picnic at the overlook above Hidden Lake. In the afternoon, continue driving east over the mountains. Stop at the **Jackson Glacier Overlook** to view one of the park's largest glaciers. Continue down; eventually the forest thins, the vistas grow broader, and a gradual transition to the high plains begins. When you reach **Rising Sun Campground,** take the one-hour St. Mary Lake boat tour to St. Mary Falls. If you'd rather hike, the 1²/₁₀-mi **Sun Point Nature Trail** also leads to the falls. (Take the boat tour if you're driving from east to west.) The Going-to-the-Sun Road is generally closed from mid-October to late May.

**16**

**Logan Pass Visitor Center.** Built of stone, this center stands sturdy against the severe weather that forces it to close in winter. Books, maps, and more are stocked inside. Rangers staff the center and give 10-minute talks on the alpine environment. ⊠ *34 mi from West Glacier, 18 mi from St. Mary* ☎ *406/888–7800* ⊙ *Mid-June–mid-Sept., daily 9–7.*

**St. Mary Visitor Center.** The park's largest visitor complex, it has a huge relief map of the park's peaks and valleys and provides a 15-minute video that orients visitors. Rangers host evening presentations during the peak summer months. Traditional Blackfeet dancing and drumming performances are offered throughout the summer. Check with the center for exact dates and times. The center has books and maps for sale, backcountry camping permits, and large viewing windows facing the 10-mi-long St. Mary Lake. ⊠ *Going-to-the-Sun Rd. off U.S. 89* ☎ *406/732–7750* ⊙ *Mid-May–mid-Oct., daily 8–4:30 with extended hours during the peak summer months.*

## Sports & the Outdoors

### Air Tours

OUTFITTER & EXPEDITIONS

**Kruger Helicopter Tours.** This outfitter offers one-hour and half-hour tours of Glacier for up to four people, weather permitting. The half-hour tour covers the park's major glaciers and lakes, while the one-hour tour encompasses the entire park. Headsets allow you to hear the pilot's narration. ⌐ *Box 235, Lakeside MT 59922* ☎ *800/879–9310* ⊕ *www. krugerhelicopters.com* ⌐ *Tours $95–$650 per person* ☉ *May–Oct.*

### Bicycling

Cyclists in Glacier must stay on roads or bike routes and are not permitted on hiking trails or in the backcountry. The one-lane, unpaved Inside North Fork Road from Apgar to Polebridge is well suited

**READ ALL ABOUT IT**

The **Waterton/Glacier Guide** contains articles on activities, special events, wildlife-interpretive programs, and religious services within the parks. It provides suggested excursions, camping information, and warnings about park hazards. The newspaper is at park entrances and visitor centers.

to mountain bikers. Two Medicine Road is an intermediate paved route, with a mild grade at the beginning, becoming steeper as you approach Two Medicine Campground. Much of the western half of Going-to-the-Sun Road is closed to bikes from 11 to 4. Other restrictions apply during peak traffic periods and road construction.

### Boating & Rafting

Glacier has many stunning lakes and rivers, making boating a popular park activity. Glacier Park Boat Company offers guided tours of Lake McDonald, St. Mary Lake, and Two Medicine Lake, as well as Swiftcurrent and Josephine lakes at Many Glacier from June to mid-September. You can rent small boats at Lake McDonald, Apgar, Two Medicine, and Many Glacier (⌐ Glacier Park Boat Company). Watercraft such as Sea-Doos or Jet Skis are not allowed in the park.

Many rafting companies provide adventures along the border of the park on the Middle and North Forks of the Flathead River. The Middle Fork has some excellent white water, while the North Fork has both slow-moving and fast-moving sections. If you bring your own raft or kayak, stop at the Hungry Horse Ranger Station in the Flathead National Forest near West Glacier to obtain a permit.

OUTFITTERS & EXPEDITIONS ★
**Glacier Park Boat Company** gives tours on five lakes. A **Lake McDonald cruise** takes you from the dock at Lake McDonald Lodge to the middle of the lake for an unparalleled view of the Continental Divide's Garden Wall. Cruises on **Swiftcurrent Lake** and **Lake Josephine** depart from Many Glacier Lodge and provide views of the Continental Divide. **Two Medicine Lake cruises** leave from the dock near the ranger station and lead to several trails. **St. Mary Lake cruises** leave from the launch near Rising Sun Campground and head to Red Eagle Mountain and other spots. The tours last 45–90 minutes. You can rent kayaks, canoes, rowboats ($12 per hour) and small motorboats ($22 per hour) at Lake McDonald, Apgar, Two Medicine, and Many Glacier. ☎ *406/257–2426* ⊕ *www.glacierparkboats.com* ⌐ *Tours $10.50–$16; rentals $12-$22 per hour* ☉ *June–Sept.*

**Glacier Guides and Montana Raft Company** will take you on raft trips through the stomach-churning white water of the Middle Fork of the

Flathead and combine it with a hike, horseback ride, or a barbecue. The company also offers guided hikes and fly-fishing trips. ⊠ *11970 U.S. 2 E, 1 mi west of West Glacier* ☎ *406/387–5555 or 800/521–7238* ⊕ *www.glacierguides.com* 🖅 *$40–$80* ☉ *May–Oct.*

**Great Northern Whitewater** offers daily white-water, kayaking, and fishing trips and rents Swiss-style chalets with views of Glacier's peaks. ⊠ *12127 U.S. 2 E, 1 mi south of West Glacier* ☎ *406/387–5340 or 800/ 735–7897* ⊕ *www.gnwhitewater.com* 🖅 *$43–$78* ☉ *May–Oct.*

⇨ Multisport Outfitters box for more options.

### Fishing

Within Glacier there's an almost unlimited range of fishing possibilities, with a catch-and-release policy encouraged. You can fish in most waters of the park, but the best fishing is generally in the least accessible spots. A fishing license is not required inside the park boundary, but you must stop by a park office to pick up a copy of the regulations. The fishing season runs from the third Saturday in May to November 30.

▓ TIP→ Fishing on both the North Fork and the Middle Fork of the Flathead River requires a Montana conservation license ($10) plus a Montana fishing license ($15 for two consecutive days or $60 for a season); they are available at most convenience stores, sports shops, and from the Montana Department of Fish, Wildlife, and Parks (☎ 406/752–5501).

### Golf

**Glacier Park Lodge** has a 9-hole, par-36 course, and a 9-hole pitch-and-putt course. Watch for moose. ⊠ *Off U.S. 2, East Glacier* ☎ *406/226– 9311.*

### Hiking

With 730 mi of marked trails, Glacier is a hiker's paradise. Trail maps are available at all visitor centers and entrance stations. Before hiking, ask about trail closures due to bear or mountain lion activity. Never hike alone. For backcountry hiking, pick up a permit from park headquarters or the Apgar backcountry office near Glacier's western entrance, (☎ 406/888–7939).

EASY **Avalanche Lake Trail.** From Avalanche Creek Campground, take this 3-mi trail leading to mountain-ringed Avalanche Lake. The walk is relatively easy (it ascends 500 feet), making this one of the most accessible backcountry lakes in the park. Crowds fill the parking area and trail during July and August, and on sunny weekends in May and June. ⊠ *15 mi north of Apgar on Going-to-the-Sun Rd.*

**Baring Falls.** For a nice family hike, try the 1³/₁₀-mi path from the Sun Point parking area. It leads to a spruce and Douglas fir wood; cross a log bridge over Baring Creek and you arrive at the base of gushing Baring Falls. ⊠ *11 mi east of Logan Pass on Going-to-the-Sun Rd.*

★ **Hidden Lake Nature Trail.** This uphill, 1½-mi trail runs from Logan Pass southwest to Hidden Lake Overlook, from which you get a beautiful

16

view of the lake and McDonald Valley. In spring, ribbons of water pour off the rocks surrounding the lake. ⊠ *Logan Pass Visitor Center.*

★ ♿ **Trail of the Cedars.** This wheelchair-accessible, ½-mi boardwalk loop through an ancient cedar and hemlock forest is a favorite of families with small children and people with disabilities. Interpretive signs describe the habitat and natural history of the rain forest. ⊠ *Avalanche Creek Campground, 15 mi north of Apgar on Going-to-the-Sun Rd.*

> **GLACIERS AWAY?**
>
> Call it Global Warming or call it a natural progression, but the glaciers at Glacier National Park are feeling the heat. By 2050, or earlier, it is estimated that all of the glaciers in the park will have melted. Currently there are 50 glaciers in the park (at one time there were between 150 and 200).

MODERATE
Fodor'sChoice
★

**Highline Trail.** From the Logan Pass parking lot, hike north along the Garden Wall and just below the craggy Continental Divide. Wildflowers dominate the 7⁷⁄₁₀ mi to Granite Park Chalet, a National Historic Landmark, where hikers with reservations can overnight. Return to Logan Pass along the same trail or hike down 4½ mi (a 2,500-foot descent) on the Loop Trail. ⊠ *Logan Pass Visitor Center.*

**Iceberg Lake Trail.** This moderately strenuous 9-mi round-trip hike passes the gushing Ptarmigan Falls, then climbs to its namesake, where icebergs bob in the chilly mountain loch. Mountain goats hang out on sheer cliffs above, bighorn sheep graze in the high mountain meadows, and grizzly bears dig for glacier lily bulbs, grubs, and other delicacies. Rangers lead hikes here almost daily in summer, leaving at 8:30 AM. ⊠ *Swiftcurrent Inn parking lot off Many Glacier Rd.*

DIFFICULT
★

**Grinnell Glacier Trail.** The strenuous 5½-mi hike to Grinnell Glacier, the park's largest and most accessible glacier, is marked by several spectacular viewpoints. You start at Swiftcurrent Lake's picnic area, climb a moraine to Lake Josephine, then climb to the Grinnell Glacier overlook. Halfway up, turn around to see the prairie land to the northeast. You can short-cut the trail by 2 mi each way by taking two scenic boat rides across Swiftcurrent and Josephine lakes. From July to mid-September, a ranger-led hike departs from the Many Glacier Hotel boat dock most mornings at 8:30. ⊠ *Josephine boat dock.*

**Two Medicine Valley Trails.** One of the least-developed parts of Glacier, the lovely southeast corner of the park is a good place for a quiet day hike, although you should look out for signs of bears. The trailhead to Upper Two Medicine Lake and Cobalt Lake begins west of the boat dock and camp supply store, where you can make arrangements for a boat pick-up or drop-off across the lake. ⊠ *Two Medicine Campground, 9 mi west of Rte. 49.*

## Horseback Riding

Horses are permitted on many trails within the parks; check for seasonal exceptions. Horseback riding is prohibited on paved roads. You can pick up a brochure about suggested routes and outfitters from any visitor

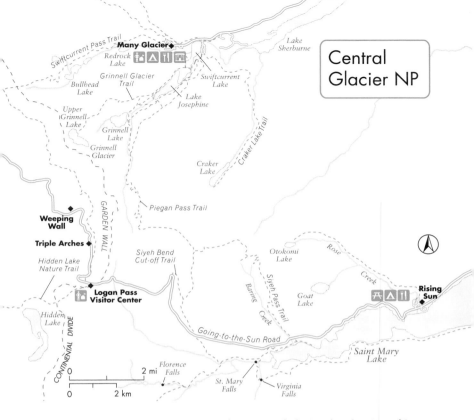

Central
Glacier NP

**Many Glacier**

*Swiftcurrent Pass Trail*

*Lake Sherburne*

*Redrock Lake*

*Grinnell Glacier Trail*

*Bullhead Lake*

*Swiftcurrent Lake*

*Upper Grinnell Lake*

*Lake Josephine*

*Grinnell Lake*

*Grinnell Glacier*

*Craker Lake*

*Craker Lake Trail*

**Weeping Wall**

*Piegan Pass Trail*

*GARDEN WALL*

**Triple Arches**

*Hidden Lake Nature Trail*

*Siyeh Bend Cut-off Trail*

*Otokomi Lake*

*Rose Creek*

**Rising Sun**

**Logan Pass Visitor Center**

*Baring Creek*

*Goat Lake*

*Siyeh Pass Trail*

*Hidden Lake*

*CONTINENTAL DIVIDE*

*Going-to-the-Sun Road*

*Saint Mary Lake*

*Florence Falls*

0 ___ 2 mi

0 ___ 2 km

*St. Mary Falls*

*Virginia Falls*

center or entrance station. The Sperry Chalet Trail to the view of Sperry Glacier above Lake McDonald is a tough 7-mi climb.

OUTFITTERS &
EXPEDITIONS

**Glacier Gateway Outfitters** offers one-hour or full-day rides in the Two Medicine area with a Blackfoot cowboy as your guide. Rides begin at Glacier Park Lodge and climb through aspen groves to high-country views of Dancing Lady and Bison mountains. You can enjoy a rodeo every Tuesday evening. All riders must be older than 7. Reservations are essential. ⬛ *Box 411, East Glacier 59434* ☎ *406/226–4408, 406/338–5560 in winter* ⬛ *$25–$175* ☽ *May–Sept.*

**Mule Shoe Outfitters** begins its rides at Apgar, Lake McDonald, and Many Glacier. Trips for beginning to advanced riders cover both flat and mountainous territory. Riders must be older than 7 and weigh less than 225 pounds. Reservations are essential. ⬛ *Box 322, West Glacier 59936* ☎ *406/888–5121, 406/732–4203, 928/684–2328 in winter* ⬛ *www.mule-shoe.com* ⬛ *$30 for an hour, $130 for a full day* ☽ *Early June to Sept. 15* ⬛ *No credit cards.*

## Skiing & Snowshoeing

Cross-country skiing and snowshoeing are increasingly popular in the park. Glacier distributes a free pamphlet entitled *Ski Trails of Glacier*

## MULTISPORT OUTFITTERS

**Glacier Raft Company and Outdoor Center.** In addition to running white-water, scenic, and fishing trips, this outfitter will set you up with camping, backpacking, and fishing gear. There's a full-service fly-fishing shop and outdoor store. You can stay in one of nine cabins that sleep from 6 to 14 people. ⊠ *11957 U.S. 2 E, West Glacier* ☎ *406/888–5454 or 800/235–6781* ⊕ *www.glacierraftco.com* ✉ *$40–$80* ⊙ *Year-round; rafting mid-May–Sept.*

**Wild River Adventures.** These guys will paddle you over the Middle Fork of the Flathead, and peddle you tall tales all the while. They also provide trail rides, and scenic fishing trips on rivers around Glacier Park. ⊠ *11900 U.S. 2 E, 1 mi west of West Glacier* ☎ *406/387–9453 or 800/700–7056* ⊕ *www. RiverWild.com* ✉ *$42–$73* ⊙ *Mid-May–Sept.*

*National Park,* with 16 noted trails. You can start at Lake McDonald Lodge and ski cross-country up Going-to-the-Sun Road. The 2½-mi Apgar Natural Trail is popular with snowshoers. No restaurants or stores are open in winter in Glacier.

OUTFITTERS & EXPEDITIONS **Glacier Park Ski Tours** leads one-day or multiday guided ski or snowshoe trips on the park's scenic winter trails. On overnight trips, you stay in snow huts or tents. ☎ *Box 4833, Whitefish 59937* ☎ *406/862–2790 or 800/646–6043 Ext. 3724* ✉ *$30–$150* ⊙ *Mid-Nov.–May.*

# Educational Offerings

### Classes & Seminars

☾ **Glacier Institute.** Based near West Glacier at the Field Camp and on the remote western boundary at the Big Creek Outdoor Education Center, this learning institute offers more than 75 field courses for kids and adults. Year-round, experts in wildlife biology, native plants, and river ecology lead treks into Glacier's backcountry on daylong and multiday programs. ☎ *Box 7457, Kalispell 59901* ☎ *406/755–1211 May–Sept.* ⊕ *www. glacierinstitute.org.*

### Kids' Camps

☾ **Adventure Camps.** Youngsters ages 6–8 can partake of one-day naturalist courses, while kids 11-13 can take weeklong hiking and rafting trips. Some camps involve backcountry camping while others are based out of the Big Creek or Glacier Park field camps. Subjects range from ecology and birding to wildflowers, predators and prey, and backcountry medicine. ⊠ *137 Main St., Box 7457, Kalispell 59904* ☎ *406/755–1211* ⊕ *www.glacierinstitute.org* ✉ *$20–$300.*

### Ranger Programs

These programs are free to visitors. Most run daily, July through Labor Day. For information on ranger programs, call 406/888–7800.

☾ **Children's Programs.** Kids learn about bears, wolves, geology, and more via hands-on activities, such as role-playing skits and short hikes. Check the Apgar Education Cabin for schedules and locations.

**Evening Campfire Programs.** Rangers lead discussions on the park's wildlife, geology, and history. The programs occur at park campgrounds, beginning at 8 or 9 PM. Topics and dates are posted at campgrounds, lodges, and the St. Mary Visitor Center.

☾ **Junior Ranger Program.** Year-round, children ages 6–12 can become a Junior Ranger by completing activities in the *Junior Ranger* newspaper.

**Naturalist activities.** Evening slide programs, guided hikes, and boat tours are among the ranger-led activities held at various sites in the park. A complete schedule of programs is listed in *Glacier Explorer.*

**Tours**

**International Peace Park Hike.** The 7⁸⁄₁₀-mi trek along Upper Waterton Lake is jointly led by Canadian and American park interpreters. Enjoy lunch at the International Border, before continuing on to Goat Haunt in Glacier National Park, Montana. Return to Waterton via boat ($22). ⊠ *Waterton Townsite* ☎ *403/859–5133* ☾ *July–Aug., Sat. 10 AM.*

★ **Sun Tours.** Tour the park and learn the Blackfeet perspective with these native guides who concentrate on how Glacier's features are relevant to the Blackfeet Nation, past and present. In summer, tours depart daily from East Glacier (8 AM) and St. Mary (9:15 AM) in air-conditioned coaches. ⊠ *29 Glacier Ave., East Glacier* ☎ *406/226–9220 or 800/786–9220* ⊕ *www.glacierinfo.com* 🎫 *$35–$45* ☾ *June–Sept., daily.*

# WATERTON LAKES

## Scenic Drives

**Akamina Parkway.** Take this winding 10-mi (16-km) road up to Cameron Lake. A relatively flat, paved, 1-mi (1⁶⁄₁₀-km) trail hugs the lake's western shore and makes a nice walk. Bring your binoculars, because it's common to see grizzly bears on the lower slopes of the mountains at the far end of the lake.

**Red Rock Parkway.** The 9-mi (15-km) route takes you from the prairie up the Blakiston Valley to Red Rock Canyon, where water has cut through the earth, exposing red sedimentary rock.

## What to See

### Historic Sites

**First Oil Well in Western Canada.** Alberta is known worldwide for its oil and gas production and the first oil well in western Canada was established in 1902 in what is now the park. Stop at this National Historic Site to explore the wellheads, drilling equipment, and remains of the Oil City boomtown. ⊠ *Along the Akamina Pkwy.*

★ **Prince of Wales Hotel.** Named for the prince who later became King Edward VIII, this lovely hotel was constructed between 1926 and 1927 and

**CLOSE UP**

# Jamming in the Park

**HARKENING BACK TO THE EARLY DAYS** of automobile touring in the parks, each summer a fleet of red jammers weaves through Glacier and Waterton Lakes national parks. Drivers began jamming gears on the vintage coaches in 1936, but today, only guides licensed with Glacier Park Inc. (☎ 406/892–2525, ⊕ www.glacierparkinc.com) operate them. Park visitors ride them for special tours, as well as to traverse the park and go up the incredible Going-to-the-Sun Road.

One of the most popular drivers is Joe Kendall, known as "Jammer Joe" to passengers. His lively narration and colorful descriptions of Glacier have endeared him to many park visitors. In fact, he has so won the hearts of fans over his 10 years of service that the park has named a pizza parlor (near Lake McDonald Lodge) after him.

Kendall's wife of 54 years, Geri, also works for Glacier Park Inc., as tour director for the dozen or so six-day Great Lodges of Glacier Tours each summer.

During the off-season, the Kendalls live in Illinois.

–Debbie Harmsen

was designated a National Historic Site in 1995. The lobby window affords a pretty view, and afternoon tea is a treat here. ⊠ *Waterton Lakes National Park, off Hwy. 5* ☎ *406/756–2444, 403/859–2231 mid-May–late Sept.* ⊕ *www.glacierparkinc.com* ⊙ *Closed late Sept.–mid-May.*

## Scenic Stops

★ **Cameron Lake.** The jewel of Waterton, Cameron Lake sits in a land of glacially carved cirques (steep-walled basins). In summer, hundreds of varieties of alpine wildflowers fill the area, including 22 kinds of wild orchids. Canoes and pedal boats can be rented here. ⊠ *Akamina Pkwy., 13 km (8 mi) southwest of Waterton Park Townsite.*

**Goat Haunt.** Reached only by foot trail or tour boat from Waterton Townsite, this spot on the U.S. end of Waterton Lake is the stomping ground for mountain goats, moose, grizzlies, and black bears. The ranger posted at this remote station gives thrice-daily 10-minute overviews of Waterton Valley history. ⊠ *South end of Waterton Lake* ☎ *406/888–7800 or 403/859–2362* ⛴ *Tour boat $22* ⊙ *Mid-May–Oct.*

★ **Waterton Townsite.** This is a decidedly low-key community in roughly the geographical center of the park. In summer it swells with tourists, and restaurants and shops open to serve them. In winter only a few motels are open, and services are limited.

### Visitor Center

**Waterton Information Centre.** Stop here on the eastern edge of Waterton Townsite to pick up brochures, maps and books. Park interpreters are on hand to answer questions and give directions. ✉ *Waterton Rd.* ☎ *403/859–5133 or 403/859–2224* ⊙ *Mid-May–mid-June, daily 8–6; mid-June–early Sept., daily 8–8; early Sept.–Oct. 8, daily 9–6.*

## Sports & the Outdoors

The park contains numerous short hikes for day-trippers and some longer treks for backpackers. Upper and Middle Waterton and Cameron lakes provide peaceful havens for boaters. A tour boat cruises across Upper Waterton Lake, crossing the U.S.–Canada border, and the winds that rake across that lake create an exciting ride for windsurfers—bring a wet suit, though; the water remains numbingly cold throughout summer.

### Bicycling

Bikes are allowed on some trails, such as the 2-mi (3 km) Townsite Loop Trail. A ride on mildly sloping Red Rock Canyon Road isn't too difficult. Cameron Lake Road is an intermediate route.

OUTFITTER **Pat's Waterton.** Choose from surrey bikes, mountain bikes, or motorized scooters. Pat's also rents tennis rackets, strollers, and binoculars. ✉ *Corner of Mt. View Rd., Waterton Townsite* ☎ *403/859–2266.*

### Boating

Nonmotorized boats can be rented at Cameron Lake in summer; private craft can be used on Upper and Middle Waterton lakes.

OUTFITTERS & **Waterton Inter-Nation Shoreline Cruise Co.** This company's two-hour EXPEDITIONS round-trip boat tour along Upper Waterton Lake from Waterton Townsite to Goat Haunt Ranger Station is one of the most popular activities in Waterton. (*Note that because Goat Haunt is in the United States, you must clear customs.*) The narrated tour passes scenic bays, sheer cliffs, and snow-clad peaks. ✉ *Waterton Townsite Marina* ☎ *403/859–2362* ⊡ *C\$27 (\$24 U.S.)* ⊙ *May–early Oct., cruises daily 2–5.*

### Hiking

There are 191 mi (225 km) of trails in Waterton Lakes that range in difficulty from short strolls to strenuous treks. Some trails connect with the trail systems at Glacier and British Columbia's Akamina-Kishenina Provincial Park. The wildflowers in June are particularly stunning along most trails.

EASY **Bear's Hump.** This 1 ⁷⁄₁₀-mi (2 ⁷⁄₁₀-km) trail climbs up the mountainside ★ ☺ to an overlook with a great view of Upper Waterton Lake and the town site. ✉ *Directly behind the Waterton Information Centre Bldg.*

☺ **Cameron Lake Shore Trail.** This relatively flat paved 1-mi (1½ km) trail is a peaceful place for a walk. Look for grizzlies on the lower slopes of the mountains at the far end of the lake. ✉ *The trailhead is located at the lakeshore in front of the parking lot, 13 km (8 mi) southwest of Waterton Townsite.*

16

## WATERTON IN ONE DAY

Begin your day with a stop at **Parks Canada's Waterton Information Centre** to pick up free maps and information about interpretive programs and schedules. Behind the reception center is the **Bear's Hump trail,** a relatively easy ⁹/₁₀-mi (1⁴/₁₀-km) path to a beautiful overlook. After the hike, drive up the hill to the historic **Prince of Wales Hotel** to enjoy the view.

Next, visit **Waterton Townsite** for an early lunch. Afterward, walk the easy 2-mi (3 km) **Townsite Loop,** stopping to view **Cameron Falls** and explore the trail behind the falls. End the day with a scenic, two-hour **Waterton International Shoreline Cruise** across the border to **Goat Haunt Ranger Station** and back.

**Crandell Lake Trail.** This easy 1 ½ mi (2½-km) trail follows an old wagon road to Oil City. ✉ *About halfway up the Akamina Pkwy.*

MODERATE **Bertha Lake Trail.** This 8-mi (13-km) trail leads from the Waterton Townsite through a Douglas fir forest to a beautiful overlook of Upper Waterton Lake, then on to Lower Bertha Falls. If you continue on, a steeper climb will take you past Upper Bertha Falls to Bertha Lake. The wildflowers are particularly stunning along this trail in June. ✉ *The trailhead is located on the south end of the town site. Head towards the lake and you will find a parking lot on the west side of the Rd.*

DIFFICULT **Crypt Lake Trail.** This awe-inspiring, 5½-mi (9-km) trail is proclaimed by
Fodor'sChoice some to be one of the most stunning hikes in the Canadian Rockies. Con-
★ quering the trail involves a boat taxi across Waterton Lake, a climb of 2,300 feet, a crawl through a tunnel that measures almost 100 feet, and a climb along a sheer rock face. The reward is a 600-foot tall cascading waterfall and the turquoise waters of Crypt Lake. ✉ *Crypt Landing is accessed by ferry from Waterton Townsite.*

### Horseback Riding

Rolling hills, grasslands, and rugged mountains make riding in Waterton Lakes a real pleasure. Scenery, wildlife, and wildflowers are easily viewed from the saddle and many of the park trails allow horses.

OUTFITTERS & **Alpine Stables.** You can arrange hourly trail rides and all-day guided ex-
EXPEDITIONS cursions within the park as well as multiday pack trips through the foothills of the Rockies. ✉ *Box 53, Waterton Lakes National Park T0K 2M0* ☎ *403/859–2463, 403/653–2449 off-season* ⊕ *www.alpinestables.com* ☼ *May–Sept.*

### Swimming

☼ **Waterton Lake.** It's chilly year-round, but it's still a great place to cool off after a long hot day of hiking. Most visitors wade, but a few join the "polar bear club" and get completely submersed. ✉ *Waterton Townsite.*

## Educational Offerings

Evening interpretive programs are offered from late June until Labor Day, at the Falls Theatre, near Cameron Falls and the town site campground. These one-hour sessions begin at 8 PM. A guided International Peace Park hike is held every Wednesday and Saturday in July and August. The 9-mi (14-km) hike begins at the Bertha trailhead, and is led by Canadian and American park interpreters. You take lunch at the International Border, before continuing on to Goat Haunt in Glacier National Park, Montana, and returning to Waterton via boat. A fee is charged for the return boat trip. You must pre-register for this hike at a Waterton Information Centre.

> ### HIKER'S SHUTTLE
>
> **Tamarack Outdoor Outfitters.** This is the headquarters for hiker shuttle services that run throughout Waterton to most of the major trailheads; they can also arrange certified hiking guides for groups. You can reserve shuttles two months in advance. ⊠ *Tamarack Village Sq., Waterton Lakes National Park* ☎ *403/859-2378* ⊕ *www. watertonvisitorservices.com* ⊘ *May–Sept.*

**16**

# WHAT'S NEARBY

## Nearby Towns & Attractions

### Nearby Towns

Early tourists to Glacier National Park first stopped in **East Glacier,** where the Great Northern Railway had established a station. Although most people coming from the east now enter by car through St. Mary, East Glacier, population about 400, attracts visitors with its quiet, secluded surroundings and lovely Glacier Park Lodge. **Browning,** 35 mi to the east of Glacier, is the center of the Blackfeet Nation, whose name is thought to have been derived from the color of their painted or dyed black moccasins; there are about 13,000 enrolled tribal members. The green waters of the Flathead River's Middle Fork and several top-notch outfitters make **West Glacier** an ideal base for river sports. The small town of **Columbia Falls,** only 15 mi west of Glacier, has restaurants, services and accommodations. The best base for the park is **Whitefish,** 25 mi west of Glacier and with a population of 6,000. The town has a well-developed nightlife scene, and good restaurants, galleries, and shops. The village of **Essex** borders the southern tip of the park and is the site of the main rail and bus terminals for visitors coming to the park. About 45 minutes from Glacier's west entrance on Flathead Lake's pristine northeast shore, **Bigfork** twinkles with decorative lights that adorn its shops, galleries, and restaurants. Just 28 mi east of Waterton **Cardston** is home to the Alberta Temple, built by the Mormon pioneers who established the town.

### Nearby Attractions

**Big Sky Waterpark.** During summer, the most popular place between the hardworking lumber town of Columbia Falls and Glacier National Park is the Big Sky Waterpark. Besides the 10 waterslides and golf course, there

## FESTIVALS & EVENTS

**JAN. Ski Fest.** This cross-country ski celebration introduces newcomers to kick-and-glide skiing. Equipment demonstrations and family activities are scheduled at the Izaak Walton Inn in Essex. ☎ *406/888–5700* ⊕ *www.izaakwaltoninn.com.*

**FEB. Whitefish Winter Carnival.** For more than 40 years, Whitefish has been the scene of outstanding winter fun, including a grand parade, and a torchlight parade on skis. ☎ *406/862–3501 or 877/862–3548.*

**JUNE Waterton Wildflower Festival.** Wildflower walks, horseback rides, hikes, watercolor workshops, photography classes, and family events help visitors and locals celebrate the annual blooming of Waterton's wildflowers. ☎ *403/859–2009 or 800/215–2395* ⊕ *www.watertonwildflowers.com.*

**JULY Canada Day.** In honor of Canada's birthday, all guests get into the national parks free of charge. Waterton also has special activities for families such as treasure hunts and street-theater performances. ☎ *403/859–5133.*

are arcade games, bumper cars, a carousel, barbecue grills, a picnic area, and food service. ⊠ *7211 U.S. 2 E, junction of U.S. 2 and Hwy. 206, Columbia Falls* ☎ *406/892–5025 or 406/892–2139* ⊕ *www.bigskywp. com* 🎫 *$20* ☉ *Memorial Day–Labor Day, daily 10–8.*

★ **Museum of the Plains Indian.** A stunning collection of artifacts from the Blackfeet, includes clothing, saddlebags, and artwork. ⊠ *U.S. 2 at U.S. 89 Browning* ☎ *406/338–2230* 🎫 *$4* ☉ *June–Sept., daily 9–4:45; Oct.–May, weekdays 10–4:30.*

## Area Activities

### Sports & the Outdoors

BICYCLING  Hill-climbing, single-track, dirt-road, or easy-cruising bike paths—northwest Montana is flush with cycling opportunities. Of the 2,000 mi of county roads, only 400 mi (640 km) are paved, leaving dirt and gravel roads and innumerable trails open for discovery. **Glacier Cyclery** (⊠ 326 E. 2nd St., Whitefish ☎ 406/862–6446 ⊕ www.glaciercyclery.com) rents bikes suitable to the terrain, and on Monday nights, group rides begin at the shop courtyard.

DOGSLEDDING  The dogs are raring to run late November to mid-April at **Dog Sled Adven-**
ᐆ  **tures** (⊠ U.S. 93, 20 mi [32 km] north of Whitefish, 2 mi [3 km] north of Olney ☎406/881–2275 ⊕www.dogsledadventuresmt.com). Your friendly musher will gear the ride to the passengers, from kids to senior citizens; bundled up in a sled, you'll be whisked through Stillwater State Forest on a 1½-hour ride over a 12-mi (19 km) trail. Reservations are necessary.

SKIING &  The **Big Mountain Ski and Summer Resort** (🏠 Box 1400, Whitefish 59937
SNOWBOARDING  ☎406/862–1900 or 800/858–4152 ⊕www.skiwhitefish.com ☉Thanks-
ᐆ  giving–early Apr. and mid-June–mid-Sept., daily 9–4:30) has been one

of Montana's top ski areas since the 1930s and remains comfortably small. Eight miles from Whitefish, it's popular among train travelers from the Pacific Northwest and the upper Midwest. A daily lift ticket is $49.

SNOWMOBILING There are more than 200 groomed snowmobile trails in the Flathead region. Unless you're an experienced snowmobiler and expert at avalanche forecasting, you should take a guided trip. **Extreme Motorsports** (✉ 803 Spokane Ave., Whitefish ☎ 406/862–8594 ⊕ www.wfmextrememotorsports.com) rents machines and leads tours.

### Arts & Entertainment

☺ **The Great Canadian Barn Dance.** When the West was young, weekend nights were reserved for community barn dances. It was an opportunity to get together with friends, enjoy live music, and kick up your heels. You can relive those times at a country barn dance and dinner almost every weekend during the summer months on a Hillspring farm, about 30 minutes east of Waterton Lakes National Park. ✇ *Box 163, Hillspring T0K 1E0* ☎ *403/626–3407 or 866/626–3407 ⊕ www.greatcanadianbarndance. com* ✉ *$23 dinner and dance ⊗ June–Sept., weekends.*

# WHERE TO STAY & EAT

16

### About the Restaurants

Steak houses featuring certified Angus beef are typical of the region; in recent years, resort communities have diversified their menus to include bison meat, fresh fish, and savory vegetarian options. Small cafés offer hearty, inexpensive meals, and you can pick up on local history through conversation with the local denizens. Trout, venison, elk, moose, and bison appear on the menus inside the park. Attire everywhere is decidedly casual.

### About the Hotels

Lodgings in the parks tend to be fairly rustic and simple, though there are a few grand lodges and some modern accommodations. There are a few modern hotels that offer facilities such as swimming pools, hot tubs, boat rentals, guided excursions, or fine dining. Although there is a limited supply of rooms within both parks, the prices are relatively reasonable. It's best to reserve well in advance, especially for July and August.

### About the Campgrounds

There are ten major campgrounds in Glacier National Park and excellent backcountry sites for backpackers. Reservations for Fish Creek and St. Mary Campgrounds are available through the National Park Reservation Service (☎ 800/365–2267 or ⊕ http://reservations.nps.gov). Reservations may be made up to 5 months in advance.

Parks Canada operates four campgrounds in Waterton Lakes that range from fully serviced to unserviced sites. There are also some backcountry campsites. Visitors can prebook campsites for a fee of C$11; to do so, visit ⊕ www.pc.gc.ca or call ☎ 905/426–4648 or 877/737–3783.

Outside the park campgrounds vary from no-services, remote state or federal campsites to upscale commercial operations. During July and August it's best to reserve a camp spot. Ask locally about bears and whether or not food must be stored inside a hard-side vehicle (not a tent).

## Where to Eat

### Inside the Parks

**$$-$$$** ✗ **Prince of Wales Dining Room.** Enjoy upmarket cuisine before a dazzling view of Waterton Lake in the dining room of this century-old chalet high on a hill. Choose from a fine selection of wines to accompany your meal. Every afternoon the lodge's main culinary event unfolds: a British high tea served in Valerie's Tea Room—tea includes finger sandwiches, scones and other pastries, and chocolate-dipped fruits. ⊠ *Waterton Townsite* ☏ *403/859–2231. $15–$29* ⊟ *D, MC, V* ☻ *Closed Oct.–May.*

**$$-$$$** ✗ **Ptarmigan Dining Room.** Sophisticated cuisine is served in the dining room of early-20th-century chalet-like Many Glacier Hotel. As the sun sets over Swiftcurrent Lake just outside the massive windows, Italian-inflected food is served amid Swiss-style decor. Each night there's a chef's special such as pork prime rib with a huckleberry demi-glace. For a true Montana creation, have a huckleberry daiquiri. ⊠ *Many Glacier Rd.* ☏ *406/732–4411 or 406/892–2525. $15–$30* ⊟ *AE, D, MC, V* ☻ *Closed late Sept.–early June.*

**¢-$$$** ✗ **Lake McDonald Lodge Restaurants.** In the Russell's Fireside Dining Room, take in a great view while choosing between standards such as pasta, steak, and salmon. Don't miss the apple bread pudding with caramel-cinnamon sauce for dessert. Across the parking lot is a cheaper alternative, **Jammer Joe's Grill & Pizzeria,** which serves burgers and pasta for lunch and dinner. ⊠ *10 mi north of Apgar on Going-to-the-Sun Rd.* ☏ *406/888–5431 or 406/892–2525. $7–$29* ⊟ *AE, D, MC, V* ☻ *Closed early Oct.–early June.*

**☺ $-$$** ✗ **Curly Bear Café & Pizza Co.** Buffalo burgers, rotisserie chicken, and pizza fill the menu. An ice-cream parlor is next door. ⊠ *St. Mary Lodge, U.S. 89 and Going-to-the-Sun Rd., St. Mary* ☏ *406/732–4431* ⊘ *Reservations not accepted. $9–$13* ⊟ *AE, D, MC, V* ☻ *Closed early Oct.–mid-May.*

PICNIC AREAS  There are picnic spots at most campgrounds and visitor centers. Each has tables, grills, and drinking water in summer.

★  **Sun Point.** On the north side of St. Mary Lake, this is one of the most beautiful places in the park for a picnic. ⊠ *Sun Point trailhead.*

### Outside the Parks

**$$-$$$$** ✗ **Glacier Park Lodge Dining Room.** Here you'll enjoy fine dining in a natural mega log structure with all the amenities of a first-class dining room that was originally a steak place. Though the restaurant now serves pasta, seafood and chicken, ribs and steaks are still the house specialties. ⊠ *Rte. 49, next to railroad station, East Glacier* ☏ *406/226–5600* ⊘ *Reservations not accepted. $16–$40* ⊟ *D, MC, V* ☻ *Closed Oct.–May.*

**¢-$$** ✗ **Serrano's.** After a day on the dusty trail, fresh Mexican food is quite a treat whether dining inside or on back patio. Make reservations during July, August, and early September. ⊠ *29 Dawson Ave., East Glacier* ☏ *406/226–9392. $7–$17* ⊟ *AE, D, DC, MC, V* ☻ *Closed Oct.–Apr.*

## Where to Stay

### Inside the Parks

★ **$$$$** ⬚ **Prince of Wales Hotel.** Perched between two lakes, with a high mountain backdrop, this hotel has the best view in town. A high steeple crowns the building, which is fantastically ornamented with eaves, balconies, and turrets. Expect creaks and rattles at night—the old hotel, built in the 1920s, is exposed to rough winds. Rates decrease by about 25% off-season. ✉ *Off Hwy. 5,* ⬚ *Glacier Park Inc., Box 33, Waterton Park T0K 2M0* ☎ *406/ 756–2444, 403/859–2231 mid-May–late Sept.* ⬚ *406/257–0384* ⊕ *www. glacierparkinc.com* ⬚ *89 rooms* ⬚ *Restaurant, no a/c, no TV. C$265–C$799* ⬚ *AE, MC, V* ☉ *Closed late Sept.–mid-May.*

**$$$-$$$$** ⬚ **Sperry Chalet.** This elegant backcountry lodge, built in 1913 by the Great Northern Railway, is accessible only by a steep, 6⁷⁄₁₀-mi (10½ km) trail with a 3,300-foot vertical rise. Either hike in or arrive on horseback. Guest rooms have no electricity, heat, or running water, but who cares when the view includes Glacier's Gunsite peak, Mt. Edwards, Lake McDonald, and mountain goats in wildflowers. Informal meals, such as turkey with the trimmings, are simple yet filling. Note that the reservations office is closed September and October. ⬚ *Box 188, Going-to-the-Sun Rd., West Glacier 59936* ☎ *406/387–5654 or 888/345–2649* ⊕ *www.sperrychalet.com. $160 per person, $150 each subsequent night ($110 for each additional adult in the same room, $100 for each subsequent night)* ⬚ *17 rooms* ⬚ *Restaurant, no a/c, no phone, no TV, no-smoking rooms* ⬚ *AE, MC, V* ☉ *Closed mid-Sept.–early July* ⬚ *FAP.*

★ **$$-$$$$** ⬚ **Glacier Park Lodge.** On the east side of the park, across from the Amtrak station, you'll find this beautiful hotel built in 1913. The full-service lodge is supported by 500- to 800-year-old fir and 3-foot-thick cedar logs. Rooms are sparsely decorated, but there are historic posters on the walls in the halls. Cottages and a house are also available on the grounds next to the golf course. If you golf on the spectacular course, watch out for moose. Entertainers delight guests with storytelling and singing in the great hall. ✉ *Off U.S. 2, East Glacier* ⬚ *Box 2025, Columbia Falls 59912* ☎ *406/892–2525 or 406/226–9311* ⬚ *406/226–9152* ⊕ *www. glacierparkinc.com* ⬚ *154 rooms* ⬚ *Restaurant, golf course, pool, bar, no a/c, no TV, no-smoking rooms. $140–$449* ⬚ *AE, D, MC, V.*

**$$-$$$$** ⬚ **Many Glacier Hotel.** The most isolated of the grand hotels—it's on Swiftcurrent Lake on the northeast side of the park—this is also one of the most scenic, especially if you nab one of the balcony rooms. There's a large fireplace in the lobby where guests gather on chilly mornings. Rooms are small and sparsely decorated. ✉ *Many Glacier Rd., 12 mi west of Babb* ⬚ *Box 2025, Columbia Falls 59912* ☎ *406/892–2525 or 406/732–4411* ⬚ *406/732–5522* ⊕ *www.glacierparkinc.com* ⬚ *211 rooms* ⬚ *Restaurant, bar, no a/c, no TV, no-smoking rooms. $132–$263* ⬚ *AE, D, MC, V.*

★ **$$-$$$** ⬚ **Lake McDonald Complex.** One of the great historic lodges of the West anchors this complex on the shore of lovely Lake McDonald. Take a room in the lodge itself, where public spaces are filled with massive timbers, stone fireplaces, and animal trophies. Cabins sleep up to four and don't have kitchens; there are also motel-style rooms separate from the lodge. ✉ *Going-to-the-Sun Rd.* ✉ *Box 2025, Columbia Falls 59912* ☎ *406/892–2525 or 406/888–5431* ⊕ *www.glacierparkinc.com* ⇦ *30 rooms, 13 cabins* ⚒ *Restaurant, bar, no-smoking rooms, no a/c, no TV.* *$110–$155* ▭ *AE, D, MC, V.*

**$$–$$$** ⊡ **Village Inn.** On Lake McDonald, this motel could use some updating, but it is very popular and offers a great view. All of the plain but serviceable rooms, some with kitchenettes, face the lake. A restaurant, bar, and coffee shop are nearby. ✉ *Apgar Village* ✉ *Box 2025, Columbia Falls 59912* ☎☎ *406/756–2444* ✉ *406/892–1375* ⊕ *www. villageinnatapgar.com* ⇦ *36 rooms* ⚒ *No a/c. $115–$184* ▭ *AE, D, MC, V.*

**$–$$** ⊡ **Granite Park Chalet.** Early tourists used to ride horses through the park 7 to 9 mi each day and stay at a different chalet each night. The Granite Park is one of two chalets still standing (the other one is the Sperry Chalet). You can reach it only by hiking trails. You must bring sleeping bags and your own food, and you need a reservation. You can park at Logan Pass Visitor Center and hike 7⁷⁄₁₀ mi or at the Loop trailhead and hike uphill 4 mi. ✉ *7⁷⁄₁₀ mi south of Logan Pass* ☎ *888/345–2649* ⇦ *12 rooms. $70 per person* ▭ *AE, D, MC, V* ☺ *Closed mid-Sept.–early July.*

CAMPGROUNDS & RV PARKS ⚠ **Apgar Campground.** This popular and large campground on the southern shore of Lake McDonald has many activities and services. From here you can hike; boat, fish, or swim; and sign up for trail rides. About 25 sites are suitable for RVs. ✉ *Apgar Rd.* ☎ *406/888–7800* ⇦ *194 sites* ⚒ *Flush toilets, pit toilets, dump station, drinking water, bear boxes, fire grates, picnic tables, food service, public telephone, general store, ranger station, swimming (lake). $15* ▭ *AE, D, MC, V* ☺ *Closed mid-Oct.–early May.*

⚠ **Avalanche Creek Campground.** This peaceful campground is shaded by huge red cedars and bordered by Avalanche Creek. Trail of the Cedars begins here, and it's along Going-to-the-Sun Road. Some campsites and the comfort stations are wheelchair accessible. There are 50 sites for RVs up to 26 feet. ✉ *Going-to-the-Sun Rd.* ☎ *406/888–7800* ⇦ *87 sites* ⚒ *Flush toilets, drinking water, fire grates, picnic tables, public telephone. $15* ▭ *AE, D, MC, V* ☺ *Closed early Sept.–early June.*

⚠ **Bowman Lake Campground.** In the remote northwestern corner of Glacier, this quiet camping spot is a fishermen's favorite for lake and stream fishing. Mosquitoes can be bothersome here, as can the potholes and ruts in the one-lane drive in from Polebridge. ✉ *Bowman Lake Rd.* ☎ *406/ 888–7800* ⇦ *48 sites* ⚒ *Pit toilets, drinking water, bear boxes, fire grates, picnic tables, ranger station, swimming (lake). $12* ▭ *AE, D, MC, V* ☺ *Closed mid-Sept.–mid-May.*

⚠ **Fish Creek Campground.** The quietest sites on Lake McDonald are surrounded by thick evergreen forest; 80 sites are suitable for RVs up to 26 feet. ✉ *2 mi north of Apgar Visitor Center on Glacier Rte. 7* ☎ *406/ 888–7800* ⇦ *180 sites* ⚒ *Flush toilets, dump station, drinking water. $20* ▭ *MC, V* ☺ *Closed late Oct.–May.*

⚠ **Kintla Lake Campground.** Beautiful and remote, this is a trout fisherman's favorite. Trails lead into the backcountry. The dirt access road is rough, so RVs are not recommended. ✉ *14 mi north of Polebridge Ranger Station on Inside North Fork Rd.* ⇦ *13 sites* ⚒ *Pit toilets, dump sta-*

*tion, bear boxes, fire grates, picnic tables* ⛺ *$12* ⚮ *Reservations not accepted* ▭ *No credit cards* ⊘ *Closed mid-Sept.–mid-May.*

★ ⛺ **Many Glacier Campground.** One of the most beautiful spots in the park is also a favorite for bears. Several hiking trails take off from here, and often ranger-led hikes climb to Grinnell Glacier. Always check posted notices for areas closed because of bears. ✉ *Many Glacier Rd.* ☎ *406/888–7800* ⛺ *110 sites* ⚮ *Flush toilets, pit toilets, drinking water, showers, bear boxes, fire grates, picnic tables, food service, public telephone, ranger station, swimming (lake). $14* ▭ *AE, D, MC, V* ⊘ *Closed Oct.–Apr.*

⛺ **Rising Sun Campground.** As the name says, you can watch the sun rise from your camp, across the peaks and grassy knolls here. The campground is near St. Mary Lake and many hiking trails. ✉ *Going-to-the-Sun Rd.* ☎ *406/888–7800 or 800/365–2267* ⛺ *83 sites* ⚮ *Flush toilets, pit toilets, drinking water, showers, bear boxes, fire grates, picnic tables, food service, public telephone, swimming (lake). $14* ▭ *AE, D, MC, V* ⊘ *Closed Oct.–Apr.*

⛺ **St. Mary Campground.** This large, grassy spot alongside the lake and stream has mountain views and cool breezes. It always seems to be the campground that fills first. ✉ *Going-to-the-Sun Rd.* ☎ *406/888–7800* ⛺ *173 sites* ⚮ *Flush toilets, pit toilets, drinking water, showers, bear boxes, fire grates, picnic tables, food service, public telephone, swimming (lake). $20* ▭ *AE, D, MC, V* ⊘ *Closed Oct.–Apr.*

⛺ **Sprague Creek Campground.** This sometimes noisy roadside camp spot for tents, RVs, and campers only (no towed units) offers spectacular views of the lake and sunsets, fishing from shore, and great rock skipping on the beach. Restaurants, gift shops, and a grocery store are 1 mi north on Going-to-the-Sun Road. ✉ *Going-to-the-Sun Rd., 1 mi south of Lake McDonald Lodge* ☎ *406/888–7800* ⛺ *25 sites* ⚮ *Flush toilets, drinking water, bear boxes, fire grates, picnic tables. $15* ⚮ *Reservations not accepted* ▭ *No credit cards* ⊘ *Closed mid-Sept.–mid-May.*

⛺ **Two Medicine Campground.** This is often the last campground to fill during the height of summer. A general store, snack bar, and boat rentals are available. ✉ *Two Medicine Rd.* ☎ *406/888–7800* ⛺ *99 sites* ⚮ *Flush toilets, pit toilets, drinking water, showers, bear boxes, fire grates, picnic tables, food service, public telephone, general store, swimming (lake). $15* ▭ *AE, D, MC, V* ⊘ *Closed Oct.–Apr.*

⛺ **Waterton Townsite Campground.** While busy, noisy, and windy, sites here are also grassy and flat, kitchen shelters, and a view down the lake into the U.S. part of the peace park. The town's restaurants and shops are within walking distance. ✉ *Waterton Ave. and Vimy Ave.* ⛺ *238 sites* ⚮ *Flush toilets, full hookups, dump station, drinking water, guest laundry, showers, fire grates, picnic tables, public telephone. $21–$33* ⚮ *www.pc.gc.ca or call* ☎ *905/426–4648 or 877/737–3783* ▭ *AE, MC, V* ⊘ *Closed early Oct.–Late Apr.*

## Outside the Parks

$$–$$$$ ⬚ **Belton Chalet.** This carefully restored 1910 railroad hotel, the original winter headquarters for the park, has a great location just outside the West Glacier entrance. Rooms are cozy and bright, with original woodwork around the windows and period furnishings. Cottages, which re-

main open in winter, are snug up against the evergreen forest behind the lodge. ⊠ *12575 U.S. 2 E, West Glacier 59936* ☎ *406/888–5000 or 888/235–8665* 🖷 *406/888–5005* ⊕ *www.beltonchalet.com* ➴ *25 rooms, 2 cottages* 🖒 *Restaurant, spa, bicycles, bar, no a/c, no phone, no TV, no smoking rooms. $135–$285* ═ *MC, V* ⫶◯⫶ *BP.*

**$$–$$$$** ⊡ **Izaak Walton Inn.** This historic lodge sits on the southern edge of Glacier and under the shadow of the Great Bear Wilderness. You can ride Amtrak to the back door and stay either in quaint lodge rooms or in refurbished train cabooses. Lodge rooms have knotty-pine paneling, lacy curtains, and simple furnishings. Caboose Cottages (three-night minimum for $723) sleep up to four people and have kitchenettes. In winter you can ski or snowshoe from the door. ⊠ *290 Izaak Walton Inn Rd. (off U.S. 2), Essex 59916* ☎ *406/888–5700* 🖷 *406/888–5200* ⊕ *www.izaakwaltoninn.com* ➴ *33 rooms, 4 caboose cottages* 🖒 *Restaurant, bicycles, bar, no a/c, no phone, no TV, no smoking rooms. $127–$242* ═ *MC, V.*

**★ $$–$$$** ⊡ **Garden Wall Inn B&B.** Most of what you see in this 1923 home is antique. All rooms are individually decorated and have down duvets. Special extras include a wake-up coffee tray delivered to your room and afternoon hors d'oeuvres in front of the fireplace. The snow bus to the ski resort stops one block away. ⊠ *504 Spokane Ave., Whitefish 59937* ☎ *406/862–3440 or 888/530–1700* ⊕ *www.gardenwallinn.com* ➴ *3 rooms, 1 suite* 🖒 *Restaurant, bicycles, parking (no fee), no a/c, no phone, no TV, no-smoking rooms. $125–$195* ═ *AE, MC, V* ⫶◯⫶ *BP.*

**CAMPGROUNDS & RV PARKS** 🛆 **Aspenwood Campground and RV Park.** A nightly bonfire and teepee rentals are some of the numerous, fun extras at this campground 10 mi west of Browning and 2 mi from Glacier. ⊠ *U.S. 89* ☎ *406/338–3009* ⊕ *www.aspenwoodcamp.com* ➴ *10 partial hookups, 9 tent sites; 3 teepees* 🖒 *Flush toilets, partial hookups (electric and water), dump station, drinking water, showers, fire pits, picnic tables, food service, electricity, public telephone, general store, play area* ☒ *$15 tent sites, $20 partial hookups, $35–$45 tepees* ═ *MC, V* ☉ *Closed Oct.–Apr.*

🛆 **Sundance RV Park and Campground.** This older campground, 6 mi south of West Glacier, was built with families in mind. It's close to a water park, and offers free Wi-Fi. Bicyclists and hikers drop in for $4 showers. ⊠ *10545 U.S. 2 E, Coram* ☎ *406/387–5016* ➴ *31 sites with partial hookups, 1 cabin* 🖒 *Flush toilets, partial hookups (electric and water), dump station, drinking water, guest laundry, showers, fire grates, picnic tables, play area. $15–$22, $35 cabin* ═ *MC, V* ☉ *Closed Oct. 15–May 15.*

# GLACIER & WATERTON ESSENTIALS

ACCESSIBILITY All visitor centers are wheelchair accessible, and most of the campgrounds and picnic areas are paved, with extended-length picnic tables and accessible restrooms. Three of Glacier's nature trails are wheelchair accessible: the Trail of Cedars, Running Eagle Falls, and the Oberlin Bend Trail, just west of Logan Pass. In Waterton, the Linnet Lake Trail, Waterton Townsite Trail, Cameron Lake day-use area, and the International Peace Park Pavilion are wheelchair accessible.

ADMISSION FEES Entrance fees for Glacier are $20 per vehicle, or $10 for one person on foot or bike, good for seven days; $20 for a one-year pass. A day pass to Waterton Lakes costs C$7 (C$3.45 per child), and an annual pass costs C$35. *Passes to Glacier and Waterton must be paid for separately.*

ADMISSION HOURS The parks are open year-round, however, most roads and facilities close October through May due to snow. The parks are in the Mountain time zone.

ATMS/BANKS You'll find cash machines at Lake McDonald, Many Glacier, St. Mary and Glacier Park lodges, and, in Waterton's Tamarack Village Square. Waterton has a full-service bank.

AUTOMOBILE SERVICE STATIONS
🚩 **Glacier Highland Store.** ✉ 12555 U.S. 2 E, West Glacier ☎ 406/888–5427 ☉ Closed mid-Oct.–Apr. **Lodge at St. Mary Exxon.** ✉ Going-to-the-Sun Rd. at U.S. 2 ☎ 406/732–4431 ☉ Closed mid-Oct.–Apr. **Pat's.** ✉ 224 Mountain View Rd., Waterton Townsite ☎ 403/859–2266.

EMERGENCIES In case of a fire or medical emergency, call 911. In summer, the West Glacier Urgent Care Clinic (☎ 406/888–9005), behind the firehouse, is open. The Royal Canadian Mounted Police (☎ 403/859–2244) has an office at the corner of Waterton Avenue and Cameron Falls Drive.

LOST AND FOUND Park headquarters in West Glacier (☎ 406/888–7800). In Waterton, the RCMP building (☎ 403/859–2044).

PERMITS At Glacier the required backcountry permit is $4 per person per day from the Apgar Backcountry Permit Center after mid-April for the upcoming summer. Advance reservations cost $20. Mail a request and a check after mid-April to Backcountry Reservations, Glacier National Park Headquarters, Box 395, West Glacier, Montana 59936.

Waterton requires backcountry camping permits for use of its 13 backcountry camp spots, with reservations available up to 90 days in advance. Buy the permit for C$6 per adult per night—reserve for an additional C$11—at the visitor reception center (☎ 403/858–5133).

POST OFFICES
🚩 **West Glacier** ✉ 110 Going-to-the-Sun Rd. ☎ 406/888–5591. **East Glacier** ✉ U.S. 2, north of town ☎ 406/226–5534. **Waterton Townsite** ✉ 102a Windflower Ave. ☎ 403/859–2294.

PUBLIC TELEPHONES Find them at Avalanche Campground, Glacier Highland Motel and Store, Apgar, St. Mary Visitor Center, Two Medicine Campstore and all lodges except Granite Park Chalet and Sperry Chalet. Cell phones do not generally work.

RELIGIOUS SERVICES In the summer, you can attend either Christian Ministry or Catholic services at Glacier, and Anglican, United, Catholic, or Mormon services in Waterton.

RESTROOMS Portable toilets are along roadside pullouts on Going-to-the-Sun Road. Restrooms also may be found at the visitor centers, and most campgrounds.

SHOPS & GROCERS
🚩 **Lake McDonald Store.** ✉ Adjacent to Lake McDonald Lodge ☎ 406/888–9953. **Rising Sun Camp Store** ✉ 6 ½ mi (11 km) from St. Mary

16

☎ 406/732-5523 **Swiftcurrent Camp Store** ✉ Near Many Glacier ☎ 406/732-5531. **Two Medicine Store** ✉ Beside Two Medicine Campground ☎ 406/226-5582. **Rocky Mountain Food Mart** ✉ 307 Windflower Ave., Waterton Townsite ☎ 403/859-2526.

### NEARBY TOWN INFORMATION

🄵 **Bigfork Area Chamber of Commerce** ✉ 8155 Hwy. 35, Bigfork, MT 59911 ☎ 406/837-5888 ⊕ www.bigfork.org. **East Glacier Chamber of Commerce** Ⓕ Box 260, East Glacier, MT 59434 ☎ 406/226-4403. **Town of Cardston** Ⓕ Box

280, Cardston, AB T0K 0K0 ☎ 888/434-3366 ⊕ www.town.cardston.ab.ca. **Whitefish Chamber of Commerce** ✉ 520 E. 2nd St., Whitefish, MT 59937 ☎ 877/862-3548 ⊕ www. whitefishchamber.org.

### VISITOR INFORMATION

🄵 **Glacier National Park** Ⓕ Box 128, West Glacier, MT 59936 ☎ 406/888-7800 ⊕ www. nps.gov/glac. **Waterton Lakes National Park** ✉ Waterton Park, AB, Canada T0K 2M0 ☎ 403/ 859-2224 or 800/748-7275 🖷 403/859-2650 ⊕ www.parkscanada.gc.ca/waterton.

# Grand Canyon National Park

**WORD OF MOUTH**

"In the Grand Canyon, Arizona has a natural wonder which, so far as I know, is in kind absolutely unparalleled throughout the rest of the world. . . . [it is] one of the great sights which every American if he can travel at all should see."

—Theodore Roosevelt

# WELCOME TO GRAND CANYON

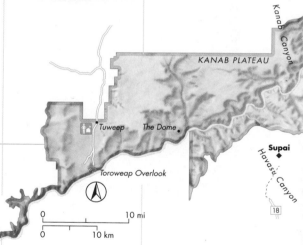

## TOP REASONS TO GO

★ **Its status.** The only natural wonder in the contiguous United States—and a UNESCO World Heritage Site. It's one place about which you really want to say, "Been there, done that!"

★ **Awesome vistas.** Painted desert, sandstone canyon walls, pine and fir forests, mesas, plateaus, volcanic features, the Colorado River, streams, and waterfalls make for some jaw-dropping moments.

★ **Year-round adventure.** Outdoor junkies can bike, boat, camp, fish, hike, ride mules, white-water raft, watch birds and wildlife, cross-country ski, and snowshoe.

★ **Continuing education.** Adults and kids can get schooled, thanks to free park-sponsored nature walks and interpretive programs.

★ **Sky-high and river-low experiences.** Visitors can experience the canyon via planes, trains, and automobiles (buses, Jeeps, and Hummers), as well as helicopters, boats, bikes, mules and, of course, on foot.

KANAB PLATEAU

Kanab Canyon

Tuweep     The Dome

Toroweap Overlook

Supai

Havasu Canyon

18

0 ——— 10 mi
0 ——— 10 km

**1** North Rim. Of the nearly 5 million people who visit the park annually, 90% enter at the South Rim, but many believe the North Rim is even more gorgeous—and worth the extra effort. Accessible only from mid-May to mid-October (or the first good snowfall), the North Rim has legitimate bragging rights: at more than 8,000 feet above sea level (and 1,000 feet higher than the South Rim), it offers precious solitude and three developed viewpoints. Rather than staring into the canyon's depths, you get a true sense of its expanse.

**2** South Rim. The South Rim, on the other hand, is where the action is: Grand Canyon Village's lodging, camping, eateries, stores, and museums, plus plenty of trailheads into the canyon. Visitor services and facilities are open and available every day of the year, including holidays. Three shuttle routes, all free, cover some-30 stops, and visitors who'd rather relax than rough it can treat themselves to comfy hotel rooms and elegant restaurant meals (lodging and camping reservations are essential).

# GETTING ORIENTED

Grand Canyon National Park is a superstar—biologically, historically, and recreationally. One of the world's best examples of arid-land erosion, the canyon provides a record of three of the four eras of geological time. In addition to its diverse fossil record, the park reveals prehistoric traces of human adaptation to an unforgiving environment. It's also home to several major ecosystems, five of the world's seven life zones, three of North America's four desert types, and all kinds of rare, endemic, and protected plant and animal species.

ARIZONA

KAIBAB PLATEAU

Colorado River

Great Thumb Mesa

Inner Gorge

HAVASUPAI INDIAN RESERVATION

Havasupai Point

North Rim Entrance Station

TO JACOB LAKE AND SOUTH RIM

67

**1** NORTH RIM

Marble Canyon

Point Imperial

Vista Encantada

Colorado River

Point Sublime

**Grand Canyon Lodge**

Visitor Center

**Bright Angel Trail**

Walhalla Overlook

Cape Royal

**Phantom Ranch**

Granite Gorge

West Rim Drive

Pima Point    Hopi Point

Hermits Rest

Mather Point

Yaki Point

Lipan Point

Desert View

Visitor Center

Grand Canyon Village

Grandview Point

East Entrance

South Entrance

Tusayan

**2** SOUTH RIM

Grand Canyon Airport

64

180

TO FLAGSTAFF, WILLIAMS

TO CAMERON AND NORTH RIM

64

# GRAND CANYON PLANNER

## When to Go

There is no bad time to visit the canyon, though **the busiest times of year are summer and spring break.** Visiting during these peak seasons as well as during holidays, requires patience and a tolerance for crowds. Note that weather changes on a whim in this exposed high-desert region. *You cannot visit the North Rim in the winter due to weather conditions and related road closures.*

### AVG. HIGH/LOW TEMPS.

SOUTH RIM

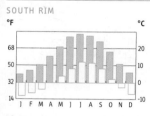

NORTH RIM

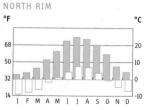

INNER CANYON

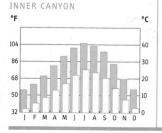

## Flora & Fauna

Eighty-eight mammal species inhabit Grand Canyon National Park, as well as 300 species of birds, 24 kinds of lizards, and 24 kinds of snakes. The rare Kaibab squirrel is found only on the North Rim—you can recognize them by their all-white tails and the long tufts of white hair on their ears. The pink Grand Canyon rattlesnake lives at lower elevations within the canyon.

Hawks and ravens are visible year-round, usually coasting on the wind above the canyon. The endangered California condor has been reintroduced to the canyon. Park rangers give daily talks on the magnificent birds, whose wingspan measures 9 feet.

In spring, summer, and fall, mule deer, recognizable by their large antlers, are abundant at the South Rim. Don't be fooled by gentle appearances, though; these guys can be aggressive. It's illegal to feed them, as it will disrupt their natural habitats—and increase your risk of getting bitten.

The South Rim's Coconino Plateau is fairly flat, at an elevation of about 7,000 feet, and covered with stands of pinyon and ponderosa pines, junipers, and Gambel's oak trees. On the Kaibab Plateau on the North Rim, Douglas fir, spruce, quaking aspen, and more ponderosa pine trees prevail. In spring you're likely to see asters, sunflowers, and lupine in bloom at both rims.

# Getting There & Around

When driving, the best access to the park from the east or south is from Flagstaff. Take U.S. 180 northwest 81 mi to the park's southern entrance and Grand Canyon Village. To go on to the North Rim, proceed north from Flagstaff on U.S. 89 to Bitter Springs. Then take U.S. 89A to the junction of Highway 67 and travel south on the highway for about 40 mi. From the west on Interstate 40, the most direct route to the South Rim is on U.S. 180 and Highway 64.

The South Rim stays open to auto traffic year-round, although access to Hermits Rest is limited to shuttle buses from March through November because of congestion. Parking is free once you pay the $25 park entrance fee, but it can be difficult to find a spot, especially during peak hours of the busiest summer weeks. Try the large lot in front of the general store near Yavapai Lodge or the Maswik Transportation Center lot, which is served by the shuttle bus. If you visit from October through April, you'll likely experience light to moderate traffic and have no problem with parking.

There are three free shuttle routes in the park. Hermits Rest Route operates March through November between Grand Canyon Village and Hermits Rest. The Village Route operates year-round in the village area from one hour before sunrise until after dark; it provides the easiest access to the Canyon View Information Center. The Kaibab Trail Route travels from Canyon View Information Center to Yaki Point, including a stop at the South Kaibab trailhead. In summer, South Rim roads are congested, and it's often easier, and sometimes required, to park your car and take the free shuttle. Running from one hour before sunrise until one hour after sunset, the shuttles arrive every 15 to 30 minutes. The roughly 30 stops are clearly marked throughout the park.

At 8,000 feet, the more remote North Rim is off limits during winter. From mid-October (or the first heavy snowfall) through mid-May, there are no services available, and Highway 67 south of Jacob Lake is closed. Weather information and road conditions for both rims, updated at 7 AM daily, can be obtained by calling 928/638–7888.

# Planning Your Time

The park is most crowded near the entrances and in parking lots and Grand Canyon Village, as well as on the scenic drives, especially the 25-mi Desert View Drive. **To avoid crowds, go further into the canyon. Hit the mostly paved Rim Trail, and you'll see that crowds generally start dropping off sharply.** For more crowd-avoidance advice, see ⇨ "Tips for Avoiding Canyon Crowds" box in this chapter. The best times of day to see the canyon are before 10 AM and after 2 PM, when the angle of the sun brings out the colors of the rock, and clouds and shadows add dimension.

*Plan ahead*, especially if you want to go down into the canyon via a mule—**mule rides require at least a six-month advance reservation,** and may even need one or two year's notice for the really busy season (they can be reserved up to 23 months in advance). Sometimes cancellations allow riders to join at the last minute, but don't count on it. For camping and lodging in the park, reservations also are essential; they are taken up to 13 months in advance.

**17**

By Jill Koch

When it comes to the Grand Canyon, there are statistics, and there are sensations. While the former are impressive—the canyon measures in at an average width of 10 mi, length of 277 mi, and depth of a mile—they don't truly prepare you for that first impression. Seeing the canyon for the first time is an astounding experience—one that's hard to wrap your head around. In fact, it's more than an experience, it's an emotion, one that is only just beginning to be captured with the superlative "Grand."

Nearly 5 million visitors come to the park each year. They can access the canyon via two main points: the South Rim and the North Rim. The width from the North Rim to the South Rim varies from 600 feet to 18 mi, but traveling between rims by road requires a 215-mi drive. Hiking arduous trails from rim to rim is a steep and strenuous trek of at least 21 mi, but it's well worth the effort. You'll travel through five of North America's seven life zones. (To do this any other way, you'd have to travel from the Mexican desert to the Canadian woods.) In total, 630 mi of trails traverse the canyon, 51 of those miles maintained.

## GRAND CANYON'S SOUTH RIM

Visitors to the canyon converge mostly on the South Rim, and mostly during the summer. Grand Canyon Village is here, with most of the park's lodging and camping, trailheads, restaurants, stores, and museums, along with a nearby airport and railroad depot. Believe it or not, the average stay in the park is a mere four hours. This is not advised! You need to spend several days to truly appreciate this marvelous place, but at the very least, give it a full day. And hike down into the canyon, or along the rim, to get away from the crowds and experience nature at its finest.

## Scenic Drive

**Hermit Road.** The Santa Fe Company built Hermit Road, formerly known as West Rim Drive, in 1912 as a scenic tour route. Ten overlooks dot this 8-mi stretch, each worth a visit. The road is filled with hairpin turns; be certain to adhere to posted speed limits. From March through November, Hermit Road is closed to private auto traffic because of congestion; during this period, a free shuttle bus will carry you to all the overlooks. Riding the bus round-trip without getting off at any of the viewpoints takes 75 minutes; the return trip stops only at Mohave and Hopi points. Take plenty of water with you for the ride—the only water along the way is at Hermits Rest.

## What to See

### Historic Sites

**Kolb Studio.** Built in 1904 by the Kolb brothers as a photographic workshop and residence, this building provides a view of Indian Gardens, where, in the days before a pipeline was installed, Emery Kolb descended 3,000 feet each day to get the water he needed to develop his prints. Kolb was doing something right; he operated the studio until he died in 1976 at age 95. The gallery here has changing exhibitions of paintings, photography, and crafts. There's also a bookstore. ⊠ *Grand Canyon Village, near Bright Angel Lodge* ☉ *Daily, 8–6.*

**17**

**Powell Memorial.** A granite statue honors the memory of John Wesley Powell, who measured, charted, and named many of the canyons and creeks of the Colorado River. It was here that the dedication ceremony for Grand Canyon National Park took place on April 3, 1920. ⊠ *About 3 mi west of Hermit Road Junction on Hermit Rd.*

### Scenic Stops

**The Abyss.** At an elevation of 6,720 feet, the Abyss is one of the most awesome stops on Hermit Road, revealing a sheer drop of 3,000 feet to the Tonto Platform, a wide terrace of Tapeats sandstone layers about two-thirds of the way down the canyon. From the Abyss you'll also see several isolated sandstone columns, the largest of which is called the Monument. ⊠ *About 5 mi west of Hermit Road Junction on Hermit Rd.*

**Desert View and Watchtower.** From the top of the 70-foot stone-and-mortar watchtower, even the muted hues of the distant Painted Desert to the east and the Vermilion Cliffs rising from a high plateau near the Utah border are visible. In the chasm below, angling to the north toward Marble Canyon, an imposing stretch of the Colorado River reveals itself. Up several flights of stairs, the Watchtower houses a glass-enclosed observatory with powerful telescopes. ⊠ *About 23 mi east of Grand Canyon Village on Desert View Dr.* ☎ *928/638–2736* ☉ *Daily 8–7, hours may vary.*

**Grandview Point.** At an elevation of 7,496 feet, the view from here is one of the finest in the canyon. To the northeast is a group of dominant buttes, including Krishna Shrine, Vishnu Temple, Rama Shrine, and Shiva Temple. A short stretch of the Colorado River is also visible. Directly below

## GREAT ITINERARIES

### GRAND CANYON IN ONE DAY

Start early, pack a picnic lunch, and take the shuttle from one of its 30-some stops to **Canyon View Information Plaza** just north of the south entrance, to pick up information and see your first incredible view at **Mather Point.** Continue east along **Desert View Drive** for about 2 mi to **Yaki Point,** your first stop. Next, hop back on the shuttle to head 7 mi east to **Grandview Point,** for a good view of the buttes Krishna Shrine and Vishnu Temple. Go 4 mi east and catch the view at **Moran Point,** then 3 mi to the **Tusayan Ruin and Museum,** where a small display is devoted to the history of the ancestral Puebloans. Continue another mile east to **Lipan Point** to view the Colorado River. In less than a mile, you'll arrive at **Navajo Point,** the highest elevation on the South Rim. **Desert View and Watchtower** are the final stops along the shuttle route.

On the return shuttle, hop off at any of the picnic areas for lunch. Once back at Grand Canyon Village, walk the paved **Rim Trail** about 1½ mi to **Maricopa Point.** Along the way, pick up souvenirs in the village and stop at the historic **El Tovar Hotel** to make dinner reservations. If you have time, take the shuttle on **Hermit Road** to **Hermits Rest,** 8 mi. It's a good place to watch the sunset.

### GRAND CANYON IN THREE DAYS

On Day 1, follow the one-day itinerary for the morning, but spend more time exploring Desert View Drive and enjoy a leisurely picnic or lunch in Grand Canyon Village.

Travel Hermit Road on your second morning, and drive to Grand Canyon Airport for a late-morning small plane or helicopter tour of the area. Have lunch in **Tusayan** and cool off during the IMAX film *Grand Canyon: The Hidden Secrets.* Back in the village, take in a free ranger-led program. On your third day, hike **Bright Angel Trail** into the canyon. It takes twice as long to hike back up, so plan accordingly. Pick up trail maps at **Canyon View Information Plaza,** and bring plenty of water.

Alternately, spend days two and three exploring **Grand Canyon West.** Fill the first day with a Hummer tour along the rim, a helicopter ride into the canyon, or a pontoon boat ride on the Colorado River, and fill up on Hualapai tacos at the Hualapai Lodge's Diamond Creek Restaurant. The next day, raft the Class V and VI rapids or hike 8 mi into **Havasu Canyon** to the small village of Supai and the Havasupai Lodge. You'll need a Havasupai tribal permit to hike here.

### GRAND CANYON IN FIVE DAYS

Between May and October, you can visit the North Rim as well as the South. Follow the three-day South Rim itinerary and, early on your fourth day, start the long but rewarding drive to the North Rim, where you can spend the last couple of days of your trip. The most popular trails here are **Transept Trail,** which starts near the Grand Canyon Lodge, and **Cliff Springs Trail,** which starts near **Cape Royal.** Before leaving the area, drive Cape Royal Road 11 mi to **Point Imperial**—at 8,803 feet, it's the highest vista on either rim.

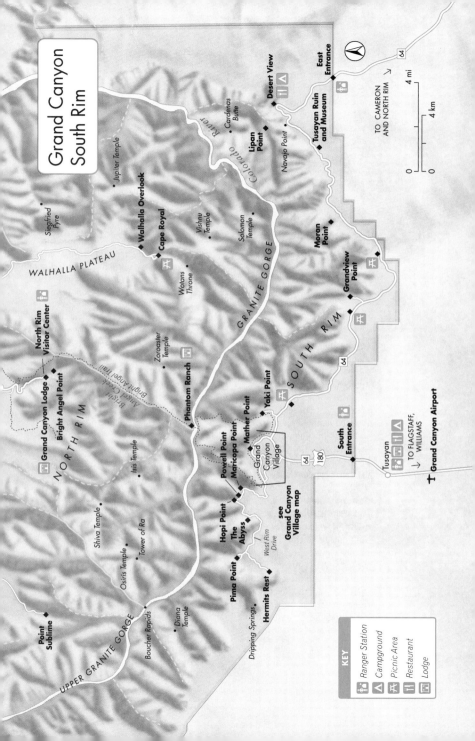

# Grand Canyon South Rim

WALHALLA PLATEAU

Colorado River

GRANITE GORGE

SOUTH RIM

UPPER GRANITE GORGE

NORTH RIM

**Point Sublime**

**Grand Canyon Lodge**
**Bright Angel Point**
**North Rim Visitor Center**

Siegfried Pyre

Jupiter Temple

Shiva Temple

Osiris Temple

Tower of Ra

Isis Temple

Diana Temple

Boucher Rapids

Dripping Springs

Bright Angel Trail

Bright Angel Creek

Zoroaster Temple

**Phantom Ranch**

Wotans Throne

Vishnu Temple

Solomon Temple

**Walhalla Overlook**
**Cape Royal**

Cardenas Butte

**Desert View**

**Lipan Point**

Navajo Point

**Tusayan Ruin and Museum**

**East Entrance**

**Moran Point**

**Grandview Point**

**Yaki Point**

**Mather Point**

**Powell Point**
**Maricopa Point**

**Hopi Point**
**The Abyss**

West Rim Drive

**Pima Point**

**Hermits Rest**

Grand Canyon Village

see Grand Canyon Village map

**South Entrance**

Tusayan

**Grand Canyon Airport**

TO FLAGSTAFF, WILLIAMS

TO CAMERON AND NORTH RIM

64

180

64

64

0   4 mi
0   4 km

## KEY

Ranger Station
Campground
Picnic Area
Restaurant
Lodge

# Tips for Avoiding Canyon Crowds

*"I find that in contemplating the natural world, my pleasure is greater if there are not too many others contemplating it with me, at the same time."–Edward Abbey*

It's hard to commune with nature while you're searching for a parking place, dodging video cams, and stepping away from strollers. However, this scenario is likely to occur only during the very peak months of mid-May through mid-October. One option is to bypass Grand Canyon National Park altogether and head to the West Rim of the canyon, tribal land of the Hualapai and Havasupai. If only the park itself will do, the following tips will help you to keep your distance and your cool.

### TAKE ANOTHER ROUTE

Avoid road rage by choosing a different route to the South Rim, foregoing the traditional highways 64 and U.S. 180 from Flagstaff. Take U.S. 89 north from Flagstaff instead, passing near Sunset Crater and Wupatki national monuments. When you reach the Cameron Trading Post at the junction with Highway 64, take a break–or stay overnight. This is a good place to shop for Native American artifacts, souvenirs, and the usual postcards, dream-catchers, recordings, and T-shirts. There are also high-quality Navajo rugs, jewelry, and other authentic handicrafts, and you can sample Navajo tacos. Highway 64 to the west takes you directly to the park's east entrance; the scenery along the Little Colorado River Gorge en route is eye-popping. It's 25 mi from the Grand Canyon east entrance to the visitor center at Canyon View Information Plaza.

### BYPASS THE SOUTH RIM ALTOGETHER

Although the North Rim is just 10 mi across from the South Rim, the trip to get there by car is a five-hour drive of 215 mi. At first it might not sound like the trip would be worth it, but the payoff is huge. Along the way, you will travel through some of the prettiest parts of the state and be granted even more stunning views than those on the more easily accessible South Rim. Those who make the North Rim trip often insist it offers the canyon's most beautiful views and best hiking. To get to the North Rim from Flagstaff, take U.S. 89 north past Cameron, turning left onto U.S. 89A at Bitter Springs. En route you'll pass the area known as Vermilion Cliffs. At Jacob Lake, take Highway 67 directly to the Grand Canyon North Rim. The road to the North Rim closes from around mid-October through mid-May because of heavy snow, but in summer months and early fall, it's a wonderful way to beat the crowds at the South Rim.

### RIDE THE RAILS

There's no need to deal with all of the other drivers racing to the South Rim. Forget the hassle of the twisting rim roads, jaywalking pedestrians, and jammed parking lots and sit back and relax in the comfy train cars of the Grand Canyon Railway. Live music and storytelling enliven the trip as you journey past the breathtaking landscape. The train departs from the depot every morning between 8:30 and 10:30 AM, depending on the season, and makes the 65-mi journey in 2¼ hours. You can do the round-trip in a single day; however, you may choose to stay overnight at the South Rim and return to Williams the following afternoon.

the point, and accessible by the steep and rugged Grandview Trail, is Horseshoe Mesa, where you can see the ruins of Last Chance Copper Mine. ⊠ *About 12 mi east of Grand Canyon Village on Desert View Dr.*

**Hopi Point.** From this elevation of 7,071 feet, you can see a large section of the Colorado River; although it appears as a thin line, the river is nearly 350 feet wide below this overlook. Across the canyon to the north is Shiva Temple, which remained

GOOD READS

Books on various aspects of the canyon—geology, history, and scenery—are for sale in the visitor centers, various gift shops, and museums at both rims, as well as through the **Grand Canyon Association** (⌕ Box 399, Grand Canyon 86023 ☎ 928/638-2481 ⊕ www.grandcanyon.org).

an isolated section of the Kaibab Plateau until 1937. That year, Harold Anthony of the American Museum of Natural History led an expedition to the rock formation in the belief that it supported life that had been cut off from the rest of the canyon. Imagine the expedition members' surprise when they found an empty Kodak film box on top of the temple. Directly below Hopi Point lies Dana Butte, named for a prominent 19th-century geologist. In 1919, an entrepreneur proposed connecting Hopi Point, Dana Butte, and the Tower of Set across the river with an aerial tramway, a technically feasible plan that fortunately has not been realized. ⊠ *About 4 mi west of Hermit Road Junction on Hermit Rd.*

**17**

★ **Hermits Rest.** This westernmost viewpoint and Hermit Trail, which descends from it, were named for "hermit" Louis Boucher, a 19th-century French-Canadian prospector who had a number of mining claims and a roughly built home down in the canyon. Views from here include Hermit Rapids and the towering cliffs of the Supai and Redwall formations. The stone building at Hermits Rest sells curios and refreshments. ⊠ *About 8 mi west of Hermit Road Junction on Hermit Rd.*

**Lipan Point.** Here, at the canyon's widest point, you can get an astonishing visual profile of the gorge's geologic history, with a view of every eroded layer of the canyon. You can also see Unkar Delta, where a creek joins the Colorado to form powerful rapids and a broad beach. Ancestral Puebloan farmers worked the Unkar Delta for hundreds of years, growing corn, beans, and melons. ⊠ *About 25 mi east of Grand Canyon Village on Desert View Dr.*

**Maricopa Point.** This site merits a stop not only for the arresting scenery, which includes the Colorado River below, but also for its view of a defunct mine. On your left, as you face the canyon, are the Orphan Mine, a mine shaft, and cable lines leading up to the rim. The mine, which started operations in 1893, was worked first for copper and then for uranium until the venture came to a halt in 1969. The Battleship, the red butte directly ahead of you in the canyon, was named during the Spanish-American War, when battleships were in the news. ⊠ *About 2 mi west of Hermit Road Junction on Hermit Rd.*

**Mather Point.** You'll likely get your first glimpse of the canyon from this viewpoint, one of the most impressive and accessible on the South Rim.

## TRIP PLANNING

Before you go, request the complimentary *Trip Planner*, updated regularly by the National Park Service, by writing to: Trip Planner, Grand Canyon National Park, Box 129, Grand Canyon, AZ 86023. You can also get the trip planner online at ⊕ www.nps.gov/grca/grandcanyon/trip_planner.htm. Several Web sites also are useful for trip planning, including the National Park Service's Web site, www.nps.gov, as well as www.thecanyon.com, a commercial site with information on lodging, dining, and general park basics.

Once you arrive at the park, pick up *The Guide,* a free newspaper with a detailed area map and a schedule of free park programs. The park also distributes *The Grand Canyon Accessibility Guide,* also free, which can be picked up at visitor centers.

Named for the National Park Service's first director, Stephen Mather, this spot yields extraordinary views of the Grand Canyon, including deep into the Inner Gorge and numerous buttes: Wotan's Throne, Brahma Temple, and Zoroaster Temple, among others. The Grand Canyon Lodge, on the North Rim, is almost directly north from Mather Point and only 10 mi away—yet you have to drive 215 mi to get from one spot to the other. ⊠ *Near Canyon View Information Plaza.*

**Moran Point.** This point was named for American landscape artist Thomas Moran, who was especially fond of the play of light and shadows from this location. He first visited the canyon with John Wesley Powell in 1873. "Thomas Moran's name, more than any other, with the possible exception of Major Powell's, is to be associated with the Grand Canyon," wrote noted canyon photographer Ellsworth Kolb. It's fitting that Moran Point is a favorite spot of photographers and painters. ⊠ *About 17 mi east of Grand Canyon Village on Desert View Dr.*

**Pima Point.** Enjoy a bird's-eye view of Tonto Platform and Tonto Trail, which winds its way through the canyon for more than 70 mi. Also to the west, two dark, cone-shape mountains—Mt. Trumbull and Mt. Logan—are visible on the North Rim on clear days. They rise in stark contrast to the surrounding flat-top mesas and buttes. ⊠ *About 7 mi west of Hermit Road Junction on Hermit Rd.*

**Yaki Point.** Stop here for an exceptional view of Wotan's Throne, a flat-top butte named by François Matthes, a U.S. Geological Survey scientist who developed the first topographical map of the Grand Canyon. ⊠ *2 mi east of Grand Canyon Village on Desert View Dr.*

**Yavapai Observation Station.** A panorama of the canyon is visible through the building's large windows. The station has new geological displays opening in 2007. ⊠ *Adjacent to Grand Canyon Village* 🎫 *Free.*

### Visitor Centers

**Canyon View Information Plaza.** The park's main orientation center near Mather Point provides pamphlets and resources to help plan your sightseeing. Park rangers are on hand to answer questions and aid in planning canyon excursions. A bookstore is stocked with books covering all topics on the Grand Canyon, and a daily schedule of ranger-led hikes and evening lectures is posted on a bulletin board inside. A shuttle bus will get you there. ⊠ *East side of Grand Canyon Village* ☏ *928/638–7888* ☉ *Daily 8–5; outdoor exhibits may be viewed anytime.*

**Desert View Information Center.** ⊠ *East entrance* ☏ *800/858–2808* ☉ *Daily 9–5; hours vary in winter.*

**Yavapai Observation Station.** Shop in the bookstore, catch the park shuttle bus, or pick up information for the Rim Trail here. ⊠ *1 mi east of Market Plaza* ☏ *928/638–7888* ☉ *Daily 8–8; hours vary in winter.*

## Sports & the Outdoors

### Air Tours

★ Flights by plane and helicopter over the canyon are offered by a number of companies, departing for the Grand Canyon Airport at the south end of Tusayan. Prices and lengths of tours vary, but you can expect to pay about $109–$120 per adult for short plane trips and approximately $130–$235 for brief helicopter tours.

OUTFITTERS & EXPEDITIONS Companies worth noting are **Air Grand Canyon** (⊠ Grand Canyon Airport, Tusayan ☏928/638–2686 or 800/247–4726 ⊕www.airgrandcanyon. com), **Grand Canyon Airlines** (⊠ Grand Canyon Airport, Tusayan ☏928/638–2407 or 866/235–9422 ⊕ www.grandcanyonairlines.com), **Grand Canyon Helicopters** (⊠Grand Canyon Airport, Tusayan ☏928/638–2764 or 800/541–4537 ⊕ www.grandcanyonhelicoptersaz.com), **Maverick-AirStar Helicopters** (⊠ *Grand Canyon Airport, Tusayan* ☏ *928/638–2622 or 800/962–3869* ⊕ *www.maverickhelicopter.com*), and **Papillon Grand Canyon Helicopters** (⊠ Grand Canyon Airport, Tusayan ☏928/638–2419 or 800/528–2418 ⊕ www.papillon.com).

### Bicycling

The South Rim's limited opportunities for off-road biking, narrow shoulders on park roads, and heavy traffic may disappoint hard-core cyclists. Bicycles are permitted on all park roads and on the multi-use Greenway System, currently under development. Bikes are prohibited on all other trails, including the Rim Trail. Mountain bikers visiting the South Rim may be better off meandering through the ponderosa pine forest on the Tusayan Bike Trail. No rentals are available at the canyon.

### Hiking

Although permits are not required for day hikes, you must have a backcountry permit for longer trips (⇨ Permits *in* the Grand Canyon Essentials section at the end of chapter). Some of the more popular trails are listed in this chapter; more detailed information and maps can be obtained from the Backcountry Information Center. Also, rangers can help design a trip to suit your abilities.

Remember that the canyon has significant elevation changes and, in summer, extreme temperature ranges, which can pose problems for people who aren't in good shape or who have heart or respiratory problems.

17

## DID YOU KNOW?

The North Rim's isolated Toroweap overlook (also called Tuweep) is perched 3,000 feet above the canyon floor: a height equal to stacking the Sears Tower and Empire State Building on top of each other!

## TALK ABOUT A CLIFFHANGER!

In 2006, on Grand Canyon's West Rim, the Hualapai Tribe expanded its tourism offerings by building the amazing new Skywalk, a cantilever-shaped glass bridge suspended 4,000 feet above the Colorado River and extending 70 feet from the edge of the Grand Canyon. The attraction opened in late March 2007.

Holding up to 120 people at a time, the Skywalk is approximately 10 feet wide, and the bridge's deck, made of tempered glass several inches thick, has five-foot glass railings on each side. A three-level, 6,000-square-foot visitor's center includes a museum, movie theater, VIP lounge, gift shop, and several restaurants and bars. The high-end Skywalk Café has an outdoor patio and rooftop seating on the edge of the canyon. Grand Canyon West packages that include the Skywalk start at $74.95.

✉ *Eagle Point* ☎ *877/716–9378* ☼ *Access to the Skywalk runs from dawn to dusk.* ⊕ *www. destinationgrandcanyon.com*

**Carry plenty of water and energy foods.** The majority of each year's 400 search-and-rescue incidents result from hikers underestimating the size of the canyon, hiking beyond their abilities, or not packing sufficient food and water.

Under no circumstances should you attempt a day hike from the rim to the river and back. Remember that when it's 80°F on the South Rim, it's 110°F on the canyon floor. Allow two to three days if you want to hike rim to rim (it's easier to descend from the North Rim, as it's more than 1,000 feet higher than the South Rim).

EASY
Fodor'sChoice
★

**Rim Trail.** The South Rim's most popular walking path is the 13-mi (one way) Rim Trail, which runs along the edge of the canyon from Mather Point (the first overlook on Desert View Drive) to Hermits Rest. This walk, which is paved to Maricopa Point, visits several of the South Rim's historic landmarks. Allow anywhere from 15 minutes to a full day; the Rim Trail is an ideal day hike, as it varies only a few hundred feet in elevation from Mather Point (7,120 feet) to the trailhead at Hermits Rest (6,640 feet). The trail also can be accessed from the major viewpoints along Hermit Road, which are serviced by shuttle buses during the busy summer months.

MODERATE
★

**Bright Angel Trail.** Well-maintained, this is one of the most scenic hiking paths from the South Rim to the bottom of the canyon (9 mi each way). Rest houses are equipped with water at the 1½- and 3-mi points from May through September and at Indian Garden (4 mi) year-round. Water is also available at Bright Angel Campground, 9¼ mi below the trailhead. Plateau Point, about 1½ mi below Indian Garden, is as far as you should attempt to go on a day hike; plan on spending six to nine hours. Bright Angel Trail is the easiest of all the footpaths into the canyon, but because the climb out from the bottom is an ascent of 5,510 feet, the

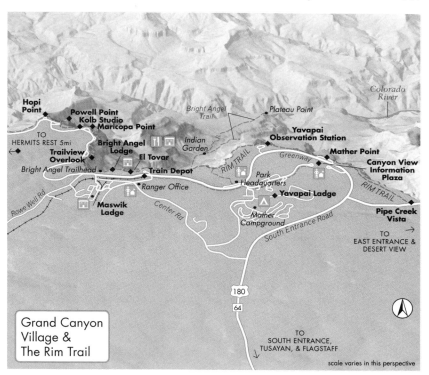

Hopi
Point

Powell Point
Kolb Studio
Maricopa Point

TO
HERMITS REST 5mi

Bright Angel
Lodge

Trailview
Overlook

El Tovar

Bright Angel Trailhead

Train Depot

Ranger Office

Maswik
Ladge

Rowe Well Rd

Center Rd

Bright Angel
Trail

Indian
Garden

RIM TRAIL

Park
Headquarters

Mather
Campground

South Entrance Road

Plateau Point

Yavapai
Observation Station

Greenway

Mather Point

Canyon View
Information
Plaza

RIM TRAIL

Yavapai Ladge

Pipe Creek
Vista

TO
EAST ENTRANCE &
DESERT VIEW

Colorado
River

180
64

TO
SOUTH ENTRANCE,
TUSAYAN, & FLAGSTAFF

scale varies in this perspective

**Grand Canyon
Village &
The Rim Trail**

17

trip should be attempted only by those in good physical condition and should be avoided in midsummer due to extreme heat. The top of the trail, a tight set of switchbacks called Jacob's Ladder, can be icy in winter. Originally a bighorn sheep path and later used by the Havasupai, the trail was widened late in the 19th century for prospectors and is now used for both mule and foot traffic. Hikers going downhill should yield to those going uphill. Also note that mule trains have the right-of-way—and sometimes leave unpleasant surprises in your path.

DIFFICULT **Clear Creek Trail.** Make this 9-mi hike only if you are prepared for a multiday trip. The trail departs from Phantom Ranch at the bottom of the canyon and leads across the Tonto Platform to Clear Creek, where drinking water is usually available, but should be treated.

**Grandview Trail.** Accessible from the parking area at Grandview Point, the trailhead is at 7,400 feet. The path heads down into the canyon for 4⁸⁄₁₀ mi to the junction and campsite at East Horseshoe Mesa Trail. Classified as a wilderness trail, the route is aggressive and not as heavily traveled as some of the more well-known trails, such as Bright Angel and Hermit; allow six to nine hours, round-trip. There is no water available along the trail, which follows a steep descent to 4,800 feet at Horseshoe Mesa, where Hopi Indians once collected mineral paints.

**Hermit Trail.** Beginning on the South Rim just west of Hermits Rest (and 8 mi west of Grand Canyon Village), this steep, 9³⁄₁₀-mi (one way) trail drops more than 5,000 feet to Hermit Creek, which usually flows year-round. It's a strenuous hike back up and is recommended for experienced long-distance hikers only; plan for six to nine hours. There's an abundance of lush growth and wildlife, including desert bighorn sheep, along this trail.

The trail descends from the trailhead at 6,640 feet to the Colorado River at 2,400 feet. Day hikers should not go past Santa Maria Springs at 4,880 feet. For much of the year, no water is available along the way; ask a park ranger about the availability of water at Santa Maria Springs and Hermit Creek before you set out. All water from these sources should be treated before drinking. The route leads down to the Colorado River and has inspiring views of Hermit Gorge and the Redwall and Supai formations. Six miles from the trailhead are the ruins of Hermit Camp, which the Santa Fe Railroad ran as a tourist camp from 1911 until 1930.

★ **South Kaibab Trail.** This trail starts at Yaki Point on Desert View Drive, 4 mi east of Grand Canyon Village. Because the trail is so steep—descending from the trailhead at 7,260 feet down to 2,480 feet at the Colorado River—and has no water, many hikers return via the less-demanding Bright Angel Trail; allow four to six hours. During this 6½-mi trek to the Colorado River, you're likely to encounter mule trains and riders. At the river, the trail crosses a suspension bridge and runs on to Phantom Ranch. Along the trail there is no water and very little shade. There are no campgrounds, though there are portable toilets at Cedar Ridge (6,320 feet), 1½ mi from the trailhead. Toilets and an emergency phone are also available at the Tipoff, 4½ mi down the trail (3 mi past Cedar Ridge). The trail corkscrews down through some spectacular geology. Look for (but don't remove) fossils in the limestone when taking water breaks.

**Tonto Trail.** A very strenuous 13⁸⁄₁₀-mi loop, Tonto Trail should be attempted only in cool weather; summer temperatures on the trail often reach 100°F. It parallels the Colorado River from South Kaibab trailhead to Bright Angel trailhead, and there's little shade.

NEED A BREAK?
If you've been driving too long and want some exercise, along with great views of the canyon, it's an easy 1¼-mi-long hike from the **Information Plaza to El Tovar Hotel.** The path runs through a quiet wooded area for about ½ mi, and then along the rim for another ¾ mi.

---

**ARRANGING TOURS**

Transportation-services desks are maintained at El Tovar, Bright Angel, Maswik Lodge, and Yavapai Lodge (closed in winter) in Grand Canyon Village. The desks provide information and handle bookings for sightseeing tours, taxi and bus services, mule and horseback rides, and accommodations at Phantom Ranch (at the bottom of the Grand Canyon). The concierge at El Tovar can also arrange most tours, with the exception of mule rides and lodging at Phantom Ranch. On the North Rim, Grand Canyon Lodge has general information about local services.

CLOSE UP

# Freebies at the Canyon

**WHILE YOU'RE HERE,** be sure to take advantage of the many freebies offered at Grand Canyon National Park. The most useful of these services is the system of free shuttle buses at the South Rim; it caters to the road-weary, with three routes winding through the park—Hermits Rest Route, Village Route, and Kaibab Trail Route. Of the bus routes, the Hermits Rest Route runs only from March through November; the other two run year-round, and the Kaibab Trail Route provides the only access to Yaki Point. Hikers coming or going from the Kaibab trailhead can catch the Hikers Express, which departs three times each morning from the Bright Angel Lodge, makes a quick stop at the Backcountry Office, and then heads out to the South Kaibab trailhead.

Ranger-led programs are always free and offered year-round, though more are scheduled during the busy spring and summer seasons. These programs might include activities such as stargazing and topics such as geology and the cultural history of prehistoric peoples. Some of the more in-depth programs may include a fossil walk or a condor talk. Check with the visitor center for seasonal programs including wildflower walks and fire ecology.

Kids ages 4 to 14 can get involved with the park's Junior Ranger program, with ever-changing activities including hikes and hands-on experiments.

Despite all of these options, rangers will tell you that the best free activity in the canyon is watching the magnificent splashes of color on the canyon walls during sunrise and sunset.

17

## Jeep Tours

OUTFITTERS & EXPEDITIONS

**Grand Canyon Jeep Tours & Safaris.** If you'd like to get off the pavement and see parts of the park that are accessible only by dirt road, a Jeep tour can be just the ticket. From March through October, Grand Canyon Outback leads daily, 1½- to 4½-hour, off-road tours within the park, as well as in Kaibab National Forest. The rides are bumpy and are not recommended for people with back injuries. Combo tours adding helicopter and airplane rides are available. ⌂ *Box 1772, Grand Canyon 86023* ☎ *928/638–5337 or 800/320–5337* ⊕ *www.grandcanyonjeeptours.com* ✆ *$45–$199* ▭ *AE, MC, V* ⚘ *Reservations essential.*

**Marvelous Marv's Private Grand Canyon Tours.** For a personalized experience, take this private tour of the Grand Canyon and surrounding sights any time of year. Rides can be rough; if you have had back injuries, check with your doctor before taking a Jeep tour. ⌂ *Box 544, Williams 86046* ☎ *928/635–4948 or 928/707–0291* ⊕ *www.marvelousmarv.com* ✆ *$85* ▭ *No credit cards* ⚘ *Reservations essential.*

## Mule Rides

★ Mule rides provide an intimate glimpse into the canyon for those who have the time, but not the stamina, to see the canyon on foot. Reservations are essential and are accepted up to 23 months in advance, or you can check the waiting list for last-minute cancellations.

These trips have been conducted since the early 1900s. A comforting fact as you ride the narrow trail: No one's ever been killed while riding a mule that fell off a cliff. (Nevertheless, the treks are not for the faint of heart or people in questionable health.)

OUTFITTERS **Grand Canyon National Park Lodges Mule Rides.** These trips delve into the canyon from the South Rim. Riders must be at least 4 feet, 7 inches tall, weigh less than 200 pounds, and understand English. Children under 15 must be accompanied by an adult. Riders must be in fairly good physical condition, and pregnant women are advised not to take these trips. The all-day ride to Plateau Point costs $142.21 (box lunch included). An overnight with a stay at Phantom Ranch at the bottom of the canyon is $369.54 ($651.80 for two riders). Two nights at Phantom Ranch, an option available from November through March, will set you back $517.82 ($879.63 for two). Meals are included. ⌂ *6312 S. Fiddlers Green Circle, Suite 600, N. Greenwood Village, CO 80111* ☎ *303/297–2757 or 888/297–2757* ⊕ *www.grandcanyonlodges.com* ⊗ *May–Sept., daily.*

## Rafting

FodorsChoice
★
Those who have taken a white-water raft trip down the Colorado River often say it's one of their most memorable life experiences. Most trips begin at Lees Ferry, a few miles below the Glen Canyon Dam near Page. There are tranquil half- and full-day float trips from the Glen Canyon Dam to Lees Ferry, as well as raft trips that run from seven to 18 days. Many of these voyages end at Phantom Ranch at the bottom of the Grand Canyon at river mile 87. You'll encounter some good white water along the way, including Lava Falls, listed in the *Guinness Book of World Records* as "the fastest navigable white-water stretch in North America."

Sixteen companies (at the time of this writing) offer motorized and oar-powered excursions, but reservations for raft trips (excluding smooth-water, one-day cruises) often need to be made more than six months in advance. Prices for river-raft trips vary greatly, depending on type and length. Half-day trips on smooth water run as low as $62 per adult/$52 for children. Trips that negotiate the entire length of the canyon and take as long as 12 days can cost more than $3,000.

OUTFITTERS & EXPEDITIONS
Worthwhile outfitters include **Arizona River Runners** (☎ 602/867–4866 or 800/477–7238 ⊕ www.raftarizona.com), **Canyoneers, Inc.** (☎ 928/526–0924, 800/525–0924 outside Arizona ⊕ www.canyoneers. com), **Diamond River Adventures, Inc.** (☎ 928/645–8866 or 800/343–3121 ⊕ www.diamondriver.com), **Grand Canyon Expeditions Company** (☎ 435/644–2691 or 800/544–2691 ⊕ www.gcex.com), **Tour West, Inc.** (☎ 801/225–0755 or 800/453–9107 ⊕ www.twriver.com), and **Wilderness River Adventures** (☎ 928/645–3279 or 800/992–8022 ⊕ www. riveradventures.com).

# Park Insider: Chuck Wahler

**WHEN CHUCK WAHLER** tells people to "take a hike," he means it in the most helpful, encouraging sense. A 16-year employee at Grand Canyon National Park, Wahler knows the lay of the land, and he encourages folks to get a feel for it on foot. A hike "either along the rim or into the canyon" ranks among his top "must-do" suggestions for park visitors.

As Chief of the Operations Branch for the park's Division of Interpretation and Resource Education, Wahler manages frontline operations for the division. "The staff that works with me operates the park visitor centers and museums, and presents interpretive programs to our visitors," he explains.

Those programs include the popular "Junior Ranger" activities, which also make Wahler's must-do list: "If there are children in your group, have them participate."

Variety is the spice of park life, as far as Wahler is concerned, and the range of activities is his favorite thing about his workplace. "It is a constantly changing place," he says, "different from minute to minute, day to day, and season to season." That diversity inspires another suggestion: "Views of the canyon from along Hermit Road are very different from those along Desert View Drive," explains Wahler. "If you have the time, plan to experience both areas of the park."

Navigating the 1,904-square-mi park is a sizeable task, but it's made easier by the free shuttle system. The buses stop at 30-some points of interest, and Wahler advocates hopping aboard whenever possible. "You'll spend more of your time exploring the park and less time looking for a place to park."

For another insider tip, he touts the park's aptly named newspaper. "*The Guide* provides visitors with all the basic information they need to plan their visit to the park. Taking a few minutes to read the newspaper will help make a visit more enjoyable." Distributed at the entrance station, *The Guide* is printed in English, French, German, Japanese, and Italian.

Wahler also urges travelers to consider coming during "the off-season" (late fall through early spring). "The weather can delightful, and the park is often less crowded than in the summer."

No matter the season, Wahler's final must-do is a simple one: "Find a quiet place along the rim, and just sit and enjoy the canyon."

**17**

### Skiing

Although you can't schuss down into the Grand Canyon, you can cross-country ski in the woods near the rim when there's enough snow, which has been lacking the last few seasons. The best time for cross-country skiing is mid-December though early March. Trails, suitable for beginner and intermediate skiers, begin ³/₁₀ mi north of the Grandview Lookout and travel through the Kaibab National Forest. Contact the **Tusayan Ranger District** (⌖ Box 3088, Grand Canyon 86023 ☎ 928/638–2443 ⊕ www.fs.fed.us/r3/kai) for details.

> #### PETS AT THE CANYON
>
> Pets are allowed in Grand Canyon National Park; however, they must be on a leash at all times. With the exception of service animals, pets are not allowed below the rim or on park shuttles. A **kennel** (☎ 928/638–0534), near the Maswik Lodge, houses cats and dogs. It's open daily from 7:30–5. Reservations are strongly recommended.

## Educational Offerings

**Grand Canyon Field Institute.** Instructors lead guided educational tours, hikes around the canyon, and weekend programs at the South Rim. Tour topics include everything from archaeology and backcountry medicine to photography and natural history. Contact GCFI for a schedule and price list. ⌖ *Box 399, Grand Canyon 86023* ☎ *928/638–2485 or 866/471-4435* ⊕ *www.grandcanyon.org/fieldinstitute* ⌗ *$95–$2,150* ⊟ *DC, MC, V* ⌖ *Reservations essential.*

**Interpretive Ranger Programs.** The National Park Service sponsors all sorts of orientation activities, such as daily guided hikes and talks, at both the North and South rims. The focus may be on any aspect of the canyon—from geology and flora and fauna to history and early inhabitants. For schedules on the South Rim, go to Canyon View Information Plaza, pick up a free copy of *The Guide* to the South Rim, or check online. ☎ *928/638–7888* ⊕ *www.nps.gov/grca* ⌗ *Free.*

**Junior Ranger Program for Families.** Children ages 4 to 14 can take part in these hands-on educational programs. ☎ *928/638–7888* ⌗ *Free.*

⟲ **Way Cool for Kids.** Rangers coordinate these free, hour-long introductions to the park for children ages 7–11, daily at 9 AM. Kids and rangers walk around the Village Rim area and talk about local plants and animals, history, or archaeology. Programs are subject to change. ⊠ *South Rim Park Headquarters, Parking Lot A* ☎ *928/638–7888* ⌗ *Free.*

### Bus Tours

**Xanterra Motorcoach Tours.** Narrated by knowledgeable guides, tours include the Hermits Rest Tour, which travels along the old wagon road built by the Santa Fe Railway; the Desert View Tour, which glimpses the Colorado River's rapids and stops at Lipan Point; and Sunrise and Sunset Tours. (⌖ 6312 S. Fiddlers Green Circle, Suite 600, N. Greenwood Village, CO 80111 ☎ 303/297–2757 or 888/297–2757 ⊕ www.grandcanyonlodges.com ⌗ $13.50 to $38 per person; children 16 and younger free when accompanied by a paying adult).

# GRAND CANYON'S NORTH RIM

The North Rim stands 1,000 feet higher than the South Rim and has a more alpine climate, with twice as much annual precipitation. Here, in the deep forests of the Kaibab Plateau, the crowds are thinner, the facilities fewer, and the views even more spectacular. Due to snow, the North Rim is off-limits in the winter.

Lodgings are available but limited. Your best bet may be to pack your camping gear and hiking boots and take several days to explore the lush Kaibab Forest. The canyon's highest, most dramatic rim views also can be enjoyed on two wheels (via primitive dirt access roads) and on four legs (courtesy of a trusty mule).

## Scenic Drive

★ **Highway 67.** Open mid-May to mid-October, (and often until Thanksgiving), the two-lane paved road climbs 1,400 feet in elevation as it passes through the Kaibab National Forest. Point Imperial and Cape Royal can be reached by spurs off this scenic drive running from Jacob Lake to Bright Angel Point.

## What to See

**17**

### Historic Site

**Grand Canyon Lodge.** Built in 1928 by the Union Pacific Railroad, this massive stone structure is listed on the National Register of Historic Places. Its huge sunroom has hardwood floors, high-beam ceilings, and a marvelous view of the canyon through plate-glass windows. On warm days, visitors sit in the sun and drink in the surrounding beauty on an outdoor viewing deck, where National Park Service employees deliver free lectures on geology and history (⇨ Educational Offerings). ⊠ *Off Hwy. 67, near Bright Angel Point.*

### Scenic Stops

★ **Bright Angel Point.** The trail, which leads to one of the most awe-inspiring overlooks on either rim, starts on the grounds of the Grand Canyon Lodge and runs along the crest of a point of rocks that juts into the canyon for several hundred yards. The walk is only ½ mi round-trip, but it's an exciting trek accented by sheer drops on each side of the trail. In a few spots where the route is extremely narrow, metal railings ensure visitors' safety. The temptation to clamber out to precarious perches to have your picture taken could get you killed—every year several people die from falls at the Grand Canyon. ⊠ *North Rim Dr., Grand Canyon.*

**Cape Royal.** A popular sunset destination, **Cape Royal** showcases the canyon's jagged landscape; you'll also get a glimpse of the Colorado River, framed by a natural stone arch called "the Angels Window." In autumn, the aspens turn a beautiful gold, adding even more color to an already magnificent scene of the forested surroundings. At Angels Window Overlook, ⅓ mi north of here, **Cliff Springs Trail** starts its 1-mi route (round-trip) through a forested ravine. The trail terminates at Cliff

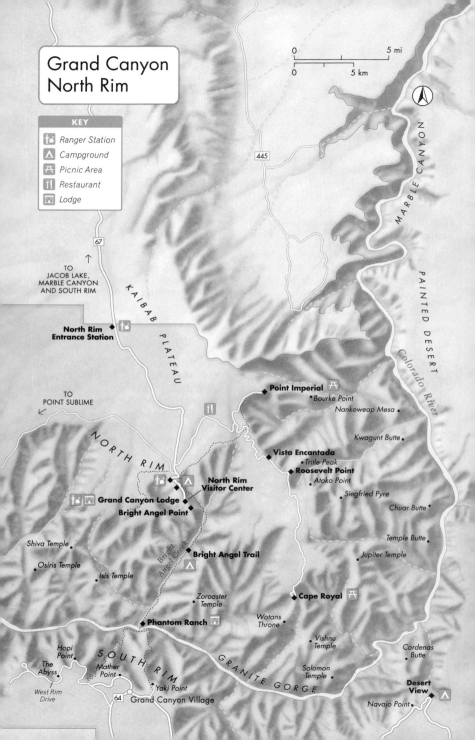

# Grand Canyon North Rim

### KEY

- 👫 Ranger Station
- ⛺ Campground
- ⛻ Picnic Area
- 🍴 Restaurant
- 🏨 Lodge

0 ——— 5 mi
0 ——— 5 km

445

MARBLE CANYON

PAINTED DESERT

Colorado River

67

TO
JACOB LAKE,
MARBLE CANYON
AND SOUTH RIM

**North Rim
Entrance Station** 👫

KAIBAB PLATEAU

TO
POINT SUBLIME

🍴

◆ **Point Imperial** ⛻
• Bourke Point
Nankoweap Mesa •

NORTH RIM

Kwagunt Butte •

◆ **Vista Encantada**
• Tritle Peak
◆ **Roosevelt Point**
Atoko Point •

👫 ⛺
**North Rim
Visitor Center**

👫🏨 **Grand Canyon Lodge**
**Bright Angel Point**

Siegfried Pyre •

Chuar Butte •

Shiva Temple •

Temple Butte •

Osiris Temple •

Isis Temple •

Bright Angel Creek

⛺ ◆ **Bright Angel Trail**

Jupiter Temple •

Zoroaster
Temple •

◆ **Cape Royal** ⛻

Wotans
Throne •

◆ **Phantom Ranch** 🏨

SOUTH RIM

Hopi
Point •

The
Abyss •

Mather
Point •

West Rim
Drive

Yaki Point •
64 **Grand Canyon Village**

GRANITE GORGE

Vishnu
Temple •

Solomon
Temple •

Cardenas
Butte •

**Desert
View** ⛺

Navajo Point •

Springs, where the forest opens to another impressive view of the canyon walls. ⊠ *Cape Royal Scenic Dr., 23 mi southeast of the Grand Canyon Lodge.*

**Point Imperial.** At 8,803 feet, Point Imperial has the highest vista point at either rim; it offers magnificent views of both the canyon and the distant country: the Vermilion Cliffs to the north, the 10,000-foot Navajo Mountain to the northeast in Utah, the Painted Desert to the east, and the Little Colorado River Canyon to the southeast. ⊠ *2⁷⁄₁₀ mi left off Cape Royal Scenic Dr., 11 mi northeast of the Grand Canyon Lodge.*

Fodor'sChoice  **Point Sublime.** Talk about solitude. Here you can camp within feet of the
★  canyon's edge. Sunrises and sunsets are spectacular. The winding road, through gorgeous high country, is only 17 mi, but it will take you at least two hours one way. The road is intended only for vehicles with high-road clearance (pickups and four-wheel-drive vehicles). It's also necessary to be properly equipped for wilderness road travel. Check with a park ranger or at the information desk at Grand Canyon Lodge before taking this journey. You may camp here only with a permit from the Backcountry Office. ⊠ *North Rim Dr., Grand Canyon; about 20 mi west of North Rim Visitor Center.*

### Visitor Center

**North Rim Visitor Center.** View exhibits, peruse the bookstore, and pick up useful maps and brochures here. Interpretive programs are often scheduled in the summer. If you're craving coffee, it's a short walk from here to the Grand Canyon Lodge. ⊠ *Near the parking lot on Bright Angel Peninsula* ☎ *928/638–7888* ☉ *Mid-May–mid-Oct., daily 8–6.*

17

## Sports & the Outdoors

### Bicycling

Mountain bikers can test the many dirt access roads found in this remote area, including the 17-mi trek to Point Sublime. It's rare to spot other people on these primitive roads. Note that you must bring your own bikes, as rentals are unavailable in the park. Bicycles and leashed pets are allowed on the 1⁷⁄₁₀ mi (one way) **Bridle Trail,** which follows the road from Grand Canyon Lodge to the North Kaibab trailhead. Watch for construction on this hard-packed trail.

### Hiking

EASY  **Cliff Springs Trail.** An easy 1-mi (round-trip), 1-hour walk near Cape Royal, Cliff Springs Trail leads through a forested ravine to an excellent view of the canyon. The trailhead begins across from Angels Window Overlook. Narrow and precarious in spots, it passes ancient dwellings, winds beneath a limestone overhang, and ends at Cliff Springs.

 ♺  **Transept Trail.** This 3-mi (round-trip), 1½-hour trail begins at 8,255 feet near the Grand Canyon Lodge's east patio. Well maintained and marked, it has little elevation change, sticking near the rim before reaching a dramatic view of a large stream through Bright Angel Canyon. The route leads to a side canyon called Transept Canyon, which geologist Clarence Dutton named in 1882, declaring it "far grander than Yosemite." Check

## People in the Park

**JOHN WESLEY POWELL**

The first European to see the canyon was Spanish explorer Garcia Lopez de Cardenas in 1540. But in 1869, American John Wesley Powell and his party became the first to brave the depths of the Grand Canyon on the Colorado River. Powell, a one-armed Civil War veteran, wrote: "Mountains of music swell in the river, hills of music billow in the creek . . . while other melodies are heard in the gorges of the lateral canyons. The Grand Canyon is a land of song." He dubbed the region "Grand Canyon," replacing the Paiute name *Kaibab* (mountain lying down).

the posted schedule to find a ranger talk along this trail; it's also a great place to view fall foliage.

MODERATE    **Ken Patrick Trail.** This primitive trail begins on the east side of the North Kaibab trailhead parking lot. It travels 10 mi one way (allow 6 hours) from the trailhead at 8,250 feet to Point Imperial at 8,803 feet. It crosses drainages and occasionally detours around fallen trees. The end of the road brings the highest views from either rim. Note that there is no water along this trail.

**Uncle Jim Trail.** This 5-mi, 3-hour loop trail starts at the North Kaibab Trail parking lot at 8,300 feet and winds south through the forest, past Roaring Springs Canyon and Bright Angel Canyon. The highlight of this rim hike is Uncle Jim Point, which, at 8,244 feet, overlooks the upper sections of the North Kaibab Trail.

**Widforss Trail.** Round-trip, Widforss Trail is 9⁹⁄₁₀ mi, with an elevation change of 200 feet. The trailhead, at 8,100 feet, is across from the North Kaibab Trail parking lot. Allow 6 hours for the hike, which passes through shady forests of pine, spruce, fir, and aspen on its way to Widforss Point, at 7,900 feet. You are likely to see wildflowers in summer, and this is a good trail for viewing fall foliage. It's named in honor of artist Gunnar M. Widforss, renowned for his paintings of national park landscapes.

DIFFICULT    **North Kaibab Trail.** At 8,250 feet, the trailhead to North Kaibab Trail is about 2 mi north of the Grand Canyon Lodge and is open only from May through October. It's recommended for experienced hikers only, who should allow four days for the full hike. The long, steep path drops 5,840 feet over a distance of 14½ mi to the Colorado River, so the National Park Service suggests that day hikers not go farther than Roaring Springs (5,020 feet) before turning to hike back up out of the canyon. After about 7 mi, Cottonwood Campground (4,080 feet) has drinking water in summer, restrooms, shade trees, and a ranger. It leads to Phantom Ranch.

### Mule Rides

OUTFITTER    **Canyon Trail Rides.** This company leads mule rides on the easier trails of the North Rim. A one-hour ride (minimum age 7) runs $30. Half-day trips on the rim or into the canyon (minimum age 10) cost $65; full-day trips (minimum age 12) go for $125. Weight limits vary from 200 to 220 pounds. Available daily from May 15 to October 15, these excursions are popular, so make reservations in advance. ☎ *435/679–8665* ⊕ *www.canyonrides.com.*

## Educational Offerings

**Interpretive Ranger Programs.** Daily guided hikes and talks may focus on any aspect of the canyon—from geology and flora and fauna to history and the canyon's early inhabitants. For schedules, go to the Grand Canyon Lodge or pick up a free copy of *The Guide* to the North Rim. ☎ *928/638–7888* ⊕ *www.nps.gov/grca.*

# WHAT'S NEARBY

The northwest section of Arizona is geographically fascinating. In addition to the Grand Canyon, it's home to national forests, national monuments, and national recreation areas. Towns, however, are small and scattered. Many of them cater to visiting adventurers, and Native American reservations dot the map.

## Nearby Towns & Attractions

**17**

### Nearby Towns

Towns near the canyon's South Rim include the park's gateway, Tusayan, 3 mi south; Williams, 58 mi south; and Flagstaff, 80 mi southeast. Tuba City is about 50 mi from the canyon's east entrance.

**Tusayan** has the basic amenities and an airport that serves as a starting point for airplane and helicopter tours of the canyon. The cozy mountain town of **Williams**, founded in 1882 when the railroad passed through, was once a rough-and-tumble joint, replete with saloons and bordellos. Today it reflects a much milder side of the Wild West, with 3,000 residents and 1,512 motel rooms. Wander along main street—part of historic Route 66, but locally named, like the town, after trapper Bill Williams—and indulge in Route 66 nostalgia inside antiques shops or souvenir and T-shirt stores. Though few travelers slow down long enough to actually explore **Flagstaff** (known as "Flag" by its 54,000 locals), they use it a base for day trips to the Native American ruins and the Navajo and Hopi reservations, as well as Petrified Forest National Park and the Painted Desert, or as a stopping point en route to the Grand Canyon. It has many fast-food outlets, but its highlight is the historic downtown district, with late Victorian, Tudor Revival, and early art-deco architecture, and historic Route 66 running right through its core. **Tuba City,** headquarters of the western portion of the Navajo Reservation, sits in the fairly isolated but beautiful Painted Desert and offers some dining and lodging options.

The communities closest to the North Rim include Fredonia, 76 mi north; Marble Canyon, 80 mi northeast; Lees Ferry, 85 mi east; and Jacob Lake, 45 mi north.

## FESTIVALS & EVENTS

**MAY Williams Rendezvous Days.** A black-powder shooting competition, 1800s-era crafts, and a parade fire up Memorial Day weekend in honor of Bill Williams, the town's namesake mountain man. ☎ 928/635-4061 ⊕ www.williamschamber.com.

**JULY Navajo Festival of Arts and Culture.** Navajo artists demonstrate jewelry-making, painting, beading, weaving, and pottery-making techniques, do traditional dances, and provide storytelling. ✉ Flagstaff ☎ 928/774-5213 ⊕ www.musnaz.org.

**SEPT. Grand Canyon Music Festival.** Three weekends of mostly chamber music fills the Shrine of Ages at Grand Canyon Village. ☎ 928/638-9215 or 800/997-8285 ⊕ grandcanyonmusicfest.org.

**NOV.-JAN. Holiday Lights Festival.** Starting with a post-Thanksgiving lighting ceremony, more than 1 million lights glow nightly through January at Flagstaff's Little America Hotel. ☎ 928/779-7979 ⊕ www.littleamerica.com/flagstaff.

**DEC. Mountain Village Holiday.** Williams hails the holidays with a parade of lights, an ice-skating rink, Polar Express train rides, and live entertainment. ☎ 928/635-4061 ⊕ www.williamschamber.com.

**Fredonia,** a small community of about 1,200, approximately an hour's drive north of the Grand Canyon, is often referred to as the gateway to the North Rim; it's also relatively close to Zion and Bryce Canyon national parks. **Marble Canyon,** to the north of Tuba City, marks the geographical beginning of the Grand Canyon at its northeastern tip. It's a good stopping point if you are driving U.S. 89 to the North Rim. En route from the South Rim to the North Rim is **Lees Ferry,** where most of the area's river rafts start their journey. The tiny town of **Jacob Lake,** nestled high in pine country at an elevation of 7,925 feet, was named after Mormon explorer Jacob Hamblin, also known as the "Buckskin Missionary." It has a hotel, café, campground, and lush mountain countryside.

### Nearby Attractions

**Planes of Fame Museum.** A good stop 30 mi north of Williams, at the junction of U.S. 180 and Highway 64 in Valle, this satellite of the Air Museum Planes of Fame in Chino, California, chronicles the history of aviation with an array of historic and modern aircraft. One of the featured pieces is a C-121A Constellation "Bataan," the personal aircraft of General MacArthur used during the Korean War. Visitors are not allowed inside the cockpits. ✉ 755 Mustang Way, Valle ☎ 928/635-1000 ⊕ www.planesoffame.org 🎟 $5.95 ☉ Daily 9–5.

★ **Vermilion Cliffs.** West from the town of Marble Canyon are these spectacular cliffs, more than 3,000 feet high in many places. Keep an eye out for condors; the giant endangered birds were reintroduced into the area in the winter of 1996–97. Reports suggest that the birds, once in captivity, are surviving well in the wilderness.

## Scenic Drives & Vistas

**U.S. 89.** The route north from Cameron Trading Post (Cameron, Ariz.) on U.S. 89 offers a stunning view of the **Painted Desert** to the right. The desert, which covers thousands of square miles stretching to the south and east, is a vision of subtle, almost harsh beauty, with windswept plains and mesas, isolated buttes, and barren valleys in pastel patterns. About 30 mi north of Cameron Trading Post, the Painted Desert country gives way to sandstone cliffs that run for miles. Brilliantly hued and ranging in color from light pink to deep orange, the **Echo Cliffs** rise to more than 1,000 feet in many places. They are essentially devoid of vegetation, but in a few high places, thick patches of tall cottonwood and poplar trees, nurtured by springs and water seepage from the rock escarpment, manage to thrive.

**U.S. 89A.** At Bitter Springs, Ariz., 60 mi north of Cameron, U.S. 89A branches off from U.S. 89, running north and providing views of **Marble Canyon,** the geographical beginning of the Grand Canyon. Like the Grand Canyon, Marble Canyon was formed by the Colorado River. Traversing a gorge nearly 500 feet deep is **Navajo Bridge,** a narrow steel span built in 1929 and listed on the National Register of Historic Places. Formerly used for car traffic, it now functions only as a pedestrian overpass.

## Area Activities

### Sports & the Outdoors

AIR TOURS   At **National Geographic Visitor Center Grand Canyon** (✉ Hwy. 64/U.S. 180, 2 mi south of the Grand Canyon's south entrance, Tusayan ☎ 928/638–2203 or 928/638–2468 ⊕ www.explorethecanyon.com ☽ Mar.–Oct., daily 8:30–8:30; Nov.–Feb., daily 10:30–6:30) you can schedule and purchase tickets for air tours and daily Colorado River trips; buy a national park pass, and access the park via special entry lanes.

BICYCLING   Pedal the depths of the Kaibab National Forest on the **Tusayan Bike Trail** (✉ Tusayan Ranger District, Tusayan ☎ 928/638–2443). Following linked loop trails at an elevation of 6,750 feet, you can bike as few as 3 mi or as many as 32 mi round-trip along old logging roads through ponderosa pine forest. Keep an eye out for elk, mule deer, hawks, eagles, pronghorn antelope, turkeys, coyote, and porcupines. Open for biking year-round (but most feasible from March through October), the trail is accessed on the west side of Highway 64, a half-mile north of Tusayan.

Cyclists also can enjoy the scenery along abandoned sections of Route 66 on the **Historic Route 66 Mountain Bike Tour.** Maps of the tour, which include the 6-mi **Ash Fork Hill Trail** and the 5-mi **Devil Dog Trail,** are available at the Williams Visitor Center.

FISHING   Fish for trout, crappie, catfish, and smallmouth bass at a number of lakes surrounding Williams. To fish on public land, anglers ages 14 and older are required to obtain a fishing license from the **Arizona Game and Fish Department** (⌂ 3500 S. Lake Mary Rd., Flagstaff 86001 ☎ 928/774–5045 ⊕ www.gf.state.az.us).

17

CLOSE UP

## Rafting Basics

SO YOU'RE READY TO TACKLE the churning white water of the Colorado River as it rumbles and hisses its way through the Grand Canyon? Well, you're in good company: The crafty, one-armed Civil War veteran John Wesley Powell first charted these dangerous rapids during the summer of 1869. It wasn't until 1938, though, that the first commercial river trip made its way down this fearsome corridor. Running the river has come a long way since then—and since Norman Neville made the first trip by kayak, in 1941, in a craft he built out of scrap lumber salvaged from an outhouse and a run-down barn.

White-water rafting still offers all the excitement of those early days—without all the danger and discomfort. Professional river runners lead journeys ranging from relaxing half-day float trips to adventurous 18-day oar excursions. Life jackets, beverages, tents, sheets, tarps, sleeping bags, wet bags, first aid, and food are provided—but you'll still need to plan ahead by packing clothing, hats, sunscreen, toiletries, and other sundries. Keep in mind that seats fill up fast due to the restricted number of visitors allowed on the river each season by the National Park Service. But once you've secured your seat, all that's left to do is pack your bags and get geared up for an experience of a lifetime. Lots of people book trips for summer's peak period: June through August. If you're flexible, take advantage of the Arizona weather; May to early June and September are ideal rafting times in the Grand Canyon.

The stretch of ice-cold, crystal-clear water at Lees Ferry off the North Rim provides arguably the best trout fishing in the Southwest. Many rafters and anglers stay the night in a campground near the river or in nearby Marble Canyon before hitting the river at dawn. Marble Canyon Lodge (☎ 928/355–2225) sells Arizona fishing licenses, as does **Lees Ferry Anglers** (✉ Milepost 547, N. U.S. 89A, Marble Canyon ☎ 928/355–2261, 800/962–9755 outside Arizona ⊕ www.leesferry.com), which also operates guided trips, starting from $300 per person per day.

RAFTING   **Arizona Raft Adventures** (✉ 4050 E. Huntington Rd., Flagstaff ☎ 928/526–8200 or 800/786–7238 ⊕ www.azraft.com) organizes 6- to 16-day paddle and/or motor trips for all skill levels. Trips, which run $1,600 to $3,450, depart from April through October.

With a reputation for high quality and a roster of 3- to 14-day trips, **Canyoneers** (✉ Box 2997, Flagstaff 86003 ☎ 928/526–0924 or 800/525–0924 ⊕ www.canyoneers.com) is popular with those who want to do some hiking as well. The five-day "Best of the Grand" trip includes a hike down to Phantom Ranch. Three- to 14-day trips, available April through September, cost between $925 and $3,150.

You can count on **Grand Canyon Expeditions** (✉ Box O, Kanab, UT 84741 ☎ 435/644–2691 or 800/544–2691 ⊕ www.gcex.com) to take you down the Colorado River safely and in style: they limit the number of people on each boat to 14, and evening meals might include filet mignon, pork chops, or shrimp. The April through mid-September trips cost $2,145 to $3,500 for 8 to 16 days.

### Educational Offerings

PROGRAMS & **Grand Canyon West** (☎ 702/878–9378 or 877/716–9378 ⊕ www. TOURS destinationgrandcanyon.com) offers packages starting at $30. Huala-pai guides will take you to attractions including Eagle Point, where the Indian Village walking tour visits authentic dwellings of the Hualapai, Havasupai, Navajo, Plains and Hopi; Hualapai Ranch, site of Western performances, cookouts, and horseback and wagon rides; and Guano Point, where the "High Point Hike" offers panoramic views of the Colorado River. Park-and-ride services are available from Dolan Springs for a nominal fee; reservations are required.

### Arts & Entertainment

At the **National Geographic Visitor Center Grand Canyon** in Tusayan, dis-cover the canyon's natural history in the 35-minute film *Grand Canyon: The Hidden Secrets,* on an IMAX screen that stands seven stories high. ⊠ *Hwy. 64/U.S. 180, 2 mi south of the south entrance, Tusayan* ☎ *928/ 638–2203 or 928/638–2468* ⊕ *www.explorethecanyon.com* ✉ *$10.65 for adults, $7.46 for children (tickets purchased online cost $7.99 for adults, $5.59 for kids)* ☉ *Mar.–Oct., daily 8:30–8:30; Nov.–Feb., daily 10:30–6:30; shows every hr on the ½ hr.*

# WHERE TO STAY & EAT

### About the Restaurants

Inside the park, you can find everything from cafeteria food to casual café fare to elegant evening specials. There's even a coffeehouse brew-ing organic joe. Reservations are accepted (and recommended) only at El Tovar Dining Room; they can be made 6 months in advance with El Tovar room reservations, 30 days in advance without. The dress code is casual across the board, but El Tovar is your best option if you're look-ing to dress up a bit and thumb through an extensive wine list. On the North Rim there is just one restaurant. Drinking water and restrooms are not available at most picnic spots. Options outside the park range from fast food to nice sit-down restaurants. Near the park, even the prici-est places allow casual dress.

### About the Hotels

The park's accommodations include three "historic rustic" facilities and four motel-style lodges. Of the 922 rooms, cabins, and suites, only 203, all at the Grand Canyon Lodge, are located at the North Rim. Out-side of El Tovar Hotel, the canyon's architectural crown jewel, frills are hard to find. Rooms are basic but comfortable, and most guests would agree that the best in-room amenity is a view of the canyon. Though rates vary widely, most rooms fall in the $125 to $136 range.

Reservations are a must, especially during the busy summer season. If you want to get your first choice (especially Bright Angel Lodge or El Tovar), make reservations as far in advance as possible; they're taken

17

up to 13 months ahead. You might find a last-minute cancellation, but you shouldn't count on it. Although lodging at the South Rim will keep you close to the action, the frenetic activity and crowded facilities are off-putting to some. With short notice, the best time to find a room on the South Rim is during winter. And though the North Rim is less crowded than the South Rim, lodging (remember that rooms are limited) is available only from mid-May through mid-October.

Outside the park, Tusayan's hotels offer a convenient location but no bargains, while Williams and Flagstaff can provide price breaks on food and lodging, as well as a respite from the crowds. Extra amenities (e.g. swimming pools and Internet access) are also more abundant. Reservations are always a good idea.

### About the Campgrounds

Inside the park, camping is permitted only in designated campsites. Some campgrounds charge nightly camping fees in addition to entrance fees, and some accept reservations up to five months in advance. Others are first come, first served. The South Rim has three campgrounds, one with RV hookups. The North Rim's single in-park campground does not offer hookups. All four campgrounds are near the rims and easily accessible. In-park camping in a spot other than a developed rim campground requires a permit from the Backcountry Information Center, which also serves as your reservation. Permits can be requested by mail or fax; applying well in advance is recommended. Call 928/638–7875 for information. Numerous backcountry campsites dot the canyon—be prepared for a considerable hike. The three established backcountry campgrounds require a trek of 4⁴⁄₁₀ to 16⁶⁄₁₀ mi.

Outside the park, two campgrounds, one with hookups, are located within 7 mi of the South Rim, and two are within about 45 mi of the North Rim. At the time of this writing one is closed for renovations; the other has hookups and accepts reservations. Developed and undeveloped campsites are available, first come, first served, in the Kaibab National Forest.

## Where to Eat

### In the Park: South Rim

**$–$$$** ✕ **Arizona Room.** The canyon views from this casual Southwestern-style steak house are the best of any restaurant at the South Rim. The menu includes chicken, steak (there's good prime rib), and seafood (including salmon), as well as vegetarian options. It's open for lunch from 11:30–3 and for dinner starting at 4:30; seating is first come, first served, so arrive early to avoid the crowds. ⊠ *Bright Angel Lodge, West Rim Dr., Grand Canyon Village* ☎ *928/638–2961* ⌂ *Reservations not accepted.* *$12–$22* ⊟ *AE, D, DC, MC, V* ⊘ *Closed Jan.–mid-Feb.*

**$–$$$** ✕ **El Tovar Dining Room.** Modeled after a European hunting lodge, this
**Fodor'sChoice** rustic 19th-century dining room built of hand-hewn logs is worth a visit.
★ Breakfast, lunch, and dinner are served beneath the beamed ceiling. The cuisine is modern Southwestern, and the menu includes such dishes as sautéed rainbow trout served with a wild rice salad and grilled New York strip steak with buttermilk-cornmeal onion rings and pepper jack au gratin

potatoes. You can even order blackened trout for breakfast. It's the best restaurant for miles. ⊠ *El Tovar Hotel, West Rim Dr., Grand Canyon Village* ☎ *303/297–2757 or 888/297–2757 (reservations only), 928/638–2961* ⋏ *Reservations essential. $11–$26* ⊟ *AE, D, DC, MC, V.*

¢–$  ⋈ **Bright Angel Restaurant and Fountain.** The specialty here is casual, affordable dining. No-surprises dishes can fill your belly at breakfast, lunch, or dinner. ⊠ *Bright Angel Lodge, Grand Canyon Village* ☎ *928/638–2961* ⋏ *Reservations not accepted. $5–$10* ⊟ *AE, D, DC, MC, V.*

¢–$  ⋈ **Canyon Cafe at Yavapai Lodge.** Stop at this refueling spot after a day of touring or to get a bite before heading out for some sightseeing. ⊠ *Yavapai Lodge, Grand Canyon Village* ☎ *928/638–2961* ⋏ *Reservations not accepted. $5–$8* ⊟ *AE, D, DC, MC, V.*

¢–$  ⋈ **Maswik Cafeteria.** You can pick up a burger or affordable Mexican fare at this food court. ⊠ *Maswik Lodge, Grand Canyon Village* ☎ *928/638–2961* ⋏ *Reservations not accepted. $5–$8* ⊟ *AE, D, DC, MC, V.*

¢  ⋈ **Yavapai Canyon Café.** Fast-food favorites here include pastries, burgers, and pizza. Open for breakfast, lunch, and dinner, the cafeteria also serves specials, chicken potpie, fried catfish, and fried chicken. ⊠ *Grand Canyon Village* ☎ *928/638–2961* ⋏ *Reservations not accepted. $4–$7* ⊟ *AE, D, DC, MC, V* ☉ *Closed mid-Dec.–Feb.*

PICNIC AREAS  **Buggeln.** This secluded, shady area is wheelchair accessible, with assistance. ⊠ *15 mi east of Grand Canyon Village on Desert View Dr.*

**South Kaibab Trailhead.** This picnic area is the closest to the park's hub; it is often filled with hikers' cars. ⊠ *On Desert View Dr., 1 mi east of Grand Canyon Village.*

### In the Park: North Rim

★ $–$$$  ⋈ **Grand Canyon Lodge Dining Room.** The historic lodge houses a huge, high-ceiling dining room with spectacular views and very good food; you might find pork medallions, red snapper, and spinach linguine with red clam sauce on the dinner menu. ⊠ *Grand Canyon Lodge, Bright Angel Point (North Rim)* ☎ *928/638–2611* ⋏ *Reservations essential. $12–$28* ⊟ *AE, D, DC, MC, V* ☉ *Closed mid-Oct.–mid-May.*

PICNIC AREAS  **Cape Royal.** This is the most popular designated picnic area on the
★  North Rim because of its panoramic views. ⊠ *23 mi south of North Rim Visitor Center.*

**Point Imperial.** If you're looking for privacy, head here, where the shade shelters you. ⊠ *11 mi northeast of the North Rim Visitor Center.*

### Outside the Park

★ $$$–$$$$  ⋈ **Cottage Place.** This small, intimate restaurant in a 1901 cottage is known for traditional dishes such as chateaubriand, charbroiled lamb chops, and rack of lamb, plus an extensive wine list. ⊠ *126 W. Cottage Ave., Flagstaff* ☎ *928/774–8431. $21–$38* ⊟ *AE, MC, V* ☉ *Closed Mon. No lunch.*

♨  ⋈ **Canyon Star Restaurant and Saloon.** Relax in the rustic dining room
★ $$–$$$  at the Grand Hotel for breakfast, lunch, or dinner. The dinner menu includes prime rib, bison, and salmon. Every evening there's entertainment: live music, karaoke, or Native American dance performances—all great

17

for families. There's even a kids' menu. In the summer, be sure to reserve a table. ⊠ *Hwy. 64/U.S. 180, Tusayan* ☎ *928/638–3333. $18–$28* ⊟ *AE, DC, MC, V.*

**$$–$$$** ✕ **The Coronado Room.** When pizza and burgers just won't do, the restaurant at the Best Western Grand Canyon Squire Inn is the best upscale choice in Tusayan. The menu encompasses everything from escargot to elk steak. Even though the Coronado Room takes pride in its fine-dining atmosphere, dress is casual and comfortable. Reservations are a good idea, particularly in the busy season. ⊠ *Hwy. 64/U.S. 180, Tusayan* ☎ *928/638–2681. $17–$25* ⊟ *AE, D, DC, MC, V* ☉ *No lunch.*

★ **$–$$** ✕ **Pancho McGillicuddy's.** Established in 1893 as the Cabinet Saloon, this restaurant is on the National Register of Historic Places. Gone are the spittoons and pipes—the smoke-free dining area now has Mexican-inspired decor and such specialties as "armadillo eggs," the local name for deep-fried jalapeños stuffed with cheese. Other favorites include fish tacos, buzzard wings—better known as hot wings—and *pollo verde* (chicken breasts smothered in a sauce of cheese, sour cream, and green chilies). On the smoking side of the restaurant, the bar has TVs tuned to sporting events and pours more than 30 tequilas. ⊠ *141 Railroad Ave., Williams* ☎ *928/635–4150. $8–$15* ⊟ *AE, D, MC, V.*

**¢–$$** ✕ **Café Tusayan.** Homemade pies and local microbrews from Sedona, Flagstaff, and Tucson brighten the menu of standard fare—omelets, salads, burgers, salmon, and prime rib—at this basic restaurant. ⊠ *Hwy. 64/U.S. 180, Tusayan* ☎ *928/638–2151. $6–$20* ⊟ *MC, V.*

☾ **¢–$$** ✕ **Cruisers Café 66.** Talk about nostalgia. Imagine your favorite 1950s-

FodorsChoice style, high school hangout—with cocktail service. Good burgers, salads,

★ and malts are family-priced, but a choice steak is available, too, for $30. Stuffed buffalo, a large mural of the town's heyday along the "Mother Road," and historic cars out front make this a Route 66 favorite. Kids especially enjoy the relaxed atmosphere and jukebox tunes. ⊠ *233 W. Rte. 66, Williams* ☎ *928/635–2445. $7–$13* ⊟ *AE, DC, MC, V.*

**¢–$** ✕ **Café Espress.** This lively natural foods restaurant offers a predominately vegetarian menu. It's known for tempeh burgers, pita pizzas, and salads, but there are usually daily chicken and fish specials. Breakfast is also available. ⊠ *16 N. San Francisco St., Flagstaff* ☎ *928/774–0541. $6–$9* ⊟ *AE, MC, V.*

**¢** ✕ **Grand Canyon Coffee Café.** You'll find good espresso drinks here, along with English-style fish-and-chips, and wonderful sandwiches on homemade focaccia. The mountain man sandwich is piled high with roast beef, cheddar, and onions. On display are a few Harley-Davidson artifacts, some for sale. ⊠ *125 W. Rte. 66, Williams* ☎ *928/635–1255. $2–$6* ⊟ *AE, MC, V* ☉ *Closed Jan. and Feb.*

**¢** ✕ **Twisters.** Kick up some Route 66 nostalgia at this old-fashioned soda fountain and gift shop. Dine on hamburgers and hot dogs, a famous Twisters sundae, Route 66 Beer Float, or cherry phosphate—all to the sounds of 1950s tunes. The adjoining gift shop is a blast from the past, with Route 66 merchandise, classic Coca-Cola memorabilia, and fanciful items celebrating the careers of such characters as Betty Boop, James Dean, Elvis, and Marilyn Monroe. ⊠ *417 E. Rte. 66, Williams* ☎ *928/635–0266* ⊕ *www.route66place.com. $3–$5* ⊟ *AE, D, MC, V.*

## Where to Stay

### In the Park: South Rim

**$$–$$$$**
Fodor'sChoice
★

**El Tovar Hotel.** A registered National Historic Landmark, El Tovar was built in 1905 of Oregon pine logs and native stone. The hotel's proximity to all of the canyon's facilities, its European hunting-lodge atmosphere, and its renowned dining room make it the best place to stay on the South Rim. It's usually booked well in advance (up to 13 months ahead), though it's easier to get a room during winter months. Three suites and several rooms have canyon views (these are booked early), but you can enjoy the view anytime from the cocktail-lounge back porch. ⊠ *West Rim Dr., Grand Canyon Village* ☎ *Box 699, Grand Canyon 86023* ☏ *303/297–2757 or 888/297–2757 (reservations only), 928/638–2961* 🖷 *303/297–3175 (reservations only)* ⊕ *www.grandcanyonlodges.com* ⇱ *70 rooms, 12 suites* ♨ *Restaurant, room service, refrigerator, bar. $134–$304* ⊟ *AE, D, DC, MC, V.*

**$$**
**Kachina Lodge.** Located on the rim halfway between El Tovar and Bright Angel Lodge, this motel-style lodge has many rooms with partial canyon views ($10 extra). Although lacking the historical charm of the neighboring lodges, these rooms are a good bet for families and are within easy walking distance of dining facilities at El Tovar and Bright Angel Lodge. There are also several rooms for people with physical disabilities. There's no air-conditioning, but evaporative coolers keep the heat at bay. Check in at El Tovar Hotel to the east. ⊠ *West Rim Dr., Grand Canyon Village* ☎ *Box 699, Grand Canyon 86023* ☏ *303/297–2757 or 888/297–2757 (reservations only), 928/638–2961* 🖷 *303/297–3175 (reservations only)* ⊕ *www.grandcanyonlodges.com* ⇱ *50 rooms* ♨ *Refrigerator, ethernet, safe, no-smoking rooms. $125–$136* ⊟ *AE, D, DC, MC, V.*

**$$**
**Thunderbird Lodge.** This motel with comfortable, no-nonsense rooms is next to Bright Angel Lodge in Grand Canyon Village. For $10 more, you can get a room with a partial view of the canyon. Rooms have either two queen beds or one king. Check in at Bright Angel Lodge, the next hotel to the west. Some rooms do not have air-conditioning, but instead have evaporative coolers. ⊠ *West Rim Dr., Grand Canyon Village* ☎ *Box 699, Grand Canyon 86023* ☏ *303/297–2757 or 888/297–2757 (reservations only), 928/638–2961* 🖷 *303/297–3175 (reservations only)* ⊕ *www.grandcanyonlodges.com* ⇱ *55 rooms* ♨ *Refrigerator, safe, no-smoking rooms, no a/c (some). $125–$136* ⊟ *AE, D, DC, MC, V.*

**☾ $–$$**
**Bright Angel Lodge.** Famed architect Mary Jane Colter designed this 1935 log-and-stone structure, which sits within a few yards of the canyon rim and blends superbly with the canyon walls. It offers a similar location to El Tovar for about half the price. Accommodations are in motel-style rooms or cabins. Lodge rooms don't have TVs, and some rooms do not have private bathrooms. Scattered among the pines, 50 cabins, some with fireplaces, have TVs and private baths. Expect historic charm but not luxury. The Bright Angel Dining Room serves family-style meals all day and a Warm Apple Grunt dessert large enough to share. The Arizona Room serves dinner only. Adding to the experience are an ice-cream parlor, gift shop, a small history museum with exhibits on Fred Harvey and Mary Jane Colter, an Internet room, and a coffee

**17**

shop. ✉ *West Rim Dr., Grand Canyon Village* ⌖ *Box 699, Grand Canyon 86023* ☎ *303/297–2757, 888/297–2757 (reservations only), 928/638–2961* 🖷 *303/297–3175 (reservations only)* ⊕ *www. grandcanyonlodges.com* ⟿ *39 rooms, 6 with shared toilet and shower, 13 with shared shower; 50 cabins* ♿ *Restaurant, bar, no a/c, no TV (some). $68–$134* ⊟ *AE, D, DC, MC, V.*

☉ **$–$$**   🏨 **Maswik Lodge.** The lodge, named for a Hopi Kachina who is said to guard the canyon, is ¼ mi from the rim. Accommodations, nestled in the ponderosa pine forest, range from rustic cabins to more modern rooms, refurbished in 2006. The cabins are the cheapest option but are available only spring through fall. Some rooms have air-conditioning, and the rest have ceiling fans. Maswik Cafeteria offers sandwiches, salads, snack foods, and a choice of several hot meals. Teenagers like the lounge, where they can shoot pool, throw darts, or watch the big-screen TV. There is also an Internet room. Kids under 16 stay free. ✉ *Grand Canyon Village* ⌖ *Box 699, Grand Canyon 86023* ☎ *303/297–2757 or 888/297–2757 (reservations only), 928/638–2961* 🖷 *303/297–3175 (reservations only)* ⊕ *www.grandcanyonlodges.com* ⟿ *250 rooms, 28 cabins* ♿ *Restaurant, bar, no-smoking rooms, no a/c (some). $78–$124* ⊟ *AE, D, DC, MC, V.*

**$–$$**   🏨 **Yavapai Lodge.** The largest motel-style lodge in the park is tucked in a pinyon and juniper forest at the eastern end of Grand Canyon Village, near the RV park. The basic rooms are near the park's general store, the visitor center (½ mi), and the rim (¼ mi). The cafeteria, open for breakfast, lunch, and dinner, serves standard park service food. An Internet room is available to guests. ✉ *Grand Canyon Village* ⌖ *Box 699, Grand Canyon 86023* ☎ *303/297–2757 or 888/297–2757 (reservations only), 928/638–2961* 🖷 *303/297–3175 (reservations only)* ⊕ *www. grandcanyonlodges.com* ⟿ *358 rooms* ♿ *Restaurant, refrigerator, no-smoking rooms. $96–$113* ⊟ *AE, D, DC, MC, V* ☉ *Closed Jan. and Feb.*

**¢–$**   🏨 **Phantom Ranch.** In a grove of cottonwood trees on the canyon floor, Phantom Ranch is accessible only to hikers and mule trekkers. The wood-and-stone buildings originally made up a hunting camp built in 1922. There are 40 dormitory beds and 14 beds in cabins, all with shared baths. Seven additional cabins are reserved for mule riders, who buy their trips as a package. The mess hall-style restaurant, one of the most remote eating establishments in the United States, serves family-style meals, with breakfast, dinner, and box lunches available. Reservations, taken up to 13 months in advance, are a must. ✉ *On canyon floor, at intersection of the Bright Angel and Kaibab trails* ☎ *303/297–2757 or 888/297–2757* 🖷 *303/297–3175 (reservations only)* ⟿ *4 dormitories and 2 cabins for hikers, 7 cabins with outside showers for mule riders* ♿ *Restaurant, no a/c, no phone, no TV. $30–$81* ⊟ *AE, D, DC, MC, V.*

CAMPGROUNDS &   △ **Mather Campground.** Mather has RV and tent sites but no hookups.
RV PARKS   No reservations are accepted from December to March, but the rest of
**$$**   the year, especially during the busy spring and summer seasons, they are
Fodor'sChoice   a good idea, and can be made up to five months in advance. Ask at the
★   campground entrance for same-day availability. ✉ *Off Village Loop Dr., Grand Canyon Village* ⌖ *National Park Reservation Service* ☎ *800/*

365–2267 ⊕ *reservations.nps.gov/index.cfm* ⊅ *308 sites for RVs and tents* ↺ *Flush toilets, public telephone, drinking water, guest laundry, showers, fire grates, picnic tables, dump station* ⊘ *Open year-round. $18; Senior and Access park pass holders pay half price.*

**$$** ⌂ **Trailer Village.** This campground in Grand Canyon Village has RV sites—but no tent-camping sites—with full hookups and bathroom facilities, though the bathrooms are ½ mi from the campground. The fee is good for two people, with an extra $2 fee for each additional person over age 16. The facility is very busy during spring and summer, so make reservations ahead of time (not accepted December through March). The dump station is closed in winter. ⊠ *Off Village Loop Dr., Grand Canyon Village* ☎ *303/297–2757, 888/297–2757 reservations only* 🖷 *303/ 297–3175 (reservations only)* ⊕ *www.xanterra.com* ⊅ *79 RV sites* ↺ *Flush toilets, full hookups, dump station, drinking water, guest laundry, showers, fire grates* ⊘ *Open year-round. $24.*

**$** ⌂ **Desert View Campground.** Popular for spectacular views of the canyon from the nearby Watchtower, this campground fills up fast in summer. Fifty RV (without hookups) and tent sites are available on a first-come, first-served basis. ⊠ *Desert View Dr., 23 mi east of Grand Canyon Village off Hwy. 64* ⌁ *Backcountry Office, Box 129, Grand Canyon 86023* ☎ *928/638–7875* 🖷 *928/638–2125* ⊅ *50 campsites* ↺ *Grills, flush toilets, drinking water, picnic tables* ⌂ *Reservations not accepted* ⊘ *Mid-May–mid-Oct. $12.*

**¢** ⌂ **Bright Angel Campground.** This campground is near Phantom Ranch on the South and North Kaibab trails, at the bottom of the canyon. There are toilet facilities and running water, but no showers. A backcountry permit, which serves as your reservation, is required to stay here. ⊠ *Intersection of South and North Kaibab trails, Grand Canyon* ⌁ *Backcountry Office, Box 129, Grand Canyon 86023* ☎ *928/638–7875* 🖷 *928/638–2125* ⊅ *32 tent sites* ↺ *Flush toilets, drinking water, picnic tables* ⌂ *Backcountry permit required* ⊘ *Open year-round. Free with backcountry permit (which costs $10, plus $5 per person per day).*

**¢** ⌂ **Cottonwood Campground.** This is the last canyon camp before you ascend to the North Rim. A backcountry permit, which serves as your reservation, is required to stay here. ⊠ *On the North Kaibab Trail, 16⁷⁄₁₀ mi from the South Rim Bright Angel trailhead and 7 mi below the North Rim, Grand Canyon* ⌁ *Backcountry Office, Box 129, Grand Canyon 86023* ☎ *928/638–7875* 🖷 *928/638–2125* ⊅ *11 tent sites* ↺ *Vault toilets, drinking water (mid-May–mid-Oct.)* ⌂ *Backcountry permit required* ⊘ *Open year-round; ranger station closed Nov. to Apr. Free with backcountry permit (which costs $10, plus $5 per person per day).*

**¢** ⌂ **Indian Garden.** Halfway down the canyon is this campground, en route to Phantom Ranch on the Bright Angel Trail. Running water and toilet facilities are available, but not showers. A backcountry permit, which serves as a reservation, is required. ⊠ *Bright Angel Trail, Grand Canyon* ⌁ *Backcountry Office, Box 129, Grand Canyon 86023* ☎ *928/638– 7875* 🖷 *928/638–2125* ⊅ *15 tent sites* ↺ *Vault toilets, drinking water, picnic tables* ⌂ *Reservations essential* ⊘ *Open year-round. Free with backcountry permit (which costs $10, plus $5 per person per day).*

**17**

## Inside the Park: North Rim

**$–$$**

**Fodor'sChoice**

★

🏨 **Grand Canyon Lodge.** This historic property, constructed mainly in the 1920s and '30s, is the premier lodging facility in the North Rim area. The main building has limestone walls and timbered ceilings. Lodging options include small, rustic cabins; larger cabins (some with a canyon view and some with two bedrooms); and newer, traditional motel rooms. You might find marinated pork kebabs or linguine with cilantro on the dining room's dinner menu ($–$$$). Dining room reservations are essential and should be made as far in advance as possible. ⊠ *Hwy. 67, North Rim, Grand Canyon National Park 86052* 🕾 *303/297–2757 or 888/297–2757(reservations only), 928/638–2611* 🖶 *303/297–3175 (reservations only)* ⊕ *www.grandcanyonnorthrim.com* 🛏 *44 rooms, 157 cabins* ♿ *Restaurant, bar, laundry facilities, no a/c, no TV, no-smoking rooms. $91–$121* ▤ *AE, D, MC, V* ⊘ *Closed mid-Oct.–mid-May.*

CAMPGROUNDS &
RV PARKS
**$$**

⚠️ **North Rim Campground.** The only designated campground at the North Rim of Grand Canyon National Park sits 3 mi north of the rim, and has 83 RV and tent sites (no hookups). You can reserve a site up to five months in advance. ⊠ *Hwy. 67, Grand Canyon* 🕾 *800/365-2267* ⊕ *reservations.nps.gov* 🛏 *83 campsites* ♿ *Flush toilets, dump station, drinking water, guest laundry, showers, fire grates, picnic tables, general store* ♿ *Reservations essential* ⊘ *Generally open mid-May–mid-Oct., possibly later, weather permitting. $18; Senior and Access park pass holders pay half price.*

## Outside the Park

**$–$$$**

**Fodor'sChoice**

★

✕🏨 **Cameron Trading Post.** Fifty-four miles north of Flagstaff, this trading post dates back to 1916. Southwestern-style rooms have carved-oak furniture, tile baths, and balconies overlooking the Colorado River. Native-stone landscaping—including fossilized dinosaur tracks—and a small, well-kept garden are pleasant. Make your reservations far in advance for high season. The dining room's delicious homemade green chili and fry bread, Navajo tacos, and hamburgers are worth the stop alone (¢–$$). Satellite TV is in the rooms. ⊠ *U.S. 89* ⌖ *Box 339, Cameron 86020* 🕾 *928/679–2231, 800/338–7385 Ext. 414 (for hotel)* 🖶 *928/ 679–2350* ⊕ *www.camerontradingpost.com* 🛏 *62 rooms, 4 suites* ♿ *Restaurant. $79–$179* ▤ *AE, D, DC, MC, V.*

**$–$$**

✕🏨 **Jacob Lake Inn.** The bustling lodge at Jacob Lake Inn is a popular stop for those heading to the North Rim; it has a grocery store, coffee shop, restaurant, and gift shop. Even if you don't stay here, stop for one of their famous malts or milk shakes (¢–$). The 5-acre complex in Kaibab National Forest has basic cabins and standard motel rooms that overlook the highways; 25 rooms added in 2006 have TVs, phones, and in-room broadband. ⊠ *Hwy. 67/U.S. 89A, Fredonia 86022* 🕾 *928/ 643–7232* ⊕ *www.jacoblake.com* 🛏 *14 rooms, 22 cabins* ♿ *Restaurant, no phone (some), no TV (some), Wi-Fi (some), Ethernet (some), no a/c (some). $75–$133* ▤ *AE, D, MC, V.*

☾
★ **$$–$$$$**

🏨 **Best Western Grand Canyon Squire Inn.** About 2 mi south of the park's south entrance, this motel lacks the historic charm of the older lodges at the canyon rim, but has more amenities, including a small cowboy museum in the lobby and an upscale gift shop. Children enjoy the bowling alley, arcade, and outdoor swimming pool. Rooms are spacious and furnished in Southwestern style. Those in the rear have a view of the woods. The Coronado Dining Room has an adventurous menu and good service. Wireless Internet service is available in the lobby, and all rooms have broadband. There also are billiards, bowling, and a video game room. ⊠ *100 Hwy. 64, Grand Canyon 86023* ☏ *928/638–2681 or 800/ 622–6966* 🖷 *928/638–2782* ⊕ *www.grandcanyonsquire.com* ⇆ *250 rooms, 4 suites* ⚥ *Restaurant, coffee shop, pool, gym, Ethernet, concierge, no-smoking rooms. $109–$225* ⊟ *AE, D, DC, MC, V.*

★ **$$$** 🖼 **The Grand Hotel.** At the south end of Tusayan, this popular hotel has bright, clean rooms decorated in Southwestern colors. The lobby has a stone-and-timber design, cozy seating areas, and Wi-Fi access. Good steaks, Mexican fare, and barbecue are on the restaurant's menu, and a Starbucks in the lobby is a bonus. At the bar, you can sit on a saddle that was once used for canyon mule trips. ⊠ *Hwy. 64/U.S. 180, Tusayan 86023* ☏ *928/638–3333* 🖷 *928/638–3131* ⊕ *www.grandcanyongrandhotel. com* ⇆ *119 rooms, 2 suites* ⚥ *Restaurant, public Wi-Fi, pool, gym, laundry facilities, bar, some pets allowed, no-smoking rooms. $169–$189* ⊟ *AE, D, DC, MC, V.*

★ **$$–$$$** 🖼 **Sheridan House Inn.** Nestled among two acres of pine trees near Route 66, this B&B has decks looking to the tall ponderosa pines and a flagstone patio with a hot tub. Average-size bedrooms all have king beds and marble bathrooms. The game room has puzzles, board games, and VCRs, and the entertainment room has a pool table and piano. Hearty breakfasts—scrambled eggs, fruit plates, bacon, sausage, potatoes, eggs Benedict and buttermilk pancakes—will ready you for the hour-long drive to the canyon. K. C. and Mary Seidner are gracious hosts who will gladly help guests plan itineraries. ⊠ *460 E. Sheridan Ave., Williams 86046* ☏ *928/635–9441 or 888/635–9345* ⇆ *6 rooms, 2 suites* ⚥ *VCR, Wi-Fi, no a/c. $145–$200* ⊟ *AE, D, MC, V* ⦿⦿ *BP.*

★ **$–$$$** 🖼 **Grand Canyon Railway Hotel and Resort.** This hotel was designed to resemble the train depot's original Fray Marcos lodge. Neoclassical Greek columns flank the grand entrance, which leads to a lobby with maple-wood balustrades, an enormous flagstone fireplace, and oil paintings of the Grand Canyon by local artist Kenneth McKenna. Original bronzes by Frederic Remington, from the private collection of hotel owners Max and Thelma Biegert, also adorn the lobby. The pleasant Southwestern-style accommodations have large bathrooms. Adjacent to the lobby is Spenser's, a pub with an ornate 19th-century hand-carved bar. ⊠ *235 N. Grand Canyon Blvd., Williams 86046* ☏ *928/635–4010 or 800/843–8724* ⊕ *www.thetrain.com* ⇆ *288 rooms, 10 suites* ⚥ *Pool, gym, bar, no-smoking rooms. $99–$189* ⊟ *AE, D, MC, V.*

**$$** 🖼 **Red Garter.** This restored saloon and bordello from 1897 now houses a small, antiques-filled B&B. Guest rooms are on the second floor; ask for the "Best Gal's Room," which has its own sitting room overlooking the train tracks. All four rooms (two are interior, with skylights) are very quiet, as the only train traffic is the Grand Canyon Railway. Even if you don't stay here, the fresh pastries served in the first-floor coffee shop are worth a stop. ⊠ *137 W. Railroad Ave., Williams 86046* ☏ *928/ 635–1484 or 800/328–1484* ⊕ *www.redgarter.com* ⇆ *4 rooms* ⚥ *Cof-*

**17**

*fee shop, Wi-Fi, ethernet, no kids under 8, no-smoking rooms. $120–$145* D, MC, V ☼ *Closed Dec.–mid-Feb.* ❑ *CP.*

◔ **$–$$** 🖼 **The Canyon Motel and Railroad RV Park.** Railcars, cabooses, and cottages make up this 13-acre property on the outskirts of Williams. The best room is the 1929 Santa Fe red caboose ($121): It's family-friendly, with two sides separated by a bathroom, giving parents a little privacy. The original wooden floor and tool equipment add to the authenticity. The other caboose looks much like a standard hotel room inside, as do the flagstone cottage rooms built from the local sandstone known for its variegated colors. A Pullman passenger car ($105) holds three rooms (railcar suites), each with its own bathroom. The motel also has a few dry campsites (no water available) and a 47-space RV park with full hookups, opened in 2006. Guests have access to hiking, horseshoes, and a playground. ✉ *1900 E. Rodeo Rd., Williams 86046* 🕾 *928/635–9371 or 800/482–3955* 🖶 *928/635–4138* ⊕ *www.thecanyonmotel.com* ↪ *18 rooms, 5 railcar suites* ♧ *Refrigerator, VCR (some), pool, no a/c (some), no phone. $74–$121* D, MC, V ❑ *CP.*

★ **$–$$** 🖼 **Marble Canyon Lodge.** This Arizona Strip lodge opened in 1929 on the same day the Navajo Bridge was dedicated. Three types of accommodations are available: rooms in the original building, standard motel rooms in the newer building, and two-bedroom apartments. You can play the 1920s piano or sit on the porch swing of the native-rock lodge and look out on Vermilion Cliffs and the desert. Zane Grey and Gary Cooper are among well-known past guests. The restaurant serves steaks, pasta, and sandwiches ($–$$$$). There is an airstrip here, too. ✉ *¼ mi west of Navajo Bridge on U.S. 89A* ⊅ *Box 6001, Marble Canyon 86036* 🕾 *928/355–2225 or 800/726–1789* 🖶 *928/355–2227* ↪ *46 rooms, 8 apartments* ♧ *Restaurant, some pets allowed. $65–$134* AE, D, MC, V.

CAMPING & RV  ⌂ **Grand Canyon Camper Village and RV Park.** More a city than a village,
PARKS  this popular RV park and campground has 200 utility hookups and 50
**$$–$$$**  tent sites. Reservations are a good idea during the busy spring and summer seasons. ✉ *Off Hwy. 64/U.S. 180, Tusayan* ⊅ *Box 490, Grand Canyon 86023* 🕾 *928/638–2887* ↪ *200 full hookups, 50 tent sites* ♧ *Flush toilets, full hookups, dump station, drinking water, showers, picnic tables, general store, play area. $22 for tents; hookups $39 for electric, $46 for water and electric, and $50 for full* ☼ *Open Mar.–Nov.*

**$** ⌂ **Cameron RV Park.** This park, open year-round, is adjacent to the Cameron Trading Post. There are 65 spaces with hookups for $15 a day. However, there are no public restrooms or showers. No reservations are accepted. ✉ *U.S. 89* ⊅ *Box 339, Cameron 86020* 🕾 *928/679–2231 or 800/338–7385* 🖶 *928/679–2350* ⊕ *www.camerontradingpost.com* ↪ *60 RV sites* ♧ *Full hookups, dump station, drinking water, food service, general store. $15.*

**$** ⌂ **Ten-X Campground.** Two miles south of Tusayan, this campground offers 70 sites with water and pit toilets but no electrical hookups or showers. Campsites are first come, first served, except for the two group sites—one accommodates 100 campers and the other 50—which require reservations. Unlike at the campgrounds in the park itself, campfires are allowed. Learn about the surrounding ponderosa pine forest on a self-guided nature trail or check out one of the evening ranger-led weekend programs. ⊠ *Kaibab National Forest, 9 mi south of the park, east of Hwy. 64/U.S. 180* ☎ *Tusayan Ranger District, Box 3088, Grand Canyon 86023* ☎ *928/638–2443* ⊕ *www.fs.fed.us/r3/kai* ⟲ *70 tent sites, 2 group sites* ⚲ *Grills, pit toilets, drinking water, fire pits, picnic tables* ⚲ *Reservations required for group sites only* ⚑ *$10* ⊘ *Open May–Sept.*

# GRAND CANYON ESSENTIALS

ACCESSIBILITY Rim Trail and all the viewpoints along the South Rim are accessible to wheelchairs. For detailed information, see *The Grand Canyon Accessibility Guide,* available free at Canyon View Information Plaza, Yavapai Information Station, Tusayan Museum, Desert View Information Center, and all entrance stations. There are free wheelchairs for use inside the park; inquire at one of the information centers. Temporary handicapped-parking permits are available at Canyon View Information Plaza, Yavapai Observation Center, and all entrance stations. Wheelchair-accessible tours are offered by prior arrangement through Grand Canyon National Park Lodges (☎ 888/297–2757). TDD phones are available as well.

ADMISSION FEES A fee of $25 per vehicle is collected at the east entrance near Cameron and at the south entrance near Tusayan; pedestrians and cyclists pay $12 per person. The fee pays for up to one week's access. The Grand Canyon Pass, available for $50, gives unlimited access to the park for 12 months from the purchase date.

ADMISSION HOURS The South Rim is open 24/7, year-round. The North Rim is open mid-May through mid-October, depending on the weather. Highway 67 from Jacob Lake is closed due to snowfall from around mid-October to mid-May, and during these times all facilities at the North Rim are closed. The entrance gates are open 24 hours, but are generally staffed from about 7 AM to 7 PM. If you arrive when there's no one at the gate, you may enter legally without paying. The park is in the Mountain time zone.

ATMS/BANKS There is an ATM at the South Rim office in Market Plaza near the General Store and at Maswik Lodge. Near the North Rim, there's an ATM at Jacob Lake Inn.

AUTOMOBILE SERVICE STATIONS
🚹 **Jacob Lake Inn** ⊠ Hwy. 67/U.S. 89A, Fredonia 86022 ☎ 928/643–7232 **Conoco Station** ⊠ Grand Canyon Village ☎ 928/638–2608.

EMERGENCIES In case of a fire or medical emergency, dial 911; from in-park lodgings, dial 9-911. To report a security problem, contact the Park Police (☎ 928/638–7805), stationed at all visitor centers. There are no pharmacies at the North or South Rim. Prescriptions can be delivered daily to the South Rim Clinic from Flagstaff. A health center is staffed by physicians from 8 AM–6 PM, seven days a week (reduced hours in winter). Emergency medical services are available 24 hours a day.
🚹 **North Country Community Health Center** ⊠ 1 Clinic Rd., Grand Canyon ☎ 928/638–2551.

LOST AND FOUND Report lost or stolen items or turn in found items at Canyon View Information Plaza or Yavapai Observation Station (928/638–7798). For items lost or found in hotels, restaurants or lounges, call 928/638–2631, Ext. 6503.

PERMITS Hikers descending into the canyon for an overnight stay need a backcountry permit ($10, plus $5 per person per night), which can be obtained in person, by mail, or faxed by request. Permits are limited, so make your reservation as far in advance as possible (they're taken up to four months ahead of arrival). A visit to the park's Web

**17**

site will go far in preparing you for the permit process. Day hikes into the canyon or anywhere else in the national park do not require a permit; overnight stays at Phantom Ranch require reservations but no permits. Overnight camping in the national park is restricted to designated campgrounds.

🔳 **Backcountry Information Center** ⬭ Box 129, Grand Canyon 86023 ☎ 928/638-7875 🖷 928/638-2125 ⊕ www.nps.gov/grca.

POST OFFICE The Market Plaza shopping center near Yavapai Lodge has a post office that is open weekdays 9 to 4:30 and Saturday 11 to 1.

PUBLIC TELEPHONES There are public telephones at all visitor centers and lodgings. Cell-phone reception is not possible in many areas of the park.

RELIGIOUS SERVICES A number of religious services are held in the park. For times, check postings at Mather Campground, the visitor centers, Shrine of the Ages, and the information kiosk between Babitt's General Store and the post office.

RESTROOMS All visitor centers, lodgings, and restaurants have restrooms.

SHOPS & GROCERS

🔳 **The Canyon Village Marketplace** ⬭ Grand Canyon Village ☎ 928/638-2262 ✉ Tusayan ☎ 928/638-2854 ✉ Desert View ☎ 928/638-2393. **The North Rim General Store** ⬭ North Rim Campground, Grand Canyon North Rim ☎ 928/638-2611.

## NEARBY TOWN INFORMATION

🔳 **Flagstaff Chamber of Commerce** ⬭ 101 W. Rte. 66, Flagstaff 86001 ☎ 928/774-4505 ⊕ www.flagstaff.az.us. **Flagstaff Visitor Center** ⬭ 1 E. Rte. 66, Flagstaff 86001-5588 ☎ 928/774-9541 or 800/842-7293 ⊕ www.flagstaffarizona.org. **Grand Canyon Chamber of Commerce** ⬭ Box 3007, Grand Canyon 86023 ☎ 928/638-2901 ⊕ www.grandcanyonchamber.com. **Navajo Nation Tourism Dept. (Tuba City)** ⬭ Box 663, Window Rock 86515 ☎ 928/871-6436 ⊕ www.discovernavajo.com. **Williams Visitor Center** ⬭ 200 W. Railroad Ave., at Grand Canyon Blvd. Williams 86046 ☎ 928/635-1418 or 800/863-0546 ⊕ www.williamschamber.com.

## VISITOR INFORMATION

🔳 **Grand Canyon National Park** ⬭ Box 129, Grand Canyon AZ 86023 ☎ 928/638-7888 🖷 928/638-7797 ⊕ www.nps.gov/grca.

# Grand Teton National Park

## WORD OF MOUTH

"Jackson Hole is a seducer. As you drive toward the valley from Dubois, conjure up the mountain men who trapped these creeks, lived and loved and died here. Then look up at the panorama of the Tetons, the sight that most people hold close forever. Go on a float trip and let the Snake River show you its beauties. Walk around Jenny Lake, and go on up the mountain—see, smell, feel. Sit on the road between Teton Village and Moose in the evening and listen to the moose move through the trees to water."  —Novelist Win Blevins

# WELCOME TO GRAND TETON

## TOP REASONS TO GO

★ **Heavenward hikes:** Trek where grizzled frontiersmen roamed. Jackson Hole got its name from mountain man David Jackson; now there are dozens of trails for you to explore.

★ **Wildlife big and small:** Keep an eye out for little fellows like short-tailed weasels and beaver, as well as bison, elk, wolves, and both black and grizzly bears.

★ **Waves to make:** Float the Snake River or take a canoe or motorboat onto Jackson Lake or Jenny Lake.

★ **Homesteader history:** Visit the 1890s barns and ranch buildings of Mormon Row or Menor's Ferry.

★ **Rare bird-watching:** Raise the binoculars—or just your head—to see more than 300 species of birds, including trumpeter swans, bald eagles, and osprey.

★ **Trout trophies:** Grab your rod and slither over to the Snake River, where cutthroat trout are an angler's delight.

**1** Antelope Flats. Buffalo and antelope frequently roam across this sagebrush-covered area of the park northeast of Moose, where homesteader barns along Mormon Row still dot the landscape. It's a popular place for wildflower viewing and leisurely bicycle rides.

**2** Jenny Lake. Nestled at the base of the Tetons, Jenny Lake is a microcosm of the park. In this developed area, you can visit a museum, purchase supplies, or talk to a ranger—plus ride a boat across the lake, hike around it, have a picnic, or camp nearby.

**3** Moose. Just north of Moose Visitor Center, this historical area is home to the Chapel of the Transfiguration, and was once the stomping grounds of early settlers at Menor's Ferry. The ferry has been recreated so you can see how it provided transportation across the Snake River before there were bridges.

**4** Oxbow Bend. This is a good place to observe the Snake River and its inhabitants, especially in early morning or near dusk. You are likely to see moose feeding in willows, elk grazing in aspen stands, and birds such as bald eagles, osprey, ducks, and American white pelicans.

## GETTING ORIENTED

Grand Teton's immense peaks jut dramatically up from the Jackson Hole valley floor. Without any foothills to soften the blow, the sight of these glacier-scoured crags is truly striking. Several alpine lakes reflect the mountains, and the winding Snake River cuts south along the eastern side of the park. The northern portion of the park is outstanding wildlife-watching territory—you can see everything from rare birds to lumbering moose to the big predators (mountain lions, and black and grizzly bears). Two main roads run through the 310,000-acre park; the Jackson Hole Highway curves along the eastern side, while Teton Park Road runs closer to the mountain range.

Snowpeaked mountains

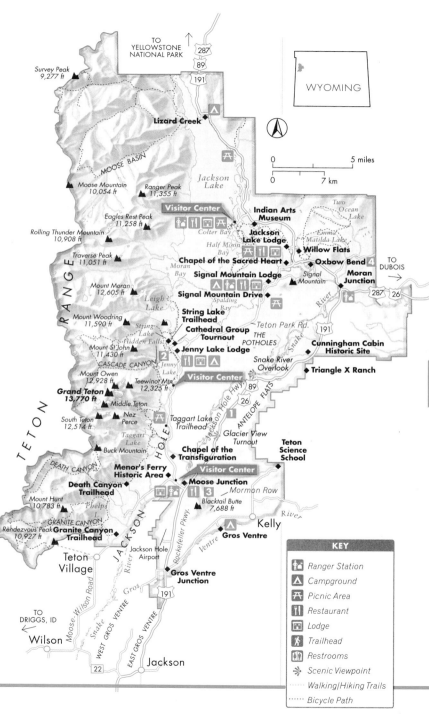

TO
YELLOWSTONE
NATIONAL PARK

287
89
191

*Survey Peak*
*9,277 ft*

WYOMING

Lizard Creek

*Jackson
Lake*

0          5 miles
0        7 km

MOOSE BASIN

*Moose Mountain
10,054 ft*

*Ranger Peak
11,355 ft*

*Eagles Rest Peak
11,258 ft*

*Rolling Thunder Mountain
10,908 ft*

**Visitor Center**

**Indian Arts
Museum**

*Two
Ocean
Lake*

*Colter Bay*

**Jackson
Lake Lodge**

*Emma
Matilda Lake*

*Traverse Peak
11,051 ft*

*Half Moon
Bay*

**Willow Flats**

*Moran
Bay*

**Chapel of the Sacred Heart**

**Oxbow Bend**    4    TO
                         DUBOIS

*Mount Moran
12,605 ft*

**Signal Mountain Lodge**

*Signal
Mountain*

**Moran
Junction**

*Leigh
Lake*

**Signal Mountain Drive**

*Spalding
Bay*

287   26

*Mount Woodring
11,590 ft*

*String
Lake*

**String Lake
Trailhead**

*Teton Park Rd.*

THE
POTHOLES

191

*Hidden Falls*

**Cathedral Group
Tournout**

*Mount St John
11,430 ft*

CASCADE CANYON

2

**Jenny Lake Lodge**

**Cunningham Cabin
Historic Site**

*Mount Owen
12,928 ft*

*Jenny
Lake*

*Snake River
Overlook*

**Triangle X Ranch**

**Grand Teton
13,770 ft**

*Teewinot Mtn
12,325 ft*

**Visitor Center**

18

*Middle Teton*

89

26

*Nez
Perce*

*South Teton
12,514 ft*

**Taggart Lake
Trailhead**

1

ANTELOPE FLATS

*Buck Mountain*

*Taggart
Lake*

**Glacier View
Turnout**

**Teton
Science
School**

DEATH CANYON

**Chapel of the
Transfiguration**

*Mount Hunt
10,783 ft*

**Menor's Ferry
Historic Area**

**Visitor Center**

**Moose Junction**

*Mormon Row*

*Phelps
L.*

GRANITE CANYON

**Death Canyon
Trailhead**

*Blacktail Butte
7,688 ft*

**Kelly**

*Rendezvous Peak
10,927 ft*

**Granite Canyon
Trailhead**

*River*

**Gros Ventre**

**Teton
Village**

**Gros Ventre
Junction**

*Jackson Hole
Airport*

TO
DRIGGS, ID

**Wilson**

22

*Gros*

*West Gros Ventre*

*East Gros Ventre*

**Jackson**

| KEY | |
|---|---|
| 🏚 | *Ranger Station* |
| ▲ | *Campground* |
| ☗ | *Picnic Area* |
| 🍴 | *Restaurant* |
| 🏠 | *Lodge* |
| 🏃 | *Trailhead* |
| 🚻 | *Restrooms* |
| ⚶ | *Scenic Viewpoint* |
| ···· | *Walking/Hiking Trails* |
| ···· | *Bicycle Path* |

# GRAND TETON PLANNER

## When to Go

In July and August all the roads, trails, and visitor centers are open, and the Snake River's float season is in full swing, but it's also the most crowded time. **To have full access to services without so many other visitors, a trip in June or September is a good plan.**

The lowest rates and smallest crowds can be found in spring and fall, but services and roads are more limited. Grand Teton Lodge Company, the park's major outfitter, winds down its activities in September, and most of Teton Park Road closes from late October through early May.

Towns just outside the park rev up in winter. Teton Village and Jackson both buzz with the energy of the Jackson Hole Mountain Resort, a skiing mecca. (Prices, accordingly, rise along with the hotel occupancy rates.) Because of this onslaught of skiers, Jackson Hole Highway remains open. It can snow in the area any month of the year.

## AVG. HIGH/LOW TEMPS.

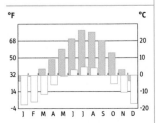

## Flora & Fauna

Grand Teton's short growing season and arid climate create a complex ecosystem and hardy plant species. The dominant elements are big sagebrush—which gives a gray-green cast to the valley—lodgepole pine trees, quaking aspen, and ground-covering wildflowers such as bluish-purple alpine forget-me-nots. In spring and early summer you will see vibrant yellow arrowleaf balsam root and delicate blue camas. The growing season in Jackson Hole is short, but gives rise to spectacular, though short-lived displays of wildflowers. The best time to see these natural displays are mid-June to early July, although the changing of the aspen and cottonwood leaves in early fall can be equally spectacular.

Your best chance to see wildlife is at dawn or dusk, along forest edges. The best place to view elk in summer is on Teton Park Road; during winter they migrate out of the surrounding mountains and about 7,500 spend the winter south of the park on the National Elk Refuge. Oxbow Bend and Willow Flats are good places to look for moose, beaver, and otter any time of year. Pronghorn antelope and bison appear in summer along Jackson Hole Highway and Antelope Flats Road. Occasionally the animals are on or crossing the road; remember in all cases they have the right-of-way. On almost any trip to Grand Teton, you will see bison, antelope, and moose. More rarely you will see a black or grizzly bear or a mountain lion or wolf. Because bears and lions do live in the park, campers should always follow safe-camping practices by storing food in bear containers and never in your tent. The park's smaller animals, yellow-bellied marmots and golden-mantled ground squirrel, as well as a variety of birds and waterfowl, are commonly seen along park trails and waterways. Seek out the water sources to see birds such as bald eagles, ospreys, ducks, and trumpeter swans.

# Getting There & Around

The best way to see Grand Teton is by car. Unlike Yellowstone's Grand Loop, Grand Teton's road system doesn't allow for easy tour-bus access to all the major sights. Only a car will get you close to Jenny Lake, into the remote east Jackson Hole hills, and to the top of Signal Mountain. You can stop at many points along the roads within the park for a hike or to take in the view. Be extremely cautious in winter, when whiteouts and ice are not uncommon. There are adequate road signs throughout the park, but a good road map will come in handy.

Jackson Hole Highway (U.S. 89/191) runs the entire length of the park, from Jackson to Yellowstone National Park's south entrance. (This highway is also called Route 26 south of Moran Junction and U.S. 287 north of Moran Junction.) This road is open all year from Jackson to Moran Junction and north to Flagg Ranch, 2 mi south of Yellowstone. Depending on traffic, the southern (Moose) entrance to Grand Teton is about 15 minutes from downtown Jackson via Jackson Hole Highway. Coming from the opposite direction on the same road, the northern boundary of the park is about 15 minutes south of Yellowstone National Park. Also open year-round, U.S. 26/287 runs east from Dubois over Togwotee Pass to the Moran entrance station, a drive of about one hour.

Grand Teton Lodge Company has shuttle service to its lodging properties, but if you drive, which is recommended, there is plenty of free parking at all developed areas and adequate parking at waysides and historic sites. Although break-ins aren't common, use good sense when leaving your vehicle for an extended period of time by locking valuables out of sight or taking them with you.

Two back-road entrances to Grand Teton require high-clearance vehicles. Both are closed by snow from November through mid-May and are heavily rutted through June. The Moose–Wilson Road (Route 390) starts at Route 22 in Wilson (west of Jackson) and travels 12 mi north past Teton Village, then turns into an unpaved road for 3 mi leading to the Moose entrance. It's closed to large trucks, trailers, and RVs. Even rougher is 60-mi Grassy Lake Road, which heads east from Route 32 in Ashton, Idaho, through Targhee National Forest. It connects with U.S. 89/287 in the John D. Rockefeller Jr. Memorial Parkway, which is actually a park, not a road, sandwiched between Grand Teton and Yellowstone.

# Festivals & Events

THROUGHOUT THE YEAR. **Grand Teton Music Festival** presents monthly concerts featuring solo performers as well as duos and groups at Walk Festival Hall in Teton Village. ☎ *307/733-1128* ⊕ *www.gtmf. org.*

MAY Jackson's **Old West Days** include a rodeo, Native American dancers, a Western swing-dance contest, and cowboy poetry readings. ☎ *307/733-3316.*

MAY–SEPT. Between Memorial Day and Labor Day, gunslingers stage **The Shootout** daily (except Sunday) in Jackson's Town Square. Don't worry, the bullets aren't real. ☎ *307/733-3316.*

JULY–AUG. During the **Grand Teton Music Festival,** a schedule of symphony orchestra performances is presented at Walk Festival Hall in Teton Village and outdoors near Jackson Hole Resort. There's also a winter concert schedule. ☎ *307/733-1128.*

SEPT.–OCT. Each year, artists in various media show and sell their work in Jackson at the **Jackson Hole Fall Arts Festival.** Special events include poetry readings and dance performances. Jackson's many art galleries have special exhibits and programs. ☎ *307/733-3316.*

**18**

By Candy
Moulton

Your jaw will probably drop the first time you see the Teton Range jabbing up from the Jackson Hole valley floor. With no foothills to get in the way, you'll have a close-up, unimpeded view of magnificent, jagged, snowcapped peaks. This massif is long on natural beauty. Before your eyes, mountain glaciers creep imperceptibly down 12,605-foot Mt. Moran. Large and small lakes gleam along the range's base. Many of the West's iconic animals (elk, bears, bald eagles) call this park home.

## Scenic Drives

**Antelope Flats Road.** Off Jackson Hole Highway, 1 mi north of Moose Junction, this narrow road wanders eastward over rolling plains and sagebrush flats. The road intersects Mormon Row, where you can see abandoned homesteaders' barns and houses from the turn of the 20th century. Less than 1 mi past Mormon Row is a four-way intersection where you can turn right to loop around past the town of Kelly and Gros Ventre campground and rejoin Jackson Hole Highway at Gros Ventre Junction. Keep an eye out for pronghorn, bison, moose—and mountain bikers.

★ **Jenny Lake Scenic Drive.** Providing the park's best roadside close-ups of the Tetons, this one-way road winds south through groves of lodgepole pine and open meadows. Roughly 2 mi down the one-way road, the Cathedral Group Turnout faces 13,770-foot Grand Teton (the range's highest peak), flanked by 12,928-foot Mt. Owen and 12,325-foot Mt. Teewinot.

**Signal Mountain Road.** This exciting drive climbs 700 feet along a 5-mi stretch of switchbacks. As you travel through forest you can catch glimpses of Jackson Lake and Mt. Moran. The trip ends with a sweeping view of Jackson Hole and the entire 40-mi Teton Range. Sunset is the most scenic time to make the climb up Signal Mountain. The road is not appropriate for long trailers.

## GRAND TETON IN ONE DAY

Begin the day by packing a picnic lunch or picking one up at a Jackson eatery. Arrive at Moose Visitor Center in time for a 9 AM, two-hour, guided Snake River float trip (make reservations in advance with one of the dozen or so outfitters that offer the trip). When you're back on dry ground, drive north on Teton Park Road, stopping at scenic turnouts—don't miss Teton Glacier—until you reach Jenny Lake Road, which is one-way headed south. After a brief stop at Cathedral Group Turnout, park at the Jenny Lake ranger station and take the 20-minute boat ride to Cascade Canyon trailhead for a short hike. Return to your car by mid-afternoon, drive back to Teton Park Road, and head north to

Signal Mountain Road to catch a top-of-the-park view of the Tetons. In late afternoon descend the mountain and continue north on Teton Park Road. At Jackson Lake Junction, you can go east to Oxbow Bend or north to Willow Flats, both excellent spots for wildlife viewing before you head to Jackson Lake Lodge for dinner and an evening watching the sun set over the Tetons. Or if you'd like to get back on the water, drive to Colter Bay Marina, where you can board a 1½-hour sunset cruise across Jackson Lake to Waterfalls Canyon. You can reverse this route if you're heading south from Yellowstone: start the day with a 7:30 AM breakfast cruise from Colter Bay and end it with a sunset float down the Snake River.

## What to See

### Historic & Cultural Sites

★ **Chapel of the Transfiguration.** This tiny chapel built in 1925 is still a functioning Episcopal church. Couples come here to exchange vows with the Tetons as a backdrop, and tourists come to take photos of the small church with its awe-inspiring view. ☒ *½ mi off Teton Park Rd., 2 mi north of Moose Junction* ⊙ *Late May–late Sept., Sun.: Eucharist 8 AM, service 10 AM.*

**Cunningham Cabin Historic Site.** At the end of a gravel spur road, an easy ¾-mi trail runs through sagebrush around Pierce Cunningham's 1890 log cabin homestead. Although you can peer inside, the building has no furnishings or displays. Watch for badgers, coyotes, and Uinta ground squirrels in the area. ☒ *½ mi off Jackson Hole Hwy., 6 mi south of Moran Junction* ⊙ *Year-round.*

**Indian Arts Museum.** This collection's standout exhibits include Plains Indian weapons and clothing. You will see Crow blanket strips with elegant beadwork, sashes from both the Shawnee and Hopi tribes, and various weapons, games and toys, flutes and drums, and a large collection of moccasins from many tribes. From June through early September, you can see crafts demonstrations by tribal members, take ranger-led tours of the museum, and listen to a daily 45-minute ranger program on Native American culture. ☒ *2 mi off U.S. 89/191/287, 5 mi north of Jackson Lake Junction inside the Colter Bay Visitor Center* ☎ *307/*

*739–3594* ✉ *Free* ⊙ *Mid-May–mid-June and Sept., daily 8–5; mid-June–Labor Day, daily 8–8.*

★ **Menor's Ferry Historic Area.** The ferry on display is not the original, but it's an accurate re-creation of the craft built by Bill Menor in the 1890s, and it demonstrates how people crossed the Snake River before bridges were built. In the cluster of turn-of-the-20th-century buildings there are historical displays, including a photo collection of historic shots taken in the area; one building has been turned into a small general store. You can pick up a pamphlet for a self-guided tour. ⊠ *½ mi off Teton Park Rd., 2 mi north of Moose Junction* ⊙ *Year-round.*

**Mormon Row Historic Area.** Settled by homesteaders from 1896–1907, this area received its name because many of them were members of the Church of Jesus Christ of Latter-day Saints, otherwise known as the Mormons. The remaining barns, homes, and outbuildings are being restored and are representative of early homesteading in the West. You can wander among the buildings, hike the row, and take photographs. ⊠ *Just off Antelope Flats Rd., 2 mi north of Moose Junction* ⊙ *Year-round.*

## Scenic Stops

**Chapel of the Sacred Heart.** This small log chapel sits in the pine forest with a view of Jackson Lake. The chapel is open only for services, but you can enjoy the view anytime. ⊠ *¼ mi east of Signal Mountain Lodge, off Teton Park Rd., 4 mi south of Jackson Lake Junction* ⊙ *Services June–Sept., Sat. 5:30 PM and Sun. 8 AM and 10 AM.*

★ **Jackson Lake.** The biggest of Grand Teton's glacier-scooped lakes, this body of water in the northern reaches of the park was enlarged by construction of the Jackson Lake Dam in 1906. You can fish, sail, and windsurf on the lake, or hike trails near the shoreline. Three marinas (Colter Bay, Leeks, and Signal Mountain) provide access for boaters, and several picnic areas, campgrounds, and lodges overlook the lake. ⊠ *U.S. 89/191/287 from Lizard Creek to Jackson Lake Junction, and Teton Park Rd. from Jackson Lake Junction to Signal Mountain Lodge.*

**Jenny Lake.** Named for the Native American wife of mountain man Beaver Dick Leigh, this alpine lake south of Jackson Lake draws boaters to its pristine waters and hikers to its tree-shaded trails. ⊠ *Off Teton Park Rd. midway between Moose and Jackson Lake.*

★ **Oxbow Bend.** This spot overlooks a quiet backwater left by the Snake River when it cut a new southern channel. White pelicans stop here on their spring migration (many stay on through summer), trumpeter swans visit frequently, and great blue herons nest amid the cottonwoods along the river. Use binoculars to search for bald eagles, ospreys, moose, beaver, and otter. The Oxbow is known for the reflection of Mt. Moran that marks its calm waters in early morning. ⊠ *U.S. 89/191/287, 2 mi east of Jackson Lake Junction.*

**Willow Flats.** You will almost always see moose grazing in the marshy area of Willow Flats, in part because it has a good growth of willow trees, which moose both eat and hide in. This is also a good place to see birds and waterfowl. ⊠ *U.S. 89/191/287, 1 mi north of Jackson Lake Junction.*

### Visitor Centers

If you plan to do any hiking or exploring on your own, it is important to stop at a visitor center to get up-to-date information about weather conditions. Rangers also will know if any trails are temporarily closed due to wildlife activity. Before beginning any backcountry explorations, you must obtain permits, which you can get at visitor centers.

★ **Colter Bay Visitor Center.** The auditorium here hosts several free daily programs about Native American culture and natural history. Also, at 11 and 3 daily, a 30-minute "Teton Highlights" ranger lecture provides tips on park activities. ⊠ *Colter Bay, off U.S. 191/287, 6 mi north of Jackson Lake Junction* ☎ *307/739–3594* ☉ *Late May–early Sept., daily 8–7; early Sept.–early Oct., daily 8–5; early May–late May, daily 8–5.*

**Jenny Lake Visitor Center.** Geology exhibits, including a relief model of the Teton Range, are on display here. ⊠ *S. Jenny Lake Junction, ½ mi off Teton Park Rd., 8 mi north of Moose Junction* ☎ *307/739–3343* ☉ *Early June–early Sept., daily 8–7; early Sept.–late Sept., daily 8–5.*

**Moose Visitor Center.** The center has exhibits of rare and endangered species and the geology and natural history of the Greater Yellowstone area. In the auditorium you can see a video called *The Nature of Grand Teton* and other videos on topics that range from geology to wolves. ⊠ *Teton Park Rd., ½ mi north of Moose Junction* ☎ *307/739–3399* ☉ *June–Aug., daily 8–7; Sept.–May, daily 8–5.*

## Sports & the Outdoors

### Bicycling

18

Teton Park Road and Jackson Hole Highway are generally flat with long, gradual inclines, and have well-marked shoulders. Grand Teton has few designated bike paths, so cyclists should be very careful when sharing the road with vehicles, especially RVs and trailers. A bike lane allows for northbound bike traffic along the one-way Jenny Lake Loop Road, a one-hour ride. The River Road, 4 mi north of Moose, is an easy four-hour mountain-bike ride along a ridge above the Snake River on a dirt road. Bicycles are not allowed on trails or in the backcountry.

In Jackson, ride the Snow King trails system that begins at Snow King resort. The Cache Creek to Game Creek loop is a 25-mi ride on dirt roads and trails. The two trails systems also link together. In addition, the surrounding Bridger-Teton National Forest has abundant mountain-biking trails and roads.

⇨ Outfitters & Expeditions box for bike rentals and expeditions.

### Bird-watching

With over 300 species of birds in the park, the Tetons make for excellent bird-watching country. Here you might spot both the calliope hummingbird (the smallest North American hummingbird) and the trumpeter swan (the world's largest waterfowl). The two riparian habitats described below draw lots of attention, but there are many other bird-busy areas as well. Birds of prey circle around Antelope Flats Road, for instance—the surrounding fields are good hunting turf for red-tailed hawks and prairie falcons. At Taggart Lake you'll see woodpeckers, bluebirds, and hummingbirds. Look for songbirds, such as pine and evening grosbeaks and Cassin's finches, in surrounding open pine and aspen forests.

**Oxbow Bend.** Some seriously impressive birds tend to congregate at this quiet spot ( ⇨ Scenic Stops). In spring, white pelicans stop by during their northerly migration; in summer, bald eagles, great blue herons, and osprey nest nearby. Year-round, you'll have a good chance of seeing trumpeter swans. Nearby Willow Flats has similar bird life, plus sandhill cranes. ⊠ *U.S. 89/191/287, 2 mi east of Jackson Lake Junction.*

**Phelps Lake.** The moderate 1⁸⁄₁₀-mi round-trip Phelps Lake Overlook Trail takes you up conifer- and aspen-lined glacial moraine to a view that's accessible only by trail. Expect abundant bird life: Western tanagers, northern flickers, and ruby-crowned kinglets thrive in the bordering woods, and hummingbirds feed on scarlet gilia beneath the overlook. ⊠ *Moose–Wilson Rd., about 3 mi off Teton Park Rd., 1 mi north of Moose Junction.*

### Boating & Water Sports

Water sports in Grand Teton are diverse. You can float the Snake River, which runs high and fast early in the season (May and June) and more slowly during the latter part of the summer. Canoes and kayaks dominate the smaller lakes and share the water with motorboats on the impressively large Jackson Lake. Motorboats are allowed on Jenny, Jackson, and Phelps lakes. On Jenny Lake, there's an engine limit of 10 horsepower. You can launch your boat at Colter Bay, Leek's Marina, Signal Mountain, and Spalding Bay.

If you're floating the Snake River on your own, you are required to purchase a permit that costs $10 per raft and is valid for the entire season, or one for $5 per raft for seven days. Permits are available year-round at Moose Visitor Center and at Colter Bay, Signal Mountain, and Buffalo (near Moran entrance) ranger stations in summer. Before you set out, check with park rangers for current conditions.

You may prefer to take one of the many guided float trips through calm-water sections of the Snake; outfitters pick you up at the float-trip parking area near Moose Visitor Center for a 10- to 20-minute drive to upriver launch sites. Ponchos and life preservers are provided. Early morning and evening floats are your best bets for wildlife viewing, but be sure to carry a jacket or sweater. Float season runs mid-April to December.

**Colter Bay Marina.** All types of services are available to boaters, including free parking for boat trailers and vehicles, free mooring, boat rentals, guided fishing trips, and fuel. ⊠ *On Jackson Lake.*

**Leek's Marina.** Both day and short-term parking for boat trailers and vehicles are available for up to three nights maximum. There are no boat rentals, but you can get fuel, and there's free short-term docking plus a pizza restaurant. This marina is operated by park concessionaire Signal Mountain Lodge. ⊠ *U.S. 89/191/287, 6 mi north of Jackson Lake Junction* ☎ *307/543–2831* ☉ *Mid-May–mid-Sept.*

**Signal Mountain Lodge Marina.** The marina rents pontoon boats, deck cruisers, motorboats, kayaks, and canoes by the hour or for full-day cruising; rates range from $12 an hour for a kayak to $62 an hour for a pontoon boat. ⊠ *Teton Park Rd., 3 mi south of Jackson Lake Junction* ☎ *307/543–2831* ⊙ *Mid-May–mid-Sept.*

⇨ Outfitters & Expeditions box for boating outfitters.

## Climbing

The Teton Range has excellent rock, snow, and ice routes for climbers of all experience levels. Unless you're already a pro, take a course from one of the area's climbing schools before tackling the tough terrain. ⇨ Outfitters & Expeditions box for outfitters.

## Fishing

Rainbow, brook, lake, and native cutthroat trout inhabit the park's waters. The Snake's 75 mi of river and tributary are world-renowned for their fishing. To fish in Grand Teton National Park, you need a Wyoming fishing license. A day permit for nonresidents is $10, and an annual permit is $65 plus a $10 conservation stamp; for state residents a license costs $15 per season plus $10 for a conservation stamp. Children under age 14 can fish free with an adult who has a license. You can buy a fishing license at Colter Bay Marina, Moose Village Store, Signal Mountain Lodge, and at area sporting-goods stores, where you will also be able to get solid information on good fishing spots and the best flies or lures to use. Or you can get one direct from **Wyoming Game and Fish Department.** ⊠ *420 N. Cache St., Box 67, Jackson 83001* ☎ *307/733–2321.*

⇨ Outfitters & Expeditions box for guided fishing expeditions.

## Hiking

Most of Grand Teton's trails are unpaved, with just a few short paved sections in the vicinity of developed areas. You can get trail maps and information about hiking conditions from rangers at the park visitor centers at Moose, Jenny Lake, or Colter Bay, where you will also find bathrooms or outhouses; there are no facilities along the trails themselves. Of the more than 250 mi of maintained trails, the most popular are those around Jenny Lake, the Leigh and String lakes area, and Taggart Lake Trail, with views of Avalanche Canyon.

Front country or backcountry, you may see moose and bears, but keep your distance. Pets are not permitted on trails or in the backcountry, but you can take them on paved front-country trails so long as they are on a leash no more than 6 feet long. Always sign in at trailheads, let someone know where you are going and when you expect to return, and carry plenty of water, snacks and a cell phone.

EASY **Cascade Canyon Trail.** Take the 20-minute boat ride from the Jenny Lake dock to the start of a gentle, ½-mi climb to 200-foot Hidden Falls, the park's most popular and crowded trail destination. With the boat ride, plan on a couple of hours to experience this trail. Listen here for the distinctive bleating of the rabbit-like pikas among the glacial boulders and pines. The trail continues ½ mi to Inspiration Point over a rocky path that is moderately steep. There are two points on the climb that afford good views of Jenny Lake and the surrounding area, but keep

18

climbing; after passing a rock wall you'll finally reach the true Inspiration Point, with the best views. To avoid crowds, try to make your way to Inspiration Point in early morning or late afternoon. To reach the Cascade Canyon trailhead, go to the Jenny Lake Visitor Center to catch a ride across Jenny Lake with **Jenny Lake Boating.** ⊠ *Jenny Lake Rd., 2 mi off Teton Park Rd., 12 mi south of Jackson Lake Junction* ☎ *307/ 734–9227* ⌨ *$5–$7* ☉ *June–early Sept.*

**Colter Bay Nature Trail Loop.** This very easy, 1¾-mi round-trip excursion treats you to views of Jackson Lake and the Tetons. As you follow the level trail from Colter Bay Visitor Center and along the forest's edge, you may see moose and bald eagles. Allow yourself two hours to complete the walk. ⊠ *2 mi off U.S. 89/191/287, 5 mi north of Jackson Lake Junction.*

**Lunchtree Hill Trail.** One of the park's easiest trails begins at Jackson Lake Lodge and leads ½ mi to the top of a hill above Willow Flats. The area's willow thickets, beaver ponds, and wet, grassy meadows make it a birder's paradise. Look for sandhill cranes, hummingbirds, and the many types of songbirds described in the free bird guide available at visitor centers. You might also see moose. The round-trip walk takes no more than half an hour. ⊠ *U.S. 89/191/287, ½ mi north of Jackson Lake Junction.*

MODERATE

★ ☺

**Jenny Lake Trail.** You can walk to Hidden Falls from Jenny Lake ranger station by following the mostly level trail around the south shore of the lake to Cascade Canyon Trail. Jenny Lake Trail continues around the lake for 6½ mi. It's an easy trail—classed here as moderate because of its length—that will take you two to three hours. You'll walk through a lodgepole pine forest, have expansive views of the lake and the land to the east, and hug the shoulder of the massive Teton range itself. Along the way you are likely to see elk, pikas, golden mantle ground squirrels, a variety of ducks and water birds, plus you may hear elk bugling, birdsong, and the chatter of squirrels. ⊠ *S. Jenny Lake Junction, ½ mi off Teton Park Rd., 8 mi north of Moose Junction.*

**Leigh Lake Trail.** The flat trail follows String Lake's northeastern shore to Leigh Lake's south shore, covering 2 mi in a round-trip of about an hour. You can extend your hike into a moderate 7½-mi, four-hour round-trip by following the forested east shore of Leigh Lake to Bearpaw Lake. Along the way you'll have views of Mt. Moran across the lake, and you may be lucky enough to spot a moose. ⊠ *String Lake trailhead, ½ mi west of Jenny Lake Rd., 14 mi north of Moose Junction.*

**String Lake Trail.** This moderate 3½-mi, three-hour loop around String Lake lies in the shadows of 11,144-foot Rockchuck Peak and 11,430-foot Mt. Saint John. This is also a good place to see moose, hear songbirds, and view wildflowers. This trail is a bit more difficult than other mid-length trails in the park, which means it is also less crowded. ⊠ *½ mi west of Jenny Lake Rd., 14 mi north of Moose.*

DIFFICULT

**Death Canyon Trail.** This 7⁹⁄₁₀-mi trail is a strenuous hike with lots of hills to traverse, ending with a climb up into Death Canyon. Plan to spend most of the day on this steep trail. ⊠ *Off Moose–Wilson Rd., 4 mi south of Moose Junction.*

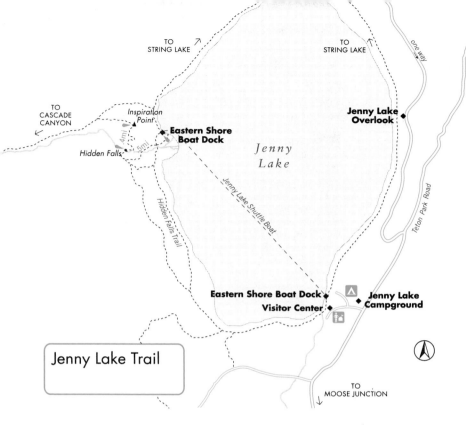

**TO STRING LAKE**

**TO STRING LAKE**

one way

**TO CASCADE CANYON**

Inspiration Point

.4mi

**Eastern Shore Boat Dock**

Hidden Falls

.5mi

*Jenny Lake*

**Jenny Lake Overlook**

Hidden Falls Trail

Jenny Lake Shuttle Boat

Teton Park Road

**Eastern Shore Boat Dock**

**Visitor Center**

**Jenny Lake Campground**

**Jenny Lake Trail**

**TO MOOSE JUNCTION**

## Horseback Riding

You can arrange a guided horseback tour at Colter Bay Village and Jackson Lake Lodge corrals or with a number of private outfitters. Most offer rides of an hour or two up to all-day excursions. If you want to spend even more time riding in Grand Teton and the surrounding mountains, consider a stay at a dude ranch. Shorter rides are almost all appropriate for novice riders, while more experienced cowboys and cowgirls will enjoy the longer journeys where the terrain gets steeper and you may wind through deep forests. For any ride, be sure to wear long pants and boots (cowboy boots or hiking boots). Because you may ride through trees, a long-sleeve shirt is also a good idea and a hat is always appropriate, but it should have a stampede string to make sure it stays on your head if the wind comes up.

⇨ Outfitters & Expeditions box for rentals and riding expeditions.

## Winter Sports

Grand Teton has some of North America's finest and most varied cross-country skiing. (And don't forget the nearby Jackson Hole Mountain Resort; ⇨ What's Nearby.) Ski the gentle 3-mi Swan Lake–Heron Pond Loop near Colter Bay Visitor Center, the mostly level 9-mi Jenny Lake Trail, or the moderate 4-mi Taggart Lake–Beaver Creek Loop and 5-mi Phelps Lake Overlook trail. Advanced skiers should head for the Teton

# OUTFITTERS & EXPEDITIONS

## BICYCLING

**Teton Cycle Works.** The oldest shop in town offers mountain- and road-bike rentals, sales, accessories, and repairs. ✉ 175 N. Glenwood St., Jackson ☎ 307/733-4386 ⊙ Mar.-Oct.

**Teton Mountain Bike Tours.** Mountain bikers of all skill levels can take guided half-, full-, or multiday tours with this company into both Grand Teton and Yellowstone national parks, as well as to the Bridger-Teton and Caribou-Targhee national forests. ⌂ Box 7027, Jackson 83002 ☎ 307/733-0712 or 800/733-0788 ⊕ www.wybike.com ✎ $55-$125 for half- to full-day trips; multiday trips $379-$400 per day ⊙ May-Sept.

## BOATING & WATER SPORTS

**Barker-Ewing Scenic Float Trips.** Travel the peaceful parts of the Snake River looking for wildlife as knowledgeable guides talk about area history, plants, and animals. ⌂ Box 100-J, Moose 83012 ☎ 307/733-1800 or 800/365-1800 ⊕ www.barkerewingscenic.com ✎ $50 ⊙ May-Sept.

**Grand Teton Lodge Company.** You can rent motorboats, row boats, and canoes at Colter Bay Marina. ✉ 2 mi off U.S. 89/191/287, 5 mi north of Jackson Lake Junction ☎ 307/543-3100, 307/543-2811, or 800/628-9988 ⊕ www.gtlc.com ✎ Motor boats $25 per hour, row boats and canoes $11 per hour ⊙ Early June-late Sept.

**Grand Teton Lodge Company Snake River Float Trips.** Choose from a scenic float trip with lunch, or an evening trip with a steak-fry dinner. Make reservations at the activities desk at Colter Bay Village or Jackson Lake Lodge. ☎ 307/543-3100 or 800/628-9988 ⊕ www.gtlc.com ✎ Scenic float $45, lunch float $53, steak-fry float $60 ⊙ June-Aug.

**Lewis and Clark River Expeditions.** Get in touch with these folks for an exhilarating wet-and-wild ride or a more leisurely scenic float. ✉ 335 N. Cache St., Box 720, Jackson 83001 ☎ 307/733-4022 or 800/824-5375 ⊕ www.lewisandclarkexpeds.com ✎ $43-$79 ⊙ Mid-May-mid-Sept.

**Mad River Boat Trips.** This company leads a variety of white-water and scenic float trips, some combined with breakfast, lunch, or dinner. ✉ 1255 S. U.S. 89 Jackson ☎ 307/733-6203 or 800/458-7238 ⊕ www.mad-river.com ✎ $44-$83 ⊙ Mid-May-Sept.

**Snake River Kayak and Canoe.** Get some instruction in the fine art of paddling here, then test yourself on the river. ⌂ Box 4311, Jackson 83001 ☎ 307/733-9999 or 800/529-2501 ⊕ www.snakeriverkayak.com ✎ Raft trips $63-$95, one-day clinics $175-$280, multiday instruction $275-$900 ⊙ Apr.-Oct.

**Triangle X Float Trips.** This company offers subdued river trips in Grand Teton National Park, including a sunset supper float. ✉ 2 Triangle X Ranch Rd., Moose ☎ 307/733-5500 or 888/860-0005 ⊕ www.trianglex.com ✎ $48-$58 ⊙ Mid-May-late Sept.

## CLIMBING

**Exum Mountain Guides.** You'll find a variety of climbing experiences here, ranging from one-day mountain climbs to ice climbing to backcountry adventures on skis and snowboards. ⌂ *Box 56, Moose 83012* ☏ *307/733-2297* ⊕ *www.exumguides.com* 🖃 *One-day climbs $200-$340, climbing schools $105-$170* ⊘ *Year-round.*

**Jackson Hole Mountain Guides.**
Mountain climbers get a leg up in the Tetons from this outfit, which offers instruction for beginning to advanced climbers in both rock and ice climbing. ⌂ *165 N. Glenwood St., Jackson* ☏ *307/733-4979 or 800/239-7642* ⊕ *www.jhmg.com* 🖃 *One-day guided climbs $195-$225, climbing classes $125-$275* ⊘ *Year-round.*

### FISHING
**Grand Teton Lodge Company.** The park's major concessionaire operates guided Jackson Lake fishing trips that include boat and tackle, and guided fly-fishing trips on the Snake River. Make reservations at the activities desks at Colter Bay Village or Jackson Lake Lodge, where trips originate. ⌂ *Colter Bay Marina or Jackson Lake Lodge* ☏ *307/543-3100 or 800/628-9988* ⊕ *www.gtlc.com* 🖃 *$130-$375 and up* ⊘ *June-Sept.*

**Signal Mountain Lodge.** A variety of guided Lake Jackson fishing trips leave from the marina here. ⌂ *Teton Park Rd., 3 mi south of Jackson Lake Junction* ☏ *307/543-2831* ⊕ *www.signalmountainlodge.com* 🖃 *$65 per hour* ⊘ *Mid-May-mid-Sept.*

### HORSEBACK RIDING
**Colter Bay Village Corral.** One- and two-hour rides leave Colter Bay Village for a variety of destinations, while half-day trips—for advanced riders only—go to Hermitage Point; some rides include a trailside breakfast or dinner. ⌂ *2 mi off U.S. 89/191/287, 5 mi north of Jackson Lake Junction* ☏ *307/543-3100 or 800/628-9988* ⊕ *www.gtlc.com*

🖃 *Short rides $30-$42, breakfast rides $50, dinner rides $56; wagon rides $30 for breakfast and $40 for dinner* ⊘ *June-Aug.*

**Jackson Lake Lodge Corral.** One-hour trail rides give an overview of the Jackson Lake Lodge area; two-hour rides go to Emma Matilda Lake, Oxbow Bend, and Christian Pond. Experienced riders can take a half-day ride to Two Ocean Lake. Some rides include breakfast or dinner eaten along the trail. ⌂ *U.S. 89/191/287, ½ mi north of Jackson Lake Junction* ☏ *307/543-3100 or 800/628-9988* 📠 *307/543-3143* ⊕ *www.gtlc.com* 🖃 *Short rides $30-$42, breakfast rides $50 ($30 by wagon), dinner rides $56 ($40 by wagon)* ⊘ *June-Aug.*

### WINTER SPORTS
**Jack Dennis Outdoor Shop.** This place stocks skis and snowboards for sale and rent, and outdoor gear for any season. ⌂ *50 E. Broadway Ave., Jackson* ☏ *307/733-3270, Jackson or 307/733-6838, Teton Village* ⊕ *www.jackdennis.com* 🖃 *Ski rental $25-$44, snowboard and boot rental $25-$35* ⊘ *Year-round.*

**Pepi Stegler Sports Shop.** You can buy or rent skis or snowboards at this Teton Village shop, conveniently located at the base of the Jackson Hole ski mountain. ⌂ *Teton Village* ☏ *307/733-4505* ⊕ *www.jackdennis.com* 🖃 *Ski rental $25-$44, snowboard and boot rental $25-$35* ⊘ *Nov.-Apr.*

**Togwotee Mountain Lodge.** You can rent a snowmobile and then ride it on an extensive trail network along the Continental Divide. ⌂ *U.S. 26/287, Box 91, Moran* ☏ *307/543-2847 or 800/543-2847* ⊕ *www.togwoteelodge.com* 🖃 *Snowmobile rentals $139-$205 per day* ⊘ *Nov.-Apr.*

18

Crest Trail. In winter overnight backcountry travelers must register at park headquarters in Moose for a free permit.

You can snowmobile on the Continental Divide snowmobile trail as well as on Jackson Lake. You must first purchase an annual $15 permit at a park entrance station. The speed limit within the park is 35 mph.

⇨ Outfitters & Expeditions box for winter-sports outfitters.

## Educational Offerings

### Classes & Seminars

**Teton Science School.** Adults can join one of the school's single- or multiday wildlife expeditions in Grand Teton, Yellowstone, and surrounding forests to see and learn about wolves, bears, mountain sheep, and other animals. Junior high and high school students can take multiweek field ecology courses while living at the school, backpacking and camping out. Weekdays, kids in grades 1–6 can join Young Naturalists programs that don't involve sleepovers. ⌂ *Box 68, Kelly 83011* ☎ *307/733–4765* ⊕ *www.tetonscience.org* ✉ *Adult programs $55–$1,950; youth programs $195–$2,950* ☉ *Year-round.*

### Programs & Tours

**Grand Teton Lodge Company Bus Tours.** Half-day tours depart from Colter Bay Village or Jackson Lake Lodge and include visits to scenic viewpoints, visitor centers, and other park sites. Interpretive guides provide information about the park geology, history, wildlife and ecosystems. Buy tickets in advance at Colter Bay Marina or Jackson Lake Lodge activities desks. Tours include Grand Teton, Yellowstone or a combination of the two parks. ⊠ *Colter Bay Village or Jackson Lake Lodge* ☎ *307/543–2811 or 800/628–9988* ✉ *$34–$72* ☉ *Mid-May–early Oct., daily.*

**Gray Line Bus Tours.** Full-day bus tours provide an overview of Grand Teton National Park. They depart from Jackson and you will learn about the park's geology, history, birds, plants, and wildlife. ⊠ *16 W. Martin La., Jackson* ☎ *307/ 733–4325 or 800/443–6133* ✉ *$65 plus park entrance fee* ☉ *Memorial Day–Sept.*

**Jackson Lake Cruises.** Grand Teton Lodge Company runs 1½-hour Jackson Lake scenic cruises from Colter Bay Marina throughout the day as well as breakfast cruises, and sunset steak-fry cruises. One cruise, known as Fire and Ice, shows how forest fires and glaciers have shaped the Grand Teton landscape. ⊠ *2 mi off U.S. 89/191/287, 5 mi north of Jackson Lake Junction* ☎ *307/543–3100, 307/543–2811, or 800/628–9988* ⊕ *www.gtlc.com*

> ### ACCESSIBLE TOURS
>
> Many Grand Teton bus tours, float trips, fishing trips, lake cruises, and wagon rides are fully or partially accessible; ask the independent operators for details. One company, **Access Tours,** caters specifically to people with physical disabilities. The company can also give you general information about places that are easily accessible in Teton, Glacier, and Yellowstone. ⌂ *Box 499, Victor, ID 83455* ☎ *208/787–2338 or 800/929–4811* ⊕ *www.accesstours.org.*

🍴 *Scenic cruise $18; breakfast cruise $30; steak-fry cruise $52* 🕐 *Late May–mid-Sept.*

**Teton Wagon Train and Horse Adventures.** Multiday covered wagon rides and horseback trips follow Grassy Lake Road on the "back side" of the Tetons. You can combine the trip with a river trip and a tour of Yellowstone and Grand Teton. ✉ *Box 10307, Jackson 83001* ☎ *307/734–6101 or 888/734–6101* ⊕ *www.tetonwagontrain.com* 🍴 *Wagon trip $795; combination trip $1,655* 🕐 *June–Aug.*

### Ranger Programs

**Campfire Programs.** Park rangers lead free nightly slide shows from June through September at the Colter Bay, Flagg Ranch Resort, Gros Ventre, and Signal Mountain amphitheaters. For schedules of topics check the park newspaper, *Teewinot*, or at visitor centers. ⊠ *Colter Bay: 2 mi off U.S. 89/191/287, 5 mi north of Jackson Lake Junction* ⊠ *Flagg Ranch Resort: John D. Rockefeller Jr. Memorial Pkwy., 4 mi north of the national park boundary* ⊠ *Gros Ventre: 4 mi off U.S. 26/89/191 and 1½ mi west of Kelly on Gros Ventre River Rd., 7 mi south of Moose Junction* ⊠ *Signal Mountain: Teton Park Rd., 4 mi south of Jackson Lake Junction* ☎ *307/739–3399 or 307/739–3594* 🕐 *June and July, nightly at 9:30; Aug. and Sept., nightly at 9.*

**Jackson Lake Lodge Ranger Talks.** Visit the Wapiti Room to hear a slide-illustrated ranger presentation on topics such as area plants and animals, geology, and natural history. Also, you can chat with the ranger on the back deck of the lodge 6:30–8 PM daily, early June through early September. ⊠ *U.S. 89/191/287, ½ mi north of Jackson Lake Junction* ☎ *307/739–3300* 🕐 *Late June–mid-Aug., nightly at 8:30.*

**Ranger Walks.** Rangers lead free walks throughout the park in summer, from a one-hour lakeside stroll at Colter Bay to a three-hour hike from Jenny Lake. The talks focus on a variety of subjects from wildlife to birds and flower species to geology. Call for itineraries, times, and reservations. ☎ *307/739–3300, 307/739–3400 TTY* 🕐 *Early June–early Sept.*

**Young Naturalist Program.** Children ages 8–12 learn about the natural world of the park as they take an easy 2-mi hike with a ranger. Kids should wear old clothes and bring water, rain gear, and insect repellent. The hike, which takes place at Jenny Lake or Colter Bay, is 1½ hours long and is limited to 12 children. ⊠ *Jenny Lake: meet at the flagpole at the visitor center; Colter Bay: meet at the visitor center* ☎ *307/739–3399 or 307/739–3594* 🕐 *Mid-June–mid-Aug., daily 1:30.*

# WHAT'S NEARBY

## Nearby Towns & Attractions

### Nearby Towns

The major gateway to Grand Teton National Park is **Jackson**—but don't confuse this with Jackson Hole. Jackson Hole is the mountain-ringed valley that houses Jackson and much of Grand Teton National Park. The town of Jackson, located south of the park, is a small community (roughly 7,000 residents) that gets flooded with more than 3 million visitors annually. Expensive homes and fashionable shops have sprung up all over, but Jackson manages to maintain at least part of its true Western character. With its raised wooden sidewalks and old-fashioned storefronts, the town center still looks a bit like a Western movie set. There's a lot to do here, both downtown and in the surrounding countryside.

If it's skiing you're after, **Teton Village,** located on the southwestern side of the park, is the place for you. This cluster of businesses centers around the facilities of the Jackson Hole Mountain Resort—a ski and snowboard area with gondola and various other lifts. There are plenty of places to eat, stay, and shop here.

On the "back side of the Tetons," as eastern Idaho is known, **Driggs** is a western gateway to Yellowstone Country and Grand Teton National Park. Easygoing and rural, Driggs resembles the Jackson of a few decades ago. From here you have to cross a major mountain pass to reach the park; note that the pass is sometimes closed in winter by avalanches. **Dubois,** about 55 mi east of Jackson, is the least known of the gateway communities to Grand Teton and Yellowstone, but this town of 1,000 has all the services of the bigger towns. You can still get a room for the night here during the peak summer travel period without making a reservation weeks or months in advance (though it's a good idea to call a week or so before you intend to arrive). About an hour to the south is **Pinedale,** another small Wyoming town with lodging, restaurants, and attractions. Energy development has made the area a hopping place these days, so be sure to plan ahead if you want to stay in town.

## Nearby Attractions

For additional nearby attractions, *see* Yellowstone chapter.

CULTURAL
VENUES **Jackson Hole Museum.** See exhibits about area homesteaders, learn how Deadman's Bar got its name, and find out about Jackson's all-female town government, one of the first such governing bodies in the nation, at this small museum. Among the exhibits are Native American, ranching, and cowboy artifacts. ✉ *Corner of Glenwood and Deloney Ave., Jackson* ☎ *307/733–2414* ⊕ *www.jacksonholehistory.org* ✉ *$3* ⊙ *Memorial Day–Sept., Mon.–Sat. 9:30–6, Sun. 10–5.*

☼ **Museum of the Mountain Man.** Tucked away in Pinedale, an hour's drive
Fodor's Choice south of Jackson, this museum preserves the history of the mountain man.
★ You'll see beaver traps, fur pelts, and an original gun once used by Jim Bridger, one of the West's most famous mountain men. The basement gallery is devoted to Sublette County pioneer and ranch history. ✉ *700 E. Hennick St., Pinedale* ☎ *307/367–4101* ⊕ *www.museumofthemountainman. com* ✉ *$4* ⊙ *May–Sept., daily 10–5.*

☼ **National Bighorn Sheep Interpretive Center.** The local variety is known as the Rocky Mountain bighorn, but you can learn about all kinds of bighorn sheep here. The center has mounted specimens and hands-on exhibits that illustrate a bighorn's body language, habitat, and characteristics. Wildlife-viewing tours are conducted in winter. ✉ *907 W. Ramshorn Ave., Dubois* ☎ *307/455–3429 or 888/209–2795* ✉ *$2* ⊙ *Memorial*

*Day–Labor Day, daily 9–8; Labor Day–Memorial Day, daily 9–5; wildlife-viewing tours mid-Nov.–Mar.*

★ **National Museum of Wildlife Art.** An impressive collection of wildlife art—most of it devoted to North American species—is displayed in the 13 galleries displaying the work of artists Karl Bodmer, Albert Bierstadt, Charles Russell, John Clymer, Robert Bateman, Carl Rungius, and others. You can also use one of the spotting scopes set up in areas overlooking the National Elk Refuge to watch wildlife in its native habitat. ✉ *2820 Rungius Rd., Jackson* ☎ *307/733–5771* ⊕ *www.wildlifeart. org* ✇ *$8* ☯ *June–Sept. and Dec.–Mar., daily 9–5; Apr., May, Oct. and Nov., Mon.–Sat. 9–5, Sun. 1–5.*

**Town Square.** You can spend an entire day wandering around Jackson's always bustling Town Square, a park-like area crisscrossed with winding paths and bedecked with arches woven from hundreds of elk antlers. Shops and restaurants surround the square, and there's often entertainment, including a melodramatic "shoot-out" summer evenings at approximately 6:30. At the southwest corner of the square, you can board a stagecoach for a ride around the area. ✉ *Jackson.*

SCENIC STOPS **Bridger-Teton National Forest.** This 3.4-million-acre forest has something for everyone: history, hiking, camping, and wildlife. It encompasses the Teton Wilderness east of Grand Teton National Park and John D. Rockefeller Memorial Parkway, and south of Yellowstone National Park, the Gros Ventre Wilderness southeast of Jackson, and the Bridger Wilderness farther south and east. No motor vehicles are allowed in the wildernesses, but there are many scenic drives, natural springs (including Granite Hot Springs) where you can swim or soak throughout the year (in winter access is on snowmobiles or dogsleds), and cultural sights like abandoned lumber camps in the national forest between the wildernesses. Get information about the forest at Jackson Hole and Greater Yellowstone Visitor Center in Jackson. ✉ *340 N. Cache St., Jackson* ☎ *307/739–5500* ⊕ *www.fs.fed.us/btnf* ✇ *Free, some picnic sites $5.*

**Caribou–Targhee National Forest.** The Targhee division of this forest includes the region primarily on the west side of the Teton Range, mainly in Idaho. Recreation includes camping, hiking, and wildlife watching. ✉ *Rte. 22 and U.S. 26 west of Jackson* ☎ *208/354–2312* ⊕ *www.fs.fed.us/r4/caribou-targhee* ✇ *Free.*

★ ☺ **National Elk Refuge.** More than 7,000 elk spend winter in the National Elk Refuge, which was established in 1912 to rescue starving herds. The animals migrate to the refuge grounds in late fall and remain until early spring. Trumpeter swans live here, too, as do bald eagles, coyotes, and wolves. In winter you can take a wagon or sleigh ride through the herd. You may see a cow lick her calf, or two bulls sparring with each other. It is just as likely that the elk will be lying down, resting as you drive by them. In summer, migration means that there are fewer big-game animals here, but you likely will see waterfowl and you can also fish on the refuge. ✉ *2820 Rungius Rd., Jackson* ☎ *307/733–9212* ✇ *Sleigh rides $13* ☯ *Year-round; sleigh rides mid-Dec.–Mar.*

18

## Area Activities

### Sports & the Outdoors

GOLF **Jackson Hole Golf and Tennis Club.** This 18-hole course redesigned by Robert Trent Jones has views of the Teton Range and is undergoing a major renovation that is slated for completion in 2007. It has been ranked as Wyoming's top course by Golf Magazine. ⊠ *5000 Spring Gulch Rd., 9 mi north of Jackson on U.S. 189 then 2 mi west at Gros Ventre Junction to Spring Gulch Rd.* ☎ *307/733–3111, 307/543–2811, or 800/628–9988* ⊕ *www.jhgtc.com* ⊙ *Early June–late Sept.*

**Teton Pines Resort and Country Tennis Club.** Designed by Arnold Palmer and Ed Seay, this relatively flat 18-hole course near Teton Village affords views of the Tetons and abundant wildlife. It's certified as an Audubon course. ⊠ *3450 N. Clubhouse Dr., Wilson* ☎ *307/733–1005 or 800/238–2223* ⊕ *www.tetonpines.com* ⊡ *$65–$175* ⊙ *Early June–late Sept.*

WINTER SPORTS Skiers and snowboarders love **Jackson Hole Mountain Resort,** one of the great skiing experiences in America. There are literally thousands of routes up and down the mountain, and not all of them are hellishly steep, despite Jackson's reputation. ⊠ *Box 290, Teton Village 83025* ☎ *307/733–2292 or 800/333–7766* ⊕ *www.jacksonhole.com.*

### Arts & Entertainment

ART GALLERIES **Trailside Galleries.** Traditional Western art including paintings by the biggest names are here—Charles M. Russell, John Clymer, and Howard Terpening—along with today's most talented Western painters including Z. S. Laing, Nancy Glazier, Bill Anton, and Tim Cox. ⊠ *1105 N. Center St., Jackson* ☎ *307/733–3186.*

Fodor'sChoice **Under the Willow Photo Gallery.** Abi Garaman has been capturing images
★ of Jackson Hole and Grand Teton National Park on film for more than half a century and has produced a wide selection of images of wildlife, mountains, barns, and both summer and winter scenes. ⊠ *50 S. Cache St., Jackson* ☎ *307/733–6633.*

**Wild By Nature Gallery.** Here you will find wildlife and landscape photography by Henry W. Holdsworth, plus books and note cards. ⊠ *95 W. Deloney Ave., Jackson* ☎ *307/733–8877.*

**Wild Exposures Gallery.** The work of Jeff Hogan, Scott McKinley, and Andrew Weller has been in National Geographic and on the BBC, and you'll find it here. Their work includes local landscapes (Mormon Row, the Tetons, and the Snake River) and wildlife (mountain sheep, coyotes, birds, and elk). ⊠ *60 E. Broadway Ave., Jackson* ☎ *307/739–1777.*

NIGHTLIFE **Million Dollar Cowboy Bar.** Everyone here dresses up in cowboy garb and tries to two-step into the Old West. You'll find locals who come here to dance and tourists who like to climb on the saddle seats. ⊠ *25 N. Cache St., Jackson* ☎ *307/733–2207.*

THEATER **Jackson Hole Playhouse.** You can attend live theater from late May to September in Jackson; some of the performances are dinner shows. ⊠ *145 W. Deloney Ave., Jackson* ☎ *307/733–6994.*

## FAMILY PICKS

**Float the Snake.** Climb aboard a big rubber raft and hang on for a float trip on the Snake River (not suitable for very young children).

**Mount a horse.** Rent a horse for a couple of hours, take a guided tour, or stay at a guest ranch where you can ride every day.

**Ride a stagecoach.** Experience the Old West with a stagecoach ride around the Town Square in Jackson.

**Take a sleigh ride.** See thousands of elk while riding a horse-drawn sleigh through the National Elk Refuge. You can watch the elk eat, sleep, and spar with each other.

## Shopping

**Jack Dennis Sports.** Jackson's premier sports shop—an internationally known fishing and sporting headquarters—is well stocked with the best in outdoor equipment for winter and summer. You can get everything from a canoe or backpack to skis and kayaks, plus clothing and other supplies. ⊠ *50 E. Broadway Ave., Jackson* ☎ *307/733–3270.*

**Jackson Hole Clothiers.** Here, there's a large selection of Western wear, belts, purses, and leather jackets for women. ⊠ *45 E. Deloney Ave., Jackson* ☎ *307/733–7211.*

# WHERE TO STAY & EAT

18

### About the Restaurants

Though the park itself has some excellent restaurants, don't miss dining in Jackson, where restaurants combine game, fowl, and fish with the enticing spices and sauces of European cuisine and the lean ingredients, vegetarian entrees, and meat cuts that reflect the desires of health-consciousness diners. Steaks are usually cut from grass-fed Wyoming beef, but you'll also find buffalo and elk on the menu; poultry and pasta are offered by most restaurants, and you'll find fresh salads and fish (trout, tilapia, and salmon are most common). Just about everywhere, you can order a burger or a bowl of homemade soup. Casual is the word for most dining both within and outside the park. An exception is Jenny Lake Lodge, where jackets and ties are recommended for dinner. Breakfast is big: steak and eggs, pancakes, biscuits and gravy; lunches are lighter, often taken in a sack to enjoy on the trail.

### About the Hotels

The choice of lodging properties is as diverse as the landscape itself. You will find simple cabins or basic motel rooms, but also can settle in to a homey B&B, or a luxurious suite in a full-service resort.

For information on lodging and dining (as well as tours) in the park, contact the park's largest concessionaire, **Grand Teton Lodge Company.** ✍ *Box 250, Moran, WY 83013* ☎ *307/543–3100, or 800/628–9988* 🖷 *307/543–3143* ⊕ *www.gtlc.com.*

You can reserve rooms near the park through two agencies. **Jackson Hole Central Reservations** (☏ 307/733–4005 or 800/443–6931 ⊕ www. jacksonholewy.com) handles hotels as well as B&Bs. **Resort Reservations** (☏ 307/733–6331 or 800/329–9205 ⊕ www.jacksonhole.net) is the place to call for reservations for most motels in Jackson.

## About the Campgrounds

You'll find a variety of campgrounds, from small areas where only tents are allowed, to full RV parks with all services. If you don't have a tent, but want to bring your sleeping bags, you can take advantage of the tent cabins at Colter Bay, where you have a hard floor, cots and canvas walls to keep the weather at bay. Standard campsites include a place to pitch your tent or park your trailer/camper, a fire pit for cooking, and a picnic table. All developed campgrounds have toilets and water; plan to bring your own firewood.

Check-in at National Park Service campsites as early as possible—sites are assigned on a first-come, first-served basis. You can camp in the park's backcountry year-round, provided you have the requisite permit and are able to gain access to your site. Between June 1 and September 15, backcountry campers in the park are limited to one stay of up to 10 days. You can reserve a backcountry site for a $15 nonrefundable fee by faxing a request to the backcountry permit office ⊟ 307/739–3438 or by writing to the office at ✉ Box 170, Moose, 83012. You can also take a chance that the site you want will be open when you show up, in which case you pay no fee. Campfires are prohibited in the backcountry except at designated lakeshore campsites.

# Where to Eat

## In the Park

★ **$$$$** ✕ **Jenny Lake Lodge Dining Room.** Elegant yet rustic, this is Grand Teton National Park's finest dining establishment, with jackets required for men. The menu is ever changing and offers fish, pasta, chicken, and beef; the wine list is extensive. Dinner is prix-fixe; lunch is à la carte. ✉ *Jenny Lake Rd., 2 mi off Teton Park Rd., 12 mi north of Moose Junction* ☏307/ 733–4647 or 800/628–9988 ⌂ *Jacket required* ⌖ *Reservations essential.* $53 ⊟ AE, MC, V ⊙ *Closed early Oct.–late May.*

★ **$$–$$$** ✕ **Dornan's.** Hearty portions of beef, beans, potatoes, short ribs, stew, and lemonade or hot coffee are the dinner standbys at Dornan's. Locals know this spot for the barbecue cooked over wood fires. At breakfast, count on old-fashioned staples such as sourdough pancakes or biscuits and gravy. You can eat your chuck wagon meal inside one of the restaurant's tepees if it happens to be raining or windy; otherwise, sit at outdoor picnic tables with views of the Snake River and the Tetons. The chuck wagon operates September–May only, but there's also a pizza parlor where lunch is served year-round. ✉ *10 Moose Rd., off Teton Park Rd. at Moose Junction* ☏ 307/733–2415. $14–$22 ⊟ MC, V.

**$$–$$$**
Fodor'sChoice
★
✕ **Jackson Lake Lodge Mural Room.** The ultimate park dining experience is found in this large room that gets its name from a 700-square-foot mural painted by Western artist Carl Roters. The mural details an 1837 Wyoming mountain man rendezvous and covers two walls of the din-

ing room. Select from a menu that includes trout, elk, beef, and pasta. The cedar plank salmon is a great choice, or try a buffalo steak. The tables face tall windows affording a panoramic view of Willow Flats and Jackson Lake to the northern Tetons. ⊠ *U.S. 89/191/287, ½ mi north of Jackson Lake Junction* ☎ *307/543–2811 Ext. 1911 or 800/628–9988. $18–$27* ⊟ *AE, MC, V* ⊘ *Closed mid-Oct.–late May.*

**$–$$$** ✕ **The Peaks.** Part of Signal Mountain Lodge, this casual room has exposed ceiling beams and big square windows overlooking southern Jackson Lake and the Tetons. The emphasis here is on fish: Rocky Mountain trout is marinated, lightly floured, and grilled, or simply grilled and topped with lemon-parsley butter. ⊠ *Teton Park Rd., 4 mi south of Jackson Lake Junction* ☎ *307/543–2831. $12–$22* ⊟ *AE, D, MC, V* ⊘ *Closed mid-Oct.–mid-May.*

**$–$$** ✕ **Chuckwagon Steak and Pasta House.** The extremely popular Chuckwagon serves both steak and pasta and has an extensive salad bar served out of a chuck wagon. The quick service and inexpensive prices make this a good choice for families or travelers on a budget. ⊠ *2 mi off U.S. 89/191/287, 5 mi north of Jackson Lake Junction* ☎ *307/543–2811. $8–$18* ⊟ *AE, MC, V* ⊘ *Closed late Sept.–late May.*

**¢–$** ✕ **Jackson Lake Lodge Pioneer Grill.** With an old-fashioned soda fountain, friendly service, and seats along a winding counter, this eatery recalls a 1950s-era luncheonette. ⊠ *U.S. 89/191/287, ½ mi north of Jackson Lake Junction* ☎ *307/543–2811 Ext. 1911. $4–$12* ⊟ *AE, MC, V* ⊘ *Closed early Oct.–late May.*

**¢–$** ✕ **John Colter Cafe Court.** At this Colter Bay Village spot you can buy hamburgers, hot and cold New York–style deli sandwiches, and ice cream. ⊠ *5 mi north of Jackson Lake Lodge* ☎ *307/543–2811. $4–$10* ⊟ *AE, MC, V* ⊘ *Closed early Sept.–early June.*

**18**

PICNIC AREAS  The park has 11 designated picnic areas, each with tables and grills, and most with pit toilets and water pumps or faucets. In addition to those listed here you can find picnic areas at Colter Bay Village Campground, Cottonwood Creek, Moose Visitor Center, the east shore of Jackson Lake, and South Jenny Lake and String Lake trailheads.

**Chapel of the Sacred Heart.** From this intimate lakeside picnic area you can look across southern Jackson Lake to Mt. Moran. ⊠ *¼ mi east of Signal Mountain Lodge, off Teton Park Rd., 4 mi south of Jackson Lake Junction.*

**Colter Bay Visitor Center.** This big picnic area, spectacularly located right on the beach at Jackson Lake, gets crowded in July and August. It's conveniently close to flush toilets and stores. ⊠ *2 mi off U.S. 89/191/287, 5 mi north of Jackson Lake Junction.*

**Hidden Falls.** Adjacent to the Jenny Lake shuttle boat dock is this shaded, pine-scented picnic site. An easy ½-mi hike takes you to the falls. Take the shuttle boat across Jenny Lake to reach the Cascade Canyon trailhead. ⊠ *At the Cascade Canyon trailhead.*

**Signal Mountain Lodge.** Slightly less crowded than the picnic area at Colter Bay Visitor Center, this lakeside picnic area can accommodate a big group. Flush toilets and stores are nearby. ⊠ *Teton Park Rd., 4 mi south of Jackson Lake Junction.*

One of the park's most isolated and uncrowded picnic sites is about 6 mi northwest of the Moran entrance station at the east end of **Two Ocean Lake.** A mile north of the entrance station turn east onto Pacific Creek Road, and about 2 mi in from U.S. 26/89/181 take a left (turning north) on the first dirt road. Two Ocean Lake is about 2 mi down the dirt road. ⊠ *Off Pacific Creek Rd., 2 mi east of U.S. 26/89/191.*

## Outside the Park

**$$–$$$$** ✕ **Mangy Moose.** Folks pour in off the ski slopes for a lot of food and talk at this two-level restaurant-plus-bar with an outdoor deck. Antiques and oddities, including a full-size stuffed caribou (complete with sleigh) suspended from the ceiling, decorate the space. The noise level is high, but you get decent fare and a chance to try the house Moose Drool beer. Beef dominates the menu, though you can also get chicken, seafood, and pasta. ⊠ *Teton Village* ☎ *307/733–4913. $13–$33* ▭ *AE, MC, V.*

★ **$$–$$$$** ✕ **Snake River Grill.** One of Jackson's best dining options, this sophisticated dining room offers creatively prepared free-range veal chops, grilled venison buffalo strip steak, elk chops, and grilled Idaho red-rainbow trout. There's an extensive wine list. ⊠ *84 E. Broadway Ave., Jackson* ☎ *307/733–0557. $19–$43* ▭ *AE, MC, V* ⊘ *Closed Apr. and Nov. No lunch.*

**$$–$$$** ✕ **Bar J Chuckwagon.** This may be the best value in Jackson Hole. You
Fodor'sChoice get a full ranch-style meal: roast beef, baked beans, coleslaw, and spiced
★ cake, plus a complete Western show featuring singing, stories, and even cowboy poetry. The dinner and show take place inside, so don't let the weather keep you away. Reservations recommended. ⊠ *Rte. 390, 6 mi north of Jackson, Jackson Hole* ☎ *307/733–3370. $18–26* ▭ *D, MC, V* ⊘ *Closed Oct.–Memorial Day.*

★ **$$–$$$** ✕ **Nani's Genuine Pasta House.** The ever-changing menu at this cozy restaurant, which was remodeled in 2006, may include braised veal shanks with saffron risotto or other regional Italian cooking. The place is almost hidden behind a motel and is designed to attract gourmets who will really appreciate the cuisine. The menu changes nightly. ⊠ *242 N. Glenwood St., Jackson* ☎ *307/733–3888. $14–$28* ▭ *MC, V.*

★ **$$–$$$** ✕ **Sweetwater Restaurant.** The log cabin atmosphere might not seem to match the globe-trotting menu, but the combination works. Start with smoked buffalo carpaccio or eggplant rouille; then go on to lamb dishes, mesquite chicken, or shrimp *spetses* (simmered in tomato and garlic with feta cheese). In the summer you can dine outside on the patio. ⊠ *85 S. King St., Jackson* ☎ *307/733–3553. $13–$26* ▭ *AE, D, MC, V.*

★ **$–$$$** ✕ **Billy's Giant Hamburgers.** Sharing an entrance with Cadillac Grille, Billy's is 1950s-style, with a few booths and a bunch of tall tables with high stools. Though you can choose from a variety of sandwiches, Billy's specialty is big—really big—burgers that are really good. ⊠ *55 N. Cache Dr., Jackson* ☎ *307/733–3279. $8–$26* ▭ *AE, MC, V.*

**$–$$** ✕ **Jedediah's House of Sourdough.** Friendly, noisy, and elbow-knocking, this restaurant a block east of Town Square in a historic home caters to the big appetite. The big meal here is breakfast. Try the sourdough pancakes, called sourjacks, or Teton taters and eggs. There's a kids' menu and outdoor deck dining for lunch where you can have a mountain man–sized burger. ✉ *135 E. Broadway Ave., Jackson* ☎ *307/733–5671. $10–$20* ⊟ *AE, D, DC, MC, V.*

¢–$$ ✕ **The Bunnery.** Tucked into a tiny spot in the Hole-in-the-Wall Mall, this is where locals go for breakfast, though you can get a great lunch or dinner as well. It's usually busy, and so there may be a short wait, but the food is worth it. Breads are home-baked, mostly of a combined grain known as OSM (oats, sunflower, millet), and they've been known to sell and ship the bread to customers throughout the world. ✉ *130 N. Cache St., Jackson* ☎ *307/733–5474. $7–$17* ⊟ *MC, V.*

## Where to Stay

### In the Park

$$$$ ⬚ **Jenny Lake Lodge.** Nestled well off Jenny Lake Road, the lodge borders a wildflower meadow, and its guest cabins are well spaced in lodgepole-pine groves. Cabin interiors, with sturdy pine beds and handmade quilts and electric blankets, live up to the elegant rustic theme, and cabin suites have fireplaces. Breakfast, bicycle and horseback riding, and dinner are included in the price. ✉ *Jenny Lake Rd., 2 mi off Teton Park Rd., 12 mi north of Moose Junction* ☎ *307/733–4647 or 800/628–9988* 🖶 *307/543–3143* ⊕ *www.gtlc.com* ⇦ *37 cabins* ⚍ *Restaurant, bicycles. $495* ⊟ *AE, DC, MC, V* ☉ *Closed early Oct.–late May* ⫶◯⫶ *MAP.*

$$$–$$$$ ⬚ **Dornan's Spur Ranch Cabins.** Near Moose Visitor Center in Dornan's all-in-one shopping–dining–recreation development, these one- and two-bedroom cabins have great views of the Tetons and the Snake River. Each of the log cabins has a full kitchen as well as a generously sized living-dining room and a furnished porch with a Weber grill in summer. ✉ *10 Moose Rd., off Teton Park Rd. at Moose Junction* ☎ *307/733–2522* 🖶 *307/733–3544* ⊕ *www.dornans.com* ⇦ *12 cabins* ⚍ *Restaurant, bar. $155–$230* ⊟ *D, MC, V.*

$$$–$$$$ ⬚ **Jackson Lake Lodge.** This large, full-service resort stands on a bluff with spectacular views across Jackson Lake to the Tetons. (And we do mean full service: there's everything from live music in the bar to in-house religious services.) The upper lobby has 60-foot picture windows and a collection of Native American artifacts and Western art. Many of the guest rooms have spectacular lake and mountain views, while others have little or no view, so ask when you book. ✉ *U.S. 89/191/287, ½ mi north of Jackson Lake Junction* ☎ *307/543–3100 or 800/628–9988* 🖶*307/543–3143* ⊕*www.gtlc.com* ⇦*385 rooms* ⚍*2 restaurants, refrigerator (some), pool, bar, airport shuttle, some pets allowed. $175–$259* ⊟ *AE, MC, V* ☉ *Closed early Oct.–mid-May.*

$$–$$$$ ⬚ **Signal Mountain Lodge.** These relaxed, pine-shaded cabins sit on Jackson Lake's southern shoreline. The main building has a cozy lounge and a grand pine deck overlooking the lake. Cabins are equipped with sleek kitchens and pine tables. The smaller log cabins are in shaded areas, and eight of them have a fireplace. Rooms 151–178 have lake views. ✉ *Teton Park Rd., 4 mi south of Jackson Lake Junction* ☎ *307/543–2831* 🖶 *307/543–2569* ⊕ *www.signalmountainlodge.com* ⇦ *47 rooms, 32*

**18**

*log cabins ⚷ 2 restaurants, kitchen, refrigerator (some), bar. $109–$280* ⊟ *AE, D, MC, V* ⊙ *Closed mid-Oct.–mid-May.*

**$–$$$**   ▣ **Moulton Ranch Cabins.** Along Mormon Row, these cabins stand a few

**Fodor'sChoice** dozen yards south of the famous Moulton Barn, which you see on

★ brochures, jigsaw puzzles, and photographs of the park. The land was once part of the T. A. Moulton homestead, and the cabins are still owned by the Moulton family. The quiet property has views of the Teton and the Gros Ventre ranges, and the owners can regale you with stories about early homesteaders. There's a dance hall in the barn, making this an ideal place for family and small group reunions. No smoking on the premises. ⊠ *Off Antelope Flats Rd., U.S. 26/89/191, 2 mi north of Moose Junction* ☎ *307/733–3749 or 208/529–2354* ⊕ *www.moultonranchcabins. com* ⤳ *5 units* ⚷ *Kitchens (some), no-smoking rooms. $95–$195* ⊟ *MC, V* ⊙ *Closed Oct.–May. No Sun. check-in.*

**¢–$$**   ▣ **Colter Bay Village.** Near Jackson Lake, this complex of Western-style cabins—some with one room, others with two or more rooms—are within walking distance of the lake. The property has splendid views and an excellent marina and beach for the windsurfing crowd (you'll need a wet suit). The tent cabins aren't fancy and they share communal baths, but they do keep the wind and rain off. There's also a 116-space RV park. ⊠ *2 mi off U.S. 89/191/287, 5 mi north of Jackson Lake Junction* ☎ *307/733–3100 or 800/628–9988* 🖷 *307/543–3143* ⤳ *166 cabins, 66 tent cabins* ⚷ *2 restaurants, bar, laundry facilities, some pets allowed. $39 tent cabins, $40–$147 1-2 bedroom cabins* ⊟ *AE, MC, V* ⊙ *Closed late Sept.–late May (shorter season for tent cabins).*

**CAMPGROUNDS &**   ⚌ **Colter Bay RV Park.** Adjacent to the National Park Service–operated

**RV PARKS** Colter Bay Campground, this concessionaire-operated campground is

**$$$** the only RV park in Grand Teton where you can get full hookups. ⊠ *2 mi off U.S. 89/191/287, 5 mi north of Jackson Lake Junction* ☎ *307/ 543–2811* ⤳ *116 RV sites with full hookups* ⚷ *Flush toilets, full hookups, dump station, drinking water, guest laundry, showers, bear boxes, fire grates, picnic tables. $44* ⚌ *Reservations not accepted* ⊟ *AE, MC, V* ⊙ *Late May–late Sept.*

**★ $**   ⚌ **Colter Bay Campground.** Busy, noisy, and filled by noon, this campground has both tent and trailer or RV sites—and one great advantage: it's centrally located. Try to get a site as far from the nearby cabin road as possible. This is the only National Park Service–operated campground in the park that has hot showers. The maximum stay is 14 days. ⊠ *2 mi off U.S. 89/191/287, 5 mi north of Jackson Lake Junction* ☎ *307/543–2100 or 800/628–9988* ⤳ *350 tent or RV-trailer sites* ⚷ *Flush toilets, dump station, drinking water, guest laundry, showers, bear boxes, fire grates, picnic tables. $14* ⚌ *Reservations not accepted* ⊟ *AE, D, MC, V* ⊙ *Late-May–late Sept.*

**$**   ⚌ **Gros Ventre.** The park's biggest campground is set in an open, grassy area on the bank of the Gros Ventre River, away from the mountains and 2 mi southwest of Kelly. Try to get a site close to the river. The campground usually doesn't fill until nightfall, if at all. There's a maximum stay of 14 days. ⊠ *4 mi off U.S. 26/89/191, 1½ mi west of Kelly on Gros Ventre River Rd., 6 mi south of Moose Junction* ☎ *307/739–3603*

🛏 *360 tent or RV sites* 🖒 *Flush toilets, dump station, drinking water, bear boxes, fire grates, picnic tables. $12* 🖒 *Reservations not accepted* 🖃 *AE, D, MC, V* 🕙 *May–mid-Oct.*

★ $ 🔥 **Jenny Lake.** Wooded sites and Teton views make this the most desirable campground in the park, and it fills early. The small, quiet facility allows tents only, and limits stays to a maximum of seven days. Maximum one vehicle per campsite no longer than 14 feet. 🖂 *Jenny Lake Rd., ½ mi off Teton Park Rd., 8 mi north of Moose Junction* 🕾 *No phone* 🛏 *49 sites* 🖒 *Flush toilets, drinking water, bear boxes, fire grates, picnic tables. $12* 🖒 *Reservations not accepted* 🖃 *No credit cards* 🕙 *Mid-May–late Sept.*

$ 🔥 **Lizard Creek.** Views of Jackson Lake, wooded sites, and the relative isolation of this campground make it a relaxing choice. There is a nearby Trails Camp Store that sells organic and natural foods, camping gear, ice, and gasoline. You can stay here no more than 14 days. No vehicles over 30 feet are allowed. 🖂 *U.S. 89/191/287, 12 mi north of Jackson Lake Junction* 🕾 *307/739–3603* 🛏 *60 tent/trailer sites* 🖒 *Flush toilets, drinking water, bear boxes, fire grates* 🛏 *$15 or $5 for campers without cars (hikers and bikers)* 🖒 *Reservations not accepted* 🖃 *No credit cards* 🕙 *Early June–early Sept.*

## Outside the Park

★ $$$$ 🏨 **Amangani.** You need truly deep pockets to stay here, but the exquisite architecture and flawless design make this "peaceful home" on a cliff edge on Gros Ventre Butte pure luxury. Huge two-story windows in the simple yet magnificent lobby overlook the Teton valley, and a generous use of redwood, sandstone, and cedar complements the natural setting. Rooms have gas fireplaces and balconies overlooking the valley, and the bathtubs offer great sunset views. You won't find more amenities, better service, or more understated elegance anywhere in the valley. 🖂 *1535 N.E. Butte Rd., Jackson 83001* 🕾 *307/734–7333 or 877/734–7333* 🖷 *307/734–7332* 🌐 *www.amangani.com* 🛏 *40 suites* 🖒 *Restaurant, room service, safe, refrigerator, VCR, tennis courts, pool, spa, bar, laundry service, airport shuttle. $750–$1,300* 🖃 *AE, D, DC, MC, V.*

$$$$ 🏨 **Lost Creek Ranch.** This luxurious dude ranch 8 mi north of Moose and right on the edge of Grand Teton Park has large, well-furnished rooms and cabins with unsurpassed views. You get entertainment in the evening, a horse to ride, a scenic Snake River float trip, a ticket to the Jackson Hole Rodeo, hiking in Grand Teton National Park, and full spa services, including the steam, weight, sauna, and aerobics rooms. For additional fees you can participate in fishing trips, white-water rafting trips, skeet shooting, and spa treatments. 🖂 *Old Ranch Rd., Box 95, Moose 83012* 🕾 *307/733–3435* 🖷 *307/733–1954* 🌐 *www.lostcreek.com* 🛏 *10 cabins* 🖒 *Restaurant, kitchen (some), refrigerators, tennis court, pool, spa, laundry service, airport shuttle. $6,015–$14,120 per week for 2–4 guests* 🖃 *AE, D, DC, MC, V* 🕙 *Closed Oct.–May* 🍴 *FAP.*

$$$$ 🏨 **Parkway Inn.** Each room has a distinctive look in oak or wicker, and FodorsChoice all are filled with antiques, from 19th-century pieces onward. The overall effect is homey and delightful—especially appealing if you plan to ★ stay several days or longer. 🖂 *125 N. Jackson St., Jackson 83001* 🕾 *307/733–3143 or 800/247–8390* 🖷 *307/733–0955* 🌐 *www.*

18

*parkwayinn.com* ⌐ *37 rooms, 12 suites* ⌂ *Pool. $199–$225 rooms; $269–$329 suites* ⊟ *AE, D, DC, MC, V* |○| *CP.*

**$$$$** 🏨 **Snake River Lodge and Spa.** From goose-down comforters and plush robes in every room to facials, salt glows, manicures, and hydrotherapy at the spa, this ski-in resort adjacent to Jackson Hole Ski Area pampers you. The indoor-outdoor pool area, where waterfalls cascade over large boulders and rocks, has a fire pit and views of the Jackson Hole ski area. The five-story Spa and Health Club has separate men's and women's floors with steam rooms and soaking tubs. ⊠ *7710 Granite Loop Rd., Teton Village 83025* ☎ *307/732–6000 or 800/445–4655* 🖷 *307/732–6009* ⊕ *www.snakeriverlodge.com* ⌐ *80 rooms, 40 condominiums* ⌂ *Restaurant, room service, refrigerator, pool, gym, spa, bar. $309–$450 rooms, $550–$1,275 condominiums* ⊟ *AE, DC, MC, V.*

**★ $$$$** 🏨 **Wort Hotel.** The locals have been gathering at this Jackson landmark half a block from Town Square since the early 1940s, and you can view the history of Jackson in the photos and clippings posted in the lobby. The spacious rooms have lodgepole furniture and comfortable armchairs. Junior suites have large sitting areas. ⊠ *50 N. Glenwood St., Jackson 83001* ☎ *307/733–2190 or 800/322–2727* 🖷 *307/733–2067* ⊕ *www. worthotel.com* ⌐ *59 rooms, 4 suites* ⌂ *Restaurant, room service, bar. $289–$329 rooms, $399–$599 suites* ⊟ *AE, D, MC, V.*

**$$–$$$$** 🏨 **Grand Targhee Ski and Summer Resort.** Perched on the west side of the Tetons, this small but modern facility has the uncrowded, stroll-around atmosphere of a small village in the Alps. The motel-style rooms have lodgepole furniture; condominiums have an adobe fireplace and a semi-private balcony. They offer lodging packages that include ski lift tickets. ⊠ *3300 Ski Hill Rd., Box SKI, Alta 83414* ☎ *307/353–2300 or 800/827–4433* 🖷 *307/353–8148* ⊕ *www.grandtarghee.com* ⌐ *65 rooms, 32 condos* ⌂ *5 restaurants, pool, spa, airport shuttle. $118–$468* ⊟ *AE, D, MC, V.*

**$$$** 🏨 **Flagg Ranch Resort.** A sprawling property 4 mi north of the park, Flagg Ranch puts up guests in cabins spread out in the pine forest. With its Western-style restaurant, plus float trips, guided snowmobile tours into Yellowstone and the surrounding area, and snow-coach tours that leave from the premises, this resort is particularly popular with families. There's a grocery store and gas station on the grounds. ⊠ *John D. Rockefeller Jr. Memorial Pkwy., 4 mi north of Grand Teton National Park boundary* ⊂Ð *P.O. Box 187, Moran 83013* ☎ *307/543–2861 or 800/ 443–2311* 🖷 *307/543–2356* ⊕ *www.flaggranch.com* ⌐ *92 cabins* ⌂ *Restaurant, bar, laundry facilities, some pets allowed. $159–$169* ⊟ *AE, D, MC, V* ☉ *Closed mid-Oct.–mid-Dec. and mid-Mar.–mid-May.*

**$–$$** 🏨 **Antler Inn.** Like real estate agents say, location, location, and location are the three things that matter, and few motels in Jackson are as convenient to Town Square as this one, just a block south. The motel rooms are standard, but some have fireplaces. ⊠ *43 W. Pearl St., Jackson 83001* ☎ *307/733–2535 or 800/522–2406* 🖷 *307/733–4158* ⌐ *110 rooms* ⌂ *Some pets allowed. $88–$150* ⊟ *AE, D, DC, MC, V.*

**$** 🏨 **Hostelx.** Although the classic hostel accommodations at this lodge-style inn are basic, you can't get any closer to Jackson Hole Mountain Resort for a better price. It's popular with young, budget-conscious people. Rooms, some of which have bunk beds, sleep two to four people. Downstairs common areas include a lounge with a fireplace, a movie room, and a ski-waxing room. ⊠ *3315 McCollister Dr., Box 546, Jackson Hole 83025* ☎ *307/733–3415* 🖷 *307/739–1142* ⊕ *www.hostelx. com* ⤳ *55 rooms* ⚴ *No a/c, no phone, no TV, bar, laundry facilities, public Internet, no-smoking rooms. $60* ⊟ *AE, MC, V.*

**$** 🖼 **Twin Pines Lodge & Cabins.** You'll climb stairs to the second-floor rooms in this log lodge that is on the National Register of Historic Places, but those stairs also provide access to a balcony area with comfortable seating and lots of reading material. The lodge rooms have tall pine beds, and small bathrooms. You can park directly in front of the cabins, which also have pine furniture and country quilts. The lodge reception area has a large fireplace, comfortable couches, and a breakfast area. ⊠ *218 W. Ramshorn Ave., Dubois 82513* ☎ *307/455–2600 or 800/550–6332* 🖷 *307/455–2608* ⤳ *5 rooms, 10 cabins. $88–$100* ⊟ *AE, D, MC, V.*

CAMPGROUNDS & RV PARKS
¢–$$
🔺 **Caribou–Targhee National Forest.** There are about 30 campgrounds here in pine forest and sometimes near streams. These campgrounds appeal to families and people who want to camp close to the areas where they will hike, bike, or fish. ⊠ *1405 Hollipark Dr., (Rte. 22 and U.S. 26 west of Jackson), Idaho Falls, ID 83403* ☎ *208/624–3151, 877/444–6777 campground reservations* ⤳ *984 sites* ⚴ *Drinking water, fire pits, picnic tables. $8–$24* ⊟ *AE, D, MC, V* ☺ *June–Sept.*

# GRAND TETON ESSENTIALS

**18**

ACCESSIBILITY The front-country portions of Grand Teton are largely accessible to people in wheelchairs. There's designated parking at most sites, and some interpretive trails are easily accessible. There are accessible restrooms at visitor centers. TDD telephones are available at **Colter Bay Visitor Center** ☎ 307/739–3544 and at **Moose Visitor Center** ☎ 307/739–3400. For an Easy Access guide to the park, stop by one of the visitor centers or contact the park (☎ 307/739–3400 TTY).

ADMISSION FEES Park entrance fees are $25 per car, truck, or RV, $15 per motorcycle or snowmobile, and $12 per person on foot or bicycle. Annual passes are $40. A winter day-use fee is $5.

ADMISSION HOURS The park is open 24/7 year-round. The park is in the Mountain time zone.

ATMS/BANKS In the park, ATMs are at Colter Bay Grocery and General Store, Dornan's, Jackson Lake Lodge, and Signal Mountain Lodge. You can also find ATMs at Flagg Ranch Resort. The nearest full-service banks are in Jackson and Dubois.

AUTOMOBILE SERVICE STATIONS Automobile service stations are located in the park at Colter Bay Village, Dornan's, Jackson Lake Lodge, and Signal Mountain Lodge. Auto and RV repair is available at Colter Bay Village.

EMERGENCIES In case of a fire, medical, or police emergency in the park, dial 911. Park law enforcement rangers are located at ranger stations (at Colter Bay, Jenny Lake, and Moose).

🚑**Grand Teton Medical Clinic** ⊠ Near the Chevron station, ½ mi north of Jackson Lake Junction ☎ 307/ 543–2514 or 307/733–8002 ☺ Mid-May–mid-Oct., daily 10–6. **St. John's Hospital** ⊠ 625 E. Broadway Ave., Jackson ☎ 307/733-3636 or 800/877-7078.

LOST AND FOUND The park's lost-and-found is at Moose Visitor Center.

PERMITS Backcountry permits, which must be obtained in person at Moose or Colter Bay visitor centers or Jenny Lake ranger station, are free and required for all overnight stays outside designated campgrounds. Seven-day boat permits, available year-round at Moose Visitor Center and in summer at Colter Bay and Signal Mountain ranger stations, cost $20 for motorized craft and $10 for nonmotorized craft and are good for 7 days. Annual permits are $40 for motorized craft and $20 for nonmotorized craft.

## POST OFFICES

🚩 **Kelly Post Office** ⊠ Kelly Rd., Kelly 83011 ☎ 307/733-8884. **Moose Post Office** ⊠ Visitor Center, Moose Village 83012 ☎ 307/733-3336. **Moran Post Office** ⊠ Moran Junction, Moran 83013 ☎ 307/543-2527.

PUBLIC TELEPHONES Public telephones may be found at park visitor centers and at Colter Bay Store, Dornan's, Jackson Lake Lodge, Leek's Marina, and Signal Mountain Lodge. Cell phones work in most developed areas and occasionally on trails.

RELIGIOUS SERVICES There are chapel services within the park on weekends late spring through early autumn. Nearby Jackson has other services. 🚩 **Chapel of the Sacred Heart** ⊠ ¼ mi east of Signal Mountain Lodge, off Teton Park Rd., 4 mi south of Jackson Lake Junction ⊙ Services June-Sept., Sat. 5:30 PM and Sun. 8 AM and 10 AM. **Chapel of the Transfiguration.** ⊠ ½ mi off Teton Park Rd., 2 mi north of Moose Junction

⊙ Late May-late Sept., Sun.: Eucharist 8 AM, service 10 AM.

RESTROOMS Public restrooms may be found at all park visitor centers, campgrounds, and ranger stations. There are restrooms at the picnic area north of Moose on Teton Park Road, and at String Lake and Colter Bay picnic areas.

## SHOPS & GROCERS

🚩 **Dornan's Moose Trading Post & Deli.** ⊠ 10 Moose Rd., off Teton Park Rd. at Moose Junction ☎ 307/733-2415 ⊙ Closed Dec.-Mar. **Hungry Jack's General Store.** ⊠ 5855 W. Hwy. 22, Wilson ☎ 307/733-3561.

## NEARBY TOWN INFORMATION

🚩 **Dubois Chamber of Commerce** ⌂ Box 632, Dubois, WY 82513 ☎ 307/455-2556 ⊕ www.duboiswyoming.org. **Eastern Idaho Visitor Information Center** ⊠ 630 W. Broadway, Box 50498, Idaho Falls, ID 83405 ☎ 208/523-1010 or 866/365-6943. **Jackson Chamber of Commerce** ⌂ Box 550, Jackson, WY 83001 ☎ 307/733-3316 ⊕ www.jacksonholechamber.com. **Jackson Hole and Greater Yellowstone Visitor Center.** ⊠ 532 N. Cache St., Jackson ☎ 307/733-3316 ⊕ www.fs.fed.us/jhgyvc ⊙ Memorial Day-Sept., daily 8-7; Oct.-Memorial Day, daily 9-5. **Jackson Lake/Colter Bay Visitor Center** ⊠ 2 mi off U.S. 89/191/287, 6 mi north of Jackson Lake Junction, Moran, WY 83013 ☎ 307/739-3594. **Pinedale Chamber of Commerce** ⊠ 32 E. Pine St., Pinedale, WY 82941 ☎ 307/367-2242 ⊕ www.pinedalechamber.com. **Teton Valley Chamber of Commerce** ⊠ 81 N. Main St. #C, Box 250, Driggs, ID 83422 ☎ 208/354-2500 ⊕ www.tetonvalleychamber.com.

## VISITOR INFORMATION

🚩 **Grand Teton National Park.** ⌂ Box 170, Moose, WY 83012 ☎ 307/739-3300, 307/739-3400 TTY ⊕ www.nps.gov/grte.

# Great Basin National Park

Bristlecone Pine and Wheeler Peak, Great Basin National Park

## WORD OF MOUTH

"The park's appeal has to do with silence and space, with the grand lonesome sweep of the country itself, with long visitas and clear air and sudden winds that roar like a locomotive and secret meadows jammed with wildflowers."

—Author Donald Dale Jackson

# WELCOME TO GREAT BASIN

## TOP REASONS TO GO

★ **Ancient Tree Spottings:** The bristlecone pines in Great Basin are thousands of years old.

★ **Being Away from It All:** Among the least visited of America's national parks, Great Basin doesn't know the meaning of the word "crowds."

★ **Wallet Stays in the Pocket:** There is no fee required to enter the park.

★ **Gather Your Pine Nuts While You May:** Come in the fall and go a little nutty, as you can gather up to three gunnysacks of pinyon pine nuts, found in abundance throughout the park and tasting oh so yummy—they're great on salads.

**1** Lehman Caves. Highlighted by the limestone cavern, this area is in some ways the heart of Great Basin. It includes a popular visitor center and two of the main campgrounds (both accessible for RVers). Nearby is the start of the Wheeler Peak Scenic Drive.

**2** Wheeler Peak. Rarely is a crown jewel truly so—but just look at this 13,063-footer when it's capped with snow. Hikers can climb the mountain via day-use-only trails, which also lead to three small alpine lakes, a glacier, and some ancient bristlecone pines.

**3** Granite Basin. This is the less-crowded part of an already sparsely visited park. Trails follow a handful of creeks around Pyramid Peak, and six primitive campgrounds line Snake Creek. A bristlecone pine grove is nearby, though far off any beaten path.

**4** Arch Canyon. A high-clearance vehicle is nice to have, and stout boots are mandatory to get to Lexington Arch, which is unusual in that it is formed of limestone, not sandstone as most arches are. This is a day-use-only area.

## GETTING ORIENTED

One of the smallest and least crowded national parks in the country (77,180 acres), Great Basin National Park, in eastern Nevada, occupies only a minute fraction of the almost 200,000 square mi of the Great Basin desert—yet it exemplifies the landscape and ecology of the region. This high desert (4,500 feet–6,200 feet in elevation), the largest desert in the United States, is bordered by the Sierra Nevada Range, the Rocky Mountains, the Columbia Plateau, and the Mojave and Sonoran deserts. It covers 75% of the state of Nevada and extends into California, Utah, and Idaho.

Bristlecone Pine

Lehman Caves

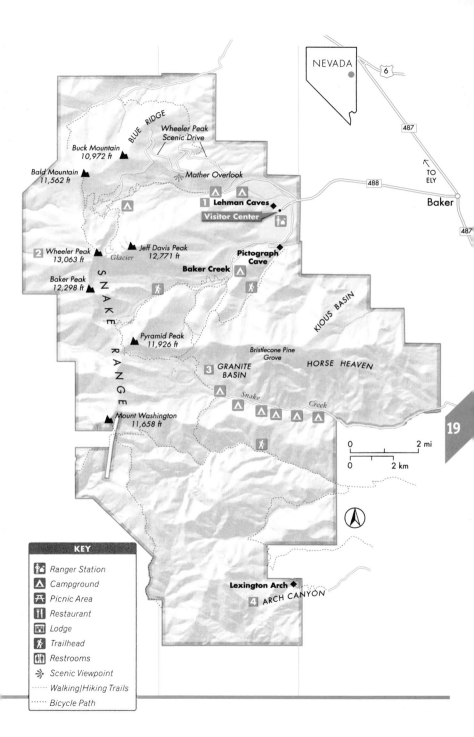

NEVADA

US 6

TO ELY

487

488

Baker

487

BLUE RIDGE

Wheeler Peak
Scenic Drive

Buck Mountain
10,972 ft

Bald Mountain
11,562 ft

Mather Overlook

**1 Lehman Caves**

**Visitor Center**

**2** Wheeler Peak
13,063 ft

Jeff Davis Peak
12,771 ft

Glacier

**Pictograph
Cave**

**Baker Creek**

Baker Peak
12,298 ft

S
N
A
K
E

R
A
N
G
E

KIOUS BASIN

Pyramid Peak
11,926 ft

Bristlecone Pine
Grove

HORSE HEAVEN

**3** GRANITE
BASIN

Snake      Creek

Mount Washington
11,658 ft

0        2 mi

0        2 km

**19**

**Lexington Arch** ◆

**4** ARCH CANYON

**KEY**

| | |
|---|---|
| 🛈 | Ranger Station |
| ⛺ | Campground |
| ⛱ | Picnic Area |
| 🍴 | Restaurant |
| 🏠 | Lodge |
| 🚶 | Trailhead |
| 🚻 | Restrooms |
| 🎋 | Scenic Viewpoint |
| ---- | Walking/Hiking Trails |
| ···· | Bicycle Path |

# GREAT BASIN PLANNER

## When to Go

As one of the least visited national parks in the country, attracting fewer than 100,000 people each year, **Great Basin National Park is never crowded.** Few visitors ensure that most any time is a fine time to visit this park, though of course much of that number will pass through the entry gates during the warmer summer months. In summer the high desert weather here is typically mild, so you'll be comfortable in shorts and T-shirts during the day—though temperatures drop at night, so bring light jackets and pants.

A winter visit can be sublime in its solitude, but the hardy visitor must be prepared for the elements, especially if the backcountry is a destination. Since winters can be harsh, with temperatures hovering in the low teens, heavy coats, jeans, and sweaters are recommended. Some roads might be impassable in winter or otherwise inclement weather; check ahead with a park ranger. The campgrounds at Baker Creek Road and the area above Upper Lehman Creek are usually closed November–June, depending on weather conditions.

AVG. HIGH/LOW TEMPS.

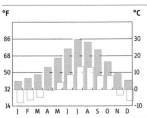

## Flora & Fauna

Despite the cold, dry conditions in Great Basin, 411 plant species thrive; 13 are considered sensitive species. The region gets less than 10 inches of rain a year, so plants have developed some ingenious methods of dealing with the desert's harshness. For instance, many flowering plants will only grow and produce seeds in a year when there is enough water. Spruces, pines, and junipers have set down roots here, and the bristlecone pine has been doing so for thousands of years.

The park's plants provide a variety of habitats for animals and for more than 230 bird species. In the sagebrush are jackrabbits, ground squirrels, chipmunks, mice, and pronghorns. Mule deer and striped skunks abound in the pygmy forest of pinyon pine and juniper trees. Shrews, ringtail cats, and weasels make their homes around the springs and streams. Mountain lions, bobcats, and sheep live on the rugged slopes and in valleys. The park is also home to coyotes, kit fox, and badgers. Treat the Great Basin rattlesnake with respect. Bites are uncommon and rarely fatal, but if you're bitten, remain calm and contact a ranger immediately.

## Getting There & Around

The entrance to Great Basin is on Route 488, 5 mi west of its junction with Route 487. From Ely, take U.S. 6/50 to Route 487. From Salt Lake City or Cedar City, UT, take I-15 South to 6/50 West; from Las Vegas, drive north on I-15 and then north on Route 93 to access U.S. 6/50. The nearest airports are in Cedar City (120 mi), Salt Lake City (240 mi), and Las Vegas (287 mi).

In the park, Baker Creek Road and portions of Wheeler Peak Scenic Drive, above Upper Lehman Creek, are closed from November to June. The road to the visitor center and the roads to the developed campgrounds are paved, but the going is tough in winter and two-wheel-drive cars don't do well. RVs and trailers aren't allowed above Lower Lehman Creek. With an 8% grade, the road to Wheeler Peak is steep and curvy, but not dangerous.

By John
Blodgett

Here, just off the Loneliest Road in America, small mountain ranges parade across farmland on the north, and a huge desert stretches south to central Utah. There are a few rivers, but in this arid land their waters evaporate in the dry air or fade into the soil quickly, adding to the sense of isolation that many visitors seek in this off-the-beaten-path park. Surface water in the Great Basin has no outlet to the sea, so it pools in more than 200 small basins throughout the steep mountain ranges. Along with these alpine lakes, the dramatic mountains shelter lush meadows, limestone caves, and ancient bristlecone pines. Within the park is the southernmost permanent glacier on the continent.

**19**

## Scenic Drives

**Baker Creek Road.** Though less popular than the Wheeler Peak Scenic Drive, this well-maintained gravel road affords gorgeous views of Wheeler Peak, the Baker Creek Drainage, and Snake Valley. The road is closed in the winter, and there are no pull-outs or scenic overlooks.

**Wheeler Peak Scenic Drive.** Less than a mile from the visitor center off Route 488, turn onto this paved road that winds its way up to elevations of 10,000 feet. The road takes you through pygmy forest in lower elevations; as you climb, the air cools. Along the way, two overlooks offer awe-inspiring views of the Snake Range mountains, and a short hiking trail leads to views of an old mining site. Turn off at Mather Overlook, elevation 9,000 feet, for the best photo ops. Allow 1½ hours for the 24-mi round-trip, not including hikes.

## What to See

### Historic Sites

★ **Lehman Caves.** In 1885, rancher and miner Absalom Lehman discovered the underground wonder that's now named after him. Although the name suggests that there's more than one cave here, Lehman is a single limestone and marble cavern ¼ mi long. Inside, stalactites, stalagmites, helictites, flowstone, popcorn, and other bizarre mineral formations cover almost every surface. Lehman Caves is one of the best places to see rare shield formations, created when calcite-rich water is forced from tiny cracks in a cave wall, ceiling, or floor. Year-round the cave maintains a constant, damp temperature of 50°F, so wear a light jacket and nonskid shoes when you take the tour. Guided tours conducted by the park service run 30–90 minutes; the full 90-minute tour route is just over ½ mi round-trip. Children under age 5 are not allowed on the 90-minute tours; those under 16 must be accompanied by an adult. Tours run four times a day. Next to the cave visitor center, peek into **Rhodes Cabin,** where black-and-white photographs of the park's earlier days line the walls. ⊠ *Lehman Caves Visitor Center* ☎ *775/234–7331* ☜ *$2–$10* ☼ *Daily 9–4.*

### Visitor Centers

**Great Basin Visitor Center.** Here you can see exhibits on the flora, fauna, and geology of the park, or ask a ranger to suggest a favorite hike. Books, videos, and souvenirs are for sale; a coffee shop is attached. ⊠ *Rte. 487, just north of Baker* ☎ *775/234–7331* ☼ *Daily.*

**Lehman Caves Visitor Center.** Regularly scheduled tours, for durations of 30, 60, and 90 minutes, depart from here. Exhibits highlight the gnarled and ancient bristlecone pine and other park flora, plus cave formations. Buy gifts for friends and family back home at the bookstore. ⊠ *Rte. 488, ½ mi inside park boundary* ☎ *775/234–7331* ☼ *Daily.*

## Sports & the Outdoors

Great Basin National Park is a great place for experienced outdoor enthusiasts. There are no outfitters to guide you, and there are no nearby shops that rent or sell sporting equipment, so bring everything you might need and be prepared to go it alone. Permits are not required to go off the beaten path, but such adventurers are encouraged to register with a ranger just in case. The effort is worth it, for the backcountry is wide open and not at all crowded no matter the time of year (just keep an eye on the weather). As with all national parks, bicycling is restricted to existing roads, but as the park sees fewer visitors than other national parks, road cyclists will find few cars to trouble them.

### Bird-watching

Great Basin National Park might not be crowded with people, but it sports an impressive list of bird species that have been sighted—238, according to the National Park Service checklist. Some species, such as the common raven and American robin, can be seen at most locations. Others, such as the red-naped sapsucker, are more commonly seen near Lehman Creek.

## GREAT BASIN IN ONE DAY

Start your visit with a tour of the fascinating limestone caverns of **Lehman Caves,** the park's most famous attraction. If you have time before or after the tour, hike the short and family friendly **Mountain View Nature Trail,** near the Lehman Caves Visitor Center, to get your first taste of the area's pinyon-juniper forests. Stop for lunch at the Lehman Caves Cafe or have a picnic near the visitor center. Then take a leisurely drive up to **Wheeler Peak,** the park's tallest mountain at just over 13,000 feet. You can stop about halfway along your drive to hike the short **Osceola Ditch Trail,** a remnant of the park's gold-mining days, or, alternatively, just enjoy the fantastic views from the two overlooks. If you're feeling energetic when you reach Wheeler Peak, hike some of the trails there, then return to the visitor center.

### Cross-Country Skiing

**Lehman Creek Trail** is the most popular cross-country skiing trail in the park. It's marked with orange flags, making it easy to find. You may need snowshoes to reach the skiable upper section.

### Hiking

You'll witness beautiful views by driving along the Wheeler Peak Scenic Drive and other park roads, but hiking allows an in-depth experience that just can't be matched. Trails at Great Basin run the gamut from relaxing ¼-mi trails to multiday backpacking specials, so everyone can find a path that matches personal ability, fitness level, and desired destination, be it mountain peak, flowered meadow, or evergreen forest. When you pick up a trail map at the visitor center, ask about weather and trail conditions (many are unpaved, and some are maintained less than others) and bring appropriate clothing when you set out from any trailhead. No matter the trail length, always carry water, and remember that the trails are at high elevations, so pace yourself accordingly. Do not enter abandoned mineshafts or tunnels, for they are unstable and potentially dangerous. Those who head out for the backcountry need not obtain a permit, but are encouraged to register at either of the two visitor centers. Though Great Basin is a high desert, winters can be harsh, so always inquire about the weather ahead of time at the visitor center.

EASY **Mountain View Nature Trail.** Just past the Rhodes Cabin on the right side of the visitor center, this short and easy trail (³⁄₁₀ mi) through pinyon pine and juniper trees is marked with signs describing the plants. The path passes the original entrance to Lehman Caves and loops back to the visitor center. It's a great way to spend a half hour or so while you wait for your cave tour to start. ⊠ *Lehman Caves Visitor Center.*

**Osceola Ditch Trail.** In 1890, at a cost of $108,223, the Osceola Gravel Mining Company constructed an 18-mi-long trench. The ditch was part of an attempt to glean gold from the South Snake Range, but water shortages and the company's failure to find much gold forced the mining operation to shut down in 1905. You can reach portions of the eastern section of the ditch on foot via the Osceola Ditch Trail, which passes through pine and fir trees. Allow 30 minutes for this easy $\frac{3}{10}$-mi round-trip hike. ⊠ *Wheeler Peak Scenic Dr.*

> **GOLD NUGGET**
>
> Gold was discovered in 1872 just 3 mi west of what is now Great Basin National Park. Fortune-seekers flocked to Osceola, creating a town of 1,500-plus. More than $3 million worth of the glittering gem was found over the next several decades. The most famous nugget weighed 24 pounds and would cash in today at $250,000.

MODERATE
★ **Wheeler Peak Trails.** From the parking area at the end of Wheeler Peak Scenic Drive, you can embark on a hike over several connecting trails. These trails are for day use only.

**Bristlecone Pine Trail.** Though the park has several bristlecone pine groves, the only way to see the ancient trees up close is to hike this trail. From the parking area to the grove, it's a moderate $1\frac{4}{10}$-mi hike that takes about an hour each way. Rangers offer guided hikes daily in season; inquire at the visitor center.

Fodor$Choice
★

Bristlecone Pine Trail leads to two other trails. To the right, as you head past the grove, is the **Alpine Lakes Loop Trail,** a moderate $2\frac{7}{10}$-mi trek that loops past stellar Stella and Teresa lakes and returns you to Bristlecone Pine Trail in about two hours. Bring your camera.

Turn left off Bristlecone Pine Trail past the grove to connect with **Glacier Trail.** The trail skirts the southernmost permanent ice field on the continent and ends with a view of a small alpine glacier, the only one in Nevada. From there it's less than 5 mi back to the parking lot. Allow $2\frac{1}{2}$ hours for the moderate hike. ⊠ *Wheeler Peak Scenic Dr., 12 mi from Lehman Caves Visitor Center.*

DIFFICULT **Baker Lake Trail.** This full-day 12-mi hike can easily be made into a two-day backpacking trip. You'll gain a total of 2,620 feet in elevation on the way to Baker Lake, a jewel-like alpine lake with a backdrop of mountainous cliffs. ⊠ *Baker Creek Rd., going south from just east of the Lehman Caves Visitor Center.*

**Wheeler Peak Summit Trail.** Begin this full-day, $8\frac{6}{10}$-mi hike early in the day so as to minimize exposure to the storms that sometimes strike the mountain in the afternoon. Most of the route follows a ridge up the mountain to the summit. Elevation gain is 2,900 feet, so hikers should have good stamina. ⊠ *Wheeler Peak Scenic Dr., Summit Trail parking area.*

## Educational Offerings

Youngsters should consider the **Junior Ranger Program.** Children who complete the program will be sworn in as Junior Rangers and receive a Great Basin Bristlecone patch.

On summer evenings the park offers **campfire programs** at two of its campgrounds, Upper Lehman Creek and Wheeler Peak. The 40–60-minute programs cover a range of subjects related to the Great Basin's cultural and natural history, and resources. Dress warmly and bring a flashlight.

Program times vary, so call for information. ⊠ *Wheeler Peak Scenic Dr., 4 mi (Upper Lehman Creek) and 12 mi (Wheeler Peak) from the Lehman Caves Visitor Center* ☎ *775/234–7331* ⊑ *Free* ⊙ *mid-June–Labor Day; check Lehman Caves Visitor Center for schedule.*

## Shopping

**Great Basin Natural History Association Book Store.** Everything you need to enrich your experience touring the park and traveling in the region is available here. ⊠ *Visitor center, Rte. 488, 1 mi from the park entrance* ☎ *775/234–7270.*

**Lehman Caves Cafe and Gift Shop.** The park's shop sells souvenirs, T-shirts, books, toys, Native American jewelry, Great Basin pottery, and travel items. ⊠ *Next to the visitor center* ☎ *775/234–7221* ⊙ *Closed mid-Oct.–mid-Apr.*

For grocery stores near the park, ⇨ Shops & Grocers *in* Essentials.

> **GOOD READS**
>
> **Hiking Great Basin National Park,** by Bruce Grubbs, will get your Great Basin trip off on the right foot.
> **Trails to Explore in Great Basin National Park,** by Rose Houk, is all about hiking in the park.
> **Geology of the Great Basin,** by Bill Fiero, or *Basin and Range,* by John McPhee, present a geological tour of the Great Basin.

# WHAT'S NEARBY

## Nearby Towns & Attractions

### Nearby Towns

An hour's drive west of the park, at the intersection of three U.S. highways, **Ely** (population 4,830) is the biggest town in the area. It grew up in the second wave of the early Nevada mining boom, right at the optimistic turn of the 20th century. For 70 years copper kept the town in business, but when it ran out in the early 1980s Ely declined fast. Then, in 1986, the National Park Service designated Great Basin National Park 68 mi to the east and the town got a boost. Ely has since been rebuilt and revitalized and is now home to a railroad museum, the county seat, and a great old hotel-casino (Hotel Nevada), as well as the basic tourist amenities. If you want to get closer to the park you can stay in tiny **Baker** (population 50), which sits at the main park entrance. Really just a cluster of small businesses a few miles south of U.S. 6/50 on Route 487, the hamlet is 5 mi from the visitor center.

### Nearby Attractions

**Cave Lake State Park.** High in the pine and juniper forest of the big Schell Creek Range that borders Ely on the east, this is an idyllic spot. You can spend a day fishing for rainbow and brown trout in the reservoir and a night sleeping under the stars. Arrive early; it gets crowded. Access may be restricted in winter. ⊠ *15 mi southeast of Ely via U.S. 50/6/93* ☎ *775/728–4460* ⊕ *parks.nv.gov/cl.htm* ⊑ *$4* ⊙ *Daily, 24 hrs.*

**19**

**Nevada Northern Railway Museum.** During the mining boom the Nevada Northern Railroad connected East Ely, Ruth, and McGill to the transcontinental rail line in the northeast corner of Nevada. The whole operation is now a museum. You can tour the depot, offices, warehouses, yard, roundhouses, and repair shops, and catch a ride on one of the trains in the summer. ⊠ *1100 Ave. A, Ely* ☏ *866/407–8326* ⊕ *nevadanorthernrailway.net* ⬚ *$3* ⊙ *Daily, 8–5.*

**Ward Charcoal Ovens State Historic Park.** In the desert south of Ely is this row of ovens. The ovens turned pinyon, juniper, and mountain mahogany into charcoal, which was used for refining local silver and copper ore. It's worth the drive from Ely to take in this well-preserved piece of Nevada mining history. ⊠ *7 mi south of Ely on U.S. 50/6/93, and 11 mi southwest on Cave Valley Rd.* ☏ *775/728–4460* ⊕ *www.parks.nv.gov/ww.htm* ⬚ *$4* ⊙ *Daily, 24 hrs.*

| FAMILY PICKS |
|---|
| **Bristlecone Pine Hike.** Take this guided hike to see one of the park's signature trees in the Wheeler Peak cirque. Bristlecone pines are ancient, often thousands of years old, and gnarled—in other words, pretty cool for kids. |
| **Fence Post Art.** All ages will enjoy exploring these whimsical pieces of art that have been popping up on random Baker fence posts since 1997, when a local man erected a glove and proclaimed it the "Permanent Wave Society." |
| **Nevada Northern Railway Museum.** Ride the rails year-round at this attraction in Ely. |

## Scenic Drive

**U.S. 93 Scenic Byway.** The 68 mi between the park and Ely make a beautiful drive with diverse views of Nevada's paradoxical geography: desert vegetation and lush mountains. You'll catch an occasional glimpse of a snake, perhaps a rattler, slithering on the road's shoulder, or a lizard sunning on a rock. A straight drive to Ely takes a little more than an hour; if you have the time to take a dirt-road adventure, don't miss the Ward Charcoal Ovens or a peek at Cave Lake.

# WHERE TO STAY & EAT

### About the Restaurants

Dining in the park itself is limited to the basic lunch fare at the Lehman Caves Cafe and Gift Shop. Nearby Baker has a handful of dining and grocery options.

### About the Hotels

There is no lodging in the park, so unless you're willing and able to snag one of the park's first-come, first-served campsites, or expect to camp in the backcountry, plan on lodging in nearby Baker or Ely.

### About the Campgrounds

Great Basin has four developed campgrounds, all easily accessible by car, but only the Lower Lehman Creek one is open year-round. One of

## FESTIVALS & EVENTS

MAY–SEPT. **Silver State Classic Challenge.** The country's largest (and longest, held) open-road race for amateur fast-car enthusiasts shows off street-legal muscle cars that zoom up to 200 mph. ⊠ *South of Ely on Route 318, from Lund to Hiko* ☎ *702/631–6166.*

AUG. **White Pine County Fair.** A hay contest; livestock, flower, and vegetable judging; carnival rides and a midway; food booths; dancing; and a buckaroo breakfast make this fair, held at the County Fairgrounds in Ely, the real thing. ☎ *775/289–8877.*

them, Grey Cliffs, is specifically for groups, and is open May through November, or until snow closes it; contact the park for details on staying there.

Primitive campsites around Snake and Strawberry creeks are open year-round and are free; however, snow and rain can make access to the sites difficult. Permits for backcountry camping are not required, though such park users are encouraged to fill out a registration form and become familiar with backcountry weather conditions at the visitor center.

None of the campgrounds in the park accept credit cards, and none have RV hookups (but RVers can stay at Whispering Elms in nearby Baker), and reservations are not accepted. Water is only provided at the developed campgrounds in summer; if you're camping in winter, bring your own. Camping parties are limited to eight people and two vehicles per site. Though not allowed on any park trails, pets can be led on a leash in the campgrounds—just be sure that the leash is no more than six feet in length. For the safety of your pet as well as that of park wildlife, stay clear of any wild animals that might cross your path.

**19**

## Where to Eat

### In the Park

⟳ ¢ ✕ **Lehman Caves Cafe and Gift Shop.** The menu here includes light breakfast, soup-and-sandwich lunches, hot drinks, soft drinks, and home-baked desserts. They hand-make large ice-cream sandwiches. ⊠ *Next to the visitor center* ☎ *775/234–7221. $4–$6* ▭ *AE, D, MC, V* ☺ *Closed Nov.–Mar. No dinner.*

PICNIC AREAS **Lehman Caves Visitor Center Picnic Area.** This full-service picnic site, with tables, fire grills, water, and restrooms (the latter two available during the summer), is a short walk from the visitor center. Summer hours are often extended beyond the standard 8 AM–4:30 PM. ⊠ *Just north of Lehman Caves Visitor Center.*

**Pole Canyon Trailhead Picnic Area.** Inaccessible in the winter when Baker Creek Road is closed, this area at the mouth of a canyon has a handful of picnic tables and fire grills but no water. It does have a restroom. Access is via an unimproved road. ⊠ *East of entrance to Grey Cliffs Group Camping site, at the mouth of Pole Canyon.*

**Upper Lehman Creek Campground.** There are a handful of sites here where you can sit down for a bite and a breather. A group picnic site requires a reservation at least two weeks in advance, but areas near the host site and amphitheater are first come, first served. Water is available. ✉ *4 mi from the Lehman Caves Visitor Center on Wheeler Peak Scenic Dr.*

### Outside the Park

**$–$$** ✕ **Red Apple Family Restaurant.** This restaurant defines "down home." The meals are home-cooked fare, ranging from three-egg omelets (your choice of ingredients) to chicken-fried steak. The most expensive item on the menu, a 12-ounce T-bone steak with all the fixings, costs $12.95. The waitstaff is ready with smiles and carafes of coffee. You can also get breakfast. ✉ *2160 Aultman St., Ely* ☎ *775/289–8585. $8–$18* ▱ *AE, D, MC, V.*

**¢–$$** ✕ **T and D's Country Store, Restaurant, and Lounge.** The bright and cheerful restaurant in this large white-brick building occupies a sunroom, where windows line the walls. Salads, hot and cold sandwiches, ribs, and chicken are the core of the menu; you can order pizza, Italian, and Mexican food as well. ✉ *1 Main St., Baker* ☎ *775/234–7264. $7–$20* ▱ *AE, D, DC, MC, V.*

**¢–$** ✕ **The Border Inn.** This part of Nevada is ranch country, so it's no surprise that meat and potatoes dominate the menu at the Border Inn. You'll find hearty fare like hamburgers, chicken-fried steak, pork chops, and, of course, steaks. Breakfast is also served. ✉ *U.S. 6/50, 13 mi east of Great Basin National Park, Baker* ☎ *775/234–7300. $5–$11* ▱ *AE, D, MC, V.*

## Where to Stay

### In the Park

CAMPGROUNDS & RV PARKS

**$** ⌂ **Baker Creek Campground.** The turnoff is just past the park entrance, on the left as you approach the Lehman Caves Visitor Center. ✉ *2½ mi south of Rte. 488, 3 mi from the visitor center* ☎ *No phone* ⇆ *32 sites* ⌂ *Pit toilets, drinking water, fire grates, picnic tables* ▱ *$12* ⌂ *Reservations not accepted* ☉ *May–Sept., depending on weather conditions.*

**$** ⌂ **Lower Lehman Creek Campground.** Other than Great Basin's primitive sites, this is the only campground in the park that is open year-round. It's the first turnoff past the Lehman Caves Visitor Center. ✉ *2½ mi from the visitor center on Wheeler Peak Scenic Dr.* ☎ *No phone* ⇆ *11 sites* ⌂ *Pit toilets, drinking water, fire grates, picnic tables* ▱ *$12* ⌂ *Reservations not accepted.*

**$** ⌂ **Upper Lehman Creek Campground.** The entrance is about a mile past the Lower Lehman Creek turnoff. ✉ *4 mi from the visitor center on Wheeler Peak Scenic Dr.* ☎ *No phone* ⇆ *24 sites* ⌂ *Pit toilets, drinking water, fire grates, picnic tables* ▱ *$12* ⌂ *Reservations not accepted* ☉ *May–Sept., depending on weather conditions.*

**$** ⌂ **Wheeler Peak Campground.** This scenic, cool campground is at the end of Wheeler Peak Scenic Drive, at an elevation of 10,000 feet. RVs cannot camp here because they cannot negotiate the twisting road past Upper Lehman Creek. In fact, nothing over 24-feet long is allowed beyond this point. The campground is closed for most of the year because of snow. ✉ *12 mi from the Lehman Caves Visitor Center on Wheeler*

Fodor'sChoice
★

*Peak Scenic Dr.* ☏ *No phone* ⇄ *37 sites* ⚸ *Pit toilets, drinking water, fire grates, picnic tables* ☏ *$12* ⚹ *Reservations not accepted* ⊘ *June–Sept., depending on weather conditions.*

## Outside the Park

¢–$ 🏨 **Hotel Nevada.** One of the oldest hotel buildings in the state, this Fodor'sChoice landmark in the middle of town is nonetheless in excellent shape. Built ★ in 1908, it's a big square brick building in downtown Ely. The luxury rooms are especially nice. The hotel has a casino. ⊠ *501 Aultman St., Ely 89301* ☏ *775/289–6665 or 888/406–3055* 🖷 *775/289–4715* ⊕ *www.hotelnevada.com* ⇄ *65 rooms* ⚸ *Restaurant, bars, some pets allowed.* $30–$85 ▱ *AE, D, DC, MC, V.*

★ 🏨 **Silver Jack Inn.** This motel surrounds a lawn with trees and a patio— ¢–$ a nice place to relax in the early evening. The motel also rents out three off-site efficiency units. The Inn's funky Lectrolux Gallery Café and Movie House serves up fresh pastries, coffee, and a surprisingly varied selection of wine, beer, and spirits. Movies are shown every Wednesday and Saturday evening. ⊠ *10 Main St., Baker 89311* ☏ *775/234–7323* ⇄ *7 rooms* ⚸ *Some pets allowed, no phone.* $45–$69 ▱ *D, MC, V.*

¢ 🏨 **The Border Inn.** Located on the Utah-Nevada border, this motel has air-conditioned rooms with twin, double, and queen beds. The only gas station in the area is right here. ⊠ *U.S. 6/50, 13 mi east of Great Basin National Park, Baker 89311* ☏ *775/234–7300* ⇄ *29 rooms* ⚸ *Restaurant, kitchen (some).* $39–$42 ▱ *AE, D, MC, V.*

CAMPGROUNDS & ⚠ **Whispering Elms Campground.** The largest camping facility close to RV PARKS but not inside the park is also the nearest to offer hookups for RVs. It $ is open year-round. ⊠ *Rte. 487, behind Great Basin Lodge, Baker* ☏ *775/234–7343* ⇄ *45 sites* ⚸ *Hookups, guest laundry, flush toilets, showers* ☏ *$17* ⚹ *Reservations not accepted* ▱ *No credit cards.*

19

# GREAT BASIN ESSENTIALS

ACCESSIBILITY Designated handicap parking spaces are available at both visitor centers, where there is a ramp over the curb. The center itself is all on one level, fully accessible to those with impaired mobility. The park slide show is captioned. At the front desk you can borrow wheelchairs to use in the center and in the first room of Lehman Caves. A cut curb provides access to a table and fire grate at the picnic area near the visitor center, which also has accessible restrooms. Three campgrounds within the park are accessible: Upper Lehman Creek Campground, Wheeler Peak Campground, and Baker Creek Campground. Note that the Upper Lehman

Creek Campground restroom access ramp is steep.

ADMISSION FEES Admission to the park is free, but if you want to tour Lehman Caves there's a fee ($4–$10, depending on age and tour length).

ADMISSION HOURS The park is open 24/7 year-round. The park is in the Pacific time zone.

ATMS/BANKS There are no ATMs in the park. The nearest ATM is in Baker, and the nearest banks are in Ely.
🏧 **The Border Inn** ⊠ U.S. 6/50, 13 mi east of Great Basin National Park entrance, Baker ☏ 775/234–7300.

AUTOMOBILE SERVICE STATIONS
🖪 **Baker Ranch Sinclair** is an unmanned, self-serve facility. ✉ Rte. 487 and Pioche St., Baker. **The Border Inn** ✉ U.S. 6/50, 13 mi east of Great Basin National Park, Baker ☎ 775/234-7300.

EMERGENCIES In case of fire or in a medical or police emergency, dial 911 or report to the ranger station at both visitor centers. The nearest hospital is in Ely.

LOST AND FOUND The park's lost-and-found is at the visitor center.

PERMITS Everyone age 12 and older needs a Nevada state fishing license to fish in Great Basin National Park. The resident license costs $13 for kids 12–15 and $29 for those 16 and older; the one-day non-resident license is $18, plus $7 for each additional day at time of purchase. For information on fishing licenses, contact the Nevada Division of Wildlife at ⊕ http://ndow.org. Backcountry hikers do not have to obtain permits, but for your own safety you should fill out a form at the visitor center before you set out.

POST OFFICES There is no mail drop in the park, but there is a post office in Baker.
🖪 **Baker Post Office** ✉ 101 Carson St., Baker, 89311 ☎ 775/234-7231.

PUBLIC TELEPHONES The only public phone in the park is at the visitor center. There is no reliable cell-phone reception.

RELIGIOUS SERVICES There are no organized religious services in the park.

RESTROOMS The visitor center has public restrooms, as does the nearby picnic area. Vault toilets are available at all the developed campgrounds: Baker Creek, Lower Lehman Creek, Upper Lehman Creek, and Wheeler Peak.

SHOPS & GROCERS While the closest full-service grocery store is 60 mi away in Ely, T and D's in Baker can supply some basics, and the Silver Jack Inn sells baked goods and lunches to go.
🖪 **T and D's Grocery Store** ✉ 1 Main St., Baker ☎ 775/234-7264 ☉ Closed Nov.-Mar. **Silver Jack Inn.** ✉ 10 Main St., Baker ☎ 775/234-7323.

**NEARBY TOWN INFORMATION**
🖪 **Ely Bristlecone Convention Center** ✉ 150 6th St., Ely, 89301 ☎ 800/496-9350 **Great Basin Business and Tourism Council** ✉ 10 Main St., Baker, 89311 ☎ No phone ⊕ www.greatbasinpark.com. **White Pine Chamber of Commerce** ✉ 636 Aultman St., Ely, 89301 ☎ 775/289-8877 ⊕ www.whitepinechamber.com.

**VISITOR INFORMATION**
🖪 **Great Basin National Park** ✉ Rte. 488, Baker, NV 89311 ☎ 775/234-7331 ⊕ www.nps.gov/grba.

# Great Sand Dunes National Park

## WORD OF MOUTH

"Their appearance was exactly that of the sea in a storm, except as to color, not the least sign of vegetation existing thereon."

–Zebulon Pike

# WELCOME TO GREAT SAND DUNES

## TOP REASONS TO GO

★ **Dune Climbing:** Trek through the 30 square mi of main dunes in this land-locked dunefield.

★ **Sand-Castle Building:** Spend a few hours constructing towering treasures in the sand with your kids.

★ **Bounty of Bison:** Take a hayride around the west end of the park, where more than 1,000 bison roam in the grasslands and wetlands.

★ **Aspens in Autumn:** If you're equipped with a 4-wheel-drive vehicle and boast good driving skills, take the rough road up to Medano Pass during fall foliage season when the aspens turn gold.

★ **Vigorous Hikes:** Pack a picnic lunch and climb up to High Dune, followed by the more strenuous stretch over to Star Dune. Enjoy the view while you nibble your nourishment.

**1** Sand Dunes. The 30-square-mi field of sand has no designated trails. The highest dune in the park—and, in fact, in North America—is 750-foot-high Star Dune.

**2** Sangre de Cristo Mountains. Named the Blood of Christ Mountains because of their ruddy color—especially at dawn—these peaks in the preserve include six that are more than 13,000 feet tall.

**3** Forest. Ponderosa pines populate the forested areas around the Sangre de Cristo Mountains in the preserve and park's eastern boundaries.

**4** Grasslands. Wildlife, such as black bears and bison, feed on the park's grassy areas, primarily found in the park's southern area and the preserve.

**5** Wetlands. Popular with sandhill cranes, wetlands form in the area around Medano creek, where cottonwood trees also thrive.

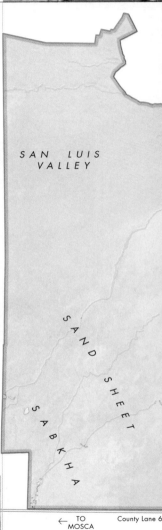

SAN LUIS VALLEY

SAND SHEET

SABKHA

← TO MOSCA          County Lane 6

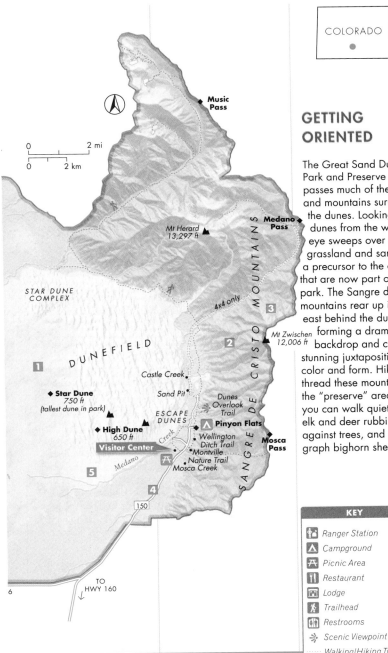

COLORADO
●

## GETTING ORIENTED

The Great Sand Dunes Park and Preserve encompasses much of the land and mountains surrounding the dunes. Looking at the dunes from the west, your eye sweeps over the grassland and sand sheet, a precursor to the dunes that are now part of the park. The Sangre de Cristo mountains rear up in the east behind the dunes, forming a dramatic backdrop and creating a stunning juxtaposition of color and form. Hiking trails thread these mountains—the "preserve" area—where you can walk quietly past elk and deer rubbing against trees, and photograph bighorn sheep.

**20**

| KEY | |
|---|---|
| 👫 | Ranger Station |
| 🔺 | Campground |
| 🍴 | Picnic Area |
| 🍴 | Restaurant |
| 🏨 | Lodge |
| 🧗 | Trailhead |
| 🚻 | Restrooms |
| ≫ | Scenic Viewpoint |
| ⋯⋯ | Walking/Hiking Trails |
| ⋯⋯ | Bicycle Path |

Music Pass

Mt Herard 13,297 ft

Medano Pass

STAR DUNE COMPLEX

SANGRE DE CRISTO MOUNTAINS

4x4 only

Mt Zwischen 12,006 ft

3

2

DUNEFIELD

1

Castle Creek

Sand Pit

Dunes Overlook Trail

◆ Star Dune 750 ft (tallest dune in park)

High Dune 650 ft

ESCAPE DUNES

🔺 Pinyon Flats

Mosca Pass

Visitor Center

Creek

Wellington Ditch Trail

Montville

Nature Trail

Mosca Creek

Medano

5

4

150

0    2 mi
0    2 km

TO HWY 160

6

# GREAT SAND DUNES PLANNER

## When to Go

Fall and spring are the prettiest times to visit. In late May, the mountains are still capped with snow, ensuring a vivid contrast to the golden dunes. In September and early October, leaves on aspen trees are turning gold. On summer afternoons, temperatures on the sand can climb to 140°F, so plan on climbing the dunes in the morning or late afternoon.

Even though only about 300,000 visitors come to the park each year, they tend to come in the summer and congregate in one area, making the park crowded June through August. In fact, in peak season, the section of the dunes closest to the parking lots sounds a lot like a playground. To avoid the seasonal crowds, hike away from the main area up to the High Dune. Or come in the winter, when the park is a place for contemplation and repose, the silence broken only by passing birds and the faint rush of water from the Medano or Sand creeks. **In addition to the summer, holiday weekends during the spring and fall are the worst times to visit because there are so many tourists.**

## Flora & Fauna

The park is spread over several ecological zones, so visitors see an amazing array of animals and plant life. The wetlands are filled with broadleaf cattail and colorful Rocky Mountain Iris. The sand sheet and grasslands are dotted with prickly pear, rabbit brush, and yucca. The dunefield looks barren from afar, but up close you see various grasses have rooted in swales among the dunes. Montane, pine, and pinyon trees grow on the lower portions of the mountain, stunted trees survive in the subalpine forest zone, and tiny flowers cling to the rock at the top.

You may see beavers and pelicans in the wetlands; short-horn lizards, elk, and mule deer in the sand sheet and grassland; and Great Sand Dunes Tiger Beetles and Ord's kangaroo rats in the dunefield. On the mountainsides, falcons fly overhead, while black bears, bobcats, and Rocky Mountain bighorn sheep graze.

■ TIP➔ **Be cautious around wild animals and never approach them. (If you're taking pictures, this is a good time to use a telephoto lense.) Campers should check with rangers about precautions to avoid bear problems.**

## Getting There & Around

Great Sand Dunes National Park and Preserve is about 230 mi from both Denver and Albuquerque, and about 170 mi from Colorado Springs and Santa Fe. The fastest route from the north is Interstate 25 south to U.S. 160, heading west to just past Blanca, to Highway 150 north. When traveling from Albuquerque, go north on Interstate 25, then merge with U.S. 285 at Santa Fe, going north to U.S. 160 to Highway 150. From the west, Highway 17 and County Lane 6 take you to the park.

The closest Amtrak train stop is in Trinidad, near the New Mexico border. Greyhound buses go to Alamosa and Blanca. Colorado Springs Airport (☎ 719/550–1972) is the largest in the south-central Colorado area.

The park itself only has one road. It's about a mile from the toll booth at the entrance to the visitor center and the Dunes Parking Lot is about a mile farther.

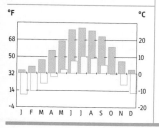

AVG. HIGH/LOW TEMPS.

By Lois
Friedland

Created by winds that sweep the San Luis Valley floor, the up to 750-foot-high sand dunes that form the heart of Great Sand Dunes National Park and Preserve are an improbable, unforgettable sight. The dunes, as curvaceous as Rubens' nudes, stretch for more than 30 square mi. The sand is as fine and feathery, making the dunes' very existence seems tenuous, as if they might blow away before your eyes, yet they're solid enough to withstand the stress of hikers and saucer-riding thrill-seekers.

## Scenic Drive

★ **Medano Pass Primitive Road.** This 22-mi road connects Great Sand Dunes with the Wet Mountain Valley and Highway 69 on the east side of the Sangre de Cristo Mountains as well as the Great Sand Dunes National Preserve via a climb to Medano Pass (10,040 feet above sea level). It is a 4-wheel-drive-only road that is best driven by someone who already has good 4-wheel-drive skills. (Your 4-wheel-drive vehicle must have high clearance and be engineered to go over rough roads.) The road has sections of deep, loose sand, and it crosses Medano creek nine times. Before you go, stop at the visitor center for a map and ask about current road conditions. Drive time pavement to pavement is 2½ to 3 hours.

## What to See

★ **Dunefield.** The more than 30 square mi of big dunes in the heart of the park is the main attraction, although the surrounding grasslands do have some smaller dunes. You can start putting your feet in the sand three mi past the main park entrance.

**High Dune.** This isn't the highest dune in the park, but it is a dune that's high enough in the dunefield so visitors can get a view of all the dunes. It's on the first ridge of dunes that you see from the main parking area.

20

## GREAT SAND DUNES IN ONE DAY

Arrive early in the day during the summertime so you can hike up to **High Dune** and get a view of the entire dunefield. Round-trip, the walk itself should take about 1½ to 2 hours (plus time to build sand castles with your kids or slide down the dunes). In the afternoon, take a nature walk or listen to a terrace talk by a ranger.

In the spring and early summer, or the fall, when the temperatures are cooler, first walk up to the High Dune to enjoy the view. If you're game to hike farther, head to **Star Dune** for a picnic lunch. Finally, hike down the ridge to the Medano creek alongside the water that nourishes a row of cottonwood trees.

If you're here on a day when there's a hayride tour to see the bison, take the tour (only available in the morning).

### Visitor Center

At the sole park visitor center you can view exhibits, browse in the bookstore, and watch a 20-minute film with an overview of the dunes. Rangers are on hand to answer questions. Facilities include restrooms and a vending machine stocked with soft drinks spring, summer and fall. Coffee is available November through February. The Great Sand Dunes Oasis, just outside the park boundary, has a café that is open year-round. ✉ *Near the park entrance* ☎ *719/378–6399.*

## Sports & the Outdoors

The park is a good choice for hikers and overnight campers. It's not for mountain bikers or other cyclists, because there aren't any mountain-bike trails and the conditions are too sandy.

### Bird Watching

In the wetlands there are migratory birds such as American white pelicans and the American avocet. On the forested sections of the mountains there are goshawks, northern harriers, gray jays, and Steller's jays. In the alpine tundra there are golden eagles, hawks, horned larks, and white-tailed ptarmigan.

### Fishing

Fly fishermen can angle for Rio Grande cutthroat trout in Medano creek, but it's catch and release. A Colorado license is required. There's also fishing in Upper and Lower Sand Creek Lake, but it's a very long hike.

### Hiking/Walking

Visitors can walk just about anywhere on the sand dunes in the heart of the park. The best view of all the dunes is from the top of High Dune. There are no formal trails because the sand keeps shifting; however, the majority of visitors trek up it, and all of those feet can create a sort of rough path in the sand.

▪ TIP➔   **Before taking any of the trails in the preserve, rangers recommend stopping at the visitor center and picking up the handout that lists the trails,** including their degree of difficulty. The dunes can get very hot in the summer, reaching up to 140°F in the afternoon. If you're hiking, carry plenty of water; if you're going into the backcountry to camp overnight, carry even more water or a water filtration system. A free permit is needed to backpack in the park. Also watch for weather changes. If there's a thunderstorm and lightning, get off the dunes or trail immediately, and seek shelter. Before hiking, leave word with someone where you're to hike and when you expect to be back. Tell that contact to call the area-wide dispatcher at 719/589-5807 if you don't show up when expected back.

EASY **Hike to High Dune.** Get a panoramic view of all the surrounding dunes. Since there's no formal path, the smartest approach is to zigzag up the dune ridgelines. High Dunes is 650 feet high, and to get there and back takes about 1½ to 2 hours. It's 1²⁄₁₀ mi each way. If you add on the walk to Star Dune, which is a few more miles, plan on another 2 hours and a strenuous workout up and down the dunes to get there. ⊠ *Start from main dunefield.*

**DID YOU KNOW?** Native Americans used to peel ponderosa pines in order to eat the inner bark (which is rich in calcium) and use the pine gum for medicinal purposes. You can view many of these "culturally modified" trees at Great Sand Dunes.

MODERATE
Fodor'sChoice
★
**Mosca Pass Trail.** This moderately easy trail follows the route laid out centuries ago by Native Americans and then the Mosca Pass toll road used in the late 1800s and early 1900s. This is a good afternoon hike, because the trail rises through the trees and subalpine meadows, often following Mosca Creek. It is 3½ miles one way, with a 1,480-foot gain in elevation. Hiking time is 2 to 3 hours each way. ⊠ *The lower end of the trail begins at the Montville Trailhead, just north of the visitor center.*

DIFFICULT **Music Pass Trail.** This steep trail offers superb views of the glacially carved Upper Sand Creek Basin, ringed by many 13,000-foot peaks and the Wet Mountain Valley to the east. At the top of the pass you are about 11,000 feet and surrounded by yet higher mountain peaks. The trail also accesses the Sand Creek Lakes Trail and the Little Sand Creek Lakes Trail, with terrain ranging from moderately difficult to very rough and requiring good route-finding ability. It's 3½ mi and a 2,000-foot elevation gain one way from the lower parking lot, and 1 mi from the upper parking lot (only reachable in a 4-wheel-drive vehicle). Depending on how fit you are and how often you stop, it could take 6 hours round-trip. ⊠ *The trailhead is reached via Hwy. 69, 4½ mi south of Westcliffe. Turn off Hwy. 69 to the west at the sign for Music Pass and South Colony Lakes Trails. At the "T" junction turn left onto South Colony Rd. At the end of the ranch fence on the right you'll see another sign for Music Pass.*

**20**

## Horseback Riding

Riding is allowed throughout the preserve and in much of the park. There are certain restrictions. For example, riding is not allowed in areas with high pedestrian traffic, such as the Pinyon Flats Campground. Camping with horses is permitted in certain areas; stop at the visitor center to pick up a horseback-riding and camping map and a free permit for camping with a horse and parking your horse trailer.

### Jeep Tours

**Great Sand Dunes Oasis.** In warmer months, you can book a Medano Pass Primitive Road Tour in an open-air, 4-wheel-drive vehicle. The tours follow a sandy road along the eastern edge of the dunes and go partway up the road then turnaround. ✉ *5400 Hwy. 150 (just outside the park), Mosca* ☎ *719/378–2222* 💲 *$21 adults; $12 children 12–18; $5 for children under 12* ◷ *10 and 2 roughly Memorial Day to Labor Day; minimum 6 people.*

## Educational Offerings

### Classes & Seminars

**Nature Conservancy.** June through August, guest speakers are on hand to lecture on all kinds of topics, from birds in the park to the region's history, and there are conservation seminars in spring, summer and fall. ✉ *Medano-Zapata Ranch* ☎ *719/378–6399 or 719/378–2356 for the Nature Conservancy workshops* 💲 *Cost varies according to program.*

### Programs & Tours

🐾 **Bison Tour and Hayride.** On these Saturday-morning tours visitors see the "Wild West" section of the park, where more than 1,000 bison roam in the grasslands and wetlands. ✉ *Tours begin at the Nature Conservancy's Medano-Zapata Ranch* ☎ *719/378–2904* 💲 *$20 adults, $10 children under 16.*

### Ranger Programs

**Interpretive Programs.** Terrace talks and nature walks designed to help visitors learn more about the park are scheduled most days from late May through September. (Contact the park in advance about any programs from October through April.) ✉ *Talks begin from the visitor center* ☎ *719/378–6399* 💲 *Free.*

**Junior Ranger Programs.** During summer months, children ages 3–12 can join age-appropriate activities to learn about plants, animals, and the park's ecology, and they can become Junior Rangers by working successfully through an activity booklet. Ask for schedules and activity booklets at the visitor center. Youngsters can learn about the park prior to their trip via an interactive online program for kids at www.nps.gov/archive/grsa/pphtml/forkids.html. ☎ *719/378–6399* 💲 *Free.*

# WHAT'S NEARBY

The vast open expanse one sees from the dunes is the San Luis Valley. At 8,000 square mi, the San Luis Valley is the world's largest alpine valley, sprawling on a broad, flat, dry plain between the San Juan and La

Garita mountains to the west and the Sangre de Cristo range to the east. The area is one of the state's major agricultural producers.

## Nearby Towns & Attractions

### Nearby Towns

**Alamosa,** the San Luis Valley's major city, is 35 mi southwest of Great Sand Dunes via U.S. 160 and Highway 150. It's a casual, central base for exploring the park and the surrounding region. The rest of the area is dotted with tiny towns, including **Mosca, Blanca,** and **Fort Garland,** to the south of the park, **Monte Vista, Del Norte,** and **Antonito** to the west. They are all within an hour or so drive from the park.

### Nearby Attractions

**Alamosa National Wildlife Refuge.** About 32 mi southwest of the park these natural and man-made wetlands bordering the Rio Grande river are an important sanctuary for myriad migrating birds. ✉ *9383 El Rancho La.* ☎ *719/589–4021* 🖥 *Free* ☾ *Daily sunrise–sunset.*

**Monte Vista National Wildlife Refuge.** From late February to mid-March, birders flock to view the migration of the sandhill cranes. Nicknamed the Valley of the Cranes, the valley is where you can see at close range these sandhill cranes gathering in large numbers as they stop and rest during their annual migration. Every morning during the mid-March Crane Festival buses shuttle visitors to the refuge from Alamosa. ✉ *6140 Hwy. 15, Monte Vista* 🖥 *Free* ☾ *Daily.*

☪ **Zapata Falls Recreation Area.** If it's a hot day, hike with the kids to Zapata Falls, just south of Great Sand Dunes National Park. It's a ½-mi hike to the 40-foot waterfall and a mildly steep trail, which includes wading in a stream and walking through a narrow gorge to view the falls. There's a picnic area and restrooms at the entrance. ✉ *The trailhead is 3½ mi off Hwy. 150 between mile markers 10 and 11.*

## Area Activities

### Sports & the Outdoors

FISHING  There are many reservoirs and lakes in the area where you can fish for trout, pike, and perch, including the Rio Grande, the Sanchez Reservoir, the San Luis lakes, and the Smith Reservoir. A Colorado fishing license is required. The park paper lists places to fish.

### Arts & Entertainment

FESTIVALS &  **Castles and Kites.** Kites soar and sand is transformed into competitive
EVENTS  sculptures at this free event in Alamosa's Cole Park the last week of June. Afterward, a concert is held. ☎ *719/378–6381.*

## Scenic Vistas

☪ **Scenic Train Rides.** Two train rides in this region take passengers through stunning scenery. Take a day trip on the **Cumbres & Toltec Scenic Railroad,** which chugs through portions of Colorado and northern New Mexico's rugged mountains that you can't reach via roads. The ride is 64 mi long, and the depot is in Antonito. The second option is **Rio Grande Scenic**

20

**Railroad,** taking riders between Alamosa and La Veta. 🚊 *$59–$72, Cumbres & Toltec; $9–$71, Rio Grande* ☎ *888/286–2737 or 877/726–7245* ⊕ *www.cumbrestoltec.com or www.alamosatrain.com* ⊙ *Late May–mid-Oct., daily.*

# WHERE TO STAY & EAT

### About the Restaurants

There are no dining establishments in the park. In the visitor center and at the campground there are vending machines with drinks that are stocked mid-spring through mid-fall. There is one picnic area in the park.

### About the Hotels

There are no hotels, motels or lodges in the park. The nearest motel is right outside the park entrance, and there are many hotels in Alamosa.

### About the Campgrounds

Great Sand Dunes has one campground that is open year-round. During the summer it often fills up with RVs and tents by mid-morning or noon. Black bears live in the preserve, so when camping there, use bear-proof containers, or hang your food, trash, and toiletries at least 10 feet above the ground and 4 feet horizontally from the tree trunk. There is one campground and RV Park near the entrance to Great Sand Dunes and others in the region and Alamosa. The campground right outside the park has a great view of the dunes.

## Where to Eat

### In the Park

PICNIC AREA **Mosca Creek.** The park's only picnic area is shaded by cottonwood trees. It has a dozen places where visitors can park a car or RV near a picnic table and a grill. ⊠ *South of the Dunes Parking Lot.*

### Outside the Park

$–$$$ ✕ **True Grits.** At this steak house, the cuts of beef are predictably good, but that's not the real draw. As the name implies, the restaurant is a shrine to John Wayne. His portraits hang everywhere: the Duke in action; the Duke in repose; the Duke lost in thought. ⊠ *Junction U.S. 160 and Highway 17, Alamosa* ☎ *719/589–9954. $11–$25* ⊟ *AE, D, MC, V.*

¢–$$ ✕ **The Oasis Cafe.** The restaurant in the Great Sand Dunes Oasis, just outside the park entrance, is open for breakfast, lunch, and dinner. The Navajo taco, and beef or chicken burritos are among the most popular items, although the menu ranges from grilled-cheese sandwiches to steaks. ⊠ *5400 Hwy. 150, Mosca* ☎ *719/378–2222. $6–$19* ⊟ *AE, MC, V.*

★ ¢ ✕ **Milagro's Coffeehouse.** The coffee is full-bodied at this combination coffeehouse, Internet café, and used-book store, where all profits go to local charities. The tuna salad sub and Reubens are especially tasty. ⊠ *529 Main St., Alamosa* ☎ *719/589–9299. $5–$7* ⊟ *MC, V.*

## Where to Stay

### In the Park

CAMPGROUNDS & RV PARKS

$

⚠ **Pinyon Flats Campground.** Set in a pinyon forest about a mile past the visitor center, this campground has a trail leading to the dunes. Sites available on a first-come, first-served basis, although groups of 10 or more might be able to reserve in advance. RVs are allowed, but there are no hookups. The campground fills up rapidly on summer weekends, and tends to have lots of families when school is out. Quiet hours start at 10 PM. Register at the kiosk. ⊠ *On the main park road, near the visitor center* ☎ *719/378–6399* ✍ *88 sites* ⚘ *Flush toilets, fire grates, picnic tables.* $14 ▭ *No credit cards.*

### Outside the Park

★ ☾ $$

⊞ **Inn of the Rio Grande.** Alamosa's largest hotel is a dog-friendly property, with comfortable rooms and suites. It's a full-service hotel, with a nice indoor pools kids will love. ⊠ *333 Santa Fe Dr., Alamosa 81101* ☎ *719/589–5833* ⊕ *www.innoftherio.com* ✍ *126 rooms* ⚘ *Refrigerator (some), ethernet, pool, gym, some pets allowed, no-smoking rooms.* $90 ▭ *AE, D, MC, V.*

$–$$

⊞ **Conejos River Guest Ranch.** On the Conejos River, this peaceful, family-friendly retreat is about 42 mi southwest of Alamosa. One of the draws is the great fishing in the area. The seven cabins and eight guest rooms are pleasantly outfitted with ranch-style decor, including lodgepole pine furnishings. Breakfast is complimentary in the lodge only. ⊠ *25390 Hwy. 17, Antonito 81120* ☎ *719/376–2464* ⊕ *www.conejosranch.com* ✍ *8 rooms, 7 cabins* ⚘ *Restaurant, kitchen (some), no a/c, no TV.* $90–$120 ▭ *D, MC, V* ☾ *Closed Dec.–Apr.*

$

⊞ **Best Western Alamosa Inn.** This sprawling, well-maintained complex is your best bet for budget lodgings. Rooms are spacious and offer the standard amenities. ⊠ *2005 Main St., Alamosa 81101* ☎ *719/589–2567* 🖷 *719/589–0767* ⊕ *www.bestwestern.com/alamosainn* ✍ *52 rooms, 1 suite* ⚘ *Pool, no-smoking rooms.* $89 ▭ *AE, D, DC, MC, V.*

CAMPGROUNDS & RV PARKS

☾ $$

⚠ **Great Sand Dunes Oasis.** Just outside the park, the Great Sand Dunes Oasis has a private, well-shaded campground with both tent and RV sites (including hookups). They sometimes have ice-cream socials on summer evenings. On the premises are a restaurant, general store, and gas station. Pets are allowed. ⊠ *5400 Hwy. 150, Mosca 81146* ☎ *719/378–2222* ⊕*www.greatdunes.com* ✍ *130 tent sites, 26 RV sites, 4 cabins.* $18 tent, $28 RV ▭ *AE, D, MC, V* ⚘ *Fire pits, picnic tables, flush toilets, showers, playarea, guest laundry* ☾ *Apr.–Oct.*

$$

⚠ **KOA Campground.** Get Wi-Fi throughout the park and access to cable TV at some of the sites at this year-round campground on Highway 160, 3½ mi east of Alamosa. Great Sand Dunes is 30 minutes away. ⊠ *6900 Juniper La., Alamosa 81101* ☎ *800/562–9157* ⊕ *www.koa. com* ✍ *15 tent sites, 56 RV sites, 3 cabins.* $22–$27 for tents, $25–$35 for RVs, $47–$57 for cabins ▭ *AE, D, DC, MC, V* ⚘ *Grills, showers, play area, RV hook-ups.*

$$

⚠ **San Luis State Park.** About 15 minutes from Great Sand Dunes on County Lane 6 North, this state park has a modern campground with

**20**

access to an abundance of water-sport options: fishing, boating, water-skiing, even windsurfing. ✍ *P.O. Box 175, Mosca 81146* ☎ *719/378–2020* ⊕ *www.parks.state.co.us* ⬛ *45 sites for RVs or tents* ⬩ *Fire pits, picnic tables, flush toilets, showers, electricity. $16 plus $8 registration fee* ⊟ *D, MC, V* ☽ *Memorial Day–Labor Day.*

$  ⚠ **Blanca RV Park & Store.** Big rigs have easy access at this year-round campground on Highway 160. Pull-through RV sites are level, with full hookups, and tent campers enjoy shaded, grassy sites. Great Sand Dunes is 30 minutes away. ✍ *521 Main St., Blanca 81123* ☎ *719/379–3201* ⬛ *10 tent sites, 26 RV sites* ⬩ *Grills, showers, dump station, public telephone, guest laundry, RV hook-ups. Tent camping $12 for 2 people; RV sites $20 for two people* ⊟ *AE, D, MC, V.*

# GREAT SAND DUNES ESSENTIALS

ACCESSIBILITY There are two wheelchairs with balloon tires that can be used on the sand. (Someone must push them.) They can be reserved by calling the visitor center in advance. There is also one handicap-accessible campsite that can be reserved in advance.

ADMISSION FEES Entrance fees are $3 per adult above age 16 and are valid for one week from date of purchase. Children are admitted free at all times. Golden Age Pass (age 62 or older) is $10 and valid at all federal fee areas for life. This includes family members traveling with pass holder.

ADMISSION HOURS The park is open 24/7. It is in the Mountain time zone.

ATMS/BANKS The park has no ATM. 🅕 **San Luis Valley Federal Bank** ✉ 401 Edison Ave., Alamosa ☎ 719/378-2904.

AUTOMOBILE SERVICE STATIONS 🅕 **Great Sand Dunes Oasis** (gas only) ✉ 5400 Hwy. 150 (about 3 mi from park entrance), Mosca ☎ 719/378-2222.

EMERGENCIES Dial 911. No clinic on-site.

LOST AND FOUND The park's lost-and-found is at the visitor center.

PERMITS Pick up camping permits ($14 per night per site at Pinyon Flats Campground) and backpacking permits (free) at the visitor center.

POST OFFICES You can mail letters from a box in front of the visitor center.

🅕 **Mosca Post Office** ✉ 9260 4th Ave., Mosca ☎ 719/378-2401.

PUBLIC TELEPHONES There are public telephones at the visitor center, the Dunes parking lot, and at the Pinyon Flats campground. Cell-phone reception is sporadic.

RELIGIOUS SERVICES There are no religious services in the park.

RESTROOMS Restrooms are located in the Dunes parking lot and at the campground.

SHOPS & GROCERS
🅕 **Great Sand Dunes Oasis.** ✉ 5400 Hwy. 150 (about 3 mi from park entrance) ☎ 719/378-2222.

**NEARBY TOWN INFORMATION**
🅕 **Alamosa Visitor Information Center & Chamber of Commerce.** ✉ 300 Chamber Dr., Alamosa, CO 81101 ☎ 800/258-7597 or 719/589-3681 ⊕ www.alamosa.org. **Antonito Chamber of Commerce.** In the summer, there's a tourist office at the junction of Highways 285 and 17, next to the train depot. ✍ 307 Main St., Antonito, CO 81120 ☎ 719/376-2277 ⊕ www.slvguide.com/Antonito/Index.htm. **Del Norte Chamber of Commerce.** ✉ 505 Grade Ave., Del Norte, CO 81132 ☎ 719/657-2845 ⊕ www.delnortechamber.org. **Monte Vista Chamber of Commerce.** ✉ 1035 Park Ave., Monte Vista, CO 81144 ☎ 719/852-2731.

**VISITOR INFORMATION**
🅕 **Great Sand Dunes National Park** ✍ 11999 Hwy. 150, Mosca, CO 81146 ☎ 719/378-6399 ⊕ www.nps.gov/grsa.

# Guadalupe Mountains National Park

Guadalupe Peak, Guadalupe Mountains National Park

**WORD OF MOUTH**

"May your trails be crooked, winding, lonesome, dangerous, leading to the most amazing view. May your mountains rise into and above the clouds."

–Edward Abbey, environmental writer and activist

# WELCOME TO GUADALUPE MOUNTAINS

## TOP REASONS TO GO

★ **Tower over Texas:** The park is home to 8,479-foot Guadalupe Peak, the highest point in the state.

★ **Fall for fiery foliage:** Though surrounded by arid desert and rocky soil, the park has miles of beautiful foliage in McKittrick Canyon. In late October, you can watch it burst into flaming colors.

★ **Hike unhindered:** The main activity at the park is hiking its rugged, remote, and often-challenging trails.

★ **Eat with elk, loll with lions:** Despite the surrounding arid region, a variety of wildlife—including shaggy brown elk, sneaky mountain lions, and shy black bears—traipses the mountains, woods, and desert here.

★ **Catch a (ghost) stagecoach:** In the late 1830s, a stagecoach line ran from St. Louis and San Francisco with a stop at what's now Guadalupe Mountains National Park. The stages are long gone, but ruins of an old station still remain in the park.

**1** Guadalupe Peak. This crude, rocky pinnacle tops 8,700 feet and towers over the rest of the park's peaks. Those who brave the seven hour-plus round-trip to the summit are rewarded with breathtaking views of New Mexico and southwestern Texas.

**2** McKittrick Canyon. In late October and early November, the lush green foliage along McKittrick Canyon's trout-filled desert stream bursts into russet, amber, and gold hues.

**3** El Capitan. El Capitan has visitors talking and hikers walking—this 3,000-foot cliff dominates the view at the southern end of the Guadalupe range. A 6- to 11-mi-plus trail winds around the base of this massive limestone formation, one of the most visible reminders of what was once the great Permian reef, exposed eons ago when the sea receded.

**4** Manzanita Spring. The area around this idyllic stream and picnic spot has a little bit of everything: a spring feeds lush grasses and trees, giving life to hundreds of wildflowers. Birds hang out here to enjoy the tasty seeds and insects that the water, shade, and vegetation provide. Plus, it's only a ⅕-mi, paved ramble from here to the Frijole Ranch Museum.

**5** Frijole Ranch Museum. This easily accessible historic ranch

El Capitan

NEW MEXICO
TEXAS

Cutoff Mountain
6,933 ft

0        2 mi

0        2 km

Texas Madrone

site houses the stone ruins of the oldest structure in the park. The recently restored Ranch House museum injects a bit of man-made history into the natural surroundings. Five nearby springs are just a refreshing stroll away.

TEXAS

137

B R O K E O F F   M O U N T A I N S

C U T O F F   R I D G E

**Dog Canyon**
🏕 🍱 🚻

Lost Peak
7,830 ft

*Pratt Cabin*

G U A D A L U P E   M O U N T A I N S

**2** 🚻

**McKittrick Canyon**

◆ **Grotto**
🍱

F R I J O L E   R I D G E

Bush Mountain
8,631 ft

Bartlett Peak
8,508 ft

Shumard Peak
8,615 ft

**5** **Frijole Ranch Museum**

Hunter Peak
8,368 ft
🏕 🍱

Guadalupe Peak
(highest point in Texas)
8,749 ft

**1** **Pine Springs** ◆
**Stay Station Ruins** ◆

🚻

**4**

**Visitor Center**

**Williams Ranch** ◆

El Capitan ▲
8,085 ft

**3**

62
180

62
180

*Williams Ranch Rd.*

Quail Mountain
4,962 ft

## GETTING ORIENTED

The park is off U.S. 62/180, 110 mi northeast of El Paso, Texas; 40 mi southwest of Carlsbad Caverns National Park; and 55 mi southwest of Carlsbad, New Mexico. White's City, New Mexico, is 35 mi northeast of the park on U.S. 62/180.

| KEY | |
|---|---|
| 🏃 | Ranger Station |
| 🏕 | Campground |
| 🍱 | Picnic Area |
| 🍴 | Restaurant |
| 🖼 | Lodge |
| 🚶 | Trailhead |
| 🚻 | Restrooms |
| ⚡ | Scenic Viewpoint |
| ---- | Walking/Hiking Trails |
| ···· | Bicycle Path |

# GUADALUPE MOUNTAINS PLANNER

## When to Go

Trails here are rarely crowded, except in fall, when foliage changes colors in McKittrick Canyon, and during Spring Break in March. Still, this is a very remote area, and you'll be unlikely to find too much congestion at any time. Hikers are more apt to explore backcountry trails in spring and fall, when it's cooler, but not too cold. Snow, not uncommon in the winter months, can linger in the higher elevations.

## Getting There & Around

Since about half of the Guadalupe Mountains is a designated wilderness, few roadways penetrate the park. Most sites are accessible off U.S. 62/180. Dog Canyon Campground on the north end of the park can be reached via Route 137, which traverses the woodlands of Lincoln National Forest.

## Flora & Fauna

Despite the constant wind and the arid conditions, more than a thousand species of plants populate the mountains, chasms, and salt dunes that make up the park's different geologic zones. Some grow many feet in a single night; others bloom so infrequently they're called "century plants." Some of the most spectacular sights, however, are seasonal. In fall, McKittrick Canyon's oaks, bigtooth maples, and velvet ashes go Technicolor above the little stream that traverses it. Barren-looking cacti burst into yellow, red, and purple bloom in spring, and wildflowers can carpet the park for thousands of acres after unusually heavy rains.

Hundreds of animal species haunt the diverse environments of the Guadalupes. At last count, there were nearly 300 different bird species, 90 types of butterflies, and 16 species of bats alone. The park's furry residents include coyotes, black bears, and badgers. You may also spot elk, which were reintroduced after nearly becoming extinct here.

Plenty of reptiles and insects make their homes here too: coachwhip snakes, diamondback rattlers, and lovelorn tarantulas (the only time you'll spy them is in the fall, when they search for mates), to name a few. Texas' famous horned lizards—affectionately called "horney toads"—can also be seen waddling across the soil in search of ants and other insects.

Despite the presence of larger predators, animal attacks are almost unheard of in the park. As one park ranger put it, "The only time you'll probably see a mountain lion is when he's running away." Despite that, rangers caution parents not to let little ones run too far ahead on the trails. Also, be mindful that rattlesnakes are common in the park. They aren't aggressive, but be sure to give a wide berth to any snakes your hear or spot.

AVG. HIGH/LOW TEMPS.

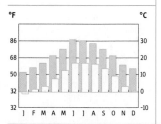

By Jennifer
Edwards

Guadalupe Mountains National Park is a study in extremes: it has arid deserts, mountaintop forests, rocky canyons, and a stream that winds through a verdant hardwood forest. The park is home to the Texas madrone tree, a lovely Ice Age relic commonly found only here and in Big Bend National Park. Guadalupe Mountains National Park also has the distinction of hosting the loftiest spot in Texas: 8,749-foot Guadalupe Peak. The mountain dominates the view from every approach, but it's just one member of a rugged range carved by wind, water, and time.

Over 86,000 acres of mountains, chasms, canyons, woods, and deserts house an incredible diversity of wildlife, including hallmark Southwestern species like roadrunners and long-limbed jackrabbits, which run so fast they appear to float on their enormous, black-tipped ears.

## Scenic Drive

**Williams Ranch Road.** You'll take in panoramic views and get an up-close look at limestone cliffs on this 7¼-mi, one-way drive over what was once the Bitterfeld Overland Mail Stage Line. The closest highway, U.S. 180, parallels the old trail. The rough route—you'll need a high-clearance, four-wheel-drive vehicle or a mountain bike—is enjoyable. To drive it, get a gate key at the visitor center and drive west on U.S. 62/180 for 8¼ mi until you see a brown metal gate on the north side with a National Park Service sign. Drive through two locked gates (be sure to lock them behind you), and follow the road to an old, lonely ranch house. James "Dolph" Williams operated this spread with his partner, an Indian named Geronimo (no relation to the historical figure). The road closes at night, though, so don't tarry too long.

## What to See

### Historic Sites

☾ **Frijole Ranch Museum.** You'll find displays and photographs depicting ranch life and early park history inside this old ranch house museum. Hiking trails are adjacent to the grounds, which have shady trees. Nearby trails, some of which are easy to travel and great for kids, lead to the **Manzanita Spring.** ⊠ *Access road 1 mi northeast of Headquarters Visitors Center* ☎ *915/828–3251* 🎫 *Free* ☉ *Call for hours.*

★ **Pinery Bitterfeld Stage Station Ruins.** In the mid-1800s, passengers en route from St. Louis or San Francisco would stop for rest and refreshment this structure, one of the stops along the old Bitterfeld Overland Mail stagecoach route. A paved ¾-mi round-trip trail leads here from the Headquarters Visitors Center, or you can drive directly here. ⊠ *½ mi east of Headquarters Visitors Center.*

### Scenic Stop

Fodor'sChoice **McKittrick Canyon.** A desert creek flows through this canyon, which is lined
★ with walnut, maple, and other trees that explode into brilliant colors each fall. You're likely to spot mule deer heading for the water here. ⊠ *4 mi off U.S. 62/180, about 7 mi northeast of Headquarters Visitor Center* ☉ *Highway gate open Nov.–Apr., daily 8–4:30; May–Sept. daily 8–6.*

### Visitor Centers

**Headquarters Visitors Center.** Exhibits and a slide show here give you a quick introduction to the park, half of which is a wilderness area. Some nicely crafted exhibits depict typical wildlife and plant scenes. ⊠ *U.S. 62/180, 55 mi southwest of Carlsbad, 110 mi northeast of El Paso* ☎ *915/ 828–3251* 🖶 *915/828–3269* ☉ *June–Aug., daily 8–6; Sept.–May, daily 8–4:30; closed Christmas Day.*

**McKittrick Contact Station.** Poster-size illustrations in a shaded, outdoor patio area tell the geologic story of the Guadalupe Mountains, an area carved from an ancient sea. You can also hear the recorded memoirs of oilman Wallace Pratt, who donated his ranch and surrounding area to the federal government for preservation. ⊠ *4 mi off U.S. 62/180, 7 mi northeast of Headquarters Visitor Center* ☎ *915/828–3251 (Headquarters Visitor Center)* ☉ *June–Aug., daily 8–6; Sept.–May, daily 8–4:30.*

## Sports & the Outdoors

### Bird-watching

More than 300 species of birds have been spotted in the park, including the ladder-backed woodpecker, Scott's oriole, Say's Phoebe, and white-throated swift. Many non-native birds stop at Guadalupe during spring and fall migrations. **Manzanita Springs,** located near the Frijole Ranch Museum, is an excellent birding spot. As with hiking, there aren't any local guides, but rangers at the Dog Canyon and Pine Springs stations can help you spot some native species. Books on birding are available at the Pine Springs station; visitors might find the Natural History Association's birding checklist for Guadalupe Mountains National Park especially helpful. It will be easy to spot the larger birds of prey circling overhead, such

# GUADALUPE MOUNTAINS IN ONE DAY

Start your tour at **Headquarters Visitor Center,** where a year-round exhibit and slide show acquaint you with the park's wildlife and geology. Nearby is the ¾-mi round-trip, handicapped-accessible **Pinery Trail,** which rambles to the Pinery Bitterfeld Stage Station ruins. Take in the sites, but be sure not to touch the fragile walls; the site is more vulnerable than most. Next, head to the **Frijole Ranch Museum,** built in 1876 and preserved through several renovations.

Once you're done gawking at the old structures, stroll to the calming waters of **Manzanita Spring.** Turn onto the paved trailhead behind the ranch house for the ⅕-mi trek to the spring. Manzanita is one of five springs that gurgle within only a couple of miles of the museum. Park staff call such areas riparian zones; they are the oases that supply the fragile wildlife here, and can sometime look like Pre-Raphaelite paintings, with mirrored-surface ponds and delicate flowers and greenery.

Afterwards, pay a visit to the famed **McKittrick Canyon.** Regardless of the season, the dense foliage and basin stream are worth the hike—though it's best to visit it in late October and early November when the trees burst into color. There isn't a direct route, but you can get there quickly by driving northeast from the visitor center on U.S. 62/180. Follow it to the gate at the western turnoff, which is locked at sunset. Head northwest, ignoring the service road, and you'll arrive at the canyon.

Take your time walking the **McKittrick Canyon Trail** that leads to Pratt Lodge, or the strenuous but rewarding 8⁴⁄₁₀-mi **Permian Reef Trail,** which takes you up thousands of feet, past monumental geological formations. Or traverse the easy, short (less than 1 mi) **McKittrick Canyon Nature Trail.**

as keen-beaked golden eagles and swift, red-tailed hawks. Be on the lookout for owls in the **Bowl** area, and watch for swift-footed roadrunners in the desert areas (they're not as speedy as their cartoon counterpart).

## Hiking

No matter which trail you select, be sure to pack wisely—the park doesn't sell anything. This includes the recommended gallon of water per day per person, as well as sunscreen and hats. The area has a triple-whammy as far as sun ailments are concerned: it's very open, very sunny, and the high altitude makes sunburns more likely. So slather up. And be sure to leave Fido at home—few of the park's trails allow pets. The staff at the **Dog Canyon ranger station** can help you plan your hikes (☎ 505/981–2418). The bookstore at the **Pine Springs ranger station** also sells hiking guides. These and other guides also can be found at www.ccgma.org.

EASY The **Indian Meadows Nature Trail** in Dog Canyon is a very easy, mostly level ½-mi hike that crosses an arroyo into meadowlands. It's a good way to spend about 45 minutes savoring the countryside.

**FodorśChoice**
★

The easiest McKittrick trail is a 1-mi **McKittrick Nature Loop**. Signs along the way explain the geologic and biological history of the area. The trail is handicapped accessible and great for little ones. Plus, you can see the canyon's signature foliage.

**OUTFITTERS**

The staff at **Dog Canyon ranger station** can help you plan your hikes. ☎ 505/981-2418. Visit **Headquarters Visitor Center** 🖃 HC 60, Box 400, Salt Flat, TX 79847 ☎ 915/828-3251 ⊕ www.nps.gov/gumo for hiking advice.

MODERATE    **Bush Mountain**, a moderate 4½-mi round-trip, rewards you with a panoramic view of West Dog Canyon. It will take about half a day to complete. ⊠ Rte. 137, 60 mi southwest of U.S. 285.

The moderate **Devil's Hall Trail** runs through about 4 mi of Chihuahuan Desert habitat thick with spiked agave plants, prickly pear cacti, giant boulders, and Devil's Hall, a narrow canyon about 10 feet wide and 100 feet deep. This moderate hike, which begins at the Pine Springs trailhead, will take about a day if you travel at a leisurely pace.

★    The **El Capital/Salt Basin Overlook Trails** form a popular loop through the low desert. El Capital skirts the base of El Capital peak for about 3½ miles, leading to a junction with Salt Basin Overlook. The 4½-mi trail begins at the Pine Springs trailhead and has views of the stark, white salt flat below and loops back onto the El Capital Trail. Though moderate, the 11³⁄₁₀-mi round-trip is not recommended during the intense heat of summer, since there is absolutely no shade. ⊠ Behind Headquarters Visitor Center at Pine Springs campground.

The **Frijole/Foothills Trail**, which branches off the Frijole Ranch trailhead, leads to the Pine Springs campground behind Headquarters Visitors Center. The moderate, 5½-mi round-trip through desert vistas takes about five hours.

The 6¾-mi round-trip to the **Grotto Picnic Area** starts at the McKittrick contact station. It affords views of a flowing stream and surface rock that resembles formations in an underground cave, with jagged overhangs. Plan on about five hours for a leisurely walk.

You can view stream and canyon woodland areas along the **Pratt Lodge Trail**, a 4½-mi round-trip excursion that leads to the now vacant Pratt Lodge. Plan on at least two hours at a fast pace on this moderate trail, but give yourself another hour or two if you want to take your time. ⊠ 4 mi off U.S. 62/180, about 7 mi northeast of Headquarters Visitor Center.

The **Smith Spring Trail** also departs from the Frijole Ranch trailhead. The trail, a round-trip walk of 2²⁄₁₀ mi, takes you through a shady oasis where you're likely to spot mule deer alongside a spring and a small waterfall. Allow 1½ hours to complete the walk. This is a good hike for older kids, whose legs won't tire as easily. ⊠ Access road 1 mi northeast of Headquarters Visitors Center.

DIFFICULT
★

Cutting through forests of pine and Douglas fir, **The Bowl** is considered one of the most gorgeous trails in the park. The strenuous 9-mi round-trip—which can take up to 10 hours, depending on your pace—begins at the Pine Springs trailhead. This is where rangers go when they want to enjoy themselves. Don't forget to drink lots of water!

The 8½-mi **Guadalupe Peak Trail** is a strenuous workout over a steep grade, but it offers some great views of exposed cliff face. The hike begins at the Pine Springs trailhead and can take up to eight hours to complete.

The somewhat strenuous **Lost Peak Trail** in Dog Canyon is 6½ mi round-trip, which will take about six hours to complete if your pace is slower; it leads from Dog Canyon into a coniferous forest.

> ## PUBLICATIONS
>
> The Guadalupe Mountains' natural features and history are the subjects of the illustrated **The Guadalupes,** by Dan Murphy, a booklet published by the Carlsbad Caverns Guadalupe Mountains Association. Other booklets include **Trails of the Guadalupes,** by Don Kurtz and William D. Goran; and **Hiking Carlsbad Caverns and Guadalupe Mountains National Parks,** by Bill Schneider. These and other publications are available at the visitor center. Also, check out the park's excellent Web site, www.nps.gov/gumo, for at-home planning.

If you're in shape and have a serious geological bent, you may want to hike the **Permian Ridge Geology Trail.** The 8½-mi round-trip climb heads through open, expansive desert country to a forested ridge with Douglas fir and ponderosa pines. You'll have panoramic views of McKittrick Canyon and the surrounding mountain ranges and see the many rock layers that built up over the eons. Begin at the McKittrick Contact Station, and set aside at least eight hours for this trek.

### Mountain Biking

If you've got a mountain bike or a high-clearance, four-wheel-drive vehicle, cruise to the **Williams Ranch Trail.** Skittering down it will only take about an hour one way (for vehicles), and will lead you to the **Williams Ranch House,** which sits alone at the base of a 3,000-foot cliff. ■ TIP➔ **Before you set out, check out the gate key at the Headquarters Visitor Center.** Then head west on Highway 62/180. Drive 8¼ mi to the brown metal gate with National Park signs; be sure to lock the gate behind you once you're through. Proceed for another ¾ mi to another gate; lock this one as well once you're through it. Follow the worn dirt road—which runs past arid scenery and cacti that bloom in the spring months—to the Ranch House, and enjoy a close-up El Capitan, second-largest peak in the park. Be sure to leave before sundown, and don't forget to return the key to the visitor center.

## Educational Offerings

### Ranger Program

 **Junior Ranger Program.** The park offers a self-guided Junior Ranger Program: kids choose activities from a workbook—including taking nature hikes and answering questions based on park exhibits—and earn a patch and certificate once they've completed three. If they complete six, they earn an additional patch. ✉ *Headquarters Visitor Center* ☎ *915/828–3251 Ext. 118* 🚮 *Free* ☉ *June–Aug., daily 8–6; Sept.–May, daily 8–4:30.*

# WHAT'S NEARBY

### Nearby U.S. Towns

Tiny **White's City, New Mexico**, 35 mi to the northeast off U.S. 62/180, is more a crossroads than a town. The town of **Carlsbad, New Mexico**, 55 mi northeast of the park, has more amenities. For more information about both cities, including dining, lodging, and attractions, ⇨ Carlsbad Caverns National Park.

# WHERE TO STAY & EAT

### About the Restaurants

Dining in the park is a do-it-yourself affair. Ranger stations don't serve meals or sell picnic items, though nearby White's City offers some basics—sodas, snacks, and the like—to help you plan a picnic.

### About the Hotels

The Best Western in White's City is your best local option. For information on lodging near the park, ⇨ Carlsbad Caverns National Park.

### About the Campgrounds

Visitors haul their supplies across miles to stretch out on the unsoiled land of several backcountry sites, but the only two developed campsites in the park are located at the Pine Springs Headquarters and Dog Canyon.

## Where to Eat

### In Guadalupe Mountains

PICNIC AREAS   The park has no snack bars or restaurants, but several picnic areas are available. Wood and charcoal fires are not allowed anywhere in the park. If you want to cook a hot meal, bring a camp stove.

**Dog Canyon Campground.** Thirteen campsites have picnic tables, which you can use during the day for free. This is a lovely shaded area where you're very likely to see mule deer. Drinking water and restrooms are available at the site. This area is about 2½ hours from Headquarters Visitor Center. ⊠ *Off Rte. 137, 65 mi southwest of Carlsbad.*

**Frijole Ranch Museum.** This area is much cooler than nearby Pine Springs campground. Two picnic tables are set up under tall trees; restrooms are available at the ranch house museum. ⊠ *Access road 1 mi northeast of Headquarters Visitor Center.*

**Pine Springs Campground.** Shade varies depending on the time of day, and it can be hard to find a cool spot in hot summer. You will find drinking water and restrooms here, though. ⊠ *Behind Headquarters Visitor Center.*

### Outside the Park

For more dining options near the park, ⇨ Carlsbad Caverns National Park.

★ ¢   ✕ **Cornudas Café.** Your first thought when you see the colorful flags flapping outside this remote roadside café may be "How did this get here?"

Food has been served at this site for almost a century, dating from the construction of the first roadway through the area. Try the café's famous green-chili hamburgers, and enjoy the quirky, ornery ambience. Levi and boot-clad cowboys often hold up the tables. ⊠ *Off U.S. 62/ 180, 63 mi east of El Paso and 103 mi southwest of Carlsbad, NM* ☎ *915/964–2409. $4–$7* ⊟ *AE, D, DC, MC, V.*

¢ ✕ **Nickel Creek Café.** This tiny stop is the only option within 35 mi of the main park entrance (it's 5 mi from Headquarters Visitor Center). American fare is served diner style, and many customers are lured by the savory chili sauce accompanying Tex-Mex dishes like burritos and fajitas. ⊠ *U.S. 62/180, 15 mi northeast of junction with Rte. 54, Pine Springs* ☎ *915/828–3295. $4–$7* ⊟ *No credit cards* ⊙ *Closed Sun.*

## Where to Stay

The park has two developed campgrounds that charge fees and a number of designated primitive, backcountry sites where you can camp for free. Check with the visitor center about primitive camping. Wood and charcoal fires are prohibited throughout the park, but you can use your camp stove. The same rules apply for backcountry sites; however, no restrooms are provided. Visitors may dig their own privies, but toilet paper and other paper waste should be packed out. There are no hotels within the park. For information on lodging near the park, ⇨ Carlsbad Caverns National Park.

### In Guadalupe Mountains

¢ ⛺ **Dog Canyon Campground.** This campground is remote and a little tricky to find, but well worth the effort. Located on the north side of Guadalupe National Park, it can be accessed by turning west on County Road 408 off U.S. 62/180, about 9 mi south of Carlsbad. Drive 23 mi on this county road; then turn south on Highway 137. Travel 43 mi through Lincoln National Forest until the road dead-ends just at the park boundary, at the New Mexico–Texas state line. Here, you find a very well-maintained camping area in a coniferous forest, with hiking trails nearby. ⊠ *Guadalupe Mountains National Park, off Rte. 137, 65 mi southwest of Carlsbad* ☎ *505/981–2418* ⇴ *4 RV sites, 9 tent sites* ⚬ *Flush toilets, drinking water, picnic tables, public telephone, ranger station. $8* ⊟ *AE, D, MC, V.*

¢ ⛺ **Pine Springs Campground.** You'll be snuggled amid pinyon and juniper trees at the base of a tall mountain peak at this site behind the Guadalupe Mountains National Park Visitors Center. Wood and charcoal fires are prohibited, although camp stoves are allowed. Shade here can be a bit sparse in the intense summer heat. Advance reservations are accepted for group sites only. ⊠ *Guadalupe Mountains National Park, off U.S. 62/180* ☎ *915/828–3251* ⇴ *20 tent sites, 18 RV sites, 1 wheelchair-accessible site, 2 group sites* ⚬ *Flush toilets, drinking water, picnic tables, public telephone, ranger station. $8* ⊟ *AE, D, MC, V.*

# GUADALUPE MOUNTAINS ESSENTIALS

You can find more basic services in the town of Carlsbad ( ⇨ Carlsbad Caverns National Park).

ACCESSIBILITY The wheelchair-accessible Headquarters Visitor Center has a wheelchair available for use. The ¾-mi round-trip Pinery Trail from the visitor center to Butterfield Stage Ruins is wheelchair accessible, as is McKittrick contact station.

ADMISSION HOURS The park is open 24 hours daily, year-round.

ADMISSION FEES An admission fee of $8 is collected at the visitor center.

ATMS/BANKS
🏧 **Best Western Cavern Inn** ✉ 17 Carlsbad Caverns Hwy., White's City ☎ 505/785-2291.

AUTOMOBILE SERVICE STATION
🏧 **White's City 24-Hour Texaco** ✉ 17 Carlsbad Caverns Hwy., White's City ☎ 505/785-2291.

EMERGENCIES There are no fire boxes in this largely wilderness park, but cell phones with far-reaching service can pick up signals at key points along trails. Rangers have emergency medical technician training and are also law enforcement officers. To reach them, call 911 or contact Headquarters Visitor Center or Dog Canyon ranger station.

LOST AND FOUND The park's lost-and-found is at Headquarters Visitor Center.

PERMITS For overnight backpacking trips, you must get a free permit from either Headquarters Visitor Center or Dog Canyon ranger station.

POST OFFICE
🏧 **Dell City Post Office** ✉ Ranch Rd. 1437, 13 mi north of junction with Rte. 62, Dell City, TX 79837 ☎ 915/964-2626 ⊗ Weekdays 7-11:30 and 12:30-3.

PUBLIC TELEPHONES AND RESTROOMS Dog Canyon ranger station, Headquarters Visitor Center, McKittrick contact station, and Pine Springs campground all have public phones and restrooms.

**VISITOR INFORMATION**
The Carlsbad Cavern Guadalupe Mountains Association, a nonprofit that sells books and other publications about both parks, has information at http://www.ccgma.org. The Carlsbad Chamber of Commerce, which supplies maps and information about lodging, events, entertainment, and other areas of interest, is at www.carlsbadchamber.com.
🏧 **Headquarters Visitor Center** ⌂ HC 60, Box 400, Salt Flat, TX 79847 ☎ 915/828-3251 ⊕ www.nps.gov/gumo.

# Jasper
# National Park

Maligne Lake, Jasper National Park

## WORD OF MOUTH

"The view that lay before us in the evening light was one that does not often fall to the lot of modern mountaineers. A new world was spread at our feet; to the westward stretched a vast ice-field probably never before seen by human eye, and surrounded by entirely unknown, un-named, and unclimbed peaks."

–J. Norman Collie, British scientist and mountaineer

# WELCOME TO JASPER

## TOP REASONS TO GO

★ **Larger than life:** Almost as large as the entire state of Connecticut, Jasper is the largest of the Canadian Rocky Mountain national parks, and one of the world's largest protected mountain ecosystems.

★ **Spectacular scenery:** Jasper's scenery is rugged and mountainous. Within its boundaries are crystal-clear mountain lakes, thundering waterfalls, jagged mountain peaks, and ancient glaciers.

★ **Wonderful wildlife:** The Canadian Rockies provide a diverse habitat for 277 bird species and 69 species of mammals, including deer, elk, moose, sheep, goats, and bears.

★ **Columbia Icefield:** The largest ice field south of Alaska, the Columbia Icefield is also the hydrographic apex of North America, with water flowing to three different oceans from one point.

**1 Yellowhead Corridor.** Trans-Canada Highway 16 (Yellowhead Highway) travels through the foothills and main ranges of the Canadian Rockies. Highlights are views of the Jasper Lake sand dunes (Km 27), Disaster Point Animal Lick (Km 39.5), Pocahontas Townsite (Km 39.5), the Coal Mine Interpretive Trail (Km 39.5), and Miette Hot Springs (Km 43).

**2 Maligne Valley.** Highlights here include the Athabasca Valley Lookout (Km 5.8), Maligne Canyon (Km 7), Medicine Lake (Km 20.7), and Maligne Lake (Km 45), where the paved road ends.

**3 Jasper Townsite.** Shops, restaurants, nightclubs, and the main park information center are here. Just outside town are Lac Beauvert, Lake Annette, and Lake Edith, plus Old Fort Point, and Whistlers Tramway.

**4 Cavell Road.** The road is just past the Astoria River bridge (Km 11.7) on Highway 93A, south of Jasper Townsite. Depending on weather conditions, it's open from early June to mid-October. Highlights include Astoria Valley Viewpoint, Mt. Edith Cavell, and Cavell Meadows.

**5 Icefield Parkway.** Highway 93 spans 130 mi (210 km) between Jasper Townsite and Lake Louise and is one of the world's most spectacular drives. Highlights include Athabasca Falls (Km 31), Sunwapta Falls (Km 55), Columbia Icefield (Km 103), Sunwapta Pass (Km 108), and the Weeping Wall (Km 125).

Athabasca Glacier

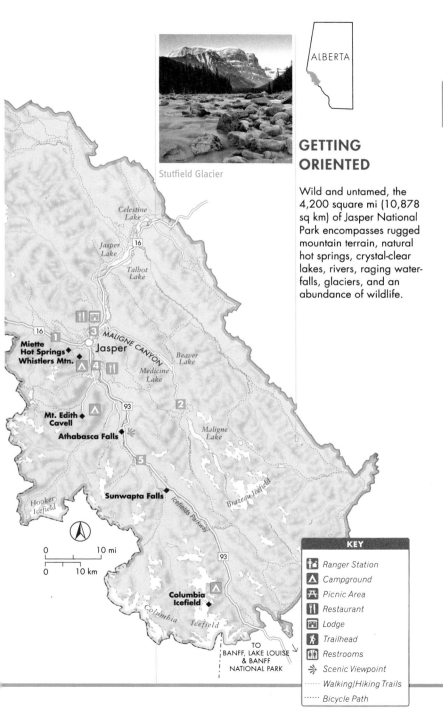

Stutfield Glacier

ALBERTA

## GETTING ORIENTED

Wild and untamed, the 4,200 square mi (10,878 sq km) of Jasper National Park encompasses rugged mountain terrain, natural hot springs, crystal-clear lakes, rivers, raging waterfalls, glaciers, and an abundance of wildlife.

Celestine Lake

Jasper Lake

Talbot Lake

Miette Hot Springs
Whistlers Mtn.

Jasper

MALIGNE CANYON

Beaver Lake

Medicine Lake

Mt. Edith Cavell

Athabasca Falls

Maligne Lake

Sunwapta Falls

Hooker Icefield

Icefields Parkway

Brazeau Icefield

Columbia Icefield

Columbia Icefield

| 0 | | 10 mi |
| 0 | | 10 km |

TO
BANFF, LAKE LOUISE
& BANFF
NATIONAL PARK

| KEY | |
|-----|--|
| 🏠 | Ranger Station |
| △ | Campground |
| 🛆 | Picnic Area |
| 🍴 | Restaurant |
| 🏨 | Lodge |
| 🚶 | Trailhead |
| 🚻 | Restrooms |
| 🔅 | Scenic Viewpoint |
| ····· | Walking/Hiking Trails |
| ····· | Bicycle Path |

# JASPER PLANNER

## When to Go

An old saying in the Canadian Rockies states: "If you don't like the weather, just wait a minute." The weather in Jasper National Park is unpredictable and ever changing, so you need to prepare for all weather conditions, especially when hiking. The summer months can be hot enough for swimming in Lake Edith one day and icy cold the next. Temperatures in winter are usually well below freezing, but occasionally warm Chinook winds blow in and begin to melt the snow.

**July and August are the peak travel months for visitors and the best time for hiking and viewing wildflowers.** If you are traveling then, book accommodations well in advance and expect to pay a bit more.

Temporary road closures may occur due to adverse weather conditions—especially in winter.

AVG. HIGH/LOW TEMPS.

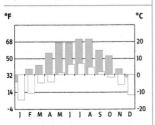

## Flora & Fauna

In Jasper it is possible to stand in a field of wildflowers, hike through a thick subalpine forest, and revel in the solitude of the fragile alpine zone all in one day. A wide array of plants occupies the parks' three life zones of montane, alpine, and subalpine. In fact, about 1,300 species of plants and 20,000 types of insects and spiders are part of the complex web of life in the Canadian Rockies.

Jasper's vast wilderness is one of the few remaining places with a full range of carnivores, such as grizzly bears, black bears, wolves, coyotes, cougars, and wolverines. There are also large populations of elk, deer, bighorn sheep, and mountain goats among the park's nearly 53 species of mammals—which are often seen right from the roadsides. Each year hundreds of animals are killed along Jasper's highways, so it is vital to observe all speed limits and especially to slow down in special animal-sighting speed-zone areas. When hiking, keep your distance from wild animals and make a lot of noise as a means of avoiding contact with large mammals, especially bears.

## Getting There & Around

Jasper National Park is in central Alberta in the Canadian Rockies. It is 110 mi (178 km) north of Banff Townsite and 31 mi (50 km) east of Jasper Townsite. The closest international airports are in Edmonton, 225 mi (362 km) to the east, and Calgary, 300 mi (480 km) to the southeast. Car rental agencies are available at both airports, as well as in Jasper. Driving is the easiest way to get from Edmonton to Jasper (on Yellowhead Highway 16).

Alternatively, train service is available three times per week (Monday, Thursday, and Saturday) from Edmonton to Jasper with VIA Rail Canada (☎ 888/842–7245). Also, Greyhound Canada Transportation (☎ 800/661–8747 or 800/231–2222 in the U.S.) provides regular service to Jasper from Calgary, Edmonton, and Vancouver; and Brewsters Transportation and Tours (☎ 800/661–1152) provides transportation between Calgary International Airport and Jasper.

22

By Debbie Olsen

Jagged mountain peaks, shimmering glaciers, and crystal-clear lakes are just part of the incredible scenery that make up the largest and wildest of Canada's Rocky Mountain parks. Situated along the eastern slopes of the Rockies in west-central Alberta, Jasper National Park encompasses 4,200 square mi (10,878 square km) of land and is home to an astonishing variety of wildlife.

## Scenic Drives

Scenic drives skirt the base of glaciers, stunning lakes, and exceptional wildlife-viewing areas. The 142-mi (230-km) **Icefields Parkway** that connects Jasper with Banff provides access to the largest ice field south of Alaska and takes you to the very edge of the treeless alpine tundra. For more details on the parkway *see* the Banff National Park chapter. Within Jasper, **Maligne Lake Road** and **Pyramid Lake Road** are good scenic drives, south and north of the town site, respectively.

## What to See

### Historic Sites

There are five National Historic Sites within the boundaries of Jasper National Park: Jasper Information Centre, Athabasca Pass, Yellowhead Pass, Jasper House, and Henry House.

### Scenic Stops

★ ⟲  At **Athabasca Falls** (✉ Icefields Pkwy. and Hwy. 93A, 19 mi [31 km] south of Jasper), the Athabasca River is compressed through a narrow gorge, producing a violent torrent of water. Trails and overlooks provide good viewpoints.

**Disaster Point Animal Lick** (✉ Hwy. 16, 33 mi [53 km] northeast of Jasper), less than 3 mi (5 km) before Highway 16 from Jasper reaches the turn for Miette Hot Springs, is the most easily accessible spot in the park for encountering bighorn sheep; it's a rare summer moment when the sheep haven't descended from the adjacent steep slopes to lick up the mineral-rich mud, wandering back and forth across the road. You're likely to see numerous cars stopped by the side of the road.

★ ☾ The **Jasper Tramway** whisks you 3,191 vertical feet up the steep flank of Whistlers Mountain to an impressive overlook of the town site and the surrounding mountains. The seven-minute ride takes you to the upper station, above the tree line (be sure to bring warm clothes). A 30- to 45-minute hike from here takes you to the summit, which is 8,085 feet above sea level. Several unmarked trails lead through the alpine meadows beyond. ⊠ *Whistlers Mountain Rd., 2 mi (3 km) south of Jasper off Hwy. 93* ☏ *780/852–3093* ⊕ *www.jaspertramway.com* ☜ *C$20 round-trip* ☉ *Apr., May, and Oct., daily 9:30–4:30; June–early Sept., daily 8:30 AM–10 PM; rest of Sept., daily 9:30–6:30.*

★ ☾ The Maligne River cuts a 165-foot-deep gorge through limestone bedrock at **Maligne Canyon** (⊠ Maligne Lake Rd., 7 mi [11 km] south of Jasper). An interpretive trail winds its way along the river, switching from side to side over six bridges as the canyon progressively deepens. The 2½-mi (4-km) trail along the canyon can be crowded, especially near the trailhead. Just off the path, at the Maligne Canyon teahouse, are a restaurant and a good Native American crafts store.

★ ☾ The remarkably blue, 14-mi-long (22-km-long) **Maligne Lake** (⊠ Maligne Lake Rd., 27 mi [44 km] southeast of Jasper ⊕ www.malignelake.com) is one of the largest glacier-fed lakes in the world. The first outsider known to visit the lake was Henry MacLeod, a surveyor looking for a possible route for the Canadian Pacific Railway, in 1875. You can explore the lake on a 1½-hour tour with **Maligne Lake Scenic Cruises** or in a rented canoe. A couple of day hikes (approximately four hours round-trip), with some steep sections, lead to alpine meadows that have panoramic views of the lake and the surrounding mountain ranges. You can also take horseback-riding and fishing trips, and there's an excellent cafeteria. **Tour reservations** ⊠ *Maligne Lake Scenic Cruises, 627 Patricia St., Jasper* ☏ *780/852–3370 or 780/852–4803* ☜ *Boat tour C$35* ☉ *June and Sept.–early Oct., daily 10–4; July and Aug., daily 10–5; tours every hr on the hr.*

The naturally heated mineral waters of **Miette Hot Springs** originate from three springs and are cooled to 104°F (40°C) to allow bathing in the two hot pools. There's also an adjacent cold pool—especially liked by the younger crowd—which is definitely on the cool side, at about 59°F (15°C). A short walk leads to the remnants of the original hot-springs facility, where several springs still pour hot sulfurous water into the adjacent creek. Day passes and bathing suit, locker, and towel rentals are available. ⊠ *Miette Hot Springs Rd., off Hwy. 16, 36 mi (58 km) northeast of Jasper* ☏ *780/866–3939* ⊕ *www.parkscanada.gc.ca/hotsprings* ☜ *C$6.25* ☉ *Mid-May–late June and early Sept.–early Oct., daily 10:30–9; late June–early Sept., daily 8:30 AM–10:30 PM.*

☾ **Mt. Edith Cavell,** the highest mountain in the vicinity of Jasper, towers at 11,033 feet and shows its permanently snow-clad north face to the town. Fodor'sChoice ★ It's named after a World War I British nurse who stayed in Belgium to

## JASPER IN ONE DAY

Make a stop at the **Jasper Information Centre** to get maps of the park and information about any special activities before driving up to **Mt. Edith Cavell.** The 1 km (½-mi) trail from the parking lot leads to the base of an imposing cliff where you can see the stunning Angel Glacier. If you are feeling energetic, take the steep 3-km (2-mi) trail that climbs up the valley to **Cavell Meadows,** which are carpeted with wildflowers from mid-July to mid-August. Return to the Jasper Townsite for lunch. In the afternoon, take the 45-minute drive southeast of the town site to beautiful **Maligne Lake,** the second-largest glacier-fed lake in the world. Explore the lake and make a stop at **Spirit Island** on a 1½-hour guided boat tour with **Maligne Lake Scenic Cruises.** Return to the town site for supper and end your day by participating in a free ranger-led evening interpretive program at **Whistlers Outdoor Theatre,** south of the Jasper Townsite at Whistlers Campground.

treat wounded Allied soldiers after Brussels fell to the Germans; she was executed for helping prisoners of war escape. The mountain is arguably the most spectacular site in the park reachable by car. From Highway 93A, a narrow, winding 9-mi (14½-km) road (often closed until the beginning of June) leads to a parking lot at the base of the mountain. Trailers are not permitted on this road, but they can be left at a separate parking lot near the junction with 93A. Several scenic lookouts along the route offer access to trails leading up the **Tonquin Valley,** a premier hiking area. ⊠ *Off Hwy. 93A, 17 mi (27 km) south of Jasper.*

### Visitor Center

**Jasper Information Centre.** A registered National Historic Site, this information center is in the Jasper Townsite and is worth a stop even if you don't need advice. Completed in 1914, this building was designed by Edmonton A. M. Calderon and is constructed of cobblestone and timber and is one of the finest examples of rustic architecture in Canada's national parks. You can pick up maps, informative brochures, and other materials to help you explore the parks and its trails. A small gift shop and restroom facilities are also inside the building. Parks Canada also operates an information desk at the Icefields Centre 64 mi (103 km) south of Jasper Townsite. ⊠ *500 Connaught Dr.* ☎ *780/852–6176 or 780/852–6177 (trail office)* ⊕ *www.pc.gc.ca/pn-np/ab/jasper* ☯ *Apr.–June 14 and Oct., daily 9–5; June 15–Sept. 4, daily 8:30–7; Sept. 5–30, daily 9–6; Nov.–Mar., daily 9–4.*

## Sports & the Outdoors

In the northern half of the park, backpacking and horse-packing trips offer wilderness seclusion, while the park's southern half rewards trekkers with dramatic glacial scenery. Day hikes are popular around Mt. Edith Cavell, Miette Hot Springs, and Maligne Lake; Pyramid Lake and the Fairmont Jasper Park Lodge are destinations for horseback riding.

---

## READ ALL ABOUT IT

You will receive *The Mountain Guide* upon entry to the park. This has maps and good general information such as points of interest, safety messages, programs and events, camping information, and fees. It is online at www.pc.gc.ca/jasper.

At the Jasper Information Centre you can pick up a *Points of Interest* map to help you find your way to major points of interest in the park and the town site. A *Summer Trails Guide* contains both maps and details hiking, mountain biking, and horseback riding trails, while the *Winter Trails Guide* provides maps and details cross-country skiing and snowshoeing trails. The *Backcountry Visitor's Guide* provides an overview of backcountry options.

---

### Air Tours

OUTFITTERS & EXPEDITIONS **High Country Helicopter Tours Ltd.** Contact this outfitter to enjoy a helicopter tour of the park, or to arrange heli-hiking or snowshoeing. Flights take off from Jasper Hinton Airport, just outside the park. ☎ *877/777–4354 or 780/852–0125* ✆ *Tours $189–$834 per person* ⊕ *www.hcheli.com.*

### Bicycling

There are hundreds of miles of mountain bike trails and scenic roadways to enjoy in the park. Riders are expected to stick to designated trails. ⇨ the Multisport Outfitters box for bike rentals and expeditions.

### Bird-watching

An astonishing 277 species of birds make their home in the Canadian Rockies. The golden eagle migration, which occurs in the spring and fall, is the biggest birding event in the park. In late September and early October, you may be able to see more than 200 eagles in one day at the east end of the park (Pocahontas area). At other times of year, the best place to observe birds is at **Cottonwood Slough** along Pyramid Lake Road. This spot is a good place to find Barrow's goldeneye, warblers, snipes, soras and hummingbirds, and red-necked grebe.

OUTFITTER & EXPEDITIONS **On-Line Sport & Tackle.** Stop in at this outdoor store to arrange a guided birding trip. ⊠ *600 Patricia St.* ☎ *780/852–4245.*

### Boating & Rafting

Boating in rowboats and canoes is allowed on most of the ponds and lakes in the park. Boats with electric motors without on-board generators are allowed on most road-accessible lakes, but the use of gas-powered motors is restricted. It's always wise to ask park staff about restrictions before launching your boat.

The rafting season runs from May through September and children as young as six years of age can participate on some of the float trips. The Athabasca River has Class II white-water rapids; the Sunwapta and Fraser rivers have Class III rapids.

OUTFITTERS & EXPEDITIONS **Jasper Raft Tours** (☎ 780/852–3613 ⊕ www.jasperrafttours.com) runs half-day float trips on the Athabasca. **Maligne Tours** (⊠ Maligne Lake

☎ 780/ 852–3370 or 866/625–4463 ⊕ www.mra.ab.ca) rents boats on beautiful Maligne Lake, and offers rafting on the Athabasca, Sunwapta, and Fraser rivers. **Rocky Mountain River Guides** (☎780/852–3777 ⊕ www. rmriverguides.com) conducts a variety of rafting trips for different levels of rafters. **Whitewater Rafting (Jasper) Ltd.** (☎ 780/852–7238 or 800/ 557–7238) offers half-day trips on the Athabasca and Sunwapta rivers.

*See* ⇨ the Multisport Outfitters box for additional boating outfitters.

## Golf

The **Fairmont Jasper Park Lodge** (✉ Off Hwy. 16 ☎ 780/852–6090) has a championship 18-hole, par-71 course that was voted the best golf resort in Canada by *Score Magazine.*

## Hiking

Long before Jasper was established as a national park, a vast network of trails provided an essential passageway for wildlife, First Nations people, explorers, and fur traders. More than 660 mi (1,060 km) of hiking trails in Jasper provide an opportunity to truly experience wilderness, and hardcored backpackers will find multiday loops of more than 100 mi (160 km).

A few of these trails are restricted to pedestrians, but hikers, mountain bikers, and equestrian users may share most of them. There are several paved trails that are suitable for wheelchairs, while others are rugged backcountry trails designed for backpacking trips. Bathrooms are found along the most used day-use trails. You may see elk, bighorn sheep, moose, and mountain goats along the way. It is never a good idea to surprise a large animal such as an elk or bear, so make plenty of noise as you go along, avoid hiking alone, and stick to designated trails. The trails at Mt. Edith Cavell and Maligne Canyon should not be missed.

EASY **Lake Annette Loop.** This short loop trail with interpretive signage is paved and mostly level and was designed especially for wheelchair use. Toilets are at two locations, and there is a shelter halfway around the 1½-mi (2⁴⁄₁₀-km) loop that will take an hour to complete.

★ ☘ **Maligne Canyon.** This 1³⁄₁₀-mi (2¹⁄₁₀-km), one-way trail 5 mi (8 km) east of Jasper Townsite leads to views of Jasper's famous limestone gorge and will take one to two hours to complete. Six bridges stretch across the canyon and a winding trail gains about 328 feet in elevation. Signage lines the trail that leads to a waterfall at the head of the canyon.

**Old Fort Point Loop.** Shaped by glaciers, Old Fort Point is a bedrock knob that provides an excellent view of Jasper. It will take one to two hours to complete the 2²⁄₁₀-mi (3½-km) loop trail. There is a wide, easy path that begins behind the trail information kiosk and leads to a section of trail that is very steep. The trail passes the oldest rock in Jasper National Park, but the real highlight is the view from the top.

★ ☘ **Path of the Glacier Loop.** This short 1-mi (1⁶⁄₁₀-km) trail only takes about an hour and is a must-do. The start of the trail is paved and runs across a rocky landscape that was once covered in glacial ice. Eventually you come to Cavell pond, which is fed by Cavell Glacier. Small icebergs often

**DID YOU KNOW?**

Beargrass isn't actually consumed by bears. It also isn't a grass, but rather a lily that blooms with fist-sized clusters of cream-colored flowers every few years. Plants can reach heights of up to five feet.

float in the water. Across the valley, you will have a good view of the Angel glacier resting her wings between Mt. Edith Cavell and Sorrow Peak. Follow the trail back along Cavell Creek to the parking lot.

**Valley of the Five Lakes.** It will take 2–3 hours to complete the 2³⁄₁₀ mi (4²⁄₁₀ km) of this family-friendly hike just 5⁶⁄₁₀ mi (9 km) south of Jasper Townsite. Five small lakes are the highlight of the trip, which takes you through a lodgepole pine forest, across the Wabasso Creek wetlands, and through a flowery meadow. Watch for birds, beavers, and other wildlife along the way. Note: You can turn this into a moderate hike by continuing another 6²⁄₁₀ mi (10 km) to Old Fort Point.

MODERATE

Fodor'sChoice

★

**Cavell Meadows Loop.** This moderately steep 5-mi (8-km) trail will take four to six hours. The upper section is not recommended in early summer, but from mid-July to mid-August you can enjoy the carpet of wildflowers. There's also an excellent view of the Angel Glacier.

DIFFICULT

**Opal Hills Loop.** Near Maligne Lake, this 5¹⁄₁₀-mi (8²⁄₁₀-km) hike is relatively steep and will take four to six hours to complete. There are excellent views of Maligne Valley on this hike and many opportunities to observe wildlife including moose and bears. Be sure to make noise as you hike and keep your distance from the wildlife. During the summer months, there is often an abundance of wildflowers along the trail.

★

**Wilcox Pass.** Excellent views of the Athabasca Glacier are the highlight of this strenuous 5-mi (8-km) hike near the Icefield Centre. This pass was originally used by explorers and First Nations people and is fairly steep. Keep an eye out for wildflowers and bighorn sheep. Be sure to dress in warm layers, because this pass can be snowy until late July.

WILDERNESS
HIKING

The backcountry is some of the wildest and most pristine of any mountain park in the world. For information on overnight camping quotas on the Skyline and Tonquin Valley trails or on any of the hundreds of hiking and mountain-biking trails in the area, contact the park information center. The **Skyline Trail** meanders for 27 mi (44 km) past some of the park's best scenery, at or above the tree line. **Tonquin Valley,** near Mt. Edith Cavell, is one of Canada's classic backpacking areas. Its high mountain lakes, bounded by a series of steep rocky peaks known as the Ramparts, attract many hikers in high summer.

## Horseback Riding

Several outfitters offer one-hour, half-day, full-day, and multiday guided trips within the park. Participants must be at least age 6 to participate in a riding trip, but pony rides are available for younger children. It's wise to make your reservations well in advance, especially during the peak summer months and for multiday journeys. Horses can be boarded at the commercial holding facilities available through the Cottonwood Corral Association at Pyramid Riding Stables.

OUTFITTER &
EXPEDITIONS

**Pyramid Riding Stables** offers rides and full-day excursions in the hills overlooking Jasper; there are also pony and carriage rides. ✉ *Pyramid Resort, Pyramid Lake Rd.* ☎ *780/852–3562.*

**Skyline Trail Rides** offers lessons and one-hour to half-day rides. Multiday trips into the backcountry are also available. ✉ *Fairmont Jasper*

## MULTISPORT OUTFITTERS & EXPEDITIONS

22

The **Boat House** (✉ Fairmont Jasper Park Lodge, off Hwy. 16 ☎ 780/852–5708) rents adult and children's mountain bikes, as well as paddleboats and canoes.

**Gravity Gear** (✉ 618A Patricia St. ☎ 780/852–3155 or 888/852–3155) can arrange for ice climbing, backcountry skiing, and mountaineering trips led by certified guides.

**Jasper Source for Sports** (✉ 406 Patricia St. ☎ 780/852–3654 ⊕ www.jaspersports.com) rents bikes, fishing and camping equipment, as well as ski and snowboard equipment.

**Pyramid Lake Boat Rentals** (✉ Pyramid Lake Resort ☎ 780/852–4900 or 800/717–1277) rents canoes, kayaks, electric boats, and paddleboats. They also sell fishing licenses and have rod and reel rentals.

**Tonquin Valley Adventures** (☎ 780/852–1188) arranges hiking, skiing, and horseback trips into the Tonquin Valley. In winter there's a private cabin with cooking equipment provided; in the summer there's a cook at the cabin. Reservations for backcountry huts in Tonquin Valley can be made through **Tonquin Valley Pack and Ski Trips** (☎ 780/852–3909 ⊕ www.tonquinvalley.com); call well in advance.

**Totem Ski Shop** (✉ 408 Connaught Dr. ☎ 780/852–3078 or 800/363–3078) sells summer and winter sports equipment and clothing.

*Park Lodge, off Hwy. 16 ☎ 780/852–4215, 780/852–3301 Ext. 6189, or 888/852–7787.* **Tonquin Valley Adventures** is a smaller outfitter that arranges five-day horseback trips into the Tonquin Valley and offers some trail rides. ☎ *780/852–1188.*

### Swimming

☺ **Lakes Annette and Edith** (✉ Near Fairmont Jasper Park Lodge, off Hwy. 16) have sandy beaches and water that reaches the low 20s°C/70s°F during warm spells.

☺ **Jasper Aquatic Center** has a 180-foot indoor waterslide, a kids' pool, and a 25-meter regular pool. A steam room and a hot tub are also on-site, and towel and suit rentals are available. ✉ *401 Pyramid Lake Rd.* ☎ *780/852–3663* 🎟 *C$6.50* ☼ *Public swimming daily 2–9.*

### Winter Sports

There is a wide choice of groomed and natural trails for skiing and snowshoeing, and equipment and local guides can be arranged through local ski shops. Current cross-country ski information is available at the park visitor center. Snowmobiling is not allowed in the park, but can be experienced in the nearby town of Hinton. **Pyramid and Patricia lakes** (✉ Pyramid Lake Rd.) have excellent groomed cross-country trails. **Marmot Basin** (✉ Off Hwy. 93A ☎ 780/852–3816), near Jasper, has a wide mix of downhill skiing terrain (75 runs, 9 lifts, and a snowboard park with all the toys), and the slopes are a little less crowded than those around Banff, especially on weekdays. This area has three day lodges, two of which are at mid-mountain; the vertical drop is 2,944 feet.

OUTFITTER & EXPEDITIONS  You cannot ride a snowmobile through the national park, but **Canadian Rockies Adventures** (☎ 780/865–7380 or 866/666–7823 ✉ Tours $95–$300 per person ⊕ www.canadianrockiesadvent.com) has guided tours that take you through stunning scenery just outside the park.

For more winter sports outfitters, ⇨ the Multisport Outfitters box.

## Educational Offerings

### Interpretive Programs

★ **Jasper Institute.** Seminars and multiday programs, including weekend courses, are offered through the Jasper Institute by the Friends of Jasper National Park. The courses are given by naturalists and other experts; in conjunction with the programs, reasonably priced accommodations and food can be provided. Contact the Friends of Jasper National Park (☎ 780/852–4799) for a list of seminars and programs. ✉ *Jasper Information Centre, 500 Connaught Dr.* ☎ *780/852–4799* ✉ *C$60–C$150* ⊗ *May–Aug.*

★ ☾ **Mountain World Heritage Theatre.** Parks Canada's troupe of professional actors put on entertaining and educational performances for park guests. Tickets are available at The Friends of Jasper Store, DO Travel, and at the door. For show times, check at the information center. ✉ *Jasper Heritage Railway Station* ☎ *780/852–4767* ✉ *$10* ⊗ *July and Aug.*

★ ☾ **Whistlers Outdoor Theatre.** Interpretive programs are offered daily through the summer months at this Whistlers Campground theater. Programs are appropriate for both children and adults, and a schedule of seminars and activities is available at the information center. ✉ *Whistlers Campground* ✉ *Free* ⊗ *Late June–early Sept.*

### Tours

**Currie's Guiding.** Currie's offers four- to six-hour driving tours, as well as a "wildlife search" tour. Prices begin around C$59. Fishing tours to Maligne Lake start at C$169. ✉ *406 Patricia St.* ☎ *780/852–5650.*

★ ☾ **Friends of Jasper National Park.** This nonprofit organization offers courses on discovering Jasper through guided hikes, nature photography, and wildlife viewing. Local experts lead the sessions at very reasonable prices. Courses also include discount accommodations and meals at the Jasper Palisades Centre, a park facility usually reserved for visiting park wardens and professors. The Friends also loan out free hiking kits with binoculars, maps, first-aid materials, and other useful items. Kits can be picked up at the Friends store in the information center. ✉ *Jasper Information Centre, 500 Connaught Dr.* ☎ *780/852–4767* ⊕ *www. friendsofjasper.com* ✉ *Free or nominal fee.*

☾ **Jasper Adventure Centre.** Guided tours, birding trips, ice walks, and snowshoeing tours are all available here. Rates start at C$45 per person, with

## FESTIVALS & EVENTS

Jasper National Park celebrates its 100th birthday in 2007, marked by activities and centennial events throughout the year. The official birthday celebration takes place the weekend of September 14. ☎ 780/852-6176.

**JAN. Jasper in January.** Fun events for the entire family include an ice-sculpting contest, wine tasting, great live music, a chili cook-off, Taste of the Town, outdoor contests, and more. Accommodation deals and reduced ski lift ticket prices are available. ☎ *780/852-3858.*

**JULY Canada Day.** July 1, Canada's birthday, is celebrated with a parade, a full day of activities, and fireworks at dusk. ☎ *780/852-6176.*

**Parks Day.** Celebrating national parks, this annual event takes place in mid-July. There are activities for the whole family, a fair on the Information center lawn in the middle of town and free guided hikes to some of Jasper National Park's most interesting spots. ☎ *780/852-6176.*

**NOV.–DEC. Jasper Welcomes Winter.** Jasper's annual winter kick-off festival marks winter's arrival. Special activities for the entire family include the Santa Claus Parade, the Christmas Craft Fair, and shopping festivities. Special hotel rates are available. Watch for the opening of Jasper's Marmot Basin ski resort in 2007. ☎ *780/852-3858.*

most tours lasting three hours. The center also handles bookings for other adventure companies (canoeing, rafting, and other sports). ⊠ *604 Connaught Dr.* ☎ *780/852–5595* ⊕ *www.jasperadventurecentre.com.*

# WHAT'S NEARBY

Jasper National Park is 178 mi (287 km) north of Banff National Park, 248 mi (400 km) northwest of the city of **Calgary,** 224 mi (360 km) west of the city of **Edmonton,** and 34 mi (55 km) west of the town of **Hinton** and the Jasper/Hinton Airport. Most visitors arrive through either Calgary or Edmonton, where the major highway and the two major international airports are located.

⇨ Banff National Park chapter for more activities in the Canadian Rockies.

# WHERE TO STAY & EAT

### About the Restaurants

Jasper's casual restaurants offer a wide variety of cuisines, including Greek, Italian, Japanese, French, and North American. Regional specialties include Alberta beef, lamb, pheasant, venison, elk, bison, trout, and BC (British Columbia) salmon. For the best views in town, try the cafeteria-style Treeline Restaurant at the top of the Jasper Tramway, 7,500 feet above sea level.

### About the Hotels

Accommodations in this area include luxury resorts, fine hotels, reasonably priced motels, rustic cabins, and backcountry lodges. Reserve your accommodations in advance if you are traveling during the peak summer season.

### About the Campgrounds

Parks Canada operates 10 campgrounds in Jasper National Park that have a total of 1,772 available sites during the peak season. There is winter camping only at Wapiti campground. Hookup sites are available at Whistlers and Wapiti campgrounds only, so reserve a site in advance if you are traveling during the peak summer season. Reservations can only be made at **Pocahontas, Whistlers, Wapiti, and Wabasso campgrounds** (☎ 877/737–3783 ⊕ www.pccamping.ca), and there is a C$10.80 reservation fee. Other campgrounds work on a first-come, first-served basis and campers line up for sites early in the morning. You can pay using a credit card, but at remote campsites, you may wish to pay cash so that you don't have to wait for the mobile truck to come around to take your credit card payment. If your campsite has a fire pit, you will need to purchase a fire permit for C$7.80 before using it.

If you arrive at the park without a reservation and cannot obtain a serviced (with hookup) site, you may choose to take an unserviced site for the first night; campground staff can advise you on how to go about getting a hookup site for the rest of your stay. Another option is to travel to nearby Hinton, outside the park, where there are a number of serviced campsites and several good campgrounds. For general campground information, call ☎ 780/852–6176.

## Where to Eat

**$$$–$$$$** ✕ **Edith Cavell.** This sophisticated restaurant overlooks the impressive mountain of the same name. The menu focuses on fine regional cuisine with local nuances; signature dishes include bison and Alberta rack of lamb. The wine list is extensive. A tasting menu is offered with (C$140) and without (C$90) wine pairings. ⊠ *Fairmont Jasper Park Lodge, off Hwy. 16, 7 km (4½ mi) northeast of Jasper* ☎ *780/852–3301 or 800/441–1414* ⊸ *Reservations essential. C$25–C$35* ▭ *AE, D, DC, MC, V* ⊘ *No lunch.*

★ **$$–$$$$** ✕ **Becker's Gourmet Restaurant.** Many visitors to Jasper miss Becker's because of its out-of-town location, but it's a favorite with locals. Spectacular panoramic views of the Athabasca River and Mt. Kerkeslin from a glass-enclosed dining room are a suitable accompaniment to the fine French food. After dinner you can stroll along the upper bank of the Athabasca River. There's a breakfast buffet from 8 to 11. ⊠ *Beside Becker's Chalets, Hwy. 93, 5 km (3 mi) south of Jasper* ☎ *780/852–3535. C$16–C$36* ▭ *AE, MC, V* ⊘ *Closed Nov.–Apr. No lunch.*

**$$–$$$$** ✕ **Fiddle River.** Candles, dried flowers, and plenty of wood decorate this cozy, second-floor dining room. Seafood is the star and fresh Canadian fish, including salmon, halibut, trout, northern pike, and pickerel, appear on the menu when available. Alberta beef, bison, pork, and chicken are available for landlubbers. ⊠ *620 Connaught Dr., Jasper* ☎ *780/852–3032. C$16–C$34* ▭ *AE, MC, V* ⊘ *No lunch.*

**22**

**$$–$$$$**  ✕ **Moose's Nook Northern Grill.** The cuisine is contemporary Canadian at this seasonally open restaurant in the Fairmont Jasper Park Lodge. Live music plays every night during the summer. Wild game, AAA Alberta beef tenderloin, and fresh fish are some of the highlights. ✉ *Fairmont Jasper Park Lodge, off Hwy. 16, 4½ mi (7 km) northeast of Jasper* ☎ *780/852–3301 or 800/441–1414* ⌖ *Reservations essential.* C$16–C$36 ▤ *AE, D, DC, MC, V* ☾ *Closed Nov.–Apr. No lunch.*

**$$–$$$$**  ✕ **Villa Caruso.** Alberta is ranch country and this steak house is a good place to sample the products of the cattle industry. Entrées include flame-grilled grain-fed Alberta AAA Angus beef cuts, such as tenderloin, New York steak, and prime rib. Pasta, fish, chicken, pork tenderloin, lamb, and ribs round out the menu. There's also a children's menu. Cozy up for cocktails next to one of the two fireplaces. ✉ *640 Connaught Dr., Jasper* ☎ *780/852–3920. C$19–C$35* ▤ *AE, MC, V.*

**$$–$$$**  ✕ **Andy's Bistro.** This intimate bistro in downtown Jasper is known for
Fodor'sChoice its fresh market ingredients. Chef and owner Andy Allenbach is Swiss
★ born and trained and is one of only 700 certified Chefs de Cuisine in Canada. His dishes have a European flare and regional influence, and include in-season organic fruits and vegetables, wild game, and fresh herbs. From November to April enjoy a three-course table d'hôte for $28. ✉ *606 Patricia St., Jasper* ☎ *780/852–4559* ⌖ *Reservations essential. C$19–C$27* ▤ *AE, MC, V.*

**¢–$**  ✕ **Soft Rock Café.** Jasper's first Internet café is not only a great place to send an e-mail but also a good place to get a quick bite to eat. The café serves baked goods, ice cream, all-day breakfast, and homemade sandwiches made to order. In the evenings you can enjoy inexpensive Thai food. ✉ *622 Connaught Dr., Jasper* ☎ *780/852–5850* ⌖ *Reservations not accepted. C$4–C$10* ▤ *MC, V.*

PICNIC AREAS  **Airport picnic area.** This large area has a shelter and is ideal for family reunions, because it can be reserved in advance. ✉ *Off Hwy. 16 E, 9 mi (15 km) from Jasper Townsite.*

**Athabasca Falls picnic area.** Dine beside the stunning Athabasca Falls. ✉ *Off Icefields Pkwy., 19 mi (30 km) from Jasper Townsite.*

☾ **Lake Annette.** Beside Lake Annette, this picnic area has shelters and tables and is a favorite with families who come to the lake to swim. ✉ *Near the junction of Maligne Lake Rd. and Hwy. 16.*

**Sixth Bridge.** This picnic area is right beside the Maligne River just before it flows into the Athabasca River. There are no shelters, but it is a preferred picnic areas with locals because of the scenic location. ✉ *Off Maligne Lake Rd., 1³⁄₁₀ mi (2²⁄₁₀ km) from the Hwy. 16 junction.*

## Where to Stay

### In the Park

**$$$$**  ⌂ **Fairmont Jasper Park Lodge.** With abundant on-site recreational ameni-
Fodor'sChoice ties, this lakeside resort, 4½ mi (7 km) northeast of Jasper, is a destina-
★ tion in itself, whether or not you stay overnight. Accommodations vary from cedar chalets and log cabins to specialty cabins with up to eight bedrooms. Rooms include down duvets, and all have either a porch, patio,

or balcony. Winter guests love the year-round outdoor swimming pool, which is heated to 86°F/30°C in winter. Canoe rentals and horseback riding are available in the summer months and sleigh rides are offered in the winter. The golf course was voted the "best golf resort in Canada" by readers of *Score Magazine* in 2005, and nearby Marmot Basin has world-class skiing. It's located off Old Fort Point Road, 1½ km (1 mi) from the Highway 93A junction. ⌂ *Box 40, Jasper T0E 1E0* ☎ *780/852–3301 or 800/441–1414* 🖷 *780/852–5107* ⊕ *www.fairmont.com* 🛏 *446 rooms, 100 suites* ♻ *9 restaurants, room service, ethernet, Wi-Fi, golf course, tennis courts, pool, gym, bicycles, bar, no a/c.* *C$549–C$789* 🖃 *AE, D, DC, MC, V.*

★ **$–$$$$** ▦ **Patricia Lake Bungalows.** Five minutes north of Jasper, this is one of the few remaining bargain accommodations near Jasper. Though the motel rooms are the least expensive accommodation, the cabins—at a 20% premium over the motel units—are the most popular. Ten luxury cabins are also available. Rates decrease by up to 50% off-season. ⌂ *Off Pyramid Lake Road, Box 657, Jasper T0E 1E0* ☎ *780/852–3560* 🖷 *780/852–4060* ⊕ *www.patricialakebungalows.com* 🛏 *6 rooms, 6 suites, 39 cabins* ♻ *Bicycles, laundry facilities, no a/c, no phone.* *C$81–C$285* 🖃 *AE, MC, V* ☻ *Closed mid-Oct.–Apr.*

♻ **$$–$$$** ▦ **Pine Bungalows.** On the banks of the Athabasca River, this property is ideal for families because it has 72 modern cabins with outdoor barbecues, picnic tables, and tubs with showers. Many cabins have fireplaces and most have kitchens; there are laundry facilities on-site. ✉ *Approximately 1¼ mi (2 km) east of Jasper Townsite, 2 Cottonwood Creek Rd., Jasper T0E 1E0* ☎ *780/852–3491* 🖷 *780/852–3432* ⊕ *www.pinebungalows.com* 🛏 *72 cabins* ♻ *Kitchen, laundry facilities, no a/c, no TV, no phone.* *C$120–C$190* 🖃 *AE, MC, V* ☻ *Closed mid-Oct.–Apr.*

**$–$$$** ▦ **Becker's Chalets.** On the Icefields Parkway, 3 mi (5 km) south of the town of Jasper, this quaint family-run log cabin resort is set in a picturesque forest glade along the shores of the Athabasca River. Cabins range from one-bedroom cottages to four-room chalets and have fireplaces and kitchenettes. There are also some inexpensive, motel-style rooms. Its restaurant is one of the best in Jasper. ⌂ *Box 579, Jasper T0E 1E0* ☎ *780/852–3779* 🖷 *780/852–7202* ⊕ *www.beckerschalets.com* 🛏 *118 rooms* ♻ *Restaurant, refrigerator, laundry facilities, no a/c, no phone.* *C$95–C$160* 🖃 *AE, MC, V* ☻ *Closed mid-Oct.–May.*

**¢–$** ▦ **HI-Jasper Hostel.** This chalet-style hostel rests at the foot of Whistlers Mountain just 4 mi (7 km) from Jasper. There is an easily accessible trail from the hostel to the summit of Whistlers Mountain. The hostel has mountain-bike rentals, volleyball court, campfire pit, Internet access, and free parking. Linen rentals are $1 per day. There are 74 dorm-style beds and 3 private rooms, including one family room with a queen-sized bed and bunk beds. ⌂ *Box 387, Jasper T0E 1E0* ☎ *877/852–0781 or 780/852–3215* 🖷 *780/852–5560* ⊕ *www.hihostels.ca/jasper* 🛏 *74 dorm-room beds, 3 private rooms* ♻ *Kitchen, refrigerator, bicycles, laundry facilities, no a/c, no phone.* *C$27–C$70* 🖃 *AE, MC, V.*

**CAMPGROUNDS &** ⚠ **Pocahontas Campground.** Near Miette Hot Springs at the park's east
**RV PARKS** end, the campground is close to good hiking trails, including the Poca-
**$$** hontas Mine Trail. ✉ *⅗ mi (1 km) off Hwy. 16 on Miette Rd.* ☎ *877/*

737–3783 ⌁ *140 sites* ⌂ *Drinking water, public telephone, picnic tables, fire pits. C$19–C$26* ▱ *AE, MC, V* ⊘ *Closed early Oct. to mid-May.*

⟳ **$$** ⌂ **Wabasso Campground.** Families flock to this campground because of its playground and many amenities. ⊠ *10 mi (16 km) south of Jasper Townsite on Hwy. 93A* ☎ *877/737–3783* ⌁ *238 sites* ⌂ *Drinking water, flush toilets, dump station, public telephone, play area. C$19–C$27* ▱ *AE, MC, V* ⊘ *Closed early Sept. to late June.*

⟳ **$$** ⌂ **Whistlers Campground.** This campground is the largest and has the most amenities. It's the number-one choice for families because of the on-site interpretive programs at Whistlers Theatre. ⊠ *2 mi (3 km) south of Jasper Townsite on Hwy. 93* ☎ *877/737–3783* ⌁ *781 sites* ⌂ *Flush toilets, drinking water, showers, dump station, electricity, public telephone. C$24–C$35* ▱ *AE, MC, V* ⊘ *Closed early Oct to mid-May.*

**$-$$** ⌂ **Wapiti Campground.** Close to Jasper, this campground is near a number of good hiking trails. There are 53 unserviced sites that are open during the winter season. ⊠ *3 mi (5 km) south of Jasper Townsite on Hwy. 93* ☎ *877/737–3782* ⌁ *366 sites* ⌂ *Public telephones, drinking water, showers, dump station, electricity, flush toilets. C$15–C$28* ▱ *AE, MC, V.*

**$** ⌂ **Columbia Icefield Campground.** This rustic campground is near a creek and has great views of the Columbia Icefield. Warm camping gear is recommended. ⊠ *66 mi (106 km) south of Jasper on Hwy. 93* ☎ *780/852–6176* ⌁ *33 sites* ⌂ *Drinking water* ⌂ *Reservations not accepted. C$14* ▱ *AE, MC, V* ⊘ *Closed early Oct. to mid-May.*

**$** ⌂ **Jonas Creek Campground.** This small, primitive campground is in a quiet spot along a creek off the Icefields Parkway. ⊠ *47 mi (75 km) south of the Jasper Townsite* ☎ *780/852–6176* ⌁ *25 sites* ⌂ *Public telephone, picnic tables* ⌂ *Reservations not accepted. C$14* ▱ *AE, MC, V* ⊘ *Closed early Sept. to mid-May.*

**$** ⌂ **Mt. Kerkeslin Campground.** This is a very basic campground with few facilities. Tent camping is available, and there are fire pits for cooking. ⊠ *22 mi (35 km) south of Jasper Townsite on Hwy. 93* ☎ *780/852–6176* ⌁ *45 sites* ⌂ *Fire pits* ⌂ *Reservations not accepted. C$14* ▱ *AE, MC, V* ⊘ *Closed early Sept. to early June.*

**$** ⌂ **Snaring River Campground.** This east-side campground on the Snaring River tends to be warmer than many of the park's other campgrounds. ⊠ *10 mi (16 km) east of Jasper Townsite on Hwy. 16 N* ☎ *780/852–6176* ⌁ *66 sites (tent only)* ⌂ *Picnic tables* ⌂ *Reservations not accepted. C$14* ▱ *AE, MC, V* ⊘ *Closed mid Sept. to mid-May.*

**$** ⌂ **Wilcox Creek Campground.** Near the Columbia Icefield, this tent campground is at a high elevation, so bring equipment and clothing suitable for cold weather. ⊠ *69 mi (111 km) south of Jasper Townsite on Hwy. 93* ☎ *780/852–6176* ⌁ *46 sites* ⌂ *Drinking water, public telephone, picnic tables* ⌂ *Reservations not accepted. C$15* ▱ *AE, MC, V* ⊘ *Closed mid Sept. to early June.*

## Outside the Park

CAMPGROUNDS & RV PARKS

**$–$$$** ⌂ **Hinton/Jasper KOA Campground.** This campground is 15 minutes from the east entrance of Jasper National Park and about five minutes from the town of Hinton. It's situated in a meadow bordered by three creeks and has many amenities, including 81 fully serviced sites, rustic camping cabins, camper kitchen, and handicap-accessible showers and washrooms. Horseback riding, hayrides, and hiking trails are nearby. ⊠ *Hwy. 16, 2½ mi (4 km) west of Hinton* ☎ *780/865–5061 or 888/ 562–4714* ⊕ *www.koa.com* ⇆ *106 sites* ⟳ *Flush toilets, showers, fire pits, picnic tables, play area. C$15–C$38* ⊟ *MC, V.*

# JASPER ESSENTIALS

ACCESSIBILITY Miette Hot Springs has wheelchair-accessible washrooms and changing rooms and a ramp descending into the pool with a railing. Several trails, scenic viewpoints, and day-use areas are paved. Whistlers Campground has two paved sites, each with adapted picnic tables and fireboxes. Ask for a key at the kiosk for wheelchair-accessible showers. Other campgrounds have various facilities for disabled access.

ADMISSION FEES A park entrance pass is C$8.90 per person or C$17.80 maximum per vehicle per day. Larger buses and vans pay a group rate. An annual pass costs $62.40 per adult or $123.80 per family or group.

ADMISSION HOURS The park is open 24/7, year-round. It is in the Mountain time zone.

ATMS/BANKS
🚩 **Alberta Treasury Branch** ⊠ 404 Patricia St., Jasper ☎ 780/852-3297. **Canada Trust TD** ⊠ 606 Patricia St., Jasper ☎ 780/852-6270. **CIBC** ⊠ 416 Connaught Dr., Jasper ☎ 800/465-2422.

AUTOMOBILE SERVICE STATIONS
🚩 Licensed technicians offer automobile service and repairs at **Jasper Shell.** ⊠ 638 Connaught Dr., Jasper ☎ 780/852-3022. Gas is also available at the following stations: **Avalanche Esso** ⊠ 702 Connaught Dr., Jasper ☎ 780/852-4721. **Jasper Petro Canada** ⊠ 300 Connaught Dr., Jasper ☎ 780/852-3366. **Mountain Esso** ⊠ 84 Connaught Dr., Jasper ☎ 780/852-3688.

EMERGENCIES For all emergencies dial 911. Call 780/852-6155 for a park warden. 🚩 **Cottage Medical Clinic.** ⊠ 505 Turret St., Jasper ☎ 780/852-4885. **Seton General Hospital.** ⊠ 518 Robson St., Jasper ☎ 780/852-3344.

LOST AND FOUND ☎ 780/852-6176.

PERMITS Permits are required for back-country camping and certain other activities in the park ☎ 780/852-6177. Backcountry camping permits (C$8.90 per day), day-use permits (C$6.90 per day), fire permits (C$7.90 per day), dumping station permits (C$6.90 per day), and fishing permits (C$8.90 per day) are available at the information center.

POST OFFICES
🚩 **Canada Post Office.** ⊠ 502 Patricia St., Jasper ☎ 780/852-3041. **More Than Mail.** ⊠ 620 Connaught Dr., Jasper ☎ 780/852-3160.

PUBLIC TELEPHONES Look in the Jasper Townsite, at the information center, outside the IGA grocery store, by the Shell gas station, and inside hotels. Also at the Icefields Centre, along some roadways, and at major sites such as Athabasca Falls, Sunwapta Falls, and Mt. Christie picnic area. Cell phones generally only work in and around the town of Jasper.

RELIGIOUS SERVICES There are seven chapels offering services in the Jasper Townsite. Denominations represented are: Anglican, Baptist, Catholic, Lutheran, Pentecostal, Presbyterian, and United.

RESTROOMS Restrooms are located throughout the park at all major day-use areas.

SHOPS & GROCERS
🚩 **Robinson's IGA** ⊠ 218 Connaught Dr., Jasper ☎ 780/852-3195. **Super A Foods** ⊠ 601 Patricia St., Jasper ☎ 780/852-3200.

## VISITOR INFORMATION
🚩 **Jasper National Park** 🗁 Box 10, Jasper, AB T0E 1E0 ☎ 780/852-6176 ⊕ www.pc.gc.ca/pn-np/ab/jasper.

# Joshua Tree
# National Park

## WORD OF MOUTH

"Take your time here, too, and let the desert take hold of you. Joshua Tree National Park provides a haven from everyday routines, space for self-discovery, a refuge for the human spirit, and a sense of place in the greater scheme of things."

—Ed Zahniser, National Park Service

# WELCOME TO JOSHUA TREE

## TOP REASONS TO GO

★ **Rock Climbing:** Joshua Tree is a world-class site with challenges for climbers of just about every skill level.

★ **Peace and Quiet:** Savor the solitude of one of the last great wildernesses in America.

★ **Stargazing:** You'll be mesmerized by the Milky Way flowing across the dark night sky. For spectacular natural fireworks, visit in mid-August during the Perseid meteor shower and watch shooting stars streak overhead.

★ **Wildflowers:** In spring, the hillsides explode in a patchwork of yellow, blue, pink, and white.

★ **Sunsets:** Twilight is a special time here, especially during the winter, when the setting sun casts a golden glow on the mountains.

**Map labels:**
247
Yucca Valley
Twentynine Palms Hwy
62
Yucca Trail
Joshua Tree
62
Entrance Station
West Entrance Station
Black Rock Canyon
Visitor Center
Twentynine Palms
Fortynine Palms Oasis
Oasis of Mara 4
Utah Trail Rd.
North Entrance Station
Park Boulevard
Keys Ranch
Barker Dam
QUEEN VALLEY
Hidden Valley 2
LOST HORSE VALLEY
California Riding Trail
Ryan Mtn
LITTLE SAN BERNARDINO MTS
Desert Hot Springs
Keys View 1
Lost Horse Mine
Geology Tour Road
PLEASANT VALLEY
TO LOS ANGELES
Dillon Road
10
0   5 mi
0   5 km

**1** **Keys View.** This is the most dramatic overlook in the park—on clear days you can see the Signal Mountains in Mexico.

**2** **Hidden Valley.** Crawl between the big rocks and you'll understand why this boulder-strewn area was once a cattle rustlers' hideout.

**3** **Cholla Cactus Gardens.** Come here in the late afternoon, when the spiky stalks of the bigelow (jumping) cholla cactus is back-lit against an intense blue sky.

**4** **Oasis of Mara.** Walk the nature trail around this desert oasis, which the first settlers, the Serrano, dubbed "the place of little springs and much grass."

Joshua Tree Artist in Residence Program

Joshua tree

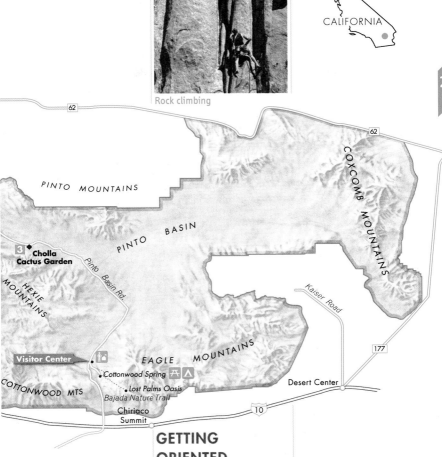

Rock climbing

PINTO MOUNTAINS

PINTO BASIN

COXCOMB MOUNTAINS

3 ◆ **Cholla Cactus Garden**

HEXIE MOUNTAINS

Pinto Basin Rd.

Kaiser Road

177

**Visitor Center** →

Cottonwood Spring

EAGLE MOUNTAINS

Desert Center

COTTONWOOD MTS

Lost Palms Oasis
Bajada Nature Trail

Chiriaco Summit

10

62

62

## GETTING ORIENTED

Dagger-like tufts grace the branches of the namesake of Joshua Tree National Park in southeastern California, where the arid Mojave Desert meets the sparsely vegetated Colorado Desert (part of the Sonoran Desert, which lies within California and Northern Mexico).

Passenger cars are fine for paved areas, but you'll need four-wheel drive for many of the rugged back-country roadways. At the park's most popular sites, parking is limited. Joshua Tree does not have public transportation.

| KEY |
| --- |
| 🏕 *Ranger Station* |
| ▲ *Campground* |
| 🍴 *Picnic Area* |
| 🍴 *Restaurant* |
| 🏨 *Lodge* |
| 🚶 *Trailhead* |
| 🚻 *Restrooms* |
| ☀ *Scenic Viewpoint* |
| ----- *Walking/Hiking Trails* |
| ••••• *Bicycle Path* |

# JOSHUA TREE PLANNER

## When to Go

**October through May, when the desert is cooler, is when most of Joshua Tree's visitors arrive.** Daytime temperatures range from the mid-70s in December and January to mid-90s in October and May. Lows can dip to near freezing in mid-winter, and in some years you may even encounter snow at the higher elevations. Summers can be torrid, with daytime temperatures reaching 110°F.

### FESTIVALS & EVENTS

FEB. **Riverside County Fair & National Date Festival.** Come to Indio for camel and ostrich races. ☎ 800/811-3247.

MAY **Pony Express Ride and Barbecue.** This reenactment of the historic mail delivery service runs from Twentynine Palms or Joshua Tree (depending on year) to Pioneertown. ☎ 760/365-6323.

OCT. **Pioneer Days.** Outhouse races, beard contests, and arm-wrestling mark this annual celebration in Twentynine Palms. ☎ 760/367-3445.

### AVG. HIGH/LOW TEMPS.

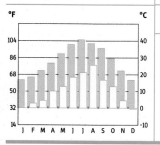

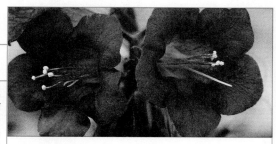

## Flora & Fauna

Joshua Tree will shatter your notions of the desert as a vast wasteland. Life flourishes in this land of little rain, as flora and fauna have adapted to heat and drought. In most areas you'll be walking among native Joshua trees, ocotillos, and yuccas. One of the best spring desert wildflower displays in Southern California blooms here in March, April, and May. You'll see plenty of animals—reptiles such as nocturnal sidewinders, birds like golden eagles or burrowing owls, and occasionally mammals like coyotes and bobcats.

## Getting There & Around

A rarity these days, Joshua Tree National Park is an isolated island of pristine wilderness within a short drive of 11 million Southern California residents. Most visitors, in fact, make the two-hour drive from the Los Angeles area to enjoy a weekend of solitude in 585,000 acres of untouched desert. The urban sprawl of Palm Springs is 45 mi away, but gateway towns Joshua Tree and Twentynine Palms are just north of the park. You can see the park's highlights in about a day, but you'll need to spend two or three days here to truly experience the quiet beauty of the desert.

## Great Reads

If you want a general introduction to hiking in Joshua Tree, try *On Foot in Joshua Tree,* by Patty Furbush, which lists more than 90 trails in the park. Adventurers setting out to conquer Joshua Tree's peaks should thumb through the *Climber's Guide to Joshua Tree* by Alan Bartlett or the *Joshua Tree Climber's Guide* by Randy Vogel.

23

By Bobbi Zane  Ruggedly beautiful desert scenery attracts nearly 2 million visitors each year to Joshua Tree National Park, one of the last great wildernesses in the continental United States. Its mountains support mounds of enormous boulders and jagged rock; natural cactus gardens and lush oases shaded by tall fan palms mark the meeting place of the Mojave (high) and Sonora (low) deserts. Extensive stands of Joshua trees give the park its name; the plants (really shrubs) reminded early white settlers of the biblical Joshua, with their thick, stubby branches representing the prophet raising his arms toward heaven.

The park stands at 1,239 square mi, most of it roadless wilderness. Elevation in some areas of the park exceeds 5,000 feet, and light snowfalls and cold, strong north winds are common in winter. There are no services within the park and little water, so you should carry at least a gallon of water per person per day. Apply sunscreen liberally at any time of the year.

## Scenic Drives

**Geology Tour Road.** Some of the park's most fascinating landscapes can be observed from this 18-mi dirt road. Parts of the journey are rough, so make sure you have a 4×4. Sights to see include a 100-year-old stone dam called Squaw Tank, defunct mines, and a large plain with an abundance of Joshua trees. There are 16 stops along the way, so give yourself about two hours to make the round-trip. ⊠ *South of Park Blvd., west of Jumbo Rocks.*

★ **Park Boulevard.** Traversing the most scenic portions of Joshua Tree, this well-paved road connects the north and west entrances in the park's high desert section. Along with some sweeping desert views, you'll see jum-

## JOSHUA TREE IN ONE DAY

Enter through the North Entrance in Twentynine Palms and follow Park Boulevard south. Head to the **Oasis Visitor Center** for information on special events, then stroll through the palm-shaded **Oasis of Mara.** Stop for a picnic lunch at **Live Oak Springs,** where you'll see boulders randomly piled on top of each other, like the contents of a mixed bowl of fruit. Drive through **Queen Valley** where the stands of Joshua trees are particularly alluring in spring, then take a detour south to survey the entire valley from **Keys**

**View.** Return to Park Boulevard, where you can crawl through the boulders at **Hidden Valley**—where cattle rustlers hid their animals a century ago.

If you have time, take the 60-minute guided **Keys Ranch tour.** Then enjoy the stunning desert drive through Pinto Basin, stopping at the **Cholla Cactus Garden** and at the **Ocotillo Patch.** Follow Pinto Basin Road south toward Cottonwood Spring, and exit the park onto Interstate 10.

bles of splendid boulder formations, extensive stands of Joshua trees, and Hidden Valley and Barker Dam, remnants of the area's wild and woolly past. From the Oasis Visitor Center, drive south. After about 5 mi, the road forks; turn right and head west toward Jumbo Rocks (clearly marked with a road sign).

**Pinto Basin Road.** This paved road takes you from high desert to low desert. From the Oasis Visitor Center, drive south. After about 5 mi, the road forks; take a left and continue another 9 mi to the Cholla Cactus Garden, where the sun fills the cactus needles with light. Past that is the Ocotillo Patch, filled with spindly plants bearing razor-sharp thorns. Side trips from this route require a 4×4.

## What to See

### Historic Sites

**Barker Dam.** Built around 1900 by ranchers and miners to hold water for cattle and mining operations, the dam now collects rainwater and is used by elusive bighorn sheep and other wildlife. ✉ *Barker Dam Rd., off Park Blvd., 14 mi south of West Entrance.*

**Hidden Valley.** This legendary cattle-rustlers hideout is set among big boulders, which kids love to scramble over and around. ✉ *Park Blvd., 14 mi south of West Entrance.*

★ **Keys Ranch.** This 150-acre ranch once belonged to William and Frances Keys and illustrates one of the area's most successful attempts at homesteading. The couple raised five children under extreme desert conditions. Most of the original buildings, including the house, school, store, and workshop, have been restored to the way it was when William died in 1969. The only way to see the ranch is on one of the 60-minute, ranger-led walking tours, offered weekdays between October and May. ✉ *2 mi north of Barker Dam Rd.* ☎ *760/367–5555* ♿ *Reservations essen-*

*tial* ⬛$5 ⊙ *Oct.–May, tours week-days* 10 *and* 1.

**Lost Horse Mine.** This historic mine illustrates the gold prospecting and mining activities that took place here in the late 1800s. The site is accessed via a fairly strenuous 2-mi hike. ⊠ *Keys View Rd., about 15 mi south of West Entrance.*

> **LOOK, DON'T TOUCH–REALLY**
>
> Some cactus needles, like those on the cholla, can become embedded in your skin with just the slightest touch. If you do get zapped, use tweezers to gently pull it out.

23

## Scenic Stops

**Cholla Cactus Garden.** This stand of bigelow cholla (sometimes called jumping cholla, since its hooked spines seem to jump at you) is best seen and photographed in late afternoon, when the backlit spiky stalks stand out against a colorful sky. ⊠ *Pinto Basin Rd., 20 mi north of Cottonwood Visitor Center.*

**Cottonwood Spring Oasis.** Noted for its abundant birdlife, this is an example of the palm-shaded oases that were a welcome sight to prospectors traveling through the area. The remains of an *arrastra,* a primitive type of gold mill, can be found nearby. Bighorn sheep frequent this area in winter. Take the 1-mi paved trail that begins at sites 13A and 13B of the Cottonwood Campground. ⊠ *Cottonwood Visitor Center.*

**Fortynine Palms Oasis.** Sights within the oasis include stands of fan palms, interesting petroglyphs, and evidence of fires built by early Native Americans. Since animals frequent this area, you may spot a coyote, bobcat, or roadrunner. ⊠ *End of Canyon Rd., 4 mi west of Twentynine Palms.*

★ **Keys View.** At 5,185 feet, this point affords a sweeping view of the Coachella Valley, the mountains of the San Bernardino National Forest, and—on a rare clear day—Signal Mountain in Mexico. Sunrise and sunset are magical times, when the light throws rocks and trees into high relief before bathing the hills in brilliant shades of red, orange, and gold. ⊠ *Keys View Rd., 21 mi south of West Entrance.*

**Lost Palms Oasis.** More than 100 palms comprise the largest group of the exotic plants in the park. A spring bubbles from between the rocks, but disappears into the sandy, boulder-strewn canyon. As you hike along the 4-mi trail, you might spot bighorn sheep. ⊠ *Cottonwood Visitor Center.*

**Ocotillo Patch.** Stop here for a roadside exhibit on the dramatic display made by the red-tipped succulent after even the shortest rain shower. ⊠ *Pinto Basin Rd., about 3 mi east of Cholla Cactus Gardens.*

## Visitor Centers

**Cottonwood Visitor Center.** Exhibits in this small center, staffed by rangers and volunteers, illustrate the region's natural history. ⊠ *Pinto Basin Rd.* ☎ *No phone* ⊕ *www.nps.gov/jotr* ⊙ *Daily 8–4.*

**Joshua Tree Visitor Center.** This visitor center, opened in summer 2006, holds exhibits illustrating park geology, cultural and historic sites, and hiking and rock-climbing activities. There's also a small bookstore.

✉ *6554 Park Blvd. Joshua Tree* ☎ *760/367–5500* ⊕ *www.nps.gov/jotr*
⊘ *Daily 8–5.*

**Oasis Visitor Center.** Exhibits here illustrate how Joshua Tree was formed,
reveal the differences between the two types of desert within the park,
and demonstrate how plants and animals eke out an existence in this
arid climate. Take the ½-mi nature walk through the nearby Oasis of
Mara, which is alive with cottonwood trees, palm trees, and mesquite
shrubs. ✉ *74485 National Park Dr., Twentynine Palms* ☎ *760/367–
5500* ⊕ *www.nps.gov/jotr* ⊘ *Daily 8–4:30.*

## Sports & the Outdoors

Fall, winter, and spring are the best times to indulge in active sports;
heat and high altitude make these dangerous activities in summer.

### Bicycling

Mountain biking is a great way to see Joshua Tree. With newer routes
opened in backcountry areas, there are plenty of trails waiting to be explored. Keep in mind that all except Thermal Canyon are also open to
horseback riding.

**Black Eagle Mountain Road.** This dead-end, 9-mi road peppered with defunct mines runs along the edge of a former lake bed, then crosses a number of dry washes before navigating several of Eagle Mountain's canyons.
✉ *Off Pinto Basin Rd., 6½ mi north of Cottonwood Visitor Center.*

**Covington Flats.** This 4-mi trail leads you past some of the park's most
impressive Joshua trees as well as pinyon pines, junipers, and areas of
lush desert vegetation. It's tough going toward the end, but once you
reach 5,516-foot Eureka Peak, you'll have great views of Palm Springs,
the Morongo Basin, and the surrounding mountains. ✉ *Covington
Flats picnic area, La Contenta Rd., 10 mi south of Rte. 62.*

**Old Dale Road.** The first 11 mi of this 23-mi route run across Pinto Basin
to the Old Dale Mining District, where several side roads head off toward dusty old shafts. Here you'll find Mission Well, dug to provide
water for the area's mines and mills. The vegetation is remarkably varied, including tiny yellow chinchweed and desert willows. ✉ *Off Pinto
Basin Rd., 7 mi north of Cottonwood Visitor Center.*

**Pinkham Canyon Road.** This challenging 20-mi trail follows Smoke Tree
Wash, then descends into Pinkham Canyon. Be careful—the route
crosses some soft sand. ✉ *Starts at Cottonwood Visitor Center.*

**Queen Valley.** This 13⅖-mi network of mostly level dirt roads winds
through one of the park's most impressive groves of Joshua trees. Bike
racks at the Barker Dam and Hidden Valley trailheads allow you to park
your ride and go hiking. ✉ *Hidden Valley Campground.*

**Thermal Canyon Bike Trail.** This newly opened 10-mi trail—intended for
mountain bikers who want a wilderness experience—follows a rigorous route along Berdoo Canyon Road through a rugged portion of the
Cottonwood Mountains; the views are lovely. ✉ *Off Geology Tour Rd.*

**Big Wheel Tours.** Based in Palm Desert, Big Wheel offers occasional combination Jeep/bike excursions through the park. ⊠ *PO Box 4188, Palm Desert 92261* ☎ *760/779–1837* ⊕ *www.bwbtours.com* ✍ *$150 per person.*

### Bird-watching

Birding is a popular pastime in Joshua Tree. During the fall migration, which runs from mid-September through mid-October, there are several reliable sighting areas. At Barker Dam you might spot white-throated swifts, several types of swallows, or red-tailed hawks. Lucy's warbler, lesser goldfinches, and Anna's hummingbirds cruise around Cottonwood Spring, a serene tree-shaded setting where you'll likely see the largest concentrations of birds in the park. At Black Rock Canyon and Covington Flats, you're likely to see LaConter's thrashers, ruby crowned kinglets, and warbling vireos. Rufus hummingbirds, Pacific slope fly-catchers, and various warblers are frequent visitors to Indian Cove. Lists of birds found in the park, as well as information on recent sightings, are available at visitor centers.

### Hiking

There are more than 50 mi of hiking trails in Joshua Tree, ranging from quarter-of-a-mile treks to 35-mi journeys. Many cross each other, so you can design your own desert maze. Remember that drinking water is hard to come by—you won't find water in the park except at the entrances. Bring along at least a gallon per person for all but the shortest hikes, more if the weather is hot. Before striking out on a hike or apparent nature trail, check out the signage. Hiking trails are marked with a hiking figure; similar signs without the hiking figure identify rock-climbing routes.

EASY    **Bajada All Access.** Learn all about what plants do to survive in the desert on this easy, wheelchair accessible ¼-mi loop. ⊠ *South of Cottonwood Visitor Center, ½ mi from park entrance.*

**Cap Rock.** This ½-mi wheelchair accessible loop—named after a boulder that sits atop a huge rock formation like a cap—winds through fascinating rock formations and has signs that explain the geology of the Mojave Desert. ⊠ *Junction of Park Blvd. and Keys View Rd.*

**Indian Cove Trail.** Look for lizards and roadrunners along this ½-mi loop that follows a desert wash. This easy trail has signs with interesting facts about these and other animals of the Mojave Desert. ⊠ *West end of Indian Cove Campground.*

**Skull Rock Trail.** The ¼-mi loop guides hikers through boulder piles, desert washes, and a rocky alley. It's named for what is perhaps the park's most famous rock formation, which resembles a human head. ⊠ *Jumbo Rocks Campground.*

MODERATE    **California Riding and Hiking Trail.** This well-traveled route stretches for 35 mi between the Black Rock Canyon Entrance and the North Entrance. No need to hike the entire trail, however. Start at any point along the way, including where it crosses major roads near Ryan Campground or Belle Campground, for hikes from 4 to 11 mi. ⊠ *Trailheads at Covington Flats, Keys View, and Squaw Tank.*

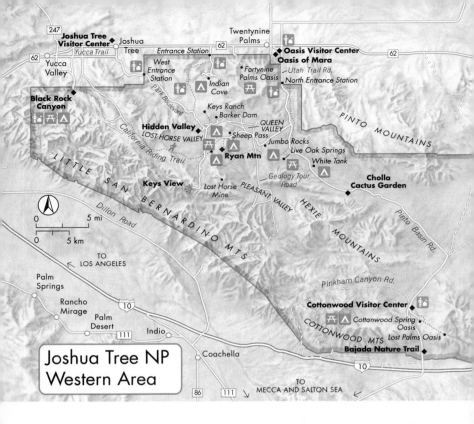

Joshua Tree NP
Western Area

**High View Nature Trail.** This 1³⁄₁₀-mi loop climbs nearly to the top of 4,500-foot Summit Peak. The views of nearby Mt. San Gorgonio make the moderately steep journey worth the effort. ⊠ ½ *mi west of Black Rock Canyon Campground.*

Fodor'sChoice ★ **Ryan Mountain Trail.** The payoff for hiking to the top of 5,461-foot Ryan Mountain is one of the best panoramic views of Joshua Tree. From here you can see Mt. San Jacinto, Mt. San Gorgonio, Lost Horse Valley, and the Pinto Basin. You'll need two to three hours to complete the 3-mi round-trip. ⊠ *Ryan Mountain parking area, 16 mi southeast of West Entrance or Sheep Pass, 16 mi southwest of Oasis Visitor Center.*

DIFFICULT **Boy Scout Trail.** The moderately strenuous 16-mi trail, suitable for back-packers, runs through the westernmost edge of the Wonderland of Rocks, passing through a forest of Joshua trees, past granite towers, and around willow-lined pools. Completing the round-trip journey requires camping along the way, so you may want to hike only part of the trail or have a car waiting at the other end. ⊠ *Between Quail Springs Picnic Area and Indian Cove Campground.*

**Fortynine Palms Oasis Trail.** Allow three hours for this moderately strenuous 3-mi trek. The trail makes a steep climb into the hills, then it drops down into a canyon where you'll find an oasis lined with fan palms.

There's plenty of evidence of Native Americans in this area, from traces of cooking fires to rocks carved with petroglyphs. ⊠ *End of Canyon Rd., 4 mi west of Twentynine Palms.*

**Lost Horse Mine Trail.** This fairly strenuous 4-mi round-trip hike follows a former mining road to a well-preserved mill that was used in the 1890s to crush gold-encrusted rock mined from the nearby mountain. The operation was one of the area's most successful, and the mine's cyanide settling tanks and stone buildings are the area's best preserved. From the mill area, a short but steep 10-minute side trip takes you to the top of a 5,278-foot peak with great views of the valley. ⊠ *1¼ mi east of Keys View Rd.*

**Lost Palms Oasis Trail.** Allow four to six hours for the moderately strenuous, 7½-mi round-trip, which leads to the most impressive oasis in the park. You'll find more than 100 fan palms and an abundance of wildflowers here. ⊠ *Cottonwood Spring Oasis.*

★ **Mastodon Peak Trail.** Some boulder scrambling is required on this 3-mi hike up 3,371-foot Mastodon Peak, but the journey rewards you with stunning views of the Salton Sea. The trail passes through a region where gold was mined from 1919 to 1932, so be on the lookout for open mines. The peak draws its name from a large rock formation that early miners believed looked like the head of a prehistoric behemoth. ⊠ *Cottonwood Spring Oasis.*

OUTFITTERS & EXPEDITIONS **Joshua Tree Hike and Fitness.** Joshua Tree Hike and Fitness leads easy to moderate hikes to park destinations such as Willow Hole, Juniper Flats, Keys View, and Wall Street Mill; they also offer custom trips. Most hikes are four to six hours. ⊠ *PO Box 1088, Joshua Tree 92252* ☎ *760/366-7985* ⊕ *www.joshuatreehike.com* ⊠ *$50–$240 per person depending upon number in party and duration* ☉ *Daily.*

## Horseback Riding

More than 200 mi of equestrian trails are gradually being added as part of a backcountry and wilderness management plan at Joshua Tree, and visitors are welcome to bring their own animals. Trail maps are available at visitor centers. Ryan and Black Rock campgrounds have designated areas for horses and mules.

## Rock Climbing

Fodor'sChoice ★ With an abundance of weathered igneous boulder outcroppings, Joshua Tree is one of the nation's top winter climbing destinations and offers a full menu of climbing experiences—from bouldering for beginners in the Wonderland of Rocks to multiple-pitch climbs at Echo Rock and Saddle Rock. The best-known climb in the park is Hidden Valley's Sports Challenge Rock. A map inside the *Joshua Tree Guide* shows locations of selected wilderness and nonwilderness climbs.

OUTFITTERS & EXPEDITIONS **Backcountry Found** conducts two-day backpacking/rock-climbing excursions. Climbing gear, instructions, group camping, and most meals are included. They also offer custom-designed trips. ⊠ *221 Noe St. #200, San Francisco* ☎ *415/626–6240* ⊠ *$750 per person* ☉ *Apr. and Nov.*

**Joshua Tree Rock Climbing School** offers several programs, from one-day introductory classes to multiday programs for experienced climbers. The

## GUIDED TOURS

**Desert Adventures.** Red Jeep tours combine excursions on roads less traveled with hikes and nature walks. ⊠ *74794 Lennon Pl., Suite A, Palm Desert* ☎ *888/440-5337* ⊕ *www.red-jeep.com* ▦ *$150 per person* ⊙ *Daily in fall, winter, spring.*

**Elite Land Tours.** This luxury outfitter conducts half-day Hummer tours through the backcountry of the park to the world's largest Joshua tree. Evening excursions that utilize night-vision equipment are also available. Tours include hotel pick up and refreshments. Gourmet picnics are available for an extra charge. ⊠ *555 S. Sunrise Way, Suite 200, Palm Springs* ☎ *760/318-1200* ⊕ *www.elitelandtours.com* ▦ *$150 per person* ⊙ *Daily.*

school provides all needed equipment. Beginning classes are limited to six people age 13 or older. ⌂ *Box 3034, Joshua Tree, 92252* ☎ *760/366-4745 or 800/890-4745* ⊕ *www.joshuatreerockclimbing.com* ▦ *$110 for beginner class* ⊙ *Aug.–June.*

**Vertical Adventures Climbing School** trains about 1,000 climbers each year in Joshua Tree National Park. Classes meet at a designated location in the park, and all equipment is provided. ☎ *800/514-8785* ⊕ *www.verticaladventures.com* ▦ *$105 per person for one-day class* ⊙ *Sept.–June.*

## Educational Offerings

The Desert Institute of the Joshua Tree National Park Association offers a full calendar of lectures, field trips, and seminars during the fall and spring months at many locations in and around the park; some offer college credit.

### Ranger Programs

**Campfire Coffee.** Bring your own mug for the coffee (or hot chocolate) served at informative Sunday morning meetings led by rangers who answer questions and help plan your day. It's brewing at Cottonwood Campground and Hidden Valley Campground. ▦ *Free* ⊙ *Oct.–Apr., Sun. at 8.*

**Evening Programs.** Rangers present hour-long Saturday evening lectures at Black Rock Canyon Nature Center, Cottonwood Amphitheater, Indian Cove Amphitheater, and Jumbo Rocks Campground. Topics range from natural history to local lore. The schedule is posted at the visitor centers. ▦ *Free* ⊙ *Oct.–Apr., Sat. at 7; May, Sat. at 8.*

# WHAT'S NEARBY

## Nearby Towns & Attractions

### Nearby Towns

**Palm Springs,** about a 45-minute drive from the North Entrance Station at Joshua Tree, serves as the home base for most park visitors. This city of 43,000 has 95 golf courses, 600 tennis courts, and 30,000 swimming pools. A hideout for Hollywood stars since the 1920s, Palm Springs offers a glittering array of shops, restaurants, and hotels. Stroll down Palm Canyon Drive and you're sure to run into a celebrity or two. About 9 mi north of Palm Springs and closer to the park is **Desert Hot Springs,** which has more than 1,000 natural hot mineral pools and 40 health spas ranging from low-key to luxurious. **Yucca Valley** is the largest and fastest growing of the communities straddling the park's northern border. The town boasts a handful of motels, supermarkets, and a Wal-Mart. Tiny **Joshua Tree,** the closest community to the park's West Entrance, is where the serious rock climbers make their headquarters. **Twentynine Palms,** known as "two-nine" by locals, is sandwiched between the Marine Corps Air Ground Task Force Center to the north and Joshua Tree National Park to the south. Here you'll find a smattering of coffeehouses, antiques shops, and cafés.

## Nearby Attractions

**Coachella Valley Museum and Cultural Center.** Displays at this former farmhouse explain how dates are harvested and ways in which the desert can be irrigated. You'll also find a smithy and an old sawmill on the grounds. ☒ *82-616 Miles Ave., Indio* ☎ *760/342–6651* 🏷 *$2* ☉ *Sept.–June, Wed.–Sat. 10–4, Sun. 1–4.*

**Hi-Desert Nature Museum.** Check out this small zoo containing creatures that make their homes in Joshua Tree, including scorpions, snakes, ground squirrels, and chuckawallas (a type of lizard). There's also a collection of rocks, minerals, and fossils from the Paleozoic era, a Native American collection, and a children's room. ☒ *57–116 Twentynine Palms Hwy. Yucca Valley* ☎ *760/369–7212* ⊕ *www.yucca-valley.org* 🏷 *Free* ☉ *Tues.–Sun. 10–5.*

**Oasis of Murals.** This collection of 17 murals painted on the sides of buildings depicts the history of Twentynine Palms and the daily lives of its citizens. If you drive around town, you can't miss them, but you can also pick up a free map from the **Action Council for 29 Palms** (☒ 6455B Mesquite Ave., Twentynine Palms ☎ 760/361–2286).

**Pioneertown.** A hangout built by movie stars Roy Rogers, Gene Autry, and Russ Hayden in the 1940s, this 1880s-style Old West movie set is complete with hitching posts, a saloon, and an OK Corral. Although filming still takes place here, you can stroll the wooden sidewalks past false-fronted stores, clapboard houses and a historic bowling alley. Pappy & Harriett's old-time saloon and eatery is a popular venue for local and touring bands and singers. Gunfighters face off Old-West style in the dusty Mane Street on weekend afternoons. ☒ *4 mi north of Yucca Valley on Pioneertown Rd.* ⊕ *www.pioneertown.com.*

---

### FAMILY PICKS

- Walk in the footsteps of "real" spaghetti-western movie cowboys on Mane Street in Pioneertown.

- See a family-oriented live show at Theatre 29 in Twentynine Palms.

- Get in the swim of things at Knotts Soak City in Palm Springs, with 13 waterslides and a huge wave pool.

## Area Activities

### Educational Offerings

**The Desert Institute of Joshua Tree National Park Association.** This organization offers a full schedule of educational lectures on topics like the birds of Joshua Tree National Park, wildflower wanderings, the desert night sky, and basket weaving. University credit is available for some lectures. Classes meet at various locations; many include field trips within the park. Call for current schedule and prices. ✉ *74485 National Park Dr., Twentynine Palms* ☎ *760/367–5535* ⊕ *www.joshuatree.org.*

# WHERE TO STAY & EAT

### About the Restaurants

Dining options in the gateway towns around Joshua Tree National Park are extremely limited—you'll mostly find fast-food outlets in Yucca Valley and Twentynine Palms and a few casual cafés that cater to locals and park visitors. The exception is the restaurant at 29 Palms Inn, which has an interesting California cuisine menu that features lots of veggies. Still, you'll have to travel to the Palm Springs desert resort area for a fine-dining experience.

### About the Hotels

Lodging choices in the Joshua Tree National Park area are limited to a few motels, chain hotels, and a couple of bed-and-breakfast establishments in the gateway towns. In general, most offer few amenities and are modestly priced. Book ahead for the spring wildflower season—reservations may be difficult to obtain then.

### About the Campgrounds

Camping is the best way to experience the stark, exquisite beauty of Joshua Tree. You'll also have a rare opportunity to sleep outside in a semi-wilderness setting. The campgrounds, set at elevations from 3,000 to 4,500 feet, have only primitive facilities; few have drinking water. With the exception of Black Rock and Indian Cove campgrounds—which accept reservations up to five months in advance (☎ 800/365–2267)—campsites are on a first-come basis. During the busy fall and spring weekends, plan to arrive early in the day to ensure a site, or if you have an organized group, reserve one of the group sites in advance. Temperatures can drop at night during any part of the year—bring a sweater or light jacket. If you plan to camp in late winter or early spring, be prepared for the gusty Santa Ana winds that may sweep through the park. Backcountry camping is permitted in certain wilderness areas of Joshua Tree. You must sign in at a backcountry register board if you plan to stay overnight. For more information, stop at the visitor centers or ranger stations.

## Where to Eat

### In the Park

PICNIC AREAS **Black Rock Canyon.** Set among Joshua trees, pinyon pines, and junipers, this popular picnic area has barbecue grills and drinking water. It's one

23

of the few with flush toilets. ⊠ *End of Joshua Lane at the Black Rock Canyon Campground.*

**Cottonwood Spring.** Shady trees make this a pleasant place to picnic. It has drinking water and restrooms with flush toilets. ⊠ *On Pinto Basin Rd., adjacent to visitor center.*

**Covington Flats.** This is a great place to get away from crowds. There's just one table, and it's surrounded by flat open desert dotted here and there by Joshua trees. ⊠ *La Contenta Rd., 10 mi from Rte. 62.*

**Hidden Valley.** Set among huge rock formations, with picnic tables shaded by dense trees, this is one of the most pleasant places in the park to stop for lunch. ⊠ *Park Blvd., 14 mi south of the West Entrance.*

**Indian Cove.** The view here is rock formations that draw thousands of climbers to the park each year. This isolated area is reached via Twentynine Palms Highway. ⊠ *End of Indian Cove Rd.*

**Live Oak Springs.** Tucked among piles of boulders, this picnic area in the midst of interesting rock formations is near a stand of Joshua trees. ⊠ *Park Blvd., east of Jumbo Rocks.*

### Outside the Park

$–$$  ✕ **Pappy & Harriet's Pioneertown Palace.** Smack in the middle of a Western-movie-set town is this Western-movie-set saloon, where you can have dinner, dance to live country-and-western music, or just relax with a drink at the bar. The food ranges from Tex-Mex to Santa Maria barbecue to steak and burgers—no surprises but plenty of fun. It may be in the middle of nowhere, but you'll need reservations for dinner on weekends. ⊠ *53688 Pioneertown Rd., Pioneertown* ☎ *760/365–5956* ⊕ *www. pappyandharriets.com. $10–$17* ⊟ *AE, D, MC, V* ☺ *No lunch Mon.–Wed.*

$  ✕ **Edchada's.** Rock climbers who spend their days in Joshua Tree swear by the margaritas at this Mexican restaurant, which also has a location in Twentynine Palms. Specialties include prodigious portions of fajitas, carnitas, seafood enchiladas, and fish tacos. ⊠ *56805 Twentynine Palms Hwy., Yucca Valley* ☎ *760/365–7655* ⊠ *73502 Twentynine Palms Hwy., Twentynine Palms* ☎ *760/367–2131. $9–$12* ⊟ *AE, D, MC, V.*

¢  ✕ **Park Rock Café.** If you're on your way to the national park on Highway 62, stop in the town of Joshua Tree to stoke up on a hearty breakfast bagel sandwich and order a bag lunch to take with you. The café creates some unusual sandwiches such as roast beef with Philly cheese or chicken Parmesan. Outside dining is pleasant here. ⊠ *6554 Park Blvd., Joshua Tree* ☎ *760/366–3622. $6–$8* ⊟ *MC, V* ☺ *Closed Sun.—Thurs.*

## Where to Stay

### In the Park

CAMPGROUNDS & RV PARKS

$$–$$$

⚠ **Sheep Pass Campground.** At 4,500 feet, Sheep Pass is the highest campground in the park. It's also the smallest—it has only six sites, all designated for groups. The campsites, set among boulders and relatively dense vegetation, are fairly private. ⊠ *Park Blvd., 16 mi from Oasis of Mara* ☎ *760/367–5500, 800/365–2267 for reservations* ⊕ *www.nps. gov/jotr* ↪ *31 group sites* ⚲ *Pit toilets, fire pits, picnic tables. $20–$35* ⚐ *Reservations essential* ☺ *Year-round* ⊟ *D, MC, V.*

**$** ⚠ **Black Rock Canyon Campground.** Set among juniper bushes, cholla cacti, and other desert shrubs, Black Rock Canyon is one of the prettiest campgrounds in Joshua Tree. South of Yucca Valley, it's the closest campground to most of the desert communities. Located on the California Riding and Hiking Trail, it has facilities for horses and mules. ⊠ *Joshua Lane, south of Hwy. 62 and Hwy. 247* ☎ *760/367–5500, 800/365–2267 for reservations* ⊕ *www.nps.gov/jotr* ↩ *100 sites* ⚲ *Flush toilets, dump station, drinking water, fire pits, picnic tables, ranger station. $10* ⊟ *D, MC, V* ⊘ *Year-round.*

**$** ⚠ **Cottonwood Campground.** In spring this campground, the southernmost one in the park (and therefore often the last to fill up), is surrounded by some of the desert's finest wildflowers. Reservations are not accepted. ⊠ *Pinto Basin Rd., 32 mi south of North Entrance Station* ☎ *760/ 367–5500* ⊕ *www.nps.gov/jotr* ↩ *62 sites, 3 group sites* ⚲ *Flush toilets, dump station, fire pits, picnic tables, ranger station. $10, $25 for groups* ⊟ *D, MC, V* ⊘ *Year-round.*

**$** ⚠ **Indian Cove Campground.** This is a very sought-after spot for rock climbers, primarily because it lies among the 50 square mi of rugged terrain at the Wonderland of Rocks. Popular climbs near the campground include Pixie Rock, Feudal Wall, and Corral Wall. Call ahead to reserve one of the 13 group sites. ⊠ *Indian Cove Rd., south of Hwy. 62* ☎ *760/ 367–5500, 800/365–2267 for reservations* ⊕ *www.nps.gov/jotr* ↩ *101 sites, 13 group sites. $10, $20–$35 for groups* ⚲ *Pit toilets, fire pits, picnic tables* ⚲ *Reservations essential* ⊘ *Year-round* ⊟ *D, MC, V.*

**¢** ⚠ **Belle Campground.** This small campground is popular with families, as there are a number of boulders kids can scramble over and around. Campsites here are small and not recommended for recreational vehicles. ⊠ *9 mi south of Oasis of Mara* ☎ *760/367–5500* ⊕ *www.nps.gov/ jotr* ↩ *18 sites* ⚲ *Pit toilets, fire pits, picnic tables. $5* ⊘ *Year-round.*

**¢** ⚠ **Hidden Valley Campground.** This campground is a favorite with rock climbers, who make their way up valley formations that have names like the Blob, Old Woman, and Chimney Rock. RVs are permitted, but there are no hookups. ⊠ *Off Park Blvd., 20 mi southwest of Oasis of Mara* ☎ *760/367–5500* ⊕ *www.nps.gov/jotr* ↩ *39 sites* ⚲ *Pit toilets, fire pits, picnic tables. $5* ⚲ *Reservations not accepted* ⊘ *Year-round.*

**¢** ⚠ **Jumbo Rocks.** Each campsite at this well-regarded campground tucked among giant boulders has a bit of privacy. It's a good home base for visiting many of Joshua Tree's attractions, including Geology Tour Road. ⊠ *Park Blvd., 11 mi from Oasis of Mara* ☎ *760/367–5500* ⊕ *www.nps.gov/jotr* ↩ *125 sites* ⚲ *Pit toilets, fire pits, picnic tables. $5* ⚲ *Reservations not accepted* ⊘ *Year-round.*

**¢** ⚠ **Ryan Campground.** At the foot of Ryan Mountain, this primitive campground is east of the turnoff leading to Keys Views and Lost Horse Mine. Although there are no facilities for them, horses are permitted here. ⊠ *16 mi south of West Entrance* ☎ *760/367–5500* ⊕ *www.nps. gov/otr* ↩ *31 sites* ⚲ *Pit toilets, fire pits, picnic tables. Free* ⚲ *Reservations not accepted* ⊘ *Year-round.*

**¢** ⚠ **White Tank.** This small, quiet campground is popular with families because a nearby trail leads to a natural arch. Campsites are small and not recommended for RVs or trailers. ⊠ *Pinto Basin Rd., 11 mi south of Oasis* *of Mara* ☎ *760/367–5500* ⊕ *www.nps.gov/jotr* ↩ *15 sites* ⚐ *Pit toilets, fire pits, picnic tables. $5* ⚐ *Reservations not accepted* ⊙ *Year-round.*

### Outside the Park

**$–$$$$** ⊞ **Casa Cody.** An excellent headquarters for families, the Casa Cody has spacious simply furnished studios and one- and two-bedroom suites that have kitchens. The homey rooms are situated in four buildings surrounding courtyards lushly landscaped with bougainvillea and citrus. Continental breakfast is included in the rates. ⊠ *175 S. Cahuilla Rd., Palm Springs, 92262* ☎ *760/325–2639* 🖷 *760/325–8610* ⊕ *www.casacody. com* ↩ *16 rooms, 7 suites, 2 cottages* ⚐ *Kitchen (some), refrigerator, dial-up, pool, some pets allowed, no-smoking rooms. $69–$279* ▤ *AE, D, MC, V* ⦿ *CP.*

**$$–$$$** ⊞ **Homestead Inn.** Run by a salt-of-the-earth innkeeper who keeps a flock of roadrunners as pets, this little lodge is set on 15 acres outside the park. Three of the comfortable rooms have private patios; two have fireplaces and whirlpool tubs. ⊠ *74153 Two Mile Rd., Twentynine Palms 92277* ☎ *760/367–0030 or 877/367–0030* ⊕ *www. joshuatreelodging.com* ↩ *6 rooms* ⚐ *Refrigerator, VCR. $125–$160* ▤ *AE, MC, V.*

**$$–$$$** ⊞ **Rimrock Ranch Cabins.** The quiet beauty of the surrounding desert attracts Hollywood writers, artists, and musicians to these four circa-1940s housekeeping cabins. Owners Szu and Dusty Wakeman have restored the cabins to their original condition, complete with knotty-pine paneling, vintage Wedgwood stoves, artisan tiles, and antique furnishings. Special touches include outdoor fireplaces and espresso machines in the fully equipped kitchens. The grounds include a stargazing deck, campfire pit, and a deep-pit barbecue. ⊠ *50857 Burns Canyon Rd., Pioneertown 92268* ☎ *760/228–1297* 🖷 *818/557–6383* ⊕ *www.rimrockranchcabins. com* ↩ *4 cabins* ⚐ *Kitchen, VCR, pool, some pets allowed, no phone, no TV, no-smoking rooms. $102–$156* ▤ *AE, MC, V.*

**★ $$–$$$** ⊞ **Roughley Manor.** Cost was no object for the wealthy pioneer who erected this stone mansion, now a B&B. A 50-foot-long planked maple floor is the pride of the great room, the carpentry on the walls throughout is intricate, and huge stone fireplaces warm the house on the rare cold night. Original fixtures still gleam in the bathrooms, and bedrooms hold pencil and canopy beds and some fireplaces. The innkeepers serve afternoon tea and evening dessert. An acre of gardens shaded by Washingtonia palms surrounds the house. ⊠ *74–744 Joe Davis Rd., Twentynine Palms 92277* ☎ *760/367–3238* 🖷 *760/367–6261* ⊕ *www.roughleymanor. com* ↩ *2 suites, 7 cottages* ⚐ *Kitchen, ethernet (some), no-smoking rooms. $135–$160* ▤ *DC, MC, V* ⦿ *BP.*

CAMPGROUNDS & RV PARKS
**$$–$$$$** ⚠ **Twentynine Palms RV Resort.** This well-equipped RV park caters to snowbirds in winter who stay two or three months at a time to enjoy warm weather, an active social life, and an array of amenities. ⊠ *4949 Desert Knoll Ave, Twentynine Palms 92277* ☎ *760/367–3320* 🖷 *760/367–2351* ⊕ *www.29palmsgolfresort.com* ↩ *197 RV sites, 26 cottages* ⚐ *Swimming (pool), guest laundry. $33 for RVs, $80 for cottages* ▤ *MC, V.*

# JOSHUA TREE ESSENTIALS

ACCESSIBILITY Black Rock Canyon and Jumbo Rocks campgrounds each have one accessible campsite. Nature trails at Oasis of Mara, Bajada, Keys View, and Cap Rock are accessible. Some trails at roadside viewpoints can be negotiated by those with limited mobility.

ADMISSION FEES $15 per car, $5 per person on foot. The Joshua Tree Pass, good for one year, is $30.

ADMISSION HOURS The park is open every day, around the clock. Oasis Visitor Center is open daily 8–5; Cottonwood Visitor Center, daily 8–4:40; Joshua Tree Visitor Center, daily 8–5; park 24 hours. The park is in the Pacific time zone.

ATMS/BANKS There are no banks in Joshua Tree, but ATMs can be found in nearby gas stations.
⛽ **Beacon Gas Station** ✉ 73777 29 Palms Hwy., Twentynine Palms ☎ 760/367–9807. **Circle K** ✉ 61920 29 Palms Hwy., Joshua Tree ☎ 760/366–8513.

AUTOMOBILE SERVICE STATIONS
⛽ **Beacon Gas Station** ✉ 73777 29 Palms Hwy., Twentynine Palms ☎ 760/367–9807 ☉ Daily 6 AM–midnight. **Circle K** ✉ 61920 29 Palms Hwy., Joshua Tree ☎ 760/366–8513 ☉ Open 24 hrs.

EMERGENCIES Emergency assistance within Joshua Tree is limited; call San Bernardino Dispatch at (909)383-5651, or dial 911. Emergency-only phones are at Intersection Rock at the entrance to Hidden Valley Campground and Indian Cove Campground.

LOST AND FOUND Report any lost or found items at any of the park's visitor centers.

PERMITS Free permits—available at all visitor centers—are required for rock climbing.

POST OFFICES There is no place in the park to mail letters or buy stamps. Nearby towns have full-service post offices.
📮 **Yucca Valley** ✉ 57280 Yucca Trail, 92284 ☎ 800/275–8777 ☉ Weekdays 9–5, Sat. 10–1.

**Joshua Tree** ✉ 61416 29 Palms Hwy., 92252 ☎ 800/275–8777 ☉ Weekdays 9–5, Sat. 9–noon. **Twentynine Palms** ✉ 73839 Gorgonio Dr., 92277 ☎ 800/275–8777 ☉ Weekdays 8:30–5.

PUBLIC TELEPHONES Pay phones are at Oasis Visitor Center and Black Rock Canyon Campground. There are no telephones in the interior of the park, and cell phones don't work in most areas.

SHOPS & GROCERS
🛒 **Coyote Corners.** ✉ 6535 Park Blvd, Joshua Tree ☎ 760/366–9683 ⊕ www. joshuatreecoyotecorner.com ☉ Daily 9–6. At **Joshua Tree Outfitters** ✉ 61707 Hwy. 62, Joshua Tree ☎ 760/366–1848 or 888/366–1848 ⊕ www. joshuatreeoutfitters.com ☉ Thurs., Fri., and Mon. 11–5, weekends 9–5.

**NEARBY TOWN INFORMATION**
**Desert Hot Springs Chamber of Commerce** ✉ 11-711 West Dr., Desert Hot Springs, 92240 ☎ 760/329–6403 🖷 760/329–2833 ⊕ www. deserthotsprings.com. **Joshua Tree Chamber of Commerce** ✉ 61325 Twentynine Palms Hwy., Suite F, Joshua Tree, 92252 ☎ 760/366–3723 🖷 760/366–2573 ⊕ www.joshuatreechamber. org. **Palm Springs Bureau of Tourism** ✉ 2901 N. Palm Canyon Dr., Suite 201, Palm Springs, 92262 ☎ 800/348–7746 🖷 760/323–3021 ⊕ www.palm-springs.org. **Twentynine Palms Chamber of Commerce** ✉ 73660 Civic Center, Suite C and D, Twentynine Palms, 92277 ☎ 760/ 367–3445 🖷 760/367–3366 ⊕ www.29chamber. com. **Yucca Valley Chamber of Commerce** ✉ 55569 Twentynine Palms Hwy., Yucca Valley, 92284 ☎ 760/365–6323 🖷 760/365–0763 ⊕ www.yuccavalley.org.

**VISITOR INFORMATION**
🏞 **Joshua Tree National Park** ✉ 74485 National Park Dr., Twentynine Palms, CA 92277 ☎ 760/367–5500 🖷 760/367–6392 ⊕ www.nps. gov/jotr.

# Lassen Volcanic National Park

Bumpass Hell, Lassen Volcanic National Park

## WORD OF MOUTH

"Miles of its flanks are reeking and bubbling with hot springs, many of them so boisterous and sulphurous they seem ever ready to become spouting geysers . . . "

–John Muir

# WELCOME TO LASSEN VOLCANIC

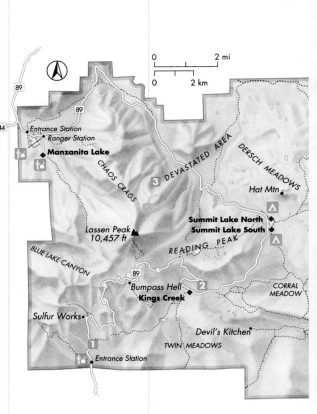

Cliff Lake

## TOP REASONS TO GO

★ **To hike a volcano:** The 2½ mi trek up Lassen Peak rewards you with a spectacular view of far northern California.

★ **To spot a rare bloom:** The Lassen Smelowskia, a small white-to-pinkish flower, grows only in Lassen Volcanic National Park, mainly on Lassen Peak.

★ **To find four in one:** All four types of volcanoes found in the world—shield, plug dome, cinder cone, and composite—are represented in Lassen Volcanic National Park.

★ **To hear inner earth:** The park's thumping mudpots and venting fumaroles roil, gurgle, and belch a raucous symphony from beneath the earth's crust.

★ **To escape the crowds:** Lassen, in sparsely populated far northern California, is one of the least-visited national parks.

**1** Southwest. Geothermal activity is greatest in the southwest area; you'll see evidence on hikes to Bumpass Hell and Devil's Kitchen. Walkways beside the former Sulphur Works on Lassen Park Road, just past the entrance station, provide easy access to smelly, belching fumaroles.

**2** Middle. Marsh meadows and stunning falls highlight the Kings Creek area in the park's southern midsection. Further north, Summit Lake—in the midst of a red fir forest at an elevation of about 6,700 ft.—has two campgrounds and a trail leading to several smaller lakes.

**3** Northwest. Lassen Park Road winds past the barren rubble of Devastated Area, providing stunning views of Lassen Peak and passing Chaos Jumbles before reaching lush, wooded Manzanita Lake.

**4** Eastern. Among the delights found in the least-accessible and least-visited part of the park are Cinder Cone and Ash Butte, lava beds, and meadows, plus beautiful Snag and Juniper Lakes and the many creeks that flow out of them.

CALIFORNIA

# GETTING ORIENTED

**24**

From gurgling mud pots and hissing steam vents, to tranquil lakes and lily-covered ponds, to jagged mountain peaks bordered by flowering meadows, Lassen Volcanic National Park's varied landscapes are certain to soothe, awe, and intrigue. Whether you want to climb to the top of a dormant volcano or simply loll at the water's edge as birdsongs drift down from tall pines, you'll find unexpected pleasures in this park formed by molten lava.

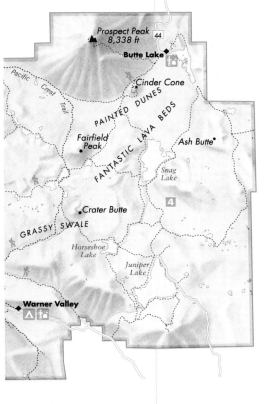

Prospect Peak
8,338 ft
44
**Butte Lake**

Pacific Crest Trail

Cinder Cone

PAINTED DUNES

FANTASTIC LAVA BEDS

Fairfield
Peak

Ash Butte

Snag
Lake

**4**

Crater Butte

GRASSY SWALE

Horseshoe
Lake

Juniper
Lake

**Warner Valley**

Fumarole

| KEY | |
|---|---|
| 🏠 | Ranger Station |
| ⛺ | Campground |
| 🌲 | Picnic Area |
| 🍴 | Restaurant |
| 🏨 | Lodge |
| 🚶 | Trailhead |
| 🚻 | Restrooms |
| ⤳ | Scenic Viewpoint |
| ⋯⋯ | Walking/Hiking Trails |
| ⋯⋯ | Bicycle Path |

# LASSEN VOLCANIC PLANNER

## When to Go

The park is open year-round, though most roads are closed from late October to mid-June due to snow. **Peak season is mid-July to mid-September, when days are sunny, warm, and mostly dry, and nights are cool.**

## Getting There & Around

From the north, take the Hwy. 44 exit off I-5 and travel east about 48 mi to Route 89. Turn right and drive 1 mi to the Northwest Entrance Station. From the south, take the second Red Bluff exit off the freeway, head east, and turn left onto Route 36. Drive approximately 45 miles, and turn left onto Route 89 just past the town of Mineral. Drive north about 8 mi to reach the park's Southwest Entrance Station.

The 30-mi main park road, known as both Lassen Park Road and Route 89, starts at the park's southwest entrance, broadly loops around three sides of Lassen Peak, and exits the park on the northwest side.

AVG. HIGH/LOW TEMPS.

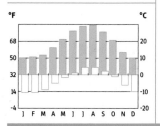

## Flora & Fauna

Because of its varying elevations, Lassen has several different ecological habitats. Below 6,500 feet you can find ponderosa pine, Jeffrey pine, sugar pine, white fir, and several species of manzanita, gooseberry, and ceanothus. Wildflowers—wild iris, spotted coralroot, pyrola, violets, and lupine—surround the hiking trails in spring and early summer.

The Manzanita Lake area has the best bird-watching opportunities, with pygmy and great horned owls, white-headed and downy woodpeckers, golden-crowned kinglets, and Steller's jays. The area is also home to rubber boas, garter snakes, brush rabbits, Sierra Nevada red foxes, black-tailed deer, coyotes, and the occasional mountain lion.

At elevations of 6,500–8,000 feet are red fir forests populated by many of the same wildlife as the lower regions, with the addition of black-backed three-toed woodpeckers, blue grouse, snowshoe hare, pine martens, and the hermit thrush.

Above 8,000 feet the environment is harsher, with bare patches of land between subalpine forests. You'll find whitebark pine, groves of mountain hemlock, and the occasional wolverine. Bird-watchers should look for gray-crowned rosy finches, rock wrens, pikas, golden eagles, falcons, and hawks. California tortoiseshell butterflies are found on the highest peaks. If you can visit in winter, you'll see one of the park's most magnificent seasonal sights: massive snowdrifts reaching 30–40 feet high.

By Christine Vovakes

A dormant plug dome, Lassen Peak is the focus of Lassen Volcanic National Park. The peak began erupting in May 1914, sending pumice, rock, and snow thundering down the mountain, and gas and hot ash billowing into the atmosphere. Lassen's most spectacular outburst was in 1915, when it blew a cloud of ash some 7 mi into the stratosphere. The resulting mudflow destroyed vegetation for miles in some directions; the evidence is still visible today, especially in Devastated Area. The volcano finally came to rest in 1921.

## Scenic Drives

**Lassen Park Road (Route 89).** The 30-mi paved road through the park weaves around Lassen Peak and passes by such important sites as Bumpass Hell, Sulphur Works, Kings Creek, Devastated Area, and Chaos Crags, before ending at Loomis Museum and Manzanita Lake.

Fodor'sChoice  **Lassen Scenic Byway.** This 185-mi scenic drive begins in Chester and loops
   ★    through the forests, volcanic peaks, geothermal springs, and lava fields of Lassen National Forest and Lassen National Park, providing for an all-day excursion into dramatic wilderness. The road is partially inaccessible in winter. From Chester, take Route 36 west to Route 89 north through the park (subject to closures due to snow), then Route 44 east to Route 36 west. ☏ *530/258–2141 Almanor Ranger District, 800/427– 7623 Caltrans.*

## What to See

The four types of volcanoes in the world—cinder cone, composite, plug dome, and shield—are all represented in the park. These, along with fumaroles, mudpots, lakes, and bubbling hot springs make for a fascinating, but dangerous, landscape. ⚠ **Stay on the trails and railed boardwalks to avoid falling into boiling water or through thin-crusted areas.**

## Historic Site

**Loomis Museum.** Here you can view artifacts from the park's 1914–1915 eruptions, including some of the original photographs taken by Benjamin Loomis, who was instrumental in the park's establishment. There also are excellent exhibits on the area's Native American heritage. In the auditorium, the museum presents two 15-minute films on the park's history. ⊠ *Lassen Park Rd. at Manzanita Lake* ☎ *530/595–4444 Ext. 5180* ⊞ *Free* ☉ *Memorial Day–late-June, Fri.–Sun. 9–5; late-June–early Sept. daily 9–5; early Sept.–late Sept., Wed.–Sun. 9–5.*

## Scenic Stops

**Boiling Springs Lake.** A worthwhile, if occasionally muddy, 1-mi hike from the Drakesbad Guest Ranch, Boiling Springs Lake is surrounded by trees, and usually shrouded in mist. Constant bubbles release sulfuric steam into the air. ⊠ *At the end of Warner Valley Rd.*

★ **Bumpass Hell.** This site's quirky name came about when a man with the last name of Bumpass was severely burned after falling into the boiling springs. A scenic, 3-mi round-trip hike brings you to the hot springs, hissing steam vents, and roiling mudpots. During the first mile of the hike there's a gradual climb of 500 feet before a steep 250-foot descent to the basin. Stay on trails and boardwalks near the thermal areas: what appears to be firm ground may be only a thin crust over scalding mud. ⊠ *Lassen Park Rd., 6 mi north of the southwest entrance station.*

**Chaos Jumbles.** More than 350 years ago, an avalanche from the Chaos Crags lava domes scattered hundreds of thousands of rocks—many of them 2–3 feet in diameter—over a couple of square miles. ⊠ *Lassen Park Rd., 2 mi north of the northwest entrance station.*

**Devastated Area.** Lassen Peak's 1915 eruptions cleared this area of all vegetation, though there are a few signs of life after all these years. An easy interpretive trail loop, less than ½-mi total, is paved and wheelchair accessible. ⊠ *Lassen Park Rd., 2½ mi north of Summit Lake.*

**Devil's Kitchen.** One of the three main geothermal areas of the park, Devil's Kitchen is a great place to view mudpots, steam vents, and boiling waters, as well as a variety of wildlife. It's much less frequented than Bumpass Hell, so you can expect more solitude during your hike; you need to drive on a partially paved road to reach the trailhead. ⊠ *Off Warner Valley Rd., at Drakesbad Guest Ranch.*

★ **Lassen Peak.** When this now-dormant plug dome volcano erupted in 1915, it spewed a mushroom cloud 7 mi into the air. A fabulous panoramic view makes the 2½ mi hike to the 10,457-foot summit worth the effort. ⊠ *Lassen Park Rd., 7 mi from the southwest entrance station.*

**Sulphur Works Thermal Area.** Proof of Lassen Peak's volatility becomes evident when you enter the park at the southwest entrance. Boardwalks go over bubbling mud and boiling springs and through sulfur-emitting steam vents. ⊠ *Lassen Park Rd., 1 mi from the southwest entrance.*

**Summit Lake.** The midpoint between the northern and southern entrances, Summit Lake is a good place to take a midday swim. A trail

## LASSEN VOLCANIC IN ONE DAY

Start your day early at the park's northwest entrance, accessible via Route 44 from Redding. Make a stop at the **Loomis Museum**, where you can view exhibits before taking the easy, 1-mi round-trip **Lily Pond Nature Trail**. Back at the museum, drive down to **Manzanita Lake**; take a mid-morning break and pick up supplies for a picnic lunch at the **Camper Store** before taking the main road toward **Lassen Peak**. As you circle the peak on its northern flank, you come upon **Devastated Area,** testimony to the damage done by the 1915 eruptions. Continue to **Summit Lake,** where you can picnic and swim, or to **Kings Creek,** an area of lush meadows and where you can hike to **Kings Creek Falls.** Allow at least 2 hours to make the 3-mi hike, which ends in a 700-foot descent to the falls. If time permits, continue to the **Sulphur Works** to walk out over the boiling springs.

24

leads around the lakeshore, and several other trails diverge toward a cluster of smaller lakes in the more remote eastern section of the park. ⊠ *Lassen Park Rd., 17½ mi from the southwest entrance station.*

### Visitor Centers

A new visitor center is scheduled to open near the southwest entrance in late 2008. Until then, obtain information from Loomis Museum at the north entrance and Park Headquarters in Mineral, south of the park.

**Park Headquarters Information Station.** Pick up maps, books, permits, and trail guides, and inquire about children's and ranger-led activities. There's a restroom and a first-aid station. ⊠ *38050 Rte. 36 E, 9 mi south of the southwest entrance station, Mineral* ☏ *530/595–4444* ☉ *Early Sept.–late June, weekdays 8–4:30; late June–early Sept., daily 8–4:30.*

## Sports & the Outdoors

Lassen is a rugged adventurer's paradise, but be prepared for sudden changes in the weather: in summer, hot temperatures can make high-altitude hikers woozy, and fierce thunderstorms drench the mountains; in winter, blizzard conditions can develop quickly.

### Bicycling

Biking is allowed on park roads, but not park trails. Cyclists under 18 must wear a helmet. Skating, skateboarding, and rollerblading are prohibited. ⇨ Outfitters & Expeditions box for tours and equipment.

### Fishing

The best place to fish is in Manzanita Lake—here it's catch and release only—or at Hat Creek. Fishing is also allowed at Butte Lake, 35 mi northwest of Susanville. A California freshwater fishing license is required to fish within the park. Pick up an application at most sporting-goods stores (call 530/225–2300 for locations), or download it from the California Department of Fish and Game's Web site ( ⊕ www.dfg.ca.gov). ⇨ Outfitters & Expeditions box for infomation on tours and equipment.

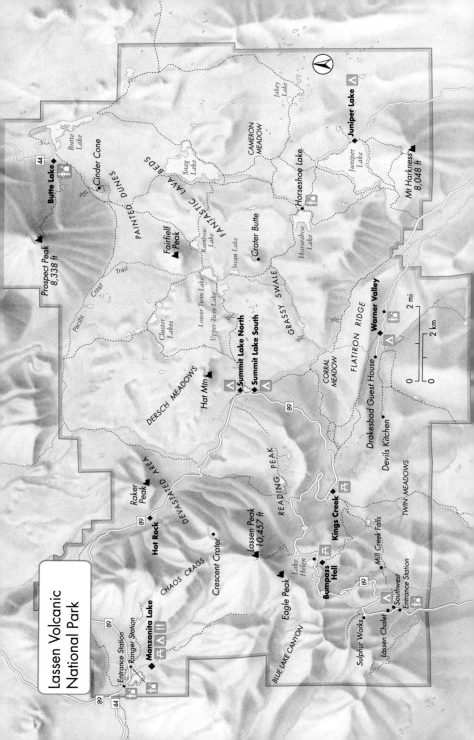

## Lassen Volcanic National Park

Butte Lake ◆
Cinder Cone ●

Prospect Peak
8,338 ft ▲

PAINTED DUNES

FANTASTIC LAVA BEDS

Fairfielf Peak ▲

Butte Lake

Snag Lake

Rainbow Lake

Crater Butte ●

Swan Lake

Jakey Lake

CAMERON MEADOW

Juniper Lake ⛺

Horseshoe Lake ●

Horseshoe Lake

Juniper Lake

Mt Harkness
8,048 ft ▲

GRASSY SWALE

Lower Twin Lake

Upper Twin Lake

Pacific    Crest    Trail

Cluster Lakes

Summit Lake North ⛺
Summit Lake South ⛺

Hat Mtn ▲

DERSCH MEADOWS

CORRAL MEADOW

FLATIRON RIDGE

Warner Valley ⛺

Drakesbad Guest House

Devils Kitchen

89

Raker Peak ▲

Hot Rock ◆

DEVASTATED AREA

CHAOS CRAGS

Crescent Crater ●

Lassen Peak
10,457 ft ▲

READING PEAK

Kings Creek ⛺

Lake Helen

Bumpass Hell ◆

Mill Creek Falls

TWIN MEADOWS

Eagle Peak ▲

89

Sulphur Works

Lassen Chalet

Southwest Entrance Station

Entrance Station

Ranger Station

Manzanita Lake ◆

89

89    44

BLUE LAKE CANYON

N

2 mi
2 km

44 ◆ Butte Lake

## Hiking

There are 150 mi of trails within the park, 17 mi of which are part of the Pacific Crest Trail. The trails vary greatly, some winding through coniferous forest, and others across alpine tundra or along waterways. ⇨ Outfitters & Expeditions box for organized hiking tours and gear.

EASY **Lily Pond Nature Trail.** This 1-mi jaunt loops past a small lake and through a wooded area, ending at a pond filled with yellow water lilies in summer. ⊠ *Loomis Museum, Lassen Park Rd., near northwest entrance.*

MODERATE
Fodor'sChoice
★

**Bumpass Hell Trail.** Boiling springs, steam vents, and mudpots highlight this 3³⁄₁₀-mi round-trip hike. Expect the loop to take about three hours. ⊠ *Lassen Park Rd., 6 mi from the southwest entrance station.*

**Crumbaugh Lake Hike.** A 3-mi round-trip hike through meadows and forests to Cold Boiling and Crumbaugh lakes, this excursion is an excellent way to view spring wildflowers. ⊠ *Kings Creek picnic area, Lassen Park Rd., 13 mi north of the southwest entrance station.*

**Kings Creek Falls Hike.** This is a good hike for nature photographers, as it takes you through forests dotted with wildflowers. A steep 700-foot descent leads to the falls. The 3-mi round-trip trail takes at least 2 hours. ⊠ *Lassen Park Rd., 12 mi from the southwest entrance station.*

**Mill Creek Falls.** Start at the Southwest Campground for a 2½-hour (4⁵⁄₁₀-mi) hike through forests and wildflowers to a watershed where waters from two thermal areas join to create the park's highest waterfall. ⊠ *Southwest Campground, near the southwest entrance station.*

DIFFICULT **Chaos Crags Hike.** This 3⁹⁄₁₀-mi round-trip hike includes a 700-foot climb to the base of the crags—protruding tubes of lava. ⊠ *Trailhead ½ mi from Loomis Museum on the road to Manzanita Lake Campground.*

**Cinder Cone Trail.** Though a little out of the way, this is one of Lassen's most fascinating trails. It's for more experienced hikers, since the 4-mi round-trip hike to the cone summit includes a steep 800-foot climb over ground that's slippery in parts with loose cinders. Pick up the trail brochure for 50¢ at Loomis Museum or the trailhead. ⊠ *West end of Butte Lake Campground, on Rte. 44, 35 mi northwest of Susanville.*

**Lassen Peak Hike.** This trail winds 2½ mi to the mountaintop. It's a tough climb—2,000 feet uphill on a steady, steep grade—but the reward is a spectacular view. At the peak you can see into the rim and view the entire park (and much of the California's far north). Bring sunscreen, water, and a jacket since it's often windy and much cooler at the summit. ⊠ *Lassen Park Rd., 7 mi north of the southwest entrance station.*

## Snowshoeing

You can try snowshoeing anywhere in the park. The gentlest places are in the northern district, while more challenging terrain is in the south. ⇨ Outfitters & Expeditions box for information on renting gear.

# Educational Offerings

If you're wondering why fumaroles fume, how lava tubes are formed, or which critter left those tracks beside the creek, check out the array

## OUTFITTERS & EXPEDITIONS

### BICYCLING

**Bikes, Etc.** A one-day rental is $20. ⌧ *2400 Athens Ave., Redding* ☏ *530/246-2453* ◷ *Mon.-Sat. 9:30-6.*

**Bodfish Bicycles & Quiet Mountain Sports.** Rent 24-gear dirt bikes at $8 an hour, with a two-hour minimum, or pay $28 a day. ⌧ *149 Main, Chester* ☏ *530/258-2338* ◷ *Tues.-Sat. 10-5.*

**Redding Sports, Ltd.** Bike rentals run $35 per day. ⌧ *950 Hilltop Dr., Redding* ☏ *530/221-7333* ◷ *Mon.-Sat. 9-7, Sun. 10-6.*

### FISHING

**Ayoobs Hardware.** Stop by for tackle, bait, and local yore. ⌧ *201 Main St., Chester* ☏ *530/258-2611* ◷ *Mon.-Sat. 7-5, Sun. 7-1.*

**The Fishin' Hole.** This bait-and-tackle shop a few miles from Shasta Lake also sells fishing licenses. Ask here about conditions. ⌧ *3844 Shasta Dam Blvd., Shasta Lake City* ☏ *530/275-4123* ◷ *Daily 6-6.*

**The Fly Shop.** Famous among fly fishers, this shop carries tackle and equipment and offers guide service. ⌧ *4140 Churn Creek Rd., Redding* ☏ *530/222-3555 or 800/669-3474* ◷ *Daily 7:30-6.*

**The Sports Nut.** Buy fishing and camping gear here. ⌧ *208 Main St., Chester* ☏ *530/258-3327* ◷ *May-Dec., Mon.-Sat. 8-5 and Sun. 8-2.*

### HIKING

**Redding Sports, Ltd.** Check here for hiking boots, poles, and other outdoor supplies. ⌧ *950 Hilltop Dr., Redding* ☏ *530/221-7333* ◷ *Mon.-Sat. 9-7, Sun. 10-6.*

### HORSEBACK RIDING

**Drakesbad Guest Ranch.** This in-park property offers guided rides to nonguests who make reservations in advance. Take a 45-minute trip to Boiling Springs, a half-day ride to Willow Lake, or an all-day, five-lake loop tour. ⌧ *End of Warner Valley Rd.* ☏ *530/529-1512 Ext. 120* ☖ *$23-$175* ◷ *Mid-June-mid-Oct.*

### SKIING & SNOWSHOEING

**Bikes, Etc.** Snowshoes are $15 per pair per day. ⌧ *2400 Athens Ave., Redding* ☏ *530/246-2453* ◷ *Mon.-Sat. 9:30-6.*

**Bodfish Bicycles & Quiet Mountain Sports.** Snowshoes, skis, boots, and poles are $16 per day. ⌧ *149 Main, Chester* ☏ *530/258-2338* ◷ *Tues.-Sat. 10-5.*

**Lassen Mineral Lodge.** Snowshoes are $12 a day. ⌧ *Rte. 36, Mineral* ☏ *530/595-4422.*

**Redding Sports, Ltd.** Snowshoes are $15 per pair per day; skis, boots, and poles are $20 per day. ⌧ *950 Hilltop Dr., Redding* ☏ *530/221-7333* ◷ *Mon.-Sat. 9-7, Sun. 10-6.*

**Snowshoe Walks.** On Saturdays from early January through early April, park rangers lead 1-2 mi snowshoe hikes exploring the park's geology and winter ecology. The hikes require moderate exertion at an elevation of 7,000 feet; children under 8 are not allowed. You can rent the shoes for $1 per person. Walks are first-come, first-served; meet by the snowshoe sign outside the Lassen Chalet. ⌧ *Lassen Park Rd. near the southwest entrance station* ☏ *530/595-4444 Ext. 5133 or 5132* ☖ *Free* ◷ *Early Jan.-early Apr., Sat. at 1:30.*

of ranger-led programs. Most groups meet outside Loomis Museum or near Manzanita Lake. Park programs are free. To learn what's available, check park bulletin boards or call 530/595–4444.

### Ranger Programs

**A GOOD READ**

**Lassen Volcanic National Park & Vicinity**, by Jeffrey P. Schaffer, is one of the most comprehensive books about the park.

**Bear Necessities.** Learn how to help keep black bears wild. ⊠ *Outside Loomis Museum* ⊗ *Wed. at 1:30.*

**Blown from a Volcano.** Explore the park's history through its rocks. ⊠ *Meet outside Loomis Museum* ⊗ *Mon. at 10:30.*

**Early Birds.** Take a morning stroll and learn about the birds of Manzanita Lake. ⊠ *Meet outside the Manzanita Lake Camp Store* ⊗ *Sat. at 8.*

**Kids Programs.** Junior Rangers, for ages 7–12, meet for two hours three times a week with rangers. Junior Firefighters gather on Thursday mornings to learn about the role wildfires have in shaping our national parks. Youngsters unable to attend the sessions can earn badges by completing certain requirements. Kids under 7 can join the Chipmunk Club and get a sticker after filling out a nature sheet. ⊠ *Outside the Loomis Museum and Manzanita Lake Amphitheater.*

**Wildlife Tracks and Trails.** Explore the lifestyles of the park's wildlife by the tracks they leave and the trails they make. ⊠ *Meet outside the Loomis Museum at the park's north entrance* ⊗ *Thurs. at 2.*

**24**

# WHAT'S NEARBY

## Nearby Towns

The tiny logging town of **Chester,** 17 mi from the park on Route 36, serves as the commercial center for the entire Lake Almanor area. It's one of the best kicking-off points for the park, but the accommodations and services are limited. **Susanville,** 35 mi east of Chester, is a high-desert town named after a pioneer's daughter. It's the area's main commercial center. Named for its vibrant cliffs, **Red Bluff** maintains a mix of Old West toughness and late 1800s gentility: restored Victorians line the streets west of Main Street, while the downtown looks like a stage set for a spaghetti Western. This small working-class city is a good place to stock up before heading into the park; it's 50 mi from Lassen's south entrance via Route 36. With a population of 90,000, **Redding** is the largest city in the extreme northern portion of California. It's 32 mi north of Red Bluff via Interstate 5 and 50 mi west of the park's north entrance via Route 44. Both Red Bluff and Redding offer the most accommodations and services in the area; each is an hour's drive from the park.

## Nearby Attractions

Fodor'sChoice **Lake Shasta Caverns.** Get an eyeful of geological formations on a one-★ hour tour that begins with a catamaran ride across Lake Shasta. It's about 21 mi from Redding. ⊠ *Shasta Caverns Rd., 2 mi off I–5* ☎ *530/238–2341 or 800/795–2283* ⊕ *www.lakeshastacaverns. com* ☞ *$20* ☉ *June–Aug., tours on the half hour, daily 9–4; Apr., May, and Sept., tours on the hour, daily 9–3; Oct.–Mar., tours at 10, noon, and 2.*

☊ **Turtle Bay Exploration Park.** Here

Fodor'sChoice you find walking trails, an arbore-

★ tum, and lots of interactive exhibits for kids, including a gold-panning area and Butterfly House. The main draw is the stunning **Sundial Bridge**, which links the Sacramento River Trail and the park's arboretum and gardens. Access to the bridge and arboretum is free, but there's a fee for the museum and gardens. ⊠ *800 Auditorium Dr., Redding* ☎ *530/243–8850* ⊕ *www.turtlebay.org* ☞ *$12; $6 for the McConnell Garden only* ☉ *Mar.–Oct., daily 9–5; Nov.–Feb., Wed.–Mon. 9–5.*

## Area Activities

Whether you want to camp in national forests, wade in creeks, watch dragonflies dip over meadows thick with wildflowers, or star gaze while listening to a chorus of crickets, the great outdoors is the draw here. When you're ready to merge with civilization, the towns near Lassen Volcanic offer shopping, movies, dining and the ever-popular activity, people watching.

### Sports & the Outdoors

BOATING & Twenty-one types of fish, including rainbow trout and salmon, inhabit
FISHING Lake Shasta. The lake area also has the state's largest nesting popula-
★ tion of bald eagles. Rent boats, Jet Skis, and windsurfing boards at marinas along the 370-mi shoreline. The Sacramento River and its numerous creeks and tributaries also attract fishing enthusiasts from across the country.

# WHERE TO STAY & EAT

### About the Restaurants

The best dining in the park might be the fresh catch any anglers in your group snag. Otherwise, you'll find simple fare at Peak Necessities Café and at the Manzanita Camper Store. Those hiking or camping near Drakesbad Guest Ranch can call ahead and reserve a place at their table (☎ 530/529–1512). A variety of dining choices, ranging from grilled steaks to ethnic specialties, can be had in Red Bluff, Redding, and Chester.

### About the Hotels

Drakesbad Guest Ranch is the only lodging available inside Lassen. It's rustic—no electricity, just old-fashioned kerosene lamps—and expensive, but reservations are often fully booked a year or more in advance. In towns surrounding the park there's everything from elegant B&Bs to chain hotels to simple, inexpensive rooms.

## FAMILY PICKS

**Butterfly House** (⊠ 800 Auditorium Dr. ☎ 530/243-8850 ⊕ www.turtlebay.org 🎫 $12; $6 for the McConnell Garden only ☉ Mar.–Oct., daily; Nov.–Feb., Wed.–Mon., flutters from late spring to early fall.

**Lariat Bowl** (⊠ 365 S. Main St., Red Bluff ☎ 530/527-2720 ☉ Weekdays noon–10, weekends

noon–1 AM) in Red Bluff has mini-golf. An added bonus is the ice-cream shop a couple of doors north.

**Riverside Plaza Cinemas,** ( ⊠ 400 S. Main, Red Bluff ☎ 530/529-5491.) and **Cinemark Movies 10,** (⊠ 980 Old Alturas Rd., Redding ☎ 530/223-7750) are the places to go for air-conditioned entertainment.

### About the Campgrounds

Sites at Lassen's eight campgrounds have wide appeal, from large groups singing around the campfire to solitary hikers seeking a quiet place under the stars. You can drive a vehicle to all campgrounds except the Southwest Walk-In; no trailers or RVs are allowed at Juniper Lake and Warner Valley campgrounds. Campfires are restricted to fire rings. Lassen has black bears, so be sure to secure your food and garbage properly by using the bear boxes provided at the park's campsites. To reserve campsites call ☎ 877/444–6777 or go to ⊕ www.reserveusa.com. To hear recorded camping information, call ☎ 530/335–7029.

## Where to Eat

### In the Park

✕ **Manzanita Lake Camper Store.** You can pick up simple prepared food items and refreshments here. ⊠ *Lassen Park Rd., near Manzanita Lake* ☎ *530/335–7557 or 530/529–1512* ☉ *Closed early Oct.–late May.*

✕ **Peak Necessities Café & Gifts.** Purchase soft drinks, coffee, hot cocoa, wine, and beer, plus sandwiches, hot dogs, and chili. ⊠ *Lassen Park Rd., 8 mi from the southwest entrance at Lassen Peak trailhead* ☎ *530/595–4444 or 530/529–1512* ▭ *MC, V* ☉ *Closed Labor Day–early June.*

PICNIC AREAS **Kings Creek.** Picnic tables are beside a creek in a shady area. There are no amenities except vault toilets. ⊠ *Off Lassen Park Rd., 11⁸⁄₁₀ mi from the southwest entrance station.*

**Lake Helen.** This site, with picnic tables and vault toilets, has views of several peaks, including Lassen Peak. ⊠ *Lassen Park Rd., 6 mi north of southwest entrance station near the Bumpass Hell trailhead.*

**Manzanita Lake.** In addition to the Camper Store, you'll find picnic tables and potable water at Manzanita Lake; restrooms are nearby. ⊠ *Lassen Park Rd., near the northwest entrance ranger station.*

### Outside the Park

$–$$$$ ✕ **Volcano Grill.** Steaks, chops, and prawns sizzling over lava rock are a fitting end to a day of hiking in Lassen. Colorful waterfall and forest murals create a relaxed atmosphere for a dinner menu that's served all day. There's also a lunch menu and lunch buffet available. Wine and microbrews are served from a mahogany bar more than 130 years old. ⊠ *384 Main St., Chester* ☎ *530/258–1000. $8–$45* ⊟ *AE, D, MC, V.*

¢–$$ ✕ **Buz's Crab.** This casual restaurant in central Redding shares space with a bustling seafood market where locals snap up ocean-fresh Dungeness crab in season. The fish-and-chips is a favorite, as are seafood combos. ⊠ *2159 East St., Redding* ☎ *530/243–2120. $7–$14* ⊟ *MC, V.*

¢–$$ ✕ **Josefina's.** Popular with the locals, this restaurant with Aztec accents makes its own salsas and tamales. The menu features traditional Mexican fare of chiles rellenos (mild, batter-fried chili peppers stuffed with cheese or a cheese-meat mixture), enchiladas, tacos, and fajitas. ⊠ *1960 Main St., Susanville* ☎ *530/257–9262. $7–$20* ⊟ *MC, V.*

¢–$$ ✕ **Kopper Kettle Cafe.** Locals return again and again to this tidy restaurant that serves savory home-cooked lunch and dinner, and breakfast whenever you've got a hankering for eggs with biscuits and gravy. ⊠ *243 Main St., Chester* ☎ *530/258–2698. $6–$15* ⊟ *MC, V.*

★ ¢ ✕ **Grand Cafe.** Walking into this downtown coffee shop, owned and operated by the same family since the 1920s, is like stepping back in time. At the old-fashioned counter, the swiveling seats have hat clips on the back; the booths have their own nickel jukeboxes. Wooden refrigerators are still used here, and if the homemade chili and fruit cobblers are any indication, they work just fine. ⊠ *730 Main St., Susanville* ☎ *530/ 257–4713. $3–$7* ⊟ *No credit cards* ⊘ *Closed Sat.–Mon.; no dinner.*

## Where to Stay

### In the Park

$$$$ ✕🏠 **Drakesbad Guest Ranch.** Near Lassen's southern border, this ranch is accessible only by a partially paved road leading out of Chester. From propane furnaces to the use of kerosene lamps in lieu of electricity, everything about this more than 100-year-old property is rustic. Meals, casual during the day and elegant in the evening, are included in the room rate. The waiting list for room reservations can be up to two years long. ⊠ *Chester–Warner Valley Rd., north from Route 36* ☍ *booking office: 2150 N. Main St., Suite 5, Red Bluff 96080* ☎ *530/529–1512* 🖨 *530/ 529–4511* ⊕ *www.drakesbad.com* ⇲ *19 rooms* ♨ *Pool. $294–$358* ⊟ *D, MC, V* ⊘ *Closed early Oct.–early June* ❖◍ *FAP.*

CAMPGROUNDS & ⚠ **Manzanita Lake.** The largest of Lassen's campgrounds accommo-
RV PARKS dates RVs up to 35 feet. Many ranger programs begin here, and a trail
$$ nearby leads to a crater that now holds Crags Lake. Summer reserva-
Fodor'sChoice tions for group sites can be made up to seven months in advance. There
★ is no running water from late September until snow closes the grounds. ⊠ *Off Lassen Park Rd., 2 mi east of junction of Route 44 and 89* ☎ *530/ 595–4444* ⇲ *148 tent/RV sites, no hookups, 31 tent sites* ♨ *Flush toilets, dump station, drinking water, showers, fire pits, picnic tables. $18* ⊟ *D, MC, V* ⊘ *Mid-May–late Sept., depending on snowfall.*

$$ ⚠ **Summit Lake North.** This completely forested campground has easy access to backcountry trails. You'll likely observe deer grazing. RVs up to 30 feet long can park here. ⊠ *Lassen Park Rd., 12 mi south of Manzanita Lake and 17½ mi north of southwest entrance* ☎ *877/444–6777*

↪ *46 tent/RV sites* ⌂ *Flush toilets, drinking water, bear boxes, fire pits, picnic tables, swimming (lake). $18* ☼ *Late June–early Sept.*

**$** ⚠ **Juniper Lake.** On the east shore of the park's largest lake, campsites are close to the water in a wooded area. To reach the campgrounds, you have to take a rough dirt road that leads 13 mi north of Chester and enters at the park's southeast corner. No trailers or RVs are allowed, and there is no potable water. ⊠ *Chester Juniper Lake Rd, 13 mi north of Rte. 36* ☎ *877/444–6777* ↪ *18 tent sites* ⌂ *Pit toilets, bear boxes, fire pits, picnic tables, swimming (lake). $10* ☼ *Late June–late Sept.*

**$** ⚠ **Southwest Walk-In.** This relatively small campground lies within a red fir forest and has views of Brokeoff Peak. From September to June no drinking water is available. RVs can park overnight in the southwest entrance parking area for $10; registser at the campground. Vehicles must stay in the parking area, a ¼-mi walk from the campsites. ⊠ *Near the southwest entrance* ↪ *21 tent sites* ⌂ *Flush and pit toilets, drinking water (summer), bear boxes, fire grates, picnic tables. $14.*

**$** ⚠ **Summit Lake South.** Less crowded than its neighbor to the north, this campground has wet meadows where wildflowers grow in the spring. RVs up to 30 feet long can park here. ⊠ *Lassen Park Rd., 12 mi south of Manzanita Lake and 17½ mi north of southwest entrance* ☎ *877/444–6777* ↪ *48 tent/RV sites* ⌂ *Pit toilets, drinking water, bear boxes, fire pits, picnic tables, swimming (lake). $16* ☼ *Late June–late Sept.*

**$** ⚠ **Warner Valley.** Accessible via a partially paved road 17 mi north of Chester, this quiet, woodsy campground is near Boiling Springs Lake. Trailers and RVs aren't allowed. ⊠ *Warner Valley Rd., 1 mi west of ranger station* ↪ *18 tent sites* ⌂ *Pit toilets, drinking water, bear boxes, fire grates, picnic tables, swimming (river). $14* ☼ *Early June–early Oct.*

## Outside the Park

**$–$$$** 🏨 **Bidwell House.** Chairs and swings on the front porch of this 1901 ranch
Fodor'sChoice house are inviting, and there are puzzles and games aplenty in the sun-
★ room. Some guest rooms have wood-burning stoves, claw-foot or Jacuzzi tubs, hardwood floors, and antiques. A separate cottage with kitchen sleeps six. The omelets and blueberry-walnut pancakes are the stars of the inn's full breakfast. ⊠ *1 Main St., Chester 96020* ☎ *530/258–3338* ⊕ *www.bidwellhouse.com* ⇨ *14 rooms, 2 with shared bath* ⌂ *No a/c, no phone (some), no-smoking rooms. $80–$170* ⊟ *MC, V* ⦿ *BP.*

**$** 🏨 **Lassen Mineral Lodge.** Rooms at this small motel, 9 mi from the park are reserved well in advance. A restaurant serves breakfast, lunch, and dinner from late May through October; the lodge is open weekends the rest of the year. A ski shop rents cross-country skis and snowshoes. There's also a general store. ⊠ *Route 36 E, Mineral 96063* ☎ *530/595–4422* ⊕ *www.minerallodge.com* ⇨ *20 rooms* ⌂ *Restaurant, bar, no a/c, no phone, no TV. $69–$80* ⊟ *AE, D, MC, V* ☼ *Year-round.*

**$** 🏨 **High Country Inn.** Rooms are spacious in this two-story, colonial-style motel on the east edge of town. Complimentary continental breakfast is provided; more extensive dining is available next door at the 24-hour Apple Peddler. ⊠ *3015 Riverside Dr., Susanville 96130* ☎ *530/257–3450* 🖷 *530/257–2460* ⊕ *www.high-country-inn.com/* ⇨ *66 rooms* ⌂ *Refrigerator, dial-up, Wi-Fi, gym, pool; no-smoking rooms. $80–$99* ⊟ *AE, D, DC, MC, V* ⦿ *CP.*

**24**

# LASSEN VOLCANIC ESSENTIALS

ACCESSIBILITY Park headquarters and the Loomis Museum are both fully accessible to those with limited mobility. The Devastated Area interpretive trail is accessible, as are most ranger programs.

ADMISSION FEES The $10 fee covers seven days. Those entering by bus, bicycle, horse, motorcycle, or on foot pay $4. U.S. residents over the age of 62 pay $10 for a lifetime pass, and permanently disabled U.S. residents are admitted free. There's also a $25 annual pass that covers both Lassen Volcanic and Whiskeytown NRA.

ADMISSION HOURS The park is open 24/7, year-round. It is in the Pacific time zone.

ATMS/BANKS

🏧 **Bank of America** ✉ 1300 Hilltop Dr. (near the junction of I-5, Rte. 299, and Rte. 44), Chester ☎ 530/246-3992 or ✉ 955 Main St., Red Bluff ☎ 800/346-7693. **Plumas Bank** ✉ 255 Main St., Chester ☎ 530/258-4161.

AUTOMOBILE SERVICE STATIONS

**Main Street Chevron** ✉ 1055 S. Main St., Red Bluff ☎ 530/527-4243. **Valero** ✉ 615 Antelope Blvd., Red Bluff ☎ 530/527-5436.

EMERGENCIES In case of a fire or medical emergency, dial 911. To reach the Park Protection Rangers, contact the park headquarters ☎ 530/595-4444 Ext. 5151 or the Loomis Ranger Station ☎ 530/595-4444 Ext. 5187.

LOST AND FOUND The main lost-and-found areas are at the Loomis Museum and park headquarters. Also try ranger stations.

PERMITS Pick up a free wilderness permit for backcountry camping; permits at the Loomis Museum, north and south entrance stations, or park's headquarters.

POST OFFICES

🏤 **Red Bluff Post Office** ✉ 447 Walnut St., Red Bluff 96080 ☎ 530/527-1455. **Redding Downtown Post Office** ✉ 1647 Yuba St., Redding 96001 ☎ 530/246-2571.

PUBLIC TELEPHONES There are public telephones at the Manzanita Camper Store and the Loomis Plaza (between ranger station and the museum). Cell phones don't work in many parts of the park.

RELIGIOUS SERVICES There are no religious services in the park.

RESTROOMS There are public restrooms at the Manzanita Camper Store and the Loomis Plaza (between ranger station and the museum). There are flush toilets at Summit Lake North campground and Manzanita Lake campground. There are vault toilets at all picnic areas and at various locations throughout the park.

SHOPS & GROCERS

🏪 **Manzanita Lake Camper Store** you can pick up food (including beer and wine), souvenirs, camping supplies, wood, and gasoline here. There are also showers and a Laundromat. ✉ Lassen Park Rd., near Manzanita Lake ☎ 530/335-7557 or 530/529-1512 ⊘ Closed early Oct-late May. In season **Peak Necessities** sells food and camping supplies as well as gifts, apparel, espresso, beer, and wine. ✉ Lassen Park Rd., near the southwest entrance station ☎ 530/529-1512 ⊘ Closed early-Oct.-mid-June.

**NEARBY TOWN INFORMATION**

🏢 **Chester & Lake Almanor Chamber of Commerce** ✉ 529 Main St., Box 1198, Chester 96020 ☎ 800/350-4838 or 530/258-2426 ⊕ www.chester-lakealmanor.com. **Lassen County Chamber of Commerce** ✉ 84 N. Lassen St., Box 338, Susanville 96130 ☎ 530/257-4323 ⊕ www.lassencountychamber.org. **Red Bluff Chamber of Commerce** ✉ 100 Main St., Box 850, Red Bluff 96080 ☎ 800/655-6225 or 530/527-6220 ⊕ www.redbluffchamberofcommerce.com. **Redding Convention and Visitors Bureau** ✉ 777 Auditorium Dr., Redding 96001 ☎ 800/874-7562 or 530/225-4100 ⊕ www.visitredding.org.

**VISITOR INFORMATION**

🏢 **Lassen Volcanic National Park** ✉ P.O. Box 100, Mineral, CA 96063-0100 ☎ 530/595-4444.

# Mesa Verde National Park

Mano (hand shaped grinding stone) with metate (slab sandstone base) next to cooking pot and bowl, Mesa Verde National Park

**WORD OF MOUTH**

"Mesa Verde National Park is America's first cultural park. . . .it celebrates a culture that slipped silently into history centuries earlier, and it is separated from today by an abyss of time."

–Author Duane A. Smith

# WELCOME TO MESA VERDE

## TOP REASONS TO GO

★ **Ancestral Mansions:** Explore Cliff Palace and the Long House, each with 150 rooms. They're among the 600 cliff dwellings tucked into Mesa Verde.

★ **Pueblo Places:** View kivas, petroglyphs, wall paintings, and more. More than 4,000 archaeological sites and 3 million objects of the ancestral Puebloans have been unearthed at Mesa Verde.

★ **Geological Goodies:** Get low and look close; the desert landscape has a story to tell. Ripple marks suggest the area was once covered with water, turtle-back weathering notes the effects of erosion, and flower-patterned solution rills reveal the power of acidic rain on the sandstone's structure.

★ **Bright Nights:** Gaze into the sky's starry depths. With no major cities nearby to reflect light at night, the Four Corners area is an ideal place to be an amateur astronomer.

**1** **Morefield Campground.** Near the entrance, this large campground is a natural center of operations for any visitor to Mesa Verde. It includes a village area with a gas station and grocery store. The park's best-known sites are farther in, but there are a few hiking trails close-by.

**2** **Far View Visitor Center.** Almost an hour's drive from Mesa Verde's entrance, the main visitor center is near the park's only overnight lodge (seasonal), and from where you can access 12-mi Wetherill Mesa Road (seasonal) to the east and 12-mi Mesa Top Loop Road to the south.

← TO CORTEZ

*Montezuma Valley Overlook*

*Park Point Overlook*

*Geologic Overlook*

NORTH RIM

**Far View Lodge**

*Far View Terrace*

**Visitor Center**

SODA CANYON

**Far View Sites**

LONG CANYON

WEST FORK

EAST FORK

*Mesa Top Road*

CHAPIN MESA

WETHERILL MESA

NAVAJO CANYON

*Cedar Tree Tower*

*Wetherill Mesa Orientation*

**Step House**

*Tram Loop Rd.*

**Chapin Mesa Museum**

*Nordenskiold Site #16*

**Badger House Community**

**Long House**

**Spruce Tree House**

**Kodak House**

*Petroglyph Point Trail*

**3**

*Cliff Palace Loop*

*Mesa Top Loop*

**Cliff Palace**

*Square Tower House*

**Sun Temple**

**Balcony House**

*Pithouses & Early Pueblo Villages*

*Mesa Top Sites*

*Hemenway House*

**3** Chapin Mesa. In many ways the heart of Mesa Verde, this southern swath is where the famous 150-room Cliff House dwelling is located.

Hopi eagle dancers at Spruce Tree House.

**4** Wetherill Mesa. This western area of the park includes sites accessible, if you so choose, by tram: the Long House, Kodak House, and Badger House Community. Also here is Step House, reached by a steep staircase.

COLORADO

160

Park Entrance Station
TO MANCOS →

**1**

Mancos Valley Overlook

Morefield Campground

Prater Ridge Trail

Tunnel

EAST RIM

PRATER CANYON

MOREFIELD CANYON

WATERS CANYON

WHITES CANYON

BIG MESA

MANCOS CANYON

EAST RIM

0 ____ 2 mi
0 ____ 2 km

Petroglyphs

## GETTING ORIENTED

Perhaps no area offers as much evidence into the ancestral Pueblo's existence as Mesa Verde National Park does. Several thousand archaeological sites have been found, and research is ongoing to discover more. The carved-out homes and assorted artifacts, displayed at the park's Chapin Mesa Archeological Museum, belonged to ancestors of today's Hopi, Zuni, and Pueblo tribes, among others. Due to the sensitive nature of these remants, hiking in the park is restricted to designated trails, and certain cliff dwellings may only be accessed under accompaniment of a ranger during the peak summer season.

| KEY | |
|---|---|
| 🏛 | Ranger Station |
| ▲ | Campground |
| 🌲 | Picnic Area |
| 🍴 | Restaurant |
| 🏨 | Lodge |
| 🚶 | Trailhead |
| 🚻 | Restrooms |
| ⛰ | Scenic Viewpoint |
| ····· | Walking/Hiking Trails |
| ······ | Bicycle Path |

# MESA VERDE PLANNER

## When to Go

The best times to visit the park are late May, early June, and most of September, when the weather is fine but the summer crowds have thinned. **Mid-June through August are Mesa Verde's most crowded months.** In July and August, lines at the museum and visitor center may last half an hour. Afternoon thunder showers are common in July and August.

The mesa gets as many as 100 inches of snow in winter. Snow may fall as late as May and as early as October, but there's rarely enough to hamper travel. In winter, the Wetherill Mesa Road and Far View Lodge are closed, but the sight of the sandstone dwellings sheltered from the snow in their cliff coves is spectacular.

## Flora & Fauna

Since 2000, wildfires have claimed thousands of Mesa Verde's acres. Visitors will see the scars for a long time, as it can take 300 years for an evergreen woodland to restore itself. In spring and summer, however, you'll still see brightly colored blossoms, like the yellow Perky Sue, sage, yucca, and mountain mahogany. Sand-loving blue lupines are seen along the roadways in the higher elevations, and bright-red Indian paintbrushes are scattered throughout the rocky cliffs.

Mule deer are the park's most frequently sighted larger animals. About 200 species of birds, including red-tailed hawks and golden eagles, live in Mesa Verde, as does the poisonous prairie rattler (give it plenty of space and it'll likely just mosey along on its way). The animals seek shade in trees and under brush, so the best time to spot them is in the early morning or just before dusk.

## Getting There & Around

The park is located off U.S. 160, between Cortez and Durango in what's known as the Four Corners. The nearest bus station and airport is 35 mi away in Durango, Colorado, a small city worth exploring.

Most of the scenic drives at Mesa Verde involve steep grades and hairpin turns, particularly on Wetherill Mesa. Vehicles over 8,000 pounds or 25 feet are prohibited on this road. Towed vehicles are prohibited past Morefield Campground. Check the condition of your vehicle's brakes before driving the road to Wetherill Mesa. For the latest road information, tune your radio to Traveler's Information at 1610 AM, or call the ranger station at ☎ 970/529–4461. Off-road vehicles are prohibited in the park.

AVG. HIGH/LOW TEMPS.

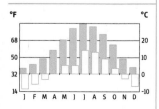

By John
Blodgett

Unlike most national parks of the West, Mesa Verde earned its status from its rich cultural history rather than its geological treasures. President Theodore Roosevelt established it in 1906 as the first national park to "preserve the works of man." The ancestral Puebloan people, who lived in the region from roughly 600 to 1300, left behind more than 4,000 archaeological sites spread out over 80 square mi. Their ancient dwellings, set high into the sandstone cliffs, are the heart of the park.

Mesa Verde, "Green Table" in Spanish, is much more than an archaeologist's dreamland, however. It's one of those windswept places where man's footprints and nature's paintbrush—some would say chisel—meet. Rising dramatically from the San Juan Basin, the jutting cliffs are cut by a series of complex canyons and covered with green, from pines in the higher elevations down to sage and other mountain brush on the desert floor. From the tops of the smaller mesas, you can look across to the cliff dwellings in the rock faces of other mesas. Dwarfed by the towering cliffs, the sand-color dwellings look almost like a natural occurrence in the midst of the desert's harsh beauty.

## Scenic Drives

**Mesa Top Loop Road.** This 12-mi drive skirts the rim of Chapin Mesa, reaching several of Mesa Verde's most important archaeological sites. Two of the park's most impressive viewpoints are also on this road, Navajo Canyon Overlook and Sun Point Overlook, from which you can see Cliff Palace, Sunset House, and other dwellings. ☉ *Daily 8 AM to sunset.*

**Park Entrance Road.** The main park road leads you from the entrance to Far View Visitor Center, on 15 mi of switchbacks, which reveal far-ranging vistas of the surrounding areas. You can stop at a couple of pretty overlooks along the way, but hold out for Park Point, which, at the mesa's highest elevation (8,572 feet), affords unobstructed 360-degree views.

## MESA VERDE IN ONE DAY

For a full experience of Mesa Verde, take at least one ranger-led tour of a major cliff dwelling site, as well as a few self-guided walks. Arrive early; it's about a 45-minute drive from the park entrance to your first stop, the **Far View Visitor Center,** where you can pick up park information and purchase tickets for Cliff Palace or Balcony House tours on Chapin Mesa. If it's going to be a hot day, you might want to take an early morning or late-afternoon tour. Drive to the **Chapin Mesa Museum** to learn about the area and its history. Just behind the museum, you can hike the ½-mi-long **Spruce Tree House trail,** which leads to the best preserved cliff dwelling in the park. Then drive to Balcony House for a ranger-led tour.

Have lunch at the Spruce Tree House cafeteria or the Cliff Palace picnic area. After lunch, take the ranger-led tour of **Cliff Palace.** Use the rest of the day to explore the overlooks and trails off the two 6-mi loops of **Mesa Top Loop Road.** Take **Petroglyph Point Trail** to see Mesa Verde's well-preserved collection of rock carvings. A leisurely walk along the mesa top's **Point Lookout Trail** will give you a beautiful bird's-eye views of the canyon below. Also stop and see the view from **Park Point** on the drive back to the entrance.

## What to See

### Historic Sites

**Badger House Community.** A self-guided walk takes you through a group of subterranean dwellings, called pithouses, and aboveground storage rooms. The community dates back to 650, the Basketmaker Period, and covers seven acres of land. Most of the pithouses and kivas—religious or ceremonial rooms—were connected by an intricate system of tunnels, some up to 41 feet long. Allow about an hour to see all the sites. ⊠ *On Wetherill Mesa Road, 12 mi from the Far View Visitor Center* ☉ *Memorial Day–Labor Day, daily, 8–4:30.*

★ ♔ **Balcony House.** The stonework of this 40-room cliff dwelling, which housed about 40 or 50 people, is impressive, but you're likely to be even more awed by the skill it took to reach this place. Perched in a sandstone cove 600 feet above the floor of Soda Canyon, Balcony House seems almost suspended in space. Even with the aid of modern steps and a partially paved trail, today's visitors must climb two wooden ladders (the first one 32 feet high) to enter. Surrounding the house are a courtyard with a parapet wall and the intact balcony for which the house is named. A favorite with kids, the dwelling is only accessible on a ranger-led tour. Youngsters love climbing the ladders, crawling through the tunnels, and clambering around its nooks and crannies. Purchase your ticket at the Far View Visitor Center. ⊠ *On Cliff Palace Loop Rd., 8½ mi southeast of the Far View Visitor Center* ☎ *$3* ☉ *Late-May–mid-Oct., daily 9–5.*

FodorśChoice **Cliff Palace.** This was the first major
★ Mesa Verde dwelling seen by cow-
boys Charlie Mason and Richard
Wetherill in 1888. It is also the
largest, containing about 150 rooms
and 23 kivas on three levels. Getting there involves a steep downhill
hike and four ladders. Purchase
tickets at the Far View Visitor Center for the one-hour, ranger-led tour
through this dwelling. ☒ *On Cliff
Palace Loop Rd., 7 mi south of the
Far View Visitor Center* 🔊 *$3*
☉ *Mid-May–mid-Oct., daily 9–5.*

> **GOOD READS**
>
> **Mesa Verde National Park: The
> First 100 Years** by Rose Houk, Faith
> Marcovecchio, and Duane A. Smith
> captures the park at its centennial.
> **Fire on the Mesa,** by Tracey Chavis
> discusses the wildfires that have
> been scarring Mesa Verde.
> **Mesa Verde: Ancient Architecture,**
> by Jesse Walter Fewkes, tells the
> stories behind Mesa Verde's
> dwellings.

**25**

**Far View Sites Complex.** This ½-
square-mi area at the top of Chapin Mesa is believed to have been one
of the most densely populated zones in Mesa Verde, comprising as
many as 50 villages. Most of the sites here were built between 900 and
1300. Begin the self-guided tour at the interpretive panels in the parking lot, then proceed down a ½-mi, level trail. The ranger-led walk
takes place daily at 4. ☒ *On the park entrance road, 1½ mi south of
the Far View Visitor Center* ☉ *Mid-May–mid-Oct., daily 8–6:30.*

**Long House.** Excavated in 1959 through 1961, this Wetherill Mesa cliff
dwelling is the second largest in Mesa Verde. It is believed that about
150 people lived in Long House, so named because of the size of its cliff
alcove. The spring at the back of the cave is still active today. The
ranger-led tour begins a short distance from the parking lot and takes
about 45 minutes. ☒ *On Wetherill Mesa Rd., 12 mi from the Far View
Visitor Center* 🔊*$3* ☉ *Memorial Day–Labor Day, daily 10–4.*

**Spruce Tree House.** The best-preserved site in the park, this dwelling contains 114 living rooms and eight kivas. It's the only dwelling where you
can actually enter a kiva, via a short ladder, just as the original inhabitants did. Tours through are self-guided, but a park ranger is on-site to
answer questions. The trail starts behind the museum and descends 170
feet—you'll find yourself puffing on the way back up, but it's worth the
effort. ☒ *On the park entrance road, 5 mi south of the Far View Visitor Center* ☉ *Mar.–Nov., daily 9–5.*

**Triple Village Pueblo Sites.** Three dwellings built atop each other from 750
to 1150 at first look like a mass of jumbled walls, but an interpretive
panel helps identify the dwellings. The 325-foot trail from the walking
area is paved and wheelchair accessible. ☒ *On Mesa Top Loop Rd., 8
mi south of the Far View Visitor Center* ☉ *Daily.*

## Scenic Stops

**Cedar Tree Tower.** A self-guided tour takes you to, but not through, a tower
and kiva built between 1100 and 1300 and connected by a tunnel. The
tower-and-kiva combinations in the park are thought to have been either religious structures or signal towers. ☒ *On the park entrance road,
4 mi south of the Far View Visitor Center* ☉ *Daily.*

**Kodak House Overlook.** Get an impressive view into Kodak House and its several small kivas from here. The house, closed to the public, was named for a Swedish researcher who absentmindedly left his Kodak camera behind here in 1891. ⊠ *On Wetherill Mesa Rd.,12 mi from the Far View Visitor Center* ☉ *Daily, Memorial Day–Labor Day.*

**Soda Canyon Overlook.** Get your best view of Balcony House here and read interpretive panels about the house and canyon geology. ⊠ *On Mesa Top Loop Rd., 9 mi south of the Far View Visitor Center* ☉ *Daily.*

### Visitor Centers

There are two visitor centers at Mesa Verde, though one is called a museum (but in fact, it serves as the official visitor center when the other closes for the season in the middle of October).

★ **Chapin Mesa Archeological Museum.** The museum tells the entire story of the cliff-dwelling people and gives as complete an understanding as possible of the Basketmaker and ancestral Puebloan cultures through detailed dioramas and exhibits, including original textiles, sandals, and kiva jars. A separate hands-on room is for children. ⊠ *On the park entrance road, 5 mi south of the Far View Visitor Center* ☎ *970/529–4465* ⊠ *Free* ☉ *Apr.–mid-Oct., daily 8–6:30; mid-Oct.–Mar., daily 8–5.*

★ **Far View Visitor Center.** Buy tickets for the Cliff Palace, Balcony House, and Long House ranger-led tours here. An extensive selection of books and videos on the history of the park are also for sale. Rangers are on hand to answer questions and explain the history of the ancestral Puebloans. ⊠ *15 mi south of the park entrance* ☎ *970/529–5036* ☉ *Mid-Apr.–mid-Oct., daily 8–5.*

## Sports & the Outdoors

Outdoor activities are restricted on account of the fragile nature of the archeological treasures contained here. Hiking is the best option, especially as a way to view some of the ancestral Puebloan dwellings.

### Bird-watching

Turkey vultures soar between April and October, large flocks of ravens hang around all summer, and ducks and waterfowl fly through Mesa Verde from mid-September through mid-October. Among the park's other large birds are red-tailed hawks, great horned owls, and a few golden eagles. The dark-blue Steller's jay frequently pierces the pinyon-juniper forest with its cries, and hummingbirds dart from flower to flower.

### Hiking

No backcountry hiking is permitted in Mesa Verde due to the fragile nature of the ancient dwellings and artifacts. However, several trails lead beyond the park's most visited sites. Most trails are easily navigable, with length being what separates the most difficult from the easiest, though a few have some elevation changes and switchbacks. Certain trails are seasonal only, so check with a ranger before heading out.

EASY **Farming Terrace Trail.** This 30-minute, ½-mi loop, beginning and ending on the spur road to Cedar Tree Tower, meanders through a series of check dams the ancestral Puebloans built to create farming terraces.

**Soda Canyon Overlook Trail.** One of the easiest and most rewarding strolls in the park, this little trail travels 1½ mi round-trip through the forest on almost completely level ground. The overlook is an excellent point from which to photograph the cliff dwellings. The trailhead is about ¼ mi past the Balcony House parking area.

MODERATE **Petroglyph Point Trail.** The highlight of this 2⁸⁄₁₀-mi loop is the largest and
Fodor'sChoice best-known group of petroglyphs in Mesa Verde. Since the trail offshoots
★ from Spruce Tree House Trail, it is only accessible when Spruce Tree House is open, March through November, daily 9–5.

**Spruce Canyon Trail.** If you want to venture down into the canyon, this is your trail. It's only 2 mi long, but you can go down about 600 feet in elevation. It is only accessible when Spruce Tree House is open, from March through November, daily 9–5, and registration is required.

DIFFICULT **Prater Ridge Trail.** This loop, which starts and finishes at Morefield Campground, is the longest hike (7⁸⁄₁₀ mi round-trip) you can take inside the park and affords fine views of Morefield Canyon to the south and the San Juan Mountains to the north.

### Stargazing

Since there are no large cities in the Four Corners area, there's little artificial light to detract from the stars in the night sky. Some ideal locations in the park for stargazing are Far View Lodge, Morefield Campground, and the Montezuma and Mancos scenic overlooks.

## Educational Offerings

### Classes & Seminars

**Cliff Palace/Sun Temple Talks.** Interpretive talks on park-related subjects are held twice daily at Cliff Palace Overlook near the Sun Temple parking area. ⊠ *Cliff Palace Overlook, Mesa Top Loop Rd.* ☎ *970/529–4465* ☾ *Memorial Day–Labor Day, daily 10–10:30, 4–4:30.*

**ARAMARK.** The park concessionaire provides all-day and half-day guided tours of the Mesa Top Loop Road sites from mid-April through mid-October. The tours depart in vans or buses from Morefield Campground and Far View Lodge. Tours cover the history, geology, and excavation process in Mesa Verde. ☞ *ARAMARK Mesa Verde, Box 277, Mancos 81328* ☎ *970/564–4300 or 800/449–2288* ⊕ *www.visitmesaverde.com* ☞ *$39–$65* ☾ *Mid-Apr.–mid-Oct., daily.*

**Cliff Palace All-Day Tour.** This guided visit of the museum, the Puebloan structures along Mesa Top Loop Road, and Spruce Tree House ends back at the museum. At Cliff Palace the tour is ranger led. Depart Morefield Campground at 9 and Far View Lodge at 9:30, and return around 5. The $65 ticket includes lunch and admission into dwellings.

25

### Ranger Programs

**Evening Ranger Campfire Program.** A park ranger presents a different 45-minute program or slide presentation each night of the week. ✉ *Morefield Campground Amphitheater, 4 mi south of the park entrance* ☎ *970/529–4465* ⊙ *Memorial Day–Labor Day, daily 9 PM–9:45 PM.*

**Junior Ranger Program.** Children ages 4–12 can earn a certificate and badge for successfully completing a two-page questionnaire about the park. ✉ *Far View Visitor Center or Chapin Mesa Museum* ☎ *970/529–4465.*

**Ranger-Led Tours.** Balcony House, Cliff Palace, and Long House can only be explored on a ranger-led tour; each lasts about an hour. Buy tickets at Far View Visitor Center the day of the tour, or at the Morefield Campground Ranger Station the evening before the tour, 5 PM to 8:30 PM. ☎ *970/529–4465* ✉ *$3 per tour* ⊙ *Mid-Apr.–mid-Oct.*

# WHAT'S NEARBY

**25**

## Nearby Towns & Attractions

### Nearby Towns

A onetime market center for sheep and cattle ranchers 30 mi from the park, **Cortez** is now the largest gateway town to Mesa Verde and a base for tourists visiting the Four Corners region of Colorado. You can still see a rodeo and cattle drive here at least once a year. **Dolores**, steeped in a rich railroad history, is set on the Dolores River, 20 mi north of Mesa Verde. Neighboring both the San Juan National Forest and McPhee Reservoir, the second-largest lake in the state, Dolores is a favorite of outdoor enthusiasts. East of Mesa Verde by 56 mi, **Durango**, the region's main hub, became a town in 1881 when the Denver and Rio Grande Railroad pushed its tracks across the neighboring San Juan Mountains.

### Nearby Attractions

★ **Anasazi Heritage Center.** More than 3 million Native American artifacts, including pottery, ornaments, and tools, were excavated from sites all over the Four Corners region and are preserved and exhibited in this state-of-the-art museum. A hands-on tour gives you the chance to grind corn, weave on a loom, and wander through a full-scale replica of an ancestral Puebloan pithouse dwelling. ✉ *27501 Rte. 184, Dolores* ☎ *970/882–5600* ⊕ *www.co.blm.gov/ahc* ✉ *$3; free Nov.–Feb.* ⊙ *Mar.–Oct., daily 9–5; Nov.–Feb., daily 10–4.*

**Crow Canyon Archaeological Center.** A one-day archaeology program explains the excavation process and the ancestral Puebloan culture through a hands-on laboratory tour and a visit to a current excavation site, with lunch included. The weeklong programs have day trips to isolated canyon sites and hands-on lessons in weaving and pottery making. The week-long excavation program requires reservations. ✉ *23390 Rd. K, Cortez* ☎ *970/565–8975 or 800/422–8975* ⊕ *www.crowcanyon.org* ✉ *$50 per day, $1150 per week* ⊙ *Mar.–Oct.*

---

## FAMILY PICKS

| | |
|---|---|
| **Durango & Silverton Narrow Gauge Railroad:** Ride the winding rails, sometimes far above the churning Animas River.<br><br>**Evening Ranger Campfire Program:** Conjure up a sense of | what dwelling in the cliffs must have been like and gaze up at bright shining stars.<br><br>**Four Corners Monument:** Find out how many ways you can straddle four states at one time. |

---

## Area Activities

### Sports & the Outdoors

FISHING **McPhee Reservoir.** The second-largest lake in Colorado provides some of the state's best boating, waterskiing, and fishing—minus the crowds. To date, McPhee Reservoir has been stocked with 4½ million fish, including trout, bass, bluegills, crappies, and kokanee salmon. The marina, where you can sign up for a fishing license, is 8 mi north of Dolores. ⊠ *Rte. 184, Dolores* ☎ *970/882–7296* ▧ *Free* ☉ *Daily.*

RAFTING Beginning in the San Juan Mountains of southwestern Colorado, the Dolores River runs north for more than 150 mi before joining the Colorado River near Moab, Utah. This is one of those rivers that tends to flow madly in spring and diminish considerably by midsummer, and for that reason rafting trips are usually run between April and June.

### Arts & Entertainment

★ The **Cortez Cultural Center** has exhibits on regional artists and ancestral Puebloan culture. Summer evening programs include Native American dances, sandpainting, rug weaving, pottery-making demonstrations, theater, and storytelling. The adjacent park contains an authentic tepee. ⊠ *25 N. Market St., Cortez* ☎ *970/565–1151* ⊕ *www.cortezculturalcenter.org* ▧ *Free* ☉ *June–Aug., weekdays 10–9, Sat. 1–9; May and Sept., Mon.–Sat. 10–6; Oct.–Apr., weekdays 10–5.*

ART GALLERIES **Toh-Atin Gallery** is one of the best galleries in Colorado, specializing in Navajo rugs and weavings. There's also a wide range of paintings, pottery, and prints. ⊠ *145 W. 9th St., Durango* ☎ *970/247–8277 or 800/ 525–0384* ⊕ *www.toh-atin.com* ☉ *Mon.–Sat. 9–6.*

NIGHTLIFE The **Diamond Belle Saloon** is still the hottest spot in town, even though it opened more than a century ago. The honky-tonk player piano and waitresses dressed as 1880s saloon girls pack them in to this spot in the Strater Hotel. ⊠ *699 Main Ave., Durango* ☎ *970/247–4431* ⊕ *www. strater.com/belle.php* ☉ *Daily.*

---

## Shopping

**Notah Dineh Trading Company and Museum** specializes in rugs, hand-carved katsinas, cradleboards, baskets, beadwork, and silver jewelry. Stop in the museum to see relics of the Old West as well as a noteworthy rug in the Two Grey Hills pattern. ✉ *345 W. Main St., Cortez* ☎ *800/444–2024* ⊕ *www.notahdineh.com* ✏ *Free* ☾ *Mon.–Sat. 9–6:30.*

# WHERE TO STAY & EAT

### About the Restaurants

Dining options in Mesa Verde are comparatively plentiful and varied, ranging from cafeterias to fine dining, all with a Southwestern flair alongside more standard American fare for the reserved diner. In surrounding communities, Southwestern and steak houses are favored.

### About the Hotels

All 150 rooms of the park's Far View Lodge, open April through October, have private balconies, are nonsmoking, and fill up quickly—so reservations are recommended, especially if you plan to visit on a weekend in the summer. Options in the surrounding area range from chain hotels to bed-and-breakfast inns. Durango in particular has a number of hotels situated in fine old buildings reminiscent of the Old West.

### About the Campgrounds

Morefield Campground is the only option within the park and is an excellent one. Reservations are accepted; it's open April through October. Nearby, Mancos has a campground with full amenities, while the San Juan National Forest offers backcountry camping.

## Where to Eat

### In the Park

★ $$ ✕ **Metate Room.** Tables in this Southwestern-style dining room are candlelit and cloth covered, but the atmosphere remains casual. A wall of windows affords wonderful Mesa Verde vistas. The menu includes American staples like steak and seafood, but game meats such as quail, venison, and rabbit occasionally appear as well. For appetizers, try Anasazi beans and mesa bread. ✉ *Far View Lodge, across from the Far View Visitor Center* ☎ *970/529–4421. $17–$20* ⊟ *AE, D, DC, MC, V* ☾ *Closed late Oct.–early Apr. No lunch.*

¢–$ ✕ **Far View Terrace.** This full-service cafeteria offers great views, plentiful choices, and reasonable prices. Fluffy blueberry pancakes are often on the breakfast menu. Dinner options might include a Navajo taco piled high with all the fixings. Don't miss the creamy malts and homemade fudge; a shot at the espresso bar will keep you going all day. ✉ *On Mesa Top Loop Rd., across from the Far View Visitor Center* ☎ *970/529–4444. $4–$8* ⊟ *D, MC, V* ☾ *Closed late Oct.–early Apr.*

¢–$ ✕ **Spruce Tree Terrace.** A limited selection of hot food and sandwiches is all you'll find at this cafeteria, but the patio is pleasant, and since it's across the street from the museum, it's convenient. The Terrace is also the only food concession open year-round. ✉ *On the park entrance road, 5 mi south of the Far View Visitor Center* ☎ *970/529–4521. $3–$8* ⊟ *AE, D, DC, MC, V* ☾ *No dinner Dec.–Feb.*

¢ ✕ **Knife's Edge Cafe.** An all-you-can-eat pancake breakfast is served every morning from 7:30 to 10, and at night there's an all-you-can-eat

**25**

barbecue dinner from 5 to 8. ⊠ *4 mi south of the park entrance* ☎ *970/ 565–2133. $4–$7* ▤ *AE, D, MC, V* ☉ *Closed Labor Day–Memorial Day. No lunch.*

PICNIC AREAS **Park Headquarters Loop Picnic Area.** This is the nicest and largest picnic ♨ area in the park. It has 40 tables under shade trees and a great view into Spruce Canyon, as well as flush toilets and running water. ⊠ *6 mi south of the Far View Visitor Center.*

**Wetherill Mesa Picnic Area.** Ten tables placed under lush shade trees, along with drinking water and restrooms, make this a very pleasant spot for lunch. ⊠ *12 mi southwest of the Far View Visitor Center.*

## Outside the Park

$$–$$$$ ✕ **Ore House.** Durango is a meat-and-potatoes kind of town, and this is Durango's idea of a steak house. The aroma of beef smacks you in the face as you walk past. This local favorite serves enormous slabs of aged Angus that are hand-cut daily. If you're watching your cholesterol, steer clear. ⊠ *147 E. College Dr., Durango* ☎ *970/247–5707* ⊕ *www. orehouserestaurant.com. $18–$35* ▤ *D, MC, V.*

★ $$ ✕ **Millwood Junction.** This rambling restaurant, made out of wood from local barns, has everything you'd want for a fun night out: good drinks, good food, and, on summer weekends, top-notch entertainment. A Friday-night seafood buffet (all you can eat for $13.95) draws folks from four states. ⊠ *U.S. 160 at Main, Mancos* ☎ *970/533–7338* ⊕ *www. millwoodjunction.com. $15–$19* ▤ *MC, V* ☉ *No lunch weekends.*

$–$$ ✕ **German Stone Oven Restaurant & Bakery.** Favorites here include Wiener schnitzel, sauerbraten, pork chops, and imported beer. There are also vegetarian dishes. Antiques and collectibles fill the dining room. You can also eat on the patio. ⊠ *811 Railroad Ave., Dolores* ☎ *970/882– 7033. $11–$16* ▤ *MC, V* ☉ *Closed Tues., Wed., and Jan.–Apr.*

¢–$ ✕ **Brickhouse Cafe & Coffee Bar.** Great lattes await at this popular little place set in a historic house with wonderful yard landscaping. Don't miss the malted buttermilk waffle, pigs in a blanket, or big burgers. Breakfast and lunch are served all day. ⊠ *1849 Main Ave., Durango* ☎ *970/247–3760* ⊕ *www.brickhousecafe.com. $4–$9* ▤ *AE, D, MC.*

¢–$ ✕ **Olde Tymer's Café.** Locals flock to this former drugstore for the hamburgers, and to bask in the feel of days gone by. The tin ceiling, artifacts, and photos give it the appearance of a 1920s dance hall. ⊠ *1000 Main Ave., Durango* ☎ *970/259–2990. $6–$9* ▤ *AE, MC, V.*

# Where to Stay

## In the Park

★ $ ▥ **Far View Lodge.** Talk about a view—all rooms have a private balcony, from which you can admire the neighboring states of Arizona, Utah, and New Mexico up to 100 mi in the distance. Otherwise, quarters are motel-style and basic, with a Southwestern touch. Talks by guest speakers on various park topics and multimedia shows on the ancestral Puebloans are held nightly. The hotel also offers enthusiastic guided tours of the park. The Metate Room, the lodge's main dining room, is acclaimed for its fine steaks and excellent Southwestern fare. ⊠ *15 mi southwest of the park entrance, across from the Far View Visitor Center* ☏ *Reser-*

CLOSE UP

# Marketing the Four Corners Monument

**THERE'S NO VIEW TO SPEAK OF** at Four Corners Monument, but it's a favorite and famous photo-op nonetheless. Set on Navajo land, about one usually dusty mile off U.S. 60, the monument is the only place in the nation where the borders of four states meet. The first permanent marker, a simple look-what's-here, was erected at the intersection of Colorado, Utah, New Mexico, and Arizona in 1912. People from all corners, not just these four, went out of their way just to come stand in such a way as to be in four states at once.

Straddle all four states at once.

People still come in droves, but Four Corners is a much larger affair these days. The monument was refurbished in 1992, and a larger marker, consisting of a bronze disk embedded in granite, was put in place. Though bigger and more ornate than the first marker, it still seems far too unassuming to have attracted the bazaar that surrounds it. In response to a ready market of tourists and trinket hounds, the perimeter of the main drive is rimmed with plywood booths hawking Ute, Navajo, Apache, and other Native American artwork, crafts, artifacts, and rugs. You can also buy fry bread and corn on the cob. It's all genuine, but the opportunistic

nature of the site—it costs $3 per vehicle just to enter—detracts from what began as the simple fascination of standing at the very point where four Southwestern states meet.

The site is pretty "out there." No major cities are nearby. Cortez, Colorado, is 40 mi away on U.S. 60; tiny Teec Nos Pos, Arizona, is 6 mi away; Shiprock, New Mexico, is about 25 mi to the east; and Bluff, Utah, is 50 mi distant.

**The Navajo Nation Parks and Recreation Department** administers the Four Corners Monument. The site is open from 7 AM to 8 PM May through mid-August and 8 to 5 mid-August through April. For more information, call ☎ *520/871-6647.*

25

---

*vations: ARAMARK Mesa Verde, Box 277, Mancos 81328* ☎ *970/564–4300 or 800/449–2288* 🖷 *970/564-4311* ⊕ *www.visitmesaverde.com* 🛏 *150 rooms* ⚒ *Restaurant, refrigerator (some), bar, laundry facilities, some pets allowed. $99* ▭ *AE, D, DC, MC, V* ⊗ *Closed Nov.–Mar.*

CAMPGROUNDS & RV PARKS
**$$**
Fodor'sChoice
★

⚠ **Morefield Campground.** With more than 400 shaded campsites, access to trailheads, and plenty of amenities, the only campground in the park is an appealing mini-city for campers. Reservations are accepted only for tent and group sites. ✉ *4 mi south of the park entrance, Box 8, Mesa Verde 81330–0008* ☎ *970/564–4300 or 800/449–2288* 🖷 *970/ 564-4311* ⊕ *www.visitmesaverde.com* 🛏 *380 sites, 15 with hookups* ⚒ *Grills, flush toilets, partial hookups, dump station, drinking water,* *guest laundry, showers, fire grates, picnic tables, food service, electricity, public telephone, general store, service station, ranger station* ⌲ *$20–$30* ▭ *AE, D, DC, MC, V* ☉ *Late-Apr.–mid-Oct.*

### Outside the Park

★ **$$–$$$$** ⬚ **New Rochester Hotel.** The rooms in this small, 19th-century hotel are decorated in an Old West style and named after some of the many Hollywood films made in Durango. Movie posters, mismatched furniture, and wagon-wheel chandeliers make for a chic but funky interior. A full gourmet breakfast includes plenty of coffee and several varieties of tempting mini-muffins and scones. ✉ *726 E. 2nd Ave., Durango 81301* ☏ *970/385–1920 or 800/664–1920* ⎙ *970/385–1967* ⊕ *www.rochesterhotel.com* ⬚ *13 rooms, 1 suite* ⟡ *Kitchen (some), refrigerator, VCR (some), some pets allowed, Wi-Fi, no smoking. $149–$229* ▭ *AE, D, DC, MC, V.*

**$$–$$$** ⬚ **Apple Orchard Inn.** This farmhouse sits on a 4½-acre apple orchard tucked into the lush Animas Valley 8 mi north of Durango. Six cottages surround a flower-bedecked pond, complete with friendly ducks. Cherrywood antiques, feather beds, and handcrafted armoires furnish the handsome rooms. The owners' experience at European cooking schools is evident in the breakfasts. ✉ *7758 Rte. 203, Durango 81301* ☏ *970/247–0751 or 800/426–0751* ⊕ *www.appleorchardinn.com* ⬚ *4 rooms, 6 cottages* ⟡ *Refrigerator, VCR (some), Wi-Fi, no smoking. $140–$160, $170–$210 cottages* ▭ *AE, D, MC, V.*

★ **$$–$$$** ⬚ **Jarvis Suite Hotel.** This former theater in the center of downtown Durango became a hotel in 1984, about a century after its curtain first went up. It's loaded with Western relics. ✉ *125 W. 10th St., Durango 81320* ☏ *970/259–6190 or 800/824–1024* ⎙ *970/259–6190* ⬚ *21 suites* ⟡ *Dial-up, Wi-Fi, kitchen, VCR (some), laundry facilities. $129–$179 suites* ▭ *AE, D, DC, MC, V.*

**$$–$$$** ⬚ **Strater Hotel.** This Victorian beauty opened in 1887 and has been lovingly restored with crystal chandeliers, beveled windows, original oak beams, flocked wallpaper, and plush velour curtains. The individually decorated rooms are swooningly exquisite: after all, the hotel owns the country's largest collection of Victorian walnut antiques and has its own wood-carving shop to create exact period reproductions. Your room might have entertained Butch Cassidy, Louis L'Amour (he wrote *The Sacketts* here), Francis Ford Coppola, John F. Kennedy, or Marilyn Monroe. ✉ *699 Main Ave., Durango 81301* ☏ *970/247–4431 or 800/247–4431* ⎙ *970/259–2208* ⊕ *www.strater.com* ⬚ *93 rooms* ⟡ *Restaurant, Wi-Fi, bar. $135–$165* ▭ *AE, D, DC, MC, V.*

FodorsChoice ★

**$** ⬚ **Anasazi Motor Inn.** This is definitely the nicest hotel in downtown Cortez, mostly because its air-conditioned rooms are spacious, carpeted, and pleasantly decorated with furniture in Southwestern colors. Outside, you'll find horseshoe and volleyball pits. ✉ *640 S. Broadway, Cortez 81321* ☏ *970/565–3773 or 800/972–6232* ⎙ *970/565–1027* ⊕ *www.anasazimotorinn.com* ⬚ *87 rooms* ⟡ *Restaurant, Wi-Fi, VCR (some), pool, bar, airport shuttle, some pets allowed. $85* ▭ *AE, D, DC, MC, V.*

**¢–$** ⬚ **National 9 Inn–Sand Canyon.** The gem in this basic, locally owned motel with simple rooms is its adjacent casual-Italian restaurant. Downtown Cortez is three blocks away. ✉ *301 W. Main St., Cortez 81321* ☏ *970/*

## FESTIVALS & EVENTS

MAY–SEPT. **Native American Dances.** The Cortez Cultural Center invites performers from the Ute, Navajo, and Hopi tribes to perform traditional dances each evening at 7:30. ☎ *970/565–1151.*

JULY **Durango Fiesta Days.** A parade, rodeo, barbecue, street dance, and pie auction come to the

La Plata County Fair Grounds in Durango on the last weekend of the month. ☎ *970/247–8835.*

OCT. **Durango Cowboy Gathering.** A rodeo, Western art exhibitions, cowboy poetry, storytelling, and a dance draw folks to Durango the first weekend in October. ☎ *970/ 247–0312 or 800/525–8855.*

*565–8562 or 800/524–9999* 🖷 *970/565–0125* ⊕ *www.sandcanyon. com* ⟿ *28 rooms* ᗉ *Restaurant, Wi-Fi, pool, bar, laundry facilities. $40–$69* ▤ *AE, D, MC, V.*

CAMPGROUNDS & RV PARKS

★ $$–$$$

⚠ **A & A Mesa Verde RV Park and Campground.** This 30-acre lot, directly across the highway from the national park, has all the facilities of a hotel. There's a modern bathhouse, recreation room, miniature golf course, sports field, a pool and hot tub, and a kennel. You can even camp in a log cabin. ⊠ *34979 U.S. 160, Mancos 81328* ☎ *800/972–6620* 🖷 *970/ 565–7141* ⊕ *www.mesaverdecamping.com* ⟿ *73 sites, 45 with hookups; 4 cabins* ᗉ *Grills, flush toilets, full hookups, dump station, drinking water, guest laundry, showers, fire grates, picnic tables, electricity, public telephone, general store, play area, swimming (pool)* ▤ *$21–$40* ▤ *D, MC, V* ☺ *Apr.–Sept.*

$

⚠ **McPhee Campground.** The largest and best-equipped campground in the San Juan National Forest, McPhee is surrounded by paved roads and has several wheelchair-accessible sites. It's at an altitude of about 7,400 feet, and many of the sites overlook McPhee Reservoir. Reach it by taking Route 184 south 7 mi from Dolores to Country Road 25, then turn north to onto Forest Road 271. ⊠ *Forest Rd. 271, 15 Burnett Ct., Durango 81301* ☎ *877/444–6777 or 970/247–4874* ⊕ *www.fs.fed.us/r2/ sanjuan* ⟿ *76 sites, 16 with hookups* ᗉ *Grills, flush toilets, partial hookups (electric and water), dump station, drinking water, showers, fire pits, picnic tables, electricity, public telephone* ▤ *$12-$17* ☺ *May–Sept.*

# MESA VERDE ESSENTIALS

ACCESSIBILITY Steep cliffs, deep canyons, narrow trails, and hard-to-reach archaeological sites mean accessibility is limited within Mesa Verde. Service dogs cannot be taken into Balcony House, Cliff Palace, or Long House because of ladders in those sites. None of these sites is accessible to those with mobility impairments. If you

have heart or respiratory ailments, you may have trouble breathing in the thin air at 7,000 to 8,000 feet. Wheelchairs with wide rim wheels are recommended on trails, some of which do not meet legal grade requirements. For the hearing impaired, park videos are open captioned and TDD services are available (970/529–

4633). Mesa Top Loop Road provides the most comprehensive and accessible view of all the archaeological sites.

ADMISSION FEES Admission is $10 per vehicle for a seven-day permit. An annual permit is $20. Ranger-led tours of Cliff Palace, Long House, and Balcony House are $3 per person.

ADMISSION HOURS The facilities open each day at 8 AM and close at sunset from Memorial Day through Labor Day. The rest of the year, the facilities close at 5. Wetherill Mesa, all the major cliff dwellings, and Morefield ranger station are open only from Memorial Day through Labor Day. Far View Visitor Center, Far View Lodge, and Morefield Campground are open mid-April through mid-October.

ATMS/BANKS There are no ATMs in the park.
🚩 **First National Bank** ✉ 178 E. Frontage Rd., Mancos ☎ 970/533–7798 ☉ Weekdays 8–6.

AUTOMOBILE SERVICE STATION
🚩 **Sinclair Service Station.** ✉ Morefield Campground, 4 mi from the park entrance ☎ 970/565–2407.

EMERGENCIES To report a fire or call for aid, dial 911 or 970/529–4465. First-aid stations are located at Morefield Campground, Far View Visitor Center, and Wetherill Mesa.

LOST AND FOUND The park's lost-and-found is at the **Chief Ranger's office** at park headquarters, 5 mi south of Far View Visitor Center ☎ 970/529–4469.

PERMITS Backcountry hiking and fishing are not permitted at Mesa Verde.

POST OFFICES
🚩 **Mancos Post Office** ✉ 291 N. Walnut St., Mancos 81328 ☎ 970/533–7754 ☉ Weekdays

9–4:30, Sat. 10–noon. **Mesa Verde National Park Post Office** ✉ *Near park headquarters, Chapin Mesa* ☎ *970/529–4554* ☉ *Weekdays 8:30–4:30.*

PUBLIC TELEPHONES Public telephones can be found at Morefield Campground and Morefield Village, Far View Visitor Center, Far View Lodge, Far View Terrace, Spruce Tree Terrace, park headquarters (5 mi from the Far View Visitor Center), and the Wetherill Mesa snack bar. Cell-phone reception in the park varies in quality.

RELIGIOUS SERVICES There are no chapel or other religious services within the park.

RESTROOMS Public restrooms may be found at Morefield Campground and Morefield Village, Far View Visitor Center, Far View Lodge, Far View Terrace, Spruce Tree Terrace, park headquarters, the Wetherill Mesa snack bar, Montezuma Valley Overlook, Cliff Palace, and Balcony House.

SHOPS & GROCERS Morefield Campground has a nicely stocked grocery store that is open 7 AM to 9 PM, mid-May to early Oct.

**NEARBY TOWN INFORMATION**
🚩 **Mesa Verde National Park** ✉ Box 8, Mesa Verde, CO 81330-0008 ☎ 970/529-4465 ⊕ www.nps.gov/meve. **Dolores Chamber of Commerce** ✉ 201 Railroad Ave., Dolores 81323 ☎ 970/882-4018 or 800/807-4712 ⊕ www.doloreschamber.com. **Durango Area Tourism Office** ✉ 111 S. Camino del Rio, Durango 81302 ☎ 970/247-0312 or 800/525-8855 ⊕ www.durango.org. **Mesa Verde Visitor Information Bureau** ✉ 928 E. Main St., Cortez 81321 ☎ 970/565-8227 or 800/253-1616 ⊕ www.swcolo.org.

**VISITOR INFORMATION**
🚩 **Mesa Verde National Park** ✉ Box 8, Mesa Verde, CO 81330-0008 ☎ 970/529-4465 ⊕ www.nps.gov/meve.

# Mount Rainier National Park

Mount Rainier National Park

**WORD OF MOUTH**

"Of all the fire mountains which like beacons, once blazed along the Pacific Coast, Mount Rainier is the noblest."

–John Muir

# WELCOME TO MOUNT RAINIER

## TOP REASONS TO GO

★ **The mountain:** Some say Mt. Rainier is the most magical mountain in America. At 14,411 feet, it is a popular peak for climbing, with more than 10,000 attempts per year—half of which are successful.

★ **The glaciers:** About 35 square mi of glaciers and snowfields encircle Mt. Rainier, including Carbon Glacier and Emmons Glacier, the largest glaciers by volume and area, respectively, in the continental United States.

★ **The wildflowers:** More than 100 species of wildflowers bloom in the high meadows here; the display dazzles from midsummer until the snow flies.

★ **Fabulous hiking:** Mt. Rainier has more than 240 mi of maintained trails that provide access to old-growth forest, river valleys, lakes, subalpine meadows, and rugged ridges.

★ **Unencumbered wilderness:** Mount Rainier National Park is one of those rare places with the ability to nurture and deeply inspire the human spirit.

**1 Longmire.** The Nisqually Gate in the southwest corner of the park was Mount Rainier's original entrance, and highlights of this area include the Longmire Historic District, Christine Falls, Glacier Bridge, and Narada Falls.

**2 Paradise.** Famous for wildflower meadows in summer and Nordic skiing in winter, there are also a number of good trails here. Be sure to visit the Jackson Memorial Visitor Center, Paradise Inn, and the Paradise Ranger Station.

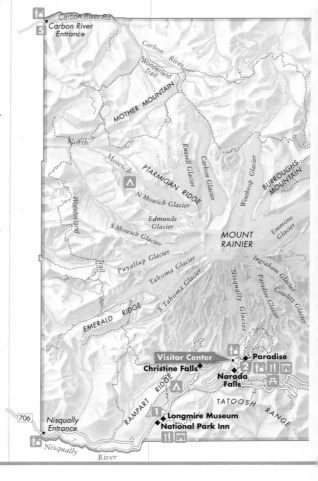

**3 Ohanapecosh.** As you approach the park from the southeast, the first stop will be Ohanapecosh. When you're here, check out the Ohanapecosh Visitor Center, the Grove of Patriarchs, and Tipsoo Lake.

**4 Sunrise/White River.** Plan to see White River Wilderness Information Center, White River Ranger Station, White River Campground, and Sunrise, the highest point you can drive to in the park.

**5 Carbon River/Mowich Lake.** Before entering the northwest corner of the park, pay your entrance fees and pick up park brochures at the Wilderness Information Center in downtown Wilkeson. Don't miss the temperate forest near Carbon River entrance station, Carbon Glacier, and Mowich Lake.

WASHINGTON

## GETTING ORIENTED

Mount Rainier is the focal point of this 337-square-mi national park. The Nisqually entrance brings you into the southwest corner of the park, where you'll find the historic Longmire District. The most popular destination in the park, Paradise, is located in the park's southern region, and Ohanapecosh, the Grove of Patriarchs, and Tipsoo Lae are in the southeastern corner. Mount Rainier National Park's eastern and northern areas are dominated by wilderness.

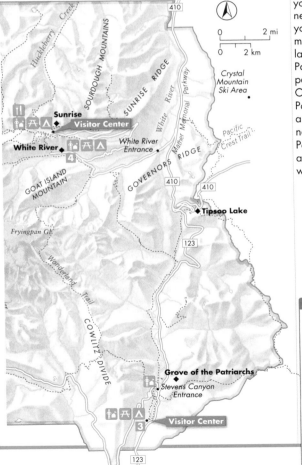

0     2 mi
0     2 km

Huckleberry Creek

SOURDOUGH MOUNTAINS

SUNRISE RIDGE

White River

Mather Memorial Parkway

410

Crystal Mountain Ski Area

Pacific Crest Trail

**Sunrise** — Visitor Center

**White River** — White River Entrance

GOVERNORS RIDGE

GOAT ISLAND MOUNTAIN

Fryingpan GI.

410    410

◆ **Tipsoo Lake**

123

Wonderland Trail

COWLITZ DIVIDE

**Grove of the Patriarchs**
◆
Stevens Canyon Entrance

Visitor Center

123

**KEY**

- Ranger Station
- Campground
- Picnic Area
- Restaurant
- Lodge
- Trailhead
- Restrooms
- Scenic Viewpoint
- Walking/Hiking Trails
- Bicycle Path

# MOUNT RAINIER PLANNER

## When to Go

**Crowds are heaviest in July, August, and September,** when the parking lots at Paradise and Sunrise often fill before noon. During this period campsites are reserved months in advance, and other lodgings are reserved as much as a year ahead. Washington's rare periods of clear winter weather bring lots of residents up to Paradise for cross-country skiing.

Rainier is the Puget Sound's weather vane: if you can see it, the weather is going to be fine. Visitors are most likely to see the summit in July, August, and September. True to its name, Paradise is often sunny during periods when the lowlands are under a cloud layer. The other nine months of the year, Rainier's summit gathers lenticular clouds whenever a Pacific storm approaches, and once it vanishes from view, not only is it impossible to see the peak, it's time to haul out rain gear.

## Flora & Fauna

Wildflower season in the meadows at and above timberline is mid-July through August, depending on the exposure (southern earlier, northern later) and the preceding winter's snowfall. Most of the park's higher-elevation trails are not snow-free until late June. You are not as likely to see Rainier's wildlife—deer, elk, black bears, cougars, and other mountain creatures—as often as you might at other parks, such as Olympic. Larger mammals tend to occupy the less accessible wilderness areas of the park and thus elude the average visitor, but squirrels, marmots, and birds are easier to spot.

As always, the best times are at dawn and dusk, when animals can often be spotted at the forest's edge. Fawns are born to the park's does in May, and the bugling of bull elk on the high ridges can be heard in late September and October, especially on the park's eastern side.

## Hours

Mount Rainier is open 24 hours a day, but with limited access in winter. Gates at Nisqually (Longmire) are staffed year-round during the day; facilities at Paradise and Ohanapecosh are open daily from late May to mid-October; and Sunrise is open daily July to early October. During off-hours you can buy passes at the gates from machines that accept credit and debit cards. Winter access to the park is limited to the Nisqually entrance, and the Jackson Memorial Visitor Center at Paradise is open on weekends and holidays in winter.

AVG. HIGH/LOW TEMPS.

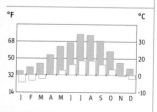

# Getting There & Around

More than two million people visit Mount Rainier National Park each year to experience the majesty of nature by hiking, camping, picnicking, skiing, and joining guided interpretive programs. Park roads are narrow and winding, with maximum speeds of 35 mph in most places, and you have to watch for pedestrians, cyclists, and wildlife. Parking can be very difficult to find during the peak summer season, especially at Paradise, Sunrise, the Grove of Patriarchs, and at the trailheads between Longmire and Paradise; it's best to arrive early in the day if you plan to visit these sites.

The major roads that reach Mount Rainier National Park—Highways 410, 706, and 123—are paved and well-maintained state highways. The Nisqually entrance is on Highway 706, 14 mi east of Route 7; the Ohanapecosh entrance is on Route 123, 5 mi north of U.S. 12; and the White River entrance is on Route 410, 3 mi north of the Chinook and Cayuse passes.

As these highways reach Rainier, they become mountain roads and wind up and down many steep slopes—cautious driving is essential. Vehicles hauling large loads should gear down, especially on downhill sections. Even drivers of passenger cars should take care not to overheat brakes by constant use. Because they traverse the shoulders of a mountain with tempestuous weather, these roads are subject to storms any time of year—even in midsummer—and are almost always being repaired in summer from winter damage and washouts. Expect to encounter road-work delays several times if you are circumnavigating the mountain.

The side roads that wind their way into the park's western slope are all narrower, unpaved, and subject to frequent flooding and washouts. All but Carbon River Road and Highway 706 to Paradise are closed by snow in winter. During this time, however, Carbon River Road tends to flood near the park boundary. (Route 410 is open to the Crystal Mountain access road entrance.) Cayuse Pass usually opens in late April; the Westside Road, Paradise Valley Road, and Stevens Canyon Road usually open in May; Chinook Pass, Mowich Lake Road, and White River Road open in late May; and Sunrise Road opens in late June. All these dates are subject to weather fluctuations.

All off-road vehicle use—4×4 vehicles, ATVs, motorcycles, snowmobiles—is prohibited in Mount Rainier National Park.

## Publications

The park office distributes a useful, free, four-page guide for those planning overnight trips in the backcountry, "Wilderness Trip Planner: A Hiker's Guide to the Wilderness of Mount Rainier National Park." The free, quarterly *Tahoma* newsletter lists current information on roads, campgrounds, and the like; it's available at visitor centers. The best general guide to the park, *A Traveler's Companion to Mount Rainier National Park*, is available through the Northwest Interpretative Association (NWIA). NWIA also offers a list of books and park publications, the "Catalogue of Books and Maps—Mount Rainier National Park." William H. Moir's *Forests of Mount Rainier* is a fine overview if you're interested in the flora, fauna, and geology of the park. For a concise and useful map and guide to Rainier's trail system, buy *50 Hikes in Mount Rainier National Park*, by Ira Spring and Harvey Manning, published by Seattle's famed Mountaineers. If you're curious about glaciers, pick up Carolyn Driedger's pamphlet "Visitor's Guide to Mount Rainier's Glaciers."

26

By Debbie Olsen

Like a mysterious, white-clad woman, often veiled in clouds even when the surrounding forests and fields are bathed in sunlight, Mt. Rainier is the centerpiece of its namesake park. The impressive volcanic peak stands at an elevation of 14,411 feet, making it the fifth-highest peak in the lower 48 states. More than 2 million visitors a year enjoy spectacular views of the mountain and return home with a lifelong memory of its image.

The mountain holds the largest glacial system in the contiguous United States, with more than two dozen major glaciers. On the lower slopes you'll find silent forests made up of cathedral-like groves of Douglas fir, Western hemlock, and Western red cedar, some more than 1,000 years old. Water and lush greenery are everywhere in the park, and dozens of thundering waterfalls, accessible from the road or by a short hike, fill the air with mist.

## Scenic Drives

★ **Chinook Pass Road.** Route 410 (the highway to Yakima) follows the eastern edge of the park to Chinook Pass, where it climbs the steep, 5,432-foot pass via a series of switchbacks. At its top, you'll see broad views of Rainier and the east slope of the Cascades.

★ **Mowich Lake Road.** In the northwest corner of the park, this 24-mi mountain road begins in Wilkeson and heads up the Rainier foothills to Mowich Lake, traversing beautiful mountain meadows along the way. Mowich Lake is a pleasant spot for a picnic; there's also a peaceful walk-in campground.

**Paradise Road.** This 9-mi stretch of Highway 706 winds its way up the mountain's southwest flank from Longmire to Paradise, taking you from lowland forest to the ever-expanding vistas of the mountain above.

Visit on a weekday if possible, especially in peak summer months, when the road is packed with cars. The route is open year-round.

**Route 123 and Stevens Canyon Road.** At Chinook Pass you can pick up Route 123 and head south to its junction with Stevens Canyon Road. Take this road west to its junction with the Paradise–Nisqually entrance road, which runs west through Longmire and exits the park at Nisqually. The route winds among valley-floor rain forest and uphill slopes; vistas of Puget Sound and the Cascade Range appear at numerous points along the way.

> **FLOOD DAMAGE**
>
> On November 6–7, 2006, 18 inches of rain fell in Mount Rainier National Park over a 36 hour period. The subsequent flooding caused severe damage to much of the park's infrastructure (roads, trails, and campsites), and the extent of closures for the 2007 season and beyond were unknown at this writing. Please be sure to confirm site and road openings with one of the park's visitor centers before your trip.

**Sunrise Road.** This popular (read: crowded) scenic road carves its way 11 mi up Sunrise Ridge from the White River Valley on the northeast side of the park. As you top the ridge there are sweeping views of the surrounding lowlands. The road is open late June to October.

**26**

## What to See

### Historic Sites

**National Park Inn.** Even if you don't plan to stay overnight, stop by to observe the architecture of this 1917 inn, which is listed on the National Register of Historic Places. While you're here, relax in front of the fireplace in the lounge, shop at the gift shop, or dine at the restaurant. ⊠ *Longmire Visitor Complex, Hwy. 706, 10 mi east of Nisqually entrance, Longmire 98304* ☎ *360/569–2411.*

### Scenic Stops

**Christine Falls.** These two tiered falls were named in honor of Christine Louise Van Trump, who climbed to the 10,000-foot level on Mt. Rainier in 1889 at the age of nine, despite having a crippling nervous-system disorder. ⊠ *Next to Hwy. 706, about 2½ mi east of Cougar Rock Campground.*

Fodor'sChoice ★ **Grove of the Patriarchs.** Protected from the periodic fires that swept through the surrounding areas, this small island of 1,000-year-old trees is one of Mount Rainier National Park's most memorable features. A 1½-mi loop trail heads through the old-growth forest of Douglas fir, cedar, and hemlock. ⊠ *Rte. 123, west of the Stevens Canyon entrance.*

★ **Narada Falls.** A steep but short trail leads to the viewing area for these spectacular 168-foot falls, which expand to a width of 75 feet during peak flow times. In winter the frozen falls are popular with ice climbers. ⊠ *Along Hwy. 706, 1 mi west of the turnoff for Paradise, 6 mi east of Cougar Rock Campground.*

## MOUNT RAINIER IN ONE DAY

The best way to get a complete overview of Mount Rainier in a day or less is to enter via Nisqually and begin your tour by browsing in **Longmire Museum.** When you're done, get to know the environment in and around Longmire Meadow and the overgrown ruins of Longmire Springs Hotel on the ½-mi **Trail of the Shadows** nature loop.

From Longmire, Highway 706 E. climbs northeast into the mountains toward Paradise. Take a moment to explore gorgeous **Christine Falls,** just north of the road 1½ mi past Cougar Rock Campground, and **Narada Falls,** 3 mi farther on; both are spanned by graceful stone footbridges. Fantastic mountain views, alpine meadows crosshatched with nature trails, a

welcoming lodge and restaurant, and the excellent **Jackson Memorial Visitor Center** combine to make lofty Paradise the primary goal of most park visitors. One outstanding (but challenging) way to explore the high country is to hike the 5-mi round-trip **Skyline Trail** to Panorama Point, which rewards you with stunning 360-degree views.

Continue eastward on Highway 706 E. for 21 mi and leave your car to explore the incomparable, thousand-year-old **Grove of the Patriarchs.** Afterward, turn your car north toward White River and **Sunrise Visitor Center,** where you can watch the alpenglow fade from Mt. Rainier's domed summit.

Ⓒ **Tipsoo Lake.** The short, pleasant trail that circles the lake here—ideal for families—provides breathtaking views. Enjoy the subalpine wildflower meadows during the summer months; in early fall there is an abundant supply of huckleberries. ⊠ *Off Cayuse Pass east on Hwy. 410.*

### Visitor Centers

**Jackson Memorial Visitor Center.** High on the mountain's southern flank, this center houses exhibits on geology, mountaineering, glaciology, winter storms, and alpine ecology; multimedia programs repeat at half-hour intervals. This is the park's most popular visitor destination, and it can be quite crowded in summer. ⊠ *Hwy. 706 E., 19 mi. east of the Nisqually park entrance* ☏ *360/569–2211 Ext. 2328* ☉ *May–mid-Oct., daily 9–5; Nov.–Apr., weekends and holidays 10–5.*

★ **Longmire Museum and Visitor Center.** Glass cases inside this museum preserve plants and animals from the park—including a large, friendly-looking stuffed cougar—and historical photographs and geographical displays provide a worthwhile overview of the park's history. The visitor center, next door to the museum, has some perfunctory exhibits on the surrounding forest and its inhabitants, as well as pamphlets and information about park activities. ⊠ *Hwy. 706, 17 mi east of Ashford* ☏ *360/569–2211 Ext. 3314* 🎫 *Free* ☉ *Daily 9–4:30.*

**Ohanapecosh Visitor Center.** Learn about the region's dense old-growth forests through interpretive displays and videos at this visitor center, located near the Grove of the Patriarchs. ⌂ *Rte. 123, 11 mi north of Packwood* ☎ *360/569–6046* ☺ *Late May–Oct., daily 9–6.*

**Sunrise Visitor Center.** Exhibits at this center explain the region's sparser alpine and subalpine ecology. A network of nearby loop trails leads you through alpine meadows and forest to overlooks that afford broad views of the Cascades and Rainier. Evening programs are offered at White River Campground on Thursday through Saturday nights in summer. ⌂ *Sunrise Rd., 15 mi from the White River park entrance* ☎ *360/663–2425* ☺ *Early July–Labor Day, daily 9–6.*

**WHAT'S IN A NAME?**

Mount Rainier's Native American name, Tahoma (also rendered Takhoma), means "the mountain that was God." Various unsuccessful attempts have been made to restore the aboriginal name to the peak (Peter Rainier was an obscure British admiral of no significance to Northwest history). However, to most Puget Sound residents, Rainier is simply "the mountain."

## Sports & the Outdoors

**26**

### Bird-watching

★ Watch for kestrels, red-tailed hawks, and, occasionally, golden eagles on snags in the lowland forests. Also present at Rainier, but rarely seen, are great horned owls, spotted owls, and screech owls. Iridescent rufous hummingbirds flit from blossom to blossom in the drowsy summer lowlands, and sprightly water ouzels flutter in the many forest creeks. Raucous Steller's jays and gray jays scold passersby from trees, often darting boldly down to steal morsels from unguarded picnic tables. At higher elevations, look for the pure white plumage of the white-tailed ptarmigan as it hunts for seeds and insects in winter. Waxwings, vireos, nuthatches, sapsuckers, warblers, flycatchers, larks, thrushes, siskins, tanagers, and finches are common throughout the park.

### Boating

Nonmotorized boating is permitted on all lakes inside the park except Frozen, Ghost, Reflection, and Tipsoo lakes. Mowich Lake, in the northwest corner of the park, is the only lake easily accessible to canoes and kayaks. There are no boat rentals inside the park.

### Hiking

★ Although the mountain can seem remarkably benign on calm summer days, hiking Rainier is not a city-park stroll. Dozens of hikers and trekkers annually lose their way and must be rescued—and lives are lost on the mountain each year. Weather that approaches cyclonic levels can appear quite suddenly, any month of the year. With the possible exception of the short loop hikes listed below, all visitors venturing far from vehicle access points should carry day packs with warm clothing, food, and other emergency supplies.

EASY **Nisqually Vista Trail.** Equally popular in summer and winter, this trail is a 1¼-mi round-trip through subalpine meadows to an overlook point for Nisqually Glacier. The gradually sloping path is a favorite venue for

Mount Rainier,
Looking North

KEY
– – – Hiking Trails
· · · · · Climbing Routes

MOUNT RAINIER

Liberty Cap
14,122ft
Columbia Crest
14,411ft
Disappointment
Cleaver
Little Tahoma Peak
11,138ft
Ingraham Glacier
CATHEDRAL ROCKS
Anvil Rock
9,584ft
Paradise Glaciers
McClure Rock
7,385ft
Camp Muir
10,188ft
Muir Snowfield
Gibraltar Rock
12,660ft
Point Success
14,153ft
Nisqually Glacier
Panorama Point
6,800ft
Skyline Trail
Alta Vista
Paradise
Wilson Glacier
Henry M. Jackson
Memorial Visitor Center
Pinnacle
Peak
6,562ft
The Castle
Louise
Lake
Reflection
Lakes
Unicorn Peak
6,917ft
SUNSET
AMPHITHEATER
St. Andrews Rock
10,992ft
Van Trump Glaciers
SUCCESS CLEAVER
Success Glacier
KAUTZ GLACIER
WAPOWETY CLEAVER
CUSHMAN CREST
Plummer Peak
6,370ft
Lane Peak
6,012ft
TATOOSH RANGE
Tokaloo Rock
7,684ft
PUYALLUP CLEAVER
Tahoma Glacier
GLACIER
ISLAND
South Tahoma Glacier
SUCCESS DIVIDE
Pyramid Glaciers
Mildred Point
VAN TRUMP
PARK
Chutla Peak
Wahpenayo Peak
6,231ft
EMERALD RIDGE
Iron Mountain
6,283ft
Pyramid Peak
6,937ft
PYRAMID
PARK
Eagle Peak
5,958ft
Rampart Ridge Trail
PYRAMID RIDGE
Cougar Rock
Pyramid Creek
RAMPART
THE RAMPARTS
Longmire

cross-country skiers in winter; in summer, listen for the shrill alarm calls of the area's marmots. ⊠ *Jackson Memorial Visitor Center, Rte. 123, 1 mi north of Ohanapecosh, at the high point of Hwy. 706.*

**Sourdough Ridge Self-Guiding Trail.** The mile-long loop of this easy trail takes you through the delicate subalpine meadows near the Sunrise Visitor Center. A gradual climb to the ridgetop yields magnificent views of Mt. Rainier and the more distant volcanic cones of Mts. Baker, Adams, Glacier, and Hood. ⊠ *Sunrise Visitor Center, Sunrise Rd., 15 mi from the White River park entrance.*

**Trail of the Shadows.** This ½-mi trek is notable for its glimpses of meadowland ecology, its colorful soda springs (don't drink the water), James Longmire's old homestead cabin, and the foundation of the old Longmire Springs Hotel, which was destroyed by fire around 1900. ⊠ *Hwy. 706, 10 mi east of Nisqually entrance.*

MODERATE
Fodor'sChoice
★
**Skyline Trail.** This 5-mi loop, one of the highest trails in the park, beckons day-trippers with a vista of alpine ridges and, in summer, meadows filled with brilliant flowers and birds. At 6,800 feet, Panorama Point, the spine of the Cascade Range, spreads away to the east, and Nisqually Glacier grumbles its way downslope. ⊠ *Jackson Memorial Visitor Center, Rte. 123, 1 mi north of Ohanapecosh at the high point of Hwy. 706.*

26

**Van Trump Park Trail.** You gain an exhilarating 2,200 feet on this trail while hiking through a vast expanse of meadow with views of the southern Puget Sound. The 5-mi trail provides good footing, and the average hiker can make it up in three to four hours. ⊠ *Hwy. 706 at Christine Falls, 4⁴/₁₀ mi east of Longmire.*

DIFFICULT
★
**Burroughs Mountain Trail.** Starting at the south side of the Sunrise parking area, this three-hour, 7-mi round-trip hike offers spectacular views of the peak named in honor of naturalist and essayist John Burroughs. The challenging trail passes Shadow Lake before climbing to an overlook of the White River and Emmon's Glacier. As you continue on, you'll reach First Burroughs Mountain and Second Burroughs Mountain. This area on the northeast slope of Mt. Rainier has some of the most accessible tundra in the Cascades, and you can observe the delicate slow-growing plants that survive in this harsh environment. Note: early-season hiking on this trail can be particularly hazardous due to snow and ice on the steep mountain slopes; check trail conditions before starting out.

Fodor'sChoice
★
**Wonderland Trail.** All other Mt. Rainier hikes pale in comparison to this stunning 93-mi trek, which completely encircles the mountain. The trail passes through all the major life zones of the park, from the old-growth forests of the lowlands to the alpine meadows and goat-haunted glaciers of the highlands. Be sure to pick up a mountain-goat sighting card from a ranger station or information center to help in the park's ongoing effort to learn more about these elusive animals. Wonderland is a rugged trail; elevation gains and losses totaling 3,500 feet are common in a day's hike, which averages 8 mi. Most hikers start out from either Longmire or Sunrise and take 10–14 days to cover the 93-mi route. Snow lingers on the high passes well into June (sometimes July), and you can count on rain any time of the year. Campsites are wilderness trailside

## OUTFITTERS & EXPEDITIONS

### HIKING

**Rainier Mountaineering Inc.** Reserve a private hiking guide through this mountaineering outfitter. ⊠ *30027 Hwy. 706 E, Ashford* ☎ *888/892–5462 or 360/569–2227* ⊕ *www.rmiguides.com* ⌑ *$805 (three-day summit climb package).*

**Whittaker Mountaineering.** You can rent hiking gear and outdoor equipment here, or arrange for a private hiking guide. ⊠ *30027 Hwy. 706 E, Ashford* ☎ *800/238–5756 or 360/569–2142* ⊕ *www. whittakermountaineering.com.*

### MOUNTAIN CLIMBING

**Rainier Mountaineering Inc.** The highly regarded concessionaire teaches the fundamentals of mountaineering at one-day classes held from mid-May through late September; participants are evaluated on their fitness for the climb and must be able to withstand a 16-mi round-trip hike with a 9,000-ft gain in elevation. ⊠ *30027 Hwy. 706 E, Ashford* ☎ *888/892–5462 or 360/569–2227* ⊕ *www.rmiguides.com* ⌑ *$805 (three-day summit climb package).*

**Whittaker Mountaineering.** This all-purpose Rainier Base Camp outfitter rents climbing equipment. ⊠ *30027 Hwy. 706 E, Ashford* ☎ *800/238–5756 or 360/569–2142* ⊕ *www.whittakermountaineering. com.*

### SKIING & SNOWSHOEING

**Paradise Ski Area.** Here you can cross-country ski or, in the Snowplay Area north of the upper parking lot at Paradise, sled using inner tubes and soft platters from December to April. Check with rangers for any restrictions.

⊠ *Accessible from Nisqually entrance at park's southwest corner and from Stevens Canyon entrance at park's southeast corner (summer only)* ☎ *360/569–2211* ⊕ *www.nps. gov/mora* ☉ *May–mid-Oct., daily, sunrise–sunset; mid-Oct.–Apr., weekends sunrise–sunset.*

**Rainier Mountaineering Inc.** This mountaineering outfitter offers winter ski programs and seminars; they also arrange private cross-country skiing and snowshoeing guides. ⊠ *30027 Hwy. 706 E, Ashford* ☎ *888/892–5462 or 360/569–2227* ⊕ *www.rmiguides.com.*

**Rainier Ski Touring Center.** Adjacent to the National Park Inn, this company rents cross-country ski equipment and provides lessons from mid-December through Easter, depending on snow conditions. ⊠ *Hwy. 706, 10 mi east of Nisqually entrance, Longmire* ⊕ *http://www. mashell.com/~mtrretail/Skiing.htm* ☎ *360/569–2411, 360/569–2271 Mon.–Fri.*

**Snowshoe Walks.** Park rangers lead snowshoe walks that start at Jackson Memorial Visitor Center at Paradise and cover 1¼ mi in about two hours. Check park publications for exact dates. ⊠ *1 mi north of Ohanapecosh on Rte. 123, at the high point of Hwy. 706* ☎ *360/569–2211 Ext. 2328* ⌑ *Free* ☉ *Late Dec.–Apr., weekends and holidays.*

**Whittaker Mountaineering.** You can rent outdoor equipment, skis, snowshoes, and snowboards through this outfitter, which also arranges for private cross-country skiing guides. ⊠ *30027 Hwy. 706 E, Ashford* ☎ *800/238–5756 or 360/569–2142* ⊕ *www. whittakermountaineering.com.*

areas with pit toilets and water that must be purified before drinking. Only hardy, well-equipped, and experienced wilderness trekkers should attempt this trip, but those who do will be amply rewarded. Wilderness permits are required, and reservations are strongly recommended. ⚠ Parts of the Wonderland Trail were severely damaged in the Nov. 2006 floods, and some sections may remain closed in 2007. Be sure to check with one of the park's visitor centers for the trail's current status. ✉ *Longmire Visitor Center, Hwy. 706, 17 mi east of Ashford; Sunrise Visitor Center, Sunrise Rd., 15 mi west of the White River park entrance.*

For information on tours and equipment, ⇨ Outfitters & Expeditions box.

## Mountain Climbing

★ Climbing Mt. Rainier is not for amateurs; each year, climbers die on the mountain, and many climbers become lost and must be rescued. Near-catastrophic weather can appear quite suddenly, any month of the year. If you're experienced in technical, high-elevation snow, rock, and ice-field adventuring, Mt. Rainier can be a memorable experience. Experienced climbers can fill out a climbing card at the Paradise, White River, or Carbon River ranger stations and lead their own groups of two or more. Climbers must register with a ranger before leaving and check out upon return. A $30 annual climbing fee applies to anyone venturing above 10,000 feet or onto one of Rainier's glaciers. During peak season, it is recommended that you make a climbing reservation in advance. The reservation fee is $20 per group, and reservations are taken by fax beginning on April 1 on a first-come first-served basis. For more information on climbing Mt. Rainier or for a reservation form and fax number, visit the park's Web site ⊕ www.nps.gov/mora/climb/climb.htm. For information on tours and equipment, ⇨ Outfitters & Expeditions box.

## Skiing

Mt. Rainier is a major Nordic ski center. Although trails are not groomed, those around Paradise are extremely popular. If you want to ski with fewer people, try the trails in and around the Ohanapecosh–Stevens Canyon area, which are just as beautiful and, because of their more easterly exposure, slightly less subject to the rains that can douse the Longmire side, even in the dead of winter. You should never ski on the plowed main roads, especially in the Paradise area—the snowplow operator can't see you. No rentals are available on the eastern side of the park. For information on tours and equipment, ⇨ Outfitters & Expeditions box.

## Snowshoeing

★ Deep snows make Mt. Rainier a snowshoeing Mecca. The network of trails in the Paradise area makes it the best choice for snowshoers. The park's east side roads, Routes 123 and 410, are unplowed and provide another good snowshoeing venue, although you must share the main parts of the road with snowmobilers. For information on tours and equipment, ⇨ Outfitters & Expeditions box.

# Educational Offerings

FodorśChoice **Gray Line Bus Tours.** This company conducts sightseeing tours of Seattle, and one-day and longer tours from Seattle to Mount Rainier and

Olympic national parks, Mt. St. Helens, the North Cascades, and the Washington Wine Country (Yakima Valley). ✉ *4500 Marginal Way SW, Seattle* ☎ *206/624–5077 or 800/426–7532* ⊕ *www.graylineofseattle. com* 📠 *Call for prices and schedules.*

★ **Ancient Forest Walks.** Park naturalists help visitors learn to identify different rain-forest trees and plants on forest walks. For exact schedules, consult bulletin boards at visitor centers, ranger stations, and campgrounds. ✉ *Ohanapecosh Visitor Center: Rte. 123, 11 mi north of Packwood* ☎ *360/569–6046* 📠 *Free* ☉ *June–Sept., hours and days vary according to staffing schedules.*

# WHAT'S NEARBY

## Nearby Towns

**Ashford** sits astride an ancient trail across the Cascades used by the Yakama Indians to trade with the coastal tribes of western Washington. The town began as a logging railway terminal; today, it's the main gateway to Mount Rainier—and the only year-round access point to the park—catering to visitors with lodges, restaurants, groceries, and gift shops. Surrounded by Cascade peaks, **Packwood** is a pretty mountain village on U.S. 12, below White Pass. Between Mt. Rainier and Mt. St. Helens, it's a perfect jumping-off point for exploring local wilderness areas.

## Nearby Attractions

★ **Coldwater Ridge Visitor Center.** Exhibits at this multimillion-dollar facility document the great blast of Mt. St. Helens and its effects on the surrounding 150,000 acres, which were devastated but are in the process of a remarkable recovery. A ¼-mi trail leads from the visitor center to Coldwater Lake, which has a recreation area. ✉ *Rte. 504, 43 mi east of I–5* ☎ *360/274–2131* 📠 *Free* ☉ *Daily 10–6.*

**Crystal Mountain Ski Area.** Washington State's biggest and best-known ski area is also open in summer for chairlift rides that afford sensational views of Rainier and the Cascades. ✉ *Crystal Mountain Blvd., off Rte. 410, Crystal Mountain* ☎ *360/663–2265* ⊕ *www.skicrystal.com* 📠 *$15* ☉ *Memorial Day–Labor Day, weekends and holidays 10–4.*

★ **Goat Rocks Wilderness.** The crags in Gifford Pinchot National Forest, south of Mt. Rainier, are aptly named: you'll often see mountain goats here, especially when you hike into the backcountry; Goat Lake is a particularly good spot for viewing the elusive creatures. You can see the goats without backpacking by taking Forest Road 2140 south from U.S. 12 near Packwood to Stonewall Ridge (ask for exact directions in Packwood, or ask a national forest ranger). The goats will be on Stonewall Ridge looming up ahead of you. ✉ *10600 N.E. 51st St. Circle, Vancouver, Wilderness entrance points along U.S. 12, 2–10 mi east of White Pass* ☎ *360/ 891–5000* ⊕ *www.fs.fed.us/gpnf* 📠 *Free* ☉ *Call for weather conditions.*

**Johnston Ridge Observatory.** With the most spectacular views of the crater and lava dome of Mt. St. Helens, this observatory also has exhibits that interpret the geology of the mountain and explain how scientists monitor an active volcano. ⊠ *Rte. 504, 53 mi east of I–5, Mount St. Helens* ☎ *360/274–2140* ☒ *Free* ⊙ *Daily 10–6.*

★ ⊙ **Mount Rainier Scenic Railroad.** Beginning at Elbe, 11 mi west of Ashford, the train takes you southeast through lush forests and across scenic bridges, covering 14 mi of incomparable beauty. Seasonal theme trips, such as the Halloween Ghost Train and the Christmastime Snowball Express, are also available. ⊠ *Rte. 7, Elbe* ☎ *888/783–2611* ⊕ *www.mrsr.com* ☒ *$15* ⊙ *Memorial Day–July 4, weekends; early July–Labor Day, daily; remainder of Sept., weekends; Dec. (Snowball Express), weekends. Call for hrs.*

**Mount St. Helens Visitor Center.** This facility, one of three visitor centers along Route 504 on the west side of the mountain, has exhibits documenting the eruption, plus a walk-through volcano. ⊠ *Rte. 504, 5 mi east of I–5, Silver Lake* ☎ *360/274–2100* ⊕ *http://www.parks.wa.gov/mountsthelens. asp* ☒ *$3* ⊙ *Late Oct.–Mar., daily 9–4; Apr.–late Oct., daily 9–5.*

★ **Northwest Trek Wildlife Park.** One of the pioneers in modern zoo operation, this park consists of large, natural enclosures where native animals such as elk, caribou, moose, and deer roam free. Five miles of nature trails meander near the enclosures, and the hands-on Cheney Discovery Center provides an up-close wildlife experience. Hop on a tram for a narrated tour of the park; another tour lets you accompany keepers while they feed the wildlife. ⊠ *Rte. 161, about 35 mi west of Mount Rainier National Park, Eatonville* ☎ *360/832–6122* ⊕ *www.nwtrek.org* ☒ *$12* ⊙ *Mid-Feb.–Oct., daily 9:30–6; Nov.–mid-Feb., Fri.–Sun. 9:30–6.*

**26**

# WHERE TO STAY & EAT

### About the Restaurants

There are a limited number of restaurants inside the park, and a few worth checking out lie beyond its borders. Mount Rainier's picnic areas are justly famous, especially in summer, when wildflowers fill the meadows and friendly yellow pine chipmunks dart hopefully about in search of handouts.

### About the Hotels

The Mount Rainier area is remarkably bereft of quality lodging. Rainier's two national park lodges, at Longmire and Paradise, are attractive and well maintained. They ooze considerable history and charm, especially Paradise Inn, but unless you've made summer reservations a year in advance, getting a room can be a challenge. Be aware that Paradise Inn is closed in 2007 for a major renovation and is not expected to reopen until the spring of 2008. There are dozens of motels and cabin complexes near the park entrances, but the vast majority are plain, overpriced, or downright dilapidated. With just a few exceptions, you're better off camping.

### About the Campgrounds

There are five drive-in campgrounds in the park—Cougar Rock, Ipsut Creek, Ohanapecosh, Sunshine Point, and White River—with almost

700 sites for tents and RVs. None of the park campgrounds has hot water or RV hookups; showers are available at Jackson Memorial Visitor Center. ⚠ **The Sunshine Point Campground was severely damaged in the Nov. 2006 floods; be sure to check with one of the park's visitor centers for its current status.**

For backcountry camping, you must obtain a free wilderness permit at one of the visitor centers. Primitive sites are spaced at 7- to 8-mi intervals along the Wonderland Trail. ⚠ **Parts of the Wonderland Trail were severely damaged in the Nov. 2006 floods, and some sections may remain closed in 2007. Be sure to check with one of the park's visitor centers for the trail's current status.** A copy of *Wilderness Trip Planner: A Hiker's Guide to the Wilderness of Mount Rainier National Park,* available from any of the park's visitor centers or through the superintendent's office, is an invaluable guide if you're planning backcountry stays. Reservations for specific wilderness campsites are available from May 1 to September 30 for $20; for details, call the Wilderness Information Center at 360/569–4453.

## Where to Eat

### In Mount Rainier

★ **$–$$$** ✕ **Paradise Inn.** Where else can you get a decent Sunday brunch in a historic heavy-timbered lodge halfway up a mountain? Tall, many-paned windows provide terrific views of Rainier, and the warm glow of native wood permeates the large dining room. The lunch menu is simple and healthy—grilled salmon, salads, and the like. For dinner, there's nothing like a hearty plate of the inn's signature bourbon buffalo meat loaf. At press time, Paradise Inn was closed for extensive renovations; the inn is expected to reopen in May 2008. ✉ *Paradise* ☎ *360/569–2413* ⚵ *Reservations not accepted. $12–$25* ▭ *MC, V* ☉ *Closed Oct.–late May.*

★ **$–$$** ✕ **National Park Inn.** Photos of Mt. Rainier taken by some of the Northwest's top photographers adorn the walls of this inn's large dining room, a bonus on the many days the mountain refuses to show itself. Meals, served family-style, are simple but tasty: maple hazelnut chicken, tenderloin tip stir-fry, and grilled red snapper with black bean sauce and corn relish. For breakfast, don't miss the home-baked cinnamon rolls with cream-cheese frosting. ✉ *Longmire* ☎ *360/569–2411* ⚵ *Reservations not accepted. $12–$20* ▭ *MC, V.*

☾ ¢ ✕ **Jackson Memorial Visitor Center.** Traditional grill fare such as hot dogs, hamburgers, and soft drinks are served daily from May through early October at this visitor center and on weekends and holidays during the rest of the year. ✉ *Rte. 123, 1 mi north of Ohanapecosh at the high point of Hwy. 706* ☎ *360/569–2211. $3–$5* ▭ *No credit cards* ☉ *Closed weekdays early Oct.–Apr.*

☾ ¢ ✕ **Sunshine Day Lodge & Visitor Center.** A cafeteria and grill at this visitor center serves inexpensive hamburgers, chili, hot dogs, and snacks from early July to early September. ✉ *Sunrise Rd., 15 mi from the White River park entrance* ☎ *360/663–2425. $3–$6* ▭ *No credit cards* ☉ *Closed early Sept.–early July.*

PICNIC AREAS   All Mount Rainier picnic areas are open July through September only.

**Carbon River Picnic Ground.** You'll find a half-dozen tables in the woods, near the park's northwest boundary. ⊠ *Carbon River Rd., 1½ mi east of park entrance.*

**Paradise Picnic Area.** This site has great views on clear days. After picnicking at Paradise, you can take an easy hike to one of the many waterfalls in the area—Sluiskin, Myrtle, or Narada, to name a few. ⊠ *Hwy. 706, 11 mi east of Longmire.*

**Sunrise Picnic Area.** Set in an alpine meadow that's filled with wildflowers in July and August, this picnic area provides expansive views of the mountain and surrounding ranges in good weather. ⊠ *Sunrise Rd., 11 mi west of the White River entrance.*

**Sunshine Point Picnic Area.** A small group of picnic tables at the Sunshine Point Campground sits in an open meadow along the burbling Nisqually River. ⚠ **The Sunshine Point Campground was severely damaged in the Nov. 2006 floods; be sure to check with one of the park's visitor centers for its current status.** ⊠ *Hwy. 706, 1 mi east of the Nisqually entrance.*

### Outside the Park

★ **$–$$$** ✕ **Alexander's Country Inn.** Without a doubt, this classic, woodsy Northwest country inn built in 1912 serves some of the best food in the area. Ceiling fans and wooden booths lining the walls make it look like a country kitchen. Try the steak or trout (freshly caught from the pond on the grounds); the homemade bread is fantastic, and the blackberry pie is a must for dessert. You can dine inside or outside on a patio overlooking the trout pond and a waterfall. The Inn also prepares box lunches for adventurers upon request. ⊠ *37515 Hwy. 706, Ashford* ☎ *360/569–2323 or 800/654–7615.* *$10–$25* ▭ *MC, V* ☺ *Closed Nov.–Mar., Mon.–Thurs.*

♺ ¢ ✕ **Scaleburgers.** This 1939 state weigh station has been converted into a popular restaurant serving hamburgers, fries, milk shakes, and ice cream, all made from only the finest ingredients. Eat outside on tables overlooking the hills and scenic railroad. The restaurant is 11 mi west of Ashford. ⊠ *54109 Mountain Hwy. E, Elbe* ☎ *360/569–2247.* *$3–$4* ▭ *No credit cards.*

## Where to Stay

### In Mount Rainier

★ **$–$$** ✕ **National Park Inn.** A large stone fireplace sits prominently in the common room of this country inn, the only one of the park's two lodgings that's open year-round. Rustic details such as wrought-iron lamps and antique bentwood headboards adorn the rooms. Simple American fare is served in the restaurant ($–$$). The inn is operated as a B&B from October through April. ⊠ *Longmire Visitor Complex, Hwy. 706, 10 mi east of Nisqually entrance, Longmire 98304* ☎ *360/569–2275* 🖷 *360/569–2770* ⊕ *www.guestservices.com/rainier* ⤳ *25 rooms, 18 with bath* ⚴ *Restaurant, no a/c, no phone. $100–$134* ▭ *MC, V.*

**$–$$** ✕ **Paradise Inn.** With its hand-carved Alaskan cedar logs, burnished
FodorśChoice  parquet floors, stone fireplaces, Indian rugs, and glorious mountain views,
★  this 1917 inn is a sterling example of national park lodge architecture.

German architect Hans Fraehnke designed the decorative woodwork. In addition to the full-service dining room ($–$$$), there's a small snack bar and a snug lounge. At press time, Paradise Inn was closed for extensive renovations; the inn is expected to reopen in May 2008. ⊠ *Hwy. 706, Paradise* ⌖ *c/o Mount Rainier Guest Services, Box 108, Star Rte., Ashford 98304* ☎ *360/569–2275* 🖷 *360/569–2770* ⊕ *www.guestservices. com/rainier* ⇆ *127 rooms, 96 with bath* ⚭ *Restaurant, bar, no phone, no TV.* *$75–$150* ▤ *MC, V* ⊗ *Closed Nov.–mid-May.*

**CAMPGROUNDS**

★ $ ⛺ **Cougar Rock Campground.** A secluded, heavily wooded campground with an amphitheater, Cougar Rock is one of the first to fill up. You can reserve group sites for $3 per person, per night, with a minimum of 12 people per group. Reservations are accepted for summer only. ⊠ *2½ mi north of Longmire* ☎ *301/722–1257 or 800/365–2267* ⊕ *reservations.nps.gov* ⇆ *173 sites* ⚭ *Flush toilets, dump station, drinking water, fire grates, ranger station.* *$12–$15* ▤ *AE, D, MC, V* ⊗ *Closed mid-Oct.–Apr.*

★ $ ⛺ **Ohanapecosh Campground.** This lush, green campground in the park's southeast corner has a visitor center, amphitheater, and self-guided trail. It's one of the first campgrounds to open. Reservations are accepted for summer only. ⊠ *Ohanapecosh Visitor Center, Hwy. 123, 1½ mi north of park boundary* ☎ *301/722–1257 or 800/365–2267* ⊕ *reservations.nps.gov* ⇆ *188 sites* ⚭ *Flush toilets, dump station, drinking water, fire grates, ranger station.* *$12–$15* ▤ *AE, D, MC, V* ⊗ *Closed late-Oct.–Apr.*

$ ⛺ **Sunshine Point Campground.** This pleasant, partly wooded campground near the river fills up fast. ⚠ **The campground was severely damaged in the Nov. 2006 floods; be sure to check with one of the park's visitor centers for its current status.** ⊠ *5 mi past the Nisqually entrance* ☎ *360/569–2211* ⇆ *18 sites* ⚭ *Drinking water, fire grates, pit toilets.* *$10* ▤ *AE, D, MC, V* ⚭ *Reservations not accepted.*

$ ⛺ **White River Campground.** At an elevation of 4,400 feet, White River is one of the park's highest and least-wooded campgrounds. Here you can enjoy campfire programs, self-guided trails, and partial views of Mt. Rainier's summit. ⊠ *5 mi west of White River entrance* ☎ *360/569–2211* ⇆ *112 sites* ⚭ *Flush toilets, drinking water, fire grates, dump station, ranger station.* *$10* ▤ *AE, D, MC, V* ⚭ *Reservations not accepted* ⊗ *Closed mid-Sept.–early June.*

¢ ⛺ **Ipsut Creek Campground.** The quietest park campground is also the most difficult to reach. It's in the park's northwest corner, amid a wet, green, and rugged wilderness; many self-guided trails are nearby. The campground is theoretically open year-round, though the gravel Carbon River Road that leads to it is subject to flooding and potential closure at any time. Reservations aren't accepted here. ⊠ *Carbon River Rd., 4 mi east of the Carbon River entrance* ☎ *360/569–2211* ⇆ *30 sites* ⚭ *Running water (non-potable), fire grates, pit toilets.* *$8 summer, free in winter* ▤ *AE, D, MC, V.*

★ ¢ ⛺ **Mowich Lake Campground.** This is Rainier's only lakeside campground. Located at 4,959 feet, it's also peaceful and secluded. Note that the campground is accessible only by 5 mi of convoluted gravel roads, which are subject to weather damage and potential closure at any time. ⊠ *Mowich Lake Rd., 6 mi east of the park boundary* ☎ *360/568–2211* ⇆ *30 sites*

⚲ *Pit toilets, running water (non-potable), fire grates, picnic tables, ranger station. Free* ⚲ *Reservations not accepted* ⊘ *Closed Nov.–mid July.*

### Outside the Park

★ **$$–$$$** ✕⊡ **Alexander's Country Inn.** Serving guests since 1912, Alexander's offers premier lodging just a mile from Mt. Rainier. Antiques and fine linens lend the main building romance; there are also two adjacent guesthouses. Rates include a hearty breakfast and evening wine. The cozy restaurant ($–$$; closed to off-site guests weekdays in winter) is the best place in town for lunch or dinner. ⊠ *37515 Hwy. 706 E, 4 mi east of Ashford, Ashford 98304* ☏ *360/569–2323 or 800/654–7615* ⊕ *www. alexanderscountryinn.com* ⊷ *12 rooms, 2 3-bedroom houses* ⚲ *Restaurant, spa, DVD. $120–$175* ═ *MC, V* ⊙⏐ *BP.*

★ **$–$$$** ⊡ **Wellspring.** In the woodlands outside Ashford, the accommodations here include tastefully designed log cabins, a tree house, and a room in a greenhouse. Rooms are individually decorated: a queen-size feather bed suspended by ropes beneath a skylight highlights the Nest Room; the Tatoosh lodge, which can accommodate up to 14 people, has a huge stone fireplace. This collection of units, the only property of its kind in the area, is the creation of a massage therapist; a variety of spa-like amenities are available. ⊠ *54922 Kernehan Rd., Ashford, 98304* ☏ *360/569–2514* ⊷ *1 lodge, 6 cabins, 3 tent cabins,1 treehouse, 1 cottage* ⚲ *Kitchen (some), refrigerator (some), spa, no phone, no TV (some), no a/c, no-smoking rooms. $85–$175* ═ *MC, V* ⊙⏐ *CP, EP.*

**$–$$** ⊡ **Inn of Packwood.** Mt. Rainier and the Cascade Mountains tower above this inn, which is located in the center of Packwood. Pine paneling and furniture lend the rooms rustic charm, and you can swim in an indoor heated pool beneath skylights or have a picnic beneath a weeping willow. A Continental breakfast is included. ⊠ *13032 U.S. 12, Packwood, 98361* ☏ *877/496–9666 or 360/494–5500* ⊟ *360/494–5503* ⊕ *www.innofpackwood.com* ⊷ *33 rooms* ⚲ *Kitchen (some), refrigerator (some), pool. $60–$150* ═ *AE, MC, V* ⊙⏐ *CP.*

**$** ⊡ **Nisqually Lodge.** Fires in the grand stone fireplace lend warmth and cheer to the great room of this hotel, located a few miles west of Mount Rainier National Park. Guest rooms are comfortable and have standard motel decor. ⊠ *31609 Hwy. 706 E, 98304* ☏ *360/569–8804 or 888/674–3554* ⊟ *360/569–2435* ⊕ *www.escapetothemountains.com* ⊷ *24 rooms* ⚲ *Laundry facilities, no-smoking rooms. $76–$80* ═ *AE, MC, V* ⊙⏐ *CP.*

# MOUNT RAINIER ESSENTIALS

**Accessibility** The only trail in the park that is fully accessible to those with impaired mobility is Kautz Creek Trail, a ½-mi boardwalk that leads to a splendid view of the mountain. Parts of the Trail of the Shadows at Longmire and the Grove of the Patriarchs at Ohanapecosh are also accessible. Campgrounds at Cougar Rock, Ohanapecosh, and Sunshine Point have several accessible sites. All main visitor centers, as well as National Park Inn at Longmire, are accessible.

**Admission Fees & Permits** The entrance fee is $15 per vehicle, which covers everyone in the vehicle for seven days; motorcycles and bicycles pay $5. Annual passes are available for $30. Climbing permits are $30 per person per climb or glacier trek. Wilderness camping permits, which must be obtained for all backcountry trips, are free, but advance reservations are highly recommended and cost $20 per party.

**Admission Hours** Mt. Rainier National Park is open 24 hours a day year-round, but with limited access in winter. Gates at Nisqually (Longmire) are open 24 hours a day year-round, but may only be staffed during the day. The Carbon River Ranger Station is open 24 hours a day year-round; the White River Ranger Station is open 24 hours a day from June through September; and the Stevens Canyon entrance by Ohanapecosh is open 24 hours a day from late May to late September. The Jackson Memorial Visitor Center is open from late May to late September 9-5 daily, and from October to April 10–5 weekends and holidays. Sunrise Visitor Center is open daily 9–6, and the Longmire Museum is open daily 9–5 year-round.

**ATMs/Banks** There are no ATMs in the park. Numerous ATMs are available at stores, gas stations, and bank branches in Ashford, Packwood, and Eatonville. In Ashford there are ATMs at Ashford Valley Grocery and Suver's General Store.
🟥 **First Community Bank** ⊠ 121 Washington Ave. N, Eatonville ☎ 360/832-7200. **Key Bank** ⊠ 101 Center St. E, Eatonville ☎ 360/832-6125.

**Automobile Service Stations** Gas and automotive services are not available in Mount Rainier National Park. Ashford and Packwood, with several stations each, are the closest outlets.
🟥 **Mill Town Chevron** ⊠ 236 Center St. E, Eatonville ☎ 360/832-6476.

**Emergencies** For all park emergencies, dial 911.

**Lost and Found** The park's lost and found is located at the park headquarters office in Ashford. You can call or visit in person to see if your missing item has been found, or fill out a form, and park staff will call you when your item is recovered.
🟥 **Lost and Found** ⊠ 55210 238th Ave E., Ashford 98304 ☎ 360/569-2211 ext. 2334.

**Post Offices**
🟥 **The National Park Inn Post Office** ⊠ Longmire Visitor Complex, Hwy. 706 E., 10 mi east of Nisqually entrance, Longmire, 98304 ☎ No phone. **Paradise Inn Post Office** ⊠ Jackson Memorial Visitor Center, Paradise 98304 ☎ No phone.

**Public Telephones and Restrooms** Public telephones and restrooms are located at all park visitor centers (Sunrise, Ohanapecosh, and Paradise), at the National Park Inn at Longmire, and at Paradise Inn at Paradise.

**Shops & Grocers**
🟥 **Eatonville Market.** ⊠ 210 Center St., Eatonville ☎ 360/832-4551. **General Store at Longmire's National Park Inn.** ⊠ Longmire Visitor Complex, Longmire ☎ 360/569-2411. **Plaza Market.** ⊠ 201 Center St., Eatonville ☎ 360/832-6151.

**NEARBY TOWN INFORMATION**
🟥 **Destination Packwood Association** 🗂 Box 64, Packwood 98361 ☎ 360/494-2223 or 800/963-7898 ⊕ www.destinationpackwood.com. **Mount Rainier Business Association** 🗂 Box 214, Ashford 98304 ☎ 360/569-0910 or 877/617-9950 ⊕ www.mt-rainier.com.

**VISITOR INFORMATION**
🟥 **Mount Rainier National Park** ⊠ Tahoma Woods, Star Rte., Ashford, WA 98304 ☎ 360/569-2211 ⊕ www.nps.gov/mora.

# North Cascades National Park

Hiker in Maple Pass, North Cascades National Park

**WORD OF MOUTH**

"Climb the mountains and get their good tidings. Nature's peace will flow into you as sunshine flows into trees. The winds will blow their own freshness into you and the storms their energy, while care will drop off like autumn leaves."

–John Muir

# WELCOME TO NORTH CASCADES

## TOP REASONS TO GO

★ **Pure Wilderness:** Nearly 400 mi of mountain and meadow trails immerse hikers in pristine natural panoramas, with sure sightings of bald eagles, deer, elk, and other wildlife.

★ **Majestic Glaciers:** The North Cascades are home to 318 moving ice masses, more than half of the glaciers in the United States.

★ **Splendid Flora:** A bright palette of flowers blankets the hillsides in midsummer, while October's colors paint the landscape in vibrant autumn hues.

★ **Thrilling Boat Rides:** Lake Chelan, Lake Ross, and the Stehekin River are the starting points for kayaking, white-water rafting, and ferry trips.

★ **19th-Century History:** Delve into the state's farming, lumber, and logging pasts in clapboard towns and homesteads around the park.

**1** North Unit. The park's creek-cut northern wilderness, centered on snowy Mount Challenger, stretches north from Highway 20 over the Picket Range toward the Canadian border. It's an endless landscape of pine-topped peaks and ridges, hemmed in by sinewy Ross Lake to the east and the western slopes of the Mt. Baker Ski Area.

**2** South Unit. Hike the South Unit's lake-filled mountain foothills in summer, where you'll take in a panorama of blue skies and flower-filled meadows. Waterfalls and wildlife are abundant here.

**3** Ross Lake National Recreation Area. Drawing a thick line from British Columbia all the way down to the North Cascades Scenic Highway, placid Ross Lake is edged with pretty bays that draw swimmers and boaters.

**4** Lake Chelan National Recreation Area. Ferries steam between small waterfront towns along this pristine waterway, while kayakers and hikers follow quiet trails along its edges. This is one of the Northwest's most popular summer escapes, where simple country life, nature-bound activities, and rustic accommodations all focus on the pleasures of the outdoors.

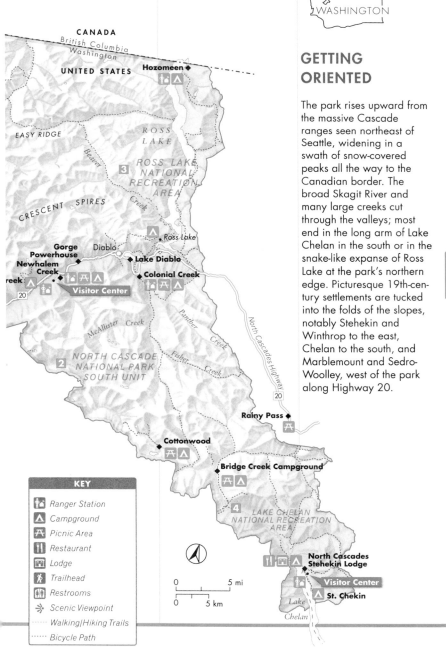

## GETTING ORIENTED

The park rises upward from the massive Cascade ranges seen northeast of Seattle, widening in a swath of snow-covered peaks all the way to the Canadian border. The broad Skagit River and many large creeks cut through the valleys; most end in the long arm of Lake Chelan in the south or in the snake-like expanse of Ross Lake at the park's northern edge. Picturesque 19th-century settlements are tucked into the folds of the slopes, notably Stehekin and Winthrop to the east, Chelan to the south, and Marblemount and Sedro-Woolley, west of the park along Highway 20.

WASHINGTON

CANADA
British Columbia
Washington

UNITED STATES

Hozomeen

EASY RIDGE

ROSS LAKE

ROSS LAKE NATIONAL RECREATION AREA

CRESCENT SPIRES

Beaver

Creek

Ross Lake

Gorge
Powerhouse
Newhalem
Creek

Diablo

Lake Diablo

Colonial Creek

Visitor Center

20

McAllister Creek

Panther Creek

North Cascades Highway

NORTH CASCADE NATIONAL PARK SOUTH UNIT

Fisher Creek

20

Rainy Pass

Cottonwood

Bridge Creek Campground

LAKE CHELAN NATIONAL RECREATION AREA

### KEY

| | |
|---|---|
| 🏠 | Ranger Station |
| ⬛ | Campground |
| ⛱ | Picnic Area |
| 🍴 | Restaurant |
| 🏨 | Lodge |
| 🚶 | Trailhead |
| 🚻 | Restrooms |
| ⚜ | Scenic Viewpoint |
| ---- | Walking/Hiking Trails |
| ······ | Bicycle Path |

0        5 mi
0        5 km

North Cascades
Stehekin Lodge

Visitor Center

St. Chekin

Lake Chelan

# NORTH CASCADES PLANNER

## When to Go

The spectacular, craggy peaks of the North Cascades—often likened to the Alps—are breathtaking in any season. **Summer is short and glorious in the high country, extending from snowmelt (late May to July, depending on the elevation and the amount of snow) to early September. This is peak season for the North Cascades,** especially along the alpine stretches of Route 20; weekends and holidays can be crowded. The North Cascades Highway is a popular autumn drive in September and October, when the changing leaves (on larches, the only conifer that sheds its leaves, as well as aspen, vine maple, huckleberry, and cottonwood) put on a colorful show. The lowland forest areas, such as the complex around Newhalem, can be visited almost any time of year. These can be wonderfully quiet in early spring or late autumn on mild, rainy days, when you can experience the weather that makes the old-growth forest possible. Snow closes the North Cascades Highway November through mid-April; exact dates depend on snow conditions.

## AVG. HIGH/LOW TEMPS.

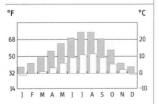

## Flora & Fauna

Bald eagles are present year-round along the Skagit River and the various lakes—although in December, hundreds flock to the Skagit to feed on a rare winter salmon run; they remain through January. Black bears are often seen in spring and early summer along the roadsides in the high country, feeding on new green growth. Deer and elk can often be seen in early morning and late evening, grazing and browsing at the forest's edge. Other mountain residents include beaver, marmots, pika, otters, skunks, opossums, and smaller mammals, as well as a variety of forest and field birds.

## Getting There & Around

Highway 20, the North Cascades Highway, splits the park's north and south sections. The gravel Cascade River Road, which runs southeast from Marblemount, splits off Highway 20; Sibley Creek/Hidden Lake Road (USFS 1540) breaks off Cascade River Road to the Cascade Pass trailhead. Thornton Creek Road is another rough four-wheel-drive track. For the Ross Lake area in the north, the unpaved Hozomeen Road (Silver–Skagit Rd.) provides access between Hope, British Columbia; Silver Lake; and Skagit Valley provincial parks. From Stehekin, the Stehekin Valley Road continues to High Bridge, Car Wash Falls, Bridge Creek, and Cottonwood campgrounds—although seasonal floods may cause washouts. Note that a day trip isn't nearly enough to make a thorough exploration of the park: roads are narrow and closed from October to June, many sights are mostly off the beaten path, and the scenery is so spectacular that, once you're in it, you won't want to hurry through anyway.

By Holly S. Smith

Countless snow-clad mountain spires dwarf narrow glacial valleys in this 505,000-acre expanse of the North Cascades, which actually encompasses three diverse natural areas. North Cascades National Park is the core of the region, flanked by Lake Chelan National Recreation Area to the south and Ross Lake National Recreation Area to the north; all are part of the Stephen T. Mather Wilderness Area. This is an utterly spectacular gathering of snowy peaks, glacial meadows, plunging canyons, and cold, deep-blue lakes. Traditionally the lands of several Native American tribes, it's fitting that it's still a completely wild—and wildlife-filled—stretch of earth, which is all but inaccessible most of the year.

**27**

## Scenic Drives

★ **North Cascades Highway.** Also known as Highway 20, this classic scenic route first winds through the green pastures and woods of the upper Skagit Valley, the mountains looming in the distance. Beyond Concrete, a former cement-manufacturing town, the highway climbs into the mountains, passes the Ross and Diablo dams, and traverses Ross Lake National Recreation Area. Here several pullouts offer great views of the lake and the surrounding snowcapped peaks. From June to September, the meadows are covered with wildflowers, and from late September through October, the mountain slopes flame with fall foliage. The pinnacle point of this stretch is 5,477-foot-high Washington Pass: look east, to where the road descends quickly into a series of hairpin curves between Early Winters Creek and the Methow Valley. Remember, this section of the highway is closed from roughly November to April, depending on snowfall. From the Methow Valley, Highway 153 takes the scenic route along the Methow River's apple, nectarine, and peach orchards to Pateros, on the Columbia River; from here, you can continue east to Grand Coulee or south to Lake Chelan.

## What to See

### Historic Sites

**Buckner Homestead.** Founded in 1912, this pioneer farm includes an apple orchard, farmhouse, barn, and many ranch buildings, which are slowly being restored by the National Park Service. ⊠ *Stehekin Valley Rd., 3½ mi from Stehekin Landing, Stehekin* ☎ *360/856–5700 Ext. 340 then press 14* ☉ *June–Sept., daily 9–5.*

**Diablo Dam.** From the tour center in Diablo, Seattle City Lights operates a 2½-hour tour that takes you across Diablo Dam by motor coach and then on a boat cruise of Diablo Lake. Purchase snacks at the Skagit General Store or pack a picnic lunch for the trip. Note that increased security has closed public access to Ross Powerhouse, the Incline Railway, and Diablo Dam (except on tours). ⊠ *500 Newhalem St., Rockport* ☎ *206/ 684–3030* ⊠ *$25* ⊕ *www.ci.seattle.wa.us/light/tours/skagit* ☉ *Daily June–Sept.; tours June–Aug., Fri.–Sun. at 12:45; Sept., Sat. at 12:45.*

### Scenic Stops

**Gorge Powerhouse/Ladder Creek Falls and Rock Gardens.** A powerhouse is a powerhouse, but the rock gardens overlooking Ladder Creek Falls, 7 mi west of Diablo, are beautiful and inspiring. ⊠ *Rte. 20, 2 mi east of North Cascades Visitor Center, Newhalem* ☎ *206/684–3030* ⊠ *Free* ☉ *Daily May–Sept.*

Fodor'sChoice
★
**Stehekin.** One of the most beautiful and secluded valleys in the Pacific Northwest, Stehekin was homesteaded by hardy souls in the late 19th century. It's actually not a town, but rather a small community set at the northwest end of Lake Chelan, accessible only by boat, floatplane, or trail. Year-round residents, who have intermittent outside communications, boat-delivered supplies, and just two dozen cars between them, enjoy a wilderness lifestyle—and only around 200 visitors make the trek here during the peak summer season.

### Visitor Centers

**Chelan Ranger Station.** The base for the Chelan National Recreation Area and Wenatchee National Forest has an information desk and a shop selling regional maps and books. ⊠ *Foot of Lake Chelan, Chelan* ☎ *360/ 682–2549* ☉ *Mon.–Sat. 7:45–4:30.*

**Glacier Public Service Center.** This office doubles as a headquarters for the Mt. Baker–Snoqualmie National Forest; it has maps, a book and souvenir shop, and a permits desk. The center is also right on the way to some of the park's main trailheads. ⊠ *Mt. Baker Hwy., east of Glacier* ☎ *360/599–2714* ☉ *Mid-Mar.–mid-Oct., daily 8:30–4:30.*

**Golden West Visitor Center.** Rangers here offer guidance on hiking, camping, and other activities, as well as audiovisual and children's programs and bike tours. There's also an arts and crafts gallery. Maps and con-

## NORTH CASCADES IN ONE DAY

The **North Cascades Highway,** with its breathtaking mountain and meadow scenery, is one of the most memorable drives in the United States. Although many travelers first head northeast from Seattle into the park and make this their grand finale, if you start out from Winthrop, at the south end of the route, traffic is lighter and there's less morning fog. Either way, the main highlight is **Washington Pass,** the road's highest point, where an overlook affords a sensational panorama of snow-covered peaks.

**Rainy Pass,** where the road heading north drops into the west slope valleys, is another good vantage point. Old-growth forest begins to appear, and after about an hour you reach **Gorge Creek Falls overlook** with its 242-foot cascade. Continue west to Newhalem and stop for lunch, then take a half-hour stroll along the **Trail of the Cedars.** Later, stop at the **North Cascades Visitor Center** and take another short hike. It's an hour drive down the Skagit Valley to Sedro-Woolley, where bald eagles are often seen along the river in winter.

**27**

cise displays explain the complicated ecology of the valley, which encompasses in its length virtually every ecosystem in the Northwest. Note that access is by floatplane, ferry, or trail only. ⊠ *Stehekin Valley Rd., ¼ mi north of Stehekin Landing, Stehekin* ☎ *360/856–5700 Ext. 340 then press 14* ☉ *Mid-Mar.–mid-Oct., daily 8:30–5.*

**North Cascades Environmental Learning Center.** Come here for information on park hiking, wildlife watching, horseback riding, climbing, boat rentals, and fishing, as well as classroom education and hands-on nature experiences. Guided tours staged from the center include mountain climbs, pack-train excursions, and float trips on the Skagit and Stehekin rivers. There's even a research library, a dock on Lake Diablo, an amphitheater, and overnight lodging. ⊠ *Sedro-Woolley; along Route 20, near Diablo Dam* ☎ *360/856–5700 Ext. 209.*

**North Cascades National Park Headquarters Information Station.** This is the park's major administrative center, and the place to pick up passes, permits, and information about current conditions. ⊠ *810 Rte. 20, Sedro-Woolley* ☎ *360/856–5700 Ext. 515* ☉ *Memorial Day through Oct., daily 8–4:30; Nov.–Memorial Day, weekdays 8–4:30.*

**North Cascades Visitor Center.** The main visitor facility for the park complex has extensive displays on surrounding landscape. Learn about the history and value of old-growth trees, the many creatures that depend on the rain forest ecology, and the effects of human activity on the ecosystem. Park rangers frequently conduct programs; check bulletin boards for schedules. ⊠ *Milepost 20, N. Cascades Hwy., Newhalem* ☎ *206/ 386–4495 Ext. 11* ☉ *Daily 9–6.*

**Wilderness Information Center.** The main stop to secure backcountry and climbing permits for North Cascades National Park and the Lake Chelan and Ross Lake recreational areas, this office has maps, a bookshop, and nature exhibits. Note that if you arrive after hours, there's a self-register permit stop outside. ⊠ *Ranger Station Rd., off Milepost 105.9, N. Cascades Hwy., Marblemount* ☎ *360/873–4500 Ext. 39* ☉ *Sun.–Thurs. 8–6, Fri. and Sat. 7 AM–8 PM.*

## Sports & the Outdoors

### Bicycling

Mountain bikes are permitted on all highways, unpaved back roads, and a few designated tracks around the park; however, you can't take a bike on any footpaths. Ranger stations have details on the best places to ride in each season, as well as notes on spots that are closed due to weather, mud, or other environmental factors. Note that it's $15 round-trip to bring your own bike on the Lake Chelan ferry.

OUTFITTERS & EXPEDITIONS **Discovery Bikes.** You can rent mountain bikes at a self-serve rack in front of the Courtney Log Office in Stehekin for $5 per hour, $15 a day; helmets are provided. ☎ *509/682–3014.*

**North Cascades Stehekin Lodge.** Bikes rent for $5 per hour or $25 per day, and seasonal trips can be arranged. ☎ *509/682–4494* ⊕ *www. stehekin.com.*

**Stehekin Valley Ranch.** Group cycling tours are offered 3½ mi from Stehekin Landing. ⊠ *Stehekin Valley Rd., Stehekin* ☎ *509/682–4677 or 800/536–0745.*

### Boating

The boundaries of North Cascades National Park touch two long and sinewy expanses: Lake Chelan in the far south, and Ross Lake, which runs toward the Canadian border. Boat ramps, some with speed- and sailboat, paddleboat, kayak, and canoe rentals, are situated all around Lake Chelan, and passenger ferries cross between towns and campgrounds. Hozomeen, accessible via a 39-mi dirt road from Canada, is the boating base for Ross Lake; the site has a large boat ramp, and a boat taxi makes drops at campgrounds all around the shoreline. Diablo Lake, in the center of the park, also has a ramp at Colonial Creek. Gorge Lake has a public ramp near the town of Diablo.

OUTFITTERS & EXPEDITIONS **Seattle City Light.** The company offers a 2½-hour cruise around Diablo Lake. ☎ *360/734–6771* ⊕ *www.seattlecitylight.com.*

**Skagit Tours.** Diablo Lake excursions include transportation from Seattle. ☎ *206/684–3026* ⊕ *www.skagittours.com.*

### Hiking

⚠ **Black bears are often sighted along trails in the summer; DO NOT approach them!** Back away carefully, and report sightings to the Golden West Visitor Center. Cougars, which are shy of humans and well aware of their presence, are rarely sighted in this region. Still, keep kids close and don't let them run ahead too far or lag behind on a trail. If you do spot a cougar, pick up children, have the whole group stand close together, and make yourself look as large as possible.

EASY **Happy Creek Forest Walk.** Old-growth forests are the focus of this kid-friendly boardwalk route, which loops just ⅓ mi through the trees right off the North Cascades Highway. Interpretive signs provide details about flora along the way. ⊠ *Milepost 135, Hwy. 20.*

**Rainy Pass.** An easy and accessible 1-mi paved trail leads to Rainy Lake, a waterfall, and glacier-view platform. ⊠ *Hwy. 20, 38 mi east of visitor center at Newhalem.*

**Rock Shelter Trail.** This short trail—partly boardwalk—leads to a campsite used 1,400 years ago by Native Americans; interpretive signs tell the history of human presence in the region. ⊠ *Off Hwy. 20.*

★ **Skagit River Loop.** Take this flat and easy, 1⅘-mi, wheelchair-accessible trail down through stands of huge, old-growth firs and cedars toward the Skagit River. ⊠ *Near North Cascades Visitor Center.*

**Sterling Munro Trail.** Starting from the North Cascades Headquarters and Information Station, this popular introductory stroll follows a boardwalk path to a lookout above the forested Picket Range peaks. ⊠ *810 Hwy. 20.*

★ **Trail of the Cedars.** Only ½ mi long, this trail winds its way through one of the finest surviving stands of old-growth Western Red Cedar in Washington. Some of the trees on the path are more than 1,000 years old. ⊠ *Near North Cascades Visitor Center.*

MODERATE
Fodor'sChoice
★
**Cascade Pass.** The draws of this extremely popular 3⅔-mi, four-hour trail are stunning panoramas from the great mountain divide. Dozens of peaks line the horizon as you make your way up the fairly flat, hairpin-turn track, the scene fronted by a blanket of alpine wildflowers from July to mid-August. Arrive before noon if you want a parking spot at the trailhead. ⊠ *End of Cascade River Rd., 14 mi from Marblemount.*

**Diablo Lake Trail.** You can explore nearly 4 mi of waterside terrain on this moderate route, which is accessed from the Sourdough Creek parking lot. An excellent alternative for parties with small hikers is to take the Seattle City Light Ferry one way. ⊠ *Milepost 135, Hwy. 20.*

DIFFICULT **Thornton Lakes Trail.** A 5-mi climb into an alpine basin with two pretty lakes, this steep and strenuous hike takes about 5–6 hours round-trip. ⊠ *Hwy. 20, 3 mi west of Newhalem.*

OUTFITTERS &
EXPEDITIONS
**Alpine Ascents.** The Seattle company makes North Cascades National Park one of its prime excursions. ☎ *206/378–1927.*

**American Alpine Institute.** Based in Bellingham, WA, the organization conducts training trips and guided tours of the park. ☎ *360/671–1505.*

**Evergreen Adventure Travel.** Just south of the park in Leavenworth, the agency organizes overnight hikes and multisport adventures in the Cascades. ☎ *509/264–1516.*

27

### DID YOU KNOW?

Cyclists at North Cascades National Park can drop in at a ranger station to get the skinny on the best routes, or visit the Golden West Visitor Center to join a group tour. Enthusiasts should plan to visit in April to catch the Lake Chelan Mountain Bike Festival.

**North Cascades Mountain Guides.** Mazama, one of the towns closest to the park, is a hiking and mountaineering center; this outfitter provides training and tours. ☎ 206/378–1927.

**Pacific Crest Trail Association.** The National Pacific Crest Hiking Track stretches from the western Canadian border all the way down to Mexico, passing through North Cascades National Park and Lake Chelan National Recreation Area along the way. The organization provides maps, route advice, and tour suggestions. ☎ 916/349–2109 ⊕ www.pcta.org.

**Pacific Northwest Trail Association.** Some 60 mi of the magnificent Pacific Northwest Trail, which links Glacier National Park in Montana to Cape Alava on the Washington coast of Olympic National Park, passes right through North Cascades National Park and the Ross Lake National Recreation Area. Sights along the way include Ross Lake, Big Beaver Trail, and the Whatcom and Hannegan passes. The managing association has all sorts of resources, including advice on tours and independent travel. ☎ 877/854–9415 ⊕ www.pnt.org.

## Horseback Riding

Many hiking trails and backwoods paths are also popular horseback-riding routes, particularly around the park's southern fringes.

OUTFITTERS & EXPEDITIONS  **Cascade Corrals.** This company organizes three-hour horseback trips to Coon Lake. Costs depend on experience, and English- and Western-style riding lessons are also available. Reservations are taken at the Courtney Log Office at Stehekin Landing. ☎ 509/682–7742 ⊕ www.cascadecorrals.com ☞ $40–$50 ☉ June–mid.-Sept, daily at 8:30 and 2:15.

**Stehekin Adventure.** This group specializes in horseback-riding excursions and overnight pack trips through the Stehekin Valley. ☎ 509/682–7742.

**Stehekin Valley Ranch.** Enjoy the view as a team of horses pulls your group's wagon through the countryside. You can also book Cascade Corrals horseback trips from here. ☎ 509/682–4677 or 800/536–0745.

## Kayaking

The park's tangles of waterways offer access to remote areas inaccessible by road or trail; here you'll find some of the most pristine and secluded mountain scenes on the continent. Bring your own kayak and you can launch from any boat ramp or beach; otherwise, companies in several nearby towns and Seattle suburbs offer kayak and canoe rentals, portage, and tours. The upper basin of Lake Chelan (at the park's southern end) and Ross Lake (at the top edge of the park) are two well-known kayaking expanses, but there are dozens of smaller lakes and creeks between. The Stehekin River also provides many kayaking possibilities.

OUTFITTERS & EXPEDITIONS  **Outward Bound West.** Based in the mountain-sports center of Mazama, this group stages canoe expeditions on Ross Lake. ☎ 360/385–3605.

**Ross Lake Resort.** The resort rents kayaks and offers portage service for exploring Ross Lake; a water-taxi service is also available. ☎ 206/386–4437.

**Stehekin Adventure Company.** Book a two-hour trip along the lake's upper estuary and western shoreline, or just hire a kayak and set out on your own. You can make a reservation at the Stehekin Log Office. *Box 36, Stehekin 98852* ☎ *509/682–4677* ⛵ *Tour $30* ☾ *June–Sept. tours daily at 10, rentals 10–4.*

## Rafting

June through August is the park's white-water season, and rafting trips run through the lower section of the Stehekin River. Along the way you'll take in views of cottonwood and pine forests, glimpses of Yawning Glacier on Magic Mountain, and placid vistas of Lake Chelan.

OUTFITTERS & EXPEDITIONS **Downstream River Runners.** This outfitter covers rafting throughout the Northwest. ✉ *13414 Chain Lake Rd., Monroe* ☎ *360/805–9899.*

**North Cascades River Expeditions.** This outfitter focuses on the Stehekin and other regional rivers. *Box 116, Arlington 98223* ☎ *360/435–0796.*

**Orion River Expeditions.** White-water tours are available on the Stehekin and other area rivers. ✉ *5111 Latona Ave., Seattle* ☎ *206/547–6715.*

**Stehekin Valley Ranch.** Guided trips on the class III Stehekin River leave from here. ✉ *Stehekin Valley Rd., 3½ mi from Stehekin Landing, Stehekin* ☎ *509/682–4677 or 800/536–0745* ⛵ *$35–$75* ☾ *June–Sept.*

**Wildwater River Tours.** Exciting half- and full-day rafting excursions include transportation and a picnic. *Box 3623, Federal Way 98063* ☎ *253/939–3337.*

## Winter Sports

Mt. Baker, just off the park's far northwest corner, is one of the Northwest's premier skiing, snowboarding, and snowshoeing regions—the area set a U.S. record for most snow in a single season during the winter of 1998–99 (1,140 inches). The Mt. Baker Highway (Route 542) cuts through the slopes toward several major ski sites; main access is 17 mi east of the town of Glacier, and the season runs roughly from November to April. Salmon Ridge, 46 mi east of Bellingham at exit 255, has groomed trails and parking.

Stehekin is another base for winter sports. The Stehekin Valley alone has 20 mi of trails; some of the most popular are around Buckner Orchard, Coon Lake, and the Courtney Ranch (Cascade Corrals).

OUTFITTERS & EXPEDITIONS **Mt. Baker.** Off the park's northwest corner, this is the closest winter-sports area, with facilities for downhill and Nordic skiing, snowboarding, and other recreational ventures. The main base is the town of Glacier, 17 mi west of the slopes. Equipment, lodgings, restaurants, and tourist services are on-site. ✉ *Mt. Baker Hwy. 542, 62 mi east of Bellingham* ☎ *360/734–6771, 360/671–0211 for snow reports* ⊕ *www.mtbaker. us* ⛵ *All-day lift ticket weekends and holidays $36, weekdays $29* ☾ *Nov.–Apr.*

**Silver Bay Inn Resort.** The resort rents ski and snowshoe equipment, and puts on winter bonfires and other events for day-trippers and guests. ☎ *509/682–2212 or 800/555–7781* ⊕ *www.silverbayinn.com.*

**Stehekin Valley Lodge.** This well-known winter-sports base offers equipment rentals, tours, and activities. ☎ *509/682–4677 or 800/536–0745* ⊕ *www.courtneycountry.com.*

## Educational Offerings

### Guided Tours

**North Cascades Institute (NCI).** This group runs the North Cascades Environmental Learning Center and offers classes, field trips, seminars, and wilderness adventures from its Diablo base. Choices range from forest ecology and backpacking trips to explorations of the Cascades hot springs. ✉ *810 Rte. 20, Sedro-Woolley* ☎ *360/856–5700 Ext. 209* ⊕ *www.ncascades.org.*

**Seattle City Light Information and Tour Center.** Based at a history museum that has exhibits about the onset of electric power through the Cascade ranges, this company offers several tours and programs during summer. Several trails start at the building, and the group offers boat tours on Diablo Lake ($25–$55). The facility is open May through September. ☎*206/684–3030* ⊕*www.cityofseattle.net/light/tours/skagit* ☉ *May–Sept.*

# WHAT'S NEARBY

## Nearby Towns

**27**

Heading into North Cascades National Park from Seattle on Interstate 5 to Highway 2, **Sedro-Woolley** (pronounced "seedro wooley") is the first main town you'll encounter. A former logging and steel-mill base settled by North Carolina pioneers, the settlement still has a 19th-century ambience throughout its rustic downtown buildings. Surrounded by farmlands, it's a pretty spot to stop and has basic visitor services like hotels, gas stations, and groceries. It's also home to the North Cascades National Park Headquarters. From here, it's about 40 mi to the park's western edges. Along the way, you still have a chance to stop for supplies in **Concrete,** about 20 mi from the park along Highway 2.

**Marblemount** is 10 mi further east, about 12 mi west of the North Cascades Visitor Center. It's another atmospheric former timber settlement nestled into the mountain foothills, and its growing collection of motels, cafés, and tour outfitters draw outdoor enthusiasts each summer. The park's base town, though, is **Newhalem,** tucked right along the highway between the north and south regions. This is the place to explore the visitor center and its surrounding trails, view exhibits, and pick up maps, permits, and tour information.

Still traveling east on Highway 20, it's about 5 mi from Newhalem to **Diablo,** where the local lake, dam, and overlook are all good reasons to stop. Keep going until the road turns south along the park's eastern side: this is the famed North Cascades Scenic Highway. From top to bottom, including Rainy Pass and the curve through the chilly Washington Pass overlook, this section is about 20 mi.

**Winthrop,** a relaxed and rustic rodeo town, is about a 6-mi drive east of Washington Pass. This is also an outdoor-recreation base, offering activities that range from cross-country skiing to hiking, mountain biking, and white-water rafting. Less than 10 mi southeast of Winthrop, the tiny town of **Twisp** is settled into the farmlands and orchards, its streets lined with a few small lodgings and cafés.

The resort town of **Chelan,** lakeside about 40 mi due south of Winthrop along Highway 153, is a serene summer getaway. Boating and swimming are the main activities, but it's also an access point for other small villages and campgrounds along the shoreline. **Stehekin,** at the lake's northern end, is a favorite tourist stop for its remoteness—without road connections, your only options for getting here are by boat, floatplane, or trail. A regular ferry runs between Chelan and Stehekin year-round.

## Nearby Attractions

★ **Lake Chelan.** This sinewy, 55-mi-long fjord—Washington's deepest lake—works its way southeast between the towns of Chelan, at its south end, and Stehekin, at the far northwest edge. The scenery is unparalleled, the flat blue water encircled by plunging gorges, with a vista of snow-slathered mountains beyond. No roads access the lake except for Chelan, so a floatplane or boat is needed to see the whole thing. Resorts dot the warmer eastern shores. ✉ *Alt. 97, Chelan* ☎ *360/856–5700 Ext. 340, then 14* ⊕ *www.nps.gov/lach* 🎫 *Free* ⊙ *Daily.*

**Stehekin Boat Co.** Come aboard to tour Lake Chelan. Voyages range from 2-hour high-speed catamaran jaunts up-lake to leisurely 4½-hour cruises through the changing scenery. Although most summer passengers are tourists, these are also working boats that haul supplies, mail, cars, and construction material to Stehekin. The vessel also makes drops and pick-ups at lakeshore trailheads. ✉ *1418 Woodin Ave., Chelan* ☎ *509/682–4584 or 509/682–2224* ⊕ *www.ladyofthelake.com* 🎫 *$25–$89* ⊙ *Daily; call for schedule.*

## Area Activities

### Educational Offerings

**Skagit River Bald Eagle Interpretive Center** (✉ Albert St., Rockport ☎ 509/853–7283 ⊕ www.skagiteagle.org) schedules monthly programs, including lectures, classes, workshops, and performances. This is also the site of the annual Upper Skagit Bald Eagle Festival. From December to February you can tour the on-site Fish Hatchery, which houses all five species of Northwest salmon. The facility is open 10 to 4 Friday through Sunday, Monday holidays, and daily the same hours December 26 to 31; free guided tours run weekends at 10:30, 11:30, 1:30, and 2:30.

TOURS  **Lake Chelan Boat Company** (✉ 1418 W. Woodin Ave., Chelan 98816 ☎ 509/682–4584 ⊕ www.ladyofthelake.com) connects Chelan to Stehekin and stops at lakeside campgrounds along the way. The *Lady of the Lake* makes the journey 8:30 to 6 from May to October; tickets are $29.50 one way, $42 round-trip for adults, half price for those ages 2 to 11. The company's speedy catamaran, *Lady Express,* also runs between Stehekin, Holden Village, the national park, and Lake Chelan. Connections run daily 10 to 3:50 from June to October; on Monday, Wednesday, Friday, and Sunday from November to mid-March; daily through April, and 8:30 to 2:30 on weekends in May.

The **Lake Chelan Tour Boat** (✉ 1228 W. Woodin Ave., Chelan 98816 ☎ 509/682–8287) makes scheduled and individually tailored excursions around the lake. Three-hour dinner cruises and charters around Lake Chelan take place year-round on the local yacht *Innamorata* (☎ 509/682–9500).

# WHERE TO STAY & EAT

## About the Restaurants

There are no formal restaurants in North Cascades National Park, just a lakeside café at the North Cascades Environmental Learning Center. The only other place to eat out is in Stehekin, at the Stehekin Valley Ranch dining room or the Stehekin Pastry Company; both serve simple, hearty, country-style meals and sweets. Towns within a few hours of the park on either side all have a few small eateries, and some lodgings have small dining rooms. Don't expect fancy decor or gourmet frills—just friendly service and generally delicious homemade stews, roasts, grilled fare, soups, salads, and baked goods.

## About the Hotels

Accommodations in North Cascades National Park are rustic, cozy, and comfortable. Options range from plush Stehekin lodges and homey cabin rentals to spartan Learning Center bunks and campgrounds. Expect to pay roughly $50 to $200 per night, depending on the rental size and the season—you'll be out of luck if you don't book at least three months in advance, or even a year in advance for popular accommodations in summer. Outside the park, you'll find numerous resorts, motels, bed-and-breakfasts, and even overnight boat rentals in Chelan, Concrete, Glacier, Marblemount, Sedro-Woolley, Twisp, and Winthrop.

## About the Campgrounds

Tent campers can choose between forest sites, riverside spots, lake grounds, or meadow spreads encircled by mountains. Here camping is as easy or challenging as you want to make it; some campgrounds are a short walk from ranger stations, while others are miles from the highway. Note that many campsites, particularly those around Stehekin, are completely remote and without road access anywhere—so you'll have to walk, boat, ride a horse, or take a floatplane to reach them. Most don't accept reservations, and spots fill up quickly May through September. If there's no ranger on-site, you'll often sign in yourself—be sure to always check in at a ranger station before you set out overnight. Note that some areas are occasionally closed due to flooding, forest fires, or other factors. Outside the park, each town has several managed camping spots, which can be at a formal campgrounds or in the side yard of a motel.

**27**

## Where to Eat

### In North Cascades

**$–$$** ✕ **Stehekin Valley Ranch.** Meals in the rustic log ranch house, served at long, polished log tables, include buffet dinners of steak, ribs, hamburgers, salad, beans, and dessert. Note that breakfast is served 7 to 9, lunch is noon to 1, and dinner is 5:30 to 7; show up later, and you're out of luck until the next meal. Transportation from Stehekin Landing is included for day visitors. ⊠ *Stehekin Valley Rd., 9 mi north of Stehekin Landing, Stehekin* ☎ *509/682–4677 or 800/536–0745. $11–$20* ▭ *No credit cards* ☉ *Closed Oct.–mid-June.*

**¢** ✕ **Stehekin Pastry Company.** As you enter this lawn-framed timber chalet, you'll be immersed in the tantalizing aromas of a European bakery. Glassed-in display cases are filled with trays of homemade baked goods, and the pungent espresso is eye-opening. Sit down at a window-side table and dig into an over-filled sandwich or rich bowl of soup—and you'll never taste a better slice of pie, with fruit fresh-picked from local orchards. Although it's outside of town, the shop is conveniently en route to Rainbow Falls and adjacent to the Norwegian Fjord Horses stables, which also makes it a popular summertime ice-cream stop for sightseers. ⊠ *Stehekin Valley Rd., about 2 mi from Stehekin Landing, on the way to Rainbow Falls, Stehekin* ☎ *509/682–4677. $2–$4* ▭ *No credit cards* ☉ *Closed mid-Oct.–mid-May.*

PICNIC AREAS    Developed picnic areas at Rainy Pass (Route 20, 38 mi east of the park visitor center) and Washington Pass (Route 20, 42 mi east of the visitor center) each have a half-dozen picnic tables, drinking water, and pit toilets. The vistas of surrounding peaks are sensational at these two overlooks. More picnic facilities are located near the visitor center in Newhalem and at Colonial Creek Campground 10 mi east of the visitor center on Highway 20.

### Outside the Park

**$$$–$$$$** ✕ **Dining Room at Sun Mountain Lodge.** Cozy tables are surrounded by a woodsy decor in this spacious restaurant, where you can enjoy the mountain scenery while you dine. Farm-fresh produce, Washington beef, and locally caught seafood highlight the excellent menu, which includes such delicacies as rich forest-mushroom strudel; melt-in-your-mouth pork chops with caramelized apples and onions; and parchment-wrapped halibut cheeks served with saffron, orange, and basmati pilaf. Desserts range from seven-course cheese tastings to dark rum chocolate cake. The 5,000-bottle wine cellar is one of the best in the region. ⊠ *Patterson Lake Rd., Winthrop* ☎ *509/996–2211. $28–$42* ▭ *AE, DC, MC, V.*

**¢–$$** ✕ **Heenan's Burnt Finger Bar-B-Q & Steak House.** You can't get more authentic than a barbecue joint that serves slow-smoked sauce-slathered ribs and chicken right out of an old Conestoga wagon. Sidled up to the Methow River, the corral-style restaurant provides sweeping views of the water, the valley, and the farmlands beyond. Creamy coleslaw, crisp corn on the cob, and an assortment of salads and chilies round out the menu. Diners can relax inside the cozy dining rooms or outside by the grill, where evenings bring campfires and guitar-strumming cowboys.

✉ *940 Hwy. 20 S, Winthrop* ☎ *509/996–8221. $6–$16* ▤ *MC, V* ◴ *Closed Oct.–Memorial Day weekend.*

¢ ✕ **Ship 'n' Shore Drive/Boat In.** The casual "dining room" here consists of dockside picnic tables, where big hamburgers and taco salads are local favorites. On hot days, kids line up for ice cream. ✉ *1230 W. Woodin Ave., Chelan* ☎ *509/682–5125. $5–$7* ◴ *Closed Labor Day–Memorial Day.*

## Where to Stay

### In North Cascades

$$$–$$$$ ▦ **Silver Bay Inn.** Perched on a private little slip of land at the head of Lake Chelan, Silver Bay enjoys water and mountain views. Spacious timber cabins for two each have a loft, full kitchen, and wraparound cedar deck; the Riverview Room also has a kitchen and a deck over the Stehekin. The luxury two-bedroom Lakeview House is a Northwest-style escape with a sunroom, two baths, and lots of artistic touches. Guests share a huge lawn, a waterside hot tub, and nightly bonfire cheer. Hiking, swimming, and relaxing are the top activities; you can also set out on a free bike or canoe. Note that kids must be at least 8. ✉ *Silver Bay Rd., Box 85, Stehekin 98852* ☎ *509/687–3142 or 800/555–7781* ⊕ *www.silverbayinn.com* ⤸ *1 room, 2 cabins, 1 house* ⚐ *Kitchen, bicycles, no a/c, no phone, no TV. $165–$265* ▤ *AE, MC, V.*

$$$ ▦ **Stehekin Valley Ranch.** Nestled along pretty meadows at the edge of pine forest, this classic ranch is a center for hikers and horseback riders. Big, barnlike cabins have cedar paneling, tile floors, and a private bath; the canvas-roof tent cabins have bunk beds, kerosene lamps, and shared facilities. Enormous breakfasts and meaty dinner buffets are turned out family-style at picnic tables in the rustic wood restaurant ($–$$). Rates include accommodations, linens, meals, and transport from Stehekin Landing. Credit cards are accepted only by phone. ⊡ *Box 881, Chelan 98816* ✉ *Stehekin Valley Rd., 9 mi north of Stehekin Landing, Stehekin* ☎ *509/682–4677 or 800/536–0745* ⊕ *www.courtneycountry.com* ⤸ *32 cabins* ⚐ *Restaurant, kitchen (some), bicycles, no a/c, no phone, no TV. $160–$180* ▤ *MC, V* ◴ *Closed Oct.–mid-June* ⑪ *FAP.*

$$ ▦ **North Cascades Stehekin Lodge.** Large log cabins welcome you with crackling fires and Lake Chelan views. Standard rooms are in the Alpine House, which has a shared lounge and a lakeside deck; larger rooms in the Swiss Mont building each have a private deck overlooking the water. Hearty American fare and light snacks are served in the restaurant, which is open all day in high season (lunch only October through April). For deep discounts, check out the lodge's seasonal packages, which combine accommodations, round-trip boat fare across Lake Chelan, a bus tour, parking, and sports equipment (like snowshoes). ✉ *About 5 mi south of Stehekin Landing on Lake Chelan* ⊡ *Box 457, Stehekin Landing, Chelan 98816* ☎ *509/682–4494* ⊕ *www.stehekin.com* ⤸ *28 rooms* ⚐ *Restaurant, kitchen (some), no a/c, no phone, no TV. $101–$114* ▤ *D, MC, V.*

27

CAMPING & RV
FACILITIES

🏕 **Ross Lake National Recreation Area.** The National Park Service maintains three upper Skagit Valley campgrounds near Newhalem. ☎ *360/856–5700 Ext. 515* ⚒ *Reservations not accepted* 🚫 *No credit cards.*
Colonial Creek Campground. In a valley setting amid old-growth forest, this campground is close to Route 20 services and Diablo Lake. A boat ramp affords easy access to the lake, and several hiking trails that lead into the park begin at the campground. ✉ *10 mi east of Newhalem on Rte. 20* 🏕 *130 tent sites, 32 RV sites* ⚒ *Flush toilets, dump station, drinking water, fire grates, picnic tables. $12* ☉ *Mid-May–Sept.*
Goodell Creek Campground. This forested site lies across the Skagit River from Newhalem Creek Campground, near the North Cascades Visitor Center. It's more primitive than Newhalem Creek, with pit toilets and no programs. No water is available in winter. ✉ *Rte. 20, ½ mi west of park visitor center turnoff* ☎ *360/873–4590* 🏕 *21 tent sites* ⚒ *Pit toilets, drinking water, fire grates, picnic tables. $10 , free mid-Oct.–mid-Apr.*
Newhalem Creek Campground. With three loops, a small amphitheater, a playground, and a regular slate of ranger programs in summer, Newhalem Creek is the main North Cascades park complex campground. Perched on a bench above the Skagit River, in old-growth forest, it's adjacent to the North Cascades Visitor Center, and close to several forest and river trails. ✉ *Rte. 20, along the access road to the park's main visitor center* ☎ *360/873–4590* 🏕 *111 RV sites* ⚒ *Flush toilets, dump station, drinking water, fire grates, picnic tables, public telephone, ranger station, play area. $12* ☉ *Mid-May–mid-Oct.*

¢ 🏕 **Lake Chelan National Recreation Area.** Many backcountry camping areas are accessible via park shuttles or boat. All require a free backcountry permit; 12 boat-in sites also require a $5 per day dock fee. Everything you bring must be hung on bear wires, so rethink those big coolers. Purple Point, the most popular campground due to its quick access to Stehekin Landing, has just seven tent sites, bear boxes, and nearby road access. Note that group requests must be made in writing. ✉ *Stehekin Landing, NPS, Box 7, Stehekin, WA 98852* ☎ *360/856–5700 Ext. 360 then Ext. 14* ⊕ *www.nps.gov/noca/focus/focus5.htm* 🏕 *63 tent sites* ⚒ *Pit toilets, drinking water, bear boxes. Free* ⚒ *Reservations not accepted* 🚫 *No credit cards.*

## Outside North Cascades

$$$$ ✕🏨 **Campbell's Resort.** This sand-colored apartment-style resort sits on landscaped grounds alongside Lake Chelan; it's been open for more than a century. Every room has a balcony with mountain and beach views; some have a kitchen or fireplace. Two-bedroom cabins with a kitchen and porch are on the east side of the property, near the marina. The elegant House Café ($–$$), with hardwood walls and a nautical feel, serves Northwest fare and wines in an elegant atmosphere; the second-floor Pub and Veranda, with views over the lake, dishes out simpler meals. The park-like, family-friendly setting includes pristine beaches, picnic areas, barbecues, and lots of room to romp. ✉ *104 W. Woodin Ave., Chelan 98816* ☎ *509/682–2561 or 800/553–8225* 🖨 *509/682–2177* ⊕ *www.campbellsresort.com* 🛏 *172 rooms, 2 cottages* ⚒ *Restaurant,*

*kitchen (some), refrigerator, dial-up, Wi-Fi (some), pools, gym, spa, bar, children's programs (ages 4–15). $202–$288 ☐ AE, MC, V.*

★ $$$–$$$$ ✕◻ **Sun Mountain Lodge.** A hilltop location gives guests panoramic views of the Cascade Mountains and Methow Valley; some rooms face Mt. Gardner or Mt. Robinson. Accommodations mirror the lodge-style elegance of the main building; many have a fireplace, kitchen facilities, CD player, and a private deck. Luxury cabins are off-site, 1½ mi below on the Patterson lakefront. There are 100 mi of hiking, horse-back-riding, and ski trails nearby; afterward, you can indulge your sore muscles at the spa. The restaurant ($$–$$$$), with snowy mountain views from every table, serves Northwest fare and has a private wine cellar. ⊠ *Patterson Lake Rd., Winthrop 98862* ☎ *509/996–2211 or 800/572–0493* 🖷 *509/996–3133* ⊕ *www.sunmountainlodge.com* 🛏 *98 rooms, 17 cabins* ↺ *Restaurant, room service, kitchen (some), refrigerator (some), Wi-Fi, tennis court, pools, spa, bicycles, bar, children's programs (ages 4–10), no TV, no-smoking rooms. $185–$365* ☐ *AE, DC, MC, V.*

$$–$$$$ ◻ **Freestone Inn.** Set at the heart of a 120-acre farm amid more than 2 million acres of forest, this rustic resort will make you feel like a pioneer—albeit with more luxuries at your disposal. Tucked into the massive log-cabin inn are simple, spacious guest rooms, each done in Northwest colors and enhanced with a gas fireplace, hot tub, and balcony. Several spacious lodges stand lakeside, and wood-paneled cabins snuggle up to Early Winters Creek; some have stone fireplaces, others have wrought-iron fireplaces and decks over the water. The inn houses a vast library, a Great Room with a three-story fireplace, and a restaurant serving Northwest cuisine. Jack's Hut Adventure Center organizes everything from hot-air balloon trips and mountaineering expeditions to sleigh rides and children's activities. Note that this is also one of the Northwest's top heli-skiing bases. ⊠ *31 Early Winters Dr., Mazama 98833* ☎ *509/996–3906 or 800/639–3809* 🖷 *509/996–3907* ⊕ *www. freestoneinn.com* 🛏 *21 rooms, 15 cabins, 3 lodges* ↺ *Restaurant, kitchen (some), refrigerator, VCR, dial-up, pool, bicycles, some pets allowed, no a/c (some), no-smoking rooms. $129–$320* ☐ *AE, MC, V.*

$–$$ ◻ **Skagit River Resort.** The Clark Family runs this rambling resort at the western entrance to the North Cascades. Many of the clapboard cabins with kitchens have a gas or log fireplace; you can also stay in one of the charming second-floor bed-and-breakfast rooms, RVs with kitchens, or campsites along the Skagit River. You can also book adventure tours, rent DVD and VCR players, enjoy the spacious picnic grounds, and try "bunny-hole golf" on a course dug by local rabbits. The Eatery—a quaint, country-style restaurant and museum fronted by a huge sawmill mural—serves up homemade cinnamon rolls and chicken-fried steak amid exhibits of 19th-century pioneer memorabilia. Savory pies are made by Tootsie Clark herself, whose grandmother arrived here in 1888 by Indian canoe and later named Marblemount. ⊠ *58468 Clark Cabin Road (Milepost 103.5 on North Cascades Highway), Rockport 98283* ☎ *360/873–2250 or 800/273–2606* ⊕ *www.northcascades.com* 🛏 *32 cabins, 4 B&B rooms with shared bath, 5 trailers, 30 RV sites, 15 tent sites. $79–$149* ↺ *Restaurant, kitchen (some), bicycles, laundry facilities* ☐ *MC, V.*

27

# NORTH CASCADES ESSENTIALS

ACCESSIBILITY All visitor centers along North Cascades Highway, including the main facility in Newhalem, are accessible to those with mobility impairments. Accessible hikes along the highway include Sterling Munro, River Loop, and Rock Shelter, three short trails into lowland old-growth forest, all at Mile 120 along Route 20 near Newhalem; and the Happy Creek Forest Trail at Mile 134.

ADMISSION FEES A Northwest Forest Pass, required for use of various park and National Forest facilities, such as trailheads, is $5 per vehicle for one calendar day or $30 for one year. A free wilderness permit is required for all overnight stays in the backcountry; these are available in person only. Dock permits for boat-in campgrounds are also $5 per day. Passes and permits are sold at visitor centers and ranger stations around the park area.

ADMISSION HOURS The park never closes, but access is limited by snow in winter. Route 20 (North Cascades Highway), the major access to the park, is partially closed from mid-November to mid-April.

ATMS/BANKS There are no ATMs in the park. Marblemount, Winthrop, and Chelan have banks with 24-hour ATMs.

AUTOMOBILE SERVICE STATIONS There are no gas or service stations available between Marblemount and Mazama. Marblemount has several gas and service stations.

EMERGENCIES Dial 911 for all emergencies.

LOST AND FOUND The park's lost and found is at the visitor center in Newhalem.

POST OFFICES There are no post offices in the park.
🚩 **Marblemount Post Office** ✉ 60096 Rte. 20, Marblemount 98267 ☎ 360/873-2125

PUBLIC TELEPHONES AND RESTROOMS Public telephones and restrooms are found at the North Cascades Visitor Center and Skagit Information Center in Newhalem; and at the Golden West Visitor Center and North Cascades Stehekin Lodge in Stehekin.

TRANSPORTATION
🚩 **Chelan Air.** ✍ Box W, Chelan 98816 ☎ 509/682-5555 ⊕ www.chelanairways.com ✈ $120 round-trip. **Destinations Unlimited.** ☎ 509/682-4571 or 800/642-7336. At **Lake Chelan Boat Company.** ✉ 1418 W. Woodin Ave., Chelan ☎ 509/682-4584, 509/682-4444 info line ⊕ www.ladyofthelake.com ✈ $38-$102. **Mountain Transporter.** ☎ 509/996-8294 or 866/638-4691 ⊕ www.mountaintransporter.com. **Stehekin Adventures Shuttle Bus.** ☎ 360/856-5700 Ext. 340 then press 14 ⊕ www.nps.gov/noca/focus/focus.htm ✈ $5 one way ▭ No credit cards ☉ Mid-May-mid-Oct. **Stehekin Pastry Company.** ⊕ www.stehekinvalley.com/pastryco.htm ✈ $1 ▭ No credit cards ☉ Mid-May-mid-Oct.

**NEARBY TOWN INFORMATION**
🚩 **Lake Chelan Chamber of Commerce** ✉ 102 E. Johnson, Chelan, 98816 ☎ 509/682-3500 or 800/424-3526 ⊕ www.lakechelan.com. **North Cascades Chamber of Commerce** ✉ 59831 Rte. 20, Marblemount ✍ Box 175, Marblemount 98267 ☎ 360/873-2106 or 877/875-2448 ⊕ www.marblemount.com. **Sedro-Woolley Chamber of Commerce** ✉ 714-B Metcalf St., Sedro-Woolley 98284 ☎ 360/855-1841 or 888/225-8365 ⊕ www.sedro-woolley.com. **Twisp Visitor Information Center and Chamber of Commerce** ✉ 201 S. Methow Valley Hwy., Twisp 98856 ☎ 509/997-2926 ⊕ www.twispinfo.com. **Winthrop Chamber of Commerce** ✉ 202 Hwy. 20, Winthrop 98862 ☎ 509/996-2125 or 888/463-8469 ⊕ www.winthropwashington.com.

**VISITOR INFORMATION**
🚩 **North Cascades National Park Headquarters and Information Station** ✉ 810 Rte. 20, Sedro-Woolley, WA 98284 ☎ 360/856-5700 ⊕ www.nps.gov/noca, www.north.cascades.national-park.com/.

# Olympic
# National Park

## WORD OF MOUTH

"If future generations are to remember us with gratitude rather than contempt, we must leave them something more than the miracles of technology. We must leave them a glimpse of the world as it was in the beginning, not just after we got through with it."

–President Lyndon B. Johnson
upon signing the Wilderness Act, 1964.
Today 95% of Olympic National Park is
designated wilderness.

# WELCOME TO OLYMPIC

## TOP REASONS TO GO

★ **Exotic rain forest:** A rain forest in the Pacific Northwest? Olympic National Park is one of a few places in the world with this unique temperate landscape.

★ **Beachcombing:** Miles of spectacular, rugged coastline dotted with tidal pools, sea stacks, and driftwood hem the edges of the Olympic Peninsula.

★ **Nature's hot tubs:** Take a relaxing dip in the wooded heart of the park at the Sol Duc hot springs, a series of geothermal mineral pools.

★ **Lofty vistas:** The Olympics have plenty of peaks you can climb—or you just drive up to Hurricane Ridge for endless views over the ranges.

★ **A sense of history:** The first evidence of humans on the Olympic Peninsula dates back 12,000 years. Today, eight tribes still have traditional ties to lands in Olympic National Park, and there are ample opportunities for exploring Native American history in and around the region.

**1 Coastal Olympic.** Here the Pacific smashes endlessly into the rugged coastline, carving out some of the park's most memorable scenes in the massive, rocky sea stacks and islets just offshore. Back from the water are beaches and tide pools full of starfish, crabs, and anemones.

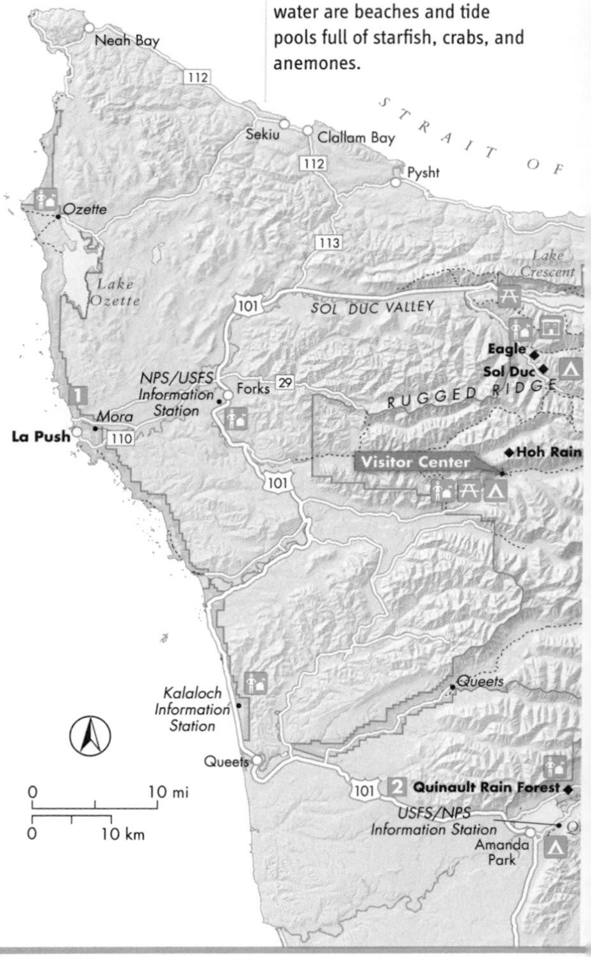

Neah Bay

STRAIT OF

112

Sekiu   Clallam Bay

112

Pysht

113

Ozette

Lake Crescent

Lake Ozette

101   SOL DUC VALLEY

Eagle

Sol Duc

RUGGED RIDGE

NPS/USFS Information Station

Forks   29

**La Push**   Mora

110

Visitor Center

♦ **Hoh Rain**

101

Kalaloch Information Station

Queets

0        10 mi

0        10 km

Queets

101   **2 Quinault Rain Forest**

USFS/NPS Information Station

Amanda Park

**2** The Rain Forest. Centered on the Hoh, Queets, and Quinault river valleys, this is the region's most unique landscape. Fog-shrouded Douglas firs and Sitka spruces, some at more than 300 feet tall, huddle in this moist, pine-carpeted area, shading fern- and moss-draped cedars, maples, and alders.

**3** The Mountains. Craggy gray peaks and snow-covered summits dominate the skyline. Low-level foliage and wildflower meadows make for excellent hiking in the plateaus. Even on the sunniest days, temperatures are brisk. Some roads are closed in winter months.

Hikers at Marymere Falls

**4** Alpine Meadows. In mid-summer, the swathe of colors is like a Monet canvas spread over the landscape, and wildlife teems within the honeyed flowers. Trails are never prettier, and views are crisp and vast.

WASHINGTON

# GETTING ORIENTED

The Olympic peninsula's elegant snowcapped and forested landscape is edged on all sides by water: to the north, the Strait of Juan de Fuca separates the United States from Canada, while a network of Puget Sound bays laces the east, the Chehalis River meanders along the southern end, and the massive gray Pacific Ocean guards the west side.

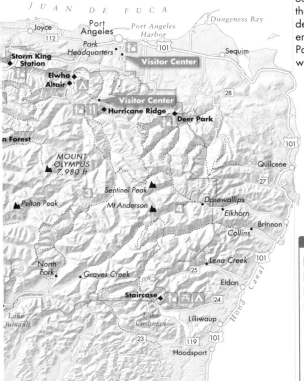

| KEY | |
|---|---|
| 🏨 | Ranger Station |
| ⛺ | Campground |
| 🎪 | Picnic Area |
| 🍴 | Restaurant |
| 🏨 | Lodge |
| 🚶 | Trailhead |
| 🚻 | Restrooms |
| ⤳ | Scenic Viewpoint |
| ----- | Walking/Hiking Trails |
| ...... | Bicycle Path |

# OLYMPIC PLANNER

## When to Go

Summer, with its long stretches of sun-filled days, is prime touring time for Olympic National Park, perfect for taking in sweeping mountaintop vistas and dazzling Northwestern beaches. **June through September are peak months,** when more than 75% of park visitors stream into the area; popular stops like Hurricane Ridge, the Hoh Rain Forest, Lake Crescent, and Ruby Beach are bustling by 10 AM.

Late spring and early autumn are also good bets for clear weather; any time between April and October, and you'll have a good chance of fair skies. Between Thanksgiving and Easter, it's a toss-up as to which days will turn out fair; prepare for heavy clouds, rain showers, and chilly temperatures, then hope for the best.

That said, winter is a great time to visit if you enjoy isolation. Locals are usually the only hardy souls exploring the park's winter scenes, except for weekend skiers heading to the snowfields around Hurricane Ridge. Many visitor facilities have limited hours or are closed from October to April.

AVG. HIGH/LOW TEMPS.

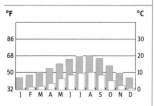

## Flora & Fauna

Along the high mountain slopes hardy cedar, fir, and hemlock trees stand tough on the rugged land; the lower montane forests are filled with thickets of silver firs; and valleys stream with Douglas firs and Western hemlock. The park's famous temperate rain forests are on the peninsula's western side, marked by broad Western red cedars, towering red spruces, and ferns festooned with strands of mosses and patchwork lichens. This lower landscape is also home to some of the Northwest's largest trees: massive cedar and Sitka spruce near Lake Quinault can measure more than 700 inches around, and Douglas firs near the Queets and Hoh rivers are nearly as wide.

These landscapes are home to a variety of wildlife, including many large mammals and 15 creatures found nowhere else in the world. Hikers often come across Roosevelt's elk, black-tailed deer, mountain goats, beavers, raccoons, skunks, opossums, and foxes; Douglas squirrels and flying squirrels populate the heights of the forest. Less common are black bears (most prevalent from May through August); wolves, bobcats, and cougar are rarely seen. Birdlife includes bald eagles, red-tailed hawks, osprey, and great horned owls. Rivers and lakes are filled with freshwater fish, while beaches hold crabs, starfish, anemones, and other shelled creatures. Get out in a boat on the Pacific to spot seals, sea lions, and sea otters—and perhaps a pod of porpoises, orcas, or gray whales.

Beware of jellyfish around the shores—beached jellyfish can still sting. In the woods, check for ticks after every hike and after each shower. Biting nasties include black flies, horseflies, sand fleas, and the ever-present mosquitoes. Yellow jacket nests populate tree hollows along many trails—signs along Hoh Rain Forest trails warn hikers to move quickly through these sections. If one or two chase you, remain calm and keep walking; these are just "guards" making sure you're keeping away from the hive. Poison oak is common, so familiarize yourself with its appearance. Bug repellent, sunscreen, and long pants and sleeves will go a long way toward making your experience more comfortable.

## Getting There & Around

U.S. 101 essentially encircles the main section of Olympic National Park, and a number of roads lead from the highway into the park's mountains and toward its beaches. You can reach U.S. 101 via Interstate 5 at Olympia, via Route 12 at Aberdeen, or via Route 104 from the Washington State ferry terminals at Bainbridge or Kingston. The ferries are the most direct route to the Olympic area from Seattle; call **Washington State Ferries** (☎ 800/843–3779 or 206/464–6400) for information. You can enter the park at a number of points, though access roads do not penetrate far, since the park is 95% wilderness. The best way to get around and to see many of the park's key sites is on foot.

**Grays Harbor Transit** (☎ 360/532–2770 or 800/562–9730 ⊕ www.ghtransit.com) runs free daily buses between Forks and Amanda Park, to the south on the west end of Lake Quinault as does **West Jefferson Transit** (☎ 800/436–3950 ⊕ www.jeffersontransit.com).

## Good Reads

Robert L. Wood's **Olympic Mountain Trail Guide** is a bible for both day hikers and those planning longer excursions. Stephen Whitney's **A Field Guide to the Cascades and Olympics** is an excellent trailside reference, covering more than 500 plant and animal species found in the park.

The park's newspaper, the *Bugler,* is a seasonal guide for activities and opportunities in Olympic National Park. You can pick it up at the visitor centers. A handy mail-order catalog of books and maps about the park is available from the **Northwest Interpretive Association (NWIA).** ✉ 3002 Mount Angeles Rd., Port Angeles ☎ 360/565–3195 ⊕ http://nwpubliclands.com.

## Festivals & Seasonal Events

APR. **Rainfest.** A celebration of arts and crafts, inspired by the huge annual rainfall of 100-plus inches, takes place mid-April in downtown Forks. ☎ *800/443-6757.*

MAY **Irrigation Festival.** Highlights of this Sequim festival include an antique-car show, logging demonstrations, arts and crafts, dancing, and a parade. ☎ 360/683-6197. **Juan de Fuca Festival of the Arts.** Port Angeles comes alive each May with four days of music, dance, and theater from around the world, as well as children's programs. ☎ *360/457-5411.*

JUNE–AUG. **Centrum Summer Arts Festival.** A former aircraft hangar in Port Townsend is the arena for this summerlong music and performance festival. ☎ 360/385-3102.

JUNE–SEPT. **Olympic Music Festival.** Led by the Philadelphia String Quartet, some of the country's most prestigious summer classical music events take place in and around a barn near Port Townsend. ☎ *206/ 527-8839.*

JULY **Fourth of July.** A salmon bake, a parade, a demolition derby, and arts and crafts exhibits mark Forks' four-day-long celebration. ☎ *800/ 443-6757.*

SEPT. **Wooden Boat Festival.** Hundreds of antique boats sail into Port Townsend. ☎ 360/385-3628.

OCT. **Forks Heritage Days.** Logging skills contests, parades, pancake breakfasts, and other events bring Forks' pioneer past to life. ☎ *800/ 443-6757.*

28

By Holly S. Smith

One of the country's most fascinating environments lies at its far northwestern corner, within the heart-shaped Olympic Peninsula. Edged on all sides by water, the elegant snow-capped and forested landscape is remote and pristine. The endless sharpened ridges of the towering Olympic Mountains are visible for 50 mi inland. Big lakes cut pockets of blue in the rugged blanket of pine forests, and hot springs gurgle up from the foothills. Along the coast the sights are even more amazing: wave-sculpted boulders, tidal pools teeming with sea life, and tree-topped sea stacks.

## Scenic Drives

★ **Port Angeles Visitor Center to Hurricane Ridge.** Climbing steeply—from thick fir forests in the foothills and subalpine meadow below the ridge, to alpine meadow at the top—this is the premier scenic drive in Olympic National Park. At the top, the visitor center at Hurricane Ridge has some truly spectacular views of the heart of the mountains and across the Strait of Juan de Fuca. (Backpackers note wryly that you have to hike a long way in other parts of the park to get the kinds of views you can drive to at Hurricane Ridge.) Hurricane Ridge also has an uncommonly fine display of wildflowers in spring and summer.

## What to See

Most of the park's attractions are found either far off Highway 101 or down trails that require hikes of 15 minutes or longer. The west coast beaches are linked to the highway by downhill trails; the number of cars parked alongside the road at the start of the paths indicate how crowded the beach will be.

## OLYMPIC IN ONE DAY

Start at the **Lake Quinault Lodge,** in the park's southwest corner. From here, drive a half hour into the Quinault Valley via **South Shore Road.** Tackle the forested **Graves Creek Nature Trail,** then head up **North Shore Road** to the Quinault Rain Forest Interpretive Trail. Next, head back to Highway 101 and drive to **Ruby Beach,** where a shoreline walk presents a breathtaking scene of sea stacks and sparkling, pink-hued sands.

Forks, and its **Timber Museum,** are your next stop; have lunch here, then drive 20 minutes to the beach

at **La Push.** Next, head to **Lake Crescent,** around the corner to the northeast, where you can rent a boat, take a swim, or enjoy a picnic next to the sparkling teal waters. Drive through **Port Angeles** to **Hurricane Ridge Road;** count on an hour's drive from bottom to top if there aren't too many visitors. At the ridge, explore the visitor center or hike the 3-mi loop to 5,757-foot **Hurricane Hill,** where you can see over the entire park north to Vancouver Island and south past Mt. Olympus.

### Historic Sites

**La Push.** At the mouth of Quileute River, La Push is the tribal center of the Quileute Indians. In fact, the town's name is a variation on the French *la bouche,* which means "the mouth." Offshore rock spires known as sea stacks dot the coast here, and you may catch a glimpse of bald eagles nesting in the nearby cliffs. ⊠ *Rte. 110, 14 mi west of Forks.*

★ **Lake Ozette.** The third-largest glacial impoundment in Washington anchors the coastal strip of Olympic National Park at its north end. The small town of Ozette, home to a coastal tribe, is the trailhead for two of the park's better one-day hikes. Both 3-mi trails lead over boardwalks through swampy wetland and coastal old-growth forest to the ocean shore and uncrowded beaches. ⊠ *At the end of Hoko-Ozette Rd., 26 mi southwest of Hwy. 112 near Sekiu* ☎ *360/963–2725.*

### Scenic Stops

Fodor'sChoice
★ **Hoh River Rain Forest.** South of Forks, an 18-mi spur road links Highway 101 with this unique temperate rain forest, where spruce and hemlock trees soar to heights of more than 200 feet. Alders and big-leaf maples are so densely covered with mosses they look more like shaggy prehistoric animals than trees, and elk browse in shaded glens. Be prepared for precipitation: the region receives 140 inches or more each year (that's 12 feet and up). ⊠ *From Hwy. 101, at about 20 mi north of Kalaloch, turn onto Upper Hoh Rd. 18 mi east to Hoh Rain Forest Visitor Center* ☎ *360/374–6925.*

Fodor'sChoice
★ **Hurricane Ridge.** The panoramic view from this 5,200-foot-high ridge encompasses the Olympic range, the Strait of Juan de Fuca, and Vancouver Island. Guided tours are given in summer along the many paved and unpaved trails, where wildflowers and wildlife such as deer and mar-

**28**

mots flourish. ✉ *Hurricane Ridge Rd., 17 mi south of Port Angeles* ☎ *360/565–3130* ☉ *Visitor center daily 10–5.*

**Kalaloch.** With a lodge, a huge campground, miles of coastline, and easy access from the highway, this is another popular spot. Keen-eyed beachcombers may spot sea otters just offshore; they were reintroduced here in 1970. ✉ *Hwy. 101, 32 mi northwest of Lake Quinault* ☎ *360/ 962–2283.*

**Lake Crescent.** Visitors see Lake Crescent as Highway 101 winds along its southern shore, giving way to gorgeous views of azure waters rippling in a basin formed by Tuscan-like hills. In the evening, low bands of clouds caught between the surrounding mountains often linger over its reflective surface. ✉ *Hwy. 101, 16 mi west of Port Angeles and 28 mi east of Forks* ☎ *360/928–3380.*

★ **Lake Quinault.** This glimmering lake, 4½ mi long and 300 feet deep, is the first landmark you'll reach when driving the west-side loop of U.S. 101. The rain forest is densest here, with moss-draped maples and alders, and towering spruce, fir, and hemlock. Enchanted Valley, high up near the Quinault River's source, is a deeply glaciated valley that's closer to the Hood Canal than to the Pacific Ocean. A scenic loop drive circles the lake and travels around a section of the Quinault River. ✉ *Hwy. 101, 38 mi north of Hoquiam* ☎ *360/288–2444* ☉ *Ranger station May–Sept., daily 8–5.*

**Second and Third Beaches.** During low tide, the pools here brim with life, and you can walk out to some sea stacks. Gray whales play offshore during their annual spring migration, and most of the year the waves are great for surfing and kayaking (bring a wet suit). ✉ *Hwy. 101, 32 mi north of Lake Quinault* ☎ *360/374–5460.*

**Sol Duc.** Sol Duc Valley is one of those magical, serene places where all the Northwest's virtues seem at hand—lush lowland forests, a sparkling river, salmon runs, and quiet hiking trails. Here, the popular Sol Duc Hot Springs area includes three sulfuric pools ranging in temperature from 98°F to 104°F. ✉ *Sol Duc Rd. south of U.S. 101, 1 mi past the west end of Lake Crescent* ☎ *360/374–6925.*

**Staircase.** Unlike the forests of the park's south and west sides, Douglas fir is the dominant tree on the east slope of the Olympic Mountains. Fire has played an important role in creating the majestic forest here, as the Staircase Ranger Station explains in interpretive exhibits. ✉ *At end of Rte. 119, 15 mi from U.S. 101 at Hoodsport* ☎ *360/877–5569.*

## Visitor Centers

**Forks Recreation and Information Center.** The office has park maps and brochures; they also provide permits and rent bear-proof containers. ✉ *Hwy. 101, Forks* ☎ *360/565–3100* ⊕ *www.nps.gov/olym* ☉ *June–Aug., daily 9–4.*

**Hoh Rain Forest Visitor Center.** Pick up park maps and pamphlets, permits, and activities lists in this busy, woodsy chalet; there's also a shop and exhibits on natural history. Several short interpretive trails and

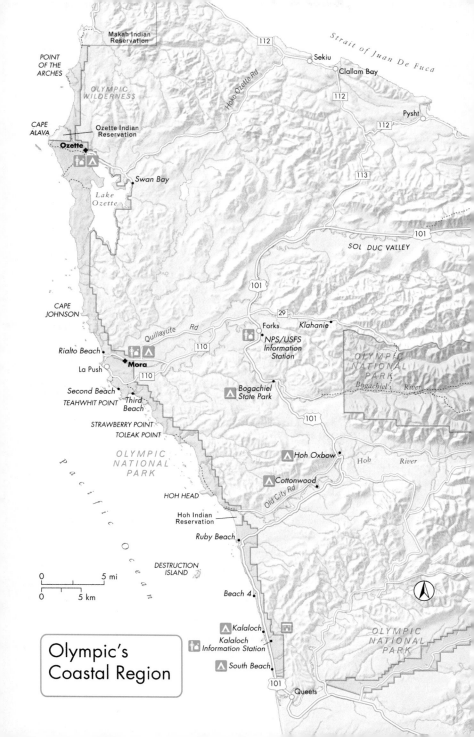

Makah Indian
Reservation

POINT
OF THE
ARCHES

*Strait of Juan De Fuca*

112

Sekiu

Clallam Bay

OLYMPIC
WILDERNESS

Hoko Ozette Rd

112

112

Pysht

CAPE
ALAVA

Ozette Indian
Reservation

113

Ozette

Swan Bay

*Lake
Ozette*

101

*SOL DUC VALLEY*

CAPE
JOHNSON

*Quillayute Rd*

29

Forks

Klahanie

Rialto Beach

110

NPS/USFS
Information
Station

OLYMPIC
NATIONAL
PARK

*Bogachiel River*

Mora

La Push

110

Second Beach

TEAHWHIT POINT

*Third
Beach*

Bogachiel
State Park

STRAWBERRY POINT
TOLEAK POINT

101

OLYMPIC
NATIONAL
PARK

Hoh Oxbow

*Hoh        River*

HOH HEAD

Cottonwood

Old City Rd

Hoh Indian
Reservation

Ruby Beach

*P
a
c
i
f
i
c*

0        5 mi

0        5 km

*O
c
e
a
n*

DESTRUCTION
ISLAND

Beach 4

Kalaloch

OLYMPIC
NATIONAL
PARK

Kalaloch
Information Station

South Beach

101

Queets

Olympic's
Coastal Region

longer wilderness treks start from here. ⊠ *Upper Hoh Rd., Forks* ☎ *360/374–6925* ⊕ *www.nps.gov/olym* ☉ *Sept.–June daily 9–4, July and Aug. daily 9–6:30.*

**Hurricane Ridge Visitor Center.** The upper level of this visitor center has exhibits, a gift shop, and a café; the lower level has open seating and nice views. Guided walks and programs start in late June, and you can also get details on the surrounding Winter Use Area ski and sledding slopes. ⊠ *Hurricane Ridge Rd., Port Angeles* ☎ *360/565–3131* ⊕ *www. nps.gov/olym* ☉ *Memorial Day–Labor Day, daily 9–7; Dec.–Apr., Fri.–Sun. 9–4.*

**Olympic National Park Visitor Center.** This modern, well-organized facility, staffed by park rangers, provides everything: maps, trail brochures, campground advice, listings of wildlife sightings, educational programs and exhibits, information on road and trail closures, and weather forecasts. ⊠ *3002 Mount Angeles Rd., Port Angeles 98362* ☎ *360/565–3130* ⊕ *www.nps.gov/olym* ☉ *May–Sept., daily 9–4; Oct.–Apr., daily 10–4.*

**South Shore Quinault Ranger Station.** This office at the Lake Quinault Lodge has maps, campground information, and program listings. ⊠ *S. Shore Lake Quinault Rd., Lake Quinault* ⊕ *www.nps.gov/olym* ☉ *Memorial Day–Labor Day, weekdays 8–4:30, weekends 9–4.*

**Wilderness Information Center (WIC).** Located behind Olympic National Park Visitor Center, this facility provides all the information you'll need for a trip in the park, including trail conditions, safety tips, and weather bulletins. The office also issues camping permits, takes campground reservations, and rents bear-proof food canisters for $3. ⊠ *3002 Mount Angeles Rd., Port Angeles* ☎ *360/565–3100* ⊕ *www.nps.gov/olym* ☉ *Late June–Labor Day, Sun.–Thurs. 7:30–6, Fri. and Sat. 7:30–7.*

## Sports & the Outdoors

### Beachcombing

★ The wild, pebble- and shell-strewn Pacific coast teems with tide pools and clawed creatures. Crabs, sand dollars, anemones, starfish, and all sorts of shellfish are exposed at low tide, when flat beaches can stretch out for hundreds of yards. Note that the most easily accessible sand-strolling spots are Rialto; Ruby; First and Second near Mora and La Push; and beaches No. 2 and No. 4 in the Kalaloch stretch.

The Wilderness Act and the park's code of ethics strongly encourage visitors to leave all non-living materials where they are for others to enjoy.

### Bicycling

The rough gravel car tracks to some of the park's remote sites were meant for four-wheel-drive vehicles, but can double as mountain-bike routes. The Quinault Valley, Queets River, Hoh River, and Sol Duc River roads have bike paths through old-growth forest. Graves Creek Road, in the southwest, is a mountain-bike path; Lake Crescent's north side is also edged by the bike-friendly Spruce Railroad Trail. More bike trails run through the adjacent Olympic National Forest. Note that Highway 101 has heavy traffic and isn't recommended for cycling, although the western side has broad roads with beautiful scenery and can be biked off-season. Bikes are not permitted on foot trails. For bike rentals and guides ⇨ Outfitters & Expeditions box.

## Climbing

At 7,980 feet, Mt. Olympus is the highest peak in the park and the most popular climb in the region. To attempt the summit, participants must register at the Glacier Meadows Ranger Station. Mt. Constance, the third-highest Olympic summit at 7,743 feet, has a well-traversed climbing route that requires technical experience; reservations are recommended for the Lake Constance stop, which is limited to 20 campers. Mt. Deception is a third possibility, though tricky snows have caused several fatalities and injuries in the last decade. Climbing season runs late June through September. Note that crevasse skills and self-rescue experience are highly recommended. Climbers must register with park officials and purchase wilderness permits before setting out. The best resource for climbing advice is the Wilderness Information Center in Port Angeles. For guides and equipment ⇨ Outfitters & Expeditions box.

## Fishing

Bodies of water throughout the park offer numerous fishing possibilities. Lake Crescent is home to cutthroat and rainbow trout, as well as petite kokanee salmon; Lake Cushman, Lake Quinault, and Ozette Lake have trout, salmon, and steelhead; and Lake Mills has three trout varieties. As for rivers, the Bogachiel and Queets have steelhead salmon in season. The glacier-fed Hoh River is home to chinook salmon April to November, and coho salmon from August through November; the Sol Duc River offers all five species of salmon, plus cutthroat and steelhead trout. Rainbow trout are also found in the Dosewallips, Elwha, and Skykomish rivers. Other places to go after salmon and trout include the Duckabush, Quillayute, Quinault, and Salmon rivers. A Washington State punch card required during salmon-spawning months; general fishing regulations vary throughout the park. Licenses are available from sporting goods and outdoor supply stores. For guides ⇨ Outfitters & Expeditions box.

## Hiking

Caution: know your tides, or you might be trapped by high water. Tide tables are available at all visitor centers and ranger stations. Remember that a wilderness permit is required for all overnight backcountry visits. For guides ⇨ Outfitters & Expeditions box.

EASY **Hoh Valley Trail.** Leaving from the Hoh Visitor Center, this rain forest jaunt takes you into the Hoh Valley, wending its way alongside the river, FodorśChoice through moss-draped maple and alder trees, and past open meadows ★ where elk roam in winter. ⊠ *Hoh Visitor Center, 18 mi east of U.S. 101.*

**Hurricane Ridge Trail.** A ¼-mi alpine loop, most of it wheelchair-accessible, leads through wildflower meadows overlooking numerous vistas of the interior Olympic peaks to the south and a panorama of the Strait of Juan de Fuca to the north. ⊠ *Hurricane Ridge Rd., 17 mi south of Port Angeles.*

**28**

# OUTFITTERS & EXPEDITIONS

### BICYCLING

**Bicycle Adventures** (☎ 360/786-0989 or 800/443-6060 ⊕ www.bicycleadventures.com), an Olympia bike tour outfit, stages trips in and around the park area, including up Hurricane Ridge. **Mike's Bikes** (✉ 150 W. Sequim Bay Rd., Sequim ☎ 360/681-3868 ⊕ www.mikes-bikes.net), a bike, gear, and repair shop, is a great resource for advice on routes around the Olympic Peninsula. **Peak 6** (✉ 4883 Upper Hoh Rd., Forks ☎ 360/374-5254), an adventure store on the way to the Hoh Rain Forest Visitor Center, rents mountain bikes. **Sound Bike & Kayak** (✉ 120 E. Front St., Port Angeles ☎ 360/457-1240 ⊕ www.soundbikeskayaks.com) rents and sells biking equipment.

### CLIMBING

**Alpine Ascents** (✉ 121 Mercer St., Seattle ☎ 206/378-1927 ⊕ www.alpineascents.com) leads tours of the Olympic ranges. **Mountain Madness** (✉ 4218 SW Alaska St., Ste. 206, Seattle ☎ 206/937-8389 ⊕ www.mountainmadness.com) offers adventure trips to summits around the Olympic Peninsula. **Olympic Mountaineering** (✉ 140 W. Front St., Port Angeles ☎ 360/452-0240 ⊕ www.olymtn.com) sells mountaineering gear and organizes climbs and hikes in the park.

### FISHING

**Bob's Piscatorial Pursuits** (☎ 866/347-4232 ⊕ www.piscatorialpursuits.com), based in Forks, offers year-round fishing trips around Olympic. **Blue Sky Outfitters** (✉ 9674 50th Ave. SW, Seattle ☎ 800/228-7238 ⊕ www.blueskyoutfitters.com), in Seattle, organizes custom-tailored fishing trips. White-water rafting trips are another specialty. **Kalaloch Lodge** (✉ 157151 U.S. 101, Forks ☎ 360/962-2271 or 866/525-2562 ⊕ www.visitkalaloch.com) organizes guided fishing expeditions around the Olympic Peninsula.

### HIKING

**Peak 6** (✉ 4883 Upper Hoh Rd., Forks ☎ 360/374-5254) runs guided hiking and camping trips. **Timberline Adventures** (☎ 800/417-2453 ⊕ www.timbertours.com) offers weeklong excursions around the Olympic Peninsula.

### KAYAKING & CANOEING

**Fairholm General Store** (✉ U.S. 101, Fairholm ☎ 360/928-3020) rents rowboats and canoes on Lake Crescent for $10 to $45. It's at the lake's west end, 27 mi west of Port Angeles. **Lake Crescent Lodge** (✉ 416 Lake Crescent Rd. ☎ 360/928-3211) rents rowboats for $8.50 per hour and $35 per day. **Log Cabin Resort** (✉ Piedmont Rd., off U.S. 101 ☎ 360/928-3325), 17 mi west of Port Angeles, has boat rentals for $10 to $30. The dock provides easy access to Lake Crescent's northeast section. **Rain Forest Paddlers** (✉ 4882 Upper Hoh Rd., Forks ☎ 360/374-5254 or 866/457-8398 ⊕ www.rainforestpaddlers.com) takes kayakers down the Lizard Rock and Oxbow sections of the Hoh River.

### RAFTING

**Olympic Raft and Kayak** (☎ 360/452-5268 or 888/452-1443 ⊕ www.raftandkayak.com), based in Port Angeles, is the only rafting outfit allowed to venture into Olympic National Park.

SKIING & SNOWSHOEING

**Hurricane Ridge Visitor Center** (✉ Hurricane Ridge Rd., Port Angeles ☎ 360/565-3131 information, 360/565-3136 tour reservations ⊕ www.nps.gov/olym) rents ski equipment December through March; prices are $15 to $35. Free 90-minute snowshoe tours also depart from here every weekend from late December through March. Group bookings are at 10:30, with informal group tours at 2; sign-ups are at 1:30 and are first-come, first-served. A $5 per person donation is requested to cover trail and equipment maintenance. **Lost Mountain Lodge** (✉ 303 Sunny View Dr., Sequim ☎ 360/683-2431 or 888/683-2431 ⊕ www.lostmountainlodge.com), in Sequim, offers weekend Olympic Mountains snowshoe packages; gear rental and an in-room, fireside fondue are included.

MODERATE **Boulder Creek Trail.** The 5-mi round-trip walk up Boulder Creek leads to a half-dozen hot spring pools of varying temperatures; some are clothing-optional. ✉ *End of the Elwha River Rd., 4 mi south of Altair Campground.*

★ ☺ **Cape Alva Trail.** Beginning at Ozette, this 3-mi trail leads from the forest to wave-tossed headlands. ✉ *End of the Hoko-Ozette Rd., 26 mi south of Hwy. 112, west of Sekiu.*

**Graves Creek Trail.** This 6-mi-long moderately strenuous trail climbs from lowland rain forest to alpine territory at Sundown Pass. Due to spring floods, a fjord halfway up is often impassable in May and June. ✉ *End of S. Quinault Valley Rd., 23 mi east of U.S. 101.*

☺ Fodor'sChoice ★ **Sol Duc Trail.** The 1½-mi gravel path off Sol Duc Road winds through thick Douglas fir forests toward the thundering, three-chute Sol Duc Falls. Just ¹⁄₁₀ mi from the road, below a wooden platform over the Sol Duc River, you'll come across the 70-foot Salmon Cascades. In late summer and autumn, thousands of salmon negotiate 50 mi or more of treacherous waters to reach the cascades and the tamer pools near Sol Duc Hot Springs. The popular 6-mi **Lovers Lane Loop Trail** links the Sol Duc falls with the hot springs. You can continue up from the falls 5 mi to the **Appleton Pass Trail**, at 3,100 feet. From there you can hike on to the 8½-mi mark, where views at the High Divide are from 5,050 feet. ✉ *Sol Duc Rd., 11 mi south of U.S. 101.*

DIFFICULT **High Divide Trail.** A 9-mi hike in the park's high country defines this trail, which includes some strenuous climbing on its last 4 mi before topping out at a small alpine lake. A return loop along High Divide wends its way an extra mile through alpine territory, with sensational views of Olympic peaks. This trail is only for dedicated, properly equipped hikers who are in good shape. ✉ *End of Sol Duc River Rd., 13 mi south of U.S. 101.*

## Kayaking & Canoeing

Lake Crescent, a serene expanse of teal-colored waters surrounded by thick, deep-green forests, is one of the park's best boating areas. Note that the west end is for swimming only; no speedboats are allowed here.

28

Lake Quinault has boating access from a gravel ramp on the north shore. From U.S. 101, take a right on North Shore Road, another right on Hemlock Way, and a left on Lakeview Drive. There are plank ramps at Falls Creek and Willoughby campgrounds on South Shore Drive, $\frac{1}{10}$ mi and $1\frac{1}{5}$ mi past the Quinault Ranger Station, respectively.

Lake Ozette, with just one access road, is a good place for overnight trips. Only experienced canoe and kayak handlers should travel far from the put-in, since fierce storms occasionally strike—even in summer. For equipment and guides ⇨ Outfitters & Expeditions box.

### Rafting

Olympic has excellent rafting rivers, with Class II to Class V rapids. The Elwha River is a popular place to paddle, with some exciting turns. The Hoh is better for those who like a smooth, easy float. For guides ⇨ Outfitters & Expeditions box.

### Winter Sports

Hurricane Ridge is the central spot for winter sports. Miles of downhill and Nordic ski tracks are open late December through March, and a ski lift, tow ropes, and ski school are open 10 to 4 weekends and holidays. Tubing areas for adults and children are open Friday through Sunday across from Hurricane Ridge Lodge. For equipment and guides ⇨ Outfitters & Expeditions box.

## Educational Offerings

### Classes & Seminars

**Olympic Park Institute.** This first-class educational facility offers talks and excursions focusing on park ecology and history. Trips range from two-hour canoe trips ($20) to five-day camping, kayaking, and climbing excursions ($200 to $400 per person; family discounts are offered). ⊠ *111 Barnes Point Rd., Port Angeles* ☎ *360/928–3720 or 800/775–3720* ⊕ *www.olympicparkinstitute.org* ⊙ *Weekdays 8:30–4:30.*

# WHAT'S NEARBY

## Nearby Towns

Although most Olympic Peninsula towns have evolved from their exclusive reliance on timber, **Forks,** outside the national park's northwest tip, remains one of the region's logging capitals. Washington State's wettest town (100 inches or more of rain a year), it's a small, friendly place with just 3,500 residents and a modicum of visitor facilities. **Port Angeles,** a town of 19,000 now focuses on its status as the main gateway to Olympic National Park and Victoria, BC. Set below the Strait of Juan de Fuca and looking north to Vancouver Island, it's an enviably scenic site filled with attractive, Craftsman-style homes. The Pacific Northwest has its very own "Banana Belt" in the waterfront community of **Sequim,** 15 mi east of Port Angeles along Highway 101. The town of 6,000 is located in the rain shadow of the Olympics and receives only 16 inches of rain per year (compared to the 40 inches that drench the Hoh Rain Forest just 40 mi away).

## Nearby Attractions

**Fodor'sChoice** ★ **Dungeness Spit.** Curving 5½ mi into the Strait of Juan de Fuca, the longest natural sand spit in the United States is a wild, beautiful section of shoreline. More than 30,000 migratory waterfowl stop here each spring and fall, but you'll see plenty of birdlife any time of year. The entire spit is part of the Dungeness National Wildlife Refuge. At the end of the Dungeness Spit is the towering white **Dungeness Lighthouse** (☎ 360/683–9166 ⊕ www.newdungenesslighthouse.com); tours are available, though access is limited to those who can hike or kayak out 5 mi to the end of the spit. ⊠ *Kitchen Rd., 3 mi north from U.S. 101, 4 mi west of Sequim* ☎ *360/457–8451 wildlife refuge, 360/683–5847 campground* 📷 *$3 per family* ☉ *Wildlife refuge daily sunrise–sunset.*

# WHERE TO STAY & EAT

### About the Restaurants

The major resorts are your best bets for eating out in the park. Each has a main restaurant, café, and/or kiosk, as well as casually upscale dinner service, with regional seafood, meat, and produce complemented by a range of microbrews and good Washington and international wines. Reservations are either recommended or required.

Outside the park, Port Angeles is the place to go for a truly spectacular meal; several restaurants are internationally renowned by diners and chefs alike, and most are run by famous former chefs. Dozens of small, easygoing eateries offering hearty American-style fare line the main thoroughfares in Forks and Sequim.

**28**

### About the Hotels

Major park resorts run from good to terrific, with generally comfortable rooms, excellent facilities, and easy access to trails, beaches, and activity centers. Midsize accommodations, like Sol Duc Hot Springs Resort, are often shockingly rustic—but remember, you're here for the park, not for the rooms.

The towns around the park have motels, hotels, and resorts for every budget. For high-priced stays with lots of perks, base yourself in Port Angeles. Sequim has many attractive, friendly B&Bs, plus lots of inexpensive chain hotels and motels. Forks is basically a motel town, with a few guesthouses around its fringes.

### About the Campgrounds

Note that only a few places take reservations; if you can't book in advance, you'll have to arrive early to get a place. Each site usually has a picnic table and grill or fire pit, and most campgrounds have water, toilets, and garbage containers; for hookups, showers, and laundry facilities, you'll have to head into the towns. Firewood is available from camp concessions, but if there's no store you can collect dead wood within 1 mi of your campsite. Dogs are allowed in campgrounds, but not on trails or in the backcountry. Trailers should be 21 feet long or less (15 feet or less at Queets Campground). There's a camping limit of two weeks.

If you have a backcountry pass, you can camp virtually anywhere throughout the park's forests and shores. Overnight wilderness permits are $5—plus $2 per person per night—and are available at visitor centers and ranger stations. Note that when you camp in the backcountry, you must choose a site at least ½ mi inside the park boundary.

## Where to Eat

### In Olympic National Park

★ $$–$$$$ ✕ **Lake Crescent Lodge.** Part of the original 1916 lodge, the fir-paneled dining room overlooks the lake; you also won't find a better spot for a view of the sunset. Entrées include crab cakes, grilled salmon, halibut fish-and-chips, classic American steaks, and elk ribs. A good Northwest wine list complements the menu. Note that meals are only offered during set hours; if you arrive between midday and dinner, the restaurant offers a "Missed Lunch" option in the lobby bar. ✉ *416 Lake Crescent Rd., Port Angeles* ☎ *360/928–3211* ⚐ *Reservations essential. $15–$32* ▭ *AE, D, DC, MC, V* ⊘ *Closed mid-Oct.–May.*

★ $$–$$$ ✕ **Kalaloch Lodge.** A tranquil country setting and ocean views create the perfect backdrop for savoring local dinner specialties like cedar-planked salmon, fresh shellfish, wild mushrooms, and well-aged beef. Note that seating is every half hour after 5, and reservations are recommended. Hearty breakfasts and sandwich-style lunches are more casual. ✉ *157151 Hwy. 101, Kalaloch* ☎ *360/962–3391 or 866/525–2562. $14–$29* ▭ *AE, MC, V.*

$–$$$ ✕ **The Springs Restaurant.** The main Sol Duc Hot Springs Resort restaurant is a rustic, fir-and-cedar paneled dining room surrounded by trees. Big breakfasts are turned out daily 7:30 to 10:30, while dinner is served daily between 5 and 9 (lunch and snacks are available at the Poolside Deli or Espresso Hut). Evening choices include Northwest seafood and game highlighted by fresh-picked fruits and vegetables. ✉ *12076 Sol Duc Rd., at U.S. 101, Port Angeles* ☎ *360/327–3583. $12–$22* ▭ *AE, D, MC, V* ⊘ *Closed mid-Oct.–mid-May.*

PICNIC AREAS    All Olympic National Park campgrounds have adjacent picnic areas with tables, some shelters, and restrooms, but no cooking facilities. The same is true for major visitor centers, such as Hoh Rain Forest. Drinking water is available at ranger stations, interpretive centers, and inside campgrounds.

**East Beach Picnic Area.** Set on a grassy meadow overlooking Lake Crescent, this popular swimming spot has six picnic tables and vault toilets. ✉ *Hwy. 101, 17 mi west of Port Angeles, at the far east end of Lake Crescent.*

**La Poel Picnic Area.** Tall firs lean over a tiny gravel beach at this small picnic area, which has five picnic tables and a splendid view of Pyramid Mountain across Lake Crescent. ✉ *Hwy. 101, 22 mi west of Port Angeles.*

**North Shore Picnic Area.** This site lies beneath Pyramid Mountain along the north shore of Lake Crescent; a steep trail leads from the eight-table picnic ground to the mountain top. ✉ *North Shore Rd., 3 mi east of Fairholm.*

**Rialto Beach Picnic Area.** Relatively secluded at the end of the road from Forks, this is one of the premier day-use areas in the park's Pacific coast segment. This site has 12 picnic tables, fire grills, and vault toilets. ⊠ *Rte. 110, 14 mi west of Forks.*

### Outside the Park

**$$$–$$$$**
**Fodor'sChoice**
**★**
✕ **C'est Si Bon.** Far more Euro-savvy than is typical on the Olympic Peninsula, this first-rate restaurant stands out for its decor as well as for its food. The fanciful dining room is done up in bold red hues, with crisp white linens, huge oil paintings, and glittering chandeliers; the spacious solarium takes an equally formal approach. The changing menu highlights homemade onion soup, Cornish hen, filet mignon, and lobster tail. The wine list is superb, with French, Australian, and Northwest choices to pair with everything. ⊠ *23 Cedar Park Rd., Port Angeles* ☎ *360/452–8888* ⌔ *Reservations essential. $25–$39* ⊟ *AE, DC, MC, V* ⊘ *Closed Mon. No lunch.*

**★ $–$$$**
✕ **Three Crabs.** An institution since 1958, this large crab shack on the beach, 5 mi north of Sequim, specializes in Dungeness's famed crustacean. Although the clawed creatures are served many ways here, these crabs are so fresh that it's best to simply have them with lemon and butter. ⊠ *11 Three Crabs Rd., Sequim* ☎ *360/683–4264. $10–$22* ⊟ *MC, V* ⊘ *Closed Tues. in winter.*

**★ $–$$**
✕ **Marina Restaurant.** With tremendous views of John Wayne Marina and Sequim Bay, this family restaurant is a fun place to watch the ships placidly sail by. The menu includes seafood, pasta, salads, and sandwiches, but the emphasis is on steak—especially prime rib, which is served on Saturday night. ⊠ *2577 W. Sequim Bay Rd., Sequim* ☎ *360/681–0577. $11–$18* ⊟ *AE, D, MC, V* ⊘ *Closed Tues. in winter.*

**¢–$$**
✕ **La Casita.** This family-run Mexican restaurant overlooking Port Angeles harbor leans heavily on old standbys and combination plates, but what sets it apart is its artful use of local fish. Try the seafood chimichanga, a crisp-fried burrito filled with Dungeness crab, bay shrimp, fresh cod, Monterey jack cheese, tomato, and chilies. ⊠ *203 E. Front St., Port Angeles* ☎ *360/452–2289. $7–$14* ⊟ *AE, D, MC, V.*

## Where to Stay

### In Olympic National Park

**$$–$$$$**
✕▤ **Kalaloch Lodge.** A two-story cedar lodge overlooking the Pacific, Kalaloch has cozy rooms with sea views. The surrounding log cabins have a fireplace or woodstove, knotty-pine furnishings, earth-tone fabrics, and kitchenettes; waterfront cottages have deep couches and picture windows overlooking the sea. Guests have pool privileges at the Lake Quinault Resort; towels are provided. The restaurant's ($$–$$$) menu changes seasonally, but usually includes local oysters, crab, and salmon. ⊠ *157151 U.S. 101* ⌂ *HC 80, Box 1100, Forks 98331* ☎ *360/962–2271 or 866/525–2562* ⊠ *360/962–3391* ⊕ *www.visitkalaloch. com* ⇆ *10 lodge rooms, 6 motel rooms, 3 motel suites, 44 cabins* ⌂ *Restaurant, coffee shop, kitchen, bar, some pets allowed, no phone, no TV. $149–$265* ⊟ *AE, MC, V.*

**$–$$$$**
✕▤ **Lake Crescent Lodge.** Deep in the forest at the foot of Mt. Storm King, this comfortable lodge, built in 1916, has a wraparound veranda and picture windows that frame the lake's sapphire waters. Rooms in the

**28**

rustic Roosevelt Cottage have polished wood floors, stone fireplaces, and lake views, while Tavern Cottage quarters resemble modern motel rooms. The historic lodge has second-floor rooms with shared baths. The lodge's fir-paneled dining room ($$–$$$$) overlooks the lake, and the adjacent lounge is often crowded with campers. Seafood dishes like grilled salmon or steamed Quilcene oysters highlight the restaurant menu; reservations are required. ⊠ *416 Lake Crescent Rd., Port Angeles 98363* ☎ *360/928–3211* 📠 *360/928–3253* ⊕ *www.lakecrescentlodge.com* ⇌ *30 motel rooms, 17 cabins, 5 lodge rooms with shared bath* ⟡ *2 restaurants, no phone, no TV. $85–$211* ▭ *AE, DC, MC, V* ⊙ *Closed Nov.–Apr.*

**$$–$$$**  ✕▦ **Lake Quinault Lodge.** On a lovely glacial lake in Olympic National Forest, this beautiful early-20th-century lodge complex is within walking distance of the lakeshore and hiking trails in the spectacular old-growth forest. A towering brick fireplace is the centerpiece of the great room, where antique wicker furnishings sit beneath ceiling beams painted with Native American designs. In the rooms, modern gadgets are traded in for old-fashioned comforts, such as claw-foot tubs, fireplaces, and walking sticks. The lively bar is a good place to unwind after a day outdoors, and the restaurant ($$–$$$) serves upscale seafood entrées like baked salmon with capers and onions. ⊠ *South Shore Rd., Box 7, Quinault 98575* ☎ *360/288–2900 or 800/562–6672* 📠 *360/288–2901* ⊕ *www.visitlakequinault.com* ⇌ *92 rooms* ⟡ *Restaurant, VCR (some), pool, bar, some pets allowed, no phone, no TV (some). $117–$183* ▭ *AE, D, MC, V.*

**$$–$$$**  ✕▦ **Sol Duc Hot Springs Resort.** Deep in the brooding forest along the Sol Duc River, this remote 1910 resort is surrounded by 5,000-foot-tall mountains. The main draw is the pool area, which surrounds a gathering of soothing mineral baths, and has a freshwater swimming pool. Some forest cabins have kitchens, but all are spartan; however, after a day's hike, a dip, and dinner at The Springs Restaurant ($–$$$), you'll hardly notice. The attractive fir-and-cedar-paneled dining room serves unpretentious meals all day, drawing on top Northwest seafood and produce. ⊠ *12076 Sol Duc Rd.* ⟁ *Box 2168, Port Angeles 98362* ☎ *360/327–3583 or 866/476–5382* 📠 *360/327–3398* ⊕ *www.visitsolduc.com* ⇌ *32 rooms, 6 cabins* ⟡ *Restaurant, kitchen (some), pool, massage, bar, no a/c (some), no phone (some), no TV (some). $125–$155* ▭ *AE, DC, MC, V* ⊙ *Closed mid-Oct.–mid-Apr.*

**$–$$**  ▦ **Log Cabin Resort.** This rustic hotel has an idyllic setting at the northeast end of Lake Crescent. Settle into one of the A-frame chalet units, standard cabins, "camping cabins" (wooden tents with shared bathroom), motel units, or RV sites, which include full hookups. Some rooms have full kitchens. Twelve of the units are on the lake. You can rent paddleboats or kayaks to use by the day. ⊠ *3183 E. Beach Rd., Port Angeles 98363* ☎ *360/928–3325* ⊕ *www.logcabinresort.net* ⇌ *28 units, 4 cabins, 40 RV sites* ⟡ *Restaurant, laundry facilities, no a/c, no phone, no TV. $55–$139* ▭ *D, MC, V* ⊙ *Closed Nov.–Mar.*

**CAMPGROUNDS &**  ⚠ **Lake Quinault Rain Forest Resort Village Campground.** Stretching along
**RV PARKS**  the south shore of Lake Quinault, this campground has many recreation
**$$**  facilities, including beaches, canoes, ball fields, and horseshoe pits. ⊠ *3½ mi east of U.S. 101, South Shore Rd., Lake Quinault* ☎ *360/288–*

2535 or 800/255–6936 ⊕ *www.rainforestresort.com* ⊲ *31 sites* ⚹ *Grills, flush toilets, full hookups, drinking water, showers, picnic tables, electricity, public telephone, general store.* $21.50 RVs ⊟ AE, D, MC, V ⊗ *Apr.–Oct.*

**$–$$** ⚲ **Kalaloch Campground.** Kalaloch is the biggest and most popular Olympic campground, and it's open all year. Its vantage of the Pacific is unmatched on the park's coastal stretch—although the campsites themselves are set back in the spruce fringe. ⊠ *U.S. 101, ½ mi north of the Kalaloch Information Station, Olympic National Park* ☏ 360/962–2271 *group bookings* ⊲ *175 sites* ⚹ *Flush toilets, dump station, drinking water, fire grates, public telephone, ranger station.* $18 *mid-June–Aug., otherwise* $14 ⊟ MC, V ⊗ *Year-round.*

**$** ⚲ **Altair Campground.** This small campground sits amid an old-growth forest by the river in the rather narrow Elwha River Valley. The 3-mi West Elwha Trail leads downstream from the campground. ⊠ *Elwha River Rd., 8 mi south of U.S. 101, Olympic National Park* ☏ *No phone* ⊲ *30 sites* ⚹ *Flush toilets, drinking water, fire grates.* $12 ⊗ *Apr.–Oct.*

**$** ⚲ **Deer Park Campground.** At 5,400 feet, this is the park's only drive-to alpine campground. The part-gravel access road is steep and winding; RVs are prohibited. ⊠ *Deer Park (Blue Mountain) Rd., 21 mi south of U.S. 101, Olympic National Park* ☏ *No phone* ⊲ *14 sites* ⚹ *Pit toilets, drinking water, fire grates.* $10 ⊗ *May–Sept.*

**$** ⚲ **Dosewallips Campground.** Popular with hikers—and hunters in the fall—this small, remote campground lies beneath Mt. Constance in old-growth forest along the river. The long gravel access road is not suitable for RVs. ⊠ *Dosewallips River Rd., 15 mi west of Brinnon, Olympic National Park* ☏ *No phone* ⊲ *30 sites* ⚹ *Pit toilets, fire grates.* $10 ⊟ MC, V ⊗ *May–Oct.*

**$** ⚲ **Elwha Campground.** The larger of the Elwha Valley's two campgrounds, this is one of Olympic's year-round facilities. Two campsite loops lie in an old-growth forest. ⊠ *Elwha River Rd., 7 mi south of U.S. 101, Olympic National Park* ☏ *No phone* ⊲ *40 sites* ⚹ *Pit toilets, drinking water (summer only), fire grates, public telephone, ranger station.* $12 ⊟ MC, V ⊗ *Year-round.*

**★ $** ⚲ **Fairholme Campground.** One of just three lakeside campgrounds in the park, Fairholm is near the Lake Crescent Resort. There is an on-site boat launch. ⊠ *U.S. 101, 28 mi west of Port Angeles, on the west end of Lake Crescent, Olympic National Park* ☏ *No phone* ⊲ *88 sites* ⚹ *Flush toilets, dump station, drinking water, fire grates, public telephone, swimming (lake).* $12 ⊗ *Apr.–Oct.*

**$** ⚲ **Graves Creek Campground.** At the junction of its namesake creek and the east fork of the Quinault, this campground lies deep in an old-growth rain forest. The access road includes an 11-mi stretch of gravel that is prone to washouts. Nearby is the Graves Creek trailhead, the start of one of the park's best alpine day hikes. ⊠ *S. Quinault Valley Rd., 22 mi east of U.S. 101, Olympic National Park* ☏ *No phone* ⊲ *30 sites* ⚹ *Pit toilets, drinking water, fire grates, ranger station.* $12 ⊗ *Apr.–Oct.*

**$** ⚲ **Heart O' the Hills Campground.** At the foot of Hurricane Ridge in a grove of tall firs, this popular year-round campground offers a regular slate of summer programs. The trade-off is a distinct lack of peace and

28

quiet. ⊠ *Hurricane Ridge Rd., 4 mi south of the main park visitor center in Port Angeles, Olympic National Park* 🕾 *No phone* 🛏 *105 sites* ⚎ *Flush toilets, drinking water, fire grates, public telephone, ranger station. $12* ⊘ *Year-round.*

$ ⚠ **Hoh Campground.** Crowds flock to this rain-forest site, near the Hoh Visitor Center under a canopy of moss-draped maples and towering spruce trees. ⊠ *Hoh River Rd., 17 mi east of U.S. 101, Olympic National Park* 🕾 *No phone* 🛏 *88 sites* ⚎ *Flush toilets, dump station, drinking water, fire grates, public telephone, ranger station. $12* ⊟ *MC, V* ⊘ *Year-round.*

$ ⚠ **July Creek Campground.** This walk-in campground overlooks Lake Quinault and the rugged mountains beyond. Lake access is less than 100 yards away. ⊠ *North Shore Rd., 3 mi east of U.S. 101, Port Angeles* 🕾 *No phone* 🛏 *28 sites* ⚎ *Pit toilets, drinking water (no water in winter), fire grates, swimming (lake). $10* ⊘ *Apr.–Oct.*

★ $ ⚠ **Mora Campground.** Along the Quillayute estuary, this campground doubles as a popular staging point for hikes northward along the coast's wilderness stretch. ⊠ *Rte. 110, 13 mi west of Forks, Olympic National Park* 🕾 *No phone* 🛏 *94 sites (1 walk-in)* ⚎ *Flush toilets, dump station, drinking water, fire grates, public telephone, ranger station. $12* ⊘ *Year-round.*

$ ⚠ **North Fork Campground.** The park's smallest campground is for self-sufficient travelers who want to enjoy the rain forest in peace. It's deep, wet woods here; RVs are not advised. ⊠ *N. Quinault Valley Rd., 19 mi east of U.S. 101, Olympic National Park* 🕾 *No phone* 🛏 *7 sites* ⚎ *Pit toilets, fire grates, ranger station. $10* ⊘ *May–Sept.*

$ ⚠ **Ozette Campground.** Hikers heading to Cape Alava, a scenic promontory that is the westernmost point in the lower 48 states, use this lakeshore campground as a jumping-off point. There's a boat launch and a small beach. ⊠ *Hoko-Ozette Rd., 26 mi south of Hwy. 112, Olympic National Park* 🕾 *No phone* 🛏 *15 sites* ⚎ *Pit toilets, fire grates, ranger station. $12* ⊟ *MC, V* ⊘ *Year-round, but call ahead in winter.*

$ ⚠ **Queets Campground.** Set amid lush old-growth forests in the southwestern corner of the park near Olympic's largest Douglas fir tree, this campground is not suitable for camp trailers or RVs. ⊠ *Queets River Rd., 12 mi east of U.S. 101, Olympic National Park* 🕾 *No phone* 🛏 *20 sites* ⚎ *Pit toilets, fire grates, ranger station. $10* ⊘ *Apr.–Oct.*

$ ⚠ **Sol Duc Campground.** Sol Duc resembles virtually all Olympic campgrounds save one distinguishing feature—the famed hot springs are a short walk away. ⊠ *Sol Duc Rd., 11 mi south of U.S. 101, Olympic National Park* 🕾 *360/327–3534* 🛏 *82 sites* ⚎ *Flush toilets, dump station, drinking water, fire grates, public telephone, ranger station, swimming (hot springs). $14* ⊘ *May–Oct.*

$ ⚠ **South Beach Campground.** The first campground travelers reach as they enter the park's coastal stretch from the south, this is basically an overflow campground for the more popular and better-equipped Kalaloch a few miles north. There is no water. ⊠ *2 mi south of the Kalaloch Information Station at the southern boundary of the park, U.S. 101, Olympic National Park* 🕾 *No phone* 🛏 *50 sites* ⚎ *Pit toilets, fire grates. $10* ⊟ *No credit cards* ⊘ *Apr.–Oct.*

**$** ⛺ **Staircase Campground.** In deep woods away from the river, this campground is a popular jumping-off point for hikes into the Skokomish River Valley and the Olympic high country. ✉ *Rte. 119, 16 mi northwest of U.S. 101, Olympic National Park* ☎ *No phone* ⛺ *56 sites* ♿ *Flush toilets, drinking water, fire grates, public telephone, ranger station. $12* ☉ *Year-round.*

### Outside the Park

**$$$-$$$$** 🏠 **Colette's Bed & Breakfast.** A contemporary mansion curving around
Fodor'sChoice 10 acres of gorgeous waterfront property, this B&B offers more space,
★ service, and luxury than any other property in the area. Leather sofas and chairs and a river-rock fireplace make the front room a lovely spot to watch the water through expansive 20-foot windows. The suites, which have such names as Iris, Azalea, and Cedar, also overlook the water and have fireplaces, balconies, CD and DVD players, and two-person hot tubs. A specially-made outdoor fireplace means you can enjoy the deck even in winter. Multicourse breakfasts include espresso-based drinks and fresh fruit. ✉ *339 Finn Hall Rd., 10 mi east of town, Port Angeles 98362* ☎ *360/457–9197 or 888/457–9777* 🖨 *360/452–0711* ⊕ *www.colettes. com* ⛺ *5 suites* ♿ *Restaurant, refrigerator, VCR, no kids. $175–$235* 🍽 *MC, V* ⵊ⧠ *BP.*

★ **$-$$$** 🏠 **Greywolf Inn.** On a 5-acre hilltop overlooking the town and bay, this country retreat among the trees is right on the Olympic Discovery Trail. A gazebo, Japanese-style hot tub, and warm front room encourage convivial gatherings. Berry bushes and occasionally elk dot the 5 acres of wild grounds. Room themes are inspired by diverse places and cultures like the south of France, the African savanna, and Bavaria. One room has a fireplace, another has a feather bed, and two have magnificent views. The glass-enclosed dining room and deck overlook a meadow. ✉ *395 Keeler Rd., Sequim 98392* ☎ *360/683–5889 or 800/914–9653* 🖨 *360/ 683–1487* ⊕ *www.greywolfinn.com* ⛺ *5 rooms* ♿ *Restaurant, Wi-Fi, no phone, no kids. $95–$175* 🍽 *MC, V* ⵊ⧠ *BP.*

**$-$$$** 🏠 **Quality Inn.** South of town, at the green edge of the Olympic Mountain foothills, this inn has mountain and harbor views. Perks include nightly cookies. ✉ *101 E. 2nd St., Port Angeles 98362* ☎ *360/457–9434 or 800/858–3812* 🖨 *360/457–5915* ⊕ *www.qualityinnportangeles.com* ⛺ *51 rooms* ♿ *Kitchen (some),refrigerator, Wi-Fi, no-smoking rooms. $79–$179* 🍽 *AE, D, DC, MC, V* ⵊ⧠ *BP.*

28

# OLYMPIC ESSENTIALS

**ACCESSIBILITY** There are wheelchair-accessible facilities—including trails, campgrounds, and visitor centers—throughout the park; contact visitor centers for more information.

**ADMISSION HOURS** Six park entrances are open 24/7; gate kiosk hours (for buying passes) vary widely according to season and location, but most kiosks are staffed during daylight hours. Olympic National Park is located in the Pacific time one.

**ATMS/BANKS**
🏧 **Bank of America** ✉ 481 S. Forks Ave., Forks ☎ 360/374-2261 ✉ 134 W. 8th St., Port Angeles

☎ 360/457-2747 ✉ 102 E. Front St., Port Angeles ☎ 360/457-2737 ⊕ www.bankofamerica.com. **Washington Mutual Bank** ✉ 101 W. Front St., Port Angeles ☎ 360/452-8981 ✉ 680 W. Washington St., Sequim ☎ 360/683-7242 ⊕ www.wamu.com.

AUTOMOBILE SERVICE STATIONS
🏢 **Fairholm General Store** ✉ 416 Lake Crescent Rd., Lake Crescent ☎ 360/928-3020. **Port Angeles Chevron** ✉ 402 Marine Dr., Port Angeles ☎ 360/457-6350.

EMERGENCIES For all park emergencies, dial 360/565-3000 (7 AM–midnight in summer, 7–5:30 off-season); after hours dial 911. Park rangers are on duty during daylight hours at Port Angeles Visitor Center, Hoh Rain Forest Visitor Center, and Hurricane Ridge Visitor Center. Other ranger stations are staffed daily in summer, staff levels permitting; off-season schedules vary.

ADMISSION FEES Seven-day vehicle admission fee is $10, plus $5 for each individual; an annual family pass is $30. Parking at Ozette, the trailhead for one of the park's most popular hikes, is $1 per day.

LOST AND FOUND
🏢 **Olympic National Park Visitor Center** ✉ 3002 Mount Angeles Rd., Port Angeles ☎ 360/565-3130 ⊕ www.nps.gov/olym.

PERMITS An overnight wilderness permit, available at visitor centers and ranger stations, is $5 (covers registration of your party for up to 14 days), plus $2 per person per night. A frequent-hiker pass, which covers all wilderness use fees, is $30 per year. Fishing in freshwater streams and lakes within Olympic National Park does not require a Washington State fishing license; however, anglers must acquire a salmon-steelhead punch card when fishing

for those species. Ocean fishing and harvesting shellfish and seaweed require licenses, which are available at sporting goods and outdoor supply stores.

POST OFFICES
🏢 **Forks Post Office** ✉ 61 S. Spartan Ave., Forks 98331 ☎ 360/374-6303. **Port Angeles Post Office** ✉ 424 E. 1st Ave., Port Angeles 98362 ☎ 360/452-9275.

PUBLIC TELEPHONES There are public telephones at the Olympic National Park Visitor Center, Hoh River Rain Forest Visitor Center, and the lodging properties within the park—Lake Crescent, Kalaloch, and Sol Duc Hot Springs. Fairholm General Store also has a phone. Note that there is no cell phone reception in wilderness areas.

RESTROOMS Visitor centers, interpretive centers, and ranger stations within the park have public restroom facilities, as do picnic grounds, campgrounds, and the lodging properties within the park: Lake Quinault, Lake Crescent, Kalaloch, and Sol Duc Hot Springs.

## NEARBY TOWN INFORMATION
🏢 **Forks Chamber of Commerce Visitor Center** ✉ 1411 S. Forks Ave. (U.S. 101), Forks 98331 ☎ 800/443-6757 ⊕ www.forkswa.com. **Port Angeles Chamber of Commerce Visitor Center** ✉ 121 E. Railroad Ave., Port Angeles 98362 ☎ 360/452-2363 ⊕ www.cityofpa.com. **Sequim-Dungeness Chamber of Commerce** 🖃 Box 907, Sequim 98382 ☎ 360/693-6197 or 800/737-8462 ⊕ www.cityofsequim.com.

## VISITOR INFORMATION
🏢 **Olympic National Park** ✉ 600 E. Park Ave., Port Angeles, WA 98362 ☎ 360/565-3130 ⊕ www.nps.gov/olym.

# Petrified Forest National Park

Petroglyphs, Wilderness Area of Petrified Forest National Park

## WORD OF MOUTH

"An enchanted spot to stand on the glass of a gigantic kaleidoscope,
over whose sparkling surface the sun breaks in infinite rainbows . . ."

–Charles F. Lummis

# WELCOME TO PETRIFIED FOREST

Petrified wood

## TOP REASONS TO GO

★ **Terrific Timber:** Be mesmerized by the clusters of petrified (fossilized) wood. The trees look like they're made of colorful stone.

★ **Triassic Treasures:** Find an oasis of water in the desert, or at least evidence it once existed. Clam fossils indicate that waterways once prevailed where sand, stone, and trees now define the land.

★ **Walls with Words:** Don't just scratch the surface, but see how others did. Ancestors of the Hopi, Zuni, and Navajo left their mark in petroglyphs cut, scratched, or carved into stone.

★ **Route 66 Kicks:** Put the top down on the Chevrolet. A section of the fabled road is preserved in the park at the rim of Painted Desert.

★ **Corps Creations:** Say thanks to FDR. The Painted Desert Inn, a National Historic Landmark, was renovated by the Civilian Conservation Corps (CCC) during the throes of the Great Depression.

Vibrant four o'clock

**1 Painted Desert Visitor Center.** The main section of the park, the northern section, is where park headquarters, the Painted Desert Inn, and Route 66 are located. It's also the best place for hiking. A permit is required for overnight camping in the wilderness area, but day users need not obtain one. The 28-mi park road begins here, off Interstate 40.

**2 Blue Mesa.** In the heart of the Painted Desert, this 1-mi loop trail begins off a loop road accessed from the park road. Petrified trees lay amid hills of bluish bentonite clay.

**3 Rainbow Forest Museum.** Get a trail guide here for the short Giant Logs trail located behind the museum, and keep an eye out for "Old Faithful," a log almost 10 feet wide. The southern terminus for the park road is here.

The Painted Desert Inn

Petrified wood along the Giant Logs Trail

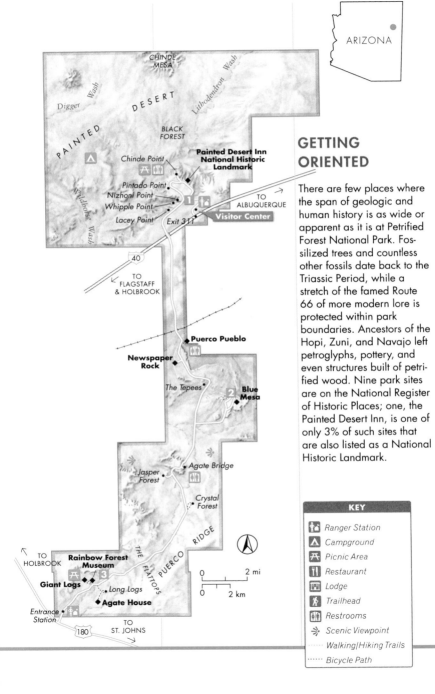

ARIZONA

## GETTING ORIENTED

There are few places where the span of geologic and human history is as wide or apparent as it is at Petrified Forest National Park. Fossilized trees and countless other fossils date back to the Triassic Period, while a stretch of the famed Route 66 of more modern lore is protected within park boundaries. Ancestors of the Hopi, Zuni, and Navajo left petroglyphs, pottery, and even structures built of petrified wood. Nine park sites are on the National Register of Historic Places; one, the Painted Desert Inn, is one of only 3% of such sites that are also listed as a National Historic Landmark.

29

**KEY**

| 👫 | Ranger Station |
| 🔺 | Campground |
| 🪑 | Picnic Area |
| 🍴 | Restaurant |
| 🏨 | Lodge |
| 🚶 | Trailhead |
| 🚻 | Restrooms |
| ⇘ | Scenic Viewpoint |
| ⋯⋯ | Walking/Hiking Trails |
| ⋯⋯ | Bicycle Path |

# PETRIFIED FOREST PLANNER

## When to Go

The park is rarely crowded. Weather-wise, **the best time to visit is in the autumn,** when nights are chilly, but daytime temperatures hover near 70°F. Half of all yearly rain falls be-tween June and August, so it's a good time to spot blooming wild-flowers. The park is least crowded in winter because of cold winds and occasional snow, though daytime temperatures are in the 50s and 60s.

## Festivals & Events

**June Old West Celebration.** Shoot-out reenactments, music, and kids' activities occur at Holbrook's Old West Courthouse. ☎ 800/524-2459.

**June–Aug. Native American Indian Dances.** Young people perform Navajo dances at Holbrook's Old West Courthouse. ☎ 800/524-2459.

**July Prescott Frontier Days and Rodeo.** Started in 1888, it's the world's oldest rodeo–though Pecos, Texas, says otherwise. ☎ 800/266-7534.

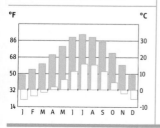

AVG. HIGH/LOW TEMPS.

## Flora & Fauna

Engelmann asters and sunflowers are among the blooms in the park each summer. Juniper trees, cottonwoods, and willows grow along Puerco River Wash, providing shelter for all manner of wildlife. You might spot mule deer, coy-otes, prairie dogs, and foxes, while other inhabitants, like porcupines and bobcats, tend to hide. Bird-watchers should keep an eye out for mockingbirds, red-tailed and Swainson's hawks, roadrunners, swallows, and humming-birds. Look for all three kinds of lizards—collared, side-blotched, and southern prairie—in rocks.

Beware of rattlesnakes. They are common but can gener-ally be avoided if using common sense: Watch where you step, and don't step anywhere you can't see. If you do come across a rattler, give it plenty of space, and let it go its way before you continue yours. Other reptiles—and there are plenty—are just as common but not as worrisome. The gopher snake looks similar to a rattlesnake, but is non-poisonous. The collared lizard, with its yellow head, can be seen scurrying out of your way just about everywhere in bursts measured at up to 15 mph. They are not poisonous, but will bite in the rare instance of being caught.

## Getting There & Around

The nearest major airports are in Phoenix, AZ (259 mi away via U.S. 17 and U.S. 40) and Albuquerque, NM (204 mi distant via U.S. 40). Holbrook, the nearest larger town, is roughly 20 mi from either of the park's two en-trances on U.S. 40. The closest towns you can get to by bus are Show Low (via White Mountain Passenger Lines ☎ 928/537-4539) and Winslow (via Greyhound ☎ 928/289-2171). By train you can get to Flagstaff and Winslow (Amtrak ☎ 928/774-8679).

Parking is free, and there's ample space at all trailheads, as well as at the visitor center and the museum. The main park road extends 28 mi from the Painted Desert Visitor Center (north entrance) to the Rainbow Forest Museum (south entrance). For park road condition information, call ☎ 928/524-6228.

By John
Blodgett

Petrified logs scattered about a vast lunarlike landscape resemble a fairly-tale forest turned to stone at Petrified Forest National Park. The park's 218,533 acres, which include portions of the Painted Desert, are covered with petrified tree trunks whose wood cells were fossilized over centuries by brightly hued mineral deposits—silica, iron oxide, carbon, manganese, aluminum, copper, and lithium. The park holds plenty of other fossils; remnants of humans and their artifacts have been recovered at more than 500 sites in the park.

**29**

## Scenic Drive

**Painted Desert Scenic Drive.** This 28-mi drive takes you through the park from one entrance to the other. From the north, the first 5 mi leads you along the edge of a high mesa, with spectacular views of Painted Desert. After the 5-mi point, the road crosses Interstate 40, then swings south toward Perco River across a landscape covered with sagebrush, saltbrush, sunflowers, and Apache plume. Past the river, the road climbs onto a narrow mesa leading to Newspaper Rock, a panel of Pueblo Indian rock art. Then the road bends southeast, enters a barren stretch, and passes tepee-shape buttes in the distance. Next you come to Blue Mesa, roughly the park's midpoint and a good place to stop for views of petrified logs. The next stop on the drive is Agate Bridge, really a 100-foot log over a wide wash. The remaining overlooks are Jasper Forest and Crystal Forest. ⊠ *Begins at Painted Desert Visitor Center.*

## What to See

Though named for its famous fossilized trees, Petrified Forest has something to see for history buffs of all stripes, from a segment of Route 66 to ancient dwellings to even more ancient fossils. And the good thing is, much of Petrified Forest's treasures can easily be viewed without a

## PETRIFIED FOREST IN ONE DAY

A nonstop drive through the park (28 mi) takes only 45 minutes, but you can spend most of a day exploring if you stop along the way. From almost any vantage point you can see the multicolored rocks and hills that were home to dinosaurs.

Entering the park from the north, stop at **Painted Desert Visitor Center** and see a 20-minute introductory film. **Painted Desert Inn's visitor center,** 2 mi south of the north entrance, provides further orientation in the form of guided ranger tours. Drive south 8 mi to reach **Puerco Pueblo,** a 100-room pueblo built before 1400. To the south of this are Puebloan petroglyphs at **Newspaper Rock** and, just beyond, **The Teepees,** cone-shaped rock formations covered with manganese and other minerals.

**Blue Mesa** is roughly the midpoint of the drive, and the start of a 1-mi, moderately steep loop hike that leads you around badland hills made of bentonite clay. Drive on for 5 mi until you come to **Jasper Forest,** just past **Agate Bridge. Crystal Forest,** 18 mi south of the north entrance, is named for the smoky quartz, amethyst, and citrine along the $^{8}/_{10}$-mi loop trail. **Rainbow Forest Museum,** at the park's south entrance, has restrooms, a bookstore, and exhibits. Just behind the museum is **Giant Logs,** a $^{4}/_{10}$-mi loop that goes by "Old Faithful," the largest log in the park, an estimated 44 tons.

great amount of athletic conditioning. By combining a drive with a short hike here and there, much can be seen in as short as half a day.

### Historic Sites

**Agate House.** This eight-room pueblo is thought to have been built entirely of petrified wood 700 years ago. Researchers believe it might have been used as a temporary dwelling by seasonal farmers or traders from one of the area tribes. ⊠ *Rainbow Forest Museum parking area.*

**Newspaper Rock.** See huge boulders covered with petroglyphs believed to have been carved by the Pueblo Indians more than 500 years ago. ⊠ *6 mi south of Painted Desert Visitor Center on the main park road.*

**Painted Desert Inn National Historic Site.** Here there are cultural history exhibits, as well as the murals of Fred Kabotie, a popular 1940s artist whose work was commissioned by Mary Jane Colter. Native American crafts are also displayed. ⊠ *2 mi north of Painted Desert Visitor Center on the main park road.* ☎ *928/524–6228* ☜ *Free* ☉ *Daily 8–4.*

**Puerco Pueblo.** This is a 100-room pueblo, built before 1400 and said to have housed ancestral Puebloan people. Many visitors come to see petroglyphs, as well as a solar calendar. ⊠ *10 mi south of the Painted Desert Visitor Center on the main park road.*

### Scenic Stops

★ **Agate Bridge.** See a 100-foot log spanning a 40-foot-wide wash. ⊠ *19 mi south of Painted Desert Visitor Center on the main park road.*

# The Writing on the Wall

**THE ROCK ART OF EARLY NATIVE AMERICANS** is carved or painted on basalt boulders, on canyon walls, and on the underside of overhangs throughout eastern Arizona. Designs pecked or scratched into the stone are called petroglyphs; those that are painted on the surface are pictographs. Few pictographs remain because of the deleterious effects of weathering, but the more durable petroglyphs number in the thousands. No one knows the exact meaning of these signs, and interpretations vary from use in shaman or hunting rituals to clan signs, maps, or even indications of visits by extra-terrestrials.

It's just as difficult to date a "glyph" as it is to understand it. Archaeologists try to determine a general time frame by judging the style, the date of the ruins and pottery in the vicinity, the amount of patination (formation of minerals) on the design, or the superimposition of newer images on top of older ones. Most of eastern Arizona's rock art is estimated to be at least 1,000 years old, and many of the glyphs were created even earlier.

Some glyphs depict animals like big horn sheep, deer, bear, and mountain lions; others are geometric patterns. The most unusual are the anthropomorphs, strange humanlike figures with elaborate headdresses. A concentric circle is a common design. A few of these circles served as solstice signs, indicating summer and winter solstice and other important dates. Many solstice signs are in remote regions, but you can visit the Petrified Forest National Park around June 20 to see a concentric circle illuminated during the summer solstice. The glyph, reached by paved trail just a few hundred yards from the parking area, is visible year-round, but a finger of light shines directly in the center during the week of the solstice. The phenomenon occurs at 9 AM.

Do not touch petroglyphs or pictographs—the oils from your hands can cause damage to the image.

–Janet Webb Farnsworth

29

**Crystal Forest.** The fragments of petrified wood strewn here once held clear quartz and amethyst crystals. ⊠ *20 mi south of Painted Desert Visitor Center on the main park road.*

★ **Giant Logs.** A short walk leads you past the park's largest log, known as "Old Faithful." It's considered the largest because of its diameter (9 feet, 9 inches), as well as how tall it once was. ⊠ *28 mi south of Painted Desert Visitor Center on the main park road.*

**Jasper Forest.** More of an overlook than a forest, this spot has a large concentration of petrified trees in jasper or red. ⊠ *17 mi south of Painted Desert Visitor Center on the main park road.*

**The Tepees.** Witness the effects of time on these cone-shape rock formations colored by iron, manganese, and other minerals. ⊠ *8 mi south of Painted Desert Visitor Center on the main park road.*

## Visitor Centers

**Painted Desert Visitor Center.** This is the place to go for general park information and an informative 20-minute film. Proceeds from books purchased here will fund park research and interpretive ac-

| DON'T LIFT IT! |
| --- |
| "Old Faithful," the largest log in the park, weighs an estimated 44 tons. |

tivities. ⊠ *North entrance, off I–40, 27 mi east of Holbrook* ☎ *928/524–6228* ⊕ *www.nps.gov/pefo* ☯ *Daily 8–5.*

**Rainbow Forest Museum and Visitor Center.** More museum than visitor center, this structure houses artifacts of early reptiles, dinosaurs, and petrified wood. Be sure to see Gurtie, a skeleton of a phytosaur, a crocodile-like carnivore. ⊠ *South entrance, off U.S. 180, 18 mi southeast of Holbrook* ☎ *928/524–6228* ⊟ *Free* ☯ *Daily 8–5.*

# Sports & the Outdoors

As with visits to all national parks, you don't get the full experience unless you take time to smell the roses—or in this case, get close enough to see the multihued lines streaking a petrified log. However, because the park goes to great pains to maintain the integrity of the fossil- and artifact-strewn landscape, outdoor options in the park are limited. Off-highway activity is restricted to on-trail hiking and horseback riding.

## Hiking

All trails begin off the main road, with restrooms at or near the trailheads. Most maintained trails are relatively short, paved, clearly marked, and, with a few exceptions, easy to moderate in difficulty. Hikers with greater stamina can make their own trails in the wilderness area, located just north of the Painted Desert Visitor Center. Watch your step for rattlesnakes, which are common in the park—if left alone and given a wide berth, they are easily enough passed.

EASY **Crystal Forest.** The easy ⁸⁄₁₀-mi loop leads you past petrified wood that once held quartz crystals and amethyst chips. ⊠ *20 mi south of the Painted Desert Visitor Center.*

**Giant Logs.** At ⁴⁄₁₀ mi, Giant Logs is the park's shortest trail. The loop leads you to "Old Faithful," the park's largest log—it's 9 feet, 9 inches at its base, weighing 44 tons. ⊠ *Directly behind Rainbow Forest Museum, 28 mi south of Painted Desert Visitor Center.*

**Long Logs.** The easy ⁶⁄₁₀-mi loop reveals the largest concentration of wood in the park. ⊠ *26 mi south of Painted Desert Visitor Center.*

☻ **Puerco Pueblo.** A relatively flat and paved ³⁄₁₀-mi trail takes you past remains of an ancestral home of the Pueblo people. The trail is handicapped accessible. ⊠ *10 mi south of Painted Desert Visitor Center.*

MODERATE
Fodor'sChoice
★
**Agate House.** A fairly flat 1-mi trip takes you to an eight-room pueblo sitting high on a knoll ( ⇨ Historic Sites, What to See). ⊠ *26 mi south of Painted Desert Visitor Center.*

**Blue Mesa.** Although it's only 1 mi long and it's significantly steeper than the rest, this trail at the park's midway point is quite popular.

✉ *14 mi south of Painted Desert Visitor Center.*

**Painted Desert Rim.** The 1-mi trail is at its best in early morning or late afternoon, when the sun accentuates the brilliant red, blue, purple, and other hues of the desert and petrified forest landscape. ✉ *Tawa Point and Kachina Point, 1 mi north of Painted Desert Visitor Center.*

DIFFICULT **Kachina Point.** A 1-mi trail leads to the Wilderness Area, and from there you're on your own. With no developed trails, hiking here is cross-country style, but expect to see strange formations, beautifully colored landscape, and maybe even a pronghorn antelope. ✉ *On the northwest side of the Painted Desert Inn Museum.*

### Horseback Riding

Horseback riding in Petrified Forest is limited mostly to the wilderness area (paved roads and trails are off-limits), but that doesn't mean it's a limiting experience. You can load/unload and park your trailer on the northwest side of Painted Desert Inn, 2 mi north of the Painted Desert Visitor Center. There are no maintained trails in the park's wilderness, but riders are advised to stick to dry washes as much as possible so as to minimize impact to the fragile desert ecosystem. The first switchback into the Wilderness Area is steep, sometimes unstable, and often exposed; some riders lead their horses down on foot. Once you reach the desert floor, the grade is relatively flat and easy to ride. There is no fee to camp overnight, but a free permit is required and available at either visitor center. Group camping is limited to eight people and four horses.

> ### GUILT TRIPS
>
> In 1906, President Theodore Roosevelt made the area a national monument to protect the petrified wood, which many looters were hauling away in large quantities. Since then, it has been illegal to remove even a small sliver of petrified wood from the park. Those who have say it's brought them all sorts of problems. "Guilt Books" at the park's Rainbow Forest Museum preserve letters from guilt-riddled former visitors anxiously returning their purloined souvenirs and detailing directly attributable hexes—from runs of bad luck to husbands turning into "hard-drinking strangers."

## Educational Offerings

### Ranger Programs

Children 12 and younger can learn more about the park's extensive human, animal, and geologic history as they train to become a **Junior Ranger**.

Park rangers lead regular **20-minute tours** along the Great Logs trail, inside the Painted Desert Inn Museum, and to the Puerco Pueblo. Ask at either visitor center for the availability of **special tours,** such as the after-hours lantern tour of the Painted Desert Inn Museum.

# WHAT'S NEARBY

Surrounding much of Petrified Forest, particularly to the south and east, edging up to the New Mexico border, are Arizona's White Mountains. Here you can hike amid the world's largest stand of ponderosa pines, fish for trout in babbling brooks, swim in clear reservoirs fed by unsullied mountain streams, and, at night, camp under a million stars. In winter, you can ski, snowboard, snowshoe, or snowmobile. It is a wilderness area, and past volcanic activity has strewn the ground with cinder cones. The eastern region of Arizona is, in fact, bounded by the Mogollon Rim (pronounced muh-gee-on)—a 200-mi geologic upthrust that splits the state—made famous as the "Tonto Rim" in Zane Grey's books.

## Nearby Towns & Attractions

### Nearby Towns

If you want to be closer to the park, your best bet is to stay in **Holbrook,** 20 minutes west of Petrified Forest on historic Route 66. Before the "Mother Road" rolled into Holbrook and turned it kitsch, the town was a notorious hangout for cowboys from the vast Aztec Land and Cattle Company, better known as the Hashknife Outfit, after the shape of their brand. The ranching town of 6,000 is now mostly a base for exploring the sights of northeastern Arizona. **Show Low,** to the south, is the commercial center for this high-country area and a good stopping point on your way to the Painted Desert or Petrified Forest. **Pinetop-Lakeside,** at 7,200 feet, is surrounded by the world's largest stand of ponderosa pines. The modest year-round population is 4,200, but in summer months it can jump as high as 30,000. It has gorgeous scenery, excellent multiuse trails, premier golf courses, and temperatures rarely exceeding 85°F. Nearby **Alpine** has a variety of winter sports and is a popular destination for hiking and fishing in summer. A section of historic Route 66 passes through the center of **Winslow,** about an hour west of the park.

### Nearby Attractions

**Bucket of Blood Saloon.** Come have a look at this classic Western saloon with the gory name that has remained virtually untouched since it was built in the 1800s. Although it's not open for inside tours, you can get a good view of the old saloon from the street. ⊠ *S.E. Central St., Holbrook* ☎ *928/524–6558* ☉ *Daily (from outside only).*

★ **Canyon de Chelly National Monument.** In Arizona's northeast corner, Canyon de Chelly (pronounced d'shay) is a place of spectacular beauty. Its two main gorges have dramatically red sandstone walls, some as high as 1,000 feet. Ancient pictographs adorn the cliffs. The park is also noteworthy for its ruins of Indian villages (built between 350 and 1300); some of the park's 7,000 archaeological sites date back 4,500 years. ⊠ *3 mi east of Chinle on Navajo Rte. 7, Box 588, Chinle* ☎ *928/674–5500* ⊕ *www.nps.gov/cach* ☒ *Free* ☉ *Daily 8–5.*

★ **Homolovi Ruins State Park.** The Hopi believe their ancestors inhabited this "place of the little hills" and hold the site to be sacred. They welcome visitors, believing that each potentially brings rain. On the grounds are four major ancestral pueblos thought to have been occupied between 1200 and 1425, 40 ceremonial kivas dating from 900, and two pueblos containing more than 1,000 rooms. Rangers give guided tours, and on weekdays in June and July archaeologists work the site. The visitor center has a small museum with ancestral Puebloan artifacts; it also hosts workshops on native art and traditional foods. ✉ *4 mi northeast of Winslow, off AZ 87* ☎ *928/289–4106* ⊕ *www.pr.state.az.us* ⊠ *$5 per vehicle up to 4 persons; additional persons $1 each* ⊙ *Daily 8–5.*

★ **The Old Courthouse Museum.** This museum holds memorabilia from the Route 66 heyday along with Old West and railroad records. Near the railroad tracks, models of bright green dinosaurs glare down at you. ✉ *Corner of Arizona St. and Navajo Blvd., Holbrook* ☎ *800/524–2459* ⊕ *www.ci.holbrook.az.us* ⊠ *Free* ⊙ *Weekdays 8–5, weekends 8–4.*

Fodor'sChoice ★ **Rock Art Ranch.** The ancestral Puebloan petroglyphs here are startlingly vivid, even after 1,000 years. Brantly Baird, owner of this working cattle ranch, will guide you along the ¼-mi trail, explaining Western and archaeological history. It's mostly easy walking, except for the climb in and out of Chevelon Canyon, where there are handrails. Baird houses his Native American artifacts and pioneer farming items in his own private museum. It's out of the way and on a dirt road, but you'll see some of the best rock art in northern Arizona. Reservations are required. ✉ *Off AZ 87, 13 mi southeast of Winslow* ✉ *Box 224, Joseph City 85032* ☎ *928/288–3260* ⊠ *$20* ⊙ *May–Oct. by appointment only.*

## Area Activities

### Sports & the Outdoors

FISHING **Show Low Lake,** south of Show Low and 1 mi off AZ 260, holds the state record for the largest walleye catch and is well stocked with largemouth bass, bluegill, and catfish. Some anglers have pulled out 9-pound rainbow trout. Facilities include a bait shop, marina with boat rentals, and campsites with bathrooms and showers. ✉ *Show Low Lake Rd., Show Low* ☎ *928/537–4126.*

GOLF **Alpine Country Club.** At 8,500 feet above sea level, this is one of the highest golf courses in the Southwest. Even if you don't play golf, stop in for Mexican food and breathtaking scenery at the club's Aspen Room Restaurant. Closed for winter. ✉ *Off U.S. 180, 3 mi east of U.S. 191, Alpine* ☎ *928/339–4944.*

Fodor'sChoice ★ **Silver Creek Golf Club.** This 18-hole championship golf course is 5 mi east of Show Low on U.S. 60, then 7½ mi north on Bourdon Ranch Road. Voted by the PGA as one of the top 10 golf courses in Arizona, it's also one of the more affordable. Given its lower elevation, this course is usually a few degrees warmer than Show Low and stays open year-round. Green fees change seasonally. ✉ *2051 Silver Lake Blvd., Show Low* ☎ *928/537–2744* ⊕ *www.silvercreekgolfclub.com.*

HIKING ★ Ranked No. 3 in the country's "Top 10 Trail Towns" by the American Hiking Society, **Pinetop-Lakeside** is the primary trailhead for the White Mountains Trails System, made up of roughly 200 mi of interconnecting multiuse loop trails spanning the White Mountains. Trails are open to hikers, mountain bikers, and horseback riders.

**Apache-Sitgreaves National Forest.** You can get trail brochures and a $2 booklet on the White Mountains Trail System at the forest's Lakeside Ranger Station.

29

**Mogollon Rim Interpretive Trail.** This well-traveled and very easy route follows a small part of the 19th-century **Crook Trail** along the Mogollon Rim; the ¼-mi path, with a trailhead just west of the Pinetop-Lakeside city limits, is well marked with placards describing local wildlife and geography. ✉ *2022 W. White Mountain Blvd., Lakeside 85929* ☎ *928/368–5111.*

**Panorama Trail.** This 8-mi route, rated moderate, affords astonishing views from the top of extinct double volcanoes known as the Twin Knolls and passes through a portion of designated wildlife habitat area. ✉ *6 mi east on Porter Mountain Rd. off AZ 260, Pinetop-Lakeside.*

> **FAMILY PICKS**
>
> ■ **Bucket of Blood Saloon.** Take a peek at this Old West relic; with a name like this, the kids are sure to be pleased.
>
> ■ **The Old Courthouse Museum.** See memorabilia from the heyday of car travel on Route 66 and train travel on the rails.

## Shopping

**Harvest Moon Antiques** (✉ 392 W. White Mountain Blvd., Pinetop ☎ 928/367–6973 ☉ Memorial Day through Thanksgiving weekend) specializes in Old West relics, ranging from buckskins and Apache wares to old guns and U.S. Cavalry items. This is an excellent place to find affordable Navajo rugs and jewelry; look for the tepees outside.

Fodor'sChoice ★ **McGees Beyond Native Tradition** (✉ 2114 E. Navajo Blvd., Holbrook ☎ 928/524–1977 ⊕ www.hopiart.com ☉ Weekdays 9–5:30, Sat. 9–4) is the area's premier source of high-quality Native American jewelry, rugs, Hopi baskets, and Kachina dolls. The owners have longstanding, personal relationships with reservation artisans and a knowledgeable staff that adroitly assists first-time buyers and seasoned collectors alike.

# WHERE TO STAY & EAT

### About the Restaurants

Dining in the park is limited to a cafeteria in the Painted Desert Visitor Center and snacks in the Rainbow Forest Museum. In and around the Navajo and Hopi reservations, be sure to sample Indian tacos, an authentic treat made with scrumptious fry bread, beans, and chilies.

### About the Hotels

There is no lodging within Petrified Forest. Outside the park, lodging choices include modern resorts, rustic cabins, and small bed-and-breakfasts. Air-conditioning is *not* a standard amenity in the mountains, where the nights are cool enough for a blanket even in summer. Closer to the Navajo and Hopi reservations, many establishments are run by Native Americans, tribal enterprises intent on offering first-class service and hospitality.

### About the Campgrounds

There are no campgrounds in the park. Backcountry camping is allowed if you obtain a free permit at the visitor center or museum. The only camping allowed in the park is minimal-impact camping in a designated zone north of Lithodendron Wash in the Wilderness Area. Group size is limited to 8. RVs are not allowed. There are no fire pits or designated sites, nor is any shade available. Also note that if it rains, that pretty Painted Desert formation turns to sticky clay. The campgrounds listed here are open year-round unless the listing states otherwise.

## Where to Eat

### In the Park

¢ ✕ **Painted Desert Visitor Center Cafeteria.** The only place in the park to get a full meal, it offers standard cafeteria fare. ⊠ *North entrance, off I–40, 27 mi east of Holbrook* ☎ 928/524–6228. *$4–$8* ▭ *MC, V.*

PICNIC AREAS **Chinde Point Picnic Area.** This small area near the north entrance has tables and restrooms. ⊠ *2 mi north of Painted Desert Visitor Center.*

**Rainbow Forest Museum Picnic Area.** This small area has picnic tables and restrooms. ⊠ *South entrance, off I–40, 27 mi east of Holbrook.*

### Outside the Park

★ $$–$$$ ✕ **Christmas Tree.** Year-round festive lights and ornaments highlight a theme at work here since 1977. Chicken and dumplings is the big draw, but the kitchen also serves elegant dishes like lamb chops and honey duck with fried apples, plus a children's menu. The fresh fruit cobbler is a must. ⊠ *455 N. Woodland Rd., near AZ 260, Lakeside* ☎ *928/367– 3107. $13–$30* ▭ *D, MC, V* ⊗ *Closed 3rd wk in Oct.–Thanksgiving. Closed Mon., Tues. No lunch* ⌦ *Reservations recommended.*

$–$$ ✕ **Charlie Clark's Steak House.** Prime rib is the house specialty at this log cabin–style restaurant. The chicken-fried steak is also deservedly popular. ⊠ *1701 White Mountain Blvd., Alpine* ☎ *928/367–4900 or 888/ 333–0259. $10–$19* ▭ *AE, D, MC, V.*

★ ¢–$$ ✕ **Licano's Mexican Food and Steakhouse.** Licano's serves what locals claim are the best enchiladas on the mountain, along with prime rib and lobster tail. The spacious lounge, with a weekday happy hour 4:30–6:30, stays open to 9:30 nightly. ⊠ *573 W. Deuce of Clubs, Show Low* ☎ *928/537–8220. $4–$18* ▭ *AE, D, DC, MC, V.*

¢–$ ✕ **High in the Pines Deli.** Locals flock to this intimate coffeehouse and deli for tasty specialty sandwiches—the roasted pork tenderloin sandwich is out of this world. European-style charcuterie includes selections of pâtés, meats, and cheeses served with a fresh baguette. On a cold day, try the Show Low hot chocolate or steaming homemade soups. Box lunches are available. ⊠ *1191 E. Hall, Show Low* ☎ *928/537–1453. $3–$13* ▭ *AE, D, MC, V* ⊗ *Closed Sun. No dinner.*

## Where to Stay

### In the Park

CAMPGROUNDS & **Wilderness Area.** Minimal-impact camping is allowed year-round in a RV PARKS designated zone with a free permit. ⊠ *North of Lithodendron Wash* ☎ *928/524–6228* ⌂ *No fire pits. Free.*

### Outside the Park

$–$$ ▭ **Northwoods Resort.** Surrounded by mountain pines, each cabin has a full kitchen, covered porch, and grill. Some have in-room hot tubs;

**29**

two-story cabins can accommodate up to 18 people. ✉ *165 E. White Mountain Blvd., Pinetop 85935* ☎ *928/367–2966 or 800/813–2966* 🖷 *928/367–2969* ⊕ *www.northwoodsaz.com* ⇨ *15 cabins* ⚭ *Pool, some pets allowed, no phone, no a/c. $99–$149* ⊟ *AE, D, MC, V.*

$ 🖫 **Tal Wi Wi Lodge.** Facing a lush meadow 4 mi north of Alpine, this lodge's setting is unparalleled in the area for value, quietude, and views. Rooms are simple and clean; three have wood-burning stoves. The bar has satellite TV. ✉ *40 County Rd. 2220, Alpine 85920* ☎ *928/339–4319 or 800/476–2695* 🖷 *928/339–1962* ⊕ *www.talwiwilodge.com* ⇨ *20 rooms* ⚭ *Restaurant, bar, no phone, no TV, no a/c. $69* ⊟ *AE, MC, V* ⦿⦿ *CP (weekends only).*

¢–$ 🖫 **KC Motel.** Victorian decor, including four-poster beds, and large rooms make this a not-so-typical motel. There's also a hot tub. ✉ *60 W. Deuce of Clubs, Show Low 85901* ☎ *928/537–4433 or 800/531–7152* ⊕ *www.kcmotelinshowlow.com* ⇨ *63 rooms* ⚭ *Refrigerator, ethernet. $68–$72* ⊟ *AE, D, DC, MC, V* ⦿⦿ *CP.*

★ ⚙ ¢ 🖫 **Wigwam Motel.** Classic Route 66, this motel consists of 15 bright white concrete "tepees" (built in the 1940s), where you can sleep inexpensively, in a quirky environment. Inside they're ordinary motel rooms, though are phoneless. A small lobby museum exhibits Native American, Mexican, and military relics collected by the owner's family. The 180-pound, polished petrified wood sphere is one of the largest in the Southwest. ✉ *811 W. Hopi Dr., Holbrook 86025* ☎ *928/524–3048* ⊕ *www.galerie-kokopelli.com/wigwam* ⇨ *15 rooms* ⚭ *Some pets allowed, no phone. $48* ⊟ *MC, V.*

CAMPGROUNDS & RV PARKS    ⚠ **Apache-Sitgreaves National Forest.** Many of the local campgrounds are maintained by the Apache-Sitgreaves National Forest, a 2-million acre area covering the east-central Arizona White Mountains and Mogollon Rim. Credit cards (AE, D, MC, V) are accepted for online or phone reservations only. ✑ *USFS P.O. Box 640, Springerville 85938* ☎ *928/333–4301 or 877/444–6777* ⊕ *www.fs.fed.us/r3/asnf.*

$ ⚠ **East Fork Recreation Area.** Six adjacent campgrounds (Aspen, Buffalo Crossing, Horse Spring, Diamond Rock, Deer Creek, and Racoon Campground) form this large, popular camping area near the trout-stocked Black River, in the Apache-Sitgreaves National Forest. Sites at Aspen are small, but Buffalo Crossing has large enough ones to accommodate RVs. Diamond Rock Campground has 12 Adirondack-style three-sided shelters. ✉ *Forest Rd. 276, 6 mi south of Forest Rd. 249, 5 mi west of U.S. 191, Alpine* ☎ *877/444–6777* ⇨ *77 tent sites, 16 RV sites* ⚭ *Pit toilets, drinking water, fire grates. $10 plus $5 per each additional vehicle* ⦿ *May–Oct.*

$ ⚠ **Fool Hollow Lake Recreation Area.** Fool Hollow has been called "the Rolls Royce of campgrounds" and has more amenities—including RV hook-ups and modern bathrooms—than any other in the area. ✉ *Fool Hollow Lake Rd. ⁹⁄₁₀ mi off Old Linden Rd. and Rte. 260, Show Low* ☎ *928/333–4301* ⇨ *31 tent sites, 92 RV sites with full hookups* ⚭ *Flush toilets, dump station, drinking water, showers, fire pits, public telephone, play area, swimming (lake), full hookups. $12–$15 without hookups, $19–$25 with hookups per night per vehicle.*

Fodor'sChoice ★

$ ⚠ **Rolfe C. Hoyer Campground.** This 100-site campground in Apache-Sitgreaves National Forest is popular with families and senior citizens.

Most sites are suited for tent or RV and are well maintained and shaded by tall ponderosa pines. ⊠ *Rte. 373, 2 mi north of Greer, Greer* ☏ *877/444–6777* ⌂ *100 sites* ♿ *Flush toilets, dump station, drinking water, showers, fire grates. $16, $8 each additional vehicle,* ☼ *May–Oct.*

¢ ⚠ **Benny Creek Campground.** Camping sites are in the open, under a thin canopy of ponderosa pine, and can accommodate tents and small trailers. The grounds are within walking distance of Greer Lake. ⊠ *Off Rte. 373, 2½ mi north of Greer* ☏ *877/444–6777* ⌂ *24 tent sites* ♿ *Pit toilets, drinking water, fire grates. $8 plus $4 per each additional vehicle* ☼ *May–Sept.*

# PETRIFIED FOREST ESSENTIALS

ACCESSIBILITY The visitor center, museum, and overlooks on the scenic drive are wheelchair accessible. All trails are paved, and all are accessible except Blue Mesa, which is very steep. For more information, call the park switchboard at 928/524–6228.

ADMISSION FEES Entrance fees are $10 per car for seven consecutive days or $5 per person on foot, bicycle, motorcycle, or bus.

ADMISSION HOURS The park is open daily 8 AM–5 PM year-round, except for Christmas Day and New Year's Day. Hours are extended in summer, but vary (call for information). The park is in Mountain time zone.

ATMS/BANKS The park has no ATMs. 🏧 **Wells Fargo Bank** ⊠ 266 Navajo Blvd., Holbrook ☏ 928/524–6275 ☼ Bank Mon.–Thurs. 9–5, Fri 9–6; ATM, 24 hrs.

AUTOMOBILE SERVICE STATIONS
🏧 **Painted Desert Oasis**. ⊠ Near Painted Desert Visitor Center, off I-40, 27 mi east of Holbrook ☏ 928/524–3756 ☼ Daily 7–6. **Scotty & Son Towing & Auto** ⊠ 405 Navajo Blvd., Holbrook ☏ 928/524–2500 ☼ Weekdays 8–5; Sat. 8–2.

EMERGENCIES In case of emergency, dial 911. Crystal Forest, Blue Mesa, and Puerco Pueblo have free emergency call boxes. The park switchboard (928/524–6228) can connect you with park police or a ranger, who can provide emergency medical assistance.

LOST AND FOUND The lost-and-found is at Painted Desert Visitor Center.

PERMITS Permits are required for backcountry hiking and camping, and are free (limit of 15 days) at Painted Desert Visitor Center or the Rainbow Forest Museum before 4 PM.

POST OFFICES Visitors can mail letters and buy stamps (cash only) at the Painted Desert Visitor Center.
🏧 **Painted Desert Visitor Center** ⊠ North entrance, off I-40 ☏ 928/524–6228 ☼ Post office open weekdays 11–1. **Greer Post Office** ⊠ 74 Main St., Greer ☏ 928/735–7322 ☼ Weekdays 8–3, Sat. 8:30–9:30 AM.

PUBLIC TELEPHONES The Painted Desert Visitor Center and the museum near the south entrance have public phones. Cell-phone reception generally works in much of the park.

RELIGIOUS SERVICES There are no chapels or religious services in the park.

RESTROOMS From north to south, you'll find restrooms at Painted Desert Inn National Historic Landmark, Painted Desert Visitor Center, Chinde Point, Puerco Pueblo, Agate Bridge, and Rainbow Forest Museum.

SHOPS & GROCERS Snacks and supplies such as sunscreen and bottled water are available at the Painted Desert Visitor Center and the Rainbow Forest Museum.

**29**

**Safeway Stores** ✉ 702 W. Hopi Dr., Holbrook ☎ 928/524-3313.

## NEARBY TOWN INFORMATION

**Alpine Chamber of Commerce** ✉ Box 410, Alpine, AZ 85920 ☎ 928/339-4330 ⊕ www.alpinearizona.com. **Holbrook Chamber of Commerce** ✉ 100 E. Arizona Ave., Holbrook, AZ 86025 ☎ 928/524-6558 or 800/524-2459 ⊕ www.ci.holbrook.az.us. **Pinetop-Lakeside Chamber of Commerce** ✉ 6102-C W. White Mountain Blvd., Pinetop, AZ 85929 ☎ 800/573-4031 ⊕ www.pinetoplakesidechamber.com.

**Show Low Chamber of Commerce** ✉ 81 E. Deuce of Clubs, Show Low, AZ 85901 ☎ 928/537-2326 or 888/746-9569 ⊕ www.showlowchamberofcommerce.com. **Winslow Chamber of Commerce** ✉ 101 E. 2nd St. Winslow, AZ 86047 ☎ 928/289-2434 ⊕ www.winslowarizona.org.

## VISITOR INFORMATION

**Petrified Forest National Park** ✉ 1 Park Rd., Box 2217, Petrified Forest, AZ 86028 ☎ 928/524-6228 ⊕ www.nps.gov/pefo.

# Redwood National Park

Redwood National Park

**WORD OF MOUTH**

"The redwoods, once seen, leave a mark or create a vision that stays with you always . . .From them comes silence and awe . . .They are not like any trees we know. They are ambassadors from another time."

–John Steinbeck, *Travels with Charley*

# WELCOME TO REDWOOD

## TOP REASONS TO GO

★ **Giant trees:** These mature coast redwoods are the tallest trees in the world.

★ **Hiking to the sea:** The park's trails wind between majestic redwood groves, and many connect to the Coastal Trail running along the western edge of the park.

★ **Step back in time:** Hike the Fern Canyon Trail, which weaves through a prehistoric scene of lush vegetation and giant ferns.

★ **Rare wildlife:** Mighty Roosevelt elk favor the park's flat prairie and open lands; seldom-seen black bears roam the backcountry; trout and salmon leap through streams, and Pacific gray whales swim along the coast during their biannual migrations.

★ **Cheeps, not beeps:** Amid the majestic redwoods you're out of range for cell-phone service—and in range for the soothing sounds of warblers and burbling creeks.

**1** **Del Norte Coast Redwoods State Park.** The rugged terrain of this far northwest corner of California combines stretches of treacherous surf, steep cliffs, and forested ridges. On a clear day it's postcard-perfect; with fog, it's mysteriously mesmerizing.

**2** **Jedediah Smith Redwoods State Park.** Gargantuan old growth redwoods dominate the scenery here. The Smith River cuts through canyons and spills across boulders, carrying salmon to the inland creeks where they spawn.

**3** **Prairie Creek Redwoods State Park.** The forests here give way to spacious, grassy plains where abundant wildlife thrives. Roosevelt elk are a common sight in the meadows and down to Gold Bluffs Beach.

**4** **Orick Area.** The highlight of the southern portion of Redwood National Park is the Tall Trees Grove. It's difficult to reach and requires a special pass, but it's worth the hassle—this section has the tallest coast redwood trees, with a new record-holder discovered in 2006.

Wild Sweet Pea

# GETTING ORIENTED

Highway 101 weaves through the southern portion of the park, skirts around the center, and then slips back through redwoods in the north and on to Crescent City. Kuchel Visitor Center, Prairie Creek Redwoods State Park and Visitor Center, Tall Trees Grove, Fern Canyon, and Lady Bird Johnson Grove are all in the park's southern section. The graveled Coastal Drive curves along ocean vistas and dips down to the Klamath River in the park's central section. To the north you'll find Mill Creek Trail, Enderts Beach, and Crescent Beach Overlook in Del Norte Coast Redwoods State Park as well as Jedediah Smith Redwoods State Park, Stout Grove, Little Bald Hills, and Simpson-Reed Grove.

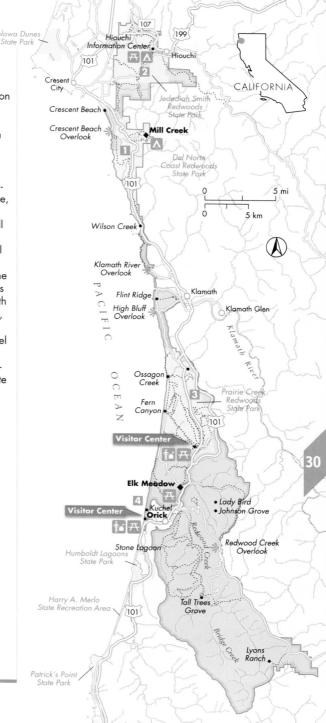

Tolowa Dunes State Park

107

199

Hiouchi Information Center

Hiouchi

101

Crescent City

CALIFORNIA

Crescent Beach

**Mill Creek**

Crescent Beach Overlook

2

Jedediah Smith Redwoods State Park

1

Del Norte Coast Redwoods State Park

101

0      5 mi

0      5 km

Wilson Creek

Klamath River Overlook

P A C I F I C

Flint Ridge

Klamath

High Bluff Overlook

Klamath Glen

Klamath River

O C E A N

Ossagon Creek

3

Prairie Creek Redwoods State Park

Fern Canyon

101

**Visitor Center**

**Elk Meadow**

Lady Bird Johnson Grove

30

4

Kuchel

Redwood Creek

Redwood Creek Overlook

**Visitor Center**

**Orick**

Stone Lagoon

Humboldt Lagoons State Park

Harry A. Merlo State Recreation Area

101

Tall Trees Grove

Bridge Creek

Lyons Ranch

Patrick's Point State Park

| KEY | |
|---|---|
| 👫 | Ranger Station |
| 🅐 | Campground |
| 🌲 | Picnic Area |
| 🍴 | Restaurant |
| 🏨 | Lodge |
| 🚶 | Trailhead |
| 🚻 | Restrooms |
| ⟫ | Scenic Viewpoint |
| ·········· | Walking/Hiking Trails |
| ······ | Bicycle Path |

# REDWOOD PLANNER

## When to Go

**Campers and hikers flock to the park from mid-June to early September.** Crowds disappear in winter, but you'll have to contend with frequent rains and nasty potholes. Temperatures fluctuate widely throughout the park: the foggy coastal lowland is much cooler than the higher-altitude interior. The average annual rainfall here is 90 to 100 inches.

## Getting There & Around

U.S. 101 runs north–south along the park, and Highway 199 cuts east–west through its northern portion. Access routes off 101 include Bald Hills Road, Davison Road, Newton B. Drury Scenic Parkway, Coastal Drive, Requa Road, and Enderts Beach Road. From 199 take South Fork Road to Howland Hill Road. Many of the park's roads aren't paved and winter rains can turn them into obstacle courses; sometimes they're closed completely. RVs and trailers aren't permitted on some routes or beyond certain points on others.

AVG. HIGH/LOW TEMPS.

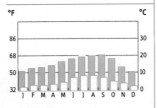

## Flora & Fauna

Coast redwoods, the world's tallest trees (a new record holder, topping out at 379 feet, was found within the park in 2006) grow in the moist, temperate climate of California's North Coast. These ancient giants, whose botanical ancestors date back to the Jurassic era 160 million years ago, thrive in an environment that exists in only a few hundred coastal miles along the Pacific Ocean. They commonly live 600 years—though some have been around for 2,000 years.

A healthy redwood forest is diverse and includes Douglas firs, Western hemlocks, tan oaks, and madrone trees. The complex soils of the forest floor support a verdant profusion of ferns, mosses, and fungi, along with numerous shrubs and berry bushes. In spring, California rhododendron bloom throughout the forest, providing a dazzling purple and pink contrast to the dense greenery.

Redwood National Park holds 45% of all California's old-growth redwood forests. Of the original 3,125 square mi (2 million acres) in the Redwoods Historic Range, only 4% remain following the logging that began in 1850; 1% is privately owned and managed, and 3% is on public land.

In the park's backcountry, you might spot mountain lions, black bears, black-tailed deer, river otters, beavers, and minks. Roosevelt elk roam the flatlands, and the rivers and streams teem with salmon and trout. Gray whales, seals, and sea lions cavort near the coastline. And thanks to the area's location along the Pacific Flyway, an amazing 402 species of birds have been sighted here.

### GOOD READS

Joseph Brown's *Monarchs of the Mist* is a brief and readable history of the coast redwood and the parks. Richard Rasp's *Redwood: The Story Behind the Scenery* is a photo essay on the forest. Bill Schneider uses simple text and enchanting watercolors to describe big trees to small readers in *The Tree Giants*. If you plan on hiking, stop at one of the visitor centers and purchase an inexpensive *Redwood National Park Trail Guide* which details more than 200 mi of trails. You can also pick up a free large-scale color map at any of the visitor centers.

By Christine Vovakes

Soaring to more than 300 feet, the coastal redwoods that give this park its name are miracles of efficiency—some have survived hundreds of years (a few live for more than 2,000 years). These massive trees glean nutrients from the rich alluvial flats at their feet and from the moisture and nitrogen trapped in their uneven canopy. Their huge, thick-barked trunks can hold thousands of gallons of water, reservoirs that have helped them withstand centuries of firestorms. The area averages 90–100 inches of annual rainfall, and during dry summer months thick fog rolling in from the Pacific veils the forests, giving redwoods a large portion of their moisture intake.

## Scenic Drives

★ **Coastal Drive.** This 8-mi, partially paved road is closed to trailers and RVs and takes about 45 minutes to drive one way. The slow pace alongside stands of redwoods offers close-up views of the Klamath River and expansive panoramas of the Pacific. From here you'll find access to the Flint Ridge section of the Coastal Trail.

**Howland Hill Road/Stout Grove.** Take your time as you drive this 10 mi route along Mill Creek, which winds through old-growth redwoods and past the Smith River. Trailers and RVs are prohibited on this route.

**Newton B. Drury Scenic Parkway/Big Tree Wayside.** This 10-mi track, open to all non-commercial vehicles, threads through Prairie Creek Redwoods State Park and old-growth redwoods. Just north of the Prairie Creek Visitor Center you can make the ⅕-mi walk to Big Tree Wayside and observe Roosevelt elk in the prairie.

30

## What to See

### Scenic Stops

**Crescent Beach Overlook.** The scenery here includes ocean views and, in the distance, Crescent City and its working harbor; this is a good place for a picnic. The overlook is known as a good spot to see gray whales that migrate November through December and March through April. ⊠ *2 mi south of Crescent City off Enderts Beach Rd.*

**Fern Canyon.** Enter another world and be surrounded by 60-foot canyon walls covered with sword, maidenhair, and five-finger ferns. Allow an hour to explore the ¼-mi long vertical garden along a 1½-mi round-trip trail. From the north end of Gold Bluffs Beach it's an easy walk, although you'll have to wade across a small stream several times (in addition to driving across streams on the way to the parking area). But the lush surroundings are otherworldly, and worth a visit when creeks aren't running too high. Be aware that RVs longer than 24 feet and all trailers are not allowed here. ⊠ *10 mi northwest of Prairie Creek Visitor Center, via Newton B. Drury Scenic Pkwy. (U.S. 101) and Davison Rd.*

**Lady Bird Johnson Grove.** This section of the park was dedicated by, and named for, the former first lady. A 1-mi, wheelchair-accessible nature loop follows an old logging road through a mature redwood forest. Allow 45 minutes to complete the trail. ⊠ *5 mi east of Kuchel Visitor Center, along U.S. 101 and Bald Hills Rd.*

**Redwoods State Parks.** The three state parks have miles of trails that lead to magnificent redwood groves and overlooks with views of sea lion colonies and migrating whales. Birds inhabit bluffs, lagoons, and offshore rocks. All three parks are open year-round and have ranger programs for children, as well as ranger-led talks. Admission is $6 per day.

**Del Norte Coast Redwoods State Park.** Seven miles southeast of Crescent City via U.S. 101, this park contains 15 memorial redwood groves. The growth extends down steep slopes almost to the shore. ⊠ *Crescent City Information Center, 1111 2nd St., off U.S. 101, Crescent City* ☎ *707/465–7306* ⊕ *www.parks.ca.gov* ☉ *Mid-Feb.–Mid-Nov., daily 9–5; mid-Nov.–mid-Feb., daily 9–4.*

**Jedediah Smith Redwoods State Park.** Home to the Stout Memorial Grove, this park is named after a trapper who, in 1826, became the first white man to explore northern California's interior. You'll find 20 mi of hiking and nature trails and a seasonal visitor center here. The park is 2 mi west of Hiouchi and 9 mi east of Crescent City off Highway 199. ⊠ *Jedediah Smith Visitor Center, Highway 199, Hiouchi* ☎ *707/465–2144* ⊕ *www.parks.ca.gov* ☉ *Mid-May–mid-Sept., daily 9–5; mid-Sept.–mid-May, Sat.–Sun. 10–5.* ⊠ *Hiouchi Information Center, Highway 199, Hiouchi* ☎ *707/458–3209* ⊕ *www.nps.gov/redw* ☉ *Mid-June–mid-Sept., daily 9–5.*

**Prairie Creek Redwoods State Park.** Spectacular redwoods and lush ferns make up this park 5 mi north of Orick and 50 mi south of Crescent City. Extra space has been paved alongside the parklands, providing fine

## REDWOOD IN ONE DAY

Head south on Highway 101. About a mile south of Klamath, detour onto the 8-mi-long, partially paved **Coastal Drive** (trailers and RVs not allowed), which loops north before reaching the ocean. Along the way, you'll pass the old **Douglas Memorial Bridge,** destroyed in the 1964 flood. Coastal Drive turns south above Flint Ridge. In less than a mile you'll reach the **World War II Radar Station,** which looks like a farmhouse, its disguise in the 1940s. Continue south to the intersection with Alder Camp Road, stopping at the **High Bluff Overlook.**

From the Coastal Drive turn left to reconnect with Highway 101, or turn right onto **Newton B. Drury Scenic Parkway,** a 10-mi drive through an old-growth redwood forest with access to numerous trailheads. (This road is open to all non-commercial vehicles). Along the way stop at **Prairie Creek Visitor Center,** housed in a small redwood lodge crafted in 1933. Enjoy a picnic lunch and an engaging tactile walk in a grove behind the lodge on the Revelation Trail, which was designed for people with diminished sight. Head north less than a mile and drive out unpaved **Cal-Barrel Road** (trailers and RVs not allowed),

which leads east from the parkway through redwood forests. Return to the parkway, continue south about 2 mi to reconnect with Highway 101, and turn west on **Davison Road.** It's partially unpaved; RVs longer than 24 feet and all trailers are prohibited. In about 30 minutes you'll reach **Gold Bluffs Beach.** Turn right and drive north, crossing a narrow creek a number of times, to the terminus at **Fern Canyon.**

Return to Highway 101, and drive south to the turnoff for the **Kuchel Information Center.** Pick up free permits to visit the **Tall Trees Grove,** and then head north on Highway 101 to the turnoff for **Bald Hills Road,** a steep route that doesn't allow trailers or RVs (park them at the trailhead or the information center). If you visit the grove, allow about four hours round-trip from the information center. You could also bypass the turnoff to the grove and continue south on Bald Hills Road to 3,097-foot **Schoolhouse Peak.** For a simpler jaunt, turn onto Bald Hills Road and follow it for 2 mi to the **Lady Bird Johnson Grove Nature Loop Trail.** Take the footbridge to the easy 1-mi loop, which follows an old logging road through a mature redwood forest.

**30**

places to observe herds of Roosevelt elk in adjoining meadows. ⊠ *Prairie Creek Information Center, Newton B. Drury Scenic Pkwy., Orick* ☎ *707/ 465–7354* ⊘ *Mid-Feb.–mid-Nov., daily 9–5; mid-Nov.–mid-Feb., daily 9–4.* ⊠ *Kuchel Visitor Center, U.S. 101, Orick* ☎ *707/465–7765* ⊘ *Mid-Feb.–mid-Nov., daily 9–5; mid-Nov.–mid-Feb., daily 9–4.*

★ **Tall Trees Grove.** From the Kuchel Visitor Center, you can get a free permit to make the drive up the steep 17-mi Tall Trees Access Road (the last 6 mi are gravel) to the grove's trailhead (trailers and RVs not allowed). Access to the popular grove is first-come, first-served, and a maximum of 50 permits are handed out each day. ⊠ *Access road is 10 mi drive east of Kuchel Visitor Center, via U.S. 101 and Bald Hills Rd.*

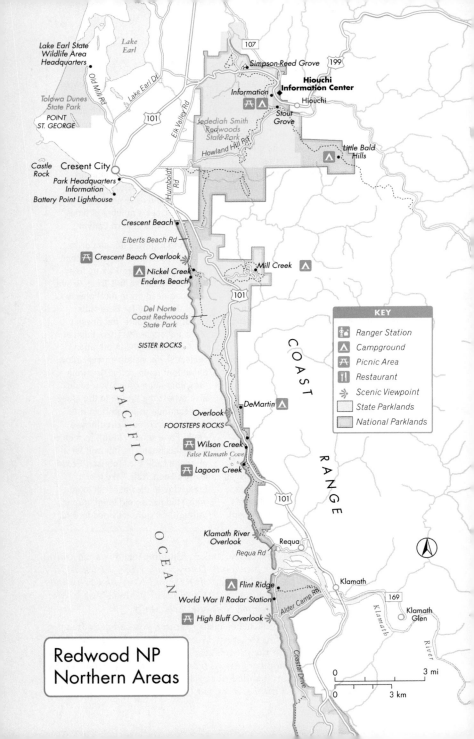

Redwood NP
Northern Areas

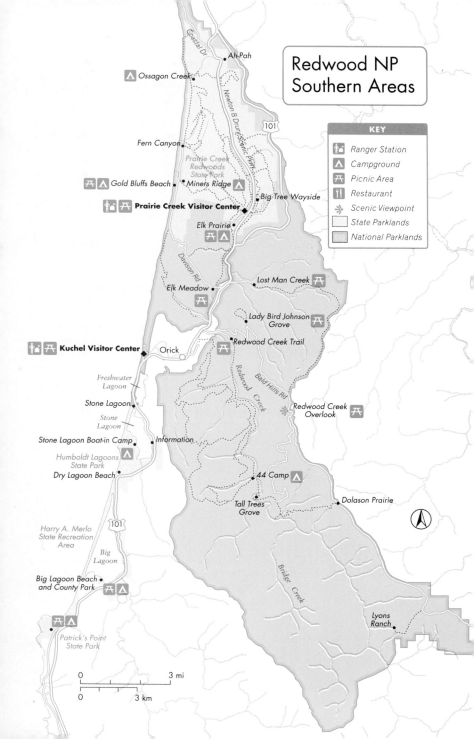

# Redwood NP
# Southern Areas

Coastal Dr.

Ah-Pah

△ Ossagon Creek

Newton B Drury Scenic Pkwy

101

Fern Canyon

*Prairie Creek Redwoods State Park*

🖰 △ Gold Bluffs Beach
Miners Ridge

Big Tree Wayside

🖰 🖰 **Prairie Creek Visitor Center**

Elk Prairie
🖰 △

Davison Rd.

Lost Man Creek 🖰

Elk Meadow
🖰

Lady Bird Johnson Grove 🖰

🖰 Redwood Creek Trail

🖰 🖰 **Kuchel Visitor Center**  Orick

*Freshwater Lagoon*

Bald Hills Rd.

Redwood Creek

Stone Lagoon

*Stone Lagoon*

Redwood Creek Overlook 🖰

Stone Lagoon Boat-in Camp

Information

*Humboldt Lagoons State Park*

Dry Lagoon Beach

44 Camp △

Tall Trees Grove

Dolason Prairie

*Harry A. Merlo State Recreation Area*

101

*Big Lagoon*

Bridge Creek

🖰 Big Lagoon Beach and County Park 🖰 △

Lyons Ranch

🖰 △

*Patrick's Point State Park*

| KEY | |
|---|---|
| 🖰 | Ranger Station |
| △ | Campground |
| 🖰 | Picnic Area |
| 🍴 | Restaurant |
| ⇒ | Scenic Viewpoint |
| | State Parklands |
| | National Parklands |

0 ——— 3 mi

0 ——— 3 km

### Visitor Centers

The **Hiouchi Information Center** (⊠ Hiouchi Information Center, Highway 199, Hiouchi ☎ 707/458–3209 ⊕ www.nps.gov/redw) is open daily, 9–5, mid-June to mid-September in Jedediah Smith Redwoods State Park. The park is 2 mi west of Hiouchi and 9 mi east of Crescent City off Highway 199.

**Jedediah Smith Visitor Center** (⊠ Off Highway 199, Hiouchi ☎ 707/465–2144 ⊕ www.parks.ca.gov), open late May to mid-September, daily 9–5, and Friday to Sunday 10–6 the rest of the year, has information about ranger-led walks and evening campfire programs held in summer in Jedediah Smith Redwoods State Park.

**Crescent City Information Center.** (⊠ Off U.S. 101 at 2nd and K Sts., Crescent City ☎ 707/465–7306 ⊕ www.nps.gov/redw)—open mid-Feb.–mid-Nov., daily 9–5; mid-Nov.–mid-Feb., daily 9–4—is the park's headquarters. It's the main information stop if you're approaching the redwoods from the north.

**Prairie Creek Visitor Center,** (⊠ Off southern end of Newton B. Drury Scenic Pkwy., Orick ☎ 707/465–7354 ⊕ www.parks.ca.gov/), open mid-February–mid-November, daily 9–5, and mid-November through mid-February, daily 9–4, is housed in a redwood lodge with a massive stone fireplace built in 1933. Stretch your legs with an easy stroll along Revelation Trail, a short loop behind the lodge. Pick up information about programs held during the summer in Prairie Creek Redwoods State Park.

At the **Thomas H. Kuchel Visitor Center** (⊠ Off U.S. 101, Orick ☎ 707/465–7765 ⊕ www.nps.gov/redw) open mid-February–mid-November, daily 9–5, and mid-November–mid-February, daily 9–4, you can get brochures, advice, and a free permit to drive up the access road to Tall Trees Grove. Whale-watchers will find the deck of the visitor center an excellent observation point, and bird-watchers will enjoy the nearby Freshwater Lagoon, a popular layover for migrating waterfowl.

## Sports & the Outdoors

### Bicycling

Besides the roadways, you can bike on several trails. Your best bets include the 11-mi Lost Man Creek Trail that begins 3 mi north of Orick; the 12-mi round-trip Coastal Trail (Last Chance Section), which starts at the south end of Enderts Beach Road and becomes steep and narrow as it travels through dense slopes of foggy redwood forests; and the 20-mi, single-track Ossagon Trail Loop, where you're likely to see elk as you cruise through redwoods before ending up ocean side for the last leg of the trail. For information on tours and equipment, ⇨ Outfitters & Expeditions box.

### Fishing

Both deep-sea and freshwater fishing are popular sports here. Anglers often stake out sections of the Klamath and Smith rivers in their search for salmon and trout. (A single fishing license covers both ocean and river fishing.) Less serious anglers can go crabbing or clamming on the

## OUTFITTERS & EXPEDITIONS

### BICYCLING

**Bikes & Trikes.** Rent a mountain bike for $25 per day. Also check out their summer biking tours to city landmarks and coastal sites. ✉ *260 "I" St., Crescent City* ☎ *707/465-6560* ⊕ *www.bikesandtrikes.net.*

### FISHING

**Coast True Value.** This is a good place to get fishing licenses (good for both river and ocean fishing; $34.90 for California residents; two-day and 10-day licenses for $17.60 and $34.90 can also be purchased by nonresidents). The store sells fishing gear plus bait and tackle. ✉ *900 Northcrest Dr., Crescent City* ☎ *707/464-3535.*

**Lunker's.** You can buy bait, rent fishing gear, and arrange for a fishing guide ($175) here. Lunker's is open daily except for parts of September and October as well as April and May; call ahead in these months. ✉ *2095 Highway 199, Hiouchi* ☎ *707/458-4704 or 800/248-4704* ☺ *Early Sept.-late May, daily 8-5; Memorial Day-Labor Day, daily 6 AM-8 PM.*

### KAYAKING

**Lunker's.** You can rent inflatable and hard shell kayaks for $25-$65 a day; another $10-$100 gets you transportation to and from various put-in points on the Smith River (make reservations a day or two in advance). Lunker's is open daily except for parts of September and October as well as April and May; call ahead in these months. ✉ *2095 Highway 199, Hiouchi* ☎ *707/458-4704 or 800/248-4704* ☺ *Early Sept.-late May daily 8-5; Memorial Day-Labor Day, daily 6 AM-8 PM.*

coast, but check the tides carefully. For information on tours and equipment, ⇨ Outfitters & Expeditions box.

### Hiking

★ **Coastal Trail.** Although this trail runs along most of the park's length, smaller sections—of varying degrees of difficulty—are accessible via frequent, well-marked trailheads. The somewhat difficult DeMartin section leads past 5 mi of mature redwoods and through prairie. If you're up for a real workout, you'll be well rewarded with the brutal but stunning Flint Ridge section, a 4½-mi stretch of steep grades and numerous switchbacks that leads past redwoods and Marshall Pond. The 4-mi-long Hidden Beach section connects the Lagoon Creek picnic area with Klamath Overlook and provides coastal views and whale-watching opportunities. ✉ *Flint Ridge trailhead: Douglas Bridge parking area, north end of Coastal Dr.*

**West Ridge-Friendship Ridge-James Irvine Loop.** For a moderately strenuous trek, try this 12½-mi loop. The West Ridge segment passes redwoods looming above a carpet of ferns. The Friendship Ridge portion slopes down toward the coast through forests of spruce and hemlock. The James Irvine Trail portion winds along a small creek and amid old-growth redwoods. ✉ *Prairie Creek Redwoods State Park information center, off Newton B. Drury Scenic Pkwy.*

## DID YOU KNOW?

Moss, which covers this tree in Redwood National Park, grows best in damp, shady environments. In portions of the forest that get some sunlight, more moss will grow on a rock or tree's north side than on its south side, since the north side of the tree gets less sun.

### DID YOU KNOW?

Crater Lake, which is actually a flooded caldera (collapsed volcano), is the deepest lake in the United States, the second deepest lake in the Western Hemisphere, and the seventh deepest lake in the world. It's 1,932 feet to the very bottom.

### Kayaking

With many miles of often shallow rivers and streams in the area, kayaking is a popular pastime in the park. For information on tours and equipment, ⇨ Outfitters & Expeditions box.

### Whale-watching

Good vantage points for whale-watching include Crescent Beach Overlook, the Kuchel Visitor Center in Orick, points along the Coastal Drive, and the Klamath River Overlook. Late November through January are the best months to see their southward migrations; February through April they return and generally pass closer to shore.

# WHAT'S NEARBY

## Nearby Towns

**Crescent City,** north of the park, is Del Norte County's largest town (pop. 7,500) and home to the Redwood National and State Park headquarters. Though it curves around a beautiful stretch of ocean and radiates small-town charm, rain and bone-chilling fog often prevail. Roughly 50 mi south of Crescent City, **Trinidad**'s cove harbor attracts fishermen and photographers, while campers head to nearby Patrick's Point State Park. **Arcata** began life in 1850 as a base camp for miners and lumberjacks. Today this town of 17,000 residents is also home to the 7,500 students of Humboldt State University. Activity centers around Arcata Plaza, which is surrounded by restored buildings. Pick up the "Victorian Walking Tour" map at the chamber of commerce. **Eureka,** south of Arcata, may be filled with strip malls, but this city of 25,500 residents has some history. In 1850 it was a place to stock up on mining supplies; indeed, it was named after a gold miner's hearty exclamation. Old Town has a new waterfront boardwalk, a few good restaurants and shops, and the chamber of commerce has a free driving map to Victorian homes.

## Nearby Attractions

**Battery Point Lighthouse.** At low tide, you can walk from the pier across the ocean floor to this working lighthouse, which was built in 1856. It houses a museum with nautical artifacts and photographs of shipwrecks, and even a resident ghost. Call ahead for guided group tours. ⊠ *A St., Crescent City* ☎ *707/464–3089* ✉ *$3; $1 for students* ⊙ *Apr.–Oct., Wed.–Sun. 10–4; Nov.–Mar., weekends at low tide.*

★ **California Western Railroad Skunk Train.** Following the same coastal route between Fort Bragg and Willits since 1885, the Skunk Train winds along the Noyo River, crosses some 30 bridges and passes through two tunnels in this scenic trip into the redwoods. The gas-powered locomotive replaced the steam engine on this train in 1925. Locals say, "You can smell 'em before you can see 'em." Hence, the nickname. You can take a 90-minute or half-day trip. ⊠ *100 W. Laurel St., Fort Bragg* ☎ *707/ 964–6371 or 800/777–5865* ⊕ *www.skunktrain.com* ✉ *$28–$45* ⊙ *Mar.–Nov.*

**Northcoast Marine Mammal Center.** This nonprofit organization rescues and rehabilitates stranded, sick, or injured seals, sea lions, dolphins, and porpoises. You can see the rescued creatures through a fence enclosing individual pools, and learn about marine mammals and coastal ecosystems. ⊠ *424 Howe Dr., Crescent City* ☎ *707/465–6265* ⊕ *www. northcoastmarinemammal.org* ⊠ *Free* ☉ *Gift shop daily noon–4.*

# WHERE TO STAY & EAT

### About the Restaurants

If you're an angler, fresh catch of the day is your best bet, since there are no dining facilities in the park itself. The seasonal Steelhead Lodge in Klamath Glen serves huge barbecued portions of steak, ribs, chicken, and fish. To sample ethnic cuisine, pub fare, and seafood delights, head to the towns north or south of the park. Crescent City and Eureka offer the broadest selections.

### About the Hotels

There's only one lodging option—a hostel—within park boundaries. Orick and Klamath, the two towns on Highway 101 near the park, have basic motels, plus the rustic Requa Inn, a two-story B&B on Requa Road beside the Klamath River. In towns north and south of the park you'll find numerous options, from elegant Victorians to seaside inns to no-frills rooms. Reservations at all lodgings should be made far in advance for summer visits.

### About the Campgrounds

Within a 30-minute drive of Redwood National and State parks there are nearly 60 public and private camping facilities. None of the four primitive areas in Redwood—DeMartin, Flint Ridge, Little Bald Hills, and Nickel Creek—is a drive-in site. Although you don't need a permit at these four hike-in sites, stop at a ranger station to inquire about availability. You will need to get a permit from a ranger station for camping along Redwood Creek in the backcountry. Bring your own water, since drinking water isn't available in any of these sites.

If you'd rather drive than hike in, Redwood has four developed campgrounds—Elk Prairie, Gold Bluffs Beach, Jedediah Smith, and Mill Creek—that are within the state park boundaries. None has RV hookups, and some length restrictions apply. Fees range from $15 to $20 in state park campgrounds. For details and reservations, call 800/444–7275 or check ⊕ www.reserveamerica.com.

## Where to Eat

### In Redwood

PICNIC AREAS **Crescent Beach.** This beach has a grassy picnic area with tables, fire pits, and restrooms. There's an overlook south of the beach. ⊠ *2 mi south of Crescent City Visitor Center, on Enderts Beach Rd.*

**Elk Prairie.** In addition to many elk, this spot has a campground, a nature trail, and a ranger station. ⊠ *On Newton B. Drury Scenic Pkwy. in Prairie Creek Redwoods State Park.*

**Gold Bluffs Beach.** Fern Canyon is nearby this spot on a beach where Roosevelt elk stroll. ☒ *End of Davison Rd., off U.S. 101 in Prairie Creek Redwoods State Park.*

**High Bluff.** This picnic area's sunsets and whale-watching are unequaled. A ½-mi trail leads from here to the beach. ☒ *On Coastal Dr. about 2 mi from U.S. 101, south of Golden Bear Bridge over the Klamath River via Alder Camp Rd.*

**Jedediah Smith.** Old-growth coast redwoods provide shade and scenery at the picnic areas in this campground. ☒ *8 mi east of Crescent City on Highway 199.*

**Lagoon Creek.** Here, you can beachcomb, fish the freshwater lagoon, or hike along a trail. ☒ *Off U.S. 101, 14 mi south of Crescent City Visitor Center.*

### Outside the Park

**$$–$$$$** ✕ **Harbor View Grotto.** The fish comes straight from the boat, into this casual eatery's kitchen, and onto your plate. Not surprisingly, the dining room has large windows overlooking the Pacific. Note that the white two-story building off U.S. 101 is marked only by a neon RESTAURANT sign—keep your eyes open. ☒ *150 Starfish Way, Crescent City* ☎ *707/464–3815. $14–$34* ▭ *MC, V.*

**$$–$$$$** ✕ **Steelhead Lodge.** Come hungry to this rustic lodge where huge portions of beef, ribs, chicken, and fish are barbecued over a roaring hardwood fire outside the restaurant's back door. Stop at the lounge with its curved wooden bar, distinctive "riffle" floor tiles, and anglers perched on stools casting yarns. ☒ *330 Terwer Riffle Rd., Klamath* ☎ *707/482–8145. $15–$38* ▭ *MC, V* ☉ *Closed weekdays mid-Feb.–mid-May; weekdays Sept.–Nov.; Nov.–mid-Feb.*

**¢–$$$** ✕ **Cafe Waterfront.** This airy local landmark serves a solid basic menu of burgers and steaks, but the real standouts are the daily seafood specials—lingcod, shrimp, and other treats fresh from the bay across the street. The building, listed on the National Register of Historic Places, was a saloon and brothel until the 1950s. Named after former ladies of the house, two Victorian-style B&B rooms ($$$–$$$$) are available upstairs. ☒ *102 F St., Eureka* ☎ *707/443–9190. $8–$21* ▭ *MC, V.*

**$–$$** ✕ **Apple Peddler.** This busy eatery serves breakfast around the clock, plus burgers, steaks, and seasonal seafood. ☒ *308 U.S. 101 S, Crescent City* ☎ *707/464–5630. $10–$16* ▭ *D, MC, V.*

**¢–$$** ✕ **Humboldt Brewing Co.** This laid-back watering hole caters to a college crowd with burgers, sandwiches, and microbrews. There's live music six nights a week. ☒ *856 10th St., Arcata* ☎ *707/826–2739* ⚐ *Reservations not accepted. $7–$16* ▭ *D, MC, V.*

**$** ✕ **Trinidad Bay Eatery and Gallery.** This combination diner-gift shop a few doors down from the bay serves up hearty morning fare like pecan waffles; try the Country Boy Breakfast. They're famous for homemade blackberry cobbler, and seafood dishes come fresh from the harbor to the table. Try crab specialties in season at market price. ☒ *Trinity and Parker Sts., Trinidad* ☎ *707/677–3777. $8–$12* ▭ *AE, D, MC, V.*

**★ ¢–$** ✕ **Good Harvest Cafe.** Not only does the Good Harvest have a funky atmosphere, but it serves the best breakfasts in town. A lunch menu of salads, hamburgers, sandwiches and vegetarian specialties is served after

11 AM, and an espresso bar is open all day long. ⊠ *700 Northcrest Dr., Crescent City* ☎ *707/465–6028. $5–$10* ▭ *D, MC, V* ☉ *No dinner.*

## Where to Stay

### In Redwood

¢ 🖼 **Hostels International–Redwood.** Travelers of all ages are welcome at this vintage 1908 Edwardian-style hostel. Perks include an enthusiastic staff and a location across the highway from the ocean, but beware the 10 AM to 5 PM lockout. There are three dorm rooms and three private rooms; linens are included. A wood-burning stove warms the common room, and kitchen and laundry facilities are available. ⊠ *14480 U.S. 101, Klamath* ☎ *707/482–8265* ⊕ *www.norcalhostels.org/redwoods/* ↪ *30 beds. $17–$49* ▭ *AE, D, MC, V* ☉ *Mar.–Dec.*

CAMPGROUNDS &
RV PARKS
⚠ **DeMartin Campground.** This primitive hike-in area occupies a grassy prairie with a panoramic ocean view. ⊠ *3 mi from Coastal Trail along U.S. 101* ☎ *707/465–7306* ↪ *10 sites* ⚲ *Pit toilets, fire pits, picnic tables. Free.*

⚠ **Elk Prairie Campground.** Adjacent to a prairie and old-growth redwoods, this campground is popular with Roosevelt elk. To park here, RVs can be no longer than 27 feet, trailers no longer than 24 feet. ⊠ *On Newton B. Drury Scenic Pkwy. in Prairie Creek Redwoods State Park* ☎ *800/444–7275* ↪ *75 RV or tent sites* ⚲ *Flush toilets, dump station, drinking water, showers, bear boxes, fire pits, picnic tables, public telephone, ranger station. $20* ▭ *AE, D, MC, V.*

⚠ **Flint Ridge Campground.** In old-growth forest with excellent wildlife-viewing opportunities, this primitive site is accessible from two trailheads along Coastal Drive: from the west, it's a ½-mi hike; from the east, it's 4½ mi. ⊠ *On Coastal Trail south of Klamath River estuary* ☎ *707/465–7306* ↪ *10 sites* ⚲ *Pit toilets, bear boxes, fire pits, picnic tables. Free.*

Fodor'sChoice
★
⚠ **Gold Bluffs Beach Campground.** You can camp in tents or RVs right on the beach at this Prairie Creek Redwoods State Park campground near Fern Canyon. Keep your eyes open for Roosevelt elk. Note that RVs must be less than 24 feet long and 8 feet wide, and trailers aren't allowed on the access road. ⊠ *At end of Davison Rd., 5 mi north of Redwood Information Center off U.S. 101* ☎ *800/444–7275* ↪ *26 tent or RV sites* ⚲ *Flush toilets, drinking water, showers, fire pits, picnic tables. $15* ▭ *AE, D, MC, V.*

⚠ **Jedediah Smith Campground.** This is one of the few places to camp—in tents or RVs—within groves of old-growth redwood forest. The length limit on RVs is 36 feet; for trailers it's 31 feet. ⊠ *8 mi northeast of Crescent City on Highway 199* ☎ *800/444–7275* ↪ *106 RV or tent sites* ⚲ *Flush toilets, dump station, drinking water, bear boxes, fire pits, picnic tables, public telephone, ranger station, play area, swimming (river). $20* ▭ *AE, D, MC, V.*

⚠ **Little Bald Hills Campground.** You can hike, bike, or horseback ride the 4½ mi through old-growth forest and prairies lined with fir and pine to this primitive area and its ridgetop vistas. There's a corral and horse troughs. ⊠ *East end of Howland Hill Rd.* ☎ *707/465–7306* ↪ *5 sites* ⚲ *Pit toilets, bear boxes, fire pits, picnic tables. Free.*

30

⚠ **Mill Creek Campground.** Mill Creek is the largest of the state park campgrounds. ⊠ *West of U.S. 101, 7 mi southeast of Crescent City* ☎ *800/444–7275* ⌦ *145 tent or RV sites* ♿ *Flush toilets, dump station, drinking water, showers, bear boxes, fire pits, picnic tables. $20* ▣ *AE, D, MC, V* ⊙ *May–Labor Day.*

⚠ **Nickel Creek Campground.** An easy hike gets you to this primitive site, which is near tide pools and has great ocean views. ⊠ *On Coastal Trail ½ mi from end of Enderts Beach Rd.* ☎ *707/465–7306* ⌦ *5 sites* ♿ *Pit toilets, bear boxes, fire pits, picnic tables. Free.*

## Outside the Park

★ **$$$–$$$$** ✕▣ **Carter House & Restaurant 301.** According to owner Mark Carter, his staff has been trained always to say "Yes." Whether it's breakfast in bed or an in-room massage, someone here will make sure you get what you want. Richly painted and aglow with wood detailing, rooms blend modern and antique furnishings in two main buildings and several cottages. Eureka's most elegant restaurant ($$-$$$$; dinner only) uses ingredients hand-selected from the farmers' market, local cheese makers and ranchers, and the on-site gardens. Dishes are prepared with a delicate hand and a sensuous imagination—the ever-changing menu has featured sturgeon with house-made mushroom pasta, braised fennel, and white-wine sauce. ⊠ *301 L St., Eureka 95501* ☎ *707/444–8062 or 800/404–1390* 🖷 *707/444–8067* ⊕ *www.carterhouse.com* ⌦ *21 rooms, 11 suites* ♿ *Restaurant, kitchen (some), VCR, ethernet, laundry service, concierge; no-smoking rooms. $185–$295* ▣ *AE, D, DC, MC, V* ⦿ *BP.*

★ **$$–$$$$** ▣ **Cornelius Daly Inn.** In the heart of Eureka's historic area, this three-story B&B was built in 1905 as the home of department store magnate Cornelius Daly. Period touches include Victorian gardens, ornate floral wallpaper, a ballroom, and many antiques. Innkeepers Donna and Bob Gafford serve complimentary refreshments in the afternoon. Four rooms have wood-burning fireplaces; two rooms share a bath. ⊠ *1125 H St., Eureka 95501* ☎ *707/445–3638 or 800/321–9656* ⊕ *www.dalyinn.com* ⌦ *3 rooms, 2 suites* ♿ *Laundry facilities, Wi-Fi; no phone, no-smoking rooms, no a/c. $125–$225* ▣ *AE, D, MC, V* ⦿ *BP.*

**$$–$$$** ▣ **Abigail's Elegant Victorian Mansion.** This meticulously restored Eastlake mansion in a residential neighborhood lives up to its name. Each room is completely decked out in period furnishings, down to the carved-wood beds, fringed lamp shades, and pull-chain commodes. You can also arrange for a guided tour of local Victoriana in an antique automobile. The lowest rates do not include breakfast. ⊠ *1406 C St., Eureka 95501* ☎ *707/444–3144* ⊕ *www.eureka-california.com* ⌦ *4 rooms, 2 with shared bath* ♿ *Tennis court, bicycles, laundry service; no-smoking rooms. $125–$195* ▣ *MC, V* ⦿ *BP.*

**$–$$$** ▣ **Historic Requa Inn.** Neither TVs nor phones disrupt the serenity of this 12-room B&B that overlooks the Klamath River a mile east of where it meets the ocean. Set near the park's central section, the inn is within easy reach of numerous trails and scenic drives. Breakfast is included; dinner reservations—the restaurant is also open to the public—secure a spot in Bailey's Dining Room for the evening meal. ⊠ *451 Requa Rd., Klamath 95548* ☎ *707/482–1425 or 866/800–8777* ⊕ *www.requainn.com* ⌦ *12 rooms. $85–$155* ▣ *AE, D, MC, V* ⊙ *Closed mid-Dec.–Jan.* ⦿ *BP.*

Fodor'sChoice ★

**$-$$$**  🏠 **Trinidad Inn.** These quiet cottage rooms nestled in the redwoods are 2 mi north of Trinidad Bay's harbor, restaurants, and shops. Individually decorated, most rooms have full kitchens. It's an ideal home base from which to explore the park. ✉ *1170 Patrick's Point Dr., Trinidad 95570* ☎ *707/677–3349* ⊕ *www.trinidadinn.com* ⬎ *10 rooms* ⚫ *VCR (some), no-smoking rooms. $95–$155* ▭ *AE, MC, V* ⭐ *CP.*

**$-$$**  🏠 **Ravenwood Motel.** The tidy rooms in this centrally located motel come with a Continental breakfast. Standard double rooms are $58 year-round while a few large kitchen suites suitable for families cost more. ✉ *151 Klamath Blvd., Klamath 95548* ☎ *707/482–5911* ⊕ *ravenwoodmotel.com* ⚫ *Refrigerator (some). $58–$105* ▭ *AE, D, MC, V* ⭐ *CP.*

**$**  🏠 **Crescent Beach Motel.** Simple and clean, this motel is directly on the beach with half of its rooms facing the water. An adjacent 3-bedroom oceanfront house is also available. ✉ *1455 Hwy. 101 S, Crescent City 95531* ☎ *707/464–5436* ⊕ *www.crescentbeachmotel.com* ⬎ *27 rooms* ⚫ *No phone, no a/c. $70–$99* ▭ *AE, MC, V* ⭐ *CP.*

**¢-$**  🏠 **Curly Redwood Lodge.** A single redwood tree produced the 57,000 feet of lumber used to build this lodge in 1957. Furnishings make the most of that tree, with paneling, platform beds, and built-in dressers. ✉ *701 Redwood Hwy. S, Crescent City 95531* ☎ *707/464–2137* 🖨 *707/464–1655* ⊕ *www.curlyredwoodlodge.com* ⬎ *36 rooms, 3 suites* ⚫ *Wi-Fi, no-smoking rooms; No a/c. $45–$65* ▭ *AE, DC, MC, V.*

# REDWOOD ESSENTIALS

ACCESSIBILITY Park maps indicate which camping, picnic, and other areas are wheelchair accessible. Such spots include all the visitor centers as well as Crescent Beach, Crescent Beach Overlook, Lagoon Creek, Klamath Overlook, High Bluff Overlook, Big Tree Wayside, and picnic areas of Lost Man Creek.

ADMISSION FEES Admission to the national park portion of Redwood National and State parks is free. There's a $6 day-use fee to enter one or all of the state parks.

ADMISSION HOURS The park is open year-round, 24 hours a day.

ATMS/BANKS
🏦 **Bank of America** ✉ 240 H St., Crescent City ☎ 800/237-8052. **Washington Mutual** ✉ 803 3rd St., Crescent City ☎ 707/464-4106.

AUTOMOBILE SERVICE STATIONS
🏦 **Crescent City Chevron** ✉ 315 Hwy. 101 S, Crescent City ☎ 707/465-3825. **Pete's Auto and**

**Marine** ✉ 1305 2nd St., Crescent City ☎ 707/464-2538.

EMERGENCIES In an emergency call 911 or go to the nearest visitor center.

LOST AND FOUND To find whatever you've lost, head to the nearest visitor center.

PERMITS To visit Tall Trees Grove, you must get a free permit at the Kuchel Information Center in Orick. Permits are also needed to camp in Redwood Creek backcountry.

POST OFFICE
🏦 **Crescent City Post Office** ✉ 751 2nd St., Crescent City 95531 ☎ 707/464-2151.

PUBLIC TELEPHONES There are no public phones at any of the visitor centers.

RESTROOMS You'll find restrooms at all the visitor centers and state park campgrounds and at some picnic areas. There's also a restroom at the wayside station in Elk Meadow on Davison Road.

**30**

SHOPS & GROCERS

Orick Market. ⊠ 121175 U.S. 101, Orick ☎ 707/488-3225. Rite Aid Drugstore. ⊠ 575 M St., Crescent City ☎ 707/465-3981. Safeway. ⊠ 475 M St., Crescent City ☎ 707/465-3353. Wildberries Marketplace. ⊠ 747 13th St., Arcata ☎ 707/822-0095 ⊕ www.wildberries.com.

## NEARBY TOWN INFORMATION

Arcata Chamber of Commerce. ⊠ 1635 Heindon Rd., Arcata 95521-5800 ☎ 707/822-3619 ⊕ www.arcatachamber.com/. Crescent City/Del Norte County Chamber of Commerce. ⊠ 1001 Front St., Crescent City 95531 ☎ 707/464-3174 or 800/343-8300 ⊕ www.northerncalifornia.net. Eureka/Humboldt County Convention and Visitors Bureau ⊠ 1034 2nd St., Eureka 95501-0541 ☎ 707/443-5097 or 800/346-3482 ⊕ www.redwoodvisitor.org. Trinidad Chamber of Commerce ⊠ Box 356, Trinidad 95570 ☎ 707/677-1610 ⊕ www.trinidadcalif.com.

## VISITOR INFORMATION

Redwood National Park. ⊠ 1111 2nd St., Crescent City, CA 95531 ☎ 707/465-7306 ⊕ www.nps.gov/redw.

# Rocky Mountain National Park

Coyote pups, Rocky Mountain National Park

**WORD OF MOUTH**

"I've seen it rainin' fire in the sky,
   You can talk to God and listen to the casual reply,
   Rocky Mountain high . . ."

–John Denver, "Rocky Mountain High"

# WELCOME TO ROCKY MOUNTAIN

## TOP REASONS TO GO

★ **Gorgeous scenery:** Peer out over dozens of lakes, gaze up at majestic mountain peaks, and look around at pine-scented woods that are perfect for whiling away an afternoon.

★ **350 mi of trails:** Hike to your heart's content on mostly moderate trails crisscrossing the park.

★ **Continental Divide:** Straddle this great divide, which cuts through the western part of the park and separates water's flow to either the Pacific or Atlantic Ocean.

★ **Awesome ascents:** Trek to the summit of Longs Peak or go rock climbing on Lumpy Ridge. In winter, you can even ice climb.

★ **Wildlife wonders:** Spot elk and bighorn sheep; there are more than 3,000 and 800 of them, respectively.

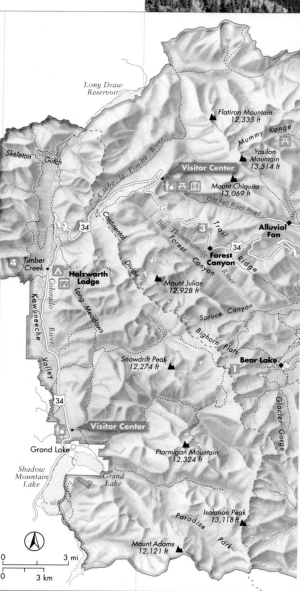

Long Draw Reservoir

Flatiron Mountain
12,335 ft

Mummy Range

Skeleton Gulch

Ypsilon Mountain
13,514 ft

Cache la Poudre River

**Visitor Center**

Mount Chiquita
13,069 ft

Old Fall River Road

34

Continental Divide

Big Thompson

Trail Ridge

**Alluvial Fan**

34

Forest Canyon

**Forest Canyon**

Timber Creek

4

**Holzwarth Lodge**

Mount Julian
12,928 ft

Colorado River

Long Meadows

Spruce Canyon

Kawuneeche Valley

Bighorn Flats

Snowdrift Peak
12,274 ft

**Bear Lake**

1

34

**Visitor Center**

Glacier Gorge

Grand Lake

Ptarmigan Mountain
12,324 ft

Shadow Mountain Lake

Grand Lake

Isolation Peak
13,118 ft

Paradise Park

Mount Adams
12,121 ft

0        3 mi

0        3 km

**1** Bear Lake. One of the most photographed places in the park, Bear Lake is the hub for many trailheads. It gets crowded in the summer.

**2** Longs Peak. The highest peak in the park and the toughest to climb, this fourteener pops up in many park vistas. If you want to reach the summit on a day-long trek, it's recommended you begin at 3 AM.

**3** Trail Ridge Road. The alpine tundra of the park is the highlight here as the road climbs beyond the timber line.

**4** Timber Creek. The park's western area is much less crowded, though it has its share of amenities and attractions, including a campground, historic sites, and a visitor center.

**5** Wild Basin Area. Far from the crowds, the park's southeast quadrant consists of lovely expanses of subalpine forest punctuated by streams and lakes.

COLORADO

## GETTING ORIENTED

Rocky Mountain National Park's 416 square mi wilderness of meadows, mountains, and mirror-like lakes lie just 65 mi from Denver. The park is nine times smaller than Yellowstone, yet it receives almost as many visitors—3.5 million a year.

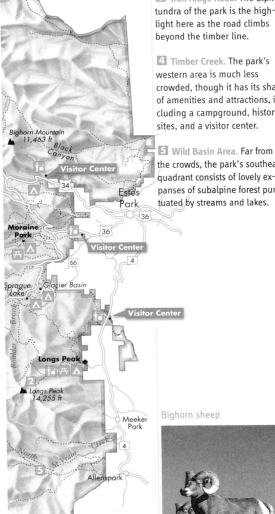

Bighorn Mountain 11,463 ft
Black Canyon
Visitor Center
34
Estes Park
36
Moraine Park
36
66
4
Sprague Lake
Glacier Basin
Visitor Center
Boulder Brook
Longs Peak
2
Longs Peak 14,255 ft
Meeker Park
North St. Vrain Creek
4
5
Allenspark

Bighorn sheep

| KEY | |
|---|---|
| 🏠 | Ranger Station |
| △ | Campground |
| ⊼ | Picnic Area |
| 🍴 | Restaurant |
| 🏨 | Lodge |
| 🏃 | Trailhead |
| 🚻 | Restrooms |
| ≋ | Scenic Viewpoint |
| ---- | Walking/Hiking Trails |
| ····· | Bicycle Path |

# ROCKY MOUNTAIN PLANNER

## When to Go

Visiting Rocky Mountain is pleasurable any season, though **more than two-thirds of the park's annual 3.5 million visitors come in summer.** But there is a good reason to put up with summer crowds: only from Memorial Day to mid-October can you make the unforgettable drive over Trail Ridge Road. (It also closes occasionally in summer due to weather.) **For thinner high-season crowds, come in early June or late August,** when many students are in school.

Spring is capricious—75°F one day and a blizzard the next (snowfall is the highest in March). June conditions can range from hot to cool and rainy. July typically ushers in high summer, which can last through September. Up on Trail Ridge Road and the Continental Divide, temperatures can be 15-20 degrees cooler. Spring and summer are the best times for wildlife viewing and fishing. In early fall, the trees blaze with brilliant foliage. Winter, when backcountry snow can be four feet deep and the wind brutal at high elevations, is the time for skiing, snowshoeing, and ice fishing.

AVG. HIGH/LOW TEMPS.

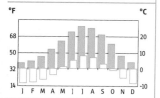

## Flora & Fauna

Volcanic uplifts and the savage clawing of receding glaciers have brought about Rocky Mountain's majestic landscape. You'll find three distinct ecosystems here—verdant mountain valleys towering with proud ponderosa pines and Douglas firs; higher and colder subalpine mountains with wind-whipped trees (krummholz) that grow at right angles; and harsh, unforgiving alpine tundra with dollhouse-size versions of familiar plants and wildflowers. The high, wind-whipped ecosystem of alpine tundra is seldom found outside the Arctic, yet it makes up one-third of the park's terrain. Few plants can survive at the tundra's elevation, but many beautiful wildflowers—including alpine forget-me-nots—bloom briefly in late June or early July.

The park has so much wildlife that you can often enjoy prime viewing from the seat of your car. Fall, when many animals begin moving down from higher elevations, is an excellent time to spot the park's animal residents. This is also when you'll hear the male elk bugle mating calls (popular "listening" spots are Horseshoe Park, Moraine Park, and Upper Beaver Meadows).

May through mid-October is the best time to see the bighorn sheep that congregate in the Horseshoe Park–Sheep Lakes area, just past the Fall River entrance. If you want to glimpse a moose, try Kawuneeche Valley, on the park's western side. Other animals you may see in the park include elk, mule deer, squirrels, chipmunks, and marmots. Common birds are broad-tailed and rufous hummingbirds, peregrine falcons, woodpeckers, mountain bluebirds, and Clark's nutcracker, as well as the white-tailed ptarmigan, spotted year-round on the alpine tundra.

Mountain lions, black bear, and bobcats also inhabit the park but are rarely spotted by visitors. Altogether, the park is home to 65 species of mammals and 260 bird species.

# Getting There & Around

Estes Park and Grand Lake are Rocky Mountain's gateway communities; from these you can enter the park via U.S. 34 or U.S. 36. The closest commercial airport is Denver International Airport (DEN). Its **Ground Transportation Information Center** (☎ 800/247–2336 or 303/342–4059) assists visitors with car rentals, door-to-door shuttles, wheelchair services, and limousine services. From the airport, the eastern entrance of the park is 80 mi (about 2 hours). **Estes Park Shuttle** (☎ 970/586–5151; reservations essential) serves Estes Park and Rocky Mountain from Denver, the airport, and Boulder. Greyhound Lines serve Denver, Boulder, and Fort Collins, and Amtrak's *California Zephyr* stops in downtown Denver, Winter Park/Fraser, and Granby.

U.S. 36 runs from Denver through Boulder, Lyons, and Estes Park to the park; the portion between Boulder and Estes Park is heavily traveled—especially on summer weekends. Colorado routes 119, 72, and 7 have much less traffic. If you're driving directly to Rocky Mountain from the airport, the E–470 tollway connects Peña Boulevard to Interstate 25.

The Colorado Department of Transportation plows roads efficiently, but winter snowstorms can slow traffic and create wet or icy conditions. For road conditions, call **CDOT Road Information** (☎ 303/639–1111 or 877/315–7623).

The main thoroughfare in the park is Trail Ridge Road; in winter, it's plowed up to Many Parks Curve on the east side and the Colorado River trailhead on the west side. Gravel-surfaced, extremely curvy Old Fall River Road is open from July to September. Pulled trailers and vehicles longer than 25 feet are prohibited.

Two free park shuttle bus routes operate along the park's popular Bear Lake Road from mid-June to mid-October. Unless you arrive early enough to get one of the few parking spaces beyond the park-and-ride, you must take the shuttle to access this area of the park. One bus line runs every 30 minutes between 7:30 AM and 7:30 PM from near the Fern Lake trailhead to the Moraine Park Museum and on to Glacier Basin Campground. The other runs every 15 minutes between 7 AM and 7 PM from the campground to the Bear Lake trailhead. There is also a new summer-only shuttle bus running from the Estes Park Visitor Center to the park. The Estes Park shuttle is free, but you must have a park pass to board.

# Festivals & Events

**FEB. Discovery Snowshoe Festival.** A 5K snowshoe race, snowshoe demos, a kids' obstacle course, and guided hikes in the park are among this event's activities. ☎ 970/586–4431 or 800/443–7837 ✉ Estes Park.

**JUNE Chili Cook-off.** Sponsored by the Grand Lake Fire Department, this competition draws entrants from all over Colorado and New Mexico. ☎ 970/627–8428 ✉ Town Park, Grand Lake.

**JULY Rooftop Rodeo.** A tradition for more than 75 years, the six-day event features a parade, nightly rodeos, and an arts-and-crafts fair. ☎ 970/586–6104 ✉ Estes Park.

**SEPT. Longs Peak Scottish/Irish Highland Festival.** A traditional tattoo kicks off this three-day fair of athletic competitions, Celtic music, dancing, a parade, and seminars on topics such as heraldry and scotch whisky. It's held the weekend after Labor Day. ☎ 970/586–6308 or 800/903–7837 ⊕ www.scotfest.com ✉ Estes Park.

**OCT. Elk Fest.** The event includes seminars on photographing and tracking wildlife, archery demonstrations, bugling contests, and a wildlife art exhibit. ☎ 970/586–6104 ✉ Estes Park.

By Debbie Harmsen & Molly Moker

Anyone who delights in alpine lakes, mountain peaks, and an abundance of wildlife—not to mention dizzying heights—should consider Rocky Mountain National Park. Here, a single hour's drive leads from a 7,800-foot elevation at park headquarters to the 12,183-foot apex of the twisting and turning Trail Ridge Road. More than 350 mi of hiking trails take you to the park's many treasures: meadows flushed with wildflowers, cool dense forests of lodgepole pine and Engelmann spruce, and the noticable presence of wildlife, including elk and bighorn sheep.

## Scenic Drives

**Bear Lake Road.** This 9-mi drive offers superlative views of Longs Peak (14,255-foot summit) and the glaciers surrounding Bear Lake, winding past shimmering waterfalls perpetually shrouded with rainbows. ⊠ *Runs from the Beaver Meadow entrance station to Bear Lake.*

**Old Fall River Road.** A one-way 11-mi loop up to the Alpine Visitor Center and back down along Trail Ridge Road is a scenic alternative to driving Trail Ridge Road twice. Start at West Horseshoe Park, which has the park's largest concentrations of sheep and elk, and head up the paved and gravel Old Fall River Road, passing Chasm Falls. Early visitors to the park traveled Old Fall River Road before Trail Ridge Road was built.

**Trail Ridge Road.** This is the park's star attraction and the world's highest continuous paved highway, topping out at 12,183 feet. The 48-mi road connects the park's gateways of Estes Park and Grand Lake. The views around each bend—of moraines and glaciers, and craggy hills framing emerald meadows carpeted with columbine and Indian paintbrush—are truly awesome. As it passes through three ecosystems (montane, subalpine, and arctic tundra), the road climbs 4,300 feet in elevation. As you drive the road, take your time at the numerous turnouts to gaze over verdant valleys—brushed with yellowing aspen in fall—that slope between the glacier-etched granite peaks. **Many Parks Curve** affords views of the crest of the Continental Divide and of the **Alluvial Fan,** a huge gash a vicious flood created after an earthen dam broke in 1982. ■ TIP➔ **Pick up a copy of the** *Trail Ridge Road Guide,* **available at visitor centers, for an overview of what you will be seeing as you drive the road.** In normal traffic, it's a two-hour drive across the park, but it's best to give yourself three to four hours to allow for leisurely breaks at the overlooks. Note that the middle part of the road closes by mid-October, though you can still drive up about 10 mi from the west and 8 mi from the east. ⊠ *Trail Ridge Rd. (U.S. 34)* ☉ *June–mid-Oct.*

## What to See

### Historic Sites

Rocky Mountain has more than 100 sites of historic significance. In order to be nominated for the National Register of Historic Places, a park building must tie in strongly to the park's history in terms of architecture, archaeology, engineering, or culture. Most buildings at Rocky Mountain are done in the rustic style, a design preferred by the National Park Service's first director, Stephen Mather. The rustic style is a way to incorporate nature within man-made structures.

☺ **Holzwarth Historic Trout Lodge.** A scenic ½-mi interpretive trail leads you over the Colorado River to the original "dude ranch" that the Holzwarth family ran between the 1920s and 1950s. Allow about an hour to explore the buildings and chat with a ranger. It's a great place for families to learn about homesteading. ⊠ *Trail Ridge Rd., about 13 mi west of the Alpine Visitor Center* ☜ *Free* ☉ *Daily 10–4.*

**Lulu City.** A few remnants of cabins and mining equipment are all that's left of this onetime silver mining town, established in 1880. Reach it by hiking the 3⁶⁄₁₀-mi Colorado River Trail. Look for wagon ruts from the old Stewart Toll Road and the ruins of cabins in Shipler Park. The Colorado River is a mere stream at this point, flowing south from its headwaters at nearby La Poudre Pass. ⊠ *Off Trail Ridge Rd., 10½ mi north of Grand Lake.*

**Moraine Park Museum.** Lectures, slide shows, and displays explain the park's geology, botany, and history. ⊠ *Bear Lake Rd., off U.S. 36* ☜ *Free* ☉ *May–Sept., daily 9–5.*

### Scenic Stops

**Alluvial Fan.** On July 15, 1982, the 79-year-old dam at Lawn Lake burst, and water roared into Estes Park, killing three people and causing major flooding. The flood created the alluvial fan, a pile of glacial and streambed debris up to 44 feet deep on the north side of Horseshoe Park. A ½-mi trail allows you to explore it up close. You also can view it from the Rainbow Curve lookout on Trail Ridge Road. ⊠ *Fall River Rd., 3 mi from the Fall River entrance station.*

★ **Bear Lake.** Thanks to its picturesque location, easy accessibility, and the good hiking trails nearby, this small alpine lake below Flattop Moun-

## ROCKY MOUNTAIN IN ONE DAY

Begin your adventure with a hearty breakfast at the **Bighorn Restaurant** in Estes Park. While you're enjoying your short stack with apple-cinnamon-raisin topping, you can put in an order for a packed lunch.

Drive west on U.S. 34 into the park, and stop at the **Fall River Visitor Center** to watch the orientation film and pick up a park map. Also inquire about road conditions on Trail Ridge Road, which you should plan to drive either in the morning or afternoon, depending on the weather. If possible, save the drive for the afternoon, and use the morning to get out on the trails before any afternoon lightening threatens your safety.

For a beautiful and invigorating hike, follow the route that takes you from the trailhead at **Bear Lake** to **Nymph Lake** (an easy ½-mi hike),

then onto **Dream Lake** (an additional ⁶/₁₀ mi with a steeper ascent), and finally to **Emerald Lake** (an additional ⁷/₁₀ mi of moderate to challenging terrain). You can stop at several places along the way. The trek down is much easier, and quicker, than the climb up.

■ TIP→ **If you prefer a shorter, simpler, yet still scenic walk, consider the Bear Lake Nature Trail,** a ⁶/₁₀-mi loop that is partially wheelchair and stroller accessible.

You'll need the better part of your afternoon to drive the scenic **Trail Ridge Road.** If you're heading to Grand Lake and destinations west, take Trail Ridge Road west, over the Continental Divide; otherwise, after you reach the top, take it back east and end your day with a ranger-led talk or **evening campfire program.**

tain and Hallett Peak is one of the most popular destinations in the park. Free park shuttle buses can take you here. ⊠ *Bear Lake Rd., 10 mi southwest of Beaver Meadows Visitor Center.*

**Forest Canyon Overlook.** Beyond the classic U-shape glacial valley lies a high-alpine circle of ice-blue pools (the Gorge Lakes) framed by ragged peaks. ⊠ *Trail Ridge Rd., 14 mi east of Alpine Visitor Center.*

### Visitor Centers
**Alpine Visitor Center.** At the top of Trail Ridge Road, this visitor center is open only when that road is navigable. There's a snack bar inside. ⊠ *Trail Ridge Rd. at Fall River Pass, 22 mi from the Beaver Meadows entrance station* ☎ *970/586–1206* ☺ *Memorial Day–mid-Oct., daily 9–5.*

★ **Beaver Meadows Visitor Center.** Housing park headquarters, this visitor center was designed by students of the Frank Lloyd Wright School of Architecture at Taliesen West using the park's popular rustic style, which integrates buildings into their natural surroundings. Completed in 1966, it was named a National Historic Landmark in 2001. The surrounding utility buildings are also on the National Register and are noteworthy examples of the rustic-style buildings that the Civilian Conservation Corps constructed during the Depression. The park has a terrific orientation film and a large relief map of the park. ⊠ *U.S. 36,* *before the Beaver Meadows entrance station* ☎ 970/586–1206 ⊙ *Mid-June–Labor Day, daily 8–9; early Sept.–mid-June, daily 8–5.*

**Fall River Visitor Center.** The Discovery Room, which houses everything from old ranger outfits to elk antlers, coyote pelts, and bighorn sheep skulls for hands-on exploration, is a favorite with kids (and adults) at this northeast center. ⊠ *U.S. 34, at the Fall River entrance station* ☎ 970/586–1206 ⊙ *Mid-June–Labor Day, daily 9–6; winter hrs vary.*

**GOOD READS**

**A Lady's Life in the Rocky Mountains** by Isabella Bird has long been a favorite with Colorado residents and visitors to the park. **Hiking Rocky Mountain National Park** by Kent and Donna Dannen is what Rocky Mountain rangers use as their park hiking guide. **Magnificent Mountain Women** by Janet Robertson gives historical accounts or early pioneers.

**Kawuneeche Visitor Center.** The park's only west-side source of visitor information has exhibits on the plant and animal life of the area, as well as a large three-dimensional map of the park. ⊠ *U.S. 34, before the Grand Lake entrance station* ☎ 970/586–1206 ⊙ *Mid-June–mid-Aug., daily 8–6; mid-Aug.–mid-June, daily 8–4:30.*

**Never Summer Ranch.** On the site of the original Holzwarth homestead and a rustic 1920s resort and dude ranch—Holzwarth's Trout Lodge—buildings have been restored to serve as an interpretive center. You can take a free tour to view the lodge, workshops, icehouse, and taxidermy building. Reaching the ranch involves an easy ½-mi hike. ⊠ *Off Trail Ridge Rd., 9 mi north of Grand Lake* ⊙ *Mid-June to Labor Day, daily 10–4.*

## Sports & the Outdoors

### Bird-watching

Spring and summer, early in the morning, are the best times for bird-watching in the park. **Lumpy Ridge** is a nesting ground for raptors such as golden eagles, red-tailed hawks, and peregrine falcons. Migratory songbirds from South America have summer breeding grounds near the **Endovalley Picnic Area.** The **alpine tundra** is habitat for white-tailed ptarmigan. The **alluvial fan** is the place for viewing broad-tailed hummingbirds, hairy woodpeckers, ouzels, and the occasional raptor.

### Fishing

Rocky Mountain is a wonderful place to fish, especially for trout—German brown, brook, rainbow, cutthroat, and greenback cutthroat—but check at a visitor center about regulations and information on specific closures, catch-and-release areas, and limits on size and possession. No fishing is allowed at Bear Lake. Rangers recommend the more remote backcountry lakes, since they are less crowded. Anyone older than 16 needs a Colorado fishing license, which you can obtain at local sporting-goods stores. See ⊕ www.wildlife.state.co.us/fishing for details.

OUTFITTERS & EXPEDITIONS **Scot's Sporting Goods.** Scot's gives half- and full-day fishing instruction from May through September. Clinics, geared toward first-timers, focus on casting, reading the water, identifying insects for flies, and properly presenting natural and artificial flies to the fish. Half-day excursions into the park are available for three or more people. You can also rent and buy gear here. ⊠ *2325 Spruce Ave., Estes Park* ☎ *970/586–2877* ☎ *$100–$190* ☉ *May–Sept., daily 8–8; Oct.–Apr., daily 9–5.*

## Hiking

Fodor'sChoice
★

Rocky Mountain National Park contains 350 mi of hiking trails, so you could theoretically wander the park for weeks. Most visitors explore just a small portion of these trails, so some of the park's most accessible and scenic paths can resemble a backcountry highway on busy summer days. The high-alpine terrain around Bear Lake is the park's most popular hiking area, and it's well worth exploring. However, for a truly remote experience, hike one of the trails in the far northern end of the park or in the Wild Basin area to the south. Keep in mind that trails at higher elevations may have some snow on them even in July. And because of afternoon thunderstorms on most summer afternoons, an early morning start is highly recommended; the last place you want to be when a storm approaches is on a peak or anywhere above tree line.

All trails are round-trip unless stated otherwise.

EASY
★

**Bear Lake.** The virtually flat nature trail around Bear Lake is an easy, 1-mi walk that's wheelchair accessible. Sharing the route with you will likely be plenty of other hikers as well as songbirds and chipmunks. ⊠ *Trailhead: Bear Lake, Bear Lake Rd.*

☺ **Copeland Falls.** The $^6/_{10}$-mi hike to the Wild Basin area falls is a good option for families, as the terrain is relatively flat (only a 15-foot elevation gain). ⊠ *Trailhead: Wild Basin.*

**Cub Lake.** This 4$^6/_{10}$-mi, three-hour hike takes you through meadows and stands of aspen trees and up 540 feet in elevation to a lake with water lilies. ⊠ *Trailhead: Cub Lake. Take Bear Lake Rd. to Moraine Park Campground, turn right, then left at road to trailhead.*

**East Inlet Trail.** You can get to **Adams Falls** in about 15 minutes on this $^1/_3$-mi route with an 80-foot climb in elevation. The trail to the falls will likely be packed with visitors, so if you have time, continue east on the trail past the falls to enjoy more solitude, see wildlife, and catch views of Mt. Craig from near the East Meadow Campground. Note, however, that beyond the falls the elevation climbs between 1,500 and 1,900 feet, making it a challenging hike. ⊠ *Trailhead: East Inlet, end of W. Portal Rd.; W. Portal Rd. spurs off Trail Ridge Rd. by entrance to Grand Lake village. Stay left at junction with Grand Ave.*

**Glacier Gorge Trail.** The 5-mi hike to **Mills Lake** can be crowded, but the reward is one the park's prettiest lakes, set against the breathtak-

> ### ACCESSIBLE HIKES
>
> **Alluvial Fan**–$^2/_{10}$-mi interpetive trail
> **Bear Lake**–$^6/_{10}$-mi loop nature trail
> **Coyote Valley**–1-mi loop on gravel; look for elk and moose
> **Lily Lake**–$^7/_{10}$-mi loop on gravel; view wildflowers
> **Sprague Lake**–$^1/_2$-mi loop walk; view the Continental Divide

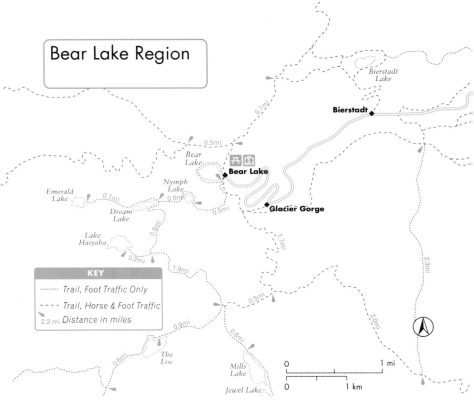

## Bear Lake Region

**KEY**

- ⋯⋯ *Trail, Foot Traffic Only*
- – – – *Trail, Horse & Foot Traffic*
- 2.2 mi *Distance in miles*

ing backdrop of Longs Peak, Pagoda Mountain, and the Keyboard of the Winds. There's a modest elevation gain of 700 feet. About 1 mi in, you pass **Alberta Falls,** a popular destination in and of itself. The hike travels along Glacier Creek, under the shade of a subalpine forest. Give yourself at least four hours for hiking and lingering time. ⊠ *Off Bear Lake Rd., 9 mi south of the Beaver Meadows entrance station.*

★ **Sprague Lake.** With virtually no elevation gain, this 1-mi, pine-lined path is wheelchair accessible and provides views of Hallet Peak and Flattop Mountain. ⊠ *Trailhead: Sprague Lake, Bear Lake Rd.*

MODERATE
Fodor'sChoice
★

**Bear Lake to Emerald Lake.** This scenic, calorie-burning hike begins at Bear Lake and takes you first on a moderately level, ½-mi journey to **Nymph Lake.** From here, the trail gets steeper, with a 425-foot elevation gain, as it winds around for 6/10 mi to **Dream Lake.** The last stretch is the most arduous part of the hike, an almost all-uphill 7/10-mi trek to lovely **Emerald Lake,** where you can perch on a boulder and enjoy the view. Round-trip, the hike is 3 3/10 mi, with an elevation gain of 605 feet. Allow two hours or more, depending on stops. ⊠ *Trailhead: Bear Lake, off Bear Lake Rd.*

**Colorado River Trail.** This walk to the ghost town of Lulu City on the west side of the park is excellent for looking for the bighorn sheep, elk, and moose that reside in the area. Part of the former stagecoach route that went from Granby to Walden, the 7⁷⁄₁₀-mi trail parallels the infant Colorado River to the meadow where Lulu City once stood. Elevation gain is 350 feet. ⊠ *Trailhead: Colorado River, Trail Ridge Rd.*

**Fern Lake Trail.** Heading to Odessa Lake from the north involves a steep hike, but usually you'll encounter fewer fellow hikers than if you begin at Bear Lake. Along the way, you'll come to the Arch Rocks; The Pool, an eroded formation in the Big Thompson River; two waterfalls; and Fern Lake (4 mi from your starting point). Odessa Lake itself lies at the foot of Tourmaline Gorge, below the craggy summits of Gabletop Mountain, Little Mat-

> **SHUTTLE TO THE TRAILS**
>
> The many trails in the Bear Lake area of the park are so popular that parking areas at the trailheads usually cannot accommodate all of the hikers' cars. Shuttle buses connect a large park-and-ride facility at the Glacier Basin Campground with the Cub Lake, Fern Lake, Glacier Gorge Junction, Sprague Lake, and Bear Lake trailheads. Buses run daily between mid-June and mid-September. The Bear Lake shuttle runs approximately every 15 minutes between 7 AM and 7 PM; the Moraine Park shuttle runs approximately every 30 minutes between 7:30 AM and 7:30 PM.

terhorn, Knobtop Mountain, and Notchtop Mountain. For a full day of spectacular scenery, continue past Odessa to Bear Lake (8½ mi total), where you can pick up the shuttle back to the Fern Lake trailhead. Total elevation gain is 1,375 feet. ⊠ *Off Bear Lake Rd., about 1½ mi south of the Beaver Meadows entrance station.*

DIFFICULT **Chasm Lake Trail.** Nestled in the shadow of Longs Peak and Mt. Meeker, Chasm Lake offers one of Colorado's most impressive backdrops, so en route to it, expect to encounter plenty of other hikers. The 4³⁄₁₀-mi Chasm Lake Trail, reached via the Longs Peak Trail, has a 2,360-foot elevation gain. Just before the lake, you'll need to climb a small rock ledge, which can be a bit of a challenge for the less sure-footed; follow the cairns for the most straightforward route. Once atop the ledge, you'll catch your first memorable view of the lake. ⊠ *Off Rte. 7, 9 mi south of Estes Park.*

★ **Longs Peak Trail.** Climbing this 14,255-foot mountain (one of 54 "fourteeners" in Colorado) is an ambitious goal for many people—but only those who are very fit and acclimated to the altitude should attempt it. The 16-mi round-trip hike up Longs requires a predawn start (3 AM is ideal) so that you're off the summit before the typical summer afternoon thunderstorm hits. Also, the last 2 mi or so of the trail are very exposed—you have to traverse narrow ledges with vertigo-inducing dropoffs. That said, summiting Longs can be one of the most rewarding hikes you'll ever attempt. The Keyhole route is the traditional means of ascent, and the number of people going up it on a summer day can be astounding given the rigors of the hike. Though just as scenic, the Loft route, between Longs and Mt. Meeker from Chasm Lake, is not clearly marked and is therefore difficult to navigate. ⊠ *Off Rte. 7, 9 mi south of Estes Park.*

## Horseback Riding

Horses and riders can access 260 mi of trails in Rocky Mountain.

OUTFITTERS & **Allenspark Livery.** The stable offers three-hour to all-day rides into the
EXPEDITIONS Wild Basin area in the park's southeast corner. ✉ *211 Main St., Allenspark* ☎ *303/747–2551* ✉ *$45–$85* ☼ *June–mid-Sept.*

**Sombrero Ranches, Inc.** Sombrero offers guided rides into the wilderness
and national park, including scenic and relaxing early-morning breakfast rides. The Boulder-based company also gives guided fishing trips
to remote streams and lakes, winter sleigh rides, and private camping
trips. Guided horseback riding trips last two to eight hours. **Grand Lake
Stables** ✉ *304 W. Portal Rd., Grand Lake* ☎ *970/627–3514* ⊕ *www.
sombrero.com* ✉ *$35–$80* ☼ *Mid-May–late Sept.* **Glacier Creek Stables**
✉ *Off Bear Lake Rd., near Sprague Lake* ☎ *970/586–3244.* **Moraine
Park Stables** ✉ *Off Bear Lake Rd.* ☎ *970/586–2327.*

## Rock Climbing

★ Expert rock climbers as well as novices can try hundreds of classic
climbs here. The burgeoning sport of ice climbing also thrives in the park.
The Diamond, Lumpy Ridge, and Petit Grepons are the places for rock
climbing, while well-known ice-climbing spots include Hidden Falls, Loch
Vale, and Emerald and Black lakes.

OUTFITTER **Colorado Mountain School** is the oldest continuously operating U.S. guide
service and an invaluable resource. You can take introductory half-day
and two-day courses on climbing and rappelling technique, or sign up
for guided introductory trips, full-day climbs, and longer expeditions.
Make reservations as far as six weeks in advance for summer climbs.
The school also runs a 16-bed hostel. ✉ *351 Moraine Ave., Estes Park*
☎ *970/586–5758 or 888/267–7783* ⊕ *www.cmschool.com* ✉ *$35–$80.*

## Winter Sports

Each winter, the popularity of snowshoeing in the park increases. It's a
wonderful way to experience Rocky Mountain's majestic winter side, when
the jagged peaks are softened with a blanket of snow and the summer
hordes are nonexistent. You can snowshoe any of the summer hiking trails
that are accessible by road; many of them also become well-traveled cross-
country ski trails.

Backcountry skiing within the park ranges from gentle cross-country
outings to full-on telemarking down steep chutes and glaciers. Come
spring, when avalanche danger decreases, the park has some classic
ski descents for those on telemark or alpine touring equipment. Ask
a ranger about conditions and gear up as if you were spending the night.
If you plan on venturing off-trail, take a shovel, probe pole, and avalanche transceiver. Two trails to try are Tonahutu Creek Trail (near
Kawuneeche Visitor Center) and the Colorado River Trail to Lulu City
(start at the Timber Creek Campground).

Only on the west side of the park are you permitted to snowmobile, but
you must register at Kawuneeche Visitor Center before traveling up the
unplowed section of Trail Ridge Road up to Milner Pass. Check the park
newspaper, *High Country Headlines,* for ranger-guided tours.

CLOSE UP

## Longs Peak: The Northernmost Fourteener

AT 14,255 FEET ABOVE SEA LEVEL, Longs Peak has long fascinated explorers to the region. Isabella L. Bird wrote of it, "It is one of the noblest of mountains, but in one's imagination it grows to be much more than a mountain. It becomes invested with a personality."

It was named after Major Stephen H. Long, who led an expedition in 1820 up the Platte River to the base of the Rockies. Long never ascended the mountain—in fact, he didn't even get within 40 mi of it—but a few decades later, in 1868, the one-armed Civil War veteran John Wesley Powell climbed to its summit.

In the park's southeast quadrant, Longs Peak is northernmost of the 54 mountains in Colorado that reach above the 14,000-foot mark, and one of more than 114 named mountains in the park higher than 10,000 feet. You can see its distinctive flat-top, rectangular-shape summit from many spots on the park's east side and Trail Ridge Road.

If you want to make the ambitious climb to Longs summit—and it's only recommended for those who are strong climbers and well acclimated to the altitude—you should begin by 3 AM so that you're down from the summit when the typical afternoon thunderstorm hits.

OUTFITTERS & EXPEDITIONS

**Estes Park Mountain Shop.** Rent snowshoes and skis here, as well as fishing, hiking, and climbing equipment. The store gives half- and full-day guided fly-fishing trips into the park year-round for all levels. ⊠ *2050 Big Thompson Ave., Estes Park* ☎ *970/586–6548 or 866/303–6548* ⊕ *www.estesparkmountainshop.com.*

**Grand Lake Snowmobile Rental.** Located at Elk Creek Campground, this snowmobile rental company has been doing it longer than anyone else in Grand Lake. Rentals are available for two, four, or eight hours. ⊠ *143 County Rd. 48, Grand Lake* ☎ *970/627–8502* ⊠ *$65–$160* ☉ *Late Nov.–mid-Apr.*

**Never Summer Mountain Sports** (⊠ 919 Grand Ave., Grand Lake ☎ 970/ 627–3642) rents cross-country skis, boots, and poles, and sells hiking and climbing gear.

**Outdoor World** (⊠ 156 E. Elkhorn Ave., Estes Park ☎ 970/586–2114 ⊠ $8) has daily snowshoe rentals, which include poles.

## Educational Offerings

### Art Program

**Artist-in-Residence.** Professional writers, sculptors, composers, and visual and performing artists can stay in a rustic cabin for two weeks in the summer while working on their art. During their stay they must do two park presentations, and donate a piece of original work to Rocky Mountain that relates to their stay. Applications must be received by December for requests for the following summer. ☎ 970/586–1206.

### Classes & Seminars

★ **Rocky Mountain Field Seminars.** The Rocky Mountain Nature Association sponsors some 100 hands-on seminars for adults and children on such topics as natural history, geology, bird-watching, wildflower identification, wildlife biology, photography, sketching, and Native American handiwork. The classes, which usually run three hours, are taught by expert instructors. College students often receive academic credit. ✉ *1895 Fall River Rd., Estes Park* ☎ *970/586–3262 or 800/748–7002* ⊕ *www.rmna.org* ✎ *$15–$65 per day* ☉ *Jan.–Oct.*

### Ranger Programs

☾ **Junior Ranger Program.** Pick up a Junior Ranger activity book (in English or Spanish) at any visitor center. Program content has been developed for children ages 6–12 and focuses on environmental education, identifying birds and wildlife, and outdoor safety skills. Once a child has completed all of the activities, a ranger will look over the book and award a Junior Ranger badge. ☎ *970/586–1206* ✎ *Free.*

★ ☾ **Ranger-Led Programs.** With more than 150 programs each summer, there are many opportunities to join in on free hikes, talks, and activities conducted by those who know the park best. Topics may include the wildlife, geology, vegetation, or park history. At night, storytelling, slide shows, and talks may be part of the evening campfire program, held in summer at park campgrounds and at Beaver Meadows Visitor Center. There are also evening hikes and stargazing sessions. On Friday, stories, songs, and marshmallow roasts take place at Never Summer Ranch. In winter, rangers lead snowshoeing and cross-country ski tours. Special programs for kids include "Ranger for a Day," "Skins and Skulls," and "Tales for Tots" (for preschool-age kids with an accompanying adult). Look for the extensive program schedule in the park's guide, *High Country Headlines.* ☎ *970/586–1206* ✎ *Free.*

# WHAT'S NEARBY

## Nearby Towns & Attractions

### Nearby Towns

**Estes Park,** 5 mi east of Rocky Mountain, is the park's primary gateway. The town sits at an altitude of more than 7,500 feet, with 14,255-foot Longs Peak and a chorus of surrounding mountains as its stunning backdrop. Many of the small hotels lining the roads are mom-and-pop outfits that have been passed down through several generations. Estes Park's quieter cousin, **Grand Lake,** 1½ mi outside the park's west entrance, gets busy in summer, but overall has a low-key, Western graciousness. In winter it's *the* snowmobiling capital and ice-fishing destination for Coloradans. At the park's southwestern entrance are Arapaho National Forest, Arapaho National Recreational Area, and the small town of **Granby,** the place to go for big-game hunting, mountain biking, and skiing at nearby SolVista resort, Winter Park, and Mary Jane.

## FODOR'S FIRST PERSON: THE CALL OF THE ELK

**Barbara Colligan**
*Colorado resident*

In September and October, there are traffic jams at the park as people drive up to listen to the elk bugling. It's a lot of fun. The rangers and park volunteers keep track of where the elk are and direct visitors to the mating spots. The bugling is high-pitched, and if it's light enough, you can see the elk put his head in the air. He really puts his whole head and shoulders into it, and his throat puffs out. It's

fascinating to listen to. It echoes across the forest.

The call is to let the other bulls know "These are my females. You other males stay away." They sometimes have clashes. I've seen a big elk chase a smaller one off. The females are grouped around the bulls. Once I saw a female start to move away and the bull pushed her back into line. That was annoying.

Having binoculars really makes a difference, too. With those I could see the elk even when it got dark.

### Nearby Attractions

**The Stanley Hotel.** Genius entrepreneur F. O. Stanley, inventor of the Stanley Steamer automobile and several photographic processes, constructed this regal hotel on a promontory overlooking Estes Park in 1907, after his doctors said he would soon die of tuberculosis. Stanley went on to live another 30-odd years, an extension that he attributed to the area's fresh air. The hotel soon became one of the most glamorous resorts in the Rockies, a reputation it holds to this day. The hotel was the inspiration for Stephen King's *The Shining*, part of which he wrote while staying here. ⊠ *333 East Wonderview Ave., Estes Park* ☎ *970/586–3371 or 800/976–1377* ⊕ *www.stanleyhotel.com.*

**State Forest State Park.** Rugged peaks, thick forests, and burbling streams make up this 71,000-acre park. Fish for trout, boat the azure alpine lakes, ride horseback, hike or bicycle 130 mi of trails, and explore a few four-wheel-drive roads with views of the 12,000-foot Medicine Bow and Never Summer mountain ranges. Yurts are available in the winter (call 970/723–4070) so you can explore the 70 mi of groomed snowmobiling trails or the 50 mi of groomed and signed cross-country skiing and snowshoeing trails. ⊠ *56750 Hwy. 14, Walden, Drive 53 mi north of Granby on U.S. 40 and Rte. 125 to Walden and 21 mi east on Rte. 14 to park* ☎ *970/723–8366* ⊕ *www. parks.state.co.us* ⊠ *$5 a day per vehicle* ⊙ *Year-round.*

## Area Activities

### Sports & the Outdoors

BIRD-WATCHING    **Windy Gap Wildlife Viewing Area.** On migration routes for geese, pelicans, swans, eagles, and osprey, this reservoir has information kiosks, viewing scopes, viewing blinds, a picnic area, and a wheelchair-accessible nature trail. ✉ *2 mi west of Granby on U.S. 40 where it meets Rte. 125* ☎ *970/725–6200* ◷ *May–Sept., daily dawn–dusk.*

FISHING Anglers in the Grand Lake and Granby area enjoy plentiful trout, mackinaw, and kokanee salmon. Ice fishers will not want to miss the big contest held the first weekend in January on Lake Granby, where winners collect $20,000 in cash and prizes. The Big Thompson River, east of Estes Park along U.S. 34, has a good stock of rainbow and brown trout. Anyone older than 16 needs a Colorado fishing license, which you can obtain at local sporting-goods stores (visit ⊕ www.wildlife.state.co.us/fishing for locations and details). **Rocky Mountain Adventures** (☎ 970/586–6191 or 800/858–6808) offers guided fly- and float-fishing trips on the Cache la Poudre River. **Trail Ridge Marina** (✉ Shadow Mountain Lake, 4 mi south of Grand Lake on U.S. 34 ☎ 970/627–3586) rents pontoons, runabouts, and fishing boats by the hour.

GOLF **Grand Elk Golf Club.** You might share a tee with an elk here. Designed ★ by PGA great Craig Stadler, the challenging course is reminiscent of traditional heathland greens in Britain. ✉ *1321 Tenmile Dr., Granby* ☎ *970/887–9122 or 877/389–9333* ⊕ *www.grandelk.com* ⅄ *18 Holes. Yards: 7,144/5,095. Par: 71/71. Greens Fee: $60/$99.*

WINTER SPORTS Many consider Grand Lake to be Colorado's snowmobiling capital, ★ with more than 300 mi of trails (150 mi groomed), many winding through virgin forest. If you're visiting during the winter holidays, make reservations about three weeks ahead. **Grand Adventures LLC** (✉ 304 W. Portal Rd. ☎ 970/627–3098 or 800/726–9247 ⊕ www.grandadventures. com) arranges unguided rentals. **Never Summer Mountain Products** (✉ 919 Grand Ave. ☎ 970/627–3642) rents cross-country skis and snowshoes. **On The Trail** (✉ 1447 County Rd. 491 ☎ 970/627–0171 or 888/627–2429 ⊕ www.onthetrailrentals.com) rents snowmobiles. **Spirit Lake Polaris** (✉ 347 W. Portal Rd. ☎ 970/627–9288) sells snowmobiles and rents ATVs.

### Arts & Entertainment

The **Rocky Ridge Music Center** (✉ 465 Longs Peak Rd., 9 mi south of Estes Park off Hwy. 7 ☎ 970/586–4031 ⊕ www.rockyridge.org) holds classical concerts June through August.

NIGHTLIFE The **Lariat Saloon** (✉ 1121 Grand Ave., Grand Lake ☎ 970/627–9965) is the Grand Lake local hot spot with live rock music almost every night. Look for the talking buffalo. Blues and rock bands play at **Lonigans** (✉ 110 W. Elkhorn Ave., Estes Park ☎ 970/586–4346) on weekends. **The Tavern** (✉ Marys Lake Lodge, 2625 Mary's Lake Rd., Estes Park ☎ 970/586–5958) has live entertainment nightly in summer and fives nights a week in winter.

## Scenic Drive

★ **Peak-to-Peak Highway.** Winding from Central City through Nederland to Estes Park, this route is not the quickest way to get to the eastern gateway to Rocky Mountain National Park, but it's certainly the most scenic. You pass through the old mining towns of Ward and Allenspark and enjoy spectacular mountain vistas and, in fall, golden stands of aspen.

Mt. Meeker and Longs Peak rise magnificently behind every bend in the road, and the descent into Estes Park provides grand vistas of snow-covered alpine peaks and green valleys. ⊠ *From Nederland drive north on Hwy. 72. Turn left at intersection with Hwy. 7 and continue to Estes Park.*

# WHERE TO STAY & EAT

### About the Restaurants

Restaurants in north-central Colorado run the gamut from simple diners with tasty, homey basics to elegant establishments with extensive wine lists. Some restaurants take reservations, but many—particularly mid-range spots—seat on a first-come, first-served basis. In the park itself, there are no real dining establishments, though you can get snacks and light fare at the top of Trail Ridge Road. The park also has a handful of scenic picnic areas, all with tables and pit or flush toilets.

### About the Hotels

Bed-and-breakfasts and small inns in north-central Colorado vary from old-fashioned cottages to sleek, modern buildings with understated lodge themes. If you want some pampering, there are guest ranches and spas. In Estes Park, Grand Lake, and nearby towns, the elevation keeps the climate cool, and you'll have a tough time finding air-conditioned lodging. For a historic spot, try the Stanley Hotel in Estes Park—with its stately structure, it would fit right in on Mackinac Island in Michigan. The park has no hotels or lodges.

### About the Campgrounds

Five top-notch campgrounds in the park meet the needs of campers, whether you're staying in a tent, trailer, or RV (only two campgrounds accept reservations; the others fill up on a first-come, first-served basis). Backcountry camping requires advance reservations or a day-of-trip permit; contact **Backcountry Permits, Rocky Mountain National Park** (⊠ Beaver Meadows Visitor Center, U.S. 36 southwest of Estes Park ☎ 970/586–1242 ☉ May–Sept., daily 7–7, Oct.–Apr., daily 8–4:30) before starting out.

## Where to Eat

### In the Park

¢ ✕ **Trail Ridge Store Snack Bar.** Pick up snacks and sandwiches, burgers, and soups at the Alpine Visitor Center. ⊠ *Trail Ridge Rd.* ☎ *970/586–3097. $1–$5* ▭ *AE, D, MC, V* ☉ *Closed mid-Oct.–May.*

PICNIC AREAS **Endovalley** (⊠ U.S. 34, at the beginning of Old Fall River Rd.), with 32 tables and 30 fire grates, is the largest picnic area in the park. The views here are of aspen groves, Fall River Pass, and a beautiful lake.

**Hollowell Park** (⊠ Off Bear Lake Rd., between the Moraine Park Museum and Glacier Basin Campground), in a meadow near Mill Creek, is a lovely spot for a picnic. The Mill Creek Basin trailhead is nearby. There are nine tables, no running water, and no fire grates.

☾ **Sprague Lake** (⊠ ⁶⁄₁₀ mi from the intersection of Bear Lake Road and U.S. 36) has 23 tables, all wheelchair accessible, and restrooms.

## Outside the Park

**$$–$$$$** ✕ **Hunter's Chophouse.** This popular steak house fills up quickly in the evening, and for good reason. Locals head here for the savory and spicy barbecue: steaks, venison, buffalo, chicken, and seafood. If you're not hungry enough for a 20-ounce porterhouse steak, try one of their gourmet burgers, such as the Gorgonzola pancetta burger. There's a good kids' menu, too, with fish-and-chips, a junior sirloin, and a mini Chophouse burger. ⊠ *1690 Big Thompson Ave., Estes Park* ☎ *970/586– 6962* ⚏ *Reservations essential. $14–$33* ▭ *MC, V.*

**$–$$$** ✕ **Mama Rose's.** After an active day in the park head here for a $13 four-course meal, including all the salad, soup, bread, and spaghetti you can eat, with a good portion of spumoni to top it off. The lasagna and tricolor baked pasta are popular entrées, as are veal- or chicken parmigiana and fettuccine Alfredo. There's also a kids' menu. ⊠ *338 E. Elkhorn Ave., Estes Park* ☎ *970/586–3330. $8–$21* ▭ *AE, D, DC, MC, V* ⊘ *Closed Jan.–mid Feb. No lunch.*

**★ $–$$$** ✕ **The Other Side.** View ducks from your table and listen to easy jazz at this delightful, rustic, high-ceilinged restaurant on Estes Park's west side. Specialties include trout, crab cakes, Alfredo chicken breast, and cowboy steak (a 16-ounce rib eye). Entrées come with soup or salad, and bread—you won't leave hungry. ⊠ *900 Moraine Ave., Estes Park* ☎ *970/ 586–2171* ⊕ *www.theothersideofestes.com. $9–$25* ▭ *AE, D, MC, V.*

**$–$$$** ✕ **Sagebrush BBQ & Grill.** Barbecue ribs, chicken, and catfish draw local and out-of-town attention to this homey café. Comforting sides such as baked beans, corn bread, cole slaw, and potatoes top off the large plates; meals can be sized for smaller appetites. They also serve breakfast. ⊠ *1101 Grand Ave., Grand Lake* ☎ *970/627–1404. $8–$22* ▭ *AE, D, DC, MC, V.*

**★ $–$$** ✕ **Bighorn Restaurant.** An Estes Park staple since 1972, this family-run outfit is where the locals go for breakfast. As early as 6 AM, you can get a double-cheese omelet, huevos rancheros, or grits before heading into the park. Owners Laura and Sid Brown are happy to pack a lunch for you—just place your order with breakfast, and your sandwich, chips, homemade cookie, and drink will be ready to go when you leave. This homey spot also serves lunch and dinner. ⊠ *401 W. Elkhorn Ave., Estes Park* ☎ *970/586–2792. $10–$14* ▭ *D, MC, V.*

**$–$$** ✕ **Longbranch Restaurant.** This smoke-free, Western-style coffee shop has a warm fireplace, rustic wood interior, and wagon-wheel chandeliers. It serves delicious German food: bratwurst, goulash, schnitzel, and sauerbraten. The traditional German desserts are authentic; the strudel gets particularly high marks. The bar serves many domestic and foreign beers, as well as a few microbrews. ⊠ *185 E. Agate Ave., U.S. 40, Granby* ☎ *970/887–2209. $8–$18* ▭ *D, MC, V.*

**★ $–$$** ✕ **Sweet Basilico Café.** This tiny, homey place is the local favorite for basic Italian classics like lasagna, manicotti, and eggplant Parmesan. Sandwiches made with homemade focaccia are delicious, and the minestrone is wonderfully satisfying. ⊠ *430 Prospect Village, Estes Park* ☎ *970/ 586–3899* ⚏ *Reservations essential. $8–$15* ▭ *AE, D, MC, V.*

**¢–$$** ✕ **The Bear's Den.** The menu at this rustic, log restaurant includes Rocky Mountain oysters, New York strip steak, and seafood. But the standouts here are the nightly specials—especially the fried chicken and chicken-fried steak, cooked in cast-iron skillets for homemade flavor. ⊠ *612 Grand Ave., Grand Lake* ☎ *970/627–3385. $7–$20* ▭ *D, MC, V.*

¢–$$ ✕ **Ed's Cantina and Grill.** Zesty 12-inch burritos and tasty burgers are what make this Estes Park hangout so popular. The decor is bright, with light woods and large windows, and the bar is well stocked. Try to get patio seating by the river. ⊠ *390 E. Elkhorn Ave., Estes Park* ☎ *970/586–2919. $5–$14* ▭ *AE, D, MC, V.*

¢–$$ ✕ **Poppy's Pizza & Grill.** The spinach, artichoke, and feta pie with sun-dried tomato sauce at this family-friendly pizzeria is excellent. Try a pizza with Rocky Mountain smoked trout, capers, and cream cheese, or create your own specialty from the five sauces and more than 40 toppings on the menu. A portion of the profits go to local charities. ⊠ *342 E. Elkhorn Ave., Estes Park* ☎ *970/586–8282. $5–$20* ▭ *AE, D, DC, MC, V* ☉ *Closed Jan.*

## Where to Stay

### In the Park

CAMPGROUNDS & RV PARKS

$$ ⚠ **Aspenglen Campground.** This quiet east side spot near the north entrance is set in open pine woodland along Fall River. It doesn't have the views of Moraine Park or Glacier Basin, but it's small and peaceful. There are a few excellent walk-in sites for those who want to pitch a tent away from the crowds but still be close to the car. All sites accommodate RVs, tents, trailers, or campers. Firewood and ice are for sale. ⊠ *Drive past Fall River Visitor Center on U.S. 34 and turn left at the campground Rd.* ☎ *877/444–6777* ◔ *54 sites* ♿ *Flush toilets, drinking water, fire grates, public telephone* ♿ *Reservations not accepted. $20* ▭ *AE, D, MC, V* ☉ *Mid-May–late Sept.*

$$ ⚠ **Glacier Basin Campground.** Rest in the shade of lodgepole pines on the banks of Glacier Creek and take in views of the Continental Divide. There's easy access to a network of popular trails, and rangers come here for campfire programs. All sites accommodate RVs, tents, trailers, or campers. Firewood and ice are for sale. ⊠ *Drive 5 mi south from U.S. 36 along Bear Lake Rd.* ☎ *877/444–6777* ◔ *150 sites* ♿ *Flush toilets, dump station, drinking water, fire grates, public telephone* ♿ *Reservations essential. $20, $3 per person for the group sites* ▭ *AE, D, MC, V* ☉ *Memorial Day weekend–late-Sept.*

$$ ⚠ **Longs Peak Campground.** Hikers going up Longs Peak can stay at this year-round, tent-only campground. Sites are limited to eight people; ice and firewood are sold in summer. ⊠ *9 mi south of Estes Park on Rte. 7* ☎ *877/444–6777* ◔ *26 tent sites* ♿ *Flush toilets, pit toilets, drinking water (mid-May–mid-Sept.), fire grates, ranger station* ♿ *Reservations not accepted. $20 in summer, $14 in winter* ▭ *AE, D, MC, V.*

★ $$ ⚠ **Moraine Park Campground.** This popular campground hosts ranger-led campfire programs and is near hiking trails. You'll hear elk bugling if you camp here in September or October. Sites accommodate RVs, tents, trailers, and campers, but are limited to eight people (except at group sites). Reservations are essential from mid-May to late September. ⊠ *Drive south on Bear Lake Rd. from U.S. 36 ¾ mi to campground* *entrance* ☎ 877/444–6777 ⇱ *247 sites* ⚒ *Flush toilets, pit toilets, dump station, drinking water (mid-May–mid-Sept.), fire grates, public telephone. $20 in summer, $14 in winter, $3 per person for group sites* 🖃 *AE, D, MC, V.*

**$$** ⚠ **Timber Creek Campground.** Anglers love this spot on the Colorado River, 10 mi from Grand Lake village. In the evening you can sit in on ranger-led campfire programs. All sites accommodate RVs, tents, trailers, or campers, and are limited to eight people. Firewood is sold here. ⊠ *Trail Ridge Rd. 12 mi west of Alpine Visitor Center* ☎ 877/444–6777 ⇱ *98 sites* ⚒ *Flush toilets, pit toilets, dump station, drinking water (mid-May–mid-Sept.), fire grates, public telephone* ⚒ *Reservations not accepted. $20 in the summer, $14 in winter* 🖃 *AE, D, MC, V.*

### Outside the Park

**$$$$** ⊞ **C Lazy U Guest Ranch.** Secluded in a broad, verdant valley, this deluxe guest ranch attracts an international clientele, including Hollywood royalty and the real thing. Guests enjoy luxurious Western-style accommodations, fine meals, live entertainment, and any outdoor activity they can dream up—and their own personal horse. The instructors are top-notch, and the children's programs are unbeatable. The minimum stay is three days with arrival on Wednesday or Saturday in the summer, and two nights in winter. All meals are included. ⊘ *Box 379, Granby 80446* ✛ *3½ mi north on Rte. 125 from U.S. 40 junction* ☎ 970/887–3344 🖷 970/887–3917 ⊕ *www.clazyu.com* ⇱ *40 rooms, 20 cabins* ⚒ *Tennis courts, pool, gym, bar, children's programs (ages 3–17), no a/c, no phone, no TV. $360–$580* 🖃 *AE, MC, V* ☉ *Mid-Sept–early Dec. and mid-Feb. to late May* ⦿ *FAP.*

**$$$–$$$$**

Fodor'sChoice
★

⊞ **The Stanley Hotel.** Perched regally on a hill with a commanding view of the town, the Stanley is one of Colorado's great old hotels, impeccably maintained in its historic state, yet with all the modern conveniences. F. O. Stanley (the inventor of the Stanley Steamer) began construction in 1907, and when it opened in 1909 it was the first hotel in the world with electricity and the first in the United States with in-room telephones. Be sure to take one of the daily historical and ghost tours (the Stanley inspired Stephen King's novel *The Shining*). Many of the sunny rooms have mountain views and are decorated with antiques and period reproductions. ⊠ *333 East Wonderview Ave., Estes Park 80517* ☎ 970/586–3371 *or* 800/976–1377 🖷 970/586–3673 ⊕ *www.stanleyhotel. com* ⇱ *138 rooms* ⚒ *Restaurant, Wi-Fi, pool, bar, no a/c. $169–$249* 🖃 *AE, D, DC, MC, V.*

**$$–$$$$** ⊞ **Valhalla Resort.** Away from the touristy bustle of Estes Park's main downtown area, this tucked-away resort allows you to relax in large cabins with modern amenities—in fact, the larger ones feel more like condos. Look out your window and it's quite likely you'll see an elk grazing. The resort is often booked in summer and early fall during the elk bugling, so be sure to reserve far in advance. All cabins have kitchen, living room, and deck or patio with a grill. Resort activities include shuffleboard, miniature golf, and horseshoes. There's also a lounge with video games and a hot tub. If you're 62 or older, you get a 10% discount. Also, prices drop in the shoulder season. ⊠ *2185 Eagle Cliff Rd., Estes Park*

*80517* ☎ *970/586–3284 or 800/522–3284* 🖨 *970/522–3284* ⊕ *www. valhallaresort.com* ⇨ *52 rooms, 25 1- to 4-bedroom cabins* ♨ *Pool, no-smoking rooms. $101–$487 per cabin* 🖃 *AE, MC, V.*

**$$–$$$** 🏨 **Marys Lake Lodge.** This 1913 chalet-style lodge overlooks Marys Lake a couple miles south of town. Original woodwork and antiques adorn the rooms; look for the Victorian floral lamps in the hallways. Some rooms have claw-foot tubs; others have Jacuzzi tubs. ⊠ *2625 Marys Lake Rd., Estes Park 80517* ☎ *970/586–5958 or 877/442–6279* ⊕ *www. maryslakelodge.com* ⇨ *16 suites, 40 condos* ♨ *2 restaurants, public Wi-Fi, no-smoking rooms. $149–$169* 🖃 *AE, D, MC, V* ⊌❙ *CP.*

**$–$$$** 🏨 **Estes Park Center/YMCA of the Rockies.** This 890-acre, family-friendly property has a wealth of attractive lodging options among its seven lodges and many cabins. A couple can rent a simple, rustic pine cabin, and an extended family (up to 40) has plenty of space in the newer cabins, which have modern kitchen appliances and televisions. Lodge rooms can be outfitted with queen beds or bunk beds. There's a Frisbee–golf course, and a climbing wall. ⊠ *2515 Tunnel Rd., Estes Park 80511* ☎ *303/ 448–1616* 🖨 *970/586–6078* ⊕ *www.ymcarockies.org* ⇨ *688 rooms, 220 cabins* ♨ *Restaurant, tennis court, pool, gym, no a/c, no TV. $75–$110 rooms, cabins $91–$300* 🖃 *MC, V* ⊌❙ *MAP.*

♨ **$–$$** 🏨 **Glacier Lodge.** Families are the specialty at this secluded, 19-acre guest resort on the banks of the Big Thompson River. The kids will take home plenty of fun memories from the twice-weekly "soda saloons," nature walks, arts-and-crafts kids' programs, and Tuesday evening campfire stories. Once a week there's a "mountain breakfast" with omelets and flapjacks before a guided trail ride, usually into Roosevelt National Forest. You can stay in former Colorado governor James Peabody's (in office 1902–04) family summer residence. There's a minimum stay of four nights in the summer and two nights in spring and fall. ⊠ *2166 Hwy. 66, Box 2656, Estes Park 80517* ☎ *970/586–4401 or 800/523–3920* ⊕ *www.glacierlodge.com* ⇨ *24 single-family cabins, 4 cabins for 12–30* ♨ *Kitchens, pool, no a/c, public Wi-Fi. $80–$150* 🖃 *AE, D, MC, V* ⊘ *Closed mid-May–mid-Oct.*

**$–$$** 🏨 **The Historic Rapids Lodge & Restaurant.** This 1915 lodgepole-pine

Fodor'sChoice structure on the Tonahutu River has seven lodge rooms—each with ceil-
★ ing fan—done in the Rocky Mountain rustic style with a mix of antique furnishings, such as claw-foot tubs. The innkeepers also rent newer condos for large groups. The delightful Rapids Restaurant ($$$–$$$$; reservations advised) is Grand Lake's most romantic for fine dining, with stained glass and timber beams. The specialty is an 8-ounce filet mignon with artichokes and béarnaise sauce. ⊠ *209 Rapids La., Grand Lake 80447* ☎ *970/627–3707* ⊕ *www.rapidslodge.com* ⇨ *7 rooms, 8 suites, 5 cabins, 11 condos* ♨ *Restaurant, kitchen (some), bar, no a/c, no-smoking rooms. $75–$125* 🖃 *AE, MC, V* ⊘ *Closed Apr. and Nov.*

★ **$–$$** 🏨 **Mountain Lakes Lodge.** The scent of the pine forest welcomes you to these charming log cabins. All cabins have private decks and charcoal grills. Dogs are enthusiastically welcomed, and have their own private fenced yards. Cabins accommodate two to seven people. ⊠ *10480 U.S. 34, Grand Lake 80447* ☎ *970/627–8448* ⊕ *www.mountainlakeslodge.*

*com* ⟲ *11 cabins* ⚇ *Kitchens, some pets allowed, no a/c, no phone.*
*$75–$145* ▭ *MC, V.*

$ ☷ **Riverview Pines.** Fish in the Fall River or just sit and read on the ex-
pansive lawn at this peaceful motel. The simple, recently updated rooms
have coffeemakers. The luxury, log-style, duplex cabins accommodate
up to six persons, have full kitchens, fireplaces, DVD/VCRs, and decks
that face the river. A two-night stay is required for rooms; cabins have
a four-night minimum. ✉ *1150 W. Elkhorn Ave., Box 690, Estes Park*
*80517* ☎ *970/586–3627 or 800/340–5764* ⊕ *www.riverviewpines.*
*com* ⟲ *18 rooms, 8 cabins* ⚇ *Kitchen (some), refrigerator, laundry fa-*
*cilities, no a/c, no-smoking rooms. $95, $169–$229 cabins* ▭ *AE, D,*
*MC, V.*

CAMPGROUNDS &   ⚠ **Mary's Lake Campground and RV Park.** The campground is across the
RV PARKS   road from Mary's Lake; no swimming is allowed in the lake, but you
$$-$$$   can fish for trout. There's also a pool, basketball court, horseshoe pits,
and rec room with pool tables, air hockey, and video games. Prices are
based on two people per site; each additional person is $3 extra. ✉ *2120*
*Mary's Lake Rd., Estes Park 80517* ☎ *970/586–4411 or 800/445–*
*6279* 🖷 *970/586–4493* ⊕ *www.maryslakecampground.com* ⟲ *150*
*sites (60 with full hookups, 30 with partial hookups)* ⚇ *Flush toilets,*
*full hookups, partial hookups (electric and water), dump station, drink-*
*ing water, sewer, guest laundry, showers, fire pits, picnic tables, public*
*telephone, general store. $25–$40* ▭ *D, MC, V* ⊙ *May–mid-Sept.*

$-$$   ⚠ **Arapaho National Recreation Area.** Five lakeside campgrounds—Still-
water, Cutthroat Bay, Green Ridge, Arapaho Bay, and Sunset Creek—
keep you close to recreational activities. Stillwater has showers. ✉ *South*
*of Grand Lake on U.S. 34* ☎ *970/887–0056 or 877/444–6777* ⊕ *www.*
*reserveusa.com* ⟲ *21 partial hookups (water and electricity), 272 multi-*
*use sites, 29 tent sites, 3 group sites* ⚇ *Flush toilets, pit toilets, dump*
*station, drinking water, fire grates, picnic tables, public telephone. $5*
*vehicle entrance fee, partial hookups $22, tent sites $14–$17, $70 group*
*site* ▭ *No credit cards* ⊙ *Memorial Day–Labor Day.*

$   ⚠ **National Recreation Reservation Service.** West of Lyons and south of
Estes Park, three campgrounds—Camp Dick, Olive Ridge, and Peaceful Valley—are tucked away in quiet forests. Although reservations can
be made, half of the sites in these campgrounds are not reservable and
are filled on a first-come, first-served basis. Weekends are popular, so
if you don't have a reservation, the rangers recommend arriving before
noon on Friday. For campground details, *see* ⊕ www.fs.fed.us/r2/arnf.
When making a reservation online only, you can pay by credit card (AE,
D, MC, V). ☎ *877/444–6777* ⊕ *www.reserveusa.com* ⟲ *17–56 sites*
⚇ *Pit toilets, drinking water, fire grates, picnic tables. $14* ⊙ *Mid-*
*May–mid-Oct.*

# ROCKY MOUNTAIN ESSENTIALS

ACCESSIBILITY All visitor centers are fully accessible to mobility-impaired people. The Sprague Lake, Bear Lake, Coyote Valley, and Lily Lake trails are hard-packed gravel, ½- to 1-mi, accessible loops. A backcountry campsite at Sprague Lake accommodates up to 12 campers, including six in wheelchairs. Bear Lake shuttles are wheelchair accessible.

ADMISSION FEES Entrance fees are $20. If you enter on bicycle, motorcycle, horseback, or on foot, you pay $10 for a weekly pass. An annual pass costs $30.

ADMISSION HOURS The park is open 24/7, year-round; some roads close in winter. It is in the Mountain time zone.

ATMS/BANKS The park has no ATM. 🏧 **Country Supermarket** ⊠ 900 Moraine Ave., U.S. 36, next to the Conoco, Estes Park ☎ 970/586-2702. **Lone Eagle gas station** ⊠ 720 Grand Ave., Grand Lake ☎ 970/627-3281. **WestStar Bank** ⊠ 363 E. Elkhorn Ave., Estes Park ☎ 970/586-4412.

AUTOMOBILE SERVICE STATIONS
🔧 **Conoco-National Park Village** ⊠ 900 Moraine Ave., U.S. 36, Estes Park ☎ 970/586-2139. **Lakeview General Store** ⊠ 14626 U.S. 34, Grand Lake ☎ 970/627-3479.

EMERGENCIES Call 911. You can also call the park's dispatch office at 970/586-1203. There are emergency phones at Cow Creek, Lawn Lake, Longs Peak, and Wild Basin trailheads. Medical assistance is available at visitor centers and ranger stations at Longs Peak and Wild Basin (daily in summer, weekends only in winter). Estes Park and Grandy have medical centers.

🆘 LOST AND FOUND It's at the backcountry office next to Beaver Meadows Visitor Center (970/586-1242), or, on the west side of the park, at Kawuneeche Visitor Center (970/586-1206).

PERMITS From May through October, the backcountry camping cost is $15 per party

(it's free the rest of the year, but you'll still need the permit). You can pick up the permit at the backcountry office, east of Beaver Meadows Visitor Center, or at Kawuneeche Visitor Center. Phone reservations for backcountry campsites can be made between March 1 and May 15 and after October 1 by calling the backcountry office at 970/586-1242. To fish in the park, you must have a valid Colorado fishing license if you're more than 16 years old. Licenses are available from sporting goods stores.

POST OFFICES
📮 **Estes Park Post Office** ⊠ 215 W. Riverside Dr., Estes Park ☎ 970/586-0170. **Grand Lake Post Office** ⊠ 520 Center Dr., Grand Lake ☎ 970/627-3340.

PUBLIC TELEPHONES These may be found at the Beaver Meadows, Kawuneeche, and Fall River visitor centers and at most park campgrounds. Cell-phone reception is good in much of the park.

RELIGIOUS SERVICES For services, look in Estes Park and Grand Lake.

RESTROOMS Public restrooms may be found at all visitor centers and campgrounds, at several picnic areas, and at Bear Lake, Sprague Lake, Lawn Lake trailhead, Timber Lake trailhead, and Milner Pass.

SHOPS & GROCERS Most park campgrounds sell ice and firewood; for groceries, head to Estes Park or Grand Lake.

### NEARBY TOWN INFORMATION
🏛 **Estes Park Convention and Visitors Bureau** ⊠ 500 Big Thompson Ave., Estes Park 80517 ☎ 800/443-7837 ⊕ www.EstesParkCVB.com. **Grand Lake Area Chamber of Commerce** ⊠ 14700 U.S. 34, Grand Lake 80447 ☎ 800/531-1019 ⊕ www.grandlakechamber.com.

### VISITOR INFORMATION
🏛 **Rocky Mountain National Park** ⊠ 1000 U.S. 36, Estes Park, CO 80517-8397 ☎ 970/586-1206 ⊕ www.nps.gov/romo.

# Saguaro National Park

Saguaro Cactus, Saguaro National Park

**WORD OF MOUTH**

"Nothing so symbolizes the Southwestern lowlands as a single plant, the saguaro."

–Nature writer Carle Hodge

# WELCOME TO SAGUARO

## TOP REASONS TO GO

★ **Saguaro sightseeing:** Hike, bike, or drive through dense saguaro stands for an up-close look at this king of all cacti.

★ **Wildlife watching:** Diverse wildlife roams the park, including such ground dwellers as javelinas, coyotes, and rattlesnakes, and winged residents ranging from the migratory lesser long-nosed bat to the diminutive elf owl.

Ferruginous Hawk

★ **Ancient artwork:** Get a glimpse into the past at the numerous rock-art sites where ancient peoples etched into the stones as far back as 5,000 BC.

**1** Tucson Mountain District. Also called Saguaro West, this more-visited district makes up less than one-third of the park. Here you'll find a Native American video orientation to hiking trails, an ancient Hohokam petroglyph site at Signal Hill, and a scenic drive through dense desert growth.

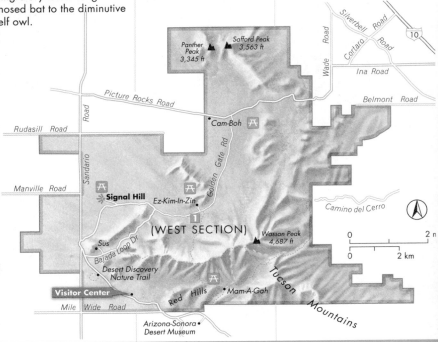

ARIZONA

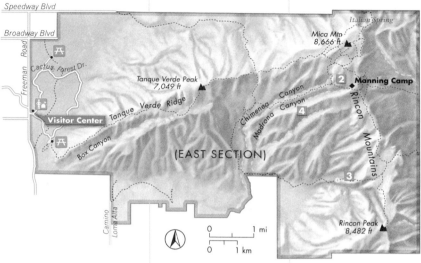

Speedway Blvd

Broadway Blvd

Freeman Road

Cactus Forest Dr.

Italian Spring

Mica Mtn
8,666 ft

Tanque Verde Peak
7,049 ft

**Manning Camp**
2

**Visitor Center**

Tanque Verde Ridge

Chimenea Canyon

Madrona Canyon

Rincon Canyon

4

Rincon Mountains

Box Canyon

(EAST SECTION)

3

Camino Loma Alta

Rincon Peak
8,482 ft

0        1 mi

0        1 km

**2** Rincon Mountain District. On the eastern side of Tucson in the Rincon Mountains, Saguaro East encompasses 57,930 acres of designated wilderness area, an easily accessible scenic loop drive, several easy and intermediate trails through the cactus forest, and opportunities for adventure and backcountry camping at six rustic campgrounds.

**3** Rincon Valley Area. This 4,011-acre expansion along the southern border of Saguaro's Rincon Mountain District offers access to the riparian area along Rincon Creek.

**4** Saguaro Wilderness Area. In the Rincon Mountain District, this backcountry area travels from desert scrublands at 3,000 feet to mixed conifer forests at 9,000 feet.

## GETTING ORIENTED

Saguaro preserves some of the densest stands of these massive cacti, which can live up to 200 years and weigh up to two tons. Today more than 90,000 acres include habitats stretching from the arid Sonoran Desert up to high mountain forests. The park is split into two sections, with Tucson, Arizona, sandwiched in the middle. The urban base proves useful, but the park is no less rugged. More than half of it is designated wilderness area.

| KEY | |
|---|---|
|  | |
| 👫 | Ranger Station |
| ⛺ | Campground |
| 🌲 | Picnic Area |
| 🍴 | Restaurant |
| 🏨 | Lodge |
| 🚶 | Trailhead |
| 🚻 | Restrooms |
| ⇗ | Scenic Viewpoint |
| ·········· | Walking/Hiking Trails |
| ·········· | Bicycle Path |

# SAGUARO PLANNER

## When to Go

Saguaro never gets crowded; however, **most people visit in milder weather, December through April.** December through February is cool and prone to gentle afternoon rain showers. The spring months from March through May offer bright, sunny days and desert wildflowers in bloom. Because of high temperatures, it's best to visit the park in the early morning or late afternoon from June through August. The intense heat puts off most hikers, at least at lower elevations, and lodging prices are much cheaper—rates at top resorts in Tucson drop by as much as 70%. The cooler temperatures in September, October and November are perfect for hiking and camping throughout the park.

The wildlife, from bobcats to jackrabbits, is most active in early morning and at dusk. In spring and summer lizards and snakes are out and about, but keep a low profile during the midday heat.

## Flora & Fauna

The saguaro may be the centerpiece of Saguaro National Park, but more than 1,200 plant species, including 50 types of cactus, thrive in the park. Among the most common cacti here are the prickly pear, barrel cactus, and teddy bear cholla—named so because it appears cuddly, but rangers advise packing a comb to pull its barbed hooks from unwary fingers.

For many of the desert fauna, the saguaro functions as a high-rise hotel. Each spring, the Gila woodpecker and gilded flicker create holes in the cactus and then nest there. When they give up their temporary digs, elf owls, cactus wrens, sparrow hawks, and other avians move in, as do dangerous Africanized honeybees.

You're not likely to encounter the six species of rattlesnake and the Gila monster, a venomous lizard, that inhabit the park, but avoid sticking your hands or feet under rocks or into crevices. If you do get bitten, get to a clinic or hospital as soon as possible.

## Getting There & Around

Saguaro National Park's two distinct sections flank the city of Tucson. Both districts are about a half-hour drive from central Tucson. To reach Rincon Mountain District (east section) from Interstate 10, take exit 257 or exit 275 then go east on Speedway Boulevard to Old Spanish Trail and turn right. To reach Tucson Mountain District from Interstate 10, take exit 242 or exit 257, then Speedway Boulevard (the name will change to Gates Pass Road) west to Kinney Road and turn right.

In the western section, Bajada Loop Drive takes you through the park and to various trailheads; Cactus Forest Drive does the same for the eastern section.

AVG. HIGH/LOW TEMPS.

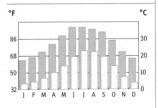

32

By Carrie
Miner

Standing sentinel in the desert, the towering saguaro is perhaps the most familiar emblem of the Southwest. Known for their height (often 50 feet) and arms reaching out in weird configurations, these slow-growing giants can take 15 years to grow a foot high and up to 75 years to grow their first arm. They are found only in the Sonoran Desert, and the largest concentration is in Saguaro National Park. In late spring (usually May), the succulent's top is covered with tiny white blooms—the Arizona state flower. The cacti are protected by state and federal laws, so don't disturb them.

## Scenic Drives

**Bajada Loop Drive.** This 6-mi drive winds through thick stands of saguaros and offers two picnic areas and a few short hikes, including one to a rock-art site. Although the road is unpaved and moderately bumpy, it's a worthwhile trade-off for access to some of the park's densest desert growth. It's one way between Hugh Norris Trail and Golden Gate Road, so if you want to make the complete circuit, travel counterclockwise. The road is susceptible to flash floods during the monsoon season, so check road conditions at the visitor center before proceeding. ⊠ *Saguaro West.*

★ **Cactus Forest Drive.** This paved 8-mi drive provides a great overview of all Saguaro has to offer. The one-way road, which circles clockwise, also has several turnouts that make it easy to stop and linger over the scenery or stop at one of two picnic areas or three easy nature trails. This road was repaved in 2006 and now offers more scenic pullouts, new roadside displays, and wider bicycle lanes. This road is open from 7 AM to sunset daily. ⊠ *Saguaro East.*

## SAGUARO IN ONE DAY

Before setting off, choose which section of the park to visit today, and pack a lunch. Also bring plenty of water—you are likely to get dehydrated and you can't depend on finding water in the park.

In the western section, start out by watching the 15-minute slide show at the **Red Hills Visitor Center,** then stroll along the ½-mi-long **Desert Discovery Trail.**

In your car, head north along Kinney Road, then turn right onto the graded dirt **Bajada Loop Drive.** Before long you'll soon see a turnoff for the **Hugh Norris Trail** on your right. Hike up, and after about 45 minutes, you'll reach a perfect spot for a picnic. Hike back down and drive along the Bajada Loop Drive until you reach the turnoff for **Signal Hill.** From here, it's a short walk to the **Hohokam petroglyphs.**

Alternatively, in the eastern section, pick up a free map of the hiking trails at the **Saguaro East Visitor Center.** Drive south along the paved **Cactus Forest Drive** to the Javelina picnic area, where you'll see signs for the **Freeman Homestead Trail,** an easy 1-mi loop that winds through a stand of mesquite as interpretive signs describe early inhabitants in the Tucson basin. If you're reasonably fit you might want to tackle part of the **Tanque Verde Ridge Trail,** which affords excellent views of saguaro-studded hillsides.

Along the northern loop of the Cactus Forest Drive is **Cactus Forest Trail,** which branches off into several fairly level paths. You can easily spend the rest of the afternoon strolling among the saguaro.

## What to See

### Historic Site

**Manning Camp.** The summer home of Levi Manning, onetime Tucson mayor, was a popular gathering spot for the city's elite in the early 1900s. The cabin can be reached via one of several challenging high-country trails: Douglas Spring Trail to Cow Head Saddle Trail (12 mi), Turkey Creek Trail (7½-mi), and Tanque Verde Ridge Trail (15⁴⁄₁₀-mi). The cabin itself is not open for viewing. ⊠ *Douglas Spring Trail (6 mi) to Cow Head Saddle Trail (6 mi).*

### Scenic Stop

**Signal Hill.** The most impressive petroglyphs, and the only ones with explanatory signs, are on the Bajada Loop Drive in Saguaro West. An easy 5-minute stroll from the signposted parking area takes you to one of the largest gatherings of rock carvings in the Southwest. You'll have a close-up view of the designs left by the Hohokam people between AD 900 and 1200, including large spirals some believe are astronomical markers. ⊠ *4½ mi north of visitor center on Bajada Loop Dr.*

### Visitor Centers

Neither center serves coffee; they do sell bottled water.

**Red Hills Visitor Center.** Take in gorgeous views of nearby mountains and the surrounding desert from the center's large windows and shaded outdoor terrace. A spacious gallery is filled with educational exhibits and a lifelike display simulates the flora and fauna of the region. A 15-minute slide show, "Voices of a Desert," offers a poetic, Native American perspective of the saguaro. Park rangers and volunteers provide maps and suggest hikes to suit your interests. A nicely appointed gift shop and bookstore add to the experience. ⊠ *2700 N. Kinney Rd., Saguaro West* ☎ *520/733–5158* ☉ *Daily 9–5.*

**Saguaro East Visitor Center.** Stop here to pick up free maps and printed materials on various aspects of the park, including maps of hiking trails and backcountry camping permits (Red Hills Visitor Center does not offer permits). Exhibits at the center are comprehensive, and a relief map of the park lays out the complexities of this protected landscape. A 15-minute "Home in the Desert" slide-show program gives the history of the region, and there is a short self-guided nature hike along the Cactus Garden Trail. A small, select variety of books and other gift items are sold here too. ⊠ *3693 S. Old Spanish Trail, Saguaro East* ☎ *520/733–5153* ☉ *Daily 9–5.*

## Sports & the Outdoors

### Bicycling

**Cactus Forest Drive.** Expansive vistas of saguaro-covered hills in Saguaro East highlight this paved 8-mi loop road. Go slowly during the first few hundred yards because of an unexpectedly sharp curve. Snakes and javelinas traverse the roads. ⊠ *Saguaro East Visitor Center.*

**Cactus Forest Trail.** Accessed from Cactus Forest Drive, the 2½-mi trail near Saguaro East Visitor Center is a sand, single track with varied terrain. It's good for both beginning and experienced mountain bikers who don't mind sharing the path with hikers and the occasional horse, to whom bikers must yield. You'll see plenty of wildlife and older, larger saguaro alongside palo verde and mesquite trees. ⊠ *1 mi south of Saguaro East Visitor Center on Cactus Forest Dr.*

OUTFITTERS & EXPEDITIONS **Tucson Bicycles.** In the Tucson foothills, this shop organizes group rides of varying difficulty, and rents road and mountain bikes. ⊠ *4743 E. Sunrise Dr., Tucson* ☎ *520/577–7374.*

### Bird-watching

To check out the more than 200 species of birds living or migrating through the park, begin by focusing your binoculars on the limbs of the saguaros, where many birds make their home. In general, early morning and early evening are the best times for sightings. In winter and spring volunteer-led birding hikes begin at the visitor centers.

The finest areas to flock to in the Rincon Mountain District are the Desert Ecology Trail, where you may find rufous-winged sparrow, verdins, and Cooper's hawks along the washes, and the Javelina picnic area, where you will most likely spot canyon wrens and black-chinned sparrows. At the Tucson Mountain District, sit down on one of the visitor center benches and look for ash-throated flycatchers, Say's phoebes, curve-billed

---

## GOOD READS

| | |
|---|---|
| **All About Saguaros** by Carle Hodge sports fabulous color photos of the cactus. | **Story Behind the Scenery** by Christopher L. Helms give general park introductions. |
| **Saguaro National Park** by Doris Evans and **Sonoran Desert: The** | The **Tucson Hiking Guide** by Betty Leavengood is full of day hikes. |

---

thrashers, and Gila woodpeckers. During the cooler months keep a lookout for the wintering neotropical migrants such as hummingbirds, swallows, orioles, and warblers.

OUTFITTERS & EXPEDITIONS **Audubon Nature Shop.** Run by the Tucson Audubon Society, this shop carries field guides, binoculars, and other items of interest to birders. It can provide a list of local independent guides who will take you out birding. The society also operates a 24-hour recorded message about sightings of rare or interesting birds. ⊠ *300 E. University Blvd., Tucson* ☏ *520/ 629–0510 shop, 520/798–1005 recording.*

**Borderlands.** This organization conducts weeklong birding tours about three times yearly in southeastern Arizona, with trips originating in Tucson. ⊠ *2550 W. Calle Padilla, Tucson* ☏ *520/882–7650.*

**Nature Conservancy.** Contact this national organization's local branch about bird-watching trips in nature preserves. ⊠ *1510 E. Fort Lowell Rd., Tucson* ☏ *520/622–3861.*

### Hiking

The park has more than 100 mi of trails. The shorter hikes, such as the Desert Discovery and Desert Ecology trails, are perfect for those looking to learn about the desert ecosystem without expending too much energy.

Rattlesnakes are commonly seen on trails; so are coyotes, javelinas, roadrunners, Gambel's quail, and desert spiny lizards. Hikers should keep their distance from all wildlife.

EASY **Cactus Garden Trail.** This 100-yard paved trail in front of the Red Hills Visitor Center is wheelchair accessible and has resting benches and interpretive signs about common desert plants.

**Desert Discovery Trail.** Learn about plants and animals native to the region on this paved path in Saguaro West. The ½-mi loop is wheelchair accessible and has resting benches and ramadas (wooden shelters that supply shade for your table). ⊠ *1 mi north of Red Hills Visitor Center.*

**Desert Ecology Trail.** Exhibits on this ¼-mi loop near the Mica View picnic area explain how local plants and animals subsist on a limited supply of water. ⊠ *2 mi north of Saguaro East Visitor Center.*

**Freeman Homestead Trail.** Learn a bit about the history of homesteading in the region on this 1-mi loop. Look for owls living in the cliffs above as you make your way through the lowland vegetation. ⊠ *2 mi south of Saguaro East Visitor Center at Javelina picnic area.*

### DID YOU KNOW?

Great horned owls can be heard from several miles away. They have a wide range of calls, from the high-pitched screech of owl young to adults' classic low hoots. Listen for horned owls just before dawn and from dusk until midnight.

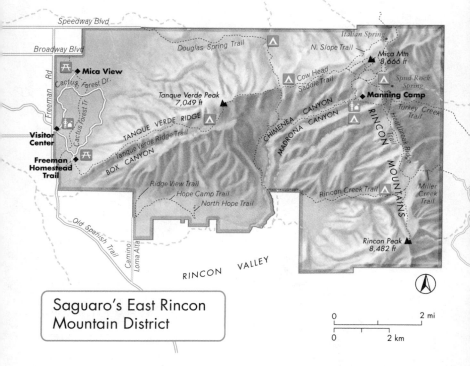

## Saguaro's East Rincon Mountain District

**MODERATE**  **Douglas Spring Trail.** This challenging 6-mi trail leads almost due east into the Rincon Mountains. After a half mile through a dense concentration of saguaros you reach the open desert. About 3 mi in is Bridal Wreath Falls, worth a slight detour in early spring when melting snow creates a larger cascade. Blackened tree trunks at the Douglas Spring Campground are one of the few traces of a huge fire that swept through the area in 1989. ⊠ *Eastern end of Speedway Blvd.*

**Fodor'sChoice**  **Hope Camp Trail.** Well worth the 5⁹⁄₁₀-mi round-trip trek, this Rincon Val-
★  ley Area hike offers gorgeous views of the Tanque Verde Ridge and Rincon Peak. ⊠ *From the Camino Loma Alta trailhead to Hope Camp.*

**Valley View Overlook Trail.** On clear days you can spot the distinctive slope of Picacho Peak from this 1½-mi trail in Saguaro West. Even on an overcast day you'll be treated to splendid vistas of Avra Valley. ⊠ *3 mi north of Red Hills Visitor Center on Bajada Loop Dr.*

**DIFFICULT**  **Hugh Norris Trail.** This 10-mi trail through the Tucson Mountains is one
**Fodor'sChoice**  of the most impressive in the Southwest. It's full of switchbacks and some
★  sections are moderately steep, but at the top of 4,687-foot Wasson Peak you'll enjoy views of the saguaro forest spread across the *bajada* (the gently rolling hills at the base of taller mountains). ⊠ *2½ mi north of Red Hills Visitor Center on Bajada Loop Dr.*

★ **Tanque Verde Ridge Trail.** Be rewarded with spectacular scenery on this 15⁴/₁₀-mi trail through desert scrub, oak, alligator juniper, and pinyon pine at the 6,000-foot peak, where views of the surrounding mountain ranges from both sides of the ridge delight. ⊠ *2 mi south of Saguaro East Visitor Center at Javelina picnic area.*

**32**

### Horseback Riding

More than 100 mi of trails in the park are open to use by livestock (mules, donkeys, and horses); however, animals are prohibited from off-trail travel and require a special permit, which can be obtained in person at one of the visitor centers or by mail. No grazing is allowed in the park.

OUTFITTERS & EXPEDITIONS  **Corcoraque Ranch** (⊠ Mile Wide Rd., Tucson ☎ 520/682–8594) wranglers lead riders into Saguaro West.

**Pantano Riding Stables** (⊠ 4450 South Houghton Rd., Tucson ☎ 520/298–8980) is a reliable operator offering one- and two-hour rides.

## Educational Offerings

**Junior Ranger Programs.** Offered several times in June, for 2-3 days at a time, a **camp** for kids 5–12 includes daily hikes and workshops on pottery and petroglyphs. In the **Junior Ranger Discovery program,** young visitors can pick up an activity pack and complete it within an hour or two. ⊠ *Saguaro East Visitor Center* ☎ *520/733–5153* ⊠ *Red Hills Visitor Center* ☎ *520/733–5158.*

**Orientation Programs.** Daily programs introduce the desert. You might find slide shows on bats, birds, or desert blooms, naturalist-led hikes, and in the summer only, films. ⊠ *Saguaro East Visitor Center* ☎ *520/733–5153* ⊠ *Red Hills Visitor Center* ☎ *520/733–5158* ⊠ *Free* ☉ *Daily.*

**Ranger Talks.** Hear about wildlife, geology, and archaeology. ⊠ *Saguaro East Visitor Center* ☎ *520/733–5153* ⊠ *Red Hills Visitor Center* ☎ *520/733–5158* ⊠ *Free* ☉ *Nov.–mid-Apr.*

# WHAT'S NEARBY

While Saguaro stands as a protected desert oasis, metropolitan **Tucson,** Arizona's second-largest city, lies between the two park sections. Spread over 195 mi, and with a population of more than 900,000, Tucson averages 340 days of sunshine and only 12 inches of rain annually.

## Nearby Attractions

### Tucson Attractions

☺ **Arizona–Sonora Desert Museum.** The name "museum" is misleading; this
Fodor'sChoice  delightful site is a beautifully planned zoo and botanical garden featur-
★  ing the animals and plants of the Sonoran Desert. The coyote and javelina exhibits have "invisible" fencing that separates humans from animals, and the Riparian Corridor section affords great underwater views of otters and beavers. ⊠ *2021 N. Kinney Rd., Tucson* ☎ *520/883–2702* ⊕ *www.desertmuseum.org* ⊠ *June–Aug., $9; Sept.–May, $12*

☉ *Mar.–Sept., daily 7:30–5; Oct.–Feb., daily 8:30–5. Last ticket sales 1 hr before closing.*

**Old Tucson Studios.** This film studio–cum–theme park, originally built for the 1940 motion picture *Arizona,* has been used to shoot countless movies, such as *Rio Bravo* (1959) and *The Quick and the Dead* (1994), and the TV shows *Gunsmoke, Bonanza,* and *Highway to Heaven.* Actors in Western garb perform and roam the streets, talking to visitors. Youngsters enjoy the simulated gunfights, rides, stunt shows, and petting farm, while adults might appreciate the screenings of old Westerns. ⊠ *Tucson Mountain Park, 201 S. Kinney Rd., Tucson* ☎ *520/883–0100* ⊕ *www.oldtucson.com* ᐧ *$14.95* ☉ *Sun.–Fri. 10–3, Sat. 10–4.*

★ **Sabino Canyon.** Come to this oasis in Coronado National Forest to hike, picnic, and enjoy the waterfalls, streams, swimming holes, and shade trees. No cars are allowed, but a narrated tram ride (about 45 minutes round-trip) takes you up a WPA-built road to the top of the canyon; you can hop off and on at any of the nine stops or hike any of the numerous trails. There's also a tram ride to Bear Canyon, where a rewarding hike leads to Seven Falls. The 7⁷⁄₁₀-mi round-trip hike is moderately easy and fun, crisscrossing the stream several times on the way up the canyon. Kids enjoy the boulder-hopping, and all are rewarded with pools and waterfalls as well as views at the top. ■ TIP→ **If you're in Tucson near a full moon, take the special night tram and watch the desert come alive with nocturnal critters.** ⊠ *5700 N. Sabino Canyon Rd., at Sunrise Dr., Tucson* ☎ *520/749–2861 recorded tram information, 520/749–8700 visitor center* ⊕ *www.fs.fed.us/r3/coronado* ᐧ *$5 per vehicle per day or $20 for an annual pass; tram $7.50; Bear Canyon tram $3* ☉ *Visitor center weekdays 8–4:30, weekends 8:30–4:30; call for tram schedules.*

**St. Augustine Cathedral.** Construction began in 1896 on this striking white-and-beige Spanish-style building modeled after the Cathedral of Queretaro in Mexico. ■ TIP→ **For a distinctly Southwestern experience, attend the mariachi mass celebrated Sunday at 8 AM.** ⊠ *192 S. Stone Ave., Tucson* ☎ *520/623–6351* ᐧ *Free* ☉ *Daily 7–6.*

### Nearby Attraction

**Colossal Cave Mountain Park.** Guides discuss the fascinating crystal formations of this limestone grotto and relate the many romantic tales surrounding the cave, including the legend that an enormous sum of money stolen in a stagecoach robbery is hidden here. Cave tours last 45 minutes and include 363 steps. ⊠ *Intersection of Colossal Cave Rd. and E. Old Spanish Trail, Vail (20 mi east of Tucson)* ☎ *520/647–7275* ⊕ *colossalcave.com* ᐧ *$3 per car* ☉ *Mid-Sept.–mid-Mar., Mon.–Sat. 9–5, Sun. and holidays 9–6; mid-Mar.–mid-Sept., Mon.–Sat. 8–6, Sun. and holidays 8–7.*

## Area Activities

### Sports & the Outdoors

BALLOONING  **Fleur de Tucson Balloon Tours** (⌂ 4635 N. Caida Pl., Tucson 85718 ☎ 520/529–1025) flies over the Tucson Mountains and Sagauro West, or over the Avra Valley.

32

## FESTIVALS & EVENTS

**JAN.-FEB. Tucson Gem, Mineral and Fossil Showcase.** This huge trade show, the largest of its kind in the world, offers everything from precious stones to geodes to beads. It's held at the Tucson Convention Center. ☎ *800/638-8350.*

**FEB. La Fiesta de los Vaqueros.** America's largest outdoor midwinter rodeo, with more than 600 events, takes place on the Tucson Rodeo Grounds. ☎ *520/741-2233.*

**APR. Fiesta de Saguaro.** A celebration of the Hispanic culture and heritage is held at the Rincon Mountain District in Saguaro National Park. ☎ *520/733-5153.*

**JULY Saguaro Harvest Celebration.** This celebration at Colossal Cave Mountain Park in Vail, AZ, centers on the majestic saguaro and the summer harvest of its fruit. ☎ *520/647-7121.*

BASEBALL    Spring training brings the **Arizona Diamondbacks,** the **Chicago White Sox,** and the **Colorado Rockies** to Tucson from mid-February until the end of March. The Diamondbacks and White Sox play at Tucson Electric Park (✉ 2400 E. Ajo Way, Tucson ☎ 520/434–1367), and the Rockies play at Hi Corbett Field (✉ 3400 E. Camino Campestre, Tucson ☎ 520/327–9467).

BIRD-WATCHING    Naturalist and illustrator Roger Tory Peterson (1908–96) considered Tucson one of the country's top birding spots. Sabino Canyon is alive with cactus and canyon wrens, hawks, and quail. Spring and summer, when species of migrants come in from Mexico, are great hummingbird seasons. In the nearby Santa Rita Mountains and Madera Canyon, you can see elegant trogons nesting in early spring.

### Tour Options

ADVENTURE & ECOTOURS    **Sunshine Jeep Tours** (☎ 520/742–1943) and **Trail Dust Adventures** (☎ 520/747–0323) arrange trips into the Sonoran Desert.

MISSION TOURS    In the spring and fall, those interested in visiting the area's historic missions can contact **Kino Mission Tours** (☎ 520/628–1269), which has professional historians and bilingual guides on staff.

## Arts & Entertainment

Tucson has a symphony, opera, theater, and ballet. The free *Tucson Weekly* (⊕ www.tucsonweekly.com) and the "Caliente" section of the *Arizona Daily Star* (⊕ www.azstarnet.com) list town happenings.

## Shopping

**Summit Hut.** This is an excellent place to pick up any hiking or camping supplies you may have forgotten. It also carries snakebite kits. ✉ *5045 E. Speedway Blvd.* ☎ *520/325–1554* ⊕ *www.summithut.com.*

**Western Warehouse** (✉ 3719 N. Oracle Rd., ☎ 520/293–1808 ✉ 6701 E. Broadway Blvd., ☎ 520/885–4385) is the place if you want to go where native Tucsonans shop for their everyday Western duds.

# WHERE TO STAY & EAT

### About the Restaurants

At Saguaro, you won't find more than a Southwest sampling of jams, hot sauces, and candy bars at the two visitor centers' gift shops. However, five picnic areas in the West district, and two in the East, offer scenery and shade. Tucson, sandwiched neatly between the two districts, offers some of the best Mexican and Southwestern cuisine in the country.

### About the Hotels

While there are no hotels within the park, its immediate proximity to Tucson makes finding a place to stay easy. Some ranches and smaller accommodations close during the hottest months of summer, but many inexpensive B&Bs and hotels are open year-round.

### About the Campgrounds

There's no drive-up camping in the park; all six primitive campgrounds require a hike to reach—the shortest hikes are to Douglas Spring Campground (6-mi) and to Happy Valley (5-mi). All are open year-round. Pick up your backcountry camping permit ($6 per night) at the Saguaro East Visitor Center. Before choosing a camping destination, look over the relief map of hiking trails and the book of wilderness campground photos taken by park rangers. You can camp in the backcountry for a maximum of 14 days. Each site can accommodate up to six people. Reservations can be made via mail or in person up to two months in advance. Hikers are encouraged to set out before noon. Several more relaxed camping opportunities exist within just a few miles of the park.

## Where to Eat

### In the Park

PICNIC AREAS   Each picnic area has a wheelchair-accessible pit toilet.

**Cam-Boh.** More locals than tourists are found at this "countryside" spot with lovely views of the Tucson Mountain range. ⊠ *Picture Rocks Rd. near Golden Gate Rd., Saguaro West.*

**Ez-Kim-In-Zin.** Named after an Apache chief, this picnic area is set on a rocky hillside at the start of the Sendero Esperanza Trail. ⊠ *1 mi from Bajada Loop Dr. on Golden Gate Rd., Saguaro West.*

**Mam-A-Gah.** This is the most isolated picnic area in Saguaro West. It's on King Canyon Trail, a good area for birding and wildflower viewing. It's about a mile walk to reach the site, and the undeveloped trail is not wheelchair accessible. ⊠ *King Canyon Trail, 1 mi from Kinney Rd.*

**Mica View.** Talk about truth in advertising: This picnic area gives you an eyeful of Mica Mountain, the park's highest peak. None of the tables are in the shade. ⊠ *2 mi north of Saguaro East Visitor Center on Cactus Forest Dr.*

**Signal Hill.** Because of the nearby petroglyphs, this is the park's most popular picnic site. Its many picnic tables, sprinkled around palo verde and mesquite trees, can accommodate large groups. ⊠ *4½ mi north of Red Hills Visitor Center on Bajada Loop Dr.*

## Outside the Park

**$$$–$$$$** ✕ **The Grill at Hacienda del Sol.** Tucked into the foothills and surrounded by flowering gardens, this special-occasion restaurant, a favorite for locals to take out-of-town visitors, provides an alternative to the chili-laden dishes of most Southwestern nouvelle cuisine. Wild mushroom bisque, pecan-grilled buffalo, and pan-seared sea bass are among the menu choices. Tapas (and most items on the full menu) can be enjoyed on the more casual outdoor patio, accented by live flamenco guitar music. ⊠ *Hacienda del Sol Guest Ranch Resort, 5601 N. Hacienda del Sol Rd., Tucson* ☎ *520/529–3500. $21–$39* ▭ *AE, DC, MC, V.*

**$$–$$$** ✕ **Soleil.** Watch the sun set over the Tucson Mountains from the outdoor terrace or the panoramic picture window inside—then gaze at the twinkling city lights below as you feast on contemporary fare like caramelized sea scallops or filet mignon with sweet corn and shiitake mushrooms. A full vegetarian menu with vegan options also shines. ⊠ *El Cortijo, 3001 E. Skyline Dr., Foothills* ☎ *520/299–3345. $17–$26* ▭ *AE, D, MC, V* ☉ *Closed Mon.*

**$$–$$$** ✕ **Vivace.** Decorated in warm gold and rust tones, this Italian bistro in the lovely St. Philip's Plaza has long been a favorite with locals. Wild mushrooms and goat cheese in puff pastry is hard to resist as a starter. Follow this with the fettuccine with grilled salmon. For dessert, the molten chocolate cake with spumoni ice cream is worth the 20 minutes it takes to create. ⊠ *4310 N. Campbell Ave., Tucson* ☎ *520/795–7221. $14–$30* ▭ *AE, D, MC, V* ☉ *Closed Sun.*

**★ $–$$** ✕ **Zona 78.** Fresh food takes on a whole new meaning at this contemporary bistro emphasizing inventive pizzas, pastas, and salads. The casual interior's focal point is a huge stone oven, where the pies are fired with toppings like Australian blue cheese, kalamata olives, sausage, and even chicken with peanut sauce. Whole-wheat crust is an option. ⊠ *78 W. River Rd., Central* ☎ *520/888–7878. $9–$18* ▭ *AE, D, MC, V* ☉ *No lunch Sun.*

**¢–$** ✕ **Mi Nidito.** A favorite among locals (be prepared to wait awhile), Mi
Fodor'sChoice Nidito—"my little nest"—has hosted its share of celebrities. Following
★ President Clinton's lunch here, the rather hefty "Presidential Plate" (bean tostada, taco with barbecued meat, chiles rellenos, chicken enchilada, and beef tamale with rice and beans) was added to the menu. Top that off with the mango chimichangas for dessert, and you're talking executive privilege. ⊠ *1813 S. 4th Ave., Tucson* ☎ *520/622–5081. $4–$11* ▭ *AE, DC, MC, V* ☉ *Closed Mon. and Tues.*

**¢–$** ✕ **Tony's.** En route to Saguaro East, stop at this deli to pick up some supplies—a prosciutto and provolone hero, say, accompanied by imported olives and potato salad. For comfort food after hiking, come by for lasagna on the way back. ⊠ *6219 E. 22nd St., Tucson* ☎ *520/747–0070. $5–$11* ▭ *AE, D, MC, V* ☉ *Closed Sun.*

## Where to Stay

### In the Park

CAMPGROUNDS & RV PARKS

⚠ **Douglas Spring.** Getting to this 4,800-foot-elevation campground takes a not-too-rough 6-mi hike up the Douglas Spring Trail. ✉ *6 mi on Douglas Spring Trail, off Speedway Blvd.* ☎ *No phone* ⌁ *3 sites.*

⚠ **Grass Shack.** This pretty campground is among juniper and small oak trees in a transitional area midway up Mica Mountain. ✉ *10³/₁₀ mi via Douglas Spring Trail to Manning Camp Trail* ☎ *No phone* ⌁ *3 sites.*

⚠ **Happy Valley.** The 5-mi hike to this isolated campground begins at the Miller Creek trailhead and continues south on Rincon Creek Trail. To reach it, take the Mescal, J-Six Ranch exit (no. 297) off Interstate 10 and go north on USFS Route 35. Sixteen miles north of Interstate 10 is a sign for the Miller Creek Trail. Turn left and travel ²/₁₀ mi to the trailhead. ✉ *5 mi via Miller Creek Trail and Rincon Creek Trail* ☎ *No phone* ⌁ *3 sites.*

⚠ **Juniper Basin.** Vegetation here is oak forest, and the expansive views are worth the challenging, 7-mi ascent. ✉ *7 mi on Tanque Verde Ridge Trail* ☎ *No phone* ⌁ *3 sites.*

⚠ **Manning Camp.** Of the park's campgrounds, only this one has water year-round, but it has to be treated. Reach it via a 12-mi hike up the Douglas Spring Trail and Cow Head Saddle Trail, the 7½-mi Turkey Creek Trail or the Tanque Verde Ridge Trail. ✉ *6 mi on Douglas Spring Trail, then 6 mi on Cow Head Saddle Trail* ☎ *No phone* ⌁ *6 sites. Free.*

⚠ **Spud Rock Camp.** Set in the same higher-elevation forest as Manning Camp, this campground has a spring with intermittent water, which must be treated. ✉ *7 mi on Turkey Creek Trail* ☎ *No phone* ⌁ *3 sites. Free.*

## Outside the Park

$$$$
Fodor'sChoice
★

🏨 **Arizona Inn.** This 1930 inn on the National Register of Historic Places boasts spacious rooms in pink adobe-style casitas spread over 14 acres of beautifully landscaped lawns and gardens. Most have private patios, and some have fireplaces. The resort also has two luxurious two-story houses with their own heated pools and full hotel service. The main building houses a library, a fine restaurant, and a cocktail lounge where a jazz pianist plays. ✉ *2200 E. Elm St., Tucson 85719* ☎ *520/325–1541 or 800/933–1093* 🖷 *520/881–5830* ⊕ *www.arizonainn.com* ⌁ *70 rooms, 16 suites, 3 casitas* ⌂ *2 restaurants, public Internet, room service, tennis courts, pool, gym, bar, laundry services, no-smoking rooms.* *$239–$429* ▤ *AE, DC, MC, V.*

☾ $$$$
Fodor'sChoice
★

🏨 **Tanque Verde Ranch.** The most upscale of Tucson's guest ranches and one of the oldest in the country, the Tanque Verde sits on 640 beautiful acres in the Rincon Mountains next to Saguaro National Park East. Rooms in one-story casitas have tasteful Western-style furnishings, fireplaces, and picture-window views of the desert. Breakfast and lunch buffets are huge, and barbecues add sizzle to the daily dinner menu. Horseback excursions into the national park are offered for every skill level (lessons are included in rates), and children can participate in day-long activity programs, from riding to tennis to crafts, leaving parents to their leisure. ✉ *14301 E. Speedway Blvd., Tucson 85748* ☎ *520/296–*

6275 or 800/234–3833 ⊜ 520/721–9426 ⊕ www.tanqueverderanch. com ⟿ 49 rooms, 23 suites, 2 casitas ⌂ Tennis courts, pools, gym, bicycles, children's programs (ages 4–11), no-smoking rooms, no TV. $340–$430 ▭ AE, D, MC, V ⫯⊙⫯ FAP.

**$$$$** ⫯⊙⫯ **White Stallion Ranch.** A number of scenes from *High Chaparral* were
Fodor'sChoice shot on this working, family-run cattle ranch that sits on 3,000 acres
★ abutting Saguaro West. Run by the hospitable True family since 1965,
this place is the real deal. You can ride up to four times daily and join
longer excursions into the national park (on Tuesday and Thursday),
hike in the mountains, enjoy a hayride cookout, and compete in team
cattle penning. Most rooms have original Western furniture, and newer
deluxe rooms have whirlpool baths or fireplaces. Rates include all
meals, riding, and daily entertainment such as rodeos, country dancing,
telescopic stargazing, and campfire sing-alongs. ⊠ 9251 W. Twin Peaks
Rd., Northwest, Tucson 85743 ☎ 520/297–0252 or 888/977–2624
⊜ 520/744–2786 ⊕ www.wsranch.com ⟿ 24 rooms, 17 suites ⌂ Tennis courts, pool, gym, bar, Wi-Fi, airport shuttle, no phone, no TV. $300
▭ No credit cards ⊙ Closed June–Aug. ⫯⊙⫯ FAP.

★ **$$–$$$$** ⫯⊙⫯ **Hacienda del Sol Guest Ranch Resort.** Designed in classic Mexican hacienda style, this former finishing school for girls attracted stars like Clark
Gable, Katharine Hepburn, and Spencer Tracy when it was converted
to a guest ranch during World War II. Some of the one- and two-bedroom casitas have fireplaces and private porches, where you can watch
the sun set over the Tucson Mountains. The property has a no-smoking policy. The superb Grill at Hacienda del Sol is part of the resort.
⊠ 5601 N. Hacienda del Sol Rd., Tucson 85718 ☎ 520/299–1501 or
800/728–6514 ⊜ 520/299–5554 ⊕ www.haciendadelsol.com ⟿ 22
rooms, 8 suites ⌂ Restaurant, pool, no-smoking rooms. $150–$225
▭ AE, D, MC, V.

★ **$$—$$$** ⫯⊙⫯ **Casa Tierra.** Rooms in this lovely B&B with hacienda-style lodging,
5 minutes from Saguaro National Park West, all have private terraces
overlooking a central courtyard and dense desert foliage. The Southwestern-style furnishings include Mexican *equipales* (chairs with pigskin
seats), cool tile floors, and beamed ceilings. A full vegetarian breakfast
served on fine china is included, and there's a media room for those who
can't stand the quiet. There's a minimum stay of two nights and there's
no smoking. ⊠ 11155 W. Calle Pima, Tucson 85743 ☎ 520/578–3058
or 866/254–0006 ⊜ 520/578–8445 ⊕ www.casatierratucson.com ⟿ 3
rooms, 1 suite ⌂ Refrigerator, gym, no TV, no-smoking rooms.
$135–$175 ▭ AE, MC, V ⊙ Closed mid-June–mid-Aug. ⫯⊙⫯ BP.

**$$** ⫯⊙⫯ **Rimrock West.** About 7 mi north of Saguaro National Park East, this
B&B on 20 acres has a panoramic view of Tucson. The artwork in the
adobe ranch house is all by the innkeepers and their son; their studio is
on the property. Attractive rooms open onto a sunny brick courtyard;
a kidney-shape pool occupies its own walled enclosure. Take Catalina
Highway and turn on Prince Street, where the B&B's road is signposted. ⊠ 3450 N. Drake Pl., Tucson 85749 ☎ 520/749–8774 ⟿ 2
rooms, 1 cottage ⌂ Pool. $120 ▭ No credit cards ⫯⊙⫯ BP.

CAMPGROUNDS & ⚠ **Colossal Cave Campground.** The closest non-wilderness camping to
RV PARKS Saguaro East, this first-come, first-served campground still *feels* like the

wilderness. It has no electrical hookups, and the entrance gates close for the night at 6 PM (5 PM in winter) and open at 8 AM (9 AM in winter). ⊠ *Old Spanish Trail, Tucson* ☎ *520/647–7275* 🖷 *520/647–3299* ⊕ *www.colossalcave.com* ⤳ *50 sites* ⚭ *Pit toilets, drinking water, fire grates, picnic tables, public telephone. $5 parking fee* ▭ *No credit cards.*

⚠ **Gilbert Ray Campground.** Slumber amid saguaros at this pleasant spot 4 mi south of the park's West district and just down the road from the Arizona–Sonora Desert Museum. There are no reservations, and no showers, and there's a seven-day limit for stays. ⊠ *W. Kinney Rd., Tucson* ☎ *520/883–4200* ⤳ *130 sites* ⚭ *Grills, flush toilets, drinking water, picnic tables, electricity, dump station. $10, $20 with hookups.*

# SAGUARO ESSENTIALS

ACCESSIBILITY In the western section, the Red Hills Visitor Center and two nearby nature trails are wheelchair accessible. The eastern district's visitor center is accessible, as is the paved Desert Ecology Trail.

ADMISSION FEES Admission to Saguaro is $10 per vehicle and $5 for individuals on foot or bicycle; it is good for seven days from purchase. Annual passes cost $25.

ADMISSION HOURS The park opens at 7 AM and closes at sunset. It is in the Mountain time zone.

ATMS/BANKS
🏧 Circle K ⊠ Ajo Rd. and Kinney Rd., 5 mi south of Saguaro West, Tucson ☎ 520/883–4515. Qwikmart ⊠ Golf Links Rd. and Harrison Rd., 3 mi northwest of Saguaro East, Tucson ☎ 520/298–9120.

AUTOMOBILE SERVICE STATIONS
🚗 Qwikmart ⊠ Golf Links Rd. and Harrison Rd., 3 mi northwest of Saguaro East, Tucson ☎ 520/298–9120 ✉ Sandario Rd. and Picture Rocks Rd., 5 mi north of Saguaro West, Avra Valley ☎ 520/682–7798.

EMERGENCIES To report an emergency, call ☎ 520/733–5158 or ☎ 520/733–5153. After hours, call 911.

LOST AND FOUND Inquire about lost items at the visitor centers.

PERMITS Obtain a required backcountry permit for $6 nightly per campsite from the Saguaro East Visitor Center up to two months in advance.

POST OFFICES
🏤 Tucson Main Post Office ⊠ 1501 Cherrybell St., Tucson 85726 ☎ 800/275–8777 🕓 Weekdays 8:30–8, Sat. 9–1

PUBLIC TELEPHONES There are telephones at the visitor centers. Cell-phone reception is generally good in the eastern district but is unreliable in the western district.

RELIGIOUS SERVICES There are a variety of options in Tucson.

RESTROOMS Public restrooms are available at the visitor centers and at all picnic areas in both sections.

SHOPS & GROCERS There is no place in the park to buy groceries or camping supplies. Plenty of stores are available in Tucson.

**NEARBY TOWN INFORMATION**
🏤 Metropolitan Tucson Convention and Visitors Bureau ⊠ 110 S. Church Ave., Tucson 85701 ☎ 800/638–8350 ⊕ visittucson.org.

**VISITOR INFORMATION**
🏤 Saguaro National Park ⊠ 3693 S. Old Spanish Trail, Tucson AZ 85730 ☎ 520/733–5158 Saguaro West, 520/733–5153 Saguaro East ⊕ nps.gov/sagu.

# Sequoia & Kings Canyon National Parks

Isosceles and Columbine Peak, Dusy Basin, Kings Canyon National Park

## WORD OF MOUTH

"Who of all the dwellers of the plains and prairies and fertile home forests of round-headed oak and maple, hickory and elm, ever dreamed that earth could bear such growths—trees that the familiar pines and firs seem to know nothing about, lonely, silent, serene, with a physiognomy almost godlike; and so old, thousands of them still living had already counted their years by tens of centuries when Columbus set sail from Spain."

–John Muir, *Our National Parks*

# WELCOME TO SEQUOIA & KINGS CANYON

## TOP 5 REASONS TO GO

★ **Gentle giants:** You'll feel small—in a good way—walking among some of the world's largest living things in Sequoia's Giant Forest and Kings Canyon's Grant Grove.

★ **Because it's there:** You can't even glimpse it from the main part of Sequoia, but the sight of majestic Mount Whitney is worth the trek to the eastern face of the High Sierra.

★ **Underground exploration:** Far older even than the giant sequoias, the gleaming limestone formations in Crystal Cave will draw you along dark, marble passages.

★ **A Grander-than-Grand Canyon:** Drive the twisting Kings Canyon Scenic Byway down into the jagged, granite Kings River Canyon, deeper in parts than the Grand Canyon.

★ **Regal solitude:** To spend a day or two hiking in a subalpine world of your own, pick one of the 11 trailheads at Mineral King.

**1** Giant Forest–Lodgepole Village. The most heavily visited area of Sequoia lies at the base of the "thumb" portion of Kings Canyon National Park and contains major sights such as Giant Forest, General Sherman Tree, Crystal Cave, and Moro Rock.

**2** Grant Grove Village–Redwood Canyon. The "thumb" of Kings Canyon National Park is its busiest section, where Grant Grove, General Grant Tree, Panoramic Point, and Big Stump are the main attractions.

**3** Kings River Canyon–Cedar Grove Village. Most visitors to the huge, high-country portion of Kings Canyon National Park don't go farther than Roads End, a few miles east of Cedar Grove on the canyon floor. Here, the river runs through Zumwalt Meadow, surrounded by magnificent granite formations.

**4** Mineral King. In the southeast section of Sequoia, the highest road-accessible part of the park is a good place to hike, camp, and soak up the unspoiled grandeur of the Sierra Nevada.

**5** Mount Whitney. The highest peak in the Lower 48 stands on the eastern edge of Sequoia; to get there from Giant Forest you must either backpack eight days through the mountains or drive nearly 400 mi around the park to its other side.

Climbing Bubbs Creek wall

| KEY | |
|---|---|
| 🚹 | *Ranger Station* |
| ⛺ | *Campground* |
| 🏕 | *Picnic Area* |
| 🍴 | *Restaurant* |
| 🏨 | *Lodge* |
| 🚶 | *Trailhead* |
| 🚻 | *Restrooms* |
| ⚜ | *Scenic Viewpoint* |
| ⋯⋯ | *Walking/Hiking Trails* |
| ⋯⋯ | *Bicycle Path* |

# GETTING ORIENTED

The two parks comprise 865,952 acres, mostly on the western flank of the Sierra. A map of the adjacent parks looks vaguely like a mitten, with the palm of Sequoia National Park south of the north-pointing, skinny thumb and long fingers of Kings Canyon National Park. Between the western thumb and eastern fingers, north of Sequoia, lies part of Sequoia National Forest, which includes Giant Sequoia National Monument.

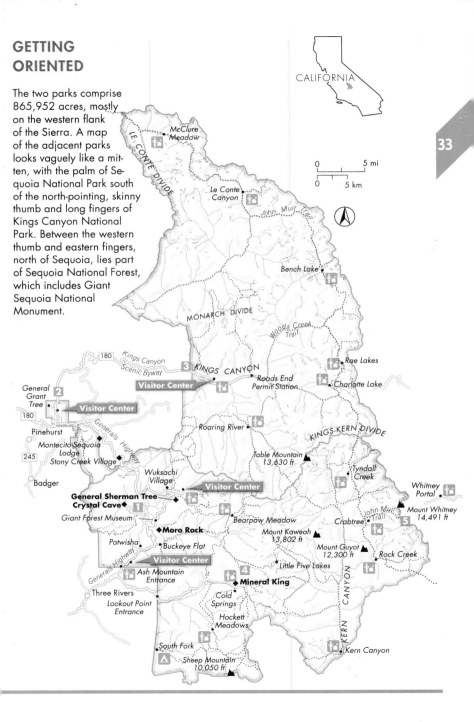

CALIFORNIA

0 ___ 5 mi
0 ___ 5 km

McClure Meadow

LE CONTE DIVIDE

Le Conte Canyon

John Muir Trail

Bench Lake

MONARCH DIVIDE

Woods Creek Trail

Rae Lakes

180  Kings Canyon Scenic Byway

3  KINGS CANYON
Visitor Center

Roads End Permit Station

Charlotte Lake

General Grant Tree  2
Visitor Center

180

Pinehurst

Generals Highway

Roaring River

KINGS-KERN DIVIDE

Montecito-Sequoia Lodge
Stony Creek Village

245

Table Mountain 13,630 ft

Tyndall Creek

Whitney Portal

Badger

Wuksachi Village

Visitor Center

General Sherman Tree
Crystal Cave  1

Giant Forest Museum

Moro Rock

Bearpaw Meadow

Mount Kaweah 13,802 ft

Crabtree

John Muir Trail

Mount Whitney 14,491 ft

5

Potwisha

Buckeye Flat

Mount Guyot 12,300 ft

Rock Creek

Visitor Center

Generals Highway

Ash Mountain Entrance

4  Mineral King

Little Five Lakes

KERN CANYON

Three Rivers

Lookout Point Entrance

Cold Springs

Hockett Meadows

South Fork

Sheep Mountain 10,050 ft

Kern Canyon

# SEQUOIA & KINGS CANYON PLANNER

## When to Go

The best times to visit are late spring and early fall, when temperatures are moderate and crowds are thin. **Summertime can draw hoards of tourists to see the giant sequoias, and the few, narrow roads mean congestion at peak holiday times.** If you must visit in summer, go during the week. By contrast, in wintertime you may feel as though you have the parks all to yourself. But because of heavy snows, sections of the main park roads can be closed without warning, and low-hanging clouds can move in and obscure mountains and valleys for days. Check road and weather conditions before venturing out mid-November to late April.

Temperatures in the chart below are for the mid-level elevations, generally between 4,000 and 7,000 feet. At higher elevations, temperatures drop and precipitation rises; at lower elevations, temperatures rise—by as much as 20°F in summer—and annual precipitation drops.

## Flora & Fauna

The parks can be divided into three distinct zones. In the west (1,500–4,500 feet) are the rolling, lower elevation foothills, covered with shrubby chaparral vegetation or golden grasslands dotted with oaks. Chamise, red-barked manzanita, and the occasional yucca plant grow here. Fields of white popcorn flower cover the hillsides in spring, and the yellow fiddleneck flourishes. In summer, intense heat and absence of rain cause the hills to turn golden brown. Wildlife includes the California ground squirrel, noisy blue-and-gray scrub jay, black bears, coyotes, skunks, and gray fox.

At middle elevations (5,000–9,000 feet), where the giant sequoia belt resides, rock formations mix with meadows and huge stands of evergreens—red and white fir, incense cedar, and ponderosa pines, to name a few. Wildflowers, including yellow blazing star and red Indian paintbrush, bloom in spring and summer. Golden-mantled ground squirrels, Steller's jays, mule deer, and black bears (most active in fall) inhabit the area, as does the Douglas squirrel, or chickaree.

The high alpine section of the parks is extremely rugged, with a string of rocky peaks reaching above 13,000 feet to Mt. Whitney's 14,494 feet. Fierce weather and scarcity of soil make vegetation and wildlife sparse. Foxtail and whitebark pines have gnarled and twisted trunks, the result of high wind, heavy snowfall, and freezing temperatures. In summer you can see yellow-bellied marmots, pikas, weasels, mountain chickadees, and Clark's nutcrackers. Leopard lilies and shooting stars grow near streams and meadows.

## AVG. HIGH/LOW TEMPS.

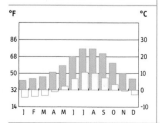

| °F | | °C |
|---|---|---|
| 86 | | 30 |
| 68 | | 20 |
| 50 | | 10 |
| 32 | | 0 |
| 14 | | -10 |
| | J F M A M J J A S O N D | |

## Getting There & Around

Sequoia is 36 mi east of Visalia on Route 198; Kings Canyon is 53 mi east of Fresno on Route 180. There is no automobile entrance on the eastern side of the Sierra. Routes 180 and 198 are connected by Generals Highway, a paved two-lane road that's open year-round. Ongoing improvements to Generals Highway can cause delays of up to an hour at peak times, and the road is extremely narrow and steep from Route 198 to Giant Forest. Keep an eye on your engine temperature gauge, as the incline and congestion can cause vehicles to overheat; to avoid overheated brakes, use low gears on downgrades.

If you are traveling in an RV or with a trailer, study a map of the parks and the restrictions on these vehicles. Do not travel beyond Potwisha Campground with an RV longer than 22 feet on Route 198; take straighter, easier Route 180 instead. Maximum vehicle length on Generals Highway is 40 feet, or 50 feet combined length for vehicles with trailers.

Snowstorms are common late October–April. Unless you have four-wheel drive with snow tires, always carry chains and know how to apply them to the tires on the drive axle. Generals Highway between Lodgepole and Grant Grove is sometimes closed by snow. The Mineral King Road from Route 198 into southern Sequoia National Park is closed 2 mi below Atwell Mill either on November 1 or after the first heavy snow. The Buckeye Flat–Middle Fork Trailhead Road is closed mid-October–mid-April when the Buckeye Flat Campground closes. The lower Crystal Cave Road is closed when the cave closes in November. Its upper 2 mi, as well as the Panoramic Point and Moro Rock–Crescent Meadow roads, are closed with the first heavy snow. Because of the danger of rockfall, the portion of Kings Canyon Scenic Byway east of Grant Grove closes in winter. For current conditions, call the park at 559/565–3341 Ext. 4.

## Publications

**The Guide: Sequoia and Kings Canyon National Parks** is a free newspaper available at park entrance gates or by contacting the parks directly; www.nps.gov/seki has current and back issues. For information on planning a backcountry hiking trip, download **Backcountry Basics** at www.nps.gov/seki.

## Festivals & Events

DEC. **Annual Trek to the Tree.** On the second Sunday, thousands of Christmas carolers, many of whom arrive en masse from Sanger, gather at the base of General Grant Tree, the nation's official Christmas tree. ☎ 559/565–4307.

MAR. **Blossom Days Festival.** The first Saturday of March, communities along Fresno County's Blossom Trail celebrate the flowering of the area's many orchards, citrus groves, and vineyards. You can drive the 62-mi trail any time of year, but peak blossom season is late February–mid-March. ☎ 559/262–4271 ⊕ www.driveblossomtrail.com.

APR. **Jazzaffair.** Held just south of the parks in the town of Three Rivers, a festival of mostly swing jazz takes place at several locations, with shuttle buses between sites. The festival is usually the second weekend of the month. ☎ 559/561–4592 or 559/561–3105 ⊕ www.jazzaffair.info.

MAY **Woodlake Rodeo.** A weekend-long event thrown by the Woodlake Lions, this rodeo draws large crowds to Woodlake (near Three Rivers) on Mother's Day weekend. ☎ 559/564–8555 ⊕ www.woodlakelionsrodeo.com.

SEPT. **Celebrate Sequoias Festival.** On the second Saturday of the month, rangers guide field trips to the lesser known groves of Sequoia National Park. ☎ 559/565–4307 Grant Grove Visitor Center.

OCT. **Big Fresno Fair.** The Fresno Fairgrounds come alive with an old-fashioned county fair that includes a midway, agriculture and livestock shows, horse races, and big-name entertainment. ☎ 559/650–3247.

By Constance Jones

The silent giants of Sequoia and Kings Canyon, surrounded by vast granite canyons and towering snowcapped peaks, strike awe in everyone who sees them. No less than famed naturalist John Muir proclaimed the sequoia tree "the most beautiful and majestic on earth." The largest living things on the planet, *Sequoiadendron giganteum* trees are not as tall as the coast redwoods (*Sequoia sempervirens*), but they're more massive and, on average, older. Exhibits at the visitor centers explain why they can live so long and grow so big, as well as the special relationship between these trees and fire (their thick, fibrous bark helps protect them from flames and insects, and their seeds can't germinate until they first explode out of a burning pinecone).

Sequoia and Kings Canyon share a boundary and are administered together. They encompass 1,353 square mi, rivaled only by Yosemite in rugged Sierra beauty. The topography ranges from the western foothills at an elevation of 1,500 feet to the towering peaks of the Great Western Divide and the Sierra Crest. The Kings River cuts a swath through the backcountry and over the years has formed a granite canyon that, in places, towers nearly 4,000 feet above the canyon floor. From Junction Overlook, on the drive to Cedar Grove, you can see the 8,200-foot drop from Spanish Mountain to the Kings River, as well as the confluence of the Middle and South forks of the Kings River. Mt. Whitney, the highest point in the contiguous United States, is the crown jewel of the eastern side.

# SEQUOIA

## Scenic Drives

★ **Generals Highway.** Connecting the two parks from Grant Grove to Giant Forest and the foothills to the south, this narrow, twisting road runs past Stony Creek, Lost Grove, Little Baldy, General Sherman Tree, Amphitheater Point, and Foothills Visitor Center. Stop to see the Giant Forest Museum, which focuses entirely on the ecology of the sequoia. Also stop at the Lodgepole Visitor Center, which has excellent exhibits and audiovisual programs describing the Sierra Nevada and the natural history of the area. Under normal conditions it takes two hours to complete the drive one way, but when parks are crowded in summer, traffic can slow to a crawl in some areas.

**Mineral King Road.** Accessible from Memorial Day weekend through October (weather permitting), this small, winding, rough, steep road begins outside the park south of the Ash Mountain entrance, off Route 198. Trailers and RVs are prohibited. The exciting 25-mi drive ascends approximately 6,000 feet to a subalpine valley, where there are a ranger station and limited facilities. Bring a picnic lunch. Many backpackers use this as a trailhead, and you can take a fine day hike from here as well. Allow 90 minutes for the one-way drive.

## What to See

### Scenic Stops

**Auto Log.** At one time, cars drove right on top of this giant fallen sequoia. Now it's a great place to pose for pictures. ⊠ *Moro Rock–Crescent Meadow Rd., 1 mi south of Giant Forest.*

**Crescent Meadow.** Walk on fallen logs and trails through spectacular fields of summertime wildflowers. ⊠ *End of Moro Rock–Crescent Meadow Rd., 2⁰∕₁₀ mi east off Generals Hwy.*

★ **Crystal Cave.** Ten thousand feet of passageways in this marble cave were created from limestone that metamorphosed under tremendous heat and pressure. Formations are relatively undisturbed. The standard tour is 50 minutes in length. In summer, Sequoia Natural History Association offers a four- to six-hour "wild cave" tour (reservations required) and a 90-minute discovery tour, a less-structured excursion with fewer people. Tickets are not available at the cave; purchase them by 2:30 PM, and at least 90 minutes in advance, from the Lodgepole or Foothills visitor center. ⊠ *Crystal Cave Rd., 6 mi west off Generals Hwy.* ☎ *559/565–3759* ⊕ *www.sequoiahistory.org* ✉ *$10.95* ⊙ *Mid-May–mid-Oct., daily 10–4.*

★ **General Sherman Tree.** The world's largest living tree is estimated to be about 2,100 years old. ⊠ *Generals Hwy. (Rte. 198), 2 mi south of Lodgepole Visitor Center.*

**Mineral King.** This subalpine valley sits at 7,800 feet at the end of a steep, winding road, the highest point to which you can drive in the park. ⊠ *End*

## SEQUOIA IN ONE DAY

From late spring through early fall, you can see most of the major sights in Sequoia in less than a day. Start out on Route 198 and enter Sequoia National Park in early morning. Head for **Foothills Visitor Center**; a half hour here gives you a good overview of the area and an idea of what you'll want to see in the parks. If you are visiting in summer, pick up tickets for the tour of Crystal Cave; tickets are not available at the cave itself. Follow Generals Highway north to the **Crystal Cave** turnoff and take the 50-minute tour. Next, head north and turn onto Moro Rock–Crescent Meadow Road. If you are able, climb the steep ¼-mi staircase leading to the summit of **Moro Rock**, a large granite dome from which you can gaze out over the western end of Sequoia National Park. Even from a short distance up, you can get a wonderful view. From there, check out the midsummer wildflower show at **Crescent**

**Meadow.** A 2-mi round-trip hike from the meadow leads to Tharp's Log, the summer home of Hale Tharp, built inside a fallen sequoia.

Return to Generals Highway, bypass Giant Forest, and drive north to Lodgepole Village for lunch. Afterward, tour the **Lodgepole Visitor Center,** which has excellent park history exhibits. Backtrack on Generals Highway and continue south to the Wolverton Road turnoff to reach **General Sherman Tree,** the world's largest living tree, which is a short but steep walk downhill from the parking area. If you have time to spare, stroll down **Congress Trail,** a 2-mi loop through the heart of the sequoia forest that takes one to two hours to complete.

Return to your car, and drive south for about 2 mi to reach **Giant Forest.** After walking the ⁷⁄₁₀-mi **Big Trees Trail,** which passes through forest and meadow in an easy loop, stop at the **Giant Forest Museum.**

---

of Mineral King Rd., 25 mi east of Generals Hwy. (Rte. 198), east of Three Rivers.

★ **Moro Rock.** Climb the steep 400-step staircase 300 feet to the top of this granite dome for spectacular views of the Great Western Divide and the western regions of the park. To the southwest you look down the Kaweah River to Three Rivers, Lake Kaweah, and—on clear days—the Central Valley and the Coast Range. To the northeast are views of the High Sierra. Thousands of feet below lies the middle fork of the Kaweah River. ⊠ Moro Rock–Crescent Meadow Rd., 2 mi east off Generals Hwy. (Rte. 198) to parking area.

**Tunnel Log.** You can drive your car through this tunnel carved in a fallen sequoia. There's a bypass for larger vehicles. ⊠ Moro Rock–Crescent Meadow Rd., 2 mi east of Generals Hwy. (Rte. 198).

### Visitor Centers

★ **Beetle Rock Family Nature Center.** At Beetle Rock Education Center, across the road from Giant Forest Museum, the Sequoia Natural History Association operates a nature center with interactive exhibits and a chil-

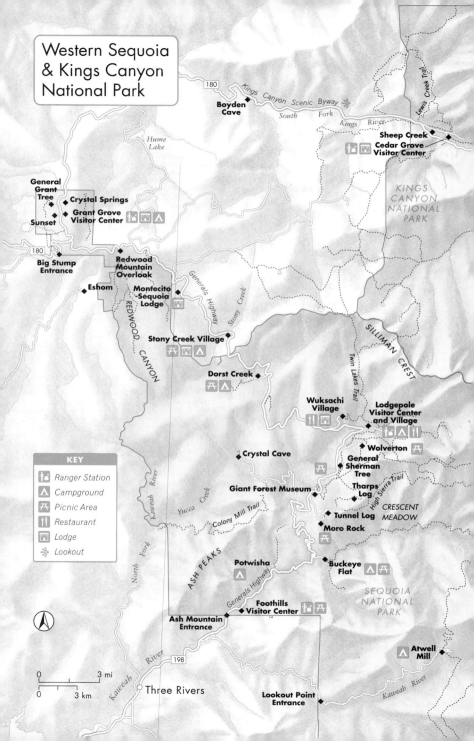

# Western Sequoia & Kings Canyon National Park

**180**

Kings Canyon Scenic Byway

**Boyden Cave**

*South Fork* *Kings River*

Lewis Creek Trail

**Sheep Creek**
**Cedar Grove Visitor Center**

Hume Lake

KINGS CANYON NATIONAL PARK

**General Grant Tree**
**Crystal Springs**
**Grant Grove Visitor Center**
**Sunset**

**180**

**Big Stump Entrance**

**Redwood Mountain Overlook**

**Eshom**

**Montecito-Sequoia Lodge**

REDWOOD CANYON

Generals Highway

Stony Creek

SILLIMAN CREST

**Stony Creek Village**

**Dorst Creek**

Twin Lakes Trail

**Wuksachi Village**

**Lodgepole Visitor Center and Village**

**Crystal Cave**

**Wolverton**

**General Sherman Tree**

Kaweah River

Yucca Creek

**Giant Forest Museum**

**Tharps Log**

High Sierra Trail

CRESCENT MEADOW

Colony Mill Trail

**Tunnel Log**
**Moro Rock**

North Fork

**Potwisha**

ASH PEAKS

**Buckeye Flat**

SEQUOIA NATIONAL PARK

Generals Highway

**Foothills Visitor Center**

**Ash Mountain Entrance**

## KEY

| | |
|---|---|
| Ranger Station | |
| Campground | |
| Picnic Area | |
| Restaurant | |
| Lodge | |
| Lookout | |

**198**

Kaweah River

**Atwell Mill**

Three Rivers

0 — 3 mi
0 — 3 km

**Lookout Point Entrance**

Kaweah River

dren's bookstore with science-oriented games, books, and toys. ⊠ *Generals Hwy., 4 mi south of Lodgepole Visitor Center* ☎ *559/565–4251* ▣ *Free* ☉ *July–Aug. 19, daily 10–4.*

**Foothills Visitor Center.** Exhibits focusing on the foothills and resource issues facing the parks are on display here. You can also pick up books, maps, and a list of ranger-led walks, and get wilderness permits. ⊠ *Generals Hwy. (Rte. 198), 1 mi north of the Ash Mountain entrance* ☎ *559/565–3135* ☉ *Oct.–mid-May, daily 8–4:30; mid-May–Sept., daily 8–5.*

★ **Giant Forest Museum.** You'll find outstanding exhibits on the ecology of the giant sequoia at the park's premier museum. Though housed in a historic building, it's entirely wheelchair accessible. ⊠ *Generals Hwy., 4 mi south of Lodgepole Visitor Center* ☎ *559/565–4480* ▣ *Free* ☉ *Daily 8–5.*

**Lodgepole Visitor Center.** The center has exhibits on the early years of the park and a slide program on geology and forest life. Books and maps are sold here. ⊠ *Generals Hwy. (Rte. 198), 21 mi north of Ash Mountain entrance* ☎ *559/565–4436* ☉ *Daily June–Oct. 7–6; weekends only Nov.–May 7–6.*

**Mineral King Ranger Station.** The small visitor center here houses a few exhibits on the history of the area; wilderness permits and some books and maps are available. ⊠ *End of Mineral King Rd., 25 mi east of East Fork entrance* ☎ *559/565–3768* ☉ *Late May–mid-Sept., daily 8–4:30.*

☾ **Walter Fry Nature Center.** The hands-on nature exhibits here are designed primarily for children. ⊠ *Lodgepole Campground, ½ mi east of Lodgepole Visitor Center* ☎ *559/565–4436* ▣ *Free* ☉ *July–mid-Aug., weekends noon–5.*

## Sports & the Outdoors

### Bird-watching

Not seen in most parts of the United States, the white-headed woodpecker and the pileated woodpecker are common in most mid-elevation areas here. There are also many hawks and owls, including the renowned spotted owl. Species are diverse in both parks due to the changes in elevation, and range from warblers, kingbirds, thrushes, and sparrows in the foothills to goshawk, blue grouse, red-breasted nuthatch, and brown creeper at the highest elevations. Ranger-led bird-watching tours are held on a sporadic basis. Call the parks at 559/565–3341 for information.

Contact the **Sequoia Natural History Association** (🖎 HCR 89, Box 10, 93271 ☎ 559/565–3759 ⊕ www.sequoiahistory.org) for information on bird-watching in the southern Sierra.

### Cross-country Skiing

For a one-of-a-kind experience, cut through the groves of mammoth sequoias in Giant Forest. Some of the Crescent Meadow trails ( ⇨ Hiking) are suitable for skiing as well. None of the trails is groomed. You can park at Giant Forest. Note that roads can be precarious in bad weather. Some advanced trails begin at Wolverton.

**Pear Lake Ski Hut.** Primitive lodging is available at this backcountry hut, reached by a steep and extremely difficult 7-mi trail from Wolverton. Only expert skiers should attempt this trek. Space is limited; make reservations well in advance. ⊠ *Trailhead at end of Wolverton Rd., 1½ mi northeast off Generals Hwy. (Rte. 198)* ☎ *559/565–3759* ⊠ *$20* ⊗ *Mid-Dec.–mid-Apr.*

**Wuksachi Lodge.** Rent skis here. Depending on snowfall amounts, there may also be instruction available. Reservations are recommended. Marked trails cut through Giant Forest, which sits 5 mi south of the lodge. ⊠ *Off Generals Hwy. (Rte. 198), 2 mi north of Lodgepole* ☎ *559/565–4070* ⊠ *$15–$20 ski rental* ⊗ *Nov.–May (unless no snow) daily 9–4.*

## Fishing

There's limited trout fishing in the creeks and rivers from late April to mid-November. The Kaweah River is a popular spot; check at visitor centers for open and closed waters. Some of the park's secluded backcountry lakes have good fishing. A California fishing license is $11.30 for one day, $17.60 for two days, $34.90 for 10 days (discounts are available for state residents) and is required for persons 16 and older. For park regulations, closures, and restrictions, call the parks at 559/565–3341 or stop at a park visitor center. Licenses and fishing tackle are usually available in Lodgepole. Among many other functions, the **California Department of Fish and Game** (☎ 916/653–7661 ⊕ www.dfg.ca.gov) supplies fishing licenses.

## Hiking

Carry a hiking map—available at any visitor center—and plenty of water. Check with rangers for current trail conditions, and be aware of rapidly changing weather. As a rule of thumb, plan on trekking 1 mph. For books about hikes in Sequoia National Park, contact the **Sequoia Natural History Association** (⊠ 47050 Generals Hwy., Three Rivers ☎ 559/565–3759 ⊕ www.sequoiahistory.org).

EASY **Big Trees Trail.** The Giant Forest is known for its trails through sequoia groves. You can get the best views of the big trees from the meadows, where flowers are in full bloom by June or July. The ⁷⁄₁₀-mi trail—the park's only wheelchair-accessible trail—circles Round Meadow. ⊠ *Off Generals Hwy. (Rte. 198), near the Giant Forest Museum.*

★ **Congress Trail.** This easy 2-mi trail is a paved loop that begins near General Sherman Tree and winds through the heart of the sequoia forest. Watch for the groups of trees known as the House and Senate, and the individual trees called the President and McKinley. ⊠ *Off Generals Hwy. (Rte. 198), 2 mi north of Giant Forest.*

Fodor'sChoice **Crescent Meadow Trails.** John Muir reportedly called Crescent Meadow
★ the "gem of the Sierra." Brilliant wildflowers bloom here by midsummer, and a 1⁸⁄₁₀-mi trail loops around the meadow. A 1⁶⁄₁₀-mi trail begins at Crescent Meadow and leads to Tharps Log, a cabin built from a fire-hollowed sequoia. ⊠ *End of Moro Rock–Crescent Meadow Rd., 2⁶⁄₁₀ mi east off Generals Hwy. (Rte. 198).*

## Mt. Whitney

**AT 14,494 FEET, MT. WHITNEY** is the highest point in the contiguous United States and the crown jewel of Sequoia National Park's wild eastern side. The peak looms high above the tiny, high-mountain desert community of Lone Pine, where numerous Hollywood Westerns have been filmed. Despite its scale, you can't see the mountain from the more traveled west side of the park, because it is hidden behind the Great Western Divide. The only way to access Mt. Whitney from the main part of the park is to circumnavigate the Sierra Nevada via a 10-hour, nearly 400-mi drive outside the park ( ⇨ Chapter 15, Death Valley, *for* Mt. Whitney). No road ascends the peak; the best vantage point from which to catch a glimpse of the mountain is at the end of Whitney Portal Road. The 13 mi winding road leads from U.S. 395 at Lone Pine to the trailhead for the hiking route to the top of the mountain. Whitney Portal Road is closed in winter.

The most popular route to the summit, the **Mt. Whitney Trail,** can be conquered by fit and moderately experienced hikers, unless there is snow on the mountain; then it is a challenge for expert mountaineers only. Day hikers must have a permit to hike the trail beyond Lone Pine Lake, about 2½ mi from the trailhead; all overnighters must have a permit. Reservations for climbing Mt. Whitney May through October are difficult to obtain because of a daily limit on the number of hikers allowed. You can apply for overnight and day permits by lottery each February. In May, if other hikers have canceled, a few permits may become available. Contact the **Wilderness Permit Office of Inyo National Forest** ( ☎ 760/873–2485 wilderness information line, 760/873–2483 reservation line ⊕ www.fs.fed.us/r5/inyo).

**Muir Grove Trail.** An easy 2-mi hike with some distant views brings you to a sequoia grove where you might well find some solitude. Give yourself a couple of hours to make the round-trip. ⊠ *Dorst Creek Campground, Generals Hwy. (Rte. 198), 8 mi north of Lodgepole Visitor Center.*

MODERATE **Little Baldy Trail.** Climbing 700 vertical feet in 1¾ mi of switchbacking, this trail ends at a granite dome with a great view of the peaks of the Mineral King area and the Great Western Divide. The walk to the summit and back takes about four hours. ⊠ *Little Baldy Saddle, Generals Hwy. (Rte. 198), 11 mi north of Giant Forest.*

**Tokopah Falls Trail.** This moderate trail follows the Marble Fork of the Kaweah River for 1¾ mi one way and dead-ends below the impressive granite cliffs and cascading waterfall of Tokopah Canyon. It takes 2½ to 4 hours to make the 3½-mi round-trip journey. The trail passes through a mixed-conifer forest. ⊠ *Off Generals Hwy. (Rte. 198), ¼ mi north of Lodgepole Campground.*

DIFFICULT **Marble Falls Trail.** The 3⁷⁄₁₀-mi, moderately strenuous hike to Marble Falls crosses through the rugged foothills before reaching the cascading water.

Plan on three to four hours one way. ⊠ *Off the dirt road across from the concrete ditch near site 17 at Potwisha Campground, off Generals Hwy. (Rte. 198).*

**Mineral King Trails.** Many trails to the high country begin at Mineral King. At 7,800 feet, this is the highest point accessible by car in either of the parks, and the Great Western Divide runs right above this area. Get a map and provisions, and check with rangers about conditions. ⊠ *Trailhead at end of Mineral King Rd., 25 mi east of Generals Hwy. (Rte. 198).*

## Horseback Riding

Scheduled trips take you through redwood forests, flowering meadows, across the Sierra, or even up to Mt. Whitney. Costs per person range from $25 for a one-hour guided ride to around $200 per day for fully guided trips.

**Grant Grove Stables** ( ⇨ Kings Canyon) is the stable to choose if you want a short ride.

**Horse Corral Pack Station.** Hourly, half-day, full-day, or overnight trips through Sequoia are available for beginning and advanced riders. ⊠ *Off Big Meadows Rd., 12 mi east of Generals Hwy. (Rte. 198) between Sequoia and Kings Canyon national parks* ☎ *559/565–3404 in summer, 559/564–6429 in winter* ⊕ *www.horsecorralpackers.com* ▭ *$25–$95 day trips* ⊗ *May–Sept.*

**Mineral King Pack Station.** Day and overnight tours in the high-mountain area around Mineral King are available here. ⊠ *End of Mineral King Rd., 25 mi east of East Fork entrance* ☎ *559/561–3039 in summer, 520/855–5885 in winter* ⊕ *mineralking.tripod.com* ▭ *$25–$75 day trips* ⊗ *July–late Sept. or early Oct.*

## Sledding

The Wolverton area, on Route 198 near Giant Forest, is a popular sledding spot, where sleds, inner tubes, and platters are allowed. You can buy sleds and saucers, starting at $8, at the Wuksachi Lodge (559/565–4070), 2 mi north of Lodgepole.

## Snowshoeing

You can rent snowshoes at the Giant Forest Museum or Wuksachi Lodge and strike out on your own, or you can join a guided goup on Saturdays and holidays. Snowshoers may stay at the Pear Lake Ski Hut ( ⇨ Cross-country Skiing). You can rent snowshoes for $15–$20 at the Wuksachi Lodge (559/565–4070), 2 mi north of Lodgepole. Naturalists lead snowshoe walks around Giant Forest and Wuksachi Lodge, conditions permitting, on Saturdays and holidays. Snowshoes are provided for a $1 donation. Make reservations and check schedules at Giant Forest Museum (559/565–4480) or Wuksachi Lodge.

## Swimming

Drowning is the number-one cause of death in both Sequoia and Kings Canyon parks. Though it is sometimes safe to swim in the parks' rivers in the late summer and early fall, it is extremely dangerous to do so in the spring and early summer, when the snowmelt from the high country causes swift currents and icy temperatures. Stand clear of the water when the rivers are running, and stay off wet rocks to avoid falling in. Check with rangers if you're unsure about conditions or to learn the safest locations to wade in the water.

## Educational Offerings

### Classes & Seminars

**Evening Programs.** In summer, the park shows documentary films and slide shows, and has evening lectures. Locations and times vary; pick up a schedule at any visitor center or check bulletin boards near ranger stations. ☎ *559/565–3341.*

★ **Seminars.** Expert naturalists lead seminars on a range of topics, including birds, wildflowers, geology, botany, photography, park history, backpacking, and pathfinding. Some courses offer transferable credits. Reserve in advance. For information and prices, pick up a course catalogue at any visitor center or from Sequoia Natural History Association. ☎ *559/565–3759* ⊕ *www.sequoiahistory.org.*

**Sequoia Sightseeing Tours.** The only licensed tour operator in either park offers daily interpretive sightseeing tours in a 10-passenger van with a friendly, knowledgeable guide. Reservations are essential. They also offer private tours of Kings Canyon. ☎ *559/561–4489* ⊕ *www.sequoiatours.com.*

# KINGS CANYON

## Scenic Drives

★ **Kings Canyon Scenic Byway.** Winding alongside the powerful Kings River (the byway along Route 180, east of Grant Grove), this drive leads below the towering granite cliffs and past two tumbling waterfalls in the Kings River Canyon. One mile past the Cedar Grove Village turnoff, the U-shape canyon becomes broader, and you can see evidence of its glacial past and the effects of wind and water on the granite. Four miles farther is Grand Sentinel Viewpoint, where you can see the 3,500-foot-tall granite monolith and some of the most interesting rock formations in the canyon. The drive dead-ends in the canyon, so you must double back. It's about one hour each way.

## What to See

### Historic Sites

★ **Fallen Monarch.** No matter how tall you are, you could theoretically walk through the entire 100-foot length of this burned-out, fallen sequoia near the General Grant Tree. (In order to protect it, access to the log's interior is prohibited indefinitely.) Early explorers, cattle ranchers, and Native Americans used the log for shelter, and soldiers who began patrolling the area in the late 1880s used it to stable their horses. ⊠ *Trailhead 1 mi north of Grant Grove Visitor Center.*

## KINGS CANYON IN ONE DAY

You can see the major sights of Kings Canyon in a day. Enter the park from Route 180 east, or from Sequoia National Park via Generals Highway north. Your first stop is **Grant Grove Village.** Tour the visitor center to pick up maps and learn about the geological history of Kings Canyon. While in the village, you can also buy supplies for a picnic lunch. Continue ¾ mi to the parking lot for **General Grant Tree,** which has been standing for about 2,000 years. Reach the tree, which President Calvin Coolidge ordained as the nation's Christmas tree in 1926, via a ½-mi loop trail. Nearby, a 2³/₁₀-mi (one way) spur road−not recommended for trailers or RVs− leads to the **Panoramic Point Trail,** where a short uphill hike from the parking lot rewards you with views of a jagged escarpment of granite

peaks looming some 20 mi in the distance.

Return to Route 180 east and drive through the **Sequoia National Forest.** The road leads along the **Kings Canyon Scenic Byway,** affording great views of the Kings River Canyon, which in places is deeper than the Grand Canyon. About 30 mi east of Grant Grove (allow one hour for the drive on this extremely winding road), the road enters the eastern portion of Kings Canyon National Park (closed in winter) and descends to **Cedar Grove,** where there is a tiny visitor center and a market−snack bar. Drive through the glacial U-shape valley, ringed by huge granite cliffs and monoliths, toward Road's End (you can't drive any farther east) and walk the **Zumwalt Meadow Trail.**

**33**

**Gamlin Cabin.** Built as a summer cabin in 1867, this building was used primarily for storage. Listed on the National Register of Historic Places, the cabin was returned to an area close to its original site in 1931 and rehabilitated in 1981. The roof and lower timber are giant sequoia. ✉ *Trailhead 1 mi north of Grant Grove Visitor Center.*

**Knapp's Cabin.** During the Roaring '20s, wealthy Santa Barbara business-man George Knapp commissioned extravagant fishing expeditions into the Kings River Canyon. To store gear, he built this small cabin. ✉ *Kings Canyon Scenic Byway, 2 mi east of Cedar Grove Village turnoff.*

### Scenic Stops

**Canyon View.** The glacial history of the Kings River Canyon is evident from this viewpoint. Note the canyon's giant "U" shape, which sparked John Muir to compare it to Yosemite. ✉ *Kings Canyon Scenic Byway (Rte. 180), 1 mi east of the Cedar Grove turnoff.*

**General Grant Tree.** The nation's Christmas tree, this is also the world's third-largest living tree. ✉ *Trailhead 1 mi north of Grant Grove Visitor Center.*

★ **Redwood Mountain Grove.** This is the largest grove of giant sequoias in the world. As you head south through Kings Canyon toward Sequoia on Generals Highway, several paved turnouts allow you to look out over

# Kings Canyon's Cedar Grove Area

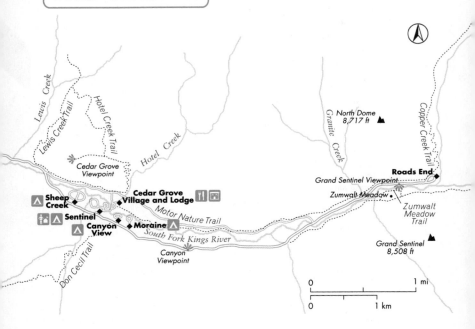

the treetops. The grove itself is accessible only on foot or by horseback, but the drive to the trailhead, on a twisting, rutted dirt road down a steep gorge, is dramatic in itself. ✉ *Drive 5 mi south of Grant Grove on Generals Hwy. (Rte. 198), then turn right at Quail Flat; follow it 1½ mi to the Redwood Canyon trailhead.*

## Visitor Centers

**Cedar Grove Visitor Center.** This tiny, historic log ranger station provides information and sells books and maps. ✉ *Kings Canyon Scenic Byway, 30 mi east of park entrance* ☎ *559/565–3793* ☼ *Spring–fall, daily 9–4.*

**Grant Grove Visitor Center.** A film and extensive exhibits on the park's sequoia and human history provide an engaging introduction to Kings Canyon. Books, maps, and wilderness permits are for sale. ✉ *Generals Hwy. (Rte. 198), 3 mi northeast of Rte. 180, Big Stump entrance* ☎ *559/565–4307* ☼ *Summer, daily 8–6; spring and fall, daily 9–4:30; winter, daily 9:30–4:30.*

**Road's End Permit Station.** If you're planning to hike the backcountry, you can pick up a permit and information on the backcountry here. You can also rent or buy bear canisters, a must for campers. When the station is closed, you can still complete a self-service permit form. ✉ *5 mi east* *of Cedar Grove Visitor Center, at the end of Kings Canyon Scenic Byway* ⊙ *Late May–late Sept., daily 7–3:30* ☏ *No phone.*

## Sports & the Outdoors

### Bird-watching

For information on bird-watching in Sequoia and Kings Canyon national parks, ⇨ Sports & the Outdoors *in* Sequoia National Park.

### Cross-Country Skiing

Roads to Grant Grove are easily accessible during heavy snowfall, making the trails here a good choice over Sequoia's Giant Forest when harsh weather hits.

**Grant Grove Ski Touring Center.** The Grant Grove Market doubles as the ski-touring center, where you can rent cross-country skis in winter. This is a good starting point for a number of marked trails, including the Panoramic Point Trail and the General Grant Tree Trail (⇨ Hiking). ⊠ *Grant Grove Market, Generals Hwy. (Rte. 198), 3 mi northeast of Rte. 180, Big Stump entrance* ☏ *559/335–2665* ⊟ *$6–$11* ⊙ *Daily 9–6.*

### Fishing

There is limited trout fishing in the park from late April to mid-November, and catches are minor. Still, Kings River is a popular spot. Some of the park's secluded backcountry lakes have good fishing. Licenses ($10.75 for two days, $29.40 for 10 days, less for state residents) are required for those over 16, and are available, along with fishing tackle, in Grant Grove and Cedar Grove. Only Grant Grove is open year-round. Fishing licenses are issued by the **California Department of Fish and Game** (☏ 916/653–7661 ⊕ www.dfg.ca.gov).

### Hiking

Carry a hiking map—available at any visitor center—and plenty of water. Check with rangers for current trail conditions, and be aware of rapidly changing weather.

EASY **Big Stump Trail.** A walk along this 1-mi trail graphically demonstrates the toll heavy logging takes on the wilderness. ⊠ *Trailhead near Rte. 180, Big Stump Entrance.*

**General Grant Tree Trail.** One of the shortest trails in the parks is the one that leads to General Grant Tree, the third-largest living tree in the world. The trail is only ³⁄₁₀ mi, but it passes Gamlin Cabin and Fallen Monarch. It's paved and fairly level. ⊠ *Trailhead off Generals Hwy. (Rte. 198), 1 mi northwest of Grant Grove Visitor Center.*

**Roaring River Falls Walk.** Take a shady five-minute walk to this forceful waterfall that rushes through a narrow granite chute. The trail is paved and mostly accessible. ⊠ *Trailhead 3 mi east of Cedar Grove Village turnoff from Kings Canyon Scenic Byway.*

Fodor'sChoice **Zumwalt Meadow Trail.** Walk beneath high granite walls and along the
★ meandering Kings River, en route to the lush Zumwalt Meadow. The

1½-mi trail involves a little rock-hopping. ☒ *Trailhead 4½ mi east of Cedar Grove Village turnoff from Kings Canyon Scenic Byway.*

MODERATE **Big Baldy.** This hike climbs 600 feet and 2 mi up to the 8,209-feet sum-
★ mit of Big Baldy. Your reward is the view of Redwood Canyon. The round-trip hike is 4 mi. ☒ *Trailhead 8 mi south of Grant Grove on Generals Hwy. (Rte. 198).*

**Mist Falls Trail.** This sandy trail follows the glaciated South Fork Canyon through forest and chaparral, past several rapids and cascades, to one of the largest waterfalls in the two parks. Nine miles round-trip, the hike is relatively flat, but climbs 600 feet in the last mile. It takes four to five hours to complete. ☒ *Trailhead at end of Kings Canyon Scenic Byway, 5½ mi east of Cedar Grove Village.*

**Panoramic Point Trail.** A steep ¼-mi walk from the parking lot leads to a viewpoint where you can see the High Sierra from Mt. Goddard in northern Kings Canyon National Park to Eagle Scout Peak in Sequoia. Trailers and RVs are not permitted on the steep and narrow road. ☒ *End of Panoramic Point Rd., 2³⁄₁₀ mi from Grant Grove Village.*

★ **Redwood Canyon Trail.** Depending on whether you hike the perimeter of two adjoining loops or take only one of them, this 6- or 10- mi trek in Redwood Canyon leads through the world's largest grove of sequoias. Take in the cascades, the quiet pools of Redwood Creek, and the mixed conifer forest on a short walk, day hike, or overnight backpacking trip. ☒ *Drive 5 mi south of Grant Grove on Generals Hwy. (Rte. 198), then turn right at Quail Flat; follow it 1½ mi to the Redwood Canyon trailhead.*

DIFFICULT **Buena Vista Peak.** For a 360-degree view of Redwood Canyon and the High Sierra, make the 2-mi ascent to Buena Vista. ☒ *Trailhead off Generals Hwy. (Rte. 198), south of Kings Canyon Overlook, 7 mi southeast of Grant Grove.*

**Don Cecil Trail.** This trail climbs the cool north-facing slope of the Kings River Canyon, passes Sheep Creek Cascade, and provides several good views of the canyon and the 11,000-foot Monarch Divide. The trail leads to Lookout Peak, which affords an incredible panorama of the park's backcountry. It's a strenuous, all-day hike—13 mi round-trip—and climbs 4,000 feet. ☒ *Trailhead off Kings Canyon Scenic Byway, across from parking lot, ²⁄₁₀ mi west of Cedar Grove Village.*

★ **Hotel Creek Trail.** For gorgeous canyon views, take this trail from the canyon floor at Cedar Grove up a series of switchbacks until it splits. Follow the route left through chaparral to the forested ridge and rocky outcrop known as Cedar Grove Overlook, where you can see the Kings River Canyon stretching below. This strenuous 5-mi round-trip hike gains 1,200 feet and takes three to four hours to complete. For a longer hike, return via Lewis Creek Trail for an 8-mi loop. ☒ *Trailhead at Cedar Grove pack station, 1 mi east of Cedar Grove Village.*

## Horseback Riding

One-day destinations by horseback out of Cedar Grove include Mist Falls and Upper Bubb's Creek. In the backcountry, many equestrians head for Volcanic Lakes or Granite Basin, ascending trails that reach elevations of 10,000 feet. Costs per person range from $25 for a one-hour guided ride to around $200 per day for fully guided trips.

**Cedar Grove Pack Station.** Take a day or overnight trip along the Kings River Canyon. Popular routes include the Rae Lakes Loop and Monarch Divide. ⊠ *Kings Canyon Scenic Byway, 1 mi east of Cedar Grove Village* ☏ *559/565–3464 in summer, 559/337–2314 off-season* 🖾 *Call for prices* ◷ *May–Oct.*

**33**

**Grant Grove Stables.** A one- or two-hour trip through Grant Grove is a good way to get a taste of horseback riding in Kings Canyon. ⊠ *Rte. 180, ½ mi north of Grant Grove Visitor Center, near Grant Grove Village* ☏ *559/335–9292 mid-June–Sept., 559/594–9307 Oct.–mid-June* 🖾 *$25–$40* ◷ *June–Labor Day, daily 8–6.*

### Sledding

In winter, Kings Canyon has a few great places to play in the snow. Sleds, inner tubes, and platters are allowed at both the Azalea Campground area on Grant Tree Road, ¼ mi north of Grant Grove Visitor Center, and at the Big Stump picnic area, 2 mi north of the lower Route 180 entrance to the park.

**Grant Grove Market.** Purchase sleds, saucers and other snowplay gear here. ⊠ *Generals Hwy. (Rte. 198), 3 mi northeast of Rte. 180, Big Stump entrance* ☏ *559/335–2665* ◷ *Daily 9–6.*

### Snowshoeing

Snowshoeing is good around Grant Grove, where you can take naturalist-guided snowshoe walks on Saturdays and holidays mid-December through mid-March as conditions permit.

**Grant Grove Market.** If you prefer to take a self-guided walk, you can rent snowshoes here. ⊠ *Generals Hwy. (Rte. 198), 3 mi northeast of Rte. 180, Big Stump entrance* ☏ *559/335–2665* ◷ *Daily 9–6.*

**Grant Grove Visitor Center.** For a $1 donation, the visitor center rents out snowshoes for ranger-led walks. ⊠ *Generals Hwy. (Rte. 198), 3 mi northeast of Rte. 180, Big Stump entrance* ☏ *559/565–4307* ◷ *Daily 9:30–4:30.*

### Swimming

Swimming in the parks is generally quite dangerous. For more information, ⇨ Swimming *in* Sequoia.

# WHAT'S NEARBY

## Nearby Towns & Attractions

### Nearby Towns

In the foothills of the Sierra along the Kaweah River, **Three Rivers** is a leafy hamlet whose livelihood depends largely on tourism from Sequoia and Kings Canyon. Close to Sequoia's Ash Mountain and Lookout Point (Mineral King) entrances, this is a good spot to find a room when park lodgings are full. **Visalia**, a city of 93,000, lies 46 mi east of Sequoia and 55 mi west of Kings Canyon on the edge of the San Joaquin Valley. Its vibrant downtown contains several good restaurants and bed-and-breakfasts. Closest to Kings Canyon's Big Stump entrance, **Sanger** lies on the Kings River where it emerges from the foothills, about 40 minutes from the park. The agricultural community calls itself "the Nation's Christmas Tree City" and celebrates the holiday each year with a caravan to the General Grant Tree. **Fresno**, the main gateway to the Southern Sierra region, is about 55 mi west of Kings Canyon and about 65 mi southwest of Yosemite. California's sixth-largest city has all the amenities you'd expect of a major crossroads.

## What to See

**Project Survival's Cat Haven.** Take the rare opportunity to glimpse a Siberian lynx, a cloud leopard, a Bengal tiger and other endangered wild cats at this conservation facility. ⊠ *38257 E. Kings Canyon Rd. (Rte. 180), 15 mi west of Kings Canyon National Park, Dunlap* ☎ *559/338–3216* ⊕ *www.cathaven.com* ⌦ *$8.50* ☉ *May–Sept., Weds.–Mon. 10–5; Oct.–Apr., Thurs.–Mon. 10–4. Last tour leaves 1 hr before closing.*

★ **Sequoia National Forest & Giant Sequoia National Monument.** Covering 1,139,500 acres, this forest is tucked north of Sequoia National Park between the two sections of Kings Canyon National Park. Of the world's sequoia groves, more than half are in the part of the forest that has been further protected as a national monument. Three National Recreation Trails and a section of the Pacific Crest Trail wind through the landscape. Four streams are designated National Wild and Scenic Rivers; some of the nation's liveliest white water is found on the Forks section of the Kern. Lake Isabella (11,000 acres) is one of the area's largest reservoirs. There's cross-country skiing and snowmobiling in winter, and 900 mi of trail for hiking, camping, and picnicking.

Anglers go for 10- to 12-inch trout on **Hume Lake** (⊠ Hume Lake Rd., 3 mi. south of Rte. 180) in Sequoia National Forest, also ideal for swimming and boating. At the **Hume Lake Forest Service District Office** (⊠ 35860 Kings Canyon Scenic Byway [Rte. 180] ☎ 559/338–2251), pick up maps and books on the Hume Lake area. It's open weekdays 8–4:30 and Saturday 8–4:30 in summer. ⊠ *Entrances: Forest Rd. off Generals Hwy. (Rte. 198), 7 mi southeast of Grant Grove; Hume Lake Rd. between Generals Hwy. (Rte. 198) and Kings Canyon Scenic Byway (Rte. 180); Kings Canyon Scenic Byway (Rte. 180) between Grant Grove and Cedar Grove* ☎ *559/784–1500* ⊕ *www.fs.fed. us/r5/sequoia.*

# WHERE TO STAY & EAT

## About the Restaurants

Dining in the Southern Sierra is generally a simple affair, with even the fanciest restaurants offering little in the way of culinary excitement. In the parks, fare is extremely humble except at the Wuksachi Lodge Dining Room; it's the only restaurant in the area where you really need reservations, but even there you can wear jeans and order a burger. Outside the parks, you have to come down from the hills and into Visalia if you're in the mood for memorable food.

## About the Hotels

Except for Wuksachi Lodge in Sequoia, in-park accommodations are no-frills. You'll nonetheless pay a premium to stay in the parks, but it is well worth it to spare yourself the long drive from even the closest towns. Summer is peak season, and you should reserve as far ahead of your visit as you can. A room is easier to come by outside the parks, where you can generally find a last-minute place to lay your head if you're not too particular.

## About the Campgrounds

The campgrounds within Sequoia and Kings Canyon afford pretty settings for a relaxed getaway. Many do not accept reservations or cash, and none has full-service bells and whistles (or even RV hookups), but there are plenty of options that don't require you to hike in. Those around Lodgepole and Grant Grove get quite busy in summer with vacationing families, while Cedar Grove sites attract a younger, crunchier set. Permits are required for backcountry camping.

# Where to Eat

## In Sequoia

★ **$–$$$**  ✕ **Wuksachi Village Dining Room.** In the high-ceiling dining room at Sequoia's only upscale restaurant, huge windows run the length of the room, providing a view of the surrounding trees. The dinner menu lists everything from sandwiches and burgers to steaks and pasta. Breakfast and lunch are also served. ☒ *Wuksachi Village* ☎ *559/565–4070* ⌦ *Reservations essential. $12–$26* ▭ *AE, D, DC, MC, V.*

**$**  ✕ **Wolverton Barbecue.** All-you-can-eat barbecue ribs and chicken, hot dogs and hamburgers, and lots of sides and desserts are whipped up outdoors overlooking Wolverton Meadow Friday through Sunday evenings. After the meal is a ranger talk, campfire sing-along, or living history demonstration. Buy tickets at Wuksachi Lodge or Lodgepole Market. ☒ *Wolverton Rd., 1½ mi northeast off Generals Hwy. (Rte. 198)* ☎ *559/565–4070 or 559/565–3301. $19 prix fixe* ▭ *AE, D, DC, MC, V* ⊘ *No lunch. Closed Mon.–Thurs. and early Sept.–mid-June.*

**¢**  ✕ **Lodgepole Market and Snack Bar.** Visit the market for pre-packaged sandwiches and salads to go or to assemble the components of a picnic. In summer, there's a deli for sandwiches and a snack bar for breakfast, pizza, and hamburgers. ☒ *Next to Lodgepole Visitor Center* ☎ *559/565–3301. $4–$6* ▭ *AE, D, DC, MC, V* ⊘ *Closed early Sept.–mid-Apr.*

PICNIC AREAS  **Crescent Meadow.** This area near Moro Rock has vistas over the meadows. Tables are under the giant sequoia, off the parking area. There are restrooms and drinking water. Fires are not allowed. ☒ *End of Moro Rock–Crescent Rd., 2⁹⁄₁₀ mi east off Generals Hwy. (Rte. 198).*

**Foothills Picnic Area.** Near the parking lot at the southern entrance of the park, this small area has tables on grass. Drinking water and restrooms are available. ☒ *Near Foothills Visitor Center.*

**Halstead Meadow.** Tables are at the edge of the meadow at this area off the main road and a short walk from parking. Grills and restrooms are provided, but there's no drinking water. The Dorst Campground is nearby. ⊠ *Generals Hwy. (Rte. 198), 4 mi north of Lodgepole junction.*

**Hospital Rock.** Native Americans once ground acorns into meal at this site; outdoor exhibits tell the story. Tables are on grass a short distance from the parking lot. Grills, drinking water, and restrooms are available. The Buckeye Flat Campground is nearby. ⊠ *Generals Hwy. (Rte. 198), 6 mi north of Ash Mountain entrance.*

**Pinewood Picnic Area.** Picnic in Giant Forest, among the giant sequoia trees. Drinking water, restrooms, and grills are provided. ⊠ *Generals Hwy. (Rte. 198), 2 mi north of Giant Forest Museum, halfway between Giant Forest Museum and General Sherman Tree.*

**Wolverton Meadow.** At a major trailhead to the backcountry, this is a great place to stop for lunch before a hike. The area sits in a mixed-conifer forest adjacent to parking. Drinking water, grills, and restrooms are available. ⊠ *Wolverton Rd., 1½ mi northeast off Generals Hwy. (Rte. 198).*

### In Kings Canyon

**$–$$$** ✕ **Grant Grove Restaurant.** Come here year-round for simple family-style dining. The restaurant serves full breakfasts, and hot entrées and sandwiches for lunch and dinner. Take-out service is available. ⊠ *Grant Grove Village* ☎ *559/335–5500. $10–$30* ▭ *AE, D, MC, V.*

**¢–$$** ✕ **Cedar Grove Restaurant.** This snack bar with counter service serves eggs at breakfast, sandwiches and hamburgers at lunch and dinner, and several evening specials like chicken-fried steak. Take your tray onto the deck overlooking the Kings River. ⊠ *Cedar Grove Village* ☎ *559/565–0100. $5–$20* ▭ *AE, D, MC, V* ☉ *Closed Oct.–May.*

**¢–$** ✕ **Cedar Grove Market.** You can pick up sandwiches and salads to go at this market, as well as a range of grocery items. It's open daily 8–8. ⊠ *Cedar Grove Village* ☎ *559/565–0100. $3–$10* ▭ *AE, D, MC, V* ☉ *Closed late Oct.–mid-Apr.*

PICNIC AREAS **Big Stump.** At the edge of a logged sequoia grove, some trees still stand at this site. Near the park's entrance, the area is paved and next to the road. It's the only picnic area in either park that is plowed in the wintertime. Restrooms, grills, and drinking water are available, and the area is entirely accessible. ⊠ *Just inside Rte. 180, Big Stump entrance.*

**Columbine.** This grassy picnic area near the sequoias is relatively level. Tables, restrooms, drinking water, and grills are available. ⊠ *Grant Tree Rd., just off Generals Hwy. (Rte. 198), ½ mi northwest of Grant Grove Visitor Center.*

**Grizzly Falls.** A short walk from the parking area leads to a grassy picnic spot near the bottom of a canyon. The area is not level. Tables and restrooms are available, grills and water are not. ⊠ *Off Rte. 180, 2½ mi west of Cedar Grove entrance.*

### Outside the Parks

**$$–$$$** ✕ **Gateway Restaurant and Lodge.** The patio of this raucous roadhouse overlooks the roaring Kaweah River as it plunges out of the high country, and though the food is nothing special, the location makes up for it. Standouts include baby back ribs and eggplant parmigiana; there's also a cocktail lounge, and guest rooms are available for overnight visitors. Breakfast isn't served weekdays; dinner reservations are essential on weekends. ☒ *45978 Sierra Dr., Three Rivers* ☎ *559/561–4133. $14–$28* ⊟ *AE, D, MC, V.*

**$–$$** ✕ **Hummingbird Café.** The Kaweah River flows within view of the many windows at this restaurant that, true to its name, attracts hummingbirds with its windowside feeders. The food is American: steaks, chicken, salads, and pastas for dinner; burgers, sandwiches, salads, and homemade soup for lunch; and omelets, eggs Benedict, and steak and eggs for breakfast. ☒ *41775 Sierra Dr., Three Rivers* ☎ *559/561–0140. $10–$18* ⊟ *AE, D, MC, V* ⊙ *No dinner Mon.*

**$–$$** ✕ **Stony Creek Restaurant.** This family-style restaurant in Sequoia National Forest serves soups, sandwiches, and burgers at lunch, and pasta, salads, fish, and steaks in the evening. ☒ *Generals Hwy. (Rte. 198), between Sequoia and Kings Canyon parks, 12 mi south of Grant Grove, Sequoia National Forest* ☎ *559/565–3909. $8–$16* ⊟ *AE, D, MC, V* ⊙ *Closed mid-Oct.–May.*

## Where to Stay

### In Sequoia

**$$$–$$$$**
FodorsChoice
★
🏨 **Wuksachi Lodge.** These cedar-and-stone lodge buildings, which blend with the landscape, house comfortable rooms with modern amenities. The village is 7,200 feet above sea level; many of the rooms have spectacular views of the surrounding mountains. ☒ *Wuksachi Village 93262* ☎ *559/565–4070 front desk, 559/253–2199 or 888/252–5757 reservations* 🖷 *559/456–0542* ⊕ *www.visitsequoia.com* ⬐ *102 rooms* ♨ *Restaurant, refrigerator, dial-up, Wi-Fi, bar, no a/c, no-smoking rooms. $155–$219* ⊟ *AE, D, DC, MC, V.*

**☾ $–$$$** 🏨 **Silver City Resort.** High on the Mineral King Road, this resort provides an excellent alternative to the crowded properties at the parks' lower elevations. Lodgings range from modern Swiss-style chalets to traditional rustic alpine cabins with woodstoves and central bathing facilities. There is a small general store, a bakery serving homemade pies, and a modestly priced restaurant on-site, though the latter serves Thursday through Monday only. Some cabins share a central shower and bath. ☒ *Mineral King Rd., 20 mi east of Hwy. 198, 93271* ☎ *559/561–3223 or 805/528–2730* ⊕ *www.silvercityresort.com* ⬐ *13 units, 8 with shared bath* ♨ *Restaurant, kitchen, refrigerator (some), dial-up, no a/c, no phone (some), no TV, no-smoking rooms. $75–$200* ⊟ *MC, V* ⊙ *Closed Nov.–May.*

CAMPGROUNDS & RV PARKS

**$$** ⛺ **Buckeye Flat Campground.** This tents-only campground at the southern end of Sequoia National Park is smaller—and consequently quieter—than campgrounds elsewhere in the park. Because of its low elevation (2,800 feet), it scorches in summer. ☒ *Generals Hwy., 6 mi north of Foothills Visitor Center* ☎ *559/565–3341* ⬐ *28 tent sites* ♨ *Flush toilets, drinking water, bear boxes, fire grates, picnic tables* ♨ *Reservations not accepted. $18* ⊟ *No credit cards* ⊙ *Apr.–early Sept.*

**$$** ⛺ **Dorst Creek Campground.** This large campground is at 6,700 feet. Use the bear boxes: this is a popular area for the furry creatures to raid. Reservations, made by mail or through the Web site, are essential in summer. There are accessible sites here. ⊠ *Generals Hwy. (Rte. 198), 8 mi north of Lodgepole Visitor Center, near Kings Canyon border* ☎ *301/722– 1257 or 800/365–2267* 🖷 *301/722–1174* ⊕ *http://reservations.nps. gov* ⤢ *204 tent and RV sites* ⚸ *Flush toilets, dump station, drinking water, bear boxes, fire grates, picnic tables, public telephone.* $20 ▤ *D, MC, V* ☻ *Memorial Day–Labor Day.*

**$$** ⚠ **Lodgepole Campground.** The largest Lodgepole-area campground is also the noisiest, though things do quiet down at night. Restrooms are nearby. Reservations are essential up to five months in advance for stays between mid-May and mid-October. ⊠ *Off Generals Hwy. beyond Lodgepole Village* ☎ *559/565–3341 Ext. 2 for information, 800/365– 2267 reservations* ⊕ *http://reservations.nps.gov* ⤢ *214 tent and RV sites* ⚸ *Flush toilets, dump station (summer only), drinking water, guest laundry (summer only), showers (summer only), bear boxes, fire grates, picnic tables, public telephone, general store.* $20 ▤ *D, MC, V* ☻ *Year-round.*

**$$** ⚠ **Potwisha Campground.** On the Marble Fork of the Kaweah River, this midsize campground with attractive surroundings sits at 2,100 feet— which means it gets no snow in winter and can be hotter in summer than campgrounds at higher elevations. RVs up to 30 feet long can camp here. ⊠ *Generals Hwy., 4 mi north of Foothills Visitor Center* ☎ *559/565– 3341* ⤢ *42 tent and RV sites* ⚸ *Flush toilets, dump station, drinking water, bear boxes, fire grates, picnic tables, public telephone* ⚸ *Reservations not accepted.* $18 ▤ *No credit cards* ☻ *Year-round.*

**$** ⚠ **Atwell Mill Campground.** At 6,650 feet, this tents-only campground is just south of the Western Divide. There are telephones and a general store is ½ mi away at the Silver City Resort. Reservations are not accepted. ⊠ *Mineral King Rd., 20 mi east of Hwy. 198* ☎ *559/565–3341* ⤢ *23 tent sites* ⚸ *Pit toilets, drinking water, showers, bear boxes, fire grates, picnic tables.* $12 ▤ *No credit cards* ☻ *May–Oct.*

**$** ⚠ **South Fork Campground.** At 3,600 feet, this tiny campground is at the southernmost corner of Sequoia. At the end of a dirt road, it best accommodates tent campers. ⊠ *End of South Fork Rd., 12 mi east of Generals Hwy. (Rte. 198)* ☎ *No phone* ⤢ *10 tent sites* ⚸ *Pit toilets, running water (non-potable), bear boxes, fire grates, picnic tables* ⚸ *Reservations not accepted.* $12 *May–Labor Day; free rest of the year* ▤ *No credit cards* ☻ *Year-round.*

## In Kings Canyon

**$$** 🏨 **Cedar Grove Lodge.** This lodge manages to deliver peace and quiet, because the hardcore hiking types who stay here go to bed early. It's not particularly attractive or clean, but it's the only accommodation out in Kings River Canyon. Book far in advance—the lodge has only 21 rooms. Each has two queen-size beds, and three have kitchenettes and patios. ⊠ *Kings Canyon Scenic Byway* ⅅ *Sequoia Kings Canyon Park Services Co., 5755 E. Kings Canyon Rd., Suite 101, Fresno 93727* ☎ *559/335– 5500 or 866/522–6966* 🖷 *559/335–5507* ⊕ *www.sequoia-kingscanyon. com* ⤢ *21 rooms* ⚸ *Snack bar, some kitchenettes, laundry facilities, no phone, no TV, no-smoking rooms.* $109–$125 ▤ *AE, D, MC, V* ☻ *Closed mid-Oct.–mid-May.*

**$$$** ⌂ **John Muir Lodge.** This modern, timber-sided lodge is nestled in a wooded area near Grant Grove Village. The rooms and suites all have queen beds and private baths, and there's a comfortable common room with low-pile carpeting and a stone fireplace where you can play cards and board games. Though it's little more than a good motel, this is the finest place to stay in Grant Grove. ⊠ *Kings Canyon Scenic Byway, ¼ mi north of Grant Grove Village* ◌ *Sequoia Kings Canyon Park Services Co., 5755 E. Kings Canyon Rd., Suite 101, Fresno 93727* ☎ *559/ 335–5500 or 866/522–6966* 🖷 *559/335–5507* ⊕ *www.sequoia- kingscanyon.com* 🛏 *24 rooms, 6 suites* ♿ *No a/c, no TV. $159* 🗖 *AE, D, MC, V.*

**$–$$** ⌂ **Grant Grove Cabins.** Some of the wood-panel cabins here have heaters, electric lights, and private baths, but most have woodstoves, battery lamps, and shared baths. Those who don't mind roughing it might opt for the tent cabins. In winter, only the cabins that have private baths remain open. ⊠ *Kings Canyon Scenic Byway in Grant Grove Village* ◌ *Sequoia Kings Canyon Park Services Co., 5755 E. Kings Canyon Rd., Suite 101, Fresno 93727* ☎ *559/335–5500 or 866/522–6966* 🖷 *559/335–5507* ⊕ *www.sequoia-kingscanyon.com* 🛏 *36 cabins, 9 with bath; 19 tents* ♿ *Coffee shop; no a/c, no room phones, no room TVs. $5–$18. $58–$115* 🗖 *AE, D, MC, V.*

CAMPGROUNDS
& RV PARKS

**$$** ⛰ **Azalea Campground.** Of the three campgrounds in the Grant Grove area (the others are Sunset and Crystal Springs), Azalea is the only one open year-round. It sits at 6,500 feet amid giant sequoias, yet is close to restaurants, stores, and other facilities. Some sites at Azalea are wheelchair accessible. The campground can accommodate RVs up to 30 feet. ⊠ *Kings Canyon Scenic Byway, ¼ mi north of Grant Grove Village* ☎ *559/565–3341* 🛏 *113 tent and RV sites* ♿ *Flush toilets, drinking water, showers, bear boxes, fire grates, picnic tables, public telephone, general store. $18 May–mid-Oct.; free rest of year* 🗖 *No credit cards* ☼ *Year-round.*

**$$** ⛰ **Canyon View Campground.** One of four sites near Cedar Grove, this campground is near the start of the Don Cecil Trail, which leads to Lookout Point. The elevation of the camp is 4,600 feet along the Kings River. There are no accessible sites. ⊠ *Off Kings Canyon Scenic Byway, ½-mi east of Cedar Grove Village* ☎ *No phone* 🛏 *37 tent sites* ♿ *Flush toilets, drinking water, bear boxes, fire grates, picnic tables, public telephone* ♿ *Reservations not accepted. $18* 🗖 *No credit cards* ☼ *Late May–late Sept., as needed.*

**$$** ⛰ **Crystal Springs Campground.** Near the Grant Grove Village and the towering sequoias, this camp is at 6,500 feet. There are accessible sites here. ⊠ *Off Generals Hwy. (Rte. 198), ¼-mi north of Grant Grove Visitor Center* ☎ *No phone* 🛏 *62 tent and RV sites* ♿ *Flush toilets, drinking water, bear boxes, fire grates, picnic tables, public telephone* ♿ *Reservations not accepted. $18* 🗖 *No credit cards* ☼ *Memorial Day–Labor Day.*

**$$** ⛰ **Sentinel Campground.** Of the three campgrounds in the Cedar Grove area (the other two are Sheep Creek and Moraine, both open June–September only), Sentinel is open the longest. At 4,600 feet and within walking distance of Cedar Grove Village, it fills up fast in the summer. Some sites are wheelchair accessible, and the campground can accommodate RVs up to 30 feet. Nearby are laundry facilities, a restaurant, a general store, and a ranger station. ♿ *Flush toilets, drinking water, showers (nearby), bear boxes, fire grates, picnic tables, public telephone* ⇨ *82 tent and RV sites)* ⊠ *Kings Canyon Scenic Byway, ¼-mi west of Cedar Grove Village* ☎ *559/565–3341. $18* ⊸ *Reservations not accepted* ⊟ *No credit cards* ⊙ *May–Oct.*

**$$**   ⚠ **Sheep Creek Campground.** Of the overflow campgrounds, this is one

**Fodor$Choice** of the prettiest. The camp, like the adjacent Cedar Grove, is at 4,600

★ feet along the Kings River. ⊠ *Off Kings Canyon Scenic Byway, 1 mi west of Cedar Grove Village* ☎ *No phone* ⇨ *111 tent and RV sites* ♿ *Flush toilets, drinking water, bear boxes, fire grates, picnic tables, public telephone* ⊸ *Reservations not accepted. $18* ⊟ *No credit cards* ⊙ *Late May–late Sept., as needed.*

**$$**   ⚠ **Sunset Campground.** Many of the easiest trails through Grant Grove are adjacent to this large camp, near the giant sequoias at 6,500 feet. ⊠ *Off Generals Hwy. (Rte. 198), near Grant Grove Visitor Center* ☎ *No phone* ⇨ *200 tent and RV sites* ♿ *Flush toilets, drinking water, bear boxes, fire grates, picnic tables, public telephone* ⊸ *Reservations not accepted. $18* ⊟ *No credit cards* ⊙ *Memorial Day–late Sept.*

### Outside the Parks

The only lodging immediately outside the parks is in Three Rivers. Numerous chain properties operate in Visalia or Fresno, about an hour from the south and north entrances, respectively.

If none of the properties listed here suits your needs, check with the **Three Rivers Reservation Center** (☎ 559/561–0410).

**$$–$$$**   🏨 **Cinnamon Creek Bed and Breakfast.** Rooms have mountain views and a vegan breakfast is served at this remote 10-acre ranch with resident donkeys. One room has a private terrace overlooking the river. Reservations are required. ⌖ *Box 54, Three Rivers 93271* ☎ *559/561–1107* ⇨ *2 rooms, 2 cabins* ♿ *Some kitchens, in-room VCRs, hot tub, hiking; no room TVs, no a/c. $110–$180* ⊟ *AE, D, MC, V* ⦿ *CP.*

**$$–$$$**   🏨 **Montecito-Sequoia Lodge.** A summer-camp atmosphere prevails all year long at this rustic, family-oriented resort just south of Kings Canyon National Park. Specializing in all-inclusive vacations, it offers everything from skiing and snowboarding in winter to sailing and horseback riding in summer. From mid-June to early September there's normally a six-night minimum, but you can book a one-night stay on Saturdays. ⊠ *8000 Generals Hwy., 11 mi south of Grant Grove, Kings Canyon National Park 93633* ☎ *559/565–3388, 800/227–9900 reservations* 🖷 *650/967–0540* ⊕ *www.montecitosequoia.com* ⇨ *32 rooms, 13 cabins* ♿ *Restaurant, tennis court, pool, bicycles, children's programs (ages 2–18), no a/c, no phone, no TV. $145–$200* ⊟ *AE, D, MC, V* ⦿ *FAP.*

**$–$$**   🏨 **Buckeye Tree Lodge.** Every room at this two-story motel has a patio facing a sun-dappled grassy lawn, right on the banks of the Kaweah River. Accommodations are simple and well kept, and the lodge sits a mere quarter mile from the park gate. Book well in advance. ⊠ *46000 Sierra Dr. (Hwy. 198), Three Rivers 93271* ☎ *559/561–5900* ⊕ *www.*

*buckeyetree.com* 🖨 *11 rooms, 1 cottage* ⚒ *VCR, pool, some pets allowed, no-smoking rooms. $100–$115* ▭ *AE, D, DC, MC, V* ⵏⵓ *CP.*

**$–$$** ⵏ **Lazy J Ranch Motel.** Surrounded by 12 acres of green lawns and a split-rail fence, the Lazy J is a modest, well-kept compound of freestanding cottages near the banks of the Kaweah River. Some rooms have gas fireplaces; all have coffeemakers. ✉ *39625 Sierra Dr., Hwy 198, Three Rivers 93271* ☎ *559/561–4449 or 888/315–2378* 🖷 *559/561–4889* ⊕ *www.bvilazyj.com* 🖨 *11 rooms, 7 cottages* ⚒ *Kitchen (some), refrigerator, VCR, pool, laundry facilities, some pets allowed, no-smoking rooms. $95–$125* ▭ *AE, D, DC, MC, V* ⵏⵓ *CP.*

**$–$$** ⵏ **Sequoia Motel.** An old-fashioned single-story mom-and-pop motel, the Sequoia stands out with such extra touches as country-style quilts and mismatched Americana furnishings that lend a retro charm to the rooms. The on-site owners keep the rooms meticulously clean. There are also one- and two-bedroom cottages with full kitchens. ✉ *43000 Sierra Dr. (Hwy. 198), Box 145, Three Rivers 93271* ☎ *559/561–4453* 🖷 *559/561–1625* ⊕ *www.sequoiamotel.com* 🖨 *11 rooms, 3 cottages* ⚒ *Kitchen (some), VCR (some), Wi-Fi, pool, laundry facilities, no phone, no-smoking rooms. $95–$120* ▭ *AE, D, MC, V.*

**33**

# SEQUOIA & KINGS CANYON ESSENTIALS

ACCESSIBILITY: All of the visitor centers, the Giant Forest Museum, and Big Trees Trail are wheelchair-accessible, as are some short ranger-led walks and talks. General Sherman Tree can be reached via a paved, level trail near a parking area. None of the caves is accessible, and wilderness areas must be reached by horseback or on foot. Some picnic tables are extended to accommodate wheelchairs. Many of the major sites are in the 6,000-foot range, and thin air at high elevations can cause respiratory distress for people with breathing difficulties. Carry oxygen if necessary. Contact the park's main number for more information.

ADMISSION FEES The vehicle admission fee is $10 and valid for seven days in both parks. Those who enter by bus, on foot, bicycle, motorcycle, or horse pay $5 for a seven-day pass. Senior citizens who are U.S. residents over the age of 62 pay $10 for a lifetime pass, and permanently disabled U.S. residents are admitted free.

ADMISSION HOURS The parks are open daily 24 hours. Sequoia and Kings Canyon National Parks are in the Pacific time zone.

ATMS/BANKS

ⵏ **Bank of America** ✉ 212 E. Main St., Visalia ☎ 559/635–3160. **Bank of the Sierra** ✉ 40884 Sierra Dr., Three Rivers ☎ 559/561–5910. **Grant Grove Village Gift Shop** ✉ Grant Grove Village, Kings Canyon National Park. **Lodgepole Market** ✉ Next to Lodgepole Visitor Center, Sequoia National Park.

AUTOMOBILE SERVICE STATIONS

ⵏ **Hume Lake Christian Camps Gas Station** ✉ Hume Lake Rd., off Rte. 180, 11 mi east of Grant Grove ☎ 559/335–2000 Ext. 279. **Pat O'-Connell's Service** ✉ 41500 Sierra Dr., Three Rivers ☎ 559/561–4776. **Three Rivers Chevron** ✉ 41907 Sierra Dr., Three Rivers ☎ 559/561–3835.

EMERGENCIES Call 911 from any telephone within the park in an emergency. Rangers at the Cedar Grove, Foothills, Grant Grove, and Lodgepole visitor centers and the Mineral King ranger station are trained in first aid. National Park rangers have legal jurisdiction within park boundaries: contact a ranger station or visitor center for police matters. For nonemergencies, call the parks' main number, 559/565-3341.

LOST AND FOUND Report lost items or turn in found items at any visitor center or ranger station. Items are held at a central location and are handled by park rangers. For more information, call park headquarters at 559/565-3181.

PERMITS If you plan to camp in the backcountry, your group must have a backcountry camping permit, which costs $15 for hikers or $30 for stock users (horseback riders, etc.). One permit covers the entire group. Availability of permits depends upon trailhead quotas. Advance reservations are accepted by mail, fax, or e-mail for a $15 processing fee, beginning March 1, and must be made at least three weeks in advance. Without a reservation, you may still get a permit on a first-come, first-served basis starting at 1 PM the day before you plan to hike. For more information on backcountry camping or travel with pack animals (horses, mules, burros, or llamas), contact the Wilderness Permit Office or visit www.nps.gov/seki/resform.htm.
🛈 **Wilderness Permit Office** ☎ 530/565-3761. **Wilderness Permit Reservations** ⌂ HCR 89 Box 60, Three Rivers 93271 ☎ 559/575-3766 🖷 559/565-4239.

POST OFFICES
🛈 **Kings Canyon National Park Branch** ✉ 86724 Rte. 180, Grant Grove Village, Kings Canyon National Park 93633 ☎ 559/335-2499. **Sequoia National Park Branch** ✉ Lodgepole Village, Sequoia National Park 93262 ☎ 559/565-3468. **Three Rivers Main Post Office** ✉ 40857 Sierra Dr., Three Rivers 93271 ☎ 559/561-4261.

PUBLIC TELEPHONES Public telephones may be found at the park entrance stations, vis-itor centers, ranger stations, some trail-heads, and at all restaurants and lodging facilities in the park.

RESTROOMS Public restrooms may be found at all visitor centers and campgrounds. Additional locations include Big Stump, Columbine, Grizzly Falls, Hospital Rock, Wolverton, Crescent Meadow, Giant Forest Museum, and Crystal Cave.

### NEARBY TOWN INFORMATION
🛈 **Fresno Convention & Visitors Bureau** ✉ 848 M St., Fresno 93721 ☎ 559/445-8300 ⊕ www.fresnocvb.org. **Fresno County Office of Tourism** ✉ 2220 Tulare St., Fresno 93721 ☎ 559/262-4271 ⊕ www.gofresnocounty.com. **Sanger Chamber of Commerce** ✉ 1789 Jensen Ave., Sanger 93657 ☎ 559/875-4575 ⊕ www.sanger.org. **Sequoia Foothills Chamber of Commerce** ✉ 42268 Sierra Dr., Three Rivers 93271 ☎ 559/561-3300 ⊕ www.threerivers.com. **Visalia Chamber of Commerce & Visitors Bureau** ✉ 220 N. Santa Fe Ave., Visalia 93291 ☎ 559/734-5876 or 877/847-2542 ⊕ www.visaliachamber.org.

### VISITOR INFORMATION
🛈 **Delaware North Park Services** ⌂ Box 89, Sequoia National Park, CA 93262 ☎ 559/565-4070 or 888/252-5757 ⊕ www.visitsequoia.com. **Sequoia and Kings Canyon National Parks** ✉ 47050 Generals Hwy. (Rte. 198), Three Rivers, CA 93271-9651 ☎ 559/565-3341 or 559/565-3134 ⊕ www.nps.gov/seki. **Sequoia Natural History Association** ⌂ HCR 89 Box 10, Three Rivers, CA 93271 ☎ 559/565-3759 ⊕ www.sequoiahistory.org. **U.S. Forest Service, Sequoia National Forest** ✉ 900 W. Grand Ave., Porterville, CA 93527 ☎ 559/784-1500 ⊕ www.fs.fed.us/r5/sequoia. **Kings Canyon Park Services** ⌂ Box 909, Kings Canyon National Park, CA 93633 ☎ 559/335-5500 or 866/522-6966 ⊕ www.sequoia-kingscanyon.com.

# Theodore Roosevelt National Park

Wild Horses, Theodore Roosevelt National Park

**WORD OF MOUTH**

"I grow very fond of this place, and it certainly has a desolate, grim
beauty of its own, that has a curious fascination for me."

–Theodore Roosevelt

# WELCOME TO THEODORE ROOSEVELT

## TOP REASONS TO GO

★ **The Granddaddy Trail:**
Hike the Maah Daah Hey
Trail, which means "grandfather" It's one of the most
popular and well-main-
tained trails in western
North Dakota.

★ **Views from Above:** Get
a 360-degree view of the
badlands from Buck Hill.

★ **History Lessons from the
Frontier:** View Maltese
Cross Ranch Cabin, once
part of Theodore Roo-
sevelt's Dakota Terrority
property.

★ **Badlands Broadway:**
Come experience a theatrical tribute to the history
and personalities that
make up the Old West at
the Medora Musical.

★ **Great Clubbing—Golf
That Is:** Perfect your swing
at Bully Pulpit Golf Course
in Medora, one of Amer-
ica's best courses near a
national park.

★ **Away from It All:** As
one of the most isolated
parks, you're unlikely to
encounter many other souls
here.

**1** **North Unit.** Visitors looking
to enjoy the great outdoors
should be sure to travel along
the 14-mi scenic tour and stop at
one of the many hiking trailheads along the way. These
trailheads give easy access to
the backcountry of the North
Unit.

**2** **South Unit.** Often considered
the main unit of Theodore Roosevelt National Park and adjacent to the famous town of
Medora, the South Unit is the
home to some of the former
president's personal artifacts
and even his cabin.

**3** **Elkhorn Ranch.** This area
of the park is the actual location
of Teddy Roosevelt's ranch in
the badlands. None of the ranch
buildings are still standing, but
signs mark their former location.

## GETTING ORIENTED

The Little Missouri River
winds throughout this western North Dakota park, and
plenty of bison, deer, antelope, coyote, prairie dogs,
and bald eagles inhabit the
land. Climb the peaks and
you will get exceptional
views of the canyons,
caprocks, petrified forest,
and other bizarre geological formations that make up
the badlands.

Badlands formations.

| KEY | |
|---|---|
| 👣 | *Ranger Station* |
| △ | *Campground* |
| 🔀 | *Picnic Area* |
| 🍴 | *Restaurant* |
| 🏠 | *Lodge* |
| 🚶 | *Trailhead* |
| 🚻 | *Restrooms* |
| ⇘ | *Scenic Viewpoint* |
| ------- | *Walking/Hiking Trails* |
| ⋯⋯ | *Bicycle Path* |

NORTH DAKOTA

**North Unit**

Man and Grass Overlook
Bentonitic Clay Overlook
Scenic Drive
Buckhorn Trail
Caprock Coulee Trailhead
Long X Trailhead
**Visitor Center**
Oxbow Overlook
Achenbach Trail
Little Missouri River
Juniper Campground
Slump Block Pullout
GCC Campground
NORTH UNIT
Achenbach Trail
Achenbach Hills

85
94

0        2 mi
0        2 km

Maah Daah Hey Trail

**South Unit**

Little Missouri River
Mike Auney Bottom
◆ **Horse Camp**
Petrified Forest Plateau
Big Plateau
Scenic Loop Drive
Beef Corral Pullout
**Peaceful Valley Ranch** ◆
Boicourt Overlook
**Cottonwood**
Halliday Well Site
Prairie Dog Town
SOUTH UNIT
2
River Woodland Overlook
North Dakota Badlands Overlook
◆ **Buck Hill**
Maltese Cross Ranch Cabin
3
Medora
**Visitor Center**
Ridgeline Trail
Prairie Dog Town
Chateau DeMores State Historic Site
Prairie Dog Town
**Sully Creek State Park** ◆
Sully Creek State Park
10
94
**Visitor Center**

0        2 mi
0        2 km

# THEODORE ROOSEVELT PLANNER

## When to Go

The park is open year-round, and people can hike year-round. But, North Dakota winters can be brutal—very cold, windy, and snowy; not the most desirable conditions for hiking. Portions of some roads close during winter months, depending on snowfall. Rangers discontinue their outdoor programs when autumn comes, and they recommend that only experienced hikers do any winter explorations.

**Though July and August tend to be the busiest months, it's rarely crowded.** Fewer than 500,000 people visit the park each year, with the South Unit receiving the greater number of visitors. The best times of year to see wildlife and hike comfortably are May through October. December through February the park is all but desolate, but it's a beautiful time to see the wildlife as they cope with the snow and ice. Also in winter, sunsets can be very vivid as the colors reflect off the snow and ice. The park gets an average of 30 inches of snow per year.

AVG. HIGH/LOW TEMPS.

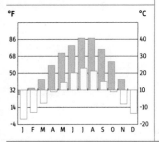

## Flora & Fauna

The park's landscape is one of prairies marked by cliffs and rock chasms made of alternating layers of sandstone, siltstone, mudstone, and bentonite clay. In spring the prairies are awash with tall grasses, wildflowers, and shrubs including the ubiquitous poison ivy. The pesky plant also inhabits the forests, where you find box elders, elms, and junipers among the trees. To avoid the rash-inducing plant—and scrapes and bruises that may come from rocks and thick undergrowth—it's always advisable to hike with long pants and sturdy boots.

More than 500 American bison, live in the park. These normally-docile beasts look tame, but with a set of horns, up to a ton of weight and legs that will carry them at speeds in excess of 35 mph, they could be the most dangerous animals within park boundaries. Park rangers will tell you repeatedly not to approach them. A small population of mountain lions also lives in the park, but they're rarely seen. The same goes for prairie rattlers.

On the less-threatening side of the park's fauna, a herd of 300–400 elk live only in the South Unit, favoring the Buck Hill area. Wild horses are also in the South Unit only, usually in the eastern section. The North Unit has a herd of longhorns that are often found in the bison corral area about 2½ mi west of the visitor center.

## Getting There & Around

Getting to and from the park is relatively easy due to its close proximity to Medora, as well as exceptional signage. The South Unit entrance and visitor center is just off I-94 in Medora at exits 23 and 27. The Painted Canyon Visitor Center is 7 mi east of Medora at exit 32. The North Unit entrance is south of Waterford City on U.S. 85. Bus transportation is available along I-94, with a stop in Medora that is only three blocks from the park entrance. Planes fly into the North Dakota towns of Bismarck, Dickinson, and Williston. Amtrak serves Williston.

There's ample parking space at all trailheads, and parking is free. Some roads are closed in winter. Be careful of buffalo and other wildlife on the roadway.

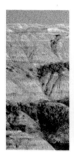

**34**

By T.D. Griffith

Across the open plains of North Dakota, you can travel for miles without seeing a house or business. Then you spy craggy ravines, tablelands, and gorges, and know at once you're in the badlands. The terrain has remained virtually unchanged since Theodore Roosevelt stepped off the train here in 1883, 24 and eager to shoot his first bison. Within two weeks, Roosevelt purchased an open-range cattle ranch, and the following year he returned to buy a second; both are a part of the 110-square-mi national park that bears his name.

The 26th president became dedicated to preserving the animals and land he saw devastated by hunting and overgrazing. He established the U.S. Forest Service and signed into law 150 national forests, 51 bird reserves, four game preserves, and five national parks. Theodore Roosevelt National Park was established in 1947 to commemorate his efforts.

## Scenic Drives

**North Unit Scenic Drive.** The 14-mi, two-way North Unit drive follows rugged terrain above spectacular views of the canyons, and is flanked by more than a dozen turn-outs with interpretive signs. Notice the slump blocks, massive segments of rock that have slipped down the cliff walls over time. Farther along you'll pass through badlands coulees, deep-water clefts that are now dry. There's always a good chance of meeting bison, mule deer, and longhorns along the way. The drive goes from the entrance to the Oxbow Overlook. Keep an eye out for longhorn cattle, just like the ones you would see in Texas.

★ **South Unit Scenic Loop Drive.** A 36-mi, two-way scenic loop takes you past prairie dog towns, coal veins, trailheads, and panoramic views of the badlands. Information on the park's natural history is posted at the various overlooks—be sure to stop at all of the interpretive signs to learn more about the park's natural and historical phenomena. Some of the best views can be seen from Scoria Point Overlook, Boicourt Overlook, North Dakota Badlands Overlook, Skyline Vista, and Buck Hill. If you hit the road at dusk, be prepared to get caught in a buffalo traffic jam, as the huge creatures sometimes block the road and aren't in any hurry to move. Don't get out of your car or honk at them—they don't like it (think Pamplona with you in their path).

# What to See

### Historic Sites

**Elkhorn Ranch.** This unit of the park is composed of the 218 acres of ranch-land Theodore Roosevelt purchased in 1884. Today there are no buildings here, but foundation blocks outline the original structures. Check with one of the visitor centers about river fording and road conditions before you go. ☒ *35 mi north of the South Unit Visitor Center.*

★ **Maltese Cross Ranch Cabin.** Seven mi from its original site in the river bottom sits the cabin Theodore Roosevelt commissioned to be built on his Dakota Territory property. Inside are Roosevelt's original writing table and rocking chair. Interpretive tours are held on the half hour every day June–September. ☒ *South Unit entrance, exits 24 and 27 off I–94.*

### Scenic Stops

Fodor'sChoice **Buck Hill.** At 2,855 feet, this is one of the highest points in the park and
★ provides a spectacular 360-degree view of the badlands. Come here for the sunset. ☒ *17 mi east of the South Unit Visitor Center.*

**Oxbow Overlook.** The view from this spot at the end of the North Unit drive looks over the unit's westerly badlands and the Little Missouri River, where it takes a sharp turn south. This is the place to come for stargazing. ☒ *14 mi west of the North Unit Visitor Center.*

For the best view of the Little Missouri River's 90-degree angle, hike a 1 ½-mi round-trip trail to **Sperati Point,** 430 feet above the riverbed. ☒ *14 mi west of the North Unit Visitor Center.*

★ **Painted Canyon Scenic Overlook.** Catch your first glimpse of badlands majesty here—the South Unit canyon's colors change dramatically with the movement of the sun across the sky. ☒ *Exit 32 off I–94.*

**Petrified Forest.** Although bits of petrified wood have been found all over the park, the densest collection is in the South Unit's west end, reached on foot or horseback via the Petrified Forest Loop Trail from Peaceful Valley Ranch (10 mi round-trip) or the park's west boundary (3 mi round-trip). ☒ *Trailheads: Peaceful Valley Ranch; west boundary (10 mi north of exit 23 off I–94/U.S. 10, via an unpaved road).*

### Visitor Centers

**North Unit Visitor Center.** A bookstore, gift shop, and small auditorium where you can watch park films acquaint you with the park. ☒ *North Unit entrance, off U.S. 85* ☎ *701/842–2333* ☉ *Daily 9–5:30.*

**Painted Canyon Visitor Center.** Easily reached off Interstate 94, this visitor center has a gift shop and bookstore, a hands-on exhibit for kids

## THEODORE ROOSEVELT IN ONE DAY

Focus on the South Unit. Arrive early at the **Painted Canyon Scenic Overlook** near the visitor center for a sweeping and colorful vista of the canyon's rock formations. Stay awhile to watch the effect of the sun's progress across the sky, or come back in the evening to witness the deepening colors and silhouettes in the fading sunlight. Continue to Medora's **South Unit Visitor Center** to tour the Theodore Roosevelt exhibit and the Maltese Cross Cabin. Circle the 36-mi **Scenic Loop Drive** twice: once to stop and walk a few trails and visit the overlooks, and once at night to watch the wildlife. Your first time around, go counterclockwise. Stop at **Scoria Point Overlook** and hike ⁶/₁₀ mi on **Ridgeline Nature Trail**. Continue around the loop, stopping at the North Dakota Badlands and Boicourt overlooks to gaze at the strange, ever-changing terrain. When you pass through Peaceful Valley, look for prairie dog towns.

Return to your car at least an hour before sunset, and drive slowly around Scenic Loop Drive, clockwise this time, to view the wildlife. Plan to be at **Buck Hill** for one of the most spectacular sunsets you'll ever see. Bring a jacket; it's windy and gets chilly as the sun sets. After dark, drive carefully—elk may still be on the road.

**34**

about park wildlife, and a large display on badlands topography. ⊠ *Exit 32 off I–94* ☎ *701/575–4020* ⊙ *Mid-June–Labor Day, daily 8–6; Apr.–mid-June and early Sept.–mid-Nov., daily 8:30–4:30.*

★ **South Unit Visitor Center.** Sometimes called the Medora Visitor Center, this building houses a large auditorium for films about the park, plus an excellent exhibit on Theodore Roosevelt's life. On display are artifacts such as the clothing Roosevelt wore while ranching in the Dakota Territory, his firearms, and several of his writings reflecting his thoughts on the nation's environmental resources. A bookstore and public restrooms are available. ⊠ *South Unit entrance, exits 24 and 27 off I–94* ☎ *701/623–4466* ⊙ *June–Sept., daily 8–8; Oct.–May, daily 8–4:30.*

## Sports & the Outdoors

Theodore Roosevelt offers an array of activities for even the most adventurous outdoors enthusiasts. During the summer, the park is best seen either by foot or bike. Hiking and biking will give visitors a better opportunity to take in the subtle and intricate details the park has to offer. If visitors want to take in the park the way the West's original settlers did, there are ample opportunities to saddle up and view the park on horseback.

### Bicycling

Bikes are allowed on paved interior roads and on most designated trails, but not off-road. Cyclists on the multiuse Maah Daah Hey Trail aren't allowed on the portions of the trails within the park.

OUTFITTERS & EXPEDITIONS **Dakota Cyclery Adventures.** This company rents bikes and provides shuttle service to both units of the park and guided tours of the Maah Daah Hey Trail. ✉ *275 3rd Ave., Medora* ☎ *701/623–4808 or 888/321–1218* ⊕ *www.dakotacyclery.com* ⊙ *Memorial Day–Labor Day.*

## Boating

A float trip via canoe down the Little Missouri River, a designated State Scenic River, is an ideal way to experience the beauty and solitude of the North Dakota badlands and Theodore Roosevelt National Park. It takes three or four days to canoe the 110 mi from the North Unit to the South Unit. The river ice generally breaks up by early April, so May and June are the best months for float trips; and in fact, canoeing is generally not practical after June, since the river gets too shallow.

Jet Skis are not allowed on the river. Boats with outboard motors are allowed but not advised, as there are portions that are too shallow for safe boat use. Boats must be registered with the state with current tags.

Camping along the river is allowed, but backcountry use permits are required and campers must get permission to camp on private land. Open fires are not allowed in the park at any time.

OUTFITTERS & EXPEDITIONS **Wayne's Sport Center.** Gear and boats of all sizes are available for rent here. Wayne or a member of his staff will give you a ride to the river. ✉ *Rte. 23 E, Watford City* ☎ *701/842–3294.*

## Fishing

Catfish, little suckers, northern pikes, and goldeneyes are among the underwater inhabitants of the Little Missouri River. If you wish to fish in the park or elsewhere in the state and are over age 16, you must obtain a North Dakota fishing license. For out-of-state residents, a three-day permit is $11, a seven-day permit is $15, and a one-year permit is $25. For in-state residents, a one-year permit is $11. The **Medora Convenience Store** (✉ 200 Pacific Ave., at the entrance to the South Unit ☎ 701/623–4479) sells fishing licenses.

OUTFITTERS & EXPEDITIONS **Greg Simonson Fishing Services.** A champion of several regional and state fishing tournaments, the owner of this outfitter leads individuals or groups on expeditions through the park and the outlying grasslands. ✉ *13892 U.S. 85 N, Alexander* ☎ *701/828–3425.*

## Hiking

Particularly the South Unit, where there are numerous opportunities to jump on a trail right from the park road. The North and South units are connected by the 96-mi Maah Daah Hey Trail.

Backcountry hiking is allowed, but you'll need a permit (free from any visitor center) to camp in the wild. Park maps are available at all three visitor centers. If you plan to camp overnight, be sure to let several people know about where you plan to pitch your tent, since there are no fire call boxes in the park and cell-phone services can be extremely limited. You should inquire about river conditions, maps, regulations, trail updates, and water sources before setting out.

EASY **Buckhorn Trail.** A thriving prairie dog town is just 1 mi from the trailhead of this 11-mi North Unit trail. It travels over level grasslands, then it loops back along the banks of Squaw Creek. If you're an experienced hiker, you'll complete the entire trail in about a half day. Novices or families might want to plan on a whole day, however.

**34**

★ **Little Mo Nature Trail.** Flat and only $1\frac{1}{10}$-mi long, this trail starts at the Juniper Campground and passes through badlands and woodlands to the river's edge. The first $\frac{7}{10}$ mi is wheelchair accessible. It's a great way to see the park's diverse terrain and wildlife, and because it shouldn't take you longer than an hour, it's a great trail for families with children.

MODERATE **Achenbach Trail.** This 16-mi round-trip, moderate-to-difficult trail begins at the North Unit's Juniper Campground, climbs through the Achenbach Hills, descends to the river and ends at Oxbow Overlook. Check with rangers about river-fording conditions. For a shorter (6-mi) hike to Oxbow, begin at the River Bend Overlook. This is an all-day trail.

Fodor'sChoice **Maah Daah Hey Trail.** Hike, bike, or ride horseback on the 96-mi Maah Daah Hey Trail, the most popular and well-maintained trail in western North Dakota. Its name means "grandfather" or "been here long" in the Mandan language. The trail starts at Sully Creek State Primitive Park (3 mi south of the South Unit visitor center) and traverses all three park units and the Little Missouri National Grasslands. Maps are available at the park visitor centers and from the U.S. Forest Service (701/225–5151). Walking the entire trail is a true wilderness adventure, and will probably take you five days. If you want to do something shorter, such as a two- or three-hour hike, leave from the South Unit and walk an hour or hour and a half in one direction, and then return. (Note that you are *not* allowed to bike the portions of the trail that are within the national park.) For maps and information, contact the **Maah Daah Hey Trail Association.** ⊠ *Box 156, Bismarck, 58501* ☎ *701/628–2747.*

DIFFICULT **Upper Caprock Coulee Trail.** This trail begins on the scenic drive about 8 mi west of the North Unit visitor center and follows a $4\frac{1}{3}$-mi loop around the pockmarked lower-badlands coulees (dry water gulches). There's a slow incline that takes you up 300 feet. Portions of the trail are slippery. Beginners should plan a half day for this trail.

## Horseback Riding

The best way to see many of the park's sights is on horseback. You are allowed to bring your own horse to the park, or you can sign up for a guided trip. Horses are only allowed on the 80 mi of marked horse trails or cross-country. Backcountry riding is allowed but as with any other campers, riders must obtain free backcountry-use permits. Riders taking multiday trips through the park must also have a permit and must camp in the Round-Up Group Horse Camp (☎ 701/623–4466) or in the backcountry. Horses are not allowed on park roadways, in developed campgrounds, picnic areas, or on developed nature trails. Overnight parties in the backcountry are limited to a maximum of 8 horses and 8 riders per group. Horse must be tied down securely when not being ridden. Be sure to bring enough water for the animals.

OUTFITTERS & **Little Knife Outfitters.** Take a guided one-day, two-day, or weeklong
EXPEDITIONS horseback trip on the Maah Daah Hey Trail. Knowledgeable guides will tell you all you want to know about the ecology and cultural history of the area. Beginners are welcome. ⌂ *Box 82, Watford City, 58584* ☎ *701/842–2631* ⊕ *www.littleknifeoutfitters.com* ☉ *May–Sept.*

**Peaceful Valley Ranch Horse Rides.** Experienced guides help you to see the park the way trappers, ranchers, and pioneers did a century ago. Rides are 90 minutes to five hours long. ⊠ *Scenic Loop Dr., South Unit* ☎ *701/623–4568.*

### Winter Sports

Cross-country skiing and snowshoeing are allowed in the park, although no outfitters provide services in the area. Snowmobiling is allowed on a very limited basis along the frozen bed of the Little Missouri.

## Educational Offerings

Parents and children alike will find numerous educational opportunities within the park. All three visitor centers show *T.R. Country,* a film focusing on the unique beauty and breathtaking landscape of North Dakota's badlands. In addition, several short films play throughout the day that give insight into the park's wildlife and the area's cultural history.

### Ranger Programs

Visitors seeking expert advice from those who know the area best will enjoy several of the ranger programs offered at the park. At 10 AM and 2 PM daily, mid-June to Labor Day, join a park ranger at the Medora Visitor Center for a discussion of the history and culture of the park. Park rangers also lead evening wildlife viewing walks. Check with a visitor center for details. ⇨ Nightlife for information on stargazing.

**Evening Campfires.** Rangers host hour-long slide presentations and discussions on such subjects as park history, archaeology, forest and brush fires, and wildlife, following the Evening Ranger Hike. Look for times and subjects posted at park campgrounds. ☉ *June–mid-Sept., daily.*

**Ranger-Led Walks.** Rangers lead one-hour walks and full- and half-day hikes on trails in both units and through the backcountry and Elkhorn Ranch, discussing such subjects as geology, paleontology, wildlife, and natural history. Check at campground entrances or at the visitor centers for times, topics, departure points, and destinations. ☉ *June–Labor Day, daily.* From June through mid-September, there's a one-hour **Naturalist's Choice Hike** in the North Unit at 2 PM focused on plant life and a one-hour ranger-led hike in the evening. ☉ *June–mid-Sept., daily.*

**Visitor Center Ranger Presentations.** Rangers conduct oral presentations at the South Unit Visitor Center on subjects such as cowboy clothing, seasonal changes in the park, and the history of cattle ranching. Presentation times vary. ▣ *Free* ☉ *June–mid-Sept., daily.*

### Film

***TR Country.*** This 13-minute film (shown every half hour) takes you on a visual tour of the wildlife, scenery, and history of western North Dakota and is narrated with Roosevelt's own words. ⊠ *South Unit, North Unit, and Painted Canyon visitor centers* 🖼 *Free* ☉ *Daily.*

## Arts & Entertainment

### Nightlife

**Stargazing Party.** The air at Theodore Roosevelt National Park has been officially certified to be at least 80% pure, making the park ideal for astronomical observation. On an early August weekend, the Northern Sky Astronomical Society sets up telescopes for an all-night star-watching party. ☏ *No phone* ⊕ *www.und.edu/org/nsas* 🖼 *Free.*

# WHAT'S NEARBY

## Nearby Towns & Attractions

### Nearby Towns

**Medora,** gateway to the park's South Unit, may only have a population of 96, but it is a walkable town with several museums, tiny shops and plenty of restaurants and places to stay. Its Wild West history is reenacted in a madcap musical production each night in summer. To the east is **Dickinson** (pop. 17,700), the largest town near the national park. North of Dickinson and about 35 mi east of the park's North Unit, **Killdeer** (pop. about 700) is known for its Roundup Rodeo—North Dakota's oldest—and its gorgeous scenery. Killdeer is the place to fill your tank, since there isn't another gas station around for 40 mi. **Williston** (pop. about 13,000) is 60 mi north of the North Unit, just over the Missouri River. The Amtrak stop nearest to the national park is here.

> **FAMILY PICKS**
>
> ▪ Horseback Riding
> ▪ Medora Musical
> ▪ Stargazing Party

### Nearby Attractions

★ **Dakota Dinosaur Museum.** A huge triceratops casting stands guard at the entrance. The museum houses dozens of dinosaur bones, fossilized plants and seashells, and local rocks and minerals. ⊠ *200 Museum Dr., Dickinson* ☎ *701/225–3466* ⊕ *www.dakotadino.com* 🖼 *$6* ☉ *May–Labor Day, daily 9–5.*

**Fort Buford State Historic Site.** Built near the confluence of the Missouri and Yellowstone rivers, this military post was the site of Sitting Bull's surrender in 1881. See the restored officers' quarters and the unusual, sometimes humorous, tombstones in the soldiers' cemetery. ⊠ *15349 39th La. NW, Williston* ☎ *701/572–9034* 🖼 *$5* ☉ *Mid-May–mid-Sept., daily 8–6; mid-Sept.–mid-May, weekends by appointment only.*

★ **Little Missouri State Park.** Called "Mako Shika" or "where the land breaks" by the Sioux, the unusual land formations here create the state's

## FESTIVALS & EVENTS

JULY **Killdeer Mountain Roundup Rodeo.** Begun in 1923, this is North Dakota's oldest PRCA (Professional Rodeo Cowboys Association)–sanctioned rodeo. The community goes all out, hosting a Native American and frontier encampment, classic car show, parade, fireworks display, and street dance on July 4th at the Killdeer rodeo grounds. ☎ 701/764–5777.

AUG. **Founder's Day.** You can enter Theodore Roosevelt National Park for free on August 25 to commemorate the establishment of the National Park Service on that date in 1916. The visitor centers host lectures and slide shows and serve cookies and lemonade ☎ 701/623–4466.

DEC. **Old-Fashioned Cowboy Christmas.** Held the first full weekend in December in downtown Medora, the festivities begin with a wreath-hanging ceremony at the community center, followed by Christmas poetry readings, a holiday doll show, sleigh rides, and a dance. ☎ 701/623–4910.

most awe-inspiring scenery. The beehive-shape rock formations resulted from the erosion of sedimentary rock deposited by streams flowing from the Rocky Mountains. Undeveloped, this wilderness area has primitive camping and 75 mi of horse trails. ⊠ *Off Rte. 22, 15 mi north of Killdeer* ☎ *701/764–5256 summer, 701/794–3731 winter* ⊕ *www.ndparks.com/Parks/Little_Mo/Home.htm* 🎫 *$5 per vehicle* ☉ *Daily.*

## Area Activities

### Sports & the Outdoors

GOLF **Bully Pulpit Golf Course.** This impressive course weaves its way through the badlands buttes, giving players a truly breathtaking backdrop. In 2005, it was voted the number-one affordable public golf course in the nation by *Golf Digest*. ⊠ *East River Rd., Medora* ☎ *701/623–4653* 🎫 *$49* ☉ *Mid-Apr.–Oct., daily, dawn to dusk.*

### Arts & Entertainment

**Burning Hills Amphitheater.** This seven-story amphitheater 1 mi west of Medora is the area's most beloved performance space, hosting all kinds of concerts and performances. If you sit near the top, you can enjoy a panoramic view of the badlands. ⊠ *3422 Chateau Rd., Medora* ☎ *701/623–4444 or 800/633–6721* ☉ *Early June–Labor Day.*

★ **Medora Musical.** This is a worthwhile theatrical tribute to the Old West, its history, and its personalities. ☎ *701/623–4444 or 800/633–6721* 🎫 *$24–$30* ☉ *Early June–Labor Day, daily 8:30 PM.*

# WHERE TO STAY & EAT

### About the Restaurants

One does not visit Theodore Roosevelt for the fine dining. In fact, the only venues within park are the picnic areas, and provided you've prepared, this can be a perfectly simple and satisfying way to experience the open spaces and natural wonder of the badlands. In the towns near the park you'll find casual, down-to-earth family establishments that largely cater to the locals. Expect steak and potatoes, and lots of them. Fortunately, the beef here is among the best in the country.

### About the Hotels

If you're set on sleeping within the park, be sure to pack your tent. Outside the park are mostly small chain hotels catering to interstate travelers—largely retired couples in RVs and young families in minivans. However, there are a handful of historic properties and working ranches that offer guests a truly Western experience. It's usually a good idea to book ahead during summer months.

### About the Campgrounds

For the adventurous traveler, camping in Theodore Roosevelt is well worth the effort. The unadulterated isolation, epic views, and relationship with nature afforded by the spartan campgrounds within the park create an experience you'll be hard-pressed to find elsewhere in the United States. Just remember that the park's campgrounds are relatively undeveloped—you'll need to pack in everything you need. If you pick a campsite in the surrounding wilderness, you'll need to obtain a backcountry camping permit (available free) from a visitor center first.

Campgrounds outside the park are more developed, and typically attract an older and more laid-back crowd—usually retirees with massive RVs. These commercial operations also attract a fair number of young families, who prefer the extra amenities. Reservations are usually not required, but probably a wise choice in the summer months.

## Where to Eat

### In the Park

PICNIC AREAS **Cottonwood.** This is in a lovely valley near the river. There are fire pits, drinking water, restrooms, eight open tables, and eight covered tables. ⊠ *5½ mi north of the South Unit Visitor Center.*

**Juniper.** This area has 28 tables (8 of which are sheltered), grills, drinking water, and restrooms. ⊠ *5 mi west of North Unit Visitor Center.*

**Painted Canyon Visitor Center** has eight covered tables, drinking water, restrooms, and a spectacular view. ⊠ *Exit 32 off I–94.*

### Outside the Park

★ **$$** ✕ **Pitchfork Steak Fondue.** Rib-eye steaks are prepared on the tines of pitchforks in classic Western style. A full buffet accompanies the meat, all of it served with a view of the badlands and live musical entertainment. ⊠ *Tjaden Terrace, Medora* ☎ *701/623–4444 or 800/633–6721.* $20 ⊟ *AE, D, MC, V* ⊘ *Closed early Sept.–May.*

☾ **$–$$** ✕ **Georgia's and the Owl.** The family's pet owl, which once reigned in this restaurant, is deceased, but stuffed owls and other owl paraphernalia makes Georgia's a fun place to visit. Try the prime rib dinner or the steak. ⊠ *U.S. 85 at Main St., Amidon* ☎ *701/879–6289. $12–$20* ⊟ *No credit cards* ☉ *Closed Sun. and Oct.–May.*

**$–$$**
**Fodor's Choice**
★

✕ **Iron Horse Restaurant.** Great breakfasts, burgers, and tenderloin sandwiches draw locals to this independently owned restaurant with roughhewn benches and barn-wood walls. A spiral staircase leads to an upstairs dining room. ⊠ *201 Main St., Medora* ☎ *701/623–9894. $8–$15* ⊟ *AE, D, MC, V.*

★ **¢–$$** ✕ **Buckskin Bar and Grill.** This steak house, with saloon and dance hall, seats 350. Stuffed critters are mounted on the walls in one room; the other rooms have photographs of local cowboy celebrities who dine here. Steak and seafood are the kitchen's focus, with prime rib a specialty. For dessert, the homemade apple cobbler is a must. Kids' menu. ⊠ *416 Central Ave., Killdeer* ☎ *701/764–5321. $7–$20* ⊟ *MC, V.*

**¢–$$** ✕ **Gramma Sharon's Cafe.** For great omelets and biscuits try Gramma's, but don't come for the atmosphere: it's attached to a gas station. Kids' menu. No alcohol. ⊠ *U.S. 2 and U.S. 85 W, Williston* ☎ *701/572–1412. $6–$13* ⊟ *D, MC, V.*

★ **¢** ✕ **Cowboy Cafe.** This cozy, locally owned café specializes in homemade soups, caramel rolls, and delicious roast beef specials. Be prepared for a short wait since the restaurant is popular with both locals and visitors. ⊠ *215 4th St., Medora* ☎ *701/623–4343. $4–$7* ⊟ *No credit cards.*

## Where to Stay

### In the Park

**CAMPGROUNDS &**
**RV PARKS**
★ **$**

⚠ **Cottonwood Campground.** Nestled under juniper and cottonwood trees on the bank of the Little Missouri River, this is a wonderful place to watch buffalo and elk drink from the river at sunrise and just before sunset. Flush toilets are available May–September; pit toilets the remainder of the year. ⊠ *5½ mi north of the South Unit Visitor Center* ☎ *701/623–4466* ⟲ *78 sites* ♿ *Grills, flush toilets, drinking water, picnic tables* ▦ *$10* ♿ *Reservations not accepted* ⊟ *No credit cards.*

**$** ⚠ **Juniper Campground.** The sites here are surrounded by junipers, hence the name. Don't be surprised if you see a bison herd wander through on its way to the Little Missouri River. Drinking water and flush toilets are available May–September; pit toilets are available the remainder of the year. No RV hookups. ⊠ *5 mi west of the North Unit Visitor Center* ☎ *701/842–2333* ⟲ *50 sites* ♿ *Grills, flush toilets, drinking water, picnic tables* ▦ *$10* ♿ *Reservations not accepted* ⊟ *No credit cards.*

### Outside the Park

⟳ **$–$$** ⊡ **Custer's Cottage.** The two separate units and big yard of this home are ideal for families. Mary, the owner and lifelong resident of Medora, will gladly entertain you with stories. ⊠ *156 E. River Rd. S, Medora 58645* ☎ *701/623–4378 or 800/783–6366 Ext. 0749* ⊕ *www.custerscottage.com* ⟲ *2 units* ♿ *Kitchen, laundry facilities. $50–$105* ⊟ *No credit cards.*

**$–$$**
Fodor'sChoice
★   🏨 **Rough Riders Hotel.** Second-floor rooms have country-style, Western antiques, brass beds, patchwork quilts, and red velvet drapes. Guests have pool privileges at a nearby motel. ☒ *301 3rd Ave., Medora 58645* ☎ *701/623–4444 or 800/633–6721* 📠 *701/623–4494* 🛏 *9 rooms (7 with shower only)* ⚐ *Restaurant. $80–$105* 🖃 *AE, D, MC, V.*

🐾 **$**   🏨 **Naard Creek Ranch.** A secluded log cabin on a 340-acre plot 21 mi northwest of Killdeer, accommodates up to 10 people. ☒ *11580 6th St. NW, Killdeer 58640* ☎ *701/863–6911* ⊕ *www.naardcreek.com* 🛏 *1 cabin* ⚐ *Refrigerator, no phone. $75–$100* 🖃 *No credit cards.*

CAMPGROUNDS &
RV PARKS
**$–$$**
🏕 **East View Campground.** Deer and wild turkey are your neighbors in this extremely secluded campground with incredible views of buttes and badlands. The owners bring you drinking water in coolers. ☒ *10460 Ken St., NW, Killdeer 58645* ☎ *701/764–5219* 🛏 *15 sites (10 with partial hookups)* ⚐ *Grills, flush toilets, showers, picnic tables, electricity* 🗺 *$15–$20* ⚐ *Reservations not accepted* 🖃 *No credit cards.*

🐾 **$**   🏕 **Medora Campground.** This shaded campground in west Medora is within walking distance of downtown. Basketball and volleyball courts are nearby. ☒ *195 3rd Ave., off Pacific Ave., Medora 58645* ☎ *701/623–4444 or 800/633–6721* 🛏 *200 sites (105 with hookups)* ⚐ *Grills, flush toilets, full hookups, dump station, drinking water, guest laundry, showers, picnic tables, electricity, public telephone, general store, pool* 🗺 *$15 tents, $21–$25 RVs* 🖃 *AE, D, MC, V* ☉ *May–Sept.*

**$**   🏕 **Red Trail Campground.** Live country music is performed every night from June through Labor Day in front of the store at this campground six blocks from downtown Medora. It was built especially for RVs. ☒ *250 E. River Rd. S, off Pacific Ave., Medora 58645* ☎ *701/623–4317 or 800/621–4317* 🛏 *104 sites (100 with hookups)* ⚐ *Grills, flush toilets, full hookups, dump station, drinking water, guest laundry, showers, picnic tables, electricity, public telephone, general store, play area* 🗺 *$14 tents, $20–$26 RVs* 🖃 *MC, V* ☉ *May–Sept.*

¢–$   🏕 🏨 **Bar X Ranch.** Catering to horseback riding, mountain biking, and hiking enthusiasts, this guest ranch and campground is south of Medora via East River Road and adjacent to the Maah Daah Hey trail. ☎ *Box 103, Medora 58645* ☎ *701/623–4300* 🛏 *2 cabins, 15 sites* ⚐ *Flush toilets, partial hookups, drinking water, showers, fire pits, picnic tables* 🗺 *$7–$13 tents or campers, $75 cabins* 🖃 *No credit cards.*

¢   🏕 **Sully Creek State Campground.** On an 80-acre park at the head of the Maah Daah Hey Trail, this campground complete with horse corrals is perfect if you're planning a bike or horseback trip on the trail, or a canoe trip on the Little Missouri River. You'll find squeaky clean pit toilets and solar-powered showers. ☒ *East River Rd., 3 mi south of Medora* ☎ *4480 Fort Lincoln Rd., Mandan 58554* ☎ *701/623–4496* 🛏 *45 sites* ⚐ *Pit toilets, showers, fire pits, picnic tables, swimming (river)* 🗺 *$5 per horse, $9* ⚐ *Reservations not accepted* 🖃 *No credit cards.*

**34**

# THEODORE ROOSEVELT ESSENTIALS

ACCESSIBILITY The flat terrain of this park allows for relatively easy access for people with mobility impairments. The visitor centers, campgrounds, and historic sites such as Roosevelt's cabin, are all wheelchair accessible, and films at the visitor centers are close-captioned. The first part of the Little Mo Nature Trail in the North Unit and the ¼-mi Skyline Vista Trail in the South Unit are both paved.

ADMISSION FEES The entrance pass is $5 per person or $10 maximum per vehicle and is good for seven days. A $20 annual pass allows admission to the park for an entire year.

ADMISSION HOURS The park is open year-round. The North Unit is in the Central time zone. The South Unit and the Painted Canyon Visitor Center are in the Mountain time zone.

ATMS/BANKS There are no ATMs in the park. The nearest ATM and bank is in Medora.

**First State Bank** ⊠ 365 3rd Ave., Medora ☎ 701/623–5000. **Medora Convenience Store** ⊠ 200 Pacific Ave., at the South Unit entrance, Medora ☎ 701/623–4479.

AUTOMOBILE SERVICE STATIONS You can get gas at the entrance to the South Unit of the park, but the nearest full-service station is 17 mi away in Belfield.

**Medora Convenience Store** ⊠ 200 Pacific Ave., Medora ☎ 701/623–4479.

EMERGENCIES In case of a fire or medical emergency dial 911 or the Billings County Sheriff's Office at 701/623–4323. You should also phone the rangers in each unit: 701/623–4379, 701/623–4466, or 701/623–4562 (after hours) in the South Unit; 701/842–2580, 701/842–2333, or 701/842–4266 (after hours) in the North Unit.

LOST AND FOUND There's a lost-and-found in each visitor center.

PERMITS A backcountry permit, free from the visitor centers, is required for overnight camping away from campgrounds.

POST OFFICES
**Medora Post Office** ⊠ 311 3rd Ave., 58645 ☎ 701/623–4385.

PUBLIC TELEPHONES Public telephones can be found at the South Unit's Cottonwood Campground, at the Painted Canyon Visitor Center, and at the North Unit Visitor Center. Cell phone reception occurs in some areas of the park, but most places receive no signal.

RELIGIOUS SERVICES There are no chapel or other religious services in the park.

RESTROOMS Each of the visitor centers and park campgrounds have public restrooms.

SHOPS & GROCERS
**Medora Convenience Store.** Purchase your fishing license, gas up the car, rent a canoe, and buy snacks and camping supplies at this store outside the South Unit's entrance. ⊠ 200 Pacific Ave., Medora ☎ 701/623–4479.

**NEARBY TOWN INFORMATION**
**Dickinson Convention and Visitors Bureau** ⊡ Box 181, 58601 ☎ 701/483–4988 or 800/279–7391 ⊕ www.dickinsonnd.com. **Killdeer City Hall** ⊠ 214 Railroad St., 58640 ☎ 701/764–5295 ⊕ www.killdeer.com. **Medora Chamber of Commerce** ⊠ 272 Pacific Ave., Box 186, 58645 ☎ 701/623–4910 ⊕ www.medorand.com. **Williston Convention and Visitors Bureau** ⊠ 10 Main St., 58801 ☎ 701/774–9041 or 800/615–9041 ⊕ www.willistonnd.com.

**VISITOR INFORMATION**
**Theodore Roosevelt National Park** ⊡ Box 7, Medora, 58645-0007 ☎ 701/623–4466 South Unit, 701/842-2333 North Unit, 701/575-4020 Painted Canyon ⊕ www.nps.gov/thro.

# Wind Cave National Park

## AND THE BLACK HILLS

Wind Cave National Park

**WORD OF MOUTH**

"Have given up the idea of finding the end of Wind Cave."
— Explorer Alvin McDonald

# WELCOME TO WIND CAVE

## TOP REASONS TO GO

★ **Underground Exploring:** Visitors can get their hands and feet dirty on a four-hour guided tour through one of American's longest and most complex caves.

★ **The Call of the Wild:** Wind Cave National Park boasts a wide variety of animals: bison, coyote, deer, antelope, elk, prairie dogs, and 37 species of birds, to name just a few.

★ **Education by Candlelight:** Numerous educational and interpretive programs include the Candlelight Cave Tour, where guests explore the cave only by candlelight.

★ **Noteworthy Neighbors:** On the north border of Wind Cave sits Custer State Park, one of South Dakota's can't-miss areas. With its close proximity to numerous other national parks, state parks, and other monuments and memorials, including Mount Rushmore, Wind Cave is perfectly situated to explore some of American's greatest national treasures.

**1** The Surface. Wind Cave lies at the confluence of Western mountains and central plains, which blesses the park with a unique landscape. A series of established trails weaves in and out of forested hillsides and grassy meadows, providing treks of varying difficulty.

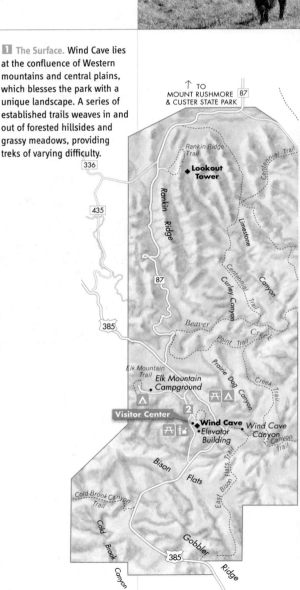

↑ TO MOUNT RUSHMORE & CUSTER STATE PARK  87

336

Rankin Ridge Trail

◆ **Lookout Tower**

Centennial Trail

Rankin Ridge

435

Limestone

87

Centennial Trail

Curley Canyon

Canyon

385

*Beaver*

Point Trail

*Creek*

Creek Trail

Elk Mountain Trail

Elk Mountain Campground

**Visitor Center**  2

◆ **Wind Cave**

Prairie Dog Canyon

Wind Cave Canyon

Canyon Trail

◆ Elevator Building

*Bison*

*Flats*

East Bison Flats Trail

Cold Brook Canyon Trail

Cold Brook

*Gobbler*

385

*Ridge*

Canyon

**2** The Cave. With an explored maze of caverns totaling 121 mi, Wind Cave is considered one of the largest caves in the world. Notably, scientists estimate that only 5% of the cave has been explored to date. It is also estimated that 95% of the world's boxwork formations are found in Wind Cave, which means that visitors here are treated to some of the rarest geological features on the planet.

Whitetail Deer

SOUTH DAKOTA

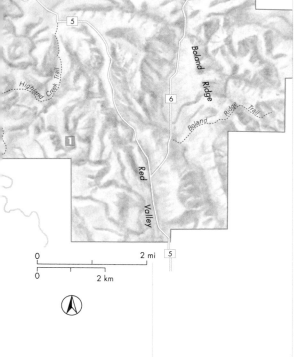

# GETTING ORIENTED

Bounded by Black Hills National Forest to the west and windswept prairie to the east, Wind Cave National Park, in southwestern South Dakota, encompasses the transition between two distinct ecosystems: mountain forest and mixed-grass prairie. Abundant wildlife, including bison and elk, roam the 28,295 acres of the park's diverse terrain. Underground, a year-round 53°F temperature gives summer visitors a cool oasis—and winter visitors a warm escape.

0        2 mi

0        2 km

| KEY | |
|---|---|
| 📛 | Ranger Station |
| ⛺ | Campground |
| 🍽 | Picnic Area |
| 🍴 | Restaurant |
| 🏨 | Lodge |
| 🚶 | Trailhead |
| 🚻 | Restrooms |
| ⇘ | Scenic Viewpoint |
| ---- | Walking/Hiking Trails |
| ····· | Bicycle Path |

# WIND CAVE PLANNER

## When to Go

The heaviest crowds come to Wind Cave from June to September, but the park and surrounding Black Hills are large enough to diffuse the masses. **Neither the cave nor grounds above are ever too packed, except during the first full week in August, when the Black Hills play host to one of the world's largest biker gatherings.** The Sturgis Motorcycle Rally brings half a million people to the region, clogging highways for miles around. Most hotels within a 100-mi radius are booked up to a year in advance.

The colder months are the least crowded, though you can still explore underground, thanks to the cave's constant 53°F temperature. The shoulder seasons are also unpopular, though autumn is a perfect time to visit. The days are warm, the nights are cool, and in late September/early October the park displays its incredible fall colors. Your only competition for space will be small groups of sportsmen and the occasional photographer.

## Flora & Fauna

About three-quarters of the park is grasslands. The rest is forested, mostly by the ponderosa pine. Poison ivy and poison oak are common in wetter, shadier areas, so wear long pants and boots when hiking.

The convergence of forest and prairies makes an attractive home for bison, elk, coyotes, pronghorn antelope, and mule deer. Wild turkey, prairie dogs, marmots, and squirrels are less obvious, but commonly seen by the observant hiker. Mountain lions also live in the park; while usually shy, they will attack if surprised or threatened. Make noise while hiking to prevent chance encounters. Bison appear docile but can be dangerous. The largest land mammal in North America, they weigh up to a ton and run at speeds in excess of 35 mph. When park rangers tell you not to approach them, it's wise to heed their warning.

## Getting There & Around

Wind Cave is 56 mi from Rapid City, via U.S. 16 and Highway 87, which runs through the park, and 73 mi southwest of Badlands National Park. The nearest commercial airport is in Rapid City. Bus lines service Rapid City, Jefferson and Wall. **Gray Line of the Black Hills** (☎ 605/342-4461 ⊕ www.blackhillsgrayline.com) offers regional tours.

U.S. 385 and Highway 87 travel the length of the park on the west side. Additionally, two unpaved roads, Forest Service Roads 5 and 6, traverse the northeastern part of Wind Cave. Forest Service Road 5 joins Highway 87 at the park's north border. There's ample free parking at the visitor center, although it can get full in midsummer.

AVG. HIGH/LOW TEMPS.

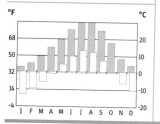

By T.D. Griffith & Dustin D. Floyd

35

If you don't get out of your car at Wind Cave, you haven't scratched the surface—literally. The park has more than 121 mi of underground passageways. Curious cave formations include 95% of the world's mineral boxwork, gypsum beard so sensitive it reacts to the heat of a lamp, and delicate helictite balloons that would burst at the touch of a finger. Some are partly hollow, some are partly filled with minerals. No one seems to have a clear understanding of how exactly these intriguing formations are created. Wind Cave is the fourth-longest cave in the world, and experts believe 95% of it is yet to be mapped.

## Scenic Drives

**Bison Flats Drive (South Entrance).** Entering the park from the south on U.S. 385 will take you past Gobbler Ridge and into the hills commonly found in the southern Black Hills region. After a couple of miles, the landscape gently levels onto the Bison Flats, one of the mixed-grass prairies on which the park prides itself. You might see a herd of grazing buffalo between here and the visitor center. You'll also catch panoramic views of the parklands and surrounding hills, and limestone bluffs.

★ **Rankin Ridge Drive (North Entrance).** Entering the park across the north border via Highway 87 is perhaps the most beautiful drive into the park. As you leave behind the grasslands and granite spires of Custer State Park and enter Wind Cave, you see the prairie, forest, and wetland habitats of the backcountry and some of the oldest rock in the Black Hills. The silvery twinkle of mica, quartz, and feldspar crystals dot Rankin Ridge east of Highway 87, and gradually give way to limestone and sandstone formations.

## WIND CAVE IN ONE DAY

Pack a picnic lunch, then head to the visitor center to purchase tickets for a morning tour of Wind Cave. Visit the exhibit rooms in the center before or after the tour. By the time you complete your tour, you will probably be ready for lunch. Drive or walk the quarter mile to the picnic area north of the visitor center. The refreshing air and deep emerald color of the pine woodlands will flavor your meal.

In the afternoon, take a leisurely drive through the parklands south of the visitor center, passing through Gobbler Pass and Bison Flats, for an archetypal view of the park and to look for wildlife. On the way back north, follow U.S. 385 east toward Wind Cave Canyon. If you enjoy bird-watching, park your car at a turnout and hike the 1⁸⁄₁₀-mi trail into the canyon, where you can spot swallows and great horned owls in the cliffs and woodpeckers in the dead trees at the bottom. Next, get back on the highway going north, take a right on Highway 87, and continue a half mile to the turnout for Centennial Trail. Hike the trail about 2 mi to the junction with Lookout Point Trail, turn right and return to Highway 87. The whole loop is about 4³⁄₄ mi. As you continue driving north to the top of Rankin Ridge, a pullout to the right serves as the starting point for 1¹⁄₄-mi Rankin Ridge Trail. It loops around the ridge, past Lookout Tower—the park's highest point and a great place to view the whole park—and ends up back at the pullout. This trail is an excellent opportunity to enjoy the fresh air, open spaces, and diversity of wildlife in the park. Conclude your day by exiting the park on Highway 87 and driving through Custer State Park.

## What to See

**Rankin Ridge Lookout Tower.** Some of the best panoramic views of the park can be seen from this 5,013-foot tower. Hike the 1-mi Rankin Ridge loop to get there. ⊠ *6 mi north of the visitor center on Hwy. 87.*

★ **Wind Cave.** Discovered by the Bingham brothers in 1881, Wind Cave was named for the strong currents of air that blow in or out of the entrance. This is related to the difference in atmospheric pressure between the cave and the surface. When the atmospheric pressure is higher outside than inside the cave, the air blows in, and vice versa. With more than 100 mi of known passageway divided into three different levels, Wind Cave ranks the sixth longest worldwide. It's host to an incredibly diverse collection of geologic formations, including more boxwork than any other known cave, plus a series of underground lakes. The cave tours sponsored by the National Park Service allow you to see examples of unusual and beautiful formations with names such as button popcorn, starburst, Christmas trees, frostwork, nail quartz, helictite bushes, and gypsum flowers. ⊠ *U.S. 385 to Wind Cave Visitor Center.*

### Visitor Center

The park's sole visitor center is the primary place to get general information. Located on top of the cave, it has three exhibit rooms, with dis-

## GEAR UP!

**Edge Sports—Lead.** On the way to the ski slopes in the northern Black Hills, it maintains a good stock of winter sports equipment. ✉ *32 Baltimore St., Lead* ☎ *605/722-7547.*

**Edge Sports—Rapid City.** Rock climbers and hikers will find a good selection of equipment. Cavers will find a solid inventory of clothing and gear. ✉ *922 Main St., Rapid City* ☎ *605/716-9912.*

**Granite Sports.** Several miles north of the park, this outfitter sells hiking boots, Gore-Tex jackets, packs, water bottles, and more. ✉ *201 Main St., Hill City* ☎ *605/574-2121.*

**Scheels All Sport.** In Rushmore Mall, Scheels carries a wide selection of all-weather hiking clothes and binoculars suitable for bird-watchers. ✉ *2200 N. Maple Ave., Rapid City* ☎ *605/342-9033.*

**35**

plays on cave exploration, the Civilian Conservation Corps, park wildlife, and resource management. ✉ *Off U.S. 385, 3 mi north of the park's southern border* ☎ *605/745-4600* ⊕ *www.nps.gov/wica* ✉ *Free* ☉ *Mid-Apr.–mid-Oct., daily 8–5; mid-Oct.–early Apr., daily 8–4:30.*

## Sports & the Outdoors

### Bird-watching

★ **Wind Cave Canyon.** Here's one of the best birding areas in the park. The limestone walls of the canyon are ideal nesting grounds for cliff swallows and great horned owls, while the standing dead trees on the canyon floor attract red-headed and Lewis woodpeckers. As you hike down the trail, the steep-sided canyon widens to a panoramic view east across the prairies. ✉ *About ½ mi east of the visitor center.*

**Rankin Ridge.** See large birds of prey here, including turkey vultures, hawks, and golden eagles. ✉ *6 mi north of the visitor center on Hwy. 87.*

### Hiking

There are more than 30 mi of hiking trails within the boundaries of the park, covering ponderosa forest and mixed-grass prairie. The landscape has changed little over the past century, so a hike through the park is as much a historical snapshot of pioneer life in the 1890s as it is exercise. Hiking into the wild, untouched backcountry is perfectly safe, provided you have a map and a good sense of direction.

EASY ★ **Wind Cave Canyon Trail.** This easy 1⁸⁄₁₀-mi trail follows Wind Cave Canyon to the park boundary fence. The canyon, with its steep limestone walls and dead trees, provides the best opportunity in the park for bird-watching. Be especially vigilant for cliff swallows, great horned owls, and red-headed and Lewis woodpeckers. Deer, marmots, least chipmunks, and other small animals also are attracted to the sheltered environment of the canyon. Even though you could probably do a round-trip tour of this trail in less than an hour and a half, be sure to spend more time here to observe the wildlife. This trail represents one of your best chances for seeing the park's animal inhabitants, and a little patience will almost cer-

tainly be rewarded. ⊠ *Begins on the east side of Hwy. 385, 1 mile north of the southern access road to the visitor center.*

MODERATE

☺ **Cold Brook Canyon Trail.** Starting on the west side of U.S. 385, 2 mi south of the visitor center, this 1½-mi, mildly strenuous hike runs past a former prairie dog town, the edge of an area burned by a controlled fire in 1986, and through Cold Brook Canyon to the park boundary fence. Experienced hikers will conquer this trail and return to the trailhead in an hour or less, but more leisurely visitors will probably need more time. ⊠ *Begins on the west side of U.S. 385, 2 mi south of the visitor center.*

DIFFICULT

**Boland Ridge Trail.** Get away from the crowds for half a day via this strenuous 2½-mi round-trip hike. The panorama from the top is well worth it, especially at sunset. ⊠ *The trailhead is off Forest Service Rd. 6, 1 mi north of the junction with Forest Service Rd. 5.*

**Highland Creek Trail.** This difficult, roughly 8½-mi trail is the longest and most diverse trail within the park, traversing mixed-grass prairies, ponderosa pine forests, and the riparian habitats of Highland Creek, Beaver Creek, and Wind Cave Canyon. Even those in good shape will need a full day to cover this trail round-trip. ⊠ *The southern trailhead stems from Wind Cave Canyon trail 1 mi east of U.S. 385. The northern trailhead is on Forest Service Rd. 5.*

## Spelunking

★ You may not explore the depths of Wind Cave on your own, but you can choose from five ranger-led cave tours, available from June through August; the rest of the year, only one or two tours are available. On each tour you pass incredibly beautiful cave formations, including extremely well-developed boxwork. The least crowded times to visit in summer are mornings and weekends. The cave is 53°F year-round, so bring a sweater. Note that the uneven passages are often wet and slippery. Rangers discourage those with heart conditions and physical limitations from taking the organized tours. However, with some advance warning (and for a nominal fee) park rangers can arrange private, limited tours for those with physical disabilities. The park provides hard hats, knee pads, and gloves, and all cavers are required to have long pants, a long-sleeved shirt, and hiking boots or closed-toe shoes with nonslip soles. If you prefer lighted passages and stairways to dark crawl spaces, a tour other than the Wild Caving Tour might appeal to you.

Tours depart from the visitor center. A schedule can be found online at ⊕ www.nps.gov/wica. To make a reservation, call 605/745–4600.

EASY

**Garden of Eden Cave Tour.** You don't need to go far to see boxwork, popcorn, and flowstone formations. Just take the relatively easy, one-hour tour, which covers about ¼ mi and 150 stairs. It's available seven times daily, early June through Labor Day, and three times daily, October through early June. The cost is $7.

**Natural Entrance Cave Tour.** This 1¼-hour tour takes you ½ mi into the cave, over 300 stairs (most heading down), and out an elevator exit. Along the way are some significant boxwork deposits on the middle level. The tour costs $9 and leaves nine times daily from early June through Labor

35

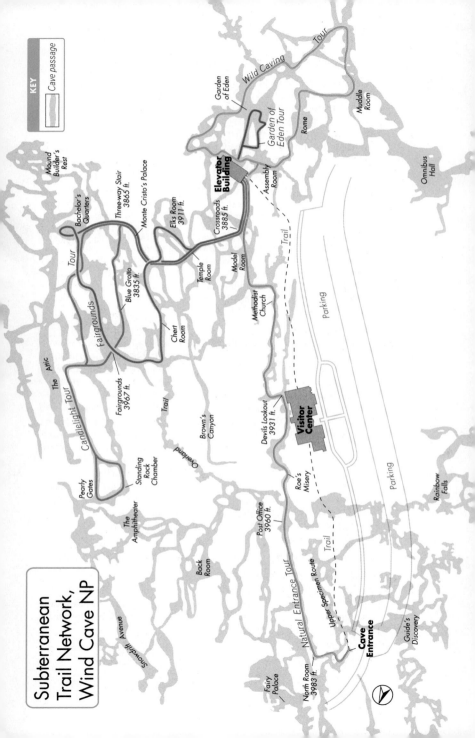

# Subterranean Trail Network, Wind Cave NP

**KEY**

Cave passage

Mound Builder's Rest

Bachelor's Quarters

Three-way Stair 3865 ft.

Monte Cristo's Palace

Garden of Eden

Wild Caving Tour

Tour

Rome

Middle Room

Omnibus Hall

Elks Room 3911 ft.

Crossroads 3885 ft.

**Elevator Building**

Assembly Room

Garden of Eden Tour

Temple Room

Model Room

Blue Grotto 3835 ft.

Fairgrounds

Tour

Chert Room

Methodist Church

The Attic

Candlelight Tour

Fairgrounds 3967 ft.

Overland

Trail

Brown's Canyon

Devils Lookout 3931 ft.

**Visitor Center**

Parking

Trail

Pearly Gates

Standing Rock Chamber

The Amphitheater

Back Room

Roe's Misery

Parking

Rainbow Falls

Snowhill Avenue

Post Office 3960 ft.

Natural Entrance Tour

Upper Specimen Route

Trail

Fairy Palace

North Room 3983 ft.

**Cave Entrance**

Guide's Discovery

Day, and seven times daily for the rest of September.

MODERATE ★ **Candlelight Cave Tour.** Available twice daily, early June through Labor Day, this tour goes into a section of the cave with no paved walks or lighting. Everyone on the tour carries a lantern similar to those used in expeditions in the 1890s. The $9 tour lasts two hours and covers 1 mi; reservations are essential. Children under 8 are not admitted.

**Fairgrounds Cave Tour.** View examples of nearly every type of calcite formation found in the cave on this 1½-hour tour, available five times daily, early June through Labor Day. There are some 450 steps, leading up and down; the cost is $9.

> ### HATS OFF TO THE CAVE
>
> Homesteaders Jesse and Tom Bingham first discovered Wind Cave when they heard air whistling through the rocky opening. Legend goes that the airflow was so strong that day that it knocked Tom's hat clean off his head. Jesse came back a few days later to show the trick to some friends, but it didn't happen quite as he'd planned. The wind, now flowing in the opposite direction, stole Jesse's hat and vacuumed it into the murky depths of the cave.

**35**

DIFFICULT
Fodor'sChoice ★

**Wild Caving Tour.** For a serious caving experience, sign up for this challenging, extraordinary, four-hour tour. After some basic training in spelunking, you crawl and climb through fissures and corridors, most lined with gypsum needles, frostwork, and boxwork. Expect to get dirty. Wear shoes with good traction, long pants, and a long-sleeve shirt. The park provides knee pads, gloves, and hard hats with headlamps. You must be at least 16 to take this tour, and 16- and 17-year-olds must show signed consent from a parent or guardian. Tours cost $23 and are available at 1 PM daily, early June through mid-August, and at 1 PM weekends mid-August through Labor Day. Reservations are essential.

## Educational Offerings

### Ranger Programs

**Campfire Program.** A park ranger lectures for about 45 minutes on topics such as wildlife, park management, and cave history. ✉ *Elk Mountain Campground amphitheater* ☽ *June–Labor Day, nightly 8 or 9 PM; Sept., Tues., Thurs., Sat. 7 PM.*

**Junior Ranger Program.** Kids 12 and younger can earn a Junior Ranger badge by completing activities that teach them about the park's ecosystems, the cave, the animals, and protecting the environment. Pick up the Junior Ranger guidebook for $1.50 at the Wind Cave Visitor Center.

**Prairie Hike.** This two-hour exploration of parkland habitats begins with a short talk at the visitor center, then moves to a trailhead. ☽ *Early June–mid-Aug., daily 9 AM.*

# WHAT'S NEARBY

Wind Cave is part of South Dakota's Black Hills, a diverse region of alpine meadows, ponderosa pine forests, and creek-carved, granite-

## CAVEMEN SPEAK

Sound like a serious spelunker with this cavemen cheat-sheet. These *Speleothems* (cave formations) are ones you may see in Wind Cave.

**Cave balloons:** Thin-walled formations resembling partially deflated balloons, usually composed of hydromagnesite.

**Boxwork:** Composed of interconnecting thin blades that were left in relief on cave walls when the bedrock was dissolved away.

**Flowstone:** Consists of thin layers of a mineral deposited on a sloping surface by flowing or seeping water.

**Frostwork:** Sprays of needles that radiate from a central point that are usually made of aragonite.

**Gypsum beard:** Composed of bundles of gypsum fibers that resemble a human beard.

**Logomites:** Consists of popcorn and superficially resembles a hollowed-out stalagmite.

**Pool Fingers:** Deposited underneath water around organic filaments.

**Ribbons:** Thin, layered formations found on sloping ceilings or walls that resemble curtains or scarves.

**Stalagmites:** Mineral deposits that build up on a cave floor from dripping water.

**Stalactites:** Carrot-shaped formations that hang down from a cave ceiling and are formed from dripping water.

---

walled canyons covering 2 million acres in the state's southwest quadrant. This mountain range contrasts sharply with the sheer cliffs and dramatic buttes of the badlands to the north and east, and the wide, windswept plains of most of the state. The Black Hills' crown jewel is Mount Rushmore National Memorial, visited by nearly 3 million visitors each year. U.S. 385 is the backbone of the Black Hills.

## Nearby Towns & Attractions

### Nearby Towns

**Hot Springs,** a small and historic community of about 4,000 residents, is the gateway to Wind Cave National Park. About 30 mi north, on U.S. 85, is the town of **Custer,** where George Armstrong Custer and his expedition first discovered gold in 1874, leading to the gold rush of 1875–76. Founded in the 1880s by prospectors searching the central Black Hills for gold deposits, the small town of **Keystone,** just 2 mi from Mount Rushmore, has an abundance of restaurants, shops, and attractions. To serve the millions of visitors passing through the area, there are 700 hotel rooms—more than twice the town's number of permanent residents. Because it's such a touristy town, we don't recommend it for your Black Hills base. Instead, you may want to stay in quiet **Hill City,** the gateway to Mount Rushmore.

Its brick-paved streets lined with Victorian architecture, **Deadwood** owes its historical character to casinos. Gaming halls, restaurants, and hotels occupy virtually every storefront on Main Street, just as they did back in Deadwood's late-19th-century heyday. You can walk in the footsteps of Wild Bill Hickok and Calamity Jane, who swore she could outdrink, outspit, and outswear any man—and usually did. The central Black Hills is anchored by **Rapid City,** South Dakota's second-largest city (population 60,876) and the largest urban center in a 350-mi radius. It is a good base from which to explore the treasures of the state's southwestern corner, including Mount Rushmore and Wind Cave National Park, 25 mi and 50 mi to the south respectively.

## Nearby Attractions

☕ **Adams Museum.** There are three floors of displays, including the first locomotive used in the area, photographs of the town's early days, and a reproduction of the largest gold nugget (7¾ troy ounces) ever discovered in the Black

> ### AN OUNCE OF GOLD
>
> A troy ounce is a unit used almost exclusively in mining. It's about 1¹/₁₀ ounces or 31 grams.

Hills. ⊠ *54 Sherman St., Deadwood* ☎ *605/578–1714* ⊕ *www. adamsmuseumandhouse.org* ✉ *Donations accepted* ☉ *Memorial Day–Labor Day, Mon.–Sat. 9–7, Sun. noon–5; Labor Day–Memorial Day, Mon.–Sat. 10–4.*

☕ **Big Thunder Gold Mine.** You can take a guided tour through an underground gold mine, get some free gold ore samples, and do a little gold panning yourself. ⊠*Rte. 40, Keystone* ☎*605/666–4847 or 800/314–3917* ⊕*www. bigthundermine.com* ✉*$8* ☉ *May–mid-Oct., daily 9–5.*

**Black Hills Wild Horse Sanctuary.** Hundreds of wild mustangs inhabit this 11,000-acre preserve of rugged canyons, forests, and grasslands along the Cheyenne River. Take a guided tour or hike, and sign up for a chuck-wagon dinner. Drive 14 mi south of Hot Springs until you see signs off Route 71. ⊠ *Rte. 71, Hot Springs* ☎ *605/745–5955 or 800/252–6652* ⊕*www.gwtc.net/~iram* ✉*$15* ☉ *Memorial Day–Labor Day, Mon.–Sat. 9:30–5; tours at 10, 1, and 3.*

☕ **Broken Boot Gold Mine.** You can pan for gold and even if you don't find any, you'll leave with a souvenir stock certificate. ⊠ *U.S. 14A, Deadwood* ☎ *605/578–9997* ⊕ *www.brokenbootgoldmine.com* ✉ *Tour $5, gold panning $5* ☉ *May–Aug., daily 8–5:30; Sept., daily 9–4:30.*

★ **Crazy Horse Memorial.** Designed to be the world's largest sculpture (641 feet long by 563 feet high), this tribute to Crazy Horse, the legendary Lakota leader who defeated General Custer at Little Bighorn, is a work in progress. So far the warrior's head has been carved out of the mountain, and the head of his horse is starting to emerge; when work is underway you can expect to witness frequent blasting. Self-taught sculptor Korczak Ziolkowski conceived this memorial to Native American heritage in 1948, and after his death in 1982 his family took on the project. The completion date is unknown, since activity is limited by weather and funding. Near the work site stands a very good orientation center, the Indian Museum of North America, Korczak's studio/home and workshop, indoor and outdoor sculpture galleries, and a restaurant. ⊠ *Along Hwy. 385, about 3 mi north of Custer* ☎ *605/673–4681*

35

## America's Shrine of Democracy

ABRAHAM LINCOLN WAS TALL in real life—6 feet, four inches, though add a few more for his hat. But as one of the nation's most famous icons, Honest Abe, along with Presidents George Washington, Thomas Jefferson, and Theodore Roosevelt, towers over the Black Hills in a 60-foot-high likeness. The four images look especially spectacular at night, June through mid-September, when a special lighting ceremony dramatically illuminates the carving.

Like most impressive undertakings, Mount Rushmore's path to realization was one of personalities and perseverance.

When Gutzon Borglum, a talented and patriotic sculptor, was invited to create a giant monument to Confederate soldiers in Georgia in 1915, he jumped at the chance. The son of Danish immigrants, Borglum was raised in California and trained in art in Paris, even studying under Auguste Rodin, who influenced his style. Georgia's Stone Mountain project was to be massive in scope—encompassing the rock face of an entire peak—and would give Borglum the opportunity to exercise his artistic vision on a grand scale.

But the relationship with the project backers and Borglum went sour, causing the sculptor to destroy his models and flee the state as a fugitive. Fortunately, state officials in South Dakota had a vision for another mountain memorial, and Borglum was eager to jump on board. His passion and flamboyant personality were well-matched to the project, which involved carving legends of the Wild West on a gigantic scale. In time, Borglum convinced local officials to

think larger, and the idea of carving a monument to U.S. presidents on a mountainside was born.

On a massive granite cliff, at an elevation of 5,725 feet, Borglum began carving Mount Rushmore in 1927 with the help of some 400 assistants. In consultation with U.S. Senator Peter Norbeck and State Historian Doane Robinson, Borglum chose the four presidents to signify the birth, growth, preservation, and development of the nation. In six and a half years of carving over a 14-year period, the sculptor and his crew drilled and dynamited a masterpiece, the largest work of art on Earth. Borglum died in March, 1941, leaving his son, Lincoln, to complete the work only a few months later—in the wake of the gathering storm of World War II.

Follow the Presidential Trail through the forest to gain excellent views of the colossal sculpture, or stroll the Avenue of Flags for a different perspective. Also on-site are an impressive museum, indoor theaters where films are shown, an outdoor amphitheater for live performances, and concession facilities. The nightly ranger program and lighting of the memorial is reportedly the most popular interpretive program in all of the national parks system.

The **Mount Rushmore Information Center,** between the park entrance and the Avenue of Flags, has a small exhibit with photographs of the presidents' faces as they were being carved. There's also an information desk here, staffed by rangers who can answer questions about the memorial or the surrounding Black Hills. A nearly identical building across from the information center houses restrooms,

35

telephones, and soda machines.
✉ *Beginning of Ave. of Flags* ☎ *605/574-2523* ⊕ *www.nps.gov/moru* 📷 *Free; parking $8* ⊘ *May–Sept., daily 8 AM–10 PM; Oct.–Apr., daily 8–5.*

**MOUNT RUSHMORE ATTRACTIONS**

■ **Avenue of Flags.** Running from the entrance of the memorial to the museum and amphitheater at the base of the mountain, the avenue represents each state, commonwealth, district, and territory of the United States.

■ **Lincoln Borglum Museum.** This giant granite-and-glass structure underneath the viewing platform has permanent exhibits on the carving of the mountain, its history, and its significance. There also are temporary exhibits, a bookstore, and an orientation film. Admission is free and it is open year-round.

■ **Presidential Trail.** This easy hike along a boardwalk and down some stairs leads to the very base of the mountain. Although the trail is thickly forested, you'll have more than ample opportunity to look straight up the noses of the four giant heads. The trail is open year-round, so long as snow and/or ice don't present a safety hazard.

■ **Sculptor's Studio.** Built in 1939 as Gutzon Borglum's on-site workshop, it displays tools used by the mountain carvers, a $\frac{1}{12}$-scale model of the memorial, and a model depicting the unfinished Hall of Records. Admission is free. Open May–September only.

⊕ *www.crazyhorse.org* ✉ *$10 per adult or $24 per carload for more than 2 adults* ⊙ *May–Sept., daily 7 AM–9 PM; Oct.–Apr., daily 8–4:30.*

Fodor'sChoice   **Custer State Park.** This 71,000-acre park is considered the crown jewel
★   of South Dakota's state park system. Here, scenic backcountry is watered by clear trout streams. Elk, antelope, mountain goat, bighorn sheep, mountain lion, wild turkey, prairie dog, and the second-largest (behind the one in Yellowstone National Park) publicly owned herd of bison in the world walk the pristine land. Scenic drives roll past fingerlike granite spires and panoramic views (try the Needles Highway). Each year at the Buffalo Roundup and Arts Festival, thousands of spectators watch the park's 1,450 bison thunder through the hills at the start of a Western-themed art and food expo. Take the 18-mi Wildlife Loop Road to see prairies teeming with animals. ⊠ *U.S. 16A, 4 mi east of Custer* ☎ *605/255–4515* ⊕ *www. custerstatepark.info* ✉ *$2.50–$23* ⊙ *Year-round.*

C   **Flintstones Bedrock City.** Step into Bedrock at this Stone Age fun park with rides on the Flintmobile. Play areas, a theater, camping, and brontoburgers and dinodogs at the drive-in round out the experience. ⊠ *U.S 385 at U.S. 16, Custer* ☎ *605/673–4079* ⊕ *www.flintstonesbedrockcity. com* ✉ *$8* ⊙ *Mid-May–mid-Sept., daily 8:30–8.*

**Ft. Hays *Dances with Wolves* Movie Set.** Although it was released in the early 1990s, *Dances with Wolves* continues to generate interest in the Black Hills. View photo displays and a video of the making of the film. A chuck-wagon dinner show ($15) is offered Memorial Day through Labor Day. ⊠ *Ft. Hays Dr. and U.S. 16, Rapid City* ☎ *605/394–9653* ✉ *Free* ⊙ *Mid-May–mid-Sept., daily 7:30 AM–8 PM.*

★   **Jewel Cave National Monument.** Even though its 125 mi of surveyed passages make this cave the world's second largest (Kentucky's Mammoth Cave is the largest), it isn't the size of Jewel Cave that draws visitors, it's the rare crystalline formations that abound in the cave's vast passages. Wander the dark passageways, and you'll be rewarded with the sight of tiny crystal Christmas trees, hydromagnesite balloons that would pop if you touched them, and delicate calcite deposits dubbed "cave popcorn." Year-round, you can take ranger-led tours, from a simple half-hour walk to a lantern-light or wild caving tour. ⊠ *U.S. 16, 15 mi west of Custer* ☎ *605/673–2288* ⊕ *www.nps.gov/jeca* ✉ *$4–$27* ⊙ *Sept.–Apr., daily 8–4:30; May–Aug., daily 8–7.*

★ C   **Reptile Gardens.** On the bottom of a valley between Rapid City and Mount Rushmore is western South Dakota's answer to a zoo. In addition to the world's largest private reptile collection, the site also has a raptor rehabilitation center. No visit is complete without watching some alligator wrestling or letting the kids ride the giant tortoises. ⊠ *8955 S. U.S. 16, Rapid City* ☎ *605/342–5873* ⊕ *www.reptilegardens.com* ✉ *$12* ⊙ *Memorial Day–Labor Day, daily 8–7.*

**South Dakota Air & Space Museum.** See a model of a Stealth bomber that's 60% actual size. Also here are Gen. Dwight D. Eisenhower's Mitchell B-25 bomber and more than two dozen other planes, and a once-operational missile silo. Tours are not available in winter. ⊠ *2890 Davis*

*Dr., Box Elder* ☎ *605/385–5188* 📧 *Free, tour $5* ☉ *Mid-May–mid-Sept., daily 8:30–6; mid-Sept.–mid-May, daily 8:30–4:30.*

## Area Activities

### Sports & the Outdoors

FISHING  The Black Hills are filled with tiny mountain creeks, especially on the wetter western and northern slopes, that are ideal for fly-fishing. Rapid Creek, which flows down from the Central Hills into Pactola Reservoir and finally into Rapid City, is a favorite fishing venue for the city's anglers, both because of its regularly stocked population of trout and for its easy accessibility. Besides the local chambers of commerce, **South Dakota Game, Fish, and Parks** (✉ 523 E. Capitol Ave., Pierre 57501 ☎ 605/773–3485 ⊕ www.state.sd.us/gfp/) is your best bet for updated information on regional fishing locations and their conditions.

HIKING & BICYCLING  Beginning in Deadwood and running the length of the Black Hills from north to south, the **Mickelson Trail** (⊕ www.ridethetrail.com), part of the rails-to-trails program, incorporates more than 100 converted railroad bridges and four tunnels in its 117-mi-long course. Although the grade seldom exceeds 4%, parts of the trail are strenuous. A $2 day pass lets you hike or bike on the trail ($10 for an annual pass); passes are available at self-service stations along the trail, some state park offices, and through the South Dakota Game, Fish, and Parks Web site. A portion of the trail is open for snowmobiling in winter.

WINTER SPORTS  Heavy snowfalls and lovely views make the Black Hills prime cross-country skiing territory. Many trails are open to snowmobilers as well as skiers. Trade and travel magazines consistently rank the Black Hills among the top snowmobiling destinations in the country for two simple reasons: dramatic scenery and an abundance of snow.

**Big Hill Trails.** The trees are gorgeous, ranging from the ubiquitous ponderosa and Black Hills spruce to quaking aspen and paperbark birch. The towering canyon walls, abundant wildlife, and stark contrast between the evergreens and bare trees make this particularly outstanding. ✉ *7 mi south of Spearfish on Tinton Rd. Black Hills National Forest* ☎ *605/673–9200.*

**Deer Mountain Ski Area.** This slope has a massive beginner's area and the only night skiing in the Black Hills. ✉ *3 mi south of Lead on U.S. 85* ☎ *605/717–0422* ⊕ *www.skideermountain.com.*

**Terry Peak Ski Area.** Perched on the sides of a 7,076-foot mountain, Terry Peak claims the Black Hills' second-highest mountain summit. The runs are challenging for novice and intermediate skiers and should keep the experts entertained. From the top, on a clear day, you can see into Wyoming, Montana, and North Dakota. ✉ *2 mi south of Lead on U.S. 85* ☎ *800/456–0524* ⊕ *www.terrypeak.com.*

### Arts & Entertainment

THE ARTS  The **Rushmore Plaza Civic Center Fine Arts Theater** (✉ 444 Mt. Rushmore Rd. N ☎ 800/468–6463) hosts about a half-dozen touring Broadway shows in winter. It's also the venue for the Vucurevich Speaker Series, which has

35

## FESTIVALS & EVENTS

JUNE **Crazy Horse Volksmarch.** This 10-km (6⅕-mi) hike up the mountain where the giant Crazy Horse Memorial is being carved is the largest event of its kind. It's held the first full weekend in June. ☎ *605/673–4681.*

JULY **Gold Discovery Days.** A parade, carnival, balloon rally, firemen's ball, and more, are all part of the fun in late July in Custer. ☎ *800/992–9818.* **Days of '76.** This Deadwood festival has earned PRCA honors as Best Small Outdoor Rodeo numerous times. Rodeo performances, two parades with vintage carriages and coaches,

street dances, and Western arts and crafts make this one of the best events in South Dakota. ☎ *800/999–1876.*

SEPT. **Deadwood Jam.** The Black Hills' premier music event showcases the top in country, rock, and blues. ☎ *800/999–1876.*

OCT. **Custer State Park Buffalo Roundup.** The nation's largest buffalo roundup is one of South Dakota's most exciting events. Cowboys and park crews saddle up and corral the park's 1,400 head of bison so that they may later be vaccinated. ☎ *605/255–4515.*

attracted prominent names such as the humorist Dave Barry, late astronomer Carl Sagan, and former Secretary of State Colin Powell.

ENTERTAINMENT
★ Billing itself as a "museum with a bar," the **Old Style Saloon No. 10** (✉ 657 Main St., Deadwood ☎ 605/578–3346) is where you want to come to drink, listen to music, and socialize. Thousands of artifacts, vintage photos, and a two-headed calf set the scene—plus the chair in which Wild Bill Hickok was supposedly shot. A reenactment of his murder takes place four times daily in the summer.

**Tours**

**Gray Line of the Black Hills** (✉ 1600 E. St. Patrick St., Rapid City SD ☎ 605/ 342–4461 ⊕ www.blackhillsgrayline.com) offers bus tours of the region.

## Shopping

One of the world's top collections of Plains Indian artwork and crafts makes **Prairie Edge Trading Company and Galleries** (✉ 6th and Main Sts., Rapid City ☎ 605/342–3086 or 800/541–2388) seem more like a museum than a store and gallery. The collection ranges from books and CDs to artifact reproductions and artwork representing the Lakota, Crow, Cheyenne, Shoshone, Arapaho, and Assiniboin tribes of the Great Plains.

## Scenic Drives

**Spearfish Canyon Scenic Byway.** The easiest way to get from Deadwood to Rapid City and the central Black Hills is east through Boulder Canyon on U.S. 14A, which joins Interstate 90 in Sturgis. However, it's worth looping north and taking the long way around on this 20-mi scenic route past 1,000-foot limestone cliffs and some of the most breathtaking scenery in the region. Cascading waterfalls quench the thirst of quaking aspen, gnarled oaks, sweet-smelling spruce, and the ubiquitous ponderosa pine, which grow right off the edges of rocky precipices. The canyon is home to deer, mountain goats, porcupines, and bobcats. Near its middle is the old sawmill town of Savoy, a jumping-off point for scenic hikes to Spearfish Falls and Roughlock Falls.

# WHERE TO STAY & EAT

### About the Restaurants

If you're determined to dine in Wind Cave National Park, be sure to pack your own meal, because the only dining venues inside park boundaries are the two picnic areas near the visitor center and Elk Mountain Campground. The towns beyond the park offer additional options—in fact, Deadwood claims some of the best-ranked restaurants in South Dakota. Buffalo, pheasant, and elk are relatively common ingredients in the Black Hills. No matter where you go, in this part of the world, beef is king.

**35**

### About the Hotels

While Wind Cave claims a singular campground, you'll have to look outside park boundaries if you want to bed down in something more substantial than a tent. New chain hotels with modern amenities are plentiful in the Black Hills, but when booking accommodations consider a stay at one of the area's historic properties.

It may be difficult to obtain quality accommodations during summer—and downright impossible during the Sturgis Motorcycle Rally, held the first full week of August every year—so plan ahead and make reservations (three or four months out is a good rule of thumb) if you're going to travel during peak season. To find the best value, choose a hotel far from Interstate 90.

### About the Campgrounds

Camping is one of this region's strengths. While there is only one primitive campground within the park, there are countless campgrounds in the Black Hills. The public campgrounds in the national forest are accessible by road but otherwise secluded and undeveloped; private campgrounds typically have more amenities. If you're up for a more adventurous experience, most of the public land within the Black Hills is open for backcountry camping, provided that you don't light any fires and obtain a permit (usually free) from the appropriate park or forest headquarters. Note that the Black Hills don't have any native bears, but there is a significant population of mountain lions.

## Where to Eat

### In the Park

PICNIC AREAS **Elk Mountain Campground Picnic Area.** You don't have to be a camper to use this well-developed picnic spot, which has more than 70 tables, fire pits, and restrooms with running water. Some of the tables are on the prairie, others are amidst the pines. ⊠ *½ mi north of the visitor center.*

**Wind Cave Picnic Area.** On the edge of a prairie and grove of ponderosa, this is a peaceful, pretty place. Small and simple, it is equipped with a dozen tables and a potable-water pump. ⊠ *¼ mi north of the visitor center.*

### Outside the Park

★ **$$–$$$** ✕ **Deadwood Thymes Bistro.** Located across from the historic courthouse, away from the Main Street casinos, this has a quieter, more intimate feel than other town restaurants—and the food is among the best. The menu changes frequently, but expect dishes like brioche French toast, salmon quiche, Parisian grilled ham and Swiss, Thai burrito with peanut sauce, and lamb chops marinated in white wine and mustard and served with parsley-gin sauce. The wine list features imports, and desserts are incredible. You might find raspberry cheesecake, or chocolate angel food cake with a whiskey-bourbon sauce. ⊠ *87 Sherman St., Deadwood* ☎ *605/578–7566. $15–$25* ▤ *MC, V.*

★ **$$–$$$** ✕ **Jakes.** This restaurant owned by actor Kevin Costner is among South Dakota's classiest dining experiences. Cherrywood pillars inlaid with etched-glass lights, white-brick fireplaces, and a pianist add to the elegance of the atrium dining room. Among the menu's eclectic offerings are buffalo roulade, Cajun seafood tortellini, filet mignon, and fresh fish. ⊠ *677 Main St., Deadwood* ☎ *605/578–1555* ⚏ *Reservations essential. $18–$30* ▤ *AE, D, DC, MC, V.*

**$–$$$** ✕ **Deadwood Social Club.** On the second floor of historic Saloon No. 10,
Fodor'sChoice   this warm restaurant surrounds you with wood and old-time photographs
★   of Deadwood's past. Light jazz and blues play over the sound system. The decor is Western, but the food is northern Italian, a juxtaposition that keeps patrons coming back. The menu stretches from wild-mushroom pasta-and-seafood nest with basil cream to chicken piccata and melt-in-your-mouth Black Angus rib eyes. The wine list had nearly 200 selections at last count. Reservations are a good idea. ⊠ *657 Main St., Deadwood* ☎ *605/578–1533. $9–$22* ▤ *AE, MC, V.*

**$$** ✕ **Blue Bell Lodge and Resort.** Feast on fresh trout or buffalo, which you can have as a steak or a stew, in this rustic log building within the boundaries of Custer State Park. There's a kids' menu. On the property, hayrides and cookouts are part of the entertainment, and you can sign up for trail rides and overnight pack trips on old Indian trails with the nearby stable. ⊠ *About 6 mi south of U.S. 16A junction on Hwy. 87, in Custer State Park, Custer* ☎ *605/255–4531 or 800/658–3530. $19–$20* ▤ *AE, D, MC, V* ☉ *Closed mid-Oct.–mid-May.*

★ **$–$$** ✕ **Botticelli Ristorante Italiano.** With a wide selection of delectable veal and chicken dishes as well as creamy pastas, this Italian eatery provides a welcome respite from the traditional Midwestern meat and potatoes. The artwork and traditional Italian music in the background give the place a European air. ⊠ *523 Main St., Rapid City* ☎ *605/348–0089. $9–$20* ▤ *AE, MC, V.*

**¢–$** ✕ **Buffalo Dining Room.** The only restaurant within the bounds of the memorial affords commanding views of Mount Rushmore and the surrounding ponderosa pine forest, and exceptional food at a reasonable price.

The menu includes New England pot roast, buffalo stew, and homemade rhubarb pie. It's open for breakfast, lunch, and dinner. ⊠ *Beginning of Ave. of Flags* ☎ *605/574–2515. $6–$11* ▭ *AE, D, MC, V* ☽ *No dinner mid-Oct.–early Mar.*

## Where to Stay

### In the Park

CAMPGROUNDS & RV PARKS

★ ¢–$

⚠ **Elk Mountain Campground.** If you prefer a relatively developed campsite and relative proximity to civilization, Elk Mountain is an excellent choice. You can experience the peaceful pine forests and wild creatures of the park without straying too far from the safety of the beaten path. Most of the campers who stay here pitch tents, but there are 25 pull-through sites for RVs, and Sites 24 and 69 are reserved for campers with disabilities. Note that water is shut off during winter. ⊠ *½ mi north of the visitor center* ☎ *605/745–4600* ⮣ *75 sites* ⚠ *Flush toilets, running water (non-potable), fire grates, public telephone. $5–$10* ▭ *No credit cards* ☽ *Apr.–late Oct.*

35

### Outside the Park

$–$$$$

Fodor'sChoice

★

▣ **Franklin Hotel.** Built in 1903, this imposing hotel has housed many famous guests in its time, including John Wayne, Teddy Roosevelt, and Babe Ruth. It still has its original banisters, ceilings, and fireplace. The guest rooms are Victorian style, with reproduction furniture, lace on hardwood tables, and flowery bedspreads. A bar on the second floor spills out onto the veranda above the white-columned hotel entrance, affording a great view down Main Street. The fabled Franklin reopened in spring 2006 following a major face-lift. ⊠ *700 Main St., Deadwood 57732* ☎ *605/578–2241 or 800/688–1876* ⎙ *605/578–3452* ⊕ *www.silveradofranklin.com* ⮣ *81 rooms* ⚠ *Room service, bar, no-smoking rooms. $95–205* ▭ *AE, D, DC, MC, V.*

$–$$$$

✕▣ **State Game Lodge and Resort.** Once the Summer White House for President Coolidge, and host to President Eisenhower as well, this stately stone-and-wood lodge has well-appointed rooms and isolated pine-shaded cabins, many right on the banks of a creek. The cabins are simple and spartan, the motel rooms are comfortable, and the lodge rooms are almost stately, with elegant hardwood furniture and massive stone fireplaces. You can arrange for Jeep rides into the buffalo area. The excellent, upscale Pheasant Dining Room ($$–$$$) is known for pheasant and buffalo specialties. ⊠ *16 mi east of Custer on U.S. 16A, Custer* ⌂ *HCR 83, Box 74, Custer 57730* ☎ *605/255–4541 or 800/658–3530* ⎙ *605/255–4706* ⊕ *www.custerresorts.com* ⮣ *7 lodge rooms, 40 motel rooms, 33 cabins* ⚠ *Restaurant, kitchen (some), bar, some pets allowed, no a/c (some), no phone (some), no TV, no-smoking rooms. $75–$315* ▭ *AE, D, MC, V* ☽ *Closed Oct.–Mother's Day.*

★ ☾

$–$$$$

✕▣ **Sylvan Lake Resort.** This spacious stone-and-wood lodge in Custer State Park affords fantastic views of pristine Sylvan Lake and Harney Peak beyond. The rooms in the lodge are large and modern, and there are rustic cabins, some with fireplaces, scattered along the cliff and in the forest. The Lakota Dining Room ($–$$) has an exceptional view of the lake; its lovely veranda constructed of native stone is the perfect place to sip tea and watch the sunrise. On the menu are buffalo selections and rainbow trout. You can canoe, fish, and swim in the lake, and numerous hiking trails make this a great choice for active families. ✉ *16 mi east of Custer on U.S. 16A, Hill City* ⌂ *HC 83, Box 74, Custer 57730* ☎ *605/574–2561 or 800/658–3530* 🖷 *605/574–4943* ⊕ *www. custerresorts.com* ⇒ *35 rooms, 31 cabins* ⚬ *Restaurant, no-smoking rooms. $82–$215* ▭ *AE, D, MC, V* ⊙ *Closed Oct.–Mother's Day.*

★ **$$$** 🏠 **Spearfish Canyon Lodge.** Located about midway between Spearfish and Deadwood, near the bottom of Spearfish Canyon, this lodge-style hotel commands some of the best views in the Black Hills. Limestone cliffs rise nearly 1,000 feet in all directions. The rush of Spearfish Falls is only a ¼-mi hike away, while the gentle flow of Roughlock Falls is a mi-long hike through pine, oak, and aspen from the lodge's front door. The rooms are furnished in natural woods, and fabrics are dark maroon and green. ✉ *10619 Roughlock Falls Rd., Lead 57754* ☎ *877/975–6343 or 605/584–3435* 🖷 *605/584–3990* ⊕ *www.spfcanyon.com* ⇒ *54 rooms* ⚬ *Restaurant, room service, ethernet (fee), bar, laundry facilities, no smoking. $159–$199* ▭ *AE, D, MC, V.*

★ **$$–$$$** 🏠 **Audrie's Bed & Breakfast.** Victorian antiques and the hint of romance greet you at this out-of-the-way B&B, set in a thick woods 7 mi west of Rapid City. Suites, cottages, and creek-side cabins sleeping two come with old-world furnishings, fireplaces, private baths, hot tubs, and big-screen TVs. Bicycles and fishing poles can be obtained free from the office. ✉ *23029 Thunderhead Falls Rd., Rapid City 57702* ☎ *605/342–7788* ⊕ *www.audriesbb.com* ⇒ *2 suites, 7 cottages and cabins* ⚬ *Bicycles, no kids, no smoking. $115–$175* ▭ *No credit cards* ⏐◯⏐ *BP.*

**$$** 🏠 **Buffalo Rock Lodge B&B.** A large, native-rock fireplace surrounded by hefty logs adds to the rustic quality of this lodge decorated with Western artifacts. There's an extensive view of Mount Rushmore from an oversize deck surrounded by a plush pine forest filled with wildflowers. ✉ *Playhouse Rd., Box 641, Keystone 57751* ☎ *605/666–4781 or 888/564–5634* ⊕ *buffalorock.net* ⇒ *3 rooms* ⚬ *Some pets allowed, no TV, no-smoking rooms. $125–$150* ▭ *DC, MC, V* ⏐◯⏐ *CP.*

**$$** ✕🏠 **Deadwood Gulch Resort.** Pine-clad hills, a little creek, and a deck from which to view the mountains are at your disposal at this family-style resort about a mile from downtown. A trolley stops here to take you to sites in Deadwood. The Creekside Restaurant (¢–$$) serves hearty breakfasts and some of the best burgers in town. The giant salads are also favorites, largely because of the side of sunflower bread and the homemade apricot dressing. ✉ *U.S. 85, Deadwood 57732* ☎ *605/ 578–1294 or 800/695–1876* 🖷 *605/578–2505* ⊕ *www.deadwoodgulch. com* ⇒ *98 rooms* ⚬ *Restaurant, ethernet (fee), bar, no-smoking rooms, some pets allowed. $109* ▭ *AE, D, DC, MC, V* ⏐◯⏐ *BP.*

**$–$$** 🏠 **French Creek Guest Ranch B&B.** Soak up views of the Needles formation while you sit on the porch of this luxurious B&B. On a 25-acre working horse ranch, French Creek is designed to meet the needs of the traveling horse owner: the stable has eight wooden box stalls each with its own run. Horses may be boarded for an additional fee. Facilities are also available for a horse trailer or camper hookup. The ranch is 1½ mi from Custer State Park. ✉ *Rte. 16A, Custer 57730* ☎ *605/673–4790*

*or 877/673–4790* 🖷 *605/673–4767* ⊕ *www.frenchcreekranch.com*
🛏 *3 rooms* ⚖ *Restaurant, refrigerator, tennis court, no kids under 13.*
*$65–$145* ▤ *D, MC, V* ⦿❘ *BP.*

★ **$–$$** ▦ **Strutton Inn B&B.** Set on 4 acres, this three-story Victorian home a few
miles from Crazy Horse has a 140-foot veranda with a gazebo on each
corner looking out over a lovely garden and the Black Hills beyond. Most
of the guest rooms of the well-furnished retreat are decorated with pas-
tels, frills, and floral patterns. The rooms have king-size beds but no TVs;
there is, however, a 46-inch big-screen TV in the common room. ⊠ *U.S.*
*16* ⌂ *R.R. 1, Box 55 S, Custer 57730* ☎ *605/673–2395 or 800/226–*
*2611* 🖷 *605/673–2395* ⊕ *www.struttoninn.com* 🛏 *9 rooms* ⚖ *No*
*phone, no TV, no smoking. $89–$145* ▤ *MC, V* ⦿❘ *BP.*

CAMPGROUNDS &
RV PARKS
**$$–$$$**

⌂ **Berry Patch Campground.** This well-developed, grassy campground,
which is open year-round, is especially convenient for RVs. Bus tours
to area sights depart from the campground daily. Take exit 60 off Interstate 90. ⊠ *1860 E. North St., Rapid City 57701* ☎ *605/341–5588*
🛏 *150 sites (123 with full hookups, 27 with partial hookups)* ⚖ *Flush*
*toilets, full hookups, partial hookups, dump station, drinking water, show-*
*ers, fire grates, picnic tables, electricity, public telephone, general store,*
*play area, swimming (pool). $20–$38.*

★ ☾ **$$** ⌂ **Mount Rushmore KOA–Palmer Gulch Lodge.** This huge commercial
campground on Route 244 west of Mount Rushmore offers shuttles to
the mountain, bus tours, horse rides, and car rentals. There are also large
furnished cabins and primitive camping cabins, as well as a new lodge
shadowed by the massive granite ramparts of Harney Peak. With its pools,
waterslide, outdoor activities, and kids' programs, this is a great place
for families, and parents will appreciate the three hot tubs. A free shut-
tle takes you to Mount Rushmore and Crazy Horse. ⊠ *12620 Rte. 244,*
*Hill City 57745* ☎ *605/574–2525* 🖷 *605/574–2574* ⊕ *www.palmergulch.*
*com* 🛏 *500 sites (130 with full hookups, 192 with partial hookups),*
*85 cabins* ⚖ *Flush toilets, full hookups, partial hookups (electric and*
*water), dump station, drinking water, guest laundry, showers, fire grates,*
*restaurant, picnic tables, kitchen (some), electricity, service station, play*
*area, pool, some pets allowed, no a/c (some), no phone (some), Wi-Fi.*
*$25–$30 tent sites, $35–$40 partial hookups, $40–$55 full hookups,*
*lodge $110–$165, cabins $57–$415* ⊙ *May–Sept.*

☾ **$–$$** ⌂ **Whispering Pines Campground and Lodging.** Block party–style cookouts are followed by movies every night here as long as the weather is
good. Located 16 mi west of Rapid City in Black Hills National Forest, the campground lies exactly midway between Deadwood (22 mi to
the north) and Mount Rushmore (22 mi to the south). In addition to
RV and tent sites, cabins are available at a reasonable price. ⊠ *22700*
*Silver City Rd., Rapid City 57702* ☎ *605/341–3667* 🖷 *605/341–3667*
⊕ *www.blackhillscampresort.com* 🛏 *26 full hookups, 2 partial hookups,*
*45 tent sites; 5 cabins* ⚖ *Flush toilets, partial hookups (elec-*
*tric and water), dump station, drinking water, guest laundry, showers,*
*fire pits, picnic tables, food service, electricity, public telephone, gen-*
*eral store, play area, swimming (lake). $15 tent sites, $20 partial*
*hookups, $22 full hookups, $33–$40 cabins* ⚖ *Reservations essential*
▤ *D, MC, V* ⊙ *May–Sept.*

**35**

# WIND CAVE ESSENTIALS

ACCESSIBILITY The visitor center is entirely wheelchair accessible, but only a few areas of the cave itself are navigable by those with limited mobility. Arrangements can be made in advance for a special ranger-assisted tour for a small fee.

ADMISSION FEES There's no fee to enter the park; cave tours cost $7–$23.

ADMISSION HOURS The park is open year-round. It is in the Central time zone.

ATMS/BANKS
🏧 **Wells Fargo Bank** ✉ 101 S. Chicago St., Hot Springs ☎ 605/745-4120.

AUTOMOBILE SERVICE STATIONS
🏧 **Big D Oil Company** ✉ 381 U.S. 16, Custer ☎ 605/673-2262. **Norton's Sinclair** ✉ 1845 University Ave., Hot Springs ☎ 605/745-3219.

EMERGENCIES Dial 911 for emergencies, then call the visitor center at 605/745–4600. Rangers can provide basic first aid. Further medical attention is available at Custer Community Hospital in Custer, Southern Hills Hospital in Hot Springs, or Rapid City Regional Hospital.

LOST AND FOUND The park's lost-and-found is at the visitor center.

PERMITS The requisite backcountry camping and horseback riding permits are both free from the visitor center.

POST OFFICES
🏧 **Custer Post Office** ✉ 643 Mt. Rushmore Rd., Custer 57730 ☎ 605/673-4248. **Hot Springs Post Office** ✉ 146 N. Chicago St., Hot Springs 57747 ☎ 605/745-4117.

PUBLIC TELEPHONES Public telephones may be found at the visitor center and Elk Mountain Campground. Cell-phone reception is hit and miss in the park.

RELIGIOUS SERVICES There is no chapel or other religious service within the park.

RESTROOMS Public restrooms may be found at the visitor center and Elk Mountain Campground.

SHOPS & GROCERS There are no stores within the park. You can find basic groceries and camping supplies at shops in Custer or Hot Springs.

## NEARBY TOWN INFORMATION
🏧 **Black Hills, Badlands and Lakes Association.** ✉ 1851 Discovery Circle, Rapid City, SD 57701 ☎ 605/355-3600 ⊕ www.blackhillsbadlands.com.

## VISITOR INFORMATION
🏧 **Wind Cave National Park** ✉ U.S. 385 (Box 190), Hot Springs, SD 57747 ☎ 605/745-4600 ⊕ www.nps.gov/wica.

# Yellowstone National Park

Beauty Pool, Yellowstone National Park

## WORD OF MOUTH

"A thousand Yellowstone wonders are calling. Look up and down and round about you."

–John Muir, *Our National Parks*

# WELCOME TO YELLOWSTONE

## TOP REASONS TO GO

★**Going-off geysers:** With over 10,000 thermal features, Yellowstone is a natural war zone of hot geysers, the most famous being Old Faithful.

★ **Fisherman's dream:** Thousands of miles of streams and lakes, home to several types of trout, grayling, and mountain whitefish, make Yellowstone a fisherman's dream.

★ **Winter wonderland:** Yellowstone can be a truly amazing place during the winter months, and navigating the park by snowmobile allows visitors to see all the park's main attractions.

★ **Volcanic ventures:** A combination of thinner-than-normal crust depth and a huge magma chamber beneath the park result in the surface being active with geysers, steaming pools, hissing fumaroles, bubbling mud pots, and warm seeps.

★ **Nature-calling:** With its mix of wildlife, mountains, geysers, and water, Yellowstone showcases nature at her best.

**1** Grant Village/West Thumb. Named for President Ulysses S. Grant, Grant Village is located on the western edge of Yellowstone Lake. Early explorers thought the lake was shaped like a human hand, thus it's also called West Thumb.

**2** Old Faithful area. One of the most recognizable images in U.S. pop culture, Old Faithful erupts every 94 minutes or so.

**3** Madison. Here, the Madison River is formed by the joining of the Gibbon and Firehole rivers. Fly fisherman will find healthy stocks of brown and rainbow trout and mountain whitefish.

**4** Norris. In the hottest and most changeable part of Yellowstone, geysers can suddenly stop flowing and new ones can appear.

**5** Mammoth Hot Springs. The springs are a result of several key ingredients; rock fractures in the limestone allow heat and water to escape the earth's surface.

**6** Tower-Roosevelt. This least-visited area is the place to go for solitude, or at least a less crowded atmosphere.

Mammoth Hot Springs

**7** Canyon area. Scientists believe that the Yellowstone area is home to one of the largest volcanic eruptions in history, which resulted in the formation of a large caldera and several canyons. Receding glaciers left the area in its current state.

**8** Yellowstone Lake area. The largest body of water within the park, Yellowstone Lake is believed to have once been 200 feet higher than the present-day lake. In the winter months, the lake freezes over with ice depths ranging from a few inches to several feet.

WYOMING

## GETTING ORIENTED

At more than 2.2 million acres, Yellowstone National Park is considered one of America's most scenic and diverse national parks. Established in 1872 in what is now the northwest corner of Wyoming, Yellowstone was the first national park in the world and was named for its location at the head of the Yellowstone River. Yellowstone is every bit as wonderous today as it was over 130 years ago.

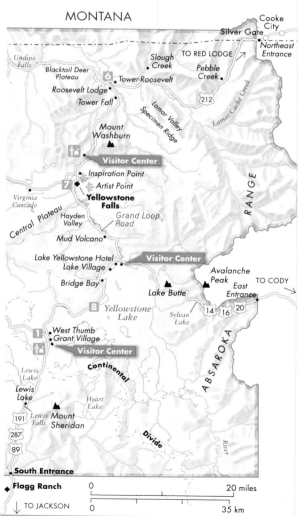

MONTANA

Cooke City
Silver Gate
Northeast Entrance

Undine Falls
Blacktail Deer Plateau
**6** Tower-Roosevelt
Slough Creek
Pebble Creek
TO RED LODGE
Roosevelt Lodge
Tower Fall
212

Mount Washburn
Lamar Valley
Specimen Ridge
Lamar Cache Creek

Visitor Center

Inspiration Point
**7** Artist Point
Virginia Cascade
**Yellowstone Falls**
Central Plateau
Hayden Valley
Grand Loop Road
Mud Volcano

RANGE

Lake Yellowstone Hotel
Lake Village
Visitor Center
Bridge Bay
Lake Butte
Avalanche Peak
East Entrance
TO CODY

**8** Yellowstone Lake
Sylvan Lake
14 16 20

West Thumb
Grant Village
Visitor Center

Lewis Lake
Continental
Lewis Lake
Heart Lake
191 Lewis Falls Mount Sheridan
287
89
Divide

ABSAROKA

**South Entrance**
Flagg Ranch
0    20 miles
0    35 km

↓ TO JACKSON

| KEY | |
|---|---|
| 👫 | Ranger Station |
| ⛺ | Campground |
| 🧺 | Picnic Area |
| 🍴 | Restaurant |
| 🏠 | Lodge |
| 🚶 | Trailhead |
| 🚻 | Restrooms |
| ⇌ | Scenic Viewpoint |
| ---- | Walking/Hiking Trails |
| ..... | Bicycle Path |

# YELLOWSTONE PLANNER

## When to Go

There are two seasons in Yellowstone: summer (May–September), when warm days give way to brisk evenings, and when by far the majority of visitors come; and winter (mid-December–February), when fewer people come. Most of the park closes from October to mid-December and again from March to late April or early May.

**You'll find the really big crowds from mid-July to mid-August.** There are fewer people in the park the month or two before and after this peak season, but there are also fewer dining and lodging facilities open. There's also a bit more rain, especially at the lower elevations. Snowy conditions mean most roads are closed to most vehicles from early November to early May. Snow is possible the entire year. If you've visited Yellowstone many times in the summer, you might not recognize it after the first snowfall. Rocky outcroppings are smoothed over and waterfalls are transformed into jagged sheets of ice. The most satisfying—and often the only—way to explore is by snowshoe, ski, or snowmobile.

AVG. HIGH/LOW TEMPS.

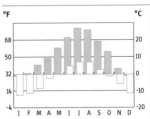

## Flora & Fauna

Yellowstone's scenery is astonishing any time of day, though the play of light and shadow makes the park most appealing in early morning and late afternoon. That is exactly when you should be out looking for wildlife, as most are active around dawn and dusk, when animals move out of the forest in search of food and water. May and June are the best months for seeing baby bison, moose, and other young arrivals. Spring and early summer find the park covered with wildflowers, while autumn is a great time to visit because of the vivid reds and golds of the changing foliage. Winter visitors are the ones who see the park at its most magical, with steam billowing from geyser basins to wreath trees in ice, and elk foraging close to roads transformed into ski trails.

Bison, elk, and coyotes populate virtually all areas; elk and bison particularly like river valleys and the geyser basins. Moose like marshy areas along Yellowstone Lake and in the northeast corner of the park. Wolves roam throughout the region but are most common in the Lamar Valley and areas south of Mammoth, while bears are most visible in the Pelican Valley–Fishing Bridge area, near Dunraven Pass, and near Mammoth. Watch for trumpeter swans and other waterfowl along the Yellowstone River and for sandhill cranes near the Firehole River and in Madison Valley.

Controversy swirls around the park's wolves, which were reintroduced in 1995, as well as its bison, which sometimes roam outside the park in winter. Both draw headlines because neighboring cattle ranchers see the creatures as a threat to their herds.

# Getting There & Around

Yellowstone National Park is served by airports in nearby communities, including Cody, Wyoming, one hour east; Jackson, Wyoming, one hour south; Bozeman, Montana, 90 minutes north; and West Yellowstone, Montana, just outside the park's west gate, which has only summer service. The best places to rent cars in the region are at airports in Cody, Jackson, Bozeman, and West Yellowstone. There is no commercial bus service to Yellowstone.

Yellowstone is well away from the interstates, so drivers make their way here on two-lane highways that are long on miles and scenery. From Interstate 80, take U.S. 191 north from Rock Springs; it's about 177 mi to Jackson, then 60 mi north to Yellowstone. From Interstate 90, head south at Livingston, Montana, 80 mi to Gardiner and the park's north entrance. From Bozeman travel south 90 mi to West Yellowstone.

Yellowstone has five primary entrances. The majority of visitors arrive through the south entrance, north of Grand Teton National Park and Jackson, Wyoming. Other entrances are the east entrance, with a main point of origin in Cody, Wyoming; the west entrance at West Yellowstone, Montana (most used during winter); the north entrance at Gardiner, Montana; and the northeast entrance at Cooke City, Montana, which can be reached from either Cody, Wyoming, via the Chief Joseph Scenic Highway, or from Red Lodge, Montana, over the Beartooth Pass.

**The best way to keep your bearings in Yellowstone is to remember that the major roads form a figure eight, known as the Grand Loop, which all entrance roads feed into.** It doesn't matter at which point you begin, as you can hit most of the major sights if you follow the entire route.

The 370 mi of public roads in the park used to be riddled with potholes and had narrow shoulders—a bit tight when a motor home was pulled over to the side to capture wildlife or scenery on film. But due to the park's efforts to upgrade its roads, most of them are now wide and smooth. Road work is ongoing in a few areas, including a segment of the East Entrance Road over Sylvan Pass, with half-hour delays most days and complete nighttime closures through 2007. On holiday weekends, road construction halts so there are no construction delays for travelers. Check with park rangers to determine where you'll encounter delays or closures. Snow is possible any time of year in almost all areas of the park.

# Winter Driving

All roads except those between Mammoth Hot Springs and the north entrance, and Cooke City and the Northeast Entrance are closed to wheeled vehicles from mid-October to mid-April; they are only open (and groomed accordingly) to over-snow vehicles from mid-December to mid-March. And come spring, the roads don't open at the same time. The road from Mammoth Hot Springs to Norris generally opens mid-April. The West Entrance opens in mid-April, while the East and South entrances open in early May. The last to open is the road from Tower Fall to Canyon Village, which sees its first traffic at the end of May.

Contact the Wyoming Department of Transportation ( ☎ 307/772-0824 or 800/996-7623) for road and travel reports October–April. For emergency situations dial 911 or contact the Wyoming Highway Patrol.

At present, you can ride a snowmobile in winter, as long as you have a guide and a four-stroke machine. But the controversy over snowmobile use in the park has continued for several years and further restrictions could be implemented. Snow coaches are the only certain means of motorized winter transportation into the park. They range from old-style, bright yellow Bombardier coaches to modern vans with their wheels converted to tracks so they can travel over the snow. Snow coaches carry from six to a dozen passengers, make frequent stops, have guides to interpret the park's attractions, and serve as both tour vehicles and shuttles within the park.

36

By T. D. Griffith & Dustin D. Floyd

Few places in the world can match Yellowstone National Park's collection of accessible wonders—a "window on the Earth's interior" is how one geophysicist described it. As you visit the park's hydrothermal areas, you'll be walking on top of Yellowstone Caldera, a 28-by-47-mi collapsed volcanic cone. The geyser basins, hot mud pots, fumaroles (steam vents), and hot springs are kept bubbling by an underground pressure cooker filled with magma. Above ground, the terrain yields rugged mountains, lush meadows, pine forests, free-flowing rivers, and the largest natural high-elevation lake in the United States.

If you're not here for the geysers or beautiful scenery, chances are you've come for the teeming wildlife, from grazing bison to cruising trumpeter swans. To see a spectacularly different Yellowstone than that experienced by most of the 3 million annual visitors, come in winter. Even in the depths of a deep freeze, the park is never totally still: mud pots bubble, geysers shoot skyward, and wind soughs through the pines. Above these sounds, the cry of a hawk, the yip of a coyote, or even the howl of a wolf may pierce the air.

The park has five entrances, each with its own attractions: the south has the Lewis River canyon; the east, Sylvan Pass; the west, the Madison River valley; the north, the beautiful Paradise Valley; and the northeast, the spectacular Beartooth Pass. Along the park's main drive—the Grand Loop—are eight primary "communities" or developed areas. Grant Village, near West Thumb, is the farthest south; Old Faithful and Madison are on the western side of the Lower Loop; Norris and Canyon Village are in the central part of the park, where the two loops intersect; Mammoth Hot Springs and Tower Roosevelt Fall lie at the northern corners of the Upper Loop; and the Yellowstone Lake area is along the eastern segment of the Lower Loop.

## PLANNING YOUR TIME

If you plan to spend just one full day in the park, you will have to strategize wisely to get a good glimpse of the park's wonders. Your best approach would be to concentrate on one or two of the park's major areas. Many visitors head for the two biggest attractions: Old Faithful geyser, and Grand Canyon of the Yellowstone.

With more time you can really sink your teeth into Yellowstone. If you want to study a geyser terrace and see elk, go to Mammoth. Head to Roosevelt for hiking in open meadows, a horseback or stagecoach ride, and a cookout, as well as the chance to see or hear wolves and examine the remnants of a petrified forest. In the Lake Yellowstone area, you can fish, watch buffalo and often see grizzly bears, especially in the Pelican Valley. Grant has its own small geyser basin that abuts Lake Yellowstone.

Spend as much time as possible out of the car to immerse yourself in this natural place. Take a hike on some of the park's dozens of trails, which range from extremely easy and suitable for people with impaired mobility to rigorous enough to challenge hard-core backpackers.

Another good way to learn about the park is to participate in a ranger-led tour or discussion. Take a sunset cruise on Lake Yellowstone or a ride to LeHardy Rapids in a classic 1937 touring bus. In winter there are guided snowmobile or snow-coach trips with options for cross-country skiing or snowshoeing through geyser basins and along the canyon. If you seek greater solitude, explore Yellowstone's backcountry either on your own or on a guided backpacking or horse-packing trip. For days on end, you might not see a visitor center and you might not sleep in a bed with four walls around you, but you will gain an appreciation for the park's unspoiled wilderness—without running into hordes of other people. Some backcountry campsites are accessible for people with disabilities.

*From south to north, these are the five areas of the western part of the Grand Loop, as shown on the western Yellowstone map (see page 757):*

**Grant Village,** along the western edge of Lake Yellowstone, is the first community you encounter from the South Entrance. It has lodging and dining facilities and provides access to the West Thumb Geyser Basin.

★ **Old Faithful,** the world's most famous geyser, is the centerpiece of this area, which has extensive boardwalks through the Upper Geyser Basin and equally extensive visitor services. In winter it's the one area of the park that offers dining and lodging.

**Madison,** the area around the junction of the West Entrance Road and the Lower Loop, is a good place for a break, because you will almost always see bison grazing along the Madison River; elk are often in the area as well. Limited visitor services are here—just an amphitheater for programs, a bookstore, a picnic area, and a campground.

**Norris,** at the western junction of the Upper and Lower Loops, has the most active geyser basin in the park. The underground plumbing occasionally reaches such high temperatures—the ground itself has heated up in areas to nearly 200°F—that a portion of the basin is periodically closed for safety reasons. Consult with rangers at the Norris Geyser Basin Museum to learn when geysers are expected to erupt. Visitor services are limited to two museums, a bookstore, and a picnic area.

**Mammoth Hot Springs** is known for its massive natural terraces, where mineral water flows continuously. You'll almost always see elk grazing here. In the park's early days, it was the site of Fort Yellowstone, and the brick buildings from that era are still used for park activities. The Albright Visitor Center displays some of the paintings Thomas Moran created on a government expedition to Yellowstone in 1871. A range of visitor services are here.

*From north to south, these are the three main areas of eastern Grand Loop, as shown on the Eastern Yellowstone map (see page 760):*

**Tower-Roosevelt,** the northeast region of Yellowstone, is the least-visited part of the park, making it a great place to explore without running into lots of other people. Sights in the area include a petrified tree and a ridge filled with fossil specimens. This is where wolves were first reintroduced to the park; packs are often seen in the Lamar Valley.

**Canyon** has waterfalls and steep canyon walls surrounding the Yellowstone River. This central part of the park is one of Yellowstone's most spectacular places. You will find all types of visitors' services and lots of hiking opportunities—as well as lots of visitors.

**Yellowstone Lake area,** in the park's southeastern segment, is permeated by the massive Yellowstone Lake. Near Fishing Bridge you might see grizzly bears. They like to hunt for fish spawning or swimming near the lake's outlet to the Yellowstone River. Visitor services include Lake Yellowstone Hotel, Fishing Bridge RV Park (for hard-sided vehicles only), and Bridge Bay Campground, the park's largest, with 432 sites.

## Scenic Drives

**Blacktail Deer Plateau Drive.** Keep an eye out for coyotes on this dirt road that traverses sagebrush-covered hills and forests of lodgepole pines. ✉ *Begins east of Mammoth Hot Springs.*

**East Entrance Road.** Crossing the Absaroka Range, this 16-mi drive meanders through beautiful alpine setting. At the top of Sylvan Pass are spectacular views of Yellowstone Lake. ✉ *Begins at the East Entrance.*

**Firehole Canyon Drive.** This one-way, 2-mi detour off Grand Loop Road runs in a southerly direction just south of Madison Junction. The road twists through the 700- to 800-foot-deep canyon and passes the 40-foot Firehole Falls. ✉ *1 mi south of Madison off Grand Loop Rd.*

**Firehole Lake Drive.** This one-way, 3-mi road runs past Great Fountain Geyser, which shoots out jets of water occasionally as high as 200 feet. In winter, watch for bison. ✉ *Begins 8 mi north of Old Faithful.*

## GREAT ITINERARIES

### YELLOWSTONE IN ONE DAY

There's no way you can see everything in just one day. So concentrate on a single area of the park. If you enter the park from the south or west, focus on the geyser basins around Old Faithful, Norris Geyser, and the Grand Canyon of the Yellowstone. Start with an early morning trip to **Old Faithful,** then head north, taking a detour onto the Firehole Lake Drive to see Great Fountain Geyser. When you reach **Norris Geyser Basin,** walk ¼ mi out to Steamboat Geyser, the world's tallest of its kind (it seldom erupts; the last time was in 2000). You can easily spend all afternoon at Norris enjoying the sights and poking through the geyseriana at Norris Geyser Basin Museum, or you can head east to **Canyon Village** to hike the trails in the late afternoon.

If you're arriving from the east, start with sunrise at **Lake Butte,** then spend the early morning viewing wildlife in Hayden Valley. Drive counterclockwise around Grand Loop Road to **Canyon Village,** viewing the spectacular **Grand Canyon of the Yellowstone.** In early afternoon stop at **Old Faithful,** then head southeast to **Yellowstone Lake** for a boat ride at Bridge Bay and an elegant dinner at the **Lake Yellowstone Hotel.**

If you're entering through the North or Northeast entrance, begin at dawn looking for wolves and other animals in Lamar Valley, then head to **Tower-Roosevelt** and take a horseback ride into the surrounding forest. After your ride, continue west to **Mammoth Hot Springs,** where you can hike the **Lower Terrace Interpretive Trail.** If you

drive 1½ mi south of the visitor center you will reach the **Upper Terrace Drive,** where you'll be treated to close-ups of hot springs. In the late afternoon, drive south, keeping an eye out for wildlife as you go—you're almost certain to see elk, buffalo, and possibly even a bear. When you reach **Old Faithful,** you can place the famous geyser into context by walking the 1½-mi **Geyser Hill Loop** or a variety of other trails. Wait for the next eruption. Do it from the deck of the **Old Faithful Inn.**

### YELLOWSTONE IN THREE DAYS

On your first day, enter the park through the East Gate, heading over Sylvan Pass. Take a break at **Fishing Bridge** (the ice cream at the old Hamilton Store is great on a hot day) and watch for the grizzly bears that like to fish here. Stop for lunch at the **Lake Yellowstone Hotel** before turning north through Hayden Valley to **Canyon Village.** There you can view the **Grand Canyon of the Yellowstone** from Inspiration Point or Artist Point, then hike along the canyon rim. Spend the night at Canyon Village.

On your second day, spend the morning exploring **Norris Geyser Basin,** then continue south to **Old Faithful** and have lunch at the **Old Faithful Inn** or the **Old Faithful Snow Lodge.** In the afternoon, explore the surrounding area and spend the night in either the Inn or the Snow Lodge.

On your third day, head toward the north entrance and the small town of Gardiner, Montana, where you can hook up with an outfitter and explore some white-water rapids.

**36**

**Northeastern Grand Loop.** This 19-mi byway passes some of Yellowstone's finest scenery, twisting beneath a series of leaning basalt towers 40–50 feet high. The behemoth to the east is 10,243-foot Mt. Washburn. ⊠ *Grand Loop Rd., between Canyon Village and Roosevelt Falls.*

**South Entrance Road.** The sheer black lava walls of the Lewis River Canyon make this a memorable drive. Turn into the parking area at the highway bridge for a close-up view of the spectacular Lewis River Falls. ⊠ *Begins at the South Entrance.*

**Upper Terrace Loop Drive.** Five-hundred-year-old limber pines line this 1½-mi loop. You can spot a variety of mosses growing through white travertine, composed of lime. ⊠ *Near Mammoth Hot Springs.*

**West Entrance Road.** Following the Madison River for 14 mi, this route is especially good for a sunset drive. In winter you'll see lots of bison and elk, and occasionally even swans. ⊠ *Begins at the West Entrance.*

## What to See

### Historical Sites

**Fort Yellowstone.** The oldest buildings at Mammoth Hot Springs served as Fort Yellowstone from 1886 to 1918, the period when the U.S. Army managed the park. The redbrick buildings cluster around an open area reminiscent of a frontier-era fort parade ground. You can pick up a self-guided tour map of the area. ⊠ *Mammoth Hot Springs.*

Fodor'sChoice
★
**Lake Yellowstone Hotel.** Completed in 1891, this structure on the National Register of Historic Places is the oldest lodging in any national park. Spiffed up for its centennial in 1991, it feels fresh and new; from the lounge, you can relax in white wicker chairs and watch the waters of Yellowstone Lake through massive windows. ⊠ *Lake Village Rd., Lake Yellowstone area* ☎ *307/344–7901* ⊗ *Mid-May–late Sept.*

**Museum of the National Park Ranger.** The former Norris Soldier Station is now a museum where you can see a movie about the National Park Service and exhibits related to military service in Yellowstone. ⊠ *Grand Loop Rd., Norris* ⊗ *June–Sept., daily 10–5.*

**Norris Geyser Basin Museum.** Stop in to have a look at the exhibits on geothermal geology, life in thermal areas, and the features of the basin. The museum building, erected 1929–30, is a National Historic Landmark. ⊠ *Grand Loop Rd., Norris* ⊗ *Late May–early Oct., daily 10–5.*

Fodor'sChoice
★
**Old Faithful Inn.** This historic hotel has served as a lodging property for Yellowstone visitors since opening in 1904. Even if you don't plan to spend a night at this massive log structure, take a walk through it to admire its massive open-beam lobby and rock fireplace, where a 45-minute guided tour begins. Writing desks grace the second-floor balcony, and during evening hours a pianist plays. From the outdoor deck, reached from the second floor, you can watch Old Faithful geyser as it erupts. Call ahead to confirm tour times. ⊠ *Old Faithful Bypass Rd., Old Faithful* ☎ *307/344–7901* ⊠ *Free* ⊗ *Late June–mid Oct.; tours daily 9:30, 11, 2, and 3:30 (subject to change).*

# WHAT TO SEE BY COMMUNITY

### CANYON AREA
- Artist Point
- Grand Canyon of the Yellowstone
- Grand View Point
- Inspiration Point
- Lookout Point
- Upper Falls View

### GRANT VILLAGE
- Lake Overlook
- West Thumb Geyser Basin

### MADISON
- Gibbon Falls

### MAMMOTH HOT SPRINGS
- Fort Yellowstone
- Mammoth Hot Springs Terraces

### NORRIS
- Back Basin
- Museum of the National Park Ranger
- Norris Geyser
- Norris Geyser Museum
- Porcelain Basin
- Roaring Mountain

### OLD FAITHFUL AREA
- Biscuit Basin
- Black Sand Basin
- Geyser Hill Loop
- Grand Prismatic Spring
- Great Fountain Geyser
- Lower, Midway, and Upper Geyser basins
- Morning Glory Pool
- Old Faithful Geyser & Inn

### TOWER-ROOSEVELT
- Lamar Valley
- Petrified Tree
- Specimen Ridge
- Tower Fall

### YELLOWSTONE LAKE
- Fishing Bridge
- Lake Butte
- Lake Yellowstone Hotel
- LeHardy Rapids
- Mud Volcano
- Natural Bridge
- Sulphur Caldron
- Yellowstone Lake

**36**

## Scenic Stops

★ **Artist Point.** The most spectacular view of the Lower Falls of the Yellowstone is seen from this point, which has two different viewing levels, one of which is accessible for people with disabilities. The South Rim Trail goes right past this point, and there is a nearby parking area open in both summer and winter. ⊠ *East end of South Rim Rd., Canyon.*

**Back Basin.** The basin's most famous geyser, Steamboat, performs rarely—sometimes going for years without an eruption—but when it does, it shoots a stream of water nearly 400 feet, making it the world's tallest geyser. Meanwhile, another Back Basin geyser, Echinus, erupts 50–100 feet every 35–75 minutes. Access the area via the 1½-mi loop of Back Basin Trail. ⊠ *Norris Geyser Basin, Grand Loop Rd., Norris.*

**Biscuit Basin.** This is an active geyser basin—sometimes there are even steam vents popping through the asphalt in the parking lot. The 2½-mi boardwalk loop trail takes you across the Firehole River to Sapphire Pool. This basin is also the trailhead for the Mystic Falls Trail. ⊠ *3 mi north of Old Faithful on Grand Loop Rd., Old Faithful.*

**Black Sand Basin.** There are a dozen hot springs and geysers in this basin near the cloverleaf entrance from Grand Loop Road to Old Faithful. ⊠ *North of Old Faithful on Grand Loop Rd., Old Faithful.*

## A GOOD TOUR: OLD FAITHFUL

At Old Faithful Village you're in the heart of the **Upper Geyser Basin,** a 1-mi-square area with about 140 geysers, the biggest being **Old Faithful,** which spouts up to 180 feet every 94 minutes or so. After watching Old Faithful erupt, begin to explore the larger basin with a hike around **Geyser Hill Loop,** where you'll see a variety of wildlife as well as thermal features. Heading the list of attractions is the **Morning Glory Pool,** with its unique flower shape. Next, head to **Black Sand Basin,** which has a dozen or so hot springs and geysers.

From Black Sand Basin, return to your car and drive north 3 mi to **Biscuit Basin,** where you'll find the trailhead for the Mystic Falls Trail. There's a boardwalk through the Biscuit Basin geyser area, and you can get views of the basin and the Upper Geyser Basin from atop the hill on the Mystic Falls Trail. Return to your car and drive farther north along **Firehole Lake Drive** through an area that's sometimes populated by bison and has access to more thermal areas. Continue north to the **Lower Geyser Basin** to see the Great Fountain Geyser, White Dome Geyser, and **Fountain Paint Pots.**

**Geyser Hill Loop.** Along the 1³⁄₁₀-mi Geyser Hill Loop boardwalk you can see active thermal features such as violent Giantess Geyser. When it erupts—only a few times each year—it spouts 100–250 feet high for five to eight minutes once or twice each hour for a period of 12 to 43 hours. Nearby Doublet Pool consists of two adjacent springs whose complex ledges and deep-blue waters are highly photogenic. Anemone Geyser starts as a gentle pool, overflows, bubbles, and finally erupts 10 feet or more, repeating the cycle every three to eight minutes. The loop boardwalk brings you close to the action, making it especially appealing to children intrigued with the sights and sounds of the geyser basin. To reach Geyser Hill, head counterclockwise around the Old Faithful boardwalk ³⁄₁₀ mi from the Old Faithful Visitor Center, crossing the Firehole River and entering Upper Geyser Basin. ☒ *Old Faithful.*

**Gibbon Falls.** Water rushes over the caldera rim in this 84-foot waterfall on the Gibbon River. ☒ *4 mi east of Madison on Grand Loop Rd.*

**Fodor'sChoice**
★ **Grand Canyon of the Yellowstone.** Along with Yosemite's El Capitan and the view from Grand Canyon National Park's South Rim, this is arguably one of the most amazing vistas in the United States. A rushing river and waterfall carved this 24-mi-long canyon. The red-and-ochre canyon walls are topped with an emerald-green forest. ☒ *Canyon.*

**Grand Prismatic Spring.** Yellowstone's largest hot spring—370 feet in diameter—is deep blue in color, with yellow and orange rings formed by bacteria that give it the effect of a prism. ☒ *Midway Geyser Basin off Grand Loop Rd., Old Faithful.*

**Grand View Point.** View the Lower Falls of the Yellowstone from this spot on the north canyon rim. ☒ *Off North Rim Dr., Canyon.*

## A GOOD TOUR:
## THE GRAND CANYON OF YELLOWSTONE

Most visitors catch their first view of the **Grand Canyon of the Yellowstone** from **Artist Point,** where there are two viewing levels, the lower one accessible by wheelchair. After you have peered into the canyon, take at least a short hike along the rim; then return to your vehicle and backtrack along **South Rim Drive** to the Uncle Tom's parking area. If your schedule allows, park there and hike along the **South Rim Trail,** which has impressive views of the yellow walls above the river.

After your explorations from the South Canyon rim, return to the Grand Loop Road and proceed to the Canyon Village. Begin at the

**Canyon Visitor Center,** where park rangers can give you details about hiking opportunities. From the village, travel south on the one-way **North Rim Drive,** which gives you access to **Inspiration Point, Grand View Point,** and **Lookout Point.** Farther south you'll find a spur road leading to the **Upper Falls View.**

For a great early-morning or late-evening side trip with opportunities to see a variety of wildlife, travel south into the open meadows of the **Hayden Valley.**

Depending on how much hiking you do, it can take anywhere from half a day to a couple of days to explore the Canyon area.

**36**

**Great Fountain Geyser.** This geyser erupts twice a day; rangers predict a time (within two hours) when it will shoot some 200 feet into the air. Should you see Great Fountain spew, you'll be rewarded with a view of waves of water cascading down the terraces that form the edges of the geyser. ⊠ *Firehole Lake Dr., north of Old Faithful.*

**Inspiration Point.** A short loop walk off a spur road takes you to this point, from which you can see Grand Canyon of the Yellowstone. ⊠ *Off Spur Rd. and North Rim Dr., Canyon.*

**Lake Butte.** This wooded promontory rising 615 feet above Yellowstone Lake is a prime spot for watching the sun set over the lake. ⊠ *2 mi east of Fishing Bridge on a spur off East Entrance Rd.*

**Lake Overlook.** From this hilltop northwest of West Thumb you get an expansive view of the southwest portion of Yellowstone. You reach the promontory by taking a 1½-mi hiking trail through forest still recovering from the massive fires of 1988; the clearing caused by the fire makes this a prime area for sighting elk. ⊠ *1½ mi northwest of Grant Village.*

**Lamar Valley.** The Northeast Entrance Road between Cooke City and Roosevelt slices through this broad valley, where you're likely to see an abundance of wildlife, including the park's main wolf-watching activities, which occur here during early-morning and late-evening hours year-round. ⊠ *Northeast Entrance Rd. between Cooke City and Roosevelt.*

**LeHardy Rapids.** Take an evening drive to this point, where Yellowstone Lake feeds into the Yellowstone River. Watch for waterfowl. ⊠ *3 mi north of Fishing Bridge, Lake Yellowstone area.*

**Lookout Point.** Located midway on the North Rim Trail, or accessible via the one-way North Rim Drive, Lookout Point gives you a view of the Grand Canyon of the Yellowstone from above the falls. From there you can descend a steep trail to stand above the lower falls. The best time to hike it is early morning, when sunlight reflects off the mist from the falls to create a rainbow. ⊠ *Off North Rim Dr., Canyon.*

**Lower Geyser Basin.** Shooting more than 150 feet, the Great Fountain Geyser is this basin's most spectacular sight. Less impressive but more regular is White Dome Geyser, which shoots from a 20-foot-tall cone. You'll also find pink mud pots and blue pools at the basin's Fountain Paint Pots. ⊠ *Between Old Faithful and Madison on Grand Loop Rd.*

**Mammoth Hot Springs Terraces.** Multicolored travertine terraces formed by slowly escaping hot mineral water mark this geological formation. It constantly changes as a result of shifts in water flow. Explore the terraces via an elaborate network of boardwalks—the best is the Lower Terrace Interpretive Trail. If you start at Liberty Cap, in the north end, and head uphill, you'll pass bright and ornately terraced Minerva Spring. ⊠ *Northwest corner of Grand Loop Rd., Mammoth Hot Springs.*

**Midway Geyser Basin.** Called "Hell's Half Acre" by writer Rudyard Kipling, this is a favorite stop of visitors, particularly in winter. A series of boardwalks wind their way through this extension of the Lower Geyser Basin. Here you'll find the richly colored pools of Grand Prismatic Spring and Excelsior Geyser, two of the world's largest hot springs. ⊠ *Between Old Faithful and Madison on Grand Loop Rd.*

**Morning Glory Pool.** Shaped somewhat like a morning glory flower, this beautiful pool was once a deep blue and one of the park's most glorious sites. But tourists dropping coins and other debris into it clogged the plumbing vent. As a result, the color is no longer as striking. Even so, the pool is worth viewing. To reach it, follow the boardwalk past Geyser Hill Loop and stately Castle Geyser, which has the biggest cone in Yellowstone. It erupts every 10 to 12 hours, to heights of 90 feet, for as much as an hour at a time. It's about 2 mi from the Old Faithful Visitor Center. ⊠ *At the north end of Upper Geyser Basin at Old Faithful.*

☼ **Mud Volcano.** A ¾-mi round-trip interpretive trail loops gently around seething, sulfuric mud pots with names such as Black Dragon's Cauldron and Sizzling Basin and makes its way around Mud Volcano itself, a boiling pot of brown goo. ⊠ *10 mi south of Canyon; 4 mi north of Fishing Bridge on Grand Loop Rd., Lake Yellowstone area.*

**Natural Bridge.** You can take an easy 1-mi hike or bicycle ride from Bridge Bay Campground to Natural Bridge, formed by erosion of a rhyolite outcrop by Bridge Creek. The top of the bridge is about 50 feet above the creek, and there is a trail to it; travel over the bridge itself is restricted. ⊠ *1 mi west of Bridge Bay Campground, Yellowstone Lake area.*

CLOSE UP

# A World of Geological Wonders

SPOUTING GEYSERS, bubbling mud pots, and hissing steam vents have earned fame for Yellowstone, which has the greatest concentration of thermal features in the country—nearly 10,000 of them all told.

The past eruptions of cataclysmic volcanoes helped to create the steaming, vaporous landscape of Yellowstone today. The heat from the magma (molten rock) under the Yellowstone Caldera continues to fuel the park's most famous geyser basins—West Thumb, Upper, Lower, Midway, and Norris—which contain most of Yellowstone's 200 to 250 active geysers.

Other traces of the geological past include the basaltic columns near Tower and the steam that hisses from Roaring Mountain. The molten lava beneath the Yellowstone Caldera, one of the world's most active volcanoes, has created two resurgent domes: Sour Creek, forming the eastern edge of Hayden Valley, and Mallard Lake, which overlooks Old Faithful from the Upper Geyser Basin, at Observation Point. In Firehole Canyon, the Firehole River runs between two lava flows; at West Thumb, a minor eruption created the Lake Yellowstone bay lined with hydrothermal features; in the park's forests, volcanic soils nurture lodgepole pine.

The superheated underground means Yellowstone is a constantly changing landscape. A geyser that is active one month may go dormant while a nearby thermal feature suddenly becomes quite intense. This potential for change makes Yellowstone a place where you can see something new and different each time you visit.

36

**Norris Geyser Basin.** The oldest geyser basin in Yellowstone, Norris is also the most volatile—some geysers might suddenly stop flowing, while new ones blow and hiss to life. Thermal features sport such colorful names as Black Growler Steam Vent, Whirligig Geyser, and Whale's Mountain. The area is accessible via an extensive system of boardwalks, some of them suitable for people with disabilities. ⊠ *Grand Loop Rd., Norris.*

FodorśChoice ★

**Old Faithful.** The world's most famous geyser is Yellowstone's star attraction. It's not the park's largest or most regular geyser, but it's the most predictable. It sometimes reaches 180 feet, though it averages 130 feet. When it doesn't shoot as high, the eruptions usually last longer. The mysterious natural plumbing of Yellowstone has lengthened Old Faithful's cycle somewhat in recent years, to every 94 minutes or so. To find out when Old Faithful is likely to erupt, check at the visitor center, or area lodging properties. You can view the eruption from a bench just yards away, from the lodge cafeteria, or a guest room at Old Faithful Inn. ⊠ *Southwest segment, Old Faithful Bypass Rd.*

FodorśChoice ★

**Petrified Tree.** This redwood is thought to be altered from minerals in volcanic ash. Reach it by a short walk from the Petrified Tree parking area. ⊠ *Grand Loop Rd., 1 mi west of Tower-Roosevelt.*

**Porcelain Basin.** The ground bulges and belches from the underground pressure at this geothermal field in the Norris Geyser Basin. You'll find bubbling pools, some milky white and others ringed in orange because of the minerals in the water. Reach the area by a ¾-mi-long boardwalk. ⊠ *Between Madison and Old Faithful Village on Grand Loop Rd.*

**Roaring Mountain.** This bare mountain north of Norris is a good place for spotting bears, and it's known for steam vents that can be seen all across the acidic hillside. ⊠ *4 mi north of Norris on Grand Loop Rd.*

**Specimen Ridge.** The world's largest concentration of standing petrified trees is on this ridge in the park's northeast region, southwest of the Lamar Valley. There are also plenty of unusual fossils, such as impressions of leaves on rocks. Access is via a difficult 3²/₁₀-mi (one way) hike. ⊠ *About 2 mi east of Tower-Roosevelt on Northeast Entrance Rd.*

**Sulphur Caldron.** Hissing steam escapes from a moonscape-like surface as superheated bubbling mud—you can smell the sulfur before you even leave your car. ⊠ *9½ mi south of Canyon; 4½ mi north of Fishing Bridge on Grand Loop Rd., Lake Yellowstone area.*

★ **Tower Fall.** View volcanic pinnacles in the area of the 132-foot Tower Fall, one of the major waterfalls on the Yellowstone River. From the lookout point, the ½-mi (round-trip) Tower Fall Trail switchbacks down through pine trees matted with luminous green wolf lichen to the base of the waterfall. ⊠ *2 mi south of Roosevelt on Grand Loop Rd.*

**Upper Falls View.** A spur road gives you access to the west end of the North Rim Trail and takes you down a fairly steep trail for a view of Upper Falls from above. ⊠ *¼ mi south of Canyon, off Grand Loop Rd.*

**Upper Geyser Basin.** This 1-mi-square basin contains Old Faithful and about 140 other geysers—one-fifth of the world's known geysers. It's an excellent place to spend a day or more exploring. ⊠ *Old Faithful.*

**West Thumb Geyser Basin.** This area, full of geysers and hot springs, is particularly popular with winter visitors who take advantage of the nearby warming hut before continuing their trip via snowmobile or snow coach. The unusual name comes from its location along a digit-like projection of Yellowstone Lake. ⊠ *Grand Loop Rd., 22 mi north of South Entrance, Grant Village.*

**Yellowstone Lake.** This alpine lake, one of the world's largest, at 136 square mi, was formed from glaciers melting into a caldera—a crater formed by a volcano. Along the 110 mi of shoreline, much of it followed by the East Entrance Road and Grand Loop Road, you'll often see moose, elk, and waterfowl. In winter you can sometimes see otters and coyotes stepping gingerly on the

> **CAUTION: A WILD PLACE**
>
> As you explore the park keep this thought in mind: Yellowstone is not an amusement park. Animals may seem docile or tame, but they are wild, and every year careless visitors are injured, sometimes even killed, when they venture too close. Particularly dangerous are female animals with their young, and bison, which can turn and charge in an instant. (Watch their tails—when they're standing up or crooked like a question mark, the bison is agitated.)

ice along the edge. ⊠ *Intersection of East Entrance Rd. and Grand Loop Rd., between Fishing Bridge and Grant Village.*

## Visitor Centers

**Albright Visitor Center.** Once serving as quarters for cavalry officers, this red-roof building now holds a museum and theater. Thomas Moran paintings of park sites are on display. ⊠ *Mammoth Hot Springs* ☎ *307/344–2263* ⊗ *June–Aug., daily 8–7; Sept., daily 9–6; Oct.–May, daily 9–5.*

**Canyon Visitor Education Center.** At this state-of-the-art center, which opened in August 2006, interact with hands-on exhibits especially devoted to Yellowstone's geology and the "supervolcano" beneath the park. ⊠ *Canyon Village* ☎ *307/242–2552* ⊗ *June–Sept., daily 8–7.*

**Fishing Bridge Visitor Center.** With a distinctive stone-and-log design, this building, dating from 1931, has been designated a National Historic Landmark. It has exhibits on Yellowstone birds and other wildlife. Take note, particularly, of the overhead light made from the skulls and horns of Rocky Mountain bighorn sheep. ⊠ *East Entrance Rd., 1 mi from Grand Loop Rd.* ☎ *307/242–2450* ⊗ *Memorial Day–Sept., daily 8–7.*

**Grant Village Visitor Center.** Closest to the park's South Entrance, this center shows a video on the role of fire in Yellowstone. ⊠ *Grant Village* ☎ *307/242–2650* ⊗ *June–Aug., daily 8–7; Sept., daily 9–6.*

**Madison Information Center.** Find basic information and meet here for evening ranger programs. ⊠ *Grand Loop Rd. at West Entrance Rd.* ☎ *307/344–2821* ⊗ *June–Aug., daily 8–7; Sept.–early Oct., daily 9–5.*

**Old Faithful Visitor Center.** This A-frame building has one of the best views of Old Faithful. Here you can watch a movie about geysers, talk to rangers, and purchase books. The backcountry office is nearby. ⊠ *Old Faithful Bypass Rd.* ☎ *307/545–2750* ⊗ *June–Aug., daily 8–7; Sept., daily 8–6; Oct., daily 9–5.*

**West Thumb Information Station.** This little log cabin has a bookstore and, in winter, doubles as a warming hut. Restrooms are in the parking area. ⊠ *West Thumb* ☎ *307/242–2452* ⊗ *June–Aug., daily 9–5; Sept., daily 9–6; Dec.–Feb., daily 8–5.*

**36**

# Sports & the Outdoors

In summer, hiking, biking, and fishing are the best ways to enjoy the park. In winter, the activities of choice are snowmobiling and skiing.

## Bicycling

Despite the heavy traffic, large vehicles, and narrow, shoulderless roads, more and more visitors tour Yellowstone by bicycle every year. To be on the safe side, ride single file and wear a helmet and reflective clothing. Bikes are prohibited on most hiking trails and in the backcountry.

**Blacktail Plateau Drive.** Running parallel to Grand Loop Road, this gravel road is one-way traffic for cars traveling east, but bicycles are allowed in both directions. The road meanders through forest, where you might see deer, coyotes, or elk. The western entrance is 9 mi east of Mammoth

Hot Springs; the eastern entrance is 2 mi west of Tower-Roosevelt. Mountain bikes are recommended. ✉ *Tower-Roosevelt.*

**Fountain Freight Road.** Fountain Flats Drive departs the Grand Loop Road south of the Nez Perce picnic area and follows the Firehole River to a trailhead 1½ mi away. From there, the Fountain Freight Road continues along the old roadbed, giving bikers access to the Sentinel Meadows Trail and the Fairy Falls Trail. The overall route is 5½ mi. Mountain bikes are recommended; you'll share Fountain Flats Drive with one-way automobile traffic and the Freight Road with hikers. ✉ *Madison.*

**Natural Bridge Road.** Leading off Grand Loop Road at Bridge Bay along Yellowstone Lake's western shore, this easy 1-mi loop leads to Natural Bridge, a 50-foot cliff cut by Bridge Creek. ✉ *Yellowstone Lake area.*

**Old Faithful to Morning Glory Pool.** This paved 2-mi trail starts at the Hamilton Store at Old Faithful Village, loops near Old Faithful geyser, and ends at Morning Glory Pool. The entire route is through a geyser basin, so stay on the trail. Watch for elk and buffalo. ✉ *Old Faithful.*

OUTFITTER &
EXPEDITIONS
**Free Heel and Wheel.** This outfitter just outside the West Entrance rents bikes and dispenses advice, plus sells hiking and cross-country skiing gear. ✉ *40 Yellowstone Ave., West Yellowstone, MT 59758* ☎ *406/646-7744* ⊕ *www.freeheelandwheel.com* ✉ *$5 per hour, $20 per day.*

## Boating

Yellowstone Lake attracts the most attention, but the park is filled with pristine waters waiting to be explored. Most of its 175 lakes—except for Sylvan, Eleanor, and Twin lakes—are open for boating. Jet skis, airboats, submersibles, and similar vessels are prohibited. You must purchase a permit—$20 (annual) or $10 (7 day) for motorized vessels and $10 (annual) or $5 (7 day) for nonmotorized vessels; they are available at Bridge Bay Ranger Station, Grant Village Backcountry Office, the South Entrance, and Lewis Lake Campground (non-motorized permits are also available at additional locations). Yellowstone honors permits issued at Grand Teton, but owners still need to register their vessels with the park. A Coast Guard approved personal flotation device must be worn.

OUTFITTER &
EXPEDITIONS
**Xanterra Parks & Resorts.** Rent watercraft such as rowboats and powerboats by the hour or the day. Throughout the day, one-hour **Yellowstone Lake Scenic Cruises** on the *Lake Queen II* make their way from Bridge Bay Marina to Stevenson Island and back. ✉ *Bridge Bay Marina, 2 mi south of Lake Village* ☎ *307/344-7311* ✉ *$10–$45 per hour, rentals; $12.50 for cruises* ⊙ *Mid-June–mid-Sept., daily 8 AM–9:30 PM.*

## Fishing

Between Memorial Day weekend and late November, thousands find a favorite spot along the park's rivers and streams. Many varieties of trout—cutthroat, brook, lake, and rainbow—along with grayling and mountain whitefish inhabit Yellowstone's waters. Sportfishing is done on the Gardner and Yellowstone rivers as well as Soda Butte Creek, but the top fishing area in the region is Madison River, known to fly fishermen throughout the country. Catch and release is the policy. Pick up a copy of fishing regulations at any park visitor center. Permits (available at ranger

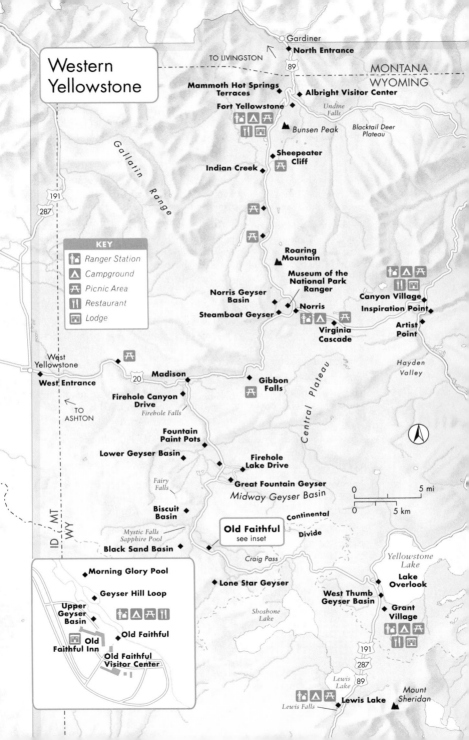

stations, visitor centers, and general stores) are required for people over age 16; they cost $15 (3 days), $20 (7 days) or $35 (season). Anglers ages 12 to 15 must have a nonfee permit; those younger than 12 don't need a permit but must be with an adult who knows the regulations.

OUTFITTER & EXPEDITIONS **Xanterra Parks & Resorts.** Guided fishing charters on 22- and 34-foot cabin cruisers can accommodate up to three anglers. The cost includes guide plus fishing gear. ⊠ *Bridge Bay Marina, 2 mi south of Lake Village* ☏ *307/344–7311* 🖃 *$75–$95 per hour* ☉ *Mid-June–early Sept.*

## Hiking

Before starting any hike, pick up a trail map at any park visitor center. Pack proper amounts of water, as drinking water in the park can be hazardous, and dress in layers, as weather in the area can change very quickly.

OUTFITTER & EXPEDITIONS **Yellowstone Association Institute.** To help visitors learn about the flora, fauna, and geology of the park, the institute offers daylong hiking excursions; multiday "Lodging and Learning" trips geared around hikes, some of them designed for families (some have age restrictions); and full-blown backcountry backpacking trips. ⊕ *Box 117, Yellowstone National Park, WY 82190* ☏ *307/344–2293* ⊕ *www.yellowstoneassociation. org* 🖃 *$150–$350, guided trips; $299–$999, Lodging and Learning trips.*

EASY **Back Basin Trail.** A 1½-mi loop passes Emerald Spring, Steamboat Geyser, Cistern Spring (which drains when Steamboat erupts), and Echinus Geyser. The latter erupts 50–100 feet every 35–75 minutes, making it Norris's most dependable big geyser. ⊠ *Grand Loop Rd. at Norris.*

**Fountain Paint Pots Nature Trail.** Take this ½-mi loop to see fumaroles (steam vents), blue pools, pink mud pots, and minigeysers. It's popular in both summer and winter because it's right next to Grand Loop Road. ⊠ *Lower Geyster Basin, between Old Faithful and Madison.*

**Cascade Lake Trail.** This 4½-mi round-trip hike passes through meadows, over creeks, and bursts with the color of wildflowers. Rain can make it muddy. ⊠ *1½-mi north of Canyon Junction, on Tower-Canyon Rd.*

**Mud Volcano Interpretive Trail.** This ¾-mi round-trip trail loops around Mud Volcano and seething, sulfuric mud pots like Black Dragon's Cauldron. ⊠ *Grand Loop Rd., 10 mi south of Canyon Village.*

Fodor'sChoice ★ **Old Faithful Geyser Loop.** Old Faithful and its environs in the Upper Geyser Basin are rich in short-walk options, starting with three connected loops departing from the Old Faithful Visitor Center. The ¾-mi loop simply circles the benches around Old Faithful. ⊠ *Old Faithful.*

**Porcelain Basin Trail.** This ¾-mi, partial-boardwalk loop leads from the north end of Norris Museum through whitish geyserite stone and past geysers like extremely active Whirligig. ⊠ *Grand Loop Rd., Norris.*

★ **Storm Point Trail.** Well marked and mostly flat, this 1½-mi loop, leaves the south side of the road for a perfect beginner's hike out to Yellowstone Lake. The trail rounds the western edge of Indian Pond, then passes moose habitat on its way to Yellowstone Lake's Storm Point, named for its frequent afternoon windstorms and crashing waves. As you head west along the shore, you'll likely hear the shrill chirping of yellow-bellied marmots,

## HIKING TRAILS BY COMMUNITY

**CANYON AREA**
- Brink of the Lower Falls Trail
- Cascade Lake Trail
- Mud Volcano Interpretive Trail
- North & South Rim Trails

**GRANT VILLAGE**
- Heart Lake–Mt. Sheridan Trail

**MAMMOTH HOT SPRINGS**
- Beaver Ponds Loop Trail
- Bunsen Peak Trail
- Osprey Falls Trail
- Skyline Trail
- Specimen Creek Trail

**MADISON**
- Purple Mountain Trail
- Two Ribbons Trail

**NORRIS**
- Back Basin Trail
- Porcelain Basin Trail

**OLD FAITHFUL AREA**
- Biscuit Basin Trail
- Fountain Paint Pots Nature Trail
- Mystic Falls Trail
- Observation Point Loop
- Old Faithful Geyser Loop
- Shoshone Lake–Shoshone Geyser Basin Trail

**TOWER-ROOSEVELT**
- Slough Creek Trail

**YELLOWSTONE LAKE**
- Avalanche Peak Trail
- Storm Point Trail

rodents that grow as long as 2 feet. Look for ducks, pelicans, and swans. ⊠ *3 mi east of Lake Junction on East Entrance Rd., Yellowstone Lake.*

**Two Ribbons Trail.** This accessible, boardwalked path runs along the Madison River for 1½ mi round-trip. ⊠ *5 mi east of the West Entrance.*

MODERATE **Beaver Ponds Loop Trail.** This 2½-hour, 5-mi (round-trip) trail starts at Liberty Cap and climbs 400 feet through ½ mi of spruce and fir, passing through open meadows and past beaver ponds (look for their dams). It has spectacular views of Mammoth Terraces. Moose, antelope, and bears may be sighted. ⊠ *Grand Loop Rd. at Old Gardiner Rd.*

Fodor'sChoice **Brink of the Lower Falls Trail.** Especially scenic, this trail branches off the ★ North Rim Trail at the Brink of the Upper Falls parking area. The steep ½-mi one-way trail switchbacks 600 feet down to within a few yards of the top of the Yellowstone River's Lower Falls. The spectacular and strenuous 700-step **Uncle Tom's Trail,** ½ mi east of Chittenden Bridge, descends 500 feet from the parking area to the roaring base of the Lower Falls of the Yellowstone. Much of this walk is on steel sheeting, which can have a film of ice on early summer mornings or anytime in spring and fall. ⊠ *1 mi south of Canyon Village.*

**Bunsen Peak Trail.** This moderate-to-difficult trail is a 4-mi, three-hour round-trip climb 1,300 feet to Bunsen Peak for a panoramic view of Blacktail Plateau, Swan Lake Flats, the Gallatin Mountains, and the Yellowstone River valley. (A topographical map can help you find these landmarks.) ⊠ *Grand Loop Rd., 1½ mi south of Mammoth Hot Springs.*

**Mystic Falls Trail.** From the Biscuit Basin boardwalk's west end, Mystic Falls Trail gently climbs 1 mi (3½ mi round-trip from Biscuit Basin parking area) through heavily burned forest to the lava-rock base of 70-foot

36

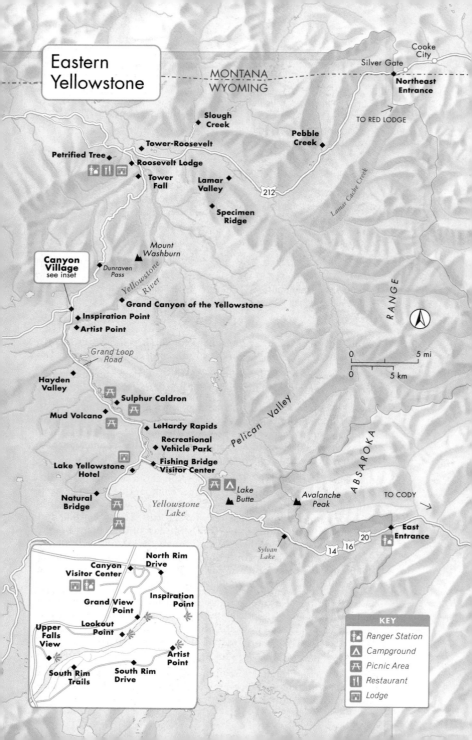

Mystic Falls. It then switchbacks up Madison Plateau to a lookout with the park's least-crowded view of Old Faithful and Upper Geyser Basin. ⊠ *3 mi north of Old Faithful Village off Grand Loop Rd.*

★ **North Rim Trail.** Take in great views of the Grand Canyon of the Yellowstone on this 1¾-mi trail from Inspiration Point to Chittenden Bridge. You can wander along small sections of the trail, or combine it with the South Rim Trail. ⊠ *1 mi south of Canyon Village.*

**Observation Point Loop.** Old Faithful and its environs in the Upper Geyser Basin are rich in short-walk options, starting with three connected loops that depart from Old Faithful Visitor Center. Observation Point Loop, a 2-mi round-trip from the visitor center, leaves Geyser Hill Loop boardwalk and becomes a trail shortly after the boardwalk crosses the Firehole River; it circles a picturesque overview of Geyser Hill with Old Faithful Inn as a backdrop. ⊠ *Old Faithful Village.*

**Purple Mountain Trail.** Climbing a steady 1,500 feet from start to finish, this 6-mi round-trip trail takes you through lodgepole-pine forest. At the end of the trail catch views of Firehole and Gibbon valleys. ⊠ *¼ mi north of Madison Junction, on Madison-Norris Rd.*

**Shoshone Lake–Shoshone Geyser Basin Trail.** This 22-mi, 11-hour, moderate-to-difficult overnight trip combines several shorter trails. The trail starts at DeLacy Creek Trail, gently descending 3 mi to the north shore of Shoshone Lake. On your way to the lake, look for sandhill cranes and moose. At the lake, turn right and follow the North Shore Trail for 8 mi, first along the beach and then through lodgepole-pine forest. Make sure you've reserved one of the good backcountry campsites—reservations can be made at any ranger station. Take time to explore the Shoshone Geyser Basin, reached by turning left at the fork at the end of the trail and walking about ¼ mi. In the morning, turn right at the fork, follow Shoshone Creek for 2 mi, and make the gradual climb over Grant's Pass. At the 17-mi mark the trail crosses the Firehole River and divides; take a right onto Lone Star Geyser Trail and continue past this fine coned geyser through the backcountry to Lone Star Geyser trailhead. ⊠ *On Grand Loop Rd., 8 mi east of Old Faithful Village.*

**Slough Creek Trail.** Starting at Slough Creek Campground, this route climbs steeply for the first 1½ mi before reaching expansive meadows and prime fishing spots, where moose are common and grizzlies sometimes wander. From this point the trail, now mostly level, meanders 9½ mi north. ⊠ *7 mi east of Tower-Roosevelt off Northeast Entrance Rd.*

**South Rim Trail.** Partly paved and fairly flat, this 4½-mi loop along the south rim of the Grand Canyon of the Yellowstone affords impressive views and photo opportunities of the canyon and falls of the Yellowstone River. It starts at Chittenden Bridge. Along the way you can take a break for a snack or a picnic but you'll need to sit on the ground, as there are no picnic tables. Beyond Artist Point, the trail crosses a high plateau and meanders through high mountain meadows, where you're likely to see bison grazing. ⊠ *Off South Rim Dr., Canyon.*

**36**

**Specimen Creek Trail.** Starting at Specimen Creek trailhead, follow the trail 2½ mi and turn left at the junction, passing petrified trees to your left. At the 6½-mi mark, turn left again at the fork and start climbing 1,400 feet for 2 mi up to Shelf Lake, one of the park's highest bodies of water, at 9,200 feet. Stay at one of the designated backcountry campsites, which you can reserve at any ranger station. Just past the lake the Skyline Trail begins. Watch for bighorn sheep as you approach Bighorn Peak's summit. The trail's most treacherous section is just past the summit, where it drops 2,300 feet in the first 2½ mi of descent; take a left where the trail forks at the big meadow just past the summit to reach Black Butte Creek Trail. Moose and elk can be seen along this last 2½-mi stretch. ⊠ *U.S. 191, 27 mi north of West Yellowstone.*

DIFFICULT **Avalanche Peak Trail.** Starting across from a parking area, this difficult 4-mi, four-hour round-trip climbs 2,150 feet to the peak's 10,566-foot summit, from which you'll see the rugged Absaroka Mountains running north and south. Some of these peaks have patches of snow year-round. Look around the talus and tundra near the top of Avalanche Peak for alpine wildflowers and butterflies. Don't try this trail before late June or after early September—it may be covered in snow. At any time of year, carry a jacket: the winds at the top are strong. ⊠ *19 mi east of Lake Junction on the north side of East Entrance Rd., Yellowstone Lake.*

**Heart Lake–Mt. Sheridan Trail.** This very difficult 24-mi, 13-hour round-trip route provides one of Yellowstone's top backcountry experiences. After traversing 5½ mi of partly burned lodgepole-pine forest, the trail descends into Heart Lake Geyser Basin and reaches Heart Lake at the 8-mi mark. This is one of the park's most active thermal areas—the biggest geyser here is Rustic Geyser, which erupts 25–30 feet every 15 minutes. Circle around the northern tip of Heart Lake and camp at one of five designated backcountry sites on the western shore (get your permit beforehand). Leave all but the essentials here as you take on the 3-mi, 2,700-foot climb to the top of 10,308-foot Mt. Sheridan. To the south, if you look carefully, you can see the Tetons. ⊠ *1 mi north of Lewis Lake on the east side of South Entrance Rd., Grant Village.*

**Osprey Falls Trail.** This 4-mi trail, a two-hour round-trip, has a series of switchbacks, which drop 800 feet to the bottom of Sheepeater Canyon and the base of the Gardner River's 151-foot Osprey Falls. At Tower Fall, the canyon walls are basalt columns formed by ancient lava flow. ⊠ *Bunsen Peak Rd., 3 mi south of Mammoth Hot Springs.*

**Skyline Trail.** In the park's northwest corner, this extremely difficult 16½-mi, 10-hour trip is a combination trail that climbs up and over numerous peaks, whose ridgelines mark the park's northwest boundary, before looping sharply back down via Black Butte Creek. For much of its length the trail follows the ridgetops, with steep drop-offs on either side. ⊠ *U.S. 191, 25 mi north of West Yellowstone.*

## Horseback Riding

Horses are not allowed in front-country campgrounds, but are permitted in certain backcountry campsites. For information on planning a backcountry trip with stock, call the Backcountry Office at 307/344–2160.

## FODOR'S FIRST PERSON

**Orestes Ruffin**
*Camper*

Elevation, time of day, and even what side of the mountain you're on will have a dramatic effect on the weather, including how quickly it can change.

In 2003, my wife, Christy, and I went to Yellowstone and camped in a nice campground next to a meadow. We spent the day in shorts and T-shirts, and the mountain meadow was in full spring bloom. The next morning we woke up to three inches of snow on our tent. We did our hiking that day in snowshoes.

**OUTFITTERS & EXPEDITIONS**

**Xanterra Parks & Resorts**. Yellowstone's in-park concessionaire provides one- and two-hour horse rides in Canyon Village, Mammoth Hot Springs, and Tower-Roosevelt. Reservations are recommended. Xanterra also offers horseback or wagon rides to a Old West cookout site for a steak dinner. Advance reservations are required. To ride horses, you must weigh less than 250 pounds, be at least 48 inches tall, and be at least 8 years old (kids 8–11 must be accompanied by an adult). ☎ *307/344–7311 or 307/344–7901* ⊕ *www.travelyellowstone.com* ✉ *$37, one-hour rides, $57 two-hour rides; $56–$79, Old West Cookouts.*

**Gunsel Horse Adventures**. Since 1968, this South Dakota-based outfitter has provided 1-, 4-, 7-, and 10-day excursions into Yellowstone's backcountry. The trips are a great way to see moose, bear, deer, elk, and wolves. ☎ *605/343–7608* ⊕ *www.gunselhorseadventures.com* ✉ *$250 per day; $1,400–$1,500 multiday trips.*

**Rimrock Dude Ranch**. Outfitter Gary Fales has been leading multiday pack trips into Yellowstone for decades, operating out of this ranch west of Cody. Regular trips include treks between the Cody area and Jackson. Trips last a week and include backcountry camping, fishing, hiking, and horseback activities. All food and camping items are provided. ☎ *307/587–3970* ⊕ *www.rimrockranch.com* ✉ *$1,475 per person.*

### Skiing, Snowshoeing & Snowmobiling

Snowmobiling is an exhilarating way to experience Yellowstone. It's also controversial because of the pollution and the disruption to animal habitats. Regulations are subject to change, but at the time of this writing, the daily number of riders is limited, and you must have a reservation, a guide, and a four-stroke engine (it's less polluting than the two-stroke variety). When you need a break from the cold, you can stop at strategically located warming huts, open 24 hours. Huts at West Thumb, Madison, and Canyon Village are intermittently staffed; huts at Indian Creek, Old Faithful Village, and Fishing Bridge are unstaffed.

For skiing, **Lone Star Geyser Trail** is an easy $2\frac{3}{10}$ mi to the Lone Star Geyser, starting south of Keppler Cascades. ✉ *Shuttle at Old Faithful Snow Lodge; trailhead 3½ mi west of Old Faithful Village.* Alternatively, five ski trails begin at the **Madison River Bridge** trailhead. The shortest is 4 mi and the longest is 14 mi. ✉ *West Entrance Rd., 6 mi west of Madison.*

OUTFITTER &
EXPEDITIONS

**American National Park Adventures.** This Jackson-based outfitter conducts one-day and multiday snowmobile trips into Yellowstone, centering on Canyon and Old Faithful. Trips include meals; multiday trips also include lodging. ☎ *307/733–1572 or 800/255–1572* ✉ *155 W. Broadway, Jackson, WY* ⊕ *www.anpatours.com* 💲 *$230–$250 day trip ($100 extra per adult passenger), $325 per day for multiday trips.*

**Free Heel and Wheel.** Rent cross-country skis and snowshoes from this outfitter just outside the West Entrance. Ski lessons are also available. ✉ *40 Yellowstone Ave., West Yellowstone, MT* ☎ *406/646–7744* 💲 *$5 per hour, $20 per day rentals.*

**Xanterra Parks & Resorts.** Rent skis, snowshoes, and snowmobiles at Mammoth Hot Springs Hotel and Old Faithful Snow Lodge. You also can sign up for a snowmobile tour through the park. ☎ *307/344–7901* 💲 *$10–$30 skis and snowshoes, $115–$150 snowmobile rentals.*

**Yellowstone Association Institute.** This in-park organization offers daylong cross-country skiing treks as well as multiday "Lodging and Learning" ski and snowshoe trips. ☎ *307/344–2293* ⊕ *www.yellowstoneassociation. org* 💲 *$150–$255, day trips; $673–823, Lodging and Learning trips.*

**Yellowstone Tour & Travel.** Rent snowmobiles here or reserve a spot on a guided trip into the park. ✉ *211 Yellowstone Ave., West Yellowstone, MT* ☎ *406/646–9310 or 800/221–1151* ⊕ *www.yellowstonetravel.com* 💲 *$119–$180 per day.*

## Swimming

Numerous waterways delight kids; however, unless you come during July and August, you'll likely want to forego swimming due to the extremely cold water. Streams and lakes seldom have a chance to warm up in this climate, where nights can be fairly cool even in summer.

# Educational Offerings

## Classes & Seminars

**"Expedition: Yellowstone!"** This four- to five-day residential program is for grades 4–8. The curriculum includes hikes, discussions, journal keeping, and presentations as students go out in the field to learn about the natural and cultural history of Yellowstone, and the issues affecting its ecosystem. ✉ *Lamar Buffalo Ranch or Youth Conservation Corps facilities* ⊙ *September through May.*

**Yellowstone Institute.** Stay in a log cabin in Lamar Valley while taking a courses about the park's ecology, history, or wildlife. Search with a historian for the trail the Nez Perce Indians took in their flee a century ago from the U.S. Army, or get the perfect shot with tips from professional photographers. Facilities are fairly primitive—guests do their own cooking and camp during some of the courses—but prices are reasonable. Some programs are designed specifically for young people and families. ✉ *North Park Rd., between Tower-Roosevelt and Northeast Entrance* ☎ *307/344–2294* ⊕ *www.yellowstoneassociation.org/institute* ⊙ *Year-round, programs vary with season.*

## GOOD READS

**The Yellowstone Story,** by Aubrey L. Haines, is a park classic.

Explaining the park's geological processes are William R. Keefer's **The Geologic Story of Yellowstone National Park** and Robert B. Smith and Lee J. Siegel's **Windows into the Earth: The Geologic Story of Yellowstone and Grand Teton National Parks**.

Alston Chase's controversial **Playing God in Yellowstone**

chronicles a century of government mismanagement.

Three other excellent titles are:

**Roadside History of Yellowstone Park** by Winfred Blevins

**Roadside Geology of the Yellowstone Country** by William J. Fritz

**Yellowstone Ecology: A Road Guide** by Sharon Eversman and Mary Carr.

### Film

*Yellowstone Revealed.* A 100-seat auditorium at the Old Faithful Visitor Center provides daily showings of this 14-minute film that explores newly discovered life forms and the associated benefits to society through new breathtaking footage of the park. Ranger-led programs are available at all visitor centers. ✉ *Old Faithful Visitor Center* ☎ *307/545–2750.*

### Ranger Programs

Yellowstone offers a busy schedule of guided hikes, talks, and campfire programs. For dates and times, check the park's *Discover Yellowstone* newsletter, available at all entrances and visitor centers.

**Campfire Programs.** Gather around the campfire at various park campgrounds to hear fascinating tales about Yellowstone's history during hour-long programs. ☉ *June–Aug., nightly 9 or 9:30.*

**Daytime Programs.** Ranger-led programs run during both the winter and summer seasons. Summer programs are held at Canyon Village, Grant Village, Madison, West Yellowstone, Norris Geyser, Lake Village, Old Faithful, and Mammoth. Winter programs are held at West Yellowstone, Old Faithful, and Mammoth. Contact visitor centers for schedules.

**Junior Ranger Program.** The Junior Ranger Program is available in the summer. Pick up an activity booklet at any visitor center.

### Tours

**Grub Steak Expeditions and Tours.** These tours, ranging from half a day to several days in length, focus on topics such as photography, geology, history, and wildlife. They're led by a former Yellowstone park ranger, professional photographer, and retired teacher. ⌂ *Box 1013, Cody, WY 82414* ☎ *307/527–6316 or 800/527–6316* ⊕ *www.grubsteaktours.com* ▱ *$200–$300.*

**LeHardy Rapids-Lake Butte Bus Tour.** If you feel like letting someone else do the driving, you can opt for this bus tour. The sunset tour originates at the Lake Yellowstone Hotel, where you board a 1937 touring bus to

# Park Ranger Mary Wilson

FOR YELLOWSTONE NATIONAL PARK RANGER MARY WILSON, every day is an adventure and, even after two decades of working in some of the nation's most pristine preserves, she never tires of assisting visitors who have come to explore America's natural treasures.

"Almost every day, I am approached by visitors who, in awe of the wonderful and exciting things they have experienced in the parks, tell me that these places are the most beautiful and inspiring places they have ever seen or been," she says. "Somehow, these places help foster memories and feelings that last a lifetime."

Visitors have left lasting impressions that Wilson has incorporated into her instruction of new park rangers. One of the most poignant occurred while she was working in the mid-1980s as an interpretive ranger at Grand Canyon National Park.

"I came across an elderly woman sitting near the south rim of the canyon who was just sobbing," Wilson recalls. "Thinking that she may have been hurt, sick or missing someone, I approached and asked if I could help her. She told me she was fine, but that she was from New York City, had raised five kids, and that this was the first time she had ventured out of her home state. She told me that the one thing she had wanted to see more than anything else in the world in her entire life was the Grand Canyon. I told her it was so great that she was here now, to which she responded, 'Yes, but it makes me wonder how many other beautiful places I may have missed in my life. . . and will never get to see.' I sat down on the bench next to her and began to cry with her. It reminded me of the power these very special places we call national parks have on our lives; how they offer us a chance to reflect upon our relationship with nature, the importance of beauty and solitude, and how lucky we are to have them preserved for everyone to enjoy."

Wilson's passion for animals, combined with a love for the outdoors and helping people turned her professional interests toward the National Park Service. "Serving as a park ranger was a way to achieve a little of all of those worlds," says Wilson, who grew up in Muncie, Ind., before earning her bachelor's and master's degrees from Purdue University.

After serving stints as a student volunteer in South Dakota's Custer State Park and Montana's Glacier National Park, working side by side with rangers, Wilson was hired by the National Park Service in Glacier. Since then, she's taken assignments at Rocky Mountain, Grand Canyon, and Sequoia/Kings Canyon national parks, and Montezuma Castle National Monument. At her job at Yellowstone she supervises other rangers as well as assists visitors.

## RANGER WILSON'S TOP 10 TIPS FOR VISITING YELLOWSTONE

1. Before your trip, go online to get information from the park's official Web site, www.nps.gov/yell.

2. Upon arrival at the park, stop at the nearest visitor center for information and updates.

3. Pack for all types of weather no matter what time of year.

4. Avoid the crowds by getting an early start to your day in the park.

5. Stay at least 75 feet away from wildlife (300 feet for bears).

6. Stay on geyser basin boardwalks to prevent serious thermal burns.

7. Drive defensively, and allow more time than you think you need.

8. Try to be to your destination before dark to avoid hitting wildlife on park roads.

9. Take a friend when you go hiking; it's safer and a lot more fun!

10. Don't try to see and do everything. You need 2 to 3 days just to visit the park highlights.

**36**

travel to the rapids and then on to the Lake Butte Overlook in time to watch the sun go down over the western mountains. The driver delivers a narrative of historical and natural information as you travel along the shores of Yellowstone Lake. You'll likely spot a variety of wildlife, such as bison, elk, waterbirds, and coyotes. The tour takes a couple of hours. ⊠ *Lake Yellowstone Hotel* ⊠ *$25* ☽ *Daily, sunset.*

**Xanterra Parks & Resorts.** The company that runs most of concessions in Yellowstone offers bus, boat, horseback, and stagecoach tours of the park in summer, and skiing, snowmobiling, and snowshoeing treks in winter. ⊠ *Mammoth Hot Springs* ☎ *307/344–7901.*

**Yellowstone Alpen Guides.** Choose from six one-day tours of Yellowstone, Grand Teton, and the surrounding area via motor coach. The company also leads ski trips and winter park tours—it's a quieter way than snowmobiling to sight buffalo herds, trophy-size bull elk, and moose. ⊠ *555 Yellowstone Ave., West Yellowstone, MT* ☎ *406/646–9374 or 800/ 858–3502* ⊕ *www.yellowstoneguides.com* ⊠ *$40–$50* ☽ *Apr.–mid-Oct.*

# WHAT'S NEARBY

Yellowstone National Park is a destination, not something to see as you pass through the area; however, there are several upscale resorts in nearby towns for those who appreciate sleeping on beds, and there are literally thousands of possible campsites for those looking to rough it. Plan on spending several days in the park to see all that it has to offer.

## Nearby Towns & Attractions

### Nearby Towns

Named for William F. "Buffalo Bill" Cody, the town of **Cody** sits near the park's East Entrance. It is a good base for hiking trips, horseback

## DID YOU KNOW?

Grizzly bears can run up to 40 mph and live 30 years in the wild. These 350- to 800-pound omnivores can stretch to 8 feet tall. In Yellowstone, their diets commonly include elk, bison, cutthroat trout, ants, dandelions, strawberries, and whitebark pine seeds swiped from red squirrels' caches.

# Ever-Changing Yellowstone

**YELLOWSTONE IS DEFINITELY NOT** a world of slumbering wonders. The national park truly feels alive when you see (and hear, and sometimes even smell) the mud pots, steam vents, fumaroles, and paint pots. Beyond the geysers' activity, seasonal changes in wildlife and vegetation make Yellowstone fascinating to visit time and time again.

Even Old Faithful, which spews routinely, has changed in recent years. The geyser now erupts about every 94 minutes (up from 78 minutes in 1990), and each eruption may look different. Sometimes it shoots higher and faster, whereas other times it lasts longer but doesn't reach so high in the sky.

Other geyser basin features aren't so reliable. The force and nature of the various geysers depend on several factors, including the complex underground geology at Yellowstone. Rangers say the greatest threats to the geyser basin activity are earthquakes (small ones occur regularly in the region) and the impact caused by people—in past years, for example, people threw hundreds of coins into the bright blue Morning Glory Pool; the coins eventually clogged the pool's water vents, causing it to change to a sickly green color.

Besides the park's unique geology, the ongoing ecological development of the region draws widespread interest and debate. The reintroduction of wolves to the park and the efforts to control the movement of bison (to keep them from wandering out of the park in the winter in search of food) are two examples of issues that divide opinions on the management of Yellowstone.

When wolves were brought back to Yellowstone in 1995, they acclimated so well that they quickly formed several packs, some of which have ventured outside the park's boundaries. (Wolves from Yellowstone's packs have been spotted as far south as northern Utah and Colorado.) Their presence has had a lasting effect on wildlife populations. The wolves feed on both elk and buffalo, and researchers have noted a significant decline in elk calf survival throughout the region as a result of wolf predation. Park rangers have also reported a significant decline in Yellowstone's coyote population—since the wolves are bigger and stronger than coyotes, they kill them or drive them to look for new territory.

Bison leave the park in winter—mainly through the north and west entrances—in part because of overpopulation and the need to find adequate feed. Their movements are sometimes made easier by the winter grooming of Yellowstone roads for use by over-snow vehicles.

When massive wildfires tore through Yellowstone in 1988, some believed it would take generations for the park to recover. But the pessimists were in for a suprise. Within a short time, the park had begun to renew itself. When you visit Yellowstone now you will see reminders of fires from 1988 and more recent fires in 2001 and 2002, but you will also see new growth. Lodgepole-pine forests need fire to release their seeds, and once seeds get a start, trees grow quickly. The new growth provides excellent cover for animals, making it harder for visitors to see wildlife such as elk, deer, and bears.

riding excursions, and white-water rafting on the North Fork of the Shoshone or the Clarks Fork of the Yellowstone. Because of its proximity to both Grand Teton and Yellowstone, **Jackson** is the region's busiest community in the summer and has the widest selection of dining and lodging options. Meanwhile, the least well-known gateway, the little town of **Dubois,** is a great base if you want to be far from the madding crowds. Jackson and Dubois are near the park's South Entrance.

> **FAMILY PICK**
>
> West Yellowstone is the place for families. It has a movie theater, IMAX theater, live theater, fun center, Old Time photos, rodeos, and Bear World, an animal attraction, among other things.

The most popular gateway from Montana, particularly in winter, is **West Yellowstone,** near the park's West Entrance. This is where the open plains of southwestern Montana and northeastern Idaho come together along the Madison River Valley. Affectionately known among winter recreationists as the "snowmobile capital of the world," this town of 1,000 is also a good place to go for fishing, horseback riding, and downhill skiing. Bustling all year long is **Gardiner.** Though it only has a population of 800, the town stays busy because it is near the park's North Entrance, the only Yellowstone entrance that's open all year. Gardiner's Roosevelt Arch has marked this park entrance since 1903, when President Theodore Roosevelt dedicated it. The Yellowstone River slices through town, beckoning fishermen and rafters. North of Gardiner is **Livingston,** a town of 7,500 known for its charming historic district.

With both Yellowstone and the Absaroka-Beartooth Wilderness at its back door, the village of **Cooke City** is a good place for hiking, horseback riding, mountain climbing, and other outdoor sports. However, some 50 mi to the east, **Red Lodge** provides a lot more options for dining and lodging. Cooke City and Red Lodge guard the park's Northeast Entrance—though it's the least used of all entry points to the park, it's by far the most spectacular. Driving along the Beartooth Scenic Byway between Red Lodge and Cooke City, you'll cross the southern tip of the Beartooth range, literally in the ramparts of the Rockies.

### Nearby Attractions

★ **Buffalo Bill Historical Center.** This sprawling complex, sometimes called the Smithsonian of the West, contains the Whitney Gallery of Western Art, the Plains Indian Museum, the Cody Firearms Museum, the Draper Museum of Natural History, and the Harold McCracken Research Library. Plan to spend at least four hours here. ⊠ *720 Sheridan Ave., Cody, WY* ☎ *307/587–4771* ⊕ *www.bbhc.org* 🎫 *$15* ☉ *May–Sept., daily 8–8; Oct., daily 8–5; Nov.–Mar., Tues.–Sun. 10–3; Apr., daily 10–5.*

**Grizzly and Wolf Discovery Center.** You can get up close to the grizzlies and other endangered species that live a this nonprofit center devoted to protecting their natural habitat. ⊠ *201 S. Canyon, West Yellowstone, MT* ☎ *406/646–7001 or 800/257–2570* 🎫 *$9.75* ☉ *Daily 8 AM–dusk.*

⇨ the Grand Teton National Park chapter for more area attractions.

**36**

## FESTIVALS & EVENTS

**FEB. Buffalo Bill Birthday Ball.**
Hundreds of folks don their turn-of-the-20th-century attire and dance in Cody until the wee hours. ☎ *307/587-0500.*

**MAR. World Snowmobile Expo.**
Top-notch racing is combined with a sneak peek at next year's hot models. The SnowWest SnoCross attracts racers to West Yellowstone from throughout the snowbelt. ☎ *406/646-7701.*

**JUNE–AUG. Cody Nite Rodeo.**
Some Western towns host a rodeo now and then, but come summer Cody has one every night. The action includes bronco busting and bull riding. ☎ *307/587-5155.*

**SEPT. Old Settler's Days.**
Celebrating Livingston's pioneer history, this event in Clyde Park includes an art show, a quilt display, and entertainment. ☎ *406/686-4409.*

# WHERE TO STAY & EAT

### About the Restaurants

When traveling in Yellowstone it's always a good idea to bring along a cooler—that way you can carry some snacks for a picnic and not have to worry about making it to one of the more developed areas of the park. Generally you'll find burgers and sandwiches at cafeterias and full meals at restaurants. There is a good selection of entrées such as free-range beef and chicken; game meats such as elk, venison, and trout; plus organic vegetables. At the several delis and general stores in the park you can purchase picnic items, snacks, and sandwiches.

### About the Hotels

Park lodgings range from two of the national park system's magnificent old hotels to simple cabins to bland modern motels. Make reservations at least two months in advance for July and August for all park lodgings. Old Faithful Snow Lodge and Mammoth Hot Springs Hotel are the only accommodations open in winter; rates are the same as in summer. Ask about the size of beds, bathrooms, thickness of walls, and room location when you book, especially in the older hotels, where accommodations vary and upgrades are ongoing. Telephones have been put in some rooms, but there are no TVs. All park lodging is no smoking. There are no roll-away beds available.

### About the Campgrounds

Yellowstone has a dozen campgrounds scattered around the park. Most have flush toilets; some have coin-operated showers and laundry facilities. Most are operated by the National Park Service and are available on a first-come, first-served basis. Those campgrounds run by Xanterra Parks & Resorts—Bridge Bay, Canyon, Fishing Bridge, Grant Village, and Madison—accept bookings in advance. To reserve, call 307/344-7311. Larger groups can reserve space in Bridge Bay, Grant, and Madison from late May through September.

There are about 300 backcountry sites available in the park; camping outside designated areas is prohibited, except during the winter season (October 15–May 15). All overnight backcountry camping requires a free backcountry-use permit, which must be obtained in person from the Backcountry Office no more than 48 hours before the planned trip. (In summer you can usually obtain the permits seven days a week, from 8 AM to 4:30 PM, at most visitor centers and ranger stations.) Sites can be reserved for $20, regardless of the duration of the stay or the number in the group. Reserve a site by visiting any ranger station or mailing the Backcountry Office, Box 168, Yellowstone National Park, Wyoming 82190. All backcountry campsites have restrictions on group size and length of stay. Pit fires are prohibited at certain campsites.

## Where to Eat

### In the Park

**$–$$$$**  ✕ **Lake Yellowstone Hotel Dining Room.** This double-colonnaded dining room off the hotel lobby will have you gazing through the big square windows overlooking the lake. Because this is one of the park's most elegant restaurants, it tends to attract an older clientele. The menu includes steak, pasta, seafood, and buffalo prime rib. Reservations are required for dinner. ⊠ *Lake Village Rd.* ☎ *307/344–7311. $12–$32* ☰ *AE, D, DC, MC, V* ☉ *Closed early Oct.–mid-May.*

Fodor'sChoice ★

**36**

**$–$$$$**  ✕ **Old Faithful Inn Dining Room.** Lodgepole-pine walls and ceiling beams, a giant volcanic rock fireplace graced with a painting of Old Faithful, and green-tinted windows etched with scenes from the 1920s set the mood here. Soaked in history, the restaurant has always been a friendly place where servers find time amid the bustle to chat with diners. Don't pass up the prime rib or elk medallions, although you can also get a burger or seafood. ⊠ *Old Faithful Village* ☎ *307/344–7311* ⚐ *Reservations essential. $12–$30* ☰ *AE, D, DC, MC, V* ☉ *Closed late Oct.–early May.*

**$–$$$$**  ✕ **Old Faithful Snow Lodge.** From the wood-and-leather chairs etched with figures of park animals to the intricate lighting fixtures that resemble snowcapped trees, there's lots of atmosphere at Old Faithful Snow Lodge. The huge windows give you a view of the Old Faithful area, and you can sometimes see the famous geyser as it erupts. Aside from Mammoth Hot Springs Dining Room, this is the only place in the park where you can enjoy a full lunch or dinner in winter. The French onion soup will warm you up on a chilly afternoon; among the main courses, look for elk, beef, or salmon. ⊠ *Old Faithful Village, far end of Old Faithful Bypass Rd.* ☎ *307/344–7311. $12–$33* ☰ *AE, D, DC, MC, V* ☉ *Closed mid-Oct.–mid-Dec. and mid-Mar.–mid-May.*

Fodor'sChoice ★

**$–$$$**  ✕ **Grant Village Restaurant.** The floor-to-ceiling windows here provide views of Yellowstone Lake through the thick stand of pines. The most contemporary of the park's restaurants, it makes you feel at home with pine-beam ceilings and cedar-shake walls. Dishes range from pork and duck to prime rib; late in the season there's a sandwich buffet on Sundays. ⊠ *Grant Village* ☎ *307/344–7311* ⚐ *Reservations essential. $11–$24* ☰ *AE, D, DC, MC, V* ☉ *Closed late Sept.–late May.*

**$–$$$**  ✕ **Mammoth Hot Springs Dining Room.** A wall of windows overlooks an expanse of green that was once a military parade and drill field at Mammoth Hot Springs. The art deco–style restaurant, decorated in shades of gray, green, and burgundy, has an airy feel with its bentwood chairs. Beef, pork, and chicken are on the menu as well as a selection of pasta and vegetarian dishes. ⊠ *Mammoth Hot Springs* ☎ *307/344–7311* ⚜ *Reservations essential. $9–$24* ⊟ *AE, D, DC, MC, V* ⊘ *Closed mid-Oct.–mid-Dec. and mid-Mar.–mid-May.*

**$–$$$** ✕ **Roosevelt Lodge Dining Room.** At this rustic log cabin set in a pine forest, the menu ranges from barbecued ribs and Roosevelt beans to hamburgers and french fries. For a real Western adventure, call ahead to join a chuck-wagon cookout ($$$$) that includes an hour-long trail ride or a stagecoach ride. ⊠ *Tower-Roosevelt* ☎ *307/344–7311. $10–$22* ⊟ *AE, D, DC, MC, V* ⊘ *Closed early Sept.–early June.*

**¢–$$** ✕ **Canyon Lodge Cafeteria.** The park's busiest lunch spot serves such traditional American fare as country-fried steak and hot turkey sandwiches. For early risers, it also has a full breakfast menu. ⊠*Canyon Village* ☎*307/344–7311. $4–$16* ⊟*AE, D, DC, MC, V* ⊘ *Closed mid-Sept.–early June.*

**⟳ ¢–$$** ✕ **Lake Lodge Cafeteria.** This casual eatery, popular with families, serves hearty lunches and dinners such as spaghetti, pot roast, and fried chicken. It also has a full breakfast menu. ⊠ *Lake Village Rd.* ☎ *307/344–7311. $4–$14* ⊟ *AE, D, DC, MC, V* ⊘ *Closed mid-Sept.–early June.*

**⟳ ¢–$$** ✕ **Old Faithful Lodge Cafeteria.** Serving kid-friendly fare such as pizza, this noisy, family-oriented eatery has some of the best views of Old Faithful. ⊠ *South end of Old Faithful Bypass Rd.* ☎ *307/344–7311. $4–$14* ⊟ *AE, D, DC, MC, V* ⊘ *Closed mid-Sept.–mid-May.*

**¢–$** ✕ **Bear Paw Snack Shop.** When the kids are hungry, stop by this spot off the lobby of Old Faithful Inn for burgers, sandwiches, and french fries any time of day. ⊠ *Old Faithful Village* ☎ *307/344–7311. $5–$10* ⊟ *AE, D, DC, MC, V* ⊘ *Closed early Oct.–late May.*

**¢–$** ✕ **Terrace Grill.** Although the exterior looks rather elegant, this restaurant in Mammoth Hot Springs serves only fast food, ranging from biscuits and gravy for breakfast to hamburgers and veggie burgers for lunch and dinner. ⊠ *Mammoth Hot Springs* ☎ *307/344–7311. $3–$9* ⊟ *AE, D, DC, MC, V* ⊘ *Closed late Sept.–mid-May.*

PICNIC AREAS    There are 49 picnic areas in the park, ranging from secluded spots with a couple of tables to stops with a dozen or more tables plus other amenities. Only nine areas—Snake River, Grant Village, Spring Creek, Nez Perce, Old Faithful East, Bridge Bay, Cascade Lake Trail, Norris Meadows, and Yellowstone River—have fire grates. In other areas, only gas stoves may be used. None have running water; most have pit toilets.

Keep an eye out for wildlife; you never know when a herd of bison might decide to march through. In that case, it's best to leave your food and move a safe distance away.

**Firehole River.** The Firehole River rolls past and you might see elk

---

**PACKING A PICNIC**

You can stock up your cooler at any of the general stores in the park; there is one in each major developed area. It is also possible to purchase box lunches from restaurants within Yellowstone. Boxed lunches include drinks, snacks, sandwiches, and fruit, or vegetarian selections.

grazing along its banks. This picnic area has 12 tables and one pit toilet. ⊠ *Grand Loop Rd., 3 mi south of Madison.*

**Fishing Bridge.** This picnic area has 11 tables within the busy Fishing Bridge area. It's walking distance to the amphitheater, store, and visitor center. ⊠ *East Entrance Road, 1 mi from Grand Loop Rd.*

**Gibbon Meadows.** You're likely to see elk or buffalo along the Gibbon River from one of nine tables at this area, which has a handicapped-accessible pit toilet. ⊠ *Grand Loop Rd., 3 mi south of Norris.*

### Outside the Park
⇨ Grand Teton National Park chapter for more area dining options.

**$$–$$$** ✕ **Proud Cut Saloon.** Some of the best prime rib in northwest Wyoming is served in this cowboy-style restaurant and bar decorated with historic photographs of cowboys working at the huge TA Ranch near Meeteetse. Owner Del Nose says he serves "kick-ass cowboy cuisine," which means steak, shrimp, crab legs, and ½-pound cheeseburgers. ⊠ *1227 Sheridan Ave., Cody, WY* ☎ *307/527–6905. $13–$24* ▭ *D, MC, V.*

**$–$$$** ✕ **Stephan's.** Locals praise this intimate restaurant with burlap tablecloths. Good bets are shrimp, halibut, and filet mignon stuffed with Gorgonzola, sun-dried tomatoes, and portobello mushrooms. ⊠ *1367 Sheridan Ave., Cody, WY* ☎ *307/587–8511. $11–$22* ▭ *AE, D, MC, V.*

**$–$$$** ✕ **Trapper's Inn.** Eat like a mountain man with this popular restaurant's massive breakfasts, featuring sourdough pancakes, biscuits, and rolls. Trout with eggs will fortify you for a day of exploring. Lunch standouts are buffalo burgers, while hearty steaks are a dinnertime favorite. ⊠ *315 Madison Ave., West Yellowstone, MT* ☎ *406/646–9375. $11–$22* ▭ *AE, D, MC, V.*

**☚ $–$$$** ✕ **Yellowstone Mine.** Decorated with mining equipment such as picks and shovels, this is a place for casual family-style dining. Town residents come in for the steaks and seafood. ⊠ *U.S. 89, Gardiner, MT* ☎ *406/848–7336. $10–$24* ▭ *AE, D, MC, V* ⊘ *No lunch.*

## Where to Stay

### In the Park
**★ $$–$$$$** 🏨 **Lake Yellowstone Hotel.** This distinguished hotel, dating from 1891, is popular with older visitors, who gather in the sunroom each afternoon to gaze at the lake while a pianist plays. Others browse behind the etched green windows of the expensive Crystal Palace gift shop or warm themselves on chilly days before the tile-mantel fireplace in the colonnaded lobby. Rooms have white wicker furnishings, giving them a light, airy feeling; some have lake views. There is one two-room suite with lake views that has been used as accommodations for more than one U.S. president. ⊠ *Lake Village Rd.* ☎ *307/344–7901* 🖷 *307/344–7456* ⊕ *www.travelyellowstone.com* ⇴ *158 rooms* ⚴ *Restaurant, bar, no a/c, no TV, no-smoking rooms* ❏ *CP. $137–$211, hotel rooms; $516, suite* ▭ *AE, D, DC, MC, V* ⊘ *Closed late Sept.–mid-May.*

**$–$$$$** 🏨 **Old Faithful Inn.** When you push open the massive, iron-latched front door, you enter the log-pillared lobby of one of the most distinctive national park lodgings. From the main building, where many gables dot

Fodor'sChoice
★

the wood-shingled roof, you can watch Old Faithful erupt. Rooms in the 1904 "Old House" have brass beds, and some have deep claw-foot tubs. Rooms in the 1927 west wing contain antique cherrywood furniture, and those in the 1913 east wing have Stickley furniture and tremendous four-poster beds. First-floor rooms in the Old House are the hotel's noisiest, so ask for a rear-facing room if you are seeking some quiet. Some of the rooms in the older sections share hallway bathrooms, though they do have sinks. Renovations to the inn are underway; a lobby renovation and roof repairs were completed in 2005 and other work will continue until 2007. The inn remains open, but its historic ambience is compromised by the construction. ⊠ *Old Faithful Village* ☎ *307/344–7901* 🖷 *307/344–7456* ⊕ *www.travelyellowstone.com* ⤳ *327 rooms, 6 suites* ⟁ *Restaurant, bar, no a/c, no phone (some), no TV, no-smoking rooms* ⦿ *CP. $90–$216, rooms; $320–$449, suites* ⊟ *AE, D, DC, MC, V* ⊘ *Closed late Oct.–early May.*

**$$$** ▦ **Cascade Lodge.** Pine wainscoting and brown carpets set the tone in this newer motel-style facility in the trees above the Grand Canyon of the Yellowstone. The lodge is at the farthest edge of the Canyon Village, which means it's quite a hike to the nearest dining facilities, but it's quiet because it's away from the major traffic at Canyon. ⊠ *North Rim Dr. at Grand Loop Rd.* ☎ *307/344–7901* 🖷 *307/344–7456* ⊕ *www.travelyellowstone.com* ⤳ *40 rooms* ⟁ *Bar, no a/c, no TV, no-smoking rooms* ⦿ *CP. $151* ⊟ *AE, D, DC, MC, V* ⊘ *Closed early Sept.–early June.*

**★ $$$** ▦ **Old Faithful Snow Lodge.** Built in 1998, this massive structure brings back the grand tradition of park lodges by making good use of heavy timber beams and wrought-iron accents in a distinctive facade. Inside you'll find soaring ceilings, natural lighting, and a spacious lobby with a stone fireplace. Nearby is a long sitting room where writing desks and overstuffed chairs invite you to linger. Rooms combine traditional style with modern amenities. This is one of only two lodging facilities open in winter, when the only way to get here is on over-snow vehicles. Snow Lodge also has older cabins with basic amenities. ⊠ *Far end of Old Faithful Bypass Rd.* ☎ *307/344–7901* 🖷 *307/344–7456* ⊕ *www.travelyellowstone.com* ⤳ *95 rooms, 33 cabins* ⟁ *Restaurant, bar, no a/c, no TV, no-smoking rooms. $171* ⊟ *AE, D, DC, MC, V* ⊘ *Closed mid-Oct.–mid-Dec. and mid-Mar.–May.*

**$–$$$** ▦ **Canyon Cabins.** With clusters of plain pine-frame cabins that are all duplex or fourplex units surrounding a main lodge building, this is one of Yellowstone's most bare-bones places to stay. Cabins have beds but no other amenities to speak of. Most have no running water; instead you use a bathhouse at the main lodge. ⊠ *North Rim Dr. at Grand Loop Rd.* ☎ *307/344–7901* 🖷 *307/344–7456* ⊕ *www.travelyellowstone.com* ⤳ *532 cabins* ⟁ *2 restaurants, bar, no a/c, no TV, no-smoking rooms. $65–$155* ⊟ *AE, D, DC, MC, V* ⊘ *Closed Sept.–May.*

**$$** ▦ **Dunraven Lodge.** This motel-style lodge with pine wainscoting and brown carpets is in the pine trees at the edge of the Grand Canyon of the Yellowstone, adjacent to the essentially identical Cascade Lodge. It's at the farthest edge of the Canyon Village, so it's a distance to the nearest dining facilities. ⊠ *North Rim Dr. at Grand Loop Rd.* ☎ *307/344–7901* 🖷 *307/344–7456* ⊕ *www.travelyellowstone.com* ⤳ *41 rooms*

⚴ *Bar, no a/c, no TV, no-smoking rooms. $125* ▭ *AE, D, DC, MC, V* ⊘ *Closed early Sept.–early June.*

**$$** 🏨 **Grant Village Lodge.** The six humble lodge buildings that make up this facility have rough pine exteriors painted gray and rust. Reminiscent of a big-city motel, the complex offers basic rooms with few features beyond a bed and nightstand. ⊠ *Grant Village* ☎ *307/344–7901* 🖷 *307/ 344–7456* ⊕ *www.travelyellowstone.com* ⤵ *300 rooms* ⚴ *2 restaurants, bar, no a/c, no TV, no-smoking rooms. $131* ▭ *AE, D, DC, MC, V* ⊘ *Closed mid-Sept.–late May.*

**$$** 🏨 **Lake Yellowstone Hotel Cabins.** Set unobtrusively in the trees behind the Lake Yellowstone Hotel, these pine-paneled cabins with yellow exteriors provide basic accommodations. ⊠ *Lake Village Rd.* ☎ *307/ 344–7901* 🖷 *307/344–7456* ⊕ *www.travelyellowstone.com* ⤵ *102 cabins* ⚴ *Restaurant, bar, no a/c, no TV, no-smoking rooms. $109* ▭ *AE, D, DC, MC, V* ⊘ *Closed mid-Sept.–mid-June.*

**$–$$** 🏨 **Lake Lodge.** Among the pines not far from Lake Yellowstone Hotel, this lodge was built in 1920 but has been modernized so that the accommodations resemble those of a fairly standard motel. There are views of the lake from the lodge but not from the rooms. ⊠ *Lake Village Rd.* ☎ *307/344–7901* 🖷 *307/344–7456* ⊕ *www.travelyellowstone.com* ⤵ *186 rooms* ⚴ *Restaurant, bar, no a/c, no TV, no-smoking rooms. $65–$145* ▭ *AE, D, DC, MC, V* ⊘ *Closed mid-Sept.–mid-June.*

**$–$$** 🏨 **Lake Lodge Cabins.** Located near Yellowstone Lake, these older cabins, brightened up with yellow paint, provide basic, no-frills accommodations. ⊠ *Lake Village Rd.* ☎ *307/344–7901* 🖷 *307/344–7456* ⊕ *www. travelyellowstone.com* ⤵ *186 cabins* ⚴ *No a/c, no TV, no-smoking rooms. $65–$130* ▭ *AE, D, DC, MC, V* ⊘ *Closed mid-Sept.–mid-June.*

**$–$$** 🏨 **Mammoth Hot Springs Hotel and Cabins.** Built in 1937, this hotel has a spacious art deco lobby, where you'll find an espresso cart after 4 PM. The rooms are smaller and less elegant than those at the park's other two historic hotels, but the Mammoth Hot Springs Hotel is less expensive and usually less crowded. In summer the rooms can get hot, but you can open the window and there are fans. Some rooms do not have bathrooms, so you must use a bathroom down the hall. The cabins, set amid lush lawns, are the nicest inside the park. This is one of only two lodging facilities open in winter. Some cabins have hot tubs, a nice amenity after a day of cross-country skiing or snowshoeing. ⊠ *Mammoth Hot Springs* ☎ *307/344–7901* 🖷 *307/344–7456* ⊕ *www. travelyellowstone.com* ⤵ *97 rooms, 67 with bath; 2 suites; 115 cabins, 76 with bath* ⚴ *Restaurant, bar, no a/c, no TV, no-smoking rooms. $75–$108, hotel; $68–$102, cabins; $351, suite* ▭ *AE, D, DC, MC, V* ⊘ *Closed mid-Sept.–mid-Dec. and mid-Mar.–late May.*

**$–$$** 🏨 **Old Faithful Lodge Cabins.** These older cabins located behind the Old Faithful Lodge are a good budget option. They're small and plainly decorated and have no views of Old Faithful geyser. Many do not have bathrooms—guests must use the bathrooms in the lodge. ⊠ *South end of Old Faithful Bypass Rd.* ☎ *307/344–7901* 🖷 *307/344–7456* ⊕ *www. travelyellowstone.com* ⤵ *97 cabins* ⚴ *Restaurant, no a/c, no TV, no-smoking rooms* ⦿ *CP. $66–$102* ▭ *AE, D, DC, MC, V* ⊘ *Closed mid-Sept.–mid-May.*

36

**¢–$$**   ⊞ **Roosevelt Lodge.** Near the beautiful Lamar Valley in the park's north-east corner, this simple lodge dating from the 1920s surpasses some of the more expensive options. Nearby cabins set around a pine forest require that you bring your own bedding. Some cabins have bathrooms, but most do not; there is a bathhouse nearby. Some rooms also have woodstoves. You can make arrangements for horseback and stagecoach rides. ⊠ *Tower-Roosevelt Junction on Grand Loop Rd.* ☎ *307/344–7901* 🖷 *307/344–7456* ⊕ *www.travelyellowstone.com* 🛏 *80 cabins, 12 with bath* ⚱ *Restaurant, no a/c, no TV, no-smoking rooms. $59–$102* ⊟ *AE, D, DC, MC, V* ⊗ *Closed early Sept.–early June.*

CAMPGROUNDS &   If the kids enjoy camping and spending time in the great outdoors, any
RV PARKS   of the properties listed below will be good. Fishing Bridge RV Park is the only campground offering water, sewer, and electrical hookups, and it is for hard-sided vehicles only (no tents or tent-trailers are allowed).

★   ⚠ **Bridge Bay.** The park's largest campground, Bridge Bay rests in a wooded grove. You can rent boats at the nearby marina, take guided walks, or listen to rangers lecture about the history of the park. Don't expect solitude, as there are more than 400 campsites. Generators are allowed from 8 AM to 8 PM. Hot showers and laundry are 4 mi north at Fishing Bridge. ⊠ *3 mi southwest of Lake Village on Grand Loop Rd.* ☎ *307/344–7311* 🖷 *307/344–7456* ⊕ *www.travelyellowstone. com* 🛏 *432 sites* ⚱ *Flush toilets, dump station, drinking water, showers, bear boxes, fire pits, picnic tables, public telephone, ranger station. $17* ⊟ *AE, D, DC, MC, V* ⊗ *Late May–mid-Sept.*

★ ☾   ⚠ **Canyon.** The campground is accessible to Canyon's many short trails, which makes it a hit with families. The location is near laundry facilities and the visitor center. Generators are allowed from 8 AM to 8 PM. ⊠ *North Rim Dr., ¼ mi east of Grand Loop Rd.* ☎ *307/344–7311* 🖷 *307/344–7456* ⊕ *www.travelyellowstone.com* 🛏 *272 sites* ⚱ *Flush toilets, drinking water, guest laundry, showers, bear boxes, fire pits, picnic tables, public telephone, ranger station. $17* ⊟ *AE, D, DC, MC, V* ⊗ *Early June–early Sept.*

⚠ **Fishing Bridge RV Park.** Near Bridge Bay Marina, this is the only facility in the park that caters exclusively to recreational vehicles. Because of bear activity in the area, only hard-sided campers are allowed. Liquid propane is available. Generators are allowed from 8 AM to 8 PM. There is no boat access here. ⊠ *East Entrance Rd. at Grand Loop Rd.* ☎ *307/344–7311* 🖷 *307/344–7456* ⊕ *www.travelyellowstone.com* 🛏 *344 sites* ⚱ *Flush toilets, full hookups, dump station, drinking water, guest laundry, showers, bear boxes, picnic tables, public telephone, ranger station. $34* ⊟ *AE, D, DC, MC, V* ⊗ *Mid-May–late Sept.*

⚠ **Grant Village.** The park's second-largest campground has some sites with great Yellowstone Lake views. Some sites are wheelchair accessible. The campground has a boat launch but no dock. Generators are allowed from 8 AM to 8 PM. ⊠ *South Entrance Rd., 2 mi south of West Thumb* ☎ *307/344–7311* 🖷 *307/344–7456* ⊕ *www.travelyellowstone. com* 🛏 *425 sites* ⚱ *Flush toilets, dump station, drinking water, guest laundry, showers, bear boxes, picnic tables, public telephone, ranger station. $17* ⊟ *AE, D, DC, MC, V* ⊗ *Late June–late Sept.*

⚠ **Indian Creek.** In a picturesque setting next to a creek, this campground sits amid prime wildlife-viewing area. Some sites accommodate trailers of up to 45 feet. ✉ *8 mi south of Mammoth Hot Springs on Grand Loop Rd.* ☎ *307/344–2017* ⟟ *75 sites* ⚑ *Pit toilets, bear boxes, fire pits, picnic tables. $12* ▭ *No credit cards* ☾ *Early June–mid-Sept.*

⚠ **Lewis Lake.** It's a bit off the beaten track, which means this campground south of Grant Village is quieter than most. Also, it's a good choice for boaters who don't want to fight the crowds, because it's the only campground besides Bridge Bay and Grant Village that has a boat launch. ✉ *6 mi south of Grant Village on South Entrance Rd.* ☎ *307/344–2017* ⟟ *85 sites* ⚑ *Pit toilets, drinking water, bear boxes, fire pits, picnic tables. $12* ▭ *No credit cards* ☾ *Late June–early Nov.*

⚠ **Madison.** This campground is beside the Madison River, with plenty of hiking trails nearby. It can accommodate trailers up to 45 feet. ✉ *Grand Loop Rd. at Madison* ☎ *307/344–7311* 🖶 *307/344–7456* ⊕ *www.travelyellowstone.com* ⟟ *277 sites* ⚑ *Flush toilets, dump station, drinking water, bear boxes, fire pits, picnic tables, public telephone, ranger station. $17* ▭ *AE, D, DC, MC, V* ☾ *Early May–mid-Oct.*

⚠ **Mammoth Hot Springs.** The sagebrush-covered hillside where the sites are located often attracts elk and mule deer. There are plenty of things to do at the nearby visitor center, including evening talks by park rangers. The campground is more exposed than most, so it gets hot on summer days. There are wheelchair-accessible sites at this campground. ✉ *North Entrance Rd. at Mammoth Hot Springs* ☎ *307/344–2017* ⟟ *85 sites* ⚑ *Flush toilets, drinking water, bear boxes, fire pits, picnic tables, public telephone, ranger station. $14* ▭ *AE, D, DC, MC, V.*

⚠ **Norris.** This campground adjoins the Gibbon River, making it a favorite among anglers—brook trout and grayling are the prizes catches. It can accommodate trailers up to 45 feet. Generators are allowed from 8 AM to 8 PM. ✉ *Grand Loop Rd. at Norris* ☎ *307/344–2177* ⟟ *116 sites* ⚑ *Flush toilets, drinking water, bear boxes, fire pits, picnic tables, ranger station. $14* ▭ *No credit cards* ☾ *Mid-May–late Sept.*

⚠ **Pebble Creek.** Near a 10,554-foot peak called the Thunderer, sites here offer some unforgettable views. It's also smaller than most, which means it tends to be a little quieter. It allows trailers up to 45 feet. ✉ *Northeast Entrance Rd., 22 mi east of Tower-Roosevelt Junction* ☎ *307/344–2017* ⟟ *32 sites* ⚑ *Pit toilets, bear boxes, fire pits, picnic tables. $12* ▭ *No credit cards* ☾ *June–late Sept.*

⚠ **Slough Creek.** Reached by a little-used spur road, this creek-side campground is about as far from the beaten path as you can get without actually camping in the backcountry. Fishing aficionados come here for the trout. ✉ *Northeast Entrance Rd., 10 mi east of Tower-Roosevelt Junction* ☎ *307/344–2017* ⟟ *29 sites* ⚑ *Pit toilets, bear boxes, fire pits, picnic tables. $12* ▭ *No credit cards* ☾ *Late May–late Oct.*

⚠ **Tower Fall.** It's within hiking distance of the roaring waterfall, so this campground gets a lot of foot traffic. It can accommodate shorter trailers. Hot water and flush toilets are at Tower Store restrooms nearby. ✉ *3 mi southeast of Tower-Roosevelt on Grand Loop Rd.* ☎ *307/344–2017* ⟟ *32 sites* ⚑ *Pit toilets, bear boxes, fire pits, picnic tables. $12* ▭ *No credit cards* ☾ *Mid-May–late Sept.*

**36**

### Outside the Park

⇨ Grand Teton National Park for more area lodging and camping.

**$–$$** ✕▥ **Three Bear Lodge.** Earth-tone walls, carpets, and draperies and pine furnishings help set a casual and woodsy mood at this lodge. You can eat a hearty breakfast, arrange an all-day snowmobile tour, then return to this log lodge for a dinner ($–$$, no lunch) of prime rib, steak, or buffalo burgers. They don't serve lunch, but will pack a boxed meal for your day in the park. ⊠ *217 Yellowstone Ave., West Yellowstone, MT 59758* ☎ *406/646–7353 or 800/646–7353* ☐ *406/646–4767* ⊕ *www. threebearlodge.com* ⇦ *73 rooms* ⌂ *Restaurant, Wi-Fi, pool, bar, no-smoking rooms. $9–$17. $70–$143* ▭ *AE, D, MC, V.*

**$$$$** ▥ **Rimrock Dude Ranch.** One of the oldest ranches on the North Fork of the Shoshone River, year-round Rimrock offers snowmobile and horse-back riding trips into the surrounding mountains. Lodging is in small cabins with views of the North Fork Valley. ⊠ *2728 North Fork Hwy., Cody, WY 82414* ☎ *307/587–3970 or 800/208–7468* ☐ *307/527–5014* ⊕ *www.rimrockranch.com* ⌂ *Restaurant, refrigerator, pool, air-port shuttle, no a/c* ⇦ *9 cabins. $1,475 for 7-day minimum* ▭ *MC, V.*

**$–$$** ▥ **Pahaska Tepee Resort.** Just 2 mi from Yellowstone's East Entrance, this was Buffalo Bill's original getaway in the high country. The cabins, some of which stand alone and some of which are grouped together, have two, four, or six bedrooms. With seven bedrooms and a kitchen, the Re-union Lodge is ideal for big groups. ⊠ *183 Yellowstone Hwy., Cody, WY 82414* ☎ *307/527–7701 or 800/628–7791* ☐ *307/527–4019* ⊕ *www.pahaska.com* ⇦ *48 cabins, 1 lodge* ⌂ *Restaurant, bar, no-smoking rooms, no a/c, no TV. $85–$150* ▭ *D, MC, V.*

CAMPGROUNDS & RV PARKS ⛺ **Flagg Ranch Village.** In a wooded area near the Snake River, this sprawl-ing complex is 2 mi from the south entrance of Yellowstone. On site is a main lodge, convenience store and gas station. ⊡ *PO Box 187, Moran, WY 83013* ☎ *307/733–8761 or 800/443–2311* ⇦ *171 tent/RV sites, 95 cabins* ⌂ *Flush toilets, full hookups, drinking water, guest laundry, showers, fire pits, food service, public telephone. $20–$45, $150–$170 cabins* ▭ *AE, D, MC, V* ☉ *Mid-May–mid-Oct.*

⛺ **Ponderosa Campground.** This campground and RV park has shaded sites. Camp in one of the tepees for a change of pace. ⊠ *1815 8th St., Cody, WY 82414* ☎ *307/587–9203* ⇦ *140 tent/RV sites, 9 tepees* ⌂ *Flush toilets, partial hookups, dump station, drinking water, guest laundry, showers, public telephone, general store, play area. $25–$36, $25 tepees* ▭ *No credit cards* ☉ *May–Oct.*

⛺ **Wagon Wheel Campground and Cabins.** Located within West Yellow-stone a few blocks west of the park, this campground has tent and RV sites along with cozy cabins with porches, barbecue grills, and cable TV. No pets are allowed, and there's no smoking in the cabins. Two cabins are open year-round. ⊠ *408 Gibbon Ave., West Yellowstone, MT 59758* ☎ *406/646–7872* ⊕ *www.wagonwheelrv.com* ⇦ *40 RV sites, 8 tent sites; 9 cabins* ⌂ *Flush toilets, full hookups, drinking water, guest laun-dry, showers, public telephone. $26–$36 tent and RV sites, $55 cabins (2 persons, $5 each additional person), 3-day and 5-day minimum rental* ▭ *No credit cards* ☉ *Memorial Day–Sept. 15.*

# YELLOWSTONE ESSENTIALS

**ACCESSIBILITY:** Yellowstone has long been a National Park Service leader in providing for people with disabilities. Restrooms with sinks and flush toilets designed for those in wheelchairs are in all developed areas except Norris and West Thumb, where more rustic facilities are available. Accessible campsites and restrooms are at Bridge Bay, Canyon Village, Madison, and Grant Village campgrounds, while accessible campsites are found at both Lewis Lake and Slough Creek campgrounds. Ice Lake has an accessible backcountry campsite. An accessible fishing platform is about 3½ mi west of Madison at Mt. Haynes Overlook. For details, contact the accessibility coordinator at ☎ 307/344–2018 or 307/344–2386 (TDD), or pick up a free copy of *Visitor Guide to Accessible Features in Yellowstone National Park,* available at all park visitor centers.

**ADMISSION FEES:** A fee of $25 per car and $12 per visitor arriving on a bus, motorcycle, or snowmobile covers seven days in Yellowstone and Grand Teton. An annual pass to the two parks is $50.

**ADMISSION HOURS:** Depending on weather, Yellowstone is generally open late April to October and mid-December to early March. In winter, only one road, going from the Northeast entrance at Cooke City to the north entrance at Gardiner, is open to regular vehicles; other roads are used by over-snow vehicles. The park is in the Mountain time zone.

**ATM/BANKS:** ATMs are at Lake Yellowstone Hotel, Old Faithful Inn, Old Faithful Snow Lodge, Old Faithful Upper Store, and the Canyon Lodge, and Canyon, Fishing Bridge, Grant Village, and Mammoth general stores.

**AUTOMOBILE SERVICE STATIONS** There are two Chevron gas stations in the park: the one at Panther Junction does minor work (oil and tires), and the Rio Grande Village one offers gas, and propane for camp stoves. 🖬 **Panther Junction Chevron** ✉ 26 mi south of park north entrance ☎ 432/477–2294. **Rio Grande Village Chevron** ✉ 22 mi southeast of Panther Junction ☎ 432/477–2293. **Terlingua Auto** ✉ Off Highway 170 in the Terlingua business district Terlingua Texas 79852 ☎ 432/371-2223.

**AUTOMOBILE SERVICE STATIONS:** Service stations, which are closed in winter (and fall, in some cases), are found at Canyon Village, Fishing Bridge, Grant Village, Mammoth Hot Springs, Old Faithful, and Tower Junction.

**EMERGENCIES:** In case of emergency, dial 911 or 307/344–7381. There are ranger stations in Canyon Village, Fishing Bridge, Grant Village, Lake Village, Mammoth Hot Springs, and Old Faithful Village. Yellowstone has three clinics. 🖬 **Lake Clinic,** behind the Lake Hotel (open mid-May to mid-October, 8:30-8:30); **Mammoth Clinic,** next to the Mammoth Hot Springs post office (open weekdays, 8:30-1 and 2-5); **Old Faithful Clinic,** in the parking lot behind Old Faithful Inn (open mid-May to mid-October, 8:30-5). There are hospitals with 24-hour emergency rooms in Jackson, Cody, and Bozeman.

**LOST AND FOUND:** You can turn in any found item or search for a lost object at any ranger station or visitor center.

**PERMITS:** Fishing permits are required if you want to take advantage of Yellowstone's abundant lakes and streams. Live bait is not allowed, and for all native species of fish, a catch-and-release policy stands. Anglers 16 and older must purchase a $15 three-day permit, a $20 seven-day permit, or a $35 season permit; Those 12 to 15 need a free permit, and those 11 and under do not need a permit but must be supervised by an adult. Camping outside of designated campgrounds requires a free

**36**

backcountry permit. Horseback riding also requires a free permit. Permits are available at ranger stations and visitor centers.

POST OFFICES:
🚩 **Canyon Village Post Office** ✉ Canyon Village, 82190 ☎ 307/242-7323 ⊙ Closed early Sept.-mid-May. **Grant Village Post Office** ✉ Grant Village, 82190 ☎ 307/242-7338 ⊙ Closed early Sept.-mid-May. **Lake Post Office** ✉ Lake Village, 82190 ☎ 307/242-7383 ⊙ Closed early Sept.-mid-May. **Mammoth Hot Springs Post Office** ✉ Mammoth Hot Springs, 82190 ☎ 307/344-7764. **Old Faithful Post Office** ✉ Old Faithful, 82190 ☎ 307/545-7252 ⊙ Closed early Sept.-mid-May.

PUBLIC TELEPHONES: Public telephones are near visitor centers and major park attractions. Cell-phone reception in the park is hit or miss; in general, don't count on it.

RELIGIOUS SERVICES: Religious services are held at several park locations as well as in the communities surrounding the park during the summer and on some holidays. For times and locations, check at visitor centers or lodging front desks.

RESTROOMS: Public restrooms may be found at all visitor centers. They are also located at Old Faithful Village beside the Hamilton Store and at Snow Lodge and the Old Faithful Inn, in Tower-Roosevelt beside the Hamilton Store, and in Madison and West Thumb near the information station and winter warming hut.

SHOPS & GROCERS: All of the grocery stores listed here carry the basics.
🚩 **Bridge Bay Marina Store** ✉ Bridge Bay Marina ☎ 307/242-7326. **Canyon General Store** ✉ Canyon Village ☎ 307/242-7377. **Fishing Bridge General Store** ✉ Fishing Bridge ☎ 307/242-7200. **Grant Village General Store** ✉ Grant Village ☎ 307/242-7266. **Grant**

**Village Mini Store** ✉ Grant Village ☎ 307/242-7390. **Lake General Store** ✉ Lake Village ☎ 307/242-7563. **Mammoth General Store** ✉ Mammoth Hot Springs ☎ 307/344-7702. **Roosevelt Store** ✉ Tower-Roosevelt ☎ 307/344-7779. **Tower Fall Store** ✉ Tower Fall ☎ 307/344-7786. **Yellowstone General Store #300** ✉ Old Faithful Village ☎ 307/545-7282. **Yellowstone General Store #301** ✉ Old Faithful Village ☎ 307/545-7237. **Yellowstone Nature Store** ✉ Old Faithful Village ☎ 307/344-7757.

### NEARBY TOWN INFORMATION

🚩 **Cody Country Chamber of Commerce** ✉ 836 Sheridan Ave., Box 2777, Cody, WY 82414 ☎ 307/587-2297 ⊕ www.codychamber.org. **Cooke City Chamber of Commerce** ✆ Box 1071, Cooke City, MT 59020 ☎ 406/838-2495 ⊕ www.cookecitychamber.org. **Dubois Chamber of Commerce** ✉ 616 W. Ramshorn, Dubois, WY 82513 ☎ 307/455-2556 ⊕ www.duboiswyoming.org. **Gardiner Chamber of Commerce** ✉ 221 Park St., Gardiner, MT 59030 ☎ 406/848-7971 ⊕ www.gardinerchamber.com. **Jackson Hole Chamber of Commerce** ✉ 990 W. Broadway, Box E, Jackson, WY 83001 ☎ 307/733-3316 ⊕ www.jacksonholeinfo.com. **Livingston Chamber of Commerce** Livingston, MT 59047 ☎ 406/222-0850 ⊕ www.livingston.avicom.net. **Park County Travel Council (Cody)** ✉ 836 Sheridan Ave., Box 2777, Cody, WY 82414 ☎ 307/587-2297 ⊕ www.pctc.org. **Red Lodge Chamber of Commerce** ✉ 601 N. Broadway, Red Lodge, MT 59068 ☎ 406/446-1718 ⊕ www.redlodge.com. **West Yellowstone Chamber of Commerce** ✉ 30 Yellowstone Ave., West Yellowstone, MT 59758 ☎ 406/646-7701 ⊕ www.westyellowstonechamber.com.

### VISITOR INFORMATION

🚩 **Yellowstone National Park** ✆ Box 168, Mammoth, WY 82190-0168 ☎ 307/344-7381, 307/344-2386 TDD ⊕ www.nps.gov/yell.

# Yosemite National Park

Yosemite National Park

## WORD OF MOUTH

"Awful in stern, immovable majesty, how softly these rocks are adorned, and how fine and reassuring the company they keep: their feet among beautiful groves and meadows, their brows in the sky, a thousand flowers leaning confidingly against their feet, bathed in floods of water, floods of light, while the snow and waterfalls, the winds and avalanches and clouds shine and sing and wreathe about them as the years go by."

–John Muir, *The Yosemite.*

# WELCOME TO YOSEMITE

## TOP REASONS TO GO

★ **Feel the earth move:** An easy stroll brings you to the base of Yosemite Falls, America's highest, where thundering springtime waters shake the ground.

★ **Tunnel to heaven: :** Winding down into Yosemite Valley, Wawona Road passes through a mountainside and emerges before one of the park's most heart-stopping vistas.

★ **Touch the sky:** Watch clouds scudding across the bright blue dome that arches above the High Sierra's Tuolumne Meadows, a wide-open alpine valley ringed by 10,000-foot granite peaks.

★ **Walk away from it all:** Early or late in the day, leave the crowds behind and take a forest hike on a few of Yosemite's 800 mi of trails.

★ **Powder your nose:** Winter's hush floats into Yosemite on snowflakes. Wade into a fluffy drift, lift your face to the sky, and listen to the trees.

**1** Yosemite Valley. In the southern third of the park, east of the High Sierra, beats Yosemite's heart. This is where you'll find the park's most famous sights and biggest crowds.

**2** Wawona and Mariposa Grove. The park's southeastern tip holds Wawona, with its grand old hotel and pioneer history center, and the Mariposa Grove of Big Trees, filled with giant sequoias. These are closest to the South Entrance, 35 mi (a 1½-hour drive) south of Yosemite Village.

**3** Glacier Point. Take in the entire valley with one glance from Glacier Point, south of the valley, about 16 hilly, twisting miles east of Wawona Road (Route 41). November–May, Glacier Point Road is only open between Wawona Road and Badger Pass Ski Area, where you can play in the snow.

**4** Tuolumne Meadows. The highlight of east-central Yosemite is this wildflower-strewn valley with hiking trails, nestled between sharp, rocky peaks. It's a two-hour drive northeast of Yosemite Valley along Tioga Road (closed November–May).

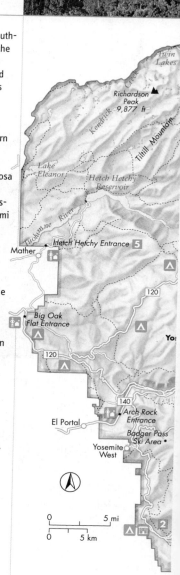

**5** Hetch Hetchy. The most remote, least-visited part of Yosemite accessible by automobile, this glacial valley is dominated by a reservoir and veined with wilderness trails. It's near the park's western boundary, about half an hour's drive north of Big Oak Flat Entrance.

CALIFORNIA

## GETTING ORIENTED

Except for its southwestern quadrant and a narrow strip across its mid-section, Yosemite—a park the size of Rhode Island—is wild country seen only by backpackers and horse-packers. Most visitors spend their time along the park's southwestern border, between Wawona and Big Oak Flat Entrance; a bit farther east in Yosemite Valley and Badger Pass Ski Area; and along the east-west corridor of Tioga Road, which spans the park north of Yosemite Valley and bisects Tuolumne Meadows.

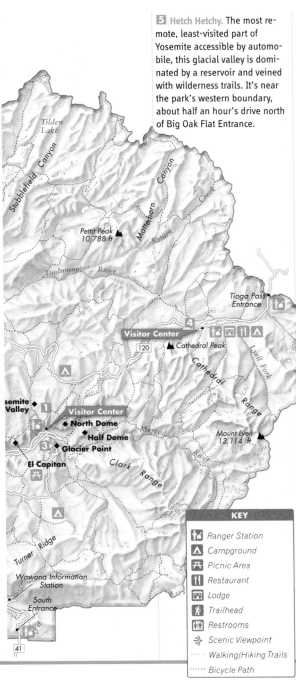

Tilden Lake

Stubblefield Canyon

Pettit Peak
10,788 ft

Tuolumne River

Matterhorn Canyon

Return Creek

Tioga Pass Entrance

Visitor Center
120
Cathedral Peak

Cathedral Range

Lyell Fork

semite Valley **1**
Visitor Center
**♦ North Dome**
**3 ♦ Half Dome**
**♦ Glacier Point**
Mercede

Mount Lyell
13,114 ft

**El Capitan**

Clark Range

River

Turner Ridge

Wawona Information Station

South Entrance

41

**KEY**

| | |
|---|---|
| 🏕 | Ranger Station |
| ⛺ | Campground |
| ⛱ | Picnic Area |
| 🍴 | Restaurant |
| 🏨 | Lodge |
| 🚶 | Trailhead |
| 🚻 | Restrooms |
| ⋇ | Scenic Viewpoint |
| ⋯⋯ | Walking/Hiking Trails |
| ⋯⋯ | Bicycle Path |

# YOSEMITE PLANNER

## When to Go

During extremely busy periods—like the 4th of July—you may experience delays at the entrance gates. If you can only make it here in the warmest months, try to visit midweek.

In winter, heavy snows occasionally cause road closures, and tire chains or four-wheel drive may be required on the roads that remain open. Tioga Road is closed from late October through the end of May or middle of June, depending on the snowmelt. The road to Glacier Point beyond the turnoff for Badger Pass is closed after the first major snowfall—usually in late October—through May; Mariposa Grove Road is typically closed for a shorter period in winter.

**The ideal time to visit is from mid-April through Memorial Day and from mid-September through October,** when the park is only moderately busy and the days are usually sunny and clear.

The chart below is for Yosemite Valley. In the high country, temperatures are cooler—by as much as 10–20°F in Tuolumne Meadows—and precipitation is greater.

## Flora & Fauna

Dense stands of incense cedar and Douglas fir—as well as ponderosa, Jeffrey, lodgepole, and sugar pines—cover much of the park, but the stellar standout, quite literally, is the *Sequoia sempervirens,* the giant sequoia. Sequoias grow only along the west slope of the Sierra Nevada between 4,500 and 7,000 feet in elevation. Starting from a seed the size of a rolled-oat flake, each of these ancient monuments assumes remarkable proportions in adulthood; you can see them in the Mariposa Grove of Big Trees. In late May the Valley's dogwood trees bloom with white, starlike flowers. Wildflowers, such as black-eyed Susan, bull thistle, cow parsnip, lupine, and meadow goldenrod, peak in June in the Valley and in July at higher elevations. Yosemite's waterfalls are at their most spectacular in May and June. By summer's end, some falls, including the mighty Yosemite Falls, dry up. They begin flowing again in late fall, and in winter they may be hung dramatically with ice. Visit the park during a full moon, and you can stroll in the evening without a flashlight and still make out the silhouettes of the giant granite monoliths and ribbons of falling water. Regardless of the season, sunset casts a brilliant orange light onto Half Dome, a stunning sight.

The most visible animals in the park are the mule deer, the only kind of deer in Yosemite. Though sightings of bighorn sheep are infrequent in the park itself, you can sometimes see them on the eastern side of the Sierra Crest, just off Route 120 in Lee Vining Canyon. The American black bear, which often has a brown, cinnamon, or blond coat, is the only species of bear in Yosemite (the California grizzlies were hunted to extinction in the 1920s), though few people ever see them. Watch for the blue Steller's jay along trails, in campgrounds, and around public buildings. Golden eagles are sometimes seen soaring above the Valley.

AVG. HIGH/LOW TEMPS.

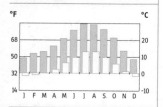

## Getting There & Around

To get to Yosemite, take Route 120 east to the Big Oak Flat entrance or west to the Tioga Pass entrance (summer to late fall only); Route 140 east to the Arch Rock entrance; or Route 41 to the South entrance. Yosemite Valley is 180 mi from Kings Canyon National Park and 340 mi from Lassen Volcanic National Park. Driving distance from San Francisco is about 200 mi; from Reno or Los Angeles it is roughly 300 mi; and from Las Vegas it is nearly 500 mi.

When it's especially crowded, some roads are closed to private vehicles; the road to Happy Isles and the Mist Trail are only accessible by shuttle. You can avoid traffic jams, save time, and take in more of the scenery by leaving your car at any of the designated lots and taking the free hybrid diesel-electric shuttle bus. Shuttles serve eastern Yosemite Valley between Camp 4 and Happy Isles year-round, every day. From May to September, shuttles run from 7 AM to 10 PM; the rest of the year, shuttles run from 9 AM to 10 PM. In summer, shuttles also operate between the visitor center and El Capitan, between Wawona and the Mariposa Grove, and between the Tioga Pass entrance and Olmstead Point. In winter, a shuttle runs between Yosemite Valley and Badger Pass Ski Area. For more information on shuttles within the park, visit ⊕ www.nps.gov/yose/trip/shuttle.htm or call ☎ 209/372-1240.

There are few gas stations within Yosemite (near the entrances), so fuel up before you reach the park. From late fall until early spring, the weather is unpredictable, and driving can be treacherous. You should carry chains; they are often mandatory on Sierra roads in snowstorms. Pick chains up before you arrive—if you buy them in the Valley, you'll pay twice the normal price. For information about road conditions, call ☎ 800/427-7623 or 209/372-0200 from within California or go to ⊕ www.dot.ca.gov.

## Good Reading

Write or call the park to obtain *Yosemite: Your Complete Guide to the Park,* an indispensable booklet that lists everything from trip planning to seasonal activities. It's also available online at www.americanparknetwork.com and in person upon your arrival. For a detailed calendar of activities, including the operating hours of all facilities, send for *Yosemite Today* or pick up a copy when you arrive; it's online at ⊕ www.nps.gov/archive/yose/now/today.htm.

## Bears

The Sierra Nevada is home to thousands of bears, and you should take all necessary precautions to keep yourself—and the bears—safe. Bears that acquire a taste for human food can become very aggressive and destructive and often must be destroyed by rangers. The national parks' campgrounds and some campgrounds outside the parks provide food-storage boxes that can keep bears from pilfering your edibles (portable canisters for backpackers can be rented in most park stores). It's imperative that you move all food, coolers, and items with a scent (including toiletries, toothpaste, chewing gum, and air fresheners) from your car (including the trunk) to the storage box at your campsite; day-trippers should lock food in bear boxes provided at parking lots. If you don't, a bear may break into your car by literally peeling off the door or ripping open the trunk, or it may ransack your tent. The familiar tactic of hanging your food from high tree limbs is not an effective deterrent, as bears can easily scale trees. In the Southern Sierra, bear canisters are the only effective and proven method for preventing bears from getting human food.

37

By Constance
Jones

You can lose your perspective in Yosemite. This is a land where everything is big. Really big. There are big rocks, big trees, and big waterfalls. The park has been so extravagantly praised and so beautifully photographed that some people wonder if the reality can possibly measure up. For almost everyone it does: here, you will remember what *breathtaking* really means.

With 1,189 square mi of parkland—94.5% of it undeveloped wilderness accessible only to the backpacker and horseback rider—Yosemite is a nature lover's wonderland. The western boundary dips as low as 2,000 feet in the chaparral-covered foothills; the eastern boundary rises to 13,000 feet at points along the Sierra Crest. Yosemite Valley has many of the park's most famous sites and is easy to reach, but take the time to explore the high country above the Valley and you'll see a different side of the park; the fragile and unique alpine terrain is arresting. Wander through this world of wind-warped trees, scurrying animals, and bighorn sheep, and you'll come away with a distinct sense of peace and solitude.

The Miwok, the last of several Native American peoples to inhabit the Yosemite area (they were forced out by gold miners in 1851), named the Yosemite Valley *Ahwahnee*, which is thought to mean "the place of the gaping mouth." Abraham Lincoln established Yosemite Valley and the Mariposa Grove of Giant Sequoias as public land in 1864, when he deeded the land to the state of California. This grant was the first of its kind in America, and it laid the foundation for the establishment of national and state parks. The high country above the Valley, however, was not protected. John Muir, concerned about the destructive effects of overgrazing on subalpine meadows, rallied together a team of dedicated supporters and lobbied for expanded protection of lands surrounding Yosemite Valley. As a result of their efforts, Yosemite National Park was established by Congress on October 1, 1890.

# GREAT ITINERARIES

## YOSEMITE IN ONE DAY

Your first stop as you enter Yosemite Valley from the west is the graceful 620-foot cascade of **Bridalveil Fall.** As you continue east, you'll spot 3,593-foot **El Capitan,** the world's largest granite monolith, across the Valley. Follow signs to **Yosemite Village,** and stop in at the **Valley Visitor Center** to pick up maps and brochures. Behind the center, walk through a small, re-created **Ahwahneechee village.** For more Native American lore, take a quick peek at the **Yosemite Museum** next door, where there's an impressive collection of baskets. If you're a photography buff, the nearby **Ansel Adams Gallery** is a must-see. Next, amble over to **Sentinel Bridge,** walk to its center, and take in the best view of **Half Dome,** with its reflection in the Merced River. Before you leave the Village, stop at the Village Store or a snack bar to pick up provisions for a picnic lunch.

Return to your car, drive over Sentinel Bridge, turn left, and continue on Southside Drive toward **Curry Village.** Hardy hikers may want to go straight to the day-use lot, walk to the end of the shuttle-bus road, and climb the moderately steep trail to the footbridge overlooking 317-foot **Vernal Fall** (1½ mi round-trip; allow 1½ hours). Looping back toward Yosemite Village, follow signs to the **Ahwahnee Hotel.**

Back on the main road heading west, drive to **Yosemite Falls,** the highest waterfall in North America. If you have time at the end of the day, drive up to **Glacier Point** for a sunset view of the Valley and the surrounding peaks.

## YOSEMITE IN THREE DAYS

If you have three days, start at the **Valley Visitor Center.** Head west for a short hike to **Yosemite Falls.** Afterward, continue driving west for a valley view of giant, granite **El Capitan.** Continue west on Northside Drive, and follow signs for **Route 41 (Wawona Road)**; head south. At the Chinquapin junction, make a left turn onto Glacier Point Road (summer only). From **Glacier Point,** you'll get a phenomenal bird's-eye view of the entire Valley, including **Half Dome, Vernal Fall,** and **Nevada Fall.** If you want to avoid the busloads of tourists at Glacier Point, stop at **Sentinel Dome** instead.

On Day 2, head south on Route 41 and visit the **Mariposa Grove of Big Trees** and the **Pioneer Yosemite History Center.** Stop at the historic **Wawona Hotel** and have lunch. Return to Yosemite Valley on Route 41, stopping at the **Tunnel View** pullout to take in the breathtaking panorama of the Valley, with the afternoon sun lighting up the peaks. Back in the Valley, stop at **Bridalveil Falls** on the right side of the road. Then, head to the **Ahwahnee Hotel.**

On the third day, have breakfast near the Valley Visitor Center in **Yosemite Village,** then see the **Ansel Adams Gallery,** the re-created **Ahwahneechee Village,** and the **Yosemite Museum.** Pick up light provisions before hiking to **Vernal Fall** or **Nevada Fall.** Picnic on the trail or in the Valley, then visit **Tuolumne Meadows,** 55 mi east of the Valley on **Tioga Road (Route 120)** (summer only).

37

## Scenic Drives

**Route 41.** From the South entrance station, curvy Route 41 provides great views and stopover points en route to the Valley. Just past the gate, an offshoot to the right leads to the Mariposa Grove of Big Trees (it's closed once there's snow on the ground). A few miles north on Route 41 is Wawona, where you can stop for lunch. Drive another 15 mi, and you'll come to the turnoff for Glacier Point. Farther along on Route 41, you'll pass through a tunnel, after which you can pull off the road and park. "Tunnel View" is one of the most famous views of Yosemite Valley, with El Capitan on the left, Bridalveil Fall on the right, and Half Dome as a backdrop. Continue another 5 mi on Route 41 until you reach Yosemite Valley. From beginning to end, drive time alone is about an hour; with stops it will take a minimum of three hours to complete this tour.

**Tioga Road.** In summer, a drive up Tioga Road (Route 120) to the high country will reward you with gorgeous alpine scenery, including crystal-blue lakes, grassy meadows dotted with wildflowers, and high-alpine peaks. Keep a sharp eye out for the neon colors of rock climbers, who seem to defy gravity on the cliffs. Wildflowers peak in July and August. The one-way trip to Tioga Pass takes approximately 1½ hours.

## What to See

Yosemite is so large that you can think of it as five different parks. Yosemite Valley, famous for waterfalls and cliffs, and Wawona, where the giant sequoias stand, are open all year. Hetch Hetchy, home of less-used backcountry trails, closes after the first big snow and reopens in May or June. The subalpine high country, Tuolumne Meadows, is open for summer hiking and camping; in winter it's accessible only via cross-country skis or snowshoes. Badger Pass Ski Area is open in winter only.

### Historic Sites

★ **Ahwahnee Hotel.** Built in 1927, this stately lodge of granite and concrete beams stained to look like redwood is a perfect man-made complement to Yosemite's natural majesty. Even if you aren't a guest, take time to visit the immense parlors with walk-in hearths and priceless, antique Native American rugs and baskets. The dining room, its high ceiling interlaced with massive sugar-pine beams, is extraordinary. Dinner is formal; breakfast and lunch are more casual. ⊠ *Ahwahnee Rd., about ¾ mi east of Yosemite Valley Visitor Center, Yosemite Village* ☎ *209/372–1489.*

**Ahwahneechee Village.** Tucked behind the Valley Visitor Center, a short loop trail of about 100 yards circles through a re-creation of an Ahwahneechee Native American village as it might have appeared in 1872, 21 years after the Native Americans' first contact with Europeans. Markers explain the lifestyle of Yosemite's first residents. Allow 30 minutes to see it all. ⊠ *Northside Dr., Yosemite Village* 🖼 *Free* ☉ *Daily sunrise–sunset.*

**Ansel Adams Gallery.** This shop displays and sells original and reproduction prints by the master Yosemite photographer, as well as work by other landscape photographers. Its elegant camera shop conducts photography workshops and sometimes holds private showings of fine prints on Saturdays. ✉ *Northside Dr., Yosemite Village* ☎ *209/372–4413 or 888/361–7622* ⊕ *www.anseladams.com* ⌑ *Free* ☉ *Apr.–Oct., daily 9–6; Nov.–Mar. daily 9–5.*

**Curry Village.** Opened in 1899 by David and Jenny Curry, Curry Village offers tented lodgings for a modest price. There are also several stores, an evening campfire program in summer, and an ice-skating rink in winter. If you want to rent rafts or bicycles, this is the place. ✉ *Southside Dr., about ½ mi east of Yosemite Village.*

**Pioneer Yosemite History Center.** Yosemite's first buildings, relocated here from around the park, make up this historic collection near the Wawona Hotel—you'll even enter on the covered bridge that welcomed the park's first tourists. There's a homesteader's cabin, a blacksmith's shop, a bakery, and a U.S. Cavalry headquarters, all from the late-19th or early 20th centuries. Costumed docents play the roles of the pioneers Wednesday through Sunday in summer; ask about ranger-led walks and horse-drawn carriage rides, which happen sporadically. ✉ *Rte. 41, Wawona* ☎ *209/375–9531 or 209/379–2646* ⌑ *Free* ☉ *Building interiors are open mid-June–Labor Day, Wed. 2–5, Thurs.–Sun. 10–1 and 2–5.*

★ **Wawona Hotel.** In the southern tip of Yosemite, the park's first lodge was built in 1879. With a whitewashed exterior and wraparound verandas, this National Historic Landmark is a fine example of Victorian resort architecture—a blend of rusticity and elegance. The Wawona is an excellent place to stay or to stop for lunch when making the drive from the South entrance to the Valley, but be aware that the hotel is closed in January. ✉ *Rte. 41, Wawona* ☎ *209/375–1425.*

**Yosemite Museum.** This museum's collection and demonstrations in beadwork, basket weaving, and other traditional activities elucidate the cultural history of Yosemite's Miwok and Paiute people. ✉ *Yosemite Village* ☎ *209/372–0299* ⌑ *Free* ☉ *Daily 9–noon and 1–4:30.*

## Scenic Stops

★ **El Capitan.** Rising 3,593 feet—more than 350 stories—above the Valley, El Capitan is the largest exposed-granite monolith in the world. It's almost twice the height of the Rock of Gibraltar. Look for climbers scaling the vertical face. ✉ *Off Northside Dr., about 4 mi west of the Valley Visitor Center.*

Fodor'sChoice **Glacier Point.** A Yosemite hot spot for its sweeping, bird's-eye views, Glacier Point looms 3,214 feet above the Valley. From the parking area, walk a few hundred yards and you'll see waterfalls, Half Dome, and other mountain peaks. It's a tremendous place to watch the sun set. Glacier Point is also a popular hiking destination. You can make the strenuous hike up, or take a bus ($15) to the top and hike down. The bus runs June through October, weather permitting; call 209/372–1240 for schedules. ✉ *Glacier Point Rd., 16 mi northeast of Rte. 41.*

★ **Half Dome.** Though you may have seen it on countless postcards and calendars, it's still arresting to see Half Dome, the Valley's most recognizable formation, which tops out at an elevation of 8,842 feet. The

37

afternoon sun lights its face with orange and yellow shades that are reflected in the Merced River; stand on the Sentinel Bridge at sunset for the best view.

**Hetch Hetchy Reservoir.** The Hetch Hetchy Reservoir, which supplies water and hydroelectric power to San Francisco, is about 40 mi from Yosemite Valley. Some say John Muir died of heartbreak when this grand valley was dammed and flooded beneath 300 feet of water in 1913. Almost from the start, environmental groups such as the Sierra Club have lobbied the government to drain the reservoir; in 2006 the State of California issued a report stating that restoration of the valley is a "feasible" possibility. ⊠ *Hetch Hetchy Rd., about 15 mi north of the Big Oak Flat entrance station.*

**High Country.** The above–tree line, high-alpine region east of the Valley—land of alpenglow and top-of-the-world vistas—is often missed by crowds who come to gawk at the Valley's more publicized splendors. If you've never seen Sierra high country, go. If you've already been there, you know why it's not to be missed. Summer wildflowers, which usually spring up mid-July through August, carpet the meadows and mountainsides with pink, purple, blue, red, yellow, and orange. On foot or on horseback are the best ways to get here. For information on trails and backcountry permits, check with the visitor center.

★ **Mariposa Grove of Big Trees.** Mariposa is Yosemite's largest grove of giant sequoias. The Grizzly Giant, the oldest tree here, is estimated to be 2,700 years old. You can visit the trees on foot or, in summer, on a one-hour tram tour. If the road to the grove is closed in summer—which happens when Yosemite is crowded—park in Wawona and take the free shuttle (9 AM to 4:30 PM) to the parking lot. The access road to the grove may also be closed by snow for extended periods from November to mid-May; you can still usually walk, snowshoe, or ski in. ⊠ *Rte. 41, 2 mi north of the South entrance station.*

**Sentinel Dome.** The view from here is similar to that from Glacier Point, except you can't see the Valley floor. A 1¹⁄₁₀-mi path climbs to the viewpoint from the parking lot. The trail is long and steep enough to keep the crowds away, but it's not overly rugged. ⊠ *Glacier Point Rd., off Rte. 41.*

★ **Tuolumne Meadows.** The largest subalpine meadow in the Sierra, at 8,600 feet, is a popular way station for backpack trips along the Sierra-scribing Pacific Crest and John Muir trails. No wonder: the cracklingly clear air and dramatic sky above the river-scored valley can make even the most jaded heart soar. The colorful wildflowers peak in mid-July and August. Tioga Road provides easy access to the high country, but the highway closes when snow starts to fall, usually in mid-October. ⊠ *Tioga Rd. (Rte. 120), about 8 mi west of the Tioga Pass entrance station.*

WATERFALLS    When the snow starts to melt (usually peaking in May), almost every rocky lip or narrow gorge becomes a spillway for streaming snowmelt churning down to meet the Merced River. But even in drier months, the waterfalls can be breathtaking. If you choose to hike any of the trails

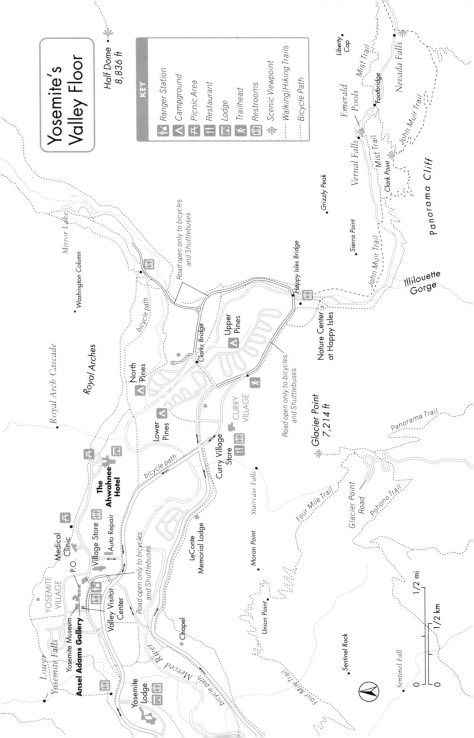

to or up the falls, be sure to wear shoes with good, no-slip soles; the rocks can be extremely slick. Stay on trails at all times.

**Bridalveil Fall,** a filmy fall of 620 feet that is often diverted as much as 20 feet one way or the other by the breeze, is the first marvelous view of Yosemite Valley you will see if you come in via Route 41.

Climb Mist Trail from Happy Isles for an up-close view of 594-foot **Nevada Fall,** the first major fall as the Merced River plunges out of the high country toward the eastern end of Yosemite Valley. If you don't want to hike, you can see it—distantly—from Glacier Point.

At 1,612 feet, **Ribbon Fall** is the highest single fall in North America. It's also the first valley waterfall to dry up in summer; the rainwater and melted snow that create the slender fall evaporate quickly at this height. Look just west of El Capitan from the Valley floor for the best view of the fall from the base of Bridalveil Fall.

Fern-covered black rocks frame 317-foot **Vernal Fall,** and rainbows play in the spray at its base. Take Mist Trail from Happy Isles to see it—or, if you'd rather not hike, go to Glacier Point for a distant view.

Fodor'sChoice ★  **Yosemite Falls**—which form the highest waterfall in North America and the fifth-highest in the world—are actually three falls, one on top of another. The water from the top descends a total of 2,425 feet, and when the falls run hard, you can hear them thunder all across the Valley. When they dry up, as often happens in late summer, the Valley seems naked without the wavering tower of spray. To view the falls up close, head to their base on the trail from Camp 4.

## Visitor Centers

**Le Conte Memorial Lodge.** A cute stone cottage from the outside and a dramatic mini-cathedral on the inside, the Valley's first visitor center is now operated by the Sierra Club. You can browse its substantial library, small children's library, and environmental exhibits, and attend evening programs. It's across from Housekeeping Camp. ⊠ *Southside Dr., about ½ mi west of Curry Village* ⊘ *Memorial Day–Labor Day, Wed.–Sun. 10–4.*

**Nature Center at Happy Isles.** Named after the pair of little islands in the Merced River where it enters Yosemite Valley, this family-oriented center has books, dioramas, and interactive exhibits on the park, with special attention paid to recent natural phenomena, such as recurring rock slides. ⊠ *Off Southside Dr., about ¾ mi east of Curry Village* ⊠ *Free* ⊘ *Mid-May–Oct., 10–noon and 12:30–4.*

**Valley Visitor Center.** A thorough overhaul, slated for completion by summer of 2007, is to make the museum here state-of-the-art, with interactive and high-tech exhibits. Be sure to stop by and learn a little about the park; you can also pick up maps, guides, and information from park rangers. ⊠ *Yosemite Village* ☎ *209/372–0299* ⊕ *www.yosemitepark. com* ⊠ *Free* ⊘ *Memorial Day–Labor Day, daily 8–6; Labor Day–Memorial Day, daily 9–5.*

**Wilderness Center.** The staff at the Wilderness Center in Yosemite Village provides free wilderness permits for overnight camping, maps, and advice to hikers heading into the backcountry. When the center is closed, go to the Valley Visitor Center next door. ⊠ *Yosemite Village* ⊘ *Memorial Day–Labor Day, daily 7:30–6.*

## Sports & the Outdoors

### Bicycling

There may be no more enjoyable way to see Yosemite Valley than to ride a bike beneath its lofty granite monoliths. The eastern valley has 12 mi of paved, flat bicycle paths across meadows and through woods, with bike racks at convenient stopping points. For a greater challenge, you can ride on 196 mi of paved park roads—but bicycles are not allowed on hiking trails or in the backcountry. Kids under 18 must wear a helmet. For information on renting equipment ⇨ Outfitters & Expeditions box.

### Bird-watching

More than 200 bird species have been spotted in the park, including the sage sparrow, pygmy owl, blue grouse, and mountain bluebird. Park rangers lead free bird-watching walks in Yosemite Valley one day each week in summer; check at a visitor center or information station for times and locations. Binoculars are sometimes available for loan. For information on tours ⇨ Outfitters & Expeditions box.

### Fishing

The waters in Yosemite are not stocked; trout, mostly brown and rainbow, live here but are not plentiful. Yosemite's fishing season begins on the last Saturday in April and ends on November 15. Some waterways are off-limits at certain times; be sure to inquire at the visitor center about regulations.

A California fishing license is required; licenses run $11.30 for one day, $17.60 for two days, and $34.90 for 10 days. Full season licenses cost $30.70 for state residents, and a whopping $82.45 for nonresidents.

Buy your license in season at Yosemite Village Sport Shop (☎ 209/372–1286) or at the Wawona Store (☎ 209/375–6574). You can also obtain a license by writing the **California Department of Fish and Game.** ⊠ *3211 S St., Sacramento 95814* ☎ *916/227–2245* ⊕ *www.dfg.ca.gov.* For information on tours ⇨ Outfitters & Expeditions box.

### Golf

Wawona Golf course is one of the country's few organic golf courses; it's also an Audubon Cooperative sanctuary for birds. You can play a round or take a lesson from the pro here.

**Wawona Golf Course.** The 9-hole, par-35 course at Wawona has different tee positions per side, providing 18 holes at par 70. The pro shop rents out electric golf carts, rents and sells other equipment, and sells golf clothing. ⊠ *Rte. 41, Wawona* ☎ *209/375–6572 Wawona Golf Shop* ⊕ *www.yosemitepark.com* 🔄 *$18.50–$29.50* ⊘ *Mid-Apr.–Oct., daily.*

**37**

**DID YOU KNOW?**

Yosemite Falls, one of the world's tallest, is composed of three separate waterfalls. Upper Yosemite Fall, pictured here, plunges 1,430 feet, while the drops for the Middle cascades (675 feet) and Lower Yosemite Fall (320 feet) are significantly shorter.

## Hiking

For information on tours ⇨ Outfitters & Expeditions box.

EASY **"A Changing Yosemite" Interpretive Trail.** This self-guided, wheelchair- and stroller-accessible walk begins about 75 yards in front of the Valley Visitor Center, where you can pick up an informative pamphlet that explains the continually changing geology visible along the walk. The trail follows the road, then circles through Cook's Meadow on a paved path. ⊠ *Across from the Valley Visitor Center.*

★ **Yosemite Falls Trail.** This is the highest waterfall in North America. The upper fall (1,430 feet), the middle cascades (675 feet), and the lower fall (320 feet) combine for a total of 2,425 feet and, when viewed from the valley, appear as a single waterfall. The ¼-mi trail leads from the parking lot to the base of the falls. Upper Yosemite Fall Trail, a strenuous 3½-mi climb rising 2,700 feet, takes you above the top of the falls. ⊠ *Northside Dr. at Camp 4.*

MODERATE **Mist Trail.** You'll walk through rainbows when you visit 317-foot Vernal Fall. The hike to the bridge at the base of the fall is moderately strenuous and less than 1 mi long. It's another steep (and often wet) ¾-mi grind up to the top. From there, you can continue 2 mi to the top of Nevada Fall, a 594-foot cascade as the Merced River plunges out of the high country. The trail is open late spring to early fall, depending on snowmelt. ⊠ *Happy Isles.*

★ **Panorama Trail.** Starting at Glacier Point, the trail circles 8½ mi down through forest, past the secluded Illilouette Falls, to the top of Nevada Fall, where it connects with Mist Trail and the John Muir Trail. You'll pass Nevada, then Vernal Fall on your way down to the Valley floor for a total elevation loss of 3,200 feet. Arrange to take the early-morning hiker bus to Glacier Point, and allow a full day for this hike. ⊠ *Glacier Point.*

DIFFICULT **Chilnualna Falls Trail.** This Wawona-area trail runs 4 mi one way to the top of the falls, then leads into the backcountry, connecting with miles of other trails. This is one of the park's most inspiring and secluded— albeit strenuous—trails. Past the tumbling cascade, and up through forests, you'll emerge before a panoramic vista at the top. ⊠ *Chilnualna Falls Rd., off Rte. 41, Wawona.*

**Four-Mile Trail.** You can take the hiker bus up to Glacier Point ($15), and then descend from there, zigzagging through the forest to the Valley floor, where you can catch a free shuttle back to your starting hiker-bus stop. If you decide to hike up Four-Mile Trail and back down again, allow about six hours for the challenging 9½-mi round-trip (the original 4-mi-long trail was lengthened to make it less steep). The Valley floor trailhead is on Southside Drive near Sentinel Beach, and the elevation change is 3,220 feet. ⊠ *Glacier Point.*

Fodor'sChoice **John Muir Trail to Half Dome.** Ardent and courageous trekkers can continue on from the top of Nevada Fall, off Mist Trail, to the top of Half Dome. Some hikers attempt this entire 10- to 12-hour, 16¾-mi round-

# Q & A with Ranger Scott Gediman

**What's your favorite thing to do in the park?**

I really enjoy hiking in Yosemite; in my opinion there's no better way to see the park. My favorite is the classic hike up the Mist Trail to Vernal Fall. I've done it literally hundreds of times—I've got family photos of my folks pushing me up the trail in a stroller. If you can only take one hike in Yosemite, do this one, especially in spring and summer.

**Which time of year is best for visiting Yosemite?**

The spring is wonderful, with the waterfalls going full blast and the meadows so green. The fall colors are beautiful, too. But in winter, the weather is great. The most stunning time in the valley is when a winter storm clears and there are incredible blue skies above the granite rocks, and the snow. There's a feeling you get seeing Half Dome with snow on it, or doing a winter hike on the Four-Mile Trail, Yosemite Falls Trail, or the Glacier Point trails.

**What's there to do here in winter?**

There's the ice skating rink at Curry Village, and up at Badger Pass there's a wonderful ski school that specializes in teaching kids. There's cross-country skiing on groomed tracks along Glacier Point Road. Snowshoeing is really catching on. It's fun, it's easy, families can do it. You don't need special skills or a bunch of gear to go hiking through the snow; just put some snowshoes on your sneakers or hiking boots, and you're off. Every morning from about mid-December to mid-March, park rangers lead free snowshoe walks from Badger Pass. We talk about winter ecology and

adaptations animals make, or we hike up the old Badger Summit for some fantastic views.

**What about summer?**

There's a misperception that the crowds are unmanageable, but it's not true. It's very easy to get away from the crowds in the Valley. One easy way is to hike the Valley Loop Trail, which a lot of people don't even know about. It goes all around the valley perimeter. Five minutes from Yosemite Lodge, and you won't see anybody.

**How crowded does the Valley really get?**

At the busiest time, probably Memorial Day Weekend, there can be as many as 25,000 people in the park at one time, many of them in the Valley. The biggest mistake people make in summer is to drive everywhere. It's frustrating because of the traffic, and it takes longer even than walking. Park your car in the day-use lot or leave it at your hotel, and take the free shuttle around. The shuttle goes to all the popular spots in the Valley.

37

# OUTFITTERS & EXPEDITIONS

### BICYCLING

**Yosemite Bike Rentals.** You can rent bikes by the hour ($7.50) or by day ($24.50) from either Yosemite Lodge or Curry Village bike stands. Bikes with child trailers, baby-jogger strollers, and wheelchairs are also available. ⊠ *Yosemite Lodge or Curry Village* ☎ *209/372-1208* ⊕ *www.yosemitepark.com* 🚲 *$7.50 (hour)/$24 (day)* ⊙ *Apr.-Oct.*

### BIRD-WATCHING

**Birding Seminars.** The Yosemite Association sponsors one- to four-day seminars for beginner and intermediate birders. ☎ *209/379-2321* ⊕ *www.yosemite.org* 🚲 *$82-$254* ⊙ *Apr.-Aug.*

### FISHING

**Southern Yosemite Mountain Guides** (☎ 800/231-4575 ⊕ www.symg.com) offers fly-fishing lessons and day- and weekend trips deep in Yosemite's backcountry.

### HIKING & BACKPACKING

The staff at the **Wilderness Center** (⊠ Yosemite Village 🏕 Yosemite Wilderness Reservations, Box 545, Yosemite 95389 ☎ 209/372-0740 ⊕ www.nps.gov/yose) provides free wilderness permits, which are required for overnight camping (advance reservations are available for $5 and are highly recommended for popular trailheads from May through September and on weekends). They also provide maps and advice to hikers heading into the backcountry. **Yosemite Mountaineering School and Guide Service** (⊠ Yosemite Mountain Shop, Curry Village ☎ 209/372-8344 ⊕ www.yosemitepark.com) can take you on guided two-hour to full-day treks from April through November.

### HORSEBACK RIDING

**Tuolumne Meadows Stables** (⊠ Off Tioga Rd., about 2 mi east of Tuolumne Meadows Visitor Center ☎ 209/372-8427 ⊕ www.yosemitepark.com) runs two-, four-, and eight-hour trips—which cost $53, $69, and $96, respectively—and High Sierra four- to six-day camping treks on mules, which begin at $625. Reservations are essential. **Wawona Stables** (⊠ Rte. 41, Wawona ☎ 209/375-6502) has two- and five-hour rides, starting at $53 (reservations essential). You can tour the valley and the start of the high country on two-hour, four-hour, and all-day rides at **Yosemite Valley Stables** (⊠ At entrance to North Pines Campground, 100 yards northeast of Curry Village ☎ 209/372-8348 ⊕ www.yosemitepark.com). You must reserve in advance for the $53, $69, and $96 trips.

### RAFTING

The per-person rental fee at **Curry Village Raft Stand** covers the raft (4- to 6-person), two paddles, and life jackets, plus a shuttle to the launch point on Sentinel Beach. ⊠ *South side of Southside Dr., Curry Village* ☎ *209/372-8319* ⊕ *www.yosemitepark.com* 🚣 *$20.50* ⊙ *Late May-July.*

### ROCK CLIMBING

The one-day basic lesson at **Yosemite Mountaineering School and Guide Service** includes some bouldering and rappelling, and three or four 60-foot climbs. Climbers must be at least 10 (kids under 12 must be accompanied by a parent or guardian) and in reasonably good physical condition. Intermediate and advanced classes include instruction in belays, self-rescue, summer snow climbing, and free climbing. ⊠ *Yosemite Mountain Shop, Curry Village* ☎ *209/372–8344* ⊕ *www. yosemitepark.com* 🎟 *$80–$190* 🕙 *Apr.–Nov.*

### SKIING & SNOWSHOEING

California's first ski resort, **Badger Pass Ski Area** (⊠ Badger Pass Rd., off Glacier Point Rd., 18 mi from Yosemite Valley ☎ 209/372–8430 ☞ 35% beginner, 50% intermediate, 15% advanced. Longest run ³/₁₀ mi, base 7,200 feet, summit, 8,000 feet. Lifts: 5) has 10 downhill runs, 90 mi of groomed cross-country trails, and two excellent ski schools. Free shuttle buses from Yosemite Valley operate during ski season (December–early April, weather permitting). Lift tickets are $38, downhill equipment rents for $24, and snowboard rental with boots is $35. The gentle slopes of Badger Pass make **Yosemite Ski School** (☎ 209/372–8430) an ideal spot for children and beginners to learn downhill skiing or snowboarding for as little as $28 for a group lesson. The highlight of Yosemite's cross-country skiing center is a 21-mi loop from Badger Pass to Glacier Point. You can rent cross-country skis for $21.50 per day at the **Cross-Country Ski School** (☎ 209/372–8444), which also rents snowshoes ($19.50 per day), telemarking equipment ($29), and skate-skis ($24). **Yosemite Mountaineering School** (⊠ Badger Pass Ski Area ☎ 209/ 372–8344 ⊕ www.yosemitepark. com) conducts snowshoeing, cross-country skiing, telemarking, and skate-skiing classes starting at $30.

**37**

trip trek from Happy Isles in one day; if you're planning to do this, remember that the 4,800-foot elevation gain and the 8,842-foot altitude will cause shortness of breath. Another option is to hike to a campground in Little Yosemite Valley near the top of Nevada Fall the first day, then climb to the top of Half Dome and hike out the next day; it's highly recommended that you get your wilderness permit reservations at least a month in advance. Be sure to wear hiking boots and bring gloves. The last pitch up the back of Half Dome is very steep—the only way to climb this sheer rock face is to pull yourself up using the steel cable handrails, which are in place only from late spring to early fall. Those who brave the ascent will be rewarded with an unbeatable view of Yosemite Valley below and the high country beyond. Before heading out, check conditions with rangers, and don't attempt the final ascent if there are any storm clouds overhead. ⊠ *Happy Isles.*

### Horseback Riding

Reservations for guided trail rides must be made in advance at the hotel tour desks or by phone. For overnight saddle trips, which use mules, call ☎ 559/253–5673 on or after September 15 to request a lottery application for the following year. Scenic trail rides range from two hours to a full day; six-day High Sierra saddle trips are also available. For information on tours ⇨ Outfitters & Expeditions box.

### Ice-Skating

Winter visitors have skated at the outdoor **Curry Village ice-skating rink** for decades, and there's no mystery why: it's a kick to glide across the ice while soaking up views of Half Dome and Glacier Point. ⊠ *South side of Southside Dr., Curry Village* ☎ *209/372–8319* ☞ *$6.50 per 2½ hrs, $3.25 skate rental* ☉ *Mid-Nov.–mid-Mar. afternoons and evenings daily, morning sessions weekends.*

### Rafting

Rafting is permitted only on designated areas of the Middle and South Forks of the Merced River. Check with the Valley Visitor Center for closures and other restrictions. For information on equipment ⇨ Outfitters & Expeditions box.

### Rock Climbing

FodorsChoice ★   The granite canyon walls of Yosemite Valley are world-renowned for rock climbing. El Capitan, with its 3,593-foot vertical face, is the most famous and difficult, but there are many other options here for all skill levels. For information on classes ⇨ Outfitters & Expeditions box.

### Skiing & Snowshoeing

The beauty of Yosemite under a blanket of snow has long inspired poets and artists, as well as ordinary folks. Skiing and snowshoeing activities in the park center on Badger Pass Ski Area, California's oldest snow-sports resort, which is about 40 minutes away from the valley on Glacier Point Road. Here you can rent equipment, take a lesson, have lunch, join a guided excursion, and take the free shuttle back to the valley after a drink in the lounge. For information on lessons and equipment ⇨ Outfitters & Expeditions box.

### Swimming

The pools at Curry Village and Yosemite Lodge are open to nonguests. Several swimming holes with small sandy beaches can be found in midsummer along the Merced River at the eastern end of Yosemite Valley. Find gentle waters to swim; currents are often stronger than they appear, and temperatures are chilling. To conserve riparian habitats, step into the river at sandy beaches and other obvious entry points. Do not attempt to swim above or near waterfalls or rapids; fatalities have occurred.

Nonguests can swim in the pool at **Curry Village** (☎ 209/372–8324 ⊕ www.yosemitepark.com) for $2. The pool is open late May–early September.

The pool at **Yosemite Lodge** (☎ 209/372–1250 ⊕ www.yosemitepark.com), open Late May-mid-September, is available to nonguests for $2.

## Educational Offerings

### Classes & Seminars

**Art Classes.** Professional artists conduct workshops in watercolor, etching, drawing, and other mediums. Bring your own materials or purchase the basics at the Art Activity Center, next to the Village Store. Call to verify scheduling. On the Web site, look for Activities, then Fun Park Activities. ⊠ *Art Activity Center, Yosemite Village* ☎ *209/372–1442*

⊕ *www.yosemitepark.com* ▨ *Free* ☉ *Early Apr.–early Oct., Mon.–Sat., 10 AM–2 PM.*

**Yosemite Outdoor Adventures.** Naturalists, scientists, and park rangers lead multi-hour to multiday educational outings on topics from woodpeckers to fire management to pastel painting. Most sessions take place spring through fall, but a few focus on winter phenomena. ⊠ *Various locations* ☎ *209/379–2321* ⊕ *www.yosemite.org* ▨ *$82–$465.*

### Ranger Programs

**Junior Ranger Program.** Children 3–13 can participate in the informal, self-guided Little Cub and Junior Ranger programs. A park activity handbook ($5) is available at the Valley Visitor Center or the Nature Center at Happy Isles; once your child has completed the book, a ranger will present him or her with a certificate and a badge. ⊠ *Valley Visitor Center or The Nature Center at Happy Isles* ☎ *209/372–0299.*

**Ranger-Led Programs.** Rangers lead walks and hikes and give informative and entertaining talks on a range of topics at different locations several times a day from spring through fall. The schedule is reduced in winter, but most days you can usually find a ranger program somewhere in the park. In the evenings at Yosemite Lodge and Curry Village, lectures by rangers, slide shows, and documentary films present unique perspectives on Yosemite. On summer weekends, Camp Curry and Tuolumne Meadows Campground host sing-along campfire programs. There's usually at least one ranger-led activity each night in the Valley; schedules and locations are posted on bulletin boards throughout the park and published in *Yosemite Today.*

### Tours

★ **Ansel Adams Photo Walks.** Photography enthusiasts shouldn't miss these two-hour guided camera walks offered by professional photographers. Some walks are hosted by the Ansel Adams Gallery, others by Delaware North Corporation; meeting points vary. All are free, but participation is limited—call up to 10 days in advance or visit the gallery. In-depth information about the walks can be found at www.anseladams.com. ☎ *209/372–4413 or 800/568–7398* ⊕ *www.yosemitepark.com* ▨ *Free* ⌂ *Reservations essential.*

**Big Trees Tram Tour.** This open-air tram tour of the Mariposa Grove of Big Trees takes one hour. The trip does not include transportation from the Valley to the Grove, so plan to drive or take the shuttle. ☎ *209/372–1240* ▨ *$16* ☉ *Usually June–Oct., depending on snowfall.*

**Glacier Point Tour.** This four-hour trip takes you from Yosemite Valley (you're picked up from your hotel) to the Glacier Point vista, 3,214 feet above the Valley floor. ☎ *209/372–1240* ▨ *$32.50* ⌂ *Reservations essential* ☉ *June–Oct.*

**Grand Tour.** For a full-day tour of the Mariposa Grove and Glacier Point, try the Grand Tour. The tour stops for lunch at the historic Wawona Hotel, but the meal is not included in the tour price. ☎ *209/372–1240* ▨ *$55 ($7 additional for lunch)* ⌂ *Reservations essential* ☉ *June–Thanksgiving.*

37

# Yosemite in Black & White: The Work of Ansel Adams

**WHAT JOHN MUIR DID FOR YOSEMITE** with words, Ansel Adams did with photographs. His photographs have inspired millions of people to visit Yosemite, and his persistent activism has helped to ensure the park's conservation.

Born in 1902, Adams first came to the valley when he was 14, photographing it with a Box Brownie camera. He later said his first visit "was a culmination of experience so intense as to be almost painful. From that day in 1916 my life has been colored and modulated by the great earth gesture of the Sierra." By 1919 he was working in the valley, as custodian of LeConte Memorial Lodge, the Sierra Club headquarters in Yosemite National Park.

Adams had harbored dreams of a career as a concert pianist, but the park sealed his fate as a photographer in 1928, the day he shot "Monolith: The Face of Half Dome," which remains one of his most famous works. Adams also married Virginia Best in 1928, in her father's studio in the valley (now the Ansel Adams Gallery).

As his photographic career took off, Yosemite began to sear itself into the American consciousness. David Brower, first executive director of the Sierra Club, later said of Adams' impact, "That Ansel Adams came to be recognized as one of the great photographers of this century is a tribute to the places that informed him."

In 1934 Adams was elected to the Sierra Club's board of directors; he would serve until 1971. As a representative of the conservation group, he combined his work with the club's mission, showing his photographs of the Sierra to influential officials such as Secretary of the Interior Harold L. Ickes, who showed them to President Franklin Delano Roosevelt. The images were a key factor in the establishment of Kings Canyon National Park.

In 1968, the Department of the Interior granted Adams its highest honor, the Conservation Service Award, and in 1980 he received the Presidential Medal of Freedom in recognition of his conservation work. Until his death in 1984, Adams continued not only to record Yosemite's majesty on film but to urge the federal government and park managers to do right by the park.

In one of his many public pleas on behalf of Yosemite, Adams said, "Yosemite Valley itself is one of the great shrines of the world and—belonging to all our people—must be both protected and appropriately accessible." As an artist and an activist, Adams never gave up on his dream of keeping Yosemite wild yet within reach of every visitor who wants to experience that wildness.

**Moonlight Tour.** A late-evening version of the Valley Floor Tour takes place on moonlit nights, depending on weather conditions. ☎ *209/372–1240* ✉ *$20.50* ⊙ *Apr.–Sept.*

**Tuolumne Meadows Tour.** For a full day's outing to the high country, opt for this ride up Tioga Road to Tuolumne Meadows. You'll stop at several overlooks, and you can connect with another shuttle at Tuolumne Lodge. This service is mostly for hikers and backpackers who want to reach high-country trailheads, but anyone can ride. ☎ *209/372–1240* ✉ *$23* ⌖ *Reservations essential* ⊙ *July–Labor Day.*

**Valley Floor Tour.** Take a 26-mi, two-hour tour of the Valley's highlights, with narration on area history, geology, and plant and animal life. Tour vehicles are either trams or enclosed motor coaches, depending on weather conditions. ☎ *209/372–1240* ✉ *$22* ⊙ *Year-round.*

**Wee Wild Ones.** Designed for kids 6 and under, this 45-minute program includes animal-theme games, songs, stories, and craft activities. The event is held outdoors before the regular Yosemite Lodge or Curry Village evening programs in summer and fall; children gather in daytime before the Ahwahnee's big fireplace in winter and spring. All children must be accompanied by an adult. ☎ *209/372–1240* ✉ *Free.*

## Arts & Entertainment

### Arts Venues
**Yosemite Theater.** Theatrical and musical presentations are offered at various times throughout the year. One of the best-loved is Lee Stetson's portrayal of John Muir in *Conversation with a Tramp, John Muir's Stickeen and Other Fellow Mortals,* and *The Spirit of John Muir.* Tickets should be purchased in advance at the Valley Visitor Center. Unsold seats are available at the door at performance time, 8 PM. ⊠ *Valley Visitor Center auditorium; Yosemite Lodge Theater* ☎ *209/372–0299* ✉ *$8–$10.*

### Entertainment
**Vintage Music of Yosemite.** From spring through fall, a pianist/singer performs four hours of live old-time music at the Wawona Hotel (call for schedule). ⊠ *Wawona Hotel, Rte. 41, Wawona* ☎ *209/375–1425* ✉ *Free* ⊙ *5:30.*

## Shopping

**The Ahwahnee Gift Shop.** Featuring signature Ahwahnee china, jewelry, and Native American crafts, this is the swankiest gift shop in the park. ⊠ *Ahwahnee Hotel* ☎ *209/372–1409.*

**Ansel Adams Gallery.** Here you'll find original photographic and fine art prints, Native American crafts, literature, photography supplies, and camera rentals. ⊠ *Yosemite Village* ☎ *209/372–4413 or 800/568–7398.*

**Habitat Yosemite.** An animal theme permeates this shop, which peddles everything from black bear–patterned socks to mountain lion chocolate bars. ⊠ *Yosemite Village* ☎ *209/372–1253* ⊙ *Nov.–Apr.*

37

**Yosemite Bookstore.** An extensive selection of maps and books is available at this store in the Valley Visitor Center. ⊠ *Yosemite Village* ☎ *209/372–0299.*

**Yosemite Lodge Nature Shop.** Here you'll find sculpture, music, videos, and apparel. ⊠ *Yosemite Lodge, Northside Dr. about ¾ mi west of the visitor center, Yosemite Village* ☎ *209/372–1438.*

**Yosemite Museum Shop.** In addition to books on California's Native Americans, the museum shop sells traditional arts and crafts. ⊠ *Yosemite Village* ☎ *209/372–0295.*

# WHAT'S NEARBY

## Nearby Towns

Marking the southern end of the Sierra's gold-bearing mother lode, **Mariposa** is the last moderate-sized town before you enter Yosemite on Route 140. In addition to a mining museum, Mariposa has numerous shops, restaurants, and service stations. Motels and restaurants dot both sides of Route 41 as it cuts through the town of **Oakhurst,** a boomtown during the Gold Rush that is now a magnet for fast-food restaurants and chain stores. Oakhurst has a population of about 13,000 and sits 15 mi south of the park. The gracious city of **Sonora,** 70 mi west of the park via Routes 120 and 49, retains evidence of its own vibrant, Gold Rush history. Stroll Washington Street and see Old West storefronts with second-story porches and 19th-century hotels. The tiny town of **Lee Vining** is home to the eerily beautiful Mono Lake, where millions of migratory birds nest. You'll pass through Lee Vining if you're coming to Yosemite through the eastern entrance (which is closed in winter). Visit **Mammoth Lakes,** about 40 mi southeast of Yosemite's Tioga Pass entrance, for excellent skiing and snowboarding in winter, with fishing, mountain biking, hiking, and horseback riding in summer. Nine deep-blue lakes form the Mammoth Lakes Basin, and another hundred dot the surrounding countryside. Devils Postpile National Monument sits at the base of Mammoth Mountain.

## Nearby Attractions

★ **Bodie Ghost Town.** Old shacks and shops, abandoned mine shafts, a Methodist church, the mining village of Rattlesnake Gulch, and the remains of a small Chinatown are among the sights at this fascinating ghost town, which sits at an elevation of 8,200 feet. The town boomed from about 1878 to 1881, but by the late 1940s, all its residents had departed. A state park was established in 1962, with a mandate to preserve the town in a state of "arrested decay," but not to restore it. Evidence of Bodie's wild past survives at an excellent museum, and you can tour an old stamp mill (where ore was stamped into fine powder to extract gold and silver) and a ridge that contains many mine sites. No food, drink, or lodging is available in Bodie; the nearest picnic area is ½ mi away. The town is 23 mi from Lee Vining, north on U.S. 395, then east on Route 270; the last 3 mi are unpaved. Snow may close Route 270 late fall through early spring,

# FESTIVALS & EVENTS

NOV.–DEC. **Vintners' Holidays.** Free two- and three-day seminars by California's most prestigious vintners are held midweek in the Great Room of the Ahwahnee Hotel in Yosemite Village and culminate in an elegant—albeit pricey—banquet dinner. Arrive early for seats in the free seminars; book early for lodging and dining packages. ☎ 559/253–5641 ⊕ www.yosemitepark.com.

DEC. **The Bracebridge Dinner.** Held at the Ahwahnee Hotel in Yosemite Village every Christmas since 1928, this 17th-century-themed madrigal dinner is so popular that you must book in mid-May to secure a seat. ☎ 559/252–4848 ⊕ www.yosemitepark.com.

JAN.–FEB. **Chefs' Holidays.** Celebrated chefs present cooking demonstrations and five-course meals at the Ahwahnee Hotel in Yosemite Village on weekends from early January through early February. Special lodging packages are available; space is limited. ☎ 559/253–5641 ⊕ www.yosemitepark.com.

MAY **Fireman's Muster.** North of Sonora in the old mining town of Columbia, history springs to life at this festival of antique fire engines, with hose-spraying contests and a parade of the old pumpers. ☎ 209/536–1672. **Mother Lode Roundup Parade and Rodeo.** On Mother's Day weekend the town of Sonora celebrates its gold-mining, agricultural, and lumbering heritage with a parade, rodeo, entertainment, and food. ☎ 209/532–7428 or 800/446–1333.

JULY **Mammoth Lakes Jazz Jubilee.** This festival, founded in 1989, is hosted by the local Temple of Folly Jazz Band and takes place in 10 venues, most with dance floors. ☎ 760/934–2478 or 800/367–6572 ⊕ www.mammothjazz.org. **Mother Lode Fair.** Sonora was settled by miners from Mexico, and the town has never forgotten its gold-mining roots. This fair at Mother Lode Fairgrounds celebrates this unique time in California history. ☎ 209/532–7428 or 800/446–1333.

AUG. **Bluesapalooza.** For one long weekend every summer, Mammoth Lakes hosts a blues and beer festival—with an emphasis on the beer tasting. ☎ 760/934–0606 or 800/367–6572 ⊕ www.mammothmountain.com.

OCT. **Sierra Art Trails.** The work of more than 100 artists is on display in studios and galleries throughout eastern Madera and Mariposa counties. Purchase the catalog of locations and hours at area shops. ☎ 559/658–8844 ⊕ www.sierraarttrails.org. **Oakhurst Fall Chocolate and Wine Festival.** Dessert judging, vendor booths, a beauty pageant, and more celebrate the glories of the world's most beloved sweet. ☎ 559/683–1993 ⊕ www.wildwonderfulwomen.net.

37

but you can ski the 13 mi from the highway to the park. ✉ *Main and Green Sts., Bodie* ☎ *760/647–6445* 🎫 *Park $2; museum free* ☉ *Park: Memorial Day–Labor Day, daily 8–7; Sept.–May, daily 8–4. Museum: Memorial Day–Labor Day, daily 9–6; Sept.–May, hrs vary.*

**California State Mining and Mineral Museum.** Displays on Gold Rush history here include a faux hard-rock mine shaft, a miniature stamp mill, and a 13-pound chunk of crystallized gold. ✉ *Mariposa County Fairgrounds, Mariposa* ☎ *209/742–7625* ⊕ *www.parks.ca.gov* 🎫 *$3* ☉ *May–Sept., daily 10–6; Oct.–Apr., Wed.–Mon. 10–4.*

★ **Devils Postpile National Monument.** East of Mammoth Lakes lies this rock formation of smooth, vertical basalt columns sculpted by volcanic and glacial forces. A short, steep trail winds to the top of the 60-foot cliff for a bird's-eye view of the columns. Follow Route 203 west from U.S. 395 to Mammoth Mountain Ski Area to board the shuttle bus to the monument, which you must take if you are a day-use visitor entering the monument between 7:30 AM and 5:30 PM mid-June through early September. A 2-mi hike past Devils Postpile leads to the monument's second scenic wonder, **Rainbow Falls,** where a branch of the San Joaquin River plunges more than 100 feet over a lava ledge. When the water hits the pool below, sunlight turns the resulting mist into a spray of color. Scenic picnic spots dot the banks of the river. ✉ *Minaret Rd., Mammoth Lakes* ☎ *760/934–2289, 760/934–0606 shuttle* ⊕ *www.nps.gov/depo* 🎫 *$7* ☉ *Mid-June–Oct., 24 hrs.*

**Hot Creek Geologic Site.** Forged by an ancient volcanic eruption, the Hot Creek Geologic Site is a landscape of boiling hot springs, fumaroles, and geysers about 10 mi southeast of the town of Mammoth Lakes. You can walk along boardwalks through the canyon to view the steaming volcanic features. Fly-fishing for trout is popular upstream from the springs. En route to Hot Creek Geologic Site is the **Hot Creek Fish Hatchery,** the breeding ponds for most of the fish (3–5 million annually) the state uses to stock eastern Sierra lakes and rivers. ✉ *Hot Creek Hatchery Rd. east of U.S. 395, Mammoth Lakes* ☎ *760/934–2664* 🎫 *Free* ☉ *June–Oct., daily 8–4, depending on snowfall.* ✉ *Hot Creek Hatchery Rd. east of U.S. 395, Mammoth Lakes* ☎ *760/924–5500* 🎫 *Free* ☉ *Daily sunrise–sunset.*

★ **Mono Lake.** Since the 1940s the city of Los Angeles has diverted water from the streams that feed this lake, lowering its water level and exposing striking towers of tufa, or calcium carbonate. Court victories by environmentalists have forced a reduction of the diversions, and the lake is rising again. Millions of migratory birds nest in and around Mono Lake. If you join the naturalist-guided **South Tufa Walk,** bring your binoculars. Tours depart the South Tufa parking lot 5 mi east of U.S. 395 on Route 120 and last about 1½ hours. ☎ *760/647–3044* ⊕ *www.monolake.org* 🎫 *$3* ☉ *Weekends 1 pm.* ✉ *South of Lee Vining on U.S. 395.*

**Railtown 1897.** Have a look at the roundhouse, turntable, shop rooms and old locomotives and rail cars at this site, which is operated by the California State Railroad Museum. A steam train makes 40-minute journeys on weekends April through October. ✉ *5th Ave. and Reser-*

*voir Rd., Jamestown* ☎ *209/984–3953* ⊕ *www.csrmf.org* ✉ *Tour $2;*
*train ride $6* ⊙ *Daily 9:30–4:30.*

**Yosemite Mountain–Sugar Pine Railroad.** Travel back to a time when powerful locomotives hauled massive log trains through the Sierra. This
4-mi, narrow-gauge, steam-powered railroad excursion takes you near
Yosemite's south gate; there's also a moonlight special, with dinner and
entertainment. Take Route 41 south from Yosemite about 8 mi to the
departure point. ✉ *56001 Rte. 41, Fish Camp* ☎ *559/683–7273*
⊕ *www.ymsprr.com* ✉ *$13–$36.50* ⊙ *Mar.–Oct., daily.*

## Area Activities

### Sports & the Outdoors

BOATING &
RAFTING
**Bass Lake Water Sports and Marina**
(☎ 559/642–3565), on the Bass
Lake Reservoir, 3 mi north and 6
mi east of Oakhurst, rents ski boats,
patio boats, and fishing boats. In
summer, the noisy reservoir is
packed shortly after 8 AM, when it
opens. There's also a restaurant
and snack bar.

**Zephyr Whitewater Expeditions**
(☎ 800/431–3636 ⊕ www.zrafting.
com), in Columbia, conducts half-
day to three-day white-water trips
on the Tuolumne, Merced, and
American rivers for paddlers of all
experience levels.

HIKING, ROCK
CLIMBING &
MOUNTAINEERING
**Southern Yosemite Mountain Guides**
(☎ 831/459–8735 or 800/231–
4575 ⊕ www.symg.com) leads multiday adventure trips into the southern High Sierra backcountry.

SKIING
★
**Mammoth Mountain** (✉ Rte. 203 off U.S. 395, Mammoth Lakes ☎ 800/
626–6684 ⊕ www.mammothmountain.com), one of the nation's premier ski resorts, offers more than 3,500 acres of skiable boulevards,
canyons, and bowls, and a 3,100-foot vertical drop. Ski season starts
in November and can run through June. There's a ski school, cross-country trails, snowboarding, snowmobiling, and dogsledding. You can rent
or buy equipment. The resort has extensive lodging, dining, and shopping options in the Village at Mammoth.

---

**FAMILY PICKS**

- Rent a boat, splash around in
the water, and watch bald eagles
teach their young how to fish at
**Bass Lake Recreation Area.**

- Wander once-bustling Gold
Rush streets and peer into sa-
loons and miners' shacks at
**Bodie Ghost Town.**

- Listen to the vintage steam engine huff and puff as you ride
into logging history on the narrow-gauge **Yosemite Mountain
Sugar Pine Railroad.**

- Schuss through **Mammoth
Mountain** powder, then warm
up with a hot chocolate.

**37**

---

# WHERE TO STAY & EAT

### About the Restaurants

For the most part, food service in Yosemite is geared toward handling
a large number of visitors—that is, it's often fast, plain, and sometimes
not very good. The three notable exceptions are the full-service dining

rooms at the Ahwanee, Wawona, and Yosemite Lodge at the Falls, which strive to present imaginative American dishes prepared with fresh—often local and organic—ingredients. Spring through fall, it's a good idea to make dinner reservations. All food concessions are run by the Delaware North Corporation.

Outside the park, the situation is much the same, with casual dining the rule and exceptional food the rarity. Typical American cuisine predominates, with dashes of Mexican, Italian, and Asian thrown in. Except at the higher-end spots, reservations are generally not necessary, although they're advisable on weekends in season.

## About the Hotels

Lodgings in Yosemite range from canvas tent-cabins without heat or bath to luxury suites with room service. All have lovely, if not spectacular, settings, though those in the valley are far from peaceful in summer. In season, rooms of any description are expensive and hard to come by; if you can, make your reservations a year in advance—call the day your chosen dates open for booking. All lodging concessions, except Redwoods Guest Cottages, are run by Delaware North Corporation.

Out-of-park lodgings get busier and pricier the closer you get to Yosemite. These run the gamut from the humblest of motel rooms to moderately fancy, or charmingly wholesome, resorts. Prices rise to painfully high levels in season, but you'll find great bargains when the crowds leave. You can generally find a room near the park, but if you don't book ahead you might not land choice accomodations.

## About the Campgrounds

Camping in Yosemite is the most popular lodging choice; it's relatively inexpensive, and it can be a great outdoor experience. The park has lots of camping sites (nearly 2,000 in summer, 400 year-round), and though none have RV hookups, they fill up quickly, especially in the Valley. Near the park are a number of appealing, readily accessible campgrounds for tents and RVs. Most get very busy in fine weather, and many don't accept reservations.

All campgrounds listed here are front-country spots you can reach with a car. The park's backcountry and the surrounding wilderness have some unforgettable campsites that can be reached only via long and often difficult hikes or horseback rides. Delaware North Corporation operates five High Sierra Camps with comfortable, furnished tent cabins in the remote reaches of Yosemite; rates include breakfast and dinner service. The park concessionaire books the extremely popular backcountry camps by lottery each December for the following late June to early September season. Phone ☎ 559/253–5674 for more information.

Overnight hiking is restricted in Yosemite's backcountry to limit human impact on natural areas, and you'll need a wilderness permit to camp there. It's a good idea to make reservations for wilderness permits, especially if you visit May through September. (Note that making a request for a reservation does not guarantee you'll get one.) You can reserve two days to 24 weeks in advance by calling ☎ 209/372–0740, logging on to ⊕ www.nps.gov/yose/wilderness, or by writing to Wilderness Permits, Box 545, Yosemite, 95389. Include your name, address, daytime phone, the number of people in your party, trip date, alternative dates, starting and ending trailheads, and a brief itinerary. There's a $5 per person processing fee for reservations; permits are free if obtained in person at wilderness permit offices at Big Oak Flat, Hetch Hetchy, Tuolumne, Wawona, the Wilderness Center, and Yosemite Valley in summer; fall through spring, visit the Valley Visitor Center.

## Where to Eat

### In the Park

In addition to the dining options listed here, you'll find fast-food grills and cafeterias, plus temporary snack bars, hamburger stands, and pizza joints lining park roads in summer. Many dining facilities in the park are open summer only.

**$$$–$$$$**
Fodor'sChoice
★
✕ **Ahwahnee Hotel Dining Room.** This is the most dramatic dining room in Yosemite, if not California. The massive room has a 34-foot ceiling supported by immense sugar-pine beams, and floor-to-ceiling windows. In the evening, everything glows with candlelight. Specialties on the often-changing menu highlight sustainable, organic produce and include salmon, duckling, and prime rib. Collared shirts and long pants (no jeans) are required for men at dinner. ⊠ *Ahwahnee Hotel, Ahwahnee Rd., about ¾ mi east of Yosemite Valley Visitor Center, Yosemite Village* ☎ *209/ 372–1489* ⌂ *Reservations essential. $21–$38* ▭ *AE, D, DC, MC, V.*

★ **$$–$$$** ✕ **Mountain Room.** Though remarkably good, the food becomes secondary when you see Yosemite Falls through this dining room's wall of windows—almost every table has a view. The chef makes a point of using locally sourced, organic ingredients, so you can be assured of fresh salad and veggies here. Grilled trout and salmon, steak, pasta, and several children's dishes are also on the menu. ⊠ *Yosemite Lodge, North-side Dr. about ¾ mi west of the visitor center, Yosemite Village* ☎ *209/ 372–1281* ⌂ *Reservations essential. $18–$30* ▭ *AE, D, DC, MC, V* ⊘ *No lunch.*

**$$–$$$** ✕ **Tuolumne Meadows Lodge.** Adjacent to the Tuolumne River under a giant tent canopy, this restaurant serves hearty American fare at breakfast and dinner. ⊠ *Tioga Rd. (Rte. 120)* ☎ *209/372–8413* ⌂ *Reservations essential. $13–$22* ▭ *AE, D, DC, MC, V* ⊘ *No lunch. Closed late Sept.–Memorial Day.*

★ **$$–$$$** ✕ **Wawona Hotel Dining Room.** Watch deer graze on the meadow while you dine in the romantic, candlelit dining room of the whitewashed Wawona Hotel, which dates from the late 1800s. The American-style cuisine favors fresh California ingredients and flavors; trout is a menu staple. There's also a Sunday brunch Easter through Thanksgiving, and a barbeque on the lawn Saturday evenings in summer. A jacket is required at dinner. ⊠ *Wawona Hotel, Rte. 41, Wawona* ☎ *209/375–1425* ⌂ *Reservations essential. $17–$27* ▭ *AE, D, DC, MC, V* ⊘ *Closed Jan. and Feb.*

**$–$$** ✕ **Pavillion Buffet.** Come to this Curry Village restaurant for a hot, cafeteria-style meal. Bring your tray outside to the deck, and take in the views of the Valley's granite walls. ⊠ *Curry Village* ☎ *209/372–8303. $12–$15* ▭ *AE, D, DC, MC, V* ⊘ *No lunch. Closed mid-Oct.–mid-Apr.*

**37**

**$–$$** ✕ **White Wolf Lodge.** This high-country historic lodge's casual, rustic dining room fills up at breakfast and dinner. The short menu offers good, creative meat-and-potato meals. Takeout is offered at lunchtime. ⊠ *Tioga Rd. (Rte. 120), 45 minutes west of Tuolumne Meadows and 30 minutes east of Crane Flat* ☎ 209/372–8416 ⌂ *Reservations essential. $12–$20* ▤ *AE, D, DC, MC, V* ☉ *Closed late Sept.–June.*

**¢–$$** ✕ **Food Court at Yosemite Lodge.** Fast and convenient, the food court serves simple fare, ranging from hamburgers and pizzas to pastas, carved roasted meats, and salads at lunch and dinner. There's also a selection of beer and wine. At breakfast, you can get pancakes and eggs made any way you like. An espresso and smoothie bar near the entrance keeps longer hours. ⊠ *Yosemite Lodge, about ¾ mi west of the visitor center, Yosemite Village* ☎ 209/372–1265. *$5–$15* ▤ *AE, D, DC, MC, V.*

**¢–$** ✕ **Tuolumne Meadows Grill.** Serving continuously throughout the day until 5 or 6 PM, this fast-food grill cooks up breakfast, lunch, and snacks. Stop in for a quick meal before exploring the Meadows. ⊠ *Tioga Rd. (Rte. 120), 1½ mi east of Tuolumne Meadows Visitor Center* ☎ 209/372–8426. *$3–$10* ▤ *AE, D, DC, MC, V* ☉ *Closed Oct.–Memorial Day.*

**¢–$** ✕ **The Village Grill.** This family-friendly eatery in Yosemite Village serves hamburgers and grilled sandwiches from a counter. Take your tray out to the deck and enjoy your meal under the trees. ⊠ *100 yards east of Yosemite Valley Visitor Center, Yosemite Village* ☎ 209/372–1207. *$5–$9* ▤ *AE, D, DC, MC, V* ☉ *No breakfast, no dinner after 5 PM. Closed Oct.–May.*

PICNIC AREAS. Ready-made picnic lunches are available at Ahwahnee and Wawona with advance notice. Otherwise, stop at the Food Court at Yosemite Lodge for a pre-packaged salad or sandwich, or at grocery stores in the village to pick up supplies. There are 13 designated picnic areas around the park; restrooms and grills or fire grates are available only at those in the valley. Outside the valley, there are picnic areas at Cascades Falls, Glacier Point, Lembert Dome, Mariposa Grove, Wawona, Tenaya Lake, and Yosemite Creek.

**Cathedral Beach** is on Southside Drive underneath spire-like Cathedral Rocks. There are usually fewer people here than at the eastern end of the valley. No drinking water.

Tucked behind the Ahwahnee Hotel, **Church Bowl** nearly abuts the granite walls below the Royal Arches. If you're walking from the village with your supplies, this is the shortest trek to a picnic area. No drinking water.

At the western end of the valley on Northside Drive, the **El Capitan** picnic area has great views straight up the giant granite wall above. No drinking water.

On Southside Drive, **Sentinel Beach** is right alongside a running creek and the Merced River. The area is usually crowded in season. No drinking water.

East of Sentinel Beach on Southside Drive, **Swinging Bridge** is the name of a little wooden footbridge that crosses the Merced River, just past the picnic area. No drinking water.

Right next to Sentinel Beach on Southside Drive, **Yellow Pine** is named for the towering trees that cluster on the banks of the Merced River. No drinking water. No restroom.

## Outside the Park

**$$$$**
Fodor'sChoice
★
✕ **Erna's Elderberry House.** Erna Kubin, the grande dame of Château du Sureau (⇨ Where to Stay), has created a culinary oasis, stunning for its understated elegance, gorgeous setting, and impeccable service. Red walls and dark beams accent the dining room's high ceilings, and arched windows reflect the glow of candles. The seasonal six-course prix-fixe dinner can be paired with superb wines. When the waitstaff places all the plates on the table in perfect synchronicity, you'll know this will be a meal to remember. A small bistro menu is also served in the former wine cellar. ⊠ *48688 Victoria La., Oakhurst* ☎ *559/683–6800* ✍ *Reservations essential. $92* ▭ *AE, D, MC, V* ⊗ *No lunch Mon.–Sat.*

**$$–$$$$** ✕ **The Mogul.** This longtime steak house serves great prime rib, charbroiled shrimp, grilled beef, and fresh fish. There are no surprises here, just hearty, straightforward American food. Dinners come with soup or salad, and you won't leave hungry. There's also a kids' menu. ⊠ *1528 Mammoth Tavern Rd., off Old Mammoth Rd., Mammoth Lakes* ☎ *760/934–3039. $15–$35* ▭ *AE, D, MC, V* ⊗ *No lunch.*

**$$–$$$** ✕ **Nevados.** You can't go wrong at Nevados. The top choice of many locals, it serves contemporary California cuisine that draws from European and Asian cooking. The menu presents imaginative—though accessible—preparations of seafood, duck, veal, beef, and game. Everything is made in-house, and there's an excellent three-course prix-fixe menu. The atmosphere is convivial, and the bar is always bustling. ⊠ *3950 Main St. at Minaret Rd., Mammoth Lakes* ☎ *760/934–4466* ✍ *Reservations essential. $19–$26* ▭ *AE, D, DC, MC, V* ⊗ *Closed early June and late Oct.–early Nov. No lunch.*

**$$–$$$** ✕ **Ocean Sierra Restaurant.** Deep in the woods about 14 mi southeast of Mariposa, this comfortable spot serves seafood, meat, pasta, and vegetarian dishes. The owner-chef uses produce from her own garden, including the delicate crystallized rose petals that top desserts offerings—which include five different flavors of crème brûlée. From Route 49 south, take Triangle Road 2½ mi northeast. ⊠ *3292 E. Westfall Rd., Mariposa* ☎ *209/742–7050. $18–$26* ▭ *D, MC, V* ⊗ *Closed Mon.–Thurs. No lunch.*

**$–$$$** ✕ **Iron Door Grill.** If you're coming into Yosemite via Route 120, you'll pass by the Iron Door, one of the oldest operating saloons in California. Stop in for a drink. If you head next door to the grill, order something simple, such as steak or a buffalo burger—skip the fancier dishes. The saloon also has live music Friday and Saturday night. ⊠ *18751 Main St. (Rte. 120), Groveland* ☎ *209/962–6244. $10–$23* ▭ *MC, V.*

**$–$$** ✕ **Banny's Café.** A calm, pleasant environment, and hearty yet refined dishes make Banny's an attractive alternative to Sonora's noisier eateries. Try the grilled salmon fillet with scallion rice and ginger-wasabi aioli. The burgers are great, too. ⊠ *83 S. Stewart St., Sonora* ☎ *209/533–4709. $12–$15* ▭ *D, MC, V* ⊗ *No lunch Sun.*

**$–$$** ✕ **Nicely's.** Pictures of local attractions decorate this diner, which has been around since 1965 (check out the vintage signage on the street).

37

Order the blueberry pancakes and homemade sausages at breakfast. For lunch or dinner, try the chicken-fried steak or the fiesta salad. There's also a kids' menu. ⊠ *U.S. 395 and 4th St., Lee Vining* ☎ *760/647–6477. $9–$15* ▭ *MC, V* ☿ *Closed Wed. in winter.*

★ **$–$$** ✕ **Tioga Gas Mart & Whoa Nelli Deli.** This might be the only gas station in the United States that serves cocktails, but its appeal goes way beyond novelty. The mahimahi tacos are succulent, the gourmet pizzas tasty, and the herb-crusted pork loin with berry glaze elegant. Order at the counter and grab a seat inside or out. ⊠ *Rte. 120 and U.S. 395, Lee Vining* ☎ *760/647–1088. $10–$15* ▭ *AE, MC, V* ☿ *Closed mid-Nov.–mid.-Apr.*

## Where to Stay

### In the Park

Reserve your room or cabin in Yosemite as far in advance as possible—you can make a reservation up to a year before your arrival (within minutes after the reservation office makes a date available, the Ahwahnee, Yosemite Lodge, and Wawona Hotel often sell out their weekends, holiday periods, and all days between May and September). Almost all reservations for lodging in Yosemite are made through the concessionaire, **Delaware North Corporation.** ⊠ *6771 N. Palm Ave., Fresno, CA 93704* ☎ *559/252–4848* ⊕ *www.yosemitepark.com.*

**$$$–$$$$** ▤ **Redwoods Guest Cottages.** The only lodging in the park not operated by Delaware North Corporation, this collection of individually owned cabins and homes in the Wawona area is a great alternative to the over-crowded Valley. Fully furnished cabins range from small, romantic one-bedroom units to bright, resort-like, six-bedroom houses with decks overlooking the river. Most have fireplaces, TVs, and phones. The property rarely fills up, even in summer, so it's a good choice for last-minute lodging; there's a two-night minimum in the off-season and a three-night minimum in summer. ⊠ *8038 Chilnualna Falls Rd., off Rte. 41, Wawona* ☎ *209/375–6666* ▤ *209/375–6400* ⊕ *www.redwoodsinyosemite. com* ➭ *130 units* ⚬ *Kitchens, some in-room VCRs, some pets allowed, no-smoking rooms, no a/c (some), no phones (some), no TV (some). $178–$636* ▭ *AE, D, MC, V.*

**$–$$** ▤ **Curry Village.** Opened in 1899 as a place where travelers could enjoy the beauty of Yosemite for a modest price, Curry Village has plain accommodations: standard motel rooms, cabins, and tent cabins, which have rough wood frames, canvas walls, and roofs. The tent cabins are a step up from camping, with linens and blankets provided (maid service upon request). Some have heat. Most of the cabins share shower and toilet facilities. ⊠ *South side of Southside Dr., Yosemite Valley* ⌁ *Delaware North Reservations, 6771 N. Palm Ave., Fresno 93704* ☎ *559/252–4848* ⊕ *www.yosemitepark.com* ➭ *18 rooms; 183 cabins, 103 with bath; 427 tent cabins* ⚬ *3 restaurants, snack bar, pool, bicycles, bar, no-smoking rooms, no a/c, no phone, no TV. $75–$113* ▭ *AE, D, DC, MC, V.*

**$–$$** ▤ **White Wolf Lodge.** Set in a subalpine meadow, this tiny lodge offers rustic accommodations in tent cabins that share nearby baths or in wooden cabins with baths. This is an excellent base camp for hiking the backcountry. Breakfast and dinner are served in the snug, white main building. ☒ *Off Tioga Rd. (Rte. 120), 45 minutes west of Tuolumne Meadows and 30 minutes east of Crane Flat* ☼ *Delaware North Reservations, 6771 N. Palm Ave., Fresno 93704* ☎ *559/252–4848* ⚲ *24 tent cabins, 4 cabins* ♨ *Restaurant, no a/c, no phone, no TV. $82–$105* ▤ *AE, D, DC, MC, V* ☽ *Closed mid-Sept.–early June.*

**$$$$**
Fodor'sChoice
★
✕🖾 **The Ahwahnee.** This grand 1920s-era mountain lodge, a National Historic Landmark, is constructed of rocks and sugar-pine logs. Guest rooms have Native American design motifs; public spaces are decorated with art deco detailing, oriental rugs, and elaborate iron- and woodwork. Some luxury hotel amenities, including turndown service and guest bathrobes, are standard here. The Dining Room ($$$–$$$$, reservations essential) is by far the most impressive restaurant in the park, and one of the most beautiful rooms in California. If you stay in a cottage room, be aware that each cottage has multiple guest rooms. Each of the cushy cottages contains two nonadjoining guest rooms with ensuite bath. ☒ *Ahwahnee Rd., about ¾ mi east of Yosemite Valley Visitor Center, Yosemite Village Ahwahnee Rd. north of Northside Dr., Yosemite Village* ☼ *Delaware North Reservations, 6771 N. Palm Ave., Fresno 93704* ☎ *559/252–4848* ⊕ *www.yosemitepark.com* ⚲ *99 lodge rooms, 4 suites, 24 cottage rooms* ♨ *Restaurant, room service, refrigerator, Wi-Fi, tennis court, pool, bar, concierge, no a/c (some). $393* ▤ *AE, D, DC, MC, V.*

**$$–$$$**
✕🖾 **Wawona Hotel.** This 1879 National Historic Landmark sits at Yosemite's southern end, near the Mariposa Grove of Big Trees. It's an old-fashioned New England–style estate, with whitewashed buildings, wraparound verandas, and pleasant, no-frills rooms decorated with period pieces. About half the rooms share bathrooms; those that do come equipped with robes. The romantic, candlelit dining room ($$–$$$) lies across the lobby from the cozy Victorian parlor, which has a fireplace, board games, and a piano, where a pianist plays ragtime most evenings. ☒ *Hwy. 41, Wawona* ☼ *Delaware North Reservations, 6771 N. Palm Ave., Fresno 93704* ☎ *559/252–4848* ⊕ *www.yosemitepark.com* ⚲ *104 rooms, 50 with bath* ♨ *Restaurant, golf course, tennis court, pool, bar, no a/c, no phone, no TV. $126–$183* ▤ *AE, D, DC, MC, V* ☽ *Closed Jan. and Feb.*

**$$–$$$**
✕🖾 **Yosemite Lodge at the Falls.** This lodge near Yosemite Falls, which dates from 1915, looks like a 1960s motel-resort complex, with numerous brown, 2-story buildings tucked beneath the trees around large parking lots. Motel-style rooms have two double beds, and larger rooms also have dressing areas and patios or balconies. A few have views of the falls. Of the lodge's eateries, the Mountain Room Restaurant ($$–$$$) is the most formal. The cafeteria-style Food Court (¢–$) serves three meals a day. Many park tours depart from the main building. ☒ *Northside Dr. about ¾ mi west of the visitor center, Yosemite Village* ☼ *Delaware North Reservations, 6771 N. Palm Ave., Fresno 93704* ☎ *559/252–4848* ⊕ *www.yosemitepark.com* ⚲ *245 rooms* ♨ *Restaurant, Wi-Fi, pool, bicycles, bar, no-smoking rooms, no a/c. $113–$170* ▤ *AE, D, DC, MC, V.*

CAMPGROUNDS &
RV PARKS
Reservations are required at most of Yosemite's campgrounds, especially in summer. You can reserve a site up to five months in advance; book-

37

ings made more than 21 days in advance require prepayment. Unless otherwise noted, book your site through the central National Park Service reservations office. **National Park Reservation Service** ⊕ *Box 1600, Cumberland, MD 21502* ☎ *800/436–7275* ⊕ *http://reservations.nps. gov* ☐ *D, MC, V* ⊘ *Daily 7–7.*

**$$$$** ⛺ **Housekeeping Camp.** Set along the Merced River, these three-sided concrete units with canvas roofs may look a bit rustic, but they're good for travelers with RVs or those without a tent who want to camp. You can cook here on gas stoves rented from the front desk, or you can use the fire pits. Toilets and showers are in a central building, and there is a camp store for provisions. ⊠ *Southside Dr., ½ mi west of Curry Village* ⊕ *Delaware North Reservations, 6771 N. Palm Ave., Fresno 93704* ☎ *209/372–8338, 559/252–4848 reservations* ⊕ *www.yosemitepark. com* ⥲ *266 units* ⌂ *Laundry facilities, no a/c, no room phones, no room TVs. $72* ☐ *AE, D, DC, MC, V* ⊘ *Closed early Oct.–late Apr.*

**$$** ⛺ **Crane Flat.** This camp on Yosemite's western boundary, south of Hodgdon Meadow, is just 17 mi from the valley but far from its bustle. A small grove of sequoias is nearby. ⊠ *From Big Oak Flat entrance on Hwy. 120, drive 10 mi east to campground entrance on right* ☎ *800/ 436–7275 or 209/372–0265* ⊟ *209/372–0371* ⊕ *http://reservations. nps. gov* ⥲ *166 sites (tent or RV)* ⌂ *Flush toilets, drinking water, bear boxes, fire pits, picnic tables, general store, ranger station* ⊘ *Reservations essential. $20* ☐ *AE, D, MC, V* ⊘ *June–Sept.*

**$$** ⛺ **Hodgdon Meadow.** On the park's western boundary, at an elevation of about 4,900 feet, the vegetation here is similar to that in the valley— but there's no river and no development. Reservations are essential May through September. ⊠ *From Big Oak Flat entrance on Hwy. 120, immediately turn left to campground* ☎ *800/436–7275 or 209/372–0265* ⊟ *209/372–0371* ⊕ *http://reservations.nps.gov* ⥲ *105 sites (tent or RV)* ⌂ *Grills, flush toilets, drinking water, bear boxes, picnic tables, ranger station. $20* ☐ *AE, D, MC, V.*

**$$** ⛺ **Lower Pines.** This moderate-size campground sits directly along the Merced River; it's a short walk to the trailheads for the Mirror Lake and Mist trails. Expect small sites and lots of people. ⊠ *At east end of valley* ☎ *800/436–7275 or 209/372–0265* ⊟ *209/372–0371* ⊕ *http://reservations.nps.gov* ⥲ *60 sites (tent or RV)* ⌂ *Flush toilets, drinking water, bear boxes, fire grates, picnic tables, public telephone, ranger station, swimming (river)* ⊘ *Reservations essential. $20* ☐ *AE, D, MC, V* ⊘ *Mar.–Oct.*

**$$** ⛺ **North Pines.** Set along the Merced River at an elevation of 4,000 feet, this campground is near many trailheads. Sites are close together, and there is little privacy. ⊠ *At east end of valley, near Curry Village* ☎ *800/ 436–7275 or 209/372–0265* ⊕ *http://reservations.nps.gov* ⥲ *80 sites (tent or RV)* ⌂ *Flush toilets, drinking water, showers, bear boxes, fire grates, picnic tables, ranger station, swimming (river)* ⊘ *Reservations essential. $20* ☐ *AE, D, MC, V* ⊘ *Apr.–Sept.*

**$$** ⛺ **Tuolumne Meadows.** In a wooded area at 8,600 feet, just south of its namesake meadow, this is one of the most spectacular and sought-after campgrounds in Yosemite. Hot showers can be used at the Tuolumne Meadows Lodge—though only at certain strictly regulated times. Half the sites are first-come, first-served, so arrive early or make reservations.

Fodor'sChoice
★

The campground is open July–September. ⊠ *Hwy. 120, 46 mi east of Big Oak Flat entrance station* ☎ *209/372–0265 or 800/436–7275* 🖨 *209/372–0371* ⊕ *http://reservations.nps.gov* 🛏 *314 sites (tent or RV)* ⚱ *Flush toilets, dump station, drinking water, bear boxes, fire grates, picnic tables, public telephone, general store, ranger station. $20* ▤ *AE, D, MC, V* ☽ *July–Sept.*

**$$** 🏕 **Upper Pines.** This is the valley's largest campground, and the closest one to the trailheads. Expect large crowds in the summer—and little privacy. ⊠ *At east end of valley, near Curry Village* ☎ *800/436–7275* ⊕ *http://reservations.nps.gov* 🛏 *238 sites (tent or RV)* ⚱ *Flush toilets, dump station, drinking water, showers, bear boxes, fire grates, picnic tables, public telephone, ranger station, swimming (river)* 🛏 *Reservations essential. $20* ▤ *AE, D, MC, V* ☽ *Year-round.*

**$$** 🏕 **Wawona.** Near the Mariposa Grove, just downstream from a popular fishing spot, this year-round campground (reservations essential May–September) has larger, less densely packed sites than campgrounds in the valley, located right by the river. The downside is that it's an hour's drive to the valley's major attractions. ⊠ *Hwy. 41, 1 mi north of Wawona* ☎ *209/372–0265 or 800/436–7275* 🖨 *209/372–0371* ⊕ *http://reservations.nps.gov* 🛏 *93 sites (tent or RV)* ⚱ *Flush toilets, dump station, drinking water, bear boxes, fire grates, picnic tables, ranger station, swimming (river). $20* ▤ *AE, D, MC, V* ☽ *Year-round.*

**$** 🏕 **Bridalveil Creek.** This campground sits among lodgepole pines at 7,200 feet, above the valley on Glacier Point Road. From here, you can easily drive to Glacier Point's magnificent valley views. Fall evenings can be quite cold. ⊠ *From Hwy. 41 in Wawona, go north to Glacier Point Rd. and turn right; entrance to campground is 25 mi ahead on right side* ☎ *209/372–0265* 🖨 *209/372–0371* ⊕ *www.nps.gov/yose* 🛏 *74 sites (tent or RV)* ⚱ *Grills, flush toilets, drinking water, bear boxes, picnic tables, public telephone* 🛏 *Reservations not accepted. $14* ▤ *AE, D, MC, V* ☽ *July–early Sept.*

**$** 🏕 **Porcupine Flat.** Sixteen miles west of Tuolumne Meadows, this campground sits at 8,100 feet. Sites are close together, but if you want to be in the high country and Tuolumne Meadows is full, this is a good bet. There is no water available. ⊠ *16 mi west of Tuolumne Meadows on Hwy. 120* ☎ *209/372–0265* 🖨 *209/372–0371* ⊕ *www.nps.gov/yose* 🛏 *52 sites (tent or RV up to 35 feet)* ⚱ *Pit toilets, bear boxes, fire pits, picnic tables* 🛏 *Reservations not accepted. $10* ▤ *AE, D, MC, V* ☽ *July–mid-Oct.*

**$** 🏕 **Tamarack Flat.** This rather primitive campground sits in a forested area at an elevation of 6,300 feet, with lodgepole pines, red firs, and some cedars. There's no water, and only small RVs (up to 24 feet) are allowed. ⊠ *From Big Oak Flat entrance station, turn left on Tioga Rd. (Hwy. 120); 3 mi ahead turn right to enter campground, 2½ mi from Tioga Rd.* ☎ *209/372–0265* 🖨 *209/372–0371* ⊕ *www.nps.gov/yose* 🛏 *52 sites (tent or RV)* ⚱ *Pit toilets, bear boxes, fire grates, picnic tables* 🛏 *Reservations not accepted. $10* ▤ *No credit cards* ☽ *June–early Sept.*

★ **$** 🏕 **White Wolf.** Set in the beautiful high country at 8,000 feet, this is a prime spot for hikers. RVs up to 27 feet long are permitted. ⊠ *From Big Oak Flat entrance, go 15 mi east on Tioga Road (Hwy. 120); camp-*

**37**

*ground is on right* ☎ *209/372–0265* 🖷 *209/372–0371* ⊕ *www.nps.gov/ yose* ⟊ *87 sites (tent or RV)* ⚴ *Flush toilets, drinking water, bear boxes, fire grates, picnic tables, public telephone, ranger station* ⚴ *Reservations not accepted.* $14 ▭ *No credit cards* ☽ *July–early Sept.*

$ ⚠ **Yosemite Creek.** This secluded campground, set at 7,600 feet on a dirt road, is not suitable for large RVs. It's a good jumping-off point for spectacular hikes to the rim of the valley and to the top of Yosemite Falls. There is no water available. ⊠ *From Big Oak Flat entrance station, turn left onto Tioga Rd. (Hwy. 120) and continue 30 mi to the posted turnoff on right; drive 5 mi to campground* ☎ *209/372–0265* 🖷 *209/372–0371* ⊕ *www.nps.gov/yose* ⟊ *75 sites (tent or RV)* ⚴ *Pit toilets, bear boxes, fire grates, picnic tables, public telephone* ⚴ *Reservations not accepted.* $10 ▭ *No credit cards* ☽ *July–early Sept.*

¢ ⚠ **Camp 4.** Formerly known as Sunnyside Walk-In, this is the only valley campground available on a first-come, first-served basis—and the only one west of Yosemite Lodge. Open year-round, it is a favorite for rock climbers and solo campers; it fills quickly and is typically sold out by 9 AM daily spring through fall. This is a tents-only campground. ⊠ *Base of Yosemite Falls Trail, just west of Yosemite Lodge on Northside Dr., Yosemite Village* ☎ *209/372–0265* 🖷 *209/372–0371* ⊕ *www.nps.gov/ yose* ⟊ *35 sites* ⚴ *Flush toilets, drinking water, showers, bear boxes, fire grates, picnic tables, public telephone, ranger station.* $5 ▭ *AE, D, MC, V* ☽ *Year-round.*

## Outside the Park

$$$$ ▣ **Château du Sureau.** This romantic inn, adjacent to Erna's Elderberry
**Fodor's**Choice House, is straight out of a children's book. From the moment you drive
★ through the wrought-iron gates and up to the fairy-tale castle, you feel pampered. Every room is impeccably styled with European antiques, sumptuous fabrics, fresh-cut flowers, and oversize soaking tubs. Fall asleep by the glow of a crackling fire amid goose-down pillows and Italian linens, then awaken to a hearty European breakfast in the dining room. Afterward, relax with a game of chess in the piano room beneath an exquisite ceiling mural. Cable TV is available by request only. ⊠ *48688 Victoria La., Box 577, Oakhurst 93644* ☎ *559/683–6860* 🖷 *559/683– 0800* ⊕ *www.elderberryhouse.com* ⟊ *10 rooms, 1 villa* ⚴ *Restaurant, pool, bar, shop, laundry service, no kids under 12, no smoking.* $375–$575 ▭ *AE, MC, V* ⦿| *BP* ☽ *Closed two weeks, early Jan.–mid-Jan.*

$$$–$$$$ ▣ **Snowcreek Resort.** In a valley surrounded by mountain peaks, this 355-acre modern condominium and town-house community on the outskirts of Mammoth Lakes contains one- to four-bedroom units. All have kitchens, living and dining rooms, and fireplaces; some have washers and dryers. Guests have free use of the well-supplied athletic club. ⊠ *1254 Old Mammoth Rd., Mammoth Lakes 93546* ☎ *760/934–3333 or 800/ 544–6007* 🖷 *760/934–1619* ⊕ *www.snowcreek.com* ⟊ *180 condos* ⚴ *Kitchen, golf course, tennis courts, pools, health club, some pets allowed, no a/c, no smoking.* $160–$715 ▭ *AE, D, MC, V.*

$$$–$$$$ ▣ **Yosemite View Lodge.** This motel's sprawling prefab aesthetic is ameliorated by its location on the banks of the boulder-strewn Merced River and its proximity to the park entrance 2 mi east. Some rooms have river views, and many have whirlpool baths, fireplaces, and kitchenettes. The

motel complex is on the public bus route to the park, and you can fish and or go river rafting nearby. The lodge's sister property, the Cedar Lodge, sits 6 mi farther west and has similar looking, less expensive rooms without river views. ✉ *11136 Hwy. 140, El Portal 95318* ☎ *209/379–2681 or 888/742–4371* 🖷 *209/379–2704* ⊕ *www.yosemite-motels.com* ⇲ *279 rooms* ⚘ *Restaurant, pizzeria, kitchen (some), pools, bar, laundry facilities, some pets allowed, no-smoking rooms. $169–$249* ▭ *MC, V.*

★ **$$–$$$$**  🖳 **Homestead Cottages.** Serenity is the order of the day at this secluded getaway in Ahwahnee, 6 mi west of Oakhurst. On 160 acres of rolling hills that once held a Miwok village, these cottages (save one) have gas fireplaces, living rooms, fully equipped kitchens, and queen-size beds; the largest sleeps six. Hand-built by the owners out of real adobe bricks, the cottages are stocked with soft robes, oversize towels, and paperback books. If you're looking for a hideaway, this is the place. ✉ *41110 Rd. 600, 2½ mi off Hwy. 49, Ahwahnee 93601* ☎ *559/683–0495 or 800/483–0495* 🖷 *559/683–8165* ⊕ *www.homesteadcottages.com* ⇲ *5 cottages, 1 loft* ⚘ *Kitchen, no phone, no smoking. $145–$349* ▭ *AE, D, MC, V.*

★ **$–$$$$**  🖳 **Tamarack Lodge Resort.** Tucked away on the edge of the John Muir Wilderness Area, this 1924 log lodge has the most rustic and charming accommodations in the Mammoth Lakes area. Rooms in the main lodge—which is surrounded by quiet woods—can be fairly spartan, and some share a bathroom. Cross-country ski trails loop past the cozy cabins, which offer more privacy and come in a variety of sizes. Ranging from simple to luxurious, the cabins are modern, neat, and clean, with knotty-pine kitchens and private baths; some have fireplaces or wood-burning stoves. The romantic Lakefront Restaurant (no lunch early Sept.–mid-June) serves outstanding contemporary French-inspired cuisine, with an emphasis on game. ✉ *Lake Mary Rd., off Rte. 203, Mammoth Lakes 93546* ☎ *760/934–2442 or 800/237–6879* 🖷 *760/934–2281* ⊕ *www.tamaracklodge.com* ⇲ *11 rooms, 34 cabins* ⚘ *Restaurant, kitchen (some), bar, some pets allowed, no a/c, no TV, no smoking. $84–$350* ▭ *AE, MC, V.*

**$$–$$$**  🖳 **Lavender Hill.** Take in views of downtown Sonora from a porch swing on the wraparound veranda of this 1900 Victorian house, or stroll through its peaceful garden. Sunny rooms are filled with period antiques, and the gourmet country breakfast often includes fresh fruit grown on the property. ✉ *683 Barretta St., Sonora 95370* ☎ *209/532–9024 or 866/875–8637* ⊕ *www.lavenderhill.com* ⇲ *4 rooms* ⚘ *No a/c, no phone, no TV, no smoking. $120–$175* ▭ *D, MC, V* ▢| *BP.*

**$$**  🖳 **Little Valley Inn.** Pine paneling, historical photos, and old mining tools recall Mariposa's heritage at this countrified B&B, which has three comfortable guest bungalows. All rooms have modern amenities, private entrances, baths, and decks. One suite sleeps five people and includes a kitchen. ✉ *3483 Brooks Rd., off Rte. 49, Mariposa 95338* ☎ *209/742–6204 or 800/889–5444* 🖷 *209/742–5099* ⊕ *www.littlevalley.com* ⇲ *4 rooms, 1 suite, 1 cabin* ⚘ *Refrigerator, no phone. $104–$150* ▭ *MC, V* ▢| *CP.*

☾ **$–$$**  🖳 **Best Western Yosemite Gateway Inn.** The rooms at Oakhurst's best motel have attractive dark-wood American colonial–style furniture and slightly kitschy hand-painted wall murals of Yosemite. Kids love choosing between the two pools. ✉ *40530 Hwy. 41, Oakhurst 93644* ☎ *559/683–2378 or 800/545–5462* 🖷 *559/683–3813* ⊕ *www.yosemitegatewayinn.*

**37**

*com* ⟿ *122 rooms, 12 suites* ⌂ *Restaurant, refrigerators, in-room broadband, pools, exercise equipment, bar, laundry facilities, no-smoking rooms. $94–$109* ▭ *AE, D, MC, V.*

**$–$$** ▦ **Swiss Chalet.** One of the most reasonably priced motels in town, the Swiss Chalet has great views of the mountains and simple, comfortable rooms. There's also a fish-cleaning area and a freezer to keep your summer catch fresh. It's on the shuttle route. ⊠ *3776 Viewpoint Rd., Mammoth Lakes 93546* ☎ *760/934–2403 or 800/937–9477* 🖷 *760/934–2403* ⊕ *www.mammoth-swisschalet.com* ⟿ *21 rooms* ⌂ *Kitchen, some pets allowed, no a/c, no smoking. $75–$125* ▭ *AE, D, MC, V.*

**$–$$** ▦ **Tioga Lodge.** Just 2½ mi north of Yosemite's eastern gateway, this 19th-century building has been a store, a saloon, a tollbooth, and a boarding house. Now restored and expanded, it's a plain but popular lodge that's close to local ski areas and fishing spots. Ask about the summer boat tours of Mono Lake. ⊠ *54411 U.S. 395, Lee Vining 93541* ☎ *760/647–6423 or 888/647–6423* 🖷 *760/647–6074* ⊕ *www.tiogalodge.com* ⟿ *13 rooms* ⌂ *Restaurant, bar, some pets allowed, no a/c, no phone, no TV, no smoking. $79–$107* ▭ *AE, D, MC, V.*

**$** ▦ **Comfort Inn of Mariposa.** This white three-story building with a broad veranda sits on a hill above Mariposa. Some of the comfortable rooms have sitting areas. It's about an hour from Yosemite's western gate on Route 140, but a good bet if other properties in the area are booked. ⊠ *4994 Bullion St., Mariposa 95338* ☎ *209/966–4344 or 888/742–4371* 🖷 *209/966–4655* ⊕ *www.choicehotels.com* ⟿ *59 rooms, 2 suites* ⌂ *Pool. $70–$90* ▭ *AE, D, DC, MC, V* ⟋❂ *CP.*

**$$$$** ✕▦ **Tenaya Lodge.** This modern, full-service hotel—one of the region's largest—offers many creature comforts. The hulking prefab buildings and giant parking lot look out of place in the woods, but inside, the rooms are quite handsome. Ample standard rooms are decorated in pleasant earth tones, while deluxe rooms have minibars and other extras; suites have balconies. The Sierra Restaurant ($$–$$$$), with its high ceilings and giant fireplace, serves Continental cuisine. The more casual Jackalope's Bar and Grill ($–$$) has burgers, salads, and sandwiches. ⊠ *1122 Hwy. 41* ⟋ *Box 159, Fish Camp 93623* ☎ *559/683–6555 or 888/514–2167* 🖷 *559/683–0249* ⊕ *www.tenayalodge.com* ⟿ *244 rooms, 6 suites* ⌂ *2 restaurants, snack bar, room service, refrigerator, in-room broadband, Wi-Fi, pool, health club, bicycles, bar, children's programs (ages 5–12), laundry service, concierge, some pets allowed, no smoking. $285–$385* ▭ *AE, D, DC, MC, V.*

★
☞ **$–$$$$** ✕▦ **Evergreen Lodge.** It feels like summer camp at the Evergreen, where you can ditch the valley's hordes for a cozy cabin in the woods 8 mi from Hetch Hetchy. The perfect blend of rustic charm and modern comfort, cabins have sumptuous beds, comfy armchairs, candy-cane-striped pull-out sofas, and tree-stump end tables. The terrific roadhouse-style restaurant ($–$$$) serves everything from buffalo burgers to rainbow trout. After dinner, shoot pool in the old-school bar, melt s'mores, attend a lecture or film, or play Scrabble by the fire in the barn-like recreation center. There's a two–three-night minimum April through October and on holidays. ⊠ *33160 Evergreen Rd., 25 mi east of Groveland, 23 mi north of Yosemite Valley, Groveland 95321* ☎ *209/379–2606 or 800/935–6343* 🖷 *209/391–2390* ⊕ *www.evergreenlodge.com*

🛏 66 cabins ⚙ Restaurant, snack bar, refrigerator, public Wi-Fi, bicy-cles, bar, children's programs (ages 5–12), Internet room, no a/c, no phone, no TV, no smoking. $99–$259 ▭ AE, D, DC, MC, V ✿ Closed Jan.

★ $$ ✕🔲 **Narrow Gauge Inn.** All of the rooms at this well-tended, family-owned property have balconies (some shared) and great views of the surround-ing woods and mountains. For maximum atmosphere, book a room over-loooking the brook; for peace and quiet, choose a lower-level room on the edge of the forest. All are comfortably furnished with old-fashioned accents and railroad memorabilia. Be sure to reserve well ahead. The restaurant ($$–$$$$; open mid-Apr.–mid-Oct., Wed.–Sun.), which is fes-tooned with moose, bison, and other wildlife trophies, specializes in steaks and American fare; it merits a special trip. ✉ 48571 Hwy. 41, Fish Camp 93623 ☎ 559/683–7720 or 888/644–9050 🖷 559/683–2139 ⊕ www. narrowgaugeinn.com 🛏 25 rooms, 1 suite ⚙ Restaurant, VCR (some), Wi-Fi, pool, bar, some pets allowed, no a/c (some), no smoking. $120–$150 ▭ D, MC, V ❙◯❙ CP.

# YOSEMITE ESSENTIALS

**ACCESSIBILITY** Yosemite's facilities are con-tinually being upgraded to make them more accessible. Many of the Valley floor trails—particularly at Lower Yosemite Falls, Bridalveil Falls, and Mirror Lake—are wheelchair accessible, though some as-sistance may be required. The Valley Visitor Center is fully accessible, as are the shuttle buses around the Valley. A sign-language interpreter is available for ranger programs if you call ahead. For complete details, pick up the park's accessibility brochure at any visitor center or entrance, read it at ⊕ www.nps.gov/yose/access, or call the public information office at ☎ 209/372–0200. Visitors with respira-tory difficulties should take note of the park's high elevations—the Valley floor is approximately 4,000 feet above sea level, but Tuolumne Meadows and parts of the high country hover around 10,000 feet.

**ADMISSION FEES** The vehicle admission fee is $20 per car and is valid for seven days. In-dividuals arriving by bus, or on foot, bicy-cle, motorcycle, or horseback pay $10 for a seven-day pass.

**ADMISSION HOURS** The park is open daily, 24 hours a day. All entrances are open at all hours, except for Hetch Hetchy Entrance, open roughly dawn to dusk. Yosemite is in the Pacific time zone.

**ATMS/BANKS** There are ATMs inside the stores at Yosemite Village, Curry Village, Wawona, and Tuolumne Meadows, as well as in the lobby of Yosemite Lodge, and outside the Art Activity Center. 🔲 **Washington Mutual** ✉ 40003 Hwy. 49, Oakhurst ☎ 559/642-1350. **Yosemite Bank** ✉ Hwy. 140 at Hwy. 49 North, Mariposa ☎ 209/966-5444.

**AUTOMOBILE SERVICE STATIONS** There are gas stations at Crane Flat, Tuolumne Mead-ows, and Wawona. There's one garage in Yosemite Village, but it performs only basic repairs, and no gas is available there. 🔲 ☎ 209/372-8390.

**EMERGENCIES** In an emergency, call 911. You can also call the Yosemite Medical Clinic in Yosemite Village at 209/372–4637. The clinic provides 24-hour emer-gency care.

**LOST AND FOUND** To inquire about items lost or found in Yosemite's restaurants, hotels, lounges, shuttles, or tour buses, call Delaware North Corporation at 209/372–4357 or e-mail yoselost@dncinc.com. For items lost or found in other areas of

37

the park, contact the National Park Service at 209/379-1001 or e-mail yose_web manager@nps.gov.

PERMITS If you plan to camp in the backcountry, you must have a wilderness permit. Availability of permits, which are free, depends upon trailhead quotas. It's best to make a reservation, especially if you will be visiting May through September. You can reserve two days to 24 weeks in advance by phone, mail, or e-mail; a $5 per person processing fee is charged if and when your reservations are confirmed. In your request, include your name, address, daytime phone, the number of people in your party, trip date, alternative dates, starting and ending trailheads, and a brief itinerary. Without a reservation, you may still get a free permit on a first-come, first-served basis at wilderness permit offices at Big Oak Flat, Hetch Hetchy, Tuolumne, Wawona, the Wilderness Center, and Yosemite Valley in summer; fall through spring, visit the Valley Visitor Center.
🚹 **Wilderness Permits** ⌂ Box 545, Yosemite, 95389 ☎ 209/372-0740 ⊕ www.nps.gov/yose/wilderness/permits.htm.

POST OFFICES
🚹 **Curry Village Post Office** ⌂ Curry Village, 95389 ☎ 209/372-4475 ⊙ Closed Labor Day-Memorial Day. **El Portal Post Office** ⌂ 5508 Foresta Rd., El Portal 95318 ☎ 209/379-2311. **Main Post Office** ⌂ Yosemite Village, 95389 ☎ 209/372-4475. **Wawona Post Office** ⌂ Rte. 41, Wawona 95389 ☎ 209/375-6574. **Yosemite Lodge Post Office** ⌂ 95389 ☎ 209/372-4853.

PUBLIC TELEPHONES There are public telephones at park entrance stations, visitor centers, all restaurants and lodging facilities in the park, gas stations, and in Yosemite Village.

RESTROOMS Public restrooms are at visitor centers; all restaurants and lodging facilities in the park; at the Village Store, the Vernal Falls footbridge, Yosemite Falls, Tuolumne Meadows, and Glacier Point;

and at the Swinging Bridge, Cathedral Beach, Sentinel Beach, Church Bowl, and El Capitan picnic areas.

SHOPS & GROCERS
🚹 **Badger Pass Sport Shop** ⌂ Badger Pass Ski Area, Badger Pass Rd., off Glacier Point Rd., 18 mi from Yosemite Valley ☎ 209/372-8444 ⊙ Nov.-Apr. **Crane Flat Store** ⌂ Intersection of Big Oak Flat Rd. and Tioga Rd. (Rte. 120), 7 mi east of Big Oak Flat Entrance ☎ 209/379-2742. **Curry Village General Store** ⌂ Curry Village ☎ 209/372-8333. **Housekeeping Camp Store** ⌂ Southside Dr., ½ mi west of Curry Village ☎ 209/372-8338 ⊙ Open spring through fall. **Tuolumne Meadows Store and Mountain Shop** ⌂ Tioga Rd. (Rte. 120), 1½ mi east of Tuolumne Meadows Visitor Center ☎ 209/372-8428 ⊙ Closed Nov.-May. **Village Sport Shop** ⌂ Yosemite Village ☎ 209/372-1253. **Village Store** ⌂ Yosemite Village ☎ 209/372-1253. **Wawona Store and Pioneer Gift Shop** ⌂ Rte. 41, Wawoma ☎ 209/375-6574. **Yosemite Lodge Gift Shop** ⌂ Yosemite Lodge, Northside Dr. about ¾ mi west of the visitor center, Yosemite Village ☎ 209/372-1438. **Yosemite Mountain Shop** ⌂ Curry Village ☎ 209/372-8344.

**NEARBY TOWN INFORMATION**
🚹 **Lee Vining Office and Information Center** ⌂ Box 29, Lee Vining, CA 93541 ☎ 760/647-6595 ⊕ www.leevining.com. **Mammoth Lakes Visitors Bureau** ⌂ Along Rte. 203 (Main St.), near Sawmill Cutoff Rd., Box 48, Mammoth Lakes, CA 93546 ☎ 760/934-2712 or 888/466-2666 ⊕ www.visitmammoth.com. **Mariposa County Visitors Bureau** ⌂ 5158 Rte. 140, Box 967, Mariposa, CA 95338 ☎ 209/966-7082 or 888/554-9013 ⊕ www.homeofyosemite.com. **Tuolumne County Visitors Bureau** ⌂ Box 4020, Sonora, CA 95370 ☎ 209/533-4420 or 800/446-1333 ⊕ www.thegreatunfenced.com. **Yosemite Sierra Visitors Bureau** ⌂ 41969 Rte. 41, Oakhurst, CA 93644 ☎ 559/683-4636 ⊕ www.yosemitethisyear.com.

**VISITOR INFORMATION**
🚹 **Yosemite National Park** ⌂ Information Office, Box 577, Yosemite National Park, CA 95389 ☎ 209/372-0200 ⊕ www.nps.gov/yose.

# Zion
# National Park

West Fork Trail in The Subway, Zion National Park

## WORD OF MOUTH

"In an instant there flashed before us a scene never to be forgotten. In coming time it will, I believe, take rank with a very small number of spectacles each of which will in its own way, be regarded as the most exquisite of its kind which the world discloses. The scene before us was the Temples and Towers of the Virgin."

—Clarence Dutton
U.S. Geological Survey Report, 1880

# WELCOME TO ZION

## TOP REASONS TO GO

★ **To Hike Where Angels Land:** Though not for the timid or the weak, the Angels Landing Trail culminates in one of the park's most astounding viewpoints.

★ **To Leave Traffic Behind:** During the busy summer season, cars are no longer allowed in Zion Canyon, allowing for a relaxing and scenic shuttle bus ride.

★ **To Veg Out:** Zion Canyon is home to approximately 900 species of plants, more than anywhere else in Utah.

★ **To Take the Subway:** Only the hardiest of hikers venture through the pools and tunnels of the Subway in the Zion Canyon backcountry.

★ **To Experience Highs & Lows:** Zion Canyon area geography ranges from mountains to desert, offering a diverse selection of places to explore.

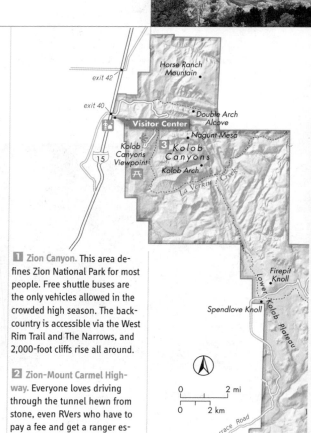

**1 Zion Canyon.** This area defines Zion National Park for most people. Free shuttle buses are the only vehicles allowed in the crowded high season. The backcountry is accessible via the West Rim Trail and The Narrows, and 2,000-foot cliffs rise all around.

**2 Zion-Mount Carmel Highway.** Everyone loves driving through the tunnel hewn from stone, even RVers who have to pay a fee and get a ranger escort. Canyon Overlook Trail provides a quick overlook of the West Temple and other majestic formations.

The Virgin River

**3 Kolob Canyons.** The quiet northwest corner of Zion, this area lets you see some of the park's attractions, such as the West Temple, from an angle many visitors never witness. Kolob Arch is easily reached via a relatively short trail.

UTAH

Hiking through the river in Zion Narrows

**4 Lava Point.** Infrequently visited, this area, has a primitive campground and nearby are two reservoirs that provide the only significant fishing opportunities in the park. Lava Point Overlook provides a view of Zion Canyon from the north.

## GETTING ORIENTED

The heart of Zion Canyon National Park is Zion Canyon itself, which follows the North Fork of the Virgin River for 6½ mi beneath cliffs that approach 2,000 feet in elevation. The Kolob area is considered by some to be superior in beauty, and you aren't likely to run into any crowds here. Both sections hint at the extensive backcountry beyond, open for those with the stamina, time, and experience to go off the park's beaten paths.

38

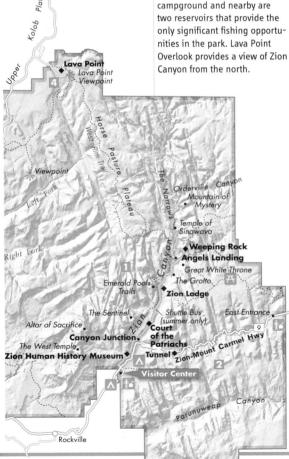

Kolob Plateau

Upper

Kolob Plateau

**Lava Point**
Lava Point
Viewpoint
4

Horse Pasture Plateau

West Rim Trail

Viewpoint

Left Fork

The Narrows

Orderville Canyon
Mountain of
Mystery

Temple of
Sinawava

Right Fork

Zion Canyon

**Weeping Rock**
**Angels Landing**
Great White Throne
The Grotto

Emerald Pools
Trails

**Zion Lodge**

The Sentinel

Shuttle Bus
(summer only)

East Entrance
9

Altar of Sacrifice

**Court
of the
Patriachs**

**Canyon Junction**

The West Temple

**Zion Human History Museum**

Tunnel

Zion-Mount Carmel Hwy

2

**Visitor Center**

Parunuweap Canyon

Rockville

| KEY | |
|---|---|
| 🏚 | Ranger Station |
| ⛛ | Campground |
| 🛆 | Picnic Area |
| 🍴 | Restaurant |
| 🏨 | Lodge |
| 🚶 | Trailhead |
| 🚻 | Restrooms |
| ⇘ | Scenic Viewpoint |
| ······ | Walking/Hiking Trails |
| ······ | Bicycle Path |

# ZION PLANNER

## When to Go

Zion is the most heavily visited national park in Utah, receiving nearly 2.5 million visitors each year. **Most visitors come between April and October,** when upper Zion Canyon is accessed only by free shuttle bus to reduce traffic congestion.

Summer in the park is hot and dry except for sudden cloudbursts, which can create flash flooding and spectacular waterfalls. Expect afternoon thunderstorms between July and September. In the summer sun, wear sunscreen and drink lots of water, regardless of your activity level.

Winters are mild at lower desert elevations, so consider planning your visit for some time other than peak season. You can expect to encounter winter driving conditions November through March, and although most park programs are suspended, winter is a wonderful and solitary time to see the canyons. During these months the shuttle does not operate.

⚠ **Extreme highs in Zion can often exceed 100°F in July and August.**

## Flora & Fauna

Zion Canyon's unique geography—the park is on the Colorado Plateau and bordered by the Great Basin and Mojave Desert provinces—supports more than 900 species of plants in environments that range from desert to hanging garden to high plateau. (Those so inclined have a variety of field guides unique to the region from which to choose in the bookstore at the Zion Canyon Visitor Center.) And yes, poison ivy is among the plant species, so ask a ranger where it is most common and keep an eye out for the itchy plant.

You are more likely to see wildlife in off-seasons because there's less human and vehicular traffic. But the introduction of the park shuttle has allowed some animals to return to the park's interior, so even in high season you can spot mule deer wandering in shady glens as you ride through the park, especially in early morning and near dusk.

The best opportunity for viewing wildlife is on the hiking trails. You'll see a large variety of lizards and you may be surprised by a Gambel's quail. Mountain lions and ringtail cats (which are not cats but are similar to raccoons) prowl the park, but you're more likely to spot their tracks than the elusive animals themselves. Black bear are rare, and when they do stumble into park boundaries, it is in the remote high country. All animals, from the smallest chipmunk to the biggest elk, should be given plenty of space.

AVG. HIGH/LOW TEMPS.

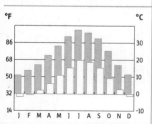

## Getting There & Around

In southwestern Utah, not far from the Nevada border, Zion National Park is closer to Las Vegas (158 mi) than to Salt Lake City (310 mi). The nearest commercial airport is 46 mi away in St. George, Utah. Off Route 9, the park is 21 mi east of Interstate 15 and 24 mi west of U.S. 89.

November through March, private vehicles are allowed on Zion's main park road, Zion Canyon Scenic Drive. From April through October, however, it is closed to private vehicles. During this time, the park's easy-to-use shuttle system ferries people into the canyon from the Zion Canyon Visitor Center, where the parking lot is typically full 10 to 3 daily, May through September. To avoid parking hassles, leave your car in Springdale and ride the town shuttle to the park entrance and connect with the park shuttle. Town shuttle stops are at Eagles Nest, Driftwood Motel, Bit & Spur Restaurant, Zion Park Inn, Bumbleberry Inn, Pizza and Noodle Company, Watchman Cafe, Flanigan's Inn, and Zion Giant Screen Theater. The shuttles are free, but you must pay the park entrance fee.

If you enter or exit Zion via the east entrance you will have the privilege of driving a gorgeous, twisting 24-mi stretch of the Zion–Mount Carmel Highway (Route 9). Two tunnels, including the highway's famous 1 1/10-mi tunnel, lie between the east park entrance and Zion Canyon. The tunnels are so narrow that vehicles more than 7 feet, 10 inches wide or 11 feet, 4 inches high require traffic control while passing through. Rangers, who are stationed at the tunnels 8 to 8 daily, April through October, stop oncoming traffic so you can drive down the middle of the tunnels. Large vehicles must pay an escort fee of $15 at either park entrance. West of the tunnels the highway meets Zion Canyon Scenic Drive at Canyon Junction, about 1 mi north of the Zion Canyon Visitor Center.

## Festivals & Events

JAN. **St. George Winter Bird Festival.** Numerous free birding field trips are the highlight of this three-day festival. The Saturday evening banquet costs $20 to attend. ☎ 435/634-5948.

MAR. **Hurricane Easter Car Show.** Classic cars from all over the West descend on Hurricane for this event, which attracts about 7,000 people each year. On Easter Sunday there's a slow Rod Run through Zion National Park. ☎ 435/635-5720.

APR. **Dixie Downs Horse Races.** For more than 25 years, St. George Lions Club has hosted two spring weekends of horse racing to prepare horses for the larger tracks in summer. ☎ 435/673-5553.

AUG. **Western Legends Roundup.** This nostalgic festival is for anyone with a love of cowboys, pioneer life, or Native American culture. For three days the small town of Kanab fills with cowboy poets and storytellers, musicians, Western arts-and-crafts vendors, and Native American dancers and weavers. Wagon making, quilt shows, and a parade are all part of the fun. ☎ 435/644-3444.

SEPT. **Dixie Roundup.** Sponsored by the St. George Lions Club, the Dixie Roundup rodeo has been a tradition for decades. The real novelty of the professional event is that it's held on the green grass of Sun Bowl stadium. ☎ 435/628-8282.

38

By John
Blodgett

The walls of Zion Canyon soar more than 2,000 feet, but it's the character, not the size, of the sandstone forms that defines the park's splendor. The domes, fins, and blocky massifs bear the names and likenesses of cathedrals and temples, prophets and angels. But for all Zion's grandeur, trails that lead deep into side canyons and up narrow ledges on the sheer canyon walls reveal a subtler beauty. Tucked among the monoliths are delicate hanging gardens, serene spring-fed pools, and shaded spots of solitude.

At the genesis of Zion is the Virgin River, a tributary of the Colorado River. It's hard to believe that this muddy little stream is responsible for carving the great canyon you see, until you witness it transformed into a rumbling red torrent during spring runoff and summer thunderstorms. Cascades pour from the cliff tops, clouds float through the canyon, and then the sun comes out and you know you are walking in one of the West's most loved and sacred places.

## Scenic Drives

Zion Canyon's grandeur is best experienced on foot whenever possible, but there is something to be said for covering a lot of ground in the car. Driving is the only way to easily access Kolob Canyon from November through March, and driving your own vehicle is the only way to access the Zion Canyon scenic drive.

★ **Kolob Canyons Road.** From Interstate 15 you get no hint of the beauty that awaits you on this 5-mi road. Most visitors gasp audibly when they get their first glimpse of the red canyon walls that rise suddenly and spectacularly out of the earth. The scenic drive winds amid these towers as it rises in elevation, until you reach a viewpoint that overlooks the whole Kolob region of Zion National Park. The shortest hike in this section of the park is the Middle Fork of Taylor Creek Trail, which is 2⁷⁄₁₀ mi one way to Double Arch Alcove, and gets fairly rugged toward the end. ⇨ Hiking in the Sports & the Outdoors section. During heavy snowfall Kolob Canyons Road may be closed. ⊠ *Kolob Canyons Rd. east of I–15, Exit 40.*

★ **Zion–Mount Carmel Highway & Tunnels.** Two narrow tunnels lie between the park's east park and Zion Canyon on this breathtaking 24-mi stretch of Route 9. As you travel through solid rock from one end of the longest (1¹⁄₁₀ mi) tunnel to the other, portals along one side provide a few glimpses of cliffs and canyons, and when you emerge on the other side you find that the landscape has changed dramatically. The tunnels are so narrow that large vehicles more than 7 feet, 10 inches wide or 11 feet, 4 inches high require traffic control to pass through, available 8–8 daily, April–October, and must pay a $15 escort fee. ⊠ *Zion–Mount Carmel Rte. 9, about 5 mi east of Canyon Junction.*

## What to See

### Historic Sites

★ **Zion Human History Museum.** Enrich your visit with a stop here, where you'll get a complete overview of the park with special attention to human history. Exhibits explain how settlers interacted with the geology, wildlife, plants, and unpredictable weather in the canyon from prehistory to the present. A 22-minute film plays throughout the day. ⊠ *Zion Canyon Scenic Dr., 1 mi north of south entrance* ☎ *435/772–3256* ⊕ *www.nps.gov/zion/HHMuseum.htm* 🖼 *Free* ⊗ *Late May–early Sept., daily 8–7; Sept. and mid-Apr.–late May, daily 8–6; Oct.–mid-Apr., daily 9–5.*

Most visitors gasp audibly when they get their first glimpse of the red canyon walls that rise suddenly and spectacularly out of the earth in Kolob Canyon.

**38**

**Zion Lodge.** The Union Pacific Railroad constructed the first Zion National Park Lodge in 1925, with buildings designed by architect Stanley Gilbert Underwood. A fire destroyed the original building, but it was rebuilt to recapture some of the look and feel of the first building. The original Western-style cabins are still in use today. Among giant cottonwoods across the road from the Emerald Pools trailhead, the lodge houses a restaurant, snack bar, and gift shop. ⊠ *Zion Canyon Scenic Dr., about 3 mi north of Canyon Junction* ☎ *435/772–7700* ⊕ *www.zionlodge.com.*

### Scenic Stops

**Checkerboard Mesa.** The distinctive pattern on this huge, white mound of sandstone was created by a combination of vertical fractures and the exposure of horizontal bedding planes by erosion. ⊠ *Zion–Mount Carmel Hwy., 1 mi west of the east entrance.*

★ **Court of the Patriarchs.** This trio of peaks bears the names of, from left to right, Abraham, Isaac, and Jacob. Mount Moroni is the reddish peak on the far right, which partially blocks your view of Jacob. You can see the Patriarchs better by hiking a half mile up Sand Bench Trail. ⊠ *Zion Canyon Scenic Dr., 1½ mi north of Canyon Junction.*

**Great White Throne.** Towering over the Grotto picnic area near Zion Lodge is this massive 6,744-foot rock peak. ✉ *Zion Canyon Scenic Dr., about 3 mi north of Canyon Junction.*

★ **Weeping Rock.** A short, paved walk leads up to this flowing rock face, where wildflowers and delicate ferns thrive near a spring-fed waterfall that seeps out of a cliff. In fall, this area bursts with color. The ⅕-mi trail to the west alcove takes about 25 minutes round-trip. It is paved, but too steep for wheelchairs. ✉ *Zion Canyon Scenic Dr., about 4 mi north of Canyon Junction.*

### Visitor Centers

Zion's two visitor centers are open year-round. The main center is at the south entrance of the park, and is larger than the one at Kolob Canyon. There is a bookstore at each location, plus rangers to answer your questions or point you to a good hike or picnic area. Both feature exhibits and photographs that cover the park's natural and cultural history. Plan to get snacks, lunch, or coffee elsewhere.

**Kolob Canyons Visitor Center.** At the origin of Kolob Canyons Road, this park office has a small bookstore plus exhibits on park geology and helpful rangers to answer questions. ✉ *Exit 40 off I–15* ☎ *435/772–3256* ⊙ *Oct.–Apr., daily 8–4:30; May–Sept., daily 8–5.*

**Zion Canyon Visitor Center.** Unlike most national park visitor centers, which are filled with indoor displays, Zion's presents most of its information in an appealing outdoor exhibit. Beneath shade trees beside a gurgling brook, displays help you plan your stay and introduce you to the area's geology, flora, and fauna. Inside, a large bookstore operated by the Zion Natural History Association sells field guides and other publications. **Ranger-guided shuttle tours** of Zion Canyon depart from the parking lot and travel to the Temple of Sinawava, with several photo-op stops along the way. The tour schedule and free tour tickets are available inside. You can also pick up backcountry permits here. ✉ *At south entrance, Springdale* ☎ *435/772–3256* ⊕ *www.nps.gov/zion* ⊙ *Apr.–Oct., daily 8–7; Nov.–Mar., daily 8–5.*

## Sports & the Outdoors

Zion has plenty of opportunities for recreation, with activities suited to all ages and abilities. Hiking is by far the most popular activity, and cyclists rejoiced when Zion Canyon was deemed off-limits to cars during the busy summer season. Some sections of the Virgin River are ideal for swimming or inner tube floating. In the winter, hiking boots can be exchanged for snowshoes and cross-country skis; check with a ranger to determine backcountry snow conditions.

### Air Tours

OUTFITTERS & EXPEDITIONS

**Bryce Canyon Airlines & Helicopters.** For a once-in-a-lifetime view of the park, join professional pilots and guides for an airplane ride over Zion, as well as Bryce Canyon National Park. Flights depart from Ruby's Inn Heliport near Bryce Canyon National Park. ☎ *435/834–5341* ⊕ *www. rubysinn.com/bryce-canyon-airlines.html* 💰 *$75.*

## ZION IN ONE DAY

Begin your visit at the **Zion Canyon Visitor Center,** where outdoor exhibits inform you about the park's geology, wildlife, and history. Catch the shuttle (or drive, depending on the season) into Zion Canyon. On your way in, make a quick stop at the **Zion Human History Museum** to watch a 22-minute park orientation program and to see exhibits chronicling the human history of the area. Board the shuttle and travel to the **Court of the Patriarchs** viewpoint to take photos and walk the short path. Then pick up the next bus headed into the canyon. Stop at Zion Lodge and cross the road to the **Emerald Pools** trailhead, and take the short hike up to the pools themselves.

Before reboarding the shuttle, grab lunch in the snack shop or dining room at **Zion Lodge.** Take the shuttle as far as **Weeping Rock** trailhead for a brief, cool walk up to the dripping,

spring-fed cascade. Ride the next shuttle to the end of the road, where you can walk to the gateway of the canyon's narrows on the paved, accessible **Riverside Walk.**

Reboard the shuttle to return to the Zion Canyon Visitor Center to pick up your car. Head out onto the beautiful **Zion–Mount Carmel Highway,** with its long, curving tunnels, making sure your camera is loaded and ready for stops at viewpoints along the road. Once you reach the park's east entrance, turn around, and on your return trip stop to take the short hike up to **Canyon Overlook.** Now you're ready to rest your feet at a screening of *Zion Canyon–Treasure of the Gods* at the **Zion Giant Screen Theater.** In the evening, you can attend a **ranger program** at one of the campground amphitheaters or at Zion Lodge, or have a relaxing dinner in **Springdale** followed with a stroll downtown.

**38**

### Bicycling

The introduction of the park shuttle has improved bicycling conditions in Zion—during the busy months, April through October, cyclists no longer share Zion Canyon Scenic Drive with thousands of cars—though two-wheelers do need to be cautious of the large buses plying the park road throughout the day. In the park, bicycles are only allowed on park roads and on the 3½-mi Pa'rus Trail, which winds along the Virgin River in Zion Canyon. You cannot ride your bicycle through the tunnels.

OUTFITTERS & EXPEDITIONS **Bicycles Unlimited.** A treasure trove of information on mountain biking in Utah, this shop rents bikes and sell parts, accessories, and guides. ✉ 90 *S. 100 East, St. George* ☎ 888/673–4492 ⊕ *www.bicyclesunlimited.com.*

**Springdale Cycles.** Rents bikes, car racks, and trailers, and can give you tips on the local trails, plus offers day- and multiday tours for both mountain bikers and road-biking enthusiasts. Ask them about the best area trails if you prefer to explore on your own. ✉ *1458 Zion Park Blvd., Springdale* ☎ *435/772–0575 or 800/776–2099* ⊕ *www.springdalecycles.com.*

### Bird-watching

Approximately 290 bird species call Zion home or else pass through its environs on occasion. Some species, such as the white-throated swift and

## GOOD READS

**Towers of Stone** by J.L. Crawford summarizes the essence of Zion National Park, its landscape, plants, animals, and human history.

**Zion National Park: Sanctuary in the Desert** by Nicky Leach gives you a photographic overview and a narrative journey through the park.

**The Zion Tunnel, From Slickrock to Switchback** by Donald T. Garate tells the fascinating story of the construction of the mile-long Zion Tunnel in the 1920s.

**Wildflowers of Zion National Park** by Dr. Stanley L. Welsh is always helpful during wildflower season.

the powerful peregrine falcon, take full advantage of the towering cliffs. Closer to the ground are the common pinyon jay and, if you look closely enough, perhaps a Gambel's quail. Wild turkeys are not only common, but some aren't very wild, venturing up to visitors looking for a handout. If you're quick, you might spot one of nine species of hummingbirds that have been spotted in the park.

### Hiking

The best way to experience Zion is to walk beneath, between and, if you can bear it (and have good balance!), along its towering cliffs. There is something for everyone, from paved and flat river strolls to precarious cliff-side scrambles. You can buy a detailed guide to the trails of Zion at the Zion Canyon Visitor Center bookstore. Whether you're heading out for a day of rock-hopping or an hour of strolling, you should carry—and drink—plenty of water to counteract the effects of southern Utah's arid climate. Wear a hat, sunscreen, and sturdy shoes or boots; make sure to bring a map, and be honest with yourself about your capabilities. Getting in over your head can have serious health consequences.

EASY **Emerald Pools Trail.** Two small waterfalls cascade (or drip, in dry weather) into pools at the top of this relatively easy trail. The way is paved up to the lower pool and is suitable for baby strollers and wheelchairs with assistance. Beyond the lower pool, the trail becomes rocky and steep as you progress toward the middle and upper pools. A less crowded and exceptionally enjoyable return route follows the Kayenta Trail connecting on to the Grotto Trail. Allow 50 minutes round-trip to the lower pool and 2½ hours round-trip to the middle and upper pools. ✉ *Zion Canyon Scenic Dr., about 3 mi north of Canyon Junction.*

**Grotto Trail.** This flat and very easy trail takes you from Zion Lodge to the Grotto picnic area, traveling for the most part along the park road. Allow 20 minutes or less for the walk. If you are up for a longer hike, and have two to three hours, connect with the Kayenta Trail after you cross the footbridge, and head for the Emerald Pools. You will begin gaining elevation, and it's a steady, steep climb to the pools. ✉ *Zion Canyon Scenic Dr., about 3 mi north of Canyon Junction.*

**Pa'rus Trail.** This 2-mi walking and biking path parallels and occasionally crosses the Virgin River, starting at South Campground and proceeding north along the river to the beginning of Zion Canyon Scenic Drive. It's paved and gives you great views of the Watchman, the Sentinel, and Towers of the Virgin. Dogs are allowed on this trail as long as they are leashed. Cyclists must follow traffic rules on this heavily used trail. ⊠ *Canyon Junction, ½ mi north of south entrance.*

**Riverside Walk.** Beginning at the Temple of Sinawava shuttle stop at the end of Zion Canyon Scenic Drive, this 1-mi round-trip stroll shadows the Virgin River. On the other side of the trail, wildflowers bloom out of the canyon wall in fascinating hanging gardens. This is the park's most trekked trail; it is paved and suitable for baby strollers and for wheelchairs with assistance. A round-trip walk takes between one and two hours. The end of the trail marks the beginning of the Narrows Trail. ⊠ *Zion Canyon Scenic Dr., 5 mi north of Canyon Junction.*

MODERATE
Fodor'sChoice
★

**Canyon Overlook Trail.** It's a little tough to locate this trailhead, but you'll find it if you watch for the parking area just east of Zion–Mount Carmel tunnel. The trail is moderately steep but only 1 mi round-trip; allow an hour to hike it. The overlook at trail's end gives you views of the West and East Temples, Towers of the Virgin, the Streaked Wall, and more. ⊠ *Rte. 9, east of Zion–Mount Carmel Tunnel.*

**Taylor Creek Trail.** In the Kolob Canyons area of the park, this trail immediately descends parallel to Taylor Creek, sometimes crossing it, sometimes shortcutting benches beside it. The historic Larsen Cabin precedes the entrance to the canyon of the Middle Fork, where the trail becomes rougher. After the old Fife Cabin, the canyon bends to the right and delivers you into Double Arch Alcove, a large, colorful grotto with a high arch towering above. The distance one way to Double Arch is 2¾ mi. Allow about four hours round-trip for this hike. ⊠ *Kolob Canyons Rd., about 1½ mi east of Kolob Canyons Visitor Center.*

DIFFICULT
Fodor'sChoice
★

**Angels Landing Trail.** Truly one of the most spectacular hikes in the park, this trail is an adventure for those not afraid of heights. On your ascent you must negotiate Walter's Wiggles, a series of 21 switchbacks built out of sandstone blocks, and traverse sheer cliffs with chains bolted into the rock face to serve as handrails. In spite of its hair-raising nature, this trail attracts many people. Small children should skip it, however, and older children should be carefully supervised. Allow 2½ hours round-trip if you stop at Scout's Lookout, and four hours if you keep going to where the angels (and birds of prey) play. ⊠ *Zion Canyon Scenic Drive, about 4½ mi north of Canyon Junction.*

★ **Narrows Trail.** On a hot, clear day there are few things more enjoyable than a walk in the river. This route does not follow a trail or path; rather, you are walking on the riverbed, no matter how much water is in it. The gateway of the Narrows admits adventurous souls deeper into Zion Canyon than most visitors go. As beautiful as it is, this hike is not for everyone. To see the Narrows you must wade upstream through chilly water and over uneven, slippery rocks. Just to cross the river, you must

38

walk deliberately and slowly using a walking stick. Be prepared to swim, as chest-deep holes may occur even when water levels are low. Like any narrow desert canyon, this one is famous for sudden flash flooding even when skies are clear. *Before attempting to hike into the Narrows, check with park rangers about the likelihood of flash floods.* A day trip up the lower section of the Narrows is 6 mi one way to the turnaround point. Allow at least five hours round-trip. ☒ *At the end of Riverside Walk.*

### Horseback Riding

Grab your hat and boots and see Zion the way the pioneers did—on the back of a horse or mule. This is a sure way to make your trip to the park memorable. Only one outfitter is licensed to guide tours within park boundaries. Easy going, one-hour and half-day trips are available, with a minimum age of 7 and 10 years respectively. Maximum weight on either trip is 220 pounds.

OUTFITTERS & EXPEDITIONS  **Canyon Trail Rides.** These friendly folks have been around for years, and they are the only outfitter for trail rides inside the park. Anyone over age 7 can participate in guided rides along the Virgin River. The horses work from late March through October; you may want to make reservations ahead of time. ☒ *Across the road from Zion Lodge* ☎ *435/679–8665* ⊕ *www.canyonrides.com* ☏ *$30–$65.*

### Swimming

Swimming is allowed in the Virgin River within and outside park boundaries, but be careful of cold water, slippery rock bottoms, and flash floods when it rains. Swimming is not allowed in the Emerald Pools. The use of inner tubes is prohibited within the park.

### Winter Sports

Cross-country skiing and snowshoeing are best experienced in the park's higher elevations during the winter, where snow stays on the ground longer. Inquire at the Zion Canyon Visitor Center for backcountry conditions. Snowmobiling is only allowed for residential access.

## Educational Offerings

### Classes and Seminars

**Zion Canyon Field Institute.** Turn Zion Canyon into a classroom by participating in a seminar on edible plants, geology, photography, adobe-brick making, or any number of other educational programs provided year-round by the Zion Canyon Field Institute, in the nature center. Classes, held outdoors throughout the park, are limited to small groups; reserve ahead to assure placement. ☎ *800/635–3959* ⊕ *www.zionpark.org* ☏ *$12–$225.*

### Ranger Programs

**Evening Programs.** Held each evening in campground amphitheaters and in Zion Lodge, entertaining 45-minute ranger-led programs cover such subjects as geology and history. You may learn about the bats that swoop through the canyons at night, the surreptitious ways of the mountain lion, or how plants and animals adapt to desert life. Programs may include a slide show or audience participation. ☎ *435/772–3256.*

☺ **Junior Ranger Program.** Kids 6–12 can have fun learning about plants, animals, geology, and archaeology through hands-on activities, games, and hikes. They can earn a certificate, pin, and patch by attending one session of the Junior Ranger Program at the Zion Nature Center and one other ranger-led activity in the park. Children 5 or younger can earn a Junior Ranger decal by completing an activity sheet available at the Zion Canyon Visitor Center. Kids can earn a Junior Ranger badge by working through an activity booklet (available at the Zion Canyon and Kolob Canyons visitor centers) during their visit to Zion. Kids need to sign up for Junior Ranger programs at the Zion Nature Center half an hour before they begin. ⊠ *Zion Nature Center, near South Campground entrance, ½ mi north of south entrance* ☎ *435/772–3256* ⊒ *Free* ☼ *Daily.*

**Morning and Afternoon Hikes.** These 1- to 2-mi ranger-led walks can greatly enhance your understanding of the geology, wildlife, and history of Zion National Park. Each park ranger selects a favorite destination, which may change daily. Inquire at the Zion Canyon Visitor Center or check park bulletin boards for locations and times. Wear sturdy footgear and bring a hat, sunglasses, sunscreen, and water.

**Shuttle Tours.** To learn about the geology, ecology, and history of Zion Canyon, join a park ranger for a two-hour narrated tour by shuttle bus. Tours depart from the Zion Canyon Visitor Center and travel to Temple of Sinawava. You'll make several stops along the way to take photographs and hear park interpretation from the ranger. Tour times are posted at the Zion Canyon Visitor Center, which is also where you can pick up your free but mandatory tour tickets. ⊠ *Zion Canyon Visitor Center* ☎ *435/772–3256* ⊒ *Free* ☼ *May–Sept., daily.*

## Arts & Entertainment

☺ **Zion Canyon Theatre.** Shown on a six-story-high screen, the 40-minute film *Zion Canyon–Treasure of the Gods* takes you on an adventure through Zion and other points in canyon country. Other films, including Hollywood features, are also regularly shown here. ⊠ *145 Zion Park Blvd., Springdale* ☎ *435/772–2400 or 888/256–3456* ⊕ *www.zioncanyontheatre.com* ⊒ *$8* ☼ *Nov.–Mar. call; Apr.–Oct. 11–8 daily.*

# WHAT'S NEARBY

## Nearby Towns & Attractions

### Nearby Towns

Hotels, restaurants, and shops keep popping up in **Springdale,** population 457, on the southern boundary of Zion National Park, yet the town still manages to maintain its small-town charm—and oh, the view! There are a surprising number of wonderful places to stay and eat, and if you take the time to stroll the main drag, or make use of frequent shuttle stops, you'll find some great shops and galleries. On Route 9 between St. George and Zion stands the small town of **Hurricane,** population 8,250. Pronounced "HUR-aken," this community on the Virgin River has ex-

38

perienced enormous growth, probably owing to the boom in nearby St. George. Hurricane is home to one of Utah's most scenic 18-hole golf courses and is a less expensive and less crowded base for exploring Zion. On Route 9, 13 mi to the east of the park is **Mount Carmel Junction,** an intersection offering some funky small-town lodging and the don't-miss studio of Maynard Dixon, the artist many consider the finest painter of the American West. Other nearby towns, much smaller in size, include **Virgin, La Verkin,** and the ghost town of **Grafton,** where there's only a stone school and dusty cemetery. It has starred in films such as *Butch Cassidy and the Sundance Kid.*

### Nearby Attractions

**Coral Pink Sand Dunes State Park.** This sweeping expanse of pink sand comes from eroding sandstone. Funneled through a notch in the rock, wind picks up speed and carries grains of sand into the area. Once the wind slows down, the sand is deposited, creating this giant playground for dune buggies, ATVs, and dirt motorcycles. A small area is fenced off for walking, but the sound of wheeled toys is always with you. Kids love to play in the sand, but before you let them loose, check the surface temperature; it can become very hot. ⊠ *Yellowjacket and Hancock Rds., 12 mi off U.S. 89, near Kanab* ☏ *435/648–2800* ⊕ *www.stateparks. utah.gov* ⊠ *$5* ☉ *Daily.*

★ **Snow Canyon State Park.** Red Navajo sandstone mesas and formations are crowned with black lava rock, creating high-contrast vistas from either end of the canyon. From the campground you can scramble up huge sandstone mounds and overlook the entire valley. About an hour from Zion, this state park is near St. George. ⊠ *1002 Snow Canyon Dr., Ivins* ☏ *435/628–2255* ⊕ *www.stateparks.utah.gov* ⊠ *$5* ☉ *Daily.*

## Area Activities

### Sports & the Outdoors

BICYCLING The mountain biking trails on **Gooseberry Mesa,** off Route 59 south of
★ Hurricane, rival those of world-famous Moab on the other side of southern Utah, yet don't have the hordes of fat-tire fanatics. Come here for solitary and technical single-track challenges.

GOLF Hurricane has **Sky Mountain** (⊠ 1030 N. 2600 West St. ☏ 888/345–5551),
★ one of the state's most scenic 18-hole golf courses. Many fairways are framed by red-rock outcroppings; the course has a front-tee view of the nearby 10,000-foot Pine Valley Mountains.

HORSEBACK The only thing more quintessentially "Old West" than the landscape itRIDING self is the animal that helped conquer it—the horse. Ranchers and explorers on horseback mapped the lands of southwestern Utah, and in many cases the trails they blazed are still used today. Ride the range for a half day, or consider a longer horse-packing route that takes four, five, or even six or more days.

**Mecham Outfitters** (🖂 Box 71, Tropic 84776 ☏ 435/679–8823 ⊕ www.mechamoutfitters.com).

### Arts & Entertainment

ART GALLERIES **Worthington Gallery.** Opened in 1980 by a single potter in a pioneer-era home near the mouth of Zion Canyon, Worthington Gallery now features more than 20 artists who create in clay, metal, glass, paint and more. ⊠ *789 Zion Park Blvd., Springdale* ☎ *800/626–9973.*

NIGHTLIFE As good as their Mexican food is, the **Bit & Spur Restaurant and Saloon** is best known as the premier place to see live music in southern Utah. Many touring rock, blues, and reggae bands go out of their way to play here. ⊠ *1212 Zion Park Blvd., Springdale* ☎ *435/772–3498.*

The **O. C. Tanner Amphitheater** (⊠ Lion Blvd., Springdale ☎ 435/652–7994 ⊕ www.dixie.edu/tanner) is set amid huge sandstone boulders at the base of the enormous red cliffs spilling south from Zion National Park. In summer, concerts are held each weekend; everything from local bands to the Utah Symphony Orchestra take to the stage.

# WHERE TO STAY & EAT

### About the Restaurants

There is only one full-service restaurant in Zion National Park, and only one lodging option, so over the years places to stay and eat have sprouted up nearby. The best and most established restaurants are in Springdale, but lodging fills up quickly and is more expensive in the high season. Many people get a room in Hurricane or Panguitch to the west, or Mount Carmel Junction to the east, and use these locales as bases for day trips into the park.

Utah does not have a signature cuisine, per se; rather, restaurants borrow from a number of sources. American cuisines are most common, followed closely by those with Mexican and Southwestern influences. Springdale has the greatest number and diversity of dining options. Because this is conservative Utah, don't presume a restaurant serves beer, much less wine or cocktails, especially in the smaller towns. Most restaurants are family friendly, and dress tends to be casual. Prices are reasonable, though they inch higher in and near the national park.

### About the Hotels

Lodging within Zion is very limited and rustic. Still, in the summer high season, you'll want to make reservations if you want to stay in or close to the park. Nearby Springdale has many lodging options to choose from, from quaint smaller motels and bed-and-breakfasts, to upscale hotels with modern amenities and riverside rooms. If you are willing to find a room upward of an hour or two away, perhaps with fewer amenities, you may be surprised not only by same-day reservations in some cases, but also much lower room rates. Panguitch and Hurricane have some particularly good options for budget and last-minute travelers.

### About the Campgrounds

Campgrounds within Zion National Park are family friendly, convenient, and quite pleasant, but in the high season they do fill up fast. Your best bet is to reserve ahead of time whenever possible. How quickly camping choices outside of the park fill up varies according to how far away

**38**

they are, but most all cater to tent campers and RVers alike, with features such as playgrounds, showers, and picnic areas. Backcountry camping in the park is an option for overnight backpackers, but make sure to get a permit at the Zion Canyon Visitor Center. The primitive Lava Point Campground has no water and is closed during the winter. Its six sites are first-come, first-served.

## Where to Eat

### In the Park

**$-$$$**  ✕ **Red Rock Grill at Zion Lodge.** This is the only full-service restaurant inside the park. A rustic reproduction of the original lodge dining room, the restaurant is hung with historic photos. You can dine on the patio overlooking the front lawn of the lodge. A good selection of steak, fish, and poultry is offered for dinner, and lunch includes sandwiches and salads. Breakfast is also served. ⊠ *Zion Canyon Scenic Dr., 3¼ mi north of Canyon Junction* ☎ *435/772–7760* ⊕ *www.zionlodge.com* ⚑ *Reservations essential. $12–$22* ⊟ *AE, D, DC, MC, V.*

**¢**  ✕ **Castle Dome Café & Snack Bar.** Right next to the Zion Lodge shuttle stop and adjoining the gift shop, this small fast-food restaurant defines convenience. Hikers on the go can grab a banana or a sandwich here, or you can while away an hour with ice cream on the sunny patio. ⊠ *Zion Canyon Scenic Dr., 3¼ mi north of Canyon Junction* ☎ *435/772–7700* ⊕ *www.zionlodge.com. $3–$7* ⊟ *AE, D, DC, MC, V.*

PICNIC AREAS  **The Grotto.** A shady lunch retreat with lots of amenities—drinking water, fire grates, picnic tables, and restrooms—the Grotto is ideal for families. A short walk takes you to Zion Lodge, where you can pick up fast food. ⊠ *Zion Canyon Scenic Dr., 3½ mi north of Canyon Junction.*

**Kolob Canyons Viewpoint.** Enjoy the views while you have your lunch at the picnic table. Restrooms and drinking water are available at the Kolob Canyons Visitor Center. ⊠ *Kolob Canyons Rd., 5 mi from Kolob Canyons Visitor Center.*

**Zion Nature Center.** On your way to or from the Junior Ranger Program feed your kids at the Nature Center picnic area. When the nature center is closed, you can use the restrooms in South Campground. ⊠ *Near the entrance to South Campground ½ mi north of the south entrance* ☎ *435/772–3256.*

## Outside the Park

**$$-$$$$**  ✕ **Sullivan's Rococo Steakhouse & Inn.** Specializing in beef and seafood, this St. George restaurant is known for its prime rib, but its vistas are worthy noting, too. It sits atop a hill overlooking town, so you can enjoy spectacular views right from your table. ⊠ *511 Airport Rd., St. George* ☎ *435/628–3671* ⊕ *www.rococo.net/steakhouse.html. $15–$42* ⊟ *AE, D, DC, MC, V.*

**$$-$$$**  ✕ **Bit & Spur Restaurant and Saloon.** This restaurant has been a legend
Fodor$Choice  in Utah for 20 years. The seasonal menu lists familiar Mexican dishes
★  like tamales, but the kitchen also gets creative. Try the chili-rubbed *bistek asado* or chipotle shrimp pasta. When the weather is nice, arrive early

so you can eat outside and enjoy the lovely grounds and views. ⌧ *1212 Zion Park Blvd., Springdale* ☎ *435/772–3498* ⊕ *www.bitandspur. com. $14–$25* ⊟ *AE, D, MC, V* ⊘ *No lunch.*

**$$–$$$** ✕ **Spotted Dog Cafe at Flanigan's Inn.** Named in honor of the family dog of Springdale's original settlers, the restaurant offers dinner entrées such as locally grown trout and a pork loin with a chipotle chili–plum sauce. Breakfast is also served, and the sidewalk patio fills quickly. ⌧ *428 Zion Park Blvd., Springdale* ☎ *435/772–3244. $14–$24* ⊟ *AE, DC, MC, V* ⊘ *No lunch.*

★ **$$–$$$** ✕ **The Switchback Grille.** Crowded with locals and tourists alike, this restaurant is known for its wood-fired pizzas, ribs, and vegetarian dishes. Try the excellent portobello sandwich for lunch. The vaulted ceilings make the dining room feel open and comfortable. ⌧ *1149 S. Zion Park Blvd., Springdale* ☎ *435/772–3700* ⊕ *www.switchbacktrading.com. $14–$30* ⊟ *AE, D, MC, V.*

**$–$$$** ✕ **Scaldoni's Grill.** At this local favorite you can't go wrong if you're hankering for Italian food. But if you're in the mood for something else, don't despair: they also serve a variety of steaks and seafood, all in delightful surroundings with good views of St. George. ⌧ *929 Sunset Blvd., St. George* ☎ *435/674–1300. $9–$23* ⊟ *AE, D, MC, V* ⊘ *Closed Sun.*

**$–$$** ✕ **Zion Pizza and Noodle Co.** The "Cholesterol Hiker" and "Good for You" pizzas put some pizzazz into the menu; you can also order pasta dishes like linguine with peanuts and grilled chicken and spaghetti with homemade marinara sauce. A selection of microbrews is served. Dine indoors or in the beer garden. The haunt occupies a former church building. ⌧ *868 Zion Park Blvd., Springdale* ☎ *435/772–3815* ⊕ *www. zionpizzanoodle.com. $8–$16* ⊟ *No credit cards* ⊘ *Closed Dec.–Feb.*

**¢–$** ✕ **Sol Foods Market and Deli.** For a quick, healthful meal any time of day, stop here. Daily specials include freshly made wraps and sandwiches. They can also prepare picnic baskets or box lunches for your day in the park. The patio seating is near the Virgin River, with views into the park. ⌧ *95 Zion Park Blvd., Springdale* ☎ *435/772–0277* ⊕ *www.solfoods. com. $5–$9* ⊟ *MC, V.*

**¢** ✕ **Main Street Café.** One of the best cups of coffee in Dixie is poured in Hurricane. A full espresso bar will satisfy "caffiends," while vegetarians and others can choose from salads, sandwiches, breakfast burritos, homemade breads, and desserts. Sit inside to admire the works of local artists, or share the patio with the hummingbirds. ⌧ *138 S. Main St., Hurricane* ☎ *435/635–9080. $3–$6* ⊟ *No credit cards* ⊘ *Closed Sun. No dinner.*

## Where to Stay

### In the Park

**$$** ▣ **Zion Lodge.** Although the original lodge burned down in 1966, the rebuilt structure convincingly re-creates the classic look of the old inn. Knotty pine woodwork and log and wicker furnishings accent the lobby. Lodge rooms are modern but not fancy, and the historic Western-style cabins have gas-log fireplaces. This is a place of quiet retreat, so there are no TVs—kids can amuse themselves outdoors on the abundant grassy lawns. The lodge is within easy walking distance of trailheads, horseback riding, and, of course, the shuttle stop, all of which are less

**38**

CLOSE UP

## Cedar Breaks National Monument

**CEDAR BREAKS NATIONAL MONUMENT**, a natural amphitheater similar to Bryce Canyon, spans almost 3 mi and plunges 2,000 feet into the Markagunt Plateau. Short alpine hiking trails along the rim and thin crowds make this a wonderful summer stop. Although its roads may be closed in winter due to heavy snow, the monument stays open for cross-country skiing and snowmobiling.

It's never crowded here, and most people who visit are content to photograph the monument from one of the handful of overlooks alongside the road—which means the intrepid hiker, skier, or snowshoer can easily find solitude along the trails. In fact, winter is one of the best times to visit, when snow drapes the red-orange formations; though call ahead for road conditions and keep in mind that all visitor facilities are closed from October through late May.

⊠ *Rte. 14, 23 mi east of Cedar City, Brian Head* ☎ *435/586-9451* ⊕ *www.nps.gov/cebr* ⊠ *$4 per person* ⊙ *Visitor center open late-May–mid-Oct., daily 8–6.*

---

than ½ mi away. Make reservations at least six months in advance. ⊠ *Zion Canyon Scenic Dr., 3¼ mi north of Canyon Junction* ☎ *888/297–2757* ⚎ *303/297–3175* ⊕ *www.zionlodge.com* ⇝ *75 rooms, 6 suites, 40 cabins* ⚭ *Restaurant, no TV. $140* ⊟ *AE, D, DC, MC, V.*

**CAMPGROUNDS & RV PARKS**

★ **$–$$**  ⚠ **Watchman Campground.** This large campground on the Virgin River operates on a reservation system between April and October, but you do not get to choose your own site. Sometimes you can get same-day reservations, but don't count on it. ⊠ *Access road off Zion Canyon Visitor Center parking lot* ☎ *435/772–3256, 800/365–2267 reservations* ⇝ *160 sites, 91 with hook-ups* ⚭ *Flush toilets, partial hookups (electric), dump station, drinking water, fire grates, picnic tables. $16 without electricity, $18 with electricity, $20 prime river sites* ⊟ *D, MC, V.*

**$**  ⚠ **South Campground.** All the sites here are under big cottonwood trees, granting campers some relief from the summer sun. The campground operates on a first-come, first-served basis, and sites are usually filled before noon each day during high season. Many of the sites are suitable for either tents or RVs, although there are no hookups. Reservations not accepted. ⊠ *Rte. 9, ½ mi north of south entrance* ⇝ *126 sites* ⚭ *Flush toilets, dump station, drinking water, fire grates, picnic tables* ☎ *435/772–3256. $16* ⊟ *No credit cards* ⊙ *Mid-Mar.–Oct.*

### Outside the Park

⟳ **$$–$$$$**  ▣ **Zion Ponderosa Ranch Resort.** This multi-pursuit resort on an 8,000-acre ranch just east of Zion National Park offers activities from horseback riding to spa treatments, and just about everything in between. Lodging options include suites that sleep 6 and luxurious mountain homes for up to 13. Hearty meals are included. ⊠ *5 mi. north of route marker 46 on North Fork Country Rd., Mount Carmel* ☎ *800/293–5444* ⊕ *www.zionponderosa.com* ⇝ *16 suites, 8 cabins, 17 houses* ⚭ *Restau-*

*rant, DVD (some), tennis courts, pool, spa. $130–$345* ⊟ *AE, D, MC, V* †○| *AP or EP* ⊘ *Closed Dec.–Feb.*

**$$$** 🖼 **Desert Pearl Inn.** By all means stay here when you visit Zion National
Fodor'sChoice  Park, but be forewarned: you won't want to leave. Every room is a suite,
★  with vaulted ceilings and thick carpets, plus cushy throw pillows, Roman
shades, oversize windows, bidets, sleeper sofas, and tiled showers with
deep tubs. The pool area is exceptionally well landscaped and fully
equipped, with a double-size hot tub and a shower-and-restroom block.
⊠ *707 Zion Park Blvd., Springdale 84767* ☎ *435/772–8888 or 888/
828–0898* 🖷 *435/772–8889* ⊕ *www.desertpearl.com* ⇲ *61 rooms*
♺ *Safe, kitchen, refrigerator, VCR, Wi-Fi, pool, no smoking. $153–$168*
⊟ *AE, D, MC, V.*

**$$** 🖼 **Best Western Zion Park Inn.** This spacious and modern facility has large
rooms. The Switchback Grille will get you going in the morning with a
hearty breakfast, and since the inn is a stop on the park shuttle route,
take one step out the door and you're on your way to Zion. ⊠ *1215
Zion Park Blvd., Springdale 84767* ☎ *435/772–3200 or 800/934–7275*
🖷 *435/772–2449* ⊕ *www.zionparkinn.com* ⇲ *114 rooms, 6 suites*
♺ *Restaurant, Wi-Fi, pool, laundry facilities, some pets allowed, no-
smoking rooms. $110* ⊟ *AE, D, DC, MC, V.*

★ **$$** 🖼 **Cliffrose Lodge and Gardens.** Comfortable rooms at this friendly,
charming lodge should keep you happy after a long hike, and from your
balcony you can continue to enjoy views of the towering, colorful cliffs.
Flowers adorn the 5-acre grounds, and the Virgin River runs right along
the property, so you can have a picnic or barbecue out back to the sound
of rushing water. It's within walking distance of the Zion Canyon Vis-
itor Center and shuttle stop. ⊠ *281 Zion Park Blvd., Springdale 84767*
☎ *435/772–3234 or 800/243–8824* 🖷 *435/772–3900* ⊕ *www.
cliffroselodge.com* ⇲ *40 rooms* ♺ *Wi-Fi, pool, no smoking. $139*
⊟ *AE, D, MC, V.*

**$–$$** 🖼 **Flanigan's Inn.** Close to the park with canyon views, this rustic country inn has contemporary furnishings. The pool area is small but sce-
nic. You can walk to the Zion Visitor Center from here (it's a few
blocks), though the shuttle to the canyon stops on the property. ⊠ *428
Zion Park Blvd., Springdale 84767* ☎ *435/772–3244 or 800/765–7787*
🖷 *435/772–3396* ⊕ *www.flanigans.com* ⇲ *34 rooms, 5 suites* ♺ *Restaurant, pool, dial-up, Wi-Fi. $99–$129* ⊟ *AE, D, MC, V.*

**$** 🖼 **Best Western Thunderbird Resort.** A quick 13 mi east of Zion National
Park, this red-adobe motel is a good option if lodging in Springdale has
filled, or if you want to be within an hour's drive of Bryce Canyon National Park as well. Surrounded by the Zion Mountains and bordered
by a scenic golf course, the rooms are spacious and bright. ⊠ *Junction
of U.S. 89 and Rte. 9, Mount Carmel Junction 84755* ☎ *435/648–2203
or 888/848–6358* 🖷 *435/648–2239* ⊕ *www.bestwestern.com* ⇲ *61
rooms, 1 suite* ♺ *Restaurant, Wi-Fi, golf course, pool, laundry facilities, no-smoking rooms. $92* ⊟ *AE, D, DC, MC, V.*

**$** 🖼 **Travelodge.** This basic motel on Hurricane's outskirts provides a
comfortable night's rest without a lot of amenities, though there is a pool.
It's a comfortable distance from Zion National Park, 35 mi. ⊠ *280 W.
State St., Hurricane 84737* ☎ *435/635–4647 or 800/578–7878* 🖷 *435/*

**38**

635–0848 ⊕ *www.travelodge.com* 📞 *63 rooms* ⚍ *Refrigerator (some), pool, some pets allowed, no-smoking rooms. $95* 🖃 *AE, D, DC, MC, V* ⦿I *CP.*

¢–$   ▥ **Golden Hills Motel.** This clean and simple establishment right at Mount Carmel Junction is an inexpensive and no-frills lodging option. Its funky pink-and-blue roadside diner serves good, basic country-style fare like country-fried steak, liver and onions, and homemade breads and pies. ✉ *Junction of U.S. 89 and Rte. 9, Mount Carmel Junction 84755* ☎ *435/648–2268 or 800/648–2268* 📠 *435/648–2558* ⊕ *www. goldenhillsmotel.com* 📞 *30 rooms* ⚍ *Restaurant, pool, laundry facilities, public Internet, some pets allowed, no-smoking rooms. $38–$52* 🖃 *AE, D, MC, V.*

¢   ▥ **Dixie Hostel.** Few hostels can boast of being listed on the National Register of Historic Places and having such proximity to a national park, with a Zion shuttle service to boot for the 35-mi trip. Built in 1929, this bright and clean facility was first a hotel and then a boarding home before becoming a hostel. Reservations are a good idea, especially if you want one of the two private rooms. Prices include tax, linens, and a Continental breakfast. ✉ *73 S. Main St., Hurricane 84737* ☎ *435/635–9000* 📞 *2 private rooms, 28 dorm beds* ⚍ *Kitchen, laundry facilities, public Internet, no TV. $15–$35* 🖃 *No credit cards* ⦿I *CP.*

CAMPGROUNDS &
RV PARKS

$$   ⚠ **Zion Canyon Campground & RV Park.** In Springdale about a half mile from the south entrance to the park, this campground is surrounded on three sides by the canyon's rock formations. Many of the sites are on the river. ✉ *479 Zion Park Blvd., Springdale* ☎ *435/772–3237* 📠 *435/ 772–3844* ⊕ *www.zioncamp.com/rv_park.html* 📞 *110 RV sites, 110 tent sites* ⚍ *Flush toilets, full hookups, dump station, drinking water, guest laundry, showers, fire grates, picnic tables, food service, electricity, public telephone, general store, play area, swimming (river). $22 tent sites, $27 full hookups* 🖃 *D, MC, V.*

$$   ⚠ **Zion River Resort RV Park & Campground.** This resort in Virgin, 8 mi east of Hurricane, has everything an RV camper could want, with the possible exception of shade. Most of the trees haven't grown up yet, but there are some premium sites along the river where the cottonwoods are mature. You can also rent a cabin, tent site, or tepee. The RV hookups include phone or modem connections. Ask about the shuttle to Zion National Park. ✉ *730 E. Rte. 9, Virgin 84779* ☎ *435/635–8594 or 888/822–8594* 📠 *435/635–3934* ⊕ *www.zionriverresort.com* 📞 *133 sites, 112 with hookups* ⚍ *Grills, flush toilets, full hookups, drinking water, guest laundry, showers, picnic tables, electricity, public telephone, general store, play area, swimming (pool). $32 tent sites, $39–$47 full hookups* 🖃 *AE, D, MC, V.*

$–$$   ⚠ **Mukuntuweep.** This shady campsite lies at the east entrance to Zion. At 6,300 feet, it's slightly cooler than the campgrounds on the other side of the park, but unlike those, Mukuntuweep has no river flowing by. ✉ *12120 W. Rte. 9, Orderville* ☎ *435/648–3011* ⊕ *www.xpressweb. com/zionpark* 📞 *230 sites, 30 with hookups* ⚍ *Flush toilets, full hookups, dump station, drinking water, public telephone. $15 for tents, $22 for RVs* 🖃 *AE, D, MC, V.*

☝ $ ⚠ **Coral Pink Sand Dunes State Park.** Roughly 25 mi from Zion, this small and pretty campground tends to be less crowded than those at the national park. Be warned, however, that it can be noisy, since most of Coral Pink's campers are here to ride their ATVs, dune buggies, and motorcycles across the sand dunes. The campground is open all year, but there's no water October–Easter. ✉ *10 mi south of Mount Carmel Junction on U.S. 89, Kanab* ☎ *435/648–2800, 800/322–3770 reservations* ⊕ *www.stateparks.utah.gov* ⟿ *22 sites* ⚭ *Flush toilets, dump station, drinking water, showers, fire grates, picnic tables, ranger station. $15* ▭ *AE, MC, V for phone and online reservations only.*

# ZION ESSENTIALS

ACCESSIBILITY Both visitor centers, all shuttle buses, and Zion Lodge are fully accessible to wheelchairs. Several campsites (sites A24 and A25 at Watchman Campground and sites 103, 114, and 115 at South Campground) are reserved for people with disabilities, and two trails—Riverside Walk and Pa'rus Trail—are accessible with some assistance.

ADMISSION FEES Entrance to Zion National Park is $20 per vehicle for a seven-day pass. People entering on foot or by bicycle or motorcycle pay $10 per person (not to exceed $20 per family) for a seven-day pass. Entrance to the Kolob Canyons section of the park costs only $10, and you receive credit for this entrance fee when you pay to enter Zion Canyon.

ADMISSION HOURS The park is open 24/7 year-round. It's in the Mountain time zone.

ATMS/BANKS The park has no ATM.
🔝 **Zions Bank** ✉ 921 Zion Park Blvd., Springdale ☎ 435/772-3274.

AUTOMOBILE SERVICE STATIONS Just outside the park and in nearby Kanab and Springdale, you can fuel up, get your tires and oil changed, and have auto-repair work done.
🔝 **Kanab Tire Center and Kwik Lube** ✉ 265 E. 300 S, Kanab ☎ 435/644-2557. **Springdale Chevron** ✉ 1593 Zion Park Blvd., Springdale ☎ 435/772-3922. **Zion's Sinclair** ✉ Rte. 9, at the east entrance to Zion National Park, Orderville ☎ 435/648-2828.

EMERGENCIES In the event of an emergency, dial 911, report to a visitor center, or contact a park ranger at 435/772-3322. The nearest hospitals are in St. George, Cedar City, and Kanab.
🔝 **Zion Canyon Medical Clinic** is open in the summer and accepts walk-in patients. ✉ 120 Zion Blvd., Springdale ☎ 435/772-3226 ⊙ June-late Sept., Mon.-Sat. 9-5.

LOST AND FOUND The park's lost-and-found is at the Zion Canyon Visitor Center.

PERMITS Permits are required for backcountry camping and overnight climbs. The maximum size of a group hiking into the backcountry is 12 people. The cost for a permit for 1–2 people is $10; 3–7 people, $15; and 8–12 people, $20. Permits and hiking information are available at the Zion Canyon Visitor Center.

POST OFFICE Within the park, you can mail letters and buy stamps at Zion Lodge.
🔝 **Springdale Branch** ✉ 625 Zion Park Blvd., Springdale 84767 ☎ 800/275-8777.

PUBLIC TELEPHONES Public telephones may be found at South Campground, Watchman Campground, Zion Canyon Visitor Center, Zion Lodge, and Zion Museum. Cell-phone reception is decent in Springdale but spotty in Zion Canyon itself.

RELIGIOUS SERVICES Interdenominational services are held during the summer at Zion Lodge and South Campground. Check bulletin boards at the Zion Canyon Visitor Center for times.

RESTROOMS Public restrooms are located at the Grotto, Kolob Canyons Visitor Center, Temple of Sinawava, Weeping Rock Trailhead, Zion Canyon Visitor Center, Zion Human History Museum, and Zion Lodge.

SHOPS & GROCERS
🚹 **Happy Camper Market** ⊠ 95 Zion Park Blvd., Springdale ☎ 435/772-3402. **Springdale Fruit Company.** ⊠ 2491 Zion Park Blvd. Springdale ☎ 435/772-3822. **Zion Park Market.** ⊠ 855 Zion Park Blvd., Springdale ☎ 435/772-3251.

**NEARBY TOWN INFORMATION**
🚹 **Color Country Travel Region (Hurricane)** ⊠ 906 N. 1400 West, Box 1550, St. George 84770 ☎ 800/233-8824. **Kane County Office of Tourism (Mount Carmel)** ⊠ 78 S. 100 East, Kanab 84741 ☎ 800/733-5263 ⊕ www.kaneutah.com. **Zion Canyon Visitors Bureau (Springdale)** ☐ Box 331, Springdale 84767 ☎ 888/518-7070 ⊕ www.zionpark.com.

**VISITOR INFORMATION**
🚹 **Zion National Park** ⊠ Springdale, UT 84767-1099 ☎ 435/772-3256 ⊕ www.nps.gov/zion.

# Driving Tours

Sequoia National Park

## WORD OF MOUTH

"Get out the map, and lay your finger anywhere down . . . around some corner I can sense a resting place . . . I'm gonna clear my head, I'm gonna drink that sun . . ."

–Indigo Girls

# PACIFIC NORTHWEST DRIVING TOUR

### North Cascades National Park

DAY 1   Start in **Sedro-Woolley,** ❶ where you can pick up information about **North Cascades National Park** ❷ at the park headquarters. From here, it's a 45-minute drive on Route 20 to the park entrance. Take your first stroll through an old-growth forest from the visitor center in Newhalem, then devote the rest of

| THE PLAN |
|---|
| DISTANCE: 1,450 mi |
| TIME: 10 days |
| BREAKS: Overnight in Yakima, Mount Rainier NP, Port Angeles, and Olympic NP, WA; and Florence, Crater Lake NP, and Ashland, OR. |

the day to driving through the **Cascades** on Route 20, stopping at the overlooks. Exit the park and continue through the **Methow Valley.** Head south on Route 20, then Route 153, then U.S. 97, then I–82 (just over 300 mi total) to **Yakima** ❸ to stay the night.

### Mount Rainier National Park

DAYS 2 & 3   On the morning of Day 2, take U.S. 12 west from Yakima 102 mi to Ohanapecosh, the southern entrance to **Mount Rainier National Park** ❹. When you arrive, take the 35-mi, three-hour drive on Sunrise Road, which reveals the "back" (northeast) side of Rainier. A room at the Paradise Inn is your base for the next two nights. On Day 3, energetic hikers can tackle one of the 4- to 6-hour trails up the park's many peaks. Another option is to hike to Panorama Point near the foot of the **Muir Snowfield** for breathtaking views of the glaciers and high ridges of Rainier overhead. After dinner at the inn, watch the sunset's alpenglow on the peak from the back porch.

### Mount St. Helens & the Olympic Foothills

DAY 4   On Day 4, follow routes 706 and 7 to U.S. 12 from Paradise, heading west to I–5. When you reach the interstate, drive south to Route 504 to spend the day at the **Mount St. Helens National Volcanic Monument** ❺ to see the destruction caused from the 1980 volcanic eruption. Return to I–5 the way you came in and head north to Olympia, where you should pick up U.S. 101 north. The highway winds through scenic Puget Sound countryside, skirting the Olympic foothills and periodically dipping down to the waterfront. Stay the next two nights at **Port Angeles** ❻, 136 mi (three hours) from the junction of Route 504 and I–5.

### Olympic National Park

DAYS 5 & 6   The next morning, launch into a full day at **Olympic National Park** ❼, exploring the **Hoh Rain Forest** and **Hurricane Ridge.** Start Day 6 with a drive west on U.S. 101 to Forks and on to **La Push** ❽ via Route 110, a total of about 45 mi. Here, an hour-long lunchtime stroll to **Second or Third Beach** will offer a taste of the wild Pacific coastline. Back on U.S. 101, head south to **Lake Quinault** (about 98 mi from Lake Crescent). Check into the Lake Quinault Lodge, then drive up the river 6 mi to one of the rain-forest trails through the lush Quinault Valley.

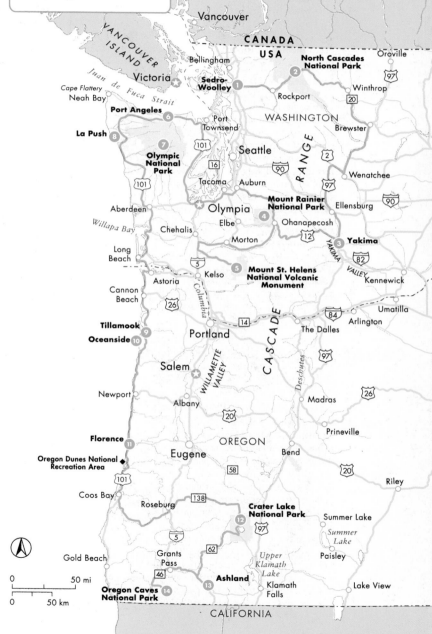

# Pacific Northwest Driving Tour

BRITISH COLUMBIA

Vancouver

CANADA
USA

VANCOUVER ISLAND

Victoria

Cape Flattery
Neah Bay

Bellingham

Sedro-Woolley ①

② North Cascades National Park

Oroville

97

Rockport

Winthrop

20

Brewster

WASHINGTON

Port Angeles ⑥

Port Townsend

101

Seattle

RANGE

Wenatchee

La Push ⑧

⑦ Olympic National Park

16

101

Tacoma

Auburn

90

97

Ellensburg

90

Aberdeen

Olympia

Elbe

④ Mount Rainier National Park

Ohanapecosh

Chehalis

Morton

12

③ Yakima

Willapa Bay

Long Beach

5

Kelso

⑤ Mount St. Helens National Volcanic Monument

YAKIMA VALLEY

82

Kennewick

Astoria

Columbia

14

84

Umatilla

Cannon Beach

26

Portland

The Dalles

Arlington

Tillamook ⑨

Oceanside ⑩

Salem

WILLAMETTE VALLEY

CASCADE

Deschutes

97

Madras

26

Newport

Albany

20

Prineville

Florence ⑪

Oregon Dunes National Recreation Area

101

OREGON

Eugene

Bend

20

Riley

58

Coos Bay

Roseburg

138

⑫ Crater Lake National Park

97

Summer Lake

Summer Lake

Gold Beach

5

62

Grants Pass

Upper Klamath Lake

Paisley

46

⑬ Ashland

Klamath Falls

Lake View

Oregon Caves National Park ⑭

CALIFORNIA

0    50 mi

0    50 km

### The Pacific Coast

DAY 7   Leave early on Day 7 for the long but scenic drive south on U.S. 101. Here the road winds through coastal spruce forests, periodically rising on headlands to offer ocean panoramas. Once you're in Oregon, seaside resort towns beckon with cafés, shops, and inns. In **Tillamook** ❾ (famous for its cheese), take a detour onto the Three Capes Loop, a stunning 35-mi byway. Stop in **Oceanside** ❿ for lunch. Back on U.S. 101, continue south to the charming village of **Florence** ⓫, 290 mi (6–8 hours) from Lake Quinault. Spend the night here.

### Crater Lake National Park

DAYS 8 & 9   From Florence, take U.S. 101 south to Reedsport, routes 38 and 138 west to Sutherlin, I–5 south to Roseburg, and Route 138 west again to **Crater Lake National Park** ⓬, 180 mi in total. Once inside the park, you can continue along Rim Drive for another half hour for excellent views of the lake. Overnight in the park or Fort Klamath. In the morning, take the lake boat tour and a hike through the surrounding forest. In the afternoon, head south on Route 62 to I–5, and on to **Ashland** ⓭, 83 mi (about two hours) from Crater Lake. Stay the night in one of Ashland's superb B&Bs. Have dinner and attend one of the **Oregon Shakespeare Festival** productions (mid-February to early November).

### Oregon Caves National Monument

DAY 10   On Day 10, head back north on I–5 from Ashland to Grants Pass, then turn south on U.S. 199. At Cave Junction, 67 mi from Ashland, you can take a three-hour side-trip to **Oregon Caves National Monument** ⓮. Guided tours of the unique marble caves last 90 minutes; in the summer the day's last tour is by candlelight, which will give you a sense of what it might have been like for early explorers.

—by John Blodgett

# CANADIAN ROCKIES DRIVING TOUR

*Note: Watch for wildlife on the highways and roads as you are driving through the mountains.*

### Jasper National Park

DAYS 1 & 2   From **Edmonton** ❶, travel 225 mi west on Yellowhead Highway 16 to **Jasper National Park** ❷. You'll pass through some stunning scenery as you move from the prairies to the foothills to the mountains. Watch for bighorn sheep, mountain goats, elk, and bears as you enter the park. Spend your afternoon exploring the shops and sites of the Jasper townsite. Stop at the Jasper Information Centre to get trail maps and information about free park interpretive programs. Take a drive to **Disaster Point Animal Lick** ❸, about 53 km (33 mi) northeast of the town of Jasper, then make a stop at nearby Miette Hot Springs and enjoy a swim in the hot mineral pools.

> **THE PLAN**
>
> **DISTANCE:** 750–1,000 mi
> **TIME:** 10 days
> **BREAKS:** Overnight in Jasper, AB; Lake Louise, AB; Emerald Lake, BC; and Banff, AB; Fairmont or Kimberley, BC; Waterton NP, AB; East Glacier, MT; and West Glacier, MT.

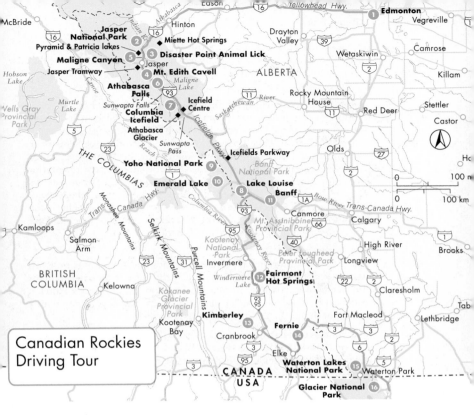

Canadian Rockies
Driving Tour

The next morning, explore **Mt. Edith Cavell,**  about 27 km (17 mi) south of Jasper. The 1-km (6/10 mi) trail from the parking lot leads to the base of an imposing cliff, where you can see the stunning Angel Glacier. A steep 3-km (2-mi) trail climbs up the valley to Cavell Meadows, carpeted with wildflowers from mid-July to mid-August. Afternoon options include hiking in **Maligne Canyon** , canoeing or horseback riding near the Jasper Park Lodge, or swimming in Lake Edith.

### Icefields Parkway

DAY 3  From Jasper townsite, proceed west along Connaught Drive. At the intersection of the Yellowhead Highway 16, proceed through the lights straight ahead to reach Highway 93, the Icefields Parkway. Make a short stop at **Athabasca Falls** , just 31 km (19 mi) south of Jasper. The 75-foot falls are some of the most powerful falls in the mountain national parks. Continue driving along the Icefields Parkway until you reach the Athabasca Glacier, one of the eight major glaciers making up the **Columbia Icefield** . This incredible ice field covers an area of approximately 325 square km (125 square mi) and is one of the largest accumulations of ice and snow south of the Arctic Circle. Enjoy lunch at the Icefield Centre, and then experience an ice explorer bus tour or a guided hike of the Athabasca Glacier. *For safety reasons, do not venture onto the glacier without a guide.* Continue driving along the Icefields Parkway, passing the Weeping Wall and stopping to stretch your legs at the Saskatchewan River Crossing and at scenic Bow Lake, before stopping for the night at **Lake Louise** ⑧.

## Lake Louise

DAY 4   Spend the morning enjoying the scenery at the beautiful Lake Louise, snapping a few pictures of the impressive Victoria Glacier flowing off the mountain at the lake's end. You can have morning tea at the classy Fairmont Chateau Lake Louise Hotel, then (June through September) ride the Lake Louise Sightseeing Gondola to the Whitehorn Lodge, where you can participate in a guided hike or interpretive presentation and enjoy lunch on an alpine plateau with a view of a dozen-plus glaciers. If time permits, take a drive 32 km (20 mi) west to **Yoho National Park** ⑨ and visit **Emerald Lake** ⑩, where you can rent a canoe, have dinner at the teahouse, or take a stroll. You can overnight at Emerald Lake Lodge or stay 57 km (35 mi) away in Banff.

## Banff National Park

DAYS 5 & 6   Spend the next morning exploring the shops and restaurants on Banff Avenue in the **Banff townsite** ⑪. Visit Canada Place in the afternoon for fun interactive activities. Stop at the Fairmont Banff Springs Hotel, a National Historic Site, and stroll the grounds. Finish your day with a late-night dip in the Banff Upper Hotsprings.

One your second day in Banff, take a short, early morning jaunt on Vermillion Lakes Drive, off the West Banff exit from Highway 1. Common wildlife sightings include elk, bighorn sheep, muskrat, and the occasional moose. When you return to town, visit the Banff Gondola for a view from the 7,500-foot summit of Sulfur Mountain. Try to take in an artistic performance at the Banff Centre in the evening, or partake of the nightlife on Banff Avenue.

## Fairmont or Kimberley, BC

DAY 7   This morning, head southwest from Banff into British Columbia on Highway 93. Stop and enjoy the hot springs in the small town of **Fairmont Hot Springs** ⑫. Consider reserving a white-water rapids excursion or a voyageur canoe trip ahead of time with Kootenay River Runners in nearby Radium (☎ 250/347–9210 ⊕ www.raftingtherockies.com). Or play a round of golf at one of the area's championship courses. Stay the night in Fairmont Hot Springs, or drive further on Highway 83 to the Bavarian-style mountain town of **Kimberley** ⑬.

## Waterton Lakes & Glacier National Parks

DAYS 8–10   Continue driving south on Highway 93 to Jaffray. Just after Jaffray, turn east onto Highway 3 towards the ski resort town of **Fernie** ⑭, which is a good place for a bite to eat. Continue driving east on Highway 3 through the scenic Crowsnest Pass into Alberta. At Pincher Creek turn south onto Highway 6 and head toward **Waterton Lakes National Park** ⑮. Explore the Waterton townsite then have dinner at the Prince of Wales Hotel.

In the morning of Day 9, take a drive southwest on the Akamina Parkway to Cameron Lake, where you can hike the trails around the lake or rent a rowboat and a fishing rod to try catching trout. If time permits, take a drive on Red Rock Parkway, followed by a walk around Red Rock Canyon.

Make your way from Waterton to Glacier via one of two routes. From mid-May to mid-September you can take Provincial Road 5 to the Chief Mountain International Highway and across the border to State 17, and then U.S. 89 to the eastern entrance of **Glacier National Park** ⑯. *Be sure to check border-crossing hours.* (When this route is closed, take Provincial Road 5 east to Cardston, then turn south on Provincial Road 2, which connects with U.S. 89.) Spend the night in East Glacier at Many Glacier Hotel or Glacier Park Lodge.

On Day 10, treat yourself to a drive up the Going-to-the-Sun Road from East Glacier to West Glacier. The road travels from the lowest elevations to the summit of the Continental Divide. Stop at the Logan Pass Visitor's Center to learn about the park's flora and fauna before taking a short hike along the scenic Skyline Trail. Snap a picture of Bird Woman Falls as you proceed toward West Glacier, and stop to take the short hike to McDonald Falls. The Lake MacDonald Lodge makes a good lunch or dinner stop, and from here you can also rent a canoe or take a guided cruise on the lake. Overnight in West Glacier.

–by Debbie Olsen

# GLACIER TO GRAND TETON DRIVING TOUR

## Glacier National Park & Montana Scenic Byways

DAY 1 After visiting **Glacier National Park** ❶, with its 1,500 square mi of exquisite ice-carved terrain, plan to spend half a day (or more, depending on stops) driving on a scenic, 160-mi route through western Montana. Start off going southwest on U.S. 2 to **Kalispell** ❷, then

**THE PLAN**

DISTANCE: 850–1,000 mi
TIME: 5 days
BREAKS: Overnight in Bozeman or Livingston, MT; and Yellowstone NP, Grand Teton NP and Jackson, WY.

**39**

south on Highway 206 and Highway 83, through the Seeley–Swan Valley, where you'll have a view of the Mission Range to the west and the Swan Range to the east. South of **Seeley Lake** ❸, turn east on Route 200, and then take Route 141 to the small town of **Avon** ❹, about 36 mi west of Helena. From here, turn west on U.S. 12 to connect with I–90. Continue southeast 10 mi to **Deer Lodge** ❺, and 41 mi to the century-old mining town of **Butte** ❻, where the lavish Copper King Mansion reveals what you could buy with an unlimited household budget back in the 1880s, when it was built. From Butte, follow I–90 to **Bozeman** ❼ or **Livingston** ❽. Either town is a good place to get a good night's sleep before exploring Yellowstone.

## Yellowstone National Park

DAYS 2 & 3 Dedicate the next two days to **Yellowstone National Park** ❾. From Bozeman, you can reach **West Yellowstone** ❿ by following I–90 west 8 mi to U.S. 287, then driving south 106 mi. (From Livingston, enter the park from the north by driving south 57 mi on U.S. 89.) Spend your first day

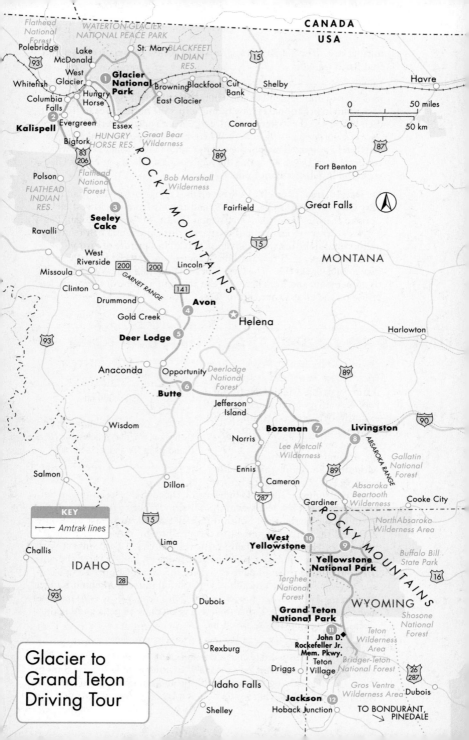

Glacier to Grand Teton Driving Tour

on the park's 142-mi Grand Loop Road. It passes nearly every major Yellowstone attraction, and you'll discover interpretive displays, overlooks, and short trails along the way. On your second day in the park, hike the park's trails, visit the geyser basins, or watch the wildlife. For your accommodations, you really can't go wrong with a stay at Old Faithful Inn, with its lodgepole walls and ceiling beams, immense volcanic rock fireplace, and green-tinted, etched windows.

### Grand Teton National Park

DAYS 4 & 5  On the final two days of your tour, experience Wyoming's other national treasure, **Grand Teton National Park** ⑪. Its northern boundary is just 7 mi from Yellowstone's south entrance. The sheer ruggedness of the Tetons makes them seem imposing and unapproachable, but a drive on Teton Park Road, with frequent stops at scenic turnouts, will get you up close and personal with the peaks. Overnight in one of the park lodges and spend your final day in the park hiking, horseback riding, or taking a river float trip, before continuing south to **Jackson** ⑫, where you'll find landmark elk antler arches in the town square, fine dining, art galleries, museums, and eclectic shopping.

*–by Candy Moulton*

# DAKOTAS' BLACK HILLS DRIVING TOUR

### Wind Cave National Park

DAY 1  Start in Hot Springs, the southern gateway to Wind Cave National Park. Here you can see historic sandstone buildings and an active dig site where the remains of 52 fossilized full-sized mammoths have been discovered at **Mammoth Site** ①. After viewing them, take a dip into **Evans Plunge** ②—the world's largest natural warm-water indoor swimming pool, holding 1 million gal-

> **THE PLAN**
>
> **DISTANCE:** 120 mi (340 mi with optional add-on)
> **TIME:** 5–7 days
> **BREAKS:** Overnight in Hot Springs, Custer, or Custer State Park, SD; Keystone, SD; Rapid City, SD; Deadwood, SD; and Medora, ND.

39

lons. After lunch, drive 6 mi north on U.S. 385 to **Wind Cave National Park** ③. The park has 28,000 acres of wildlife habitat above ground and the world's fourth-longest cave below. Take an afternoon cave tour and a short drive through the park. Overnight at nearby Custer State Park, or in one of the B&Bs around Hot Springs or Custer.

### Custer State Park

DAY 2  Spend today at **Custer State Park** ④, just 5 mi east of Custer on U.S. 16A. The 110-square-mi park has exceptional drives, lots of wildlife, and fingerlike granite spires rising from the forest floor. Relax on a hayride and enjoy a chuck wagon supper, or take a Jeep tour into the buffalo herds. Overnight in one of four enchanting mountain lodges.

### Jewel Cave National Monument & Crazy Horse Memorial

DAY 3  Today, venture down U.S. 16 to **Jewel Cave National Monument** ⑤, where you can see the beautiful nailhead and dogtooth spar crystals lining its

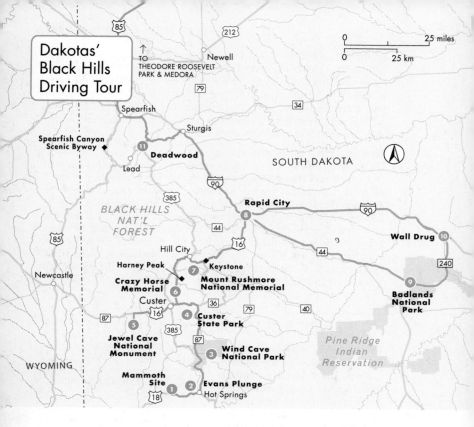

more than 100 mi of passageways. As you head from Custer State Park to Jewel Cave National Monument, you pass through the friendly community of Custer on U.S. 385. It's surrounded by some of the Black Hills' most striking scenery—picture towering rock formations spearing out of ponderosa pine forests. If you have extra time, explore Cathedral Spires, Harney Peak, and Needles Highway (Highway 87).

After visiting Jewel Cave, head back to Custer and take U.S. 16/385 toward the former gold and tin mining town of Hill City. Along the way you'll hit **Crazy Horse Memorial** ⑥, the colossal mountain carving of the legendary Lakota leader. The memorial's complex includes the Indian Museum of North America, which displays beautiful bead- and quill-work from many of the continent's native nations. Overnight at one of the hotels in and around Keystone, such as the K Bar S Lodge.

## Mount Rushmore National Memorial

DAY 4  This morning, travel just 3 mi from Keystone (10 from Hill City) on Route 244 (the Gutzon Borglum Memorial Highway) to **Mount Rushmore National Memorial** ⑦, where you can view the huge, carved renderings of presidents Washington, Jefferson, Roosevelt, and Lincoln. Afterward, head northwest on U.S. 16 to **Rapid City** ⑧, western South Dakota's largest city and the eastern gateway to the Black Hills. Overnight here.

### Badlands National Park

DAY 5  Begin your day early and drive 55 mi on Route 44 to the North Unit of **Badlands National Park** 〇. Badlands Loop Road wiggles through this moonlike landscape for 32 mi. When you've had enough of this 380-square-mi geologic wonderland, head back to the hills. Exit onto Route 240 at the northeast entrance to catch I–90. For a fun excursion, take a little detour east to Wall for its world-famous **Wall Drug** ⑩. Founded on the premise that free ice water would attract road-weary travelers, the emporium carries all manner of Westernalia.

Spend this afternoon and tonight in **Deadwood** ⑪, reached via U.S. 14 and 14A. This Old West mining town has 80 gaming halls, including Old Style Saloon No. 10, which bills itself as "the only museum in the world with a bar." Upstairs, at the Deadwood Social Club, you can discover outstanding food at reasonable prices and the best wine selection in the state. To view rare artifacts from the town's colorful past, such as items that once belonged to Wild Bill Hickock, visit Adams Memorial Museum. Overnight in Deadwood's Franklin Hotel, where past guests have included Theodore Roosevelt, Babe Ruth, and John Wayne.

### Theodore Roosevelt National Park

DAYS 6 & 7 OPTION  If you want to include Theodore Roosevelt in your tour, tack on two extra days. Begin Day 6 by traveling from the hills to the plains and then to North Dakota's badlands via U.S. 85. At the intersection with I–94, turn west. When grassy plains give way to tall ridges of fire-colored rock, you'll know you've hit Theodore Roosevelt National Park. Painted Canyon scenic overlook will give you a first tremendous view of the park. Spend the next day in the South Unit, where highlights include prairie dog towns, a petrified forest, and several overlooks. Overnight in the historic frontier town of **Medora**. It has wonderful golf, several good places to eat, and the Medora Musical, a good family activity.

–by T.D. Griffith & Dustin D. Floyd

**39**

# NORTHERN CALIFORNIA DRIVING TOUR

California's North Coast and Far North are sparsely peopled and amply forested. Driving east and south, you'll see ragged shoreline, the lush Cascade Range, and mighty Sierra Nevada peaks. This tour takes you along curving, two-lane scenic routes where the going is sometimes slow—especially if you're following a logging truck.

| THE PLAN |
| --- |
| **DISTANCE:** 750 mi<br>**TIME:** 8 days<br>**BREAKS:** Overnight in Eureka, Redding, Lassen Volcanic NP, Tahoe City, and Yosemite NP, CA. |

Distances between services can be long, and the weather is unpredictable, so keep your tank and cooler full. This tour is not recommended in winter due to wet and snowy conditions, road closures in the mountains, and park seasonality.

### Redwood National Park

DAY 1   Begin your journey in coastal Crescent City, 20 mi south of the Oregon state line, and drive south into **Redwood National Park** ❶ on Redwood Highway/U.S. 101. At the Lagoon Creek picnic area, hike the Hidden Beach section of the Coastal Trail to the Klamath Overlook. Continuing south on the highway, turn west onto Coastal Drive, a partially unpaved road that threads through the big trees and past ocean vistas. The road merges with Newton B. Drury Scenic Parkway in Prairie Creek Redwoods State Park; continue south to the visitor center at Orick. Get a free permit for Tall Trees Access Road, then backtrack north on the parkway to Bald Hills Road. The twisting route connects with the partly unpaved access road to Tall Trees Grove. After a look at some of the world's tallest redwoods, stop in Lady Bird Johnson Grove and return to the highway. Head down U.S. 101 to spend the night amid the Victorian architecture of **Eureka** ❷.

### Eureka to Redding

DAY 2   The next morning, head a few miles north on U.S. 101 and pick up Route 299 east at Arcata. The mountain road winds along the canyon of the wild and scenic Trinity River to the gold-rush town of **Weaverville** ❸. Take a stroll and take in some history, then continue east to Redding and north on I–5 to **Shasta Lake** ❹, where you can take a tour of Lake Shasta Caverns and get out on the water. Finish the day back in **Redding** ❺ with a sunset walk across Santiago Calatrava's modernist Sundial Bridge.

### Lassen Volcanic National Park

DAYS 3 & 4   On Day 3 (spring through fall), drive east on Route 44 to **Lassen Volcanic National Park** ❻. When you arrive, start at the Loomis Museum and drive the park road (Route 89) south through lava fields and past geothermal springs, stopping for hikes at Kings Creek Falls, Lassen Peak, and Bumpass Hell. This is where the Sierra Nevada meets the Cascades; plant and animal species unique to each coexist here, and the area's winters are harsh and snowy. Take Route 89 south out of the park to Route 36 east, then head north on Warner Valley Road from Chester back into the park and check into the Drakesbad Guest Ranch for two nights (make reservations far in advance). Spend Day 4 horseback riding through Lassen or hiking to thermal features near the ranch.

In winter, roads into Lassen are closed. If you're touring then, drive straight from Redding to Lake Tahoe via I–5 south and Route 50 east.

### Lake Tahoe

DAY 5 & 6   Start your fifth day by driving south on Route 89 for three hours (about 150 mi) to **Lake Tahoe** ❼. Drive around the lake and take in the dazzling views, or if it's winter, hit the slopes and enjoy Tahoe's phenomenal skiing. The town of Tahoe City on the northwest shore has accommodations ranging from rustic vacation cottages to small hotel-style resorts.

### Yosemite National Park

DAYS 7 & 8   Early on the morning of Day 7 (spring through fall), take Route 89 southeast to U.S. 395, about 85 mi or 2½ hours from Tahoe City. Turn south on U.S. 395 and drive 60 mi through the high-mountain desert of the eastern Sierra to Route 120. Drive west on Route 120 and enter **Yosemite**

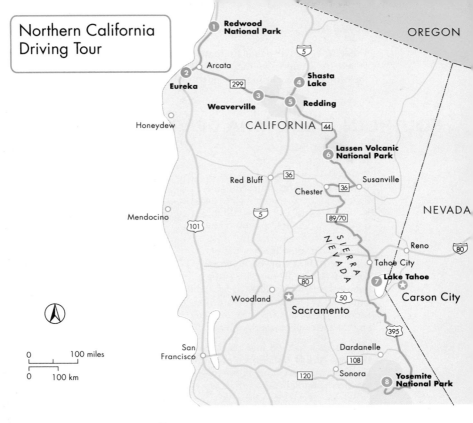

# Northern California Driving Tour

Redwood National Park ①

OREGON

Arcata ②

Shasta Lake ④

Eureka

Honeydew

Weaverville ③

Redding ⑤

CALIFORNIA 44

Lassen Volcanic National Park ⑥

Red Bluff 36

Susanville

Chester 36

Mendocino 101

5

89/70

NEVADA

Reno 80

SIERRA NEVADA

Tahoe City

Lake Tahoe ⑦

Carson City

Woodland 80

50

Sacramento

395

San Francisco

Dardanelle

108

120 Sonora

Yosemite National Park ⑧

0 — 100 miles
0 — 100 km

National Park ⑧ through its eastern gate. The 60-mi crossing through the high country takes you over Tioga Pass (9,941 feet) and along the highest stretch of road in California. Stop for lunch in Tuolumne Meadows and stretch your legs with a hike through alpine wildflowers.

Traffic through the park can move slowly in summer; plan on two full hours to reach the valley from the eastern gate. Take the hike to Yosemite Falls, and have a cocktail at the grand Ahwahnee hotel. In the evening, attend one of the fascinating ranger programs or a presentation at Yosemite Theater. If you have secured an advance reservation, stay two nights in Yosemite Valley or Wawona (closed January and February). Otherwise, get a room in Mariposa, 40 mi west of the valley on Route 140.

Ride the shuttle or rent a bike your last day in Yosemite so you don't have to fight for a parking space. Hike to Vernal Fall and to Mirror Lake, and drop in at the visitor center, museum, and Indian Village. Drive up to Glacier Point for a valley-wide view, timing your arrival for sunset. End your day with a relaxing dinner at the Wawona Hotel.

In winter, snow closes parts of Route 89 around Tahoe; Route 120 is closed east of Yosemite November through May. To get from Lake

Tahoe to Yosemite via an alternate route during these times, take U.S. 50 west to Route 49 south to Route 120 east. Route 49 takes you along the Mother Lode, through the heart of Gold Country.

*—by Constance Jones*

# SOUTHERN CALIFORNIA DRIVING TOUR

## Yosemite, Sequoia, and Kings Canyon National Parks

DAYS 1 & 2  After visiting **Yosemite National Park ❶**, leave Yosemite Valley on Route 41 south and drive 100 mi, or about two hours, to Fresno and the turn-off for Route 180 east. Ahead 50 mi, you'll reach the entrance to **Kings Canyon National Park ❷**. Follow Route 180 (summer only) along the Kings River and its giant granite canyon, well over a mile deep at some points. Stop along the way at pull-outs for long vistas of some of the highest mountains in the United States. (In winter, you'll have to head south on the Generals Highway.)

| THE PLAN |
| --- |
| **DISTANCE:** 1,200–1,600 mi |
| **TIME:** 7–9 days |
| **BREAKS:** Overnight in Yosemite NP; Sequoia or Kings Canyon NP; Death Valley NP; and Palm Springs, Los Angeles, and Ventura, CA. |

Double back to the Generals Highway and continue south to **Sequoia National Park ❸**, where some of the world's oldest and largest trees stand. Driving the winding, 40-mi-long Generals Highway takes about two hours. Book in advance and stay for two nights in either of the two parks. Spend the intervening day further exploring the parks.

## Death Valley National Park

DAYS 3 & 4  Leave Sequoia via the southern entrance and follow Route 198 about 23 mi to Route 65 south, where you'll turn left and head 60 mi toward Bakersfield. Route 65 ends at Route 99 south; get on the freeway, go one exit to Route 204 (Golden State Avenue), and turn onto Route 178 east. Follow Route 178 through the southern tip of the Sequoia National Forest, and about 35 mi from Bakersfield, you'll reach **Lake Isabella ❹**, the reservoir that catches the water from the Kern River, the major drainage for snow melting off the peaks in Sequoia National Park. The trip from Sequoia to the lake should take three hours.

Continue for about 55 mi east on Route 178 to U.S. 395. Turn north on U.S. 395 and travel about 80 mi to Route 190 east, where you'll turn right and continue 60 mi to **Death Valley National Park ❺**. Vast expanses of desert and mountain ranges extend as far as the eye can see, and you'll find the lowest point on the continent here, at 282 feet below sea level. Summer heat is brutal, and all safety precautions should be taken. Plan on spending the night here, but be sure to secure reservations in advance; this isolated area is not a place to wander around looking for a room. From Lake Isabella, the trip should take three to four hours, so expect an eight-hour, 400-mi day of driving from Sequoia. Alternatively, stop in Bakersfield for the night, or camp at Lake Isabella, and make the trip

the next day. If you make the trip in one shot, spend two nights in Death Valley and explore the park for a full day. If you stop for the night between Sequoia and Death Valley, get an early start so you can spend most of the day in the park, then overnight there.

### Mojave National Preserve & Joshua Tree National Park

DAY 5  Leave Death Valley early in the morning on Day 5. Travel east on Route 190 to Death Valley Junction and turn south onto Route 127, passing **Mojave National Preserve** 6. Drive 115 mi through the Mojave Desert to I–15, then travel south 60 mi on the interstate to **Barstow**; stop here for lunch. The town is nothing special, but you can take a short hike through a landscape of colored sedimentary rock 8 mi north of town. The trip from Death Valley to Barstow should take around four hours. From Barstow, head south for 70 mi on I–15 (follow I–215 at the split outside **San Bernardino** 7) until you hit I–10. Proceed east on I–10 for about 95 mi and turn at the exit to **Joshua Tree National Park** 8 just north of the interstate. Spend a few hours exploring the numerous, easy short hikes through a landscape that transitions between the Mojave Desert and the more arid, sparsely vegetated Colorado Desert. Overnight in Palm Springs.

### Channel Islands National Park

DAYS 6 & 7 Spend the morning of Day 6 in Joshua Tree, and then hop onto I–10 and head west toward **Los Angeles** ⑨, about 95 mi away. Pay attention: Los Angeles's freeway system uses both names and numbers, and sometimes the route number changes but the name of the freeway does not.

Spend a day hanging out in the city, or skip L.A. and head straight to **Ventura** ⑩, by taking Route 57 (Orange Freeway) north from I–10 to I–210 (Foothill Freeway) and heading west for 19 mi to Route 134 (Ventura Freeway) west. Approximately 16 mi ahead, Route 134 merges with U.S. 101 north. Though the road numbers change, you will remain on the Ventura Freeway for about 50 mi until you're in seaside Ventura, one of the gateway cities to **Channel Islands National Park** ⑪ and home to the park's visitor center. Many folks stop here but don't actually make it out to the islands; if you're planning to visit the islands themselves, you'll need a reservation for the boat.

### Ventura to San Francisco

DAYS 8 & 9 OPTION If you continue on to San Francisco you have a delightful drive ahead of you. Following U.S. 101 north you'll pass **San Luis Obispo**, home of Mission San Luis Obispo de Tolosa, and the kitschy and garish Madonna Inn. From San Luis Obispo continue north either on scenic but slow Route 1 (Pacific Coast Highway) or on speedy but nondescript U.S. 101. Either way, it's about 230 mi to **San Francisco**. Along the way, stop in **Monterey and Carmel,** where you can have lunch and visit the Monterey Bay Aquarium or the Carmel Mission.

–by Mike Nalepa

# CANYON COUNTRY DRIVING TOUR

### Zion & Bryce Canyon

DAYS 1 & 2 From Las Vegas, head up I–15, and take the Route 9 exit to **Zion National Park** ❶. Spend your afternoon in the park—if it's April to October, take the National Park Service bus down Zion Canyon Scenic Drive. Overnight in Springdale, the bustling town right next to the park. The Best Western Zion Park Inn is your best bet for getting a room in the high season. Its Switchback Grille is excellent.

> **THE PLAN**
>
> **DISTANCE:** 1,000–1,200 mi
> **TIME:** 10 days
> **BREAKS:** Overnight in Springdale, Bryce, Torrey, and Moab, UT; Cortez, CO; Monument Valley or Tuba City, AZ; Tusayan or Grand Canyon NP's South Rim, AZ.

Spend the next morning in Zion. For a nice hike, try the short and easy (read: family-friendly) Canyon Overlook Trail, where you can gaze at the massive rock formations, such as East and West Temples. It won't take very long, even if you linger with your camera, so follow it with a stroll along the Emerald Pools Trail in Zion Canyon itself, where you might come across tame wild turkeys and ravens looking for handouts.

Depart the area via Route 9, the **Zion–Mount Carmel Highway** ❷. You'll pass through a 1¹⁄₁₀-mi-long tunnel that is so narrow, RVs and towed

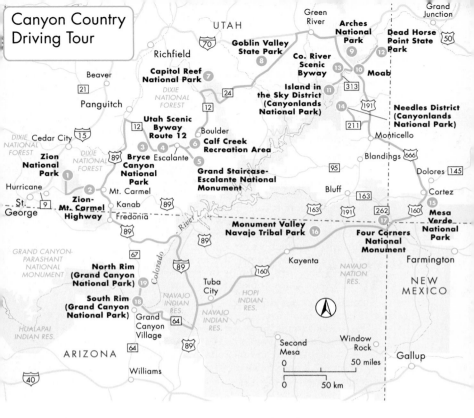

## Canyon Country Driving Tour

vehicles must pay for an escort through. When you emerge, you are in slickrock country, where huge, petrified sandstone dunes are etched by ancient waters. Stay on Route 9 for 23 mi and then turn north onto U.S. 89. After 42 mi, you will reach Route 12, where you should turn east and drive 14 mi to the entrance of **Bryce Canyon National Park** ③. The overall trip from Zion to Bryce Canyon is about 90 minutes.

Central to your tour of Bryce Canyon is the 18-mi main park road, from which numerous scenic turnouts reveal vistas of bright orange-red rock (we recommend starting with the view at Sunrise Point). You'll notice that the air is a little cooler here than it was at Zion, so get out and enjoy it. Trails most worth checking out include the Bristlecone Loop Trail and the Navajo Loop Trail, both of which easily fit into a day trip and will get you into the heart of the park with minimum effort. Listen for peregrine falcons deep in the side canyons, and keep an eye out for the species of prairie dog that only lives in these parts. Overnight in the park or at Ruby's Inn.

### Capitol Reef

DAY 3  Head out this morning on **Utah Scenic Byway–Route 12** ④. If the views don't take your breath away, the narrow, winding road with little margin for error will. Route 12 winds over and through **Grand Staircase-Es-**

calante National Monument ⑤. The views from the narrow hogback are nothing short of incredible. About 14 mi past the town of Escalante you can stop at **Calf Creek Recreation Area** ⑥ to stretch your legs or make a 5½-mi round-trip hike to a gorgeous waterfall. Route 12 continues to gain elevation as you pass over Boulder Mountain.

At the intersection of routes 12 and 24, turn east onto Route 24. You have traveled 112 mi from Bryce Canyon to reach **Capitol Reef National Park** ⑦. The crowds are smaller here than at other national parks in the state, and the scenery is stunning. Orchards in the small enclave of Fruita produce fruit—peaches, pears, and apples—in the late summer and early fall, and are close by ancient Indian rock art. If it's still daylight when you arrive, hike the 1-mi Hickman Bridge Trail if you want to explore a little, or stop in at the visitor center until 4:30 PM (later in the summer) and view pioneer and Native American exhibits, talk with rangers about geography or geology, or watch a film. Nearby Torrey is your best bet for lodging, and be sure to eat at the seasonal Cafe Diablo, serving some of Utah's finest Southwest cuisine from late April to late October. Enjoy freshly brewed coffee and baked goods at Robber's Roost Books and Beverages.

## Arches & Canyonlands

DAYS 4–6 Explore Capitol Reef more the next morning. When you leave, travel east and north for 75 mi on Route 24. If you want a break after about an hour, stop at the small **Goblin Valley State Park** ⑧, 12 mi off Route 24. Youngsters love to run around the sandstone formations known as "goblins." Return to Route 24 and take it to I–70, turn east and continue your journey.

From I-70, take exit 182 south onto U.S. 191, going about 27 mi toward **Arches National Park** ⑨, which holds the world's largest concentration of natural rock windows or "arches." Plan on spending three nights in **Moab** ⑩ while you explore the area. Adventurous types, note that the Colorado River runs near Moab; if you can squeeze in a raft trip on this legendary Western waterway, do it. Otherwise, dedicate Day 5 to Arches, perhaps including a guided hike in the Fiery Furnace, a maze of sandstone canyons and fins that is considered one of the most spectacular hikes in the park. Then on Day 6, launch your **Canyonlands National Park** ⑪ experience with the Island in the Sky District—but first take a detour to the mesa top at **Dead Horse Point State Park** ⑫ for magnificent views of the Colorado River as it goosenecks through the canyons below. To reach the state park, go 10 mi north of Moab on U.S. 191 to Route 313. Drive west for 15 mi, then turn right onto the unnamed road; continue for 6 mi to the Dead Horse fee station. To get from Dead Horse to Islands in the Sky, return to Route 313 and drive 7 mi past the Dead Horse turnoff.

On your way back to Moab, enjoy the natural scenery on the **Colorado River Scenic Byway (Route 128)** ⑬, which runs for about 44 mi along the river, or view man-made art by traveling down Route 279 (Potash Road), where Native American rock-art panels pop up after 4⁸⁄₁₀ mi from the U.S. 191 turnoff.

### Mesa Verde

DAYS 7 & 8  On Day 7, travel 42 mi south of Moab on U.S. 191. At this point, you have a choice to make. Either turn onto Route 211 and drive 34 mi to **Canyonlands' Needles District** ⓪, which is distinctly different from Island in the Sky, or skip this part of the park and drive straight to Monticello.

From Monticello, take U.S. 491 to Cortez, Colorado, and follow U.S. 160 to **Mesa Verde National Park** ⓯. The overall trip from Monticello to Mesa Verde is about 90 not particularly impressive miles. The park, however, where ancient dwellings of the ancestral Puebloan people are the highlight, is more than worth the drive. Overnight in Cortez tonight and tomorrow night while you take Day 8 to explore Mesa Verde.

### The Four Corners & Monument Valley

DAY 9  This morning, head southwest into Arizona on U.S. 160 for the spectacular, deep-red desert of **Monument Valley Navajo Tribal Park** ⓰, whose buttes and spires you will recognize from countless western movies and television commercials—if you want to do the 17-mi self-guided drive here, give yourself a couple of hours, or take a tram tour. Long before you get here, though, stop for a fun photo-op at **Four Corners National Monument** ⓱, which straddles Colorado, New Mexico, Arizona, and Utah. Call it a night at Gouldings Lodge in Monument Valley, or in Tuba City. You'll want to get a good night's sleep and start early for your finale at **Grand Canyon National Park.**

### The Grand Canyon

DAY 10  From Tuba City, you can reach the Grand Canyon via U.S. 89 and Route 64 for the South Rim, or Alternate 89 and Route 67 for the North Rim. If you have only one day, do the **South Rim** ⓲. A good hike is the South Rim Trail, part of which is paved and wheelchair accessible. You can overnight just outside the park in Tusayan or stay on the edge of the canyon in El Tovar (reserve far in advance).

To complete the loop, you can reach Zion National Park from the **North Rim** ⓳ by taking Alternate 89 north through the mountains. The road is winding and steep, but oh so beautiful. If you're heading back to Las Vegas from the South Rim take Route 64 south to Williams and then pick up I-40 west to U.S. 93 north.

–by John Blodgett

**39**

# DINOSAUR NATIONAL MONUMENT TO GREAT SAND DUNES DRIVING TOUR

### Dinosaur National Monument

DAY 1  Start your week-long driving tour at **Dinosaur National Monument** ❶, which straddles the Utah–Colorado border, 200 mi from Salt Lake City and 300 mi from Denver. In the little town of **Dinosaur, CO** ❷, a monument entrance and visitor center is located on the main drag, U.S.

---

**THE PLAN**

**DISTANCE:** 650–670 mi

**TIME:** 7 days

**BREAKS:** Overnight in Dinosaur National Monument or Rangely; Grand Lake or Rocky Mountain NP; Estes Park; Colorado Springs; Lake Pueblo State Park or Pueblo, CO.

40 (known as Brontosaurus Boulevard). Your best bets for lodging, unless you plan to camp in the monument, are in the town of **Rangely** ❸, 20 mi south of Dinosaur via Route 64.

The monument was named for its rich deposits of fossils, but there is more to do than play amateur archeologist. Here the Yampa River meets the famed Green River, so rafters, boaters, and floaters of all types have a wide selection of river-access points and bankside campgrounds from which to choose. Landlubbers can drive north from the visitor center along Harpers Corner Drive for an assortment of scenic overlooks. At road's end is the Harpers Corner Trail, an easy 2-mi round-trip stroll to a spectacular viewpoint of three canyons. *Be sure to watch where you step, for fossils of crinoids, a marine animal whose remains look plantlike, are embedded in the rock along the way.*

### En Route to the Rockies

DAY 2  The journey on Day 2 takes you across northern Colorado's ranching communities to the heart of the Rockies. From Dinosaur National Monument, play hide-and-seek with the Yampa River as you travel 130 mi east across U.S. 40 to **Steamboat Springs** ❹, best known for world-class skiing with a cowboy-chic ambience. Explore the historic downtown and have lunch at the kid-friendly Mahogany Ridge Brewery and Grill.

After lunch, continue east on U.S. 40 to **Granby** ❺ and U.S. 34. Turn north on U.S. 34 toward **Grand Lake** ❻, the western gateway to Rocky Mountain National Park. Overnight in Grand Lake or the Timber Creek campground inside the park.

### Rocky Mountain National Park

DAYS 3 & 4  Spend the next two days in north-central Colorado's crown jewel, **Rocky Mountain National Park** ❼. Begin by exploring Holzwarth Historic Site, a former guest ranch that once attracted trout fishers; then take a short hike on the paved, wheelchair-accessible Coyote Valley Trail for a chance view of elk or moose. Afterward, drive north on high-in-the-sky I–34, over the Continental Divide, and up to the Alpine Visitor Center, the only place in the park with dining services (a snack bar serves items such as chili, hot dogs, and kids' picks like PB & Js). Get a park newspaper for times and locations of the ranger programs.

This afternoon, come down the east side of Trail Ridge Road, where several turnouts let you pull over and enjoy the vistas, including that of towering 14,259-foot Longs Peak. Overnight tonight and tomorrow night in one of the park's campgrounds or in the town of **Estes Park** ❽. On Day 4 explore the park's east side, including a hike around Bear Lake.

### Denver & Colorado Springs

DAY 5  This morning, drive south via the Peak to Peak Scenic Byway, with views of the Continental Divide and its approaches, before catching I–25 at **Denver** ❾. (Note that the Peak to Peak route is 55 mi but will probably take 90 minutes.) If you have kids, a fun lunch stop in Denver is **Casa Bonita's** (⊠ 6715 W. Colfax Ave.), set in a strip mall and hard to miss with its pink facade.

After lunch, head south on I–25 for the hour drive to **Colorado Springs** ❿; overnight here in the shadow of 14,110-foot Pikes Peak.

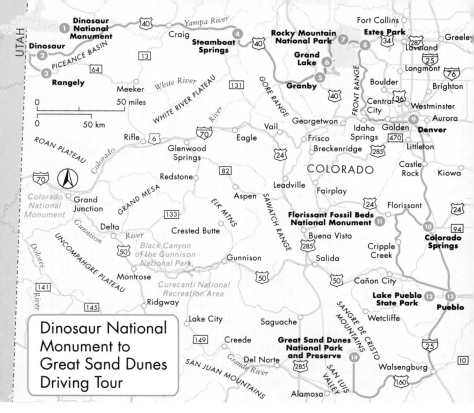

## Florissant Fossil Beds National Monument

DAY 6   Just west of Pikes Peak via U.S. 24, and about 50 mi west of Colorado
Springs, is **Florissant Fossil Beds National Monument** ⑪, where you can spend
the morning exploring petrified redwood stumps approaching 14 feet
in diameter and fossil quarries filled with ancient plants and insects. Don't
miss the "Big Stump"—once the base of a towering redwood, a whopping 38 feet in circumference. After lunch in the picnic area near the
visitor center, take the Gold Belt Tour Scenic & Historic Byway south
to U.S. 50; overnight in **Lake Pueblo State Park** ⑫ or in **Pueblo** ⑬.

## Great Sand Dunes National Park & Preserve

DAY 7   Today's drive will take you to the San Luis Valley. Drive south on I–25
until you reach U.S. 160, then head due west toward Alamosa. About
14 mi east of Alamosa turn north at Highway 150 and go 20 mi to **Great
Sand Dunes National Park and Preserve** ⑭, where North America's tallest
dunes, reaching up to 750 feet, are surrounded by some of the tallest
peaks in the United States (including the 14,000-foot Crestone Peaks to
the north). Summer travelers are advised to avoid hiking on the dunes
during midday, when the sand is hottest, but if your toes get toasty, dip
them afterward in the cool waters of Medano Creek.

–by John Blodgett

# TEXAS & NEW MEXICO DRIVING TOUR

## El Paso

DAY 1 Start in **El Paso, TX ❶**. If you want to take a peek at Old Mexico just south of the border, take the "Border Jumper" trolley the next day and visit **Juarez, Mexico ❷**. Hop off at one of the shopping stops to pick up fine jewelry and leather goods, or barter for bargains at the mercado. Spend the night in El Paso and search out one of the city's coveted

| THE PLAN |
| --- |
| **DISTANCE:** About 460 to 800 mi |
| **TIME:** 5–7 days |
| **BREAKS:** Overnight in El Paso and Lajitas, TX; and Carlsbad, NM, with a possible add-on in Albuquerque or Santa Fe, NM. |

Mexican restaurants—such as Leo's—or drive about 20 mi east on I–10 to **Fabens** to dine on juicy slabs of steak and absorb the middle-of-nowhere, badlands-bluff setting of Cattleman's Steakhouse.

## Big Bend National Park

DAYS 2 & 3 Head for the immense blue-sky country of West Texas by proceeding southeast on I–10 for about three hours or 120 mi, and dropping south at Kent onto Route 118. It takes about 2½ hours to travel about 150 mi to the west entrance of **Big Bend National Park ❸**. Before entering the park, spend the night in **Lajitas ❹**, on Route 170 about 20 mi west of the park entrance. The charming Lajitas Resort on the Rio Grande is a good alternative to the plainer lodgings closer to the park—although it's a bit more expensive. Another alternative is the park's Chisos Mountains Lodge. Accomodations here are bare-bones (you won't even find a room phone), but the peacefulness inside reflects the calm but rugged mountain beauty outside. Be sure to reserve several months in advance, especially for Spring Break stays. Pack a picnic lunch and spend the third day of your tour exploring the park via its mostly paved—though narrow and sometimes curving—roadways. Hike some of the trails and look for the succulent, thorny spikes of the lechuguilla, which is unique to the Chihuahuan Desert.

## Guadalupe Mountains National Park

DAY 4 On Day 4 head north from Big Bend on U.S. 385 about 40 mi to the tiny town of **Marathon ❺**. Take a peek at the tiled courtyards and cool gardens of the historic Gage Hotel, then dally in the nearby shops where you'll find landscapes by Southwestern artists, Central American imports, and cured cowhides. If you're shopping on Sunday, be sure to go early—most shops close by mid-afternoon. Afterward, proceed west on U.S. 90 for about 30 mi to Alpine and north on Route 118 about 75 mi to I–10. Travel west on I–10 for about 40 mi or 30 minutes. Turn north onto Route 54, a slower, two-lane highway, for about 53 mi and then northeast onto U.S. 62/180 for about 2 mi to reach **Guadalupe Mountains National Park ❻**. Including a short stop in Marathon, the drive to Guadalupe from Big Bend should take about four to five hours. Orient yourself at the park visitor center, where displays and a video will introduce you to this northernmost region of the Chihuahuan Desert. Spend a few hours hiking some of the easier trails, and if you're lucky enough

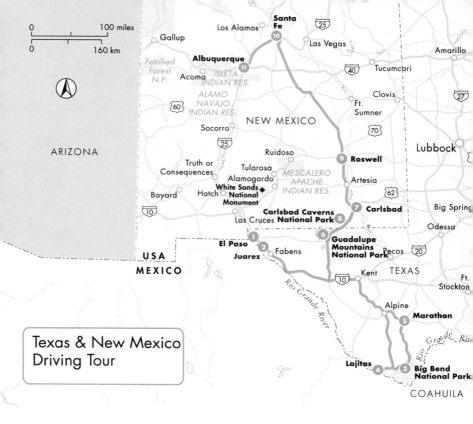

Texas & New Mexico
Driving Tour

to visit in fall, don't miss the spectacular foliage of **McKittrick Canyon**.
Stop off at the **Frijole Ranch Museum** for a healthy dose of history and
ranching culture. The museum (Frijole means bean, by the way) is about
2 mi north of the park visitor center. Because of the dearth of lodging
options nearby, plan on spending the night in **Carlsbad, NM** ⑦, about
55 mi northeast of the park on U.S. 62/180.

## Carlsbad Caverns National Park

**DAY 5** Start the next day with a visit to **Carlsbad Caverns National Park** ⑧, 27
mi southwest of town on U.S. 62/180. Plan on spending at least two
hours touring the caverns. Fill the afternoon with a swim in the Pecos
River at **Lake Carlsbad Recreation Area**, or visit the botanical and zoo-
logical displays at **Living Desert Zoo and Gardens State Park** (in order to
do justice to the 1,200 acres, plan to set aside more than a few hours
here). In summer, return to Carlsbad Caverns at sunset to witness the
swirling mass exodus of bats from the cave as they prepare to gorge on—
literally—tons of insects. Then spend another night in Carlsbad.

## Santa Fe & Albuquerque

**DAYS 6 & 7** After the bats have gone home to roost, it's time to hit the road again.
**OPTION** Take U.S. 285 north on your way to the Southwestern arts and cultural
mecca that is Sante Fe, but be sure to cleanse your palate first with an

eyeful of kitsch in **Roswell** ⑨. To get there from Carlsbad, drive 76 mi north on U.S. 285. There isn't much to this tiny town, but rumors of a UFO crash-landing and a government cover-up have made it famous. The shops are filled with alien memorabilia, and if you pop through in May, you might even see a giant alien head among the hot air balloons.

Afterward, a pleasant three-hour, 193-mi drive north on U.S. 285 brings you from Roswell to **Santa Fe** ⑩, where you can explore the adobe charms of the downtown central Plaza. Stop first at the Palace of the Governors on the Plaza's north side, and then investigate the crafts and wares of Native American outdoor vendors. East of the Plaza, check out the Romanesque-style St. Francis Cathedral. The northern New Mexico city is sometimes referred to as a "holy place" for photographers because of the luminous quality of the light here; check out some examples at the Museum of Fine Arts. Or, take in indigenous art at the Museum of Indian Arts and Culture. Treat yourself to some of the city's distinctive New Mexican cuisine in the evening.

If you're in the mood for some more old Southwest, spend an extra day in **Albuquerque** ⑪, just an hour-long, 60-mi ride from Santa Fe. Start out by strolling through the shops of Old Town Plaza, then visit the New Mexico Museum of Natural History and Science. After lunch, head north to the Indian Pueblo Cultural Center and then west to Petroglyph National Monument. Return east for a sunset ride on the Sandia Peak Aerial Tramway.

−by Jennifer Edwards

# CAMPGROUNDS AT A GLANCE

# CAMPGROUNDS AT A GLANCE

| CAMPGROUND NAME | Total # of sites | # of RV sites | # of hook-ups | Drive-to sites | Hike-to sites | Flush toilets | Pit toilets | Drinking water | Showers | Fire grates/pits | Swimming | Boat access | Playground | Dump station | Ranger station | Public telephone | Reservations possible | Daily fee per site | Dates open |
|---|---|---|---|---|---|---|---|---|---|---|---|---|---|---|---|---|---|---|---|
| **ARCHES** | | | | | | | | | | | | | | | | | | | |
| ★ Devils Garden | 52 | 52 | 0 | Y | | Y | | Y | | Y | | | | | | | | $15 | Y/R |
| **BADLANDS** | | | | | | | | | | | | | | | | | | | |
| ★ Cedar Pass Campground | 96 | 96 | 0 | Y | | | Y | Y | | | | | | Y | Y | | | $10 | Apr.–Oct. |
| ★ Sage Creek Primitive | ULP | ULP | 0 | Y | | | Y | | | | | | | | | | | Free | Y/R |
| **BANFF** | | | | | | | | | | | | | | | | | | | |
| Castle Mountain | 43 | 43 | 0 | Y | Y | Y | | Y | | Y | | | | Y | | | | $19 | May–Sept. |
| Johnston Canyon | 132 | 132 | 0 | Y | Y | Y | | Y | Y | Y | | | | Y | Y | | | $24 | June–Sept. |
| ★ 🕐 Lake Louise | 409 | 189 | 189 | Y | Y | Y | | Y | Y | Y | | | | Y | Y | Y | | $24–$28 | Y/R |
| Mosquito Creek | 32 | 32 | 0 | Y | | | Y | | | Y | | | | | | | | $14 | Y/R |
| Protection Mountain | 89 | 89 | 0 | Y | | Y | | Y | | Y | | | | Y | | | | $19 | June–Sept. |
| Rampart Creek | 50 | 50 | 0 | Y | | | Y | | | Y | | | | | | | | $14 | June–Sept. |
| ★ 🕐 Tunnel Mountain Trailer Court | 321 | 321 | 321 | Y | | Y | | Y | Y | Y | | | | Y | Y | | | $33 | May–Oct. |
| ★ 🕐 Tunnel Mountain Village 1 | 618 | 618 | 0 | Y | | Y | | Y | Y | Y | | | | Y | Y | Y | | $24 | May–Oct. |
| ★ 🕐 Tunnel Mountain Village 2 | 188 | 188 | 188 | Y | | Y | | Y | Y | Y | | | | Y | Y | Y | | $28 | Y/R |
| Two Jack Main | 380 | 380 | 0 | Y | | Y | | Y | Y | Y | | | | Y | Y | | | $19 | May–Sept. |
| Two Jack Lakeside | 74 | 0 | 0 | Y | | Y | | | | Y | Y | Y | | Y | | | | $24 | May–Sept. |
| Waterfowl Lakes | 116 | 116 | 0 | Y | | Y | | Y | | Y | Y | Y | | Y | | | | $19 | June–Sept. |
| **BIG BEND** | | | | | | | | | | | | | | | | | | | |
| Chisos Basin | 65 | | | Y | Y | Y | | Y | | Y | | | | Y | Y | Y | | $10 | Y/R |
| ★ 🕐 Rio Grande Village | 100 | | | Y | Y | Y | | Y | | Y | Y | | | Y | Y | Y | | $10 | Y/R |
| 🕐 Rio Grande RV | 25 | 25 | 25 | Y | | Y | | Y | | Y | | | | Y | Y | Y | | $21 | Y/R |
| Cottonwood | 35 | | | Y | | Y | | Y | | Y | Y | | | | Y | Y | | $10 | Y/R |

| | Sites | | | | | | | | | | | | | | Fee | Season |
|---|---|---|---|---|---|---|---|---|---|---|---|---|---|---|---|---|
| **BLACK CANYON** | | | | | | | | | | | | | | | | |
| North Rim | 13 | 13 | 0 | 13 | | | | Y | | Y | | | | | $12 | May–Oct. |
| ★ South Rim | 65 | 23 | 23* | 88 | | | | Y | | Y | | Y | | | $12, $18 | Y/R |
| **BRYCE CANYON** | | | | | | | | | | | | | | | | |
| North | 107 | 47 | 0 | Y | Y | | | Y | | Y | Y | | Y | Y | $10 | Y/R |
| Sunset | 101 | 49 | 0 | Y | Y | | | Y | Y | Y | | | Y | | $10 | May–Oct. |
| **CANYONLANDS** | | | | | | | | | | | | | | | | |
| Needles Outpost | 23 | 0 | 0 | Y | Y | Y | | Y | Y | Y | | | Y | | $15 | mid-March–Oct. |
| ★ Squaw Flat | 25 | 25 | 0 | Y | Y | | | Y | | Y | Y | | | | $10 | Y/R |
| Willow Flat | 12 | 2 | 0 | Y | | | | Y | | | Y | | Y | | $5 | Y/R |
| **CAPITOL REEF** | | | | | | | | | | | | | | | | |
| Cathedral Valley Campground | 6 | 0 | 0 | 6 | Y | | | | Y | | | | | | free | Y/R |
| Cedar Mesa Campground | 5 | 0 | 0 | 5 | | Y | | | Y | | | | | | free | Y/R |
| ★ ☺ Fruita Campground | 71 | 71 | 0 | 71 | | | Y | Y | | | | | | | $10 | Y/R |
| **CARLSBAD CAVERNS** | | | | | | | | | | | | | | | | |
| Wilderness Camping Only | | | | | | | | | | | | | | | | |
| **CHANNEL ISLANDS** | | | | | | | | | | | | | | | | |
| Del Norte | 4 | 0 | 0 | | Y | | | | Y | | | | Y | | $15 | Y/R |
| East Anacapa | 7 | 0 | 0 | | Y | | | | Y | | Y | | Y | | $15 | Y/R |
| ★ Santa Cruz | 40 | 0 | 0 | | Y | Y | | Y | Y | | | | Y | | $15 | Y/R |
| San Miguel | 9 | 0 | 0 | | Y | | | | Y | | | Y | Y | | $15 | Y/R |
| Santa Barbara | 10 | 0 | 0 | | Y | | | | Y | | | Y | Y | | $15 | Y/R |
| Santa Rosa | 15 | 0 | 0 | | Y | | Y | Y | Y | | | | Y | | $15 | Y/R |

Key:
**ULP: Unlimited Primitive**
**Y/R: Year-round**
***Partial hookups**

# CAMPGROUNDS AT A GLANCE

| CAMPGROUND NAME | Total # of sites | # of RV sites | # of hook-ups | Drive-to sites | Hike-to sites | Flush toilets | Pit toilets | Drinking water | Showers | Fire grates/pits | Swimming | Boat access | Playground | Dump station | Ranger station | Public telephone | Reservations possible | Daily fee per site | Dates open |
|---|---|---|---|---|---|---|---|---|---|---|---|---|---|---|---|---|---|---|---|
| **CRATER LAKE** | | | | | | | | | | | | | | | | | | | |
| Mazama | 211 | 211 | 0 | Y | | Y | Y | Y | Y | Y | | | | Y | Y | | Y | $18–$23 | June–Oct. |
| Lost Creek | 16 | 0 | 0 | Y | | Y | Y | Y | Y | Y | | | | | | | | $10 | July–Sept. |
| **DEATH VALLEY** | | | | | | | | | | | | | | | | | | | |
| ★ Furnace Creek | 136 | 136 | 0 | Y | | Y | | Y | Y | Y | Y | | | Y | Y | Y | | $18 | Y/R |
| Mahogany Flat | 10 | 10 | 0 | Y | | | Y | | | Y | | | | | | | | Free | Mar.–Nov. |
| Mesquite Springs | 30 | 30 | 0 | Y | | Y | | Y | | Y | | | Y | Y | | | | $12 | Y/R |
| Panamint Springs Resort | 67 | 41 | 41 | Y | | Y | | Y | Y | Y | | | Y | Y | Y | Y | Y | $15–$30 | Y/R |
| Stovepipe Wells Village | 204 | 14 | 14 | Y | | Y | | Y | Y | Y | Y | | Y | Y | Y | | | $12–$23 | Oct. 15–Apr. 15 |
| Sunset | 1,000 | 1,000 | 0 | Y | | Y | | Y | Y | Y | | Y | Y | Y | Y | | | $12 | Oct. 15–Apr. 15 |
| ★ Texas Spring | 92 | 92 | 0 | Y | | Y | | Y | Y | Y | | | Y | | | | | $14 | Oct. 15–Apr. 15 |
| Thorndike | 6 | 6 | 0 | Y | | | Y | | | Y | | | | | | | | Free | Mar.–Nov. |
| Wildrose | 23 | 23 | 0 | Y | | | Y | | | Y | | | | | | | | Free | Oct. 15–Apr. 15 |
| **GLACIER & WATERTON** | | | | | | | | | | | | | | | | | | | |
| *Glacier* | | | | | | | | | | | | | | | | | | | |
| Apgar | 194 | 25 | 0 | Y | | Y | | Y | | Y | Y | | | Y | Y | | | $15 | May–Oct. |
| Avalanche Creek | 87 | 50 | 0 | Y | | Y | | Y | | Y | Y | | | Y | Y | | | $15 | June–Sept. |
| Bowman Lake | 48 | 0 | 0 | | Y | | Y | Y | | Y | Y | | | | | | | $12 | May–Sept. |
| Fish Creek | 178 | 18 | 0 | Y | | Y | | Y | | Y | | | | Y | | Y | | $17 | June–Oct. |
| Kintla Lake | 13 | 0 | 0 | | Y | | Y | Y | | Y | | | | | | | | $12 | May–Sept. |
| ★ Many Glacier | 110 | 13 | 0 | Y | | Y | | Y | | Y | Y | | | Y | Y | | | $15 | May–Sept. |
| Rising Sun | 83 | 3 | 0 | Y | | Y | | Y | | Y | Y | | | Y | Y | | | $15 | May–Sept. |
| Sprague Creek | 25 | 0 | 0 | Y | | Y | | Y | | Y | Y | | | | | | | $15 | May–Sept. |

| Campground | Total Sites | Sites w/ Hookups | Max RV Length | Fee | Season |
|---|---|---|---|---|---|
| St. Mary | 148 | 25 | 0 | $17 | May–Sept. |
| Two Medicine | 99 | 13 | 0 | $15 | May–Sept. |
| **Waterton Lakes** | | | | | |
| Waterton Townsite | 238 | 208 | 95 | $24–$33 | Apr.–Oct. |
| Belly River | 24 | 24 | 0 | $14 | May–Oct. |
| Crandell Mountain | 129 | 129 | 0 | $19 | May–Oct. |
| **GRAND CANYON** | | | | | |
| Bright Angel | 33 | 0 | 0 | Free | Y/R |
| Desert View | 50 | 50 | 0 | $10 | mid-May–mid-Oct. |
| Indian Garden | 15 | 0 | 0 | Free | Y/R |
| ★ Mather | 319 | 319 | 0 | $15 | Y/R |
| North Rim | 83 | 83 | 0 | $15–$20 | May–Oct. |
| **GRAND TETON** | | | | | |
| ★ Colter Bay | 350 | 238 | 0 | $14 | May–Sept. |
| Colter Bay Trailer Village | 116 | 116 | 116 | $44 | May–Sept. |
| Gros Ventre | 360 | 360 | 0 | $12 | May–Oct. |
| ★ Jenny Lake | 49 | 0 | 0 | $12 | May–Sept. |
| Lizard Creek | 60 | 60 | 0 | $15 | June–Sept. |
| Signal Mountain | 86 | 86 | 0 | $15 | May–Oct. |
| **GREAT BASIN** | | | | | |
| Baker Creek | 32 | 0 | 0 | $12 | May–Sept. |
| Lower Lehman Creek | 11 | limited | 0 | $12 | Y/R |
| Upper Lehman Creek | 24 | 0 | 0 | $12 | May–Sept. |
| ★ Wheeler Peak | 37 | 0 | 0 | $12 | June–Sept. |

Key:
Y/R: Year-round
** Summer only

# CAMPGROUNDS AT A GLANCE

| CAMPGROUND NAME | Total # of sites | # of RV sites | # of hook-ups | Drive-to sites | Hike-to sites | Flush toilets | Pit toilets | Drinking water | Showers | Fire grates/pits | Swimming | Boat access | Playground | Dump station | Ranger station | Public telephone | Reservations possible | Daily fee per site | Dates open |
|---|---|---|---|---|---|---|---|---|---|---|---|---|---|---|---|---|---|---|---|
| **GREAT SAND DUNES** | | | | | | | | | | | | | | | | | | | |
| Pinyon Flats Campground | 88 | 0 | 0 | 88 | | Y | | Y | Y | Y | | | | Y | Y | Y | | $14 | Y/R |
| **GUADALUPE MOUNTAINS** | | | | | | | | | | | | | | | | | | | |
| Dog Canyon | 13 | 4 | 0 | Y | | Y | | Y | | | | | | Y | Y | Y | | $8 | Y/R |
| Pine Springs | 41 | 18 | 0 | Y | Y | Y | Y | Y | | | | | | Y | Y | Y | | $8 | Y/R |
| **JASPER** | | | | | | | | | | | | | | | | | | | |
| Columbia Icefield | 33 | 0 | 0 | Y | Y | | Y | Y | | Y | | | | | Y | | | $14 | May–Oct. |
| Honeymoon Lake | 35 | 35 | 0 | Y | | | Y | Y | | Y | Y | | | | Y | | | $14 | June–Sept. |
| Jonas Creek | 25 | 25 | 0 | Y | | | Y | Y | | Y | | | | | Y | | | $14 | May–Sept. |
| Mt. Kerkeslin | 42 | 42 | 0 | Y | | | Y | Y | | Y | | | | | | | | $14 | June–Sept. |
| Pocahontas | 140 | 130 | 0 | Y | | | Y | Y | | Y | | | | | Y | | | $19 | May–Oct. |
| Snaring River | 66 | 48 | 0 | Y | Y | | Y | Y | | Y | | | | | | Y | | $14 | May–Sept. |
| ◊ Wabasso | 228 | 228 | 0 | Y | | Y | | Y | Y | Y | | Y | Y | Y | Y | Y | Y | $19 | June–Sept. |
| Wapiti | 362 | 362 | 40 | Y | | Y | | Y | Y | Y | | | Y | Y | Y | Y | Y | $24–$28 | June–Sept. |
| ◊ Whistlers | 781 | 781 | 177 | Y | | Y | | Y | Y | Y | | Y | Y | Y | Y | Y | Y | $21–$33 | May–Oct. |
| Wilcox Creek | 46 | 46 | 0 | Y | | Y | Y | Y | | Y | | | Y | Y | Y | Y | Y | $14 | June–Sept. |
| **JOSHUA TREE** | | | | | | | | | | | | | | | | | | | |
| Belle | 18 | 0 | 0 | Y | | | Y | | | Y | | | | | | | | $5 | Y/R |
| ★ Black Rock Canyon | 100 | 100 | 0 | Y | Y | Y | | Y | | Y | | | Y | Y | Y | Y | Y | $10 | Y/R |
| Cottonwood | 65 | 65 | 0 | Y | Y | Y | | Y | | Y | | | Y | Y | Y | | | $10–$25 | Y/R |
| Hidden Valley | 39 | 39 | 0 | Y | | | Y | | | Y | | | | | | | | $5 | Y/R |
| Indian Cove | 114 | 114 | 0 | Y | | | Y | | | Y | | | | | | Y | Y | $10–$35 | Y/R |
| Jumbo Rocks | 125 | 125 | 0 | Y | | | Y | | | Y | | | | | | | | $5 | Y/R |

| Campground | | | | | | | | | | | | | | | Fee | | Season |
|---|---|---|---|---|---|---|---|---|---|---|---|---|---|---|---|---|---|
| Ryan | 31 | 31 | 0 | Y | | | | Y | | | | | | | Free | | Y/R |
| Sheep Pass | 6 | 6 | 0 | Y | | | | Y | | | | | | Y | $20–$35 | | Y/R |
| White Tank | 15 | 0 | 0 | Y | | | | Y | | | | | | | $5 | | Y/R |
| **LASSEN VOLCANIC** | | | | | | | | | | | | | | | | | |
| ★ Manzanita Lake | 179 | 148 | 0 | Y | Y** | | | Y | | Y | | Y | | | $18 | | May–Sept. |
| Summit Lake North | 46 | 46 | 0 | Y | Y | Y | | Y | | Y | | | | | $18 | | June–Sept. |
| Juniper Lake | 18 | 0 | 0 | Y | | Y | | Y | | | | | | | $10 | | June–Sept. |
| Southwest Walk-In | 21 | 0 | 0 | Y | Y** | | Y | Y | | Y | | | | | $14 | | Y/R |
| Summit Lake South | 48 | 48 | 0 | Y | Y | Y | | Y | | Y | | | | | $16 | | June–Sept. |
| Warner Valley | 18 | 0 | 0 | Y | Y | Y | | Y | | Y | | | | | $14 | | June–Oct. |
| **MESA VERDE** | | | | | | | | | | | | | | | | | |
| ★ Morefield Campground | 380 | 15 | 15 | 380 | Y | | | Y | | Y | | Y | Y | Y | $20–$30 | | Late Apr.–mid-Oct. |
| **MOUNT RAINIER** | | | | | | | | | | | | | | | | | |
| ★ Cougar Rock | 173 | 173 | 0 | Y | Y | | | Y | | Y | | Y | Y | Y | $12–$15 | | May–Oct. |
| Ipsut | 30 | 0 | 0 | Y | | Y | | Y | | Y | | Y | | | $8 | | Y/R |
| ★ Mowich Lake | 30 | 0 | 0 | | | Y | | | | | | Y | Y | Y | Free | | July–Oct. |
| ★ Ohanapecosh | 188 | 188 | 0 | Y | Y | | Y | Y | | Y | | Y | Y | | $12–$15 | | May–Oct. |
| Sunshine Point | 18 | 18 | 0 | Y | Y | | Y | Y | | Y | Y | | Y | | $10 | | Y/R |
| White River | 112 | 112 | 0 | Y | Y | | Y | Y | | Y | | Y | | Y | $10 | | June–Sept. |
| **NORTH CASCADES** | | | | | | | | | | | | | | | | | |
| Colonial Creek | 162 | 32 | 0 | Y | Y | | Y | Y | Y | Y | | Y | | | $12 | | May–Sept. |
| Goodell Creek | 21 | 0 | 0 | Y | Y** | Y | | Y | | Y | | Y | | | $10** | | Y/R |
| Newhalem Creek | 111 | 111 | 0 | Y | Y | Y | | Y | | Y | Y | | Y | | $12 | | May–Oct. |
| Lake Chelan National Recreation Area | 63 | 0 | 0 | | | Y | Y | | | | | Y | | | Free | | Y/R |

Key:
Y/R: *Year-round*
** *Summer only*

# CAMPGROUNDS AT A GLANCE

| CAMPGROUND NAME | Total # of sites | # of RV sites | # of hook-ups | Drive-to sites | Hike-to sites | Flush toilets | Pit toilets | Drinking water | Showers | Fire grates/pits | Swimming | Boat access | playground | Dump station | Ranger station | Public telephone | Reservations possible | Daily fee per site | Dates open |
|---|---|---|---|---|---|---|---|---|---|---|---|---|---|---|---|---|---|---|---|
| **OLYMPIC** | | | | | | | | | | | | | | | | | | | |
| Altaire | 30 | 30 | 0 | Y | | Y | | Y | | Y | | | | | | | | $12 | Apr.–Oct. |
| Deer Park | 14 | 0 | 0 | Y | | | Y | Y | | Y | | | | | | | | $10 | May–Sept. |
| Dosewallips | 30 | 0 | 0 | Y | | | Y | Y | | Y | | | | | Y | | | $10 | May–Oct. |
| Elwha | 40 | 40 | 0 | Y | | | Y | Y | | Y | | | | | Y | | | $10 | May–Oct. |
| ★ Fairholm | 88 | 88 | 0 | Y | | Y | | Y | | Y | Y | Y | | Y | Y | | | $12 | Y/R |
| Graves Creek | 30 | 30 | 0 | Y | | Y | | Y | | Y | | | | | | | | $12 | Apr.–Oct. |
| Heart o' the Hills | 105 | 105 | 0 | Y | | Y | | Y | | Y | | | | Y | Y | | | $12 | Apr.–Oct. |
| Hoh | 88 | 88 | 0 | Y | | Y | Y | Y | | Y | | | | Y | Y | | | $12 | Y/R |
| July Creek | 28 | 0 | 0 | | Y | | | Y | | Y | | | | | | | | $12 | Y/R |
| Kalaloch | 175 | 175 | 0 | Y | | Y | Y | Y | | Y | Y | | | Y | Y | | | $10 | Apr.–Oct. |
| Lake Quinault Resort Village | 31 | 31 | 31 | Y | | Y | Y | Y | Y | Y | | | | Y | Y | Y | Y | $14–$18 | Y/R |
| ★ Mora | 94 | 93 | 0 | Y | | Y | | Y | | Y | | | | Y | Y | Y | Y | $22 | Apr.–Oct. |
| North Fork | 7 | 0 | 0 | Y | | | Y | | | Y | | | | | Y | | | $12 | Y/R |
| Ozette | 15 | 15 | 0 | Y | | | Y | Y | | Y | | | | | Y | | | $10 | May–Sept. |
| Queets | 20 | 0 | 0 | Y | | | Y | Y | | Y | | | | | Y | | | $12 | May–Oct. |
| Sol Duc | 82 | 82 | 0 | Y | | Y | | Y | | Y | Y | | | Y | Y | | | $10 | Apr.–Oct. |
| South Beach | 50 | 50 | 0 | Y | | | Y | Y | | Y | | | | | Y | | | $14 | May–Oct. |
| Staircase | 56 | 56 | 0 | Y | | Y | | Y | | Y | | | | | Y | | | $10 | Apr.–Oct. |
| **PETRIFIED FOREST** | | | | | | | | | | | | | | | | | | | |
| Wilderness Camping Only | | | | | | | | | | | | | | | | | | | Y/R |

| Campground | | | | | | | | | | | | | | Daily fee | Open |
|---|---|---|---|---|---|---|---|---|---|---|---|---|---|---|---|
| **REDWOOD** | | | | | | | | | | | | | | | |
| DeMartin | 10 | 0 | 0 | | Y | | Y | | | | Y | | | Free | Y/R |
| Elk Prairie | 75 | 75 | 0 | Y | | | | Y | | Y | Y | | Y | Y** | $20 | Y/R |
| Flint Ridge | 10 | 0 | 0 | | Y | | Y | | | | Y | | | Free | Y/R |
| ★ Gold Bluffs Beach | 26 | 26 | 0 | Y | | Y | | Y | Y | Y | Y | | Y | | $15 | Y/R |
| Jedediah Smith | 106 | 106 | 0 | Y | | Y | | Y | Y | Y | Y | Y | Y | Y** | $20 | Y/R |
| Little Bald Hills | 5 | 0 | 0 | | Y | | Y | | | | Y | | | Free | mid-May–mid Nov. |
| Mill Creek | 145 | 145 | 0 | Y | | | | Y | Y | Y | Y | | Y | Y** | $20 | May–LD |
| Nickel Creek | 5 | 0 | 0 | | Y | | Y | | | | Y | | | Free | Y/R |
| **ROCKY MOUNTAIN** | | | | | | | | | | | | | | | |
| Aspenglen | 54 | 19 | 0 | Y | Y** | Y | | Y** | Y | Y | Y | | Y | | $20 | mid-May–late Sept. |
| Glacier Basin | 150 | 39 | 0 | Y | Y** | Y | | Y** | Y | Y | Y | Y | Y | Y | $20 | late May–early Sept. |
| Longs Peak | 26 | 0 | 0 | Y | Y** | Y** | | Y** | Y** | Y | Y | | Y | | $20 | Y/R |
| ★ Moraine Park | 247 | 65 | 0 | Y | Y** | Y** | | Y** | Y** | Y | Y | Y | Y | Y | $20 | Y/R |
| Timber Creek | 98 | 70 | 0 | Y | Y** | Y** | | Y** | Y** | Y | Y | | Y | | $20 | Y/R |
| **SAGUARO** | | | | | | | | | | | | | | | |
| Douglas Spring | 3 | 0 | 0 | | Y | | Y | | | | | | | Y | $6 | Y/R |
| Grass Shack | 3 | 0 | 0 | | Y | | Y | | | | | | | Y | $6 | Y/R |
| Happy Valley | 3 | 0 | 0 | | Y | | Y | | | | Y | | | Y | $6 | Y/R |
| Juniper Basin | 3 | 0 | 0 | | Y | | Y | | | | Y | | | | $6 | Y/R |
| Manning Camp | 6 | 0 | 0 | | Y | | Y | | | | Y | | | | $6 | Y/R |
| Spud Rock Spring | 3 | 0 | 0 | | Y | | Y | | | | Y | | | | $6 | Y/R |

Key:  
Y/R: Year-round  
** Summer only  
LD: Labor Day

# CAMPGROUNDS AT A GLANCE

| Campground Name | Total # of sites | # of RV sites | # of hook-ups | Drive-to sites | Hike-to sites | Flush toilets | Pit toilets | Drinking water | Showers | Fire grates/pits | Swimming | Boat access | Playground | Dump station | Ranger station | Public telephone | Reservations possible | Daily fee per site | Dates open |
|---|---|---|---|---|---|---|---|---|---|---|---|---|---|---|---|---|---|---|
| **SEQUOIA/KINGS CANYON** | | | | | | | | | | | | | | | | | | | |
| *Sequoia* | | | | | | | | | | | | | | | | | | | |
| Atwell Mill | 23 | 0 | | Y | | | Y | Y | | Y | | | | | | | | $12 | May–Oct. |
| Buckeye Flat | 28 | 0 | | Y | | | Y | Y | | Y | | | | | | | | $18 | Apr.–Sept. |
| Dorst Creek | 204 | 204 | | Y | Y | Y | | | | Y | | | | Y** | | | | $20 | MD–LD |
| Lodgepole | 214 | 214 | | Y | Y | Y | | Y** | | Y | | | | Y** | Y | Y | | $20 | Y/R |
| Potwisha | 42 | 42 | | Y | Y | Y | | | | Y | | | | Y | Y | Y | | $18 | Y/R |
| South Fork | 10 | 0 | | Y | | | Y | | | Y | | | | | | | | $12** | Y/R |
| *Kings Canyon* | | | | | | | | | | | | | | | | | | | |
| Azalea | 113 | 0 | | Y | | Y | | | | Y | | | | | Y | | | $18 | Y/R |
| Canyon View | 37 | 0 | | Y | | Y | | Y | | Y | | | | | Y | | | $18 | Y/R |
| Crystal Springs | 67 | 0 | | Y | | Y | | | | Y | | | | | Y | | | $18 | MD–Sept. |
| Sentinel | 82 | 0 | | Y | | Y | | | | Y | | | | | Y | | | $18 | MD–LD |
| ★ Sheep Creek | 111 | 0 | | Y | | Y | | Y | | Y | | | | | Y | | | $18 | May–Oct. |
| Sunset | 200 | 0 | | Y | | Y | | | | Y | | | | | Y | | | $18 | May–Oct. |
| **THEODORE ROOSEVELT** | | | | | | | | | | | | | | | | | | | |
| ★ Cottonwood | 78 | 30 | | Y | Y** | Y** | Y | | | Y | | | Y | | | | | $10 | Y/R |
| Juniper | 50 | 25 | | Y | Y** | Y** | Y** | | | Y | | | Y | | | | | $10 | Y/R |
| Round-Up Group Horse Camp | 10 | 0 | | Y | | | Y | | | Y | | | | | | Y | | $20 | May–Sept. |
| **WIND CAVE** | | | | | | | | | | | | | | | | | | | |
| ★ Elk Mountain Campground | 75 | 0 | Y | | | | | Y | | Y | | | | | Y | Y | Y | $6–$12 | Y/R |

## YELLOWSTONE

| Campground | | | | Price | Season |
|---|---|---|---|---|---|
| Bridge Bay | 430 | 430 | 0 | $17 | May–Sept. |
| Canyon | 272 | 272 | 0 | $17 | June–Sept. |
| Fishing Bridge RV Park | 346 | 346 | 346 | $17 | May–Sept. |
| Grant Village | 425 | 425 | 0 | $17 | June–Sept. |
| Indian Creek | 75 | 75 | 0 | $12 | June–Sept. |
| Lewis Lake | 85 | 85 | 0 | $12 | June–Oct. |
| Madison | 280 | 280 | 0 | $17 | May–Oct. |
| Mammoth Hot Springs | 85 | 85 | 0 | $14 | Y/R |
| Norris | 116 | 116 | 0 | $14 | May–Sept. |
| Pebble Creek | 32 | 32 | 0 | $12 | June–Sept. |
| Slough Creek | 29 | 29 | 0 | $12 | May–Oct. |
| Tower Fall | 32 | 32 | 0 | $12 | May–Sept. |

## YOSEMITE

| Campground | | | | Price | Season |
|---|---|---|---|---|---|
| Bridalveil Creek | 74 | 74 | 0 | $14 | July–Sept. |
| Camp 4 | 35 | 0 | 0 | $5 | Y/R |
| Crane Flat | 166 | 166 | 0 | $20 | June–Sept. |
| Hodgdon Meadow | 105 | 105 | 0 | $20 | Y/R |
| Housekeeping Camp | 266 | 266 | 0 | $72 | May–Oct. |
| Lower Pines | 60 | 60 | 0 | $20 | Mar.–Oct. |
| North Pines | 80 | 80 | 0 | $20 | Y/R |
| Porcupine Flat | 52 | 52 | 0 | $10 | July–Oct. |
| Tamarack Flat | 52 | 52 | 0 | $10 | July–Sept. |

Key:
Y/R: Year-round
** Summer only
MD: Memorial Day
LD: Labor Day

# CAMPGROUNDS AT A GLANCE

| CAMPGROUND NAME | Total # of sites | # of RV sites | # of hook-ups | Drive-to sites | Hike-to sites | Flush toilets | Pit toilets | Drinking water | Showers | Fire grates/pits | Swimming | Boat access | Playground | Dump station | Ranger station | Public telephone | Reservations possible | Daily fee per site | Dates open |
|---|---|---|---|---|---|---|---|---|---|---|---|---|---|---|---|---|---|---|---|
| ★ Tuolumne Meadows | 314 | 314 | 0 | Y | | Y | | Y | | Y | | | | Y | Y | Y | | $20 | July–Sept. |
| Upper Pines | 238 | 238 | 0 | Y | | Y | | Y | Y | Y | | | | Y | Y | Y | Y | $20 | Y/R |
| Wawona | 93 | 93 | 0 | Y | | Y | | Y | Y | Y | Y | | Y | Y | Y | | Y | $20 | Y/R |
| ★ White Wolf | 87 | 87 | 0 | Y | | Y | | Y | | Y | Y | | | Y | Y | | | $14 | July–Sept. |
| Yosemite Creek | 75 | 75 | 0 | Y | | | Y | | | Y | | | | | Y | | | $10 | July–Sept. |
| **ZION** | | | | | | | | | | | | | | | | | | | |
| South | 126 | 126 | 0 | Y | | Y | | Y | | Y | | | Y | | Y | | | $16 | Apr.–Sept. |
| ★ Watchman | 160 | 91 | 91 | Y | | Y | | Y | | Y | | | Y | Y | Y | Y | | $16–20 | Y/R |

# INDEX

## PHOTO CREDITS

227, *imagebroker/Alamy.* 231, *Jacom Stephens/Avid Creative, Inc. /iStockphoto.* **Chapter 12: Carlsbad Caverns:** 243, *W.P.Fleming/viestiphoto.com.* 244–45, *Peter Jones/NPS.* 247, *Craig Lovell/viestiphoto. com.* 250, *Karl Schatz/Aurora Photos.* 251, *Peter Jones/NPS.* **Chapter 13: Channel Islands:** 261, *Gary Crabbe/age fotostock.* 262, *Lisa Seaman Photography/Aurora Photos.* 263, *Gary Crabbe/age fotostock.* 265, *Debra Behr/Alamy.* **Chapter 14: Crater Lake:** 279, *SuperStock/age fotostock.* 280 (top), *William Blacke/age fotostock.* 280 (center), *Charles A. Blakeslee/age fotostock.* 280 (bottom), *Corey Rich/Aurora Photos.* 281, *Chris Howes/Wild Places Photography/Alamy.* 282, *SuperStock/age fotostock.* **Chapter 15: Death Valley:** 293, *P. Michael Photoz/AKA/age fotostock.* 298, *Roberto Soncin Gerometta/Alamy.* 304, *Mike Anich/age fotostock.* 305, *Greg Epperson/age fotostock.* **Chapter 16: Glacier & Waterton Lakes National Parks:** 317, *Dan Sherwood/age fotostock.* 318, *Glacier National Park/NPS.* 321, *Dan Restivo/ Glacier National Park/NPS.* 322, *Glacier National Park/NPS.* 332, *Terry Reimink/iStockphoto.* **Chapter 17: The Grand Canyon:** 345–49, *NPS.* 350, *Grand Canyon Railway.* 358, *NPS.* 359, *Danilo Donadoni/age fotostock.* 365, *Mike Weaver.* **Chapter 18: Grand Teton:** 387, *Oli Gardner/Alamy.* 388–92, *NPS.* **Chapter 19: Great Basin:** 417, *Dennis Frates/Alamy.* 418 (all), *Nevada Commission on Tourism.* 421, *Dennis Frates/Alamy.* **Chapter 20: Great Sand Dunes:** 431, *J. C. Leacock/CTO.* 432 (both), *NPS.* 435, *Stuart & Cynthia Pern/age fotostock.* **Chapter 21: Guadalupe Mountains:** 443, *Tom Till/ Alamy.* 444–47, *NPS.* **Chapter 22: Jasper:** 455–57, *Travel Alberta.* 459, *Natalia Bratslavsky/iStockphoto.* 464, *Walter Bibikow/age fotostock.* 465, *David Restivo/Glacier National Park/NPS.* **Chapter 23: Joshua Tree:** 475, *Gavin Hellier/Alamy.* 476 (top), *Loic Bernard/iStockphoto.* 476 (bottom left), *iStockphoto.* 476 (bottom right), *Richard Cummins.* 477, *Robert Holmes/CalTour.* 478, *Ron Niebrugge/Alamy.* 479, *Eric Foltz/iStockphoto.* **Chapter 24: Lassen Volcanic:** 493, *Craig Lovell/Eagle Visions Photography/Alamy.* 494–97, *NPS.* **Chapter 25: Mesa Verde:** 509–13, *NPS.* 518, *Chris Howes/Wild Places Photography/ Alamy.* **Chapter 26: Mount Rainier:** 527, *SuperStock/age fotostock.* 528–31, *Washington State Tourism.* 532, *Cornforth Images/Alamy.* **Chapter 27: North Cascades:** 547, *Alan Kearney/age fotostock.* 548 (top), *Don Geyer/Alamy.* 548 (bottom), *Washington State Tourism.* 550, *QT Luong/terragalleria.com.* 551, *Alan Kearney/age fotostock.* 556, *Colin Meagher/Aurora Photos.* **Chapter 28: Olympic:** 567, *David A. Barnes/Alamy.* 568–72, *Washington State Tourism.* 578, *SuperStock/age fotostock.* 579, *Carmel Studios.* **Chapter 29: Petrified Forest:** 591–92, *NPS.* 595, *Robert Harding Picture Library/Alamy.* **Chapter 30: Redwood:** 607, *John W. Warden/age fotostock.* 608 (top), *QT Luong/terragalleria.com.* 608 (center), *Dennis MacDonald/Alamy.* 608 (bottom), *Jean Carter/age fotostock.* 611, *North Light Images/age fotostock.* 618, *QT Luong/terragalleria.com.* 619, *Edward L. Ewert/age fotostock.* **Chapter 31: Rocky Mountain:** 627, *Stock Connection Distribution/Alamy.* 628–30, *NPS.* 632, *Eric Wunrow/CTO.* **Chapter 32: Saguaro:** 651, *Johnny Stockshooter/age fotostock.* 652 (top), *NPS.* 652 (bottom), *Visual & Written SL/Alamy.* 653, *NPS.* 654, *Eric Foltz/iStockphoto.* 655, *NPS.* 659, *Dan Leffel/age fotostock.* **Chapter 33: Sequoia & Kings Canyon National Parks:** 669, *Don Geyer/Alamy.* 670 (top), *iStockphoto.* 670 (bottom), *Greg Epperson/age fotostock.* 672, *Gary Crabbe/Alamy.* 674, *Paula Borchardt/age fotostock.* 680, *Jon Arnold Images/Alamy.* 681, *NPS.* **Chapter 34: Theodore Roosevelt:** 699, *Woodfall Wild Images/Alamy.* 700 (top), *North Dakota Tourism.* 700 (center), *Dawn Charging/North Dakota Tourism.* 700 (bottom), *Alan Majchrowicz/age fotostock.* 703, *Bruce Wendt/North Dakota Tourism.* **Chapter 35: Wind Cave:** 715–22, *South Dakota Tourism.* 729, *nagelestock.com/Alamy.* **Chapter 36: Yellowstone:** 739, *John Warden/age fotostock.* 744, *Mark Newman/age fotostock.* 768, *Mark Hamblin/age fotostock.* 769, *Oli Gardner/Alamy.* **Chapter 37: Yosemite:** 783, *Yosemite Concession Services.* 784–85, *Robert Holmes/CalTour.* 786, *Yosemite Concession Services.* 787, *Arco Images/Alamy.* 788, *Ron Yue/Alamy.* 796, *Alan Kearney/age fotostock.* 797, *Greg Epperson/age fotostock.* 799, *Bethany Gediman.* 804, *SuperStock/ age fotostock.* **Chapter 38: Zion:** 823, *True North Images/age fotostock.* 828, *True North Images/age fotostock.* **Chapter 39: Driving Tours:** 845, *Jan Paul/iStockphoto.*

# ABOUT OUR WRITERS

Since moving to Utah in 1996, writer and photojournalist John Blodgett has explored almost every corner of the Beehive State but has a particular passion for the south. It was in these silent canyons and wide-open lands of sage brush and juniper that John discovered a new muse. He has written for *Utah Business, Digital IQ, Salt Lake Magazine, Utah Home & Garden, Salt Lake City Weekly, Catalyst,* and *Fodor's Utah.*

Native Californian Cheryl Crabtree has worked as a freelance writer since 1987. She has contributed to *Fodor's California* for several years and has also written for *Resorts & Great Hotels* and *Touring and Tasting: Great American Wineries.* She currently lives in Santa Barbara with her husband, two sons, and Jack Russell terrier.

West Texas-based writer Jennifer Edwards is a senior reporter for the *Odessa American Newspaper.* During her years there, she has traveled extensively across West Texas and eastern New Mexico and spent many a weekend watching the leonid meteor showers cross over the Guadalupes and Chisos Mountains. Her stories have appeared in dozens of daily newspapers, including the *Dallas Morning News, Austin-American Statesman* and the *International Herald-Tribune,* as well as several regional magazines.

A fifth generation South Dakotan, Dustin Floyd was raised at the base of the Black Hills in Rapid City. He studied history at Oxford University before graduating magna cum laude from Coe College in Cedar Rapids, Iowa. Floyd currently serves as general manager of TDG Communications, a Deadwood, S.D.-based advertising, marketing and public relations firm, as well as executive editor of *Deadwood Magazine,* a monthly periodical that focuses on the history, culture and people of the Black Hills and the American West. He and his wife, Laura, live in the Black Hills.

Lois Friedland, adventure travel guide for About.com, is a Colorado-based freelancer who specializes in skiing, golf, and adventure travel.

Tom Griffith worked as a reporter, photographer, and managing editor of award-winning newspapers in Arizona, Montana, and South Dakota before serving as director of communications for the Mount Rushmore Preservation Fund, which raised $25 million to preserve and improve the mountain memorial. Tom is the author of five books, including *America's Shrine of Democracy* with a foreword by President Ronald Reagan, and *South Dakota,* a comprehensive guide to the state published by Random House. Tom and his wife, Nyla, make their home in South Dakota's Black Hills.

Orange County native Veronica Hill discovered California at a young age during "Sunday drives" with her family. Now a features editor at the *Daily Press* in Victorville, Calif., her articles have also appeared in *US, Rolling Stone, Food & Wine,* and *Seventeen.*

Constance Jones, formerly a Fodor's senior editor, pulled up her lifelong New York roots and relocated to California in 2004. Based in Central Coast wine country, she contributes to publications such as *National Geographic Traveler* and *The New York Times.*

Jill Koch is a Phoenix-based freelance writer and editor. Her writing has been published in *Scottsdale Magazine* and *Phoenix New Times.*

Moab-based writer Janet Lowe has explored Utah's national parks for more than a decade, and at one time headed up the publications and operations department for the Canyonlands Natural History Association. She is currently the director of the Moab Arts and Recreation Center. Janet has published two books on Arches and Canyonlands national parks and put together an Arches audio tour.

Carrie Miner, who currently splits her time between Arizona and Alaska, has wandered the wilds of the Southwest for more than a decade. She has written hundreds of travel articles and is a regular contributor to *Arizona Highways*. She also is the author of two Arizona travel books.

Janna Mock-Lopez, publisher of *Portland Family Magazine*, resides in Beaverton, Ore. Her writing has appeared in numerous publications, including Portland's daily newspaper, *The Oregonian*.

Candy Moulton, a veteran Fodor's contributor, has spent years traveling through her native state of Wyoming doing research for her travel articles and books, including *Legacy of the Tetons: Homesteading in Jackson Hole*; and *Roadside History of Wyoming*. She is the editor of *Roundup*, the official publication of Western Writers of America.

Debbie Olsen is an Alberta-based freelance travel writer who spends much of her time exploring national parks with her husband and four children. She writes travel columns for the *Red Deer Advocate* and the *Calgary Herald* and freelance travel articles for other publications.

Gary Peterson is the editor of *Home & Away* magazine, based in Omaha, Neb. His love of history and nature came together in his piece about the Roosevelts and their contributions to the National Park System.

Marge Peterson, an Omaha-based travel journalist, is the former executive editor of *Home & Away* magazine. She has traveled extensively to the national parks of the West.

Martha Schindler Connors is a freelance writer in Evergreen, Colo., where she lives with her husband, two step-daughters and three dogs. She enjoys hiking and skiing.

Seattle-based writer/editor Holly S. Smith has enjoyed far-flung Fodor's assignments to Indonesia, Australia, and Peru, but lately she's stayed closer to home covering the Pacific Northwest. Some of her previous books include *Aceh: Art & Culture* and *Adventuring in Indonesia;* her latest is *The Adventure Guide to Australia*. She is also the proud mother of three little adventurers, who often accompany her on the road.

A freelance correspondent for the *Sacramento Bee*, Christine Vovakes regularly writes news and feature stories about the region. She considers California's Far North, her home turf of 25 years, the undiscovered gem of the Golden State.

Bobbi Zane has been living in and visiting the region around Joshua Tree National Park since her childhood. Her articles on Palm Springs have appeared in the *Orange County Register* and *Westways* magazine, and she's also written for the *Los Angeles Times* and the *Los Angeles Daily News*. She recently contributed to *Fodor's San Diego, California,* and *Escape to Nature Without Roughing It*.